If graduates master these eight skills, their likelihood of long-term career success grows significantly. The Eight Skills of the Peak Performer builds on our knowledge that employers are looking for these crucial soft skills and schools need to impart them. The supplements are organized not only around Learning Outcomes, but also around these eight critical skills in order to help instructors assess and teach the topics covered in the text and the overarching skills that create a valuable employee. This is a holistic and complete package for long-term success!

Reinforcing Student Skills!

Students will reinforce the eight skills of the peak performer through assigned content in *Connect Plus* and skill vignettes, which are also available on the Online Learning Center.

Each vignette is designed to provide immediate practice and feedback on the core skills required for long-term success.

Reading directions + try method where you cover up the answer

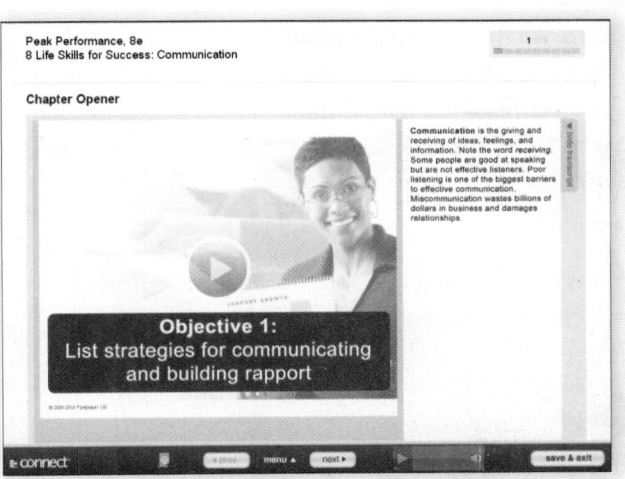

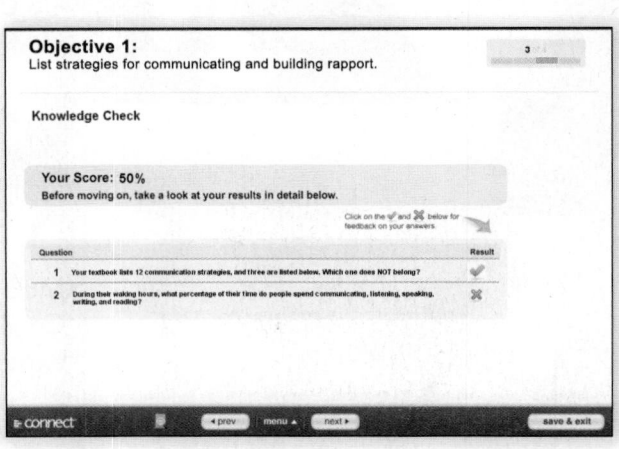

connect™ plus+

LESS MANAGING.

MORE TEACHING.

GREATER LEARNING.

What Is *Connect Plus*?

McGraw-Hill *Connect Plus* is a revolutionary online assignment and assessment solution providing instructors and students with tools and resources to maximize their success.

Through *Connect Plus*, instructors enjoy simplified course setup and assignment creation. Robust, media-rich tools and activities, **all tied to the textbook's learning outcomes**, ensure you'll create classes geared toward achievement. You'll have more time with your students and less time agonizing over course planning.

Connect Plus Features

McGraw-Hill *Connect Plus* includes powerful tools and features that allow students to access their coursework anytime and anywhere, while you control the assignments. *Connect Plus* provides students with their textbook and homework, **all in one accessible place.**

▶ *Simple Assignment Management*
Creating assignments takes just a few clicks, and with *Connect Plus*, you can choose not only which chapter to assign but also specific learning outcomes. **Videos, animations, quizzes**, and many other activities bring **active learning** to the forefront.

▶ *Smart Grading*
Study time is precious and *Connect Plus* assignments **automatically provide feedback** to you and your students. You'll be able to conveniently review class or individual student knowledge in an online environment.

▶ *Connect Plus eBooks*
McGraw-Hill has seamlessly **integrated eBooks** into their *Connect Plus* solution with **direct links to the activities and tools**—students no longer have to search for content, allowing them more time for learning.

McGraw-Hill provides live instructor orientations for *Connect Plus* to guarantee you will have a worry-free experience.

Peak Performance

eighth edition **SUCCESS IN COLLEGE AND BEYOND**

Sharon K. Ferrett, Ph.D.
Humboldt State University

Dedication

To the memory of my parents, Albert Lawrence Ferrett and Velma Mary Hollenbeck Ferrett, for setting the highest standards and their seamless expression of love.

To my husband, Sam, and my daughters, Jennifer Katherine and Sarah Angela, and my grandchildren, Emily and Caden, for making it all worthwhile.

—Sharon K. Ferrett

PEAK PERFORMANCE: SUCCESS IN COLLEGE AND BEYOND
Published by McGraw-Hill, a business unit of The McGraw-Hill Companies, Inc., 1221 Avenue of the Americas, New York, NY, 10020. Copyright © 2012 by The McGraw-Hill Companies, Inc. All rights reserved. Previous editions © 1994, 1997, 2000, 2003, 2006, 2008, and 2010. No part of this publication may be reproduced or distributed in any form or by any means, or stored in a database or retrieval system, without the prior written consent of The McGraw-Hill Companies, Inc., including, but not limited to, in any network or other electronic storage or transmission, or broadcast for distance learning.

Some ancillaries, including electronic and print components, may not be available to customers outside the United States.

This book is printed on acid-free paper.

1 2 3 4 5 6 7 8 9 0 DOW/DOW 1 0 9 8 7 6 5 4 3 2 1

ISBN 978-0-07-337519-9 (student edition)   ISBN 978-0-07-747154-5 (annotated instructor's edition)
MHID 0-07-337519-5 (student edition)   MHID 0-07-747154-7 (annotated instructor's edition)

Vice president/Editor in chief: *Elizabeth Haefele*
Vice president/Director of marketing: *John E. Biernat*
Senior sponsoring editor: *Alice Harra*
Director of development: *Sarah Wood*
Developmental editor: *Kristin Bradley*
Freelance developmental editor: *Vicki Malinee, Van Brien & Associates*
Editorial coordinator: *Vincent Bradshaw*
Senior marketing manager: *Keari Green*
Lead digital product manager: *Damian Moshak*
Digital development editor: *Kevin White*
Director, Editing/Design/Production: *Jess Ann Kosic*
Project manager: *Kathryn D. Wright*
Buyer: *Nicole Baumgartner*

Senior designer: *Anna Kinigakis*
Senior photo research coordinator: *John C. Leland*
Photo researcher: *Nancy Null, Van Brien & Associates*
Media project manager: *Brent dela Cruz*
Cover design: *Alexa R. Viscius*
Typeface: *11/14 Minion Pro*
Compositor: *Laserwords Private Limited*
Printer: *R. R. Donnelley*
Cover credit: © *Joson/Corbis*
Credits: The credits section for this book begins on page 483 and is considered an extension of the copyright page.

Library of Congress Cataloging-in-Publication Data
Ferrett, Sharon K.
    Peak performance : success in college and beyond / Sharon K. Ferrett.—8th ed.
        p. cm.
    Includes index.
    ISBN-13: 978-0-07-337519-9 (student edition : alk. paper)
    ISBN-10: 0-07-337519-5 (student edition : alk. paper)
    ISBN-13: 978-0-07-747154-5 (annotated instructor's edition : alk. paper)
    ISBN-10: 0-07-747154-7 (annotated instructor's edition : alk. paper)
    1. Academic achievement. 2. Performance. 3. Career development. 4. Success. I. Title.
LB1062.6.F47 2012
370.15'2—dc22
                                                              2010042589

The Internet addresses listed in the text were accurate at the time of publication. The inclusion of a Web site does not indicate an endorsement by the authors or McGraw-Hill, and McGraw-Hill does not guarantee the accuracy of the information presented at these sites.

www.mhhe.com

Brief Table of Contents

The 8th Edition   xiv
Secretary's Commission on Achieving Necessary Skills (SCANS)   xx
Getting Started   xxiii

PART ONE
Building Foundation Skills

1 Be a Lifelong Learner   1

2 Expand Your Emotional Intelligence   43

3 Manage Your Time   75

4 Maximize Your Resources   115

PART TWO
Basic Skills and Strategies

5 Listen and Take Effective Notes   151

6 Actively Read   179

7 Improve Your Memory Skills   217

8 Excel at Taking Tests   245

9 Express Yourself in Writing and Speech   275

PART THREE
Application

10 Become a Critical Thinker and Creative Problem Solver   305

11 Create a Healthy Mind, Body, and Spirit   343

12 Build Supportive and Diverse Relationships   379

13 Develop Positive Habits   415

14 Explore Majors and Careers   439

Glossary   480
Additional Credits   483
Features Guide   484
Index   486

Table of Contents

The 8th Edition   *xiv*
Secretary's Commission on Necessary Skills (SCANS)   *xx*
Getting Started   *xxiii*

> ## PART ONE
> ## Building Foundation Skills

1 Be a Lifelong Learner   1

What Is a "Peak Performer"?   2

Self-Management: The Key to Reaching Your Peak   3

Self-Assessment   3

PERSONAL EVALUATION NOTEBOOK 1.1: AM I A POSITIVE PERSON?   4

Critical Thinking Skills   5

Visualization and Affirmations   6

Reflection   6

PEAK PROGRESS 1.1: THE ABC METHOD OF SELF-MANAGEMENT   7

Discover Your Purpose: A Personal Mission Statement   8

Skills for School and Job Success   9

PERSONAL EVALUATION NOTEBOOK 1.2: PEAK PERFORMANCE SELF-ASSESSMENT TEST   10

Discover Your Learning Style   11

Integrate Both Sides of the Brain   12

Are You a Reader, Listener, or Doer?   12

PERSONAL EVALUATION NOTEBOOK 1.3: LEARNING STYLE INVENTORY   14

Redefining Intelligence: Other Learning Styles   16

PERSONAL EVALUATION NOTEBOOK 1.4: MULTIPLE INTELLIGENCES   18

Discover Your Personality Type   19

Carl Jung's Typology System   19

The Myers-Briggs Type Indicator   20

Connect Learning Styles and Personality Types: The Four-Temperament Profile   20

Analyzers   21

PERSONAL EVALUATION NOTEBOOK 1.5: THE FOUR-TEMPERAMENT PROFILE   22

Supporters   24

Creators   25

Directors   25

Integrate Styles to Maximize Learning   26

The Adult Learning Cycle   27

Overcome Obstacles   29

Adjust Your Learning Style to Your Instructor's Teaching Style   29

Make It Simple   30

TAKING CHARGE   32

CAREER IN FOCUS: SETTING BUSINESS GOALS   34

PEAK PERFORMER PROFILE: BLAKE MYCOSKIE   35

REVIEW AND APPLICATIONS   36

CASE STUDY: MAKING A COMMITMENT   37

WORKSHEETS

Worksheet 1.1: Applying the ABC Method of Self-Management   *38*

Worksheet 1.2: My Learning Style, Personality Types, and Temperament   *39*

Worksheet 1.3: Creating the Ideal Team   *40*

Worksheet 1.4: Applying the Four-Temperament Profile   *41*

CAREER DEVELOPMENT PORTFOLIO: AUTOBIOGRAPHY   42

2 Expand Your Emotional Intelligence   43

Emotional Intelligence and Maturity   44

Character First: Integrity, Civility, and Ethics   45

Responsibility   46

PERSONAL EVALUATION NOTEBOOK 2.1: CHARACTER AND ETHICS   47

PERSONAL EVALUATION NOTEBOOK 2.2: SKILLS AND PERSONAL QUALITIES   48

Self-Control   49

Self-Esteem and Confidence   50

PEAK PROGRESS 2.1: APPLYING THE ADULT LEARNING CYCLE TO SELF-CONTROL 50

A Positive Attitude and Personal Motivation 51

How Needs and Desires Influence Attitudes and Motivation 52

PERSONAL EVALUATION NOTEBOOK 2.3: NEEDS, MOTIVATION, AND COMMITMENT 53

The Motivation Cycle 54

Motivational Strategies 54

PERSONAL EVALUATION NOTEBOOK 2.4: SELF-TALK AND AFFIRMATIONS 55

PEAK PROGRESS 2.2: SETTING GOALS 56

PEAK PROGRESS 2.3: DIFFERENCES BETWEEN HIGH SCHOOL AND COLLEGE 57

The Benefits of Higher Education 58

PEAK PROGRESS 2.4: SKILLS FOR SCHOOL AND CAREER 60

Overcome Obstacles 60

Don't Get Discouraged 60

PEAK PROGRESS 2.5: WHAT KIND OF STUDENT/WORKER ARE YOU? 61

Create Positive Mind Shifts 62

TAKING CHARGE 64

CAREER IN FOCUS: POSITIVE ATTITUDES AT WORK 66

PEAK PERFORMER PROFILE: CHRISTIANE AMANPOUR 67

REVIEW AND APPLICATIONS 68

CASE STUDY: GETTING MOTIVATED 69

WORKSHEETS

Worksheet 2.1: Applying the ABC Method of Self-Management 70

Worksheet 2.2: My Reinforcement Contract 71

Worksheet 2.3: Self-Esteem Inventory 72

Worksheet 2.4: Learning Styles and Motivation 73

CAREER DEVELOPMENT PORTFOLIO: ASSESSMENT OF PERSONAL QUALITIES 74

3 Manage Your Time 75

Use Time Effectively 76

Where Does Your Time Go? 77

PERSONAL EVALUATION NOTEBOOK 3.1: TIME LOG 78

PERSONAL EVALUATION NOTEBOOK 3.2: HOW MUCH TIME DO YOU SPEND? 79

Where Should Your Time Go? 79

PERSONAL EVALUATION NOTEBOOK 3.3: LOOKING AHEAD: YOUR GOALS 80

Setting Priorities 81

PEAK PROGRESS 3.1: INVESTING YOUR TIME IN HIGH-PRIORITY ITEMS: THE 80/20 RULE 82

Time-Management Strategies 83

PERSONAL EVALUATION NOTEBOOK 3.4: YOUR DAILY ENERGY LEVELS 88

Time Management and Your Learning Style 89

PEAK PROGRESS 3.2: APPLYING THE ADULT LEARNING CYCLE TO TAKING CONTROL OF YOUR TIME AND LIFE 90

Overcome Obstacles 91

Stop Procrastinating 91

PERSONAL EVALUATION NOTEBOOK 3.5: PROCRASTINATION 92

Control Interruptions 93

PERSONAL EVALUATION NOTEBOOK 3.6: INTERRUPTIONS! 94

Juggling Family, School, and Job 95

PEAK PROGRESS 3.3: HOW TO SAY NO 96

PEAK PROGRESS 3.4: ONLINE LEARNING 98

PERSONAL EVALUATION NOTEBOOK 3.7: KEEPING YOUR LIFE GOALS IN BALANCE 99

TAKING CHARGE 100

CAREER IN FOCUS: FOCUS ON TASKS 102

PEAK PERFORMER PROFILE: MALCOLM GLADWELL 103

REVIEW AND APPLICATIONS 104

CASE STUDY: JUGGLING FAMILY AND SCHOOL 105

WORKSHEETS

Worksheet 3.1: Applying the ABC Method of Self-Management 106

Worksheet 3.2: My Time-Management Habits 107

Worksheet 3.3: Time Wasters 108

Worksheet 3.4: Practice Goal Setting 109

Worksheet 3.5: Map Out Your Goals 110

Worksheet 3.6: Daily Prioritizer and Planner: Your To-Do List 111

Worksheet 3.7: Weekly Planner 112

Worksheet 3.8: Month/Semester Calendar 113

CAREER DEVELOPMENT PORTFOLIO: DEMONSTRATING YOUR TIME-MANAGEMENT SKILLS 114

4 Maximize Your Resources 115

Explore Your School's Resources 116

People Resources 117

PEAK PROGRESS 4.1: HOW TO FORM A STUDY GROUP 119

Program Resources   120

Additional Online and Information Resources   123

PERSONAL EVALUATION NOTEBOOK 4.1: ACTIVITIES AND CLUBS   124

PEAK PROGRESS 4.2: STAYING SAFE   124

PEAK PROGRESS 4.3: USING TECHNOLOGY AT SCHOOL   125

Students with Disabilities   126

Commuter Students   127

Returning Students   128

PEAK PROGRESS 4.4: EXPLORE YOUR COMMUNITY'S RESOURCES   129

Manage Your Financial Resources   130

Keep a Budget   130

Research Financial Assistance   131

Avoid Credit Card Debt   131

Protect Your Identity   131

PERSONAL EVALUATION NOTEBOOK 4.2: MONEY IN/MONEY OUT   132

Save for the Future   135

PEAK PROGRESS 4.5: APPLYING THE ADULT LEARNING CYCLE TO MANAGING FINANCIAL RESOURCES   136

Get Financial Help If You're in Trouble   138

You Are a Great Resource!   139

TAKING CHARGE   140

CAREER IN FOCUS: BENEFITS OF COMMUNITY RESOURCES   142

PEAK PERFORMER PROFILE: MATTHEW FRIEDMAN AND ADAM SCOTT   143

REVIEW AND APPLICATIONS   144

CASE STUDY: USING RESOURCES   145

WORKSHEETS

Worksheet 4.1: Applying the ABC Method of Self-Management   146

Worksheet 4.2: Networking   147

Worksheet 4.3: Community Resources   148

Worksheet 4.4: Monthly Budget   149

CAREER DEVELOPMENT PORTFOLIO: MANAGING RESOURCES   150

PART TWO

Basic Skills and Strategies

5 Listen and Take Effective Notes   151

Listening to the Message: Attentive Listening Strategies   152

Prepare to Listen   152

Stay Attentive   153

Review What You Have Heard   154

Recording the Message   154

PEAK PROGRESS 5.1: APPLYING THE ADULT LEARNING CYCLE TO BECOMING AN ATTENTIVE LISTENER   155

The Cornell System of Note Taking   155

PERSONAL EVALUATION NOTEBOOK 5.1: ATTENTIVE LISTENING   156

Mind Maps   156

PEAK PROGRESS 5.2: FORMAL (TRADITIONAL) VERSUS INFORMAL (CREATIVE) OUTLINES   157

Combination Note-Taking Systems   158

Note-Taking Strategies   159

PEAK PROGRESS 5.3: GETTING THE MOST OUT OF A CLASS LECTURE   163

Assess and Review Your Notes   164

Overcome Obstacles   166

PEAK PROGRESS 5.4: TAKING NOTE OF SPECIAL CHALLENGES   167

TAKING CHARGE   168

CAREER IN FOCUS: LISTENING IN THE WORKPLACE   170

PEAK PERFORMER PROFILE: ANNA SUI   171

REVIEW AND APPLICATIONS   172

CASE STUDY: DEVELOPING ATTENTIVE LISTENING SKILLS   173

WORKSHEETS

Worksheet 5.1: Applying the ABC Method of Self-Management   174

Worksheet 5.2: Listening Self-Assessment   175

Worksheet 5.3: Mind Map a Lecture   176

Worksheet 5.4: Use the Cornell System of Note Taking   177

CAREER DEVELOPMENT PORTFOLIO: LISTENING AND NOTE TAKING IN THE WORKPLACE   178

6 Actively Read   179

The Importance of Active Reading   180

Reading Systems   181

The Five-Part Reading System   181

PEAK PROGRESS 6.1: APPLYING THE ADULT LEARNING CYCLE TO BECOMING A BETTER READER   182

The SQ3R Reading System   183

Reading Strategies   184

PERSONAL EVALUATION NOTEBOOK 6.1: USING THE SQ3R READING SYSTEM   185

PEAK PROGRESS 6.2: READING FOR DIFFERENT COURSES 187

PEAK PROGRESS 6.3: TO HIGHLIGHT OR NOT TO HIGHLIGHT? 189

Reviewing Strategies 190

PEAK PROGRESS 6.4: USING YOUR TEXTBOOK 191

PEAK PROGRESS 6.5: DIGITAL READING MATERIAL 191

Build Your Vocabulary 193

PEAK PROGRESS 6.6: LOOK IT UP! USING THE DICTIONARY 194

Manage Language Courses 195

Specialized Reading 196

Comprehending Technical Material 196

Reading Manuals 197

Completing Forms 198

Overcome Obstacles 199

Reading Difficulties 199

Create a Positive Attitude 199

PEAK PROGRESS 6.7: READING WITH CHILDREN AROUND 201

TAKING CHARGE 202

CAREER IN FOCUS: KEEPING UP-TO-DATE 204

PEAK PERFORMER PROFILE: SONIA SOTOMAYOR 205

REVIEW AND APPLICATIONS 206

CASE STUDY: EFFECTIVE READING HABITS 207

WORKSHEETS

Worksheet 6.1: Applying the ABC Method of Self-Management 208

Worksheet 6.2: Attitudes and Reading 209

Worksheet 6.3: Different Types of Reading 210

Worksheet 6.4: Summarize and Teach 211

Worksheet 6.5: Creating a Reading Outline 212

Worksheet 6.6: Analyzing Chapters 213

Worksheet 6.7: Mind Map Your Text 214

Worksheet 6.8: Breaking Barriers to Reading 215

CAREER DEVELOPMENT PORTFOLIO: DEMONSTRATING COMPETENCIES 216

7 Improve Your Memory Skills 217

The Memory Process 218

PEAK PROGRESS 7.1: APPLYING THE ADULT LEARNING CYCLE TO INCREASING YOUR MEMORY SKILLS 219

PERSONAL EVALUATION NOTEBOOK 7.1: BEING OBSERVANT 220

PEAK PROGRESS 7.2: SHORT-TERM AND LONG-TERM MEMORY 221

Memory Strategies 222

PERSONAL EVALUATION NOTEBOOK 7.2: USING A MIND MAP TO ENHANCE MEMORY 223

PERSONAL EVALUATION NOTEBOOK 7.3: MEMORY ASSESSMENT 226

PERSONAL EVALUATION NOTEBOOK 7.4: LEARNING STYLES AND MEMORY 227

PERSONAL EVALUATION NOTEBOOK 7.5: ACRONYMS AND ACROSTICS 228

PERSONAL EVALUATION NOTEBOOK 7.6: A WALK DOWN MEMORY LANE 229

Summarize, Review, and Reflect 231

PEAK PROGRESS 7.3: REMEMBERING NAMES 231

Overcome Obstacles 232

TAKING CHARGE 234

CAREER IN FOCUS: INTEGRATING LEARNING STYLES 236

PEAK PERFORMER PROFILE: DAVID DIAZ 237

REVIEW AND APPLICATIONS 238

CASE STUDY: OVERCOMING MEMORY LOSS 239

WORKSHEETS

Worksheet 7.1: Applying the ABC Method of Self-Management 240

Worksheet 7.2: Memory 241

Worksheet 7.3: Mental Pictures 243

CAREER DEVELOPMENT PORTFOLIO: APPLYING MEMORY SKILLS 244

8 Excel at Taking Tests 245

Test-Taking Strategies 246

Before the Test 246

PERSONAL EVALUATION NOTEBOOK 8.1: TEST TAKING 247

During the Test 248

PEAK PROGRESS 8.1: TAKING ONLINE EXAMS 249

After the Test 250

PEAK PROGRESS 8.2: SPECIAL STRATEGIES FOR MATH AND SCIENCE TESTS 251

Taking Different Types of Tests 252

PEAK PROGRESS 8.3: CHECKLIST FOR INCORRECT TEST ANSWERS 252

PEAK PROGRESS 8.4: USING TEST RESULTS 252

Objective Tests 253

Essay Tests 254

PEAK PROGRESS 8.5: IMPORTANT WORDS IN ESSAY QUESTIONS 256

PERSONAL EVALUATION NOTEBOOK 8.2: ESSAY TEST PREPARATION 257

Last-Minute Study Tips 257

Overcome Obstacles 258

Test Anxiety 258

PEAK PROGRESS 8.6: PREPARING FOR A PERFORMANCE APPRAISAL 260

Cheating 260

PERSONAL EVALUATION NOTEBOOK 8.3: TEST ANXIETY 261

PEAK PROGRESS 8.7: APPLYING THE ADULT LEARNING CYCLE TO IMPROVING YOUR TEST-TAKING SKILLS AND REDUCING TEST ANXIETY 263

TAKING CHARGE 264

CAREER IN FOCUS: TESTS IN THE WORKPLACE 266

PEAK PERFORMER PROFILE: ELLEN OCHOA 267

REVIEW AND APPLICATIONS 268

CASE STUDY: COPING WITH ANXIETY 269

WORKSHEETS

Worksheet 8.1: Applying the ABC Method of Self-Management 270

Worksheet 8.2: Exam Schedule 271

Worksheet 8.3: Preparing for Tests and Exams 272

CAREER DEVELOPMENT PORTFOLIO: ASSESSING YOUR SKILLS AND COMPETENCIES 274

9 Express Yourself in Writing and Speech 275

The Importance of Writing and Speaking 276

The Writing Process 276

Prepare 276

PEAK PROGRESS 9.1: HOW TO GENERATE TOPIC IDEAS 278

Organize 279

PERSONAL EVALUATION NOTEBOOK 9.1: PREPARING RESEARCH PAPERS 280

Write 281

Edit 282

PEAK PROGRESS 9.2: OVERCOMING WRITER'S BLOCK 283

PEAK PROGRESS 9.3: WRITING DO'S: THE SEVEN C 'S OF EFFECTIVE WRITING 284

PEAK PROGRESS 9.4: ONLINE WRITING 285

Review 285

PEAK PROGRESS 9.5: WRITING CITATIONS 286

Conducting Research 287

Using the Library for Research 287

PERSONAL EVALUATION NOTEBOOK 9.2: THAT'S NOT FAIR (USE) 288

PEAK PROGRESS 9.6: CHECKLISTS FOR WRITING PAPERS AND GIVING SPEECHES 289

Taking Your Search Online 290

PEAK PROGRESS 9.7: EVALUATING ONLINE INFORMATION 290

Public Speaking Strategie 291

Overcoming Speech Anxiety 292

PEAK PROGRESS 9.8: APPLYING THE ADULT LEARNING CYCLE TO IMPROVING YOUR PUBLIC SPEAKING 294

PERSONAL EVALUATION NOTEBOOK 9.3: CONTROLLING STAGE FRIGHT AND WRITER'S BLOCK 295

TAKING CHARGE 296

CAREER IN FOCUS: COMMUNICATION SKILLS 298

PEAK PERFORMER PROFILE: TONI MORRISON 299

REVIEW AND APPLICATIONS 300

CASE STUDY: LEARNING COMMUNICATION SKILLS 301

WORKSHEETS

Worksheet 9.1: Applying the ABC Method of Self-Management 302

Worksheet 9.2: Practice Paraphrasing 303

CAREER DEVELOPMENT PORTFOLIO: YOUR WRITING AND SPEAKING SKILLS 304

10 Become a Critical Thinker and Creative Problem Solver 305

Essential Critical Thinking Skills 306

Problem-Solving Steps 307

PEAK PROGRESS 10.1: FROM KNOWLEDGE TO EVALUATION 308

PERSONAL EVALUATION NOTEBOOK 10.1: THINK IT THROUGH 309

Critical Thinking and Problem-Solving Strategies 309

PERSONAL EVALUATION NOTEBOOK 10.2: USING CRITICAL THINKING TO SOLVE PROBLEMS 311

PEAK PROGRESS 10.2: ASKING QUESTIONS 312

Common Errors in Judgment 312

PERSONAL EVALUATION NOTEBOOK 10.3: INDUCTIVE VERSUS DEDUCTIVE REASONING 314

Creative Problem Solving 314

PERSONAL EVALUATION NOTEBOOK 10.4: NINE-DOT EXERCISE 316

PERSONAL EVALUATION NOTEBOOK 10.5: BRAINSTORMING NOTES 317

PERSONAL EVALUATION NOTEBOOK 10.6: MIND SETS 318

PERSONAL EVALUATION NOTEBOOK 10.7: DECISION-MAKING APPLICATION 319

PERSONAL EVALUATION NOTEBOOK 10.8: SOLVING PROBLEMS AND MAKING CHOICES 321

Math and Science Applications 323

Problem-Solving Strategies for Math and Science 323

PEAK PROGRESS 10.3: CREATIVE IDEAS CHECKLIST 324

Overcome Math and Science Anxiety 327

PEAK PROGRESS 10.4: PROBLEM-SOLVING CHECKLIST 328

PEAK PROGRESS 10.5: APPLYING THE ADULT LEARNING CYCLE TO OVERCOMING MATH AND SCIENCE ANXIETY 329

TAKING CHARGE 330

CAREER IN FOCUS: CREATIVITY AT WORK 332

PEAK PERFORMER PROFILE: SCOTT ADAMS 333

REVIEW AND APPLICATIONS 334

CASE STUDY: CONQUERING FEAR OF FAILURE 335

WORKSHEETS

Worksheet 10.1: Applying the ABC Method of Self-Management 336

Worksheet 10.2: Apply Bloom's Taxonomy 337

Worksheet 10.3: Preparing for Critical Thinking 338

Worksheet 10.4: You Can Solve the Problem: Sue's Decision 339

CAREER DEVELOPMENT PORTFOLIO: ASSESSING AND DEMONSTRATING YOUR CRITICAL THINKING SKILLS 341

11 Create a Healthy Mind, Body, and Spirit 343

Redefining Health: Connecting Mind, Body, and Spirit 344

The Mind 344

The Body 344

The Spirit 344

Awareness and Prevention 345

Strategies for Good Health Management 346

PEAK PROGRESS 11.1: EATING FOR HEALTH AND ENERGY 347

PERSONAL EVALUATION NOTEBOOK 11.1: REVIEWING YOUR HEALTH 350

PEAK PROGRESS 11.2: EATING DISORDERS 351

PERSONAL EVALUATION NOTEBOOK 11.2: GETTING PROPER REST 352

PERSONAL EVALUATION NOTEBOOK 11.3: COMMITTING TO EXERCISE 353

Manage Stress 353

PEAK PROGRESS 11.3: STRESS LEADS TO BURNOUT 354

Unhealthy Addictions 357

Alcohol Abuse 357

PEAK PROGRESS 11.4: APPLYING THE ADULT LEARNING CYCLE TO CREATING A HEALTHIER LIFESTYLE 357

Cigarette Smoking 358

PEAK PROGRESS 11.5: PARTY WITH A PLAN 358

Illegal Drug Use 359

Prescription and Over-the-Counter Medication Abuse 359

Overcoming Addictions 360

Codependency 361

Emotional Health 361

Depression 361

Suicide 362

Protecting Your Body 363

Sexually Transmitted Infections (STIs) 364

Birth Control 364

Understanding and Preventing Acquaintance Rape 366

TAKING CHARGE 368

CAREER IN FOCUS: PREVENTING STRESS AND FATIGUE AT WORK 370

PEAK PERFORMER PROFILE: MARK HERZLICH JR. 371

REVIEW AND APPLICATIONS 372

CASE STUDY: INCREASING YOUR ENERGY LEVEL 373

WORKSHEETS

Worksheet 11.1: Applying the ABC Method of Self-Management 374

Worksheet 11.2: Stress Performance Test 375

Worksheet 11.3: I Am What I Eat 377

CAREER DEVELOPMENT PORTFOLIO: INVENTORY OF INTERESTS 378

12 Build Supportive and Diverse Relationships 379

The Importance of Effective Communication and Rapport 380

Strategies for Building Communication and Rapport 380

PEAK PROGRESS **12.1:** SOCIALLY ACCEPTABLE
TECHNOLOGY **382**

Assertive Communication 383

Communicating with Instructors and Advisors 383

PERSONAL EVALUATION NOTEBOOK **12.1:** ASSERTIVE
COMMUNICATION ROLE-PLAYING **384**

Conflict 385

PEAK PROGRESS **12.2:** E-MAIL ETIQUETTE WITH
INSTRUCTORS **386**

PERSONAL EVALUATION NOTEBOOK **12.2:** OBSERVING
CONFLICT **388**

Constructive Criticism 388

PERSONAL EVALUATION NOTEBOOK **12.3:** CONFLICT
RESOLUTION **389**

Dealing with Shyness 390

PEAK PROGRESS **12.3:** MAKING SMALL TALK **391**

Overcome Obstacles to Communication 392

Build Healthy Relationships 392

Romantic Relationships 392

PERSONAL EVALUATION NOTEBOOK **12.4:** PATTERNS IN
RELATIONSHIPS **393**

Relationships with the People You Live With 394

PERSONAL EVALUATION NOTEBOOK **12.5:** HEALTHY
RELATIONSHIPS **395**

Appreciate Diversity 396

Communication Strategies for Celebrating
Diversity 397

PEAK PROGRESS **12.4:** APPLYING THE ADULT
LEARNING CYCLE TO BECOMING A BETTER
COMMUNICATOR **398**

PEAK PROGRESS **12.5:** THINKING ABOUT
DIVERSITY **399**

PERSONAL EVALUATION NOTEBOOK **12.6:** APPRECIATING
DIVERSITY **400**

PERSONAL EVALUATION NOTEBOOK **12.7:** WHAT DO YOU
WANT TO BE CALLED? **401**

Diversity in the Workplace 401

Sexual Harassment at School and Work 402

PEAK PROGRESS **12.6:** TEAM PLAYERS **402**

TAKING CHARGE 404

CAREER IN FOCUS: TEAM BUILDING AT WORK 406

PEAK PERFORMER PROFILE: CHRISTY
HAUBEGGER 407

REVIEW AND APPLICATIONS 408

CASE STUDY: SUCCESSFUL TEAMWORK 409

WORKSHEETS

Worksheet 12.1: Applying the ABC Method of
Self-Management 410

Worksheet 12.2: Study Team Relationships 411

Worksheet 12.3: Appreciating Diversity 412

Worksheet 12.4: Are You Assertive, Aggressive,
or Passive? 413

CAREER DEVELOPMENT PORTFOLIO: ASSESSING
YOUR RELATIONSHIP SKILLS 414

13 Develop Positive Habits 415

The 10 Habits of Peak Performers 417

Change Your Habits by Changing Your Attitude 419

Strategies for Creating Positive Change 420

PERSONAL EVALUATION NOTEBOOK **13.1:** MAKE A
COMMITMENT TO LEARN AND APPLY POSITIVE
HABITS **421**

Overcome Resistance to Change 423

Contract for Change 425

PEAK PROGRESS **13.1:** APPLYING THE ADULT LEARNING
CYCLE TO DEVELOPING POSITIVE HABITS **426**

PERSONAL EVALUATION NOTEBOOK **13.2:** COMMITMENT
CONTRACT **427**

TAKING CHARGE 428

CAREER IN FOCUS: GOOD HABITS IN THE
WORKPLACE 430

PEAK PERFORMER PROFILE: BEN CARSON, M.D. 431

REVIEW AND APPLICATIONS 432

CASE STUDY: SPREADING GOOD HABITS 433

WORKSHEETS

Worksheet 13.1: Applying the ABC Method of
Self-Management 434

Worksheet 13.2: Developing Positive Habits 435

Worksheet 13.3: Overcoming Resistance to Change 436

CAREER DEVELOPMENT PORTFOLIO: PLANNING
YOUR CAREER 437

14 Explore Majors and
Careers 439

Connecting School and Job Success 440

Exploring and Choosing a Major 440

PEAK PROGRESS **14.1:** SERVICE LEARNING **442**

Values, Interests, Abilities, and Skills 443

PERSONAL EVALUATION NOTEBOOK **14.1:**
YOUR VALUES **444**

Exploring Careers 445

PEAK PROGRESS **14.2:** APPLYING THE ADULT
LEARNING CYCLE TO EXPLORING MAJORS
AND CAREERS **446**

Building a Career Development Portfolio 447

When Should You Start Your Portfolio? 447

How to Organize and Assemble Your Portfolio   447

Elements of Your Portfolio   449

PERSONAL EVALUATION NOTEBOOK 14.2: TRANSFERABLE SKILLS   452

PERSONAL EVALUATION NOTEBOOK 14.3: INVENTORY OF PERSONAL QUALITIES   453

Overcome the Barriers to Portfolio Development   459

Planning the Job Hunt   460

Submitting a Cover Letter   460

Interviewing   460

Take Charge of Your Career   463

PERSONAL EVALUATION NOTEBOOK 14.4: ASSESSMENT IS LIFELONG   466

TAKING CHARGE   468

CAREER IN FOCUS: CAREER PLANNING IS LIFELONG   470

PEAK PERFORMER PROFILE: URSULA BURNS   471

REVIEW AND APPLICATIONS   472

CASE STUDY: EXPLORING CAREERS   473

WORKSHEETS

Worksheet 14.1: Applying the ABC Method of Self-Management   474

Worksheet 14.2: Checklist for Choosing a Major   475

Worksheet 14.3: Preparing Your Resumé   476

Worksheet 14.4: Informational Interview: What's the Job Like?   477

Worksheet 14.5: Informational Interview: Who Are You Looking For?   478

CAREER DEVELOPMENT PORTFOLIO: EXPLORING CAREERS   479

Glossary   480

Additional Credits   483

Features Guide   484

Index   486

The 8th Edition

Peak Performance: Success in College and Beyond continues to lead the way in showing students how to:

- **Learn how they learn best—and incorporate new ways to learn**
- **Maximize their available resources and seek out new opportunities**
- **Relate what they are exploring now to future success on the job**
- **Strive to become the best individuals they can be**

The eighth edition has been strategically revised to provide a more concise, streamlined presentation and includes new features designed to further promote critical thinking and new topics that reflect issues impacting today's student.

New Features

- **Think Fast:** Appearing in every chapter, this new critical thinking feature reinforces that we are constantly making decisions, whether we are aware of it or not, that have not only outcomes but also repercussions. These "mini-case studies" describe scenarios that readers can relate to and ask three follow-up questions that help the student think through each situation, apply material learned in the text, and offer strategies for improvement.

- **Take 3:** This new feature encourages students to focus on one task at a time for short durations of time (ideally 3 minutes) rather than attempting to multitask, which should lead to enhanced productivity and less stress and reinforce that focused effort makes a significant difference.

Sampling of New and Revised Topics

CHAPTER 1: BE A LIFELONG LEARNER

- The new section **"Make It Simple"** discusses how multitasking isn't an effective tool for handling multiple responsibilities and should be simplified by using focused effort and personal strategies.

- The retitled section **"Define Your Purpose: A Personal Mission Statement"** provides a streamlined mission statement that incorporates career aspirations.

- A new Peak Performer Profile on **Blake Mycoskie** tells how this successful entrepreneur and founder of TOMS: Shoes for Tomorrow uses his vision and skills to help others.

- The **Worksheets** have been revised to include defined spaces for providing answers. A single worksheet now focuses on personal learning styles and personality types, while another asks the student to develop the ideal team based on complementing learning styles and personality types.

CHAPTER 2: EXPAND YOUR EMOTIONAL INTELLIGENCE

- A new illustration, "Incivility in the Classroom," highlights behavior (such as texting during lecture) that is disrespectful both in class and on the job.
- The discussion of internal and external locus of control now appears with the section on responsibility, highlighting that we need to take personal responsibility for our decisions and effort.
- A connection to Chapter 9's discussion on paraphrasing has been added to the discussion of plagiarism, reinforcing that this important topic is addressed in multiple contexts within the text.
- The illustration of Maslow's hierarchy of needs now includes references to workplace satisfiers.
- The updated statistics on salaries related to educational attainment reflect the importance of higher education to increased financial success.
- The Peak Progress feature "Skills for School and Career" includes additional, relevant examples of how skills learned in school will also be used on the job.
- A new mention of being resilient in the section on overcoming obstacles reinforces that bouncing back from setbacks is key to long-term success.
- The information on why students don't graduate has been updated with recent research from Public Agenda, indicating that the challenge of juggling school and work is a major reason.

CHAPTER 3: MANAGE YOUR TIME

- A new illustration visually shows how to use typical features within a daily planner.
- A mention of PDAs and a new illustration on maximizing cell phone features for task management have been added, as most students have cell phones.

- The activity "Looking Ahead: Your Goals" has been revised to tie in with the semester calendar, helping the student put a plan into action.
- A new Peak Performer Profile on Malcolm Gladwell explores how this popular writer views aspects of time, experience, and practice.

CHAPTER 4: MAXIMIZE YOUR RESOURCES

- A streamlined section on community resources highlights key resources students should be aware of, including the 2-1-1 service offered in many areas.
- All financial statistics have been updated, including credit card use and student loan debt.
- A new example of daily spending asks students to think of all the "little" expenses that quickly add up.
- The information on financial aid has been updated and reformatted into a handy table, including useful Web site addresses for more information.
- The section on credit cards has been updated to reflect recent changes in legislation.
- A brief mention of social networking sites has been added to the section on protecting your identity, reminding students to avoid giving out personal information.
- A revised monthly budget sheet helps students realistically assess their expenses and budget accordingly.
- At the end of the text is the comprehensive form "Your School's Resources," giving students a handy guide to record contact information for useful local sources.

CHAPTER 5: LISTEN AND TAKE EFFECTIVE NOTES

- A mention of today's distractions and their impact on effective listening has been added.
- Tips on improving listening skills designed for those with learning disabilities and special needs are included in the section on overcoming obstacles.
- The illustration showing a "Combination Note-Taking System" reflects taking notes from a lecture.

- A mention of **podcasts** has been added, as many instructors also make their lectures and special presentations available for downloading.

CHAPTER 6: ACTIVELY READ

- A new box provides tips on **using a highlighter.**
- The discussion of **reading challenges** has been expanded to include topics such as speed and comprehension and possible signs and benchmarks that may signal a reading problem.
- Strategies designed for **ESL students** have also been included.
- As more students are using digital books and taking online courses, tips are provided on how to get the most out of **online reading.**
- The box "**SQ3R Reading System**" includes a more detailed example to analyze.
- A new Peak Performer Profile on **Sonia Sotomayor** highlights how early interests in reading led to her career choices.

CHAPTER 7: IMPROVE YOUR MEMORY SKILLS

- The use of **rap** has been added as a memory tool, providing cultural relevance to the topic.
- The activity on **memory assessment** includes more critical thinking questions regarding how students rate and typically use their memory.
- The activity "**A Walk Down Memory Lane**" has been revised to include a current example of setting and elements that students will relate to.

CHAPTER 8: EXCEL AT TAKING TESTS

- More examples of **potential test questions** give students practice.
- In the "**Test Taking**" assignment, study team members work together to anticipate test topics and confer with their instructor.
- A new strategy on **scanning the test** in the section "During the Test" gives tips on items to quickly look for.
- A new illustration reinforces how to effectively complete Scantron, or "**bubble," tests,** which are often used for testing in big courses and online courses with on-sight testing.

- The "after-the-test questions" to use when **evaluating test results** have been revised into a handy checklist for students to use again and again.
- A streamlined section on **performance appraisals** focuses on essential test-taking skills that also apply to performance appraisals and assessment on the job.
- The activity "**Test Anxiety**" includes a checklist of potential fears and stressors students experience.
- A mention of **cheating during tests via texting** has been added, reinforcing that this also represents academic dishonesty.
- The **Career Development Portfolio** includes additional skills and opportunities for personal assessment.

CHAPTER 9: EXPRESS YOURSELF IN WRITING AND SPEECH

- The box "**How to Generate Topic Ideas**" includes freewriting and mind mapping.
- A mention of **recording page numbers for quotations and citations** has been added to the strategy on "Taking Notes," reinforcing the importance of fully documenting sources.
- The discussion of plagiarism explains the concept of **fair use** and provides examples of what is and isn't "fair."
- Tips on how to effectively **communicate in cyberspace** have been added, including blogging and social networking sites.
- A new illustration offers tips on creating effective **PowerPoint presentations,** as this is often an integral part of delivering presentations in many courses (including speech) as well as on the job.

CHAPTER 10: BECOME A CRITICAL THINKER AND CREATIVE PROBLEM SOLVER

- A visual of the "**decision-making model**" has been added, so that students can easily refer to the steps to follow.
- A new discussion asks students to relate their learning and personality styles to their "**thinking style,**" helping them assess how they can become more effective critical thinkers.

- The "Problem-Solving Checklist" has been streamlined to provide the most effective strategies.

CHAPTER 11: CREATE A HEALTHY MIND, BODY, AND SPIRIT

- The section on awareness has been revised to focus more on **managing chronic conditions**—some of which are increasing in record numbers, such as diabetes—and recent health issues, such as H1N1.

- The section on **marijuana** use has been expanded to include harmful effects as well as the rise of products such as K2 (synthetic marijuana), which is also illegal in many states.

- All the **statistics regarding substance use** and abuse have been updated.

- A mention of **distracted driving**, including texting behind the wheel, has been added, as it is the number one cause of traffic accidents.

- A new worksheet on **dietary habits** asks students to analyze their true eating behaviors and determine if they need to make changes.

- A new Peak Performer Profile on **Mark Herzlich Jr.** highlights this college athlete's determination as he battles cancer and strives to become a better person, both on and off the field.

CHAPTER 12: BUILD SUPPORTIVE AND DIVERSE RELATIONSHIPS

- A new discussion of "**socially acceptable technology**" explores topics such as sexting and cyber bullying and positive ways to use social networking.

- New tips on **making small talk** help the student practice and develop this important communication skill essential for both personal and business success.

- The term **inclusion** has been added to the discussion of diversity.

- The new box "**What Do You Want to Be Called?**" discusses the use of "labels" in our society and the need for individuality.

- The box "**Thinking about Diversity**" includes the latest global demographics.

CHAPTER 13: DEVELOP POSITIVE HABITS

- The "**Peak Performance Success Formula**" now appears at the beginning of the chapter and frames the focus on creating life-long habits ("training").

- The activity "**Make a Commitment to Learn and Apply Positive Habits**" has been expanded, so that the student can provide personal examples of successful habits.

CHAPTER 14: EXPLORE MAJORS AND CAREERS

- A mention of being smart about **online postings** has been added, as employers are doing more Internet searches to screen potential job candidates.

- The discussion on **workplace trends** is refocused to reflect recent economic events and career marketability, including new trends such as "green" jobs and international communication.

- A new Peak Performer Profile on **Ursula Burns** explains how the CEO of Xerox made strategic academic and career choices based on her interests and strengths.

- The **informational interview** has been revised into two activities: one on finding out more about potential careers and another on getting a foot in the door at a potential employer.

Ancillaries

McGraw-Hill Connect*Plus+*™ Student Success is a Web-based assignment and assessment platform that gives students the means to better connect with their coursework, with their instructors, and with the important concepts that they will need to know for success now and in the future. With **Connect*Plus+* Student Success**, instructors can deliver assignments, quizzes, and tests online. Nearly all the questions from the text are presented in an auto-gradable format and tied to the text's learning outcomes. Instructors can edit existing questions and author entirely new problems. Track individual student performance—by question, assignment, or in relation to the class overall—with detailed grade reports. Integrate grade reports easily with Learning Management Systems (LMS) such as WebCT and Blackboard®. And much more. By choosing **Connect*Plus*+ Student Success**, instructors are providing their students with a powerful tool for improving academic performance and truly mastering course material.

Connect*Plus*+ Student Success allows students to practice important skills at their own pace and on their own schedule. Importantly, students' assessment results and instructors' feedback are all saved online—so students can continually review their progress and plot their course to success.

Connect*Plus*+ is a research-based, interactive assignment and assessment platform that incorporates cognitive science to customize the learning process. The online platform is based on McGraw-Hill's extensive, ongoing research instructional processes and students' study habits and includes a variety of digital learning tools that enable instructors to easily customize courses and allow students to learn and master content and succeed in the course. These tools, which are designed to allow students to engage with the relevant course content at their own pace, include

- online assignments with immediate, automatic feedback
- searchable recorded class lectures that can be accessed by computer or mobile device
- interactive e-books that dynamically engage students to improve learning and retention
- concise, visual snapshots of student performance
- tools that enable instructors to create and manage assignments online
- a "smart software" adaptive assessment tool that diagnoses what a student has and has not mastered, as well as how much time additional study time is needed

We have designed an extensive and convenient ancillary package that focuses on course goals, allows you to maximize your time with students, and helps students understand, retain, and apply the main principles.

- **Annotated Instructor's Edition (AIE) (0-07-747154-7).** The AIE contains the full text of the student edition of the text, along with instructional strategies that reinforce and enhance the core concepts. Notes and tips in the margin provide topics for discussion, teaching tips for hands-on and group activities, and suggestions for further reading.

- **Instructor's Resource Manual and Test Bank (0-07-747159-8).** Included in this extensive resource are chapter goals and outlines, teaching tips, additional activities, and essay exercises. Also provided is an extensive section on course planning, with sample syllabi. The extensive test bank includes matching, multiple choice, true/false, and short answer questions. The test bank is also available in an electronic format that can be downloaded from the text's Web site. The kit also includes unique resource guides that give instructors and administrators the tools to retain students and maximize the success of the course, using topics and principles that last a lifetime. Specialized sections include
  - Facilitator's Guide
  - Tools for Time Management
  - Establishing Peer Support Groups
  - Developing a Career Portfolio
  - Involving the Faculty Strategy
  - Capitalizing on Your School's Graduates
- **Online Learning Center Web site (www.mhhe.com/ferrett8e).** The book's Web site includes features for both instructors and students—downloadable ancillaries, Web links, student quizzing, Student Retention Kit, additional information on topics of interest, and much more. Access to the Web site is provided free to students.
- **Customized text options.** *Peak Performance* can be customized to suit your needs. The text can be abbreviated for shorter courses or can be expanded to include semester schedules, campus maps, additional essays, activities, or exercises, along with other materials specific to your curriculum or situation. Contact your McGraw-Hill sales representative for more information or:

Canada: 1-905-430-5034

United States: 1-800-446-8979

E-mail: FYE@mcgraw-hill.com

Thank You

We would like to thank the many instructors whose insightful comments and suggestions provided us with inspiration and the ideas that were incorporated into this new edition:

Advisory Board

Connie Warner	Baker College
Fred Martinez	Richland College
Steve Snyder	Baker College

Reviewers

Gabriel Adona	San Diego Mesa College
Lynn Akeo	Leeward College
Kendra Bolen	Marshall Community and Technical College
Daniel Brewster	Charter College
Carmen Burds	El Paso Community College
Terry Rafter Carles	Valencia Community College
Pauline Clark	West Valley College
Mary Corey	Baker College
Stephani Cuddie	Florida Institute of Technology
Charles Dickey	Beal College
Joseph Dulak	St. Mary's University of Minnesota
Sherry Dupree	Santa Fe Community College
Lisa Enright	Rivier College
Tammie Fogal	Central Michigan University
Mercedes Alafriz Gordon	Brookline College
Laurenne Grimes	Lorain County Community College
Denise Halel	St. Charles Community College
Rhonda Hall	University of West Virginia
Lois Hassan	Henry Ford Community College
Christina Havlin	ECPI
Korin Hays	McCann School of Business and Technology
James Henderson	University of Northern Colorado
Kim Jameson	Oklahoma City Community College
Gary John	Richland College
Deborah Ann Kosydar	McCann School of Business
Paul Lerdahl	Salt Lake Community College
Carrie Lunceford	University of Texas-San Antonio
John Luukkonen	TCI
Richard Marshall	Palm Beach State College
Diane Mazza	Caldwell Community College and Technical Institute
Cheryl McKnight	California State University-Dominguez Hills
Margaret Meth	William Paterson University
Raymond Navarro	California State University-San Bernardino
Greg Ochoa	Shippensburg University of Pennsylvania
Jody Owen	South Dakota State University
Elaine Pascale	Suffolk University
Gregory Pauley	Moberly Area Community College
Margaret Pinajian	County College of Morris
Kathleen Premo	Saint Bonaventure University
Adrian Rios	Newbridge College
Vicki Savino	Empire College
Phyllis Seelye	Baker College
Jacqueline Smith	Coachoma Community College
Otis Stanford	Coachoma Community College
T. C. Stuwe	Salt Lake Community College
Rosario-Montes Sutton	Grand Rapids Community College
Dorothy Swearingen	Pellissippi State Community College
Leah Tewell	Baker College
Susan Villalobos	North Lake College
Marilyn Wells	Brown Mackie College-Akron
Jamie Wyatt	Brown Mackie College-Akron

Also, I would like to gratefully acknowledge the contributions of the McGraw-Hill editorial staff—specifically, Vicki Malinee, for her considerable effort, suggestions, ideas, and insights.

—Sharon K. Ferrett

SCANS: Secretary's Commission on Achieving Necessary Skills

Competency Chart

Competencies and Foundations	Peak Performance Chapters That Address SCANS Competencies
Resources: Identifies, Organizes, Plans, and Allocates Resources	
• Managing time	Chapter 3, Take 3
• Managing money	Chapter 4
• Managing space	Chapters 3, 13
• Managing people	Chapter 2, 12
• Managing materials	Chapters 3, 4, 5, 6, 9
• Managing facilities	Chapters 4, 5, 9, 11
Information: Acquires and Uses Information	
• Acquiring information	Chapters 4, 5, 6, 9
• Evaluating information	Chapters 7, 8, 9
• Organizing and maintaining information	Chapters 3, 4, 7, 8, 9, 10, Take 3
• Using computer to process	Chapters 4, 9
Systems: Understands Complex Interrelationships	
• Understanding systems	All chapters
• Designing systems	Chapters 5, 6
• Monitoring systems	Chapters 3, 5, 6, 11
• Correcting systems	Chapters 3, 4, 5, 10
Interpersonal Skills: Works with Others	
• Positive attitudes	Chapters 2, 12, 13
• Self-control	Chapters 2, 12, 13
• Goal setting	Chapters 1, 2, 3
• Teamwork	Chapters 2, 12, 13
• Responsibility	Chapters 2, 12, 13
• Stress management	Chapter 11
Technology: Works with a Variety of Technologies	
• Selecting technology	Chapters 9, 14, Tech for Success
• Applying technology	Chapters 4, 9, 14, Tech for Success
• Maintaining technology	Chapters 9, 14
• Solving problems	Chapter 9, 10
• Staying current in technology	Chapters 4, 9, 14

Source: United States Department of Labor, 1992.

SCANS: Secretary's Commission on Achieving Necessary Skills (concluded)

Competencies and Foundations	Peak Performance Chapters That Address SCANS Competencies
Personal Qualities	
• Responsibility, character, integrity, positive habits, self-management, self-esteem, sociability	Chapters 2, 12, 13
Basic Skills	
• Reading—locates, understands, and interprets written information in prose and in documents, such as manuals, graphs, and schedules	Chapter 6, 9
• Writing—communicates thoughts, ideas, information, and messages in writing and creates documents, such as letters, directions, manuals, reports, graphs, and flowcharts	Chapter 9
• Arithmetic/mathematics—performs basic computations and approaches practical problems by choosing appropriately from a variety of mathematical techniques	Chapter 10
• Listening—receives, attends to, interprets, and responds to verbal messages and other cues	Chapters 5, 12
Thinking Skills	
• Creative thinking—generates new ideas	Chapter 10, Personal Evaluation Notebooks, Think Fast
• Decision making—specifies goals and constraints, generates alternatives, considers risks, and evaluates and chooses best alternative	Chapter 10, Case Study, Personal Evaluation Notebooks, Think Fast
• Listening—receives, attends to, interprets, and responds to verbal messages and other cues	Chapters 5, 12
• Seeing things in the mind's eye—organizes and processes symbols, pictures, graphs, objects, and other information	All chapters, with a strong emphasis in Chapter 10
• Knowing how to learn—uses efficient learning techniques to acquire and apply new knowledge and skills	Chapter 1
• Reasoning—discovers a rule or principle underlying the relationship between two or more objects and applies it when solving a problem	Chapter 10

Dear Student

Many of my students have told me I'm like a cheerleader, rooting them on to success. I know they all have what it takes to succeed, even when they have their own doubts. Why? Because I've been there, too. As I stepped onto the beautiful University of Michigan campus, I questioned whether I belonged. My small farming community seemed far away and I felt out of place. Many students had come from fancy prep schools and wealthy families. I had gone to a one-room schoolhouse and then to a tiny high school in the thumb of Michigan. I was putting myself through college with part-time jobs and baby-sitting in exchange for room and board. *Would I be able to make it here?*

Even though I was afraid, I was confident and determined. My experiences as a farm kid made me a hard worker, and I knew that no amount of effort was too great to achieve the goal of graduating from college. I was incredibly grateful for the opportunity to go to college, and I wanted to make my parents proud, since they never had the choices that I had. I visualized myself as a college graduate and held that image firmly in my mind when I was discouraged.

After I graduated with honors, I earned a teaching credential and taught for a year in the same one-room schoolhouse that I (and my father) attended. I saved enough money to travel to Europe and return to school to earn a master's degree and Ph.D. I would have never dreamed of being a college professor and an administrator when I was in high school, but, at only 24 years old, I accepted a dean position at Delta College, a large community college in Michigan. A few years later, I moved to California as Dean of Continuing Education at Humboldt State University. As a professor and an academic advisor, I developed a new program in student success. That project launched this book and became my life's work.

Throughout this book, we talk about the attributes of a "peak performer" and attempt to define success—in school, career, and life. However, in the end, *you* have to define success for yourself. Only you can determine what drives you, what makes you happy, and what will become your own life's work.

If I could give you only three pieces of advice as you journey to find your passion in life, they would be

1. **Keep it simple.** We want to do and be everything for everyone. However, success comes from a clear focus on what you value most. Don't complicate your life with unnecessary distractions, and continually take small steps to get where you want to be.

2. **Realize you are smarter than you think.** Intelligence is not defined by a score on a test but rather by how you use all your experiences, abilities, resources, and opportunities to improve your situation and find what fulfills you. Don't ever believe anyone who says you can't accomplish something for lack of skill, talent, or lot in life. You can.

3. **Be your own best friend.** Too often we dwell on the inconveniences in life rather than being grateful for the fortunes and opportunities we do have. Whenever you find yourself creating excuses, blaming others, or feeling down or hopeless, be your own cheerleader and resolve that you can—and will—succeed.

And when you need a little help developing your own "cheer" along the way, please drop me an e-mail at **sharonferrett@gmail.com.** *I believe in you!*

—**Sharon K. Ferrett**

Getting Started

Congratulations! You are about to start or restart an amazing journey of opportunity, growth, and adventure. You may be at this point in your life for a number of reasons: You may be furthering your education right after high school; you may be focusing on a specific career or trade and want to acquire the appropriate skills or certification; or you may be returning to school after years in the workforce, needing additional skills or just looking for a change.

Whatever your reasons, this is an opportunity for you to learn new things, meet new people, acquire new skills, and better equip yourself both professionally and personally for the years ahead. This book is designed to get you started on that journey by helping you (1) learn how you learn best—and incorporate new ways to learn; (2) maximize available resources and seek out new opportunities; (3) relate what you are exploring now to future success on the job; and (4) strive to become the best person you can be.

Now that you have your book in hand, you are ready to get started. Or are you really ready? What

else should you be aware of at this point? You may have already attended a basic orientation session where you learned about school and community resources and program requirements. Going through orientation, meeting with your advisor, and reviewing your catalog will help you get oriented. Additionally, this quick review is designed to outline the essentials that you will want to know, so that you not only survive but also make your first year a success. **Peak Progress 1** provides a handy checklist for the essential tasks you need to consider and accomplish the first week of school. Add to this list any tasks that are unique to your situation or school.

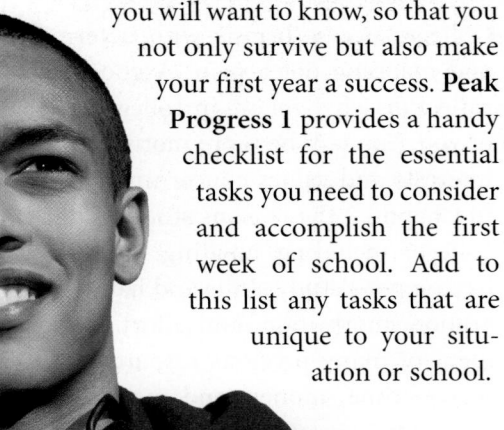

Peak Progress

①

Tasks to Accomplish the First Week of School

- Attend orientation and meet with an advisor. Ask questions and determine available resources. (See **Peak Progress 2** for questions to ask.)
- Register and pay fees on time.
- Set up an e-mail account.
- Check deadlines and procedures. *Never* just quit going to class.
- Buy books and keep receipts. Establish a record-keeping system.
- Find out the location of classrooms, parking, and campus resources.
- Know expectations and requirements. Get a syllabus for each class. E-mail instructors for clarification.
- Create an organized study area. Post instructors' names, office locations, and hours, as well as important deadlines.
- Form study teams and exchange e-mails and phone numbers. Get to know instructors and other students.
- Explore resources, such as the library, learning skills center, health center, and advising center.
- Go to all classes on time and sit in the front row.

Why Are You Here?

College success begins with determining your goals and mapping out a plan. A good place to start is to reflect on why you are in college and what is expected of you. You will be more motivated if you clarify your interests and values concerning college. You will read in Chapter 2 the reasons students don't graduate from college, including juggling multiple responsibilities, having poor study skills and habits, and lacking preparation, motivation, and effort. College is a commitment of many precious resources you can't afford to waste—time, money, and mental energies. Consider the following statements and your reasons for being in college, and share this in your study team or with students you meet the first few weeks of class:

- I value education and want to be a well-educated person.
- I want to get a good job that leads to a well-paying career.
- I want to learn new ideas and skills and grow personally and professionally.
- I want to get away from home and be independent.

- I want to make new friends.
- I want to have new experiences and stretch myself.
- I want to fulfill my goal of being a college-educated person.

Jot down what you want from college and why you're motivated to get it.

_____

_____

_____

_____

List four values that are most important to you and how college will help you achieve them.

1. _____

    _____

2. _____

    _____

3. _____

    _____

4. _____

    _____

What You Need to Know and Should Not Be Afraid to Ask

You don't want to learn the hard way that you need one more class to graduate, only to find it's offered only once a year (and you just missed it). Make your time with your advisor productive by getting answers to important questions that will help you map out your coursework. **Peak Progress 2** provides a handy checklist of common questions to get you started.

What Do You Need to Do to Graduate?

You will be more motivated and confident if you understand graduation requirements. Requirements vary among schools. Don't rely on the advice of friends. Go to orientation and meet with your advisor early and often. Check out the catalog and make certain you know what is required to graduate. Fill in the following:

GRADUATION REQUIREMENTS

- Number of units required:
- General education requirements:
- Curriculum requirements:
- Residency at the school:
- Departmental major requirements:
- Cumulative GPA required:
- Other requirements, such as special writing tests and classes:

How to Register for Classes

Find out if you have an access code and the earliest date you can register. Meet with your advisor, carefully select classes, and review general education and major requirements. Add electives that keep you active and interested. Make certain that you understand why you are taking each class, and check with your advisor that it is meeting certain requirements.

Many colleges have a purge date and, if you miss the deadline to pay your fees, your class schedule is canceled. You may not be able to get into classes and may have to pay a late fee.

Know the Grading System

Learn the minimum grade point average (GPA) that you need to maintain good standing. If your GPA falls below 2.0, you may be placed on academic probation. The GPA is calculated according to the number of credit hours each course represents and your grade in the course. In the traditional system, $A = 4$ points, $B = 3$ points, $C = 2$ points, $D = 1$ point, and $F = 0$ points (your school may have a different system, so ask to be sure). To calculate your GPA, first determine your total number of points. Following is an example:

Course	Grade Achieved	Number of Credit Hours	Points
Political Science	C	2	$2 \times 2 = 4$
Psychology	B	3	$3 \times 3 = 9$
English	A	3	$4 \times 3 = 12$
Personal Finance	A	1	$4 \times 1 = 4$
TOTAL		9	29

Then, to arrive at your GPA, you must divide your total points by your total number of credit hours:

GPA = total points divided by total number of credit hours

Thus, in this example,

GPA = 29 divided by 9 = 3.22

Monitor your progress and meet with your instructors often, but especially at midterm and before final exams. Ask what you can do to improve your grade.

Adding or Dropping Classes

Ask about the deadlines for adding and dropping classes. This is generally done in the first few weeks of classes. A withdrawal after the deadline could result in a failing grade. Also make certain before you drop the class that

- You will not fall below the required units for financial aid.
- You will not fall below the required units for playing sports.
- If required, the class is offered again before you plan to graduate.
- You don't need the class or units to meet graduation requirements.
- You are meeting important deadlines.

Peak Progress

The Most Common Questions Students Ask Advisors

1. What classes do I need to take for general education?
2. Can a course satisfy both a general education and a major requirement?
3. Can I take general elective (GE) courses for Credit/No Credit if I also want to count them for my major?
4. How can I remove an *F* grade from my record?
5. What is the deadline for dropping courses?
6. Can I drop a course after the deadline?
7. What is an "educational leave"?
8. What is the difference between a withdrawal and a drop?
9. Do I need to take any placement tests?
10. Are there other graduation requirements, such as a writing exam?
11. Where do I find out about financial aid?
12. Is there a particular order in which I should take certain courses?
13. Are there courses in which I must earn a *C*– or better?
14. How do I change my major?
15. Which of my transfer courses will count?
16. What is the minimum residency requirement for a bachelor's degree?
17. Is there a GPA requirement for the major?
18. Is there a tutoring program available?
19. If I go on exchange, how do I make sure that courses I take at another university will apply toward my degree here?
20. What is a major contract, and when should I get one?
21. When do I need to apply for graduation?
22. How do I apply for graduation?
23. What is a degree check?
24. What is the policy for incomplete grades?
25. Can I take major courses at another school and transfer them here?
26. As a nonresident, how can I establish residency in this state?
27. How do I petition to substitute a class?
28. Once I complete my major, are there other graduation requirements?
29. What is academic probation?
30. Is there any employment assistance available?
31. Is there a mentor program available in my major department?
32. Are there any internships or community service opportunities related to my major?

- You talk with the instructor first.
- You talk with your advisor.

Never simply walk away from your classes. The instructor will not drop you, nor will you be dropped automatically if you stop going to class at any time during the semester. It is your responsibility to follow-up and complete required forms.

An Incomplete Grade

If you miss class due to illness or an emergency, you may be able to take an incomplete if you can't finish a project or miss a test. Check out this option with your instructor before you drop a class. Sign a written agreement to finish the work at a specific time and stay in touch with the instructor through e-mail and phone.

Withdrawing or Taking a Leave of Absence

Some students withdraw because they don't have the money, they can't take time off from work, they lack child care, or they are having difficulty in classes. Before you drop out of college, talk with your advisor and see if you can get the support and motivation to succeed. If you want to take a leave to travel, want to explore other schools, are ill, or just need to take a break, make certain that you take a leave of absence for a semester, a year, or longer. Taking a leave means that you do not have to reapply for admission, and generally you fall under the same category as when you entered school.

Transferring

Before you transfer to another school, know the requirements, which courses are transferable, and if there is a residency requirement. If you plan to transfer from a 2-year school to a 4-year school, your advisor will help you clarify the requirements.

Expectations of Instructors

Most instructors will hand out a syllabus that out-lines their expectations for the class. Understand and clarify those expectations and the course requirements. **Worksheet 1** on page xxxii is a convenient guide to complete when checking your progress with your instructor.

The Best Strategies for Success in School

In this text, we will focus on a number of strategies that will help you determine and achieve your goals. **The Best Strategies for Success in School** provides a comprehensive list of the proven strategies you will find woven throughout this text. Apply these to your efforts in school now and through your course of study. You will find that not only are they key to your progress in school, but also they will help you develop skills, behaviors, and habits that are directly related to success on the job and in life in general.

The Best Strategies for Success in School

1. **Attend every class.** Going to every class engages you with the subject, the instructor, and other students. Think of the tuition you are paying and what it costs to cut a class.

2. **Be an active participant.** Show that you are engaged and interested by being on time, sitting in front, participating, asking questions, and being alert.

3. **Go to class prepared.** Preview all reading assignments. Highlight key ideas and main concepts, and put question marks next to anything you don't understand.

4. **Write a summary.** After you preview the chapter, close the book and write a short summary. Go back and fill in with more details. Do this after each reading.

5. **Know your instructors.** Choose the best instructors, call them by their preferred names and titles, e-mail them, and visit them during office hours. Arrive early for class and get to know them better.

6. **Know expectations.** Read the syllabus for each course and clarify the expectations and requirements, such as tests, papers, extra credit, and attendance.

7. **Join a study team.** You will learn more by studying with others than by reading alone. Make up tests, give summaries, and teach others.

8. **Organize your study space.** Create a quiet space, with a place for school documents, books, catalogs, a dictionary, a computer, notes, pens, and a calendar. Eliminate distractions by closing the door, and focus on the task at hand.

9. **Map out your day, week, and semester.** Write down all assignments, upcoming tests, meetings, daily goals, and priorities on your calendar. Review your calendar and goals each day. Do not socialize until your top priorities are completed.

10. **Get help early.** Know and use all available campus resources. Go to the learning center, counseling center, and health center; get a tutor; and talk with your advisor and instructors about concerns. Get help at the first sign of trouble.

11. **Give school your best effort.** Commit yourself to being extra disciplined the first 3 weeks—buy your textbooks early; take them to class; get to class early; keep up on your reading; start your projects, papers, and speeches early; and make school a top priority.

12. **Use note cards.** Jot down formulas and key words. Carry them with you and review them during waiting time and right before class.

13. **Review often.** Review and fill in notes immediately after class and again within 24 hours. Active reading, note taking, and reviewing are the steps that improve recall.

14. **Study everywhere.** Review your note cards before class, while you wait for class to begin, while waiting in line, before bed, and so on. Studying for short periods of time is more effective than cramming late at night.

15. **Summarize out loud.** Summarize chapters and class notes out loud to your study team. This is an excellent way to learn.

(continued)

The Best Strategies for Success in School

16. **Organize material.** You cannot remember information if it isn't organized. Logical notes help you understand and remember. Use a mind map for outlining key facts and supporting material.

17. **Dig out information.** Focus on main ideas, key words, and overall understanding. Make questions out of chapter headings, review chapter questions, and always read summaries.

18. **Look for associations.** Improve memory by connecting patterns and by linking concepts and relationships. Define, describe, compare, classify, and contrast concepts.

19. **Ask questions.** What is the obvious? What needs to be determined? How can you illustrate the concept? What information is the same and what is different? How does the lecture relate to the textbook?

20. **Pretest yourself.** This will serve as practice and reduces anxiety. This is most effective in your study team.

21. **Study when you are most alert.** Know your energy level and learning preference. Maximize reviewing during daytime hours.

22. **Turn in all assignments on time.** Give yourself an extra few days to review papers and practice speeches.

23. **Make learning physical.** Read difficult textbooks out loud and standing up. Draw pictures, write on a chalkboard, and use visuals. Tape lectures and go on field trips. Integrate learning styles.

24. **Review first drafts with your instructor.** Ask for suggestions and follow them to the letter.

25. **Pay attention to neatness.** Focus on details and turn in all assignments on time. Use your study team to read and exchange term papers. Proofread several times.

26. **Practice!** Nothing beats effort. Practice speeches until you are comfortable and confident, and visualize yourself being successful.

27. **Recite and explain.** Pretend that you are the instructor and recite main concepts. What questions would you put on a test? Give a summary to others in your study group. Make up sample test questions in your group.

28. **Take responsibility.** Don't make excuses about missing class or assignments or about earning failing grades. Be honest and take responsibility for your choices and mistakes and learn from them.

29. **Ask for feedback.** When you receive a grade, be reflective and ask questions: "What have I learned from this?" "How did I prepare for this?" "How can I improve this grade?" "Did I put in enough effort?" Based on what you learn, what new goals will you set for yourself?

30. **Negotiate for a better grade before grades are sent in.** Find out how you are doing at midterm and ask what you can do to raise your grade. Offer to do extra projects or retake tests.

31. **Always do extra credit.** Raise your grade by doing more than is required or *expected*. Immerse yourself in the subject, and find meaning and understanding.

(continued)

The Best Strategies for Success in School

32. **Take responsibility for your education.** You can do well in a class even if your instructor is boring or insensitive. Ask yourself what you can do to make the class more effective (study team, tutoring, active participation). Be flexible and adapt to your instructor's teaching style.

33. **Develop positive qualities.** Think about the personal qualities that you need most to overcome obstacles, and work on developing them each day.

34. **Stay healthy.** You cannot do well in school or in life if you are ill. Invest time in exercising, eating healthy, and getting enough sleep, and avoid alcohol, cigarettes, and drugs.

35. **Dispute negative thinking.** Replace it with positive, realistic, helpful self-talk, and focus on your successes. Don't be a perfectionist. Reward yourself when you make small steps toward achieving goals.

36. **Organize your life.** Hang up your keys in the same place, file important material, and establish routines that make your life less stressful.

37. **Break down projects.** Overcome procrastination by breaking overwhelming projects into manageable chunks. Choose a topic, do a rough draft, write a summary, preview a chapter, do a mind map, and organize the tools you need (notes, books, outline).

38. **Make school your top priority.** Working too many hours can cut into study time. Learn to balance school, your social life, and work, so that you're effective.

39. **Meet with your advisor to review goals and progress.** Ask questions about requirements, and don't drop and add classes without checking on the consequences. Develop a good relationship with your advisor and your instructors.

40. **Be persistent.** Whenever you get discouraged, just keep following positive habits and strategies and you will succeed. Success comes in small, consistent steps. Be patient and keep plugging away.

41. **Spend less than you make.** Don't go into debt for new clothes, a car, CDs, gifts, travel, or other things you can do without. Education is the best investment you can make in future happiness and job success. Learn to save.

42. **Use critical thinking, and think about the consequences of your decisions.** Don't be impulsive about money, sex, smoking, or drugs. Don't start a family until you are emotionally and financially secure. Practice impulse control by imagining how you would feel after making certain choices.

43. **Don't get addicted.** Addictions are a tragic waste of time. Ask yourself if you've ever known anyone whose life was better for being addicted. Do you know anyone whose life has been destroyed by alcohol and other drugs? This one decision will affect your life forever.

44. **Know who you are and what you want.** Visit the career center and talk with a career counselor about your interests, values, goals, strengths, personality, learning style, and career possibilities. Respect your style and set up conditions that create results.

(continued)

The Best Strategies for Success in School *(concluded)*

45. **Use creative problem solving.** Think about what went right and what went wrong this semester. What could you have done that would have helped you be more successful? What are new goals you want to set for next semester? What are some creative ways to overcome obstacles? How can you solve problems instead of letting them persist?

46. **Contribute.** Look for opportunities to contribute your time and talents. What could you do outside of class that would complement your education and serve others?

47. **Take advantage of your texts' resources.** Many textbooks have accompanying Web sites, CDs, and study materials designed to help you succeed in class. Visit this book's Web site at **www.mhhe.com/ferrett8e.**

48. **Respect yourself and others.** Be supportive, tolerant, and respectful. Look for ways to learn about other cultures and different views and ways to expand your friendships. Surround yourself with people who are positive and successful, who value learning, and who support and respect you and your goals.

49. **Focus on gratitude.** Look at the abundance in your life—your health, family, friends, and opportunities. You have so much going for you to help you succeed.

50. **Just do it.** Newton's first law of motion says that things in motion tend to stay in motion, so get started and keep working on your goals!

Progress Assessment

Course: _____

Instructor: _____

Office: _____   Office hours: _____

Phone: _____   E-mail: _____

1. How am I doing in this class?

   _____

   _____

   _____

2. What grades have you recorded for me thus far?

   _____

   _____

   _____

3. Are there any adjustments that I should make?

   _____

   _____

   _____

4. Am I missing any assignments?

   _____

   _____

   _____

5. Do you have any suggestions as to how I can improve my performance or excel in your class?

   _____

   _____

   _____

1

Be a Lifelong Learner

LEARNING OUTCOMES

In this chapter, you will learn to

1.1 List the characteristics of a peak performer

1.2 Identify self-management techniques for academic, job, and personal achievement

1.3 Create a personal mission statement

1.4 Identify skills and competencies for school and job success

1.5 Integrate learning styles and personality types

1.6 Describe the Adult Learning Cycle

SELF-MANAGEMENT

"It's the first day of class and I'm already overwhelmed. How will I manage all this?"

Are you feeling like this? Are you afraid you will never achieve your goals, or do you even know what your goals are? Instead of focusing on negative feelings, channel your energies into positive results and envision yourself being successful. In this chapter, you will learn about "self-management" and many tools—such as self-assessment, critical thinking, visualization, and reflection—you can use to become a success in all facets of life.

JOURNAL ENTRY What are you hoping to gain from your college experience? How does earning a college degree help you both personally and professionally? Consider answering the question "Why am I here?" Is your answer part of a bigger life plan? In **Worksheet 1.1** on page 38, take a stab at answering those questions. Think about the obstacles you may have faced to get to this point and what you did to overcome them. In this chapter, you'll discover that successful, lifelong learning begins with learning about yourself.

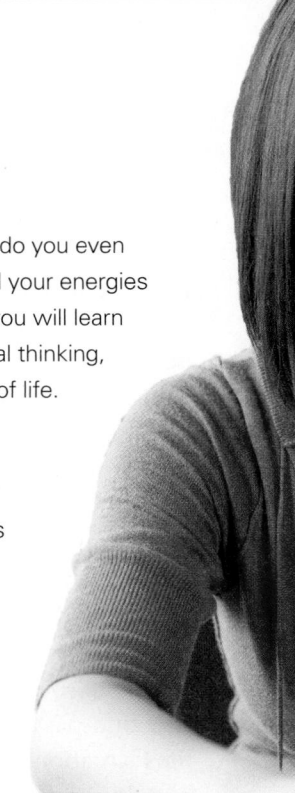

earning is a lifelong journey. People who are successful—peak performers—are on this journey. We are constantly faced with many types of changes—economic, technological, societal, and so on. These changes require us to continually learn new skills in school, on the job, and throughout life. You will meet these challenges through your study and learning strategies, in your methods of performing work-related tasks, and even in the way you view your personal life and lifestyle.

Lately, you may have been asking yourself, "Who am I?" "Why am I in school?" "What course of study should I take?" "What kind of job do I want?" "Where should I go to school?" or "What should I do with my life?" These are all important questions. Some you may have already answered—and some of those answers may change by tomorrow, next week, or next year. And that's OK. This is all part of a continual process—of learning about yourself and what you want out of life.

As you journey on the road to becoming a peak performer, this book will show you methods that will help you master self-management, set goals, and achieve success. One of the first steps is self-assessment. Self-assessment requires seeing yourself objectively. This helps you determine where you are now and where you want to go. Then, by assessing how you learn—including your learning and personality styles—you will discover how to maximize your learning potential.

The many exercises, journal entries, and portfolio worksheets throughout this text support one of its major themes—that success in school and success in your career are definitely connected! The skills, competencies, and behaviors you learn and practice today will guide your marketability and flexibility throughout your career, and will promote success in your personal life.

What Is a "Peak Performer"?

Peak performers come from all lifestyles, ages, cultures, and genders. Some are famous, such as many of the people profiled in this book. However, anyone can become a peak performer by setting goals and developing appropriate attitudes and behaviors to achieve desired results. Peak performers become masters at creating excellence by focusing on results. They know how to change their negative thoughts into positive, realistic affirmations. They focus on their long-term goals and know how to break down goals into daily action steps. They are not perfect or successful overnight. They learn to face the fear of making mistakes and working through them. They use the whole of their intelligence and abilities.

Every day, thousands of individuals quietly overcome incredible setbacks, climb over huge obstacles, and reach within themselves to find inner strength. They are successful because they know they possess the personal power to produce results and find passion in what they contribute to life. They are masters, not victims, of life's situations. They control the quality of their lives. In short, they are their own best friend.

Peak performers

- Take responsibility for their actions, behaviors, and decisions
- Know their learning styles and preferences and how to maximize their learning
- Identify and acknowledge their strengths and weaknesses
- Take risks and move beyond secure comfort zones
- Use critical thinking to solve problems creatively
- Make sound judgments and decisions
- Are effective at time management and self-management
- Seek out and utilize available resources
- Build supportive relationships
- Continually acquire new skills and competencies
- Remain confident and resilient when faced with doubt and fear
- Are motivated to overcome barriers
- Take small, consistent steps that lead to long-term goals

Self-Management: The Key to Reaching Your Peak

What is a primary strength of every peak performer? A positive attitude! Peak performers have a positive attitude toward their studies, their work, and virtually everything they do. This fundamental inclination to view life as a series of opportunities is a key to their success. Does this describe how you approach each day? Check your attitude by completing **Personal Evaluation Notebook 1.1** on page 4.

Anyone can develop the attitude of a peak performer, and it is not even difficult. It simply involves restructuring thought patterns. Instead of dwelling on problems, create options and alternatives to keep you on track. Redirecting your thought patterns in this way will give you more drive and make every task seem more meaningful and less daunting.

A positive attitude is one of the many components of **self-management.** Are you responsible for your own success? Do you believe you can control your own destiny? Think of self-management as a toolkit filled with many techniques and skills you can use to keep you focused, overcome obstacles, and help you succeed.

Along with a positive attitude (which we will discuss further in Chapter 2), some very important techniques in this toolkit are self-assessment, critical thinking, visualization, and reflection.

Self-Assessment

One of the first steps in becoming a peak performer is **self-assessment.** Out of self-assessment comes recognition of the need to learn new tasks and subjects, relate well with others, set goals, manage time and stress, and create a balanced, productive life. Self-assessment requires facing the truth and seeing yourself objectively. It isn't easy to admit you procrastinate or lack certain skills. Even when talking about your strengths, you may feel embarrassed. However, honest self-assessment is the foundation for making positive changes.

Personal Evaluation Notebook

Am I a Positive Person?

Having a positive attitude is key to effective self-management. Most people believe they are generally positive but often are not truly aware of their negative self-talk or behavior. Answer the following questions to determine your overall outlook. After you have answered the questions, ask a friend, co-worker, or family member to answer the questions about you. Were your answers the same?

	Mostly True	Sometimes True	Rarely True
I tend to look for the good in everyone.			
I look for the positive in each situation.			
I do not take offense easily.			
I welcome constructive criticism and use it to improve.			
I am not easily irritated.			
I am not easily discouraged.			
I do not take everything personally.			
I take responsibility and face problems, even when it is not comfortable.			
I don't dwell on personal mistakes.			
I don't look for perfection in myself.			
I don't look for perfection in others.			
I do not depend on others to make me happy.			
I can forgive and move on.			
I do not become overly involved or disturbed by others' problems.			
I do not make snap judgments about people.			
I praise others for their accomplishments.			
I don't start conversations with something negative.			
I view mistakes as learning experiences.			
I know that, if Plan A doesn't work, Plan B will.			
I look forward to—not worry about—what tomorrow will bring.			

Self-assessment can help you

- Understand how you learn best
- Work with your strengths and natural preferences
- Balance and integrate your preferred learning style with other styles
- Use critical thinking and reasoning to make sound decisions
- Determine your interests and what you value
- Change ineffective patterns of thinking and behaving
- Create a positive and motivated state of mind
- Work more effectively with diverse groups of people
- Handle stress and conflict
- Earn better grades
- Determine and capitalize on your strengths
- Recognize irrational and negative thoughts and behavior
- Most important, focus on self-management and develop strategies that maximize your energies and resources

The world is full of people who believe that, if only the other person would change, everything would be fine. This book is not for them. Change is possible if you take responsibility for your thoughts and behaviors and are willing to practice new ways of thinking and behaving.

Self-assessment is very important for job success. Keep a portfolio of your awards, letters of appreciation, and training program certificates, as well as the projects you have completed. Assess your expectations in terms of the results achieved, and set goals for improvement. At the end of each chapter, you will find a Career Development Portfolio worksheet, which will help you relate your current activities to future job success. This portfolio will furnish you with a lifelong assessment tool for learning where you are and where you want to go and a place for documenting your results. This portfolio of skills and competencies will become your guide for remaining marketable and flexible throughout your career. Chapter 14 further explores how to develop an effective portfolio and prepare for your future career.

Critical Thinking Skills

Throughout this book, you will be asked to apply critical thinking skills to college courses and life situations. **Critical thinking** is a logical, rational, systematic thought process that is necessary in understanding, analyzing, and evaluating information in order to solve a problem or situation. Self-management involves using your critical thinking skills to make the best decisions and solve problems.

Using critical thinking helps you

- Suspend judgment until you have gathered facts and reflected on them
- Look for evidence that supports or contradicts your initial assumptions, opinions, and beliefs
- Adjust your opinions as new information and facts are known
- Ask questions, look for proof, and examine the problem closely

- Reject incorrect or irrelevant information
- Consider the source of the information
- Recognize and dispute irrational thinking

Since critical thinking determines the quality of the decisions you make, it is an important theme throughout this book. Chapter 10 is devoted to honing your critical thinking skills and practicing creative problem solving. You use your critical thinking skills every day—from analyzing and determining your learning styles to communicating effectively with family members, classmates, and co-workers.

Make sure to complete the exercises and activities throughout this book, including the **Personal Evaluation Notebook** exercises and the end-of-chapter **Worksheets. Think Fast** case studies throughout the text highlight that we are constantly making decisions that often have many repercussions—both positive and not-so-positive. Work through these to enhance your critical thinking skills.

Visualization and Affirmations

Visualization and affirmations are powerful self-management tools that help you focus on positive action and outcomes. **Visualization** is using your imagination to see your goals clearly and to envision yourself successfully engaging in new, positive behavior. **Affirmations** are the positive self-talk—the internal dialogue—you carry on with yourself. Affirmations counter self-defeating patterns of thought with more positive, hopeful, and realistic thoughts and feelings.

Using visualization and affirmations can help you relax, boost your confidence, change your habits, and perform better on exams, in speeches, or in sports. You can use them to rehearse for an upcoming event and practice coping with obstacles.

Through self-management, you demonstrate that you are not a victim or passive spectator; you are responsible for your self-talk, images, thoughts, and behaviors. When you observe and dispute negative thoughts and replace them with positive, and realistic thoughts, images, and behaviors, you are practicing critical thinking and creativity. You are taking charge of your life, focusing on what you can change, and working toward your goals.

You can practice visualization anytime and anywhere. For example, between classes, find a quiet place and close your eyes. It helps to use relaxation techniques, such as taking several deep breaths and seeing yourself calm, centered, and focused on your goals. This is especially effective when your mind starts to chatter and you feel overwhelmed, discouraged, or stressed. Visualize yourself graduating and walking across the stage to receive your diploma. See yourself achieving your goals. Say to yourself, "I feel calm and centered. I am taking action to meet my goals. I will use all available resources to be successful."

Reflection

Another important self-management tool is **reflection.** To reflect is to think about something in a purposeful way, with the intention of making connections, exploring options, and creating new meaning. Sometimes the process causes us to reconsider our previous knowledge and explore new alternatives and ideas.

Don't confuse reflection with daydreaming. Reflection is conscious, focused, purposeful—not simply letting your mind wander. When you reflect, you direct your thoughts and use imagination. Think of your mind as an ultra-powerful database. To reflect on a new experience is to search through this vast mental database to discover—or create—relationships between experiences: new and old, new and new, old and old. As you reorganize countless experiences stored in your mental database, it becomes more complex, more sophisticated, and ultimately more useful. This ongoing reorganization is a key component of your intellectual development; it integrates critical thinking, creative problem solving, and visualization.

A convenient way to reflect is simply to write down your thoughts, such as in a journal or on your computer. In this text is ample opportunity to practice reflection and critical thinking, including a **Journal Entry** exercise at the beginning of each chapter and a follow-up **Worksheet** at the end of each chapter.

Throughout the text, we'll explore additional self-management techniques that focus on certain aspects of your schoolwork, employment, and personal life. **Peak Progress 1.1** explores the ABC Method of Self-Management, a unique process to help you work through difficult situations and achieve positive results. It uses skills such as critical thinking, visualization, and reflection to find positive outcomes.

Peak Progress

1.1

The ABC Method of Self-Management

Earlier in this chapter, you answered some questions to determine if you approach everyday life with a positive attitude. Researchers believe that positive, optimistic thinking improves your skills for coping with challenges, which may also benefit your overall health and minimize the effects of stress.

What does "negative thinking" mean? If you are negative, you may tend to

- Filter out and eliminate all the good things that happen and focus on one bad thing
- Blame yourself (or someone else) automatically when something bad happens
- Anticipate the very worst that could happen
- See things as only good or bad—there's no middle ground
- Criticize yourself—either aloud or internally—in a way you would never do to someone else
- Waste time complaining, criticizing, reliving, and making up excuses—rather than creating solutions and moving on

The good news is that anyone can become a positive thinker. First, you need to become aware of patterns of defeating thoughts that are keeping you from achieving your goals. Then you can challenge and dispute these negative and irrational thoughts.

Clear thinking will lead to positive emotions. Let's say you have to give a speech in a class and speaking in public has caused you anxiety in the past. You might be saying to yourself, "I am terrified. I just hate getting up in front of people. I just can't do this." These negative beliefs and irrational thoughts can cause severe anxiety and are not based on clear thinking. You can direct your thoughts with positive statements that will dispel anxiety: "Public speaking is a skill that can be learned with practice and effort. I will not crumble from criticism and, even if I don't do well, I can learn with practice and from constructive feedback. I will explore all the resources available to help me and I'll do well in this class."

Self-management can be as easy as ABC. These simple steps help you manage your thoughts, feelings, and behaviors, so that you can create the results you want.

A = **Actual event:** State the actual situation that affected your emotions.
B = **Beliefs:** Describe your thoughts and beliefs about the situation that created these emotions and behavior.
C = **Challenge:** Dispute the negative thoughts and replace them with accurate and positive statements.

Let's use another example. When you read the quote on page 1 of this chapter, you might have felt the same

(continued)

The ABC Method of Self-Management (concluded)

way—overwhelmed. You are in a new situation, with many new expectations. Let's apply the ABC Method to focus your energies on developing a positive outcome. For example, you might say,

A = **Actual event:** "It's the first day of class and I have a mountain of reading and lecture notes to go over."

B = **Beliefs:** "What if I fail? What if I can't keep it all straight—learning styles, personalities, temperaments? These other people are probably a lot smarter than me. Maybe I should drop out."

C = **Challenge:** "Going to college is a big change, but I have handled new and stressful situations before. I know how to overcome feeling overwhelmed by breaking big jobs into small tasks. Everyone tells me work hard, and I know I'm talented and smart in many ways. I know that going to college is a good idea, and I want to graduate. I've handled transitions in the past, and I can handle these changes, too."

When you challenge negative thoughts and replace them with positive thinking, you feel energized, and your thoughts spiral upward: "I'm excited about discovering my learning and personality styles and how I can use them to my advantage. So many resources are available to me—my instructor, my classmates, the book's Web site. I will get to know at least one person in each of my classes, and I will take a few minutes to explore at least one resource at school that can provide support. I see myself confident and energized and achieving my goals."

In the end-of-chapter **Worksheets** throughout this text, you will find opportunities to practice the ABC Method of Self-Management, as well as the self-management exercises at **www.mhhe.com/ferrett8e.**

Discover Your Purpose: A Personal Mission Statement

At the beginning of the chapter, you were asked to write about why you're in school and how it relates to your life plan. In the Getting Started section, you also explored many reasons you are attending college, such as to learn new skills, get a well-paying job, and make new friends. (If you haven't read the Getting Started, now is the perfect time.) Thinking about the answers to these and related questions gets you started on writing your mission statement.

A mission statement looks at the big picture of your life, from which your goals and priorities will flow. This written statement (which can be one or more sentences) focuses on the contributions you want to make based on your values, philosophy, and principles. When you have a sense of purpose and direction, you will be more focused, and your life will have more meaning.

In one sense, you are looking at the end result of your life. What kind of a person do you want to be when you're 95? What legacy do you want to leave? What do you want to be remembered for? What—and who—do you think will be most important to you?

Here is one example of a mission statement: "I want to thrive in a health care career that allows me to use my creativity, grow in knowledge from mentors and colleagues, advance into leadership positions, make a positive impact on my profession, and provide an effective balance with personal interests, including having a family, traveling, and participating in my community."

Think about how a college education will help you fulfill your mission in life. If you have chosen a profession (for example, nursing or teaching), you may want to include the aspects of the career that interested you (such as helping others achieve healthy lifestyles or educating and nurturing young children). It does not need to be lengthy and detailed, but it should reflect your individuality. Focusing on your mission statement will help you overcome obstacles that will challenge you.

To write your mission statement, begin by answering these (or similar) questions:

1. What do I value most in life? (List those things.)

2. What is my life's purpose?

3. What legacy do I want to leave?

Now, considering the answers to those questions, draft a personal mission statement.

My mission statement:

In Chapter 2, we'll discuss how to use goals for motivation. Then, in Chapter 3, we'll explore how your mission statement and personal goals guide you to use your time effectively. You will also review your mission statement at the end of this text. Over the years, review and update your mission statement as you change and grow personally and professionally.

Skills for School and Job Success

What does it take to succeed in a job? Many of the skills and competencies that characterize a successful student also apply to a successful employee. Over the years, employers have told educators what skills they want employees to have, resulting in the Secretary's Commission on Achieving Necessary Skills (SCANS). **Figure 1.1** illustrates the skills and competencies that are necessary not only for job success but also

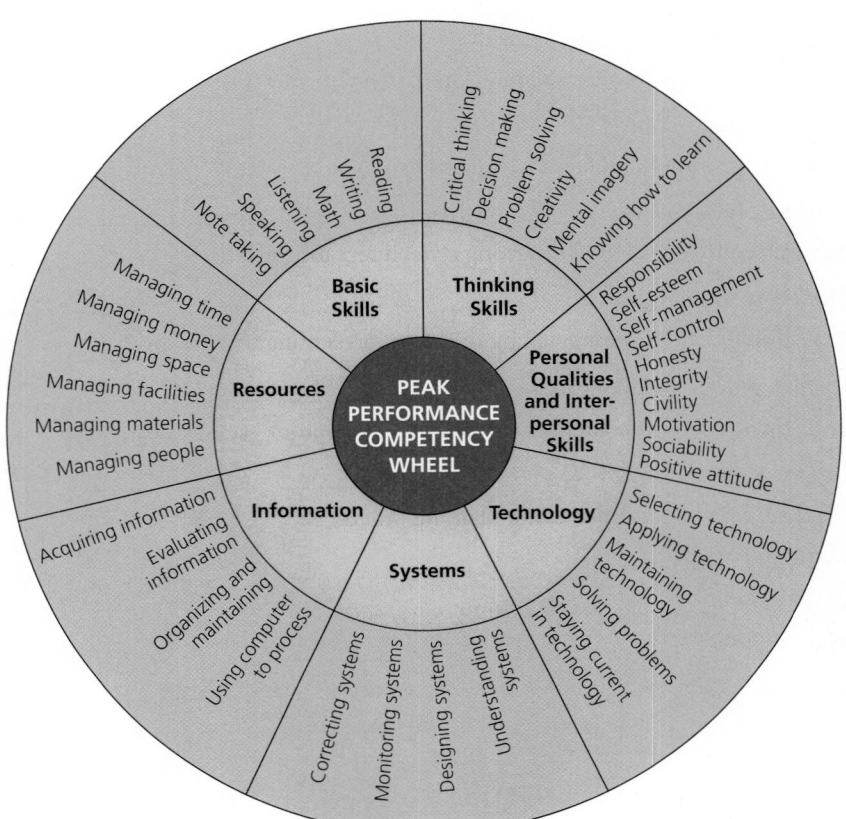

Figure 1.1
Peak Performance Competency Wheel

SCANS recommends these skills and competencies for job success. *Which of these skills have you been acquiring?*

Personal Evaluation Notebook

1.2

Peak Performance Self-Assessment Test

Assess your skills on a scale of 1 to 5 by placing a check mark. Examples are given for each. Review your answers to discover your strongest and weakest skills.

Area	Excellent 5	4	OK 3	2	Poor 1
1. Reading (e.g., comprehending; summarizing key points; reading for pleasure)	____	____	____	____	____
2. Writing (e.g., using correct grammar; presenting information clearly and concisely; documenting accurately)	____	____	____	____	____
3. Speaking (e.g., expressing main points in an interesting manner; controlling anxiety)	____	____	____	____	____
4. Mathematics (e.g., understanding basic principles and formulas; showing work)	____	____	____	____	____
5. Listening and note taking (e.g., staying focused and attentive; recording key points)	____	____	____	____	____
6. Critical thinking and reasoning (e.g., assessing facts; making decisions; linking material)	____	____	____	____	____
7. Creative problem solving (e.g., developing options; weighing alternatives)	____	____	____	____	____
8. Positive visualization (e.g., creating mental images to support goals)	____	____	____	____	____
9. Knowing how you learn (e.g., recognizing preferred learning style; integrating all styles)	____	____	____	____	____
10. Honesty and integrity (e.g., doing the right thing; telling the truth; presenting original work)	____	____	____	____	____
11. Positive attitude and motivation (e.g., being optimistic; identifying personal motivators; establishing goals)	____	____	____	____	____
12. Responsibility (e.g., keeping commitments; not blaming others)	____	____	____	____	____
13. Flexibility/ability to adapt to change (e.g., being open to new ideas; seeing the big picture)	____	____	____	____	____

(continued)

Personal Evaluation Notebook

1.2

Peak Performance Self-Assessment Test *(concluded)*

Area	Excellent 5	4	OK 3	2	Poor 1
14. Self-management and emotional control (e.g., taking ownership of thoughts and behaviors)	_____	_____	_____	_____	_____
15. Self-esteem and confidence (e.g., focusing on strengths; maintaining a positive self-image)	_____	_____	_____	_____	_____
16. Time management (e.g., setting priorities; planning; accomplishing tasks)	_____	_____	_____	_____	_____
17. Money management (e.g., budgeting; minimizing debt; saving)	_____	_____	_____	_____	_____
18. Management and leadership of people (e.g., inspiring; communicating; delegating; training)	_____	_____	_____	_____	_____
19. Interpersonal and communication skills (e.g., building rapport; listening; being an effective team member)	_____	_____	_____	_____	_____
20. Ability to work well with culturally diverse groups (e.g., respecting and celebrating differences)	_____	_____	_____	_____	_____
21. Organization and evaluation of information (e.g., assembling key points and ideas; summarizing; documenting)	_____	_____	_____	_____	_____
22. Understanding technology (e.g., using essential programs; troubleshooting basic problems)	_____	_____	_____	_____	_____
23. Commitment and effort (e.g., being persistent; working consistently toward goals)	_____	_____	_____	_____	_____

for school success. Determine how you would rate your skills by completing **Personal Evaluation Notebook 1.2**. Be honest and use critical thinking skills as you complete the assessment.

Discover Your Learning Style

Everyone processes information differently and not everyone learns the same way. There is no single right way to learn, but knowing your preferred learning style can increase your effectiveness in school or at work and can enhance your self-esteem. Knowing how you learn best can help you reduce frustration, focus on your strengths, and integrate various styles.

Integrate Both Sides of the Brain

Do you use both sides of your brain? "I use my whole brain!" you might answer—and, indeed, you do. However, you have a preference for using the left or right side of the brain for many mental and physical functions. In the 1960s, Dr. Roger Sperry and his colleagues discovered that the left and right sides of the brain specialize in different modes of thinking and perception. Dominant brain function may play a significant role in how you learn.

Studies show that the brain has two systems by which it classifies information. One is linguistic and factual (left brain), and one is visual and intuitive (right brain). Although they are interconnected, one system is usually more dominant. For example, if you are left-brain dominant, you probably like facts and order and think in a concrete manner. You use a logical, rational, and detailed thought process. If you are right-brain dominant, you are more inclined to use an intuitive and insightful approach to solving problems and processing new information. You are more comfortable with feelings and hunches and like to think abstractly and intuitively. **Figure 1.2** lists traits that are considered either left-brain or right-brain dominant.

Although you may favor one side of your brain, the key is to use all your brain power and integrate a variety of learning styles (which we'll explore next). Doing this enhances learning, memory, and recall.

Are You a Reader, Listener, or Doer?

Your brain allows you to experience the world through your senses. One way to explore how you learn best is to ask yourself if you are a reader, listener, or doer. Do you get more information from reading and seeing, talking and listening, or doing?

Figure 1.2

Left-Brain versus Right-Brain Traits

Put a check mark next to the descriptions that apply to you. *Would you consider yourself more of a left-brain dominant person or a right-brain dominant person?*

Left-Brain Dominant	Right-Brain Dominant
Feels more comfortable with facts	Feels more comfortable with feelings
Thinks rationally based on reason and logic	Thinks intuitively based on hunches and feelings
Uses concrete thinking	Uses abstract thinking
Likes a sense of order	Likes a sense of space
Uses linear, step-by-step thinking	Uses holistic, visual thinking
Uses speech and words	Uses pictures and drawings
Is more "cerebral"	Is more "physical"
Makes lists and notes	Uses visuals and colors
Is concerned about time	Lives in the moment
Analyzes parts of the whole	Looks at the whole for patterns
Likes traditional outlines	Likes mind maps or creative outlines
Likes well-organized lectures	Likes group work and open-ended class discussion

Of course, you do all these things, but your learning strength, or preferred style, may be in one of these areas. For example, you may organize information visually, favoring right-brain activities. Although such classifications may oversimplify complex brain activity and are not meant to put you in a box or category, the goal is to help you be more aware of your natural tendencies and habits and how you can use these preferences and learn new ways to enhance your success.

A person who learns better by reading possesses a visual learning style. Someone who learns better by listening is considered an auditory learner. A kinesthetic learner learns by touch and physical activity. **Personal Evaluation Notebook 1.3** on pages 14 and 15 has a Learning Style Inventory that will help you discover your learning style.

VISUAL LEARNERS

Visual learners prefer to see information and read material. They learn most effectively with pictures, graphs, illustrations, diagrams, time lines, photos, and pie charts. They like to contemplate concepts, reflect, and summarize information in writing. They might use arrows, pictures, and bullets to highlight points. Visual learners are often holistic in that they see pictures in their minds that create feelings and emotion. They often use visual descriptions in their speech, such as "It is clear . . . ," "Picture this . . . ," or "See what I mean?" Visual learners tend to

- Be right-brain dominant
- Remember what they see better than what they hear
- Try to sit close to the instructor
- Prefer to have written directions they can read
- Learn better when someone shows them rather than tells them
- Like to read, highlight, and take notes
- Keep a list of things to do when planning the week
- Be fast thinkers and gesture frequently while talking
- Communicate clearly and concisely and watch facial expressions
- Like to read for pleasure and to learn

Visual learners may enjoy being an interior designer, a drafter, a proofreader, a writer, or an artist.

AUDITORY LEARNERS

Auditory learners prefer to rely on their hearing sense. They like music, and they prefer to listen to information, as in lectures. They like to talk, recite, and summarize information aloud. Auditory learners may create rhymes out of words and play music that helps them concentrate. When they take study breaks, they listen to music or chat with a friend. They are usually good listeners but are easily distracted by noise. They often use auditory descriptions when communicating, such as "This rings true . . . ," "It's clear as a bell . . . ," or "Do you hear what you're saying?"

Personal Evaluation Notebook

1.3

Learning Style Inventory

Determine your learning preference. Complete each sentence by checking a, b, or c. No answer is correct or better than another.

1. I learn best when I
   _____ **a.** see information.
   _____ **b.** hear information.
   _____ **c.** have hands-on experience.

2. I like
   _____ **a.** pictures and illustrations.
   _____ **b.** listening to tapes and stories.
   _____ **c.** working with people and going on field trips.

3. For pleasure and relaxation, I love to
   _____ **a.** read.
   _____ **b.** listen to music.
   _____ **c.** garden or play sports.

4. I tend to be
   _____ **a.** contemplative.
   _____ **b.** talkative.
   _____ **c.** a doer.

5. To remember a zip code, I like to
   _____ **a.** write it down several times.
   _____ **b.** say it out loud several times.
   _____ **c.** doodle and draw it on any available paper.

6. In a classroom, I learn best when
   _____ **a.** I have a good textbook, visual aids, and written information.
   _____ **b.** the instructor is interesting and clear.
   _____ **c.** I am involved in doing activities.

7. When I study for a test, I
   _____ **a.** read my notes and write a summary.
   _____ **b.** review my notes aloud and talk to others.
   _____ **c.** like to study in a group and use models and charts.

8. I have
   _____ **a.** a strong fashion sense and pay attention to visual details.
   _____ **b.** fun telling stories and jokes.
   _____ **c.** a great time building things and being active.

(continued)

Personal Evaluation Notebook

Learning Style Inventory *(concluded)*

9. I plan the upcoming week by
   _____ a. making a list and keeping a detailed calendar.
   _____ b. talking it through with someone.
   _____ c. creating a computer calendar or using a project board.

10. When preparing for a math test, I like to
    _____ a. write formulas on note cards or use pictures.
    _____ b. memorize formulas or talk aloud.
    _____ c. use marbles, LEGO® blocks, or three-dimensional models.

11. I often
    _____ a. remember faces but not names.
    _____ b. remember names but not faces.
    _____ c. remember events but not names or faces.

12. I remember best
    _____ a. when I read instructions and use visual images to remember.
    _____ b. when I listen to instructions and use rhyming words to remember.
    _____ c. with hands-on activities and trial and error.

13. When I give directions, I might say,
    _____ a. "Turn right at the yellow house and left when you see the large oak tree. Do you see what I mean?"
    _____ b. "Turn right. Go three blocks. Turn left onto Buttermilk Lane. OK? Got that? Do you hear what I'm saying?"
    _____ c. "Follow me," after giving directions by using gestures.

14. When driving in a new city, I prefer to
    _____ a. get a map and find my own way.
    _____ b. stop and get directions from someone.
    _____ c. drive around and figure it out by myself.

Score: Count the number of check marks for all your choices:

Total a choices _____6_____ (visual learning style)
Total b choices _____4_____ (auditory learning style)
Total c choices _____4_____ (kinesthetic learning style)

The highest total indicates your dominant learning style. If you are a combination, that's good. It means you are integrating styles already.

Auditory learners tend to

- Be left-brain dominant
- Remember what they hear better than what they see
- Prefer to listen to instructions
- Like lectures organized in a logical sequence
- Like to listen to music and talk on the telephone
- Plan the week by talking it through with someone
- Use rhyming words to remember
- Learn best when they hear an assignment as well as see it

Auditory learners may enjoy being a disc jockey, trial lawyer, counselor, or musician.

KINESTHETIC LEARNERS

Kinesthetic learners are usually well coordinated, like to touch things, and learn best by doing. They like to collect samples, write out information, and spend time outdoors. They like to connect abstract material to something concrete. They are good at hands-on tasks. They often use phrases such as "I am getting a handle on . . . ," "I have a gut feeling that . . . ," and "I get a sense that . . ."

● Know How You Learn
Everyone has his or her own way of learning. *What type of learning style do you think best suits this person?*

Kinesthetic learners tend to

- Be right-brain dominant
- Create an experience
- Use hands-on activities
- Build things and put things together
- Use models and physical activity
- Write down information
- Apply information to real-life situations
- Draw, doodle, use games and puzzles, and play computer games
- Take field trips and collect samples
- Relate abstract information to something concrete

Kinesthetic learners may enjoy being a chef, a surgeon, a medical technician, a nurse, an automobile mechanic, an electrician, an engineer, a forest ranger, a police officer, or a dancer.

Redefining Intelligence: Other Learning Styles

Because each of us has a unique set of abilities, perceptions, needs, and ways of processing information, learning styles vary widely. Besides visual, auditory, and kinesthetic learning styles, there are other, more specific styles, and some people have more than one learning style.

Plus, intelligence has been redefined. We used to think of it as measured by an IQ test. Many schools measure and reward linguistic and logical/mathematical modes of intelligence; however, Thomas Armstrong, author of *7 Kinds of Smart: Identifying and Developing Your Many Intelligences,* and Howard Gardner, who wrote *Frames of Mind: The Theory of Multiple Intelligences,* illustrated that we all possess many different intelligences. (See **Personal Evaluation Notebook 1.4** on page 18, which includes a number of traits associated with each "intelligence.")

1. **Verbal/linguistic.** Some people are **word smart.** They have verbal/linguistic intelligence and like to read, talk, and write information. They have the ability to argue, persuade, entertain, and teach with words. Many become journalists, writers, or lawyers. **To learn best:** Talk, read, or write about it.

2. **Logical/mathematical.** Some people are **logic smart.** They have logical/mathematical intelligence and like numbers, puzzles, and logic. They have the ability to reason, solve problems, create hypotheses, think in terms of cause and effect, and explore patterns and relationships. Many become scientists, accountants, or computer programmers. **To learn best:** Conceptualize, quantify, or think critically about it.

3. **Spatial.** Some people are **picture smart.** They have spatial intelligence and like to draw, sketch, and visualize information. They have the ability to perceive in three-dimensional space and re-create various aspects of the visual world. Many become architects, photographers, artists, or engineers. **To learn best:** Draw, sketch, or visualize it.

4. **Musical.** Some people are **music smart.** They have rhythm and melody intelligence. They have the ability to appreciate, perceive, and produce rhythms and to keep time to music. Many become composers, singers, or instrumentalists. **To learn best:** Sing, chant, rap, or play music.

5. **Bodily/kinesthetic.** Some people are **body smart.** They have physical and kinesthetic intelligence. They have the ability to understand and control their bodies; they have tactile sensitivity, like movement, and handle objects skillfully. Many become dancers, carpenters, physical education teachers, or coaches and enjoy outdoor activities and sports. **To learn best:** Build a model, dance, use note cards, or do hands-on activities.

6. **Environmental.** Some people are **outdoor smart.** They have environmental intelligence. They are good at measuring, charting, and observing plants and animals. They like to keep journals, collect and classify, and participate in outdoor activities. Many become park and forest rangers, surveyors, gardeners, landscape architects, outdoor guides, wildlife experts, or environmentalists. **To learn best:** Go on field trips, collect samples, go for walks, and apply what you are learning to real life.

7. **Intrapersonal.** Some people are **self smart.** They have intrapersonal (inner) intelligence. They have the ability to be contemplative, self-disciplined, and introspective. They like to work alone and pursue their own interests. Many become writers, counselors, theologians, or self-employed businesspeople. **To learn best:** Relate information to your feelings or personal experiences or find inner expression.

8. **Interpersonal.** Some people are **people smart.** They have interpersonal intelligence. They like to talk and work with people, join groups, and solve

Personal Evaluation Notebook

Multiple Intelligences

Put a check mark on the line next to the statement that is most often true for you.
Consider what interests you or what you believe you are good at doing.

Verbal/ Linguistic	Logical/ Mathematical	Spatial	Musical	Bodily/ Kinesthetic	Environmental	Intrapersonal	Interpersonal
"Word Smart"	"Logic Smart"	"Picture Smart"	"Music Smart"	"Body Smart"	"Outdoor Smart"	"Self Smart"	"People Smart"
I like to —Tell stories —Read —Talk and express myself clearly —Persuade, argue, or negotiate —Teach or discuss topics with others —Write	I like to —Use logic to solve problems —Explore mathematics —Explore science —Observe and question how things work —Figure out how to fix things —Use logic to solve problems	I like to —Draw or sketch —Visualize —Add color —Build models —Create illustrations —Use space and spatial relationships	I like to —Use rhythms —Respond to music —Sing —Recognize and remember melodies and chords —Use songs to help me remember —Relax with music	I like to —Experience physical movement —Act things out —Use note cards and models to learn —Work with others —Touch and feel material —Be active and enjoy sports	I like to —Be outdoors —Camp and hike —Work in the earth —Collect samples —Take field trips —Appreciate nature	I like to —Be independent and work on my own —Reflect on ideas —Read and contemplate new thoughts —Go off and think through a situation alone —Be self-disciplined and set individual goals —Use personal experiences and inner expression	I like to —Inspire and lead others —Learn through discussions —Work with a group of people —"Read" other people —Hear another person's point of view —Be compassionate and helpful

Multiple Intelligences

Your goal is to try new strategies and create learning opportunities in line with each category. *What are some strategies you could easily incorporate?*

For more information, see

Frames of Mind: The Theory of Multiple Intelligences by Howard Gardner, Basic Books, 1983.
Their Own Way: Discovering and Encouraging Your Child's Personal Learning Style by Thomas Armstrong, Tarcher/Putnam, 1987.

problems as part of a team. They have the ability to work with and understand people, as well as to perceive and be responsive to the moods, intentions, and desires of other people. Many become mediators, negotiators, social directors, social workers, motivational speakers, or teachers. **To learn best:** Join a group, get a study partner, or discuss with others.

● **Learning Styles**
There is no one best way to learn. *How do you think you can develop and integrate different learning styles?*

Discover Your Personality Type

Your learning style is often associated with your personality type—your "temperament." The concepts of learning styles, personality, and temperament are not new. Early writings from ancient Greece, India, the Middle East, and China addressed various temperaments and personality types. The ancient Greek founder of modern medicine, Hippocrates, identified four basic body types and a personality type associated with each body type. Several personality typing systems grew out of this ancient view of body/mind typing.

Carl Jung's Typology System

In 1921, psychologist Carl Jung proposed, in his book *Psychological Types,* that people are fundamentally different but also fundamentally alike. He identified three main attitudes/psychological functions, each with two types of personalities:

1. *How people relate to the external or internal world.* **Extroverts** are energized and recharged by people, tending to be outgoing and social. They tend to be optimistic and are often uncomfortable with being alone. **Introverts** are energized by solitude and reflection, preferring the world of ideas and thoughts. They tend to have a small but close set of friends and are more prone to self-doubt.

2. *How people perceive and gather information.* **Sensors** learn best from their senses and feel comfortable with facts and concrete data. They like to organize information systematically. **Intuitives** feel more comfortable with theories, abstraction, imagination, and speculation. They respond to their intuition and rely on hunches and nonverbal perceptions.

3. *How people prefer to make decisions.* **Thinkers** like to analyze problems with facts, rational logic, and analysis. They tend to be unemotional and use a systematic evaluation of data and facts for problem solving. **Feelers** are sensitive to the concerns and feelings of others, value harmony, and dislike creating conflict.

Jung suggested that differences and similarities among people can be understood by combining these types. Although people are not exclusively one of these types, he maintained that they have basic preferences or tendencies.

The Myers-Briggs Type Indicator

Jung's work inspired Katherine Briggs and her daughter, Isabel Briggs Myers, to design a personality test, called the Myers-Briggs Type Indicator (MBTI), which has become the most widely used typological instrument. They added a fourth attitude/psychological function (judgment/perception), which they felt was implied in Jung's writings, focusing on *how people live.* **Judgers** prefer orderly, planned, structured learning and working environments. They like control and closure. **Perceivers** prefer flexibility and spontaneity and like to allow life to unfold. Thus, with the four attitudes/psychological functions (extroverts vs. introverts, sensors vs. intuitives, thinkers vs. feelers, and judgers vs. perceivers), the MBTI provides 16 possible personality combinations. Although we may have all 8 preferences, 1 in each pair tends to be more developed. (See **Figure 1.3**, which lists many characteristics of extroverts, introverts, sensors, intuitives, thinkers, feelers, judgers, and perceivers.)

● **Understanding Personality Types**

Psychologists have developed a variety of categories to identify how people function best. *What personality type or types might apply to the person in this photograph?*

Connect Learning Styles and Personality Types: The Four-Temperament Profile

You now are aware of your preferred learning styles and have a sense of your personality type. How are these connected? How can you use this information to improve your learning skills and participate in productive group and team situations?

The simple Four-Temperament Profile demonstrates how learning styles and personality types are interrelated. **Personal Evaluation Notebook 1.5** on page 22 includes questions that will help you determine your dominant temperament.

The following descriptions elaborate on the four temperaments in Personal Evaluation Notebook 1.5. Which is your dominant temperament: analyzer, creator, supporter, or director? Did the answer surprise you? Keep in mind that inventories provide only clues. People change over time and react differently in different situations. However, use this knowledge to discover your strengths and become a well-rounded and balanced learner. Peak performers know not only their dominant style but also the way to integrate other styles when appropriate.

Figure 1.3

Extroverts (E) vs. Introverts (I)		Sensors (S) vs. Intuitives (iN)	
Gregarious	Quiet	Practical	Speculative
Active, talkative	Reflective	Experience	Use hunches
Speak, then think	Think, then speak	See details	See the big picture
Outgoing, social	Fewer, closer friends	Sequential, work steadily	Work in burst of energy
Energized by people	Energized by self	Feet on the ground	Head in the clouds
Like to speak	Like to read	Concrete	Abstract
Like variety and action	Like quiet for concentration	Realistic	See possibilities
Interested in results	Interested in ideas	Sensible and hardworking	Imaginative and inspired
Do not mind interruptions	Dislike interruptions	Good and precise work	Dislike precise work
Thinkers (T) vs. Feelers (F)		**Judgers (J) vs. Perceivers (P)**	
Analytical	Harmonious	Decisive	Tentative
Objective	Subjective	Closure	Open-minded
Impersonal	Personal	Plan ahead	Flexible
Factual	Sympathetic	Urgency	Open time frame
Want fairness	Want recognition	Organized	Spontaneous
Detached	Involved	Deliberate	Go with the flow
Rule	Circumstances	Set goals	Let life unfold
Things, not people	People, not things	Meet deadlines	Procrastinate
Lineal	Whole	Just the facts	Interested and curious

Figure 1.3
Characteristics of Personality Types

This chart reflects information influenced by psychologists Carl Jung and Myers and Briggs. *How can understanding your own personality and temperament help you succeed in school and life?*

Source: *Please Understand Me II* by Dr. David Keirsey © 1998, Prometheus Nemesis Book Company, PO Box 2748, Del Mar, CA 92014.

Analyzers

Analyzers tend to be logical, thoughtful, loyal, exact, dedicated, steady, and organized. They like following direction and work at a steady pace. The key word for analyzers is *thinking*. (See **Figure 1.4** on page 24.)

Strengths: Creating concepts and models and thinking things through
Goal: To gain intellectual recognition; analyzers are knowledge seekers
Classroom style: Analyzers relate to instructors who are organized, know their facts, and present information logically and precisely. They dislike the ambiguity of subjects that lack right or wrong answers. They tend to be left-brained and seem more concerned with facts, abstract ideas, and concepts than with people.
Learning style: Analyzers often perceive information abstractly and process it reflectively. They learn best by observing and thinking through ideas. They like models, lectures, textbooks, and solitary work. They like to work with things and analyze how things work. They evaluate and come to a precise conclusion.

Personal Evaluation Notebook

1.5

The Four-Temperament Profile

The following statements indicate your preferences in working with others, making decisions, and learning new information. Read each statement, with its four possible choices. Mark 4 next to the choice MOST like you, 3 next to the choice ALMOST ALWAYS like you, 2 next to the choice SOMEWHAT like you, and 1 next to the choice LEAST like you.

1. I learn best when I
   - _____ **a.** rely on logical thinking and facts.
   - __✓__ **b.** am personally involved.
   - _____ **c.** can look for new patterns through trial and error.
   - _____ **d.** use hands-on activities and practical applications.

2. When I'm at my best, I'm described as
   - _____ **a.** dependable, accurate, logical, and objective.
   - _____ **b.** understanding, loyal, cooperative, and harmonious.
   - __✓__ **c.** imaginative, flexible, open-minded, and creative.
   - _____ **d.** confident, assertive, practical, and results-oriented.

3. I respond best to instructors and bosses who
   - _____ **a.** are factual and to the point.
   - _____ **b.** show appreciation and are friendly.
   - __✓__ **c.** encourage creativity and flexibility.
   - _____ **d.** expect me to be involved, be active, and get results.

4. When working in a group, I tend to value
   - _____ **a.** objectivity and correctness.
   - __✓__ **b.** consensus and harmony.
   - _____ **c.** originality and risk taking.
   - _____ **d.** efficiency and results.

5. I am most comfortable with people who are
   - _____ **a.** informed, serious, and accurate.
   - _____ **b.** supportive, appreciative, and friendly.
   - __✓__ **c.** creative, unique, and idealistic.
   - _____ **d.** productive, realistic, and dependable.

6. Generally, I am
   - _____ **a.** methodical, efficient, trustworthy, and accurate.
   - _____ **b.** cooperative, genuine, gentle, and modest.
   - _____ **c.** high-spirited, spontaneous, easily bored, and dramatic.
   - _____ **d.** straightforward, conservative, responsible, and decisive.

(continued)

Personal Evaluation Notebook

1.5

The Four-Temperament Profile *(concluded)*

7. When making a decision, I'm generally concerned with
   _____ **a.** collecting information and facts to determine the right solution.
   _____ **b.** finding the solution that pleases others and myself.
   _____ **c.** brainstorming creative solutions that feel right.
   _____ **d.** quickly choosing the most practical and realistic solution.

8. You could describe me in one word as
   _____ **a.** analytical.
   _____ **b.** caring.
   _____ **c.** innovative.
   _____ **d.** productive.

9. I excel at
   _____ **a.** reaching accurate and logical conclusions.
   _____ **b.** being cooperative and respecting people's feelings.
   _____ **c.** finding hidden connections and creative outcomes.
   _____ **d.** making realistic, practical, and timely decisions.

10. When learning at school or on the job, I enjoy
   _____ **a.** gathering facts and technical information and being objective.
   _____ **b.** making personal connections, being supportive, and working in groups.
   _____ **c.** exploring new possibilities, tackling creative tasks, and being flexible.
   _____ **d.** producing results, solving problems, and making decisions.

Score: To determine your style, mark the choices you made in each column below. Then add the column totals. Highest number in

- Column a, you are an analyzer
- Column b, you are a supporter
- Column c, you are a creator
- Column d, you are a director

	Choice a	Choice b	Choice c	Choice d
1.	_____	_____	_____	_____
2.	_____	_____	_____	_____
3.	_____	_____	_____	_____
4.	_____	_____	_____	_____
5.	_____	_____	_____	_____
6.	_____	_____	_____	_____
7.	_____	_____	_____	_____
8.	_____	_____	_____	_____
9.	_____	_____	_____	_____
10.	_____	_____	_____	_____
Total	_____	_____	_____	_____
	Analyzer	**Supporter**	**Creator**	**Director**

Figure 1.4
Profile of an Analyzer

Analyzers want things done right. Their favorite question is "What?" *Do you recognize any analyzer traits in yourself?*

Effective Traits	Ineffective Traits	Possible Majors	Possible Careers	How to Relate to Analyzers
Objective	Too cautious	Accounting	Computer programmer	Be factual
Logical	Abrupt	Bookkeeping	Accountant	Be logical
Thorough	Unemotional	Mathematics	Bookkeeper	Be formal and thorough
Precise	Aloof	Computer science	Drafter	Be organized, detached, and calm
Detail-oriented	Indecisive	Drafting	Electrician	Be accurate and use critical thinking
Disciplined	Unimaginative	Electronics	Engineer	State facts briefly and concisely
		Auto mechanics	Auto mechanic	
			Technician	
			Librarian	

Supporters

People who are supporters tend to be cooperative, honest, sensitive, warm, and understanding. They relate well to others. They value harmony and are informal, approachable, and tactful. In business, they are concerned with the feelings and values of others. The key word for supporters is *feeling*. (See **Figure 1.5.**)

> **Strengths:** Clarifying values, creating harmony, and being a loyal team player
> **Goal:** To create harmony, meaning, and cooperation; they are identity seekers
> **Classroom style:** Supporters tend to learn best when they like an instructor and feel accepted and respected. They are easily hurt by criticism. They like to integrate course concepts with their own experiences. They relate to instructors who

Figure 1.5
Profile of a Supporter

Supporters want things done harmoniously and want to be personally involved. Their favorite question is "Why?" *Do you recognize any supporter traits in yourself?*

Effective Traits	Ineffective Traits	Possible Majors	Possible Careers	How to Relate to Supporters
Understanding	Overly compliant	Counseling or therapy	Elementary teacher	Be friendly
Gentle	Passive	Social work	Physical therapist	Be positive
Loyal	Slow to act	Family and consumer science	Social worker	Be sincere and build trust
Cooperative	Naive	Nursing	Therapist	Listen actively
Diplomatic	Unprofessional	Medical assisting	Counselor	Focus on people
Appreciative	Can be overly sensitive	Physical therapy	Nurse	Focus on personal values
		Education	Medical assistant	Create a comfortable, relaxed climate
				Create an experience they can relate to

Effective Traits	Ineffective Traits	Possible Majors	Possible Careers	How to Relate to Creators
Imaginative	Unrealistic	Art	Writer	Be enthusiastic
Creative	Unreliable	English	Politician	Be involved
Visionary	Inconsistent	Music	Travel agent	Be flexible
Idealistic	Hasty	Design	Hotel manager	Be accepting
Enthusiastic	Impulsive	Hospitality	Cartoonist	of change
Innovative	Impatient	Travel	Musician	Focus on
	Fragmented	Theater	Composer	creative ideas
		Communications	Artist	Talk about dreams
			Journalist	and possibilities
			Craftsperson	
			Florist	
			Costume designer	
			Salesperson	
			Scientist	

Figure 1.6
Profile of a Creator

Creators want things done with a sense of drama and style. Their favorite question is "What if?" *Do you recognize any creator traits in yourself?*

are warm and sociable, tell interesting stories, use visuals, and are approachable. They learn best by listening, sharing ideas and feelings, and working in teams.

Learning style: Supporters perceive information through intuition and process it reflectively. They like to deal with their feelings. They prefer learning information that has personal meaning, and they are patient and likeable. They are insightful; they are imaginative thinkers and need to be personally involved.

Creators

Creators are innovative, flexible, spontaneous, creative, and idealistic. They are risk takers; they love drama, style, and imaginative design. They like fresh ideas and are passionate about their work. The key word for creators is *experience*. (See **Figure 1.6**.)

Strengths: Creating visions that inspire people

Goal: To make things happen by turning ideas into action; they are experience seekers

Classroom style: Creators learn best in innovative and active classrooms. They relate to instructors who have a passion for their work; who are challenging, imaginative, and flexible; who present interesting ideas; and who make the topic exciting.

Learning style: Creators learn by doing and being involved in active experiments. They perceive information concretely and process it actively. They like games, role-playing, stories, plays, music, illustrations, drawings, and other visual stimuli. They ask questions and enjoy acting on ideas. They are usually good public speakers. They are future-oriented and good at seeing whole systems.

Directors

Directors are dependable, self-directed, conscientious, efficient, decisive, and results-oriented. They like to be the leader of groups and respond to other people's ideas when they are logical and reasonable. Their strength is in the practical

Figure 1.7
Profile of a Director

Directors want to produce results in a practical manner. Their favorite question is "How?" *Do you recognize any director traits in yourself?*

Effective Traits	Ineffective Traits	Possible Majors	Possible Careers	How to Relate to Directors
Confident	Aggressive	Business	Lawyer	Set deadlines
Assertive	Pushy	Law enforcement	Police officer	Be responsible for your actions
Active	Insistent	Construction	Detective	Focus on results
Decisive	Overpowering	Woodworking	Consultant	Focus on achievements
Forceful	Dominating	Carpentry	Banker	Do not try to take control
Effective leader		Business management	Park ranger	Do not make excuses
Results-oriented		Wildlife conservation	Forest ranger	Have a direction
		Forestry	Administrator for outdoor recreation	Make known time or other changes in schedule

application of ideas. Because of this ability, they can excel in a variety of careers, such as law enforcement, banking, and legal professions. The key word for directors is *results*. (See **Figure 1.7.**)

Strengths: Integrating theory with practical solutions

Goal: To find practical solutions to problems; they are security seekers

Classroom style: Directors relate to instructors who are organized, clear, to the point, punctual, and results-oriented. They prefer field trips and hands-on activities.

Learning style: Directors learn by hands-on, direct experience. They learn best by practical application. They like classes that are relevant. They work hard to get things done.

Integrate Styles to Maximize Learning

Just as there is no best way to learn, there is no one instrument, assessment, or inventory that can categorize how you learn best. There are many theories about learning styles, and none of them should be regarded as air-tight explanations. Any learning style assessment or theory is, at best, a guide.

The assessment instruments discussed in this text have been adapted from various sources and are based on many years of research. They are simple, yet they provide valuable clues and strategies for determining how you learn, process information, and relate to others. They also provide clues for possible college majors and careers that fit your personality and style. Ask your instructor or learning center if there are certain assessments they recommend.

Use these inventories as a guide, not a restriction. All learning styles are connected, and we use all of them, depending on the situation, task, and people involved. Develop positive strategies based on your natural talents and abilities, and expand your effectiveness by integrating all learning styles.

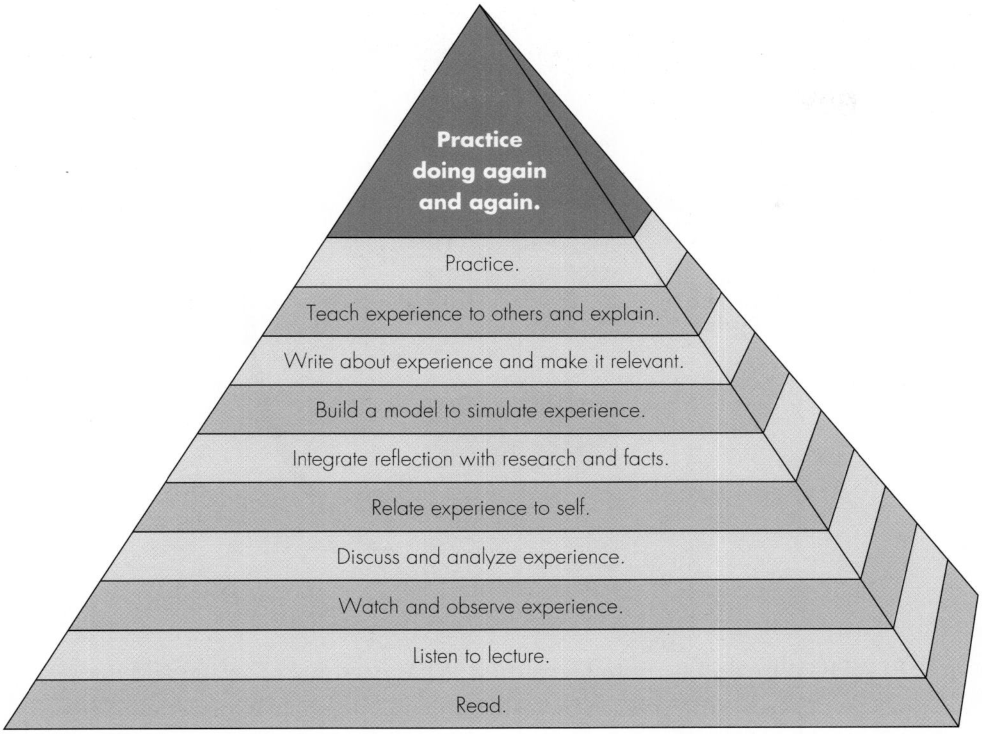
Practice doing again and again.
Practice.
Teach experience to others and explain.
Write about experience and make it relevant.
Build a model to simulate experience.
Integrate reflection with research and facts.
Relate experience to self.
Discuss and analyze experience.
Watch and observe experience.
Listen to lecture.
Read.

Figure 1.8
Peak Performance Learning Pyramid
Maximize your effectiveness by integrating various learning styles and skills as you move up the pyramid. *What additional skills and learning styles would enhance your learning ability?*

Psychologist William James believed that people use less than 5 percent of their potential. Think of what you can accomplish if you work in alignment with your natural preferences and integrate various learning styles and techniques. The Peak Performance Learning Pyramid in **Figure 1.8** illustrates how you can maximize your effectiveness by integrating learning styles and moving from passive to active, engaged learning. Now that you have assessed how you learn best—as well as new ways to learn—let's explore how learning is a never-ending cycle.

The Adult Learning Cycle

David Kolb, a professor at Case Western Reserve University, developed an inventory that categorizes learners based on how they process information:

1. Concrete experience: learn by feeling and personal experience
2. Reflective observation: learn by observing and reflecting
3. Abstract conceptualization: learn by thinking and gathering information
4. Active experimentation: learn by doing and hands-on activities

Kolb's theory about learning styles is similar to Carl Jung's four attitudes/psychological functions (feeling, intuition, thinking, and sensation). The crux of Kolb's theory is that you learn by practice, repetition, and recognition. Thus, do it, do it again, and then do it again.

The following Adult Learning Cycle is an adaptation of both Kolb's and Jung's theories. It includes a fifth stage and illustrates how they are complementary to one another. (See **Figure 1.9**.)

We Learn
10% of what we read
20% of what we hear
30% of what we see
50% of what we see and hear
70% of what we discuss with others
80% of what we do and experience
95% of what we teach others

Figure 1.9
The Adult Learning Cycle

The key to learning is practice and repetition. *Why is "Teach" an essential, unique step?*

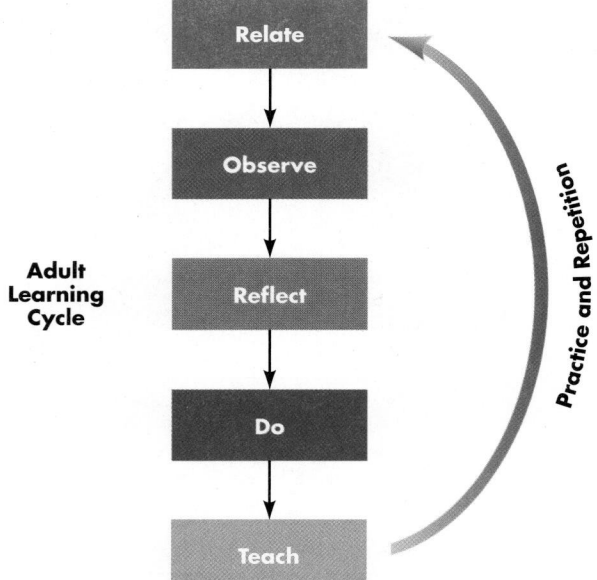

1. **RELATE. Why do I want to learn this?** What personal meaning and interest does this have for me? I learn by feeling, having personal experiences, and talking with others.
2. **OBSERVE. How does this work?** I learn by watching, listening, and experiencing.
3. **REFLECT. What does this mean?** I learn by thinking, gathering information, and reflecting.
4. **DO. What can I do with this?** I learn by doing, finding practical applications, and defining procedures.
5. **TEACH. How can I relay this information to others?** I learn by demonstrating and explaining, as well as by acknowledging and rewarding positive outcomes.

Depending on your learning style, the information to be learned, and the situation, you may find yourself starting the cycle at different stages. *The key to learning is practice and repetition.* As you repeat the stages, meaning and recall are strengthened. To make learning long-lasting, you need to find ways to make it meaningful and physical. For example, let's say you are taking a computer class:

1. **RELATE personal meaning, interests, and relevance.** Why do you want to use the computer? What are the benefits to you, your coursework, and your career? How does this relate to what you already know, such as typing skills? In what programs or skills would you like to become proficient? Think about the opportunities and talk with other people about the practical uses of a computer. Study and learn in a group.
2. **OBSERVE your instructor and watch other people using the computer.** Listen and ask questions. Talk, read, and write about your experiences. What is new and different? Jot down instructions, draw, sketch, and add color to your notes. Find music to illustrate ideas or use background music as you learn. Experience doing a task as your instructor or a friend helps you.

3. **REFLECT on problems critically and sequentially.** Build on information and qualify it. What works and doesn't work? Test new ways of doing things. Ask people when you get stuck. Find new ways to solve problems. Relate what you know to new information. Review instructions when you are stumped.

4. **DO it and learn by trial and error.** Jump in and try new tasks. Learning to use a computer is a great example of hands-on learning. Find new applications.

5. **TEACH it to others.** Demonstrate to someone else what you have learned. Answer questions and ask for feedback.

Then return to Stage 1 and reaffirm the benefits of learning this valuable new skill.

You can adapt the Adult Learning Cycle to fit your preference, but you will be most effective if you integrate all the learning styles and make learning physical and meaningful.

In each chapter, we will explore practical examples of the Adult Learning Cycle. For example, in Chapter 12, the Adult Learning Cycle will be applied to effective communication and how you can enhance your communication skills.

Overcome Obstacles

On your journey to success, you will run into stumbling blocks (or even big boulders). Maintain a positive attitude and make sure you are using your self-management tools.

Adjust Your Learning Style to Your Instructor's Teaching Style

Just as we all have different learning styles, your instructors will have a variety of teaching styles. Rather than resisting, find ways to adapt. Maximize the ways you learn best and incorporate other techniques. For example, if you prefer a highly structured lecture, focusing on facts and taking notes, you may feel uncomfortable in a student-centered course where ideas and class discussion are key and you work in small groups with little structure. The following strategies may help you succeed in this type of course:

- Ask questions and clarify expectations.
- Be flexible and try new approaches.
- Be an active participant in class, and go to every class.
- Get to know other students, and form study teams.
- Be interested in other points of view.
- See exercises and class discussions as learning opportunities.
- Visit your instructor during office hours and ask what you can do to improve.
- Do any extra-credit projects that are offered.
- Try looking at the whole of a concept before breaking it into parts.
- If the instructor jumps around a lot in a lecture or digresses, ask for main points.
- Find or ask for the theme or key points of each class.
- Focus on the learning process, not just the final product.

> ❝I have not failed. I've just found 10,000 ways that won't work.❞
>
> THOMAS EDISON
> *Inventor*

WORDS TO SUCCEED

Jenna is a medical technician student who excels in her science and math courses, but she's struggling in sociology, where her instructor likes to teach in small groups, asks a lot of open-ended questions, and has a very informal classroom style.

- What assumptions can you make about how her science and math classes may be taught?
- What are most likely Jenna's preferred learning styles?
- How can Jenna adjust her learning to adapt to her sociology class?

Let's say you prefer warm relationships and a nonstructured class. You find yourself in a traditional, content-centered, straight lecture class with few visuals or class discussion. Here are a few suggestions for adapting:

- Read the syllabus, and know expectations.
- Listen attentively, and take detailed notes.
- Clarify the weight of each test, paper, or project.
- Make certain you know and meet each deadline.
- Anticipate the lecture, and be prepared.
- Focus on the lecture, and avoid talking to others during class.
- Work in a study team, discuss lecture concepts, and predict test questions.
- Ask questions, and ask for examples from the instructor and study team.
- Take advantage of the logical sequence of material, and take notes accordingly.
- Add color, supporting examples, and drawings to your notes.
- Connect lectures to drawings, photographs, and diagrams in the textbook.
- Ask the instructor for visuals that help illustrate the points made in class.
- Have your questions ready when talking to your instructor during office hours.
- Use analytical thinking, and focus on facts and logic.
- Be precise in definitions and descriptions.

If absolutely necessary, you can drop the class and sign up for a class with an instructor who has a teaching style that matches your learning style. However, in the workplace you will interact with people who have a variety of personality types and learning styles, so it's important for you to learn coping and adapting skills now.

Make It Simple

The "M" word: **multitasking.** In our high-speed world of fast food, multimedia, and instant gratification, it's no wonder that we think we can do it all at once. Cell phone commercials boast of being able not only to chat about dinner plans but also to search the Internet for the best local sushi restaurant and make a reservation—all with your friend still on the line.

Enhanced productivity? Maybe, but many would argue that "multitasking" really means you aren't doing anything very well because you're trying to do too many things at the same time. Layering task upon task only complicates our hectic lives even more. However, few would disagree that we have more demands on our time and have to figure out the best way to accomplish as much as possible.

Rather than lumping tasks together, focus on one thing at a time for a short period of time. For example, take only three minutes right now and review what you've just read about learning styles and your instructors. Jot down each one's name and how you would characterize his or her teaching. Put an asterisk by those whose teaching style is a little more challenging for you. Write down three specific strategies you want to try during the next class. Make it simple by trying just a few techniques now to find out what works for you.

Use a watch, clock, phone—whatever is handy—to time yourself. You will be surprised how much you can accomplish in just short intervals of time. We often procrastinate or complain that there's "not enough time." If you keep to the mindset that small chunks of time make a big difference, you may discover that you can do it all—or at least most of it!

In Chapter 3, we'll tackle time management in more detail, but focusing your time and efforts and finding what works for you are essential to every topic in this book and everything you do, in both school and life. This book provides a litany of proven strategies, but it's up to you to find out what works—and to stick with it!

TAKING CHARGE

Summary

In this chapter, I learned to

- **Strive to become a peak performer.** Peak performers come from all walks of life, maximize their abilities and resources, and focus on positive results.

- **Practice self-management.** I know I am responsible for my own success, and there are self-management techniques and behaviors I can practice that will make me successful.

- **Self-assess.** Assessing and objectively seeing myself will help me recognize my need to learn new skills, relate more effectively with others, set goals, manage time and stress, and create a balanced and productive life.

- **Use my critical thinking skills.** Critical thinking is a logical, rational, and systematic thought process I can use to think through a problem or situation to make sound choices and good decisions.

- **Visualize success.** Visualization is a self-management tool I can use to see myself being successful. I will also use affirmations (positive self-talk) to focus on what's important.

- **Reflect on information.** I will think about how experiences are related and what I can learn from them, including keeping a written or online journal to record my thoughts.

- **Create a personal mission statement.** Drafting a mission statement will help me determine my values and interests and focus on my long-term goals.

- **Make connections between skills for school and job success.** The Secretary's Commission on Achieving Necessary Skills (SCANS) outlines skills and competencies that are critical to success in school as well as in the job market.

- **Determine my learning style.** Knowing my preferred learning style, such as visual, auditory, or kinesthetic, tells me how I learn best and how to incorporate features of other learning styles in order to maximize my learning opportunities.

- **Explore various personality types.** Although personality typing has been around for centuries, Jung identified extroverts vs. introverts, sensors vs. intuitives, and thinkers vs. feelers. Myers and Briggs added judgers and perceivers and developed the Myers-Briggs Type Indicator.

- **Integrate learning styles and personality types.** Once I understand my learning style(s) and personality type(s), I can incorporate features of other styles to maximize my learning. Although I tend to be either left-brain dominant (linguistic) or right-brain dominant (visual), the goal is to use all my brain power to learn new skills and information.

- **Apply the Adult Learning Cycle.** This five-step process (relate, observe, reflect, do, and teach) demonstrates that learning comes from repetition, practice, and recall.

- **Adjust to my instructor's teaching style.** If my learning style is different from my instructor's teaching style, I will try new strategies that will maximize my learning in that class.

- **Make it simple by focusing my time.** Rather than trying to tackle everything at once, I can accomplish much more by focusing my efforts in short intervals of time and finding strategies that work for me.

Performance Strategies

Following are the top 10 strategies for becoming a lifelong learner.

- Strive to become a peak performer in all aspects of your life.
- Practice self-management to create the results you want.
- Use critical thinking and honesty in self-assessment.
- Practice visualization, and state affirmations that focus on positive outcomes.
- Create a personal mission statement.
- Make the connection between school and job success.
- Discover your learning and personality styles.
- Integrate all learning styles.
- Apply the Adult Learning Cycle to maximize your learning.
- Make it simple by focusing on one task or strategy at a time.

Tech for Success

Take advantage of the text's Web site at **www.mhhe.com/ferrett8e** for additional study aids, useful forms, and convenient and applicable resources.

- **Electronic journal.** Sometimes critical thinking is easier when you write down your responses. Keeping an electronic reflection and self-assessment journal allows for easy updating and gathering of information, which can be pulled into your career portfolio later.
- **Mission statement business cards.** To keep yourself motivated and focused, print your mission statement on business cards, carry them with you, and share them with family and friends. Consider chipping in with another student or your study group and buying prescored printer paper, or simply print on a heavier paper stock and cut the cards apart.
- **Online self-assessments.** A number of online assessments can help you determine the best careers to fit your personality. Talk with your instructor, as your school may already have some available in your career center, such as the Learning and Study Strategies Inventory (LASSI).

Study Team Notes

Career*in* focus

Louis Parker
ACCOUNTANT AND FINANCIAL PLANNER

Related Majors: Accounting, Business Administration, Economics, Finance

Setting Business Goals

Louis Parker is a certified public accountant (CPA) and financial planner. In 2004, he started his own business, Parker Inc., by offering accounting services. Louis prepares taxes, financial reports, and payroll, and he does bookkeeping for individuals and small businesses. He employs three full-time and one part-time assistant but needs five full-time workers to help during peak tax season (January–April).

To get feedback on his services, Louis occasionally does a survey of his clients. The survey shows whether his clients are getting the services they want at prices they believe are reasonable. Louis uses the results of the survey to set goals and plan for the future.

One of Louis's goals is to continually increase business, as Louis believes that, without marketing and growth, his business will decline. Louis has used telemarketing services to help him set up appointments with prospective clients.

A few years ago, Louis decided to add financial planning because his clients were continually asking for his advice in financial areas. Financial planners help clients attain financial goals, such as retirement or a college education for their children. Louis was able to get certified in financial planning. Because he is affiliated with a financial services organization, he sometimes helps clients invest in the stock market, mainly in mutual funds. Currently, financial planning is only 10 percent of his business, but Louis's goal is to eventually increase that amount to 30 percent.

CRITICAL THINKING How might a survey of his clients help Louis assess his personal strengths and weaknesses? What strategies should he put in place to follow up on client feedback? How can he incorporate the feedback into his long-term goals?

Peak Performer

PROFILE

Blake Mycoskie

In just his early thirties, Blake Mycoskie has already had an "amazing race" of a life. He started his first business (a campus laundry service) while attending college at Southern Methodist University. The business was successful and, after selling it, Blake continued to create successful businesses—five altogether. It was after competing on the CBS primetime show *The Amazing Race*, however, that Mycoskie realized his true passion. He returned to all of the countries he had raced through on the show and was struck by the extreme poverty of Argentina. He decided then that he needed to do something to help.

In May 2006, Mycoskie used the skills and experiences he had acquired creating and owning a company and took a risk by doing something he had no knowledge of: making shoes. TOMS: Shoes for Tomorrow was created, a shoe company which promised that for every pair of shoes purchased, TOMS would give a pair to a child in need. His initial pledge of 250 shoes to children in Argentina quickly outpaced his expectations, and on that first Shoe Drop, TOMS gave 10,000 pairs of new shoes to children Mycoskie had met on previous visits. As of April 2010, TOMS had given over 600,000 pairs of new shoes to children in need around the world.

TOMS has been honored with many prestigious government awards, and has helped spread numerous successful community movements. Mycoskie has said that his favorite quote is by Gandhi: "Be the change you wish to see in the world." By thinking critically about his different areas of knowledge and passions, Mycoskie was truly able to understand how he could effect the change he wanted to see in the world.

PERFORMANCE THINKING How did Blake Mycoskie use the principles discussed in this chapter to create TOMS: Shoes for Tomorrow? Would the company have been as successful if Mycoskie had been unable to make the initial connection between his skills and his developing passion and new mission in life?

CHECK IT OUT TOMS "One Day Without Shoes" movement has included people from all over the world by asking them to do one thing together: walk barefoot for a day. You can find out more about the organization and its events at **www.onedaywithoutshoes.com**. Watch some of the "Bare Your Sole" videos posted on the Web site. Which one most affected you? How are online movements such as this capable of making people better understand the difficulties faced by other people in the world?

Starting Today

At least one strategy I learned in this chapter that I plan to try right away is

_____

_____

_____

What changes must I make in order for this strategy to be most effective?

_____

_____

_____

Review Questions

Based on what you have learned in this chapter, write your answers to the following questions:

1. What is a peak performer? List at least three potential characteristics.

_____

_____

2. Define visualization and how and when you can practice this self-management tool.

_____

_____

3. Explain the differences among the three types of learners (visual, auditory, kinesthetic).

_____

_____

4. Why is it important to know your learning style and personality type?

_____

_____

5. Why is it important to determine your instructor's teaching style as well as your own learning style?

_____

_____

To test your understanding of the chapter's concepts, complete the chapter quiz at **www.mhhe.com/ferrett8e**.

Making a Commitment

In the Classroom

Eric Silver is a freshman in college. He doesn't know what major to choose and isn't even sure if he wants to continue going to college. His parents are urging him to pursue his college career, but Eric wants to go to work instead. In high school, he never settled on a favorite subject, though he did briefly consider becoming a private investigator after reading a detective novel. His peers seem more committed to college and have better study habits. Eric prefers a hands-on approach to learning, and he finds it difficult to concentrate while studying or listening to a lecture. However, he enjoys the outdoors and is creative. Once he gets involved in a project he finds interesting, he is very committed.

1. What strategies from this chapter would be most useful to help Eric understand himself better and gain a sense of commitment?

   _____

   _____

2. What would you suggest to Eric to help him find direction?

   _____

   _____

In the Workplace

Eric has taken a job as a law enforcement officer. He feels more comfortable in this job than he did in school, since he knows he performs best when actively learning. He enjoys teamwork and the exchange of ideas with his co-workers. Eric also realizes that, in order to advance in his work, he needs to continue his education. He is concerned about balancing his work, school, and family life. He does admit that he did not excel in subjects he was less interested in. Eric never learned effective study habits but realizes that he must be disciplined when returning to college.

3. What suggestions would you give Eric to help him do better in school?

   _____

   _____

4. Under what category of learning style does Eric fall, and what are the ineffective traits of this style that he needs to work on most?

   _____

   _____

Applying the ABC Method of Self-Management

In the Journal Entry on page 1, you were asked to think about what you are hoping to gain from your college experience. How does earning a college degree help you both personally and professionally? Essentially, "Why are you here?" On the lines provided, indicate your answers to those questions.

_____

_____

_____

Now think about the obstacles you may have faced to get to this point and what you did to overcome them. State at least one of those obstacles:

_____

_____

_____

Now apply the ABC method to one of the obstacles.

A = Actual event:

_____

_____

B = Beliefs:

_____

_____

C = Challenge:

_____

_____

Did you use this or a similar thought process when you first encountered the obstacle? Was the obstacle not really as big as it first seemed?

PRACTICE SELF-MANAGEMENT

For more examples of learning how to manage difficult situations, see the "Self-Management Workbook" section of the Online Learning Center Web site at **www.mhhe.com/ferrett8e.**

My Learning Style, Personality Types, and Temperament

LEARNING STYLES

I am a(n) (circle one):

Visual learner

Auditory learner

Kinesthetic learner

The following learning habits make me most like this learning style:

What features of the two other learning styles should I incorporate to make me a well-rounded learner?

PERSONALITY TYPES

I am a(n) (circle one for each):

Extrovert or introvert

Sensor or intuitive

Thinker or feeler

The following characteristics make me most like these personality types:

How can I incorporate positive features of the opposite personality types?

TEMPERAMENTS

I am a(n) (circle one):

Analyzer

Supporter

Creator

Director

The following characteristics make me most like this temperament:

What positive behaviors/traits can I incorporate from the other three temperaments?

Creating the Ideal Team

In school and at work, you will often be a member of a project team. In most cases, you do not have the opportunity to select your team members but, instead, need to learn how to maximize each other's strengths.

Pretend, however, that you have the opportunity to select a four-person team to tackle an assignment. Now that you know your preferences, indicate the characteristics of three potential teammates who would be complementary. Indicate why you think each person would be an asset to the team.

PERSON #1

Learning style:

Personality type:

Temperament:

What this person will add to the team:

PERSON #2

Learning style:

Personality type:

Temperament:

What this person will add to the team:

PERSON #3

Learning style:

Personality type:

Temperament:

What this person will add to the team:

AND ME

What I add to the team:

Applying the Four-Temperament Profile

You've explored your temperament and discovered your preferred learning style and personality type. Apply this knowledge by associating with people who have various styles, and find ways to relate to and work more effectively with different people.

For example, let's say that you are assigned to a five-person team that will present a serious public health issue to your personal health class. You are a supporter type, and you find yourself having a conflict with Joe, a director type. You are in your first meeting, and Joe is ready to choose a topic for the group project, even though one team member is absent.

Apply the ABC Method of Self-Management to focus your energies on building rapport and understanding:

A = Actual event: "Joe wants to choose a topic for the group project, even though one person isn't here to voice her opinion."

B = Beliefs: "I think we are not taking the time to be sensitive to the needs of all the team members. Everyone should be present before we make a decision. Joe is trying to take control of the group and is just impatient. I'm worried that the absent group member will not like the decision or may be hurt that she wasn't involved. I resent being rushed and worry that conflict will result. Maybe this person will even quit the group."

C = Challenge: "What is the worst thing that could happen if we choose a topic today? We can always refocus later if we find this topic doesn't fit our goals. Chances are, the absent member would agree with the topic in question, anyhow. Joe is probably not impatient—he just wants to make a decision and get us moving. I'm glad our group is made up of different strengths and personalities. I'm psyched that our team members have complementary strengths and can respect and work well with each other. I know that Joe will keep us moving forward and will be sensitive to my concerns that we listen to each other and respect each other's feelings."

Are you experiencing a similar situation or conflict in your school, work, or personal life? If so, use the ABC Method to visualize a positive solution:

A = Actual event:

_____

_____

B = Beliefs:

_____

_____

C = Challenge:

_____

_____

Autobiography

The purpose of this exercise is to look back and assess how you learned skills and competencies. Write down the turning points, major events, and significant experiences of your life. This autobiography, or chronological record, will note events that helped you make decisions, set goals, or discover something about yourself. Record both negative and positive experiences and what you learned from them. Add this page to your Career Development Portfolio—for example,

Year/Event	Learned Experience
1997 Moved to Michigan.	Learned to make new friends and be flexible.
1998 First job baby-sitting.	Learned responsibility and critical thinking.
1999 Grandmother became ill.	Helped with care. Learned dependability, compassion.

Year/Event	Learned Experience

2

Expand Your Emotional Intelligence

LEARNING OUTCOMES

In this chapter, you will learn to

2.1 Describe emotional intelligence and the key personal qualities

2.2 Explain the importance of good character, including integrity, civility, and ethics

2.3 Demonstrate responsibility, self-management, and self-control

2.4 Define self-esteem and confidence

2.5 Incorporate a positive attitude and motivation

2.6 List the benefits of a higher education

SELF-MANAGEMENT

"On my commute to class, a car cut me off. I was furious and yelled at the driver. I was fuming and distracted during classes, and later I blew up at a co-worker. This just ruined my entire day. How can I handle my angry feelings in a more constructive way?"

Have you ever had a similar experience? Are you easily offended by what others do or say? Have you said things in anger that have caused a rift in a relationship? In this chapter, you will learn how to control your emotions and create a positive and resourceful state of mind.

JOURNAL ENTRY In **Worksheet 2.1** on page 70, describe a time when you were angry and lost control of your emotions. How did you feel? How did others react to your outburst? What would you do differently? Visualize yourself calm and in control, and realize you have a choice in how you interpret events.

There is a tendency to define intelligence as a score on an IQ test or the SAT or as school grades. Educators trying to predict who will succeed in college have found that high school grades, achievement test scores, and ability are only part of the picture. Emotional intelligence and maturity have more effect on school and job success than traditional scholastic measures. In fact, research has indicated that persistence and perseverance are major predictors of college success. A landmark study by the American College Test (ACT) indicated that the primary reasons for first-year students' dropping out of college were not academic but, rather, emotional difficulties, such as feelings of inadequacy, depression, loneliness, and a lack of motivation or purpose.

Employers list a positive attitude, motivation, honesty, the ability to get along with others, and the willingness to learn as more important to job success than a college degree or specific skills. In Chapter 1, you learned that SCANS identifies many personal qualities as important competencies for success in the workplace. These qualities and competencies are also essential for building and maintaining strong, healthy relationships throughout life. Essential personal qualities should be viewed as a foundation on which to build skills, experience, and knowledge.

In this chapter, you will learn the importance of emotional intelligence and why character is so important for school and job success. You will also develop personal strategies for maintaining a positive attitude and becoming self-motivated. You may realize that you are smarter than you think. You are smarter than your test scores or grades. Success in your personal life, school, and career depends more on a positive attitude, motivation, responsibility, self-control, and effort than on inborn abilities or a high IQ. Peak performers use the whole of their intelligence.

Emotional Intelligence and Maturity

Emotional intelligence is the ability to understand and manage yourself and relate effectively to others. **Maturity** is the ability to control your impulses, think beyond the moment, and consider how your words and actions affect yourself and others before you act. Researchers have demonstrated that people who have developed a set of traits that adds to their maturity level increase their sense of well-being, get along better with others, and enhance their school, job, and life success.

Emotional maturity contributes to competent behavior, problem-solving ability, socially appropriate behavior, and good communication. Being unaware of or unable to control emotions often accompanies restlessness, a short attention span, negativism, impatience, impulsiveness, and distractibility. Clearly, having emotional intelligence distinguishes peak performers from mediocre ones. Becoming more emotionally mature involves three stages:

1. Self-awareness—tuning in to yourself
2. Empathy—tuning in to others
3. Change—tuning in to results

In Chapter 1, you explored strategies to increase your self-awareness and tune in to yourself. You assessed your skills and personal qualities in the Peak Performance Self-Assessment Test on page 10. By learning personality types, you also began to tune in to others as well. The central theme of this book is that you can use self-management to begin changing your thoughts, images, and behaviors to produce the results you want in every aspect of your life. Enhancing your emotional intelligence and focusing on positive personal qualities are key to achieving those results.

Character First: Integrity, Civility, and Ethics

Good **character** is an essential personal quality for true success. A person of good character has a core set of principles that most of us accept as constant and relatively noncontroversial. These principles include fairness, honesty, respect, responsibility, caring, trustworthiness, and citizenship. Recent surveys of business leaders indicate that dishonesty, lying, and lack of respect are top reasons for on-the-job difficulties. If an employer believes an employee lacks integrity, all of that person's positive qualities—from skill and experience to productivity and intelligence—are meaningless. Employers usually list honesty or good character as an essential personal quality, followed by the ability to relate to and get along with others.

Following The Golden Rule (treating others as we want to be treated) is a simple way to weave integrity and civility into our everyday lives. The word **integrity** comes from the Latin word *integre,* meaning "wholeness." Integrity is the integration of your principles and actions. In a sense, people who have integrity "walk the talk" by consistently living up to their highest principles. Integrity is not adherence to a rigid code but, rather, an ongoing commitment to being consistent, caring, and true to doing what is right—and the courage to do it even when it is difficult.

Civility is a set of tools for treating others with respect, kindness, and good manners, or etiquette. It also includes the sacrifices we make each day so that we live together peacefully. Civility (like integrity) requires empathy—understanding of and compassion for others. You can practice civility in your classes by being on time, turning off your cell phone, staying for the entire class, and listening to the instructor and other students when they speak.

Ethics are the principles of conduct that govern a group or society. Since a company's reputation is its most important asset, most organizations have a written code of ethics that describes how people are expected to behave. It is your responsibility to know and understand the code of ethics at your place of employment and at school. Look in your school's catalog for statements regarding academic integrity, honesty, cheating, and plagiarism. **Cheating** is using or providing unauthorized help in test taking or on projects. One form of cheating is **plagiarism**, which means presenting someone else's ideas as if they were your own. The consequences of unethical behavior could result in an *F* grade, suspension, expulsion, or firing from a job. You always have the choice of telling the truth and being responsible for your own work. (We'll discuss plagiarism versus paraphrasing in Chapter 9 and the importance of giving credit and citing sources.)

> **❝** Character is like a tree and reputation like its shadow. The shadow is what we think of it; the tree is the real thing. **❞**
>
> ABRAHAM LINCOLN
> *U.S. president*

● **Become a "Class Act"**
These may seem like harmless acts, but they are clear examples of disrespect—for your instructor, your classmates, and your education. *How would an employer respond to this behavior on the job?*

Incivility in the Classroom

- Walking in late
- Ringing cell phones
- Falling asleep
- Texting
- Blurting out questions
- Interrupting classmates
- Talking during lecture
- Leaving early

Devon's midterm exam will determine 50 percent of his final grade. He's been so busy at home and his part-time job that he skipped class and study group all last week. He's afraid of bombing the exam, and someone he met in the cafeteria tells him he can buy a copy of the test.
- If he buys it, what are the repercussions if he gets caught?
- What are potential repercussions if he *doesn't* get caught?
- What would you do to prepare for the exam?

THINK
FAST

"The measure of a man's character is what he would do if he knew he never would be found out."

THOMAS MACAULAY
British writer and politician

Every day, you run into situations that test your character. **Personal Evaluation Notebook 2.1** includes questions and situations to get you thinking about your experiences. While completing this exercise, consider the personal qualities that make you smarter than you think you are, such as positive attitude, motivation, dependability, and honesty—for example, "I was raised on a farm in Michigan. What personal quality makes me smarter than my IQ or test scores?" If you answer "hard work," you're right. That one personal quality—putting in extra effort—has helped many people be more successful in life.

Personal qualities, especially honesty, are very important when you are think of hiring someone to work for a business you own. A candidate sends in an outstanding resumè. She has a college degree, experience, and a great personality, and she is positive and motivated, but you find out she stole from her last employer. No matter how bright or talented someone is, you don't want a dishonest person working for you. Complete **Personal Evaluation Notebook 2.2** on page 48 to see what qualities you would look for in a potential employee and which of those qualities you possess.

There is no universal code of ethics, and many questions about ethical issues do not have clear-cut answers. For example, taking money out of a cash drawer is clearly dishonest, but what about coming in late to work, padding your expense account, or using someone else's words without giving credit? You will be faced with situations in your personal, school, and business lives that will force you to make decisions that will be viewed as either ethical or unethical. Sometimes it is not easy. At one time or another, everyone is faced with situations that demand tough decisions. You will have to call on your own personal code of ethics. When defining your code and subsequent actions, you may find the following questions helpful:

- Is this action against the law?
- Is this action against company policy or code of behavior?
- How would this situation read if reported on the front page of the newspaper?
- How would you explain this to your mother? To your child?
- What might be the negative consequences?
- Are you causing unnecessary harm to someone?
- If unsure, have you asked a trusted associate outside of the situation?
- Are you treating others as you would want to be treated?

Remember, unethical behavior rarely goes unnoticed!

Responsibility

Peak performers take responsibility for their thoughts, state of mind, and behavior. They don't blame others for their problems but, rather, use their energy to solve them. They are persistent and patient. They know they must exert a consistently high effort to achieve their goals. They keep their word. When they say they are going to do something, they keep their commitment. People can depend on them.

Personal Evaluation Notebook

2.1

Character and Ethics

Integrity and honesty are essential qualities. It is important for you to assess and develop them as you would any skill. Use critical thinking to answer these questions.

1. What is the most difficult ethical dilemma you have faced in your life?

   _____

   _____

2. Do you have a code of ethics that helps guide you when making decisions? Explain.

   _____

   _____

3. Who have you known that is a role model for displaying integrity and honesty?

   _____

   _____

4. Do you have a code of ethics at your college? Where did you find it? (Hint: Check your school's catalog or ask the dean of students for a copy.)

   _____

   _____

Examples of being responsible include showing up prepared and on time for class, work, meetings, study teams, and so on. Responsible people own up to their mistakes and do what they can to correct them. The model in **Figure 2.1** on page 48 illustrates many important, interrelated personal responsibilities.

Other personal qualities related to responsibility include perseverance, punctuality, concentration, attention to details, follow-through, high standards, and respect for others. What you do or don't do in one area of your life affects other areas of your life and other people.

Peak performers realize they are responsible for their attitudes and actions, and they know they have the power to change. They have an **internal locus of control**, meaning they believe that they have control over their lives and that their rewards or failures are a result of their behavior, choices, or character. People with an **external locus of control** credit outside influences, such as fate, luck, or other people, with their success or failure. They are impulsive about immediate pleasures and easily swayed by the influences of others, and they often have a negative attitude and an inability to cope effectively with change, conflict, and frustration.

Learning to adjust to frustration and discouragement can take many forms. Some people withdraw or become critical, cynical, shy, sarcastic, or unmotivated. Blame, excuses, justification, and criticism of others are devices for those who

Personal Evaluation Notebook

2.2

Skills and Personal Qualities

1. Jot down the skills, personal qualities, and habits you are learning and demonstrating in each of your classes.

Skills	Personal Qualities	Habits
_____	_____	_____
_____	_____	_____
_____	_____	_____

2. Pretend that you own your own business. List the skills and personal qualities you would want in the employees you hire.

Type of business: _____

Employees' Skills	Employees' Personal Qualities
_____	_____
_____	_____
_____	_____

Figure 2.1
Personal Responsibilities

What you do or don't do in one area of life can affect other areas of your life and other people. *What one area of personal responsibility would you improve?*

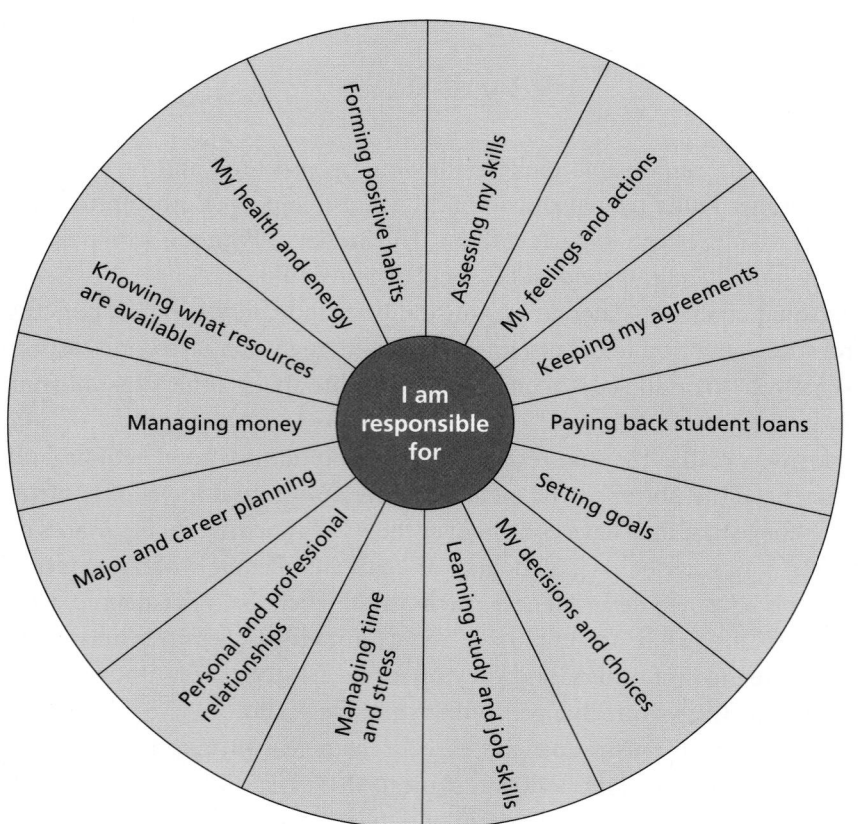

cannot accept personal responsibility. Acknowledge your feelings and attitudes. Decide if they support your goals; if they do not, choose a state of mind and actions that support you.

Being responsible creates a sense of integrity and a feeling of self-worth. For example, if you owe money to a friend, family member, or bank, or have a student loan, take responsibility for repaying the debt on schedule or make new arrangements with the lender. Not repaying can result in years of guilt and embarrassment, as well as a poor credit rating. It is important to your self-worth to know you are a person who keeps commitments and assumes responsibility.

Self-Control

If anger were a disease, there would be an epidemic in this country. Road rage, spousal and child abuse, and a lack of civility are just a few examples. Emotionally mature people know how to control their thoughts and behaviors and how to resolve conflict. Conflict is an inevitable part of school and work, but it can be resolved in a positive way. Try these tips for redirecting and transforming your anger:

1. **Calm down.** Step back from the situation and take a deep breath. Take the drama out of the situation and observe what is happening, what behavior is triggering angry emotions, and what options you have in responding appropriately and positively. If you lash out verbally, you may cause serious harm to your relationship. You cannot take back words once they are spoken. Resist the urge to overreact.

2. **Clarify and define.** Determine exactly with whom or what you are angry and why. What specific behavior in the other person is causing your anger or frustration? Determine whose problem it is. For example, your instructor may have an annoying tone and style of lecturing. If a behavior annoys only you, perhaps it is something you alone need to address.

3. **Listen with empathy and respect.** Empathy includes the ability to listen, understand, and respond to the feelings and needs of others. Take the tension out of the conflict by really listening and understanding the other person's point of view. Communicate that you have heard and understood by restating the other person's position.

4. **Use "I" statements.** Take ownership of your feelings. Using "I" statements—direct messages you deliver in a calm tone with supportive body language—can diffuse anger. Instead of blaming another person, express how a situation affects you. For example, you can say, "Carlos, when I hear you clicking your pen and tapping it on the desk, I'm distracted from studying." This is usually received better than saying, "Carlos, you're so rude and inconsiderate. You're driving me nuts with that pen!"

5. **Focus on one problem.** Don't rattle off every annoying behavior you can think of. Let's continue with the previous example: "In addition to clicking your pen, Carlos, I don't like how you leave your dishes in the sink, drop your towels in the bathroom, and make that annoying little sound when you eat." Work to resolve only one behavior or conflict at a time.

6. **Focus on win-win solutions.** How can you both win? Restate the problem and jot down as many different creative solutions as you can both agree on.

Don't let anger and conflict create more stress in your life and take a physical and emotional toll. You can learn to step back automatically from explosive situations and control them, rather than let your emotions control you. **Peak Progress 2.1** explores how you can use the Adult Learning Cycle to manage your emotions.

Self-Esteem and Confidence

Self-esteem is how you feel about yourself. People with positive self-esteem have the confidence that allows them to be more open to new experiences and accepting of different people. They tend to be more optimistic. They are more willing to share their feelings and ideas with others and are willing to tolerate differences in others. Because they have a sense of self-worth, they do not feel a need to put down or discriminate against others.

Confidence can develop from

- Focusing on your strengths and positive qualities and finding ways to bolster them. Be yourself and don't compare yourself with others.
- Learning to be resilient and bouncing back after disappointments and setbacks. Don't dwell on mistakes or limitations. Accept them, learn from them, and move on with your life.
- Using affirmations and visualizations to replace negative thoughts and images.
- Taking responsibility for your life instead of blaming others. You cannot control other people's behavior, but you have control over your own thoughts, emotions, words, and behavior.

Peak Progress

2.1

Applying the Adult Learning Cycle to Self-Control

The Adult Learning Cycle can help you increase your emotional intelligence. For example, you may have felt the same anger and frustration mentioned in the Self-Management exercise on the first page of this chapter. Maybe it happened when someone cut you off, you lost your keys, you had three papers due, or you felt so overwhelmed with responsibilities that you developed a negative attitude.

1. **RELATE. Why do I want to learn this?** What personal meaning and interest does controlling my anger have for me? Has it been a challenge? Has it hurt important relationships in my personal life or at school or work? How will controlling my anger help me in those situations?

2. **OBSERVE. How does this work?** I can learn a lot about anger management by watching, listening, and engaging in trial and error. Whom do I consider an emotionally mature person? Whom do I respect because of his or her patience, understanding, and

ability to deal with stressful events? When I observe the problems other people have, how do they exhibit their emotional maturity in general and anger specifically?

3. **REFLECT. What does this mean?** Test new ways of behaving, and break old patterns. Explore creative ways to solve problems instead of getting angry. Gather and assess information about anger management, and reflect on what works and doesn't work.

4. **DO. What can I do with this?** Learn by doing and finding practical applications for anger management. Practice the steps outlined on page 49. Apply the ABC Method of Self-Management to situations to determine positive outcomes.

5. **TEACH. Whom can I share this with?** Talk with others and share experiences. Model by example.

Now return to Stage 1 and realize your accomplishment in taking steps to control your anger better.

- Learning skills that give you opportunities and confidence in your abilities. It is not enough to feel good about yourself; you must also be able to do what is required to demonstrate that you are competent, honest, and responsible. The more skills and personal qualities you acquire, the more confident you will feel.
- Focusing on giving, not receiving, and make others feel valued and appreciated. You will increase your self-esteem when you make a contribution.
- Surround yourself with confident and kind people who feel good about themselves and make you feel good about yourself.

If you want to change your outer world and experiences for the better, you must begin by looking at your thoughts, feelings, and beliefs about yourself. Assess your self-esteem at the end of the chapter in **Worksheet 2.3** on page 72.

A Positive Attitude and Personal Motivation

There is an old story about three men working on a project in a large city in France. A curious tourist asks them, "What are you three working on?" The first man says, "I'm hauling rocks." The second man says, "I'm laying a wall." The third man says with pride, "I'm building a cathedral." The third man has a vision of the whole system. When college and work seem as tedious as hauling rocks, focus on the big picture.

A positive attitude is essential for achieving success in school, your career, and life. Your attitude, more than any other factor, influences the outcome of a task. **Motivation** is the inner drive that moves you to action. Even when you are discouraged or face setbacks, motivation can help you keep on track. You may have skills, experience, intelligence, and talent, but you will accomplish little if you are not motivated to direct your energies toward specific goals.

A positive attitude results in enthusiasm, vitality, optimism, and a zest for living. When you have a positive attitude, you are more likely to be on time, alert in meetings and class, and able to work well even on an unpleasant assignment. A positive attitude encourages

- Higher productivity
- An openness to learning at school and on the job
- School and job satisfaction
- Creativity in solving problems and finding solutions
- The ability to work with diverse groups of people
- Enthusiasm and a "can do" outlook
- Confidence and higher self-esteem
- The ability to channel stress and increase energy
- A sense of purpose and direction

A negative attitude can drain you of enthusiasm and energy. It can result in absenteeism, tardiness, and impaired mental and physical health. In addition, people who have a negative attitude may

- Feel they are victims and helpless to make a change
- Focus on the worst that can happen in a situation

> **"**It is better to light a candle than curse the darkness.**"**
>
> **ELEANOR ROOSEVELT**
> *U.S. first lady and political leader*

WORDS TO SUCCEED

- Blame external circumstances for their attitudes
- Focus on the negative in people and situations
- Believe adversity will last forever
- Be angry and blame other people

As discussed in Chapter 1, peak performers display a positive attitude even when faced with adversity. Having a positive attitude is more than simply seeing the glass as half full—it's a way of life.

How Needs and Desires Influence Attitudes and Motivation

One of the deepest needs in life is to become all that you can be by using all of your intelligence and potential. Abraham Maslow, a well-known psychologist, developed the theory of a hierarchy of needs. According to his theory, there are five levels of universal needs. **Figure 2.2** illustrates these levels, moving from the lower-order needs—physiological and safety and security needs—to the higher-order needs—the needs for self-esteem and self-actualization. Your lower-order needs must be met first before you can satisfy your higher-order needs. For example,

Figure 2.2
Maslow's Hierarchy of Needs

Maslow's theory states that most people need to satisfy the universal basic needs before considering the higher-order needs. *Which level of needs is motivating you right now?*

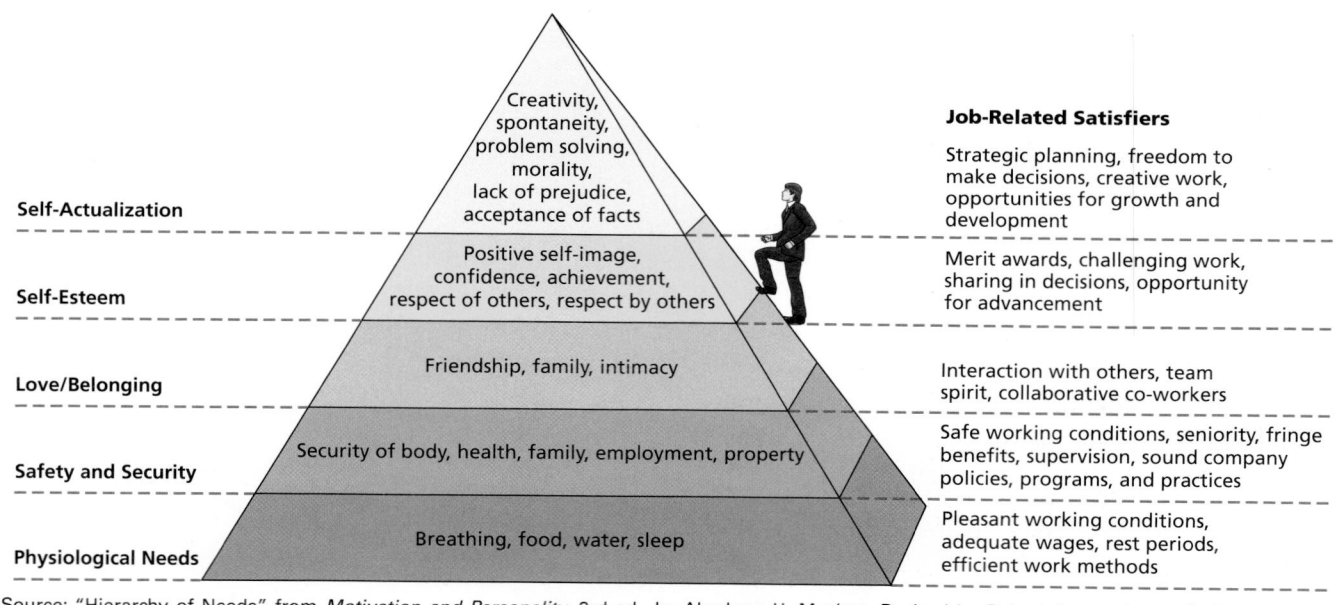

Source: "Hierarchy of Needs" from *Motivation and Personality,* 3rd ed., by Abraham H. Maslow. Revised by Robert Frager, James Fadiman, Cynthia McReynolds, and Ruth Cox. Copyright 1954, © 1987 by Harper & Row, Publishers, Inc. Copyright © 1970 by Abraham H. Maslow. Reprinted by permission of HarperCollins, Inc.

Personal Evaluation Notebook

2.3

Needs, Motivation, and Commitment

1. What needs motivate you at this time?

_____

_____

2. What do you think will motivate you in 20 years?

_____

_____

3. Complete this sentence in your own words: "For me to be more motivated, I need . . ."

_____

_____

4. Describe a time in your life when you were committed to something—such as a goal, a project, an event, or a relationship—that was important to you.

_____

_____

5. Regarding your answer to Question 4, what kept you motivated?

_____

_____

participating in hobbies that foster your self-respect is difficult if you don't have enough money for food and rent. For some people, the lower-order needs include a sense of order, power, or independence. The higher levels, which address social and self-esteem factors, include the need for companionship, respect, and a sense of belonging.

As your lower-order needs are satisfied and cease to motivate you, you begin to direct your attention to the higher-order needs for motivation. As you go up the ladder of higher-order needs, you'll find that you're learning for the joy of new ideas and the confidence that comes from learning new skills. You have more energy and focus for defining and pursuing your dreams and goals. You want to discover and develop your full potential. You not only love learning new ideas but also value emotional maturity, character, and integrity. You are well on the path to self-actualization. According to Maslow, self-actualizing people embrace the realities of the world rather than deny or avoid them. They are creative problem solvers who make the most of their unique abilities to strive to be the best they can be. Complete **Personal Evaluation Notebook 2.3** to assess what motivates you.

The Motivation Cycle

The motivation cycle in **Figure 2.3** amplifies what you learned in Chapter 1 about the power of visualization. It illustrates how your self-esteem influences what you say to yourself, which in turn influences your physical reactions—breathing, muscular tension, and posture. These physical reactions influence your behavior—both your verbal and your nonverbal responses. Isn't it amazing how the emotions, body, and mind are interrelated? If you change one part, you change the whole system. Try to remember how important affirmations and visualization are for creating a resourceful state of mind.

Motivational Strategies

Keeping yourself motivated isn't always easy when you're feeling pressures from school, work, and family. However, you can use these motivational strategies:

1. **Act as if you are motivated.** Attitude can influence behavior, and behavior can influence attitude. The way you act can affect your self-esteem, and your self-esteem can affect what you do. You can try to change your behavior anytime. You don't need to wait until your attitude changes or you feel motivated.

   For example, pretend you are performing in a movie. Your character is a positive, motivated student. How do you enter the room? Are you smiling? What are your breathing, posture, and muscle tension like? What kinds of gestures and facial expressions do you use to create this character? What kinds of friends does this person enjoy being with? If you develop positive study and work habits and do them consistently, even when you don't feel like it, you'll be successful, and this will create a positive state of mind.

2. **Use affirmations.** Any discussion of motivation must include your self-talk, what you say to yourself throughout the day. Once you start paying attention to your self-talk, you may be amazed at how much of it is negative. Countless thoughts, images, and phrases go through your brain daily almost unnoticed, but they have a tremendous influence on your mood and attitude. The first step, then, is to replace negative self-talk with affirmations (positive

Figure 2.3
The Motivation Cycle

Your emotions, body, and mind respond to what you say to yourself. *What positive message can you send to yourself?*

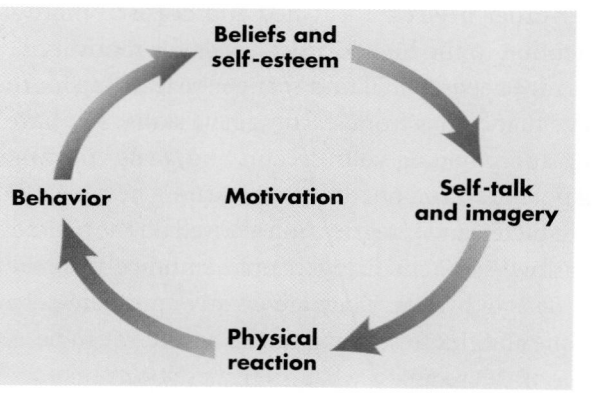

Personal Evaluation Notebook

2.4

Self-Talk and Affirmations

Listen to your self-talk for a few days. Jot down the negative thoughts you say to yourself. For example, when you first wake up, do you say, "I don't want to go to class today"?

Do your thoughts and self-talk focus on lack of time, lack of money, or other problems? Observe when you are positive. How does this change your state of mind and your physical sense of well-being? List examples of your negative self-talk and positive affirmations:

Negative Self-Talk	Positive Affirmations
1. _____	1. _____
2. _____	2. _____
3. _____	3. _____

self-talk). For example, don't say, "I won't waste my time today." Instead, affirm, "I am setting goals and priorities and achieving the results I want. I have plenty of energy to accomplish all that I choose to do, and I feel good when I'm organized and centered." Complete **Personal Evaluation Notebook 2.4** to determine if your self-talk needs to become more positive.

3. **Use visualization.** If you imagine yourself behaving in certain ways, that behavior will become real. For example, businessman Calvin Payne knows the power of visualization. Before he graduated from college, he bought his graduation cap and gown and kept them in his room. He visualized himself crossing the stage in his gown to accept his diploma. This visual goal helped him when he suffered setbacks, frustration, and disappointments. He graduated with honors and now incorporates visualization techniques in his career.

   Most right-brain dominant people are visual and use imagery a great deal. They can see scenes in detail when they read or daydream. In fact, their imagery is like a movie of themselves, with scenes of how they will react in certain situations, or a replay of what has occurred in the past. These images are rich in detail, expansive, and ongoing. Left-brain dominant people tend to use imagery less, but using imagery is a technique that can be learned.

4. **Use goals as motivational tools.** Just as an athlete visualizes crossing the finish line, you can visualize your final goal. Working toward your goal can be a great motivator; however, you first must know what your goal is. **Peak Progress 2.2** on page 56 will help you distinguish desires from goals and long-term goals from short-term goals.

   Besides visualizing goals peak performers often write them down. Try keeping yours in your wallet, taping them on your bathroom mirror, or putting them on yellow sticky notes around your computer screen. Without a specific goal, it's not easy to find the motivation, effort, and focus required to go to classes and complete assignments. Make certain your goals are

Peak Progress

Setting Goals

As the Cheshire cat said to Alice: "If you don't know where you are going, any road will take you there." The key, then, is to figure out where you are going, and then you can determine the best way to get there. Goal setting will help you do that. But goals provide more than direction and a clear vision for the future. When appropriately understood and applied, they are very effective motivators.

It is helpful first to distinguish between goals and desires. Identifying what you want out of life (that is, creating your mission statement, as discussed in Chapter 1) is certainly an important step in developing effective goals, but the goals themselves are not mere desires; rather, they are specific, measurable prescriptions for action. For example, if you want to be financially secure, you should start by identifying the actions that will help you fulfill that desire. Knowing that financial security is tied to education, you might make college graduation your first long-term goal. However, be careful how you construct this goal. "My goal is to have a college degree" is passive and vague. "I will earn my Bachelor of Science degree in computer technology from State University by June 2014" prescribes a clear course of action that you can break down into sequences of short-term goals, which then can be broken down into manageable daily tasks.

Your long-term goal always comes first. Sometimes when people are uncomfortable with long-term commitment, they try to address short-term goals first. Do not fall into this trap. Short-term goals are merely steps toward achieving the long-term goal, so they cannot even exist by themselves. To understand this better, imagine driving to an unfamiliar city and then trying to use a road map without having first determined where you are going. It cannot be done. You must know where you are going before you can plan your route (as illustrated below).

When defining your goals, remember:

- Desires and wishes are not goals.
- Goals prescribe action.
- Effective goals are specific.
- Goal setting always begins with a long-term goal.
- Short-term goals are the steps in achieving the long-term goal.
- Daily tasks are the many specific actions that fulfill short-term goals. In Chapter 3, we will explore using your goals to plan how to use your time effectively.

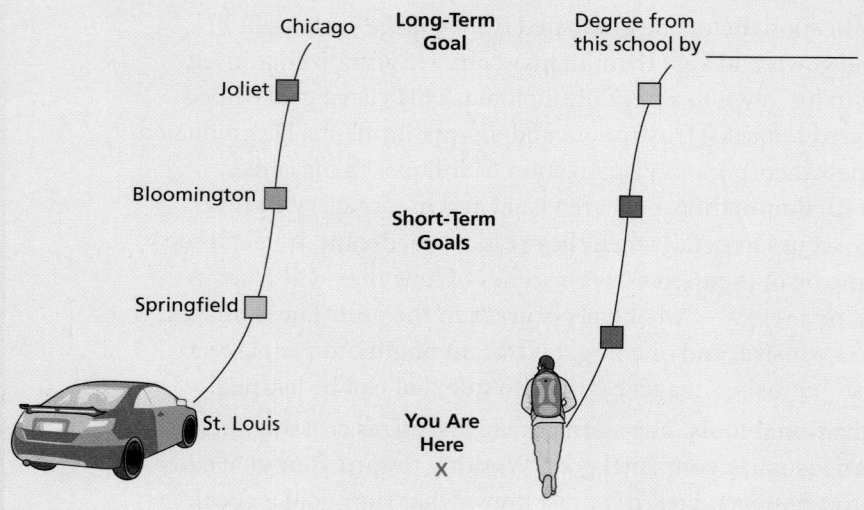

Goal Setting

Setting goals is like planning a trip—first you need to know your destination (long-term goal). Then you determine the best route to get there, including the milestones along the way (short-term goals). *If your long-term goal is to obtain your college degree, write in some of the short-term goals you need to accomplish (such as completing coursework, consulting with advisors and instructors, obtaining financial resources, and completing internships).*

Peak Progress

Differences between High School and College

Entering college brings a new level of responsibility and expectations as compared to your previous educational experiences, mimicking what is expected on the job as well as managing your personal life. For example, in college, you are expected to

- Have more responsibilities and budget your time and money
- Express your opinions logically, not just give facts
- Motivate yourself
- Handle more freedom and independence
- Attend larger classes that meet for longer periods but less often
- Be responsible for knowing procedures and graduation requirements

- Write and read more than you have before
- Think critically and logically
- Receive less feedback and be tested less often but more comprehensively
- Use several textbooks and supplemental readings
- Complete more work and turn in higher-quality work
- Interact with people of different values, cultures, interests, and religions
- Learn to be tolerant and respectful of diversity
- Encounter new ideas and critique those ideas in a thoughtful way
- Get involved in the community, school clubs, volunteer work, and internships related to your major

realistic. Achieving excellence doesn't mean attaining perfection or working compulsively toward impossible goals. Trying to be a perfectionist sets you up for frustration, which can decrease your motivation, lower productivity, increase stress, and lead to failure.

5. **Understand expectations.** You will be more motivated to succeed if you understand what is expected of you in each class. Most instructors hand out a syllabus on the first day. Read it carefully and keep a copy in your class notebook. Review the syllabus with a study partner and clarify expectations with your instructor. Meet with your academic advisor to review general college and graduation requirements. You will find that what is expected of you in college—from personal responsibility to independent thinking—is likely to be much more intense than your previous educational experiences. (See **Peak Progress 2.3.**)

6. **Study in teams.** Success in the business world depends on team skills—the sharing of skills, knowledge, confidence, and decision-making abilities. Teamwork aims for *synergy,* meaning the whole (the team's output) is greater than the sum of the parts (each member's abilities). Working as a team in school you can

- Teach each other material and outline main points.
- Read and edit each other's reports.
- Develop sample quizzes and test each other.
- Learn to get along with and value different people. (We will explore healthy relationships in more detail in Chapter 12.)

7. **Stay physically and mentally healthy.** It is difficult to motivate yourself if you don't feel well physically or emotionally. If you are ill, you will miss classes, fall behind in studying, or both. Falling behind can cause you to worry and feel

stressed. Talk out your problems, eat well, get plenty of exercise and rest, and create a balance of work and play.

8. **Learn to reframe.** You don't have control over many situations or the actions of others, but you do have control over your responses. **Reframing** is choosing to see a situation in a new way. For example, to pay for school, Joan works at a fast-food hamburger place. She could have chosen to see this negatively. Instead, she has reframed the situation to focus on learning essential job skills. She is learning to be positive, dependable, hardworking, service-oriented, flexible, and tolerant.

9. **Reward yourself.** The simplest tasks can become discouraging without rewards for progress and completion. Set up a system of appropriate rewards for finishing projects. For an easier task, the reward might be a snack, a hot shower, or a phone call to a friend. For a larger project, the reward might be going out to dinner or a movie or throwing a small party. What rewards would motivate you?

10. **Make learning relevant.** Your coursework will be more motivating if you understand how the knowledge you gain and new skills you learn will relate to your career performance. You may be attending college just because you love to learn and meet new people. However, it's more likely that you are enrolled to acquire or enhance your knowledge and skills, increasing your marketability in the workforce.

The Benefits of Higher Education

As just mentioned, you will be more motivated in your schoolwork—and more likely to graduate and excel—if you understand how attending college benefits you today and in the future.

HIGHER EDUCATION ENCOURAGES CRITICAL THINKING

Many years ago, being an educated person meant having a liberal arts education. *Liberal* comes from the Latin root word *liber,* which means "to free." A broad education is designed to free people to think and understand themselves and the world around them. The liberal arts include such areas as the arts, humanities, social sciences, mathematics, and natural sciences. Classes in philosophy, history, language, art, and geography focus on how people think, behave, and express themselves. The liberal arts integrate many disciplines and provide a foundation for professional programs, such as criminal justice, electronics, computer systems, business, medicine, and law.

Technology is no longer a separate field of study from liberal arts but is an important tool for educated people. Employers want professionals who are creative problem solvers, have good critical thinking skills, can communicate and work well with others, can adapt to change, and understand our complex technical and social world. Liberal arts classes can help make a skilled professional a truly educated professional who integrates and understands history, culture, self, and the world.

HIGHER EDUCATION IS A SMART FINANCIAL INVESTMENT

As mentioned earlier, you will be more motivated to put in long hours of studying when you feel the goal is worth it. Higher education is an excellent investment. No one can take your education away from you, and it can pay large dividends. College

"Education's purpose is to replace an empty mind with an open one."
MALCOLM FORBES
Publisher

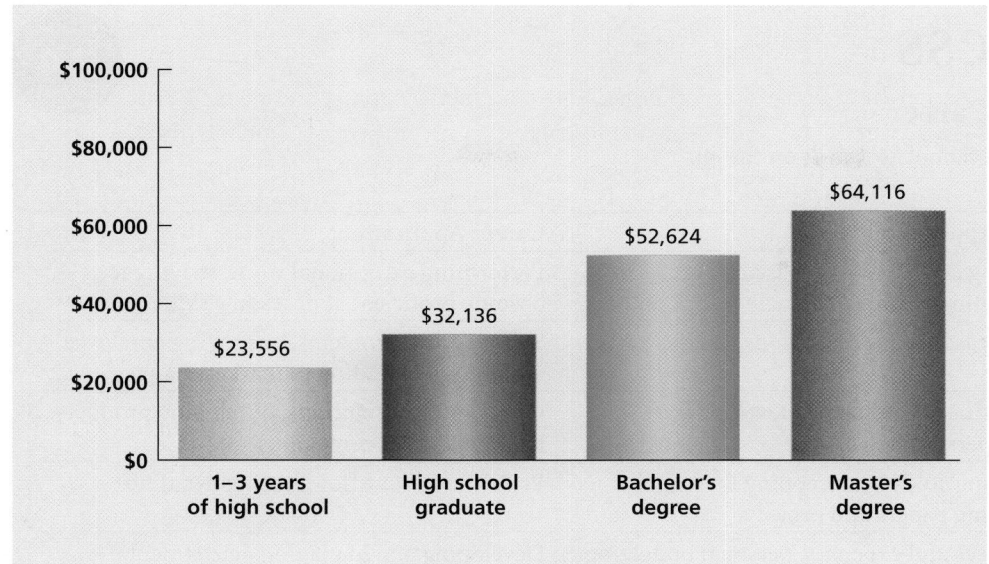

Figure 2.4

Annual Earnings and Education

Statistically, the level of your education is directly related to your income. These figures are average earnings for the U.S. population. Incomes vary within each category. *What other advantages, besides a good job and income, do you think education offers?*

Source: Bureau of Labor Statistics, Current Population Survey, 2008.

graduates earn an average of well over $800,000 more in a lifetime than do high school graduates. (See **Figure 2.4**.) Although graduating from college or a career school won't guarantee you a great job, it pays off with more career opportunities, better salaries, more benefits, more job promotions, increased workplace flexibility, better workplace conditions, and greater job satisfaction. Many college career centers are committed to helping their students find employment.

Society and the workplace benefit when people improve their literacy. Various reports from the U.S. Department of Labor indicate that people who attend at least 2 years of college tend to be more disciplined, have more self-confidence, make better decisions, and be more willing to adapt to change and learn new skills. They often have more hobbies and leisure activities, are more involved in their communities, and live longer, healthier lives.

HIGHER EDUCATION PREPARES YOU FOR LIFE ON THE JOB

What you learn in school today correlates directly with finding and keeping a job, as well as succeeding in a chosen career. As you go through school, think about how the skills, personal qualities, and habits you are learning and demonstrating in class are related to job and life success. **Peak Progress 2.4** on page 60 lists skills and qualities you are learning, practicing, and enhancing in your coursework and indicates how you will use them on the job.

As you develop your time- and stress-management skills, which we will explore in more detail later in this text, your habits in school and on the job will improve. Time management helps you show up for class on time and be prepared every day, leading to better grades. Punctuality in school will carry over to punctuality for work. Stress management may help you get along better with your roommates, instructors, or co-workers. Learning how to succeed in the school or college system can serve as a model for working effectively in organizational systems. Do you think you are maximizing your strengths, skills, and personal qualities? See **Peak Progress 2.5** on page 61 to determine what kind of student/worker you are and what you need to do to improve.

Peak Progress

Skills for School and Career

The following skills are used in school as well as on the job.

Skills	School Application	Career Application
Motivation	Attending class, being prepared and participating, submitting quality work on time	Performing exceptional work, striving to become proficient at necessary skills
Critical thinking	Solving case studies, equations, essays	Solving work problems, improving employee relations, responding to market changes
Creativity	Conducting experiments, developing term papers	Creating work solutions, developing products, launching sales campaigns
Time management	Scheduling studying, prepping for exams, completing papers and projects	Prioritizing workflow, hitting deadlines
Financial management	Paying fees and expenses, personal budgeting and saving	Developing and managing departmental budgets, projecting growth and profits
Writing	Writing papers, speeches, essay exams, e-mails, blogs	Writing reports, memos, e-mails, and product descriptions
Speeches	Giving classroom speeches, presenting research, leading and participating in class discussions	Delivering product presentations, leading and participating in meetings
Test taking	Taking quizzes and exams, applying for advanced degrees	Receiving performance reviews, certification and licensure exams
Research	Finding, evaluating, and citing information	Linking processes to results, testing new products
Learning	Learning new content to fulfill major, maximizing learning styles	Learning new job skills, adapting to changes in technology
Systems	Understanding college rules, procedures, deadlines, expectations	Understanding company rules, policies, reporting procedures
Resources	Using college resources, facilities, support services	Using work resources, training opportunities, supporting personnel
Technology	Using computers for papers, projects, research	Using computers for developing reports, communicating, managing systems

Overcome Obstacles

Don't Get Discouraged

Even peak performers sometimes feel discouraged and need help climbing out of life's valleys. To create and maintain a positive state of mind and learn self-management, you cannot just read a book, attend a lecture, or use a few strategies for a day or two. It takes time and effort. Everyone gets off course now and then, but the key is to realize that setbacks are part of life. Don't allow setbacks to make you feel as if you have failed and can no longer reach your goal. You have to become **resilient**—adapt to difficult or challenging life experiences and overcome adversity, bounce back, and thrive under pressure. Find a formula that works for you to create a positive, resourceful mind.

Peak Progress

What Kind of Student/Worker Are You?

A peak performer or an *A* student

- Is alert, actively involved, and eager to learn
- Consistently does more than required
- Consistently shows initiative and enthusiasm
- Is positive and engaged
- Can solve problems and make sound decisions
- Is dependable, prompt, neat, accurate, and thorough
- Attends work/class every day and is on time and prepared

A good worker or a *B* student

- Frequently does more than is required
- Is usually attentive, positive, and enthusiastic
- Completes most work accurately, neatly, and thoroughly
- Often uses critical thinking to solve problems and make decisions
- Attends work/class almost every day and is usually on time and prepared

An average worker or a *C* student

- Completes the tasks that are required
- Shows a willingness to follow instructions and learn
- Is generally involved, dependable, enthusiastic, and positive
- Provides work that is mostly thorough, accurate, and prompt
- Misses some work/classes

A problem worker or a *D* student

- Usually does the minimum of what is required
- Has irregular attendance, is often late, or is distracted
- Lacks a positive attitude or the ability to work well with others
- Often misunderstands assignments and deadlines
- Lacks thoroughness
- Misses many days of work/classes

An unacceptable worker or an *F* student

- Does not do the work that is required
- Is inattentive, bored, negative, and uninvolved
- Is undependable and turns in work that is incorrect and incomplete
- Misses a significant amount of work/class time

Figure 2.5 on page 62 shows reasons students have given for dropping out of college. Many of these seem out of the student's control, but many may simply be excuses for not finding a way to persevere. For example, not all classes will be exhilarating and indeed may seem boring at times—but is that a reason to give up? If you think, "I'll be more motivated as soon as I graduate and get a real job," you may never develop the necessary qualities and skills to achieve that. Starting today, you should

- Commit to being motivated and positive.
- Focus on your successes and accomplishments.
- Surround yourself with positive, supportive, and encouraging friends.
- Tell yourself, "This is a setback, not a failure."
- Learn self-control and self-management strategies.
- Make certain you are physically renewed; get more rest, exercise more, and every day do something you love.
- Replace negative and limiting thoughts and self-talk with affirmations and positive visualization.
- Collect short stories about people who were discouraged, received negative messages, and bounced back.

Create Positive Mind Shifts

Your beliefs and expectations about yourself can either limit or expand your success. Other people's expectations of you may cause you to redefine who you think you are and what you think you can achieve. You may start to believe what you tell yourself or hear from others again and again, which may limit your thinking.

Figure 2.5
Reasons Students Do Not Graduate.

Juggling the demands of work and school is a major reason why students drop out of college. Besides the reasons cited in this survey, students also struggle with poor study habits, managing their social time, and taking responsibility for their education—including asking for help. *Which "reasons" in the survey are you facing and how are you coping in order to achieve your goals?*

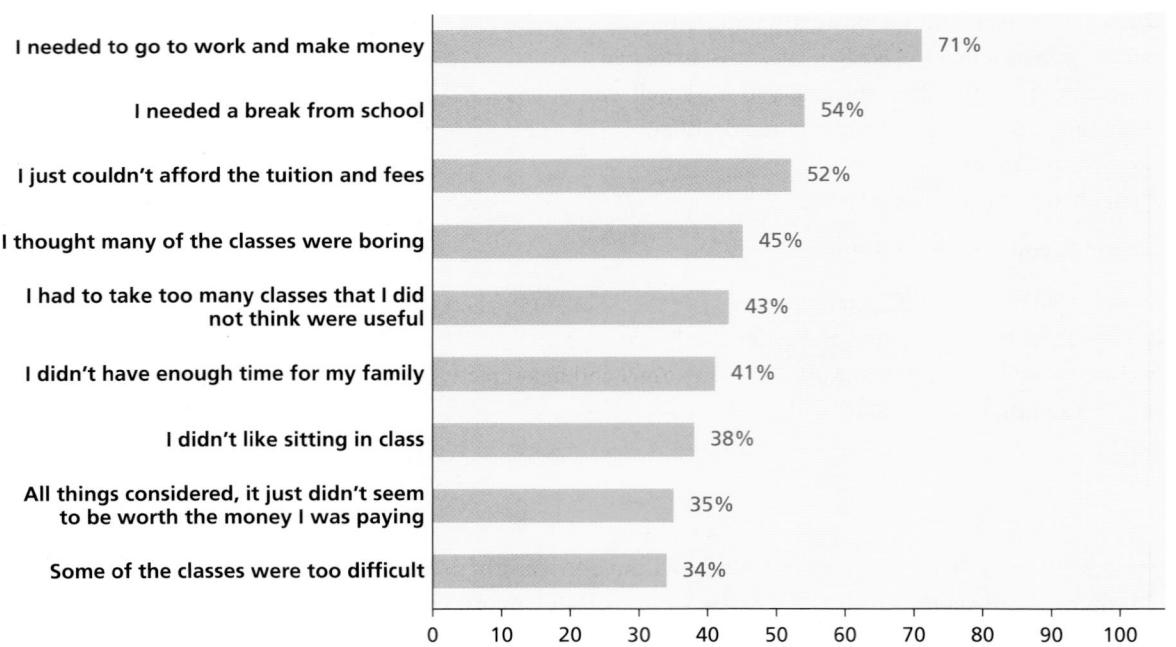

Reason	Percentage
I needed to go to work and make money	71%
I needed a break from school	54%
I just couldn't afford the tuition and fees	52%
I thought many of the classes were boring	45%
I had to take too many classes that I did not think were useful	43%
I didn't have enough time for my family	41%
I didn't like sitting in class	38%
All things considered, it just didn't seem to be worth the money I was paying	35%
Some of the classes were too difficult	34%

Source: Jean Johnson and Jon Rochkind with Amber N. Ott and Samantha DuPont, "With Their Whole Lives Ahead of Them: Myths and Realities About Why So Many Students Fail to Finish College." A Public Agenda Report for The Bill & Melinda Gates Foundation, December 20, 2009. Reprinted with permission.

For example, Steve comes from a long line of lumber mill workers. Although they have lived for generations in a college town, his family has never had anything to do with the college. Steve was expected to go to work at the mill right after high school. He never thought about other options. However, during his senior year in high school, he attended Career Day. He met instructors and students from the local college who were friendly and encouraging. His world opened up, and he saw opportunities he had never considered. Steve experienced a major mind shift. Although he had to overcome a lack of support at home, he is now a successful college student with a bright future.

College is an ideal time to develop your natural creativity and explore new ways of thinking. Try the following:

1. **Create a support system.** Without support and role models, you may question whether you can succeed. First-generation college students, women in technical programs, and men in nursing programs may feel uncomfortable and question whether they belong. Cultural minorities, veterans, and physically challenged or returning students may feel out of place. Some students may be told that they are not college material. You can find encouragement with a support system of positive, accepting people. Join a variety of clubs. Make friends with diverse groups of students, instructors, and community leaders.

2. **Reprogram your mind.** Affirmations and visualization can create a self-fulfilling prophecy. If you think of yourself as a success and are willing to put in the effort, you will succeed. Focus on your successes and accomplishments, and overcome limitations. For example, if you need to take a remedial math class, take it and don't label yourself as "dumb" or "math-impaired." Instead, focus on how improved your math skills will be.

3. **Use critical thinking.** Question limiting labels and beliefs. Where did they come from, and are they accurate?

4. **Use creative thinking.** Ask yourself, "What if?" Explore creative ways of achieving your goals. Find out how you learn best, and adopt positive habits.

5. **Take responsibility.** You are responsible for your thoughts, beliefs, and actions. You can question, think, and explore. You can achieve almost anything you dream.

6. **Learn new skills.** Focus on your strengths, but be willing to learn new skills and competencies continually. Feeling competent is empowering.

7. **Use the whole of your intelligence.** You definitely are smarter than you think you are. Use all your experiences and personal qualities to achieve your goals. Develop responsibility, self-control, dependability, sociability, character, manners, and all the other qualities necessary for school, job, and life success.

TAKING CHARGE

Summary

In this chapter, I learned to

- **Use the whole of my intelligence.** Developing emotional maturity and strong personal qualities is just as, if not more, important to my future success as learning new skills and information. Essential personal qualities include character, responsibility, self-management and self-control, self-esteem, confidence, attitude, and motivation.

- **Focus on character first.** Strong leaders have an equally strong set of values. Having personal integrity gives me the courage to do the right thing, even when it is difficult. I display civility and empathy by interacting with family, friends, and colleagues with respect, kindness, good manners, empathy, and compassion. It's important for me to have a personal code of ethics that I follow in all facets of my life.

- **Take responsibility for my thoughts, actions, and behaviors.** I don't blame others for my setbacks, and I focus my energy on positive solutions. Others can depend on me to keep my commitments.

- **Manage and control my emotions, anger, and negative thoughts.** Conflict is an inevitable part of life, but it can be resolved in a positive way. Steps I can follow to redirect my negative thoughts and anger are (1) calm down; (2) clarify and define; (3) listen with empathy and respect; (4) use "I" statements; (5) focus on one problem; and (6) focus on win-win solutions.

- **Develop self-esteem and confidence.** Through self-assessment, I understand my strengths and will continue to learn new skills and competencies that will build my confidence.

- **Maintain a positive attitude and keep myself motivated.** A positive attitude is essential for achieving success; it influences the outcome of a task more than any other factor. Motivation is the inner drive that moves me to action. Working toward goals increases my motivation. Maslow's hierarchy of needs shows that I can fulfill my higher needs for self-esteem and self-actualization only when I have fulfilled my more basic needs first. The motivation cycle further demonstrates how affirmations, visualization, and self-talk affect my physical responses and behavior.

- **Realize the benefits of higher education.** Higher education has its roots in the liberal arts. Liberal arts classes can help make me a truly educated professional by providing an integration and understanding of history, culture, ourselves, and our world. My pursuit of a higher education should pay off with more career opportunities, a higher salary, more benefits, more job promotions, increased workplace flexibility, better workplace conditions, and greater job satisfaction. I will become more prepared for life on the job.

- **Overcome the barriers to staying positive and motivated.** Discouragement is the number one barrier to motivation. Setbacks will occur, but I am resilient by focusing on my successes and accomplishments, surrounding myself with supportive and encouraging people, keeping physically renewed, and replacing negative self-talk with positive affirmations and visualization.

- **Create positive mind shifts.** My beliefs and perceptions must be realistic. If they aren't, I must refocus my expectations in order to achieve my goals. I should not allow my beliefs to limit my potential, and I will use critical thinking techniques to expand my mind and comfort zone.

Performance Strategies

Following are the top 10 strategies for expanding your emotional intelligence and personal qualities:

- Cultivate character and integrity.
- Create a personal code of ethics.
- Take responsibility for your thoughts, actions, and behaviors.
- Practice self-control.
- Develop positive self-esteem and confidence.
- Determine personal motivators.
- Use goals as motivational tools.
- Reward yourself for making progress, and strive for excellence, not perfection.
- Become resilient to bounce back from setbacks.
- Create positive mind shifts.

Tech for Success

Take advantage of the text's Web site at **www.mhhe.com/ferrett8e** for additional study aids, useful forms, and convenient and applicable resources.

- **Ethics information on the Web.** Search for articles on ethics, business etiquette, and codes of ethics. Check out different businesses, the military, government agencies, and colleges to find out if each has a code of ethics. Print some samples and bring them to class. What do the codes of ethics have in common?

- **Online discussion groups.** When you are interested in a topic or goal, it's very motivating to interact with others who share your interests. Join a discussion group or

listserv and share your knowledge, wisdom, and setbacks with others. You will learn their stories and strategies in return.

- **Goal-setting examples.** Although your goals should be personal, sometimes it helps to see how others have crafted theirs. This may inspire you to realize that setting goals isn't difficult—it just takes thinking critically about what you want out of life. A number of resources on the Web provide goal-setting ideas on everything from becoming more financially responsible to learning a second language.

Study Team Notes

Career*in* focus

Jacqui Williams
SALES REPRESENTATIVE

Related Majors: Business, Marketing, Public Relations

Positive Attitudes at Work

As a sales representative for a large medical company, Jacqui Williams sells equipment, such as X-ray and electrocardiograph (EKG) machines, to hospitals nationwide. Her job requires travel to prospective clients, where she meets with buyers to show her products and demonstrate their installation and use. Because Jacqui cannot take the large machines with her, she relies on printed materials and a laptop computer, from which she can point out new aspects of the machines she sells. The sales process usually takes several months and requires more than one trip to the prospective client.

Jacqui works on commission, being paid only when she makes a sale. Because she travels frequently, Jacqui must be able to work independently without a lot of supervision. For this reason, being personally motivated is a strong requirement for her position. Jacqui has found that what motivates her most is believing in the products she sells. Jacqui keeps up on the latest in her field by reading technical information and keeping track of the competition. She sets sales goals and then rewards herself with a short vacation.

Because personal relations with buyers are so important, Jacqui is careful about her appearance. While traveling, she keeps a positive mindset through affirmations, and she gets up early to eat a healthy breakfast and exercise in the hotel gym. She uses integrity by presenting accurate information and giving her best advice, even if it means not making a sale. Her clients would describe Jacqui as positive and helpful, someone whom they look forward to seeing and whose advice they trust.

CRITICAL THINKING In what way does having integrity, good character, and a code of ethics enhance a sales representative's business?

Peak Performer

PROFILE

Christiane Amanpour

"Amanpour is coming. Is something bad going to happen to us?"* That's how CNN's London-based chief international correspondent, Christiane Amanpour, says she's often greeted. Whether she appreciates the grim humor or not, Amanpour knows that her name and face have become linked in people's minds with war, famine, and death. But she has earned the respect of journalists and viewers around the world with her gutsy reporting from war-ravaged regions, such as Afghanistan, Iran, Israel, Pakistan, Somalia, Rwanda, and the Balkans.

Amanpour launched her career at CNN as an assistant on the international assignment desk in 1983, when some observers mockingly referred to the fledgling network as "Chicken Noodle News." "I arrived at CNN with a suitcase, my bicycle, and about 100 dollars,"* she recalls. Less than a decade later, Amanpour was covering Iraq's invasion of Kuwait, the U.S. combat operation in Somalia, and the breakup of the Soviet Union as these events unfolded.

Amanpour's globe trotting began early. Born in London, Amanpour soon moved with her family to Tehran, where her father was an Iranian airline executive. Her family fled the country and returned to England during the Islamic Revolution of 1979. After high school, Amanpour studied journalism at the University of Rhode Island. She took a job after college as an electronics graphic designer at a radio station in Providence. She

worked at a second radio station as a reporter, an anchor, and a producer before joining CNN.[†]

"I thought that CNN would be my ticket to see the world and be at the center of history—on someone else's dime,"* she says, noting that she's logged more time at the front than most military units. Fear, she admits, is as much a part of her daily life as it is for the soldiers whose activities she chronicles: "I have spent almost every working day [since becoming a war correspondent] living in a state of repressed fear."*

Amanpour worries about the changes that have transformed the television news industry in recent years, as competition for ratings and profits has heated up.

But Amanpour remains optimistic. "If we the storytellers give up, then the bad guys certainly will win," she says. "Remember the movie *Field of Dreams* when the voice said 'Build it and they will come'? Well, somehow that dumb statement has always stuck in my mind. And I always say, 'If you tell a compelling story, they will watch.'"*

PERFORMANCE THINKING Christiane Amanpour demonstrates courage, integrity, and commitment. In what ways do you speak out for freedom, justice, and equality?

CHECK IT OUT The Committee to Protect Journalists indicates that 68 journalists were killed in 2009 because of their work. Visit **www.cpj.org** to see what's being done to safeguard the lives of journalists in the world's hotspots. Use the search field to find the manual "Journalist Safety Guide" to see what precautions journalists themselves must take in high-risk situations.

*AIDA International, 2000 Murrow Awards Ceremony Speech, September 13, 2000. **www.aidainternational.nl**.
[†]CNN Anchors and Reporters: Christiane Amanpour. **www.cnn.com/CNN/anchors_reporters/amanpour.Christiane.html**.

Starting Today

At least one strategy I learned in this chapter that I plan to try right away is

_____

_____

_____

What changes must I make in order for this strategy to be most effective?

_____

_____

_____

Review Questions

Based on what you have learned in this chapter, write your answers to the following questions:

1. What personal qualities are essential to success in school and work?

_____

_____

2. Give an example of a short-term goal versus a long-term goal.

_____

_____

3. List at least five motivational strategies.

_____

_____

4. Explain how affirmations and visualization affect the motivational cycle.

_____

_____

5. Explain what a mind shift is.

_____

_____

To test your understanding of the chapter's concepts, complete the chapter quiz at **www.mhhe.com/ferret8e**.

Getting Motivated

In the Classroom

Carol Rubino is a drafting major at a community college. To pay her expenses, she needs to work several hours a week. She is very organized and responsible with her school and work obligations. Most of her peers would describe Carol as motivated because she attends every class, is punctual, and works hard in school and at work. Throughout high school, Carol participated in extracurricular activities but never really enjoyed herself. She likes college but questions the connection between school and real life. As a result, Carol sometimes feels as if she is just wasting time and postponing life until graduation.

1. What strategies in this chapter can help Carol find a strong sense of purpose and motivation?

_____

_____

2. What would you recommend to Carol for creating a more resourceful and positive attitude?

_____

_____

In the Workplace

Carol is now a draftsperson for a small industrial equipment company. She has been with the company for 10 years. Carol is a valuable employee because she is competent and well liked. Carol has a supportive family, is healthy, and travels frequently. Although she enjoys her job, Carol feels bored with the mundane routine. She wants to feel more motivated and excited on the job, as well as in her personal life.

3. What strategies in this chapter can help Carol become more enthusiastic about work or find new interest in her personal life?

_____

_____

4. What would you suggest to Carol to help her get motivated?

_____

_____

Applying the ABC Method of Self-Management

In the Journal Entry on page 43, you were asked to describe a time when you were angry and lost control of your emotions. Describe that event below and indicate how others reacted to your actions.

_____

_____

_____

_____

_____

Now apply the ABC method to the situation and visualize a situation under control:

A = Actual event:

_____

_____

B = Beliefs:

_____

_____

C = Challenge:

_____

_____

While completing this exercise, were you surprised by the amount of time you spend on negative thoughts?

PRACTICE SELF-MANAGEMENT

For more examples of learning how to manage difficult situations, see the "Self-Management Workbook" section of the Online Learning Center Web site at **www.mhhe.com/ferrett8e**.

My Reinforcement Contract

Use this example as a guide; then fill in the following contract for one or all of the courses you are taking this term.

Name *Sara Jones*

Course *General Accounting*   Date *September 2011*

If I *study for 6 hours each week in this class and attend all lectures and labs*

Then I will *reward myself with a long bike ride and picnic lunch every Saturday.*

I agree to *learn new skills, choose positive thoughts and attitudes, and try out new behaviors.*

I most want to accomplish *an "A" in this course to qualify for advanced accounting courses.*

The barriers to overcome are *my poor math skills.*

The resources I can use are *my study group and the Tutoring Center.*

I will reward myself for meeting my goals by *going out to dinner with some friends.*

The consequences for not achieving the results I want will be *to reevaluate my major.*

REINFORCEMENT CONTRACT

Name _____

Course _____ Date _____

If I _____

Then I will _____

I agree to _____

_____

I most want to accomplish _____

The barriers to overcome are _____

The resources I can use are _____

I will reward myself for meeting my goals by _____

The consequences for not achieving the results I want will be _____

Self-Esteem Inventory

Do this simple inventory to assess your self-esteem. Circle the number of points that reflects your true feelings.

4 = all the time
3 = most of the time
2 = some of the time
1 = none of the time

1.	I like myself and I am a worthwhile person.	4	3	2	1
2.	I have many positive qualities.	4	3	2	1
3.	Other people generally like me and I have a sense of belonging.	4	3	2	1
4.	I feel confident and know I can handle most situations.	4	3	2	1
5.	I am competent and good at many things.	4	3	2	1
6.	I have emotional control and I am respectful of others.	4	3	2	1
7.	I am a person of integrity and character.	4	3	2	1
8.	I respect the kind of person I am.	4	3	2	1
9.	I am capable and willing to learn new skills.	4	3	2	1
10.	Although I want to improve and grow, I am happy with myself.	4	3	2	1
11.	I take responsibility for my thoughts, beliefs, and behavior.	4	3	2	1
12.	I am empathetic and interested in others and the world around me.	4	3	2	1
	Total points	___	___	___	___

Add up your points. A high score (36 and above) indicates high self-esteem. If you have a high sense of self-esteem, you see yourself in a positive light. If your self-esteem is low (below 24), you may have less confidence to deal with problems in college or on the job. If you scored at the lower end, list some strategies you can implement that may help boost your self-esteem:

Learning Styles and Motivation

You will feel more motivated and positive when you align your efforts with your learning and personality styles. Review your preference and style and think of the factors that help motivate you.

For example, *auditory learners* may be more motivated when they listen to their favorite inspirational music and say affirmations. *Visual learners* may be more motivated when they surround themselves with pictures and practice visualizing themselves as motivated and positive. *Kinesthetic learners* may be more motivated when they work on activities, dance, hike, jog, and work with others. (See pages 12–16 for the complete discussion.)

Analyzers may be more motivated when they think, reflect, and organize information into sequential steps. *Supporters* may be more motivated when they work in a group and make information meaningful. *Creators* may be more motivated when they observe, make active experiments, and build models. *Directors* may be more motivated when they clearly define procedures and make practical applications. (See pages 20–26 for the complete discussion.)

List the ways you can motivate yourself that are compatible with your learning style and personality type:

1. _____
   _____
   _____

2. _____
   _____
   _____

3. _____
   _____
   _____

4. _____
   _____
   _____

5. _____
   _____

6. _____
   _____
   _____

Assessment of Personal Qualities

Category	Assessment	Y/N	Example
Emotional intelligence	Do I value and practice essential personal qualities?		
Character	Do I value and practice being a person of character and integrity?		
Civility	Do I treat others with respect and courtesy?		
Ethics	Do I have a code of ethics?		
Responsibility	Do I take responsibility for my thoughts and behavior?		
Self-control	Do I have self-control and know how to manage anger?		
Self-esteem	Do I have a realistic and positive sense of myself?		
Positive attitude	Do I strive to be positive and upbeat?		
Motivation	Do I create the inner drive and determination to achieve my goals?		
Self-actualization	Am I committed to growing and realizing my full potential?		
Visualization	Do I use visualization as a powerful tool for change and growth?		
Affirmation	Do I dispute and replace negative self-talk with affirmations?		
Critical thinking	Do I use critical thinking to challenge my beliefs and see new possibilities?		

The area I most want to improve is:

Strategies I will use to improve are:

3

Manage Your Time

LEARNING OUTCOMES

In this chapter, you will learn to

3.1 Determine how you use your time and how you *should* use your time.

3.2 Use personal goals to identify priorities

3.3 List time-management strategies

3.4 Work in alignment with your learning style

3.5 Overcome procrastination

3.6 Handle interruptions

3.7 Juggle family, school, and job commitments

SELF-MANAGEMENT

"It's 7:30 a.m., I'm late for class, and I can't find my keys. It always seems like there's too little time and too much to do. I feel as if I have no control over my life. How can I manage my time and get organized?"

Have you ever had a similar experience? Do you find yourself spending hours looking for things? Do you get angry at yourself and others because you feel frustrated and unorganized? In this chapter, you will learn how to take control of your time and your life and focus on priorities. Visualize yourself going through the day organized and centered. You have a clear vision of your goals and priorities, and you work steadily until tasks are finished. Feel the sense of accomplishment and completion. You are in charge of your time and your life.

JOURNAL ENTRY In **Worksheet 3.1** on page 106, describe a time or situation when you felt overwhelmed by too much to do and too little time. What were the consequences?

I n this chapter, we look at time management with a positive attitude. Instead of controlling, suppressing, or constricting your freedom, time management enables you to achieve the things you really want and frees up time to enjoy life. Peak performers use a systematic approach that allows them to

- Organize projects and achieve results
- Accomplish goals and priorities
- Be effective, not just efficient
- Avoid crises
- Remain calm and productive
- Feel a sense of accomplishment

Everyone has the same amount of time: 24 hours a day. You can't save or steal time. When it's gone, it's gone. However, you can learn to invest it wisely. This chapter will help you learn how to get control of your life by managing your time wisely and choosing to spend it on your main goals. It will also help you think about the contributions you want to make during your lifetime and the legacy you want to leave behind after you are gone. You will discover that there is always time to do what you really want to do. Too many people waste time doing things that should be done quickly (if at all) and ignoring their main goals.

As you go through this chapter, think about what you want to achieve and how you can use your time skillfully to perform at your peak level. This chapter will help you become effective, not just efficient. You are efficient when you do things faster. You are effective when you do the right things in the right way. As a wise time manager, you can avoid feeling overwhelmed and falling behind in school, at work, or in your personal life. Whether you are an 18-year-old living on campus or a 45-year-old juggling school, family, and work, the principles in this chapter can help you manage your time and your life.

Use Time Effectively

Time management is much more than focusing on minutes, hours, and days. Your attitude, energy level, and ability to concentrate have a major impact on how well you manage time. Clearly evaluate situations that may have spun out of control because you procrastinated or failed to plan and how these situations may have affected other people. Others suffer when you are late for class, miss a study group meeting, or don't do your share of a team project.

Let's look at two important questions concerning your present use of time. The answers will help you develop a plan that will fine-tune your organizational and time-management skills—ultimately leading you to become an efficient peak performer.

1. Where does your time go? (Where are you spending your time and energy?)
2. Where should your time go?

Where Does Your Time Go?

You can divide time into three types: committed time, maintenance time, and discretionary time.

- **Committed time.** Committed time is devoted to school, labs, studying, work, commuting, family, and other activities involving the immediate and long-term goals you have committed to accomplishing. Your committed time reflects what is important to your career, health, relationships, and personal growth—what you value most.

- **Maintenance time.** Maintenance time is the time you spend "maintaining" yourself. Activities such as eating, sleeping, grooming (showering, styling your hair, cleaning your contact lenses, getting dressed, etc.), cooking, cleaning/laundry, shopping, and bill paying use up your maintenance time.

- **Discretionary time.** The time that is yours to use as you please is discretionary time. Although this is your "free" time, you should spend it on the most important things in your life, such as relationships with family and friends; service to the community; intellectual development; and activities that give you joy and relaxation and that contribute to your physical, mental, and spiritual well-being. These should tie in with your long-term goals of being healthy, feeling centered and peaceful, and having loving relationships.

- **Where does fitness "fit"?**
Daily exercise can be considered committed time if it's part of your overall life plan to remain healthy. Some would consider it maintenance, and others would place it under discretionary activities. *Where would you record it?*

As you consider where your time goes, notice whether you are using most of the day for commitments. A good place to start is with an assessment of how you spend your time and energy. Complete **Personal Evaluation Notebook 3.1** on page 78 (or use the weekly planner in **Worksheet 3.7** on page 112) to track how you use your time. The far right column asks you to indicate your energy level during the day: Do you feel focused and alert, or are you distracted or tired? Many people have certain hours during the day when they are most productive.

After you have recorded your activities, review your Time Log to determine how much time you are devoting to daily tasks, such as studying, commuting, and socializing. Complete **Personal Evaluation Notebook 3.2** on page 79 and tally how much time you currently spend on various activities (and add others from your Time Log). Determining where you are currently spending your time will help you figure out the best way to use your time to achieve important goals. Even if you are juggling school, work, and family and feel you have no discretionary time, this will help you use what little discretionary time you do have to be most effective.

Personal Evaluation Notebook

Time Log

Fill in this Time Log to chart your activities throughout the day. Identify activities as committed (C), maintenance (M), or discretionary (D). Also determine your energy level throughout the day as high (H), medium (M), or low (L). Use **Worksheet 3.7** on page 112 to chart your activities for more than 1 day to see patterns in how you spend your time.

Time	Activity	Type C/M/D	Energy H/M/L
12:00–1:00 a.m.			
1:00–2:00			
2:00–3:00			
3:00–4:00			
4:00–5:00			
5:00–6:00			
6:00–7:00			
7:00–8:00			
8:00–9:00			
9:00–10:00			
10:00–11:00			
11:00–12:00 (noon)			
12:00–1:00 p.m.			
1:00–2:00			
2:00–3:00			
3:00–4:00			
4:00–5:00			
5:00–6:00			
6:00–7:00			
7:00–8:00			
8:00–9:00			
9:00–10:00			
10:00–11:00			
11:00–12:00 (midnight)			

Personal Evaluation Notebook

How Much Time Do You Spend?

Fill in this chart to determine how much time you spend on certain activities. Use the information you compiled in **Personal Evaluation Notebook 3.1.** Typical activities are listed. You may, of course, change or add activities to the list. If you recorded your activities for multiple days, include all the minutes as well as a daily average.

Activity	Time Spent	Activity	Time Spent
Attending class		Eating	
Working at a job		Sleeping	
Commuting		Cooking	
Studying		Shopping	
Working on class projects		Surfing the Internet	
Grooming		Socializing	
Exercising		Doing hobbies	
Doing household chores		Talking on the telephone	
Waiting in line		Watching television	
E-mail/texting		Recreation (including video games)	
Study group		Other	
Other		Other	

Where Should Your Time Go?

The first rule of time management is to make a commitment to what you want to accomplish—in other words, to set goals. As discussed in Chapter 2, goals are not vague wishes or far-away dreams. They are specific, measurable, observable, and realistic. A goal is a target that motivates you and directs your efforts. Goal setting is not easy; you need to think about your deepest values. Complete **Worksheet 3.2** on page 107 to assess your habits and level of commitment.

It's important to have a realistic picture of what your goals are and to observe and reflect constantly on how your daily activities are leading to larger goals. Written goals help clarify what you want and can give you energy, direction, and focus to put them into action. Goals can be short-term, intermediate, or long-term and are easier to identify when they flow out of a mission statement that defines what is most important to you. Placing goals within time frames can help you reach them. Complete **Personal Evaluation Notebook 3.3** to map out your goals. Then, in Chapter 14, revisit these goals when you are completing your Career Development Portfolio.

Personal Evaluation Notebook  **3.3**

Looking Ahead: Your Goals

Complete this activity to help you create major targets in your life—or long-term goals. From these goals, you can write intermediate goals (2 to 5 years), short-term goals (1 year), and then immediate (or semester) goals. Use **Worksheets 3.5** and **3.8** to help you map out your goals. Save this in your Career Development Portfolio.

A. MISSION STATEMENT

You'll recall from Chapter 1 that your personal mission statement summarizes the life you want to have and reflects your philosophy based on your deepest values and principles. In the blanks below, repeat (or revise) your thoughts from Chapter 1.

- What do you value most in life?

  _____

- What is your life's purpose?

  _____

- What legacy do you want to leave?

  _____

MISSION STATEMENT:

_____

_____

B. LONG-TERM GOALS (ACCOMPLISH IN 10 YEARS OR SO)

Brainstorm all the specific goals you want to accomplish during your lifetime. Include goals for all areas of your life, such as education, career, travel, financial security, relationships, spiritual life, community, and personal growth. This list will be long, and you will want to add to it and revise it every year if your goals change. Following are a few incomplete statements that might help you brainstorm:

- My dreams include _____
- I most want to accomplish _____
- The places I most want to visit are _____
- One thing I've always wanted to do is _____

C. INTERMEDIATE GOALS (ACCOMPLISH IN THE NEXT 5 YEARS)

Then, list the goals you want to accomplish in the next 5 years, such as

- I will complete my degree.
- I will graduate with honors.
- I will buy a new sports car.
- I will take a trip to Europe.

(continued)

Personal Evaluation Notebook

Looking Ahead: Your Goals (*concluded*)

D. SHORT-TERM GOALS (ACCOMPLISH THIS YEAR)

List goals you want to accomplish in the next year. Consider your answers to these questions:

- What is the major goal for which I am striving this year?
- How does this goal relate to my life's mission or purpose?
- Is this goal in conflict with any other goal?
- What hurdles must I overcome to reach my goal?
- What resources, help, and support will I need to overcome these hurdles?
- What specific actions are necessary to complete my goal?

E. SEMESTER GOALS

List goals you want to accomplish this semester—for example,

- I will preview chapters for 10 minutes before each lecture.
- I will go to all of my classes on time.
- I will jog for 30 minutes each day.

Be sure to include these goals in your daily and monthly planners. Consistently accomplishing these goals is the key to achieving your bigger goals.

Setting Priorities

There is always time for what is most important. Prioritizing helps you focus on activities that are most important to you at any given time. You want to make certain that your days are not just a treadmill of activities, crises, and endless tasks but that you focus on what is important as well as what is urgent.

Urgent priorities are pressing, deadline-driven projects or activities, such as dropping a class, paying your fees, and turning in papers. They directly affect your top goals and priorities, and not completing them on schedule can require a lot of time to fix the problem. For example, if you don't meet the deadline for adding classes, you have to pay additional fees or may not get into the class. Not paying for classes on time could result in having all your classes dropped.

Important priorities are essential activities that support your long-term goals and create the results you want—not just for today but also for future success. These activities and commitments include attending every class, creating study teams, completing homework, forming healthy relationships, planning, and exercising regularly. People who spend time daily on important items prevent crises. For example, if you build a personal fitness routine into every day, you will increase your energy, health, and overall sense of well-being and prevent medical problems that result from inactivity and weight gain. Long-term priorities must be built into your daily activities.

> **❝**Ordinary people merely think how they shall spend their time; a man of talent tries to use it.**❞**
>
> ARTHUR SCHOPENHAUER
> *German philosopher*

WORDS TO SUCCEED

Ongoing activities require continual attention and may be urgent, but they may not be important. For example, as you go through your e-mail, open mail, and answer phone calls, some messages will be urgent (needing an immediate response) but not important for your long-term goals. These activities require continual attention and follow-up and should be managed to prevent future problems. Jot down whom you need to see or call. Follow up with deadlines and determine if these activities support your top goals. For example, maybe you were pressured to join a club or community group that has been taking a lot of time. You may need to say, "This is a worthwhile project and I appreciate being inviting to attend, but I cannot participate at this time." Ask yourself if this activity meets your highest priority at this time.

Trivial activities make up all the daily stuff of life, and many are major time wasters. These unimportant activities can be fun, such as chatting online, going to parties, shopping, and surfing the Internet. They can also be annoying, such as dealing with junk mail—both real and virtual. The key is to stay focused on your important, top-priority items and schedule a certain amount of time for trivial activities. For example, since checking Facebook, Twitter, or e-mail, or texting friends can quickly eat up your discretionary time, limit these activities to just a few times each day after major tasks are done. You want a balanced life and need to socialize with friends, but sometimes a phone call or quick visit can turn into an hour-long gossip session. If this happens too often, you will not accomplish your important goals.

Setting priorities helps you focus on immediate goals. These essential, small steps lead you to your big goals. Your awareness of where your time goes becomes a continual habit of assessing, planning, and choosing tasks in the order of their importance, and this leads to success.

Ask yourself these questions: Do I have a sense of purpose and direction? Are my goals clearly defined? Are any in conflict with each other? Are they flexible enough to be modified as needed? Do I forget to write priorities and phone numbers in my planner? Do I daydream too much and have a problem with concentration? Do I invest time in high-priority tasks? Do I attend to small details that pay off in a big way? Refer to **Peak Progress 3.1** to see if the 80/20 rule applies to you.

Peak Progress

3.1

Investing Your Time in High-Priority Items: The 80/20 Rule

Whether you are a student, an executive, or an entry-level worker, your effectiveness will increase if you focus on top priorities. According to the 80/20 rule (the Pareto Principle), 80 percent of the results flow out of 20 percent of the activities—for example,

- Eighty percent of the interruptions come from 20 percent of the people.

- Eighty percent of the clothes you wear come from 20 percent of your wardrobe.
- Eighty percent of your phone calls come from 20 percent of the people you know.
- Eighty percent of a company's sales may come from 20 percent of its total customers.

(continued)

Investing Your Time in High-Priority Items: The 80/20 Rule *(concluded)*

A look at your time wasters may reveal that you are spending too much time on low-priority activities and shortchanging your top priorities. Wasting time on low-priority activities is a major reason for not accomplishing major tasks.

To produce results, focus on what is important—for example,

- Twenty percent more effort can result in an 80 percent better paper or speech.
- Twenty percent more time being involved and prepared in classes could produce 80 percent better results.

- Twenty percent more time developing positive relationships could reduce conflicts by 80 percent.
- Twenty percent more time taking care of yourself—getting enough sleep, eating healthy, exercising, and controlling stress—can result in 80 percent more effectiveness.

The 80/20 rule is just a rule of thumb. The exact percentage may change based on the circumstance. However, it reminds you to spend your time on the activities that are really important and achieve the results you want.

Time-Management Strategies

Use the following strategies to improve your time-management skills and help you achieve your goals in a balanced and effective way.

1. **Keep a calendar.** An inexpensive, pocket-size calendar is easy to carry with you and handy for scheduling commitments, such as classes, labs, and work for the entire semester. This helps you see the big picture. Review your calendar each week and list top priorities, due dates, and important school, work, and family activities. Each day, review urgent priorities that must be done by a deadline, such as paying fees, dropping a class, or paying taxes. Schedule important activities that support your goals, such as classes, exercise, study teams, and deadlines for choosing a topic. Jot down people to see or call, such as your instructor or advisor, or activities, such as meetings or social events. Remember, the shortest pencil is better than the longest memory. For example, if your advisor gives you a code for registration, put it on your calendar at the date and time for your registration. Don't just write your code on your binder or toss it into your backpack. The worksheets at the end of this chapter include handy calendars to help you plan your week, month, and semester.

2. **Create a daily to-do list.** Some people like to write a to-do list for the next day, taking some time at the end of a day to review briefly what they want to focus on for the next day. Others like to write their list in the morning at breakfast or when they first get to school or work. *List the tasks you need to accomplish during the day and map them out on a daily calendar. You may want to circle or place a number 1 by the most important priority to make sure it gets accomplished.* Make certain you build in time for family and friends. If you have children, plan special events. Bear in mind that the schedule should be flexible; you will want to allow for free time and unexpected events. Follow this schedule for 2 weeks and see how accurate it is. You can follow the format of the Time Log on page 78, or see **Worksheet 3.6** on page 111, which includes a planner for mapping out your daily to-do list. (See **Figure 3.1** for

> **"Don't start your day until you have finished it on paper first."**
>
> JIM ROHN
> *Motivational speaker*

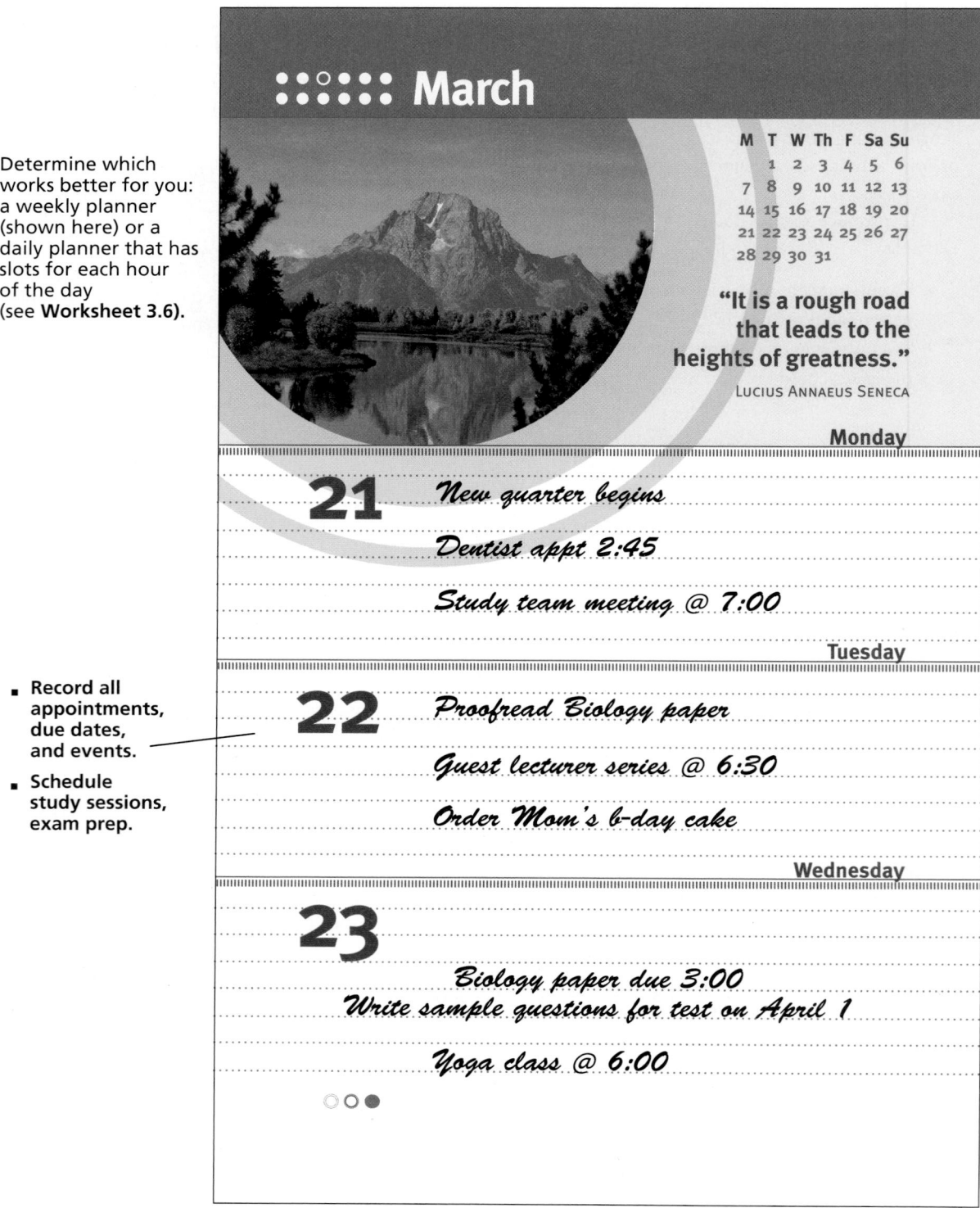

Determine which works better for you: a weekly planner (shown here) or a daily planner that has slots for each hour of the day (see **Worksheet 3.6**).

- Record all appointments, due dates, and events.
- Schedule study sessions, exam prep.

March

M	T	W	Th	F	Sa	Su
	1	2	3	4	5	6
7	8	9	10	11	12	13
14	15	16	17	18	19	20
21	22	23	24	25	26	27
28	29	30	31			

"It is a rough road that leads to the heights of greatness."

LUCIUS ANNAEUS SENECA

Monday

21
New quarter begins
Dentist appt 2:45
Study team meeting @ 7:00

Tuesday

22
Proofread Biology paper
Guest lecturer series @ 6:30
Order Mom's b-day cake

Wednesday

23
Biology paper due 3:00
Write sample questions for test on April 1
Yoga class @ 6:00

Figure 3.1
How to Use a Planner

The best way to use a planner to manage your time is to make it an essential part of your day. Some time-management experts even recommend giving your planner a name and finding it a "home" (a place in plain sight where it should always be put at the end of the day). *What name would you give your planner and where would its "home" be?*

Thursday

24

Outline Psych presentation

Lunch with Loren @ 12:15

Drop off donations at animal shelter after class

Notes — Include a "great ideas" section for recording thoughts and inspirations.

Friday

25

Financial aid forms due by 5:00!

Meet with advisor @ 11:00

Steven's soccer game @ 6:00

Size matters:
- It should be a convenient size for carrying.
- Spaces should be big enough to write in legibly.

Sat   **Sun**

26

Mom's b-day party 6:00 —pick up cake by 1:00

27

Review notes for Biology test 12:00–2:00

Study team 7:00

Contacts — Add important contacts and information (phone numbers, e-mails, office hours).

To Do

Write down priorities and tasks for the week.

Tips
- Use only 1 planner for work, school, and personal.
- Record everything in it as soon as possible.
- Carry it all the time.
- Check it 3 times a day (such as breakfast, lunch, bedtime).

○○●

tips on using a daily planner and to-do list and **Figure 3.2** on using your cell phone to help manage your time.)

Once you have written your list, do your urgent, top-priority items. Keep your commitments, such as attending every class, and don't do pleasant, fun activities until the most important ones are done. When you see important items checked off, you'll be inspired. It's OK if you don't get to everything on your list. If tasks are left over, add them to your next to-do list if they are still important. Ask yourself, "What is the best use of my time right now?"

3. **Do the tough tasks first.** Start with your most difficult subjects, while you're fresh and alert. For instance, if you are avoiding your statistics homework because it is difficult, get up early and do it before your classes begin. Start projects when they're assigned.

4. **Break projects down into smaller tasks.** Begin by seeing the whole project or each chapter as part of a larger system. Then break it into manageable chunks. You may get discouraged if you face a large task, whether it's writing a major term paper or reading several chapters. Getting started is half the battle. Sometimes working for just 15 minutes before you go to bed can yield big results. For example, preview a chapter, outline the main ideas for your term paper, or write a summary at the end of a chapter. You will find inspiration in completing smaller tasks, and you will feel more in control.

Some students find a project board helpful for long-term projects, as shown in **Figure 3.3**. Begin with today's date (or the start date), along with the due date, clearly indicated at the top. More than likely, the end date cannot change. Your start date also should be realistic—and as soon as possible. Then separate the "board" into two columns: "Key Activities" and "Date Completed." In the date column, put today's date (or start date) at the top and the project's due date at the bottom. (Some prefer to reverse that, putting the due date at the top and working backwards. Use whichever process works best for you.) With these two dates set, begin in the activities column by listing in order the project-related tasks that need to be accomplished between the start and end dates. Go back to the date column and start plugging in optimal

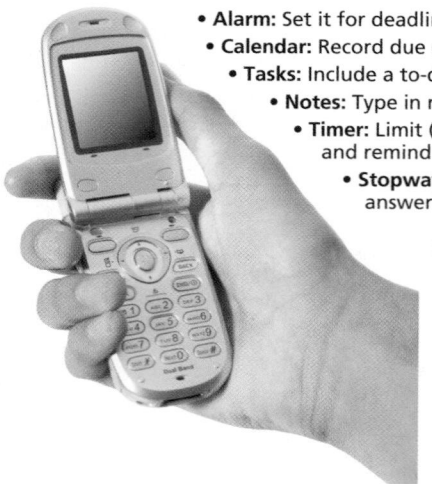

Figure **3.2**
Cell Phone 101

You don't need an expensive PDA (personal digital assistant) to help you manage your time. Almost every cell phone has these basic features. *Which ones do you already use?*

- **Alarm:** Set it for deadlines, appointments, meetings.
- **Calendar:** Record due dates for projects, exams, personal events.
- **Tasks:** Include a to-do list, errands, priorities.
- **Notes:** Type in reminders, instructions, and interesting thoughts.
- **Timer:** Limit (watching TV, texting), manage (exercising, studying), and remind (cooking, prescriptions).
- **Stopwatch:** Time tasks for future planning (reading a chapter, answering sample questions).

Many cell phones also have

- **Three-way calling:** Communicate on group projects.
- **Voice recorder:** Summarize lectures, notes, ideas.
- **Internet access:** Download podcasts, read e-books, get directions.

Project: Term Paper for Business Class 110	
Today's date: January 23, 2011	Due date: April 23, 2011
Key Activities	**Date Completed**
Explore topics	**January 23**
Finalize topic	January 28
Mind map outline	February 4
Initial library research	February 8
General outline	February 22
Library research	March 5
Detailed library research	March 10
Detailed outline	March 15
First draft	March 27
Do additional research and spell-check	April 5
Proof second draft; revise	April 10
Prepare final draft and proof	April 15
Paper finished and turned in	**April 23**

Figure 3.3
Sample Project Board

Making a project board is an effective time-management strategy. You can plan your tasks from start to end, or some people prefer to work backwards—starting with the end date. *How can you incorporate your project board into your daily planner?*

● **Study Anywhere and Everywhere**
Use your time between classes and while waiting for appointments to study and prepare for class. *What is something you can always carry with you, so that you are prepared for down time?*

dates next to the tasks, working from beginning to end. You may find that the time you think you need for each task adds up to a schedule that extends beyond your due date—obviously, that's a problem. If so, revise your dates and create a new schedule that achieves your completion date. (Allow time for proofreading and potential setbacks, such as computer problems.)

5. **Consolidate similar tasks.** Grouping similar tasks can maximize your efforts. For example, if you need to make several calls, make them all at a specific time and reduce interruptions. Set aside a block of time to shop, pay bills, and run errands. Try to answer e-mails at designated times, rather than as each one comes in. Write a list of questions for your advisor, instructor, or study team. Make certain you know expectations, so that you don't have to repeat tasks. Save your energy, and use your resources by planning and combining similar activities, such as taking a walk with a friend, thus combining exercise with socializing.

6. **Study at your high-energy time.** Know your body rhythms and study your hardest subjects during your high-energy time. Review the Time Log to determine the time of day when you have the most energy, and complete **Personal Evaluation Notebook 3.4**. Guard against interruptions, and

Personal Evaluation Notebook  3.4

Your Daily Energy Levels

Keep track of your energy levels every day for a week or more. Revisit your Time Log on page 78 to determine your daily energy levels, so that you can become more aware of your patterns.

1. What time(s) of the day are your energy levels at their peak?

   _____

2. What time(s) of the day are your energy levels at their lowest?

   _____

3. What tasks do you want to focus on during your high-energy time?

   _____

4. What can you do to increase your energy at your low-energy time?

   _____

don't do mindless tasks or socialize during your peak energy period. For example, if your peak time is in the morning, don't waste time answering mail, cleaning, or doing other routine work. Use your high-energy time to do serious studying and work that requires thinking, writing, and completing projects. Use your low-energy time to do more physical work or easy reading or previewing of chapters.

7. **Study everywhere and anywhere.** Ideally, you should choose a regular study location with few distractions, such as the library. However, you should be prepared to study anywhere, as you never know when you might get some unexpected down time. Carry note cards with you to review formulas, dates, definitions, facts, and important data. Take class notes or a book with you to review during the 5 or 10 minutes of waiting between classes, for the bus, in line at the grocery store, or for appointments. Digitally record important material and lectures and listen to them while commuting, exercising, dressing, walking, or waiting for class to begin. Even if you plan well, you will occasionally get stuck in lines, but you can make the most of this time.

8. **Study in short segments throughout the day.** Studying in short segments is much more effective than studying in marathon sessions. Your brain is much more receptive to recall when you review in short sessions at various times.

9. **Get organized.** Think of the time you waste looking for items (and the unnecessary stress it causes). Lay out your clothes and pack your lunch the night before, put your keys on the same hook, put your backpack by the door, put your mail and assignments in the same space, and keep records of bills and important information in your file. Keep an academic file that includes your

grades and transcripts. Keep a box with tests, papers, and projects. If you need to negotiate a grade, you will have the background support you will need. Make sure you save and back up any important work created on your computer and can easily retrieve it (to avoid losing hours of work).

10. **Be flexible, patient, and persistent.** Don't try to make too many changes at once, and don't get discouraged if a strategy doesn't work for you. You are striving for excellence, not perfection. Change certain aspects until a strategy fits your style. If it works, do it. If not, try something new. Give yourself at least 30 days to develop new habits. It often feels strange and uncomfortable to do any new task or vary your schedule of daily events. For example, you might discover that you have a habit of getting coffee every morning and spending an hour socializing with friends before your morning classes. Try changing this habit by doing it only once a week.

11. **Realize that you can't do it all (at least right now).** You may feel overwhelmed by too many demands and determine that some tasks are better done by others. This does not mean you can offload your responsibilities onto others, but focus on your important priorities and say no to activities that don't support your goals. Consider delegating certain tasks, joining a club later in the year, or participating in a fundraiser when you are on school break. Do social activities and return phone calls when your top-priority tasks are done.

Take 3 minutes to get organized to head out the door on time tomorrow:
- Where is the best place to put everything you'll need? Create a checklist of "must-have" items to refer to every night, if that helps.
- Is your phone charged? Are your keys, glasses, pens, and so on in your purse or backback?
- Which books, notepads, and assignments will you need for class tomorrow? Make as many piles as necessary if you'll be going back and forth to class during the day.

What else can you do in 3 minutes?
- Pack your lunch.
- Unload the dishwasher.
- Check your e-mails and respond to urgent ones.

Take 3

Time Management and Your Learning Style

Many time-management strategies are designed for people with left-brain dominance. Left-brain dominant people like routine, structure, and deadlines. They tend to be **convergent** thinkers because they are good at looking at several unrelated items and bringing order to them. Right-brain dominant people like variety, flexibility, creativity, and innovation. They are usually **divergent** thinkers because they branch out from one idea to many. They are good at brainstorming because one idea leads to another. They are able to focus on the whole picture. However, they can also learn to break the global view of the whole project into steps, break each of these steps into activities, and schedule and organize activities around the big goal. If you are right-brain dominant, you should

- **Focus on a few tasks.** It is very important for right-brain dominant people to focus their efforts on one or two top-priority items instead of being scattered and distracted by busywork. Imagine putting on blinders and focusing on one step until it is completed, and then move on to the next step. This creates discipline.

- **Write it down.** A daily calendar is vital to making certain that your activities support your short- and long-term goals. Write down phone numbers, e-mail addresses, and office hours of instructors and study team members. Highlight in color any deadlines or top-priority activities. Besides a daily calendar, use a master calendar in your study area and allow for variety and change. Make certain you review both your daily calendar with to-do items and your master calendar before you go to bed at night, so that you see the big picture.

- **Use visuals.** Right-brain dominant people often like to use visuals. One creative way to brainstorm, plan, and put your vision into action is to use a mind map (see Chapter 5, page 156). Use visual cues and sticky notes. When you think of an activity that will help you meet your goal, write it down.

- **Integrate learning styles.** Visualize yourself completing a project, and create a vision board of your goals and dreams. Use auditory cues by dictating ideas and planning your project on tape. Talk about the great feeling you will have when you complete this project. Make your project physical by adapting a hands-on approach and working with others to complete your project. Ask yourself, "Is there a way to simplify this task?" Planning is important, even if you are a creative person. **Peak Progress 3.2** explores the process of learning to take control of your time.

Peak Progress

3.2

Applying the Adult Learning Cycle to Taking Control of Your Time and Life

Applying the Adult Learning Cycle will help you establish goals and create a plan to meet them.

1. **RELATE. Why do I want to learn this?** Planning my time better and getting organized are essential for juggling the demands of school, work, and life. What are the areas where I need the most work?

2. **OBSERVE. How does this work?** I can learn a lot about time management by observing people who are on time, get their work done, work calmly and steadily, and seem to accomplish a lot in a short time. I'll also observe people who are unorganized, and often late, miss classes, and waste time blaming, complaining, and being overly involved in other people's lives. How do their problems relate to poor time management or self-management?

3. **REFLECT. What does this mean?** What strategies are working for me? What new strategies can I try? I will explore creative ways to solve problems rather than feeling overwhelmed.

4. **DO. What can I do with this?** Each day, I'll work on one area. For example, I'll choose one place to hang my keys and consistently put them there. If I find them in my purse or on the table, I'll put them on the hook until it becomes a habit.

5. **TEACH. Whom can I share this with?** I'll share my tips and experiences with others and find out their strategies in return. I should continue to reward myself, at least mentally, for making positive changes.

Now return to Stage 1 and think about how it feels to be focused, instead of rushed, by managing your time and priorities.

Overcome Obstacles

Stop Procrastinating

Procrastination is deliberately putting off tasks, and most of us have been guilty of putting off doing what we know should be done. However, a continual pattern of delaying and avoiding is a major barrier to time management.

There are many reasons for procrastination. Some people prefer to do what they enjoy rather than doing what should be done. Some people are perfectionists and don't want to do something or complete steps unless they feel the outcome is the best it can be. Other people are worriers and get weighed down with details or overwhelmed by their responsibilities. Some people are shy and avoid working with others to accomplish a task or give a speech. Others are embarrassed because they have avoided a task for too long, so they just write it off. Other people are easily distracted, blame others, or don't want to be told what to do. Some people feel they work better under extreme pressure and use it as an excuse for waiting until the last minute. Some just simply lack the discipline to sit down and complete a task. Complete **Personal Evaluation Notebook 3.5** on page 92 to determine if you procrastinate too much and, if so, why.

Self-assessment is often the key to understanding why you procrastinate and to developing strategies to help you control your life and create the results you want. Once you have identified what is holding you back, you can create solutions and apply them consistently until they are habits. To avoid procrastination, try the following strategies:

1. **Set daily priorities.** Be clear about your goals and the results you want to achieve and allow enough time to complete them. Use your to-do list to check off tasks as you complete them. This will give you a feeling of accomplishment.

2. **Break the project into small tasks.** A large project that seems overwhelming can encourage procrastination. Do something each day that brings you closer to your goal. Use a project board or write down steps and deadlines that are necessary to achieve success. For example, as soon as a paper is assigned, start that day to choose a topic, the next day do research, and so on until each step leads to an excellent paper.

3. **Gather everything you'll need to start your project.** Clear off a space, and prepare your notes and other material, such as pens, paper, and books. Reread the assignment, and clarify expectations with your instructor or study team. Having everything ready creates a positive attitude and makes it easier to start the task. This strategy is effective whether you're doing a term paper or making cookies.

4. **Focus for short spurts.** We discussed in Chapter 1 how concentrating on one task for a short period of time is more effective and helps create a positive, can-do attitude, such as "I'm going to preview this chapter for 15 minutes with full concentration." This is more effective than telling yourself you're going to

Chloe is always late. Her family, friends—everyone—continually tell her how frustrating it is that she keeps them waiting. She finally got the message when her best friend texted her that she was tired of her inconsideration and the group was leaving for a party without her. The rush she always felt from "making an entrance" was replaced with a feeling of abandonment and the realization that she had let others down.

- What negative characteristics are being demonstrated by someone who is habitually late?
- What problems does this create—in school, on the job, in personal situations?
- Give Chloe some specific strategies that might help her become more prompt and dependable.

Personal Evaluation Notebook

Procrastination

- What is something I should have accomplished by now but haven't?

- Why did I procrastinate?

- What are the consequences of my procrastination?

- What kind of tasks do I put off?

- When do I usually procrastinate?

- Where do I procrastinate? Am I more effective in the library or at home?

- How does my procrastination affect others in my life?

- Who supports, or enables, my procrastination?

study for 2 or 3 hours, which creates a mindset that says, "This is too difficult." Seeing how fully you can concentrate in a short amount of time builds confidence and uses discipline instead of guilt and willpower. Before you go to bed or when you have a few minutes during the day, use the same strategy: "I'm just going to spend 10 minutes writing a rough draft for my English paper." Ask yourself if you can do one more thing to get you started the next day.

5. **Surround yourself with supportive people.** Ask for help from motivated friends, instructors, or your advisor, or visit the Learning Center for help and

support. Sometimes talking out loud can help you clarify why you are avoiding a project. Study buddies or a study team can also help you stay on track. Sometimes just knowing that someone is counting on you to deliver is enough to keep you from procrastinating.

6. **Tackle difficult tasks during your high-energy time.** Do what is important first, while you are at your peak energy level and concentration is easiest. Once you get a difficult or unpleasant task done, you will feel more energy. When your energy dips and you need a more physical, less mentally demanding task, return phone calls and text messages or tidy up your desk.

7. **Develop a positive attitude.** Negative emotions, such as anger, jealousy, worry, and resentment, can eat up hours of time and sap your energy. Instead, resolve to have a positive attitude and use affirmations. Think, "I get to work on my project today," instead of "I have to work on this project." Feel grateful that you have the opportunity to be in college. Resourceful and positive attitudes don't just happen; they are created.

8. **Reward yourself.** Look ahead and think about how you will feel when you complete this task versus how you'll feel if you don't. Focus on the sense of accomplishment you feel when you make small, steady steps and meet your deadlines. Reward yourself with a small treat or break when you complete activities and a bigger reward (such as a nice dinner or movie) when you complete a goal. Work first and play later.

9. **Don't expect perfection.** You learn any new task by making mistakes. For example, you become a better writer or speaker with practice. Don't wait or delay because you want perfection. Your paper is not the great American novel. It is better to do your best than to do nothing. You can polish later, but avoiding writing altogether is a major trap. Do what you can today to get started on the task at hand.

Control Interruptions

Interruptions steal time. They cause you to stop projects, disrupt your thought pattern, divert your attention, and make it difficult to rebuild momentum. To avoid wasting time, take control. Set everyday priorities that will help you meet goals and reduce interruptions. Don't let endless activities e-mail, texting, and other people control you. For instance, if a friend calls, set a timer for 10 minutes or postpone the call until later, after you have previewed an assigned chapter or outlined a speech. Let calls go to voicemail if you are studying, or tell the caller that you will call back in an hour. When you return a call, chat for 5 or 10 minutes instead of 45 minutes. Combine socializing with exercising or eating lunch or dinner. If you watch a favorite program, turn the television off right after that show. The essence of time management is taking charge of your life and not allowing interruptions to control you. Complete **Personal Evaluation Notebook 3.6** on page 94 to determine the sources of your interruptions. (Also see **Worksheet 3.3** on page 108 to identify your time wasters.)

Peak performers know how to live and work with other people and manage interruptions. Try these tips to help you reduce interruptions:

> " Time is the coin of your life. It is the only coin you have, and only you can determine how it will be spent. Be careful lest you let other people spend it for you. "
>
> CARL SANDBURG
> *Author, poet*

WORDS TO SUCCEED

Personal Evaluation Notebook  3.6

Interruptions!

Keep a log of interruptions for a few days. List all the interruptions you experience and their origins. Some examples are friends, family, visitors, phone calls, and unexpected news. Also be aware of internally caused interruptions, such as procrastination, daydreaming, worry, negative thoughts, anger, and lack of concentration. Then think of possible solutions for handling the interruption the next time.

Interrupted By	Incident	Possible Solutions

1. **Create an organized place to study.** A supportive, organized study space can help you reduce interruptions and keep you focused. Have all your study tools—a dictionary, pencils, pens, books, papers, files, notes, a calendar, a semester schedule, and study team and instructor names and phone numbers—in one place, so that you won't waste time looking for items you need. Keep only one project on your desk at a time, and file everything else away or put it on a shelf. If you have children, include a study area for them, close to yours, where they can work quietly with puzzles, crayons, or books. This will allow study time together and create a lifelong study pattern for them.

2. **Determine your optimal time to study.** When you are focused, you can study anywhere, anytime. However, to increase your effectiveness, do your serious studying when your energy level is at its peak. Guard against interruptions, and use this time for serious studying.

3. **Create quiet time.** Discuss study needs and expectations with your roommates or family, and ask for an agreement. You might establish certain study hours or agree on a signal, such as closing your door or hanging a "Quiet" sign, to let each other know when you need quiet time. Make certain to balance study time with breaks to eat and socialize with your roommates or family.

4. **Study in the library.** If it is difficult to study at home, study in the library. Once you enter, your brain can turn to a serious study mode. Sitting in a quiet place and facing the wall can reduce interruptions and distractions. You can

5. **Do first things first.** You will feel more in control if you have a list of priorities every day. Knowing what you want and need to do makes it easier to say no to distractions. Make certain that these important goals include your health. Taking time to exercise, eat right, and relax not only saves time but also increases your energy and focus.

6. **Just say no.** Tell your roommates or family when an important test or project is due. If someone wants to talk or socialize when you need to study, say no. Set aside time each day to spend with your family or roommates, such as dinner, a walk, or a movie. They will understand your priorities when you include them in your plans. See **Peak Progress 3.3** on page 96 for additional tips on how to say no and still maintain a positive relationship.

Juggling Family, School, and Job

Many college students are juggling more than coursework and school activities. Many are spouses, partners, parents, caregivers (for both children and elderly parents and relatives), and co-workers. Making the decision to attend college—or return to college—may have been difficult because of these commitments and responsibilities.

Having a family involves endless physical demands, including cleaning, cooking, chauffeuring to activities, helping with homework, and nonstop picking up. Anyone who lives with children knows how much time and energy they require. Children get sick, need attention, and just want you there sometimes for them.

The following strategies can help you succeed in school while juggling many roles:

1. **Be flexible.** Around children, certain kinds of studying are realistic, and other kinds are hopeless. Carry flash cards to use as you cook dinner or while supervising children's homework or playtime. Quiz yourself, preview chapters, skim summaries, review definitions, do a set number of problems, brainstorm ideas for a paper, outline a speech, review equations, sketch a drawing, or explain a chapter out loud. Save the work that requires deeper concentration for time alone.

2. **Communicate with your family.** Let family members know that earning a college degree is an important goal and you need their support and understanding. Use every bit of time to study before you go home. Once home, let them know when you need to study and set up a specific time.

3. **Delegate and develop.** Clarify expectations, so that everyone contributes to the family. Even young children can learn to be important contributors to the family unit. Preschool children can help put away toys, set the table, and feel part of the team. Preteens can be responsible for cooking a simple meal one night a week and for doing their own laundry. When your children go to college, they will know how to cook, clean, do laundry, get up on time in the morning, and take responsibility for their lives. An important goal of being a good parent is to raise independent, capable, responsible adults.

Peak Progress

How to Say No

Some people have a hard time saying no. They are afraid they will hurt someone's feelings, send a message that they aren't interested, or miss an opportunity that may not come along again. But you can't say yes all the time and still accomplish all you need to. Following are some tips on how to say no, limit your time, and exit situations gracefully:

- **Check your to-do list:** "It doesn't fit with my schedule." It is easy to give in to the impulse to say yes to an invitation or a request from a friend or family member. However, you need to determine what priorities and commitments must be met first. You may find you have to decline the request.

- **Answer in a timely fashion:** "I can't do this right now." If you know you can't participate, let the other person know right away. Others will be more understanding if you let them know you have other commitments rather than waiting until the last minute to give a response (or no response at all).

- **Set a later date:** "I can't right now, but can we do this later?" Find another time that works better for everyone's schedule and record it on your calendar or planner.

- **Set a time limit:** "I need to leave by _____." If phone calls or lunch dates usually turn into hours of

conversation, set a time limit upfront and make it known—and then stick to it.

- **Clarify expectations:** "How much time will this involve?" It's easy to get involved in something that turns out to be more time-consuming than planned. Sometimes that's unavoidable, but make sure you ask upfront what is expected.

- **Ask for alternate responsibilities:** "I can't do this, but is there something else I can do?" The original request may require too much time (such as planning a school event), but there may be a lesser role you could take (such as lining up the speaker, contacting a caterer, or handing out flyers).

- **Sleep on it before answering:** "Let me get back to you in a day." For bigger commitments, try to take a day or two to consider if the benefits of the new opportunity outweigh the time it will take to be involved. You don't want to disappoint others by committing to a project and then not following through.

- **Don't feel guilty:** "This is the best decision for me at this time." Once you say no, don't feel guilty or have regrets. You must focus on your priorities. Be firm and polite—not defensive or overly apologetic. And definitely do not make up false excuses, which could end up causing you more stress in the long run.

4. **Find good day care.** Explore public and private day-care centers, preschools, family day-care homes, parent cooperatives, baby-sitting pools, other family members, and nannies. Line up at least two backup sources of day care. If possible, explore renting a room in the basement or attic of your house to a child-care provider. Part of the rent can be paid with child care and light housecleaning. Trade off times with other parents.

5. **Prepare the night before.** Avoid the morning rush of getting everyone out the door. The night before, do tasks such as showering, packing lunches, and checking backpacks for keys, books, notes, and supplies. Good organization helps makes the rush hour a little less stressful.

6. **Use your school's resources.** Check out resources on campus through the reentry center. Set up study teams for all your classes. Make friends with other

students who have children. (See Chapter 4 for more resources for returning students.)

7. **Communicate with your employer.** Communicate your goals to your employer, and point out how learning additional skills will make you a more valuable employee. Some companies offer tuition reimbursement programs or even allow time off to take a class.

8. **Look into online options.** See if any of your classes are offered online or at alternate times, including evenings and weekends. An online class may fit better with your schedule, but it requires just as much commitment as any other class—maybe even more. See **Peak Progress 3.4** on page 98 for tips on taking online courses.

9. **Increase your physical and emotional energy.** Focus on activities that relax you and help you recharge. Schedule time to meditate, walk, and read for pleasure. Exercise, dance, do yoga, get enough rest, and eat healthy foods. Keep a gratitude journal and remind yourself that you are blessed with a full and rewarding life.

10. **Create positive time.** Don't buy your children toys to replace spending time with them. You can enjoy each other as you study together, garden, take walks, read, play games, or watch a favorite television show. The activity is secondary to your uninterrupted presence. At bedtime, share your day, talk about dreams, read a story, and express your love and appreciation. Your children will remember and cherish this warm and special time forever, and so will you.

11. **Model successful behavior.** Returning to school sends an important message. It says learning, growing, and being able to juggle family, a job, and school are possible, worthwhile, and rewarding. It is important for children to see their parents setting personal and professional goals while knowing that the family is the center of their lives. You are modeling the importance of getting an education, setting goals, and achieving them.

12. **Balance your life.** Reflect on all areas of your life and the time you are investing in them. Decide if you are investing too much or too little in each area. Also, look at the roles you play in each area of your life. In the family area, you may be a wife, mother, daughter, and so on. In the work area, you may be a manager, a part-time worker, or an assistant. Accompanying each role in your life are certain goals. Some goals demand greater time than others. It is OK to make a trade-off for a specific goal, but realize that you may neglect a vital area of your life. For instance, you may have a big term paper due, so you trade off a family outing to accomplish this goal. Complete **Personal Evaluation Notebook 3.7** on page 99 to determine how you can achieve balance.

● **Balancing Your Life**
Balancing family with work sometimes requires making trade-offs to have a more fulfilling life. *What can you do to create a more balanced life?*

Peak Progress

Online Learning

Taking classes online can be very appealing, especially if you're juggling other demands. Most strategies that apply to taking traditional, face-to-face courses apply to online courses; however, your time-management skills may be even more critical for success. If you are considering an online course, ask yourself the following questions:

- Do I like to work independently?
- Am I persistent and self-motivated?
- Am I comfortable e-mailing or phoning my instructor if I need help?
- Am I comfortable asking questions and following up if I need more clarification?
- Am I comfortable working at a computer, including opening, storing, and sending files; participating in forums; and using e-mail and basic software programs?

If you answered yes to most of these questions, an online course may be a good option for you. The following strategies will help you navigate online courses:

1. **Keep up on the coursework.** Think of it this way: What if you crammed a semester-long, face-to-face course, including all the reading, into 1 week? Many people try taking online courses that way, waiting until the last minute to do the work. Instead, you must treat your online course as you would any other class by building it into your schedule. List due dates for assignments, tests, and projects. Build in time to read (the textbook as well as online materials) and study.

2. **Know the technology required for the course.** Make certain you have all the necessary equipment and software, and work out any bugs. Do a trial run with your computer. Verify passwords and access to course Web sites, chat rooms, and so on.

3. **Communicate with the instructor.** In an online environment, you miss the nonverbal cues often given in a traditional course, so effective communication is even more important. Clarify the expectations for the class, including reading assignments, exams, projects, and papers, as well as how to deliver finished work to the instructor. How will you know if items are received? Where will your grade be posted? Is there a set time for the class or a chat room? Learn your

instructor's office hours and the best time to respond by e-mail and phone. Ask for feedback from your instructor often, and keep track of your progress. Verify your grade with your instructor before grades are submitted. (See page 386 for tips on e-mailing your instructors.)

4. **Communicate with other students.** Create online study teams to share notes, ask questions, and study for tests. If this is your first online course, knowing there are other students out there to work with can make it less daunting. You may find that others have had the same questions about content and key points, technology problems, and so on that you do, and they may have answers.

5. **Check the school's tips.** Read any tips and frequently asked questions your school has posted about how to succeed in online courses. Many of them may be specific to the needs of the institution and its instructors.

6. **Watch for announcements.** Know how the instructor or school will alert you to any changes in assignments, tests, and upcoming events and check for them each week.

7. **Print out essential information.** If possible, print the syllabus, project assignments, and key content information, so that you can quickly refer to it, especially when you do not have access to your computer. Annotate the material with questions you need to follow up on, possible test questions, and key points to remember.

8. **Sign in early.** If your course offers or requires participation in a chat room or message board, sign in early to make sure you are involved and can keep up on the discussion. Active participation may be a percentage of your total grade.

9. **Have a computer "Plan B."** To prepare for emergencies, locate computer labs on campus and ask a friend, roommate, or family member if you can use his or her computer if yours crashes. Create organized folders, and back up important material, such as assignments and papers. Make sure you have enough paper and toner.

10. **Don't cheat.** All rules of ethics and academic honesty apply to online courses just as they do to traditional courses. Your work and responses must be your own.

Personal Evaluation Notebook

3.7

Keeping Your Life Goals in Balance

Several life areas are listed on this chart. Write one goal you have for each major area. Explain how you can commit a certain amount of time to meeting that goal and still maintain overall balance.

Life Areas	Goals
1. Career (job, earning a living)	_____
2. Education	_____
3. Spirituality (your inner being, peace of mind)	_____
4. Relationships (your family, friends, associates)	_____
5. Health (weight, exercise, food, stress, personal care)	_____
6. Recreation (hobbies, sports, interests)	_____
7. Finance	_____
8. Home	_____
9. Community involvement and service	_____
10. Personal growth and renewal	_____
11. Other	_____

TAKING CHARGE

Summary

In this chapter, I learned to

- **Assess where my time goes.** Knowing where I am already spending my time is essential for time management. I assess how much time I (1) commit to school, work, and other activities; (2) spend maintaining myself and home; and (3) devote to discretionary time.

- **Determine where my time should go.** I set goals to determine what I want to accomplish. I identify my values and priorities and use them to write a mission statement. I evaluate my dreams as I write my long-term goals. I break down my tasks and goals by short-term, intermediate, and long-term. I use a daily to-do list to stay focused on top priorities. I know what I'd like to accomplish, what I should accomplish, and what is urgent and *must be accomplished.*

- **Assess my energy level.** I know when my energy level is high and work on top-priority goals when I am alert and focused.

- **Break down projects.** I break a large project into manageable chunks. I make a project board, with deadlines for each assignment, and divide the assignment into realistic steps I can do each day. I consolidate similar tasks to maximize my efforts.

- **Study everywhere and anywhere.** I make the most of waiting time, commuting time, and time between classes. I know it is more effective to study in short segments throughout the day than to study late at night in a marathon session.

- **Get organized.** I will develop a habit of putting everything in its place and getting organized. Spending a few extra minutes organizing my space and schedule pays off later.

- **Integrate learning styles.** Left-brain dominant people tend to be convergent thinkers who like structure, whereas right-brain dominant people tend to be divergent thinkers who need more flexibility. Right-brain dominant thinkers can incorporate time-management techniques by focusing on top-priority tasks, writing down upcoming events, using visual cues, and integrating learning styles.

- **Overcome procrastination and interruptions.** By setting daily priorities, breaking large projects into manageable tasks, being positive, creating an organized place to study, and being disciplined, I can accomplish what needs to be done. I've learned to say no when necessary, and I reward myself after completing projects and finishing priorities.

- **Juggle family, school, and job responsibilities.** I communicate my educational goals to others in my life in order to establish expectations and create balance. I am flexible and creative with my time, focusing on schoolwork and involving others in the process.

Performance Strategies

Following are the top 10 strategies for time management:

- Focus on goals and priorities.
- Keep a calendar and create a to-do list.
- Break down projects and consolidate similar tasks.
- Study at the right time, in the right space, and in short segments.

- Study everywhere and anywhere.
- Get organized.
- Be flexible, patient, and persistent.
- Don't procrastinate.
- Manage interruptions.
- Create balance.

Tech for Success

Take advantage of the text's Web site at **www.mhhe.com/ferrett8e** for additional study aids, useful forms, and convenient and applicable resources.

- **Semester calendar.** It's unavoidable—most of your tests and class papers will occur around the same time. Start planning your semester now by mapping out the major events and daily tasks you'll need to accomplish. A number of planning options are available with this text (worksheets and downloadable forms), or access planners online at a variety of Web sites, such as **www.timeanddate.com.**

- **Management gurus.** Best-selling authors and popular writers and speakers—such as Stephen Covey ("habits of highly effective people"), David Allen ("getting

things done"), and Merlin Mann ("43 folders")—have developed strategies, methods, and even humorous takes on overcoming obstacles to effective time management. Visit their Web sites for advice on becoming more productive: **www.stephencovey.com; www.davidco.com; www.43folders.com.**

- **A personal time-out.** It's easy to waste hours surfing the Internet, chatting online, and perusing the latest "find" on auction sites, such as eBay. You may need to give yourself a time-out or, rather, a "time's up." Set a timer as you get online and commit to turning off the computer when the timer goes off. Use your discretionary time wisely.

Study Team Notes

Career*in* focus

Deborah Page
FOOD SCIENTIST

Related Majors: Agricultural Science, Chemistry, Microbiology, Nutrition

Focus on Tasks

Deborah Page is a food scientist for a large company in the food-processing industry. Her job is to develop new food products and ways to preserve or store foods. To do this, she engages in research and conducts tests and experiments, keeping in mind consumer demand for safety and convenience. Occasionally, she analyzes foods to determine levels of sugar, protein, vitamins, or fat.

Because her job is task-oriented, Deborah has a great deal of freedom in structuring her day. Her company allows flexible scheduling, so Deborah arrives at work at 9:30 a.m., after her children have left for school. She can work until 6:30 p.m. because her children are involved in after-school activities and her husband picks them up by 5 p.m.

Deborah finds that she does her best work in late mornings and early afternoons. She plans research and testing during those times. She schedules most calls during the first hour at work and uses the latter part of her day to organize tasks for the next day. Good planning helps her manage her time well and focus on her tasks at hand.

Deborah's job includes a fair amount of reading, and she sometimes takes work home with her for the evening. That allows her to leave work early to take her children to appointments or attend their sports activities. Giving attention to her family and personal interests helps Deborah create a balanced life.

CRITICAL THINKING Why is it important for Deborah to organize her time wisely? What are some of the prioritization strategies she uses daily to manage her time? What are some strategies to help her balance her personal and career commitments with a healthy, fulfilling lifestyle? Explore ways for Deborah to find time for herself for personal renewal.

Peak Performer

PROFILE

Malcolm Gladwell

Referred to as a "pop sociologist," international best-selling author Malcolm Gladwell constantly analyzes the way we look at everyday events and concepts of time. By studying what we often think of as "ordinary," Gladwell looks at how these issues of time shape future success.

Gladwell's background is as varied as his way of thinking. His mother was born in Jamaica as a descendant of slaves and worked as a psychotherapist. His British father was a civil engineering professor at the University of Waterloo in Ontario, Canada. Gladwell was born in England and grew up in rural Ontario, graduating with a degree in history from the University of Toronto. In his distinguished career, he has been named one of *Time Magazine*'s 100 Most Influential People. He has worked as a staff writer for *The New Yorker* magazine since 1996.

In his book *Outliers: The Story of Success,* one of the major questions Gladwell explores is why some people, such as Bill Gates and the members of the Beatles, have become outrageously successful in their professions, whereas others have not. Gladwell formulates the hypothesis of the "10,000 Hour Rule." In this rule, he states that the key to success in any field or profession is largely due to practicing a task for a total of 10,000 hours (20 hours a week for 10 years). By making this long, extended time commitment (along with other factors), individuals can fully develop their innate abilities and succeed in their chosen field. (Recall how practice and repetition are key components of the Adult Learning Cycle discussed throughout this text.)

In *The Tipping Point: How Little Things Can Make a Big Difference,* Gladwell explores, among other things, how small actions can have a ripple effect and "spread like viruses do." He explores many historical and cultural situations in which actions by just a few rapidly lead to what he calls a "tipping point" of major change. (Similarly, the **Take 3** activities throughout this text reinforce how small, focused steps can accomplish more in the end.)

In *Blink: The Power of Thinking Without Thinking,* Gladwell studies our abilities to make snap decisions. In looking at short fragments of time, Gladwell reveals the benefits of expert judgment by citing examples of how certain experts have relied on their intuition rather than studied data. (Likewise, **Think Fast** activities throughout the text exercise your critical thinking abilities to quickly solve everyday issues.)

Gladwell's writings have been considered insightful as well as controversial. However, his perceptions of time and critical thinking and the connections he finds to success and other social phenomena have spurred lively debates on the best ways to utilize time and focus efforts.

PERFORMANCE THINKING Do you think it's true that it takes 10,000 hours to become proficient in a profession? How does this idea relate to your success in a class? Have you ever relied on your intuition to solve a problem? Did you arrive at the right answer for you?

CHECK IT OUT Experts explore different approaches to thinking in the popular TED video series (**www.ted.com/**). Named for an alliance among the areas of technology, entertainment, and design (though including many more disciplines today), these brief talks challenge the world's most inspired thinkers to give the "talk of their lives." More than 500 TEDTalks are available for free viewing online, including speakers such as Malcolm Gladwell, Al Gore, and Jane Goodall. How can watching these speeches affect the way you think?

Starting Today

At least one strategy I learned in this chapter that I plan to try right away is

_____

_____

_____

What changes must I make in order for this strategy to be most effective?

_____

_____

_____

Review Questions

Based on what you have learned in this chapter, write your answers to the following questions:

1. How does time management help you achieve your goals?

_____

_____

2. What is the difference between an "urgent" priority and an "important" priority?

_____

_____

3. Name at least five time-management strategies.

_____

_____

4. What can you do to avoid procrastination?

_____

_____

5. Why is it important to control interruptions?

_____

_____

To test your understanding of the chapter's concepts, complete the chapter quiz at **www.mhhe.com/ferrett8e.**

Juggling Family and School

In the Classroom

Laura Chen is a returning part-time student. She also works full-time and takes care of her family. Her husband says he supports her goal to become a dental hygienist but does little to help with taking care of the children or housework. Their children are 12 and 14 and have always depended on Laura to help them with their homework and drive them to their activities. Laura prides herself on being efficient at home, as well as being a loving mother and wife.

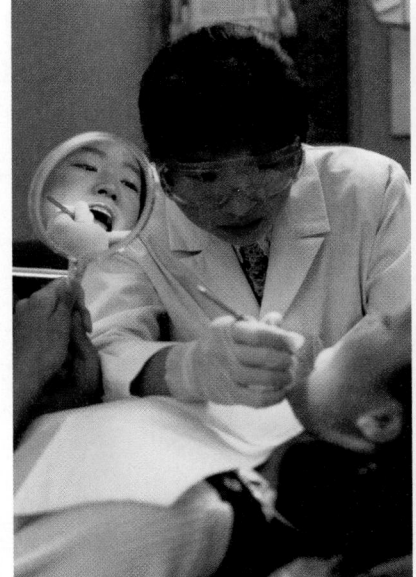

1. What can Laura do to get more control over her life?

_____

_____

2. What strategies in the chapter would be most helpful to Laura?

_____

_____

In the Workplace

Laura is now a dental hygienist. She has always had a busy schedule, but she expected to have more free time after she graduated. Instead, she is even busier than before. Her children are active in school, and she feels it is important to be involved in their activities and schoolwork. Laura also belongs to two community organizations, volunteers at the local hospital, and is active in her church. Recently, she has been late for meetings and has been rushing through her day. Because she knows her health is important, Laura has resumed her regular exercise program. Since graduation, she has had difficulty finding time for herself.

3. What strategies can help Laura gain control over her time and her life?

_____

_____

4. What areas of her life does she need to prioritize?

_____

_____

Applying the ABC Method of Self-Management

In the Journal Entry on page 75, you were asked to describe a situation when you were overwhelmed by too much to do and too little time. Describe that event below. What were the consequences?

_____
_____
_____
_____

Now apply the ABC Method and visualize a more organized situation:

A = Actual event:

_____
_____
_____
_____

B = Beliefs:

_____
_____
_____
_____

C = Challenge:

_____
_____
_____
_____

While completing this exercise, did you determine ways you can become more organized and efficient?

PRACTICE SELF-MANAGEMENT

For more examples of learning how to manage difficult situations, see the "Self-Management Workbook" section of the Online Learning Center Web site at **www.mhhe.com/ferrett8e.**

My Time-Management Habits

Complete the following statements with a Yes or No response.

                                                                                        Yes   **No**

1. I do the easiest and most enjoyable task first.
2. I do my top-priority task at the time of day when my energy is the highest and I know I will perform best.
3. I use my time wisely by doing high-return activities—previewing chapters, proofreading papers.
4. Even though I find interruptions distracting, I put up with them.
5. I save trivial and mindless tasks for the time of day when my energy is low.
6. I don't worry too much about making lists. I don't like planning and prefer to be spontaneous and respond as events occur.
7. My work space is organized, and I have only one project on my desk at a time.
8. I set goals and review them each semester and each year.
9. My workspace is open, and I like to have people wander in and out.
10. My study team socializes first, and then we work.
11. I have a lot of wasted waiting time, but you can't study in small blocks of time.
12. I block out a certain amount of time each week for my top-priority and hardest classes.

SCORING

1. Add the number of Yes responses to questions 2, 3, 5, 7, 8, 12. 5   5
2. Add the number of No responses to questions 1, 4, 6, 9, 10, 11. 2   2
3. Add the two scores together.   7

The maximum score is 12. The higher the score, the more likely you are to be practicing good time management. Which areas do you need to improve?

I need to go back & re-read chapters and look over notes when needed

Time Wasters

Getting control of your time and life involves identifying time wasters and determining your peak energy level. It also involves identifying goals, setting priorities, and creating an action plan. Use critical thinking to answer the following questions.

1. What are the major activities and tasks that take up much of your time?

   School, going to class & Homework
   also clubs and activities for my sorority.

2. What activities cause you to waste time? Some common time wasters are
   - Socializing
   - Losing things and not organizing
   - Doing what you like to do first
   - Watching television
   - Complaining and whining
   - Being overly involved with other people's problems
   - Not writing down deadlines

3. What activities can you eliminate or reduce?

   Not organizing, doing what I like to do first, TV,
   involved

4. When is your high-energy time?

   afternoon

5. When do you study?

   afternoon / anytime I can

6. Look at your committed time. Does this block of time reflect your values and goals?

   _- No_

7. Do you complete top-priority tasks first?

   Most of the time

Practice Goal Setting

Determine a personal desire or want and plan out a strategy of long-term, short-term, and daily goals that help you achieve it.

Goal-Setting Steps	Examples	Your Turn . . .
Step 1 Plainly state your *desire* or *want*.	"I want to be financially secure."	
Step 2 Develop a long-term goal that will help you fulfill your stated *desire* or *want*.	"I will earn a Bachelor of Science degree in computer technology from State University by June 2011."	
Step 3 Develop short-term goals that will help you achieve the long-term goal.	"I will enroll in all the classes recommended by my academic advisor."	
	"I will earn at least a 3.5 GPA in all my classes."	
	"I will join a small study group."	
Step 4 Develop daily objectives that focus on achieving your short-term goals.	"I will set aside 2 hours of study for every 1 hour in class."	
	"I will make note cards to carry with me and review them when I'm waiting for class."	
	"I will review the day's lecture notes with my study team to make sure I didn't miss any important points."	

Map Out Your Goals

Use this illustration as a visual guide for mapping out your goals. To get started, plug in your responses from **Personal Evaluation Notebook 3.3**.

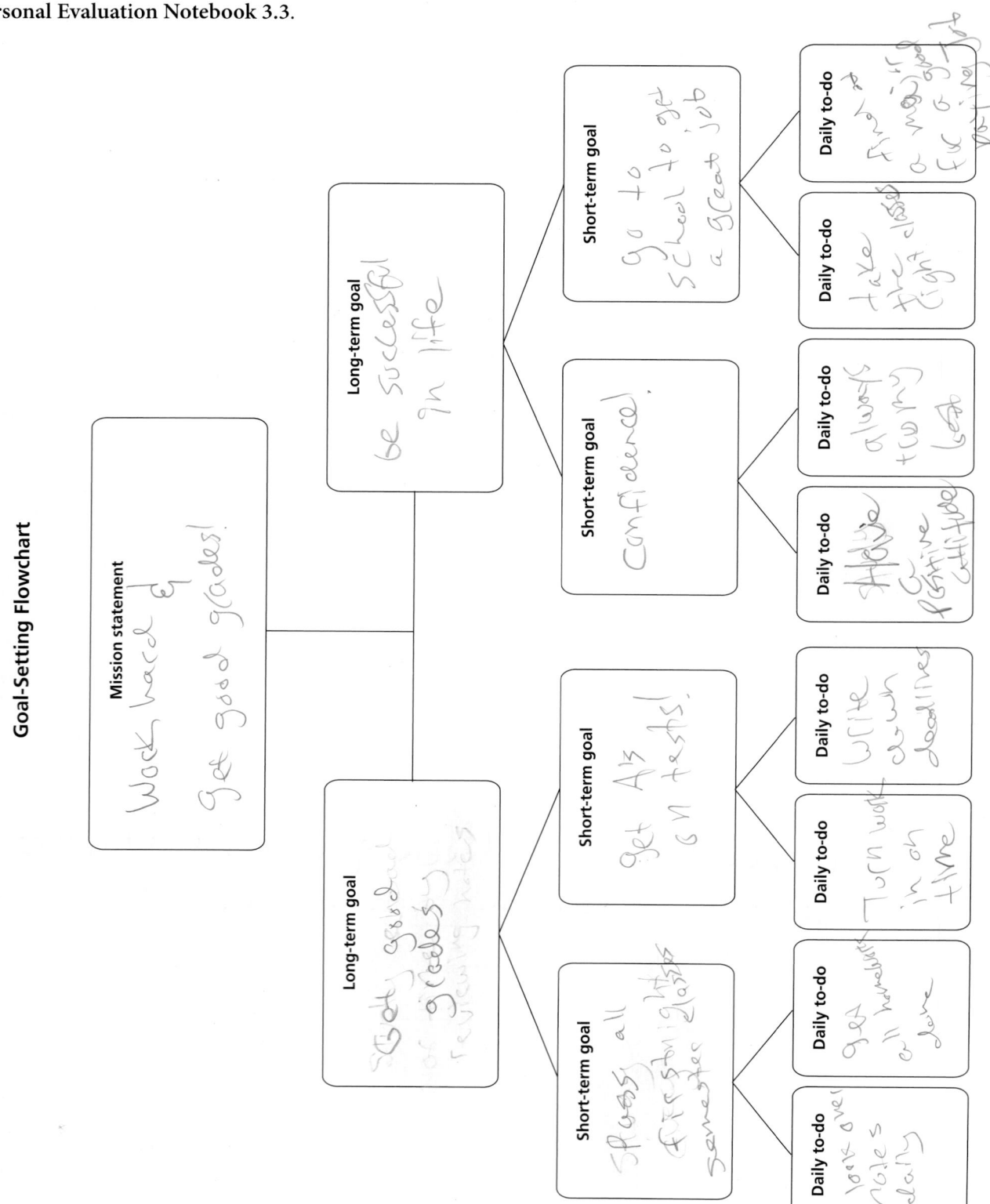

Goal-Setting Flowchart

Mission statement
Work hard & get good grades!

Long-term goal
be successful in life

Long-term goal
get good grades by reviewing notes

Short-term goal
go to school to get a great job

Short-term goal
Confidence

Short-term goal
get A's on tests!

Short-term goal
pass all firstnights classes semester

Daily to-do get good night sleep & eat right

Daily to-do take the right classes

Daily to-do shower + comb my hair

Daily to-do Have a positive attitude

Daily to-do write down deadlines

Daily to-do Turn work in on time

Daily to-do get all homework done

Daily to-do look over notes daily

Daily Prioritizer and Planner: Your To-Do List

Consider the 80/20 rule on page 82 as you use this form to prioritize your tasks and schedule your daily activities. On the left side, write down the tasks you want to accomplish during the day. Then enter those tasks in the "Activity" column, focusing on urgent and important tasks first. Also make sure you include your maintenance and committed activities. Check off your tasks on the left side once they are completed. At the end of the day, see what tasks did not get accomplished and, if need be, include them on tomorrow's to-do list.

	Time	Activity
Urgent	12:00–1:00 a.m.	studying
	1:00–2:00	sleep
	2:00–3:00	Sleep
	3:00–4:00	Sleep
	4:00–5:00	Sleep
Important	5:00–6:00	Sleep
	6:00–7:00	Sleep
	7:00–8:00	
	8:00–9:00	
	9:00–10:00	
	10:00–11:00	
	11:00–12:00 p.m.	
Ongoing	12:00–1:00	
	1:00–2:00	
	2:00–3:00	
	3:00–4:00	
	4:00–5:00	
	5:00–6:00	
Trivial	6:00–7:00	
	7:00–8:00	
	8:00–9:00	
	9:00–10:00	
	10:00–11:00	
	11:00–12:00	

Weekly Planner

Week of _____/_____/_____

Time	Sunday Activity	Monday Activity	Tuesday Activity	Wednesday Activity	Thursday Activity	Friday Activity	Saturday Activity
12:00–1:00 a.m.							
1:00–2:00							
2:00–3:00							
3:00–4:00							
4:00–5:00							
5:00–6:00							
6:00–7:00							
7:00–8:00							
8:00–9:00							
9:00–10:00							
10:00–11:00							
11:00–12:00 p.m.							
12:00–1:00							
1:00–2:00							
2:00–3:00							
3:00–4:00							
4:00–5:00							
5:00–6:00							
6:00–7:00							
7:00–8:00							
8:00–9:00							
9:00–10:00							
10:00–11:00							
11:00–12:00							

Urgent	Important	Ongoing

Month/Semester Calendar

Plan your projects and activities for the school term.

Month of _____

Appointment _____ **Date** _____

Test _____ **Date** _____

Project _____ **Due Date** _____

Demonstrating Your Time-Management Skills

List all the factors involved in time management. Indicate how you would demonstrate them to employers. Add this page to your Career Development Portfolio.

Areas	Your Demonstration
Dependability	*Haven't missed a day of work in my job*
Reliability	
Effectiveness	
Efficiency	
Responsibility	
Positive attitude	
Persistence	
Ability to plan and set goals and priorities	
Visionary	
Ability to follow through	
High energy	
Ability to handle stress	
Ability to focus	
Respect for others' time	
Ability to overcome procrastination	
Reputation as a doer and self-starter	

4

Maximize Your Resources

LEARNING OUTCOMES

In this chapter, you will learn to

4.1 Identify your school's resources

4.2 List resources of interest to students with special concerns

4.3 Describe how to use the library and technology to your advantage

4.4 Manage your financial resources and save for the future

4.5 Explain how you are your greatest resource

SELF-MANAGEMENT

"Using a credit card is easy—in fact, much too easy. Before I knew it, I rang up thousands of dollars, and I can barely handle the minimum monthly payments. In addition to credit card debt, I have student loans to pay back. I feel like I'll be in debt forever."

Are you struggling with your finances or finding it hard to make ends meet? Have you ever bought things that you didn't need or spent too much on a luxury item that you really couldn't afford? In this chapter, you will learn how to find and use your school and local resources to help you succeed in every area of your life, including financial. You will learn how to manage money, get on a debt-free track, and find ways to participate in your school and community.

JOURNAL ENTRY In **Worksheet 4.1** on page 146, write about a time when you set a financial goal, such as buying a new car. How difficult was it to achieve? What sacrifices did you have to make?

Going to college is a big change. This is true whether you are going from high school to college, leaving home, commuting, returning, or starting college later in life. The strategies and information you learn throughout this book will help you cope with major life transitions, including the transition from college to career. The more information and support you have during a transition, the more easily you'll be able to adjust and thrive. In this chapter, we will look at ways of finding and using the resources available to you, including your inner resources, to adjust to change and meet your goals. A great deal of success in life depends on solving problems through decision making. This requires knowing what resources are available and having the good sense to use them.

When you enter college or a job, you are entering a new system and culture. It is your responsibility to understand how the system and culture work. This understanding includes knowing the system's rules, regulations, deadlines, procedures, requirements, and language. As you look through the school's catalog, you'll see terms such as *GPA, accreditation, prerequisite,* and *academic freedom*—terms unique to higher education. The culture is all the written and unwritten rules of any organization. It includes the work atmosphere and the way people treat each other. In a sense, you are learning how things are done and who best can solve specific problems. Knowing the system and culture reduces stress and anxiety. Many advisors and counselors say that the top advice they would give students is to address problems as they occur and seek help when they need it.

Explore Your School's Resources

Many college graduates say they regret not having been more involved in school activities and not using the amazing resources available. Your college experience will be much more rewarding and successful if you take advantage of all the resources available to you. In fact, you can avoid many potentially big problems if you address situations as soon as they arise and know where to go for help.

You may have attended an orientation program, gone on a campus tour, and visited the bookstore and student center when you applied to or arrived at school. You may have searched the catalog, picked up a student newspaper or map, and looked at the schedule of classes. This is a good place to start. Walking around campus, finding your classrooms before classes begin, and locating your advisor's and instructors' offices can help you feel more comfortable and reduce the anxiety of the unknown. You will be amazed at the support services and resources available at most schools. The resources we'll explore in this chapter include

- People resources: advisors, faculty, classmates, and counselors
- Program resources: offices for special needs, areas of study, groups, clubs, and activities
- Online and information resources: catalogs, guides, and local news and events
- Financial resources: financial aid, credit agencies, financial planning services, and personal budgeting

Use the handy form on the inside back cover of this text to record the important information for a number of key resources. Also in the back of the text you will find an extensive list of resources that may be available at your school.

People Resources

The most important resources at school are the people with whom you work, study, and relate. Faculty, advisors, counselors, study team members, club members, sports team members, guest speakers, administrators, and all the students with whom you connect and form relationships make up your campus community. These people will provide information, emotional support, and friendship—and they may even help you find a job! They want to see you succeed as much as you do. We'll discuss a few key contacts, and others will be discussed in the section "Program Resources."

ACADEMIC ADVISOR

One of your most important contacts at school will be your academic advisor. This person will help you navigate academic life. First, read the catalog and familiarize yourself with your major's and school's requirements and procedures. Your advisor will clarify procedures, answer other academic concerns or questions, create a major contract, and refer you to offices on campus that can best meet your needs. Go to the departmental office and find out your advisor's name, office number, and posted office hours. It is best to make an appointment early in the semester and develop a good relationship. Do your part to be prepared, ask questions, and follow through on suggestions. However, if your personalities clash, check with the department about changing advisors. It is important to have an advisor who is accessible, takes time to listen, and will work closely with you to meet your academic goals. (Review **Peak Progress 2** on page xxv of the Getting Started section for questions to ask your advisor. Also see Chapter 12, page 386, for more tips on communicating with advisors and instructors.) You'll want to talk with your advisor about

- Requirements for your major and the substitutions available
- The best sequence of classes and when certain courses are offered
- Whether certain instructors are better suited to your learning style
- General education and other requirements
- Helpful suggestions concerning your academic program
- Resources at school or in the community that could be helpful
- Service learning and volunteer programs
- Internships, work study programs, and opportunities beyond the classroom
- Potential career opportunities within the major

INSTRUCTORS

Most instructors enjoy teaching and getting to know their students. At most universities and many colleges, faculty are also very involved in research, professional organizations, campus committees, community projects, and academic advising. It is important that you get to know your instructors and view them as a tremendous resource. Instructors are more supportive of students who attend class regularly, show responsibility, and are prepared and engaged in class.

MENTORS

A **mentor** is a person (such as a coach, an instructor, an employer, or a colleague) who is a role model, supports your goals, takes an interest in your professional and personal development, and helps you achieve, either directly through instruction or indirectly by example. A mentor can open doors for you and make a difference in your life. Check to see if your college has a formal mentoring program that connects students to faculty, staff, or more experienced students. Once you develop a supportive relationship, your instructor may be willing to serve as a mentor to help you make connections in your career.

PEERS

Your fellow students may be very involved in the learning community. They are active in orientation, campus tours, information and advising centers, clubs, and almost every service area on campus. Take the initiative to organize a study team or partner for each class; get to know your lab assistant, tutor, and peers in the academic advising center, clubs' offices, and so on. This is a great way to improve learning, get help, and build a network of relationships. See **Peak Progress 4.1** for tips on setting up an effective study group.

Networking, a term often used in business, simply means enriching yourself and your opportunities by building relationships with others. Not only is networking one of the best strategies for overcoming isolation and developing long-lasting relationships, but it will likely help you land a job and further your career. More than 60 percent of all jobs are found by networking—through friends, family, neighbors, co-workers, and acquaintances. At college, you have ample opportunity to build a diverse network of "who you know," including instructors, advisors, alumni, and peers. Stretch your comfort zone by getting to know people with backgrounds different from yours. (See **Worksheet 4.2** on page 147 for a handy guide.) Build a wide and diverse network at school by using these tips:

- **Get to know other students in class.** Introduce yourself and correctly write down the names of new acquaintances and try to pronounce them—ask for help if necessary. See who is interested in joining a study team.
- **Get to know students out of class.** Smile and say "hi" when you see them out of class, and take time to discuss lectures and assignments. Go to the student union, the library, and events at the multicultural and career center, and be friendly.
- **Get to know your instructors.** Throughout this book, you'll find tips for building supportive relationships with instructors. Get to know them and take an interest in their research and area of expertise.

"Mentor: Someone whose hindsight can become your foresight."

ANONYMOUS

Peak Progress

How to Form a Study Group

The old saying "Two heads are better than one" is never more true than when participating in a study group:

- Working in a study group gives you practice speaking in front of others and being an active part of a productive unit—skills that will be essential on the job.
- If someone is depending on your involvement, you are more likely to show up and come prepared. You may also become more organized, as others will get frustrated if you spend the time shuffling notes into order.
- When comparing notes, you will discover if you missed or misunderstood key points discussed in class or presented in the text.
- You are encouraged to explain things aloud to others (as in the "Teach" step in the Adult Learning Cycle). Speaking and listening to others can improve your ability to remember the information later, especially at test time.

Whether your instructor requires it or not, take advantage of the opportunity to buddy-up with classmates who are focused on excelling. But where do you start? First, notice which classmates arrive on time, stay focused, and ask thoughtful questions. Ask these individuals if they are interested in forming a study team, and exchange phone numbers and e-mail addresses.

Look for students whose learning styles complement each other (see Chapter 1 for learning styles). For example, one person may be great at taking notes, another at synopsizing the instructor's lecture, another at locating key information in the text, and another at formulating possible test questions. When you get to know each other better, you'll see each person's strength.

Determine a neutral place to meet and a consistent day and time (including starting and ending times) that accommodates everyone. An ideal study group should have no more than six members. Otherwise, maintaining focus and attendance will be a challenge.

The group should initially discuss the overall goals for the study group (such as talking through the reading assignment, comparing notes, preparing for exams, and working on a major project) and let each member comment on his or her strengths as well as weaknesses (such as "I'd like to take better notes in class"). This will encourage the members to function more as a team.

Then, keep the socializing to a minimum and focus on the group's goals. Ask questions when a point isn't clear. In the last few minutes of each meeting, develop a tentative agenda for the next get-together (such as reviewing a specific chapter or going over test results), so that each person is prepared to participate and brings the necessary materials.

If you are hesitant to line up a group yourself but see that another classmate is getting one together, politely ask to join and let that person know your strengths and what you will bring to the group. This also gives you practice selling yourself, which will better prepare you for job-hunting.

Participating in a study group can benefit anyone, especially older students who may feel out of place returning to school after an extended period. Many returning students bring practical, professional experience that offers a different perspective on the course material. It also gives nontraditional students a chance to connect more with the school and fellow classmates.

- **Join clubs.** Almost every academic department has a club, and there are clubs where you can meet students who have similar interests, such as chess, skiing, religion, or music. Does your school offer any intramural sports you enjoy? If you can't find a club that interests you, consider starting one and see if other classmates are interested in participating.
- **Work on campus.** A great way to meet people and earn extra money is to work on campus. Check out the career center for work study and student assistant jobs.

- **Perform.** Join the band, choir, jazz group, or chamber readers; perform in a play; or work in theater behind the scenes. Some campus groups serve the community by performing in local schools or reading in library story hours.
- **Join the school newspaper.** Write stories or work in the office, which will also help build your portfolio of work samples.
- **Join a political group.** Campus and community political groups are a great way to meet people, become better informed, and support a cause.
- **Attend campus events.** Go to lectures, political debates, sporting events, and the many rich cultural, musical, intellectual, and fun events that are offered.
- **Consider your living situation.** Depending on the availability and your personal situation, you may be interested in living in a learning community or housing sponsored by the Greek system.

Program Resources

Depending on the type of institution you attend, your school may have a variety of programs, departments, and offices that provide services and help, including services for specific needs. The people you meet in these offices can provide key information and help you find, evaluate, and use information of all kinds.

ADVISING CENTER

Most colleges have a central advising center to provide general education advising and answer questions about policies, procedures, graduation requirements, and deadlines. The center has **professional advisors** who work closely with other departments, such as admissions, records, registration, learning centers, exchange and study abroad programs, and the cashier's office. If you are coming from high school, you will want to verify that your advanced placement classes have been credited appropriately. If you are a transfer student, you need to know what upper-division and general education courses are required, what credits were transferred from your previous school, and whether they were accepted as general education or as electives.

While your academic advisor is responsible for helping you prepare a major contract and guide you through your major's requirements, at most schools an **evaluator** does a degree check to make certain you have met not only your major's requirements but also all the university requirements, such as general education, diversity and common ground requirements, credit and no credit guidelines, the institution's requirements, the required tests, and the number of college units. You may want to make an appointment once you have submitted your academic major contract and have applied for graduation (about three semesters before you graduate). You don't want to find out a month before graduation that you are short two units or have failed to meet a basic requirement.

ADMISSIONS, RECORDS, AND REGISTRATION

This office will have your transcripts, including information about grades, transfer credits, and the dropping or adding of classes. The registrar and staff can also assist you with graduation deadlines and requirements. You should keep your own copies of your transcripts, grades, grade changes, and other requirements.

LEARNING CENTERS

Many schools have a learning center or academic support services to help with academic problems and grade improvement. They offer workshops in test-taking skills; time management; reading skills; note taking; and math, vocabulary, and science study strategies. They may offer individual or group tutoring and study groups. They also do diagnostic testing to determine learning difficulties. If you are diagnosed with a learning disability, you may be eligible for additional time on tests, tutors, or other services. They often help students on probation by creating an academic success plan. Probation is a warning that you are doing substandard work—typically, a GPA below 2.0. If your GPA remains below 2.0 or falls to a certain level, you may be disqualified. Disqualification means being denied further school attendance until you are reinstated. Disqualified students may petition for reinstatement, usually through the office of admissions and records. Many resources are available to help you stay in school, avoid probation, and raise your GPA. Tutoring is often available for all students who want to improve their grades, not just for students on probation.

LIBRARY

The library is a rich source of books, periodicals (magazines and newspapers), encyclopedias, dictionaries, pamphlets, directories, and more. Libraries also offer many services besides the written and spoken word. They may vary in size and services, but they all have information, ideas, facts, and a mountain of treasures waiting to be explored. Librarians and media center staff are trained to find information about almost every subject. They can often order special materials from other libraries or direct you to other sources. Many libraries have electronic access to books and periodicals, and even more material is available via inter-library loans. Check out

- **The library's Web site.** Find out what the library offers and what research you can do from your own computer. (If access to materials is password protected, ask a librarian or an instructor for help.) Many libraries offer online tutorials and tips on evaluating information and citing material.

- **The catalog.** Look at the library's collection of encyclopedias, biographies, and government works, as well as all the other available materials.

- **Searchable databases.** Find out what's available on CD-ROM and online. Ask about policies regarding use of the Internet on the library's computers.

- **DVDs, CDs, and audio recordings in the media center.** This is a wonderful way to access information, especially if you are a commuter student and want to listen to recordings on your commute or watch campus speakers or special events that you missed.

- **Reserves.** Many instructors put textbooks, supplemental readings, sample tests, and study aids on reserve.

> **The library is the temple of learning, and learning has liberated more people than all the wars in history.**
>
> CARL T. ROWAN
> *Journalist, author*

● **Use the Library**
Although you can do research online, your school may have an excellent library, which you should explore. *What assistance or resources can you get at the library that would be difficult to find online?*

CHAPTER 4 Maximize Your Resources

- **Specialized libraries.** Specialized libraries may be available for your use, such as a medical or health sciences, law, journalism, or engineering library. Check the main library's Web site or ask a librarian.

CAREER CENTER

The career center is not just for seniors. If you're undecided about your major and want to explore options and find out how academic majors relate to careers, this center can help. The staff can also help you with part-time jobs and **internships** related to your major. Internship opportunities are very helpful for gaining experience and getting a job. Also, check out job placement services for summer, part-time, or full-time employment. The career center may offer career counseling, job fairs, and interview and resumé workshops. Keep a copy of personal inventories, assessments, and possible majors and careers in your binder or Career Development Portfolio.

HEALTH CENTER

Take advantage of free or low-cost medical services for illnesses, eating disorders, alcohol or drug problems, anxiety, stress, birth control, and sexually transmitted diseases. If you have a high fever, nausea, severe headache, or stiff neck, go immediately to the health center or, if closed, the emergency room, since you might have meningitis or another serious illness. Make certain you have the necessary vaccinations, or a hold may be placed on your registration.

MEDIATION AND CONFLICT RESOLUTION

You may need assistance or advice in solving conflicts with instructors, roommates, neighbors, or your landlord. Check if your school has an ombudsperson, mediation services, or legal aid.

COUNSELING CENTER

Adjusting to the demands of college life can be challenging. Most campuses have professional counselors who are trained to help with personal problems, such as loneliness, shyness, eating disorders, addictions, depression, and relationship problems. They often offer group counseling and classes, as well as individual support. They also refer students to agencies for specific problems. Many counseling centers offer classes in study skills, time and stress management, and other topics to help students succeed.

STUDENT ACTIVITIES OFFICE

Working with other offices, student services provide many programs and activities, starting with an orientation program and campus tour. Sometimes these orientation programs are offered online for first-time, transfer, and reentry students. There are usually many activities for students to participate in, such as

- **Multicultural centers.** Support, classes, activities, and events are offered to celebrate diversity and provide support for racial and ethnic groups and gays and lesbians. A women's center may offer classes and support for women.
- **International and exchange programs.** Your school may offer an exchange program, which is a great way to attend a different school without transferring.

You stay enrolled at your own school but study for a term or a year at a designated school in this country or abroad. There may also be a center for international students.

Use **Personal Evaluation Notebook 4.1** on page 124 to record activities or clubs you want to check out, and determine which ones would fit in your weekly schedule.

SERVICE LEARNING

Many schools encourage students to incorporate service learning into their education. The emphasis is on students' contributing their time and talents to improve the quality of the community and learn valuable job skills. Students often earn college credits and obtain valuable experience while integrating what they learn in classes into practical, on-the-job problem solving. Students also can create their own learning experiences through directed study and field experience. Some students tutor or work with the homeless, the elderly, or people with disabilities. (Learn more about incorporating service learning into your coursework in Chapter 14 on page 442).

STUDENT UNION

Your school may have a student union or center, which may include a dining hall, a bookstore, recreational facilities, lounges, a post office, automated teller machines, and bulletin boards for information on clubs and activities, student government, and carpooling and public transportation. It may also have information on various student vacations, special classes, religious organizations, retreats, sports, and political groups. You will also find information about on- and off-campus housing. The bookstore offers the school catalog, class schedule, textbooks, personal computers, and many general interest books and supplies.

ATHLETIC PROGRAMS AND CENTERS

Your physical health is important, and you should build exercise into your daily schedule. Check out exercise and physical activity classes, swimming, the weight room, and walking and running facilities. This is also a great way to meet other students.

ALUMNI ASSOCIATION

An alumni association offers graduates discounts, travel arrangements, benefits, and information. These services are often available to all students.

SECURITY

Many schools have security or police departments, which provide information about safety, parking, traffic rules, and lost and found items. Some provide safe escort for night-class students, classes in self-defense, and information on alcohol and drugs. See **Peak Progress 4.2** on page 124 on personal safety issues.

Additional Online and Information Resources

Technology affects every area of our lives, and many applications and resources are discussed throughout this text. Schools offer many resources on their Web site, such as the school catalog, the schedule of classes, a telephone directory, links to Web sites for departments and offices, and many financial transactions, such as financial

Personal Evaluation Notebook

Activities and Clubs

Visit the student activities office or review your school's Web site to see what clubs or activities sound interesting. Look for activities that will increase your knowledge about your field of study, help you network and build business contacts, introduce you to people with similar interests, and give you a chance to enjoy your discretionary time, physically and emotionally.

1. Club/activity: _____ Day/time: _____
   Contact person: _____ Phone/e-mail: _____
   Place: _____

2. Club/activity: _____ Day/time: _____
   Contact person: _____ Phone/e-mail: _____
   Place: _____

3. Club/activity: _____ Day/time: _____
   Contact person: _____ Phone/e-mail: _____
   Place: _____

4. Club/activity: _____ Day/time: _____
   Contact person: _____ Phone/e-mail: _____
   Place: _____

Peak Progress

Staying Safe

The topic of school-associated violence triggers many emotions: anxiety, fear, stress, shock, apathy, and grief. The rigors of academic life can be stressful enough even without the added pressure of the possibility of what, where, or when violence might occur. Fortunately, school-associated homicides are very infrequent. The School-Associated Violent Death Study found that school-associated homicide rates decreased significantly from 1992 to 2006.

Rarely does an individual just "snap." Rather, a series of behavior over time may lead to someone physically acting out. If you observe something that doesn't seem right, report it to a school counselor, official, professor, or mental health professional.

Knowing your surroundings is key to your safety in any situation, be it at school, at home, at the mall, in a parking lot, or at work. Know where exits are—from the room and the building. Plan how you would react to an emergency, be it a violent threat or natural disaster. When leaving home, always carry your cell phone and let someone know where you are going.

Many schools have implemented "e-lert" systems for contacting students regarding safety emergencies at school, through e-mail, phone, or text messages. Determine if you need to sign up to be alerted (and, if so, sign up within the first week of school or earlier if possible). Find out where at school you should go if an emergency does occur. Contact your school's public safety office for more information.

aid applications, payment of fees, and bookstore purchases. You may be able to register for classes, go through an orientation, and access your grades online. Many instructors distribute course materials, the syllabus, and assignments via e-mail or a course Web site. Online courses may include a blend of online instruction, Web sites, chat rooms, online bulletin boards, two-way audio and visual connections, podcasts, and e-mail to ask questions and respond to lectures. See **Peak Progress 4.3** for some tips on using technology to your advantage.

SCHOOL CATALOG

However you access resources—online or in print—the school catalog is a key resource, which you need to review thoroughly. The catalog includes procedures, regulations, guidelines, academic areas, basic graduation requirements, and information on most of the services offered at your school. Begin by looking at the table of contents, index, and maps. Most school catalogs contain the following information:

- Welcome from the president and a general description of the school and area
- Mission of the college and information about accreditation
- Support services and main offices in the campus community

Peak Progress

4.3

Using Technology at School

Being competent in technology means knowing how to select, understand, and apply the appropriate program to achieve the results you want, being able to solve problems with technology, and connecting to the Internet. It also means using critical thinking to evaluate information found online and determine if it is factual, current, and from a credible source. Computers can help you find useful and accurate information, create papers, stay in touch through e-mails, set goals, create calendars, keep your class schedule, create a budget, edit photos, join online groups, and create a personal Web site. If you have disabilities, technology can provide voice commands and special services.

Maximize your use of technology in these ways:

- Thoroughly search the school's main Web site and periodically review it for recent postings.
- Register for a school e-mail account and check it often.
- Investigate if your school offers online courses you may be interested in. (Remember, though, that taking online courses requires an even greater commitment,

as you will be responsible for keeping up with assignments and reading materials on your own.)

- Contact or visit the computer lab and ask about support, including available hours and any courses or workshops.
- Check to see if your school offers discounts on computers for students.
- Find out what and how technology will be used and required in your courses. Did your textbook come with a CD-ROM or Web site that will be used? Does your course require a CPS (Classroom Performance System) device, and will you reuse it in future classes?
- Make sure you understand how to do quick searches on the Internet using search engines such as Yahoo! and Google. If unclear, ask for help from another student or the computer lab.
- Don't assume that everything you see on the Internet is true. Check out sources and think through opinions versus facts. If you are unsure about the reliability of the material you find on a Web site, ask your instructor.
- Respect copyrights and credit all sources.

- Admissions information, including placement tests and estimated expenses
- Academic regulations, such as auditing of a course, credit/no credit, class level, academic standing, educational leave, drop/add, and withdrawal
- Fees and financial aid
- List of administrators, trustees, faculty, and staff
- Academic programs, minors, credentials, and graduate degrees
- Components of the degree, such as major, general education, institutions, diversity and common ground, and electives
- Course descriptions
- Expectations regarding academic honesty and plagiarism, discipline for dishonesty, class attendance, disruptive behavior, student responsibility, privacy act and access policy, grievance procedures, safety and security, substance abuse policy, and so on

Look up answers to questions before asking for help, and take responsibility for your own education. If someone gives you advice about a policy, ask where the rule is covered in the catalog, so that you can review it. Look up academic areas. What fields of study interest you most or least? Which areas are so unusual you didn't even know they existed? Sit down with a group of students and go through the catalog, so that you can build on questions, ideas, information, and understanding.

ORIENTATION GUIDE

Many colleges provide a student handbook or an orientation guide that familiarizes you with the school and basic requirements. If you attended an orientation program, keep your information packet. You may want to refer to planning guides and requirements before you register for next term's classes.

SCHEDULE OF CLASSES

Obtain a new schedule of classes each term. You will have not only a hard copy of classes to register for but also other up-to-date information, such as an exam schedule, deadlines, and a calendar of events. Most schools offer a schedule of classes online, but having a copy with you is helpful when you're planning and adjusting your schedule.

SCHOOL NEWSPAPER

The school's newspaper can inform you about campus events and activities, jobs, housing, and so on. Working for newspapers and other campus publications is a great way to develop writing and job skills and to meet new people.

Students with Disabilities

Under the Americans with Disabilities Act, colleges are legally obligated to provide services and resources for students with disabilities, including physical disabilities, mental disabilities (such as depression, anxiety, or chronic illness), physical limitations (such as visual impairment), and learning disabilities (such as dyslexia or attention deficit hyperactivity disorder). Students should be informed about their rights and ask for assistance.

1. **Check out resources.** The first step is to see what is available at your school, such as a center for students with disabilities or a learning skills center. Special services may be provided by student services or counseling. The staff will inform you of services offered by the state and resources in the library. Some students don't think they have a disability because their problem is not a physical limitation. Services to ask about include

   - Parking permits
   - Ramps and accessibility to buildings
   - Audio recordings and books in Braille
   - Extended time for test taking
   - Help in selecting courses, registering, and transcribing lectures
   - Lab course assistance
   - Availability of a Sign Language interpreter, note taker, and tutors

   A learning disability is a neurological disorder that can affect reading, writing, speaking, math abilities, and social skills. If you think you have persistent problems in these areas, you can contact the learning center or student health center for a referral to a licensed professional. Students whose learning disabilities are properly documented are entitled to certain accommodations. For more information, visit the National Center for Learning Disabilities at **www.ncld.org,** or call 1-888-575-7373.

2. **Meet with all of your instructors.** You are not asking for special favors or treatment but, rather, for alternatives for meeting your goals. You may want to sit in the front row, record the lectures, take an oral test, or use a computer instead of writing assignments longhand, or you may need extra time taking a test.

3. **Meet with your advisor.** Discuss your concerns with your academic advisor or an advisor from the learning center. It is critical that you get help early, focus on your strengths, get organized, and map out a plan for success.

4. **Be assertive.** You have a right to services and to be treated with respect. Ask for what you need and want in clear, polite, and direct language. If you don't get results, go to the next administrative level.

5. **Be positive and focus on your goals.** Realize that, even though your mountain may be steeper, you have what it takes to adapt and succeed. Use the ABC Method of Self-Management to dispute negative thinking and visualize yourself succeeding.

Take 3 minutes to connect with your advisor:
- Do you know who your major advisor is? Call him or her, schedule an appointment, and record it in your planner.
- Jot down your major educational goals. (Refer to your responses earlier in this text.)
- Create a list of potential questions to ask during your visit. (Don't forget to check the "most common questions" box on page xxv!)

What else can you do in 3 minutes?
- Stop by the career center and inquire about upcoming internships.
- Visit the student activities office and ask for a list of clubs and programs.
- Search the school's Web site to see what study tips and library resources are available online.

Commuter Students

Commuters make up the largest number of college students. To get the most out of their college experience, commuter students (all students, for that matter) should get involved with school events. Here are some tips to help them succeed:

1. **Participate in school activities.** Students who get involved and join a club are more likely to graduate and have a positive college experience. Visit the student activities office and find out what activities are offered.

2. **Use on-site resources.** Check out the library or computer center for places to check e-mail, look at class Web sites, and type documents between classes. Determine the most convenient places to study.

3. **Get support from your family.** If you live at home, talk with your parents, spouse or partner, or children about your new responsibilities. Delegate duties and ask for help and support. Let them know when you have reports, papers, and projects due or need to study for a test.

4. **Connect with others.** Build relationships with students, instructors, advisors, and staff and join study groups.

5. **Record lectures.** With your instructor's permission, record lectures or ask for recordings that would supplement your classes and make good use of your commuting time. However, never let a podcast, music, or your thoughts distract you from your main job of driving safely.

6. **Pack snacks.** Since you may be at school for most of the day, pack your lunch and take granola bars or packets of nuts or raisins that you can keep in your backpack or car.

7. **Carry an emergency kit.** If you commute by car, carry a flashlight, water, snacks, medical supplies, a blanket, pen and paper, jumper cables, a towel, a few dollars and change, extra clothes, and shoes. In the winter, pack extra gloves, a hat, boots, and even a down jacket or sleeping bag. People have been stranded for hours in snowstorms. Talk with other commuters and add items to your list.

Returning Students

If you are a returning or reentry student, you have lots of company. Over one-third of all students are over age 25, and many are well over 40. These students are sometimes referred to as **nontraditional students** (with a **traditional student** defined as 18 to 25 years old, usually going from high school directly to college). The number of nontraditional students is growing every year as more and more people return to school to complete or further their education. Some returning students are veterans or single parents, some work full-time, and almost all have other commitments and responsibilities. Returning students often do better than younger students because they have a sense of purpose, discipline, and years of experience to draw upon.

Schools are offering more and more services geared for the older, returning student, such as special orientation programs, support groups, on-campus child care, tutoring and resources for brushing-up on math or writing skills, credit for work or life experiences, and special classes. Other resources that are especially important for returning students include

- Adult reentry center
- Continuing education
- Distance learning office
- Veterans Affairs

- Office for credit for prior experience
- Women's center
- Counseling center
- Job placement center
- Information/referral services
- Financial aid office

No matter what your situation, take full advantage of all the resources available to help you succeed in school and all aspects of your life. See **Peak Progress 4.4** on community resources you should also explore.

Peak Progress

4.4

Explore Your Community's Resources

As a college student, you have a chance to get to know a city and make a contribution to the community. Even if you've always lived in the same city, you may not be aware of its rich resources and opportunities:

People Resources

- **Business professionals:** Connect with professionals in your field of study who can offer valuable information and advice, internships, scholarships, contacts, jobs, and career opportunities. Make contacts by volunteering your services or joining professional organizations. Many professional groups have student memberships.

- **Government officials:** Learn the names of your local political leaders, go to a city council meeting, or meet the mayor. Some city, county, and state governments have programs, internships, and fellowships for students. Do you know who your state senators and your state and local representatives are?

- **Political parties:** Political activity is one way to meet people, become informed about local issues, and contribute your organizational talents.

Program Resources

- **Chamber of Commerce:** The chamber of commerce has information about local attractions, special events, museums, hotels, restaurants, libraries, clubs, businesses and economic development, environmental and political issues, and organizations.

- **Clubs and organizations:** Many clubs, such as the Rotary, Lions, Elks, Soroptimist, and Kiwanis, offer scholarships. Clubs such as Toastmasters and the Sierra Club offer programs for people with specific interests. Big Brothers, Big Sisters, YWCA, YMCA, Girls Clubs, and Boys Clubs are always looking for volunteers and lecturers, and they offer many free and low-cost services.

- **Recreation centers:** Fitness centers, swimming pools, parks, and community education programs offer classes and locations to participate in enjoyable physical activity.

- **Health care:** Hospitals and health clinics may provide inexpensive vaccinations, birth control, gynecological exams, and general health care. Some may sponsor support groups and offer classes on specific health conditions, CPR training, and diet and exercise for free or a nominal charge. Counselors and therapists can help with personal problems, such as depression, excessive shyness, or destructive behavior, and are available just to talk about any problem you are having.

- **Houses of worship:** Great places to meet new friends, houses of worship hold social events, workshops, support groups, and conferences.

- **Job placement services:** Get career counseling, job listings, and help with interviewing skills and resumé writing.

- **Small Business Association (SBA):** Most cities have an SBA that provides free advice and essential con-

(continued)

Explore Your Community's Resources *(concluded)*

tacts for those getting a business off the ground or are just considering the feasibility of starting a business.

- **Crisis centers:** Hot lines are usually available 24 hours a day for such crises as suicidal feelings, physical and/or emotional abuse, rape, AIDS, and severe depression.
- **Support groups:** Whatever your needs, there may be a support group to share your concerns and offer help. Among these are support groups for alcoholism, drug addiction, friends and family of addicts or alcoholics, physical and/or emotional abuse, veterans, people making career changes, and cancer and other terminal illnesses.
- **Helping organizations:** The American Cancer Society, American Heart Association, Red Cross, Salvation Army, and animal protection agencies, such as the Humane Society and ASPCA, provide information, services, and help. These organizations always need volunteers.

Additional Online and Information Resources

- **City Web site:** Almost every community has a Web site that highlights local areas of interests, schools, housing, businesses, and upcoming events.
- **Local newspapers, magazines, and newsletters:** Learn about community events, services, seminars, clubs, auctions, art showings, sporting events, concerts, businesses, local political leaders, and current community issues. Many communities have newsletters or magazines describing the area, featuring local interest stories, and advertising community resources.
- **Libraries:** Apply for a library card at the city or county library and check out free resources, such as DVDs and music CDs, as well as special interest classes, seminars, and book clubs.
- **2-1-1:** The United Way offers a service in many communities that provides assistance and links you to related support agencies. Dial 2-1-1 or look online to see if this service is available in your area.

Manage Your Financial Resources

In this section, we will analyze how to manage a very important resource—your money. Did you know the following facts?

- The average graduating senior of a public university has more than $20,000 in student loans. Eight percent owe more than $40,000.
- The average college student has almost $3,200 in credit card debt. Almost 10 percent owe more than $7,000.
- Eighty-four percent of college students have their own credit card. About 50 percent have four or more cards.
- In 2009, there were more than 1.4 million personal bankruptcy filings in the United States, up more than 32 percent from 2008.
- The average college student spends about $600 on beer each year.

If you want to be above average at handling your finances, you must plan ahead by establishing a budget, researching financial assistance, limiting (and eliminating) your credit card debt, protecting your identity, and saving for the future.

Keep a Budget

The first step in handling your finances is to write a budget. Calculate how much you earn and how much you spend. Write a short-term monthly budget, one for the school term, and a long-term budget for a year or more. (See **Worksheet 4.4** on page 149 for samples.) You will then have a big picture of large expenses, such as tuition and will be able to monitor and modify your expenses each month. Keep receipts, bills, canceled checks, and credit card statements in a file or box, in case you want to exchange your purchases or revise your budget for accuracy. Keep a file for taxes, and file applicable receipts. **Complete Personal Evaluation Notebook 4.2** on page 132 to determine where you spend your money.

Research Financial Assistance

Most schools provide many sources of jobs and financial aid. Thousands of dollars of financial aid go unclaimed each year. Check with the financial aid office for loans, grants, scholarships, and information on programs available to students. Generally, scholarships and grants do not have to be paid back. However, student loans must be repaid. Make certain that you know the payback policy and treat your school loan with the same respect you would treat any loan. Defaulting on student loans may damage your credit, because this information appears on credit reports. Recent legislation has changed how many government loans will be distributed in the future, so make sure you thoroughly understand the necessary paperwork and payback expectations. Some sources of financial aid are included in the table on page 133.

Check with your school's financial aid office for a list of financial resources, or visit the U.S. Department of Education Web site at **www.ed.gov.** This site provides general information about the major federal student aid programs, who is eligible and how to apply, tax credits for education expenses, and other federal, state, and private sources of information.

Avoid Credit Card Debt

When used wisely, credit cards are convenient and help establish a credit rating. Unfortunately, thousands of students fall into debt every year by using a credit card for everyday expenses without backup funds or a plan for repaying the balance. Besides having to pay the interest (usually from 10 to 18 percent), you can rack up additional charges by exceeding your credit limit or making payments late (which adds up fast if you use more than one card). Some people blame the financial industry for making it too easy to obtain credit cards, but the reality is *you* filled out the application and made the purchases.

When you develop your monthly budget, don't just add the minimum balance that's due on each credit card. Plan a strategy that pays off your balances as fast as possible. If you pay just the minimum balance, interest will accrue for years. Suppose you have a credit card balance of $3,000 at a rate of 10 percent (which is at the very low end). Paying it off at $100 per month would take 3 years assuming you don't charge another dollar to the credit card. On your monthly statement, credit card companies are now required to indicate how many months it will take you to pay off your balance based on making just the minimum payments. Take a look at your statement—how long will you be in debt if you pay only the minimum?

Protect Your Identity

Incidences of identify theft are increasing. Periodically check your account balances and review your bank statements, and always review your credit card statements.

$	
Bottled water:	$1.20
Grande coffee:	$4.50
"Value" meal:	$5.39
Music download:	$1.29
Movie and popcorn:	$18
Pizza delivery:	$20

● **It All Adds Up**

Your budget needs to include not only the big expenses but also the "little" costs that quickly add up under the categories of "food" or "entertainment." *Are your daily expenses eating up too much of your budget?*

Personal Evaluation Notebook

4.2

Money In/Money Out

The following chart will help you start planning your budget. Print out a copy of this chart at **www.mhhe.com/ferrett8e** and follow the instructions.

1. Monitor your spending for a month. To keep it simple, list money in and money out. Record everything, including earnings, food, travel, and school items. At the end of the month, total your monthly income and your monthly expenses. Put them in the appropriate categories. Subtract your total expenses from your total income. The money left is your monthly surplus. If you have a deficit, you will need to explore ways of increasing revenue or decreasing expenses. Following is a sample.

Date	Money In	Money Out
Monday, Jan. 2	$28.00 (typed paper)	
Tuesday, Jan. 3		$20.00 (dinner/movie)
		$40.00 (gas for car)
Wednesday, Jan. 4	$50.00 (house cleaning)	

2. How can you increase your earnings?

_____

_____

_____

_____

3. How can you decrease your spending?

_____

_____

_____

_____

4. List all the free or inexpensive entertainment available in your community. Discuss this list with your study team.

_____

_____

_____

_____

Use **Worksheet 4.4** on page 149 as a guide for planning your budget for the school term.

Sources of Financial Aid	
Financial Aid Source	**Description**
Scholarships and Grants Financial aid awarded according to criteria as designated by donor	Scholarships and grants are awarded at most schools on the basis of academic achievement, athletics, music, art, or writing and usually do not have to be paid back. Look on your school (or department) scholarship page for scholarships offered through, or in cooperation with, your school. Many companies and organizations (such as the Rotary, Kiwanis, Lions, Elks, Soroptimist, and American Association of University Women) also offer scholarships, which fit a wide variety of interests and backgrounds. **For More Information** http://apps.collegeboard.com/cbsearch_ss/welcome.jsp www.fastweb.com www.princetonreview.com/scholarships-financial-aid.aspx https://studentaid2.ed.gov/getmoney/scholarship/scholarship_search_select.asp
Pell Grants Need-based grants that do not have to be repaid	This is the largest student aid program financed by the federal government. Students will need to complete the FAFSA before being considered for these grants. Filing for the FAFSA is free and can be done online. **For More Information** www2.ed.gov/programs/fpg/index.html www.fafsa.ed.gov http://studentaid.ed.gov
Loans Payment for school from government (or other lender) which must be repaid, usually with interest	Stafford and Perkins loans are low-interest federal loans to be repaid after you complete your education. PLUS loans and Supplemental Loans for Students (SLS) have variable interest rates; repayment of the principal and interest begins after the last loan payment. **For More Information** www.simpletuition.com/esl/glossary_full http://studentaid.ed.gov/PORTALSWebApp/students/english/studentloans.jsp https://studentaid2.ed.gov/getmoney/pay_for_college/loans_evaluate.html

(continued)

Sources of Financial Aid	
Financial Aid Source	**Description**
Work Study Aid program that allows students to work on-campus or at an approved off-campus organization to earn money to pay for college expenses	Individual colleges administer these federal funds to students participating in the Federal Work-Study (FWS) program. While on-campus, workers normally work for the school; off-campus workers may be able to work for local nonprofit organizations or in a job relevant to their course of study. Student employment, or work study, is an excellent way to earn money and gain valuable experience while still in school. **For More Information** http://studentaid.ed.gov/PORTALSWebApp/students/english/campusaid.jsp
Veterans' Programs Financial support and housing provided to military veterans for service	Bills such as the Post-9/11 GI Bill and the Montgomery GI Bill provide financial assistance for the cost of tuition (including undergraduate, graduate, and vocational/technical training), housing, and a book stipend to all eligible veterans. Apply online or at the Veterans Affairs Regional Office. Numerous scholarships are also available for veterans. **For More Information** www.fastweb.com/scholarships-directory/military-and-veteran-scholarships www.gibill.va.gov
Programs for Native American Students Aid from federal or private institutions provided to Native American students	Native American students can find financial aid from the U.S. Bureau of Indian Education or many private donors and organizations, including the American Indian College Fund. **For More Information** www.bie.edu/site_res_view_folder.aspx?id=368c58a1-2565-484a-9bcd-08ac2cbec9e4 www.indianeducation.spps.org/College_Tuition_Waivers_for_Native_American_Students.html http://studentaid.ed.gov/PORTALSWeb App/students/english/native.jsp Contact your financial aid office or search online for aid programs designed for specific cultural or ethnic groups.

Other Sources

Loans, assistance programs, and aid programs may be available if you have special needs, such as visual impairments, hearing problems, or speech difficulties; are unemployed; or have a deceased parent. Search the Internet by using key words such as *college scholarship or college loans* to find available programs. While there are many valuable financial aid resources on the Internet, some Web sites are not reliable. Be especially wary of any Web sites that ask for money or unsecured personal information.

If you handle your transactions online, carefully read the procedures on the bank's or company's Web site. Never respond to phone calls and e-mails asking for personal information, such as your Social Security number or bank account numbers, and do not post personal information on Web sites that can be viewed by persons you don't know or have only met online. Report any suspicious activity to your bank or credit card company immediately. You should also report any cases of suspected fraud to your state attorney general's office, and you can also contact the National Consumers League's Fraud Center for help at 800-876-7060 or **www.fraud.org.**

By law, you are entitled to view your credit report for free every 12 months from each of the three consumer credit reporting companies (Equifax, Experian, and Trans-Union). Check your credit report for accuracy. You can access it at 877-322-8228 or **www.annualcreditreport.com.** You do not need to sign up for additional services in order to access your credit report (although you may have to pay to view your credit score, which is optional). Be wary of look-alike sites that may charge you for your report.

Save for the Future

Getting in the habit of saving money is hard for many people. The U.S. Department of Commerce reports that most Americans save less than a penny for every $10 earned. And 35 percent of people under age 35 have less than $500 in the bank, leaving little cushion for unexpected expenses, such as car repairs or medical costs. However, there are ways to build your savings for a sound financial future. If you were to save and invest just $1 every day—the price of a small soft drink at a fast-food restaurant—you could have $90,000 in the bank at your retirement. For a traditional-aged college student, $25,000 today earning 8 percent interest will equal $800,000 at retirement. **Figure 4.1** shows how saving early—even for a shorter period of time—pays off later. (See **Peak Progress 4.5** on page 136 for applications to the Adult Learning Cycle.)

There are many ways you can cut expenses and build your savings:

1. **Pay yourself first.** If you get a paycheck, determine a percentage of your income to go directly into a savings account, your company's 401k plan, an Individual Retirement Account (IRA), or a similar investment. If your

Tonya	Ben
Invests $1,000 per year at age 21	Invests $1,000 per year at age 34
Stopped last contribution at age 31	Stopped last contribution at age 65
Number of years contributing is 10	Number of years contributing is 31
Age now is 65	Age now is 65
Total invested is $10,000	Total invested is $31,000
Total investment grew to $249,000*	Total investment grew to $136,000*

In this example, Tonya invested $1,000 a year for only 10 years (about $84 each month) in a tax-deferred retirement plan, starting at age 21. Ben waited until age 34 to begin investing and continued until retirement. At age 65, Tonya's total is much higher.
*Based on 8% annual return, compounded monthly.

Figure 4.1
The Power of Compound Interest

There is a huge benefit to saving early. *Can you figure out how much Tonya would have had if she had not stopped after 10 years but continued investing until age 65? (The answer is on page 141.)*

Peak Progress

Applying the Adult Learning Cycle to Managing Financial Resources

1. **RELATE. Why do I want to learn this?** I know if I start a habit of wise spending, successful saving, and investing now, it will pay off later. I want to stay debt-free and maintain a good credit rating.

2. **OBSERVE. How does this work?** Who do I know appears to be in good financial shape? What can I learn from resources such as investment Web sites and money counselors? What online tools can I explore to determine what my goals should be?

3. **REFLECT. What does this mean?** Where can I further limit my expenses? I'll keep track of my progress and see what strategies work for me.

4. **DO. What can I do with this?** I will practice reducing my spending every chance I get. Each day, I'll work on one area. For example, I'll pack my lunch, rather than buying it on the run.

5. **TEACH. Whom can I share this with?** I'll ask others for tips and share my progress with a financial counselor.

Make a commitment to paying your obligations on time. Investing in a wise financial plan today will pay off with big dividends later.

---

employer offers direct deposit, see if you can split it between your checking and savings accounts, so that saving is automatic. When creating your budget, add an expense entitled "me" and set a dollar amount. Unfortunately, "me" is the easiest bill not to pay—but in the end it is the most important.

2. **Shop wisely.** Research expensive purchases, such as a car, a stereo, furniture, or a computer. Take into account warranties, payment options and interest, delivery expenses, features, and what you will be using it for, and ask yourself if it is a necessity. A big screen TV may be nice to have, but you shouldn't buy it if it's beyond your means. For everyday items, refer to a list when you shop, and don't buy on impulse or just because something is on sale.

3. **Pay cash.** Limit credit card use to emergencies or special items, such as airline tickets. You will be tempted to buy more with credit, and it is difficult to monitor how much you spend. Follow this simple rule: If you don't have the money for an item, don't buy it. Also, keep your money in the bank; don't carry a large sum with you or keep it in your home. You will be less tempted to spend if money isn't readily available.

4. **Inventory your everyday expenses.** Just as you plan your monthly budget and write down anticipated expenses, jot down the many expenses you dole out each day (see your spending record from **Personal Evaluation Notebook 4.2**). Pack your lunch rather than eating out; make your coffee at home; buy in bulk and take your water bottle and snacks rather than stopping at a convenience store (and often paying twice the amount). Coffee and a bagel every morning at your corner bakery or student union can easily exceed $1,000 a year. It's easy to see how all these "little" expenses can add up.

5. **Pay bills and taxes on time.** Almost every credit card and utility bill incurs a late fee (on top of any interest) when not paid on time. The fee may be a percentage of the balance or a flat fee, which can be substantial (often $25

or more for credit cards). Besides adding up quickly, late fees can hurt your credit rating.

6. **Avoid payday loans.** Too many people opt for fast cash by borrowing against their next paycheck—and often end up extending the loan period or paying late because they don't have the funds on time. These types of loans have excessively high interest rates. For example, if you borrow $100 with the intention of paying it off when your check comes in 2 weeks, you may incur an immediate $20 interest fee—that's a 520 percent annual percentage rate (APR). If you ask for an extension and incur a $25 late fee on top of the interest, the APR goes up to 1,170 percent.

THINK *FAST*

7. **Use public transportation, if possible.** Many cities have public transportation. Biking or walking when you can is cheaper, gives you exercise, and is better for the environment. A car can be expensive, and the purchase price is only the initial cost. Also consider the cost of insurance, sales and personal property taxes, annual inspections and license plate renewal, maintenance, gasoline, and parking.

8. **Stay healthy.** Illness is costly in terms of time, energy, missed classes, and medical bills. You can avoid many illnesses by eating healthy, getting exercise and rest, and avoiding harmful substances. Not only is cigarette smoking expensive (a pack-a-day habit averages more than $31 per week), but smokers are sick more often than nonsmokers, pay higher health insurance premiums, and have more difficulty getting roommates and even employment.

9. **Look for free opportunities.** Take advantage of free concerts in the park, check out DVDs from the library, sign up for free birthday specials or frequent buyer cards, and visit your city's Web site to download discount coupons for local attractions. You may be surprised what you'll find with just a little bit of research.

10. **Conserve energy.** To save money on utilities, turn down the heat, turn off lights and switch to energy-efficient lightbulbs, unplug unused appliances, take quick showers, and turn the water off while you brush your teeth.

11. **Get a job.** You can earn extra money by working while you go to school, but make sure you are not working long hours and neglecting your education. Check with the career center or placement office for a list of on- and off-campus jobs.

12. **Exchange room and board for work.** Some students exchange room and board for lawn care, child care, or housecleaning. Since rent is expensive, an exchange situation can save you thousands of dollars over a few years. Ask around or put an ad in the newspaper or a community organization publication. Also, look for opportunities to house-sit.

13. **Spend less than you earn.** It's as simple as that. Write a budget and be absolutely firm about sticking to it. Once you have a habit of living within your means, you will reap the rewards of confidence and control.

Get Financial Help If You're in Trouble

If you are having financial problems and your credit rating might be damaged, get help.

1. **Admit that you have a problem.** Denial only makes the problem worse. There are some warning signs that you may be in financial trouble. If you experience two or more of these signs, you need to take action:

   - You make only the minimum monthly payments on credit cards.
   - You struggle to make even the minimum monthly payments on your credit card bills.
   - The total balance on your credit cards increases every month.
   - You miss loan payments or often pay late.
   - You use savings to pay for necessities, such as food and utilities.
   - You receive second or third payment-due notices from creditors.
   - You borrow money to pay off old debts.
   - You exceed the credit limits on your credit cards.
   - You've been denied credit because of a bad credit bureau report.

2. **Get professional help.** Check the yellow pages or call the local chamber of commerce and ask if your community has a consumer credit agency that helps with credit counseling. When you meet with a counselor, take all your financial information, including your budget, assets, bills, resources, loans, and any other requested items. Local branches of the Consumer Credit Counseling Service (CCCS) provide debt counseling for families and individuals, and they charge only a small fee when they supervise a debt-repayment plan. Other private and public organizations, such as

universities, credit unions, the military, and state and federal housing authorities, also provide financial counseling for a nominal fee or no charge.

You Are a Great Resource!

Your most important resource is yourself. You already possess the power to change your life; you just need to claim it and use it consistently. In college, you are surrounded by people and resources that can help you succeed—that's why they are there. But it's up to you to be resourceful and take advantage of these opportunities. Don't sit back and wait for them to come to you (chances are, they won't). "I didn't know." "Why didn't someone tell me?" "If I had only known, I would have . . . "—these statements are too easy to say in hindsight. A proactive person who asks questions, does a little research, and follows through on opportunities will achieve success.

> **❝**Few men during their lifetime come anywhere near exhausting the resources dwelling within them. There are deep wells of strength that are never used.**❞**
>
> REAR ADMIRAL RICHARD E. BYRD
> *Polar explorer*

WORDS TO SUCCEED

TAKING CHARGE

Summary

In this chapter I learned to

- **Explore and understand the campus system.** It is important to understand the rules, regulations, deadlines, policies, procedures, requirements, and resources for help at my school.

- **Seek out people resources.** I appreciate the faculty, advisors, administrators, and study team members, as well as all the students and relationships that make up the campus community. I explore and build networks with all the people who provide information, help, and support. I meet with instructors and my advisor often to review and clarify my expectations and progress. I understand that having a mentor for guidance, knowledge, and advice is essential to my personal and academic growth as a person and my field of study.

- **Use program and online resources.** I explore various programs that offer help, support, and opportunities, such as the advising center, the career development center, counseling, the tutoring and learning center, exchange programs, the job placement office, clubs, campus events, and other activities. I spend time in the library, exploring books, magazines, and newspapers. I visit the bookstore and computer labs, read through the catalog, look at school material, and read the school newspaper. I explore service learning opportunities and resources available for my special needs, such as the adult reentry center and transferring student, legal aid, and veterans programs. As a commuting student, I check out carpooling boards and look for programs that can help me be more involved in campus activities.

- **Use technology to my advantage.** I determine how technology will be used in my courses and what opportunities and resources my school provides.

- **Explore community resources.** I go to city council meetings and become familiar with community leaders and projects. I look into internships and part-time jobs. I check out the community's Web site and local publications to become familiar with local topics and opportunities for service, resources and special support groups, and agencies offering counseling and health services.

- **Manage my money.** I take full responsibility for my finances. I know how to make and stick to a budget, save money, and spend less than I earn. I limit my credit card use and seek help managing my money when necessary.

- **Explore financial resources.** I explore scholarships and grants, loans, work study, and special assistance programs. I also explore campus jobs and student assistance programs.

- **Realize that I am my greatest resource.** I know I am capable of making the most of my opportunities and must be proactive, diligent, and resourceful in order to succeed.

Performance Strategies

Following are the top 10 tips for maximizing your resources:

- Explore all available resources.
- Join clubs and activities and widen your circle of friends.
- Investigate one new campus resource each week.
- Get involved and volunteer at school and in the community.
- Seek help at the first sign of academic, financial, health, or emotional trouble.

- Know where your money goes.
- Establish a budget—and stick to it.
- Use a credit card for convenience only and don't go into debt for unnecessary items.
- Protect your identity from fraud.
- Look for creative ways to reduce spending and save money.

Tech for Success

Take advantage of the text's Web site at **www.mhhe.com/ferrett8e** for additional study aids, useful forms, and convenient and applicable resources.

- **Web sites and textbooks.** Many textbooks have accompanying Web sites that provide additional resources and study tools, such as online study guides, lab manuals, resources for research projects, and materials to study for certification exams. Many of these Web sites are free, usually when you have bought your textbook new. If you

aren't sure if your textbook has an accompanying Web site, read the book's preface (usually listed under "Ancillaries," "Supplements," or "Resources"), ask your instructor, or visit the publisher's Web site.

- **Bill paying online.** Many financial institutions offer a service that lets you pay your bills through their Web site. Would this feature help you keep up with your financial obligations?

Study Team Notes

Answer to Figure 4.1 (page 135): $385,506

Career *in* focus

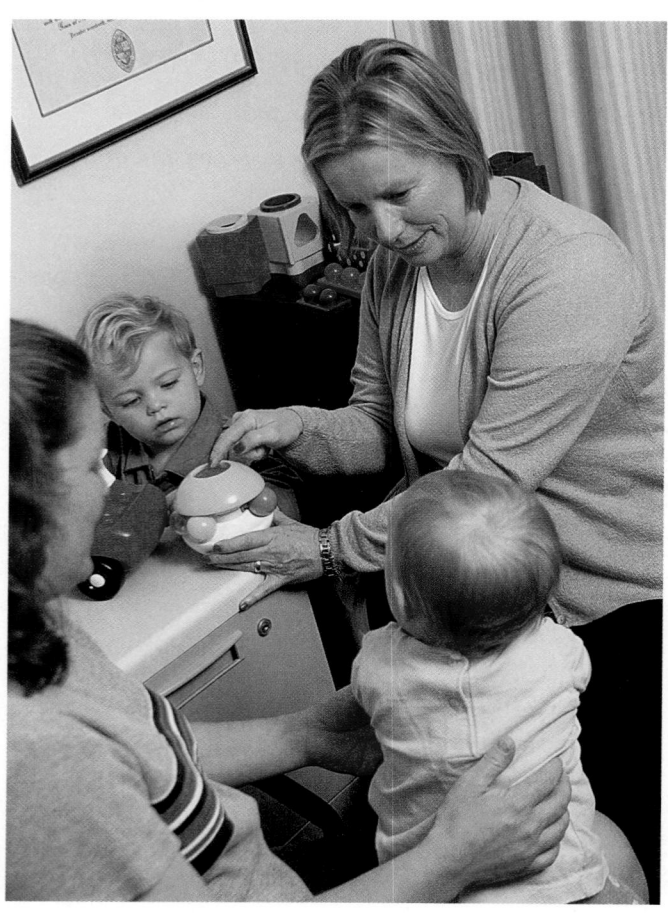

Donna Washington
SCHOOL SOCIAL WORKER

Related Majors: Social Work, Psychology, Sociology

Benefits of Community Resources

Donna Washington works as a social worker at an elementary school. School social workers help students, teachers, and parents cope with problems. Their work involves guidance and counseling regarding challenging issues in the classroom, as well as in the home. They diagnose behavior problems and advise teachers on how to deal with difficult students. They work with families to improve attendance and help working parents find after-school child care. They also help recent immigrants and students with disabilities adjust to the classroom.

A long list of community resources helps Donna provide appropriate referrals. She often uses the telephone to arrange services for children in need, such as counseling or testing. Other services on her list include legal aid societies, crisis hot lines, immigrant resource centers, and tutoring. Donna has developed her list over a 20-year career span and remains in touch with key community leaders to keep her list up-to-date.

Donna chose to be a school social worker because of a strong desire to make a difference in the lives of children. She possesses all the qualities that make her an excellent social worker: She is responsible, emotionally stable, warm and caring, and able to relate to a wide variety of clients, and she can work independently. Because of budget cuts, agencies in her district are understaffed, and Donna struggles with a huge caseload. Although she finds the work emotionally draining at times, Donna finds tremendous satisfaction when she sees the lives of her students improve due to her care.

CRITICAL THINKING What qualities make a good social worker? Why?

Peak Performer

PROFILE

Matthew Friedman and Adam Scott

Can a couple of college students make it in the restaurant business with no more than a few "hot" sauces, a single phone line, a beat-up hatchback car, and lots of ambition? Matthew Friedman and Adam Scott, co-founders of Wing Zone, proved they could when they began offering delivery of chicken wings to 40,000 students at the University of Florida in the 1990s. "There were lots of options for food on campus, but there were no restaurants that served or delivered buffalo wings," recalls Friedman. "We began with $500 and tested the concept in the frat-house kitchen." The first 2 nights in operation, they sold out, and 3 weeks later they opened their first small storefront.

Today, Wing Zone is a franchise corporation with restaurants in over 20 U.S. states and sales of more than $46 million. A high proportion of the company's franchise stores are minority owned, and Wing Zone has been actively involved in the National Minority Franchising Initiative. This program encourages minority ownership of franchise stores, especially by employees who have come up through the ranks.

Some say Friedman's generation has had an easy ride in business, compared with industry pioneers such as Ray Kroc of McDonald's and Harlan Sanders of Kentucky Fried Chicken. But Friedman disagrees with

that criticism: "I think we've had it tougher—there's more competition, customers have more choices, and they have higher expectations. We've worked hard for everything we have. It wasn't given to us on a silver platter."

Friedman has served as a role model for young people interested in starting a business of any kind. But did this busy entrepreneur manage to finish his education, too? "Both Adam and I finished college with business degrees," says Friedman. "That was very important to us and to our families, and our college diplomas hang on the walls of our offices. But it was very hectic trying to run a business and take classes at the same time."

PERFORMANCE THINKING What school and community resources might Matthew Friedman and Adam Scott have tapped into when launching their business? What inner personal qualities were important to their success?

CHECK IT OUT The latest statistics from the U.S. Census Bureau indicate that minority-owned enterprises have increased by 35 percent, whereas nonminority firms have increased by 6 percent. The International Franchise Association (IFA) has established a Diversity Institute (**www.franchise.org/diversity.aspx**) to encourage diversity recruitment and multicultural marketing. What efforts are underway in the franchise community to make ownership, recruiting, hiring, advancement, supplier selection, and marketing more inclusive?

Starting Today

At least one strategy I learned in this chapter that I plan to try right away is

_____

_____

_____

What changes must I make in order for this strategy to be most effective?

_____

_____

_____

Review Questions

Based on what you have learned in this chapter, write your answers to the following questions:

1. What are some of the benefits of participating in a study group?

_____

_____

2. What type of school programs would you contact to find a full- or part-time job while attending school?

_____

_____

3. Name two college financial resources cited in this chapter that you would like to investigate, and explain why.

_____

_____

4. How can staying healthy help you financially?

_____

_____

5. What is your most important resource? Why?

_____

_____

To test your understanding of the chapter's concepts, complete the chapter quiz at **www.mhhe.com/ferrett8e**.

Using Resources

In the Classroom

Lorraine Peterson is a returning student at a 2-year business school. She also works part-time selling cosmetics at a retail store and would like to advance to a managerial position. She was away from school for several years. During that time, she started a family and is now eager to become involved in school and its activities. On returning to school, she happily discovered other returning students. Several of them get together for coffee on a regular basis. Lorraine is especially interested in international students and global business opportunities. She also wants to learn more about available computer services, guest speakers, marketing associations, and scholarships.

1. What suggestions do you have for Lorraine about involvement in campus and community events?

_____

_____

2. How can she find out about scholarships and explore all the resources that would increase her success as a returning student?

_____

_____

In the Workplace

Lorraine has been a salesperson for several years with a large cosmetics firm. She recently was promoted to district manager for sales. Part of her job is to offer motivational seminars on the benefits of working for her firm. She wants to point out the opportunities and resources available to employees, such as training programs, support groups, demonstrations, sales meetings, and conferences. The company also donates money for scholarships and sponsors community events. An elaborate incentive system offers awards and prizes for increased sales.

3. How can Lorraine publicize these resources to her sales staff?

_____

_____

4. What strategies in this chapter would help her communicate the importance of contributing time and talents to the community and the company?

_____

_____

Applying the ABC Method of Self-Management

In the Journal Entry on page 115, you were asked to write about a time when you set a financial goal. How difficult was it to achieve? What sacrifices did you have to make?

_____

_____

Now think of a financial goal you may consider in the next few years and apply the ABC Method to work through the obstacles and create a plan for achieving that goal as well.

A = Actual event:

_____

_____

B = Beliefs:

_____

_____

C = Challenge:

_____

_____

Visualize yourself planning and saving money for investing in your goals. You feel confident about yourself, because you have learned to manage your money and your goals. See yourself feeling prosperous as you consider other aspects of wealth, such as being healthy, having supportive family and friends, having opportunities, and being surrounded by many college and community resources.

PRACTICE SELF-MANAGEMENT

For more examples of learning how to manage difficult situations, see the "Self-Management Workbook" section of the Online Learning Center Web site at **www.mhhe.com/ferrett8e.**

Networking

Using your contacts is especially important when looking for a job. Write information about your network of people on the following form. You can copy this worksheet form to extend your list of contacts.

Name _____

Company _____

Phone _____

Type of work _____

Name _____

Company _____

Phone _____

Type of work _____

Name _____

Company _____

Phone _____

Type of work _____

Name _____

Company _____

Phone _____

Type of work _____

Community Resources

Research and list the various resources your community has to offer. Make a point to visit at least a few of them, and place a check mark by those you have visited. You can copy this worksheet form to extend your list of resources.

CHECK

_____   Resource _____

Service offered _____

_____

Contact person _____

Phone number _____

_____   Resource _____

Service offered _____

_____

Contact person _____

Phone number _____

_____   Resource _____

Service offered _____

_____

Contact person _____

Phone number _____

_____   Resource _____

Service offered _____

_____

Contact person _____

Phone number _____

_____   Resource _____

Service offered _____

_____

Contact person _____

Phone number _____

Monthly Budget

Creating a budget is the first step to financial success. As you plan for your expenses, take time to reflect on your spending habits. Spending within your budget will allow you to reach your financial goals. Complete the following list and review it every month to keep track of your expenses. Many of the expenses will vary per month or will be paid periodically rather than monthly. Include monthly estimates in your budget in order to plan ahead.

Monthly Expense	Projected Cost	Actual Cost	Annual Cost
Savings account			
Housing (mortgage, rent)			
Utilities (gas, electric, water, sewer)			
Phone			
Internet/cable			
Transportation (bus, metro, car loan, taxes)			
Gasoline			
Insurance (including homeowner's, renter's, car)			
Health care (including health insurance, co-pays, prescriptions)			
Credit card(s)			
Food			
Household items			
Clothing (including laundry)			
Entertainment			
Tuition (including fees)			
Books and supplies			
Student loan			
Other			
Other			
Other			
Other			
TOTAL			
Financial Resources	**Projected Income**	**Actual Income**	**Annual Income**
Employment (include full- and part-time, work study, contract work)			
Loan(s)			
Savings			
Parental contribution			
Other			
Other			
TOTAL			

Managing Resources

Exploring your personal resources and abilities is important for your career development. Answer the following questions, and relate your community participation to your leadership skills. Add this page to your Career Development Portfolio.

1. Describe your ability to manage resources. What are your strengths in managing time, money, and information and in determining what resources are available to solve various problems?

_____

_____

_____

_____

2. Indicate how you would demonstrate to an employer that you have made a contribution to your school or community.

_____

_____

_____

_____

3. Indicate how you would demonstrate to an employer that you know how to explore and manage resources.

_____

_____

_____

_____

4. Indicate how you would demonstrate to an employer that you have learned leadership skills.

_____

_____

_____

_____

5

Listen and Take Effective Notes

LEARNING OUTCOMES

In this chapter, you will learn to

5.1 List effective listening strategies

5.2 Describe the various note-taking systems

5.3 Explain effective note-taking strategies

5.4 Refine and use your notes

SELF-MANAGEMENT

"I am having trouble staying focused and alert in my afternoon class. The instructor speaks in a monotone and I can hardly follow his lecture. How can I listen more effectively and take better notes?"

Have you had a similar experience? Do you ever daydream during class? Have you left a class feeling frustrated because you couldn't stay focused and your notes were unreadable? In this chapter, you will learn how to be an attentive listener and take clear and organized notes.

JOURNAL ENTRY In **Worksheet 5.1** on page 174, describe a time when you had difficulty making sense out of a lecture and staying alert. Are there certain classes in which it is harder for you to listen attentively?

A ttending lectures or meetings, listening, taking notes, and gathering information are a daily part of school and work. However, few people give much thought to the process of selecting, organizing, and recording information. Attentive listening and note taking are not just tools for school. They are essential job skills. Throughout your career, you will process and record information. Technology has dramatically expanded the volume of accessible information, but it has also compounded the number of distractions you may face. The career professional who can stay focused and can organize and summarize information will be valuable. This chapter addresses the fine points of attentive listening and note taking.

Listening to the Message: Attentive Listening Strategies

Before you can be an effective note taker, you must become an effective listener. Most people think of themselves as good listeners. However, listening is more than ordinary hearing. **Attentive listening** means being fully focused with the intent to understand the speaker. It is a consuming activity that requires physical and mental attention, energy, concentration, and discipline. It also requires respect, empathy, genuine interest, and the desire to understand. Researchers say we spend about 80 percent or more of our time communicating; of that time, almost half—45 to 50 percent—is spent listening, yet few of us have been trained to listen.

Not only is listening fundamental to taking good classroom notes, but it is also directly related to how well you do in college, in your career, and in relationships. Students are expected to listen attentively to lectures, to other student presentations, and in small-group and class discussions. Career professionals attend meetings, follow directions, work with customers, take notes from professional journals and lectures, and give and receive feedback. Many organizations have developed training programs to improve their employees' listening and communication habits.

Apply the following attentive listening strategies for building effective relationships at school, at work, and in the rest of your life.

Prepare to Listen

1. **Be willing to listen.** The first place to start is with your intention. You must want to be a better listener and realize that listening is an active process. Is your intention to learn and understand the other person? Or is your intention to prove how smart you are and how wrong the other person is? The best listening strategies in the world won't help if you are unwilling to listen and understand another's viewpoint. Prepare mentally by creating a positive attitude.

2. **Be open to new ideas.** Many people resist change, new ideas, or different beliefs. This resistance gets in the way of actively listening and learning. It is easy to misinterpret a message's meaning if you are defensive, judgmental, bored, or upset. Be open to different points of view, different styles of lecturing, and new ideas. With practice and discipline, you can create interest in any subject.

3. **Position yourself to listen.** In the classroom, this may mean taking a chair in the front or finding a location where you feel comfortable and able to focus on the message and create a more personal relationship with the speaker.

4. **Reduce distractions.** Avoid sitting next to a friend or someone who likes to talk or is distracting. Take a sweater if it is cold in the classroom or sit by an open window if it is warm. Carry a bottle of water with you to drink when your energy starts to lag. Don't do other activities (texting, doing math homework, making a to-do list, and so on).

5. **Show you are listening.** Attentive listening requires high energy. Sit up, keep your spine straight, and uncross your legs. Maintain eye contact and lean slightly forward. Your body language is important—whether you are in a chair or engaged in a dialogue with others.

Stay Attentive

1. **Be quiet.** The fundamental rule of listening is to be quiet while the speaker is talking. Don't interrupt or talk to classmates. The listener's role is to understand and comprehend. The speaker's role is to make the message clear and comprehensible. Don't confuse the two roles.

2. **Stay focused.** Everyone's mind wanders at times during a long lecture, but being mentally preoccupied is a major barrier to effective listening. It's up to you to focus your attention, concentrate on the subject, and bring your mind back to the present.

3. **Show empathy, respect, and genuine interest.** Focus on understanding the speaker's message and viewpoint. Look for common views and ways in which you are alike.

4. **Observe the speaker.** Watch for verbal and nonverbal clues about what information is important. If your instructor uses repetition, becomes more animated, or writes information on the board, it is probably important. Overhead transparencies or handouts may include important diagrams, lists, drawings, facts, or definitions. Pay attention to words and phrases that signal important information or transitions, such as "One important factor is . . ."

5. **Predict and ask questions.** Keep yourself alert by predicting and asking yourself questions. Is the story supporting the main topic? What are the main points? How does the example clarify the material you read prior to class? What test questions could be asked about the main points? Pretend you are in a private conversation, and ask your instructor to elaborate, give examples, or explain certain points.

6. **Integrate learning styles and use all your senses.** If you are primarily an *auditory* learner, consider recording lectures (be sure to ask the instructor first). Recite your book notes into a recorder and play them back several

times. If you are primarily a *visual* learner, the more you see, the better you remember. Visualize what your instructor is talking about, and supplement your lecture notes with drawings, illustrations, and pictures. If you are a *kinesthetic* learner, write as you listen, draw diagrams or pictures, rephrase what you hear in your own words, and take special note of material on the board, overhead transparencies, and handouts. Shift body position, so that you're comfortable.

7. **Postpone judgment.** Don't judge the speaker or the person's message based on clothes, reputation, voice, or teaching style. Listen with an open and curious mind and focus on the message, the course content, and your performance. Talk in private if you disagree, but do not embarrass or unnecessarily challenge the person in front of others. Of course, you should use critical thinking, but be respectful and open to new ideas.

Review What You Have Heard

1. **Paraphrase.** Clarify the speaker's message. After a conversation, paraphrase what you think the speaker said to you—for example, "Professor Keys, it is my understanding that the paper should be four to five pages long, is due on Friday, and should include supporting documentation. Is that correct?" Show that you understand the speaker by reflecting and paraphrasing: "Jan, do I understand that you feel you are doing more than your share of cleaning the apartment?" After a lecture, write a summary of the key points and main ideas. It is even more effective if you compare notes and summarize with your study team.

2. **Assess.** Evaluate how effective your listening skills are for recall, test taking, and studying with your study group. Reflect on conflicts, misunderstandings, and others' reactions to you. Notice nonverbal cues. If there is a misunderstanding, assess your part. Did you jump to conclusions or misunderstand nonverbal clues? Did you fail to clarify the message or to follow up? When there is a misunderstanding or something is missing, ask simple, direct questions with the intent to understand.

3. **Practice with awareness.** Changing old habits takes time. Choose one problem you want to work on. For example, do you continue to interrupt? Think about how you feel when that happens to you, and make a commitment to change. It won't happen overnight, but with consistent practice you can learn to stop annoying habits and improve your listening skills.

Peak Progress 5.1 explores how you can become a more attentive listener by applying the Adult Learning Cycle. Then, **Personal Evaluation Notebook 5.1** on page 156 asks you to think critically about your listening skills and how you can improve them.

Recording the Message

Now that you are prepared and have sharpened your listening and observation skills, let's look at how to outline your notes, so that you can organize material. **Note taking** is more than simply writing down words. It is a way to order and arrange

"He listens well, who takes notes."

DANTE
Author

Peak Progress

Applying the Adult Learning Cycle to Becoming an Attentive Listener

Learning to be an attentive listener and take good notes requires time and effort.

1. **RELATE. Why do I want to learn this?** How will being an attentive listener help me in school, work, and life? How would I rate my listening skills now? What areas do I need to improve?

2. **OBSERVE. How does this work?** I can learn a lot about attentive listening by watching others. I'll observe people who are good listeners and take good notes. I'll also observe people who are not good listeners. Do their poor listening skills cause other problems for them?

3. **REFLECT. What does this mean?** I will gather information about listening and note taking and

determine the best strategies for me to apply. What works and what doesn't? I'll explore creative ways to listen and take notes.

4. **DO. What can I do with this?** I will commit to being a more attentive listener. I'll find opportunities to try my new listening skills. Each day, I'll focus on one area and work on it. For example, I'll choose one class in which I'm having trouble listening and experiment with new strategies.

5. **TEACH. Whom can I share this with?** I'll talk with others and share my tips and experiences. I'll demonstrate and teach others the methods I've learned.

Now return to Stage 1 and think about how it feels to learn the valuable skill of attentive listening.

---

thoughts and materials to help you remember information. You can use either a formal or an informal outline (see **Peak Progress 5.2** on page 157). The point of all note-taking systems is to distinguish between major and minor points and to add order to material. Let's start with one of the most widely used and effective systems—the Cornell System of Note Taking.

The Cornell System of Note Taking

The Cornell System of Note Taking was developed in the 1950s by Walter Pauk at Cornell University. It is effective for integrating text and lecture notes. Start with a sheet of standard loose-leaf paper and label it with the class, date, and title of the lecture. Divide your notepaper into three sections ("Notes," "Cues," and "Summary") by drawing a vertical line about 2 inches from the left-hand margin; then draw a horizontal line below that. (See **Figure 5.1** on page 158.)

Notes. The right side is the largest section. Record information from class lectures in whatever format works best for you. You can use a formal system with standard Roman numerals or an informal system of indentation to distinguish between major and minor points and meaningful facts.

Cues. Then use the left side to jot down cues, main ideas, phrases, key words, or clarifications. List any pertinent examples or sample test questions from the lecture or the book. Try to pose questions that are answered by your notes. When you review, cover up the right side (the "Notes" section) and try to answer the questions you have written.

Summary. On the bottom of the page, include a "Summary" section. This is an effective way to summarize each class session in your own words. Fill in with details from the book, and elaborate after discussions with your study team or instructor.

Personal Evaluation Notebook

Attentive Listening

Use critical thinking to answer the following questions.

1. Do you go to class prepared and in a positive and receptive state of mind? Write down one tip you would be willing to try to improve your listening.

   • I should sit up straight more often
   • Keep my eyes on the speaker
   •

2. Jot down the name of a person you consider to be a good listener. Consider your feelings toward this person. It is usually easy to like a good listener. Attentive listening shows respect and caring.

   My best friend Carey is a good listener. She really tries her best to focus & makes sure she understood everything

3. Write a list of daily situations that require attentive listening, such as talking to your child about his or her day at school, listening to your spouse's or roommate's views on politics, and meeting with a community group to plan a fundraising event. What listening strategies would increase your attention and responsiveness in the situations you listed?

   Class always requires listening. Also Fashion Club we need to know important dates

The Cornell System is a great tool for reviewing and comparing notes for lectures and books. (In Chapter 6, we'll look further at taking notes while reading.) Notes can be taken sequentially to preserve the order decided upon by the lecturer. It is an effective method for study teams, since you can compare class notes, review summaries, and use the sample test questions on the left. One student can recite his or her notes on the right while another uses the cues on the left for possible test questions and examples. Each can recite his or her class and chapter summaries. Many people who are left-brain dominant prefer the logical, sequential, step-by-step Cornell System.

Mind Maps

A **mind map** (or "think link") is a visual, holistic form of note taking (see **Figure 5.2** and **Figure 5.3** on pages 159 and 160 for two examples). The advantage is that you can

Peak Progress

5.2

Formal (Traditional) versus Informal (Creative) Outlines

Your learning style, or whether you are left-brain or right-brain dominant, can affect what outline style works for you. Left-brain dominant people tend to like a traditional outline that uses a logical, step-by-step, sequential pattern of thought and focuses on words and order. **Formal outlines** use Roman numerals and capital letters to outline headings, main topics, and points, then list supporting points with lowercase letters and numbers. This system requires consistency. For example, the rules require at least two headings on the same level; if you have IA, you should also have IB. If you have IIIA1, you must also have IIIA2.

Some students find that formal outlines are too time-consuming and restrictive for classroom lectures. However, they like using an outline because it organizes ideas and illustrates major points and supporting ideas. They prefer a free-form, or **informal, outline.** This system shows headings, main points, and supporting examples and associations, but it uses a more flexible system of dashes, bullets, numbers, and/or indenting—whatever works for the note taker. Many students find an informal method easier for in-class note taking, since it lets them focus on main ideas and supporting examples instead of worrying about rules.

Following are examples of formal (top) and informal (bottom) outlines.

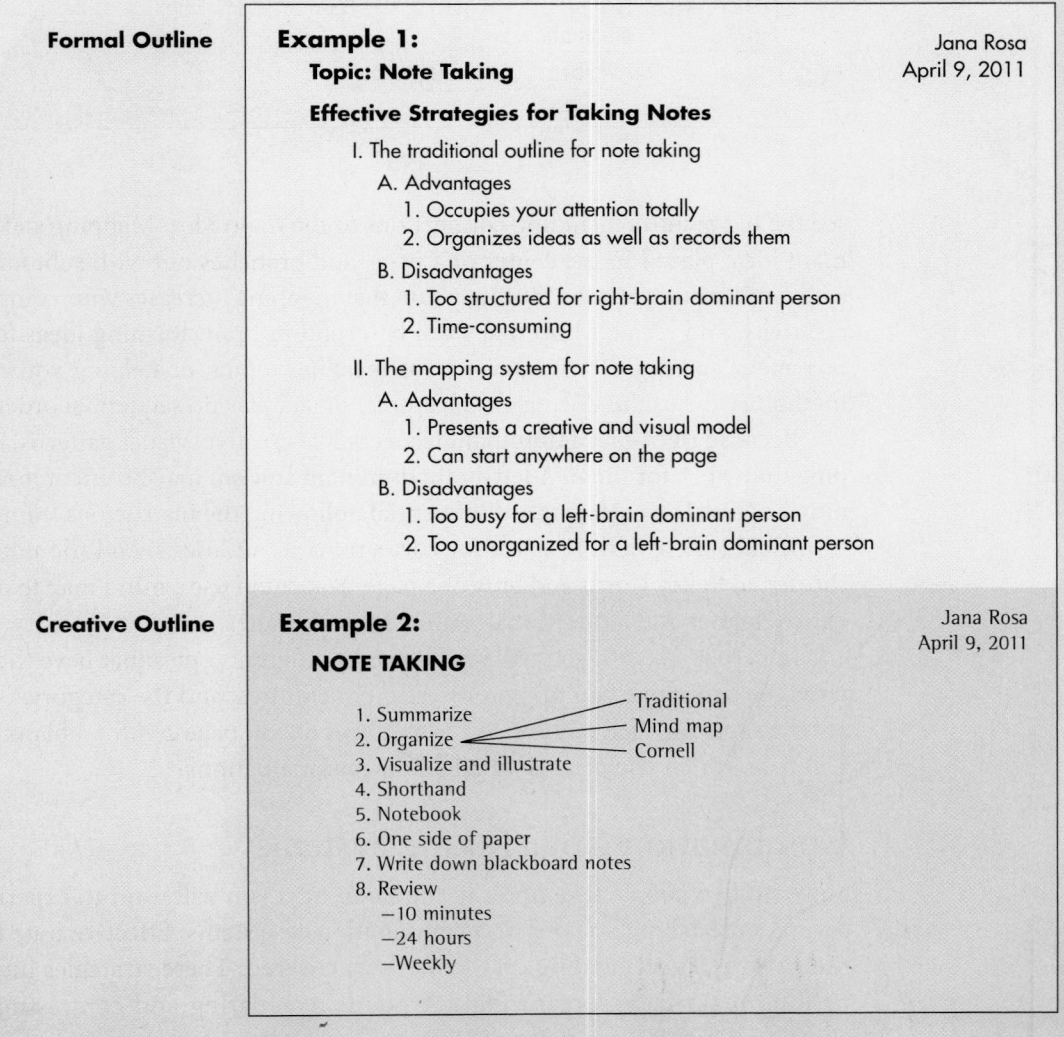

Formal Outline

Example 1:

Topic: Note Taking

Jana Rosa
April 9, 2011

Effective Strategies for Taking Notes

    I. The traditional outline for note taking
        A. Advantages
           1. Occupies your attention totally
           2. Organizes ideas as well as records them
        B. Disadvantages
           1. Too structured for right-brain dominant person
           2. Time-consuming

    II. The mapping system for note taking
        A. Advantages
           1. Presents a creative and visual model
           2. Can start anywhere on the page
        B. Disadvantages
           1. Too busy for a left-brain dominant person
           2. Too unorganized for a left-brain dominant person

Creative Outline

Example 2:

NOTE TAKING

Jana Rosa
April 9, 2011

    1. Summarize
    2. Organize —— Traditional
    —— Mind map
    —— Cornell
    3. Visualize and illustrate
    4. Shorthand
    5. Notebook
    6. One side of paper
    7. Write down blackboard notes
    8. Review
        —10 minutes
        —24 hours
        —Weekly

Figure 5.1
The Cornell System

This method integrates text and lecture notes and includes a summary section. *Which personality type might prefer the Cornell System?*

Seminar		Jana Rosa
Peak Performance 101		Oct. 2, 2011
Topic: Note taking		Tuesday

Cues:	Notes:
What is the	I. Purpose of Note Taking
purpose of	A. To accurately record information
note taking?	B. To become actual part of listening
	C. To enhance learning
Different	II. Note–Taking Systems
systems can	A. Formal outline
be combined.	B. Cornell System
	C. Mind map

Summary:
Use the note-taking system that is right for you or create a combination.
Remember to date and review.

see the big picture, including connections to the main idea. Mapping starts from the main idea, placed in the center of a page, and branches out with subtopics through associations and patterns. You may find that mapping increases your comprehension, creativity, and recall. Mind maps can be useful in brainstorming ideas for speeches or papers, serving as a framework for recalling topics, or helping you review. The method is less useful during class lectures, since it has no sequential order.

Because right-brain dominant learners like creative, visual patterns, mind mapping may work for them. A left-brain dominant student may be uncomfortable mapping because the outline is not sequential, following the instructor's train of thought is difficult, there is little space for corrections or additions, and the notes must be shortened to key words and only one page. You could use a mind map to illustrate an entire chapter and a traditional outline for daily notes.

In certain classes, you will study several different topics that have the same patterns. For example, you may study different cultures, and the categories or patterns are the same for each culture. See **Worksheet 6.**7 on page 214 for a blank mind map template, which you can use or adapt for many situations.

Combination Note-Taking Systems

Since no two people take notes in the same way, you will want to experiment with several note-taking systems or a combination of systems. Effective note takers vary their strategies, depending on the material covered. These strategies include highlighting main ideas, organizing key points, comparing and contrasting relationships, and looking for patterns. Effective note takers listen, organize, record, and review. **Figure 5.4** on page 161 shows a combination note-taking system, using a

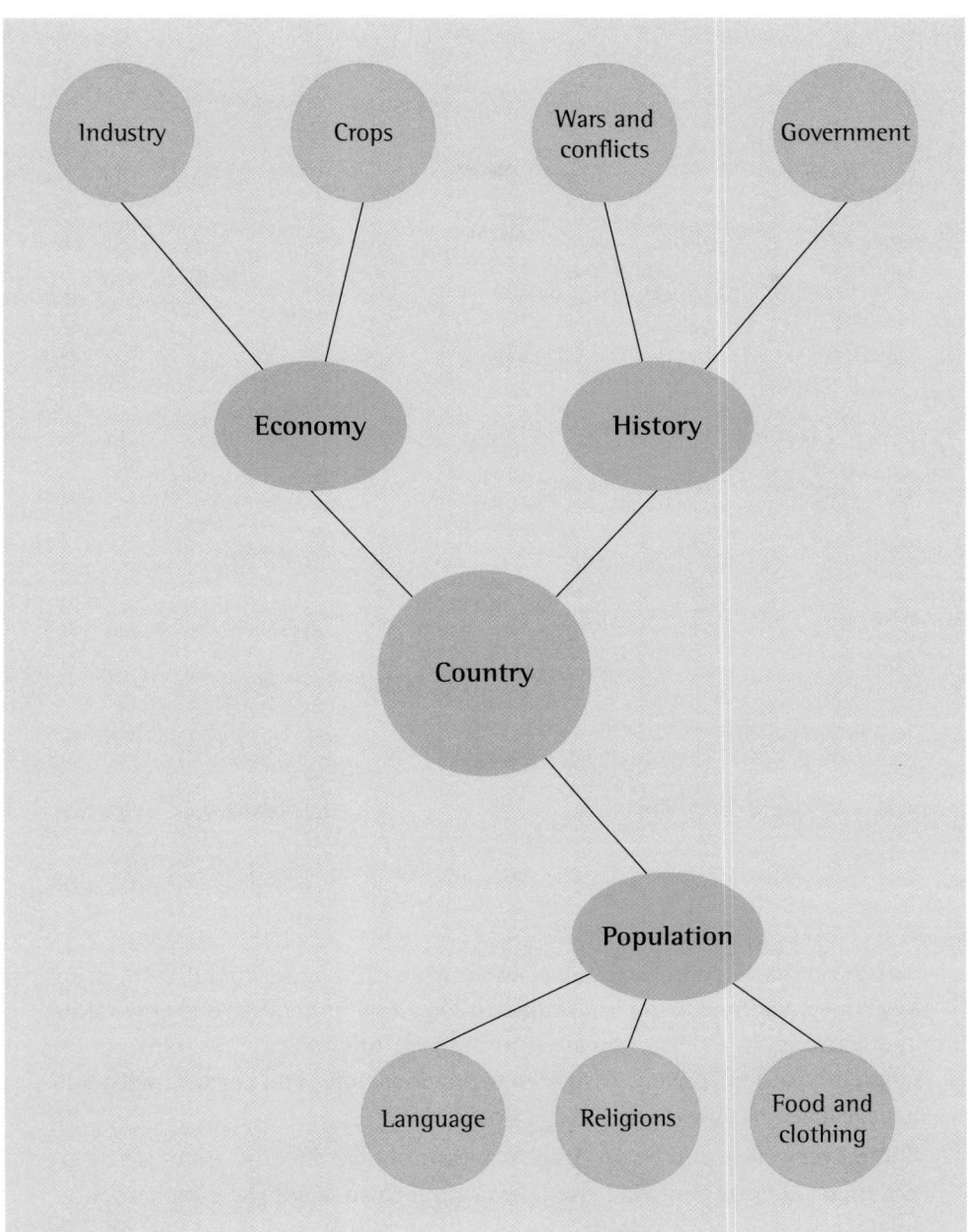

Figure 5.2
Sample Mind Map

This template can be adapted for many subjects. *In which of your courses would this format be useful for note taking?*

formal outline, mind mapping, and the Cornell System. Find your own system that supports your learning style and helps you organize and recall information easily.

Note-Taking Strategies

The following strategies will help you make the most of the note-taking system you use. Review the strategies listed at the beginning of the chapter to prepare yourself mentally and physically for listening.

1. **Preview the material.** Can you imagine going to an important class without doing your homework or lacking pen and paper? Go to classes prepared, even if you have only a few minutes to prepare the night before or right before

Figure 5.3
Another Sample Mind Map

This type of mind map uses branches to reveal concept connections and patterns. *Which mind map design do you prefer?*

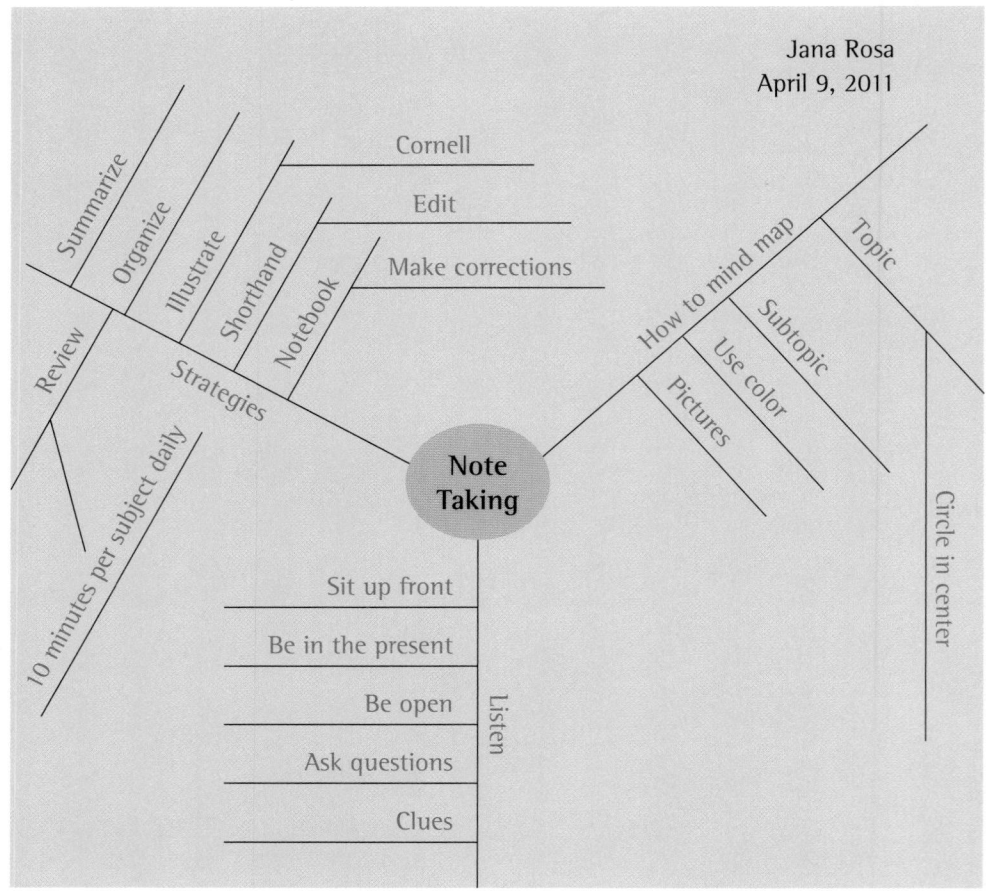

class. Preview or skim textbook chapters for main ideas, general themes, and key concepts. Previewing is a simple strategy that enhances your note taking and learning. In a sense, you are priming your brain to process information efficiently and effectively. Also review previous notes and connect what you have learned to new ideas.

2. **Go to every class and be on time.** You cannot take effective notes if you are not there. Having someone else take notes for you is not the same as being in class. Of course, this doesn't mean "If I just show up, I should get an *A*." Walking in late for class indicates a similar attitude that class is not important to you, and it disrupts the instructor and other students. Set your watch 5 minutes ahead and arrive early enough to preview your notes and get settled. Punctuality helps you prepare emotionally and mentally. You have to invest in every class by showing up—on time—prepared, alert, and ready to participate.

3. **Sit up front.** You will be more alert and will see and hear better if you sit in the front of the class. You will also be more likely to ask questions and engage the instructor in eye contact. You will be less likely to talk with other students, pass notes, or daydream. (See **Peak Progress 5.3** on page 163 for tips on getting the most out of your instructor's presentation.)

4. **Use all your senses.** Many people view note taking as an exclusively auditory activity. Actually, note taking is more effective if you integrate learning styles

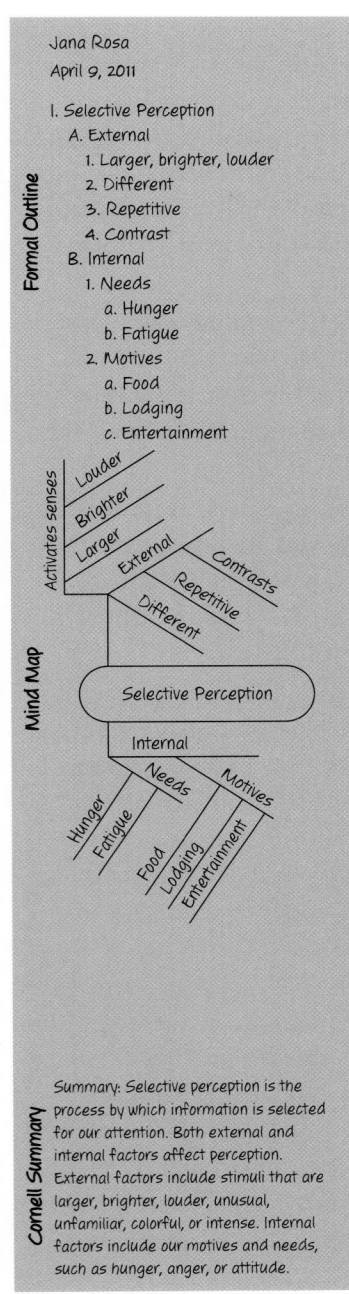

Jana Rosa
April 9, 2011

Formal Outline

I. Selective Perception
   A. External
      1. Larger, brighter, louder
      2. Different
      3. Repetitive
      4. Contrast
   B. Internal
      1. Needs
        a. Hunger
        b. Fatigue
      2. Motives
        a. Food
        b. Lodging
        c. Entertainment

Mind Map

Activates senses — Louder, Brighter, Larger
External — Contrasts, Repetitive, Different

Selective Perception

Internal
Needs — Hunger, Fatigue
Motives — Food, Lodging, Entertainment

Cornell Summary

Summary: Selective perception is the process by which information is selected for our attention. Both external and internal factors affect perception. External factors include stimuli that are larger, brighter, louder, unusual, unfamiliar, colorful, or intense. Internal factors include our motives and needs, such as hunger, anger, or attitude.

What is *Selective Perception*?

Selective perception is the *process by which certain events, objects, or information is selected for our attention*. Because of selection, we do not process the information required to make decisions or initiate behavior. Perception is selective. We all have the ability to tune out certain stimuli and focus on others or to shift our attention at will. We tend to hear and see what meets our *needs, interests, and motivation*. We fill in what is missing. We choose what we want to perceive and organize information into meaningful pictures. We block out some information and add to others. What are the factors that cause us to focus on and select certain events and ignore others? These factors fall into *two* categories: *external* and *internal*.

First let's look at *External Factors*.

External factors are *certain events* around us that determine whether we notice something or not. Many factors affect which objects will receive our attention and focus. Stimuli that activate our *senses* are noticed more (larger, brighter, louder). Anything that is out of the ordinary, colorful, or unfamiliar or that contrasts a background receives more attention. We notice what is *different* and incongruent (wearing shorts in church) and what is more *intense*. We also notice objects that are in motion and messages that are repetitive. The *more* information presented—the frequency—the greater the chances that the information will be selected.

Marketing experts study these external factors and use them in advertisements. If a message is loud or bright, it increases the chance that it will be selected. We even use external factors in our daily life. For example, John is a public relations executive and wants to be noticed at his large company. He wears expensive suits and unusual, interesting ties. Even his office is decorated in a unique, colorful, yet professional style.

The second category is *Internal Factors*.

Several internal factors affect perception. What we focus on is affected by our current *motives or needs*. If you've ever attended a meeting close to lunchtime, you may have found yourself concentrating on the smells coming from a nearby restaurant. You tend to respond to stimuli that relate to your immediate needs (hunger, fatigue). If you are driving down the highway and see a host of signs and billboards, you will notice the ones that are directed at your current motivational state, such as those for food, lodging, or entertainment.

Figure 5.4
Combination Note-Taking System

Note the various note-taking systems on the left, reflecting the lecture on the right. (The italicized words on the left denote inflection by the speaker.) *Which note-taking system do you prefer?*

and use all your senses. For example, if you are primarily a *kinesthetic* learner, you can make learning more physical by writing and rephrasing material, working with your study team or partner, collecting examples, creating stories and diagrams, using note cards, and standing when taking notes from your textbook. If you are primarily a *visual* learner, develop mental pictures and use your right-brain creativity. Draw and illustrate concepts. Practice visualizing images while the speaker is talking, form mental pictures of the topic, and associate the pictures with key words. You might try using colored pencils, cartoons, or any other illustrations that make the material come alive. Supplement your lecture notes with drawings, and take special note of

Selena loves to participate in her women's studies class—so much so that, by the end of the lecture, she has done more talking than note taking. Although she feels energized by the debates, she has little to refer to when reviewing for the weekly quizzes.

- How can Selena balance joining the discussions with taking good notes to refer to later?
- How does she know if she is listening attentively to her classmates?
- What could Selena do immediately after class to make sure she understands the main points?

material on the board, overhead transparencies, and handouts. If you are primarily an *auditory* learner, listen attentively and capitalize on this style of processing information. You might want to record lectures. Read your notes and recite aloud the main points of the lecture. Explain your notes to your study group, so that you can hear the material again.

5. **Make note taking active and physical.** Observe your body, how you hold your pen, and how your back feels against the chair. Sit up straight as slouching produces fatigue and signals the brain that this activity is not important.

6. **Link information.** Look for patterns that connect ideas as well as information that is different. Develop associations between what you are hearing for the first time and what you already know. When you link new knowledge to what you already know, you create lasting impressions. Ask yourself how this information relates to other classes or to your job.

7. **Reduce to the essential.** Students often make the mistake of trying to write down everything the instructor says. Notes are like blueprints: They represent a larger subject and highlight main details. Jot down only main points and key words. Add illustrations, statements, stories, introductions, and transitions that are important for depth, interest, and understanding. Devise a system for note taking that includes abbreviations and symbols. If you frequently text message on your cell phone, you may have already developed your own "shorthand vocabulary," which may be helpful when taking notes. See **Figure 5.5** on page 164 for common note-taking shortcuts.

8. **Organize your notes.** Use large, bold headlines for main ideas and large print for key words, important points, facts, places, and other supporting data. Write your name, the topic, and the date on each sheet of paper. Consider getting a binder for each class to organize notes, syllabi, handouts, tests, and summaries. Leave wide margins and plenty of space to make corrections, add notes, clarify, and summarize. If you crowd your words, the notes will be hard to understand. Keep all handouts you receive in class. Use a question mark if you do not understand something, so that you can ask about it later.

9. **Use note cards.** Use index cards to jot down key words, formulas, definitions, and other important information. Note cards and flash cards help you integrate all learning styles. Write down key words and main points, use them throughout the day, and review for tests.

10. **Expand on notes from others.** Many instructors lecture in conjunction with a PowerPoint presentation. Ask your instructor if the lecture outline is available as a handout, on a course Web site, or in a bookstore. Preview it before class, take a copy of the printout to class, and add notes and detail as the instructor talks. This is a handy note-taking tool that helps you follow the discussion, organize your notes, and read the text. If you missed class and borrowed notes from someone else, thoroughly review the notes, mark anything that is unclear and needs follow-up, and compare them with the textbook.

Peak Progress

Getting the Most Out of a Class Lecture

In the classroom and in meetings you attend on the job, you will come across many styles of presenters, from dynamic and succinct to agonizingly vague and verbose. As discussed in Chapter 1, you can adjust your learning style to your instructor's teaching style, just as you would need to adjust your work style to that of your boss. But what if your instructor's style presents specific challenges to your learning? Following are some tips if your instructor

- **Talks too softly.** If you can't hear your instructor, first ask other students if they are having the same problem (to make sure it's not just your hearing). Then, try a seat in the front. If you still can't hear well, tell your instructor outside of class. Your instructor may not be aware it's a problem and may be able to adjust his or her speaking level or use a microphone.
- **Talks too fast.** If you find you can't keep up with your instructor as you take notes (or you are missing points), you might be a little slower jotting down notes than others and may have to speed it up. Focus on writing just key words. If you miss a section, leave a space in your notes with a notation (such as an asterisk or "missed") and ask another student or your study group about the missing material.
- **Is hard to understand because his or her native language is different from yours.** As our world becomes more globally connected, you will encounter instructors, colleagues, physicians, neighbors, and others with various native languages, cultures, and experiences. No matter what language you or your instructor is most accustomed to, you are both in the room for the same reason—to teach and learn the material. Thus, when you don't understand a point, ask questions and be persistent until you do understand.
- **Never allows time to ask questions.** Find out your instructor's e-mail or office hours and contact him or her directly with your questions.
- **Never addresses material from the text.** Some students get frustrated when they buy a text and then the instructor doesn't cover the same material during lecture. The instructor might be expecting you to read the text on your own and is using lecture time for other topics. If you have difficulty with any of the text material, ask the instructor if you should bring that up during or outside of class.
- **Only lectures, never writes on the board or uses PowerPoint.** Listen for verbal cues (such as a louder voice) and nonverbal cues (such as hand gestures) that suggest more important points to remember. Ask for examples that illustrate key points.
- **Puts a lot of content in the PowerPoint presentation.** PowerPoint presentations can be a visual way of organizing a lecture and showing key illustrations. But some instructors get carried away and try to put the whole lecture in a few slides. Rather than scrambling to write every word, ask the instructor if the presentation is available online. If so, bring a copy to class and take notes on it. Look at slide headings for key words or phrases as the instructor speaks.
- **Never follows the lecture outline or PowerPoint.** Not everyone stays on course when speaking, especially if questions or new topics sidetrack the discussion. Remember that the PowerPoint presentation is just a blueprint, and try to balance your notes with the key points from it and the instructor's discussion.
- **Seems to ramble and never gets to a point.** Some speakers are better than others. Here's where you have to be proactive and ask clarifying questions ("So what you are saying is _____, correct?"), and confer with fellow classmates to put the pieces together.
- **Uses too many personal anecdotes that may or may not be relevant.** Everyone loves to tell old "war stories," even though the relevance may be a stretch. However, this is a chance to connect personally with the instructor, and you may find you have similar experiences. Keep an open mind and resist the urge to ask, "Will this be on the test?"

In every situation, if you still have difficulties listening and taking notes, you should promptly and politely talk with your instructor. Only with feedback does a speaker improve his or her skills, which in turn benefits listeners.

Figure 5.5
Note-Taking Shortcuts

This chart lists some common symbols and abbreviations you can incorporate into your own note-taking system. *What is the essential element in taking effective notes?*

Symbol	Meaning	Abbreviation	Meaning
>	greater than; increase	i.e.	that is
<	less than; decrease	etc.	and so forth
?	question; unclear	lb.	pound
w/	with	assoc.	association
w/o	without	info	information
V or *	important ideas	e.g.	example
+	positive; benefit; pro(s); added; additional	p.	page
—	negative; con(s); lost	pp.	multiple pages
X	times		
~	gaps in information		
→	leads to (e.g., motivation → success)		
^	bridge of concepts; insert		
#	number; end		

11. **Use your laptop.** Your instructor may allow you to take notes in class on a laptop computer. This can be a convenient way to store, organize, review, and share notes after class. However, focusing on discussions, nonverbal cues, and visual illustrations may be difficult if you are looking at your keyboard or screen. If your power fails or you forget to save your work, you may have no back-up notes. Also, your classmates or instructor may be distracted by your typing. Consider taking lecture notes on a computer only if it maximizes your learning. Another way you may be able to use your computer outside of the physical classroom is to download podcasts of lectures if the instructor makes them available. These offer a way to review lectures on your own. Use the same note-taking strategies, and follow up with your instructor if the main points are unclear.

Assess and Review Your Notes

Don't just file your notes away after class. Instead, reinforce your memory and understanding of the material by assessing and reviewing your notes. Research indicates that, even after only 1 hour, you will retain less than 50 percent of the lecture. (See **Figure 5.6.**) Thus, it's important to revisit your notes as soon as possible.

1. **Summarize in your own words.** When you finish taking text and lecture notes, summarize in your own words. You might write summaries on index cards. If you used the Cornell System, make sure you complete the summary section. Summarizing can be done quickly and can cover only main concepts. This one small action will greatly increase your comprehension and learning. It is even more effective when you read your summary out loud to others; teaching is a good way to learn.

2. **Edit and revise your notes.** Set aside a few minutes as soon as possible after the lecture to edit, fill in, or copy your notes. (If possible, avoid scheduling classes back to back, so you can spend time with your notes right after class.)

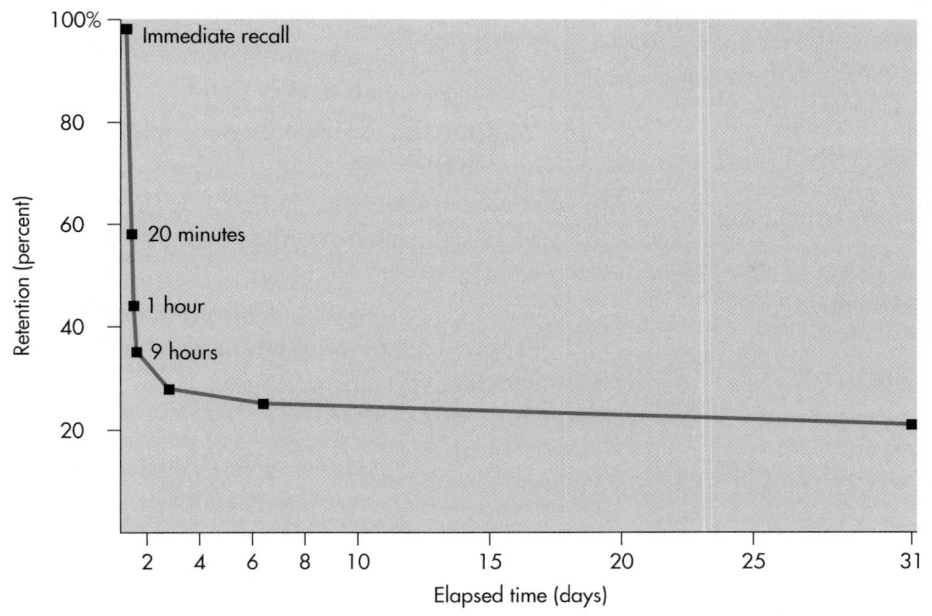

Figure **5.6**
Ebbinghaus's Forgetting Curve

German philosopher Hermann Ebbinghaus determined that after only 9 hours you remember about 36 percent of what you just learned. At 31 days, that amount drops to 21 percent. Thus, constant review is critical. *If you wait until midterm to review your lecture notes, how much will you remember from the first days of class?*

Source: Hermann Ebbinghaus, *Memory: A Contribution to Experimental Psychology, 1885/1913*. Reproduced by permission of Continuum International Publishing Group.

Underline what the instructor indicated is important. Clean up, expand, and rewrite messy or incomplete sections. Compare your notes with the material in the textbook. If you are unclear on a point, leave a space and mark it with a question mark or a colored highlighter. Ask for verification from other students or your instructor.

3. **Create a sample test.** Ask yourself what questions might be on a test and try to write a few sample test questions as if you were giving the exam. Note the correct answer and why it is correct (which may prove helpful later if there is an essay or short-answer exam).

4. **Use visual cues.** Consider drawing a mind map of your notes to display the main points and their connections. For math and science classes, creating flowcharts may help visually reinforce processes or systems.

5. **Review your notes.** Develop a review schedule that supports continual reviewing and reflects on material you have already learned. Think of how you can review your notes within the first hour, the first day, and each week. Add this to the daily planner you created in Chapter 3. There are many ways to work reviewing into your day:

- *Arrive at class early* and spend 5 minutes reviewing your notes from the previous class. Or review while the instructor passes out handouts, adjusts the overhead projector, or organizes the lecture.

- *Review right before you go to sleep,* since your mind is receptive to new information at that time.

● **Taking Notes on the Job**

Note taking is an essential skill in many professions. *What are some jobs or professions in which taking notes is a critical, daily task?*

Take 3 minutes after class today to write a brief, one-paragraph summary:
- What were the main points of the lecture?
- What examples were given?
- What parts are unclear?

What else can you do in 3 minutes?
- Compare your summary to the chapter outline.
- Create test questions out of main topics.
- Make a list of discussion topics for your study group.

Take 3

- *Compare notes with your study group members* to make sure you recorded and understood all the key points.
6. **Monitor and evaluate.** Periodically assess your note-taking system. Try different systems and strategies until you find the one that works best. Feedback from study group members, your instructor, and tests will help you assess how well your system is working. (See **Peak Progress 5.4** for note-taking tips for students who face special challenges.)

Overcome Obstacles

Some students do not realize the importance of note taking and doubt they will use this skill after they graduate from college. As a result, their notes are often disorganized, incomplete, illegible, and of little help in preparing for tests. However, effective note taking changes information you hear into information that is distinctly yours. You discard the unessential, highlight the essential, and organize information to give it meaning, relevance, and focus. Not only is mastering this process essential to improving your study skills, but it is a necessary job and life skill, whether you are learning how your job contributes to your company's objectives or listening to a presentation about employee health benefits. If you don't listen carefully and take complete, helpful notes (or any notes at all) you have nothing to fall back on if the results aren't what you expected.

Peak Progress

Taking Note of Special Challenges

For some students, note taking may be a more challenging skill. Students with learning disabilities often have more difficulty identifying the important information they should record. They often cannot write fast enough to keep up with the lecturer or decipher their notes after the lecture. Sitting through long lectures in which the instructor uses few visual cues (such as words or illustrations on the board or PowerPoint) can be especially tough, as visuals help students focus on important concepts and examples.

However, the act of taking notes has many benefits. Students with learning disabilities tend to be passive learners, and taking notes is one way to actively engage in the learning process. Note taking also encourages them to clarify confusing information and helps them recall it later.

The strategies discussed earlier in this chapter apply to all students. Also, the following tips may be helpful to those with specific challenges (although any student can benefit from trying them as well):

1. **Sit in the front of the room.** Although this is a good tip for any student, it's especially important for those who have trouble sitting or focusing for long periods of time. Put yourself where you are forced to pay attention and keep distractions, such as books, cell phones, and so on out of your hands.

2. **Use a binder instead of a traditional notebook.** This will help you keep everything organized, including lecture and reading notes, handouts, and assignments, and make studying for exams much easier. Write on loose-leaf paper, and three-hole punch everything.

3. **Put headings and dates at the top of all papers.** This makes them easier to identify and organize.

4. **Set up your paper in advance.** Create a note-taking form that helps you focus on the main points of the lecture. Include these items:
   - Today's topic
   - What you already know about the topic
   - Three to seven main points, with details of today's topic as they are being discussed (and then number each line)
   - A summary (quickly describe how the ideas are related)
   - New vocabulary or terms (write these terms in this section as they come up during class; repeat the previous sections as much as necessary)
   - The five main points of the lecture (describe each point)

5. **Cluster ideas as they are presented.** Write them with similar indentation or formatting, and separate clustered ideas by lines if that helps. Clustering information makes it easier to remember later.

6. **Leave space between notes.** Later, you can fill in comments, material you may have missed, or material from the text.

7. **Type your notes afterwards.** Typed notes are more legible to study from, and typing is an additional chance to think about the material and make sure you understand it.

8. **Clarify points with your instructor.** Students with learning disabilities often realize something is important to note after the instructor is well into the discussion, so they've already missed recording key points. Talk with your instructor outside of class and go over your notes together. Your instructor will appreciate that you are actively trying to improve your note-taking skills and may be able to provide additional tips related to his or her class.

TAKING CHARGE

Summary

In this chapter, I learned to

- **Listen attentively to the message.** Developing an interest in listening and making it meaningful to me are the first steps in becoming an attentive listener. I want to listen and am open to new information, new ideas, and different beliefs. My intent is to understand others and focus on the message.

- **Go to every class.** I know I must make a commitment to go to every class and form a relationship with my instructor and other students. I'm on time and sit in front, where I'm alert and aware. I sit up straight, maintain eye contact, and show I'm listening and involved with the speaker. I reduce distractions and focus on listening, not talking. I'm in the present and concentrate on the subject.

- **Observe my instructor and watch for verbal and nonverbal clues.** I watch for examples, words, and phrases that signal important information or transitions. I take note of handouts and transparencies. I use critical thinking to postpone judgment. I focus on the message, not the presentation. I look beyond clothes, voice, teaching style, and reputation and focus on what the person is saying. Critical thinking helps me look for supporting information and facts and ask questions.

- **Prepare before class.** I preview chapters before class, so that I have a general idea of the chapter, and I make notes of questions to ask or concepts I want the instructor to give examples of or elaborate on. I do homework and use index cards to jot down and memorize key words, formulas, and definitions.

- **Focus on essential information.** I don't try to write down everything. I look for patterns, link information, and connect ideas in a way that makes sense and organizes the information. I leave space for corrections and additions and use marks, such as "?" for questions.

- **Integrate learning styles.** I not only use my preferred learning style but also integrate all styles. I make note taking active and physical. I draw illustrations, use outlines, supplement my notes with handouts, create models, and summarize out loud.

- **Get organized.** I know that information that is not organized is not remembered. I write the date and topic on each sheet and organize notes in a folder or binder.

- **Determine the note-taking style that works best for me.** A formal outline uses my left-brain, sequential side, while an informal outline helps me see connections and the big picture. The Cornell System of Note Taking is organized into three sections: "Notes," "Cues," and "Summary." A mind map is more visual and includes main points connected to supporting points or examples. I can combine elements of various note-taking systems to determine what works best for me.

- **Summarize in my own words when I am finished taking notes in class or from the text.** This action greatly improves my comprehension and learning. I compare this summary with the material in my book, review it with my study team, and fill in essential information. I note questions to ask my instructor or study group.

- **Review, monitor, and evaluate.** I review my notes for main ideas as soon as possible after class, within 24 hours. This increases my memory and helps me make sense of my notes. I edit and add to my notes. I evaluate my note-taking skills and look for ways to improve them.

Performance Strategies

Following are the top 10 strategies for attentive listening and effective note taking:

- Postpone judgment and be open to new ideas.
- Seek to understand and show respect to the speaker.
- Reduce distractions and be alert and focused.
- Maintain eye contact and look interested.
- Observe the speaker and listen for clues, examples, signal words, and phrases.
- Predict and ask questions to clarify main points.
- Look for information that is similar to what you already know and information that is different.
- Use a note-taking system that suits your learning style.
- Summarize in your own words and review often.
- Edit and revise while information is still fresh.

Tech for Success

Take advantage of the text's Web site at **www.mhhe.com/ferrett8e** for additional study aids, useful forms, and convenient and applicable resources.

- **Your instructor's visual presentation.** Many instructors lecture in conjunction with a PowerPoint presentation. Ask your instructor if the lecture outline is available as a handout, on a course Web site, or in a bookstore. Take a copy of the printout to class with you and add notes and detail as the instructor talks. This is a handy note-taking tool that helps you follow the discussion, organize your notes, and read the text.

- **Summarize on your computer.** Some people type faster than they write. It's important to summarize your notes as soon as possible after class to make sure you understand the main points. If that sounds like a daunting task, simply write incomplete sentences first and then flesh out the sentences. If you aren't sure if you really understand the main points of the lecture, consider e-mailing your recap to your instructor and ask him or her to review it. (This may also help your instructor determine if points presented in the lecture need clarification during the next class session.)

Study Team Notes

Career *in* focus

Danielle Sievert
PSYCHOLOGIST

Related Majors: Psychology, Counseling

Listening in the Workplace

Danielle Sievert provides mental health care as an industrial-organizational psychologist for a Fortune 500 company. Most industrial-organizational psychologists hold master's degrees in psychology. Psychology is the study of human behavior and the mind and its applications to mental health. When most people think of psychologists, they think of clinicians in counseling centers or hospitals, but many large companies hire psychologists to tend to the needs of staff on all levels. Danielle and other industrial-organizational psychologists use psychology to improve quality of life and productivity in the workplace.

Danielle conducts applicant screenings to select employees who will work well within the company. She provides input on marketing research. She also helps solve human relations problems that occur in various departments. Danielle occasionally conducts individual sessions with employees who face problems within or outside the office. Danielle works a 9-to-5 schedule and is occasionally asked to work overtime. She is often interrupted to solve pressing problems.

Active listening is an important part of Danielle's job. Managers and other employees will ask for her help, she says, only when they sense that she is empathetic and wants to help. To hone her listening skills, Danielle asks questions to make sure she understands exactly what the person is saying. She also takes notes, either during or after a session. These skills help Danielle fulfill her role as a psychologist in the workplace.

CRITICAL THINKING What kinds of problems might occur at the workplace that could be addressed by a firm's psychologist?

Peak Performer

PROFILE

Anna Sui

"What should I wear?" Many people ask this question almost daily. For international fashion designer Anna Sui (pronounced *Swee*), the answer is simple: "Dress to have fun and feel great." Her first boutique, on Greene Street in Soho, New York, illustrated her attitude with a Victorian-inspired mix of purple walls, ornate clothing racks, glass lamps, and red floors.

To the second of three children and only daughter born to Chinese immigrants, the Detroit suburbs of the early 1960s were a long way from the fashion mecca of New York City. However, even then Sui seemed to be visualizing success. Whether designing tissue-paper dresses for her neighbor's toy soldiers or making her own clothes with coordinating fabric for shoes, Sui had flair.

After graduating from high school, Sui headed for the Big Apple. She eventually opened her own business after studying for 2 years at Parson's School of Design and working for years at various sportswear companies. Sui premiered her first runway show in 1991 and today has 300 stores in over 30 countries.

To create her acclaimed designs, Sui takes note of the world around her. She continues to collect her "genius files"—clippings from pages of fashion magazines—to serve as inspiration. She listens to her clients, to music, to the street, and to her own instincts. Sui is quick to say that, although her moderately priced clothes are popular with celebrities, they are also worn by her mother. It's not about age and money, she explains, but about the "spirit of the clothing." By listening actively and staying attuned to the world around her, Sui continues to influence trends and enchant with her designs.

PERFORMANCE THINKING For the career of your choice, how would attentive listening and note taking contribute to your success?

CHECK IT OUT Anna Sui's "genius files" have included people from a variety of creative professions, including photographers, illustrators, filmmakers, theater and movie actors, musicians, and, of course, fashion designers and trendsetters. She includes many of these people on her Web site at **www.annasui.com** (click on the biography and then "Anna's Favorite Things"). Consider starting your own "genius file" of people and words that inspire you. Who would you include?

Starting Today

At least one strategy I learned in this chapter that I plan to try right away is

_____

_____

_____

What changes must I make in order for this strategy to be most effective?

_____

_____

Review Questions

Based on what you have learned in this chapter, write your answers to the following questions:

1. What is attentive listening?

_____

_____

2. Why are listening and note-taking skills critical to job success?

_____

_____

3. Name two types of note-taking systems and describe how to use them.

_____

_____

4. Why is "Go to every class" an important note-taking strategy?

_____

_____

5. What should you do with your notes after attending class?

_____

_____

To test your understanding of the chapter's concepts, complete the chapter quiz at **www.mhhe.com/ferrett8e.**

Developing Attentive Listening Skills

In the Classroom

Roxanne Jackson is a fashion design student who works part-time at a retail clothing store. She has two roommates, who are also students. Roxanne is outgoing, enjoys being around people, and loves to talk and tell stories. However, Roxanne is a poor listener. In class, she is often too busy talking with the person next to her to pay attention to the class assignments. When she joins a study group, she starts off as popular but turns in assignments that are late and incorrect. Roxanne's roommates have finally confronted her. There is tension between them, because the roommates feel that Roxanne is not pulling her weight on household chores. Another major problem is that Roxanne does not take accurate phone messages. She never seems to write down the correct information.

1. What strategies in this chapter can help Roxanne be a more effective listener?

   _____

   _____

2. What should she do to improve her relationship with others and get better at taking down information?

   _____

   _____

In the Workplace

Roxanne is now a buyer for a large department store. She enjoys working with people. She is a talented, responsible employee when she is actively aware and tuned in to others. People respond to her favorably and enjoy being around her. However, she is often too busy or preoccupied to listen attentively or take correct notes. She often forgets directions, misunderstands conversations, and interrupts others in her haste and enthusiasm.

3. What would you suggest to help Roxanne become a better listener?

   _____

   _____

4. What strategies in this chapter would help her become more aware, more sensitive to others, and able to record information more effectively?

   _____

   _____

Applying the ABC Method of Self-Management

In the Journal Entry on page 151, you were asked to describe a time when you had difficulty making sense out of a lecture and staying alert. Are there certain classes in which it is more challenging for you to be an attentive listener?

_____

_____

_____

Now apply the ABC Method to the situation and visualize yourself a more attentive listener:

A = Actual event:

_____

_____

_____

B = Beliefs:

_____

_____

_____

C = Challenge:

_____

_____

_____

Practice deep breathing, with your eyes closed, for just 1 minute. Imagine that you are calm, centered, and alert. See yourself enjoying your lectures, staying alert, and taking good notes.

PRACTICE SELF-MANAGEMENT

For more examples of learning how to manage difficult situations, see the "Self-Management Workbook" section of the Online Learning Center Web site at **www.mhhe.com/ferrett8e.**

Listening Self-Assessment

This simple assessment tool will give you an idea of your attentive listening skills. Read each statement. Then, check Yes or No as to whether these statements relate to you.

	Yes	No
1. My intention is to be an attentive and effective listener.	——	——
2. I concentrate on meaning, not on every word.	——	——
3. I focus on the speaker and use eye contact.	——	——
4. I am aware of emotions and nonverbal behavior.	——	——
5. I withhold judgment until I hear the entire message.	——	——
6. I am open to new information and ideas.	——	——
7. I seek to understand the speaker's point of view.	——	——
8. I do not interrupt, argue, or plan my response; I listen.	——	——
9. I am mentally and physically alert and attentive.	——	——
10. I paraphrase to clarify my understanding.	——	——
11. When I'm in class, I sit in the front, so that I can hear and see better.	——	——
12. I mentally ask questions and summarize main ideas.	——	——
13. I increase the value of my listening by previewing the textbook before class.	——	——
14. I adapt to the instructor's speaking and teaching style.	——	——
Total Responses:	——	——

If you checked Yes to 10 or more questions, you are well on your way to becoming an attentive, effective listener. If you did not, you have some work to do to improve those skills.

Mind Map a Lecture

Create a mind map of one of your class lectures in the space provided below (see **Figure 5.2** on page 159 and **Figure 5.3** on page 160 for examples). Compare your mind maps with those drawn by other students in your class. Are there key points that you or other students missed? Did some include too much (or too little) detail?

Use the Cornell System of Note Taking

Take notes in one of your class lectures by using the Cornell System in the space provided below (see **Figure 5.1** on page 158 as a guide). Compare your notes with those from other students in your class. Are there key points that you or other students missed? Did some include too much (or too little) detail? Did you summarize your notes?

Cues: Notes:

Summary:

Listening and Note Taking in the Workplace

Write how you will demonstrate the listed listening and note-taking skills for future employers.

1. Finding meaning and interest in new information and projects

   _____

2. Showing interest and being prepared

   _____

3. Listening attentively

   _____

4. Observing and asking questions

   _____

5. Acquiring information

   _____

6. Thinking through issues

   _____

7. Organizing information and taking good notes

   _____

8. Staying alert and in the present

   _____

9. Being willing to test new strategies and learn new methods

   _____

10. Practicing attentive listening and note taking again and again

    _____

11. Teaching effective methods to others

    _____

6

Actively Read

LEARNING OUTCOMES

In this chapter, you will learn to

6.1 Describe active reading

6.2 Explain the Five-Part Reading System and SQ3R

6.3 Adopt active reading strategies

6.4 Build a better vocabulary

6.5 Manage language courses

6.6 Read technical material and manuals and complete forms

6.7 Address reading challenges

SELF-MANAGEMENT

I usually love to read, but lately I feel like I'm on information overload. Sometimes I read several pages and realize I haven't understood a word I've read. What can I do to read more effectively and actually remember what I've read?

Do you ever close a book and feel frustrated because you don't remember what you've just read? In this chapter, you will learn how to become an active reader and maximize your reading. You will visualize yourself reading quickly, comprehending, and recalling information. You will see yourself discovering new information, building on facts and concepts, developing memory skills, and feeling the joy of reading.

JOURNAL ENTRY Were you read to as a child? If so, use **Worksheet 6.1** on page 208 to describe a time when you enjoyed being read to by someone, such as a teacher, parent, or librarian. Why was the experience pleasurable? What types of books did you enjoy most? Did you have a favorite book or story? If you don't like to read, why? Are there specific obstacles that keep you from devoting more time to reading?

Some students complain about having a mountain of reading to finish each week. The challenge is not just the volume of reading required in college; you are also expected to comprehend, interpret, and evaluate what you read. **Comprehension** is the ability to understand the main ideas and details as they are written. **Interpreting** what you read means developing ideas of your own and being able to summarize the material in your own words. Interpretation requires several skills, such as noting the difference between fact and opinion, recognizing cause and effect, and drawing inferences and conclusions.

Because the amount of reading required in school can be enormous and demanding, it is easy to get discouraged and put it off until it piles up. However, as with any skill, it's important to keep a positive attitude that focuses on the benefits of improving your abilities. In this chapter, you will learn to create an effective reading system that helps you keep up with your reading assignments and increase your comprehension.

The Importance of Active Reading

When you were a child at home, you may have been told, "This is quiet time; go read a book," or "Curl up with a book and just relax." In school, your instructor may have said, "Read Chapters 1 through 5 for tomorrow's test," or "You didn't do well on the test because you didn't read the directions carefully." On the job, someone may have said to you, "I need your reactions to this report. Have them ready to discuss by this afternoon."

Whether you are reading for enjoyment, for a test, or for a project at work, to be an effective reader you must become actively involved with what you are reading. If you approach reading with a lack of interest or importance, you read only what's required and are less able to retain what you have read. **Retention** is the process by which you store information. If you think something is important, you will retain it.

Reading involves many important tasks, such as the following:

- Previewing
- Taking notes
- Outlining main points
- Digging out ideas
- Jotting down key words
- Finding definitions
- Asking and answering questions
- Underlining important points
- Looking for patterns and themes
- Summarizing in your own words
- Reviewing for recall

These tasks can greatly improve your comprehension and ability to interpret material. This is active reading because you, the reader, are purposeful, attentive, and physically active.

Reading Systems

Many factors affect your reading comprehension. Your skill level, vocabulary, ability to concentrate, and state of mind, as well as distractions, all affect what you comprehend and recall. There are a number of proven reading systems and, over the years, you may have developed a reading system that works best for you. Two helpful reading systems are the Five-Part Reading System and SQ3R.

The Five-Part Reading System

The Five-Part Reading System (see **Figure 6.1**) is similar to the Adult Learning Cycle, which is explored throughout this text (see **Peak Progress 6.1** on page 182). To remember the five parts, think of them as the five **P**s. As with many reading systems or strategies (and, in fact, many tasks in college), your first step is to prepare. Then you preview, predict questions, process information, and paraphrase and review.

1. **Prepare.** Prepare yourself mentally for reading by creating a positive, interested attitude. Look for ways to make the subject matter meaningful. Instead of telling yourself that the book is too hard or boring, say, "This book looks interesting because . . . ," or "The information in this book will be helpful because . . ." Focus on what you are about to read. Clarify your purpose and how you will use the information. Think about what you already know about the subject. Prepare yourself physically by being rested, and read during high-energy times (refer to your Time Log in Personal Evaluation Notebook 3.1).

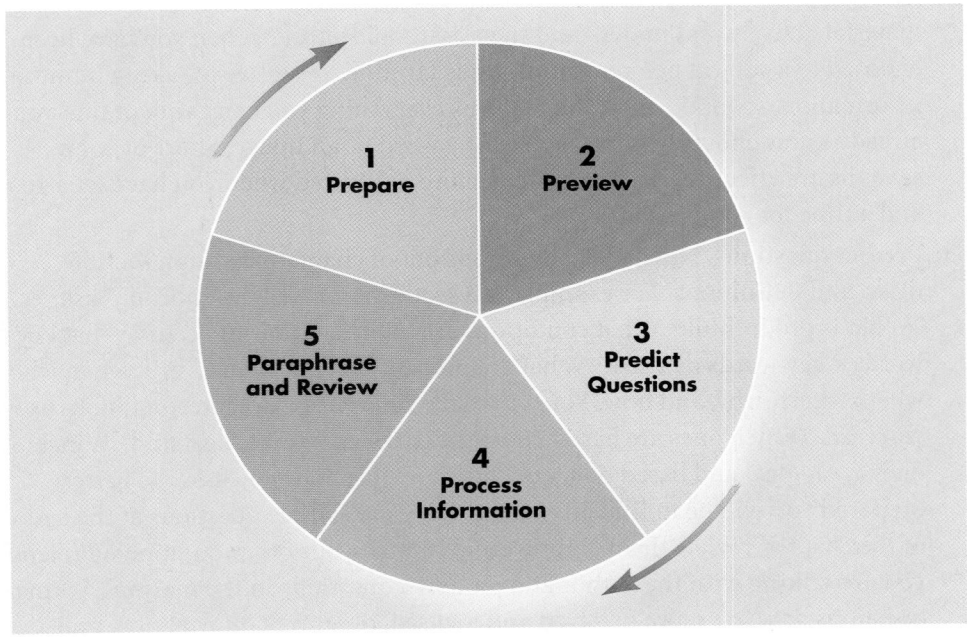

Figure **6.1**

The Five-Part Reading System

This system can be useful for increasing your reading comprehension and recall. *In what ways is this system similar to your own reading system?*

    CHAPTER 6   Actively Read

Peak Progress

Applying the Adult Learning Cycle to Becoming a Better Reader

Becoming an active reader and learning to like reading take time, effort, and practice.

1. **RELATE. Why do I want to learn this?** Being an effective reader can help me get ahead in school, work, and life. Through reading, I continually learn and explore new ideas. I can also escape through fiction, relieving the stress of the day. What do I want to improve overall about my reading?

2. **OBSERVE. How does this work?** I can learn a lot about active reading by watching, listening, and trying new things. I'll observe people who are avid readers and who remember information. I will try new techniques and strategies for active reading and mark my improvement.

3. **REFLECT. What does this mean?** Which techniques work and which ones don't work for me? Can I find creative ways to make reading more enjoyable and effective?

4. **DO. What can I do with this?** I will make a commitment to be a more active reader. I'll find practical applications for practicing my new reading skills. Each day, I'll work on one area. For example, I'll choose one class in which I'm having trouble reading and experiment with new strategies.

5. **TEACH. Whom can I share this with?** I'll talk with others and share my tips and experiences. I'll demonstrate and describe the methods I've learned. I'll read more for pleasure and read to others when possible.

Remember, the more you go through the cycle, the more interest and meaning reading will have for you.

Eliminate distractions by choosing a study area that encourages concentration. Experiment and make reading physical whenever possible. For example, take notes while reading, read while standing up, and read aloud.

2. **Preview.** A quick survey of the chapter you are about to read will give you a general overview. Pay attention to the title, chapter headings, illustrations, and key terms. Look for main ideas connecting concepts, terms, and formulas. Gaining a general understanding of the assignment prepares you to read the material actively and understand the classroom lecture. When you have been exposed to a subject before, your brain is far more receptive to taking in more information, so jot down in the margins everything you can think of that you already know about the topic, even just a word or an image. Short preview sessions are effective, and you will be more motivated when you have set a goal and a time for completion.

3. **Predict questions.** Next, make questions out of chapter headings, section titles, and definitions. For example, if a section is titled "Groupthink," ask, "What is groupthink? What conditions are required for it to occur? What key word or key words define it? What are possible test questions?" Ask what, who, when, where, why, and how. You will make **inferences** and interpretations as you read. Which ones are based on your experiences or background? Which ones are logical and based on fact? The more questions you ask, the better prepared you will be to find answers. If there are sample questions at the end of the chapter, review them and tie them in with your other questions. Pretend you are talking with the author and jot down questions in the margin. Asking questions gets you more involved and focused, organizes information, and

helps you prepare for tests. Create possible test questions on note cards and review them as you walk to classes, eat, or wait in lines. Exchange questions with your study team or partner.

4. **Process information.** Outline, underline, and highlight key words, main ideas, definitions, facts, and important concepts. Look for main ideas, supporting points, connections, and answers to the questions you have raised. Develop an outline, either a traditional outline or an informal one (such as a mind map), to help you organize the information. Integrate what you are reading into classroom lectures, notes, field trips, study group discussions, models, and graphs.

5. **Paraphrase and review.** Summarize in your own words and review. Recite your summary out loud right after class and again within 24 hours of previewing the chapter. Share it in your study group. Review several times until you understand the material and can explain it to someone else. This helps you integrate learning styles and remember the main points at the end of each major section. Review in your study group and take turns listening to each other's summary. Remember, the best way to learn is to teach. Carry your note cards, so that you can review questions and answers and can summarize often.

● **Preview Your Reading**
You get the big picture by quickly scanning through a book, and you enhance your learning. *Besides identifying key concepts, what else should you look for when previewing?*

The SQ3R Reading System

The SQ3R Reading System is a five-step method that has helped many students improve their reading comprehension since it was developed by Professor Francis Robinson in 1941. It breaks reading down into manageable segments, so that you understand the material before proceeding to the next step.

1. **S = Survey.** Survey the material before reading it. Quickly peruse the contents, scan the main heads, look at illustrations and captions, and become familiar with the special features in each chapter. Surveying, or previewing, helps you see how the chapter is organized and supports the main concept. You get an overview of where the material is going.

2. **Q = Question.** Find the main points and begin to formulate questions. Developing questions helps you determine if you really understand the material. For example, here are some questions you can ask yourself as you read:

   - What is the main idea of this chapter?
   - What is the main idea of this section?
   - What are examples that support this main idea?
   - Who are the main people or what key events are discussed in this chapter?

Take 3 minutes tonight to preview the next assigned chapter:

- What is the main topic? What are the subtopics?
- What do you already know about this topic? Have you studied it in a previous class?
- What do the supporting illustrations show? Are they clearly labeled?

What else can you do in 3 minutes?

- Preview the chapter's learning outcomes and formulate potential quiz questions.
- Check the syllabus for future reading assignments and schedule them in your planner.
- Time yourself reading the next chapter to see how many pages you read and if you can recall what the main points are.

- Why are they important?
- What are possible test questions?
- What points don't I understand?

3. **R = Read.** Actively read the material and search for answers to your questions. As you read, you will be asking more questions. Even when you read a novel, you will ask such questions as "What is the main theme of this novel? Who is this supporting character? Why did he turn up at this time in the novel? How does this character relate to the main characters? What are his motives?"

4. **R = Recite.** Recite the main ideas and key points in your words. After each section, stop and paraphrase what you have just read. Your summary should address the questions you developed for this section. Reciting promotes concentration, creates understanding, and helps raise more questions.

5. **R = Review.** Review the material carefully. Go back over your questions and make certain you have answered all of them. Review the chapter summary and then go back over each section. Jot down additional questions. Review and clarify questions with your study group or instructor.

The exercise in **Personal Evaluation Notebook 6.1** gives you an opportunity to try the SQ3R Reading System.

Reading Strategies

The Five-Part and SQ3R Reading Systems include strategies such as previewing the material and reciting or paraphrasing main concepts in your own words. You can also try the following overall reading strategies:

1. **Determine your purpose.** Clarify your purpose—how you will use the information. Reading assignments vary in terms of difficulty and purpose. Some are technical and others require imagination. (See **Peak Progress 6.2** on page 187 for tips on reading in different disciplines.) Ask yourself, "Why am I reading this?" Whether you are reading for pleasure, previewing information, looking for background information, understanding ideas, finding facts, memorizing formulas and data, or analyzing a complex subject, you will want to know your purpose.

2. **Set reading goals.** You may be assigned many chapters to read each week, preferably before walking into a lecture. You do not want to wait until the day before exams to open your textbook. Pace your reading, not only to make sure you complete it but also to give yourself time to ask questions, be sure you understand the material, and review it—again and again if necessary. Just as you map out the semester's exams, plan your reading assignments in your

(continued on page 188)

Personal Evaluation Notebook

Using the SQ3R Reading System

Follow the SQ3R Reading System on page 183 as you read the following passages. Then complete the questions that follow.

ORGANIZED INTERESTS: WHO ARE THEY?

Accomplishing broad yet shared goals is always easier when a number of people pitch in to help. Both joining with neighbors to clean up a community after a storm and banding together with friends to convince your college cafeteria to purchase "free trade" coffee are examples of cooperative action. Group activity is a hallmark of America's volunteer ethic. The same is true in politics. Organized groups are nearly always more effective in attaining common goals than individuals acting alone. The term **interest group** refers to those formally organized associations that seek to influence public policy. In America, it applies to a dizzying array of diverse organizations reflecting the broad spectrum of interests that make up our **pluralistic society**. They include corporations, labor unions, civil rights groups, professional and trade associations, and probably some of the groups with which you are associated as well.

Neighbors or Adversaries?

Theorists from Alexis de Tocqueville to Robert Putman have praised voluntary associations as training grounds for citizen involvement. De Tocqueville saw collective action as evidence of democracy at work. Putnam extols organized interests for creating social capital, the glue that binds the citizenry so they can achieve collective goals. Not all political theorists, however, share these views. In *The Federalist* No. 10, James Madison warned against factions—groups of individuals, "whether amounting to a majority or minority of the whole, who are united by some common impulse of passion, or of interest, adverse to the rights of other citizens, or to the permanent and aggregate interests of the community." Although opposed to factions, Madison felt that they could not be eliminated since they expressed the innately human drive for self-interest. Instead, he argued, the government must dilute their influence by filtering their views through elected officials and submerging their interests in a sea of competing interests. Only by countering the ambition of such groups with the ambition of others, he believed, could government fashion the compromise necessary to accommodate interests common to all.

Distinctive Features

Like the political movements of the past that advanced causes such as abolition or civil rights, interest groups seek to use the power of government to protect their concerns. However, although political movements promote wide-ranging social change, interest groups are more narrowly focused on achieving success with regard to specific policies. Where the Women's Movement of the 1960s sought to change Americans' views about the role of women at home and in the workplace, interest groups like the National Organization for Women (NOW) focus on solving specific problems faced by women in a world that has already grown more accepting of the diverse roles women play.

(continued)

Personal Evaluation Notebook

Using the SQ3R Reading System *(continued)*

Interest group causes may be purely economic, as in the case of a business seeking tax breaks or a union seeking negotiating clout; they may be ideological, as in the case of those favoring or opposing abortion rights. Some, known as **public interest groups,** advocate policies they believe promote the good of all Americans, not merely the economic or ideological interests of a few. Environmental groups such as the Sierra Club fall into this category. Some interest groups, such as trade associations and labor unions, have mass memberships; others represent institutions and have no individual membership at all. One example of the latter is the American Council on Education (ACE), a collective institution of higher education that promotes policies that benefit colleges and universities.

Source: Joseph Losco and Ralph Baker: *AM GOV 2009,* McGraw-Hill, 2009.

S—Survey

1. What is the title of the selection?

   _____

2. What is the reading selection about?

   _____

3. What are the major topics?

   _____

4. List any boldface terms.

   _____

Q—Question

5. Write a question for the first heading.

   _____

6. Write a question for the second heading.

   _____

3 Rs

R—Read

Read the selection section by section.

R—Recite

Briefly summarize to yourself what you read. Then share your summary with a study team member.

(continued)

Personal Evaluation Notebook

Using the SQ3R Reading System (*concluded*)

R—Review

7. Can you recall the questions you had for each head?   Yes _____   No _____

8. Can you answer those questions?   Yes _____   No _____

Write your answers for each section head question on the following lines.

9. Head 1

_____

10. Head 2

_____

Peak Progress

6.2

Reading for Different Courses

Sometimes even successful students cringe at the thought of reading in disciplines they find difficult or uninteresting. If you find your textbook too difficult, you might ask your instructor for supplemental reading or check out other books or sources from the library to get a different view and approach. Also try the following tips for different reading assignments.

Literature: Make a list of key figures and characters. Think about their personalities and motives. See if you can predict what they will do next. Allow your imagination to expand through your senses; taste, smell, hear, and see each scene in your mind. What is the story's main point? What are supporting points? What is the author's intent?

History: Use an outline to organize material. You may want to create a time line and place dates and events as you read. Notice how events are related. Connect main people to key events. Relate past events to current events.

Mathematics and science: When reading a math book, work out each problem on paper and take notes in the margin. Spend additional time reviewing graphs, tables, notations, formulas, and the visuals used to illustrate points and complex ideas. These are not just fillers; they are important tools you use to review and understand the concepts behind them. Ask questions when you review each visual, and write down formulas and concepts on note cards. Come up with concrete examples when you read about abstract and difficult concepts. (We will further explore critical thinking and problem solving in math and science in Chapter 10.)

Psychology and sociology: Jot down major theories and summarize them in your own words. You will be asked how these theories relate to topics in other chapters. Use the margins to analyze research conclusions. Pay attention to how the research was conducted, such as sample size and the sponsors of the research. Look for biases and arguments. Was scientific evidence presented? Was the research study duplicated? Key terms and definitions are also important for building on additional information.

Anthropology: You may want to use a mind map to compare various cultures. For example, under the culture, you may look at religion, customs, food, traditions, and so on. Ask yourself if the ideas apply to all people in all cultures or in all situations. Is the author's position based on observation, research, or assumptions? Is there a different way to look at these observations? What predictions follow these arguments?

daily planner or calendar (see Chapter 3 for many handy forms). Be realistic as to how long it takes you to read a certain number of pages, especially for difficult courses. Check off reading assignments as you complete them, and rearrange priorities if need be. Schedule blocks of time to review reading assignments and prepare for exams.

3. **Concentrate.** Whether you are playing a sport, performing a dance, giving a speech, acting in a play, talking with a friend, or focusing on a difficult book, being in the present is the key to concentration. Keep your reading goals in mind and concentrate on understanding main points as you prepare to read. Stay focused and alert by reading quickly and making it an active experience. If your mind wanders, become aware of your posture, thoughts, and surroundings and then gently bring your thoughts back to the task at hand.

4. **Create an outline.** Use a traditional or an informal outline to organize the main points. (See Chapter 5 for examples of outlines.) The outline can add meaning and structure to material, and it simplifies and organizes complex information. The physical process of writing and organizing material creates a foundation for committing it to memory. Use section titles and paragraph headlines to provide a guide. Continue to write questions in the margin. (See **Worksheet 6.5** on page 212 for a blank format to use for a formal outline.)

5. **Identify key words and concepts.** Underline and highlight key words, definitions, facts, and important concepts. Write them in the margins and on note cards. Draw illustrations (or embellish those in the book) to help clarify the text. Use graphics and symbols to indicate difficult material, connections, and questions you need go over again. (Refer to Figure 5.5 on page 164 for common symbols used in note taking and reading.) A highlighter may be useful for calling out main points and marking sections that are important to review later. (See **Peak Progress 6.3** on using a highlighter.)

6. **Make connections.** Link new information with what you already know. Look for main ideas, supporting points, connections, and answers to the questions you have raised. Integrate what you are reading into classroom lectures, notes, field trips, study group discussions, models, and graphs. Asking yourself these questions may help you make associations and jog your memory:

   - What conclusions can I make as I read the material?
   - How can I apply this new material to other material, concepts, and examples?
   - What information does and does not match?
   - What do I know about the topic that may influence how I approach the reading?

7. **Talk with the author.** Pretend you are talking with the author and jot down points with which you agree or disagree. This exercises your critical thinking skills and helps you connect new information to what you already know. If there are points you disagree with, consider bringing them up in class (if it's appropriate) and see if other students feel the same.

8. **Compare notes.** Compare your textbook notes with your lecture notes. Compare your notes with those of your study team members and clarify questions and answers. Ask your instructor for clarifications and how much

Peak Progress

To Highlight or Not to Highlight?

This is the age-old question. Fellow students may tell you not to highlight your text, as it's easier to sell back a "clean" text. Others recommend buying a used book that's already highlighted—the work is done for you.

However, these debates miss the point of highlighting. Whether you use a colored highlighter or underline words with a pen or pencil, highlighting is a very personal study strategy that can improve your ability to determine the important points within a reading. The simple act of highlighting makes you reread the information, helping you improve your comprehension, which benefits not just visual and tactile learners but also those with other learning styles as well. Highlighting helps you find key concepts more easily when reviewing and studying for exams. Research has also shown that students with learning disabilities or ADHD demonstrate a marked increase in their learning ability when they use a highlighter while reading.

Highlight?

Yes	No
• Your textbook. It's yours—use it!	• A library book; instead, make notes on stickies on the pages as well as record main points and page numbers in your notes
• Key points, names, important dates, new terms	• Highlighting too fast before you truly know the main point(s)
• Use different colors for main ideas vs. definitions vs. examples—but don't make the process too tedious or too confusing to follow	• Entire sections or paragraphs
• Use circles, arrows, and notes in the margins to make connections, add questions, etc.	• Over 10% of a page
• Read the chapter summary, which should point out the key points in case you missed them	• Relying on someone else's highlighting, especially in a used book

weight the textbook has on exams. Some instructors highlight important information in class and want students to read the text for a broad overview.

9. **Take frequent breaks.** Schedule short stretching breaks about every 40 minutes. A person's brain retains information best in short study segments. Don't struggle with unclear material now. You may need several readings to comprehend and interpret the material. Go back to the difficult areas later when you are refreshed and the creative process is not blocked.

10. **Integrate learning styles.** Read in alignment with your learning style, and integrate styles. For example, if you are a visual learner, take special note of pictures, charts, and diagrams. Develop mental pictures in your mind and actively use your imagination. Compare what you are reading with course lectures, overhead material, and notes on the board. If you are primarily an auditory learner, read out loud or into a digital recorder and then listen to it.

If you are a kinesthetic learner, read with a highlighter in hand to mark important passages and key words. Work out problems on paper and draw illustrations. Write your vocabulary, formulas, and key words on note cards. Read while standing up or recite out loud. The physical act of mouthing words and hearing your voice enhances learning. Integrate different learning styles by using all your senses. Visualize what something looks like, hear yourself repeating words, draw, and read out loud. Review your notes and summaries with your study team. This helps you integrate learning styles and increases your comprehension, critical thinking, and recall.

11. **Use the entire text.** As discussed in Chapter 4, a peak performer seeks out and uses available resources. Many textbooks include a number of resources that sometimes get overlooked, such as a glossary, chapter objectives, and study questions. Make sure you read (or at least initially scan) all the elements in your textbook, as they are included to help you preview, understand, review, and apply the material. (See **Peak Progress 6.4**.) After all, you've paid for the text, so use it! (Also see **Peak Progress 6.5** for tips on reading digital material.)

For practice on taking notes, take a look at **Figure 6.2** on page 192 and compare it with your notes for this page.

Reviewing Strategies

Reading isn't over with the turn of the last page. Take the time to review what you have read to make sure you understand and retain the information.

1. **Summarize in writing.** After you finish reading, close your book and write a summary in your own words. In just 4 or 5 minutes, write down everything you can recall about the chapter and the main topics. Writing is an active process that increases comprehension and recall. Write quickly and test yourself by asking questions such as these:
   - What is the major theme?
   - What are the main points?
   - What are the connections to other concepts?

2. **Summarize out loud.** Summarizing out loud can increase learning, especially if you are an auditory or a kinesthetic learner. Some students use an empty classroom and pretend they are lecturing. If need be, recite quietly to yourself, taking care not to disturb anyone, especially in the library or other populated areas. Review several times until you understand the material and can explain it to someone else. Review in your study teams and take turns listening to each other's summary. Remember that the best way to learn is to teach. As you recite and listen to each other, you can ask questions and clarify terms and concepts.

3. **Review and reflect.** You have previewed, developed questions, outlined main points, read actively, highlighted and underlined, written key words, and summarized in writing and aloud. Now it is important to review for understanding main ideas and to commit the information to long-term

Peak Progress

Using Your Textbook

Textbooks are developed with many features to help you preview, understand, review, and apply the material. As soon as you purchase your text, take a few minutes to flip through it to see how it is put together. Although textbooks vary many include the following elements:

Preface. At the beginning of the text, you may find a preface, and some books include two prefaces: one for the instructor who is interested in using the text in the course and the other specifically for the student. Read through the student preface, as it will provide information to help you get off on the right foot. For example, at the beginning of this text, you will find a "Getting Started" section that explores many issues you may be facing the first few weeks of school (or even before the first day of school).

It's also a good idea to review the material designed for the instructor, which may give you insights into the overall approach of the text, as well as new developments or research in the field. It may also describe challenges that your instructor faces when teaching the course, which can be helpful for you and your fellow students to know.

Preview features. Many texts include features that let you know what you will learn in the chapter, such as learning outcomes, chapter outlines, and introductory statements or quotes. *What types of preview features can you find in this text?*

Applications. More effective texts not only provide the essential information but also give you opportunities to apply it. These applications can take the form of case studies, exercises, assessments, journal activities, Web sites, and critical thinking and discussion questions. *What are some features in this text that help you apply what you are learning?*

Review material. You may find features that reinforce and help you understand and review the material, such as section or chapter summaries; glossaries; key tips, key points, or key words; bulleted lists of key information; comprehensive tables; and review questions. *What features in this text are useful for reviewing the material?*

Resources beyond the text. Many texts have accompanying Web sites, workbooks, and CD-ROMs that reinforce and apply what you are learning in the text and course. Often, connections to these resources appear in the text, reminding you to use the resource for specific information. *What resources are available with this text?*

Peak Progress

Digital Reading Material

As a student today, you have many exciting new options available through the Internet that weren't offered even just a few years ago. Books, journals, newspapers, and textbooks are often offered in an online format. Communication media, such as blogs and Wikipedia, have changed how we interact.

Digital readers are quickly becoming a popular alternative to print books. Amazon's Kindle, released in 2007, sold out in 5½ hours upon release. The device allows you to store and read digital media for use anywhere and features "electronic paper." Apple's iPad offers numerous applications, including the Internet, iTunes, and iBooks, in a portable format. Textbooks are now offered for use with these digital readers, as are subscriptions to newspapers and magazines.

As online reading becomes more popular, you may need to tweak your reading strategies. Following are a few things to consider:

- **Pace your reading.** Research indicates the average person reads from a computer screen about 10 percent slower than a printed text. If that's true for you, plan your reading schedule accordingly.
- **Adjust the page.** If you can, change the type size and font to one that is easier to read.
- **Use the built-in functions.** Learn how to use the highlighter and other note-taking features.
- **Print.** Make back-up copies of your digital notes and print key sections, in case you run into technical issues later. Annotate the hard copies to reinforce your understanding of the material.
- **Avoid ads.** Many articles are surrounded by advertisements and pop-up ads that can distract you. Turn on a pop-up blocker.
- **Protect against theft.** An iPad or Kindle is a hot commodity. Store your digital devices in a secure place.

Figure 6.2
Sample Notes

This illustration shows study notes you might take when reading page 190. Compare it with the notes you took on that page. *What are the similarities? What did you do differently? Do you have unique note-taking strategies that work for you?*

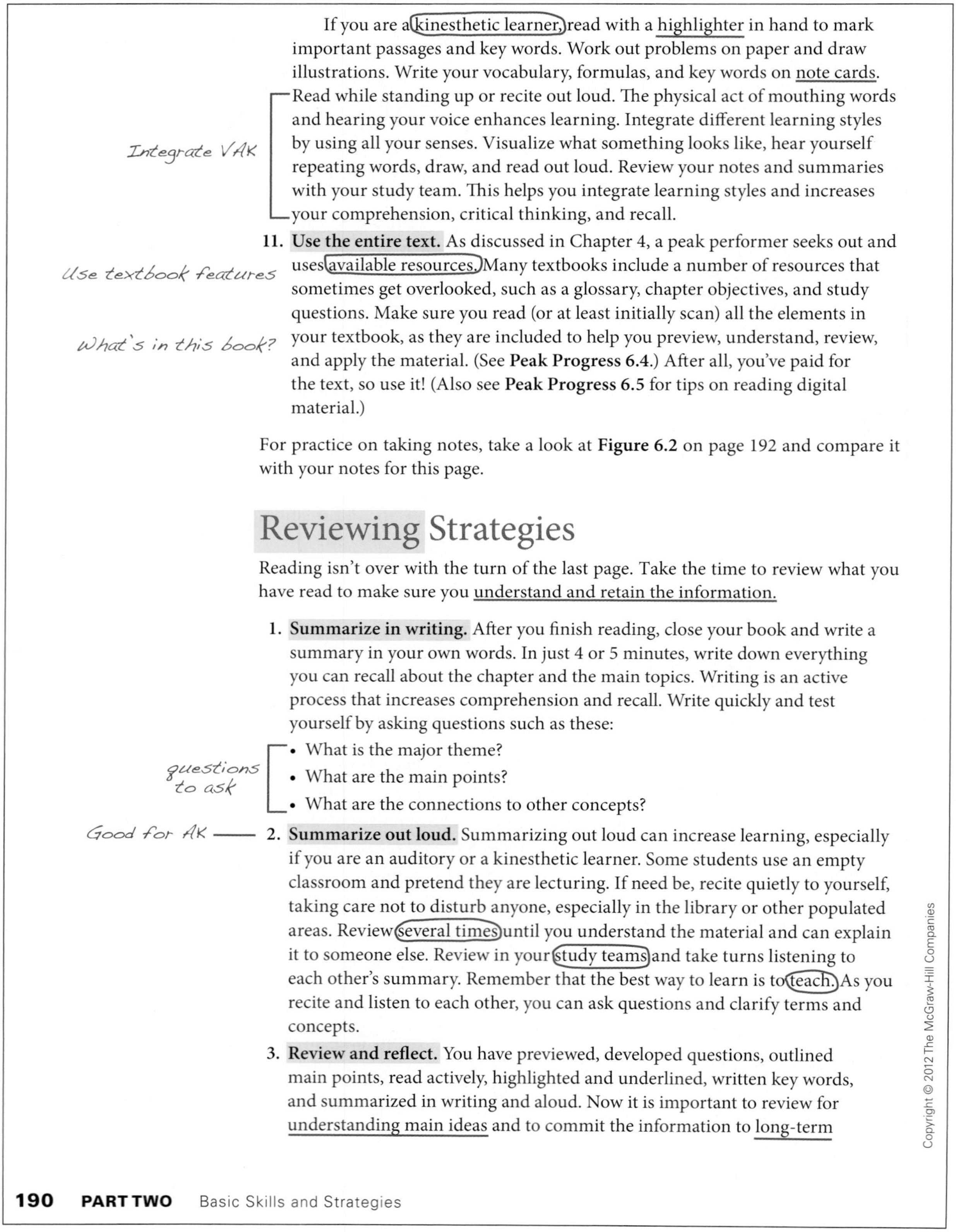

Integrate VAK

If you are a kinesthetic learner, read with a highlighter in hand to mark important passages and key words. Work out problems on paper and draw illustrations. Write your vocabulary, formulas, and key words on note cards. Read while standing up or recite out loud. The physical act of mouthing words and hearing your voice enhances learning. Integrate different learning styles by using all your senses. Visualize what something looks like, hear yourself repeating words, draw, and read out loud. Review your notes and summaries with your study team. This helps you integrate learning styles and increases your comprehension, critical thinking, and recall.

Use textbook features

What's in this book?

11. **Use the entire text.** As discussed in Chapter 4, a peak performer seeks out and uses available resources. Many textbooks include a number of resources that sometimes get overlooked, such as a glossary, chapter objectives, and study questions. Make sure you read (or at least initially scan) all the elements in your textbook, as they are included to help you preview, understand, review, and apply the material. (See **Peak Progress 6.4**.) After all, you've paid for the text, so use it! (Also see **Peak Progress 6.5** for tips on reading digital material.)

For practice on taking notes, take a look at **Figure 6.2** on page 192 and compare it with your notes for this page.

Reviewing Strategies

Reading isn't over with the turn of the last page. Take the time to review what you have read to make sure you understand and retain the information.

1. **Summarize in writing.** After you finish reading, close your book and write a summary in your own words. In just 4 or 5 minutes, write down everything you can recall about the chapter and the main topics. Writing is an active process that increases comprehension and recall. Write quickly and test yourself by asking questions such as these:

questions to ask
   - What is the major theme?
   - What are the main points?
   - What are the connections to other concepts?

Good for AK

2. **Summarize out loud.** Summarizing out loud can increase learning, especially if you are an auditory or a kinesthetic learner. Some students use an empty classroom and pretend they are lecturing. If need be, recite quietly to yourself, taking care not to disturb anyone, especially in the library or other populated areas. Review several times until you understand the material and can explain it to someone else. Review in your study teams and take turns listening to each other's summary. Remember that the best way to learn is to teach. As you recite and listen to each other, you can ask questions and clarify terms and concepts.

3. **Review and reflect.** You have previewed, developed questions, outlined main points, read actively, highlighted and underlined, written key words, and summarized in writing and aloud. Now it is important to review for understanding main ideas and to commit the information to long-term

memory. You can increase your comprehension by reviewing the material within 24 hours of your first reading session. Reflect by bringing your own experience and knowledge to what you have learned with readings lectures, field trips, and work with your study team. You should review your outline, note cards, key words, and main points. Review headings, main topics, key ideas, first and last sentences in paragraphs, and summaries. Make sure you have answered the questions you created as you read the material. Carry your note cards with you and review them when you have a few minutes before class. Your note cards are the most effective tool for reviewing information.

4. **Read and review often.** Reviewing often and in short sessions kicks the material into long-term memory. Review weekly and conduct a thorough review a week or so before a test. Keep a list of questions to ask your instructor and a list of possible test questions. The key is to stay on top of reading, so that it doesn't pile up, which should allow you enough time to review effectively.

Evan always waits until the last minute to tackle his reading assignments. At the eleventh hourly—literally—he finally plops into an easy chair near midnight and begins to read. Not a morning person, Evan is sure he can focus and whip through it, until 30 minutes later, when his eyes are half closed and he realizes he doesn't remember a word.

- If Evan truly does his best work at night, what strategies should he use while reading to make sure he's alert, focused, learning, and retaining the material?
- Do you think Evan's last-minute strategy is an effective method of reading for class? What important steps from the Five-Part Reading System might he end up skipping for time's sake?
- Does Evan really understand the purpose of reading assignments? If not, can you explain it to him?

THINK FAST

Build Your Vocabulary

You will need a fundamental vocabulary to master any subject. To succeed in a career, you must know and understand the meaning of words you encounter in conversations, reports, meetings, and professional reading. People often judge the intelligence of another person by the ability to communicate through words, and an effective speaker who has a command of language can influence others. Try the following methods for building your vocabulary:

1. **Observe your words and habits.** You may be unaware that you fill your conversations with annoying words, such as *you know, OK, like,* and *yeah.*

2. **Be creative and articulate.** Use precise, interesting, and expressive words.

3. **Associate with articulate people.** Surround yourself with people who have effective and extensive vocabularies.

4. **Look up words you don't know.** Keep a dictionary at your desk or study area. (See **Peak Progress 6.6** on page 194, which shows you how to navigate around a dictionary.)

5. **Write down new words.** Listen for new words and observe how they are used and how often you hear them and see them in print. Record them in your journal or on note cards.

6. **Practice mentally.** Say new words again and again in your mind as you read, and think of appropriate settings where you could use the words.

> **❝** If you wish to know the mind of a man, listen to his words. **❞**
> **CHINESE PROVERB**

> **❝** I was reading the dictionary. I thought it was a poem about everything. **❞**
> **STEVEN WRIGHT**
> *Comedian*

Peak Progress

Look It Up! Using the Dictionary

Here is a quick guide for using a dictionary.

Guide words: Boldface words at the top of the page indicate the first and last entries on the page.

Pronunciation: This key shows how to pronounce the word.

Part of speech: The dictionary uses nine abbreviations for the parts of speech:

n.—**noun**

adj.—**adjective**

v.i.—**intransitive verb**

adv.—adverb

conj.—conjunction

prep.—preposition

v.t.—transitive verb

pron.—pronoun

interj.—interjection

Etymology: This is the origin of the word, which is especially helpful if the word has a Latin or Greek root from which many other words are derived. Knowing the word's history can help you remember the word or look for similar words.

Syllabication: This shows how the word is divided into syllables.

Capital letters: The dictionary indicates if a word should be capitalized.

Definition: Dictionaries list definitions chronologically (oldest meaning first).

Restrictive labels: Three types of labels are used most often in a dictionary. Subject labels tell you that a word has a special meaning when used in certain fields (mus. for music, med. for medicine, etc.). Usage labels indicate how a word is used (slang, dial. for dialect, etc.). Geographic labels tell you the region of the country where the word is used most often.

Homographs: The dictionary indicates when a single spelling of a word has different meanings.

Variants: These are multiple correct spellings of a single word (example: *ax* or *axe*).

Illustrations: These are drawings or pictures used to help illustrate a word.

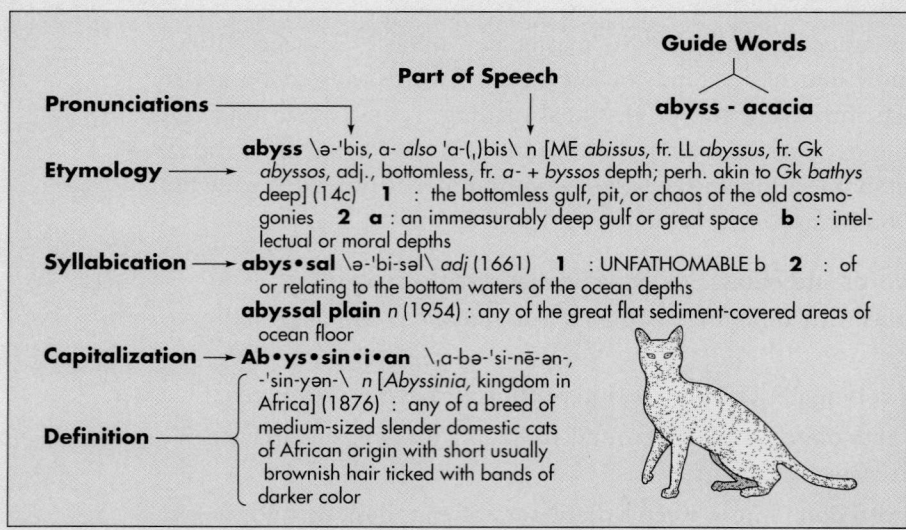

Source: By permission. From Merriam-Webster's Collegiate® Dictionary, 11th Edition © 2010 by Merriam-Webster, Incorporated (www.Merriam-Webster.com).

7. **Practice in conversation.** Use new words until you are comfortable using them.

8. **Look for contextual clues.** Try to figure out a word by the context in which it is used.

9. **Learn common word parts.** Knowing root words, prefixes, and suffixes makes it easier to understand the meaning of many new words. Also, in fields such as biology, knowing prefixes and suffixes helps you learn many new terms, such as *cardi* means "heart" (as in *cardiovascular*) and *calor* means "heat" (as in *calorie,* which is the energy content of food in the form of heat). Other examples follow:

Root	Meaning	Example
auto	self	autograph, autobiography
sub	under	submarine, submerge
circum	around	circumference, circumspect
manu	hand	manuscript, manual, manufacture

Also, learn to recognize syllables. Dividing words into syllables speeds up learning and improves pronunciation, spelling, and memory recall.

10. **Review great speeches.** Look at how Abraham Lincoln, Benjamin Franklin, Winston Churchill, and Thomas Jefferson chose precise words. Read letters written during the Revolutionary and Civil wars. You may find that the common person at that time was more articulate and expressive than many people today.

11. **Invest in a vocabulary book.** Many are available, so you may want to ask your instructor for guidance. Also, if you have decided on your future career, see if any books are written for that field.

12. **Read.** The best way to improve your vocabulary is simply to read more.

Manage Language Courses

Building vocabulary is important if you are learning a new language. Following are a number of reading and study tips.

1. **Do practice exercises.** As with math and science, doing practice exercises is critical in learning any language.

2. **Keep up with your reading.** You must build on previous lessons and skills. Therefore, it is important to keep up with your reading; preview chapters, so that you have a basic understanding of any new words; then complete your practice sessions several times.

3. **Carry note cards with you.** Drill yourself on the parts of speech and verb conjugation through all the tenses, which is a significant part of learning a new language. Keep related terms grouped together on cards (such as "In the Kitchen" or "In the Home").

4. **Recite out loud.** This is especially important in a language course, as knowing a word's pronunciation is as important as understanding its meaning. Record yourself and play it back.

5. **Form study teams.** Meet with a study team and speak only the language you are studying. Recite out loud to each other, explain verb conjugation, and use words in various contexts.

6. **Listen to CDs.** Play practice CDs while commuting, jogging, exercising, and so on.

7. **Model and tutor.** Meet with a student whose primary language is the one you are studying. Speak only his or her native language. Offer to teach the person your language in exchange for private tutoring. You can meet international students in classes for English as a second language, usually taught in local schools and communities.

8. **Have fun.** Do research on the country of the language you're studying. Invite your study group over for an authentic meal, complete with music and costumes.

The same principles and strategies you use for reading English can be applied to reading and learning a different language. Your efforts will be worthwhile, especially when you are able to speak, read, and understand another language as you communicate in the real world. Remember, as you become a better reader, you will enjoy the new language more and more. (**Figure 6.3** offers additional tips for English speakers of other languages.)

Specialized Reading

Comprehending Technical Material

Some of your courses may include technical information. Science, math, computer science, accounting, and statistics courses tend to present their data in specialized formats. You may need to interpret graphs, charts, diagrams, tables, and spreadsheets. You may read technical material, such as the directions for a chemistry experiment, a flowchart in a computer program, the steps for administering medication, or the

Figure 6.3
Tips for ESL Students

Students whose first language is not English can try additional strategies for reading success. Also, there is a wealth of resources on the Internet for ESL readers. Search "ESL reading activities" or a similar phrase in an Internet search engine. *What challenges do you face if your home language is different from a community's prominent language?*

- **Get the "gist" of it:** Don't worry about every word. Focus on main ideas, concepts, and key words.

- **Vary your reading materials:** Language "styles" vary based on the purpose, such as a textbook vs. a magazine vs. a blog. The more variety you are exposed to, the more fluent you will become.

- **Discuss in your first language:** Talk about the topic with family and friends, who will offer additional perspectives and questions to explore.

- **Make a list:** Jot down unfamiliar words that seem important and look them up.

statistical analysis of a financial statement. Such material can be complicated. Many readers get discouraged and skip over it—which is a big mistake.

Instead, try these reading strategies when you encounter graphics in your studies or on the job:

1. Identify the type of graphic you are looking at. Is it a table, chart, graph, or other type of illustration? (See **Figure 6.4**.)
2. Read each element:
   - Graphic title
   - Accompanying captions
   - Column titles
   - Labels or symbols and their interpretations
   - Data (percentages, totals, figures, etc.)
3. Identify the purpose of the graphic. Is it demonstrating similarities or differences, increases or decreases, comparisons or changes?
4. See a connection between the topic of the graphic and the chapter or section topic in which it appears.
5. Explain in your own words the information depicted on the graphic.
6. Share your interpretation of the graphic with your study group members. Do they feel your interpretation is clear and on target?

Reading Manuals

Technical writing professionals spend hundreds of hours writing instructions for everything from using your new toaster, to troubleshooting why engine lights are

Figure 6.4
Illustration Examples

The table (left) and graph (right) include the same information but present it differently. *What key elements would you look for to understand the material? Which presentation is easier to understand—the table or the graph? Which one might be easier to remember? What conclusions might you draw from this information regarding future statistics?*

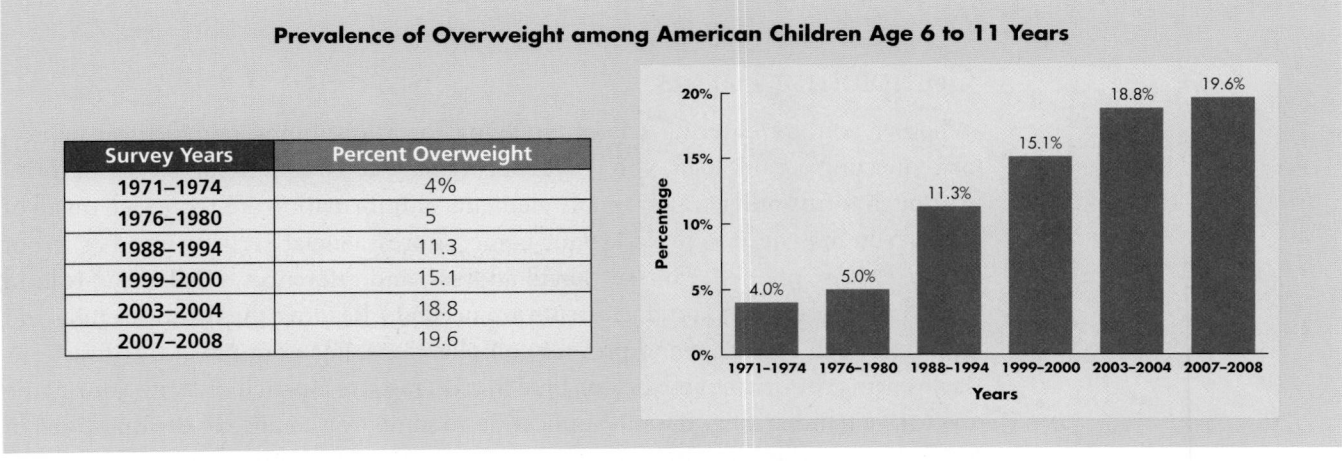

Prevalence of Overweight among American Children Age 6 to 11 Years

Survey Years	Percent Overweight
1971–1974	4%
1976–1980	5
1988–1994	11.3
1999–2000	15.1
2003–2004	18.8
2007–2008	19.6

Source: 2007–2008 National Health and Nutrition Examination Survey (NHANES).

coming on (i.e., your car's owner's manual). However, many people resist opening up the manual. We assume that, since CDs are "auto-run," shouldn't everything else be? For some, reading an instruction manual is like stopping and asking for directions: "I can figure it out on my own!" For others, deciphering a manual is like reading a foreign language. They have no idea where to begin.

Although some manuals are better than others in providing thorough, step-by-step instructions, you should invest the time to at least scan through the manual as you get started. First review the table of contents to see how the instructions are set up (such as a description or an illustration of product components, assembling or starting the product, caution or warning signs, and maintenance issues). After that, follow these time-saving tips:

1. Compare the description with what you received and make sure all the pieces are there.

2. Follow step-by-step installation or assembly instructions. Often it is helpful to read the instructions aloud to yourself or someone else as you go along. Assembling a product incorrectly can cause it to fail, break, or become dangerous.

3. Go to the index and look up key words related to problems you encounter or specific tasks you want to do. For example, if you need to change the time on your car clock, the index will show the page where the manual explains the procedure.

4. If the manual that came with the product is too brief or doesn't address a problem you are having, look online by checking the company's Web site or searching the product's name. You may find more detailed instructions, as well as tips from other users.

5. The manual (or Web site) may include a frequently asked questions (FAQs) section, which includes issues you may encounter using the product. Read this even if the product appears to be working correctly, as it may warn you of potential problems or maintenance issues.

6. If the product came with access codes or other important information, record that in the manual and keep it in a place that you'll remember later.

The key to reading manuals is to be patient and not get frustrated. Approach the task as if you were solving a puzzle—eventually, you will put the pieces together.

Completing Forms

Whether you are entering school, applying for a job, filling out medical papers, or requesting a bank loan, you will probably have to complete some type of form. Although forms differ widely, many elements of information are requested on all of them. You may need to provide your name, address, Social Security number, proof of citizenship, phone numbers, e-mail address, and references. (Call ahead to find out what information and documents are needed.) Reading the form carefully and accurately can save time and prevent complications. For example, if the directions say to print your name in black or blue ink, do not use a pencil or write your name in cursive handwriting. If a job application requires you to answer the questions in your own handwriting, do not type the application. In both examples, the forms would most likely be returned to you because you had not read the directions carefully, and you could miss a deadline or lose out on a job offer or other opportunity. These tips will help you avoid carelessness in reading forms:

1. Scan the entire form before you begin to fill it out.
2. When filling out the form, read the small print directions carefully. Often, these directions appear in parentheses below a fill-in blank.
3. Fill in all the questions that pertain to you. Pay attention when you read the directions that tell you what sections of the form or application you should fill out and what sections are to be completed by someone else.
4. Write clearly—particularly numbers.
5. Reread your responses before submitting your form or application. If you are filling out a form online, check and recheck more than once before clicking "send," since you probably can't retrieve your form.

Overcome Obstacles

Reading Difficulties

Some students have specific reading challenges to overcome. Most reading difficulties are related to decoding, comprehension, and retention, with many experts believing the root of most reading problems is decoding. **Decoding** is the process of breaking words into individual sounds. Those with decoding problems may have trouble sounding out words and recognizing words out of context, can confuse letters and the sounds they represent, and ignore punctuation while reading. Dyslexics have difficulty decoding. Experts estimate dyslexia affects as many as 15 percent of all Americans, including celebrities Jay Leno, Tom Cruise, Patrick Dempsey, and Whoopi Goldberg. Albert Einstein, Thomas Edison, George Washington, Winston Churchill, and Sir Isaac Newton were also challenged with reading difficulties.

How do you know if your reading abilities need improvement? Although reading speeds vary, the average adult reads 250 to 300 words per minute. The key, however, is to balance your pace with comprehension. Flying through pages at lightning speed will do you no good if you can't articulate the main points of what you've just read. The following concerns also could signal reading difficulties:

- Making poor grades despite significant effort
- Needing constant, step-by-step guidance for tasks
- Having difficulty mastering tasks or transferring academic skills to other tasks

The good news is that you can improve your reading abilities. As discussed in Chapter 4, many resources are available, such as your school's learning center, if you are struggling with reading. Professionals there will help you understand your difficulty and provide specific tips to help you improve. Also, your instructor or physician (or even the local elementary school) can provide advice on additional resources in your community.

Create a Positive Attitude

One of the greatest barriers to effective reading is attitude. Many people are not willing to invest the time it takes to become a better reader. If the material is difficult,

● Finding Time to Read
Investing time in reading pays off. Your reading skills improve when you read more. *How can you make time to read for pleasure?*

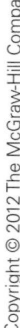
"My alma mater was books, a good library . . . I could spend the rest of my life reading, just satisfying my curiosity."

MALCOLM X
Civil rights leader

seems boring, or requires concentration, they may not complete the reading assignment. So much instant entertainment is available that it is easy to watch a movie or television program or listen to the news instead of reading a newspaper or news magazine. Reading takes time, effort, concentration, and practice.

To create a positive attitude about reading, first pinpoint and dispel illogical thoughts, such as "I have way too much reading; I can never finish it all"; "I'm just not good at math"; or "I never will understand this material!" Many students have trouble reading certain subjects and may lack confidence. It takes time and patience to learn to ski, drive a car, become proficient with computers, or become a more effective reader. Use affirmations to develop confidence: "With patience and practice, I will understand this material." Use the ABC Method of Self-Management to dispel negative thinking and create a "can do" attitude.

Some students and career professionals say they have too much required reading and too little time for pleasure reading. Returning students have difficulty juggling reading, lectures, homework, job, and kids. They can't even imagine having time to read for pleasure. However, it is important to read for pleasure, even if you have only a few minutes a day. (See **Peak Progress 6.7** for ways to fit in reading with children around.) Carry a book with you or keep one in your car. Although you shouldn't study in bed, many people like to read for pleasure each night before turning in.

The more you read, the more your reading skills will improve. As you become a better reader, you will find you enjoy reading more and more. You will also find that, as your attitude improves, so does your ability to keep up on assignments, build your vocabulary, understand and retain what you have read, and learn more about areas that interest you.

Peak Progress

Reading with Children Around

Concentrating on your reading can be challenging with children at your feet. However, it's essential to fit reading into your daily routine (as well as theirs). Try these ideas:

1. **Read in short segments.** Provide activities for your children and set a timer. Tell them that, when it goes off, you'll take a break from reading and do something enjoyable with them. Then set the timer again. In 10 or 15 minutes, you can preview a chapter, outline main ideas, recite out loud, or review. Don't fall into the trap of thinking you need 2 uninterrupted hours to tackle a chapter, or you may never get started.

2. **Read while they sleep.** Get up early and read, or try reading at night when your kids are sleeping. Even if you're tired, read actively or outline a chapter before you turn in. Resist doing the dishes or cleaning and save those activities for when reading and concentrating would be very difficult. Read a little each night and notice how it pays off.

3. **Take reading with you.** If your children are in after-school activities, such as sports or dance, take your reading with you and make the most of your waiting time. This is also a nice time to visit with other parents, but you may need to devote that time to keeping up with your reading.

4. **Read to your children.** Get your kids hooked on reading by reading to them and having them watch you read out loud. Have family reading time, when everyone reads a book. After you read your children a story, ask them to read by themselves or to each other or look at pictures while you read your assignments. Remember to approach reading with a positive attitude, so that they will connect reading with pleasure.

TAKING CHARGE

Summary

In this chapter I learned to

- **Apply the Five-Part Reading System.** Like the Adult Learning Cycle, this system is useful for increasing my comprehension and recall. The steps are (1) prepare, (2) preview, (3) predict questions, (4) process information, and (5) paraphase and review. Scanning chapters gives me a quick overview of main concepts and ideas. I look for information I already know and link it to new information. I look for key words, main ideas, definitions, facts, and important concepts. I make questions out of chapter headings and definitions. I review the chapter to find answers and write them in the margin or on note cards and compare my answers with those of my study team.

- **Apply the SQ3R Reading System.** A five-step process, this method can improve my reading comprehension: S = Survey; Q = Question; R = Read; R = Recite; R = Review.

- **Be an active reader.** I clarify how I will use the information and set goals. I concentrate on main points and general understanding. I read difficult material out loud or standing up. I write in the margins, draw illustrations, underline, sketch, take notes, and dig out key points and key words. I pretend I'm talking with the author and jot down questions.

- **Outline main points and make connections.** Organizing information in an outline creates order, meaning, and understanding and helps me recall the material. It simplifies difficult information and makes connections clear. I link new information with what I already know and look for connections to what I don't know. I look for similarities and differences. I look for examples and read end-of-chapter summaries.

- **Summarize.** Summarizing in writing and out loud are powerful reading and memory strategies. I close the book at various times to write summaries and then check my brief summaries with the book. I summarize in writing after I finish a quick read of the chapter and then fill in with details.

- **Review.** I increase my comprehension by reviewing my outline, note cards, key words, main points, and summaries within 24 hours of reading and after lectures.

- **Build a strong vocabulary.** A good vocabulary is critical to success in school and my career. I can improve my vocabulary by learning and incorporating new words into my writing and conversations, using resources such as a dictionary or vocabulary book, and observing my speech habits.

- **Manage language courses.** Many of the same vocabulary-building strategies work for second-language courses. I can focus on key words, recite out loud, carry note cards, listen to recordings, keep up with the reading assignments, and use practice exercises.

- **Tackle specialized reading.** Thoroughness and precision are critical for reading technical information, graphs, manuals, and forms. Tips for technical information include identifying the purpose of the material, looking for connections, and explaining in my own words. Tips for manuals include reviewing the table of contents, looking up key words in the index, following step-by-step instructions, and reading aloud if necessary. Tips for forms include scanning before I begin, reading the small print, knowing what pertains to me, and asking questions when I'm unsure.

- **Address reading challenges.** I know to seek help with reading difficulties and create a positive attitude about improving my reading abilities, including reading for pleasure.

Performance Strategies

Following are the top 10 strategies for active reading:

- Find interest in the material.
- Outline the main points and identify key words.
- Gather information and predict questions.
- Take breaks and make reading physical.
- Reduce distractions and stay alert.
- Make connections and link information.
- Create a relationship with the author.
- Summarize in writing in your own words.
- Review consistently and as soon as possible.
- Teach by summarizing out loud and explaining the material to others.

Tech for Success

Take advantage of the text's Web site at **www.mhhe.com/ferrett8e** for additional study aids, useful forms, and convenient and applicable resources.

- **Books online.** Many of your textbooks can be purchased online and downloaded to your computer. Most of these books are formatted to be read online, rather than printed out. Does this sound appealing, or would you rather read from a printed copy of the text? List some of the advantages and disadvantages of both options.

- **All the news that's fit to click.** What's your source for the latest news? Most major newspapers are available online and archive previous articles. Take a poll of your classmates to see who still opts for newsprint, who prefers the local and cable networks, and who relies on the Web. Discuss the pros and cons. Do your classmates' preferences match their learning styles? Which sources do the more avid readers prefer?

Study Team Notes

Career *in* focus

Brian Singer
INFORMATION TECHNOLOGY SPECIALIST

Related Majors: Computer Science, Mathematics, Information Systems

Keeping Up-to-Date

Brian Singer is an information technology specialist, or computer programmer. His job is to write instructions that computers follow to perform their functions from updating financial records to simulating air flight as training for pilots.

When writing a program, Brian must first break the task into various instructional steps that a computer can follow. Then he must code each step into a programming language. When finished, Brian tests the program to confirm it works accurately. Usually, he needs to make some adjustments, called debugging, before the program runs smoothly. The program must be maintained over time and updated as the need arises. Because critical problems can be intricate and time-consuming and must be fixed quickly, Brian usually works long hours, including evenings and weekends. Although his office surroundings are comfortable, Brian must be careful to avoid physical problems, such as eyestrain or back discomfort.

To stay current in his field, Brian reads about 500 pages of technical materials each week. Brian also took a class on reading technical information to improve his reading skills. Because he concentrates best when he is around people, Brian likes to read and study in a coffeehouse. When he has difficulty understanding what he reads, he gets on the Internet and asks for help from an online discussion group. To help him remember and better understand what he has read during the week, Brian tries to implement the new information in his work.

CRITICAL THINKING What strategies might help an information technology specialist when reading technical information?

Peak Performer
PROFILE

Sonia Sotomayor

A culmination of a successful career in law and an early love of books led Sonia Sotomayor, born and raised in the Bronx by Puerto Rican parents, to a U.S. Supreme Court nomination in 2009. In this historic appointment, Sotomayor was the first Hispanic person and third woman to become a Justice on the Supreme Court. Sotomayor believes that the law and its inherent fairness enabled her to rise from the Bronx housing project where she grew up to become a member of the Supreme Court today. She is credited as being a "role model of aspiration, discipline, commitment, intellectual prowess, and integrity."

It was a love of books that initially led Sotomayor into pursuing law. She became an avid reader when, at the age of 9, she turned to books for solace after her father died. Nancy Drew mysteries especially captivated her and inspired her to want to become a detective. She soon discovered the *Perry Mason* television show. Since the lawyers were often involved in investigative work like Nancy Drew, she decided at the age of 10 that she would become a lawyer.

Sotomayor graduated valedictorian of her high school and attended Princeton University, where she felt like "a visitor landing in alien country," given the lack of female and Hispanic students at the time. With hard work and perseverance, Sotomayor excelled in her

classes and attended Yale Law School on a scholarship, where she graduated with a J.D. in 1979.

As an assistant district attorney in New York and later as the first Latina woman on the U.S. Court of Appeals of the Second Circuit, Sotomayor was known for her preparedness, fairness, and adherence to the law. In the courthouse, she works to empower young people with her Development School for Youth program, which sponsors workshops that teach inner-city students how to function successfully in a work setting. By following her own dreams from a very early age, Sotomayor hopes to encourage the next generation of lawyers, doctors, and, perhaps, detectives.

PERFORMANCE THINKING Books and other media not only offer opportunities for escape and personal reflection but also allow us to see a different view of a particular occupation we may not have seen before. When have you learned more about a career while reading a book or an article?

CHECK IT OUT Web sites such as Flashlight Worthy Book Club Recommendations (**www.flashlightworthybooks.com/**), LitLovers Online Book Community (**www.litlovers.com/index.html**), and Book Movement Book Club Resources (**www.bookmovement.com/**) recommend books clubs and publish book reviews. Some connect members through forums, reading guides, or online courses. Find inspiration for what you'll read next. Through reading, you, too, may discover something new about yourself, as Sotomayor did with the Nancy Drew series.

Starting Today

At least one strategy I learned in this chapter that I plan to try right away is

_____

_____

_____

What changes must I make in order for this strategy to be most effective?

_____

_____

_____

Review Questions

Based on what you have learned in this chapter, write your answers to the following questions:

1. Name and describe each part of the Five-Part Reading System.

_____

_____

2. How does outlining the main points help you improve your reading?

_____

_____

3. Name three strategies for managing language courses.

_____

_____

4. Explain how building your vocabulary can be important to your career success.

_____

_____

5. What are important elements to look for when reading graphics?

_____

_____

To test your understanding of the chapter's concepts, complete the chapter quiz at **www.mhhe.com/ferrett8e.**

Effective Reading Habits

In the Classroom

Chris McDaniel struggles to keep up with her reading. She is overwhelmed by the amount of reading and the difficulty of her textbooks. She has never been much of a reader but enjoys watching television. She sometimes reads in bed or in a comfortable chair but often falls asleep. She realizes this is not the most productive way to study, but it has become a habit. Chris has noticed that, after reading for an hour or so, she can recall almost nothing. This has frustrated her, and she doubts her ability to succeed in college.

1. What habits should Chris change to improve her reading skills?

_____

_____

_____

2. Suggest one or two specific strategies Chris could implement to become a better reader.

_____

_____

_____

In the Workplace

Chris is now a stockbroker. She never thought she would work in this business, but a part-time summer job led her to a career in finance, and she really likes the challenge. She is surprised, however, at the vast amount of reading involved in her job: reports, letters, magazines, and articles. She also reads several books and blogs on money management each month.

3. What strategies in this chapter would help Chris manage and organize her reading materials?

_____

_____

4. What are some specific reading strategies that apply to both school and work?

_____

_____

Applying the ABC Method of Self-Management

In the Journal Entry on page 179, you were asked to describe a time when you enjoyed being read to. Why was the experience pleasurable? What types of books did you enjoy most? Did you have a favorite book or story?

_____

_____

_____

_____

Now think about your current experiences with reading. Do you enjoy reading? If so, what are the benefits to you? Visualize either a recent positive or a recent negative reading situation. Apply the ABC steps to visualize how the situation can enhance your reading skills.

A = Actual event:

_____

_____

B = Beliefs:

_____

_____

C = Challenge:

_____

_____

When you are in a positive state of mind, do you see yourself reading quickly and comprehending and recalling information effortlessly? Enjoy becoming an active reader.

PRACTICE SELF-MANAGEMENT

For more examples of learning how to manage difficult situations, see the "Self-Management Workbook" section of the Online Learning Center Web site at **www.mhhe.com/ferrett8e.**

Attitudes and Reading

Read the following questions and write your answers on the lines provided.

1. What is your attitude toward reading?

   I don't read much, it depends on if it interests me

2. What kind of books do you most like to read?

   I like romance novels & self help books

3. Do you read for pleasure?

   only when its something I like, magazines I do read

4. Do you read the daily newspaper?   Yes _____   No _✓_

   If yes, what sections do you read? Place a check mark.

   _✓_ Comics   _✓_ Horoscope   _✓_ Weather

   _____ Sports   _____ Classified ads   _____ World news

   _____ Business   _____ Entertainment   _____ Other

5. Do you read magazines?   Yes _✓_   No _____

   If yes, which magazines?

   Seventeen, cosmo girl

6. How would it benefit you to read faster?

   The more I read the faster

7. What techniques can you learn to read faster and remember more?

   re-reading and increasing pace

Different Types of Reading

Find a sample of each of the following sources of reading material:

- Newspaper
- Chapter from a textbook
- Instructions for an appliance, an insurance policy, or a rental contract

Read each sample. Then answer the following questions.

1. How does the reading process differ for each type of reading?

_____

_____

_____

_____

_____

_____

_____

_____

_____

2. How does knowing your purpose for reading affect how you read? Why?

_____

_____

_____

_____

_____

_____

_____

_____

_____

_____

Summarize and Teach

1. Read the following paragraphs on Title IX. Underline, write in the margins, and write a brief summary of the paragraph. Compare your work with a study partner's work. There are many ways to highlight, so don't be concerned if yours is unique.

THE IMPACT OF TITLE IX

When Title IX of the Education Amendments was passed, gender was added to the list of categories protected by federal law. From then on, schools and colleges receiving any federal funds were prohibited from discriminating against either employees or students on the basis of their sex. Despite resistance in many forms, Title IX has slowly transformed education in the United States.

When people hear the words *Title IX,* they usually think of athletics and sports facilities. Indeed, in 1972, only about 294,000 American high school girls took part in interscholastic sports; today, about 3 million girls play sports. But Title IX is much more far-reaching than sports.

Prior to Title IX, girls who became pregnant were often forced to leave school or, at best, to attend segregated—and well-hidden—classes. Title IX prohibited that practice. Although schools can still offer voluntary classes for pregnant and parenting teens, no girl can be kept out of any program, class, or extracurricular activity because of bearing a child. These were no small victories in schools where girls who became pregnant were routinely expelled.

Source: James W. Fraser, *Teach: A Question of Teaching,* McGraw-Hill, 2011.

SUMMARY

_____

_____

_____

_____

_____

_____

2. Work with a study partner in one of your classes. Read a chapter and write a summary. Compare your summary with your study partner's summary. Then summarize and teach the main concepts to your partner. Each of you can clarify and ask questions.

SUMMARY

_____

_____

_____

_____

_____

_____

Creating a Reading Outline

Outlining what you read can be a helpful study technique. Develop the habit of outlining. Use the following form as a guide. You may also develop your own form (see Chapter 5 for examples). Outline Chapter 6 on the lines below (or select another chapter in this or one of your other texts).

Course _____ Chapter _____ Date _____

I. _____   III. _____

   A. _____   A. _____

      1. _____   1. _____

      2. _____   2. _____

      3. _____   3. _____

   B. _____   B. _____

      1. _____   1. _____

      2. _____   2. _____

      3. _____   3. _____

II. _____   IV. _____

   A. _____   A. _____

      1. _____   1. _____

      2. _____   2. _____

      3. _____   3. _____

   B. _____   B. _____

      1. _____   1. _____

      2. _____   2. _____

      3. _____   3. _____

Analyzing Chapters

As you start to read the next chapter in this book, fill in this page to prepare for reading. You may need to add additional headings. List each heading and then phrase it as a question. Then summarize as you complete your reading. Use a separate sheet of paper if needed.

Course _____ Textbook _____

Chapter _____

Heading 1 _____

Question _____

Heading 2 _____

Question _____

Heading 3 _____

Question _____

Heading 4 _____

Question _____

SUMMARY OF SECTION

_____

_____

_____

_____

SUMMARY OF CHAPTER

_____

_____

_____

_____

Mind Map Your Text

Make a mind map of a section or chapter of one of your textbooks using the format provided below (and edit/change as necessary). Use **Figure 5.2** on page 159 as a guide.

For example, let's say you will map out a section from Chapter 3 of this text: "Manage Your Time." In the middle circle, you might put "Time-Management Strategies." In one of the surrounding circles, you might enter "Study everywhere and anywhere." In offshoot circles from that, you might put "Carry note cards," "Listen to taped lectures," and "Avoid peak times in the library." Compare your mind maps with those drawn by other students in your class.

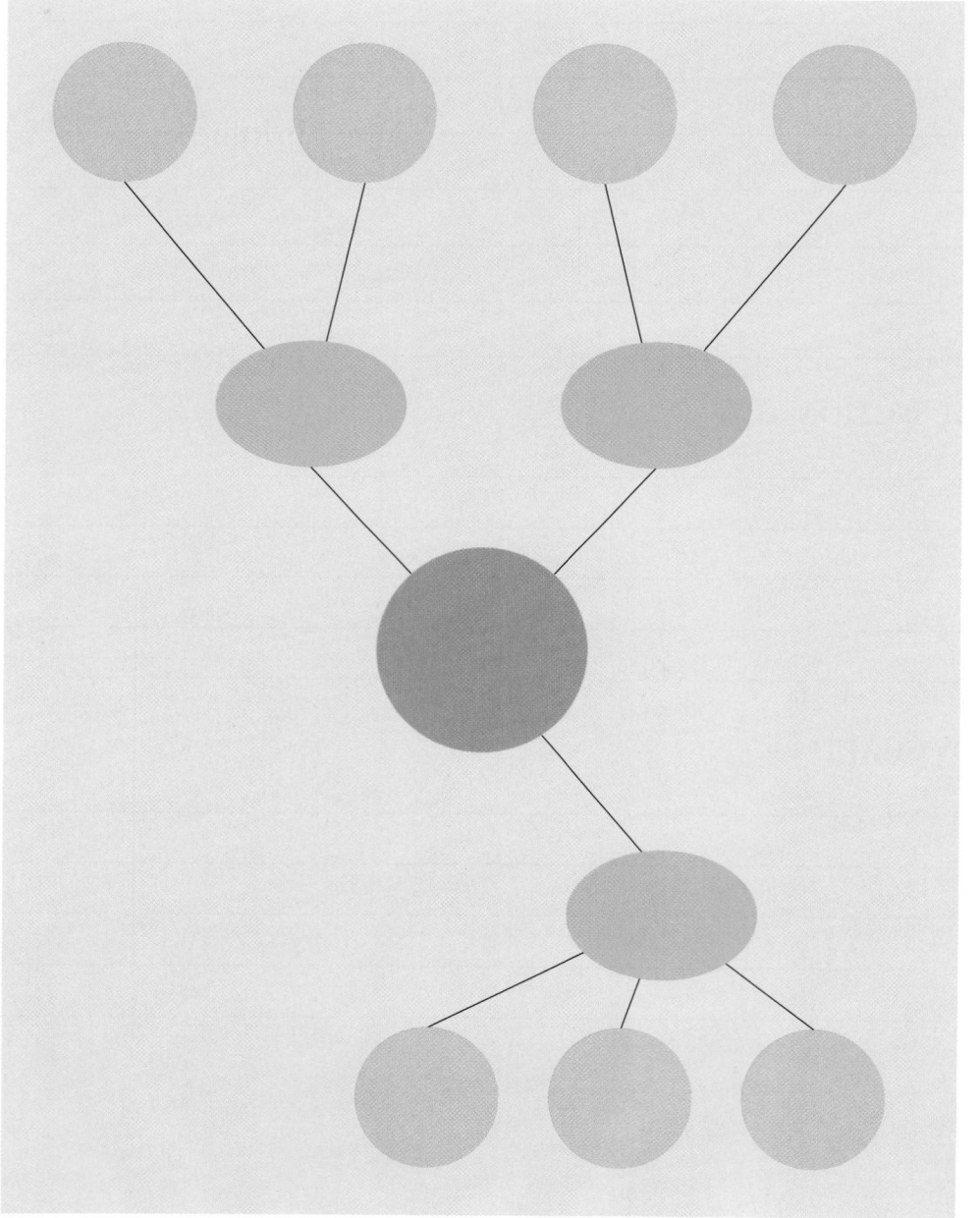

Breaking Barriers to Reading

Following is a list of the common reasons that some students use for not reading effectively. Read this list; then add to it on the lines provided. Use creative problem solving to list strategies for overcoming these barriers.

Reasons for Not Reading	Strategies for Overcoming Reading Barriers
1. My textbooks are boring.	_____
	_____
	_____
	_____
2. I can't concentrate.	_____
	_____
	_____
3. I'm easily distracted.	_____
	_____
	_____
	_____
4. I fall asleep when I read.	_____
	_____
	_____
	_____
5. I never study the right material.	_____
	_____
	_____
	_____
6. There is too much information, and I don't know what is important.	_____
	_____
	_____
7. I read for hours, but I don't understand what I have read.	_____
	_____
	_____
8. I don't like to read.	_____
	_____
	_____
	_____

Demonstrating Competencies

Follow these steps and fill in the blanks below to demonstrate your competencies. Then add this page to your Career Development Portfolio.

1. **Looking back:** Review your worksheets from other chapters to find activities from which you learned to read and concentrate.
2. **Taking stock:** Identify your strengths in reading and what you want to improve.
3. **Looking forward:** Indicate how you would demonstrate reading and comprehension skills to an employer.
4. **Documentation:** Include documentation of your reading skills.
5. **Inventory:** Make a list of the books you've read recently, including any classics. Use a separate sheet of paper.

Explain how you demonstrate these competencies:

Competencies	Your Demonstration
Active reading	_____
Critical reading	_____
Willingness to learn new words	_____
Improvement in technical vocabulary	_____
Articulation	_____
Expressiveness	_____
Ability to use a dictionary	_____
Positive attitude toward reading	_____
Technical reading	_____
Form reading	_____

7

Improve Your Memory Skills

LEARNING OUTCOMES

In this chapter, you will learn to

7.1 Apply the five-step memory process

7.2 Describe memory strategies, including mnemonic devices

7.3 Summarize, review, and reflect for better retention and recall

SELF-MANAGEMENT

"I have been meeting so many new people. I wish I could remember their names, but I just don't have a good memory. How can I increase my memory skills and remember names, facts, and information more easily?"

Do you ever feel embarrassed because you cannot remember the names of new people you've met? Do you ever get frustrated because you don't remember material for a test? In this chapter, you will learn how to increase your memory skills.

JOURNAL ENTRY In **Worksheet 7.1** on page 240, describe a situation in which you needed to learn many new names or facts for a test. How did you fare? What factors helped you remember?

Technology has provided ample ways to store and retrieve information. No longer do we memorize and recite long stories in order to pass them down, as was done hundreds of years ago. In fact, many people don't even know their best friend's phone number, since it's programmed into their cell phone.

However, you can't whip out the latest technology gadget when you take a test. Nor can you check your personal digital assistant (PDA) when you run into a business acquaintance and can't remember his name ("Is it Bob or Bill? I know it starts with a *B*."). Although you may search the Internet to find information, you still determine what the information means, how it relates to other material, and how you will use it now and in the future. For this, your brain—not your computer, cell phone, or PDA—is the most essential "device."

Do you think some people are born with better memories than others? You will discover in this chapter that memory is a complex process that involves many factors you can control, such as your attitude, interest, intent, awareness, mental alertness, observation skills, senses, distractions, memory techniques, and willingness to practice. Most people with good memories say they mastered the skill by learning and continually practicing the strategies for storing and recalling information. This chapter will describe specific strategies that help you remember information.

> "Memory . . . is the diary that we all carry about with us."
>
> OSCAR WILDE
> *Dramatist*

The Memory Process

The memory process involves five main steps:

1. Intention—you are interested and have a desire to learn and remember
2. Attention—you are attentive, observing information, and concentrating on details
3. Association—you organize and associate information to make sense of it
4. Retention—you practice until you know the information
5. Recall—you recall, teach, and share information with others

As you can see, this process is similar to the Adult Learning Cycle, which is explored throughout this text. (Read **Peak Progress 7.1** to see how you can use the Adult Learning Cycle to improve your memory skills.)

1. **Intention.** The first step in using memory effectively is to prepare mentally. As with learning any skill, your intention, attitude, and motivation are fundamental to success. Intention means being interested and willing to learn. You intend to remember by finding personal meaning and interest. Have you ever said, "I wish I could remember names," or "I can't remember formulas for math"? Instead, say, "I really want to remember JoAnne's name."

   If you make excuses or program your mind with negative self-talk, your mind refuses to learn new information. If you think a subject is

Peak Progress

Applying the Adult Learning Cycle to Increasing Your Memory Skills

1. **RELATE. Why do I want to learn this?** I must become more proficient at remembering names, facts, and information. This is critical for success not only in school but also in work and social situations. What strategies do I already use to remember information?

2. **OBSERVE. How does this work?** Who is good at remembering names and information? What tips can I pick up from him or her? Who seems to struggle with remembering important information? I'll try using new strategies and observe how I'm improving.

3. **REFLECT. What does this mean?** What strategies seem to work best for me? What strategies are ineffective? Have I eliminated negative and defeating self-talk? I continue to look for connections and associations. I use humor, songs, rhymes, and other mnemonic techniques.

4. **DO. What can I do with this?** I will practice memory skills in many different situations and make a conscious commitment to improving my skills. I'll make games out of my practice and have fun. I'll find practical applications and use my new skills in everyday life. Each day, I'll work on one area. For example, I'll choose one class in which I'm having trouble recalling information and experiment with new strategies.

5. **TEACH. Whom can I share this with?** I'll talk with others and share my tips and experiences. I'll ask if they have any strategies they find useful that I might also try.

Congratulate yourself when you make improvements. The more you go through the cycle, the more interest and meaning recall will have for you, and the better your memory skills will become.

---

boring or unimportant, you will have difficulty remembering it. Make a conscious, active decision to remember, and state your intention with positive affirmations.

2. **Attention.** The second step in the memory process is to concentrate, observe, and be attentive to details. How often have you physically been in one place but mentally and emotionally were thousands of miles away? **Mindfulness** is the state in which you are totally in the moment and part of the process. Learning occurs when your mind is relaxed, focused, receptive, and alert. Focus your attention by concentrating briefly on one thing. Visualize details by drawing mental pictures. **Personal Evaluation Notebook 7.1** on page 220 helps you practice your observation skills.

3. **Association.** Nothing is harder to remember than unconnected facts, dates, or theories. Ask about how information is interconnected: How is this information similar to other information? How is it different?

   By associating and linking new material with old material, you make it meaningful. You cannot retain or recall information unless you understand it. Understanding means being able to see connections and relationships in information and to summarize and explain the material in your own words. Make associations by looking for similarities or differences. Create understanding by finding out why this information is important and how it relates to other information. Too often, students study just enough to get by on a quiz and then forget the information. It is much better to learn a subject, so that it becomes interesting and part of your long-term memory. (See **Peak Progress 7.2** on page 221 on short-term versus long-term memory.)

> **"** An education isn't how much you have committed to memory, or even how much you know. It's being able to differentiate between what you know and what you don't. **"**
>
> ANATOLE FRANCE
> *Author*

WORDS TO SUCCEED

Personal Evaluation Notebook

Being Observant

Try the following experiments to determine if you are really observing the world around you.

EXPERIMENT 1

1. Look around the room.
2. Close your eyes.
3. Mentally picture what is in the room.
4. Open your eyes.
5. Did you remember everything? If not, what didn't you remember?

_____

_____

_____

EXPERIMENT 2

1. Look at a painting, photo, or poster for 1 minute.
2. Without looking back, write down the details you remember.
3. Compare your list of details with the painting, photo, or poster.
   a. What details did you remember? Colors? Faces? Clothing?

   _____

   _____

   _____

   b. What details didn't you remember?

   _____

   _____

   _____

   c. Did you remember the obvious things or did you remember subtle details?

   _____

   d. Why do you think those were the details you remembered?

   _____

   _____

   _____

One way to organize material to look for connections is by outlining each chapter. As discussed in Chapter 5, use the Cornell System or a mind map (or whatever outline method works for you) to organize information. (See **Personal Evaluation Notebook 7.2** on page 223 for a sample of a mind map.)

4. **Retention.** Repetition and practice help you retain information. Do it, and do it again. Repeat names or information aloud. Practice what you have learned, find new applications, and connect this information to other information you already know. Continue to ask questions and look for more examples.

5. **Recall. Memorization** is the transfer of information from short-term memory into long-term memory. Of course, the only reason to do this is so we can retrieve it in the future for use by our short-term memory. This transfer in the other direction is known as recall. To **recall** information means you not only have retained it but also can remember it when you need to.

Share information with others; introduce a person you have just met; practice giving summaries of chapters to your study team. Teach the information, write about it, talk about it, apply it to new situations, and demonstrate that you know it. This will make you more interested in the information, create more meaning for you, and build your confidence. Repeating this cycle will build your memory skills.

Peak Progress

7.2

Short-Term and Long-Term Memory

People have two basic types of memory: short-term, or active, memory and long-term, or passive, memory. Each type plays an important role in learning and the ability to respond effectively to life's challenges.

If you own a computer, you probably have heard references to its various types of memory. Your own short-term memory is very much like the memory in your computer, which you know as random access memory (RAM) (see **Figure 7.1** on page 222).

Just as the computer's central processing unit relies on RAM to perform all of its processing tasks, your own short-term memory is where your mind is able to apply, create, and evaluate. Short-term memory is where all your active thinking takes place. It is a relatively limited space, yet tremendous potential resides there.

Before short-term memory can perform its wonders, information must flow into it. This can be new information entering through your natural senses, stored information you retrieve from long-term memory, or a combination of both. Using the computer analogy, you might equate your natural senses with a keyboard or mouse, while you may think of long-term memory as your hard drive where you save your work. Just as you make choices about which work you will save on your computer, you determine which information becomes stored in your long-term memory. The information you choose to save in long-term memory has great value. It can be retrieved and used as it is, or it can be retrieved and combined with other information to create something entirely new. The possibilities are endless.

When we consider the transfer of information back and forth in our memory system, think of the mind as a vast relational database. It is not enough merely to store information; for any database to be useful; the information stored in it must be organized and indexed for retrieval. This occurs naturally when we are predisposed to remember something, but what happens when we have to memorize information we just don't care about? Not only is that information more difficult to memorize but also it becomes nearly impossible to recall. The good news is that we can make such information more memorable by personally relating to it. For example, ask yourself, "How can I use this information in my life?" Answers to such questions can create meaning, which helps our mind to naturally organize information. When it comes time to use that information, such as during an examination, it will have been naturally indexed for easier recall.

(continued)

Short-Term and Long-Term Memory *(concluded)*

Figure 7.1

Short-Term and Long-Term Memory

Think of your memory as a computer. First, you input information through your natural senses (as in inputting by way of a mouse or a keyboard). Your short-term memory is like the random access memory in your computer, which is readily available for use but can be erased if the computer suddenly crashes. Long-term memory is like information that has been stored on your hard drive, which you can retrieve (or recall) for later use. *What material from this course may be in your short-term memory? In your long-term memory?*

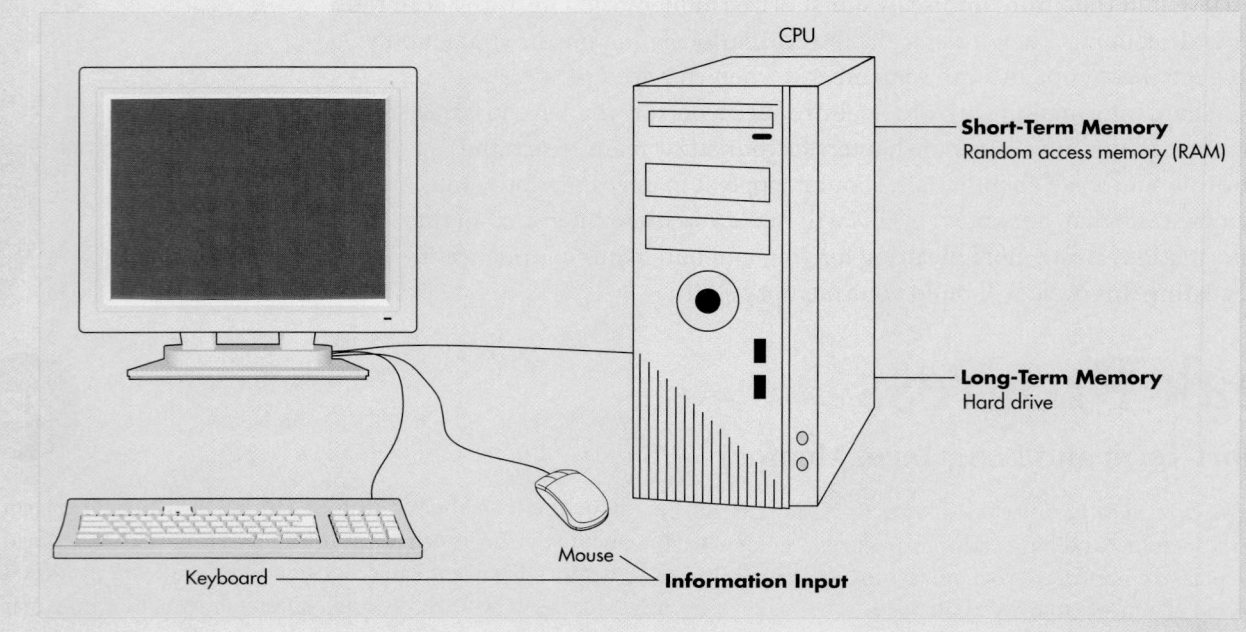

Memory Strategies

The following strategies will help you improve your memory skills.

1. **Write it down.** Writing is physical and enhances learning. When you write information, you are reinforcing learning by using your eyes, hand, fingers, and arm. Writing uses different parts of the brain than do speaking and listening.

   - Writing down a telephone number helps you remember it by providing a mental picture.
   - Planning your time in a day planner and creating a to-do list can trigger accomplishing tasks later in the day when you may have become overwhelmed with distractions.
   - Taking notes in class prompts you to be logical and concise and fills in memory gaps.
   - Underlining important information and then copying it onto note cards reinforces information.

Personal Evaluation Notebook

Using a Mind Map to Enhance Memory

Not only will a mind map help you organize information to be memorized, but also the physical act of writing will help you commit the material to memory. Use the map figure that follows as a guide, and in the space provided create a mind map of this chapter.

- Write the main topic in the middle and draw a circle or box around it.
- Surround the main topic with subtopics.
- Draw lines from the subtopics to the main topic.
- Under the subtopics, jot down supporting points, ideas, and examples.

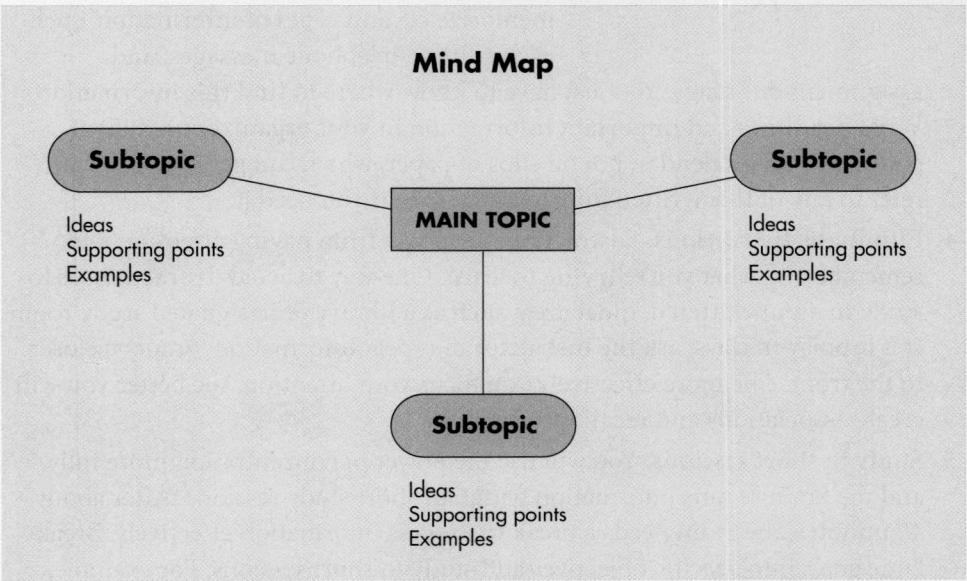

Create your own mind map.

Think of an essay question from an exam you have taken. How would using a mind map have helped you answer the question?

Take 3 minutes to organize your study area to prevent distractions:

- What assignments are completed and should be filed away?
- Which projects are due soon? Assemble all the necessary materials and put them in an accessible spot.
- Which readings must be completed this week? Pile those books together.

What else can you do in 3 minutes?

- Create file folders for all your courses.
- Scan today's lecture notes and read key points out loud.
- Empty all the trash and recycle old papers.

Take 3

- Writing a summary in your own words after reading a chapter helps transfer information to long-term memory.

2. **Go from the general to the specific.** Many people learn and remember best by looking at the big picture and then learning the details. Try to outline from the general (main topic) to the specific (subtopics). Previewing a chapter gives you an overview and makes the topic more meaningful. Your brain is more receptive to details when it has a general idea of the main topic. Read, listen, and look for general understanding; then add details.

3. **Reduce information.** You don't have to memorize certain types of information, such as deadlines, telephone messages, and assignment due dates. You just have to know where to find this information. Write deadlines and important information in your organizer or student planner or on a calendar, not on slips of paper, which can get lost. You can refer to any of this written information again if you need it.

4. **Eliminate distractions.** Distractions keep you from paying attention and remembering what you're trying to learn. One way to avoid distractions is to study in an uncluttered, quiet area, such as a library or designated study room. If it is noisy in class, ask the instructor to repeat information, or move closer to the front. The more effectively you focus your attention, the better you will create associations and recall information.

5. **Study in short sessions.** You will use the power of concentration more fully, and the brain retains information better, in short study sessions. After about 40 minutes, the brain needs a break to process information effectively. Break large goals into specific objectives and study in short sessions. For example, if you are taking a marketing course, preview a chapter in your textbook for 20 minutes and mind map the chapter for 20 minutes. Then take a 10-minute break. Stretch, drink a glass of water, or treat yourself to a small snack. Then return to complete your goal.

6. **Use all your senses.** Memory is sensory, so using all your senses (sight, hearing, touch, smell, and taste) will give your brain a better chance of retaining information.

- *Visualize.* Since much of what you learn and remember reaches you through sight, it is important to visualize what you want to remember. The art of retention is the art of attention. Be a keen observer of details and notice differences and similarities. Suppose you are taking a medical terminology or vocabulary-building course. You may want to look at pictures and visualize images with the new terms or words. Look at illustrations, pictures, and information on the board.

- *Listen.* You cannot remember a name or information in class if you are not attentive and listening. Actively listen in class, record lectures (ask for the instructor's permission), and play them back later. Recite definitions and information aloud.

- *Move.* Whether you learn best by reading or listening, you will retain information better if you use all your senses and make learning physical. Read aloud; read while standing; jot down notes; lecture in front of the classroom to yourself or your study team; draw pictures, diagrams, and models; and join a study group. Practice reciting information while doing physical activity, such as showering or jogging. The more you use all your senses, the more information you will retain.

  Complete **Personal Evaluation Notebook 7.3** on page 226 to assess your memory and how your senses relate to your childhood memories. Complete **Personal Evaluation Notebook 7.4** on page 227 to determine how to use learning styles to improve recall.

7. **Use mnemonic devices. Mnemonic** (neh-mon-nik) devices are memory tricks that help you remember information. However, mnemonic devices have limits. Developing a memory trick takes time, and the trick will be hard to remember if it is too complicated. Since mnemonic devices don't help you understand the information or develop skills in critical thinking, they are best used for sheer rote memorization. Follow up by looking for associations, making connections, and writing summaries. Some mnemonic devices are

  - *Rhymes and rhythms.* In elementary school, you might have learned the rhyme "In 1492 Columbus sailed the ocean blue" to remember the date of Columbus's voyage. Rhythms can also be helpful. Many people have learned to spell the word *Mississippi* by accenting all the *i*s and making the word rhythmic. This is similar to the technique used in rap music and poetry, in which syllables are accentuated on an established beat.

  - *Acronyms.* **Acronyms** are words formed from the first letters of a series of other words, such as HOMES for the Great Lakes (Huron, Ontario, Michigan, Erie, and Superior) and EPCOT (Experimental Prototype Community of Tomorrow).

  - *Acrostics.* **Acrostics** are similar to acronyms, but they are made-up sentences in which the first letter stands for something, such as Every Good Boy Deserves Fun for remembering the sequence of musical notes: E, G, B, D, F. Another is My Very Easy Memory Jingle Seems Useful Now, which helps you remember the order of the planets from the sun (assuming you know that the first planet is Mercury and not Mars and that Pluto is no longer considered a planet. Can you name the rest with the help of the acrostic?) Acrostics are often used in poetry, where the first letter of every line combine to spell something, such as the poem's title. (See **Personal Evaluation Notebook 7.5** on page 228 to practice creating acronyms and acrostics.)

  - *Association.* Suppose you are learning about explorer Christopher Columbus's three ships. Think of three friends whose names start with the same first letters as the ships' names: *Pinta, Santa Maria,* and *Nina* (e.g., Paul, Sandy, and Nancy). Vividly associate your friends' names with the three ships, and you should be able to recall the ships' names. Using associations can also be helpful in remembering numbers. For example, if

● **Learning Memory**
Focusing on your preferred learning style strengthens your memory skills. *How does your learning style affect the way in which you learn memory?*

❝No memory is ever alone; it's at the end of a trail of memories, a dozen trails that each have their own associations.**❞**

LOUIS L'AMOUR
Author

WORDS TO SUCCEED

Personal Evaluation Notebook

7.3

Memory Assessment

1. Sometimes your perceptions differ from reality, particularly when you are assessing your skills and personal qualities. Check Yes or No as it pertains to you.

    a. Do you remember names easily?   Yes _____   No _____
    b. Do you remember important information for tests?   Yes _____   No _____
    c. Do you often forget about due dates and appointments?   Yes _____   No _____
    d. Do you often "lose" things around the house?   Yes _____   No _____
    e. Did you use your senses more as a child?   Yes _____   No _____

2. Write a few lines about your earliest memory.

    _____

    _____

    _____

    _____

3. Does it help your memory to look at family photos or hear about your childhood? Why?

    _____

    _____

    _____

    _____

4. What smells do you remember most from home?

    _____

    _____

    _____

    _____

your ATM identification number is 9072, you might remember it by creating associations with dates. Maybe 1990 is the year you graduated from high school and 1972 is the year you were born.

- *Chunking.* **Chunking,** or grouping, long lists of information or numbers can break up the memory task and make it easier for you. Most people can remember up to seven numbers in a row, which is why phone numbers are that long.

- *Stacking technique.* Visualize objects that represent points, and stack them on top of each other. For example, if you were giving a speech on time

Personal Evaluation Notebook

7.4

Learning Styles and Memory

Answer the following questions on the lines provided.

1. How can you use your preferred learning style to enhance your memory?

_____

_____

_____

_____

_____

2. How can you incorporate other learning styles to help you improve your recall?

_____

_____

_____

_____

management, you would start with a clock with a big pencil on it to represent how much time is saved if you write information down. On top of the clock is a big calendar, which reminds you to make the point that you must set priorities in writing. On the calendar is a Time Log with the name Drucker on it. This will remind you to present a quote by Peter Drucker that you must know where your time goes if you are to be effective in managing your life. You stack an object to remind you of each of the key points in the speech.

- *Method-of-place technique.* As far back as 500 BC, the Greeks were using a method of imagery called loci—the method-of-place technique. (*Loci* is Latin for "place.") This method, which is similar to the stacking technique, is still effective because it uses imagery and association to aid memory. Memorize a setting in detail and then place the item or information you want to remember at certain places on your memory map. Some people like to use a familiar street, their home, or their car as a map on which to place their information. Memorize certain places on your map and the specific order or path in which you visit each place. Once you have memorized this map, you can position various items to remember at different points. **Personal Evaluation Notebook 7.6** on page 229 gives you a chance to practice this technique.

Personal Evaluation Notebook

Acronyms and Acrostics

An *acronym* is a word formed from the first letters of a series of other words. An *acrostic* is a made-up sentence, with the first letter of each word standing for something. Create one or more acronyms and acrostics based on information you are learning right now in your courses.

Acronym example: "NATO" stands for North Atlantic Treaty Organization.

Acronym _____

Stands for _____

Acrostic example: "Old People From Texas Eat Spiders" stands for the bones of the skull (occipital, parietal, frontal, temporal, ethmoid, sphenoid).

Acrostic _____

Stands for _____

8. **Use note cards.** On note cards, the information is condensed and written, so the act of writing is kinesthetic and holding cards is tactile. Note cards are visual and, when the information is recited out loud or in a group, the auditory element enhances learning. Note cards are a great way to organize information and highlight key words:

   - Use index cards for recording information you want to memorize. Write brief summaries and indicate the main points of each chapter on the backs of note cards.
   - Carry the cards with you and review them during waiting time, before going to sleep at night, or any other time you have a few minutes to spare.
   - Organize the cards according to category, color, size, order, weight, and other areas.

9. **Recite.** Recite and repeat information, such as a name, poem, date, or formula. When you say information aloud, you use your throat, voice, and lips, and you hear yourself recite. This recitation technique may help when you are dealing with difficult reading material. Reading aloud and hearing the material will reinforce it and help move information from your short-term memory to your long-term memory. Use the new words in your own conversations. Write summaries in your own words and read to others. Study groups are effective because you can hear each other, clarify questions, and increase understanding as you review information.

   To remember names, when you meet someone, recite the person's name several times to yourself and out loud. **Peak Progress 7.3** on page 231 provides more tips for remembering names.

10. **Practice, practice, practice!** You must practice information you want to remember. For example, when you first start driver training, you learn the

Personal Evaluation Notebook

A Walk Down Memory Lane

Creating a memory map is a visual way to enhance and practice your memory skills. The key to this method is to set the items clearly in your memory and visualize them. For example, a familiar memory map involves remembering the 13 original colonies. The memory map in this case is a garden with several distinct points. There is delicate chinaware sitting on the garden gate (Delaware); the birdbath contains a large fountain pen (Pennsylvania); in the gazebo is a new jersey calf (New Jersey); and sitting on the calf is King George (Georgia) with a cut on his finger (Connecticut). The flowerbed has a mass of flowers (Massachusetts); in the fountain, splashing, is Marilyn Monroe (Maryland); the garden sun dial is pointing south (South Carolina); a large ham is sitting on the garden bench (New Hampshire); and the gardener, named Virginia (Virginia), who is wearing an empire dress (New York), is watering the northern flowerbed (North Carolina). In the middle of the flowerbed is an island of rocks (Rhode Island) with a bottle of maple syrup. There you have the 13 original colonies in the order in which they joined the union, and it was easy to add the fourteenth state to join— Vermont.

YOUR MEMORY MAP

Create your own memory map using a familiar place, such as your neighborhood, the mall, or a store you often visit, such as a grocery store. Chances are, you navigate around these places the same way every time. You start out on the same path; you park near or enter the same door. You are very familiar with what you will see at each point. For example, you may enter the grocery store near the courtesy counter, grab a cart, and turn right towards the produce section. You can easily visualize where everything is located and what you will see along the "path." Draw a picture of your map in detail in the space provided.

(continued)

Personal Evaluation Notebook

A Walk Down Memory Lane *(concluded)*

Using your map, imagine you have a test coming up in your American government class and need to remember the first 4 (out of 10) amendments that make up the Bill of Rights:

1: Freedom of speech, press, religion, assembly, and petition

2: Right to keep and bear arms

3: Quartering of soldiers

4: Search and arrest

Now, follow these steps in the method-of-place technique:

1. Imagine your memory location, and think of each distinctive detail within the location.
2. Create a vivid image to help you remember each amendment. (If you are unfamiliar with the meaning of any of the amendments, do a quick search online or at the library.)
3. Associate each of the images representing the amendments with points in your map, and see the images at each location. Draw them in your map.
4. As you "stroll" through your map, create mental pictures of each of your items through association. Recite each one aloud as you visualize them.

To help you get started, you may think of a newspaper stand to remind you of freedom of speech or of the press, or protestors with signs to remember the right to assemble or petition. Place these images within your memory map, such as at the front door (so that you have to walk around the protestors to get in the door).

Be creative and make the images meaningful to you. If you really want to stretch your critical thinking skills, add images for Amendments 5 through 10:

5: Rights concerning prosecution in criminal cases

6: Right to a speedy and fair trial

7: Right to a trial by jury

8: Bail, fines, and punishment

9: Rights retained by the People

10: States' rights

various steps involved in driving. At first, they may seem overwhelming. You may have to stop and think through each step. After you have driven a car for awhile, however, you don't even think about all the steps required to start it and back out of the driveway. You check your mirror automatically before changing lanes, and driving safely has become a habit. Through repetition, you put information into your long-term memory. The more often you use the information, the easier it is to recall. You could not become a good musician without hours of practice. Playing sports, speaking in public, flying an airplane, and learning to drive all require skills that need to be repeated and practiced many times. Repetition puts information into long-term memory and allows for recall.

These strategies are very effective in strengthening your memory skills. Certain strategies might work better for you than others, depending on your personality and learning styles. Everyone has personal strengths and abilities. You can master the use of memory strategies with effort, patience, and practice. As you build your memory skills, you will also enhance your study habits and become more disciplined and aware of your surroundings.

Definitely a "people person," Aleah just began her nursing program and can't wait to start working with real patients. She enjoys the hands-on lab section of her anatomy and physiology course but worries she'll never master all the basic terminology—the skeletal system, the muscle groups, the endocrine system, and on and on.

- Which mnemonic devices might be helpful in remembering human anatomy?
- How could Aleah use visualization techniques to help her recall information?
- What is Aleah's preferred learning style, and how can she use it to improve her recall? How can she use other styles to complement her learning?

THINK *FAST*

Summarize, Review, and Reflect

Summarize a lecture or a section or chapter of a book in your own words as soon as possible after hearing or reading it. The sooner and more often you review

Peak Progress

7.3

Remembering Names

Techniques that help you remember names can also be used to remember material in class, such as key people and events.

1. Imagine the name. Visualize the name clearly in your mind: Tom Plum. Clarify how the name is spelled: P-l-u-m.

2. Be observant and concentrate. Pay attention to the person's features and mannerisms.

3. Use exaggeration. Caricaturing the features is a fun and effective way to remember names. Single out and amplify one outstanding feature. For example, if Tom has red hair, exaggerate it to bright red and see the hair much fuller and longer than it is.

4. Visualize the red hair and the name Tom. See this vision clearly.

5. Repeat Tom's name to yourself several times as you are talking to him.

6. Recite Tom's name aloud during your conversation. Introduce Tom to others.

7. Use association. Associate the name with something you know ("Tom is the name of my cat") or make up a story using the person's name and add action and color. Tom is picking red plums that match his hair.

8. As soon as you can, jot down the name. Use a key word, or write or draw a description.

9. Use rhyming to help you recall: "Tom is not glum, nor is he dumb."

10. Integrate learning styles. It may help if you see the name (visual), hear it pronounced (auditory), or practice saying it and writing it several times and connecting the name with something familiar (kinesthetic).

11. Ask people their names. Do this if you forget or say your name first. "Hi, I'm Sam and I met you last week." If they don't offer their names, ask.

information, the easier it is to recall. Ideally, your first review should be within the first hour after hearing a lecture or reading an assignment. Carry note cards with you and review them again during the first day. As discussed in Chapter 5, memory researchers suggest that, after only 48 hours, you may have forgotten 70 percent of what you have learned. However, if you review right after you hear it and again within 24 hours, your recall soars to 90 percent.

Go beyond studying for tests. Be able to connect and apply information to new situations. Uncover facts, interesting points, related materials, details, and fascinating aspects of the subject. Ask your instructor for interesting stories to enhance a point. If you have time, read a novel on the subject or look in the library for another textbook that explains the subject from a different view. You will remember information more easily if you take time to understand and apply it.

Overcome Obstacles

A barrier to memory is disinterest. You have to want to remember. People often say, "If only I could remember names," or "I wish I had a better memory." Avoid using words such as *try, wish,* and *hope.* Overcome the barrier of disinterest by creating a positive, curious attitude; intending to remember; using all your senses; and using memory techniques. Related to disinterest is lack of attentiveness. You must be willing to concentrate by being an attentive listener and observe. Listen for overall understanding and for details. A short period of intense concentration will help you remember more than reading for hours.

Practice becoming more observant and aware. Suppose you want to learn the students' names in all your classes. Look at each student as the instructor takes roll, copy down each name, and say each name mentally as you look around the classroom. As you go about your day, practice becoming aware of your surroundings, people, and new information.

Finally, relax. Anxiety and stress can make you forget. For example, let's return to remembering names. Suppose you see Tom when you are with a good friend. You may be so anxious to make a good impression that Tom's name is lost for a moment. Relax by being totally in the moment instead of worrying about forgetting, how you look, what others may think, or your nervousness. Take a deep breath. If you still can't remember, laugh and say, "Hi, my mind just went blank. I'm Jay; please refresh my memory."

To keep your memory skills sharp, review and assess your answers to the following questions periodically. Can you answer yes to them?

- Do I want to remember?
- Do I have a positive attitude about the information?
- Have I eliminated distractions?
- Have I organized and grouped material?
- Have I reviewed the information often?
- Have I reviewed right after the lecture? Within 24 hours?
- Have I set up weekly reviews?

- Have I visualized what I want to remember?
- Have I used repetition?
- Have I summarized material in my own words?
- Have I used association and compared and contrasted new material with what I know?
- Have I used memory techniques to help me associate key words?

TAKING CHARGE

Summary

In this chapter, I learned to

- **Apply the five-step memory process.** Similar to the Adult Learning Cycle, the memory process consists of five steps: intention, attention, association, retention, and recall.

- **Intend to remember.** People who have better memories *want* to remember and make it a priority. It's important for me to increase my memory skills, and I take responsibility for my attitude and intention. I create personal interest and meaning in what I want to remember.

- **Be observant and alert.** I observe and am attentive to details. I am relaxed, focused, and receptive to new information. I reduce distractions, concentrate, and stay focused and mindful of the present. I look at the big picture, and then I look at details. Memory is increased when I pay attention.

- **Organize and associate information.** Organization makes sense out of information. I look for patterns and connections. I look for what I already know and jot down questions for areas that I don't know. I group similarities and look for what is different.

- **Retain information.** I write summaries in my own words and say them out loud. I jot down main points, key words, and important information on note cards and review them often. I study in short sessions and review often.

- **Recall.** I recall everything I know about the subject. I increase my recall by writing down information, reciting out loud, and teaching others. Practicing and reviewing information often are key to increasing recall. I reward myself for concentration, discipline, and effort.

- **Write it down.** The simple act of writing helps me create a mental picture.

- **Go from the general to the specific.** I first look at the big picture for gaining general, overall understanding and meaning. I then focus on the details and specific supporting information.

- **Reduce information and eliminate distractions.** Some information (such as e-mail addresses and phone numbers) does not have to be memorized; I just need to know where to find it easily. I also need to eliminate distractions that affect my ability to concentrate on what I'm trying to learn and remember.

- **Take frequent breaks.** I study in 40- to 60-minute sessions, since I know that the brain retains information best in short study periods. I take breaks to keep up my motivation.

- **Use my senses and integrate learning styles.** I draw pictures and illustrations, use color, record lectures, play music, write out summaries, jot down questions, collect samples, give summaries to my study group, and recite out loud.

- **Try mnemonic devices.** I use various techniques, such as rhymes and rhythms, acronyms, acrostics, grouping, association, and the method-of-place technique to help me memorize and recall information.

- **Use note cards.** Using note cards is an easy and convenient way for me to review important facts, terms, and questions.

- **Find connections and recite.** I link new information with familiar material, and I summarize what I have learned, either out loud or in writing.

- **Practice!** If I want to understand and remember information, I must practice and review it again and again.

Performance Strategies

Following are the top 10 strategies for improving memory:

- Intend to remember and prepare yourself mentally.
- Be observant, be alert, and pay attention.
- Organize information to make it meaningful.
- Look for associations and connections.
- Write down information.
- Integrate learning styles.
- Study in short sessions.
- Use mnemonic devices.
- Summarize information in your own words.
- Practice, use repetition, and relax.

Tech for Success

Take advantage of the text's Web site at **www.mhhe.com/ferrett8e** for additional study aids, useful forms, and convenient and applicable resources.

- **Acrostics online.** Many disciplines (especially in the sciences) have well-known acrostics that students and professionals use to remember key information (such as human anatomy). There are a number of online sites you can access for free that have collected hundreds of useful acrostics.
- **Stored memory.** Your computer is one big memory tool, storing thousands of hours of your work and contact information. For example, if you use the "Favorites" feature in your Web browser to catalog Web sites, consider how long it would take for you to reconstruct this information if it were suddenly wiped out. Do you have back-up plans in case your hard drive becomes inaccessible, or if you lose your cell phone containing countless stored numbers? Use these many tools and features to help you organize and save time, but don't forget to write down or keep hard copies of very important documents and contact information.

Study Team Notes

Marla Bergstrom
JOURNALIST

Related Majors: Journalism, English, Social Studies

Integrating Learning Styles

As a journalist, Marla Bergstrom's job is to find newsworthy local issues, collect accurate information from both sides of the story, and write an article that treats the subject fairly. As a general assignment reporter for a large newspaper, she covers stories on politics, crime, education, business, and consumer affairs.

Marla works closely with her editor when selecting a topic for an article. She often investigates leads for a story, only to realize later that she does not have enough information to make a strong story. She organizes the information she gathers, not knowing how or if it will fit into the article. Marla usually works on more than one story at a time, as some stories take weeks of research. Her hours are irregular. Marla might attend an early morning political breakfast and attend a school board meeting that evening.

Each week, Marla interviews a wide variety of people, including the mayor, the police chief, the school supervisor, and other community leaders. She always says hello to people, using their names. She prides herself on being able to remember names after only one meeting. When conducting an interview, the first thing Marla does is write down the name of the person, asking for the correct spelling. By doing this, she not only checks spelling but also sees the name in print. Because Marla is a visual learner, this helps her remember it. On the way home from an interview, Marla orally reviews the names of the people she has met. After an interview, Marla types her notes and memorizes pertinent information, such as the names of people, businesses, and locations. Marla knows that having good memory skills is essential for being a capable journalist.

CRITICAL THINKING Which learning styles help Marla remember pertinent information?

Peak Performer

PROFILE

David Diaz

In first grade, David Diaz knew he wanted to be a "drawer." However, he had no idea what that meant. He knew he liked to draw. It wasn't until high school that an instructor and a sculptor became instrumental in his selection of art as his career path. The art teacher encouraged him to enter art competitions; the sculptor, Duane Hanson, demonstrated by example the life of an artist.

Diaz attended the Fort Lauderdale Art Institute before moving across the country to California to start his prolific career in graphic design and illustration. For more than 25 years, he has been illustrating for national publications, book publishers, and corporations.

Success came early in his picture-book career when he was awarded the prestigious Caldecott Medal for illustrating Eve Bunting's *Smokey Nights,* a story about a boy's point of view of the Los Angeles riots in 1992. Critics and readers continue to appreciate the honest, vibrant, painterly quality of his work.

"I'm always thinking about how to make [the book] more of an experience, not just something you read," he said. His dynamic work comes through numerous revisions of looks and feels of the characters in the stories. He keeps working over an image to get it just right.

After all this time and success, Diaz still goes back to his roots: the foundations of drawing. "All the technique in the world can't save a bad drawing. As an artist, the challenge for me is to retain the spontaneity of an initial sketch or thumbnail drawing through the creation of the final image." Here is an artist, following his instinct, education, and passion through each phase of his career.

PERFORMANCE THINKING A career in the arts is often about paying careful attention to the world around you. Unique observations and an execution of talent are two keys to garnering attention for artistic merits. How might an artist find an activity like the Memory Map on page 229 helpful to his or her work? Why might memory be important to creating a piece of artwork?

CHECK IT OUT The largest library in the world, the Library of Congress, houses more than 130 million items and 530 miles of bookshelves. Visit the Web site **www.loc.gov** to search for various print, media, and online resources. Also available on the Web site is a section called "American Memory," which showcases historical information and resources on a number of topics, such as environment/conservation, immigration/American expansion, African American history, and women's history.

Starting Today

At least one strategy I learned in this chapter that I plan to try right away is

_____

_____

_____

What changes must I make in order for this strategy to be most effective?

_____

_____

Review Questions

Based on what you have learned in this chapter, write your answers to the following questions:

1. What are the five main steps of the memory process?

_____

_____

2. Why is intending to remember so important to enhancing memory?

_____

_____

3. Why does writing down information help you remember it?

_____

_____

4. Name one mnemonic device and how it is used to help you remember. Give an example.

_____

_____

5. What is the purpose of reviewing information soon and often?

_____

_____

To test your understanding of the chapter's concepts, complete the chapter quiz at **www.mhhe.com/ferrett8e**.

Overcoming Memory Loss

In the Classroom

Erin McAdams is outgoing, bright, and popular, but she also has a reputation for being forgetful. She forgets appointments, projects, and due dates. She repeatedly loses her keys and important papers. She is often late and forgets meetings and even social events. She always tells herself, "I'm just not good at remembering names," and "I really am going to try harder to get more organized and remember my commitments." She blames her bad memory for doing poorly on tests and wishes that people would understand she's doing her best. She insists that she's tried but just can't change.

1. What would you suggest to help Erin improve her memory skills?

_____

_____

2. What strategies in this chapter would be most helpful?

_____

_____

In the Workplace

Erin is now in hotel management. She loves the excitement, the diversity of the people she meets, and the daily challenges. She has recently been assigned to plan and coordinate special events, which include parties, meetings, and social affairs. This new job requires remembering many names, dates, and endless details.

3. How can Erin learn to develop her memory skills?

_____

_____

4. Suggest a program for her that would increase her memory skills.

_____

_____

Applying the ABC Method of Self-Management

In the Journal Entry on page 217, you were asked to describe a situation when you needed to learn many new names or numerous facts for a test. How did you fare? What factors helped you remember?

_____

_____

_____

_____

Now describe a situation in which you forgot some important information or someone's name that you really wanted to remember. Work through the ABC Method and incorporate the new strategies you have learned in this chapter.

A = Actual event:

_____

_____

_____

B = Beliefs:

_____

_____

_____

C = Challenge:

_____

_____

_____

Relax, take a deep breath, and visualize yourself recalling facts, key words, dates, and information easily.

PRACTICE SELF-MANAGEMENT

For more examples of learning how to manage difficult situations, see the "Self-Management Workbook" section of the Online Learning Center Web site at **www.mhhe.com/ferrett8e.**

Memory

A. Quickly read these lists once. Read one word at a time and in order.

1	2
the	Disney World
work	light
of	time
and	and
to	of
the	house
and	the
of	packages
light	good
of	praise
care	and
the	coffee
chair	the
and	of

B. Now cover the lists and write as many words as you can remember on the lines that follow. Then check your list against the lists in Part A.

_____   praise
work   light
care   chair
chair   disney world
light   the
the   packages
care   coffee

(continued)

1. How many words did you remember from the beginning of each list? List them.

_____

_____

2. How many words did you remember from the middle of each list? List them.

_____

_____

3. How many words did you remember from the end of each list? List them.

_____

_____

4. Did you remember the term *Disney World?*   Yes _____   No _____

Most people who complete this exercise remember the first few words, the last few words, the unusual term *Disney World,* and the words that were listed more than once (*of, the,* and *and*). Did you find this to be true about yourself?   Yes _____   No _____

C. Remembering names

1. Do you have problems remembering names?   Yes _____   No _____
2. What are the benefits of remembering names now and in a career?

_____

_____

_____

D. Which memory techniques work best for you and why?

_____

_____

_____

_____

_____

_____

_____

_____

Mental Pictures

Use various techniques to recall the following information:

In World War II, the major Axis powers were Germany, Italy, and Japan. The Allied powers were led by Great Britain, the Union of Soviet Socialist Republics (USSR), and the United States of America.

1. Think of mental images that would help you remember each of the following during an exam:

Axis Powers

Germany _____

_____

Italy _____

_____

Japan _____

_____

Allied Powers

Great Britain _____

_____

USSR _____

_____

USA _____

_____

2. Create a memory map using the method-of-place technique. Either place the mental images above in the map or create new images that may work better using this technique.

3. Now create an acrostic or acronym to remember each grouping (all three Axis powers and all three Allied powers). Refer to page 225 to refresh your memory on these mnemonic devices.
   - Axis powers: _____
   - Allied powers: _____

Applying Memory Skills

Assess your memory skills by answering the following questions. Add this page to your Career Development Portfolio.

1. **Looking back:** Review an autobiography you may have written for this or another course. Indicate the ways you applied your memory skills.

   I remember things about myself, look back at what is important

2. **Taking stock:** What are your memory strengths and what do you want to improve?

   I have a great long term memory, but my short term memory is something I need to work on

3. **Looking forward:** How would you demonstrate memory skills for employers?

   I show them how to help memory while reviewing information

4. **Documentation:** Include examples, such as poems you have memorized, literary quotes, and techniques for remembering names.

   I have memorized different things for classes, acronyms help! I remember names by remembering something about them and connecting that to it

5. **Assessment and demonstration:** Critical thinking skills for memory include the following. When have you demonstrated these?

   - Preparing yourself mentally and physically
   - Creating a willingness to remember
   - Determining what information is important and organizing it
   - Linking new material with known information (creating associations)
   - Integrating various learning styles
   - Asking questions
   - Reviewing and practicing

   I have done all of these in class preparing for tests

8

Excel at Taking Tests

LEARNING OUTCOMES

In this chapter, you will learn to

8.1 Prepare for tests

8.2 Describe strategies for taking tests

8.3 Use test results

8.4 Take different types of tests

8.5 Use special tips for math and science tests

8.6 Overcome test anxiety

SELF-MANAGEMENT

" I studied very hard for my last test, but my mind went blank when I tried to answer the questions. How can I reduce my anxiety and be more confident about taking tests? "

Have you ever felt anxious and worried when taking tests? Do you suffer physical symptoms, such as sweaty palms, an upset stomach, headaches, or an inability to sleep or concentrate? Everyone experiences some anxiety when faced with a situation involving performance or evaluation. Peak performers know that the best strategy for alleviating feelings of panic is to be prepared. In this chapter, you will learn ways to decrease your anxiety and test-taking strategies that will help you before, during, and after tests.

JOURNAL ENTRY In **Worksheet 8.1** on page 270, describe a time when you did well in a performance, sporting event, or test. What factors helped you be calm, feel confident, and remember information?

Successful athletes and performers know how important it is to monitor their techniques and vary their training programs to improve results. Taking tests is part of school; performance reviews are part of a job; and tryouts and performing are part of being an athlete, a dancer, or an actor. In fact, just about any job involves some assessment of skills, attitudes, and behavior. Many fields also require you to pass rigorous exams before you complete your education (such as the LSAT for law) and certification exams (as in athletic training). In this chapter, we explore specific test-taking strategies that will help you both in school and your career.

Test-Taking Strategies

Before the Test

Test taking starts long before sitting down with pencil in hand (or in front of a computer) to tackle an exam. The following tips will help you prepare for taking a test.

1. **Start on day one.** The best way to do well on tests is to begin preparing on the first day of class. Set up a review schedule on the first day and attend all classes, arrive on time, stay until the end of class, and create a positive frame of mind about succeeding.

2. **Know expectations.** On the first day of class, most instructors outline the course and clarify the syllabus and expectations concerning grading, test dates, and types of tests. During class or office hours, ask your instructors about test formats, sample questions, a study guide, or additional material that may be helpful. Also ask how much weight the textbook has on tests. Some instructors cover key material in class and assign reading for a broad overview. Observe your instructors to see what they consider important and what points and key words they stress. As you listen to lectures or read your textbook, ask yourself what questions might be on the examination. A large part of fear and anxiety comes from the unknown, so, the more you know about what is expected, the more at ease you will be. **Personal Evaluation Notebook 8.1** gives you a handy guide for approaching your instructors about upcoming tests. (**Worksheet 8.3** on page 272 also provides a detailed guide for tracking test information.)

3. **Ask questions in class.** If you are unclear about a point, raise your hand and ask for clarification. Or ask your instructor or another student at the end of class. Don't assume all of the lecture will be covered in the textbook.

4. **Keep up.** Manage your time and keep up with daily reading and assignments. (Use your time-management strategies from Chapter 3.) Avoid waiting until the night before to prepare for an exam. (**Worksheet 8.2** on page 271 is a handy form for keeping track of your exams.)

Test-Taking Skills

1. Preparing yourself both mentally and physically
2. Determining what information is important
3. Processing information
4. Linking new material with known information
5. Creating associations
6. Creating a willingness to remember
7. Staying focused
8. Reasoning logically
9. Overcoming fear
10. Evaluating test results

Personal Evaluation Notebook

Test Taking

Your instructor will often give clues in class as to what will be covered on tests. Watch for

- Information that is repeated or emphasized
- Illustrations on the board, slide presentations, or handouts
- Intensified voice or hand gestures and eye contact
- Examples and pauses for students to take notes
- Points covered while introducing or summarizing a topic

1. With classmates or study team members, use the list of clues as a guide to create a list of topics you think might be covered on the next exam.

   _____

   _____

   _____

2. As a team, approach your instructor to see if your list is on target. Ask your instructor what kinds of questions to expect on the test. Write that information on the following lines. (See pages 253–254 for types of test questions.)

   _____

   _____

   _____

5. **Review immediately.** Start the review process by quickly previewing chapters before classes and taking a few minutes to review your notes right after class. When information is fresh, you can fill in missing pieces, make connections, and raise questions to ask later. Refer to your review schedule and make sure you have time to review notes from all your classes each day. Review time can be short; 5 or 10 minutes for every class is often enough. When reviewing each day, scan reading notes and items that need memorization. This kind of review should continue until the final exam.

6. **Review weekly.** Spend about an hour per subject to investigate and review not only the week's assignments but also what has been included thus far in the course. These review sessions can include class notes, reading notes, chapter questions, note cards, mind maps, flash cards, a checklist of items to study, and summaries written in your own words. To test your understanding, close your book after reading and write a summary; then go back and fill in missing material.

7. **Do a final review.** A week or so before a test, commit to a major review. (Some instructors recommend allocating at least 2 hours per day for 3 days before the exam.) This review should include class and book notes, note cards, and

summaries. You can practice test questions, compare concepts, integrate major points, and review and recite with your study team. Long-term memory depends on organizing the information. Fragmented information is hard to remember or recall. When you understand the main ideas and connect and relate information, you transfer the material into long-term memory.

8. **Use memory techniques.** Determine which memory techniques will help you recall information, especially if you need to remember key dates, names, or lists. (Refer to Chapter 7 for descriptions of effective memory techniques.)

9. **Create sample tests.** Pretest yourself by predicting questions and creating and taking sample tests. Chapter objectives, key concepts, summaries, and end-of-chapter questions and exercises provide examples of possible test questions. Also, many textbooks have accompanying CDs or Web sites that include sample test questions (as you will find at **www.mhhe.com/ferrett8e**). Review and rehearse until you have learned the material and feel confident. Save all quizzes, course materials, exercise sheets, and lab work. Ask if old tests or sample tests are available at the library.

10. **Summarize.** Pretend the instructor allows you to take one note card to the test. Choose the most important concepts, formulas, key words, and points, and condense them onto one note card. Chances are, you will do better on the test even if you cannot use the note card during the test. A major reason students don't do well on tests is that they don't know the material. If you go beyond memorizing facts to summarize in your own words, you will understand the material.

11. **Use your study team.** You may be tempted to skip studying one night, but you can avoid temptation if you know other people are depending on your contribution. Have each member of the study team provide 5 to 10 potential test questions. Share these questions and discuss possible answers. Word the questions in different formats—multiple-choice, true/false, matching, and essay. Then simulate the test-taking experience by taking, giving, and correcting each other's timed sample tests.

12. **Use all available resources.** If your instructor offers a review before the exam, attend it, take good notes, and ask clarifying questions. Consider getting a tutor; check with the learning center, academic departments, or student services. A tutor will expect you to attend all classes, keep up with reading and homework assignments, and be motivated to learn. Your tutor will not do your work for you but will review assignment expectations, explain concepts, help you summarize and understand terms and definitions, and help you study for tests.

13. **Assemble what you will need.** Pack sharpened pencils, pens, paper clips, and any other items you may need, such as a watch, calculator, or dictionary. Get a good night's sleep, eat a light breakfast, and make sure you set an alarm. You don't want to be frantic and late for a test. Arrive a few minutes early.

During the Test

The following strategies will help you take a test. See **Peak Progress 8.1** for specific tips on taking online exams.

1. **Read and listen to all instructions.** Many mistakes result from a failure to follow directions correctly. For example, your instructor may require that you use a pen and write on only one side of the paper. Make sure you understand what is expected in each section of the test. If you are unsure, ask your instructor immediately. (See **Figure 8.1** on page 250 on how to take a Scantron test.)

2. **Write down key information.** As soon as you get the test, write your name on it and jot down key words, facts, formulas, dates, ideas, concepts, statistics, and other memory cues in pencil on the back of your paper or in the margins. If you wait until you are reading each question, you may forget important material while under pressure.

3. **Scan the entire test.** Before you start answering questions, you need to
   - Look at the point value for each question and determine the importance of each section. For example, you will want to spend more time on an essay worth 25 points than on a multiple-choice section worth 5.

Take 3 minutes to create sample test questions for one of your courses:
- Which events, people, or ideas did the instructor stress?
- Was some material covered in the text but not in lectures (or vice versa)?
- What main points could be addressed in essay questions?

What else can you do in 3 minutes?
- Summarize the course thus far onto one note card.
- Ask your instructor what types of questions to expect on the next exam.
- Find out where the learning center is and what kinds of resources it offers.

Peak Progress

8.1

Taking Online Exams

Although the preparation may be similar, taking an online exam may involve more coordination than a traditional pencil-and-paper exam.

- Double-check your computer's settings before you start the test, so that you avoid problems.
- Unless the test must be taken at a certain time or specific date, do not wait until the last day to take it. If you have technical difficulties or lose your connection, you may not have time to solve the problem.
- Shut down all other programs not needed during the exam, including e-mail.
- If your test is timed, make sure you can easily see the timer or the computer's clock.
- If allowed, have your text and any other materials nearby and easily accessible. Put key information, dates, or formulas on sticky notes next to the screen.

- Wait until the test is fully loaded before answering questions.
- Set the window size before you start. Resizing later may refresh your screen and cause the test to reload and start over.
- To avoid being accidentally kicked out of the exam, do not click outside the test area or click the back arrow. Only use functions within the testing program to return to previous questions.
- If there is a save option, save often throughout the exam.
- If more than one question is on a page, click "Submit" or the arrow button only after all questions on that page have been answered.
- Click "Submit" only once at the end of the test, and confirm that the test was received.

Figure 8.1
Fill in the Bubbles

You have probably taken a number of Scantron tests (named after the company that distributes them), or "bubble" tests. Using a #2 pencil, you must completely fill in the circles. Fill in only one bubble per line, and completely erase any changes. Be careful not to skip a line, or all the rest of your answers may be wrong. *Would all of the answers in this figure be acceptable?*

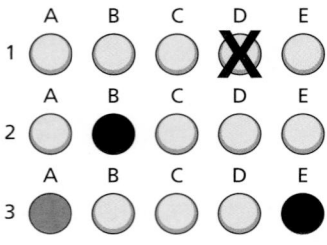

• See which questions are easiest and can be answered quickly.

• Underline or put a star by key names and themes that pop out. These may stimulate your memory for another question.

• Set a plan and pace yourself based on the amount of time allowed.

4. **Answer objective questions.** Sometimes objective questions contain details you can use for answering essay questions. Don't panic if you don't know an answer right away. Answer the easiest questions, and mark questions you want go back to later.

5. **Answer essay questions.** Answer the easiest subjective or essay questions first, and spend more time on the questions with the highest value. Underline or circle key words or points in the question. If you have time, do a quick outline in pencil, so that your answer is organized. Look for defining words, and make sure you understand what the question is asking. For example, are you being asked to justify, illustrate, compare and contrast, or explain? Write down main ideas and then fill in details, facts, and examples. Be complete, but avoid filler sentences that add nothing.

6. **Answer all remaining questions.** Unless there is a penalty for guessing, answer all questions. Rephrase questions you find difficult. It may help if you change the wording of a sentence. Draw a picture or a diagram, use a different equation, or make a mind map and write the topic and subtopics. Use association to remember items that are related.

7. **Review.** Once you have finished, reread the test carefully and check for mistakes or spelling errors. Stay the entire time, answer extra-credit and bonus questions, fill in details, and make any necessary changes. (See **Peak Progress 8.2** to learn specific strategies for math and science tests.)

After the Test

The test isn't over when you hand it in. Successful test taking includes how you use the results.

1. **Reward yourself.** Indulge yourself with a treat, such as a hot bath, a walk, an evening with friends, a special dinner—and definitely a good night's sleep.

2. **Analyze and assess.** When you receive the graded test, analyze the grade and your performance for many things, such as the following:

• *Confirm your grade.* Confirm that your score was calculated or graded correctly. If you believe there is a mistake in your grade, see your instructor immediately and ask to review it.

• *Determine common types of mistakes.* Were your mistakes due to carelessness in reading the instructions or lack of preparedness on certain topics? **Peak Progress 8.3** on page 252 identifies common reasons for incorrect answers on tests. Are there patterns in your mistakes? If so, determine how to correct those patterns.

• *Learn what to do differently next time.* Your test will provide valuable feedback, and you can learn from the experience. Be a detached, curious, receptive observer and view the results as feedback that is essential for

Peak Progress

Special Strategies for Math and Science Tests

During your years of study, you will probably take math and science courses. Following are some additional strategies for preparing to take a math or science test.

1. **Use note cards.** Write formulas, definitions, rules, and theories on note cards and review them often. Write out examples for each theorem.

2. **Write key information.** As soon as you are given the test, jot down theorems and formulas in the margins.

3. **Write the problem in longhand.** Translate into understandable words—for example, for $A = 1/2bh$, "For a triangle, the area is one-half the base times the height."

4. **Make an estimate.** A calculated guess will give you an approximate answer. This helps you when you double-check the answer.

5. **Illustrate the problem.** Draw a picture, diagram, or chart that will help you understand the problem—for example, "The length of a field is 6 feet more than twice its width. If the perimeter of the field is 228 feet, find the dimensions of the field."

Let l = the length of the field
Let w = the width of the field
Then $l = 2w + 6$

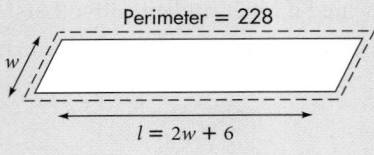

Perimeter = 228

$l = 2w + 6$

$w + 2w + 6 + w + 2w + 6 = 228$

So $6w + 12 = 228$
$(w + 2w + 6 + w + 2w + 6)$

$6w + 12 = 228$
$6w = 216$
$w = 36$
So $l = 2w + 6 = 2(36) + 6 = 78$
Translating: The width of the field is 36 ft. and its length is 78 ft.
Checking: The perimeter is $2w + 2l = 2(36) + 2(78) = 72 + 156 = 228$

6. **Ask yourself questions.** Ask, "What is being asked? What do I already know? What are the givens? What do I need to find out? How does this relate to other concepts? What is the point of the question?"

7. **Show your work.** If allowed, write down the method you used to get to the answer, which will help you retrace your steps if you get stuck. Your instructor may give you partial credit, even if the answer is incorrect. In some cases, you are expected to show your work (and will lose points for not showing complete or accurate work). Make sure you know what your instructor requires.

8. **Do a similar problem.** If you get stuck, try something similar. Which formula worked? How does this formula relate to others?

9. **State answers in the simplest terms.** For example, 4/6 instead should be answered as 2/3.

10. **Pay attention to the sign.** Note if a number is actually a negative number.

11. **Check your work.** Does your answer make sense? Is your work correct and systematic?

12. **Review.** Review your test as soon as you get it back. Where did you make mistakes? Did you read the problems correctly? Did you use the correct formulas? What will you do differently next time?

improvement. (See **Peak Progress 8.4** on page 252 for a checklist on how to assess your testing performance in order to improve your skills.)

3. **Review with your instructor.** If you honestly don't know why you received the grade you did, ask your instructor to review your answers with you. Approach the meeting with a positive attitude, not a defensive one. Ask for clarification and explain your rationale for answers. Ask for advice on preparing for the next test.

" 'Obvious' is the most dangerous word in mathematics. "

ERIC TEMPLE BELL
Mathematician, author

WORDS TO SUCCEED

Peak Progress

8.3

Checklist for Incorrect Test Answers

Following are some of the most common reasons for incorrect answers on tests. As you review your test results, see if you have recurring problems in any of the following areas.

- I did not read and/or follow the directions.
- I misread or misunderstood the question.
- I did not demonstrate reasoning ability.
- I did not demonstrate factual accuracy.
- I did not demonstrate good organization.
- My answer was incomplete.

- My answer lacked clarity.
- My handwriting was hard to read.
- I used time ineffectively.
- I did not prepare enough.
- I studied the wrong information.
- I knew the information but couldn't apply it to the questions.
- I confused facts or concepts.
- The information was not in my lecture notes.
- The information was not in the textbook.

Peak Progress

8.4

Using Test Results

Determine if your study strategy is working and what to do differently next time. Ask yourself the following questions:

1. Did I read the test before I started?
2. What were my strengths? What did I do right?
3. What questions did I miss?
4. Did I miss clues in the test? Did I ask the instructor for clarification?
5. How well did I know the content on which I was being tested?
6. What should I have studied more?
7. Did I anticipate the style and format of the questions?
8. What didn't I expect?
9. Did I have trouble with certain types of questions?
10. Did I test myself with the right questions?
11. Did I handle test anxiety well?
12. Would it have helped if I had studied with others?
13. What changes will I make in studying for the next test?

4. **Review the test with your study team.** This will help you see common errors and how others approached answering the questions, which will give you insights into how to study more effectively and answer questions better on the next test.

Remember, a test is feedback on how you are doing, not an evaluation of you as a person. You cannot change unless you understand your mistakes. Assess what you did wrong and what you will do right the next time.

Taking Different Types of Tests

The following tips will help you as you take different types of tests.

" We learn more by looking for the answer to a question and not finding it than we do from learning the answer itself. "

LLOYD ALEXANDER
Author

Objective Tests

TRUE/FALSE TESTS

1. **Read the entire question carefully before answering.** For the question to be true, the entire question must be true. If any part of the statement is false, the entire statement is false.

2. **Pay attention to details.** Read dates, names, and places carefully. Sometimes the numbers in the dates are changed around (1494 instead of 1449) or the wording is changed slightly. Any such changes can change the meaning.

3. **Watch for qualifiers.** Watch for such words as *always, all, never,* and *every.* The question is often false because there are exceptions. If you can think of one exception, then the statement is false. Ask yourself, "Does this statement overstate or understate what I know to be true?"

4. **Watch for faulty cause and effect.** Two true statements may be connected by a word that implies cause and effect, and this word may make the statement false—for example, "Temperature is measured on the centigrade scale *because* water freezes at zero degrees centigrade."

5. **Always answer every question.** Unless there is a penalty for wrong answers, answer every question. You have a 50 percent chance of being right.

6. **Trust your instincts.** Often, your first impression is correct. Don't change an answer unless you are certain it is wrong. Don't spend time pondering until you have finished the entire test and have time to spare.

MULTIPLE-CHOICE TESTS

1. **Read the question carefully.** Are you being asked for the correct answer or the best choice? Is there more than one answer? Preview the test to see if an answer is included in a statement or question.

2. **Rephrase the question.** Sometimes it helps to rephrase the question in your own words, which may trigger reading or hearing the initial discussion.

3. **Cover the potential answers.** Cover the answers (called "distractors") as you read the question and see what answer first comes to you. Then look at the answers to see if your answer is one of the choices.

4. **Eliminate choices.** Narrow your choices by reading all of them and eliminating those you know are incorrect, so that you can concentrate on real choices.

5. **Go from easy to difficult.** Go through the test and complete the questions for which you know the answers. Don't spend all your time on a few questions. With a pencil, mark the questions that you are unsure of, but make certain you mark your final answer clearly.

6. **Watch for combinations.** Read the question carefully; don't just choose what appears to be the one correct answer. Some questions offer a combination of choices, such as "all of the above" or "none of the above."

7. **Look at sentence structure.** Make sure the grammatical structure of the question matches that of your choice.

8. **Use critical thinking.** Make sure you have a good reason for changing an answer. If not, your first impulse may be right.

Sample True/False Question

You can't get skin cancer if your routine (work, hobbies, and vacations) doesn't include any outdoor activities.

_____ True
_____ False

Does this statement overstate what you know to be true?

Sample Multiple-Choice Question

Which of the following is an example of a government providing foreign aid?

A. Placing an embargo on foreign sugar

B. Signing a nuclear arms control treaty

C. Sending medical supplies to foreign doctors

D. Increasing immigration restrictions

What is the key word in the question that helps you determine the answer?

MATCHING TESTS

1. **Read carefully.** Read the question carefully before matching items, and make sure you understand what you are being asked to match.

2. **Eliminate.** Go through and match all the items you are absolutely sure of first. Cross out items as you match them unless the directions mention that an item can be used more than once.

3. **Look for clues.** Should the pair include a person's name, a date, or an event? Is chronological order important? Look for commonalities in sentence structure. Does it make sense?

FILL-IN-THE-BLANK TESTS

1. **Watch for grammatical clues.** If the word before the blank is *an,* the word in the blank generally begins with a vowel. If the word before the blank is *a,* it probably begins with a consonant.

2. **Count the number of blanks.** The number of blanks often indicates the number of words in an answer. Think of key words that were stressed in class.

3. **Watch for the length of the blank.** A longer blank may indicate a longer answer.

OPEN-BOOK TESTS

The key to an open-book test is to prepare. Students often think open-book tests will be easy, so they don't study. Generally, these tests go beyond basic recall and require critical thinking and analysis. Put markers in your book to indicate important areas. Write formulas, definitions, key words, sample questions, and main points on note cards. Bring along your detailed study sheet. You will need to find information quickly. However, use your own words to summarize—don't copy from your textbook.

Essay Tests

Being prepared is essential when taking an essay test. Make certain you understand concepts and relationships, not just specific facts. (See **Figure 8.2** for a sample essay test.) In addition, use the following strategies to help you take an essay test.

1. **Budget your writing time.** Look over the whole test, noticing which questions are easiest. Allot a certain amount of time for each essay question, and include time for review when you're finished.

2. **Read the question carefully.** Be sure you understand what the question is asking. Respond to key words, such as *explain, classify, define,* and *compare.* Rephrase the question into a main thesis. Always answer what is being asked directly—don't skirt around an issue. If you are asked to compare and contrast, do not describe, or your answer will be incorrect. **Peak Progress 8.5** on page 256 lists key words used in many essay questions.

3. **Create an outline.** Organize your main points in an outline, so that you won't leave out important information. An outline will provide a framework to help

Figure 8.2
Sample Essay Test

When answering an essay question, a detailed outline may also be required, as in this example. *In what situations would a mind map work better to develop your thoughts rather than a formal outline?*

Intro to Economics Quiz   March 16, 2011

Steve Hackett

QUESTION: Describe the general circumstances under which economists argue that government intervention in a market economy enhances efficiency.

THESIS STATEMENT: Well-functioning competitive markets are efficient resource allocators, but they can fail in certain circumstances. Government intervention can generate its own inefficiencies, so economists promote the forms of government intervention that enhance efficiency under conditions of market failure.

OUTLINE:

I.   Well-functioning competitive markets are efficient.
   A. Firms have an incentive to minimize costs and waste.
   B. Price approximates costs of production.
   C. Effort, quality, and successful innovation are rewarded.
   D. Shortages and surpluses are eliminated by price adjustment.

II. Markets fail to allocate scarce resources efficiently under some circumstances.
   A. Externalities affect other people.
      1. Negative externalities, such as pollution
      2. Positive externalities and collectively consumed goods
   B. Lack of adequate information causes failure.
   C. Firms with market power subvert the competition.

III. Government intervention can create its own inefficiencies.
   A. Rigid, bureaucratic rules can stifle innovative solutions and dilute incentives.
   B. Politically powerful groups can subvert the process.

IV. Efficient intervention policy balances market and government inefficiencies.

ESSAY RESPONSE:

Well-functioning competitive markets allocate resources efficiently in the context of scarcity. They do so in several ways. First, in market systems, firms are profit maximizers and thus have an incentive to minimize their private costs of production. In contrast, those who manage government agencies lack the profit motive and thus the financial incentive to minimize costs. Second, under competitive market conditions, the market price is bid down by rival firms to reflect their unit production costs. Thus, for the last unit sold, the value (price) to the consumer is equal to the cost to produce that unit, meaning that neither too much nor too little is produced. Third, firms and individuals have an incentive to work hard to produce new products and services preferred by consumers because, if successful, these innovators will gain an advantage over their rivals in the market-place. Fourth, competitive markets react to surpluses with lower prices and to shortages with higher prices, which work to resolve these imbalances.

Markets can fail to allocate scarce resources efficiently in several situations. First, profit-maximizing firms have an incentive to emit negative externalities (uncompensated harms generated by market activity that fall on others), such as pollution, when doing so lowers their production costs and is not prevented by law. Individual firms also have an incentive not to provide positive externalities (unpaid-for benefits) that benefit the group, such as police patrol, fire protection, public parks, and roads. A second source of market failure is incomplete information regarding product safety, quality, and workplace safety. A third type of market failure occurs when competition is subverted by a small number of firms that can manipulate prices, such as monopolies and cartels. Government intervention can take various forms, including regulatory constraints, information provision, and direct government provision of goods and services.

Government intervention may also be subject to inefficiencies. Examples include rigid regulations that stifle the incentive for innovation, onerous compliance costs imposed on firms, political subversion of the regulatory process by powerful interest groups, and lack of cost-minimizing incentives on the part of government agencies. Thus, efficient government intervention can be said to occur when markets fail in a substantial way and when the particular intervention policy generates inefficiencies that do not exceed those associated with the market failure.

Peak Progress

Important Words in Essay Questions

Analyze	Explain the key points, parts, or process and examine each part.	**Enumerate**	Present the items in a numbered list or an outline.
Apply	Show the concept or function in a specific context.	**Evaluate**	Carefully appraise the problem, citing authorities.
Compare	Show similarities between concepts, objects, or events.	**Explain**	Make an idea or a concept clear, or give a reason for an event.
Contrast	Show differences between concepts, objects, or events.	**Identify**	Label or explain.
		Illustrate	Clarify by presenting examples.
Critique	Present your view or evaluation and give supporting evidence.	**Interpret**	Explain the meaning of a concept or problem.
Define	Give concise, clear meanings and definitions.	**Justify**	Give reasons for conclusions or argue in support of a position.
Demonstrate	Show function (how something works); show understanding physically or through words.	**List**	Enumerate or write a list of points, one by one.
Describe	Present major characteristics or a detailed account.	**Outline**	Organize main points and supporting points logically.
Differentiate	Distinguish between two or more concepts or characteristics.	**Prove**	Give factual evidence and logical reasons something is true.
Discuss	Give a general presentation of the issue with examples or details to support main points.	**Summarize**	Present core ideas in a brief review that includes conclusions.

you remember dates, concepts, names, places, and supporting material. Use **Personal Evaluation Notebook 8.2** to practice outlining key words and topics.

4. **Focus on main points.** Your opening sentence should state your thesis, followed by supporting information.

5. **Write concisely and correctly.** Get directly to the point, and use short, clear sentences. Remember that your instructor (or even teaching assistants) may be grading a pile of tests, so get to the point and avoid filler sentences.

6. **Use key terms and phrases.** Your instructor may be looking for very specific information in your answer, including terms, phrases, events, or people. Make sure you include that information—don't just assume the instructor knows to whom or what you are referring.

7. **Answer completely.** Reread the question and be sure you answered it fully, including supporting documentation. Did you cover the main points thoroughly and logically?

8. **Write neatly.** Appearance and legibility matter. Use an erasable pen. Use wide margins and don't crowd your words. Write on one side of the paper only. Leave space between answers, so that you can add to an answer if time permits.

Personal Evaluation Notebook

Essay Test Preparation

Pretend you are taking an essay test on a personal topic—your life history. Your instructor has written the following essay question on the board:

Write a brief essay on your progress through life so far, covering the highs and lows, major triumphs, and challenges.

1. Before you begin writing, remind yourself of the topics you want to cover in this essay. List key words, phrases, events, and dates you would jot in the margin of your paper on the lines provided.

   _____

   _____

   _____

   _____

   _____

2. In the space below, create a mind map or an outline of the events or topics you would cover in your essay.

9. **Use all the available time.** Don't hurry. Pace yourself and use all the available time for review, revisions, reflection, additions, and corrections. Proofread carefully. Answer all questions unless otherwise directed.

Last-Minute Study Tips

Cramming is not effective if you haven't studied or attended classes. But the following activities will help you make the most of the last hours and minutes before a test.

Ashish failed his midterm. He thought he had studied enough before the test, but he quickly realized he should have paid more attention to the online readings. His mind went blank when he tried to formulate an answer to the essay question that was worth 50 percent of the total exam.

- What questions could he have asked his instructor before the test to clarify expectations?
- What could Ashish have done as he started the essay section to help him formulate his thoughts?
- How can he use the test results to improve for the final exam?

1. **Focus on a few points.** Instead of trying to cram everything into a short study session, decide what are the most important points or formulas, key words, definitions, and dates. Preview each chapter quickly; read the chapter objectives or key concepts and the end-of-chapter summary.

2. **Intend to be positive.** Don't panic or waste precious time being negative. State your intention of being receptive and open, gaining an overview of the material, and learning a few supporting points.

3. **Review your note cards.** The physical (and visual) act of reading and flipping note cards will help you review key information.

4. **Review your notes.** Look for words or topics you have highlighted or written on the side. Reread any summaries or mind maps you created after class.

5. **Affirm your memory.** The mind is capable of learning and memorizing material in a short time if you focus and apply it. Look for opportunities to connect information.

WORDS TO SUCCEED

"It's not whether you get knocked down, it's whether you get up."

VINCE LOMBARDI
Professional football coach

Overcome Obstacles

Some students see tests and performance assessments as huge mountains—one slip, and they tumble down the slope. Even capable students find that certain tests undermine their confidence. For example, even the thought of taking a math or science test causes anxiety in some people and sends others into a state of panic. A peak performer learns to manage anxiety and knows that being prepared is the road to test-taking success.

Test Anxiety

Test anxiety is a learned response to stress. The symptoms include nervousness, upset stomach, sweaty palms, and forgetfulness. Being prepared is the best way to reduce anxiety. As we discussed earlier in this chapter, you will be prepared if you have attended every class; previewed chapters; reviewed your notes; and written, summarized, and studied the material each day. Studying with others is a great way to rehearse test questions and learn through group interaction.

The attitude you bring to a test affects your performance. Approach tests with a positive attitude. Tests let you practice facing fear and transforming it into positive energy. Tests are chances to show what you have mastered. Following are more suggestions that might help:

1. **Dispute negative thoughts and conversations.** Some people have negative or faulty assumptions about their abilities, especially in courses such as math and science, and may think, "I just don't have a logical mind." Replace negative self-talk with affirmations, such as "I am well prepared and will do well on this test" or "I can excel in this subject." Talk to yourself in encouraging ways. Practice

being your own best friend! Also, avoid negative conversations that make you feel anxious—for example, if someone mentions how long he or she studied.

2. **Rehearse.** Athletes, actors, musicians, and dancers practice for hours. When they perform, their anxiety is channeled into focused energy. If you practice taking sample tests with your study team, you should be more confident during the actual test.

3. **Get regular exercise.** Aerobic exercise and yoga reduce stress and tension and promote deeper, more restful sleep. Build regular exercise into your life, and work out the day before a test, if possible.

4. **Eat breakfast.** Eat a light, balanced breakfast that includes protein, such as cheese or yogurt. Keep a piece of fruit or nuts and bottled water in your backpack for energy. Limit your caffeine intake; too much can make you more nervous or agitated.

5. **Visualize success.** See yourself taking the test and doing well. Imagine being calm and focused. Before getting out of bed, relax, breathe deeply, and visualize your day unfolding in a positive way.

6. **Stay calm.** Make your test day peaceful by laying out your clothes, books, supplies, pens, and keys the night before. Review your note cards just before you go to sleep, repeat a few affirmations, and get a good night's rest. Set an alarm, so that you'll be awake in plenty of time. Last-minute, frantic cramming creates a hectic climate and increases anxiety. To alleviate stress, practice relaxation techniques (see Chapter 11, page 355).

7. **Get to class early.** Get to class early enough that you are not rushed and can use the time before the test to take a few deep breaths and review your note cards. Deep breathing and affirmations, along with visualization, can help you relax. While waiting for the start of class, the instructor will sometimes answer questions or explain material to students who arrived early.

8. **Focus.** When your attention wanders, bring it gently back. Stay in the present moment by focusing on the task at hand. Concentrate on answering the questions, and you won't have room in your mind for worry.

9. **Keep a sense of perspective.** Don't exaggerate the importance of tests. Tests do not measure self-esteem, personal qualities, character, or ability to contribute to society. Even if the worst happens and you do poorly on one test, it is not the end of your college career. You can meet with the instructor to discuss options and possibly do extra work, retake the test, or retake the class, if necessary.

10. **Get help.** If you are experiencing severe anxiety that prevents you from taking tests or performing well, seek professional help from the learning center or see a counselor at your school. Services often include support groups, relaxation training, and other techniques for reducing anxiety. Taking tests and being evaluated are essential parts of school and work, so it's important to get your fears under control. (See **Peak Progress 8.6** on preparing for a performance appraisal.)

● **Keeping Calm**
Test anxiety can cause some people to feel overwhelmed and even panicked. *How can you reduce the feeling of anxiety before you take a test?*

Peak Progress

Preparing for a Performance Appraisal

If you are employed, at some time you will probably receive a performance appraisal. This can be a valuable tool for informing you about how your employer perceives the quality of your work, your work ethic, and your future opportunities. It also allows you to ask similar questions of your manager or reviewer. Often, employees are asked to evaluate their own performance, which is similar to answering an essay question. You want to address the question fully and provide supporting, factual evidence (and often suggest outcomes, such as new goals and challenges).

The following questions will help you focus on getting the most out of your performance appraisal.

- Review your job description, including the duties you perform. What is expected of you? What additional duties do you perform that are not listed?
- How do you view your job and the working climate?
- List your goals and objectives and the results achieved.
- What documentation demonstrates your results and achievements?
- What areas do you see as opportunities for improvement?

- What are your strengths, and how can you maximize them?
- What are your advancement possibilities?
- What additional training would be helpful for you?
- What new skills could assist in your advancement?
- How can you increase your problem-solving skills?
- How can you make more creative and sound decisions?
- What can you do to prepare yourself for stressful projects and deadlines?
- How have you specifically contributed to the company's profits?
- What relationships could you develop to help you achieve results?
- Do you work well with other people?
- What project would be rewarding and challenging this year?
- What resources do you need to complete this project?
- Do you have open and effective communication with your supervisor and co-workers?
- How does your assessment of your work compare with your supervisor's assessment?

Reflect and use critical thinking to describe your test anxiety experiences in **Personal Evaluation Notebook 8.3**. **Peak Progress 8.7** on page 263 explores how you can apply the Adult Learning Cycle to improve your test-taking skills and reduce anxiety.

Cheating

A central theme of this book is that character matters. Honesty during test taking demonstrates to your instructor, your classmates, and, most important, yourself that you are trustworthy—a person of integrity. Cheating includes

- Looking at someone's paper during a test
- Passing or texting answers back and forth
- Getting notes from someone who has just taken the same test
- Stealing tests from an office
- Using electronic devices (such as a calculator) when not allowed
- Taking or receiving pictures of test questions via cell phone
- Having someone else complete online work for you

Personal Evaluation Notebook

Test Anxiety

Read through each statement and reflect on past testing experiences. You may wish to consider all testing experiences or focus on particular subjects (history, math, science, etc.) one at a time. Indicate how often each statement describes you by choosing a number from 1 to 5.

Never	Rarely	Sometimes	Often	Always
1	2	3	4	5

___4___ I have visible signs of nervousness, such as sweaty palms and shaky hands, right before a test.

___4___ I have butterflies in my stomach before a test.

___3___ I feel nauseated before a test.

___4___ I read through the test and feel that I do not know any of the answers.

___3___ I panic before and during a test.

___3___ My mind goes blank during a test.

___3___ After I leave a testing situation, I remember the information that escaped my mind during the test.

___3___ I have trouble sleeping the night before a test.

___4___ I make mistakes on easy questions or put answers in the wrong places.

___5___ I have trouble choosing answers.

Add together your scores for each statement to find your total score. Totals will range from 10 to 50.

- **10–19 points:** You do not suffer from test anxiety. If your score was extremely low (close to 10), a little more anxiety may be healthy to keep you focused and get your blood flowing during exams.

- **20–35 points:** Although you exhibit some of the characteristics of test anxiety, the level of stress and tension you're experiencing is probably healthy.

- **Over 35 points:** You are experiencing an unhealthy level of test anxiety. Evaluate the reason(s) for the distress and determine strategies to help you handle the anxiety.

Source: From NIST. *Developing Textbook Thinking*, 5E. © 2002 Heinle/Arts & Sciences, a part of Cengage Learning, Inc. Reproduced by permission. www.cengage.com/permissions

1. In what classes do you most often experience the most anxiety? Why?

   _____

   _____

2. What physical symptoms do you most often experience? (Examples include headaches, nausea, extreme body temperature changes, excessive sweating, shortness of breath, light-headedness or fainting, rapid heartbeat, and dry mouth.)

   _____

   _____

(continued)

Personal Evaluation Notebook

Test Anxiety *(concluded)*

3. Which emotional symptoms do you most often experience? (Examples include excessive feelings of fear, disappointment, anger, depression, helplessness, or uncontrollable crying or laughing.)

_____

_____

4. Do you have different feelings about nonacademic tests, such as a driving test or a medical test, than academic tests, such as quizzes and exams? If so, why?

_____

_____

Even if you haven't fully prepared for an exam, there is no excuse for cheating. Cheating only hurts you because it

- **Violates your integrity.** You begin to see yourself as a person without integrity; if you compromise your integrity once, you're more likely to do it again.
- **Erodes confidence.** Cheating weighs on your conscience and sends you the message that you don't have what it takes to succeed. Your confidence and self-esteem suffer.

● **Cheating Only Hurts You**

There is never an excuse to cheat. *If this student is caught cheating, what are some of the repercussions he could face?*

- **Creates academic problems.** Advanced courses depend on knowledge from earlier courses, so cheating only creates future academic problems. You are paying a lot of money not to learn essential information.
- **Increases stress.** You have enough stress in your life without adding the intense pressure of worrying about being caught.
- **Brings high risks.** Possible consequences of cheating and plagiarism include failing the class, being suspended for the semester, and even being expelled from school permanently. Cheating can mess up your life. It is humiliating, stressful, and completely avoidable.

There is never a legitimate reason to cheat. Instead, be prepared, use the resources available to help you succeed, and practice the strategies offered in this book to become a peak performer.

Peak Progress

Applying the Adult Learning Cycle to Improving Your Test-Taking Skills and Reducing Test Anxiety

1. **RELATE. Why do I want to learn this?** I need to reduce my test anxiety and want to do better on tests. Knowing how to control anxiety will help me when taking tests and in other performance situations. Do I already apply specific test-taking strategies? What are some of my bad habits, such as last-minute cramming, which I should change?

2. **OBSERVE. How does this work?** Who does well on tests, and does that person seem confident when taking tests? What strategies can I learn from that person? Who does poorly on tests or seems full of anxiety? Can I determine what that person is doing wrong? I can learn from those mistakes. I'll try new strategies for test taking and observe how I'm improving.

3. **REFLECT. What does this mean?** What strategies are working for me? Have I broken any bad habits,

and am I more confident going into tests? Has my performance improved?

4. **DO. What can I do with this?** I will map out a plan before each major test, determining what I need to accomplish in order to be prepared and confident. I won't wait until the last minute to prepare. Each day, I can practice reducing my anxiety in many stressful situations.

5. **TEACH. Whom can I share this with?** I'll talk with others and share what's working for me. Talking through my effective strategies reinforces their purpose.

Now return to Stage 1 and think about how it feels to learn this valuable new skill. Remember to congratulate and reward yourself when you achieve positive results.

TAKING CHARGE

Summary

In this chapter, I learned to

- **Prepare for test taking.** The time before a test is critical. I must prepare early, starting on the first day of class. I keep up with the daily reading and ask questions in class and while I read. I review early and often, previewing the chapter before class and reviewing the materials after class. I save and review all tests, exercises, and notes and review them weekly. I rehearse by taking a pretest, and I predict questions by reviewing the text's chapter objectives and summaries. I summarize the chapter in my own words (in writing or out loud), double-checking that I've covered key points. I recite my summary to my study team and listen to theirs. We compare notes and test each other.

- **Take a test effectively.** Arriving early helps me be calm and focused on doing well. I get organized by reviewing key concepts and facts. I write neatly and get to the point with short, clear responses. I read all the instructions, scanning the entire test briefly and writing formulas and notes in the margins. I pace myself by answering the easiest questions first, and I rephrase difficult questions and look for associations to remember items. At the end, I review to make certain I've answered what was asked and check for mistakes or spelling errors. I stay the entire time that is available.

- **Follow up a test.** I should reward myself for successfully completing the test. Then I will analyze and assess how I did on the test. Did I prepare enough? Did I anticipate questions? What can I do differently for the next test? I'll use creative problem solving to explore ways to do better on future tests.

- **Be successful on different kinds of tests.** Objective tests include true/false, multiple-choice, matching, fill-in-the-blank, and open-book. I must read the question carefully, watch for clues, and look at sentence structure. Essay tests focus on my understanding of concepts and relationships. I outline my response, organize and focus on the main points, and take my time to deliver a thorough, neat, well-thought-out answer.

- **Use last-minute study tips.** I know it's not smart to wait until the last minute, but a few important things I can do include focusing on a few key points and key words, reviewing note cards, looking for connections to memorize, and not wasting time by panicking.

- **Overcome test anxiety.** A positive attitude alleviates anxiety before and during a test. I should prepare as much as possible, avoid last-minute cramming, practice taking a sample test, get to class early, stay calm, listen carefully to instructions, preview the whole test, and jot down notes.

- **Practice honesty and integrity when taking tests.** I know that cheating on exams hurts me by lowering my self-esteem and others' opinions of me. Cheating also has long-term repercussions, including possible expulsion from school. There is never an excuse for cheating.

Performance Strategies

Following are the top 10 strategies for successful test taking:

- Prepare early.
- Clarify expectations.
- Observe and question.
- Review.
- Apply memory techniques.
- Create sample tests.
- Use your study team.
- Answer easier questions first.
- Spend more time on questions worth the most points.
- Analyze your test results to learn how to improve.

Tech for Success

Take advantage of the text's Web site at **www.mhhe.com/ferrett8e** for additional study aids, useful forms, and convenient and applicable resources.

- **Online tutors.** Various organizations provide online tutors and live tutorial services. Your school or public library may also offer access to this kind of service. Often, these are paid services and may be worth the fee. However, you may be able to get limited assistance for free through a professional organization or related site.

Ask your librarian for advice and explain how much help you think you need and in what content areas.

- **Textbook accompaniments.** Many of your textbooks have accompanying Web sites that provide study materials, such as online study guides, animated flash cards, and possible essay questions. Often, this material is free when you purchase a new text. Take advantage of these resources to test your understanding of the information prior to taking the real test.

Study Team Notes

Answers to Questions on Pages 253 and 254
True/false: False
Multiple-choice: C
Matching: A/3; B/4; C/2; D/1; E/5
Fill-in-the-Blank: fair use

Career*in* focus

Carlos Fuentes
PHYSICAL THERAPIST

Related Majors: Physical Therapy, Biology

Tests in the Workplace

Carlos Fuentes is a physical therapist. A physical therapist works closely with physicians to help patients restore function and improve mobility after an injury or illness. Their work often relieves pain and prevents or limits physical disabilities.

When working with new patients, Carlos first asks questions and examines the patients' medical records, then performs tests to measure such items as strength, range of motion, balance and coordination, muscle performance, and motor function. After assessing a patient's abilities and needs, Carlos implements a treatment plan, which may include exercise, traction, massage, electrical stimulation, and hot packs or cold compresses. As treatment continues, Carlos documents the patient's progress and modifies the treatment plan.

Carlos is self-motivated and works independently. He has a strong interest in physiology and sports, and he enjoys working with people. He likes a job that keeps him active and on his feet. Carlos spends much of his day helping patients become mobile. He often demonstrates an exercise while teaching how to do it correctly. His job sometimes requires him to move heavy equipment or lift patients. Because Carlos is pursuing a master's degree in physical therapy, he works only 3 days a week.

Although his job does not require him to take tests, Carlos does undergo an annual performance appraisal with his supervisor. After 8 years of service, Carlos is familiar with the types of questions his supervisor might ask and keeps those in mind as he does his job throughout the year.

CRITICAL THINKING How might understanding test-taking skills help Carlos work more effectively with his patients? How would test-taking skills help him prepare more effectively for performance appraisals?

Peak Performer
PROFILE

Ellen Ochoa

When astronaut Ellen Ochoa was growing up in La Mesa, California, in the 1960s and early 1970s, it was an era of space exploration firsts: the first walk in space, the first man on the moon, the first space station. Even so, it would have been difficult for her to imagine that one day she would be the first Hispanic woman in space, since women were excluded from becoming astronauts.

By the time Ochoa entered graduate school in the 1980s, however, the sky was the limit. Having studied physics at San Diego State University, she attended Stanford and earned a master's of science degree and a doctorate in electrical engineering. In 1985, she and 2,000 other potential astronauts applied for admission to the National Aeronautics and Space Administration (NASA) space program. Five years later, Ochoa, 18 men, and 5 other women made the cut. The training program at the Johnson Space Center in Houston, Texas, is a rigorous mix of brain and brawn. Ochoa tackled subjects such as geology, oceanography, meteorology, astronomy, aerodynamics, and medicine. In 1991, Ochoa officially became an astronaut and was designated a mission specialist. On her first mission in 1993, Ochoa carried a pin that read "Science Is Women's Work."

From 1993 to 2002, Ochoa logged in four space shuttle missions. Her first and second missions focused on studying the sun and its impact on the earth's atmosphere. Her third mission involved the first docking of the shuttle *Discovery* on the International Space Station. Her latest flight experience was the first time crewmembers used the robotic arm to move during spacewalks.

Ochoa enjoys talking to young people about her experiences. Aware of her influence as a woman and a Hispanic, her message is that "education is what allows you to stand out"—and become a peak performer.

PERFORMANCE THINKING Ochoa had to excel in many difficult academic courses in order to realize her dream of becoming an astronaut. What are some important personal characteristics that helped her reach the top? What are some specific testing strategies she may have used to get through her coursework, as well as to prove she had the "right stuff"?

CHECK IT OUT Ochoa is among a number of space pioneers profiled by NASA at **www.nasa.gov**. This site includes a wealth of media downloads, news articles, and activities for young and old space adventurers. Also visit the "Careers@NASA" section, which describes the types of internships, cooperative programs, and positions available. According to fellow astronaut Sally Ride, the "most important steps" she followed to becoming an astronaut started with studying math and science in school.

Starting Today

At least one strategy I learned in this chapter that I plan to try right away is

_____

_____

_____

What changes must I make in order for this strategy to be most effective?

_____

_____

_____

Review Questions

Based on what you have learned in this chapter, write your answers to the following questions:

1. Describe five strategies for preparing for a test.

   _____

   _____

2. Why is it important to pace yourself while taking a test?

   _____

   _____

3. What should you do after taking a test?

   _____

   _____

4. Describe three strategies for taking math and science tests.

   _____

   _____

5. Describe three ways in which cheating hurts you.

   _____

   _____

To test your understanding of the chapter's concepts, complete the chapter quiz at **www.mhhe.com/ferrett8e.**

Coping with Anxiety

In the Classroom

Sharon Martin is a bright, hardworking student. She studies long hours, attends all her classes, and participates in class discussions. Sharon is very creative and especially enjoys her computer graphics course. When taking tests, however, she panics. She stays up late, cramming; tells herself she might fail; and gets headaches and stomach pains. Her mind goes blank when she takes the test, and she has trouble organizing her thoughts. Sharon could get much better grades and enjoy school more if she reduced her stress and applied some test-taking strategies.

1. What techniques from this chapter would be most useful to Sharon?

_____

_____

_____

2. What one habit could she adopt that would empower her to be more successful?

_____

_____

_____

In the Workplace

Sharon now works as a graphic designer for a large company. She likes having control over her work and is an excellent employee. She is dedicated, competent, and willing to learn new skills. Her job involves great pressure to meet deadlines, learn new techniques, and compete with other firms. She handles these responsibilities well unless she is being evaluated. Despite her proficiency, Sharon panics before performance appraisals. She feels pressure to perform perfectly and has trouble accepting criticism or even advice.

3. What strategies in this chapter would be most helpful to Sharon?

_____

_____

_____

4. What would you suggest she do to control her performance anxiety?

_____

_____

_____

Applying the ABC Method of Self-Management

In the Journal Entry on page 245, you were asked to describe a time when you did well in a performance, sporting event, or test. Write about that, and indicate the factors that helped you be calm, confident, and focused.

_____

_____

_____

_____

Now consider a situation in which your mind went blank or you suffered anxiety. Apply the ABC Method to visualize a result in which you are again calm, confident, and focused.

A = Actual event:

_____

_____

_____

B = Beliefs:

_____

_____

_____

C = Challenge:

_____

_____

_____

Practice deep breathing with your eyes closed for just 1 minute. See yourself calm, centered, and relaxed as you take a test or give a performance. See yourself recalling information easily. You feel confident because you have learned to control your anxiety. You are well prepared and know how to take tests.

PRACTICE SELF-MANAGEMENT

For more examples of learning how to manage difficult situations, see the "Self-Management Workbook" section of the Online Learning Center Web site at **www.mhhe.com/ferrett8e.**

Exam Schedule

Fill in the following chart to remind you of your exams as they occur throughout the semester or term.

Course	Date	Time	Room	Type of Exam
Student Success 101	November 7	2:15 p.m.	1012A	Essay

Preparing for Tests and Exams

Before you take a quiz, a test, or an exam, fill in this form to help you plan your study strategy. Certain items will be more applicable, depending on the type of test.

Course _____

Date of test _____ Test number (if any) _____

- Pretest(s)　　Date given _____　　Results _____
　　　　　　　　Date given _____　　Results _____
　　　　　　　　Date given _____　　Results _____
- Present grade in course_____
- Met with instructor　　Yes _____　No _____　Date(s) of meeting(s) _____
- Study team members　　Date(s) of meeting(s) _____

Name _____　　Phone number _____
Name _____　　Phone number _____
Name _____　　Phone number _____
Name _____　　Phone number _____

- Expected test format (circle; there can be more than one test format)

Essay　　True/false　　Multiple-choice　　Fill-in-the-blank

Other _____

- Importance (circle one)

Quiz　　Midterm　　Final exam　　Other

- Chapters covered in the test _____

Date for chapter review _____

- Chapter notes (use additional paper)

_____

_____

_____

- Date for review of chapter notes _____
- Note cards　　Yes _____　No _____　Date note cards reviewed _____
- List of key words

Word _____ Meaning _____
Word _____ Meaning _____
Word _____ Meaning _____
Word _____ Meaning _____

(continued)

- Possible essay questions
  1. Question _____
     Thesis statement _____
     Outline _____
        I. _____
          A. _____
          B. _____
          C. _____
          D. _____
        II. _____
          A. _____
          B. _____
          C. _____
          D. _____
     - Main points
       _____
       _____
     - Examples
       _____
       _____
  2. Question _____
     Thesis statement _____
     Outline _____
        I. _____
          A. _____
          B. _____
          C. _____
          D. _____
        II. _____
          A. _____
          B. _____
          C. _____
          D. _____
     - Main points
       _____
       _____
     - Examples
       _____
       _____

Assessing Your Skills and Competencies

The following are typical qualities and competencies that are included in many performance appraisals.

- Communication skills (writing, speaking, reading)
- Integrity
- Willingness to learn
- Decision-making skills

- Delegation
- Planning
- Organizational skills
- Positive attitude
- Ability to accept change

- Working with others
- Quality of work
- Quantity of work
- Personal growth and development
- Use of technology

On the following lines, describe how you currently demonstrate each of the listed skills and competencies to an employer. Consider how you can improve. Add this page to your Career Development Portfolio.

1. How do you demonstrate the listed skills?

_____

_____

_____

_____

_____

_____

_____

_____

_____

_____

2. How can you improve?

_____

_____

_____

_____

_____

_____

_____

_____

_____

_____

9

Express Yourself in Writing and Speech

LEARNING OUTCOMES

In this chapter, you will learn to

9.1 Explain the five-step writing process for developing effective papers and speeches

9.2 Research information through the library and online

9.3 Use strategies for giving effective presentations

9.4 Overcome speech anxiety

SELF-MANAGEMENT

> *I put off taking the required public speaking class because I hate getting up in front of people. My mind goes blank, I get butterflies, and my palms sweat. How can I decrease stage fright and be more confident about speaking in public?*

Have you ever had a similar experience? Do you feel anxious and worried when you have to make a presentation or give a speech? Do you suffer physical symptoms, such as sweaty palms, upset stomach, headaches, or an inability to sleep or concentrate, even days before the event? In this chapter, you will learn how to communicate effectively and develop public speaking skills.

JOURNAL ENTRY In **Worksheet 9.1** on page 302, describe a time when you did well on a speaking assignment or leading a discussion. What factors helped you remain calm and confident?

275

Famed sportswriter Red Smith once commented, "Writing is very easy. All you do is sit in front of a typewriter keyboard until little drops of blood appear on your forehead." For some people, few things in life cause as much anxiety as writing research papers and public speaking. Just the thought of speaking in front of a group can produce feelings of sheer terror. In fact, research indicates that public speaking is the greatest fear for most people, outranking even fear of death. For many students, writing not only produces feelings of doubt but also demands their focused attention, intense thinking, and detailed research. You can't avoid writing or speaking in school or at work, but you can learn strategies that will make them easier and more effective.

The Importance of Writing and Speaking

The ability to communicate clearly, both orally and in writing, is the most important skill you will ever acquire. Peter Drucker, noted management expert and author, remarked, "Colleges teach the one thing that is perhaps most valuable for the future employee to know. But very few students bother to learn it. This one basic skill is the ability to organize and express ideas in writing and speaking."

You may be asked to do research on new ideas, products, procedures, and programs and compile the results in a report. You will most likely write business letters and e-mails. You may give formal speeches before a large group, preside at meetings, or present ideas to a project team. You will be expected to present written and spoken ideas in a clear, concise, and organized manner. Writing papers and preparing speeches in school give you a chance to show initiative, use judgment, apply and interpret information, research resources, organize ideas, and polish your style. Public speaking skills also help you inform and persuade others. Good writers and speakers are not born, and there is no secret to their success. Like other skills, speaking and writing can be learned with practice and effort.

The Writing Process

This chapter will give you strategies for handling every step of the paper-writing and speech-giving process, from choosing a topic to turning in the paper or delivering the speech. Keep these five basic steps in mind as you develop your paper or speech: (1) prepare; (2) organize; (3) write; (4) edit; (5) review.

Prepare

Whether you are writing a paper or a speech, preparation includes several tasks:

1. **Set a schedule.** Estimate how long each step will take, and leave plenty of time for proofing. You may think that the bulk of your time will be spent writing your first draft (step 3). However, you should allot about half your time to Steps 1, 2 and 3 and the other half to Steps 4 and 5. To develop a schedule,

Term Paper for Criminal Justice 101, Due April 3	
Final Check. Make copy.	April 2
Edit, revise, and polish.	March 29 (Put away for one or two days)
Complete bibliography.	March 28
Revise.	March 26
Edit, review, revise.	March 24 (Confer with instructor)
Final draft completed.	March 22 (Proof and review with a good writer)
Complete second draft.	March 20
Add, delete, and rearrange information.	March 17
First draft completed.	March 15 (Share with writing group)
Write conclusion.	March 12
Continue research and flesh out main ideas.	February 16
Write introduction.	February 10
Organize and outline.	February 3
Gather information and compile bibliography and notes.	January 29
Narrow topic and write thesis statement.	January 23
Do preliminary reading.	January 20
Choose a topic.	January 16
Brainstorm ideas.	January 15
Clarify expectations and determine purpose.	January 14

Figure 9.1
Sample Schedule

This schedule for preparing a term paper starts where the paper is finished. *Why does this schedule begin at the due date of the term paper?*

consider working backward from the due date, allowing yourself ample time for each step. See **Figure 9.1** for an example.

2. **Choose a general topic.** Choose a topic that meets your instructor's requirements, interests you, and is narrow enough to handle in the time available. Talk with your instructor about any questions you have concerning expectations for the topic, length, format and style, purpose, and method of citation. Use the tips in **Peak Progress 9.1** on page 278 to help you come up with a topic.

3. **Determine your purpose.** Do you want your reader or listener to think, feel, or act differently or be called to action? Is your purpose to entertain, inform, explain, persuade, gain or maintain goodwill, gain respect and trust, or gather information?

4. **Do preliminary reading and research.** Gather general information by reviewing reference materials, such as articles or an encyclopedia. Check the list of related references at the end of reference books and reference book

Peak Progress

9.1

How to Generate Topic Ideas

- *Brainstorm.* Brainstorming is generating as many ideas as possible without evaluating their merit. You can brainstorm ideas alone, but the process works well in small groups. Your goal is to list as many creative ideas as you can in the allotted time without defending or judging ideas. Since ideas build on each other, the more ideas the better. Within 10 minutes, you can often generate a sizable list of potential topics.

- *Go to the library.* Look in the *Readers' Guide to Periodical Literature* for possible ideas. Look through newspapers, magazines, and new books.

- *Search online.* Do a number of key word searches to see what topics pop up.

- *Keep a file.* Collect articles, quotes, and a list of topics you find interesting. Listen to good speeches and collect stories or ideas from current newspapers that you could research and write about from a different perspective. Think of possible topics as you read, watch television and movies, and talk with friends. What topics are in the news? What are people talking about?

- *Complete a sentence.* Brainstorm endings to open-ended sentences such as these:

  The world would be better if _____

  Too many people _____

  In the future _____

  A major problem today is _____

  The best thing about _____

  What I enjoy most is _____

  I learned that _____

  It always makes me laugh when _____

  If I had unlimited funds, I would buy _____

  I get through a tough day by _____

- *Free write.* For one or more potential topics, start jotting down as many related items as you can as fast as you can. Include examples, descriptions, and key events. Sometimes the original topic leads to a better topic.

- *Mind map.* For a potential topic, sketch a mind map (described in Chapters 5 and 6). Include supporting points and examples.

articles. Your initial research is intended to give you an overview of the subject and key issues. Later, you will want to look at specific facts and data. You may want to develop a list of questions that can lead to new directions and additional research:

- What do I already know about the topic? What do I want to know?
- What questions do I want to explore? What interests me most?
- What is the point I want to research?

5. **Narrow your topic.** After you have finished your preliminary reading, you can focus on a specific topic. For example, instead of "health problems in America," narrow the subject to "cigarette smoking among teenage girls" or "should cigarette advertising be banned?"

6. **Write a thesis statement.** The thesis is the main point, or central idea, of a paper. In one sentence, your thesis should describe your topic and what you want to convey about it. A good thesis statement is unified and clear—for example, "Smoking among teenage girls is rising due to influences by peers and advertising that glamorizes smoking." Remember, you can always revise your thesis statement as you do more research.

7. **Take notes.** Jot down quotations and ideas that clarify your research topic. If you are using notecards, write one idea per card, so that you can organize

Copyright © 2012 The McGraw-Hill Companies

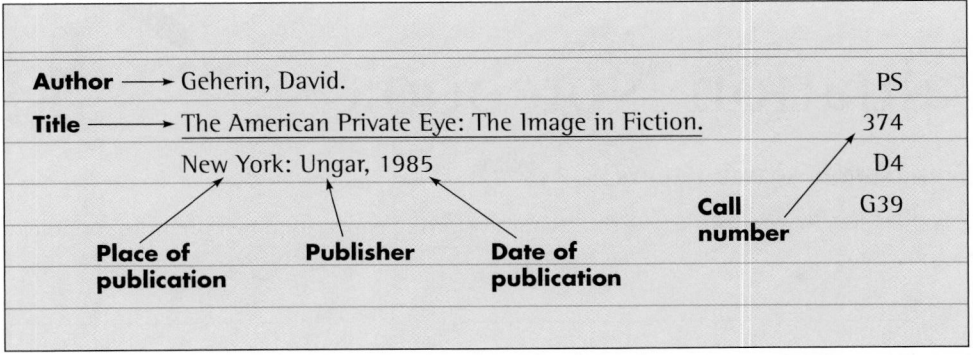

Author ──→	Geherin, David.	PS
Title ──→	The American Private Eye: The Image in Fiction.	374
	New York: Ungar, 1985	D4
		G39

Place of publication   **Publisher**   **Date of publication**   **Call number**

Source: "Bibliography card" from *MLA Handbook for Writers of Research Papers,* 4th edition, by Joseph Gibaldi. Reprinted by permission of The Modern Language Association, 1995.

Figure 9.2
Bibliography Card

As you research, write down reference information for each source, including each author's full name (last name first), the exact title (underline newspaper, magazine, and book titles and put article titles in quotations marks), the place of publication, the name of the publisher, the date of publication, and the call number. *What is the advantage of creating these cards?*

your ideas easily. (If you are creating and storing your notes on a computer, keep a back-up file or printout.) At the top of each note card, write the topic; below that, write a summary in your own words, a brief statement, or a direct quotation. If you are quoting, use quotation marks and write the words exactly as they appear and the source, including the page number. If there is an error in the text, in brackets write the term *sic,* which means "thus in the original." If you omit words, indicate missing words with ellipsis points (three dots with a space between each dot, or period). Also write each reference source on a separate card. You will need exact information for your final bibliography and footnotes and for researching material. Sorting these cards into subject divisions will help you prepare your outline. See **Figure 9.2** for a sample bibliography card.

8. **Don't just cut and paste.** As we'll discuss further in this chapter in regard to plagiarism, be careful about simply cutting and pasting material, especially from online sources. Either reword the material as you write it or make note that you will need to rework the material later when you write your paper.

9. **Prepare a bibliography.** A bibliography is a list of books, articles, Internet sources, and other resources about a subject or by a particular author that you plan to use as support for information in your paper. A bibliography page or section appears at the end of a research paper or book. Most instructors expect you to include a complete list of your sources, so record them accurately and thoroughly as you do your research. Keep note cards or a digital file as you go, so that it will be easy to assemble.

Organize

Now that you have done the preliminary legwork, you'll want to create a writing plan.

1. **Develop an outline.** Organize your note cards or digital notes into a logical order using either a traditional or mind map outline. This outline should contain main points and subtopics and serve as a road map that illustrates your entire project and keeps you focused. (See the sample outline in the margin.) Use **Personal Evaluation Notebook 9.1** to help you organize your paper.

2. **Do in-depth research.** Look for specific information and data that support your main points and thesis. Research the books and articles you noted on

Sample Outline

Thesis statement: Smoking among teenage girls is rising due to influences by peers and advertising that glamorizes smoking.

I. Smoking among teenage girls is increasing.
  A. Smoking has increased by 24 percent.
    1. Supporting information
    2. Supporting information
  B. Girls are smoking at younger ages.
    1. Supporting information
    2. Supporting information
II. Advertising targets young girls directly.
  A. Examples of advertising
    1. Supporting information
    2. Supporting information
  B. Effects of advertising
    1. Supporting information
    2. Supporting information

Personal Evaluation Notebook

Preparing Research Papers

Use this form to prepare and organize your upcoming paper. Jot down preliminary notes to get started.

Topic _____ Due Date _____

Main Point (Thesis) _____

_____

_____

How do the topic and thesis fulfill the assignment? _____

_____

_____

Review your outline and notes for these elements and provide examples or descriptions of how they will be addressed in the paper:

Main Body

- Background of topic _____
- Main points and arguments _____
- Supporting points _____
- Terminology, facts, data _____
- Key words _____

Conclusion

- Restate thesis. _____
- Summarize key points. _____
- Present a clear and strong conclusion. _____

your bibliography cards. (We will discuss research skills in more detail later in the chapter.)

3. **Revise your outline as needed.** You may also refine your writing strategy by considering how best to accomplish your purpose. What is your major topic? What subtopics do you want to include? What examples, definitions, quotations, statistics, stories, or personal comments would be most interesting and supportive? Keep looking for specific information to support your thesis.

Write

Now is the time to organize all your notes—either on computer or note cards—according to sections and headings and write your first draft in your own words according to your revised outline. Write freely and don't worry about spelling, grammar, or format. The key is to begin writing and keep the momentum going. Both papers and speeches should have three sections: an introduction, a main body, and a conclusion.

1. **Introduction.** The introduction should be a strong opening that clearly states your purpose, captures the audience's attention, defines terms, and sets the stage for the main points. Use an active, not a passive, voice. For example, "More than 450,000 people will die this year from the effects of cigarette smoking" is a stronger introduction than "This paper will present the dangers of smoking."

2. **Main body.** The main body is the heart of your paper or speech. Each main point should be presented logically and stand out as a unit (see **Figure 9.3**). Explain main points in your own words and use direct quotes when you want to state the original source. Refer often to your outline and thesis statement. Your research note cards will help you find support elements. If you find gaps, do more research.

3. **Conclusion.** Your final paragraph should tie together important points. The reader or listener should now have an understanding of the topic and believe that you have achieved your purpose. You might use a story, quotation, or call to action. You may want to refer again to the introduction, reemphasize main points, or rephrase an important position. Keep your conclusion brief, interesting, and powerful. (**Peak Progress 9.2** on page 283 provides hints on overcoming writer's block.)

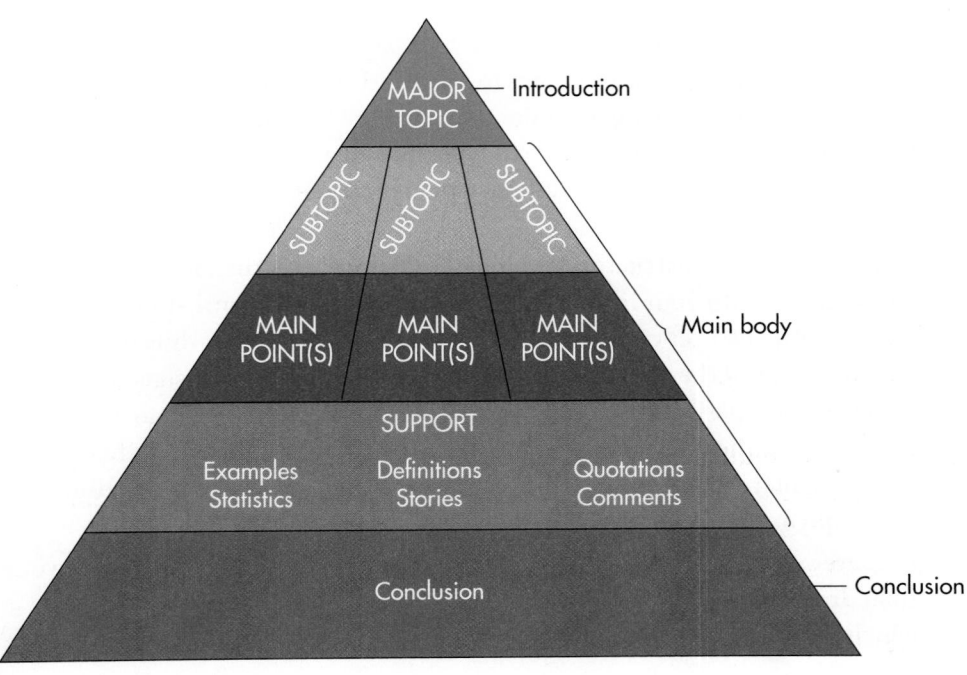

Figure 9.3
Writing Pyramid

Start at the top of the pyramid with your major topic, and move down to each subtopic and its main points. Provide support for your main points, including examples and statistics. End with a powerful conclusion that summarizes the paper or speech. *Why are "support" elements so important?*

Take 3 minutes to express your thoughts in a daily journal:

- What good things happened to you today?
- What "lessons" did you learn? Describe any negative experiences, and use the ABC Method to find positive outcomes and relieve lingering stress.
- Free write about any interesting ideas you have, and stretch your vocabulary with unusual words and phrases.

What else can you do in 3 minutes?

- Brainstorm ideas for your next writing assignment.
- Spellcheck your class paper.
- Create a writing schedule for an upcoming project.

Take.3

❝I'm not a very good writer, but I'm an excellent rewriter.❞

JAMES MICHENER
Author

Edit

A thorough edit can turn good papers into excellent papers.

1. Revise.

- Read your paper out loud to get an overall sense of meaning and the flow of words. Vary sentence lengths and arrangements to add interest and variety. For example, don't start each sentence with the subject or overuse the same words or phrases.

- Rework paragraphs for clarity and appropriate transitions. Does each paragraph contain one idea in a topic sentence? Is the idea well supported? Transitions should be smooth and unobtrusive. In a speech, they should be defined clearly, so that listeners stay focused. Take out unnecessary words. Ask yourself if a phrase or sentence contributes to your purpose.

- Recheck your outline. Have you followed your outline logically and included supporting information in the correct places? Break up the narrative with lists if you are presenting series of data. As you revise, stay focused on your purpose, not on the ideas that support your conclusion. Be sure your points are clearly and concisely presented with supporting stories, quotes, and explanations.

- Review sentence structure, punctuation, grammar, and unity of thought. Correct typographical and spelling errors, grammatical mistakes, and poor transitions. As you work, remember to save your work frequently.

2. Revise again. Set your paper aside for a day or two before you give it a final revision with a fresh view. Go through your entire paper or speech. Is your central theme clear and concise? Read your paper out loud. Does it flow? Could it use more stories or quotes to add flair? Is it too wordy or confusing? Does it have an interesting introduction and conclusion? Share your paper with a friend or member of your study team, and ask him or her to proofread your work. Others provide a fresh viewpoint and can sometimes see errors you miss.

3. Confer with your instructor. If you have not done so earlier, make an appointment with your instructor to review your paper. Some students make an appointment after completing their outline or first draft, while others like to wait until they have proofed their second draft. Most instructors will review your paper with you and make suggestions. Discuss what to add, what to revise, and the preferred method of citation. Also, many colleges have a writing center staffed with English majors who will read your rough drafts and help you revise.

4. Prepare your final draft. Following your instructor's guidelines, prepare your final draft. Leave a margin of 1 inch on all sides, except for the first page, which should have a 3-inch margin at the top of the paper. Double-space your

Peak Progress

Overcoming Writer's Block

Writer's block can be stressful and frustrating, but there are many ways to jump start your writing and keep it on track.

- **Read.** Reading will give you ideas and expand your vocabulary. Read novels, classic literature, biographies, and newspapers. Read other students' papers, and exchange papers with your study team.
- **Write in a conversational tone.** Avoid technical, artificial, or stilted language. Use everyday words as if you were talking to someone.
- **Write in short blocks of time.** You'll become discouraged if you try to write a large paper in one sitting. Write a little every day—anywhere you happen to be. Write for 5 minutes before bed, in the morning, or between classes.
- **Have a clear understanding of your purpose.** Make a list of key points you want to make, and in one or two words or phrases write what you want to accomplish.
- **Create a mind map.** If you are a visual learner, a mind map may break your writing block. Start with your central purpose and topic. Outline main points,

subtopics, and so on, and fill in with additional ideas. A map frees your ideas to flow and helps you see connections between topics. You can then use this visual map as you type your paper. Don't feel you must start with the introduction and write through to the conclusion.

- **Free write.** After you have completed your map outline, write for 30 or 40 minutes. Don't worry about spelling, organization, or grammar; just keep writing. Free writing is especially useful if you start early, let the first draft sit for a few days, and then revise.
- **Find an empty conference room or classroom.** You may need space to be alone, spread out papers, and work without interruptions.
- **Set a deadline.** Write a schedule and stick to it. Complete each task, even if it isn't perfect. You can revise later.
- **Take a break or vary your routine.** If you get frustrated, take a short break or change the pace. Skip the introduction at first, and work on your conclusion, or write about the supporting points you know the best.

---

entire paper, except for the footnotes and bibliography, which are often single-spaced. Make corrections, revise, run a spell-check, and print out a clean, corrected copy on good-quality paper. Also proofread this hard copy, because it's easy to miss errors on a computer screen. See **Peak Progress 9.3** on page 284 for writing tips. (Also see **Peak Progress 9.4** on page 285 if you are writing online.)

5. **Cite your sources.** Always cite your sources when you quote or use another person's words or ideas. **Plagiarism** is using someone else's words or ideas and trying to pass them off as your own. It can have serious consequences, such as a failing grade or expulsion from school. You can put the person's exact words in quotation marks, or you can **paraphrase** by using your own words to restate the author's ideas. You can give credit in the text of the paper or in a note, either at the bottom of the page as a footnote or at the end of the paper as an endnote. (See **Peak Progress 9.5** on page 286 for a discussion of citation styles.)

For example, you may choose to use the following source when writing a paper on the history of the funeral industry. This is the exact quote from the text along with one method of citation:

Peak Progress

Writing Do's: The Seven *C*'s of Effective Writing

Be concise. Eliminate unnecessary words. Write in plain language and avoid wordiness. Cut any phrases that do not support your purpose.

Be concrete. Use vivid action words rather than vague, general terms. The sentence "Jill wrote the paper" is in the active voice and is easy to understand; "The paper was written by Jill" is in the passive voice and sounds weak. Avoid vague adjectives and adverbs, such as *nice, good, greatly,* and *badly.*

Be clear. Make certain your message is complete and includes all the information the audience needs to understand your intent. Never assume that the audience has prior information. Avoid technical terms, clichés, slang, and jargon. If you must be technical, include simple definitions for your audience.

Be correct. Choose precise words and grammatically correct sentences. Verify that supporting details are factual and correctly interpreted. Make certain you cite another's work. Check spelling and punctuation carefully.

Be coherent. Your message should flow smoothly. Transitions between topics should be clear, logical, and varied in word choice. Also vary the length of sentences for interest and a sense of rhythm. Include stories, examples, and interesting facts.

Be complete. Include all necessary information. Will your listeners or readers understand your message? Reread your speech or paper from their point of view. What questions might the audience have? Answer any unanswered questions.

Be considerate. Respect your reader by presenting a professional paper. Neatness counts, and papers should always be typed. If you find an error in the final draft and don't have time to reprint it, it's OK to use white-out fluid or pen to make a correction. Use a respectful tone; don't talk down to your audience or use pompous or prejudiced language. Write with courtesy and consideration, and avoid using words that are biased in terms of sex, disabilities, or ethnic groups.

Instead Of	You Can Substitute
mankind	humanity, people, humankind
manmade	manufactured, handcrafted
policeman	police officer
fireman	firefighter
housewife	homemaker
crippled, disabled	physically challenged
Indian (American)	Native American
Negro	African American
Oriental	Asian
Chicano	Latino

"Simplicity to the point of starkness, the plain pine box, the laying out of the dead by friends and family who also bore the coffin to the grave—these were the hallmarks of the traditional funeral until the end of the nineteenth century."[1]

[1]Mitford, Jessica. *The American Way of Death.* New York: Simon & Schuster, 1963.

Instead, you may choose to paraphrase the information from the book:

In her book *The American Way of Death,* Jessica Mitford says one myth that is sold by the funeral industry is that today's elaborate and expensive funeral practices are part of the American

Peak Progress

Online Writing

The Internet has opened the floodgates of communication opportunities, as **blogging** (writing personal thoughts online, usually about a specific topic, for others to view and often comment on) and chatting on social networking sites have become popular writing activities. Many courses require students to manage their own blogs (for example, to report on service learning experiences) or to communicate with other class members via discussion boards.

When posting material online, the purpose is usually the same as for writing a class paper—to succinctly communicate your main message—and the techniques are very similar, including providing supporting material and examples. Following are some specific tips to help focus your online writing:

1. The point of your writing (especially with a blog) is to express your own opinion, so do it respectfully (without slander or profanity) and as briefly as possible.

2. Write a creative headline that conveys your main message.

3. Limit your words to no more than 250.

4. If your message is longer than three paragraphs, break it up with subheads, so that the post is easy to scan.

5. Use bullets for examples or to stress information, which catches the reader's attention.

6. If your goal is to attract readers to your posting, include many key terms that would pop up during word searches.

7. Link to supporting, credible Web sites.

8. Copyedit before you post. Nothing hurts your credibility more than typos and grammatical mistakes.

9. Now that you've started the line of communication, be prepared to follow up on feedback, if necessary.

---

tradition. In truth, prior to the end of the nineteenth century, the average American funeral was inexpensive and often consisted of a pine box and a simple ceremony.

You do not need to credit general ideas that are considered to be part of common knowledge, such as the suggestion that people who exercise reduce their stress levels. However, when in doubt, it's best to cite your source. Read **Personal Evaluation Notebook 9.2** on page 288 to get a better understanding of plagiarism and how to avoid it.

6. **Add a title page and page numbers.** If required, create a title page by centering the title one-third of the page from the top. Two-thirds from the top, center your name, the instructor's name, the course title, and the date. Do not number this page. Number all remaining pages in the upper right-hand corner 1/2 inch from the top of the page. Number your endnotes and bibliography as part of the text. (Refer to any guidelines your instructor may have given you regarding formatting preferences.)

Review

Proofread by carefully reading through your work one more time. **Peak Progress 9.6** on page 289 provides a handy checklist to use as you finalize. Be prepared to turn in your paper or give your speech by the due date. Delaying the date just adds to the anxiety and may result in a lower grade. Keep back-up copies (a hard copy and a digital file) of your final paper or speech, in case your instructor loses the original.

> " Proofread carefully to see if you any words out. "
> AUTHOR UNKNOWN

WORDS TO SUCCEED

Peak Progress

Writing Citations

There are many ways to write citations. Ask your instructor which documentation style is preferred. Each academic discipline has its preferred format. The Modern Language Association (MLA) of America format is often preferred for the humanities (philosophy, languages, arts, and so on). The American Psychological Association (APA) format is commonly used for the social sciences, psychology, and education. The style of the Council of Biology Editors (CBE) is primarily used for the natural and physical sciences. Computer programs are available to help you format citations according to some styles.

Reference notes can be placed at the bottom of a page as footnotes or listed together at the end of the paper as endnotes. A bibliography, which lists all the sources (such as books, articles, Web sites, and personal communication) referenced in a paper, may include works for background and further reading. A reference list, on the other hand, cites works that specifically support an article. Bibliographies and reference lists are found at the end of a paper after endnotes, if there are any. In the MLA format, the bibliography appears under the heading "Works Cited." For more information on MLA format, visit the MLA Web site at **www.mla.org/style_faq**.

The various citation formats are similar. The MLA style uses the simplest punctuation and is acceptable in many situations. The elements of an MLA citation are author, book title, place of publication, publisher, year of publication, and page number.

The APA style generally uses a combination of in-text citations and a reference list. Text citations use an author-date system (such as Nelson, 2004). Items in the reference list usually contain the following elements: author, year of publication, title of the work, place of publication, and publisher. For more information about APA style, visit the APA Web site at **www.apastyle.org/faqs.html**.

Several excellent Web sites can guide you through a generally acceptable way to cite sources. Your local or school library may also post citation information on its Web site. Following is a guide for most types of sources you will cite:

For Footnotes

MLA   1. Lee, Ann. <u>Office Reference Manual</u>. New York: Irwin, 1993.

APA   (Lee, 1993)

Note: In the APA's author-date system, the last name(s) of the author(s) and the year of publication are inserted in the text at the appropriate point.

For Reference List or Works Cited

Book: One Author

MLA   Henley, Patricia. <u>Hummingbird House</u>. Denver: MacMurray, 1999.

APA   Henley, P. (1999). *Hummingbird house*. Denver: MacMurray.

Book: Two or More Authors

MLA   Gillespie, Paula, and Neal Lerber. <u>The Allyn and Bacon Guide to Peer Tutoring</u>. Boston: Allyn, 2000.

APA   Gillespie, P., & Lerber, N. (2000). *The Allyn and Bacon guide to peer tutoring*. Boston: Allyn.

Government Publication

MLA   United States Department of Health and Human Services. <u>Pressure Ulcers in Adults: Prediction and Prevention</u>. Rockville, MD: Publisher, 1992, 28.

APA   U.S. Department of Health and Human Services. (1992). *Pressure ulcers in adults: Prediction and prevention* (AHCPR Publication No, 92-0047). Rockville, MD: Author.

Journal

MLA   Klimoski, Richard I., and Susan Palmer. "The ADA and the Hiring Process in Organization." <u>Consulting Psychology Journal: Practice and Research</u>, 45.2 (1993) 10–36.

APA   Klimoski, R. I., & Palmer, S. (1993). The ADA and the hiring process in organization. *Consulting Psychology Journal: Practice and Research*, 45(2), 10–36.

Nonprint Source (Web Site)

MLA   Stolley, Karl. "MLA Formatting and Style Guide." The OWL at Purdue. 10 May 2006.

(continued)

Writing Citations *(concluded)*

Purdue University Writing Lab. 12 May 2006 <http://owl.english.purdue.edu/owl/resource/557/01/>.

APA   Stolley, K. (2006). MLA formatting and style guide. Retrieved May 12, 2008, from Purdue University Writing Lab Web site: http://owl.english.purdue.edu/owl/resource/557/01/

Nonprint Source (Online Journal)

MLA   Wheelis, Mark. "Investigating Disease Outbreaks under a Protocol to the Biological and Toxin Weapons Convention." <u>Emerging Infectious Diseases</u> 6.6 (2000): 33 pars. 8 May 2006 <www.cdc.gov/ncidod/eid/vol6no6/wheelis.htm>.

APA   Wheelis, M. (2000). Investigating disease outbreaks under a protocol to the biological and toxin weapons convention. *Emerging Infectious Diseases*, 6. Retrieved May 8, 2006, from **www.cdc.gov/ncidod/eid/vol6no6/vvwheelis.htm**

Nonprint Source (CD-ROM)

MLA   Morgan, David E. <u>Reference Software for Smoking Studies</u>. DOS Version. CD-ROM. New York: Macmillan, 1995.

APA   Morgan, D. E. (1995). *Reference software for smoking studies* [CD-ROM]. New York: Macmillan.

Letter to the Editor

MLA   Berkowitz, A. D. Letter. "How to Tackle the Problem of Student Drinking." <u>The Chronicle of Higher Education</u>. 24 Nov 2000: B20.

APA   Berkowitz, A. D. (2000, November 24). How to tackle the problem of student drinking [Letter to the editor]. *The Chronicle of Higher Education*, p. B20.

Encyclopedia or Other Reference Work

MLA   Bergmann, Peter G. "Relativity." <u>The New Encyclopaedia Britannica</u>. 15th ed. 1993.

APA   Bergmann, P. G. (1993). Relativity. In *The new encyclopaedia britannica* (Vol. 26, pp. 501–508). Chicago: Encyclopedia Britannica.

Note: In MLA style, titles of whole works may be underlined or italicized.

Review your graded paper or speech when it is returned to you, and make sure you understand what you could have done differently to have received a better grade. If you are unsure, ask your instructor for tips on improving your work. Keep copies of your major research papers in your Career Development Portfolio to show documentation of your writing, speaking, and research skills.

Conducting Research

Conducting research requires the same skills you've been learning throughout this book: observing, recording, reviewing, and using critical thinking to assess and evaluate. The purpose of research is to find information and ideas about a topic beyond what you already know. Research helps you support opinions and information with facts and data. Your initial research will give you an overview of the subject and help you define your thesis statement. Additional research will uncover specific facts about your subject.

Using the Library for Research

As discussed in Chapter 4, the library contains a wealth of information. Besides books, libraries have newspapers, magazines, encyclopedias, dictionaries, indexes,

> **❝** Perhaps no place in any community is so totally democratic as the town library. The only entrance requirement is interest. **❞**
>
> **LADY BIRD JOHNSON**
> *U.S. first lady*

WORDS TO SUCCEED

Personal Evaluation Notebook

That's Not Fair (Use)

In 2008, 36 percent of teens surveyed said they used the Internet to plagiarize an assignment. However, it's likely that even more are committing plagiarism without realizing it because of the confusion over what constitutes plagiarism versus "fair use."

Fair use is the legal and ethical use of a direct quote from the Internet or another source, including a book, in something you claim as your own work. According to the U.S. Copyright Office, fair use is limited to the "quotation of excerpts in a review or criticism for purposes of illustration or comment; quotation of short passages in a scholarly or technical work, for illustration or clarification of the author's observations; use in a parody of some of the content of the work parodied; summary of an address or article, with brief quotations," and similar use. Even when the quotation is within the fair use guidelines, it is essential to give a reference through a footnote or other indication that these words were written by someone other than you. Because of the prevalence of plagiarism, many instructors use online services to check for it, including having students deliver their papers via an online site, such as turnitin.

To test your understanding, consider the following scenarios*:

1. This morning, you read an editorial in the local newspaper and totally agreed with the author's 10-step approach to improving high school graduation rates. You include all 10 suggestions in your presentation to your introduction to education class but reword each one slightly and don't cite the author. Is this plagiarism?

   yes _____   no _____

2. You cut and paste a lengthy article from a reputable online news service into your paper and add a new introduction and a brief summary. You include a complete citation in your source information. Is this plagiarism?

   yes _____   no _____

3. Last semester, you wrote a stellar paper for your English composition class, in which you compared and contrasted a number of local businesses. You decide to hand in the same paper this week for an economics 101 assignment. Is this plagiarism?

   yes _____   no _____

Sources: Josephson Institute Center for Youth Ethics, "The Ethics of American Youth—2008 summary," http//charactercounts.org/programs/reportcard/, accessed August 14, 2009.

U.S. Copyright Office—Fair Use, www.copyright.gov/fls/fl102.html, revised May 2009.

*Answers are on page 297.

audiovisual equipment, telephone directories, maps, catalogs, research aids, computers, and software. Reference librarians are trained to find information about every subject. They can often order materials from other libraries or direct you to other sources. Asking for their guidance at the beginning of your search can save you hours of time and frustration. When planning your research strategy, remember the basic types of sources found in most libraries:

Peak Progress

Checklists for Writing Papers and Giving Speeches

Review these checklists before submitting a paper or giving a speech.

Papers and Speeches

_____ Appropriate and focused topic

_____ Attention-getting introduction

_____ Clear thesis statement

_____ Appropriate word choice

_____ Plenty of factual support

_____ Good examples

_____ Good visuals

_____ Sources credited

_____ Smooth transitions

_____ Effective summary/conclusions

Papers

_____ Spelling and grammar checked

_____ Proofread at least twice

_____ Pages numbered

_____ Neat appearance/format

_____ Deadline met

_____ Copies made

Speeches

_____ Eye contact

_____ Appropriate voice level and tone

_____ No slang or distracting words

_____ Relaxed body language

_____ Appropriate attire

_____ Access to watch or clock

- **Books.** Books make up a large part of every library. They treat a subject in depth and offer a broad scope. In your research project, use books for historical context, detailed discussions of a subject, or varied perspectives on a topic.

- **Periodicals.** A periodical is a regularly issued publication, such as newspapers, news magazines, professional and scholarly journals, and trade and industry magazines. For your research, use periodicals when you need recent data.

- **Reference materials.** Reference materials may be in print or digital. Examples include encyclopedias, dictionaries, chronologies, abstracts, indexes, and compilations of statistics. In your research strategy, use reference materials when you want to obtain or verify specific facts.

> **A Good Source**
> Libraries provide the most research options, with books, periodicals, reference materials, online access, and trained librarians. *What's the best source for recent data?*

The *Readers' Guide to Periodical Literature* is a helpful source for locating articles. Other standard reference materials that may give you a general understanding of specific topics and help you develop questions include the *Encyclopedia Americana,* the *Encyclopaedia Britannica, and the indexes of the New York Times* and *Wall Street Journal.*

Check these sources for historical speeches:

- *Speech Index*
- *Index to American Women Speakers, 1828–1978*
- *Representative American Speeches, 1937*
- *Facts on File, 1941*
- *Vital Speeches of the Day, 1941*
- *Historic Documents of* [Year]
- *Public Papers of the Presidents of the United States*

Search by author or subject through the library's online catalog. Often, the electronic source will include only a summary, so you may need to go to the library stacks or periodicals to read the book or article.

Taking Your Search Online

Before you start a search online, think about a precise question you want to answer, such as "How does education affect smoking by college students?" Identify the key words and ideas in this question—for example, *smoking, education,* and *addiction.* Directories such as Yahoo.com (**www.yahoo.com**) are often helpful when starting your research, since they are organized by subject. Other sites, such as google.com (**www.google.com**), combine directories with search engines. Type your key words into the search box, select from the options that pop up, or hit the return key and wait for a list of Web pages to appear. If they don't answer your question, rephrase your question and search again using other key words. Each search site offers links that will explain how to do advanced searches. Bookmark Web sites that you use often.

Although searching for information on the Internet by using key words or key phrases may seem relatively easy and efficient, you must verify that what you choose to use comes from a reliable source. See **Peak Progress 9.7** for tips on evaluating

Peak Progress

9.7

Evaluating Online Information

With millions of Web pages to choose from, how do you know which sites are reliable? Use the following checklist when evaluating online information for research and personal use.

Is It Credible?

- Is the page's author clearly identified? Does he or she have the credentials for writing about this topic?
- Is the author affiliated with an organization? If so, what is the organization's nature or purpose?
- Is there a link to the organization's home page or some other way to contact the organization and verify its credibility (a physical address, phone number, or e-mail address)?
- Is the page geared for a particular audience or level of expertise?
- Is the primary purpose to provide information, sell a product, make a political point, or have fun?
- Is the page part of an edited or peer-reviewed publication?
- Does the domain name provide clues about the source of the page?
- Does the site provide details that support the data?
- Is there a bibliography or other documentation to corroborate the information? When facts or statistics are quoted, look to see whether their source is revealed.

Is It Accurate?

- Are there obvious typographical or spelling errors?
- Based on what you already know or have just learned about this subject, does the information seem credible?
- Can factual information be verified?
- Is it comprehensive, or does it focus on a narrow range of information?
- Is it clear about its focus?
- Has the site been evaluated?

Is It Timely?

- Can you tell when the information was published? Is it current?
- When was the page last updated?
- If there are links to other Web pages, are they current?

Is It Objective?

- Is the source of factual information consistent and stated clearly?
- Does the page display a particular bias? Is it clear and forthcoming about its view of a particular subject?
- If the page contains advertisements, are they clearly distinguishable from the content of the information?

Source: Used by permission of the University of Texas System Digital Library, The University of Texas at Austin.

online material. As with other sources, you must also cite material you find on the Internet.

Public Speaking Strategies

Public speaking is an essential school and job skill. In school, you will ask and answer questions in class, lead discussions, summarize topics, introduce other students, present your academic plan or thesis, and interview for internships or jobs. On the job, you may introduce a guest, present the results of a group project, make a sales pitch, demonstrate a new product, present goals and objectives, interview clients, talk with upper management, or accept an award.

Many of the strategies for choosing a topic and organizing and writing a speech are like those for writing papers. Following are additional strategies specifically for public speaking:

1. **Understand the occasion.** Why are you speaking? Is the occasion formal or informal? How much time do you have? What is your purpose? Do you want to inform, entertain, inspire, or persuade?

2. **Think about your topic.** If a topic hasn't been assigned, what are you interested in talking about? Prepare a thesis statement, such as "My purpose is to inform the Forestry Club on the benefits of our organization."

3. **Know your audience.** You don't need to know them personally, but you should have a sense of their backgrounds and why they are in the room. For example, if you are giving a speech on cutting-edge technology and the majority of your audience barely knows how to turn on a computer, chances are you are going to lose them quickly unless you present the topic at a level they can relate to, with benefits they can appreciate.

4. **Get the audience's attention.** Write an introduction that gets attention, introduces the topic, states the main purpose, and briefly identifies the main points.

5. **Get the audience involved.** Consider asking a question, which may help personalize the topic, encourage participation, or keep the audience interested.

6. **Look at the audience.** Establish eye contact and speak to the audience members. Smile, develop rapport, and notice when your audience agrees with you or looks puzzled or confused.

7. **Outline your speech.** Organize the body of your speech to include supporting points and interesting examples.

8. **Write a good conclusion.** The audience should have a clear picture of what your main point is, why it's important, and what they

Izzy's blog has become an instant hit with fans of local cuisine. Majoring in food science, Izzy loves to give (and ask for) opinions on hot spots, new chefs, menu makeovers, and dining experiences—the good and the bad. However, as much as Izzy enjoys voicing her thoughts online in elaborate detail, writing a term paper is as appealing to her as a trip to the dentist.

- How do Izzy's personality and learning styles influence her online writing success?
- If Izzy enjoys writing her blog, why does she view other writing opportunities differently? How are they different? How are they similar?
- What tips would you give Izzy to help her tackle her more structured writing projects?

THINK *FAST*

● **Eye Contact**

When you look at the audience as you speak, you create a rapport that makes everyone more comfortable. *What other strategies can help you become a good speaker?*

should do about it. You may want to end with a story, strong statement, or question.

9. **Develop visuals.** When appropriate, use overheads, a PowerPoint presentation, handouts, and demonstrations to focus attention and reinforce your speech. Make sure the projector works, and you have practiced working with the visual aids. See **Figure 9.4** for tips on creating effective PowerPoint presentations.

10. **Prepare your prompters.** Don't memorize the speech, but be well acquainted with your topic, so that you are comfortable talking about it. Prepare simple notes to prompt yourself. Write key phrases, stories, and quotes in large letters on note cards.

11. **Practice.** Rehearsal is everything! Practice the speech aloud several times in front of a mirror, an empty classroom, or friends. Practice speaking slowly, calmly, and louder than usual. Vary the pitch and speed for emphasis. Practice will also help you overcome stage fright. (See the next section on speech anxiety.)

12. **Relax.** Take a deep breath as you walk to the front of the room. During the speech, speak loudly and clearly, don't rush, and gesture when appropriate to help you communicate.

13. **Watch your time.** If you have a time limit, make sure there is a clock you can glance at during your presentation. Pace yourself, so that you finish on time.

14. **Be in the present.** Look at your audience and smile. Keep your purpose in mind, and stay focused on the message and the audience. Pause at important points for emphasis and to connect with your audience.

15. **Avoid unnecessary words.** Use clear, concise wording. Don't use pauses as fillers, irritating nonwords, or overused slang, such as *uh, ur, you know, stuff like that, sort of,* and *like.*

16. **Review your performance.** Ask your instructor and fellow students for feedback. Use the sample speech evaluation form shown in **Figure 9.5** to help you improve your performance or as you are listening to others.

See **Peak Progress 9.8** on page 294 to explore how you can apply the Adult Learning Cycle to becoming more proficient at public speaking.

Overcoming Speech Anxiety

Most beginning public speakers feel nervous about speaking in front of others. This kind of nervousness has been called speech anxiety, stage fright, or communication apprehension—and it is normal. A little apprehension is good for public speaking. It adds energy and can sharpen your awareness and focus. Too much anxiety, however, can be harmful. Speech anxiety has both mental and physical components. Mentally, you might think of all the ways you will fail. As you worry about the speech, your negative thoughts can work you into a state of real anxiety. Physical symptoms include butterflies-in-the-stomach, irregular breathing, sweaty palms, dry mouth, nausea, mental blocks, flushed skin, tense muscles, and shaky hands. Some people have even fainted. Extreme anxiety can prevent you from doing your best.

PowerPoint Tips

WORDS:
1. Title each screen with a 35-45-point font
2. Select sans-serif fonts, 24-point or larger
3. Use linear (outline) or topical organization
4. No more than 6-8 words per line
5. Bullet points:
   - 1 thought per line
   - 6 words per line maximum
   - 6 lines per slide maximum
6. Use colors, sizes, and styles (**bold**, underline) for impact

PowerPoint Tips

VISUALS:
1. Keep a consistent background
2. Use dark text on light background or light text on dark background
3. Use quality graphics sparingly
4. Avoid flashy graphics, transitions, and noisy animations
5. Limit the number of colors on a single screen

Figure 9.4
PowerPoint Presentations

When developing a PowerPoint presentation, include only essential words, and resist the urge to include too much on a slide. The text has to be big enough to be read from the back of the room. Do not read from your presentation, but use it as a guide to follow as you speak. *Do you feel more comfortable giving a presentation with or without an accompanying PowerPoint?*

You can become more confident and overcome speech anxiety with these tips:

1. **Practice.** The more prepared you are, the less nervous you're likely to be. Practice out loud, in front of a mirror, with a friend and in the room where you'll be speaking, if possible.

2. **Use visuals.** Visual aids can prompt you during the presentation and direct the spotlight away from you.

3. **Dispute irrational thoughts.** You might think, "People will laugh at me" or "My mind will go blank." In reality, others are also apprehensive (and more concerned about their own performance) and want you to do your best. Counter your "catastrophic" thinking by considering, "What's the worst thing that can happen?" and follow with affirmations. "I am well prepared. I am relaxed. I am comfortable talking with others. The audience is on my side."

Name _____ Topic _____

Introduction
___ Gained attention and interest
___ Introduced topic
___ Topic related to audience
___ Established credibility
___ Previewed body of speech

Body
___ Main points clear
___ Organizational pattern evident
___ Established need
___ Presented clear plan
___ Demonstrated practicality
___ Language clear
___ Gave evidence to support main points
___ Sources and citations clear
___ Reasoning sound
___ Used emotional appeals
___ Connectives effective

Delivery
___ Spoke at an appropriate rate
___ Maintained eye contact
___ Maintained volume and projection
___ Avoided distracting mannerisms
___ Used gestures effectively
___ Articulated clearly
___ Used vocal variety and dynamics
___ Presented visual aids effectively
___ Departed appropriately
___ Other: _____

Conclusion
___ Prepared audience for ending
___ Reinforced central idea
___ Called audience to agreement/action
___ Used a vivid ending

Suggestions
_____
_____
_____
_____
_____
_____
_____
_____

General Notes
_____
_____
_____
_____
_____
_____

Key: Superior (1), Effective (2), Average (3), Weak (4)

Figure 9.5
Speech Evaluation Form

Feedback on your speaking skills can help you improve. *How would you assess your last speech in a class?*

Peak Progress

Applying the Adult Learning Cycle to Improving Your Public Speaking

Increasing your public speaking skills takes time, effort, and practice.

1. **RELATE. Why do I want to learn this?** I admire people who are confident speaking in front of others, and I want to feel as confident, poised, and in control. Becoming an effective public speaker will be a valuable skill for both school and career. What areas do I need to work on? What are my physical symptoms of anxiety?

2. **OBSERVE. How does this work?** I can learn by observing people who confidently give effective speeches. What makes them successful? Do I understand the message? I'll also analyze ineffective speeches. Did stage fright play a role? Did the speaker seem nervous? I'll try using new techniques and strategies for dealing with stage fright and observe how I'm improving.

3. **REFLECT. What does this mean?** What strategies are working for me? Am I more confident and relaxed? Am I reducing anxiety and negative self-talk?

4. **DO. What can I do with this?** I will practice my public speaking skills whenever possible. I'll find practical applications for my new skills. Each day, I'll work on one area. For example, I'll choose less stressful situations, such as my study group or a club meeting, and offer to give a presentation on an interesting topic. I will ask for feedback.

5. **TEACH. Whom can I share this with?** I'll talk with others and share my tips and experiences and listen to theirs in return. I'll volunteer to help other students in my study group.

Now, return to Stage 1 and think about how it feels to learn this valuable new skill. Remember, the more you practice speaking in front of others, the more relaxed and confident you will become.

4. **Use stress-reduction techniques.** Relax your muscles by tensing and then quickly releasing them. Do head rolls. Put your shoulders way up and then drop them. Take deep breaths, and concentrate on expanding your stomach with each breath and exhaling fully. Don't rush right into your speech. Take several slow, deep breaths before going up to speak. Relax and smile.

If your anxiety is severe and prevents you from succeeding, see the learning center or counseling center for individualized tips. Complete **Personal Evaluation Notebook 9.3** to determine how you handle stage fright and writer's block.

Personal Evaluation Notebook

9.3

Controlling Stage Fright and Writer's Block

A. Use your critical thinking skills to answer the following questions. Be prepared to discuss your answers in your study team.

1. Describe your typical physical reaction to giving a speech.

   _____

   _____

2. What has helped you control stage fright?

   _____

   _____

3. Describe the processes of writing that are easiest for you and those that are hardest.

   _____

   _____

B. Read the following common reasons and excuses that some students give for not writing effective speeches. Use creative problem solving to list strategies for overcoming these barriers.

REASONS/EXCUSES

1. I have panic attacks before I write or give speeches.

   Strategy _____

   _____

2. I can't decide on a topic.

   Strategy _____

   _____

3. I don't know how to research.

   Strategy: _____

   _____

4. I procrastinate until the last minute.

   Strategy: _____

   _____

5. I don't know what my instructor wants.

   Strategy: _____

   _____

6. My mind goes blank when I start to write or give a speech.

   Strategy: _____

   _____

TAKING CHARGE

Summary

In this chapter, I learned to

- **Become a more effective writer and speaker.** Being a good communicator is the most important skill I will ever acquire. Although public speaking can be stressful, I can learn to reduce my anxiety and become more successful if I prepare, organize, write, edit, and review my presentation carefully.

- **Prepare effectively.** When writing a paper or presentation, I first set a schedule. I carefully and thoughtfully choose my topic and do the preliminary reading and information gathering. I can then narrow my topic and write a thesis statement that clarifies what I plan to cover. I prepare a bibliography of references and original sources, and take notes that support my topic.

- **Organize my writing plan.** I must organize my thoughts and research into a coherent outline. I continue to look for specific data that support my main points. I revise my outline as necessary as I consider the subtopics that support my main theme. I include interesting and supportive examples, definitions, quotations, and statistics.

- **Write a draft of my paper or presentation.** After finishing the preliminary research and outline, I prepare a draft, writing freely and with momentum. My draft includes an introduction, the main body, and a conclusion. The introduction clearly states the purpose or theme, captures attention, and defines terms. The main body includes the subtopics that support the main theme, as well as visual aids. The conclusion ties the important points together and supports the overall theme of the presentation.

- **Revise and edit my paper or presentation.** Now that I have prepared a draft, I must revise it often. I make sure the overall theme and supporting points are clear and revise my outline when necessary. I correct spelling and grammatical mistakes and review transitions and sentence structure. I read it out loud to make sure the writing is varied and interesting. I verify that I have accurately prepared the bibliography, and I ask my instructor to review my paper. I then finalize my paper, number the pages, and add a title page.

- **Review and assess my paper or presentation.** After a final check of my paper, I make copies and save one in my Career Development Portfolio. I deliver it on time, go over my graded results, and ask my instructor for tips for improvement.

- **Use the library and Internet for research.** The library provides a wealth of resources, including books, periodicals, and reference materials. The Internet has become the world's largest information network, providing access to a myriad of resources, including databases.

- **Incorporate new strategies for effective public speaking.** When I speak in public, it's important for me to be prepared, establish eye contact with my audience, develop visual aids, and prepare simple notes or cues to prompt myself. I avoid unnecessary words and fillers, and I connect with my audience. Rehearsing is key to a successful presentation, and I review my performance by asking others for feedback.

Performance Strategies

Following are the top 10 strategies for writing papers and giving speeches:

- Determine your purpose and set a schedule.
- Choose and narrow your topic.
- Read and research. Prepare a bibliography.
- Organize information into an outline and on note cards.
- Write a draft.
- Refine your purpose and rewrite the draft.
- Edit and proof.
- Use your study team to practice and review.
- Revise and polish.
- Practice. Practice. Practice.

Tech for Success

Take advantage of the text's Web site at **www.mhhe.com/ferrett8e** for additional study aids, useful forms, and convenient and applicable resources.

- **Visual aids.** As many of your instructors do, you will want to enhance your presentations with visual aids, such as handouts, overhead transparencies, and PowerPoint presentations. Many employers do not provide training for presentation software but knowing how to incorporate them into business meetings and presentations is often expected. Thus, learning at least the basics of PowerPoint or a similar program will be a valuable skill you can use both in school and on the job.

- **Spell-check, spell-check, spell-check.** As e-mail has replaced the traditional memo, it's much easier to send out correspondence quickly to a group of people. However, it's not uncommon to receive important e-mails that are riddled with typos and grammatical mistakes. Get in the habit of using the spell-check function before you send e-mails or any documents. The few seconds it takes to check your outgoing correspondence can save you from unnecessary embarrassment.

Study Team Notes

Answers to Personal Evaluation Notebook 9.2 on page 288:

1. Yes. Using someone else's ideas and presenting them as your own—whether from a written or a verbal source—is considered plagiarism unless credit is given to the original source.
2. Yes. Even though the source is cited, a significant amount of material has been used and is being presented as original work. The ideas can still be included in your work (as long as the source is cited), but the material should be revised in your own words.
3. Yes. This is considered "self-plagiarism," and multiple submission of material is often considered unethical in an academic situation.

Lori Benson
HUMAN RESOURCES DIRECTOR

Related Majors: Human Resources, Personnel
Administration, Labor Relations

Communication Skills

Lori Benson is the human resources director for a small advertising firm. Lori is her company's only human resources employee. Besides recruiting and interviewing potential employees, Lori also develops personnel programs and policies. She serves as her company's employee benefits manager by handling health insurance and pension plans. Lori also provides training in orientation sessions for new employees and instructs classes that help supervisors improve their interpersonal skills.

Possessing excellent communication skills is essential for Lori's job. To recruit potential employees, Lori contacts local colleges to attract recent graduates and places ads on online job search sites. In addition, Lori often sends memos and e-mails to the employees at her company to notify them about new policies and benefits. This kind of writing must be clear, accurate, and brief. Lori first writes a draft and then sets it aside for a few hours before revising it. She usually asks the CEO to review the ads and letters sent to the media.

Lori does research to find out what programs and policies other companies are offering. She uses public speaking strategies when preparing for training and other classes. First she makes notes and then writes prompts to help her remember what she wants to say. Lori practices her lecture several times and reviews her notes before each class. She keeps her notes in a file for the next time she gives a class on the same subject.

CRITICAL THINKING How does Lori incorporate the communication skills she learned in college into the workplace?

Peak Performer

PROFILE

Toni Morrison

Her books have been described as having "the luster of poetry" illuminating American reality. However, one reader once commented to acclaimed novelist Toni Morrison that her books were difficult to read. Morrison responded, "They're difficult to write." The process, Morrison sums up, "is not [always] a question of inspiration. It's a question of very hard, very sustained work."

An ethnically rich background helped provide Morrison's inspiration. The second of four children, she was born Chloe Anthony Wofford in a small Ohio steel town in 1931 during the Great Depression. The family's financial struggle was offset by a home strengthened by multiple generations and traditional ties. Storytelling was an important part of the family scene and black tradition.

In the late 1940s, Morrison headed to the East Coast. After earning a bachelor's degree in English from Howard University and a master's degree from Cornell University, she was still years away from literary recognition. While working as an editor at Random House in New York City, she began her writing career in earnest, and in 1970 her first novel, *The Bluest Eye,* was published.

Since then, Morrison has produced a body of work described as standing "among the 20th century's richest depictions of Black life and the legacy of slavery." In 1987, she won the Pulitzer Prize for her fifth novel, *Beloved.* Based on a true incident that took place in 1851, this novel has been read by millions. Then, in 1993, Morrison was awarded the Nobel Prize in Literature. She is the first black woman and only the eighth woman to receive this supreme honor.

Through Morrison's writing skills and self-expression, she has provided insight into American cultural heritage and the human condition.

PERFORMANCE THINKING The novel *Beloved* is dedicated to "Sixty Million and more." What is Morrison trying to express?

CHECK IT OUT "Toni Morrison's novels invite the reader to partake at many levels, and at varying degrees of complexity. Still, the most enduring impression they leave is of empathy, compassion with one's fellow human beings," said Professor Sture Allén as he presented Toni Morrison with the Nobel Prize for Literature for 1993. At **www.nobelprize.org**, select "Nobel Prizes" and then choose the Literature section to read about the many laureates who have received this highest honor. You can also listen to acceptance speeches and Nobel lectures, including Morrison's eloquent prose, "We die. That may be the meaning of life. But we do language. That may be the measure of our lives."

Starting Today

At least one strategy I learned in this chapter that I plan to try right away is

_____

_____

_____

What changes must I make in order for this strategy to be most effective?

_____

_____

_____

Review Questions

Based on what you have learned in this chapter, write your answers to the following questions:

1. What is the one basic skill taught in college that Peter Drucker feels is the most valuable for a future employee to know?

_____

_____

2. How should you establish a schedule to research and write a paper?

_____

_____

3. What are three questions to ask when evaluating information on the Internet?

_____

_____

4. Describe four strategies you can use to overcome writer's block.

_____

_____

5. What are five public speaking strategies?

_____

_____

To test your understanding of the chapter's concepts, complete the chapter quiz at **www.mhhe.com/ferrett8e.**

Learning Communication Skills

In the Classroom

Josh Miller is a finance student at a business college. He likes numbers and feels comfortable with order, structure, and right-or-wrong answers. As part of the graduation requirements, all students must take classes in speech and writing. Josh becomes nervous about writing reports or giving speeches and doesn't see the connection between the required class and his finance studies. One of Josh's biggest stumbling blocks is thinking of topics. He experiences writer's block and generally delays any project until the last possible minute.

1. What strategies in this chapter would help Josh think of topics and meet his deadlines?

   _____

   _____

2. What would you suggest to help him see the value of speaking and writing well?

   _____

   _____

In the Workplace

Josh has recently been promoted to regional manager for an investment firm. He feels very secure with the finance part of his job but pressured by new promotion requirements. He will need to present bimonthly speeches to top management, run daily meetings, and write dozens of reports. He must also give motivational seminars at least twice a year to his department heads. Josh wants to improve his writing skills and make his presentations clear, concise, and motivational.

3. What suggestions would you give Josh to help make his presentations more professional and interesting?

   _____

   _____

4. What strategies could he use to improve his writing?

   _____

   _____

Applying the ABC Method of Self-Management

In the Journal Entry box on page 275, you were asked to describe a time when you did well in a speaking assignment or leading a discussion. What factors helped you be calm and confident?

_____

_____

_____

Now describe a situation in which your mind went blank or you suffered stage fright. How would increasing your presentation or public speaking skills have helped you? Apply the ABC Method to visualize a result in which you are again calm, confident, and focused.

A = Actual event:

_____

_____

_____

B = Beliefs:

_____

_____

_____

C = Challenge:

_____

_____

_____

Practice deep breathing with your eyes closed for 1 minute. See yourself calm, centered, and relaxed as you give a performance or make a speech. See yourself presenting your ideas clearly, concisely, and confidently. You feel confident because you have learned to control stage fright, are well prepared, and know how to give speeches.

PRACTICE SELF-MANAGEMENT

For more examples of learning how to manage difficult situations, see the "Self-Management Workbook" section of the Outline Learning Center Web site at **www.mhhe.com/ferrett8e**.

Practice Paraphrasing

Because it's so easy to cut and paste material from the Internet, it's also too easy to pick up someone else's work and use it as your own. It's essential to paraphrase (and cite) material originally developed by others.

Read the following excerpt and then attempt to rewrite in your own words what the author has said:

Are you among the millions of Americans who take vitamin supplements? If your answer is "yes," why do you use them? Many people take multiple vitamin/mineral supplements as an "insurance policy" in case their diets are not nutritionally adequate. Other people use specific vitamin supplements because they think this practice will result in optimal health. Vitamin supplements are effective for treating people with specific vitamin deficiency diseases, metabolic defects that increase vitamin requirements, and a few other medical conditions. However, scientific evidence generally does not support claims that megadoses of vitamins can prevent or treat everything from gray hair to lung cancer.

(Source: Wendy J. Schiff: *Nutrition for Healthy Living*, 2009, McGraw-Hill.)

Now, write the essence of what the author has said:

_____

_____

_____

_____

_____

_____

_____

_____

_____

_____

_____

_____

_____

_____

_____

_____

_____

_____

Your Writing and Speaking Skills

Looking Back

1. Recall any activities and events through which you learned to write and speak. Jot down examples of classes, presentations, essays, journals, and papers.

_____

_____

2. What are your strengths in writing and speaking?

_____

_____

3. What would you like to improve?

_____

_____

4. What are your feelings about writing and speaking?

_____

_____

Looking Forward

5. How can you demonstrate to employers that you have effective writing and speaking skills?

_____

_____

6. Include in your portfolio samples of speeches you have given. List the titles on the following lines.

_____

_____

7. Include in your portfolio samples of your writing. List the titles.

_____

_____

8. Include in your portfolio samples of your research. List the titles.

_____

_____

Add this page to your Career Development Portfolio.

10

Become a Critical Thinker and Creative Problem Solver

LEARNING OUTCOMES

In this chapter, you will learn to

10.1 Define Bloom's Taxonomy

10.2 Explain the problem-solving process

10.3 Practice critical thinking and problem-solving strategies

10.4 Describe common fallacies and errors in judgment

10.5 Explain the importance of creativity in problem solving

10.6 Use problem-solving strategies for mathematics and science

10.7 Overcome math and science anxiety

SELF-MANAGEMENT

> *I dropped a class, thinking I could take it next semester, but it's offered just once a year, so I won't graduate when I had planned to. I didn't realize one decision could have such an impact.*

Have you ever made a decision without thinking through all the consequences? How does your attitude affect your thinking and creativity? In this chapter, you will learn to use your critical thinking and creative problem-solving skills and learn strategies for making sound decisions in all areas of life.

JOURNAL ENTRY In **Worksheet 10.1** on page 336, think of a decision you made that has cost you a lot of time, money, or stress. How would critical thinking and creative problem solving have helped you make better decisions?

P roblem solving—coming up with possible solutions—and **decision making**—deciding on the best solution—go hand-in-hand. You have to make decisions to solve a problem; conversely, some problems occur because of a decision you made. For example, you may decide to smoke cigarettes; later, you face the problem of nicotine addiction, health problems, and a lot of your budget spent on cigarettes. In school, a decision not to study mathematics and science because they seem too difficult will close off the chance to choose certain majors and careers. Many events in life do not just happen; they are the result of our choices and decisions. We make decisions every day; even not deciding is making a decision. For example, if you avoid going to class, that shows you have decided the class is unimportant or not worth the time. You may have not formally dropped the class or not thought through the consequences, but the result of deciding not to go to class is an *F* grade.

In this chapter, you will learn to use critical thinking and creativity to help you solve problems and make effective and sound decisions. Mathematics and science will be discussed, as these are key areas which rely on your critical thinking and problem-solving skills. You will also learn to overcome math anxiety and develop a positive attitude toward problem solving.

Essential Critical Thinking Skills

As discussed in Chapter 1, critical thinking is a logical, rational, systematic thought process necessary for understanding, analyzing, and evaluating information in order to solve a problem. In the 1956 text *Taxonomy of Educational Objectives,* Benjamin Bloom and his colleagues outlined a hierarchy of six critical thinking skills that college requires (from lowest- to highest-order): knowledge, comprehension, application, analysis, synthesis, and evaluation. (See **Figure 10.1**.)

1. **Knowledge.** In most college courses, you have to memorize lists, identify facts, complete objective tests, and recognize and recall terms and information.
2. **Comprehension.** You also need to demonstrate that you understand the material. You may be asked to state ideas in your own words, outline key ideas, and translate an author's meaning.
3. **Application.** You will be asked to apply what you've learned to a new situation. You may explore case studies, solve problems, and provide examples to support your ideas. You can learn application by applying ideas to your own life. For example, how can you apply political science concepts to issues in your community?
4. **Analysis.** You will be asked to break apart ideas and relate them to other concepts, answer essay questions, identify assumptions, and analyze values. You will compare and contrast ideas or subjects, such as economic theories or two works of art.

Evaluation	Make judgments about the information
Synthesis	Combine selected parts to create new information
Analysis	Separate understood information into parts
Application	Make practical use of the understood information
Comprehension	Understand the significance of the information
Knowledge	Recall information

CRITICAL THINKING SKILLS

Figure 10.1
Bloom's Taxonomy

Actively participating in college will require you to use six core critical thinking skills. *Which skills are you using as you complete current projects or assignments?*

5. **Synthesis.** You will be asked to integrate ideas, build on other skills, look for interconnections, create and defend a position, improve on an existing idea or design, and develop creative ideas and new perspectives. You might compose a song or research ways that a community project affects other areas of the community.

6. **Evaluation.** You will be asked to criticize a position, form conclusions and judgments, list advantages and disadvantages of a project or an idea, and develop and use criteria for evaluating a decision. You can develop evaluation skills by using standards for evaluating speeches in class, evaluating group projects, and being open to suggestions from your study group and instructors.

To excel in school and make sound decisions in life, you must move beyond simple knowledge and comprehension and be able to apply, analyze, synthesize, and evaluate questions and problems you are faced with. See **Peak Progress 10.1** on page 308 for an example of moving from knowledge to evaluation.

Problem-Solving Steps

You must exercise and apply your critical thinking skills when solving problems and making decisions. The problem-solving process can be broken down into four major steps: (1) Define the problem, (2) gather and interpret information, (3) develop and implement a plan of action, and (4) evaluate the plan.

1. **Define the problem.** Do you understand and can you clearly state the problem? What are you trying to find out? What is known and unknown? What is the situation, or context? What decision are you asked to make? Can you separate the problem into various parts? Organize the problem, or restate the decision or problem in your own words—for example, "Should I go on a study abroad exchange or do an internship?"

Peak Progress

From Knowledge to Evaluation

If you can recall the number 8675309, but you attach no significance to the number, you have mere *knowledge*. Not tremendously useful, is it?

However, if you are familiar with a particular song performed by Tommy Tutone, you may recognize this number as the telephone number of a girl named Jenny, which the songwriter had found penned on a wall. Now you have *comprehension*. Still, you wonder, "So what?"

Maybe you are intrigued enough to actually call the number to see whether Jenny answers. This is *application*. Unfortunately, unless you happen to be in an area code where this telephone number exists, you will probably get a telephone company recording.

Next you break down the number into its component parts. You see that it has a 3-digit prefix and a 4-digit suffix. The prefix is 867. You have just performed a simple *analysis*.

In order to track Jenny down, you will need to combine other bodies of information with what you already know. You know Jenny's phone number, but there could be many identical phone numbers throughout the country. What you need to find is a list of area codes that includes this number. You have then performed *synthesis*.

Before you go any further, ask yourself how important it is to find Jenny. How many matching telephone numbers did you turn up in the previous step? Are you going to dial each of them? How much is it going to cost you in long-distance charges? How much of your time will it take? Is it worth it? You have just made an *evaluation*.

Courtesy T. C. Stuwe, Salt Lake Community College, © 2002.

---

2. **Gather and interpret information.** What are all the possibilities? Be sure you have all the information you need to solve the problem and make a decision. Try to see the problem from different angles. "I have visited the career center and the study abroad office. I have listed pros and cons for each choice. I have included cost and expenses." Are there other options, such as a paid internship or student teaching abroad? When choosing a plan of action, consider all options and then narrow the list.

3. **Develop and implement a plan of action.** How would this plan work? Eventually, you need to act on your decision and choose an appropriate strategy. Ask yourself what information would be helpful. "I have gathered information and talked to people in my chosen field. Most career professionals have suggested that I go on an exchange as a way to broaden my worldview. I found out I can apply for an internship for the following term. Since I can learn a foreign language and take valuable classes, I am going on the study abroad exchange and will do everything possible to make this experience valuable." Your intention to make this decision succeed is key.

4. **Evaluate your plan.** Why is this plan better for you than other options? Is there one right answer? What consequences are likely if you choose this approach? "I made valuable contacts and am learning so much from this experience. I'll do an internship when I return. This was the best choice for me at this time." Observe the consequences of this decision over time, and reflect on what other options may have worked better. See **Personal Evaluation Notebook 10.1** to explore the consequences of everyday decisions.

Problem-Solving Steps

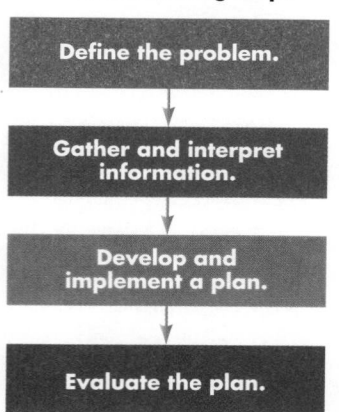

Define the problem.

Gather and interpret information.

Develop and implement a plan.

Evaluate the plan.

Personal Evaluation Notebook

10.1

Think It Through

Often we make decisions without considering the consequences. It may be because we're only thinking about the immediate result or benefit. Or maybe the decision seems so minor that the consequences are insignificant. However, a series of poor "small" decisions can lead to big problems later.

Exercise your decision-making and problem-solving skills by teaming up with classmates to consider decisions you make every day. For example, let's say you've missed a couple of classes lately. One person should state the problem or issue. Then go through the problem-solving steps, ask questions, explore possibilities, and use critical thinking to make a sound decision:

1. **Define the problem.**
   - I've missed three classes in the past 2 weeks.

2. **Gather and interpret the information.**
   - The reasons are [such as my babysitter canceled, car broke down, alarm didn't go off, or I hate 8:00 a.m. classes].
   - The consequences for missing this class are
   - If I drop the class, what could happen?
   - If I keep missing the class, what could happen?

3. **Develop and implement a plan of action.**
   - What are some creative possibilities to help me get to class?
   - What is the best plan of action?

4. **Evaluate the plan.**
   - What decision is best for my goals and priorities?
   - How will I ensure that this decision succeeds?

Come up with other situations you may encounter daily, such as relationship issues and spending decisions, and work through them using the problem-solving steps.

Critical Thinking and Problem-Solving Strategies

Critical thinking and problem solving will help you make day-to-day decisions about relationships, courses to take, jobs to apply for, places to live, ideas for speeches and papers, and resolutions to conflicts. You can apply the following strategies to ensure you are fully using your critical thinking and problem-solving capabilities:

1. **Have a positive attitude.** Critical thinking requires a willingness and passion to explore, probe, question, and search for answers and solutions. (See **Figure 10.2.**) Your attitude influences how you solve a problem or make a decision. Think of problems as puzzles to solve, rather than difficulties to

Figure 10.2

Critical Thinking Qualities

Thinking critically is important for understanding and solving problems. *Do you apply any of the attributes of a critical thinker when you need to solve a problem?*

Attributes of a Critical Thinker

- Willingness to ask pertinent questions and assess statements and arguments
- Ability to be open-minded and seek opposing views
- Ability to suspend judgment and tolerate ambiguity
- Ability to admit a lack of information or understanding
- Curiosity and interest in seeking new solutions
- Ability to clearly define a set of criteria for analyzing ideas
- Willingness to examine beliefs, assumptions, and opinions against facts

avoid. Instead of delaying, making a knee-jerk decision, or looking for the one "right answer," focus on problem-solving strategies. For example, you may have a negative attitude toward math or science, considering it irrelevant or too difficult. Choose to see a problem or situation in the best possible light. Complete **Personal Evaluation Notebook 10.2** to practice turning negatives into positives.

2. **Ask questions.** It's difficult to solve a problem without knowing all the facts and opinions—or at least as many as you can find out. **Peak Progress 10.2** on page 312 offers tips for formulating effective questions.

3. **Persistence pays off.** You won't solve every problem with your first effort. Sometimes you'll need a second or third try. Analytical thinking requires time, persistence, and patience. Sometimes it pays to sleep on an important decision instead of bowing to pressure. Effective problem solvers are not beaten by frustration but look for new ways to solve problems.

4. **Use creativity.** As we will explore later in this chapter, you should learn to think in new and fresh ways, look for interconnections, and brainstorm many solutions. Good problem solvers explore many alternatives and evaluate their strengths and weaknesses.

5. **Pay attention to details.** Effective problem solvers show concern for accuracy. They think about what could go wrong, recheck calculations, and look for errors. They gather all relevant information and proofread or ask questions. They are willing to listen to arguments, create and defend positions, and can distinguish among various points of view.

6. **See all sides of the issue.** Think critically about what you read, hear, and see in newspapers and on the Internet. As you read, question sources and viewpoints. For example, when you read an article about Social Security or tax cuts, ask yourself what biases politicians or special interest groups might have regarding these issues. Does the argument appeal to emotion rather than to logic? Talk to people who have different opinions or belong to a different political party. Really listen to their views, and ask them to explain their opinions and why they support certain issues.

7. **Use reasoning.** We are constantly trying to make sense of our world, so we make inferences to explain and interpret events. Effective problem solvers

Personal Evaluation Notebook

10.2

Using Critical Thinking to Solve Problems

Stating a problem clearly, exploring alternatives, reasoning logically, choosing the best alternative, creating an action plan, and evaluating your plan are all involved in making decisions and solving problems.

Look at the common reasons or excuses given by some students for not solving problems creatively or making sound decisions. Create strategies for overcoming these barriers.

1. I'm not a creative person.

   Strategy: _____

   _____

2. Facts can be misleading; I like to follow my gut instinct.

   Strategy: _____

   _____

3. I avoid conflict.

   Strategy: _____

   _____

4. I postpone making decisions.

   Strategy: _____

   _____

5. I worry that I'll make the wrong decision.

   Strategy: _____

   _____

check their inferences to see if they are sound, not based on assumptions, which often reflect their own experiences and biases. Ask yourself, "What makes me think this is true? Could I be wrong? Are there other possibilities?" Effective problem solvers do not jump to conclusions.

Inductive reasoning is generalizing from specific concepts to broad principles. For example, you might have had a bad experience with a math class in high school and, based on that experience, might reason inductively that all math classes are hard and boring. When you get into your college math class, you may discover that your conclusion was incorrect and that you actually like mathematics. In contrast, **deductive reasoning** is drawing conclusions based on going from the general to the specific—for example, "Since all mathematics classes at this college must be taken for credit and this class is a math class, I must take it for credit." However, don't assume that the main premise is always

Peak Progress

Asking Questions

"Why is the sky blue?" "Where do babies come from?" When we were children, our days were filled with endless questions, reflecting curiosity about the world around us. As adults, some of us have become reluctant and sometimes even nervous to ask for help or insightful answers. It's not that there are no questions left to ask—just the contrary. Attending college opens up the floodgates of new information to comprehend, process, apply, and question.

This reluctance can stem from possible embarrassment, as the information may have already been covered (and you were daydreaming, didn't read the assignment, didn't see the connections, etc.) and others will think you're behind for one reason or another. Or, when simply talking with friends, you may think asking questions will seem like you are prying or are "nosey," or behind on the latest trends.

Whatever your reasons, you must overcome your reluctance and learn how to formulate questions. Most careers require asking questions and persistence in finding answers. A sales representative asks customers what their needs are and tries to fulfill those needs with his or her product. A physician asks patients questions about their medical history, symptoms, and reactions to medications.

WHO CAN BEST ANSWER YOUR QUESTION?

Before asking a question, determine whom or what you should be consulting. Could the information be found more easily or quickly by looking it up online, in the library, or in another source? Is it a question more appropriate for your instructor, advisor, or financial aid officer? Is there a local "expert" in this area?

WHAT TYPE OF QUESTION SHOULD YOU ASK?

State your question quickly and succinctly, and provide background information only if your question isn't clear. Based on the type of response you are looking for, there are several ways to formulate your question:

- **Closed question.** Use this type of question when you want either a yes/no answer or specific details—for example, "Which planet is closer to the sun—Earth or Mars?"
- **Fact-finding question.** This is aimed at getting information on a particular subject, usually when your core materials (such as the textbook or lecture) haven't provided the information—for example, "Which battle had the most casualties, and was that considered the turning point in the war?"
- **Follow-up question.** This question clarifies a point, gathers more information, or elicits an opinion—for example, "So, what side effects might I experience from this medication?"
- **Open-ended question.** Use this to invite discussion and various viewpoints or interpretations of an issue—for example, "What do you think about the ordinance to ban smoking in local restaurants?"
- **Feedback question.** Use this when you want someone to provide you with constructive criticism—for example, "What sections of my paper supported my main points effectively, and what sections needed more back-up?"

WHEN SHOULD YOU ASK THE QUESTION?

Ask your question as soon as possible after the speaker has completed his or her point. Most likely, your instructor has guidelines for class (such as saving questions for the last 10 minutes). If so, jot down your questions during lecture, so that you can return to them or to add answers if the content is covered in the meantime. Open-ended and feedback questions may be more appropriate outside a typical class discussion but can often provide the most insightful answers.

"He who asks is a fool for five minutes, but he who does not ask remains a fool forever."

CHINESE PROVERB

true. In this example, there may be math labs, workshops, or special classes offered for no credit. Practice inductive versus deductive reasoning in **Personal Evaluation Notebook 10.3** on page 314.

Common Errors in Judgment

Some thoughts and beliefs are clearly irrational, with no evidence to support them. For example, if you believe people cannot change, you could get stuck in unhealthy situations and accept that there is no solution for your problems. Solving problems requires critical thinking and frequent self-assessment of your thoughts and beliefs. Ask questions to help clarify your thinking and apply the ABC Method of Self-Management to dispel myths and irrational thoughts.

Here are some common errors in judgment or faulty thinking that interfere with effective critical thinking:

THINK
FAST

- *Stereotypes* are judgments held by a person or group about the members of another group—for example, "All instructors are absentminded intellectuals." Learn to see individual differences between people.

- *All-or-nothing thinking* means seeing events or people in black or white, such as turning a single negative event into a pattern of defeat: "If I don't get an *A* in this class, I'm a total failure." Be careful about using the terms *always* and *never.*

- *Snap judgments* are decisions made before gathering all the necessary information or facts. An example is concluding that someone doesn't like you because of one comment or because of a comment made by someone else. Instead, find out the reason for the comment. Perhaps you misinterpreted the meaning.

- *Unwarranted assumptions* are beliefs and ideas you assume are true in different situations. For example, your business instructor allows papers to be turned in late, so you assume that your biology instructor will allow the same.

- *Projection* is the tendency to attribute to others some of your own traits in an attempt to justify your own faulty judgments or actions—for example, "It's OK if I cheat, because everyone else is cheating."

- *Sweeping generalizations* apply one experience to a whole group or issue. For example, if research has been conducted using college students as subjects, you cannot generalize the results to the overall work population.

- The *halo effect* is the tendency to label a person good at many things based on one or two qualities or actions. For example, Serena sits in the front row, attends every class, and gets good grades on papers. Based on this observation, you decide she is smart, organized, and a great student in all her classes. First impressions are important in the halo effect and are difficult to change. You can make this work for you. Suppose you start out the semester by giving it your all; you go to every class, establish a relationship with the instructor, participate in class, and work hard. Later in the semester, you may need to miss a class or ask to take an exam early. Your instructor has already formed an opinion of you as a good student and may be more sympathetic, since you have created a positive impression.

- *Negative labeling* is focusing on and identifying with shortcomings, either yours or others'. Instead of saying, "I made a mistake when I quit going to my math study group," you tell yourself, "I'm a loser." You may also pick a single negative trait or detail and focus on it exclusively. You discount positive qualities or accomplishments: "I've lost my keys again. I am so disorganized. Yes, I did organize a successful club fundraiser, but that doesn't count."

Personal Evaluation Notebook

10.3

Inductive Versus Deductive Reasoning

Practice creating inductive and deductive statements.

INDUCTIVE EXAMPLES

- No one should consider buying a car with a sunroof. Mine leaked every time it rained.
- Nadia ended up in the hospital with food poisoning the day after the party. I'm sure that's why Cara and Brendan said they were sick the next day, too.

_____

_____

_____

_____

DEDUCTIVE EXAMPLES

- Everyone who attended the review session for the first test received an *A*. If I attend the next session, I'm bound to get an *A*.
- All the men in our family are over 6 feet tall. I'm sure my baby son will be as tall when he's an adult.

_____

_____

_____

_____

“Imagination will often carry us to worlds that never were. But without it we go nowhere.”

CARL SAGAN
Astronomer, author

Creative Problem Solving

Creativity is thinking of something differently and using new approaches to solve problems. Many inventions have involved a break from traditional thinking and resulted in an "aha!" experience. For example, Albert Einstein used many unusual approaches and "riddles" that revolutionized scientific thought. (Several Web sites include "Einstein's Riddle." Locate one and test yourself to see if you can answer "who owns the fish?")

Use creativity to explore alternatives, look for relationships among different items, and develop imaginative ideas and solutions. Try the following strategies to unlock your mind's natural creativity:

1. **Expect to be creative.** Use affirmations that reinforce your innate creativity:
   - I am a creative and resourceful person.
   - I have many imaginative and unusual ideas.

- Creative ideas flow to me many times a day.
- I act on many of these ideas.
- I act responsibly, use critical thinking, check details carefully, and take calculated risks.

2. **Challenge the rules.** Habit often restricts you from trying new approaches to problem solving. Often, there is more than one solution. List many alternatives, and imagine the likely consequences of each. Empty your mind of the "right" way of looking at problems, and strive to see situations in a fresh way. How often have you told yourself you must follow certain rules and perform tasks a certain way? If you want to be creative, try new approaches, look at things in a new order, break the pattern, and challenge the rules. Practice a different approach by completing the Nine-Dot Exercise in **Personal Evaluation Notebook 10.4** on page 316.

3. **Use games, puzzles, and humor.** Rethinking an assignment as a puzzle, challenge, or game instead of a difficult problem opens your mind and encourages your creative side. Creative people often get fresh ideas while having fun engaging in an unrelated activity. When your defenses are down, your brain is relaxed and your subconscious is alive; creative thoughts can flow.

4. **Brainstorm.** Brainstorming is a common strategy for freeing the imagination. You can brainstorm alone, but a group may be more effective for generating as many ideas as possible. Brainstorming encourages the mind to explore without judging the merit of new ideas. In fact, even silly and irrelevant ideas can lead to truly inventive ideas. While brainstorming ideas for a speech, one study group started joking about the topic, and new ideas came from all directions. To exercise your brainstorming skills, complete **Personal Evaluation Notebook 10.5** on page 317.

5. **Change mindsets.** It is difficult to see another frame of reference once your mind is set. The exercise in **Personal Evaluation Notebook 10.6** on page 318 is an "aha" exercise. It is exciting to watch people see the other picture. There is enormous power in shifting your perception and gaining new ways of seeing things, events, and people. Perceptual exercises of this kind demonstrate that you see what you focus on and when you reframe. You are conditioned to see certain things, depending on your beliefs and attitudes. Rather than seeing facts, you may see your interpretation of reality. Perceptual distortion can influence how you solve problems and make decisions. For example, John was told that his Spanish instructor was aloof, not student-oriented, and boring. John went to his first class with that mindset, so he sat in the back of class and did not ask questions or get involved. He later found out that his friend had been referring to another instructor. John realized that his mindset was influencing how he viewed his instructor. He reframed his impression and developed a positive relationship with the instructor.

6. **Change your routine.** Try a different route to work or school. Read different kinds of books. Spend time with people who are different from you. Occasionally break away from your daily routine, and take time every day to relax, daydream, and renew your energy. Look at unexpected events as a chance to retreat from constant activity and hurried thoughts. Perhaps this

WORDS TO SUCCEED

"The man who has no imagination has no wings."
MUHAMMAD ALI
Professional boxer

WORDS TO SUCCEED

"It's not what you look at that matters, it's what you see."
HENRY DAVID THOREAU
Author

Personal Evaluation Notebook

Nine-Dot Exercise

Connect the following nine dots by drawing only four (or fewer) straight lines without lifting the pencil from the paper. Do not retrace any lines. The solution is on page 330.

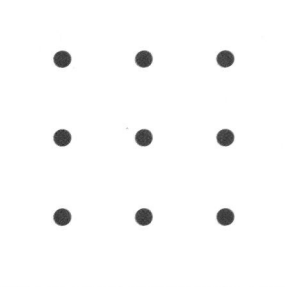

is a good time to brainstorm ideas for a speech assignment or outline an assigned paper.

7. **Use both sides of the brain.** You use the logical, analytical side of your brain for certain activities and your imaginative and multidimensional side for others. When you develop and integrate both sides of your brain, you become more imaginative, creative, and productive. Learn to be attentive to details and to trust your intuition.

8. **Acknowledge your style.** Your personality type or learning style may coincide with the way you approach problem solving. Recall Figure 1.3 on page 21, which lists the characteristics of personality types. If you tend to be a *judger*, for example, your thinking style may be to tackle problems quickly, looking for objective facts and precedents to support your decision. In contrast to a *perceiver*, you may not consider the "human toll" or circumstances that could take the decision in another direction. As in the case of learning, which you can enhance by recognizing your preferred style and mixing it up by incorporating other styles, you can enhance problem solving by adding styles to the one you prefer. To think out of the box, recognize how you normally think and respond to problems, assess if your style clouds or limits your thinking, and determine how to expand your abilities. Based on your earlier assessment of your personality type and learning style (which you may have modified since then), how would you characterize your "thinking style"?

9. **Keep a journal.** Keep a journal of creative ideas, dreams, and thoughts, and make a commitment to complete journal entries daily. Collect stories of creative people and what they do that is unique. Write in your journal about risks you take and what you have learned from the experience.

Personal Evaluation Notebook

10.5

Brainstorming Notes

Solving a problem requires more than a creative idea; you also have to convince others that your idea is the best solution. Read the following brainstorming notes. Then, on the lines that follow, write your own brainstorming notes about how Basil can sell his ideas to his staff.

Basil's Pizza   Sept. 29, 2011

Brainstorming Notes

Problem: Should I hire temporary employees or increase overtime of my regular employees to meet new production schedule?

Ideas	Evaluation	Plus + or Minus −	Solution
hire temp. employees	may lack training	−	1. hire temps
	additional benefits	−	
work regular employees			
overtime	may result in fatigue	−	2. work overtime
	extra $ for employee	+	explore further
	higher morale	+	
	possible advancement	+	
	cross training	+	
	save on overhead		
	and benefits	+	
turn down contract	not possible	−	
reduce hours store is open	not feasible	−	
reduce product line	not acceptable	−	

_____

_____

_____

_____

_____

_____

Personal Evaluation Notebook

10.6

Mind sets

Look at the following figure. Do you see an attractive young woman or an old woman with a hooked nose?

I see a(n) _____

If you saw the young woman first, it is very hard to see the old woman. If you saw the old woman first, it is just as hard to see the young woman. Why is that true?

Source: Maslow, A. "Emotional Blocks to Creativity." In S.J. Parnes, & H.F. Harding (eds), *A Sourcebook for Creative Thinking.* New York: Scribner, 1962.

10. **Evaluate.** Go through each step and examine your work. Look at what you know and don't know, and examine your hypotheses. Can you prove that each step is correct? Examine the solution carefully. Can you obtain the solution differently? Investigate the connections of the problem. What formulas did you use? Can you use the same method for other problems? Talk about problems with your study team, and see if there are other ways to solve them. Practice your decision-making skills by working through the case scenarios in **Personal Evaluation Notebook 10.7** and **10.8** on the following pages.

11. **Support, acknowledge, and reward creativity.** Get excited about new ideas and approaches, and acknowledge and reward yourself and others for creative

(continued on page 322)

Personal Evaluation Notebook

Decision-Making Application

Use critical thinking and creative problem-solving skills to evaluate the following case scenario:

I am currently attending a career school and will soon earn my associate's degree in computer-aided design. Once I obtain my degree, should I continue my education or look for a full-time job? My long-term goal is to be an architect. My wife and I have been married for 3 years, and we want to start a family soon.

- **Define the problem.** "Should I continue my education or get a job?"
- **Gather and interpret information.** Ask questions such as these: "What are the advantages and disadvantages? Whom should I talk with, such as my advisor, instructors at my current school and potential schools, family members, and career professionals?"
- **Develop and implement a plan of action.**
  1. *List the pros and cons for each choice:*"What are the factors I should consider, such as cost, opportunities, and time?"

Consider the following pros and cons for each solution, and list additional reasons that you think should be considered.

Solution: *Continue education at a local state university*

Pros	Cons
I'll get a better job with a 4-year degree.	I'll have to take out more student loans.
I'm enjoying school and the learning process.	I want to put my skills into practice in the job.
I'll meet new, diverse friends and contacts.	A lot of my time at home will be devoted to studying.

Solution: *Get a job*

Pros	Cons
I can make more money than I am now and start paying off debts.	The opportunities would be better with a 4-year degree.
We can start a family.	It will take longer to become an architect.
I get to put my skills to work.	Once I start working full-time, it may be hard to go back to school.

(continued)

Personal Evaluation Notebook

Decision-Making Application *(concluded)*

2. *Choose what you believe is the best solution:* "I have decided to get a job."

- **Evaluate the plan.** "My choice is reasonable and makes sense for me now in my situation. I won't have to work such long hours and juggle school and work, and I can pay back loans and save money. We can start our family. I can review my long-term goal and determine another way to achieve it."

Would you arrive at the same decision? What would be your decision and your main reasons?

_____

_____

Now set up a problem or decision you are facing, and follow the same steps.

- Problem

_____

- Where can I get help or information?

_____

_____

POSSIBLE SOLUTIONS AND PROS AND CONS

Solution #1: _____

_____

Pros	Cons
1. _____	_____
2. _____	_____
3. _____	_____

Solution #2: _____

_____

Pros	Cons
1. _____	_____
2. _____	_____
3. _____	_____

SOLUTION CHOSEN AND WHY

_____

_____

Personal Evaluation Notebook

10.8

Solving Problems and Making Choices

Every day you solve problems and make choices. Some problems are easy to solve: *What's for dinner?* Some problems are harder: *Can I afford to buy a car?* Some problems change a life forever: *Should I get married?*

You can use the following steps to help you review your choices to determine their impact, the risks involved, and the potential alternate choices.

Step 1 Know what the problem really is. Is it a daily problem? Is it a once-in-a-lifetime problem?

Step 2 List facts you know about the problem. List facts you don't know. Ask questions. Seek help and advice.

Step 3 Explore alternate choices.

Step 4 Think about the pros and cons for each choice. Rank them from best to worst choice.

Step 5 Pick the choice you feel good about.

Step 6 After choosing, study what happens. Are you happy about the choice? Would you make it again?

Read the following story and apply the steps in the following exercise.

JOSÉ'S CHOICE

José is 50 years old. He has a wife and three kids. He has worked as a bookkeeper for 20 years for the same company. The company is relocating. Only a few people will move with the company. Many workers will lose their jobs.

José's boss says he can keep his job, but he has to move. If he doesn't, he won't have a job. The family has always lived in this town. José's daughter is a senior in high school and wants to go to the local college next year. His twin boys are looking forward to playing next year for the ninth-grade football team. José's wife works part-time in a bakery. She has many friends, and all of her family live nearby.

The family talked about whether to take the new job and move. José's wife is afraid. His daughter doesn't want to move. The twins will miss their friends. How would you define the family's problem? What are the choices? Can you help them?

Step 1 The problem is _____

_____

_____

Is it a daily problem? _____

_____

_____

Is it a once-in-a-lifetime problem? _____

_____

_____

(continued)

Personal Evaluation Notebook

10.8

Solving Problems and Making Choices *(concluded)*

Step 2 You know _____

_____

_____

You don't know _____

_____

_____

Step 3 The other choices are _____

_____

_____

Step 4 Rank the choices. _____

_____

_____

Step 5 Pick a choice the family might feel good about. _____

_____

_____

Step 6 What might happen? _____

_____

_____

ideas. Get involved with projects that encourage you to explore and be creative. How often do you put your creative ideas into action? Is there anything you want to change but keep putting it off? What new hobby or skill have you wanted to try? If you get lazy, set a firm deadline to complete a specific project. If you are running frantically, then take an hour or so to review your life's goals and set new priorities. If you feel shy and inhibited, clear some time to socialize and risk meeting new people.

12. **Allow failure.** If you don't fail occasionally, you are not risking anything. Mistakes are stepping-stones to growth and creativity. Fear of failure undermines the creative process by forcing us to play it safe. Eliminate the fear and shame of failure experienced in earlier years, and learn to admit mistakes.

Ask yourself, "What did I learn from this mistake? How can I handle the same type of situation the next time? How can I prepare for a situation like this the next time?" Creative people aren't afraid to look foolish at times, to generate unusual ideas, and to be nonconformists. They don't take themselves too seriously. They have courage to explore new ways of thinking and risk looking different, foolish, impractical, and even wrong.

13. **Practice and be persistent.** Problem solving requires discipline and focused effort. Learning any new skill takes time, practice, and patience. **Peak Progress 10.3** on page 324 provides a handy checklist to help you think of new ways to find solutions.

Take 3 minutes right now to tackle a problem you've been putting off:
- Clearly state the problem. Why must you address it now?
- Consider rational ways to solve the problem, and list pros and cons for each. What consequences would each solution have?
- Choose one solution, and commit to implementing it and evaluating the results.

What else can you do in 3 minutes?
- Brainstorm ways to improve your study habits.
- Take a break and challenge yourself to a quick online card game.
- Flip through your journal and find good ideas to follow up on.

Take 3

Math and Science Applications

Critical thinking and creative problem solving are essential for success in mathematics, science, and computer science courses—information that is also vital for job and life success. Studying mathematics and science develops such everyday skills as interpreting interest rates on credit cards, calculating your tuition, managing your personal finances, computing your GPA, and understanding how your body and the world around you work. Basic arithmetic can help you figure out a tip at a restaurant, algebra can help you compute the interest on a loan, basic probability can help you determine the chance that a given event will occur, and statistics can help you collect, analyze, and interpret data.

Problem-Solving Strategies for Math and Science

The basic problem-solving strategies discussed earlier in this chapter, starting on page 309, also apply to math and science. Additional strategies, many of which will get you physically involved, integrate all learning styles and make learning active and personal. Included are sample problems to help you practice these strategies.

1. **Make a model or diagram.** Physical models, objects, diagrams, and drawings can help organize information and can help you visualize problem situations. Use objects, cut up a model, measure lengths, and create concrete situations—for example,

   Problem: What is the length of a pendulum that makes one complete swing in 1 second?

   Strategy: Make a model (see page 324). With a 50 cm string and some small weights, make a pendulum tied to a pencil taped to a desk. To determine the length of the pendulum, measure the distance from the pencil to the center of the weight.

Peak Progress

Creative Ideas Checklist

Use this checklist of questions to challenge your usual thought patterns. When exploring alternative approaches to problem solving, you can put each category on a separate card.

- What other idea does this situation suggest?
- How can I modify?
- What can I subtract? Can I take it apart?
- What can I streamline?
- What can I rearrange?
- Can I transfer?
- Can I combine or blend?
- What are other uses if modified?
- Have I written it out?
- Can I use another approach?
- Can I interchange components?
- Are there any opposites?

- What are the positives and negatives?
- Have I used a mind map, model, diagram, list, or chart?
- Have I used a drawing or picture?
- Have I acted it out?
- Have I talked it out?
- Have I tried it?
- Should I sleep on it?
- List some of your own suggestions for creative problem solving:

_____

_____

_____

_____

Solution: Since it is difficult to measure the time period accurately, time 10 swings and use the average. The correct answer is approximately 25 cm.

Evaluation: If the length is fixed, the amount of weight does not affect the time period. The amount of deflection does affect the period when large deflections are used, but it is not a factor for small amounts of 5 cm or less. The length of the pendulum always affects the time period.

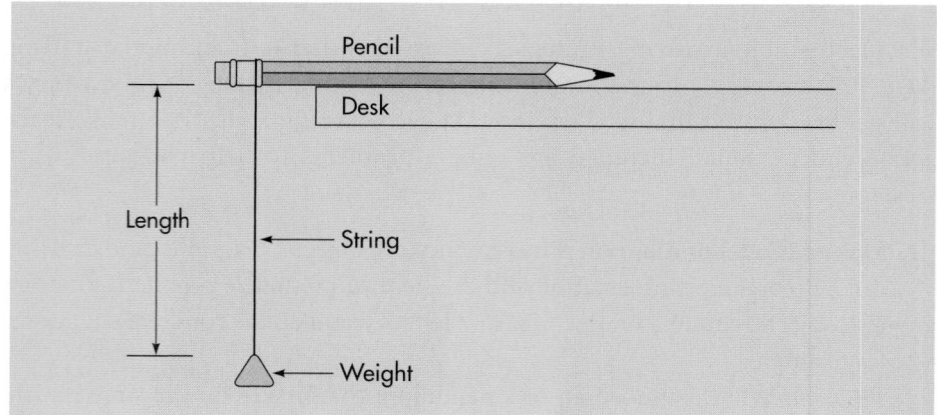

2. **Draw, illustrate, and make tables, charts, or lists.** This way of organizing data presented in a problem helps you look for patterns. For example, a fruit punch dispenser mixes 4 ml of orange juice with 6 ml of pineapple juice. How many ml of orange juice does it mix with 240 ml of pineapple juice?

			Answer
Orange juice ml	4	16	160
Pineapple juice ml	6	24	240

3. **Look for patterns and connections.** A pattern is a regular, systematic repetition that helps you predict what will come next. Field trips and laboratory work can help you find patterns and categorize information, and so can creating tables. For example, an empty commuter train is picking up passengers at the following rate: One passenger got on at the first stop, three got on at the second stop, and five got on at the third stop. How many passengers got on the train at the sixth stop?

						Answer
Stops	1	2	3	4	5	6
Number of passengers	1	3	5	7	9	11

4. **Act out the problem.** Sometimes it helps to physically act out the problem. For example, there are 5 people in your study group, and each person initiates a handshake with every member one time. How many total handshakes will there be? There will be 20 handshakes total, because each person shakes hands 4 times (since you cannot shake your own hand). Thus, 5 people times 4 handshakes equals 20 total handshakes. You multiply the total number of people times one number fewer for the handshakes.

5. **Simplify.** Sometimes the best way to simplify a problem is first to solve easier cases of the same problem. For example, simplify the problem of study group

Number of People	Each Person Initiates Handshake × Times	Total Number of Handshakes
2	1	2
3	2	
4		
5	4	20
6		

handshakes by solving it for 2 people instead of 5. When each person initiates a handshake, 2 people shake hands a total of 2 times. Using the formula determined in number 4, you see that the equation is $2 \times 1 = 2$. Fill in the rest of the table on the previous page.

Along the same lines, when working on homework, studying in your group, or taking a test, always do the easiest problems first. Confident that you can solve one kind of problem, you gain enthusiasm to tackle more difficult questions or problems. Also, an easier problem may be similar to a harder problem.

6. **Translate words into equations.** Highlight visual and verbal learning by showing connections between words and numbers. Write an equation that models that problem. For example, Sarah has a total of $82.00, consisting of an equal number of pennies, nickels, dimes, and quarters. How many coins does she have in all? You know how much all of Sarah's coins are worth and you know how much each coin is worth. (In the following equation, p = pennies, n = nickels, d = dimes, and q = quarters.)

$$p + 5n + 10d + 25q = 8,200$$

We know that she has an equal number of each coin; thus, $p = n = d = q$. Therefore, we can substitute p for all the other variables:

$$1p + 5p + 10p + 25p = 41p = 8,200, \text{ so } p = 200$$

Sarah has 200 pennies, 200 nickels, 200 dimes, and 200 quarters. Therefore, she has 800 coins.

7. **Estimate, make a reasonable guess, check the guess, and revise.** Using the example in number 6, if you were told that Sarah had a large number of coins that added up to $82.00, you could at least say that the total was no more than 8,200 (the number of coins if they were all pennies) and no less than 328 (the number of coins if they were all quarters).

8. **Work backwards and eliminate.** For example, what is the largest 2-digit number that is divisible by 3 whose digits differ by 2? First, working backwards from 99, list numbers that are divisible by 3:

99, 96, 93, 90, 87, 84, 81, 78, 75, 72, 69, 66, 63, 60, . . .

Now cross out all numbers whose digits do not differ by 2. The largest number remaining is 75.

9. **Summarize in a group.** Working in a group is the best way to integrate all learning styles, keep motivation and interest active, and generate lots of ideas and support. Explain the problem to your group and why you arrived at the answer. Talking out loud, summarizing chapters, and listening to others clarifies thinking and helps you learn.

10. **Take a quiet break.** If your group can't find a solution to the problem, take a break. Sometimes it helps to find a quiet spot and reflect. Working on another problem or relaxing for a few minutes while listening to music helps you return to the problem refreshed.

Overcome Math and Science Anxiety

Many people suffer from some math and science anxiety—having a preconceived notion that the material is difficult to learn, over their heads, or too precise (only one correct answer). As with the fear many experience with public speaking, the first step in learning any subject is to use critical thinking and creative problem solving to manage and overcome these anxieties.

Anxiety is a learned emotional response—you were not born with it. Since it is learned, it can be unlearned. In Chapter 9, we explored strategies for overcoming speech anxiety, and many apply to math and science as well. Here are some additional strategies:

1. **Do your prep work.** Don't take a math or science class if you haven't taken the proper prerequisites. It is better to spend the summer or an additional semester gaining the necessary skills, so that you don't feel overwhelmed and discouraged.

2. **Keep up and review often.** If you prepare early and often, you will be less anxious. Use the night before a test for reviewing, not learning new material.

3. **Discipline yourself.** Focus your attention away from your fears, and concentrate on the task at hand. Jot down ideas and formulas, draw pictures, and write out the problem. Reduce interruptions and concentrate fully for short periods. Time yourself on problems to increase speed and make the most of short study sessions.

4. **Study in groups.** Learning does not take place in isolation but, rather, in a supportive environment where anxiety is reduced and each person feels safe to use trial-and-error methods. Group study encourages creativity, interaction, and multiple solutions. You will build confidence as you learn to think out loud, brainstorm creative solutions, and solve problems. See **Peak Progress 10.4** on page 328 for a comprehensive checklist of questions to use as you solve problems.

5. **Have a positive attitude.** As mentioned earlier, a positive attitude is key to learning any subject. Do you get sidetracked by negative self-talk about your abilities or the reason for learning math skills? Choose to focus on the positive feelings you have when you are confident and in control. Replace negative and defeating self-talk with positive "I can" affirmations. Math anxiety, like stage fright and other fears, is compounded by negative self-talk. Approach math and science with a positive "can do," inquisitive attitude.

6. **Dispute the myths.** Many times, fears are caused by myths, such as "Men do better than women in math and science" or "Creative people are not good at math and science." There is no basis for the belief that gender determines math ability, nor is skill in math and science unfeminine. Success in math and science requires creative thinking. As mathematician Augustus De Morgan said, "The moving power of mathematics is not reasoning, but imagination."

● **Anxiety about Math and Science**

Some students are nervous about taking courses in math and science, even though the basic principles have many everyday applications. *What are some tasks you do daily that involve knowledge of basic math and science?*

> ❝Faith is taking the first step even when you don't see the whole staircase.❞
>
> MARTIN LUTHER KING, JR.
> *Civil rights leader*

WORDS TO SUCCEED

Peak Progress

Problem-Solving Checklist

When you enroll in any course, including math or science, consider these questions:

- Have you approached the class with a positive attitude?
- What do you want to know, and what are you being asked to find out?
- Have you separated essential information from the unessential?
- Have you separated the known from the unknown?
- Have you asked a series of questions: How? When? Where? What? If?
- Have you devised a plan for solving the problem?
- Have you gone from the general to the specific?
- Have you made an estimate?
- Have you illustrated or organized the problem?
- Have you made a table or a diagram, drawn a picture, or summarized data?
- Have you written out the problem?

- Have you discovered a pattern to the problem?
- Have you alternated intense concentration with frequent breaks?
- Have you tried working backwards, completing similar problems, and solving small parts?
- Have you determined if you made careless errors or do not understand the concepts?
- Have you asked for help early?
- Have you been willing to put in the time required to solve problems?
- Have you analyzed the problem? Was your guess close? Did your plan work? How else can you approach the problem?
- Have you brainstormed ideas on your own? In a group setting?
- Have you rewarded yourself for facing your fears, overcoming anxiety, and learning valuable skills that will increase your success in school, in your job, and in life?

"Man's mind, once stretched by a new idea, never regains its original dimensions."

OLIVER WENDALL HOLMES
Author

7. **Ask for help.** Don't wait until you are in trouble or frustrated. Talk with the instructor, visit the learning center, get a tutor, and join a study group. If you continue to feel anxious or lost, visit the counseling center. Try taking a summer refresher course. You'll be prepared and confident when you take the required course later.

See **Peak Progress 10.5** to apply the Adult Learning Cycle to overcoming anxiety.

Peak Progress

Applying the Adult Learning Cycle to Overcoming Math and Science Anxiety

1. **RELATE. Why do I want to learn this?** I want to be confident in math and science. Avoiding math and science closes doors and limits opportunities. More than 75 percent of careers use math and science, and these are often higher-status, better-paying jobs. This is essential knowledge I'll use in all facets of life.

2. **OBSERVE. How does this work?** I can learn a lot about applying critical thinking and creative problem solving to mathematics and science by watching, listening, and trying new things. I'll observe people who are good at math and science. What do they do? I'll also observe and learn from the mistakes of people who experience anxiety and don't do well. I'll try new critical thinking techniques for dealing with fear and observe how I'm improving.

3. **REFLECT. What does this mean?** I'll apply critical thinking to mathematics and science. What works and doesn't work? I'll think about and test new ways of reducing anxiety and break old patterns and negative self-talk. I'll look for connections and associations with other types of anxiety and apply what I learn.

4. **DO. What can I do with this?** I will practice reducing my anxiety. I'll find practical applications for connecting critical thinking and creative problem solving to math and science. Each day I'll work on one area. For example, I'll maintain a positive attitude as I approach math and science classes.

5. **TEACH. Whom can I share this with?** I'll form a study group and share my tips and experiences. I'll demonstrate and teach others the methods I've learned. I'll reward myself when I do well.

Remember, attitude is everything. If you keep an open mind, apply strategies you have learned in this chapter, and practice your critical thinking skills, you will become more confident in your problem-solving abilities.

TAKING CHARGE

Summary

In this chapter, I learned to

- **Appreciate the importance of critical thinking.** Critical thinking is fundamental to understanding and solving problems in coursework, my job, and the rest of my life. I have learned to examine beliefs, assumptions, and opinions against facts, ask pertinent questions, and analyze data.

- **Apply essential critical thinking skills.** Bloom's Taxonomy outlines the six critical thinking skills that college requires (from lowest- to highest-order): knowledge, comprehension, application, analysis, synthesis, and evaluation.

- **Use the problem-solving process.** When I problem solve, I will (1) define the problem; (2) gather and interpret information; (3) develop and implement a plan of action; and (4) evaluate the plan or solution.

- **Incorporate problem-solving strategies.** My attitude affects how I approach problem solving. I have developed a positive, inquisitive attitude and a willingness to explore, probe, question, and search for answers and solutions. I will replace negative self-talk with affirmations. I will use my critical thinking skills and be persistent in solving problems. I will participate in a supportive group environment, such as a study group.

- **Avoid errors in judgment.** I will avoid using stereotypes, all-or-nothing thinking, snap judgments, unwarranted assumptions, projection, sweeping generalizations, the halo effect, and negative labeling. I will not project my habits onto others to justify my behavior or decisions.

- **Use creative problem solving.** I will use creative problem solving to approach problems from a different direction and explore new options. What problems are similar? Is there a pattern to the problem? I will brainstorm various strategies. I will act out the problem, move it around, picture it, take it apart, translate it, and summarize it in my own words. I will solve easier problems before tackling harder problems.

- **Apply strategies to math and science courses.** What model, formula, drawing, sketch, equation, chart, table, calculation, or particular strategy will help? I choose the most appropriate strategy and outline a step-by-step plan. I show all my work, so that I can review.

- **Overcome anxiety for math and science.** If I am anxious about taking math and science courses, I will try to maintain a positive attitude, use available resources, take control, and focus on the task at hand.

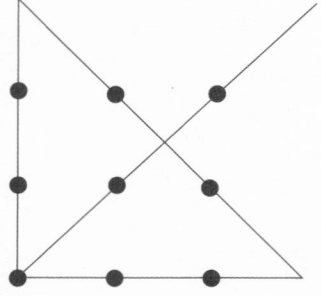

Solution to the Nine-Dot Exercise on Page 316

Most people try to solve this problem by remaining within the boundaries of the dots. However, when you move outside the confines of the dots and the boundaries are reset, you can easily solve the puzzle. This exercise helps illustrate that some problems cannot be solved with traditional thinking.

Performance Strategies

Following are the top 10 strategies for critical thinking and creative problem solving:

- Define the problem.
- Gather and interpret information.
- Develop and implement a plan of action.
- Evaluate your decisions.
- Ask questions.
- Brainstorm creative options.
- Pay attention to details.
- Consider all sides of an issue.
- Use reasoning and avoid errors in judgment.
- Have a positive attitude.

Tech for Success

Take advantage of the text's Web site at **www.mhhe.com/ferrett8e** for additional study aids, useful forms, and convenient and applicable resources.

- **Work on weak areas.** Various online programs can help you determine the mathematical areas where you need the most work. ALEKS (**www.aleks.com/highered**) is a tutorial program that identifies your less proficient areas and then focuses on improvement through practice and targeted problems.

- **Math at your fingertips.** In your studies, you will come across many standard calculations and formulas, most of which can be found online and downloaded. Although this should not replace working through the formulas yourself to make sure you understand their applications, it does make incorporating math into your everyday life much easier.

Study Team Notes

Creativity at Work

Marina Koshetz and her husband, Josef, have recently opened a small restaurant that serves foods from their homeland of Russia. Starting their restaurant was a great deal of work. They had to get the correct permits, remodel an existing building, purchase equipment, and plan the menu. The couple works long hours, 6 days a week. Before opening the restaurant at 11 a.m., Marina makes bread while Josef mixes together the traditional dishes they will serve. Then Marina remains in the kitchen to cook and prepare dishes while Josef waits tables and runs the cash register. At the end of the day, the couple washes the dishes and cleans the restaurant together. Although the restaurant is closed on Mondays, Marina and Josef use that day to plan the next week's specials and purchase food and other supplies.

Despite their hard work, the couple has made only enough money to cover costs. On a recent Monday afternoon, the two restaurateurs brainstormed ways to attract more customers. The restaurant is located in a quiet neighborhood on the edge of a district where many Russian immigrants live. So far, almost all of their customers have been Russian. Josef and Marina realized they needed to do more to attract other residents to their restaurant. They decided to host an open house and invite everyone living within a mile radius of the restaurant. Then they decided to add a couple of popular American dishes and began running ads in a local newspaper. Soon their restaurant was attracting more customers, and the business began to show a profit.

Marina and Josef Koshetz
RESTAURANT OWNERS

Related Majors: Restaurant and Food Service Management, Business

CRITICAL THINKING How did Josef and Marina use creativity and critical thinking to improve their business?

Peak Performer
PROFILE

Scott Adams

He's been described as a techie with the "social skills of a mousepad." He's not the sort of fellow you'd expect to attract media attention. However, pick up a newspaper, turn to the comics, and you'll find him. He's Dilbert. Cartoonist Scott Adams created this comic-strip character who daily lampoons corporate America and provides a humorous outlet for employees everywhere.

Though Adams was creative at a young age, his artistic endeavors were discouraged early on. The Famous Artists School rejected him at age 11. Years later, he received the lowest grade in a college drawing class. Practicality replaced creativity. In 1979, Adams earned a B.A. in economics from Hartwick College in Oneonta, New York, and, in 1986, an MBA from the University of California at Berkeley. For the next 15 years, Adams settled uncomfortably into a series of jobs that "defied description." Ironically, the frustrations of the workplace—power-driven co-workers, inept bosses, and cell-like cubicles—fueled his imagination. Adams began doodling, and Dilbert was born.

Encouraged by others, Adams submitted his work to United Media, a major cartoon syndicate. He was offered a contract in 1989, and "Dilbert" debuted in 50 national newspapers. Today, "Dilbert" appears in 2,000 newspapers in 70 countries and was the first syndicated cartoon to have its own Web site.

With such mass exposure, coming up with new ideas for cartoons could be a challenge. However, Adams found the perfect source: He has made his e-mail address available. He gets hundreds of messages a day from workers at home and abroad. His hope is that, through his creative invention, solutions will develop for the problems he satirizes.

PERFORMANCE THINKING Of the creative problem-solving strategies on pages 314–323, which one do you think has been most helpful for Scott Adams and why?

CHECK IT OUT According to Scott Adams, "Creativity is allowing yourself to make mistakes. Art is knowing which ones to keep." Adams is no stranger to taking chances and voicing his views on management—both in the workforce and in the government. At **www.dilbert.com,** you can read (and respond to, if you like) the Dilbert.blog written by Adams, and you can "mash up" one of his comics by creatively inserting your own words into the frames.

Starting Today

At least one strategy I learned in this chapter that I plan to try right away is

_____

_____

_____

What changes must I make in order for this strategy to be most effective?

_____

_____

_____

Review Questions

Based on what you have learned in this chapter, write your answers to the following questions:

1. Name six critical thinking skills necessary for success in college.

_____

_____

2. What are the attributes of a critical thinker?

_____

_____

3. What are the four steps of problem solving?

_____

_____

4. Name five strategies for becoming more creative.

_____

_____

5. Name five strategies for problem solving in math and science.

_____

_____

To test your understanding of the chapter's concepts, complete the chapter quiz at **www.mhhe.com/ferrett8e.**

Conquering Fear of Failure

In the Classroom

Gloria Ramone is a single mom who works part-time and lives and attends school in the inner city. She is eager to complete her education, begin her career, and earn a higher salary. She is an electronics student who wants her classes to be practical and relevant. Her school requires a class in critical thinking, but she is resisting it because she sees no practical application to her job. Her attitude is affecting her attendance and participation.

1. Offer ideas to help Gloria see the importance of critical thinking in decision making.

_____

_____

2. Help her connect decisions in school with job decisions.

_____

_____

In the Workplace

Gloria is now a manager in a small electronics business. She is also taking evening classes, working toward a business degree. She has received promotions quickly but knows she needs further management training. Gloria is very interested in the electronics field and loves to solve problems. New issues arise every day, and she has decisions to make. She has lots of practice predicting results and using critical thinking to solve problems. Gloria enjoys most of the business classes but dreads the classes in finance and statistics, because she has math anxiety.

3. What strategies in this chapter could help Gloria overcome math anxiety?

_____

_____

4. What are some affirmations Gloria could use to help her develop a positive attitude about math?

_____

_____

_____

Applying the ABC Method of Self-Management

In the Journal Entry on page 305, you were asked to describe a decision you made that cost you a lot of time, money, or stress. How would critical thinking and creative problem solving have helped you make better decisions?

_____

_____

_____

   Now that you know more strategies for critical thinking and creative problem solving, apply the ABC Method to a difficult situation you have encountered, such as a financial dilemma, rigorous course, or personal crisis. Use your critical thinking skills to work through the situation and arrive at a positive result.

A = Actual event:

_____

_____

_____

B = Beliefs:

_____

_____

_____

C = Challenge:

_____

_____

_____

Use positive visualization and practice deep breathing with your eyes closed for just 1 minute. See yourself calm, centered, and relaxed, learning formulas, practicing problem solving, and using critical thinking to work through problems. You feel confident because you have learned to control your anxiety and maintain a positive attitude.

PRACTICE SELF-MANAGEMENT

For more examples of learning how to manage difficult situations, see the "Self-Management Workbook" section of the Online Learning Center Web site at **www.mhhe.com/ferrett8e.**

Apply Bloom's Taxonomy

Different situations call for different levels of thinking. Although many, if not all, of these skills are required in every course you take, jot down classes or situations where you might rely more on a particular thinking skill. For example, in a speech class, you may be asked to evaluate others' speeches.

Critical Thinking Skill	Task	Class or Situation
Knowledge	Recite; recall; recognize	
Comprehension	Restate; explain; state; discuss; summarize	
Application	Apply; prepare; solve a problem; explore a case study	
Analysis	Break ideas apart and relate to other ideas; complete an essay	
Synthesis	Integrate ideas; create new ideas; improve on design	
Evaluate	Critique; evaluate; cite advantages and disadvantages	

Preparing for Critical Thinking

Brainstorm alternative approaches and solutions to the problems that arise in your day-to-day activities at school, on the job, or at home. Consider things such as the potential consequences of certain decisions, timing, and related costs.

ISSUE/PROBLEM

_____

_____

_____

_____

_____

SOLUTION #1: _____

Pros	Cons

SOLUTION #2: _____

Pros	Cons

SOLUTION #3: _____

Pros	Cons

BEST SOLUTION AND WHY:

_____

_____

_____

You Can Solve the Problem: Sue's Decision

Every day, life brings problems and choices. The kinds of choices you make can make your life easier or harder. Often, you do not know which direction to take. Use these six steps to work through the following case study:

Step 1 Know what the problem really is. Is it a daily problem? Is it a once-in-a-lifetime problem?
Step 2 List what you know about the problem. List what you don't know. Ask questions. Get help and advice.
Step 3 Explore alternate choices.
Step 4 Think about the pros and cons for the other choices. Arrange them from best to worst choice.
Step 5 Pick the choice you feel good about.
Step 6 Study what happens after you have made your choice. Are you happy about the choice? Would you make it again?

Case Study: Sue

Sue has been diagnosed with cancer. Her doctor has told her that it is in only one place in her body. The doctor wants to operate. He thinks he will be able to remove all of it, but he wants Sue to do something else. He wants her to undergo 4 months of chemotherapy, which will make her feel very sick. It will make her tired, but it may also help keep the cancer from coming back.

Sue is not sure what to do. She has two small children who are not in school. Sue's husband works days and cannot help care for the children during the day. The rest of Sue's family lives far away, and she cannot afford day care. She wonders, "How will I be able to care for my children if I'm sick?"

The doctor has told Sue that she must make her own choice. Will she undergo the chemotherapy? She will talk with her husband, and they will make a choice together.

What is Sue's problem? What are her choices? What would you decide? Apply the six steps to help Sue make a good decision by writing responses to the following questions and statements.

Step 1 The problem is

_____

_____

_____

(continued)

Step 2

   a. You know these things about the problem:

_____

_____

_____

_____

   b. You don't know these things about the problem:

_____

_____

_____

_____

Step 3   The other choices are

_____

_____

_____

_____

Step 4   Rank the choices, best to worst.

_____

_____

_____

_____

Step 5   Pick a choice the family might feel good about and explain why.

_____

_____

_____

_____

Step 6   What might happen to Sue and her family?

_____

_____

_____

_____

Assessing and Demonstrating Your Critical Thinking Skills

1. **Looking back:** Review your worksheets to find activities that helped you learn to make decisions and solve problems creatively. Jot down examples. Also, look for examples of how you learned to apply critical thinking skills to math and science.

   _____

   _____

   _____

   _____

   _____

2. **Taking stock:** What are your strengths in decision making and critical thinking? Are you creative? What areas would you like to improve?

   _____

   _____

   _____

   _____

   _____

3. **Looking forward:** How would you demonstrate critical thinking and creative problem-solving skills to an employer?

   _____

   _____

   _____

   _____

   _____

4. **Documentation:** Document your critical thinking and creative problem-solving skills. Which instructor or employer would write a letter of recommendation? Indicate here which person you'll contact. Add this letter to your portfolio.

   _____

   _____

   _____

   _____

   _____

Add this page to your Career Development Portfolio.

11

Create a Healthy Mind, Body, and Spirit

LEARNING OUTCOMES

In this chapter, you will learn to

11.1 Explain the connection among the mind, body, and spirit

11.2 Make healthy choices in your diet

11.3 Make exercise a positive habit

11.4 Manage stress and reduce anxiety

11.5 Make sound decisions about alcohol and other drugs

11.6 Recognize depression and suicidal tendencies

11.7 Protect yourself from disease, unplanned pregnancy, and acquaintance rape

SELF-MANAGEMENT

"I'm stressed out with doing so much homework and trying to juggle everything. I haven't been getting enough sleep, and I'm gaining weight from eating too much fast food and not exercising. What can I do to manage my stress and be healthier?"

Do you feel overwhelmed and stressed by too many demands? Do you lack energy from too little sleep or exercise or from excess calories? In this chapter, you will learn how to manage stress and create healthy habits to last a lifetime. You will see yourself healthy and in charge of your mental, physical, and spiritual life.

JOURNAL ENTRY In **Worksheet 11.1** on page 374, describe a time when you had lots of energy, felt healthy and rested, and were in control of your weight. What factors helped you be calm, confident, and healthy? How did your attitude help you be in control?

C reating balance, managing stress, increasing energy, and providing time for renewal are essential to becoming a peak performer. In this world of multitasking, we need to slow down, become mindful of our purpose, and focus on important priorities. In this chapter, we will present principles and guidelines to help you develop the most effective methods of maintaining your health while learning how to cope with daily demands.

Redefining Health: Connecting the Mind, Body, and Spirit

Many people think of health as the absence of disease. However, optimal health—or **wellness**—means living life fully with purpose, meaning, and vitality. Your overall wellness is largely determined by your decisions about how you live your life and the measures you take to avoid illness. Although genetics, age, and accidents also influence your health and are beyond your control, you can optimize your health by understanding the connection among your mind, body, and spirit. The habits you develop now will affect not only how long you live but also the quality of life you enjoy.

The Mind

Peak emotional and intellectual wellness requires that you develop the mind's thinking and feeling aspects. It is important to develop critical thinking and creative problem-solving skills, good judgment, common sense, and self-control. It's also important to develop and manage your emotional qualities, such as a positive attitude, optimism, confidence, coping skills, and rapport building. You need to understand and be able to express emotions, have empathy for others, manage yourself, and develop healthy relationships.

The Body

Peak physical wellness requires eating healthy foods, exercising, getting plenty of sleep, recognizing the symptoms of disease, making responsible decisions about sex, avoiding harmful habits, improving your immune system, and taking steps to prevent illness and physical harm. None of this information is new; however, many people have difficulty putting these good habits into practice.

The Spirit

Peak spiritual wellness requires thinking about and clarifying your values and questioning the purpose, beliefs, and principles that give your life meaning. Spirituality may include your religious beliefs or a belief in a higher power, but also it encompasses your willingness to serve others; your sense of ethics and honesty; your relationship to people, nature, and animals; your definition of the purpose of life; the legacy you want to leave; and how you fit into this universe. In Chapter 2, we discussed Maslow's hierarchy of needs. At the highest level, self-actualized people achieve fulfillment, creativity, and greater spiritual growth. Some physicians believe spirituality is the essence of wellness and wholeness. The body, mind, and spirit are interconnected. For example, if you are optimistic and live with love, honesty, and forgiveness, you are more likely to be physically well.

Understanding the connection among the mind, body, and spirit will help you develop skills for coping with the demands of school and work. Reports, deadlines, tests, performance reviews, conflicts, committees, commuting, family responsibilities, and presentations are all part of life. These and other demands create a great deal of stress. Stress is not an external event but part of a larger system, and it affects all aspects of your mind, body, and spirit.

Awareness and Prevention

The first step in managing your health is awareness. You may not even realize you eat every time you watch television, drink several cans of soda while you study, or nibble while you fix dinner. You may be drinking alcohol or smoking when you're under stress instead of learning healthy coping skills. Improving your health begins with observing your daily habits and replacing unproductive ones with beneficial choices.

It's also important to observe how your body feels, the thoughts going through your mind, and your stress level. Have you recently experienced discomfort or a change in your body? If you can identify symptoms and early-warning signs of an illness, you can take action to protect yourself from diseases, such as cancer. One in three people will develop cancer in his or her lifetime. At **www.cancer.org**, the American Cancer Society provides guidelines for the early detection of specific cancers, such as skin cancer, which is diagnosed more than 1 million times each year. Signs and symptoms such as unexplained weight loss of 10 pounds or more, persistent fever, fatigue, pain, and skin changes can be caused by a range of conditions, including cancer, and should be taken seriously. **Figure 11.1** on page 346 includes more specific signs and symptoms of cancer. While these are the most common, there are many other signs. If you notice any major changes in the way your body functions or looks or the way you feel, especially if it persists or gets worse, tell someone, including your doctor.

Although more than 11 million people are living with cancer in the United States, an estimated 23.6 million people (almost 8 percent of the population) have diabetes, making it one of the fastest-growing health issues. Several factors are involved (including genetics), but the rise in rates of obesity (more than 33 percent of U.S. adults over age 20 are considered obese) probably contributes to the increase in cases of diabetes. Obesity is a risk factor for many illnesses (including heart disease and cancer) and costs almost $150 billion in medical expenses each year.

● **Fighting the Flu**
In fall 2009, H1N1 flu (commonly called the "swine flu") captured worldwide attention due to related deaths, especially in Mexico, and the rush to create enough vaccine for market demand. Each year, 36,000 people in the United States die from seasonal flu-related causes, making it important to understand how to protect yourself from contracting the flu. *Do you know what to do to decrease your risk of getting the flu?*

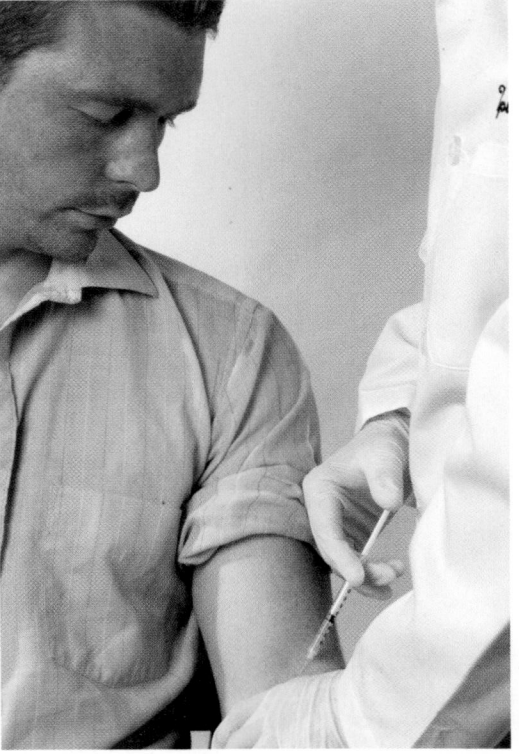

Figure 11.1

Cancer Caution Signs

Although these are the most common specific signs of cancer, they could be symptoms of other health issues. Be vigilant about monitoring your health, and discuss any concerns with your physician. *Do changes in your health always signal a serious condition?*

See your doctor if you experience any of the following
• Change in bowel habits or bladder function
• Sores that do not heal
• Unusual bleeding or discharge
• Thickening or lump in breast or other parts of the body
• Indigestion or trouble swallowing
• Recent change in a wart or mole
• Nagging cough or hoarseness

Source: American Cancer Society.

Strategies for Good Health Management

1. **Eat healthy foods.** Eat a nutritious diet daily to control your weight and blood pressure and to reduce depression, anxiety, headaches, fatigue, and insomnia. The *Dietary Guidelines for Americans,* published jointly every 5 years by the Department of Health and Human Services and the U.S. Department of Agriculture, provides authoritative advice about how good dietary habits can promote health and reduce risk for major chronic diseases. The latest edition can be found at **www.health.gov/dietaryguidelines**. Additionally, the following general guidelines will help you make healthy choices in your diet:

   - *Eat a variety of foods.* Include whole grains, lots of fruits and vegetables, milk, meats, poultry, fish, and breads and cereals in your diet. See **Peak Progress 11.1** for suggested balanced diets illustrated by the food pyramids.

   - *Eat plenty of fresh fruits and vegetables.* They are excellent sources of vitamins and disease-preventing fiber.

   - *Take a multivitamin supplement.* Many experts advise taking vitamin and mineral supplements for optimal health. Some recommend extra C, E, B-complex, and A vitamins if you are under stress.

   - *Increase your intake of whole-grain cereals and breads.* Whole grains contain fiber, vitamins, and minerals. They are also filling, so they might keep you from snacking.

   - *Reduce the amount of animal fat in your diet.* Too much animal fat can increase the level of cholesterol in your blood, which can affect your cardiovascular system, causing your body to get less oxygen.

   - *Broil or bake meats rather than frying.* If you do fry, use olive oil or another monounsaturated fat instead of butter.

   - *Cut down on sugar and refined carbohydrates.* Sugar has no nutritional value and promotes tooth decay. Eating refined sugar creates a sudden drop in blood sugar, shakiness, and a need for more glucose. This can lead to type 2 diabetes and other health problems. Maintain an even energy level rather than a quick fix. Substitute whole grains and fresh fruit and vegetables for white bread and sweets.

- *Cut down on salt.* Salt is an ingredient in many prepared foods. Be aware of how much salt you use and if it's necessary.
- *Cut down on caffeine.* A small amount of caffeine can enhance alertness and effectiveness for some people. However, many people don't stop with just one or two cups. More than 20 percent of Americans consume heavy amounts of caffeine (600 milligrams, or approximately four or more servings per day), especially with the popularity of "energy" drinks and supersized servings. Too much caffeine can make you nervous, jittery, irritable, and prone to insomnia. It may deplete your body of the B vitamins, minerals, and other nutrients it needs to cope with stress. Caffeine can also be addictive: The more you consume, the more it takes to produce the desired burst of energy. If you experience caffeine-induced symptoms, reduce your intake, but do so gradually. Headaches can result from rapid caffeine withdrawal. Try substituting decaffeinated coffee and tea (green tea is especially high in antioxidants) or plain water. Check labels to confirm that your substitutions are caffeine-free.

Peak Progress

Eating for Health and Energy

Researchers have studied the effects of diet for years and have tried to agree on the best diet for most people. In 1993, scientists and nutritionists from the United States and Europe met to look at the traditional Mediterranean diet, which may have prolonged life and prevented disease for centuries in Mediterranean countries. The experts released a model similar to that of the U.S. Department of Agriculture's (USDA's) original food guide pyramid. The Mediterranean model suggests eating more beans and legumes than animal-based proteins and advocates using olive oil daily.

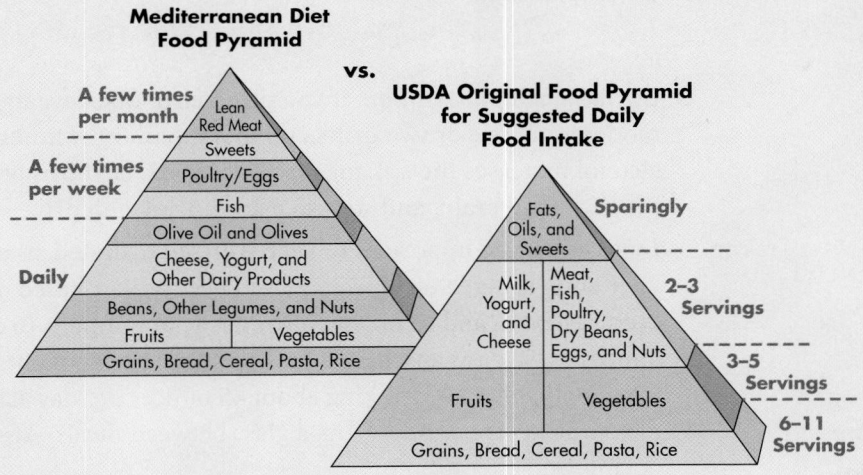

Source: U.S. Department of Agriculture, U.S. Department of Health and Human Services.

(continued)

11.1

Copyright © 2012 The McGraw-Hill Companies

Eating for Health and Energy *(concluded)*

MYPYRAMID

The food guide pyramid developed by the USDA has continued to change over the years. Because we have individual diet and exercise needs, the current pyramid, called MyPyramid, uses online technology to help you pinpoint what you should eat based on your age, sex, and activity level. Each "color" in the pyramid is tied to a specific food group (orange = grains, green = vegetables, etc.). To determine your needs and create a good eating plan, go to **www.mypyramid.gov.**

For example, the recommendations for a 25-year-old woman who exercises less than 30 minutes each day look like this (based on 2,000 calories per day):

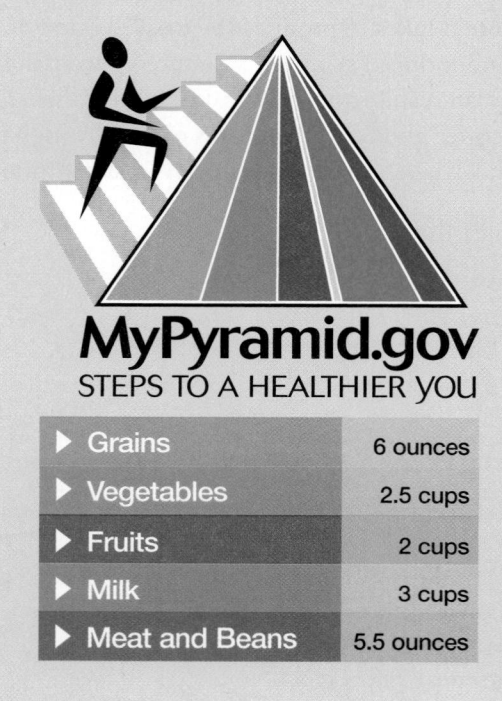

MyPyramid.gov STEPS TO A HEALTHIER YOU	
▶ Grains	6 ounces
▶ Vegetables	2.5 cups
▶ Fruits	2 cups
▶ Milk	3 cups
▶ Meat and Beans	5.5 ounces

See **www.mypyramid.gov** for a detailed diet plan.

- *Use alcohol in moderation.* If you drink alcoholic beverages, do it in moderation: one or two drinks no more than three times a week. Too much alcohol increases the risk for certain cancers, cirrhosis of the liver, damage to the heart and brain, and strokes. Never drink and drive.

- *Drink water.* It's important to keep yourself hydrated, as about 60 percent of your body is made up of water. Fluid needs differ based on overall health, exercise levels, and so on, but a good rule of thumb is to drink as many ounces of water as about 30 percent of your body weight. For a 150-pound woman, that means drinking about 45 ounces per day. Choose water as your mealtime beverage, and drink a glass between meals. Also hydrate before, during, and after exercise.

2. **Maintain your ideal weight.** People spend millions of dollars every year on diet programs, exercise equipment, and promises of a quick fix. If you need to lose weight, don't try to do it too quickly with fad diets or fasting. Consult a physician to discuss the best method for you. Slow weight loss is more effective

> " More die in the United States of too much food than of too little. "
>
> JOHN KENNETH GALBRAITH
> *Economist*

WORDS TO SUCCEED

● **Coffeehouse Blues**
The caffeine in coffee can be pleasurable in moderate amounts, but, because it is addictive, there's a downside to drinking too much. *What are some other ways to increase your energy besides consuming caffeine?*

and helps you keep the weight off longer. Support groups for weight control can also be very helpful. Building energy by nourishing and caring for the body takes a long-term commitment to good habits. The following general guidelines will help you maintain your ideal weight:

- *Exercise.* If you want to lose and keep off weight and increase your energy, build physical activity into your life. If you have time and are in a safe area, park your car a little farther out in the parking lot and walk a few extra steps. Sign up for an exercise class, or jog on a track. Find out what fitness resources are offered free by your school or community.

- *Eat only when you're hungry.* Eat to sustain your body, not because you are depressed, lonely, bored, or worried.

- *Don't fast.* When a person fasts, the body's metabolic rate decreases, so the body burns calories more slowly. At a certain point, the body has an urge to binge, which is nature's way of trying to survive famine.

- *Eat regularly.* Establish a pattern of three meals a day or five small meals. Don't skip meals, especially breakfast. You must eat regularly to stoke your metabolism, lose weight, and keep it off. If you are really rushed, carry a banana, an apple, raw vegetables, or nuts.

- *Create healthy patterns.* Eat slowly and enjoy your food. Eat in one or two locations, such as the dining room or at the kitchen table. Resist the urge to eat on the run, sample food while you are cooking, munch in bed, or snack throughout the day. Use critical thinking as you explore your eating patterns in **Personal Evaluation Notebook 11.1** on page 350.

- *Get help.* Do you have a problem with weight control, or are you overly concerned with being thin? Do you have a problem with eating too little or with fasting (such as anorexia nervosa)? Do you eat and then vomit as a way to control your weight (as with bulimia nervosa)? Anorexia and bulimia are serious illnesses that require medical treatment. You might feel isolated

Personal Evaluation Notebook

Reviewing Your Health

Read the following and write your comments on the lines provided.

1. Do you maintain your ideal weight? If not, how can you achieve your ideal weight?

   _____

   _____

   _____

2. Describe a few of your healthy eating habits.

   _____

   _____

   _____

3. Describe a few of your unhealthy eating habits.

   _____

   _____

   _____

4. Do you feel you have control over your eating? Explain.

   _____

   _____

   _____

5. What can you do to make positive and lasting changes in your eating habits?

   _____

   _____

   _____

and powerless, but many resources offer help. Confide in a friend or family member. Go to the counseling or health center. Look in the yellow pages or discuss your problem with your doctor or counselor. Don't wait to get help. (See **Peak Progress 11.2**.)

3. **Renew energy through rest.** Most people need between 6 and 9 hours of sound sleep each night. The key is not to focus on the number of hours but, rather, whether you feel rested, alert, and energized. Some people wake up rested after 5 hours of sleep; others need at least 9 hours to feel energized and refreshed. If you wake up tired, try going to bed earlier for a night or two, and then

establish a consistent bedtime. Notice if you are using sleep to escape conflict, depression, or boredom. Also find time to relax each day. Use critical thinking in **Personal Evaluation Notebook 11.2** on page 252 to assess your commitment to getting rest.

4. **Increase physical activity.** Regular aerobic exercise is essential for keeping your body at peak performance. The goal of aerobic exercise is to raise the heart rate above its normal rate and keep it there for 20 or more minutes. Aerobic exercise strengthens every organ in the body (especially the heart), reduces stress, strengthens the immune system, increases muscle strength, reduces excess fat, stimulates the lymphatic system, and increases your endurance. Exercise can also alter body chemistry by changing hormones, adjusting metabolism, and stimulating the brain to release more endorphins, which are natural chemicals in the body that affect your state of mind and increase feelings of well-being.

Melissa is determined not to succumb to the "freshman 10" and gain weight at school. In fact, she does the opposite and eats little all day before going out at night with her friends. She believes she looks good and doesn't have to worry about the extra calories she eats (and drinks) late at night since she's hardly eaten during the day.
- What negative psychological and physical patterns regarding food is Melissa displaying?
- How might her diet affect her success in school?
- What should Melissa do differently to meet her goal of a healthy weight?

THINK *FAST*

Peak Progress

11.2

Eating Disorders

Known as a perfectionist, 20-year-old Jill was a bright, social college sophomore who seemed to have it all together, coping with the stress of college and part-time work. In just a few months, however, she broke up with her boyfriend, her sister married and moved away, and she felt pressured to choose a college major before the semester ended. In addition, she lost control of her car on an icy road and her car was totaled, although she wasn't seriously hurt. She began to feel depressed and out of control. She loved to exercise, so she started running twice as much as usual. She withdrew from family and friends and didn't feel like eating, so she gradually eliminated most foods from her diet, except fruits, yogurt, and salads. She continued to lose weight until her family insisted she get counseling and weigh in at the health center every day. Jill didn't think she had an eating disorder because she wasn't obsessed with being thin, but she was diagnosed as suffering from anorexia nervosa.

Most *anorexics* are white, young, middle-class women who have a distorted body image and want to be thin. Some anorexics are perfectionists, grew up in families with high expectations, and feel overwhelmed that they cannot meet these expectations, so they turn to something they can control—their weight.

Bulimia nervosa is another eating disorder; it involves binge eating and purging through forced vomiting or the use of laxatives. It can cause long-term dental damage and chemical imbalances, both of which can lead to organ damage and failure, bone loss, and even death. Many people with eating disorders also suffer from depression, anxiety, or substance abuse.

The National Association of Anorexia Nervosa and Associated Disorders estimates that approximately 8 million people in the United States have anorexia nervosa, bulimia nervosa, and related eating disorders. Essentially, about 3 of every 100 people in this country eat in a way disordered enough to warrant treatment. Ninety percent of those dealing with eating disorders are women. Research suggests that about 4 of every 100 college-age women have bulimia nervosa.

If you are dealing with an eating disorder, or suspect a friend or a family member is struggling with a disorder, seek help immediately. To learn more, visit the National Eating Disorders Association Web site at **www.nationaleatingdisorders.org** or call (800) 931-2237.

Personal Evaluation Notebook

Getting Proper Rest

Read the following and write your comments on the lines provided.

1. Do you generally wake up in the morning feeling rested and eager to start the day or tired with little energy? _____

   _____

2. How many times do you hit the snooze button before getting out of bed? _____

   _____

3. What prevents you from getting enough rest?

   _____

   _____

4. Besides sleep, what activities can renew your body and spirit?

   _____

   _____

● **Increasing Energy**
Most people benefit from as little as 20 minutes of exercise three times a week. *What is your exercise goal?*

How much exercise you need for good physical health depends on your goals, fitness level, overall health, and your physician's advice. Most healthy people need a regular program of 20 to 30 minutes of aerobic exercise at least three times a week for optimum health. There are many ways to exercise aerobically, such as walking, swimming, bicycling, dancing, and jogging. The key is to start slowly, build up gradually, and be consistent. If you experience pain while exercising, stop and consult your physician. Assess your commitment to exercise in **Personal Evaluation Notebook 11.3.**

5. **Establish healthy relationships.** Sharing a good talk or wonderful evening with a friend is deeply satisfying. So is the sense of accomplishment after completing a team project. Indeed, other people can help us think through problems, develop self-confidence, conquer fears, develop courage, brainstorm ideas, overcome boredom and fatigue, and increase our joy and laughter. The following are some barriers to healthy relationships:

   - Getting so busy at school and work that you ignore friends and family
   - Being shy and finding it difficult to build friendships
   - Approaching friendship as a competitive sport

It takes sensitivity and awareness to value others' needs. It also takes courage to overcome shyness. The key is to see the enormous value of friendships. Friends bring great joy and fellowship to life. Life's sorrows and setbacks are

Personal Evaluation Notebook

Committing to Exercise

Read the following and write your comments on the lines provided.

1. Describe your current commitment to physical exercise.

   _____

   _____

   _____

2. What are your excuses for not exercising? What can you do to overcome these barriers?

   _____

   _____

   _____

3. Set your exercise goal.

   _____

   _____

   _____

lessened when you have friends to support you through difficult times. (We'll further discuss building healthy relationships in Chapter 12.)

Manage Stress

College students face many demands: papers, tests, deadlines, studying, finances, relationships, and conflicts. Coping with stress means being able to manage difficult circumstances, solve problems, resolve conflicts, and juggle the daily demands of school, work, and relationships. Stress is the body's natural reaction to external events (e.g., taking an exam or giving a speech) and internal events (e.g., fear, worry, or unresolved anger). Everything you experience stimulates your body to react. Stress is normal and, in fact, necessary for a vital life. With too little positive stress, many people are bored and unproductive. The key is knowing how to cope with demands and channel stress instead of dealing with stress in unproductive ways, such as the following:

- Denying, ignoring, or repressing feelings or problems, so that you don't have to face them
- Lashing out at other people
- Using alcohol, tobacco, or other drugs to reduce tension
- Eating too much or too little
- Thinking you can handle your problems without help

> **"** Man should not try to avoid stress any more than he would shun food, love, or exercise. **"**
>
> **HANS SELYE**
> *Endocrinologist*

WORDS TO SUCCEED

Life is a series of changes, and they require adaptive responses. The death of a close family member or friend, a serious illness or accident, exams, divorce, relationship changes, financial problems, and loss of a job all require adjustment and cause stress. It is important to realize, however, that your perception of and reaction to these life events determine how they affect you. Even positive events can be stressful. Marriage, a promotion, the birth of a baby, a new romantic relationship, and even vacations may be demanding for some people and therefore stressful. Public speaking may be exciting and fun for one person but causes anxiety in another. Look at the early warning signs in **Peak Progress 11.3** to see if you are under too much stress.

You can choose to see stress as a challenge or something to avoid. You can adopt a positive, optimistic outlook; use resources; and rechannel energy in productive ways. You can learn to manage stress with coping strategies:

1. **Become attuned to your body and emotions.** The transition to college forces you to become more self-sufficient, which can cause stress. Recognize if you are having physical symptoms of stress, such as frequent headaches, difficulty relaxing, or a depressed or irritable mood. Give yourself permission to feel several different emotions, but also learn strategies to pull yourself out of a slump. You might set a time limit: "I accept that I'm feeling overwhelmed or down today. I will allow a few hours to feel these emotions; then I will do what I know makes me feel better."

2. **Exercise regularly.** Exercise is one of the best ways to reduce stress, relax muscles, and promote a sense of well-being. Most people have more energy when they exercise regularly.

3. **Dispute negative thoughts.** We've discussed the importance of self-management and monitoring your self-talk. Using the ABC Method of Self-Management helps you challenge self-defeating thoughts and replace them with positive, realistic, hopeful thoughts. Pessimists tend to describe

Peak Progress

11.3

Stress Leads to Burnout

Here are early warning signs that your body is pushing too hard and too long and may be on its way to burnout. If you have more than four of the following symptoms, you should consider getting help for dealing with stress overload.

- Frequent headaches, backaches, neck pain, stomachaches, or tense muscles
- Insomnia or disturbed sleep patterns
- No sense of humor; nothing sounds like fun
- Fatigue, listlessness, or hopelessness and low energy

- Increase in alcohol or other drug use or smoking
- Depression or moodiness
- Racing heart
- Appetite changes (eating too much or too little)
- Frequent colds, flu, or other illnesses
- Anxiousness, nervousness; difficulty concentrating
- Irritability, losing your temper, and overreacting
- Lack of motivation, energy, or zest for living
- A feeling that you have too much responsibility
- Lack of interest in relationships

their stressful situations with such words as *always* and *never,* and they imagine the worst possible outcomes. Negative thinking can lead to a self-fulfilling prophecy; if you say you're going to fail, you probably will. You can change these negative thoughts to confident, positive thoughts and actions.

4. **Rest and renew your mind, body, and spirit.** Everyone needs to rest, not only through sleep but also through deep relaxation. Too little of either causes irritability, depression, inability to concentrate, and memory loss. Yoga and pilates are great ways to unwind, stretch and tone the muscles, and focus energy. Many people find that meditation is essential for relaxation and renewal. You don't have to practice a certain type of meditation; just create a time for yourself when your mind is free to rest and quiet itself. Go for a walk, listen to music, create art, dance, sing, or get a massage. Visualization is another powerful technique for relaxing your body and reducing anxiety.

   Go to the health or counseling center and ask about a method called deep relaxation—activities that relax your mind, body, and spirit. Here's a simple version:

   Sit in a quiet place and breathe deeply, fill your lungs, and exhale completely. Tense and relax your body by clenching one fist and then relaxing it; now the other fist. Then shrug your shoulders, wrinkle your forehead, squint your eyes, clench your jaw, and tighten your thighs and toes, followed by relaxing each muscle.

5. **Use breathing methods.** Deep breathing reduces stress and energizes the body. Many people breathe in short, shallow breaths, especially when under stress. Begin by sitting or standing up straight; breathe through your nose, fill your lungs completely, push out your abdomen, and exhale slowly and fully. Focus on a word, a sound, or your breathing, and give it your full attention. You can do a variation of this anytime during the day, even if you can't escape to a quiet spot.

6. **Develop hobbies and interests.** Sports, crafts, reading, and collecting can add fun and meaning to your life. Many get satisfaction from developing an interest in a cause or need, such as the environment, the elderly, politics, animals, or the homeless. Investigate volunteering opportunities in your area.

7. **Create a support system.** The support and comfort of family and friends can help you clear your mind and make better decisions. Express your feelings, fears, and problems to people you trust. A support group of people with similar experiences and goals can give you a sense of security, personal fulfillment, and motivation.

8. **Take mini-vacations.** When you are waiting on hold or in line, pull out a novel and enjoy a few moments of reading. Practice deep breathing or head rolls, or visualize the tension flowing out of your body. Get up and stretch periodically while you're studying. These mini-vacations can keep you relaxed, expand your creativity and, make you grateful for being alive.

Take 3 minutes for a stress break:

- Turn off the lights (if you can) and any other distractions. Sit in a comfortable place and close your eyes.
- Where do you feel tense? Relax your muscles and drop your shoulders.
- Concentrate on your breathing, following it from deep in your stomach all the way out your nose or mouth. (If a meditating stress break doesn't work for you, put on some music and dance around the room and sing—find what makes you peaceful and happy.)

What else can you do in 3 minutes?

- Do stomach crunches or knee-bends, or use hand weights or water bottles to do arm curls.
- Make a grocery list of healthy foods to pick up at the store.
- Boost your energy by snacking on a handful of walnuts or almonds.

Take 3

9. **Rehearse a feared event.** When you mentally rehearse a stressful event beforehand, you inoculate yourself against it. Your fears become known and manageable.

10. **Exercise and stretch the mind.** Mental exercise can refresh and stimulate your entire life. Read, complete crossword puzzles, and play challenging board games. Attend lectures, take workshops and seminars, and brainstorm creative ideas or current subjects with well-read friends. Make friends with creative people who inspire you and renew your perspective.

11. **Create balance in your life.** Peak performers recognize the importance of balance between work and play. Assess whether your activities are distractions or opportunities. Say no to requests that do not enrich your life or the lives of others. Set time limits on work, demands from others, and study; reward yourself for finishing tasks.

12. **Develop a sense of humor.** Nothing reduces stress like a hearty laugh or spontaneous fun. Discovering the child within releases our natural creativity. Laughing produces endorphins, natural chemicals that strengthen the immune system and produce a sense of well-being. Laughter also increases oxygen flow to the brain and causes other positive physiological changes.

13. **Plan; don't worry.** A disorganized life is stressful. Write down what has to be done each day; don't rely on your memory. Take a few minutes the night before to lay out your clothes, pack your lunch, and list the next day's priorities. Get up 20 minutes early, so that you don't have to rush. Set aside time each day to plan, solve problems, and explore solutions. When your time is up, leave the problems until your next scheduled session.

14. **Be assertive.** Stand up for your rights, express your preferences, and acknowledge your feelings. Assertive communication helps you solve problems, rather than build resentment and anger, and increases your confidence and control over your life.

15. **Keep a journal.** A journal can give you insight into what types of situations you find stressful and how you respond to them. Be honest with yourself, and record daily events and your reactions.

16. **Get professional help.** Grief after a loss or major transition is normal. Allow yourself time to grieve in order to experience and release your emotional pain. However, if your sadness, depression, or anger continues despite your best efforts, or if you are suicidal, get professional help. With a counselor's guidance, you can gain insight into your pattern of reacting to stress and modify your perception and behavior. (See **Peak Progress 11.4** on using the Adult Learning Cycle to create a more healthy balance.)

Unhealthy Addictions

Unfortunately, many college students turn to alcohol, other drugs, or cigarettes to relieve stress. One of the biggest concerns health professionals have about students smoking marijuana or drinking every day is that it delays developing coping skills, resulting in serious problems. Rather than looking for quick fixes, practice coping strategies, such as facing your problems head on, resolving conflicts through communication, and finding creative solutions. Unhealthy behaviors will only escalate your problems.

Alcohol Abuse

Because it is a drug, alcohol can alter moods, become habit-forming, and cause changes in the body. It depresses the central nervous system, delaying reaction times and clouding personal judgment. Examine the facts about alcohol and alcoholism in **Figure 11.2** on page 358.

There are more than 25 million alcoholics in the United States today, and most say they began drinking in high school and college. Although one in five college students report that they don't drink at all, the Core Institute, an organization that surveys college drinking practices, reports the following:

- Of today's college students, 300,000 will eventually die of alcohol-related causes, such as drunk driving accidents, cirrhosis of the liver, various cancers, and heart disease.
- Of today's first-year college students, 159,000 will drop out of school for alcohol- or other drug-related reasons.
- The average student spends $600 on alcohol each year.
- Almost one-third of college students admit to having missed at least one class because of their alcohol use.
- One night of heavy drinking can impair your ability to think abstractly for up to 30 days.

> **"**I made a commitment to completely cut out drinking and anything that might hamper me from getting my mind and body together. And the floodgates of goodness have opened upon me—both spiritually and financially.**"**
>
> DENZEL WASHINGTON
> *Actor*

WORDS TO SUCCEED

Peak Progress

11.4

Applying the Adult Learning Cycle to Creating a Healthier Lifestyle

1. **RELATE. Why do I want to learn this?** I know I must reduce my stress, control my eating habits, exercise, and maintain my ideal weight. What areas do I struggle with, and what would I like to improve? Strong physical energy will boost my mental energy.

2. **OBSERVE. How does this work?** Who do I know with a healthy lifestyle? What behaviors do I want to emulate? What benefits will motivate me to improve my health behaviors? I'll try developing new habits and using new techniques and strategies, and I'll observe how I'm improving.

3. **REFLECT. What does this mean?** What strategies are working, and where do I continue to struggle? What tools or information would keep me motivated?

4. **DO. What can I do with this?** I will make a commitment to improve my health by eating right and exercising. Each day, I'll work on one area. For example, I'll use time-management skills and find ways to build exercise into my day. I'll practice reducing my stress in different situations. I'll use my new skills in everyday life.

5. **TEACH. Whom can I share this with?** I'll look for a partner with similar interests, and we'll keep each other motivated. I'll share my tips and experiences.

Living a healthy lifestyle is a life-long commitment. You will repeat the cycle many times to stay focused and successful.

Figure 11.2
The Costs of Alcohol

Knowing the facts can help you make the right choices. *Would you allow yourself or a friend to drink and drive?*

- In 2008, 11,773 fatalities were caused by alcohol-related crashes—almost 32 percent of all fatal crashes.
- Three out of 10 Americans may be involved in an alcohol-related crash.
- In 2006, 1.46 million people were arrested in the United States for driving under the influence of alcohol or narcotics (1 out of every 139 licensed drivers).
- According to the Department of Justice, each year 37 percent of rapes and sexual assaults involve alcohol use by the offender, as do 15 percent of all robberies, 27 percent of all aggravated assaults, and 25 percent of all simple assaults.

Sources: National Highway Traffic Safety Association; National Center for Statistics and Analysis; www.factsontap.org/collexp/stats.htm; U.S. Department of Justice, *Alcohol and Crime: An Analysis of National Data on the Prevalence of Alcohol Involvement in Crime.*

For most adults, a glass of wine or a beer at dinner is not a problem, but even a small amount of alcohol can cause slowed reactions and poor judgment. See **Peak Progress 11.5** on how to "party with a plan."

Students often believe there's no problem if they drink just beer, but some alcoholics drink only beer. A six-pack of beer contains the same amount of alcohol as six drinks of hard liquor—or one beer is equivalent to one shot of hard liquor. **Binge drinking** means consuming five or more drinks in a row for men, or four or more drinks in a row for women, at least once in the previous 2 weeks. Binge drinking can lead to serious problems, including fights, injuries, academic problems, suspension, sexual assault, DUIs, and even death.

Alcoholism is a chronic disease that can be progressive and even fatal. It can begin as early as childhood and is often influenced by peer pressure. A major life lesson is to think for yourself and be responsible for your choices and behavior.

Cigarette Smoking

It is hard to believe that anyone would smoke after hearing and viewing the public awareness campaigns that present the risks of cigarette smoking, yet 46 million

Peak Progress

11.5

Party with a Plan

Motivational speaker Randy Haveson has created Party with a Plan®—a quick guide for drinking alcohol sensibly. See **www.partywithaplan.org** for a complete description.

> 0 = No drinking if you are pregnant, driving, underage, or taking medications
> 1 = No more than one drink per hour (12 oz. beer; 4 oz. wine; 1 oz. shot)
> 2 = No more than two times per week
> 3 = No more than three drinks in one day

Used by permission from Randy Speaks, Inc. copyright 2006.

adults in the United States smoke. Perhaps the billions of dollars spent to promote cigarettes each year convince them that smoking makes them sexier, cooler, and calmer. Such claims are in stark contrast to the facts shown in **Figure 11.3** below.

Illegal Drug Use

Almost 80 percent of people in their mid-twenties have tried illegal drugs. Drug addiction causes these and other social and health problems:

- The cost of drug abuse to American society is almost $50 billion a year.
- Crack addiction can occur in less than 2 months of occasional use.
- Intravenous drug use causes 24 percent of AIDS cases in the United States.
- Marijuana is the most commonly used illegal drug. Although some people think they are smoking a harmless "weed," marijuana use has many negative effects, including loss of coordination and memory and increases in heart rate and blood pressure. Besides experiencing the respiratory problems that cigarette smokers also develop, habitual marijuana users tend to inhale deeper and hold the smoke in their lungs longer, releasing five times more carbon dioxide and three times more tar into their lungs than tobacco does. K2 (also known as "spice" or synthetic marijuana) is a newer drug that is also dangerous, even though it is legal in most places and sold as incense or potpourri. Symptoms of its use mimic marijuana use, such as a rapid heartbeat, dangerously elevated blood pressure, pale skin, and vomiting. It also is believed to affect the central nervous system, causing severe, potentially life-threatening hallucinations and seizures.

Prescription and Over-the-Counter Medication Abuse

When used as directed, medications can be beneficial. However, roughly one in five people in the United States have used prescription drugs for nonmedical reasons.

- Cigarette smoking–related diseases cause about 443,600 deaths each year in the United States, killing more Americans than alcohol, car accidents, suicide, AIDS, homicide, and illegal drugs combined.
- Cigarette smoking is directly responsible for 87 percent of all lung cancer cases and causes most cases of emphysema and chronic bronchitis.
- The Environmental Protection Agency estimates that secondhand smoke causes about 3,000 lung cancer deaths and 37,000 heart disease deaths in nonsmokers each year.
- Nonsmokers married to smokers have a 30 percent greater risk for lung cancer than those married to nonsmokers.
- The effects of secondhand smoke, especially on children, include respiratory problems, colds, and other illnesses, such as cancer.
- Secondhand smoke contains over 4,000 chemicals: 200 are poisons and 63 cause cancer.
- Smoking costs the United States approximately $97.2 billion each year in health care costs and lost productivity.

Sources: American Lung Association, www.lungusa.org/tobacco.

Figure 11.3
The Costs of Cigarette Smoking

Cigarette smoking causes major health problems for those who smoke, as well as for those exposed to it through secondhand smoke. *Why do you think many people still smoke, in spite of the expense and health risks involved?*

Likewise, over-the-counter (OTC) drugs are abused for the high or other effects they produce—but often with serious consequences, especially when taken in large doses or combined with other drugs. Medicines containing dextromethorphan (DXM), such as cold medications, are the most abused OTC drugs. Excessive doses can lead to hallucinations, seizures, brain damage, and death.

Overcoming Addictions

Addictive behavior comes in many forms, not just substance abuse. Just as an alcoholic feels happy when drinking, a food addict feels comforted when eating, a sex addict gets a rush from new partners, a shoplifter feels a thrill with getting away with stealing, an addictive shopper feels excited during a shopping spree, a gambler feels in control when winning, and a workaholic feels a sense of importance while working late at night or on weekends. Addiction is an abnormal relationship with an object or event and involves repeatedly using a substance or performing a behavior. Beginning as a pleasurable act or a means of escape, it progresses until it becomes a compulsive behavior that causes significant problems. Do you have a pattern of addiction? If you don't get this under control now, it will only get worse.

A person trying to overcome an addiction may experience anxiety, irritability, or moodiness. Some people switch addictions as a way to cope and give them the illusion that they have solved the problem. For example, many former alcoholics become chain smokers. Some people take up gambling as a way to have fun and get a rush, but then it becomes a problem. Compulsive gambling can leave people deeply in debt and devastate families and careers. A key question is "Is this behavior causing ongoing disruption in my life or the lives of those close to me?" Warning signs include secrecy; a change in discipline, mood, or work habits; a loss of interest in hobbies or school; and altered eating and sleeping habits. You may become withdrawn, depressed, or aggressive. You must take the initiative to get help. Ask your school counselor or go to the health center.

Here are some additional steps to take to deal with an addiction:

- *Admit there is a problem.* The first step in solving a problem is to face it. Many people with addictions react to problems with denial. They may do well in school or hold down a job and, therefore, don't see a problem. If you think you have lost control or are involved with someone who has, admit it and take charge of your life. Look at how you handle stress and conflict. Do you solve problems, deny them, or look for an escape?

- *Take responsibility for addiction and recovery.* You are responsible for and can control your life. Several support groups and treatment programs are available for various addictions. Search the Internet or your local phone book for resources in your area, or contact the following:

   Alcoholism: Alcoholics Anonymous: **www.aa.org**

   Distracted driving: U.S. Department of Transportation Web site for Distracted Driving: **www.distraction.gov**

   Drug abuse: National Institute on Drug Abuse: **www.drugabuse.gov**

   Gambling: National Council on Problem Gambling: **www.ncpgambling.org**

Sexual behavior: The Society for the Advancement of Sexual Health: **www.sash.net**

Smoking: Centers for Disease Control and Prevention, Smoking and Tobacco Use: **www.cdc.gov/tobacco**

Codependency

Even if you do not abuse alcohol or other drugs, your life may be affected by someone who does. A common term used to describe nonaddicted people whose lives are affected by an addict is **codependency.** Codependent people exhibit numerous self-defeating behaviors, such as low self-esteem; lack of strong, emotionally fulfilling relationships; lack of self-control; and overcontrolling behavior. A codependent person may

- *Avoid facing the problem of addiction.* Denying, making excuses, justifying, rationalizing, blaming, controlling, and covering up are all games that a codependent person plays in an effort to cope with living with an addict.
- *Take responsibility for the addict's life.* This may include lying; taking over a job, an assignment, or a deadline; or somehow rescuing the addict.
- *Be obsessed with controlling the addict's behavior.* A codependent person may hide bottles; put on a happy face; hide feelings of anger; confuse love and pity; and feel that, if only he or she could help more, the addict would quit.

If you feel you have problems in your life as a result of growing up in an alcoholic family or may be codependent, get help. Organizations such as Adult Children of Alcoholics (ACA) address the issues of people who grew up in alcoholic homes. There are many agencies and groups that can make a difference.

● Addicted to Texting
Many people find it hard to put down their cell phone, even when driving. However, almost 6,000 people were killed and over 500,000 were injured in 2008 due to distracted driving. Drivers who use hand-held devices are four times more likely to get into crashes serious enough to injure themselves. *Do you text and drive?*

Emotional Health

Everyone has the blues occasionally. However, sometimes stress and emotional problems interfere with your goals or ability to cope. A variety of emotional problems affect college students and professionals in all walks of life.

Depression

Depression is an emotional state of sadness ranging from mild discouragement to utter hopelessness. Each year, over 60 million people suffer from mild depression, which is relatively short-term. Severe depression is deeper and may last months or years. Over 6 million Americans suffer serious depression that impairs their ability to function. Depression accounts for 75 percent of psychiatric hospitalizations. It can occur as a response to the following situations:

- *Loss.* The death of a loved one, divorce, the breakup of a relationship, the loss of a job, involvement in a robbery or an assault, or any other major change, loss, disappointment, or violation can trigger depression.
- *Health changes.* Physical changes, such as a serious illness, an injury, childbirth, or menopause, can produce chemical changes that can cause depression.

- *An accident.* A car accident can be very traumatic, leading to feelings of being out of control and depression. Even if you were not seriously injured, feelings of hopelessness can result from an accident.
- *Conflicts in relationships.* Unresolved conflicts in relationships can cause depression.
- *Loneliness.* Loneliness can seem like a physical illness—painful or as dark as if someone has thrown a heavy blanket over your life. It is often felt by freshmen who have left home and haven't yet rebuilt a social network. (We'll discuss loneliness in more detail in Chapter 12.) Get involved in activities on campus and in the community, get a part-time job, practice listening, and try to develop new relationships.
- *Peer pressure.* You may feel pressured to get involved in alcohol, other drugs, smoking, or sex. When you have doubts, stop and think about the consequences. Ask why you are allowing others to define your values and boundaries. When you do something you are uncomfortable with, you may experience depression or sadness as if you have lost a sense of who you really are.
- *Daily demands.* You may feel overwhelmed by too many demands, such as deadlines or the pressure to choose a major. Nontraditional, or re-entry, students often must juggle school, work, family, and care of their home. Set priorities, ask for help, and try to eliminate or reduce unimportant or routine tasks. Delegate whenever possible.

Depression can be triggered by many events. Some of these relate to certain stages in life. For example, adolescents are just beginning to realize who they are and are trying to cope with the responsibilities of freedom and adulthood. Someone facing middle age may regret the loss of youth or unrealized career goals or may miss children who are leaving home. For an elderly person, the loss of physical strength, illness, the death of friends, and growing dependency may prompt depression.

Learn to recognize some of the common symptoms of depression:

- Sleep disturbance (sleeping too much or too little, constantly waking up)
- Increase in or loss of appetite
- Overuse of alcohol or prescription and/or nonprescription drugs
- Withdrawal from family and friends, leading to feelings of isolation
- Avoidance of teachers, classmates, and co-workers and lack of attendance
- Recurring feelings of anxiety
- Anger and irritability for no apparent reason
- Loss of interest in formerly pleasurable activities
- A feeling that simple activities are too much trouble
- A feeling that other people have much more than you have

When depression causes persistent sadness and continues beyond a month, severe depression may be present.

Suicide

More than 4,000 people in the United States between ages 16 and 25 die from suicide each year, making it the third leading cause of death for young people. Suicidal thoughts occur when a feeling of hopelessness sets in and problems seem unbearable. Suicidal people think the pain will never end, but they usually respond to help. Be concerned if you or others exhibit the following warning signs:

- Excessive alcohol or other drug use
- Significant changes in emotions (hyperactivity, withdrawal, mood swings)
- Significant changes in weight or in sleeping, eating, or studying patterns
- Feelings of hopelessness or helplessness
- Little time spent with or a lack of close, supportive friends
- Nonsupportive family ties
- Rare participation in group activities
- Recent loss or traumatic or stressful events
- Suicidal statements
- A close friend or family member who committed suicide
- Attempted suicide in the past
- Participation in dangerous activities
- A plan for committing suicide or for giving away possessions

● **Severely Depressed**
If not addressed, depression can become very serious and lead to thoughts of suicide. *How can you help a friend or co-worker who is suffering from depression?*

You should be concerned if you know someone who exhibits several of these warning signs. If you do know someone who is suffering from depression and seems suicidal, take the following steps:

1. Remain calm.
2. Take the person seriously; don't ignore the situation.
3. Encourage the person to talk.
4. Listen without moralizing or judging. Acknowledge the person's feelings.
5. Remind the person that counseling can help and is confidential.
6. Remind the person that reaching out for help shows strength, not weakness.
7. Call a crisis hot line, health center, school or community counseling center, or mental health department for a list of agencies that can help. Get the name of a counselor for the person to call, or make the call with him or her.
8. Stay with the person to provide support when he or she makes the contact. If possible, walk or drive the person to the counselor.
9. Seek support yourself. Helping someone who is suicidal is stressful.

Protecting Your Body

Reliable information about sex can help you handle the many physical and emotional changes you will experience in life. Although sex is a basic human drive and natural part of life, there are dangers, including sexually transmitted infections, unplanned pregnancies, and rape. Your level of sexual activity is a personal choice and can change with knowledge, understanding, and awareness. Having been sexually active at one time does not rule out a choice to be celibate now. No one should pressure you into sexual intercourse. If you decide to be sexually active, you need to make responsible decisions and be aware of the risks.

Sexually Transmitted Infections (STIs)

Sexually transmitted infections, or STIs, are spread through sexual contact (including genital, vaginal, anal, and oral contact) with an infected partner. An infected person may appear healthy and symptom-free. See **Figure 11.4** for a list of STIs and their symptoms, treatments, and risks. Despite public health efforts and classes in health and sexuality, STIs infect significant numbers of young adults. Even if treated early, STIs are a major health risk and can have devastating effects, such as damage to the reproductive organs, infertility, or cancer.

Acquired immune deficiency syndrome (AIDS) is a fatal STI. It weakens the immune system and leads to an inability to fight infection. AIDS is transmitted through sexual or other contact with the semen, blood, or vaginal secretions of someone with human immunodeficiency virus (HIV) or by sharing nonsterile intravenous needles with someone who is HIV-positive. Occasionally, it is contracted through a blood transfusion. About 1 million people are living with HIV in the United States, with around 40,000 new infections each year. Half of new infections in the United States occur in people age 25 or younger.

AIDS is most commonly spread by heterosexual intercourse. AIDS cannot be transmitted by saliva or casual contact, such as sharing utensils or shaking hands. Therapies using a combination of drugs have succeeded in controlling the progression of the disease. Although there is currently no cure for AIDS, there is help. Go to the student health center or local health department for testing. The Public Health Service has a toll-free AIDS hot line (800-342-AIDS), and local and state hot lines are available.

To avoid contracting any STI, follow these guidelines:

- Know your partner. It takes time and awareness to develop a healthy relationship.
- Ask a prospective partner about his or her health. Don't assume anything based on looks, class, or behavior.
- No matter what the other person's health status is, explain that you always use safety precautions. (Keep in mind that, if you are having unprotected sex, you are essentially being exposed to everyone your partner has had sex with in the past.)
- Latex condoms and dental dams can help protect against most sexually transmitted diseases. However, abstinence is the only totally effective method of preventing the spread of STIs, as well as pregnancy.

Birth Control

If your relationship is intimate enough for sex, it should be open enough to discuss birth control and pregnancy if birth control fails. Both men and women need to stop and ask, "How would an unwanted pregnancy change my life?"

Many contraceptives are available, but only abstinence is 100 percent foolproof. Current contraceptives include birth control pills, condoms, diaphragms, sponges, spermicidal foams, cervical caps, intrauterine devices (IUDs), and long-term

Sexually Transmitted Infections	What Are the Common Symptoms?	What Is the Treatment?	What Are the Risks?
AIDS/HIV	No symptoms for years; some carriers can be HIV+	No known cure; medical treatments can slow the disease	Weakening of the immune system; life-threatening infections
Chlamydia	Known as the "silent" disease because most infected people have no symptoms; others may experience discharge from genitals or a burning sensation when urinating	Antibiotics	More susceptible to developing pelvic inflammatory disease and infertility, and to having premature babies; can infect baby's eyes and respiratory tract during delivery
Genital herpes	Ulcers (sores) or blisters around the genitals	No cure; antiviral medications can shorten and prevent outbreaks	Highly contagious; become more susceptible to HIV infection; can also be spread via oral sex
Genital warts	The virus (human papillomavirus, or HPV) lives in the skin or mucous membranes and usually causes no symptoms; some will get visible genital warts	No cure, although the infection usually goes away on its own; cancer-related types of HPV are more likely to persist	Higher risk of cervical cancer
Gonorrhea	Symptoms include a painful or burning sensation when urinating; men may have a white, yellow, or green discharge from the penis or painful or swollen testicles; women may have an increased vaginal discharge or vaginal bleeding between periods; however, most women have no symptoms	Antibiotics	More susceptible to pelvic inflammatory disease, infertility, and HIV
Syphilis	Early symptoms include one or multiple sores; later symptoms vary from a rash to fever, hair loss, sore throat, and fatigue	Antibiotics	Untreated, can lead to damage of internal organs, paralysis, blindness, and death
Trichomoniasis	Men may experience temporary irritation inside the penis, mild discharge, or slight burning after urination or ejaculation; women may have a yellow-green vaginal discharge with a strong odor	Prescription drugs	More susceptible to contracting HIV; giving birth to premature or underweight babies

Source: Centers for Disease Control and Prevention, Division of Sexually Transmitted Diseases, www.cdc.gov/std.

Figure 11.4
STIs: Symptoms, Treatments, and Risks

Because STIs are a serious health risk, it is important to separate fact from myth when considering your options for protection. *In what ways can knowing the facts about STIs protect you?*

implants. Douching and withdrawal do not prevent pregnancy and should not be used for birth control. Discuss birth control methods with your partner and with a qualified health professional. Make an informed decision about what is best for you.

Understanding and Preventing Acquaintance Rape

Katie, a sophomore living off campus, is on her third date with Jeff, who is in her English class. They have been having a great time together, and Jeff is attentive and loving. In fact, Katie has told friends that he puts her on a pedestal. After a movie, they are sitting on her living room couch, drinking wine, talking, and sharing hugs and kisses. Jeff's kissing becomes more aggressive, and Katie pushes his hands away several times. Finally, she tells him she feels uncomfortable, wants to take the relationship slowly, and asks him to leave. Jeff blows up, accuses her of being a tease and leading him on, holds her down, and rapes her.

A typical image about rape involves a stranger lurking around a dark corner or deserted street. Although this does occur and requires safety precautions, most sexual assaults are committed by assailants known by the victim, and many occur in the victim's home. On college campuses, 84 percent of rape is acquaintance rape; 57 percent happens on dates (i.e., date rape). According to the FBI, up to 90 percent of rapes are not reported because the victim fears retaliation and social ostracism, fears not being believed, and, like Katie, blames herself because she had too much to drink or wonders if she said or did something to give the attacker the wrong idea. Make no mistake about it—date rape is rape.

One in three women in the United States will be a victim of sexual assault in her lifetime. All women are vulnerable to rape, no matter their age, race, class, or physical appearance. Rape is an act of aggression. A rapist seeks a person he can dominate and control. Check with the counseling center, health center, or campus police for ways to protect yourself from date rape. Here are a few preventative measures:

1. **Make your expectations clear.** Send clear messages and make certain that your body language, tone of voice, and word choices match your feelings. In a direct, forceful, serious tone, let others know when their advances are not welcome. If you don't want to get physically intimate, don't allow anyone to talk you into it. Be aware of your limits and feelings, and communicate them assertively. Say, "No," loudly and clearly. Scream for help if you need it.

2. **Meet in public places.** Until you know someone well, arrange to meet where others will be around. Double date whenever possible or go out with a group of friends. Have an agreement with friends that you will not leave a party alone or with someone you do not know well.

3. **Trust your intuition.** Be aware of your surroundings, and trust your instincts. If the situation doesn't feel right, leave and get help as soon as you can. If you feel ill, get help immediately. If you plan to go to a movie, to a party, or for a walk, ask a friend to go with you. If you're on a date, tell others when you expect to be back, take your cell phone, and leave your date's name. If something doesn't feel right, contact your roommate or a friend.

4. **Take your time.** It is impossible to spot a rapist by appearance, race, occupation, or relationship to you. The attacker might be your date, your lab partner, an instructor, a friend of a friend, or a neighbor down the hall. Take time to know a person before you spend time alone with him or her. Don't

take chances because someone looks nice or knows someone you know. Don't invite anyone to your home unless you know this person well. Otherwise, make certain a roommate or friends are around. Relationships that start slowly are built on friendship and are healthier and safer.

5. **Recognize that alcohol and other drugs can be dangerous.** They can inhibit resistance, increase aggression, and impair decision-making skills. If you are intoxicated, you may not be able to protect yourself or notice the signals that should warn you of danger. In some cases, date rapists have added so-called date rape drugs, such as Rohypnol (also called Roofies), GHB, Ecstasy, or Ketamine, to the victim's drink, causing the victim to become confused, drowsy, and dizzy; to have impaired judgment; or to experience temporary amnesia. It can cause loss of consciousness and even a coma or death. Never leave your drink unattended, and do not accept drinks from a common container.

6. **Learn to read the danger signals of an unhealthy relationship.** Be concerned if you are dating someone who

   - Pressures you sexually
   - Refers to people as sex objects
   - Drinks heavily or uses drugs and pressures you to drink or take drugs
   - Doesn't respect your wants, needs, or opinions
   - Is possessive or jealous
   - Wants to make decisions for you—tells you whom you may be friends with or what clothes to wear
   - Has a temper and acts rashly
   - Is physically abusive
   - Is verbally and emotionally abusive through insults, belittling comments, or "sulking" behavior
   - Becomes angry when you say, "No"

7. **Be safe and vigilant.** Make wise choices, use common sense, and do everything possible to protect yourself. Don't go jogging alone or in isolated areas, lock your doors and windows, and don't pick up hitchhikers. Know your campus and community well, and stay out of dark, secluded areas. If you are taking a night class, find the safest place to park your car. Use a campus escort, or arrange to walk to your car with a friend or group from your class. Contact the local recreation center or campus police to learn if a self-defense course is available.

8. **Get professional help.** Unfortunately, even the most diligent and safety-minded people can be raped. Report a rape immediately by calling 911, a rape crisis center, or the local or campus police. Preserve evidence by not bathing or changing clothes. Make certain you get counseling to deal with the trauma. Remember, it is not your fault!

Rape is not just a woman's problem. Men as well as women can become victims of physical, sexual, and mental abuse. Understand how your own attitudes and actions perpetuate sexism and violence, and work to change them. Speak up against stereotypical attitudes that rape victims asked for it and that women are sex objects. You can challenge demeaning and cruel jokes and attitudes by taking a mature, caring stand against violence.

TAKING CHARGE

Summary

In this chapter, I learned to

- **Connect my mind, body, and spirit.** I envision my mind, body, and spirit as a whole system and realize that everything is connected. I observe my thoughts, how my body feels, my level of stress, my negative habits, what I eat and drink, and changes or discomfort in my body.

- **Eat a variety of healthy foods in moderation.** I increase my consumption of fresh fruits and vegetables, eat whole grains, limit animal fat, cut down on sugar and caffeine, and take a multivitamin supplement every day. This helps me maintain my ideal weight, increases my self-esteem, and gives me energy.

- **Exercise regularly.** I participate in an aerobic activity for 30 minutes three times a week. I balance rest and relaxation with active sports, such as bicycling, dancing, or swimming. Being active helps me maintain my ideal weight, gives me energy, and increases my sense of well-being.

- **Develop healthy relationships.** Spending time with friends who are supportive and share my interests is a great source of satisfaction, and it adds to my energy and enjoyment of life. Friendships bring great joy and fellowship.

- **Reduce stress.** I have developed strategies for reducing stress, including exercising, doing deep breathing, disputing negative thoughts and beliefs, developing a sense of humor, rehearsing feared events, and creating balance in my life.

- **Use critical thinking to avoid drugs.** Alcohol is a toxin. Heavy drinking can damage the brain, increase the risk of heart disease, depress the immune system, and cause liver failure. Alcohol and other drugs can cause memory loss and impair reasoning.

- **Get help for addictions.** I recognize the signs of addiction to food, gambling, and alcohol and other drugs and when to seek help. I know that campus and community resources can help me or someone I know who has a drinking or other drug problem.

- **Observe my emotional health.** Although I know life has its ups and downs, I am aware of times when I don't bounce back after a disappointment or loss. Some warning signs of depression are changes in sleep patterns and appetite, drug use, and feelings of anxiety, anger, isolation, and disinterest. Severe depression and suicidal tendencies occur when feelings are extreme.

- **Protect my body.** I protect myself from illness, sexually transmitted infections, unwanted pregnancies, and rape. I am knowledgeable, aware, and proactive. I visit the health center, use safety precautions, and learn self-defense techniques.

Performance Strategies

Following are the top 10 tips for achieving a healthy lifestyle:

- Be aware of your body, your emotions, your unhealthy habits, and unexpected changes.
- Focus on healthy eating and a balanced diet.
- Maintain your ideal weight.
- Get enough rest and renewal time.
- Increase physical activity.

- Develop supportive and healthy relationships.
- Develop coping strategies for managing stress.
- Avoid addictive substances, such as cigarettes, alcohol, and other drugs.
- Get help immediately for depression and mental distress.
- Protect yourself from sexually transmitted infections and unwanted pregnancy.

Tech for Success

Take advantage of the text's Web site at **www.mhhe.com/ferrett8e** for additional study aids, useful forms, and convenient and applicable resources.

- **Health on the Web.** More sites on the Internet are devoted to health than any other topic. However, how do you know which sites provide accurate information? Start with government, professional organization, and nonprofit sites. Many of these offer questions to ask or red flags to look for when consulting with physicians or purchasing products on the Internet.
- **Assess yourself.** You will find a vast array of free personal assessment tools on the Internet. You can explore everything from ideal body weight to your risk of developing a certain cancer. Use assessments to help you

identify patterns and behaviors you want to change. As with all information on the Internet, check the source or research behind the assessment tool.

- **Just what is in that burger?** The Web site of almost every fast-food chain provides the caloric breakdown of its most popular items. Before your next trip to your favorite restaurant, look up the calories and fat content of your usual order. Is it what you expected, or even higher? Does this information affect your selections?
- **Music to my ears.** You may enjoy listening to your iPod, but follow the 60/60 rule to preserve your hearing: no more than 60 percent volume for no more than 60 minutes at a stretch.

Study Team Notes

Career*in* focus

Tony Ferraro
FIREFIGHTER

Related Majors: Fire Science, Public Administration

Preventing Stress and Fatigue at Work

Tony Ferraro has been a member of his city's fire department for 25 years. Three years ago, he was promoted to captain. He and the other firefighters at his station respond to fire alarms using various techniques to put out fires. They also respond to medical emergencies by providing emergency medical assistance until an ambulance arrives. When not out on calls, Tony and his crew maintain their equipment, participate in drills and advanced fire fighting classes, and keep physically fit.

Tony works two or three 24-hour shifts a week, during which time he lives and eats at the fire station. Because fire fighting involves considerable risks for injury or even death, the job is stressful and demanding. Being alert, physically fit, calm, and clear-headed is critical for making sound decisions. To stay healthy mentally and physically, Tony studies a form of karate that helps him not only stay in shape but also remain calm and focused. In addition, he drinks no more than one to two cups of coffee a day and has given up smoking.

As captain of his fire station, Tony has initiated better eating habits in the kitchen by posting a food pyramid and talking to the other firefighters about reducing fat and sugar in their diet. In addition, he observes the firefighters for signs of stress and makes suggestions when needed, such as taking time off or getting more rest. The company's health insurance policy includes coverage for counseling. Once after a particularly stressful period, Tony invited a stress counselor to speak and offer services at the station.

CRITICAL THINKING Why do firefighters need to work toward goals for physical, emotional, and mental health?

Peak Performer
PROFILE

Mark Herzlich Jr.

When 23-year-old Sandon Mark Herzlich Jr. found out he had Ewing's Sarcoma, a rare form of cancer, he went home and sulked for two hours. After those two hours were over, Herzlich realized "This [cancer] has got to be something I overcome. Once I made that decision, I was ready."

Herzlich, a linebacker with the Boston College Eagles football team, had already beaten the odds in his sports career. As a college freshman, he received Freshman All-American team honorable mention from the *College Football News*. In his junior season, Herzlich was named a First-team All-American, the ACC Defensive Player of the Year, and a finalist for the Lott Trophy. He was ranked as the 45th best prospect for the 2009 NFL Draft before announcing his decision to return to Boston College the following season to finish his degree.

After his diagnosis in May 2008, Herzlich returned to school, and to the field, to provide others help during his illness. He ran with the team at the beginning of games, and served as a right-hand man for the team coach. His behind-the-scenes work was even more valuable. He spent his time providing orientation to incoming freshmen, counseling kids with cancer, and raising about $200,000 through "Uplifting Athletes," an agency which raises awareness of rare diseases.

Herzlich has said of his volunteer activities, "I like this being part of me. It's something that's exciting, in that I get to be able to help other people." He was, however, also excited for his return as a player for the

Boston College Eagles, after his cancer-free diagnosis in October of 2009. He takes care of himself by not taking any risks that could hurt his recovering body, and checks for any lingering effects of the cancer and its treatment every three months. In all areas, Herzlich defines a peak performer: in mind, body, and spirit.

PERFORMANCE THINKING How did Herzlich's refusal to "sulk" put him onto a path towards self-determination and success over cancer? How do his actions personify those characteristics of a peak performer? If you have anything troubling you in your life, how can you use Herzlich's example to help better your own situation?

CHECK IT OUT At www.mademan.com/mm/10-famous-athletes-disabilities.html, you can read about the 10 most famous athletes with disabilities. Do you recognize any of the names? What else might these athletes have overcome? Think not only of bodily limitations but the limitations of other people's perceptions, attitudes, and other regulating guidelines.

Starting Today

At least one strategy I learned in this chapter that I plan to try right away is

_____

_____

_____

What changes must I make in order for this strategy to be most effective?

_____

_____

_____

Review Questions

Based on what you have learned in this chapter, write your answers to the following questions:

1. What are five strategies for good health management?

_____

_____

2. What are some of the benefits of aerobic exercise?

_____

_____

3. Why is it important to manage your stress?

_____

_____

4. Cite two statistics or facts about alcohol.

_____

_____

5. List four symptoms of depression.

_____

_____

To test your understanding of the chapter's concepts, complete the chapter quiz at **www.mhhe.com/ferrett8e**.

Increasing Your Energy Level

In the Classroom

Danny Mendez, a business major in marketing, works part-time at a sporting goods store, is president of his fraternity, and is on the soccer team. This demanding schedule is manageable because Danny's energy is high. However, around midterm he feels overwhelmed with stress. He needs to find ways to increase his energy, maintain his good health, and manage his stress.

1. What strategies would you suggest to help Danny reduce his stress?

_____

_____

2. What could you suggest to Danny to increase his energy level?

_____

_____

In the Workplace

Danny is now a marketing manager for a large advertising agency. He often travels to meet with current and prospective clients. When Danny returns, he finds work piled on his desk—advertising campaign issues, personnel problems, and production delays. Danny's energy has always been high, but lately he eats too much fast food, has started smoking again, and rarely exercises anymore. He keeps saying he'll get back on track when he has time.

3. What habits should Danny adopt to reduce his stress and fatigue?

_____

_____

4. What strategies in this chapter can help him increase his energy?

_____

_____

Applying the ABC Method of Self-Management

In the Journal Entry on page 343, you were asked to describe a time when you had lots of energy, felt healthy and rested, and were in control of your weight. What factors helped you be calm, confident, and healthy?

_____

_____

_____

Describe a situation in which you suffered from lack of sleep, were not eating healthy, or were stressed out. Apply the ABC Method to work through the scenario and achieve a positive outcome.

A = Actual event:

_____

_____

_____

B = Beliefs:

_____

_____

_____

C = Challenge:

_____

_____

_____

Use visualization to see yourself healthy and in charge of your physical, mental, and emotional life. You feel confident because you have learned to invest time in exercising, eating well, and being rested.

PRACTICE SELF-MANAGEMENT

For more examples of learning how to manage difficult situations, see the "Self-Management Workbook" section of the Online Learning Center Web site at **www.mhhe.com/ferrett8e**.

Stress Performance Test

Read the following list of situations. Then think back over the last few months. Have you experienced these situations? If so, put a check mark in the column that best indicates how you coped with the experience.

	Overwhelmed (3)	Moderately Stressed (2)	Handled Effectively (1)	Did Not Experience/ Not Applicable (0)
1. No time for goals		✓		
2. Lack of money		✓		
3. Uncomfortable living and study areas			✓	
4. Long working hours				✓
5. Boring, uninteresting job				✓
6. Conflict with roommate, family, etc.		✓		
7. Conflict with instructors			✓	
8. Too many responsibilities		✓		
9. Deadline pressures			✓	
10. Boring classes			✓	
11. Too many changes in life			✓	✓
12. Lack of motivation				
13. Difficulty finding housing				
14. Little emotional support from family			✓	✓

(continued)

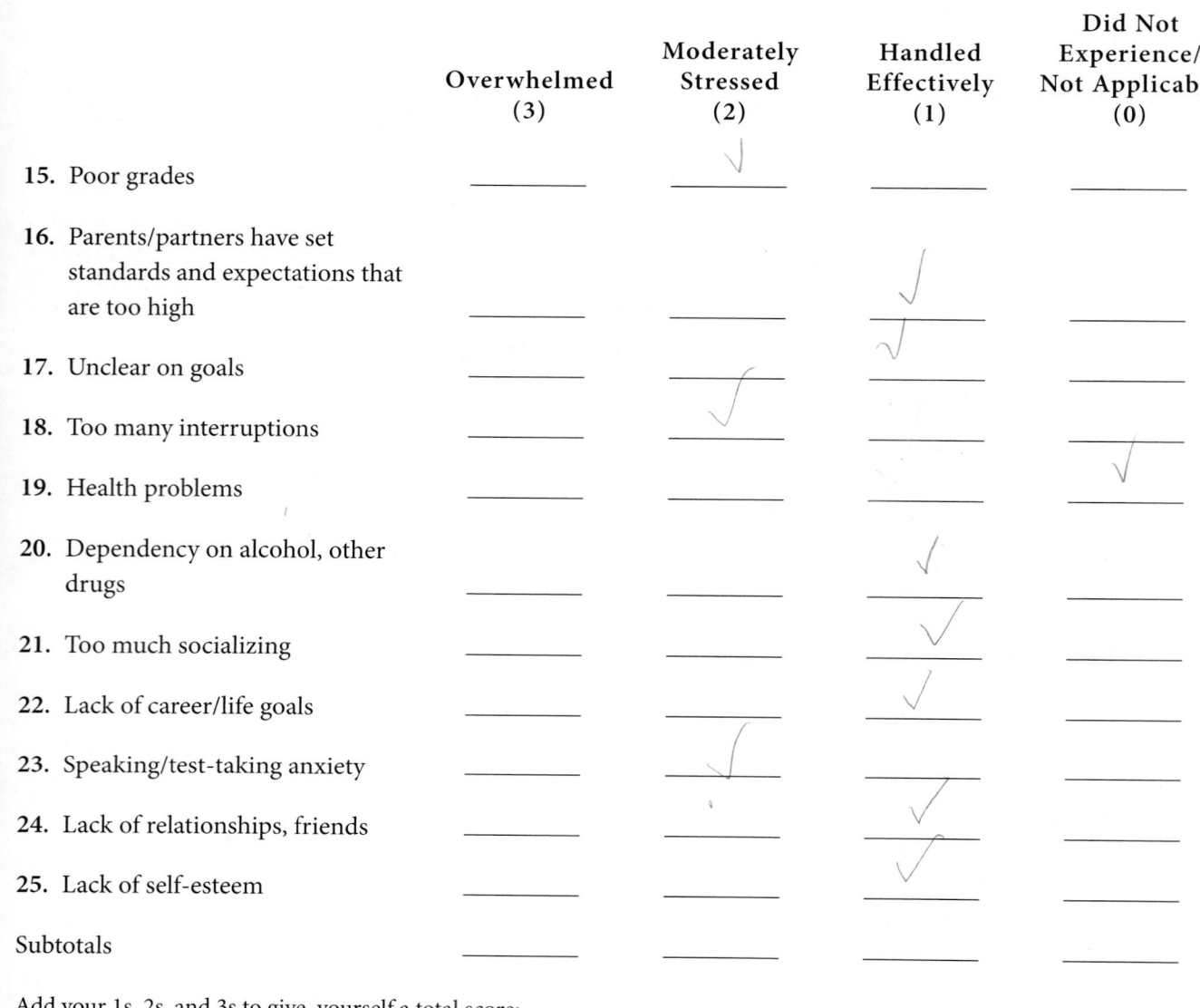

	Overwhelmed (3)	Moderately Stressed (2)	Handled Effectively (1)	Did Not Experience/ Not Applicable (0)
15. Poor grades	_____	✓	_____	_____
16. Parents/partners have set standards and expectations that are too high	_____	_____	✓	_____
17. Unclear on goals	_____	_____	✓	_____
18. Too many interruptions	_____	✓	_____	_____
19. Health problems	_____	_____	_____	✓
20. Dependency on alcohol, other drugs	_____	_____	✓	_____
21. Too much socializing	_____	_____	✓	_____
22. Lack of career/life goals	_____	_____	✓	_____
23. Speaking/test-taking anxiety	_____	✓	_____	_____
24. Lack of relationships, friends	_____	_____	✓	_____
25. Lack of self-esteem	_____	✓	_____	_____
Subtotals	_____	_____	_____	_____

Add your 1s, 2s, and 3s to give yourself a total score:

Totals O + 14 + 13 = 27

Total score

SCORES

25–36 Peak performer (you have learned how to function effectively under stress)

37–48 Persistent coper (you handle stress in most situations but have some difficulty coping and feel overwhelmed sometimes)

49–60 Stress walker (you often feel overwhelmed and exhausted, which affects your performance)

60+ Burnout disaster (you need help coping; stress is taking a toll on your health and emotions, and you risk burning out)

I Am What I Eat

This exercise aims to make you aware of your food choices. Starting on Monday, record *everything* you consume for one week, including water. Exact measurements aren't necessary. "Other" includes additional snacks, a water break, etc. (For a complete diet analysis, create a profile at **www.mypyramid.gov** or another online program designed to track and analyze your food intake and physical activity.)

Meal	Monday	Tuesday	Wednesday	Thursday	Friday	Saturday	Sunday
Breakfast							
Snack							
Lunch							
Snack							
Dinner							
Other							

1. Which type of liquid did you drink most often (water, coffee, milk, juice, etc.)? _____

2. How many soft drinks did you consume each day? (Use 12 ounces—the size of a soft drink can—as one drink, and divide by the number of days to get an average.) Are they usually diet or nondiet drinks? _____

3. How many drinks were caffeinated? _____

4. About how many times per day (or week) do you consume the following?
   - whole grains _____
   - green, leafy vegetables _____
   - fried foods _____
   - red meat _____
   - foods high in sugar _____
   - alcohol _____

5. Do you tend to eat fewer but bigger meals each day or many smaller meals? Or another pattern? _____

6. How many meals were bought at a restaurant, including via a drive thru or convenience store? _____

7. Of those meals, how many would you consider healthy choices? Did you consciously make a healthier selection versus something else you would have normally ordered? _____

8. Compare your eating and drinking habits on the weekend with the rest of the week. Are there obvious differences? If yes, explain. _____

9. Based on your food choices this week, what changes should you make to improve your diet? How easy or difficult will it be to make healthier choices? _____

Inventory of Interests

Developing outside interests can help reduce stress in your life. Interests are activities that you enjoy and pique your curiosity. Besides reducing stress, they may help you determine your life's work and career path. For example, an interest in the outdoors may lead to a major in natural resources, then to a career as a park ranger. A passion for working with cars may lead to a certificate in auto mechanics and thus to your own auto repair shop.

Fill in the following inventory to help you determine a career that coincides with activities you enjoy. Review this later to see if your interests change.

1. My interests are

_____

_____

_____

_____

2. Answer the following questions:

   a. What Web sites and blogs do I like to visit and read?

_____

_____

_____

_____

   b. What kinds of books and magazines do I like to read?

_____

_____

_____

_____

   c. When I have free time, what do I like to do? (Check the areas that interest you.)

Reading	_____	Working with people	_____
Writing	_____	Working with computers	_____
Sports	_____	Building or remodeling	_____
Outdoor activities	_____	Creating artwork	_____
Traveling	_____	Public speaking	_____

Other Activities

_____

_____

_____

Build Supportive and Diverse Relationships

LEARNING OUTCOMES

In this chapter, you will learn to

12.1 List strategies for communicating and building rapport

12.2 Practice assertive communication

12.3 Communicate effectively with instructors and advisors

12.4 Resolve conflicts

12.5 Accept and deliver criticism

12.6 Overcome shyness

12.7 Build healthy relationships

12.8 Understand and appreciate diversity

SELF-MANAGEMENT

> *I never realized I would interact with so many new people at college. It's exciting but frightening. I've been so focused on planning my coursework that I'm not prepared to think beyond my own little world.*

College offers many new experiences and exposes you to a wide variety of people with different backgrounds, opinions, and interests. It also gives you an opportunity to become a better communicator and an effective participant in social and group settings. In this chapter, you will learn how to create healthy relationships, solve conflicts, work effectively in a team, become more assertive, and handle criticism. You will see yourself communicating clearly, concisely, and confidently.

JOURNAL ENTRY In **Worksheet 12.1** on page 410, describe a difficult or confrontational situation in which you felt comfortable communicating your needs and ideas in an assertive, direct, and calm manner. What factors helped you be confident and respectful?

N o one exists in a vacuum. You can learn to read efficiently, write fluid prose, score high on tests, or memorize anything you want, but success will elude you if you cannot communicate and build rapport with different people. People spend nearly 70 percent of their waking hours communicating and interacting with others. SCANS lists interpersonal relationships, communication, an understanding of diversity, and team skills as essential for job success. In this chapter, we will discuss ways to get better at understanding and relating to people, solving conflicts, and being an effective team member.

The Importance of Effective Communication and Rapport

Communication is the giving and receiving of ideas, feelings, and information. Note the word *receiving*. Some people are good at speaking but are not effective listeners. Poor listening is one of the biggest barriers to effective communication. Miscommunication wastes billions of dollars in business and damages relationships.

What do you really want when you communicate with someone else? Do you want people to listen to you, understand your feelings, and relate to your message? Building **rapport** is more than just giving and receiving information. It is finding common ground with another person based on respect, empathy, and trust. Finding **common ground** means having an intent to focus on similarities in interests and objectives and appreciate diverse core values, seeing other viewpoints, and building bridges to understanding.

Some people have a knack for building rapport and making others feel comfortable and accepted. They are sensitive to nonverbal cues and the responses they elicit from other people. They have developed empathy and make people feel valued. They are comfortable with themselves and with people from different cultures and backgrounds. They can put their egos aside and focus on the other person with genuine interest and appreciation. You can learn this skill, too. People will want to be near you because you make them feel good about themselves, treat them as important, and create a comfortable climate. People who build rapport not only look for similarities in others but also appreciate and celebrate differences.

Strategies for Building Communication and Rapport

1. **Be willing to find common ground.** The first step in building rapport is to assess your intention to find common ground. If your goal is to build understanding, acceptance, and rapport, it will usually be reflected in your tone, body language, and style. If you are judgmental, however, this message will come through, regardless of your words. Even if you insist you want to

find common ground, others will sense your intention to prove yourself right, scold, judge, instruct, embarrass, or put down.

2. **Be an attentive listener.** In Chapter 5, we explored how to be an effective listener by using strategies such as the following:

   - *Listen; don't talk.* Don't change the subject unless the speaker is finished. Be patient and don't interrupt. Listen for feelings, undertones, and meanings in what people are saying. You can do this by observing nonverbal cues: posture, tone of voice, eye contact, body movements, and facial expressions.

   - *Put the speaker at ease.* Create a supportive, open climate by being warm and friendly, showing interest, and smiling.

   - *Withhold criticism.* Criticizing puts people on the defensive and blocks communication. Arguing almost never changes someone's mind, and it may widen the communication gap.

   - *Paraphrase.* Restating in your own words what the speaker has said shows you are interested in the other person's point. Then ask for feedback: "Did I understand you correctly?" Ask questions and seek to understand the person's point of view.

   - *Know when you cannot listen.* If you know you do not have time to pay close attention to the speaker, say so. For example, if you have a lot of studying to do and your roommate wants to talk about a date, you may want to say respectfully, "I'd like to know more about your date, but I have to read this chapter. Can we have a cup of coffee in an hour and talk about it?" You also may want to delay discussions when you are angry, tired, or stressed. Just make sure to respond in a respectful tone of voice.

3. **Pay attention to body language.** Look at the speaker and appear attentive, interested, and alert. In contrast, crossing your arms, frowning, leaning back in your chair, avoiding eye contact, sighing, and shaking your head say, "I don't like you and I don't want to listen." When your eyes wander, you appear uninterested or bored. Instead, create an attentive, supportive climate: Look at the other person, relax and uncross your arms, and lean slightly toward the person. Some experts say that 70 percent of what is communicated is done through nonverbal communication, or body language. If you intend to build rapport, your words must match your body language.

4. **Be respectful.** Many organizations are training employees in the importance of business etiquette—respect for and consideration of the feelings and needs of others. Good manners and respect are the basis of all healthy relationships. People need to feel they are getting the consideration and appreciation they deserve, whether in the classroom, on the job, or at home. See **Peak Progress 12.1** on page 382 on applying these principles to communicating online.

5. **Use warmth and humor.** Avoid sarcasm and jokes at the expense of another person's feelings, but don't take yourself too seriously. Humor puts people at ease and can dissipate tension. Wit and a sincere smile create warmth and understanding and can open the door to further effective communication.

6. **Relate to a person's personality style.** As mentioned in Chapter 1, people learn, think, and relate differently. Knowing this can help you interact and

Peak Progress

Socially Acceptable Technology

The use of technology has replaced face-to-face communication for many people. Not only has a short e-mail become more convenient than a phone call or a stroll down the hallway, but many social networking services, such as Facebook and Twitter, provide the tremendous opportunity to communicate instantly with designated groups of people. The use of these sites has exploded; for example, there are more than 400 million active users of Facebook sharing 25 billion pieces of content, including Web links, news stories, blog posts, and photos each month.

As popular and convenient as these communication sites have become, they also have their pitfalls. Because you are looking at a screen, it's easy to forget you are interacting with human beings. Misunderstandings can occur, because there are no nonverbal cues and voice inflections. More serious ramifications can happen if you don't follow some important guidelines:

- *Be respectful to others.* This may seem obvious, but many have used technology as a means to belittle, threaten, and harass others, which is considered **cyberbullying** or **cyberstalking**. The Internet should not be considered a convenient place to vent your

frustrations and anger or to torment others. If you find yourself a victim of cyber attacks, tell someone, including the site owner.

- *Do not provide personal information.* Not only could your identity be compromised financially but it also could be used by a predator to rob or physically harm you. If you are selling products on sites such as eBay or craigslist, never meet the buyer or seller alone.
- *Do not send inappropriate material.* Although **sexting** (exchanging sexually explicit material, often via cell phone) seems harmless to some, it can be considered pornography and lead to criminal prosecution, especially if a participant is a minor. Some statistics suggest that one-third of young adults have been sexted at least once, often with the embarrassing pictures forwarded to others.
- *If you think you shouldn't send it, don't.* Remember that virtual material can be available forever. If you think someone could take an e-mail or a posting the wrong way, it's better to take the time to reword it or not send it at all.

---

work more effectively with diverse groups of people. For example, if your boss has the personality of an analyzer or a thinker, you will want to base your reports on facts and deliver clear, concise, and correct presentations.

7. **Relate to a person's learning or teaching style.** For example, perhaps your instructor prefers the visual mode. She writes on the board, shows overheads and films, and uses phrases such as "Do you see what I'm saying?" For an instructor who prefers a visual mode, enhance your visual presentation. Turn in an especially attractive paper by being extra careful about neatness and spelling and using pictures and diagrams whenever appropriate. Try to maintain eye contact while this instructor is lecturing, and return visual clues, such as nods, smiles, and other reassurances.

8. **Be a team player.** You must pull your weight on a team, whether at school or at work. You build team rapport not by being fun, charming, and a good conversationalist but by being clear on expectations, deadlines, commitment, and follow-through. Excuses do not build rapport, and no one likes a slacker. Check in often with your team and know when you will meet again, what work should be accomplished by individual team members, and what resources each person needs in order to produce results. The foundation of teamwork is effective communication and responsibility.

Assertive Communication

Assertive communication is expressing yourself in a direct, above-board, and civil manner. You may not always feel you have the right to speak up for what you need, particularly in new situations where you see yourself as powerless and dependent. However, only you can take responsibility for clarifying your expectations, expressing your needs, and making your own decisions. You might tend to act passively in some situations, aggressively in others, and assertively in still others. In most situations, however, strive to communicate in an assertive and respectful manner.

- *Passive* people rarely express feelings, opinions, and desires. They have little self-confidence and low self-esteem, have difficulty accepting compliments, and often compare themselves unfavorably with others. Sometimes they feel that others take advantage of them, which creates resentment.

- *Aggressive* people are often sarcastic, critical, and controlling. They want to win at any cost and sometimes blame others for making them angry. They sometimes resort to insults and criticisms, which breaks down communication and harms relationships.

- *Passive-aggressive* people appear passive but act aggressively. For example, a passive-aggressive student will not respond in class when asked if there are any questions but will then go to the dean to complain. A passive-aggressive roommate will leave nasty notes or complain to others rather than confront you directly.

- *Assertive* people state their views and needs directly; use confident body language; and speak in a clear, strong voice. They take responsibility for their actions. Assertive people respect themselves and others.

Many of the communication strategies we've already discussed will help you be more assertive. Here are a few more tips:

1. **State the problem in clear terms.** Be clear on your position and what you want: "I cannot study with the music so loud."

2. **Express your feelings.** Use "I" messages instead of "You" messages: "I feel frustrated when the music is too loud, because I have to study for a test tomorrow."

3. **Make your request.** "Please turn the music down. I especially need it quiet after ten o'clock."

4. **Use assertive body language.** Stay calm, use direct eye contact, square your shoulders, and speak in a clear, low tone.

5. **State the consequences.** Always start with the positive: "If you will turn down the volume on your music, I can study better and our relationship will be more positive." If you don't get the results you want, try saying, "I'm going to have to go to our landlord to discuss this problem." Practice developing assertive responses in **Personal Evaluation Notebook 12.1** on page 384.

Communicating with Instructors and Advisors

Develop professional relationships with your instructors and advisors, just as you would with your supervisor at work. Try a few of these tips to increase rapport:

Personal Evaluation Notebook

Assertive Communication Role-Playing

Read the following situations. Then develop an assertive response for each one.

1. **Situation:** You receive a *B* on your test, and you think you deserve an *A*. What would you say to your instructor?

   Assertive response: _____

2. **Situation:** A friend asks you to read her term paper. She tells you it is the best paper she has ever written. However, you find several glaring errors.

   Assertive response: _____

3. **Situation:** Your roommate asks to borrow your new car. You don't want to lend it.

   Assertive response: _____

4. **Situation:** An acquaintance makes sexual advances. You are not interested.

   Assertive response: _____

5. **Situation:** You go to a party and your date pressures you to drink.

   Assertive response: _____

6. **Situation:** Your roommate's friend has moved in and doesn't pay rent.

   Assertive response: _____

7. **Situation:** Your sister borrowed your favorite sweater and stained it.

   Assertive response: _____

8. **Situation:** A friend lights up a cigarette, and you are allergic to smoke.

   Assertive response: _____

9. **Situation:** You want your roommate or spouse to help you keep the apartment clean.

   Assertive response: _____

10. **Situation:** Your mother wants you to go home for the weekend, but you have to study for a major test.

    Assertive response: _____

1. **Clarify expectations.** Make certain you understand the objectives and expectations of your instructors and advisors. Most instructors will give you extra help and feedback if you take the initiative. For instance, before a paper is due, hand in a draft and say, "I want to make sure I'm covering the important points in this paper. Am I on the right track? What reference sources would you like me to use? What can I add to make this an *A* paper?"

2. **Clarify concerns.** If you don't understand or you disagree with a grade on a test or paper, ask for an appointment with the instructor. Approach the situation with a supportive attitude: "I like this course and want to do well in it. I don't know why I got a *C* on this paper, because I thought I had met the objectives. Could you show me what points you think should be changed? Could I make

these corrections for a higher grade?" Show respect and appreciation for your instructor's time and help, as your instructor may be teaching many courses with many students. Follow basic rules of etiquette when communicating with your instructor by e-mail. (See **Peak Progress 12.2** on page 386.)

3. **Adapt to your instructor's teaching style.** Approach each class with a positive attitude, and don't expect that all instructors will teach according to your learning style. (See Chapter 1, page 29, for specific tips.)

4. **Be open to learning.** Attend every class with an inquisitive, open mind. Some instructors may be less interesting, but be as supportive of the instructor as possible. If you are a returning student, you may find that the instructor is younger than you are and may lack life experiences. Be open to learning and valuing the training, education, and knowledge the instructor brings to class. The same rule applies to the workplace.

● **Connecting with Your Instructor**

Develop a rapport with your instructor by taking the initiative to ask for feedback and help when you need it and in plenty of time to put the advice into action. *Are you working on assignments or papers right now that you should be consulting with your instructor about?*

5. **Take responsibility for your own learning.** Don't expect your instructor to feed you information. You are ultimately responsible for your own learning and career. You may be tempted to cut classes, but you will miss valuable class discussions, question-and-answer sessions, explanations, reviews of concepts, expectations about tests, contact with students, and structure to help you stay focused.

6. **Take an interest in your instructors.** Visit them during office hours to discuss your work, goals, grades, and future coursework. When appropriate, ask about your instructors' academic backgrounds as a guide for yours. Ask about degrees, colleges attended, work experience, and what projects they are working on for professional growth. A large part of building rapport is showing genuine interest, appreciation, and respect.

7. **Network.** Building your professional network begins in college. You will want to form close professional relationships with other students, your advisor, your coach, a few key instructors, club advisors, administrators, and so on. Exchange e-mails and ask people on campus (who know you well) if you may use them as a reference or if they would be willing to write a letter of recommendation for graduate school, an internship, or your first job. You can help by creating a resumé that includes your accomplishments and strengths.

Conflict

Conflicts can occur between family members, co-workers, neighbors, roommates, friends, teammates, and instructors and students. Some common causes are strong emotions, unsatisfied needs, misperceptions and stereotypes, miscommunication, repetitive negative behavior, and differing expectations, opinions, beliefs, and values. Although conflict can impede communication and damage relationships, it can also bring problems to the surface and lead to creative solutions when the conflict is understood and coped with appropriately. Use your observation and critical

Peak Progress

E-mail Etiquette with Instructors

Although you may have established a friendly, personable relationship with your instructor or advisor, you should always treat him or her with the respect due to any employer or evaluator of your performance or behavior. Because technology has allowed us to communicate more quickly, we often forget to practice the basic rules of communication etiquette that are common in written memos and face-to-face communication.

When e-mailing your instructor for help, clarification, or advice, keep in mind the following:

1. **Use proper spelling, grammar, and punctuation.** Although you may be used to text messaging in lowercase letters, proper e-mail etiquette calls for writing the e-mail just as you would a memo. Start each sentence with a capital letter, and end each sentence with punctuation (period, question mark, etc.). It's also common e-mail knowledge that you should not write in all capital letters, which designates "shouting" or intense urgency. Always use the spell-check before sending, and read it through at least once more.

2. **Avoid using slang, abbreviations, or "smileys."** Again, you wouldn't say "ADN" (for "any day now") in a memo or include little smiley faces (emoticons). Those are fine in messages to friends, but not to instructors or employers. Also, your instructor may lose your meaning because he or she doesn't know what "BTW" ("by the way") stands for.

3. **Use proper greetings.** You wouldn't start a memo to your instructor with "Hey, Dr. Smith." "Dear Dr. Smith" is appropriate; "Hello, Dr. Smith" is also acceptable in most cases.

4. **Make it clear who you are.** Since instructors interact with many people daily, they can't decipher who you are by your e-mail account (bhappy16@aol.com). Quickly make it clear who you are ("I'm Beatrice Jones in your English 305 course"). Put your full name (and phone number, if necessary) at the end of your e-mail.

5. **Be smart about your e-mail address.** Although you may think hot2trot@aol.com gets attention, it won't garner much respect (and possibly even response) from an instructor or a future employer. Plus, with the myriad of spam messages and computer viruses, your instructor may even be hesitant to open your e-mail.

6. **Be concise and to the point.** Remember that your instructor has many people to respond to during the day: students, other faculty members, and administrators (not to mention people involved in their research work, professional memberships, and consulting obligations). In your message subject line, clearly state the overall point: "Question about today's discussion on learning styles." In one or two paragraphs, briefly ask your question or make your point. Include just the essential details. If you feel your point may be lost, either put your question at the very beginning or highlight it in bold or another color.

7. **Respectfully include a "due date," if necessary.** Never say to an instructor, "I must hear from you by . . ." However, your issue may be time-sensitive for a reason, such as a registration deadline. If you need a response by a certain time, indicate that politely: "It would be great to have your response by this Friday, as I have to turn in my forms by that afternoon." If you haven't received a response, send a follow-up: "Just checking to make sure you received my e-mail." When something is urgent, e-mail may not be the appropriate mode of communication. Call the instructor, drop by his or her office, catch him or her in class, or schedule an appointment. Do not let e-mail be an excuse for not getting an important answer.

8. **Leave in the message thread.** If there has been a string of e-mails to this point, it's always better to leave them in if you can, in case the recipient needs to refresh his or her memory about the issue.

9. **Do not use graphics.** Unless necessary, do not be creative with the typeface, graphics, or backgrounds in your e-mails. They only make the e-mail harder to read (and increase the file size).

10. **Always say, "Thank you."** Get in the habit of ending e-mails with a *thank you, thanks,* or *I appreciate your help.* People will respond to you faster and more often if their efforts are acknowledged and appreciated.

thinking skills to complete **Personal Evaluation Notebooks 12.2** and **12.3** on pages 388 and 389 about conflict resolution.

The common responses to conflict are to avoid it, compromise, accommodate others, or cooperate with others. Following are a few suggestions that focus on cooperation as a means of resolving conflict.

1. **Define the conflict as a concrete problem to be solved.** Focus on the problem, not the other person: "The conflict is that Joe is doing most of the talking in my study group and I want to move on and solve the problem, so that the group can be more productive."

2. **Convert "You" statements into "I" statements.** Making "I" statements instead of "You" statements effectively communicates information without pointing the finger at the other person and putting him or her on the defensive. Instead of saying, "You talk too much," say, "I feel angry when one person does all the talking, because we need to hear the opinions of other people before we can make an informed decision." Use a three-part formula:

   "I FEEL (emotions) _____WHEN (behavior) _____ BECAUSE (reason) _____."

3. **Attentively listen to the other person's concerns and criticism.** Don't interrupt or start your defense. Really concentrate on the other person's perceptions, feelings, and expectations. Give physical cues that you are listening. Listen to what is said, how it is said, and when it is said. Listen also for what is not being said. Ask for clarification, avoid jumping to assumptions, and don't hurry the speaker.

4. **Develop empathy.** Empathy is the ability to share another's emotions, thoughts, or feelings in order to understand the person better. By taking the role of the other, you can develop the ability to see and feel the situation through his or her eyes. Sympathy is feeling compassion for a person, which can border on pity or condescension. An empathetic attitude says, "I am here with you." Empathy allows for the distance needed to maintain objectivity, so that the problem can be solved.

5. **Stay calm.** Control your emotions and don't lose your temper. Ask the other person to calm down: "I see you are upset, and I really want to know what your concerns are. Please talk more slowly." Listen to the message without overreacting or becoming defensive.

6. **Focus on the problem.** Don't use detours and attack the person—for example, "You think I'm messy. Look at your room. You're a real pig." Instead, focus on the problem: "If I do the dishes the same evening I cook, will you feel more comfortable?" Trust that you can both speak your minds calmly and nondefensively without damaging your relationship.

Take 3 minutes to thank someone for making a difference:
- Pick someone, such as a coach, teacher, boss, friend, relative, or group leader, with whom you've interacted.
- How has this person helped you or others? Has this person sacrificed personal time to fulfill the commitment?
- Write a note or an e-mail to the person, thanking him or her for the contribution, mentioning how you have been affected.

What else can you do in 3 minutes?
- Check the school's Web site or use an Internet search engine to look up information about your major instructors. See what types of research they are involved in.
- Send a "thinking of you" e-mail to a friend you haven't corresponded with lately.
- Say "hi" to everyone you pass on the way into class.

Take 3

Personal Evaluation Notebook

12.2

Observing Conflict

Read the following questions and write your answers on the lines provided.

1. Observe how others handle conflict, compliments, and criticism. What ineffective behaviors do you notice?

   _____

   _____

2. If you were a consultant in conflict resolution, what conflict resolution tips would you give?

   _____

   _____

3. What behaviors do you use under stress that you would like to change?

   _____

   _____

4. What do you intend to do the next time you are in a conflict with someone?

   _____

   _____

7. **Ask for specific details and clarification.** The key is to understand the issue at hand: "Can you describe a specific incident when you think I was rude?"

8. **Create solutions.** You might say, "I can see that this is a problem. What can I do to solve it? What procedures or options can we explore?"

9. **Apologize.** If you think the situation warrants it, apologize: "I'm sorry. I was wrong." It defuses anger and builds trust and respect.

Constructive Criticism

Part of effective communication is being open to feedback and criticism. Start with the attitude that the critic has good intentions and is offering constructive criticism—criticism meant to be supportive and useful for improvement. Unconstructive criticism is negative and harsh; it doesn't offer options and can create defensiveness and tension.

GIVING CONSTRUCTIVE CRITICISM

Your feedback will be asked for more often if you give it in a nurturing way.

1. **Establish a supportive climate.** People need to feel safe when receiving feedback or criticism. Choose a convenient time and a private place to talk. If possible, sit next to the person instead of behind a barrier, such as a desk.

Personal Evaluation Notebook

Conflict Resolution

Describe a conflict you have not yet resolved. Think of resolution techniques that would be helpful. Respond to the following statements.

1. Describe the problem.

_____

_____

2. Express your feelings.

_____

_____

3. State what you want.

_____

_____

4. Predict the consequences.

_____

_____

2. **Ask permission to offer criticism.** Don't blindside someone with your feedback. First ask if he or she would like to hear your impressions and suggestions for improvement.

3. **Focus on the behavior, not the person.** Define the specific behavior you want to change. Don't hit the person with several issues at once.

4. **Stay calm.** Look at the person, keep your voice low and calm, use positive words, and avoid threats. Be brief and to the point.

5. **Be balanced.** Let the other person know you like him or her and appreciate the person's good qualities or behaviors. Avoid words such as *always* and *never*.

6. **Explain.** Explain why the behavior warrants criticism and why a change is in order. Talk about options and offer to help.

RECEIVING CRITICISM

Learning to accept and grow from constructive criticism is important for school and job success. Here are some tips:

1. **Listen with an open mind.** Reminders that you aren't perfect are never pleasant. However, try to listen with an open mind when your instructor, boss, co-worker, roommate, spouse, or classmate points out mistakes, mentions concerns, or makes suggestions. Don't talk until you have heard all the details.

> "Minds are like parachutes. They only function when they are open."
>
> SIR JAMES DEWAR
> *Chemist and physicist*

WORDS TO SUCCEED

Think about what is being said and whether the criticism is constructive. You may want to ask for time to think it through. Do others feel the same way? Have you heard similar criticism before? If so, it may be valid.

2. **Pay attention to nonverbal cues.** Sometimes people have difficulty expressing criticism, so they express it nonverbally. If the person is aloof, angry, or sad, you might ask if you did something to offend the person. If he or she is sarcastic, perhaps there is underlying hostility. If appropriate, you can say, "You've been very quiet today. Did I do something to offend you?"

3. **Ask for clarification.** Be sure you understand the criticism—for example, "Professor Walker, you gave me a *C* on this paper. Could you explain what points you consider to be inadequate?"

4. **Ask for suggestions.** If the criticism is constructive, ask for suggestions—for example, "How can I improve this paper?" Summarize the discussion and clarify the next steps. Know what you need to do to correct the situation. Don't make excuses for your behavior. If the criticism is true, change your behavior.

5. **Explain your viewpoint.** If the criticism feels unfair, discuss it openly. Don't let resentments smolder and build. Practice saying, "Thank you for your viewpoint and your courage in telling me what is bothering you. However, I don't think the criticism is fair." Criticism reflects how another person views your behavior at a certain time. It is not necessarily reality but an interpretation. Relax and put it in perspective.

Dealing with Shyness

Shyness is common, especially on college campuses, where people are adjusting to new situations and meeting new people. Shyness is not a problem unless it interferes with your life. It is perfectly acceptable to enjoy your privacy, prefer a few close friends to many, and even embarrass easily. However, if shyness keeps you from speaking up in class, getting to know your instructors and other students, giving presentations, or making new friends, it is interfering with your success. Shyness can also add to feelings of loneliness. In school and in the workplace, it is important to ask questions, clarify assignments, and ask for help. You can overcome your shyness, build rapport, and be an effective conversationalist by following these strategies:

1. **Use positive self-talk.** Instead of saying, "I'm shy; I can't change," tell yourself, "I'm confident, people like me, and I like people. I enjoy getting to know people. I am accepted, appreciated, and admired."

2. **Use direct eye contact.** Many shy people look down or avoid eye contact. Direct eye contact reinforces your confidence and shows interest in and empathy with others. Look at your instructors and show interest in what they are presenting.

3. **Ask questions and show genuine interest.** You don't have to talk a lot to be an effective conversationalist. In fact, you don't want to deliver monologues. Ask open-ended questions, show genuine interest, and give others a chance to talk. For example, instead of asking Jennifer if she is finished with an assigned term paper (yes/no), ask her how she is progressing with the paper (open-ended

question). See **Peak Progress 12.3** for tips on making small talk and initiating conversations.

4. **Listen to other points of view.** Even if you don't agree with other people's points of view, you can listen and respond tactfully and thoughtfully. You have something to contribute, and exchanging different views is a great way to learn and grow. Ask others how they developed their point of view.

5. **Use humor.** Most people like to laugh. Poking good-natured fun at yourself lightens the conversation, as does a funny joke or story. Just make certain to be sensitive; don't tell off-color or racial jokes or stories.

6. **Focus on the benefits.** Making friends helps you develop your sense of community and belonging. It can ease the loneliness many students feel.

Peak Progress

Making Small Talk

Whether you are meeting students in class, a business client, a first date, or the patient next to you in the doctor's office, the art of small talk can help you get to know people better and overcome awkward situations.

- *Ask questions to get the conversation rolling.* Most people love to talk about themselves, and you can learn a lot about someone. Follow up on phrases. If someone answers, "How are you?" with "Excellent," respond with "It sounds like you're having a great day! May I ask why?" If the person's mood isn't positive, though, be careful about asking too much, or you will seem to be prying.
- *Mention current events.* Bring up recent happenings in the news, sports, your community, or politics. However, avoid getting into a heated debate (especially a political one).
- *Comment on a piece of clothing or an accessory you like.* Ask where it came from or the significance. Everyone appreciates honest flattery.
- *Talk about television shows, movies, books, or other pop culture.* Share your interests to see what you might have in common or can learn from each other.
- *Mention places in the community.* Ask if the person has had a chance to see the new stadium or a jazz club that just opened. What restaurant would the person recommend to someone visiting from out of town?
- *Listen and pay attention.* Not paying attention during casual conversation makes a bad impression.

The other person will think you aren't interested and are just killing time.

- *Use your body language.* Keep your arms uncrossed and relaxed. Make direct eye contact and smile.
- *Be positive and friendly.* No one likes to be around people who are negative or rude. Use appropriate humor, not sarcasm, humor that belittles others, or offensive language.
- *Use the person's name.* If this isn't your first meeting, using the person's name makes him or her feel more important. Follow up on your last conversation: "How did your son's team do in that soccer tournament?" or "Were you happy with your grade on the economics paper?" People are impressed when you remember something about them.
- *Stay on common ground.* If you are stuck trying to come up with something to say, talk about whatever you know you have in common, such as a class.
- *If all else fails, use the weather.* It may be a cliché, but initiate a conversation by talking about the surroundings or situation: "Can you believe this hot spell we're having?" Segue into related topics: "I'm sure the baseball team is feeling the heat. Do you ever go to their games?" or "I've had to use the inside track for walking lately. Do you use the rec center, too?" The weather may help you find some common interests.

7. **Take action.** Join clubs and activities. Volunteer in an organization that sponsors service learning. Join study groups or ask one of your classmates to study with you. Get a part-time job or get involved in community organizations. Try out for a play or choir—really stretch yourself. Reach out to others and make friends with a broad range of people.

Overcome Obstacles to Effective Communication

The greatest barrier to effective communication is the assumption that the other person knows what you mean. It is easy to think that what you say is what your listener hears, but communication is a complex system, with so many barriers to overcome that it is a wonder anyone ever really communicates. Other barriers include poor listening skills, the need to be right all the time, and cultural, religious, social, and gender differences.

However, communication is the lifeblood of personal relationships and the foundation of effective teams and work groups. Learning to work effectively with your study team, advisors, instructors, roommates, co-workers, and supervisors is essential for success at school, at work, and in personal relationships. Look for patterns that seem to occur in your relationships as you complete **Personal Evaluation Notebook 12.4.**

Build Healthy Relationships

Problems in relationships can consume time and energy, and they may affect your self-esteem. Because feeling good about yourself is one key to all-around success, it is important to assess how you handle relationships with partners, friends, and family.

Romantic Relationships

Success in life can be even more meaningful when you are part of a loving, supportive relationship. However, too often we define ourselves by success in romantic endeavors rather than understanding what we gain emotionally by a rewarding relationship. Following are tips for building healthy relationships.

1. **Progress slowly.** A healthy relationship progresses slowly. Take time to get to know the other person and how he or she feels and reacts to situations. Relationships that move too fast or are based on intense and instant sexuality often end quickly. Some people go from casual to intimate in one date. Solid relationships need time to develop through the stages of companionship and friendship.

2. **Have realistic expectations.** Some people think a good romantic relationship will magically improve their lives, even if they make no effort to change their thinking or behavior. If you are a poor student, are unmotivated, are depressed, or lack confidence, you will still have these problems even if you have a great relationship. A relationship can't solve life's problems; only you

"Lots of people want to ride with you in the limo, but what you want is someone who will take the bus with you when the limo breaks down."

OPRAH WINFREY
Talk show host, actor, publisher

Personal Evaluation Notebook

Patterns in Relationships

Look for patterns in your relationships. Recall situations that occur again and again. For example, you may have the same problem communicating with instructors or advisors. You may have had conflicts with several roommates, co-workers, or supervisors. Once you see the patterns and consequences of your interactions, you can begin to think and act differently. When you take responsibility for changing your inner world of beliefs and thoughts, your outer world will also change. Write about what seems to be a recurring theme or pattern in your relationships.

_____

_____

_____

_____

_____

_____

_____

_____

_____

_____

_____

can solve your problems. Put more energy into improving your life than into looking for someone else to do it.

3. **Be honest.** A healthy relationship is based on truth. You certainly don't want to reveal your entire past to a casual acquaintance or first date. At the appropriate time, however, you need to be honest about your feelings, basic values, and major life experiences. For example, if you are an alcoholic or have been married before, the other person should know that as your relationship progresses.

4. **Be supportive.** A healthy relationship is mutually supportive of the growth and well-being of each partner; an unhealthy relationship is not. No one owns another person, nor does anyone have a right to harm another physically or emotionally. An unhealthy relationship is possessive and controlling.

5. **Have respect.** A healthy relationship is based on respect for the other person's feelings and rights. An unhealthy relationship is self-centered and disrespectful.

6. **Have trust and be trustworthy.** A healthy relationship works in a relaxed, loving, and comfortable way. When a problem comes up, you have trust that it will be faced and resolved, rather than blamed on each other.

7. **Know that change can occur.** Emotionally healthy people know that not all relationships will develop into romantic and intimate commitments. Knowing how to end or let go of a relationship is as important as knowing how to form healthy relationships. It is acceptable and normal to say no to an acquaintance who asks you out or to decide you don't want a romantic relationship or friendship to continue after a few dates. No one should date, have sex, or stay in a relationship out of guilt, fear, or obligation. It is harder to terminate a relationship if it progressed too fast or if the expectations for the relationship differ. Talk about your expectations, and realize that your worth does not depend on someone's wanting or not wanting to date you.

8. **Keep the lines of communication open.** Trouble occurs in relationships when you think you know how the other person feels or would react to a situation. For example, you may assume that a relationship is intimate, but the other person may regard it as casual. Make your expectations clear.

Communication in a healthy relationship is open enough to discuss even sensitive topics, such as birth control, sexually transmitted diseases, and unplanned pregnancy. Take a moment to reflect on your relationships in **Personal Evaluation Notebook 12.5.**

Relationships with the People You Live With

If you share your living space with a roommate, partner, or family member, it's important to create an open environment for communicating needs, problems, and solutions. The following suggestions will help you create rapport and improve communication with your roommates and family members.

1. **Clarify expectations of a roommate.** List the factors you feel are important for a roommate on your housing application or in an ad. If you don't want a smoker or pets, say so. Sometimes it is best not to live with a good friend—rooming together has ruined more than one friendship. Plus, getting to know new people with different backgrounds and experiences is a great opportunity.

2. **Discuss expectations when first meeting your roommate.** Define what neatness means to you. Discuss how both of you feel about overnight guests, drinking, drugs, choice and volume of music, housework, food sharing, quiet times, and so on. Consider developing a "roommate contract," which specifies certain expectations and responsibilities (including financial ones, if need be).

3. **Clarify concerns and agree to communicate with each other.** Don't mope or whine about a grievance or leave nasty notes. Communicate honestly and kindly. It's important to understand each other's views and expectations and try to work out conflicts. If your roommate likes to have the dishes done after each meal, try to comply rather than prove that he or she is a neat freak. If you like to have friends over but your roommate goes to bed early or is studying, entertain in the early evenings, be quiet, or go out in the late evenings.

4. **Treat your roommate and family members with respect.** Don't give orders or make demands. Calmly listen to each other's needs. Treat each other with courtesy and civility. Think about your tone of voice, body language, and choice of words. Sometimes we treat family, friends, and roommates with less respect than strangers.

Personal Evaluation Notebook

12.5

Healthy Relationships

Read the following statements and questions, and respond to them on the lines provided.

1. List the factors you believe are essential for a healthy relationship.

   _____

   _____

2. What do you believe contributes to unhealthy relationships?

   _____

   _____

3. Who are your friends?

   _____

   _____

4. Describe some of your other relationships, such as in study teams and with instructors.

   _____

   _____

5. List the ways that your relationships support you and your goals.

   _____

   _____

6. List the ways that unhealthy relationships may undermine you and your goals.

   _____

   _____

   _____

5. **Don't borrow unless necessary.** A lot of problems result over borrowing money, clothes, jewelry, cars, CDs, and so on. The best advice is not to borrow. However, if you must borrow, ask permission first and return the item in good shape or replace it if you lose or damage it. Fill the tank of a borrowed car with gas, for instance. Immediately pay back all money you borrow.

6. **Take responsibility for your life.** It isn't anyone's responsibility to loan you money or food, clean up after you, entertain or feed your friends, or pay your bills.

7. **Keep your agreements.** Make a list of chores, agree on tasks, and do your share. When you say you will do something, do it. When you agree on a time, be punctual. Try to be flexible, however, so that annoyances don't build.

Max is at the breaking point. He has walked into the kitchen to make breakfast, only to find that his roommate, Jimmy, must have had the late-night munchies again, as evidenced by the dirty pans on the stove, grated cheese on the floor, and a half-eaten taco abandoned on the coffee table beside Jimmy, who is passed out on the couch.

- If you were Max, would you wake up Jimmy and discuss the situation now?
- Develop some "I" statements that Max can use to discuss the situation with his roommate.
- If Jimmy's behavior doesn't change, what should Max do?

8. **Accept others' beliefs.** Don't try to change anyone's beliefs. Listen openly and, when necessary, agree that your viewpoints are different.

9. **Accept others' privacy.** Don't enter each other's bedroom or private space without asking. Don't pry, read personal mail, or eavesdrop on conversations. Don't expect to share activities unless you are invited.

10. **Get to know each other.** Set aside time for occasional shared activities. Cook a meal, go for walks, or go to a movie. You don't need to be your roommate's best friend, but you should feel comfortable sharing a room or an apartment. Appreciate your roommate and/or family members, and try not to focus on little faults or inconveniences.

Family Ties
Balancing honesty with courtesy and respect will strengthen your relationships and improve communication. *Besides communication, what other area would you want to improve in your family relationships?*

Appreciate Diversity

Colleges and workplaces reflect the changing **diversity** in our society—in gender, race, age, ethnicity, sexual orientation, physical ability, learning styles and abilities, social and economic background, and religion. We tend to surround ourselves with people who are similar to us and to see the world in a certain way. However, college is an excellent place to fully appreciate diversity by getting to know, understand, and value other cultures and people with different life experiences, talents, and political and social views. Expand your horizons and cultivate a wide variety of friends and acquaintances who see the world differently. Communication breaks down walls, corrects false beliefs, and enriches your life.

As a contributing member of society and the workforce, it is essential that you use critical thinking to assess your assumptions, judgments, and views about people who are different from you. Cultural sensitivity is the foundation for building common ground with diverse groups. (See **Figure 12.1**.)

Communication Strategies for Celebrating Diversity

Here are some strategies you can use for developing effective communication with diverse groups of people. (See **Peak Progress 12.4** on page 398 on how to apply the Adult Learning Cycle to making the best use of your strategies.)

● **Working Together**
The composition of the workforce will continue to change and diversify. To be effective and get along with co-workers, people will need to deal with any prejudices they've learned. *What can companies do to help employees understand and appreciate diversity?*

1. **Be aware of your feelings and beliefs.** If you have a negative attitude or reaction to a group or person, examine it and see where it is coming from. (See **Figure 12.2** on page 398.) Unfortunately, **discrimination**—treating someone differently based on a characteristic—still occurs and varies by society. **Sexism** (a belief or an attitude that one sex is inferior or less valuable), **homophobia** (an irrational fear of gays and lesbians), and **racial profiling** (using racial or ethnic characteristics in determining whether a person is considered likely to commit a particular type of crime or an illegal act) are just a few examples of what we personally experience and impose on others daily. Be aware of how you talk to yourself about other people, and be willing to admit your own prejudices. This is the first step toward change and a willingness to build rapport.

2. **See the value in diversity.** We are a rich nation because of different races, cultures, backgrounds, and viewpoints. Knowledge and understanding can break through barriers. The value of education is the appreciation of different

Culturally Biased	Culturally in Denial	Culturally Aware	Culturally Sensitive and Respectful	Culturally Responsible and Active
Believes different groups have positive and negative characteristics as a whole	Believes there is no problem; everyone should be the same	Tries to understand and increase awareness; is aware that experiences differ for people based on their culture	Respects people from diverse cultural and social backgrounds; seeks out contact with people from diverse backgrounds; encourages people to value and respect their cultural identity	Acts on commitment to eliminate oppression; seeks to include full participation of diverse cultural groups in decision making

Figure 12.1
Cultural Understanding

Different categories of cultural understanding are seen in our society. *In what column do you believe you fit and why?*

Peak Progress

Applying the Adult Learning Cycle to Becoming a Better Communicator

1. **RELATE. Why do I want to learn this?** Effective communication is the most important skill I can acquire, practice, and perfect. By being more assertive, I avoid resentment and thoughts that I'm being taken advantage of. I can succinctly express my views, wants, and impressions, as well as my innovative ideas and decisions.

2. **OBSERVE. How does this work?** I admire people who are assertive and confident when expressing themselves and their views. What makes them successful? What techniques or mannerisms do they use when communicating? I'll also observe people who are passive or aggressive and learn from their mistakes. How do others respond? I'll try using new strategies for dealing with fear, resentment, and anger.

3. **REFLECT. What does this mean?** What seems to work for me? Do I feel more confident and comfortable interacting with others? Do I believe I'm presenting my ideas so that others understand my point of view? Am I more respectful of others' opinions and feelings? I'll continue to avoid negative self-talk and focus on a positive attitude and outlook.

4. **DO. What can I do with this?** I will practice being more assertive. I will make a commitment to be direct, kind, and respectful. Each day, I'll work on one area. For example, when my roommate plays music too loudly, I'll express my needs assertively and respectfully.

5. **TEACH. Whom can I share this with?** I'll ask others if they have ever felt misunderstood and what they changed to express themselves better. I'll share my experiences and the strategies that have worked for me. I'll volunteer to help other students in my study group.

Now return to Stage 1 and continue to monitor your progress and think of new ways to enhance your communication skills.

---

views and the tools for building understanding and tolerance. Learn to think instead of react. Sharing different viewpoints can teach you new and interesting ways of seeing situations and approaching problems. Shift your thinking about diversity by reviewing **Peak Progress 12.5**. Do you accept others and appreciate our diversity? Complete **Personal Evaluation Notebook 12.6** on page 400 to determine your attitudes.

3. **See and treat people as individuals.** It is important to look beyond preconceived notions and see people as individuals, not members of a particular group. Each one of us is unique. See **Personal Evaluation Notebook 12.7** on page 401 to determine your uniqueness.

Figure 12.2
Understanding the Meaning

Having a better understanding of prejudice can help reduce its effect. *Have you ever felt prejudice? How have you dealt with that feeling?*

Attitudes are thoughts and feelings. *Behaviors* are what we do—how we act out our thoughts and feelings. If we work on eliminating stereotypes and prejudices, we can affect the outcome: discrimination.

Stereotype	Prejudice	Discrimination
A mental or emotional picture held in common by members of a group that represents an oversimplified belief, opinion, or judgment about members of another group	An unjustified negative feeling directed at a person or group based on preconceived opinions, judgments, and stereotypes	An unjustified negative behavior toward a person or group based on preconceived opinions, judgments, and stereotypes

Peak Progress

Thinking about Diversity

If the world were a village of 100 people . . .

- There would be an equal number of males and females.
- 61 villagers would be Asian (including 20 who would be Chinese and 17 who would be Indian), 14 would be African, 11 would be European, 9 would be Latin or South American, and 5 would be North American.
- 33 villagers would be Christians, 20 would be Muslims, 13 would be Hindus, 6 would be Buddhists, 2 would be atheists, 12 would be nonreligious, and the remaining 14 would be members of other religions.
- 1 villager would have AIDS, 26 villagers would smoke, and 14 villagers would be obese.

- At least 18 villagers would be unable to read or write, but 33 would have cell phones and 16 would use the Internet.
- There would be 18 cars in the village.
- 63 villagers would have inadequate sanitation.
- 53 villagers would live on less than two U.S. dollars a day.
- By the end of a year, one villager would die and two new villagers would be born, increasing the population to 101.

Source: Adapted from Matt Rosenberg, "If the World Were a Village . . ." About.com, August 5, 2007; retrieved May 24, 2010 from http://geography.about.com/od/obtainpopulationdata/a/worldvillage.htm.

4. **Treat people with respect and consideration.** You can be respectful even if someone's behavior is unacceptable or you don't agree with him or her.

5. **Focus on similarities.** As human, we all experience similar emotions, fears, and needs for appreciation and respect. Don't let differences dominate your interactions. However, don't act as if people were all alike and share the same experiences. Values and experiences differ based on a person's culture, religion, background, and experiences.

6. **Get involved.** Take a cultural diversity course or workshop at college or in the community. Visit with people from other religions. Go to lectures, read, and look for opportunities to become acquainted with other cultures. Visit your campus diversity center, if you have one, or seek out various clubs and activities.

7. **Take risks.** Don't avoid contact with other cultures because you fear making a mistake, saying the wrong thing, or inadvertently offending someone. Cultivate friendships with people of different cultures, races, and viewpoints. Share your own culture's foods and customs with others. Knowledge of other cultures can help you appreciate your own roots.

8. **Apologize when you make a mistake.** Mistakes happen, even with the best intentions. Ask for clarification and apologize. Occasionally, strong feelings or misunderstandings result from past experiences with racism or sexism. Thus, don't take it personally if someone does not respond as positively as you had hoped. Sometimes bridging the gap requires an extra effort to understand. Apologize, seek to understand, and move on.

9. **Speak out.** It is not enough to be aware that values and experiences differ from culture to culture; you must act on this knowledge. Speak out whenever you hear or see discrimination in school or at work.

> **❝** People are pretty much alike. It's only that our differences are more susceptible to definition than our similarities. **❞**
>
> LINDA ELLERBEE
> *Journalist*

WORDS TO SUCCEED

Personal Evaluation Notebook  12.6

Appreciating Diversity

A. Read the following, and write your comments on the lines provided.

1. What is your attitude toward people who differ from you in gender, race, sexual orientation, or culture? Is your attitude one of acceptance or exclusion?

   _____

2. Have you ever attended a political event for a party other than the one you support? If so, what are some of your viewpoints that differed from those of the other party?

   _____

3. Would you speak up if someone's gender, cultural, racial, sexual, or ethnic background were discussed in a stereotypical manner? How?

   _____

4. Do you consider yourself to be sensitive and respectful? Why or why not?

   _____

5. How do you show a sensitive, respectful attitude even when someone sees the world differently? For example, how can you discuss abortion or gay marriage with someone who has an opposite view and find common ground?

   _____

B. Look at the excuses some students use for not meeting different people. Write strategies for overcoming these excuses.

1. **Excuse:** I'm afraid of rejection or of getting into an argument.

   Strategy: _____

2. **Excuse:** People who are different want to stick with their own kind.

   Strategy: _____

3. **Excuse:** You can't change people's minds or beliefs, so what is the point?

   Strategy: _____

4. **Excuse:** I might say something embarrassing. I feel uncomfortable around people who are different from me.

   Strategy: _____

5. **Excuse:** People who are different from me wouldn't want me in their group.

   Strategy: _____

10. **Encourage representation.** Encourage active participation by members of diverse cultural and social groups in clubs, student government, local government, college meetings and boards, community groups and boards, and decision-making groups. Don't hold a self-righteous attitude that says, "I belong to the right political party, religion, or social cause." Open your mind and explore different views with a sincere willingness to learn.

Personal Evaluation Notebook

12.7

What Do You Want to Be Called?

White, Black, Hispanic, Asian, Native American, Pacific Islander. At some point in your life, you've probably had to check off your race or ethnicity on a form. But what if none of those categories truly reflects your personal identity or accommodates those of us (the majority) who have come from multiple backgrounds? Some people of Central and South American origin prefer to be called Hispanic; others prefer Latino. Many prefer to use their specific place of origin—Guatemalan, Mexican, Puerto Rican, Cuban, and so on. In the same way, some descendents of the first residents of the United States prefer American Indian, others prefer First Peoples, and others prefer Native American. Many prefer specific tribal names, such as Sioux, Navajo, Apache, or Wampanoag. Today, many people are from families of mixed racial/ethnic origins and do not want to be called by the name of any one group. "Blasian" is now used by many of Black and Asian descent.

In general, most people agree that all people have a right to be called what they want to be called and not have a group name imposed on them by someone else. How would you "label" yourself in one (or many) words?

_____

_____

Source: James W. Fraser, *Teach: A Question of Teaching* (McGraw-Hill, 2011).

11. **Study abroad.** Look into a national or an international exchange program. A semester or year abroad is a tremendous learning experience. You can also get to know students on your campus from other countries or states. Attend events sponsored by the exchange programs. Volunteer to help with tutoring students in English. Check out internships in different countries or states.

Diversity in the Workplace

As the workplace has become more diverse, it has become a more inclusive environment. **Inclusion** is a sense of belonging—feeling respected and valued for who you are. You feel you have support and commitment from others, so that you can do your best work. Attitudes and behavior from top management can set this tone for the whole company. Many top managers approach this by asking themselves, "How can I instruct others to tolerate differences in race, gender, religion, and sexual orientation?" Perhaps a better question would be "How can I set an example, create a climate of respect, and encourage people to value differences?"

As a result of our cultural explosion, many organizations offer diversity awareness training to help employees relate comfortably to each other and appreciate diversity. These programs give employees a chance to develop and strengthen critical thinking skills and reduce stereotypical thinking and prejudice. Firm guidelines clearly communicate the consequences for discrimination, which is illegal and can be grounds for court action.

Organizations are obligated to ensure that all employees know what behaviors are illegal and inappropriate, as well as the consequences for such behavior. Top managers are responsible for establishing procedures and need to offer a safe atmosphere for complaints. In short, companies must provide education, create guidelines and procedures, and set a tone of serious concern and respect for differences in the workplace. Think about what you learned about personality and team styles in Chapter 1. Diversity can have many positive effects on team effectiveness. Consider your study or work teams as you complete **Peak Progress 12.6**.

Sexual Harassment at School and Work

Sexual harassment is behavior that is unwelcome, unwanted, and degrading. It can be destructive to the school and work climate. It is also costly. Employee turnover, loss of productivity, expensive lawsuits, and a negative work environment are just some of the consequences. Think about your attitudes, beliefs, and behaviors. Err on the side of discretion, and avoid being too chummy or touchy or disclosing too many details about your personal life. If you aren't sure if a remark or joke is appropriate, don't say it.

Organizations are responsible for establishing guidelines. Most campuses and companies employ someone to talk to if you have a complaint or concern. Organizations with more than 25 employees are legally required to have written procedures concerning sexual harassment.

Peak Progress

12.6

Team Players

Evaluate the effectiveness of a work team, a study team, or any other team using the following list of skills. Score each item from 1 to 10 (10 = most effective).

Team Function
- Commitment to tasks
- Oral communication skills
- Listening skills
- Writing skills
- Conflict-resolution skills
- Decision-making skills
- Creative problem solving
- Openness to brainstorming and new ideas
- Team spirit and cohesiveness
- Encouragement of critical thinking
- Interest in quality decisions
- Professionalism
- Team integrity and concern for ethics
- Punctuality in starting and ending meetings

When a score is totaled, the team can discuss answers to these questions:

1. How can this team be more effective?

   _____

   _____

   _____

2. What can individual members do to strengthen the team?

   _____

   _____

   _____

If you feel uncomfortable in a situation or are being sexually harassed, you should

1. **Confront the harasser.** State what you believe the harasser has done, identifying the unwanted behavior, and insist that the harassment stop immediately. (Do not approach the harasser if you fear for your safety.)

2. **Document the harassment.** Keep a log of incidents, including the dates, behavior, witnesses, and the like. Keep copies of any inappropriate e-mails or other correspondence, even if they are anonymous.

3. **Document your performance.** The harasser may be someone who evaluates your work and may retaliate by giving you poor marks. Keep copies of performance evaluations, papers, exams, and memos that support the quality of your work.

4. **Read the organization's sexual harassment policy.** All reports of harassment will be followed up on, so you should know the procedures and who may become involved in the investigation.

5. **Contact the appropriate authorities.** At school, this may be the affirmative action or student affairs office, dean of students, or ombudsman. At work, consult with the human resources department.

6. **Mention the harassment to others.** Chances are, others have experienced harassment from the same person and will join your grievance.

7. **Do not make excuses for the harasser.** It is the harasser's behavior that is unwarranted, not your reactions to it.

Everyone's goal should always be to create a supportive, respectful, and productive environment—one that makes all colleagues feel comfortable and valued.

TAKING CHARGE

Summary

In this chapter, I learned to

- **Build rapport with others.** To build rapport, I must first clarify my intention and use corresponding body language. I must be an attentive listener who puts the speaker at ease, contains my criticisms, restates the speaker's point, and declines respectfully if the timing is not good for communicating. I am respectful and considerate, and I use humor when appropriate. I relate to different learning and personality styles, understanding that people differ in how they process and learn information and see the world. I look for the best in others and appreciate the strengths of different styles. I focus on people's strengths, not weaknesses.

- **Be assertive.** I express myself in a direct, above-board, and respectful manner. I can express feelings and opinions calmly, confidently, and authentically without offending others. I do not use sarcasm or criticism to express myself. I can say no to inappropriate behavior that is unwelcome.

- **Communicate with instructors and advisors.** I meet with my instructors often to clarify expectations, get help with homework, consult on drafts of papers or speeches, discuss ways to prepare for tests, get advice about project requirements, and discuss grades or assignments. I attend every class, adapt to my instructor's teaching style, and am positive and open to learning. I take an interest in my instructor's research or area of expertise. Since I have built rapport with my instructor, I feel comfortable asking for a letter of reference.

- **Accept feedback and criticism.** I know that, to grow and learn, I must be open to feedback. I do not take offense when criticism is offered in the spirit of helpfulness. I listen, stay calm, and ask for clarification and suggestions. My intent is to grow in all areas of my life. If I make mistakes, I apologize and try to make amends.

- **Overcome shyness.** When shyness interferes with making friends, speaking in front of groups, working with others, or getting to know my instructors, I must learn to be more confident and outgoing. I use visualization and affirmations to dispute negative self-talk. I use direct eye contact, am warm and friendly, ask questions, and listen. I relax, am able to laugh at myself, and use humor when it is appropriate.

- **Clarify miscommunications.** I do not assume I know what the other person thinks or says. I clear up misunderstandings by asking for clarification and paraphrase what I think I've heard. I focus on listening and seek to understand, rather than to be right. I want to be a better listener and communicator.

- **Develop healthy relationships.** I value friendships and take time to get to know others. My relationships are built on honesty, trust, respect, and open communication. I support others' goals and values, and I expect them to respect and support mine. I talk about expectations with friends, both casual and romantic.

- **Communicate with roommates and family.** To improve communication, I clarify and discuss expectations concerning guests, smoking, neatness, noise, borrowing, food, bills, privacy, and other issues that could cause problems. We agree to talk and get to know each other but also to respect each other's beliefs, views, and space.

- **Appreciate diversity.** We are diverse by our race, age, ethnicity, gender, learning and physical abilities, and social, economic, and religious backgrounds. I value different cultures and seek to build rapport with diverse people. By sharing different backgrounds, experiences, values, interests, and viewpoints, I can learn new and interesting ways of seeing situations and solving problems. I look for ways to become acquainted with other cultures and opportunities to work with a variety of people.

- **Recognize sexual harassment.** Sexual harassment is behavior that is unwelcome, unwanted, degrading, and detrimental to school and work.

Performance Strategies

Following are the top 10 tips for building supportive, diverse relationships:

- Find common ground.
- Attentively listen to understand.
- Use body language and eye contact.
- Use warmth and humor.
- Communicate in an assertive, clear, calm, and direct yet kind manner.
- Solve conflicts through cooperation.
- Learn to receive and give constructive criticism.
- Make time to develop diverse, supportive, and healthy relationships.
- Clarify relationship expectations.
- Seek interactions with people from various backgrounds.

Tech for Success

Take advantage of the text's Web site at **www.mhhe.com/ferrett8e** for additional study aids, useful forms, and convenient and applicable resources.

- **Happy virtual birthday.** People love being remembered on their birthdays (even if they are perpetually 29). If you are constantly forgetting or don't have the time to drop a card in the mail, send an e-card instead. Many free e-card sites are available, and many subscription-based sites offer reminder features.

- **Are you smiling?** If you are frustrated by e-mails that include smiley faces (emoticons) and are not sure what each one means, consult online sites that include mini-glossaries and instructions on how to create them. Use search words such as "e-mail smileys" and you'll receive many options.

Study Team Notes

Careerin focus

Kathy Brown
MARINE BIOLOGIST

Related Major: Biological Science

Team Building at Work

Kathy Brown is a marine biologist who manages teams researching saltwater organisms outside Monterey, California. Currently, she is head of a project to gain more knowledge on the navigation techniques of gray whales during migration.

Although Kathy is a top-rate biologist and researcher with a Ph.D., she can accomplish her project goals only by building teams of researchers who work together effectively. To do this, she carefully considers the personalities and leadership styles of each researcher while forming teams. Kathy provides preproject training in communication skills, group decision making, diversity, and conflict resolution. She lets teams brainstorm ideas and come up with solutions for studying wild animals in a controlled experiment. Kathy also has teams rate their effectiveness in several key functions, including creative problem solving and team spirit.

Finally, the teams are sent to sea to set up labs and conduct research from ocean vessels. Kathy travels from vessel to vessel to encourage teamwork, check research procedures, and help solve problems. She ensures that each team knows how to reach her at all times, day and night.

Because teamwork is so important to the overall results, Kathy will not rehire anyone who cannot work as a part of a team. She knows that even the most educated and skillful researchers will fail if they cannot work effectively and cooperatively with a variety of people.

CRITICAL THINKING Why do you think team building is an important part of a science research project?

Peak Performer

PROFILE

Christy Haubegger

At first glance, the glossy magazine looks like many others on the newsstands. The front cover offers a snapshot of the current issue: a profile of a famous celebrity, beauty and fashion tips, and a self-help article to improve the inner being. The big, bold letters across the top, however, spell the difference. This is *Latina,* the first bilingual magazine targeted at Hispanic American women and the inspiration of founder Christy Haubegger. More than 3 million bilingual, bicultural women are avid readers of this popular magazine.

Born in Houston, Texas, in 1968, Haubegger has described herself as a "chubby Mexican-American baby adopted by parents who were tall, thin, and blond." As a teenager during the mega-media 1980s, she was especially sensitive to the lack of Hispanic role models in women's magazines. It was a void waiting to be filled. At the age of 20, Haubegger received a bachelor's degree in philosophy from the University of Texas. At 23, she earned her law degree from Stanford, where she joined the editorial staff of the *Law Review,* rising to the position of senior editor: "My experience as senior editor gave me a start in the worlds of journalism and publishing."

Haubegger also took a course in marketing. In that class, she had to write a business plan for a favorite enterprise. *Latina* magazine was born. As one of the best-known publications for Hispanic American women, *Latina* covers issues such as health, politics, family, and finance, as well as beauty and entertainment.

Named as one of *Advertising Age*'s "Women to Watch" and *Newsweek*'s "Women of the New Century," Haubegger was tapped by President Obama, along with 27 other distinguished Americans, for the President's Commission on White House Fellowships. Her work through *Latina* and other ventures has definitely given Hispanic women a voice and reminds them that they are part of the American Dream.

PERFORMANCE THINKING If you were assessing the characteristics that make Christy Haubegger a successful entrepreneur, which would you say are the most important?

CHECK IT OUT Go to **www.latina.com** to see the numerous online features the magazine offers of interest to the U.S. Latin community.

Starting Today

At least one strategy I learned in this chapter that I plan to try right away is

_____

_____

_____

What changes must I make in order for this strategy to be most effective?

_____

_____

_____

Review Questions

Based on what you have learned in this chapter, write your answers to the following questions:

1. Describe five strategies for building rapport.

_____

_____

2. How do assertive people communicate?

_____

_____

3. Describe three ways to handle conflict.

_____

_____

4. Name a barrier to effective communication and how to overcome it.

_____

_____

5. List three strategies for creating rapport and improving communication with people you live with.

_____

_____

To test your understanding of the chapter's concepts, complete the chapter quiz at **www.mhhe.com/ferrett8e.**

Successful Teamwork

In the Classroom

Brian Chase is an electronics student who works part-time in an electronics firm. He likes working with his hands and enjoys his technical classes. However, one marketing class is difficult for him. The instructor has formed permanent class teams with weekly case studies to present to the class and a final team project to complete. Brian dislikes relying on others for a final grade and gets frustrated trying to keep the team members focused on their tasks. Some people are late for meetings, others don't do their share of the work, and two team members have a personality conflict.

1. What suggestions do you have for Brian to help him work more effectively with others?

   _____

   _____

2. What strategies in the chapter would increase Brian's listening and team-building skills?

   _____

   _____

In the Workplace

Brian is now a manager of service technicians for a large security company that provides security equipment and alarm systems for banks, hotels, and industrial firms. His department must work closely with salespeople, systems design specialists, clerical staff, and maintenance personnel. Brian is having trouble convincing his technicians that they are part of the team. Sometimes they don't listen to the advice of the salespeople, clerical staff, or each other, which results in miscommunication and frustration.

3. How might Brian build rapport within and among various departments?

   _____

   _____

4. What strategies in this chapter could help create a solid team?

   _____

   _____

Applying the ABC Method of Self-Management

In the Journal Entry on page 379, you were asked to describe a difficult or confrontational situation in which you felt comfortable communicating your needs and ideas assertively, directly, and calmly. What factors helped you be confident and respectful?

_____

_____

_____

Now think of a confrontational situation in which you were passive or aggressive. Apply the ABC Method to explore how you can achieve a positive outcome.

A = Actual event:

_____

_____

_____

B = Beliefs:

_____

_____

_____

C = Challenge:

_____

_____

_____

See yourself calm, centered, and relaxed as you state your needs, ideas, or rights. See yourself talking in a clear, concise, and confident manner. You feel confident because you have learned to communicate in an assertive and direct manner.

PRACTICE SELF-MANAGEMENT

For more examples of learning how to manage difficult situations, see the "Self-Management Workbook" section of the Online Learning Center Web site at **www.mhhe.com/ferrett8e.**

Study Team Relationships

List some strategies for helping your study team be more organized and effective.

1. **Before the Meeting**

   _____

   _____

   _____

   _____

2. **During the Meeting**

   _____

   _____

   _____

   _____

3. **After the Meeting**

   _____

   _____

   _____

   _____

4. Think of effective ways to deal with the following list of challenges.

Challenges	Solutions
Latecomers or no-shows	_____
Passive members	_____
Negative attitudes	_____
Low energy	_____
Arguments	_____
Lack of preparation	_____
Socializing	_____
Members who dominate	_____

Appreciating Diversity

Assess your appreciation for diversity and check Yes or No for each of the following comments.

	Yes	No
1. I am committed to increasing my awareness of and sensitivity to diversity.	_____	_____
2. I ask questions and don't assume that I know about various groups.	_____	_____
3. I use critical thinking to question my assumptions and examine my views.	_____	_____
4. I strive to be sensitive to and respectful of differences in people.	_____	_____
5. I listen carefully and seek to understand people with different views and perspectives.	_____	_____
6. I realize I have biases, but I work to overcome prejudices and stereotypes.	_____	_____
7. I do not use offensive language.	_____	_____
8. I readily apologize if I unintentionally offend someone. I do not argue or make excuses.	_____	_____
9. I celebrate differences and see diversity as positive.	_____	_____
10. I speak up if I hear others speaking with prejudice.	_____	_____
11. I try to read about other cultures and customs.	_____	_____
12. I do not tell offensive jokes.	_____	_____
13. I encourage members of diverse cultural and social groups to participate in clubs and decision-making groups.	_____	_____

As you review your responses, think of areas where you can improve. List at least one of those areas and possible strategies you could use:

Are You Assertive, Aggressive, or Passive?

Next to each statement, write the number that best describes how you usually feel when relating to other people.

3 = mostly true   2 = sometimes true   1 = rarely true

_____ 1. I often feel resentful because people use me.

_____ 2. If someone is rude, I have a right to be rude, too.

_____ 3. I am a confident, interesting person.

_____ 4. I am shy and don't like speaking in public.

_____ 5. I use sarcasm if I need to make my point with another person.

_____ 6. I can ask for a higher grade if I feel I deserve it.

_____ 7. People interrupt me often, but I prefer not to bring their attention to it.

_____ 8. I can talk louder than other people and can get them to back down.

_____ 9. I feel competent with my skills and accomplishments without bragging.

_____ 10. People take advantage of my good nature and willingness to help.

_____ 11. I go along with people, so that they will like me or will give me what I want.

_____ 12. I ask for help when I need it and give honest compliments easily.

_____ 13. I can't say no when someone wants to borrow something.

_____ 14. I like to win arguments and control the conversation.

_____ 15. It is easy for me to express my true feelings directly.

_____ 16. I don't like to express anger, so I often keep it inside or make a joke.

_____ 17. People often get angry with me when I give them feedback.

_____ 18. I respect other people's rights and can stand up for myself.

_____ 19. I speak in a soft, quiet voice and don't look people in the eyes.

_____ 20. I speak in a loud voice, make my point forcefully, and can stare someone in the eye.

_____ 21. I speak clearly and concisely and use direct eye contact.

Scoring

Total your answers to questions 1, 4, 7, 10, 13, 16, 19 (passive):

Total your answers to questions 3, 6, 9, 12, 15, 18, 21 (assertive):

Total your answers to questions 2, 5, 8, 11, 14, 17, 20 (aggressive):

Your highest score indicates your prevalent pattern.

Are you more passive, assertive, or aggressive—or a combination?

Has your tendency towards one behavior helped or hurt you in situations?

What can you do to become more assertive and communicate effectively?

Assessing Your Relationship Skills

Skills in building diverse and healthy relationships are essential for success in school and throughout your career. Take stock of your relationship skills, and look ahead as you do the following exercises. Add this page to your Career Development Portfolio.

1. **Looking back:** Review your worksheets to find situations in which you learned to build rapport, listen, overcome shyness, resolve conflict, work with diversity, and be assertive. List the situations on the lines provided.

   _____

   _____

   _____

   _____

   _____

2. **Taking stock:** Describe your people skills. What are your strengths in building relationships? What areas do you want to improve?

   _____

   _____

   _____

   _____

   _____

3. **Looking forward:** Indicate how you would demonstrate to an employer that you can work well with a variety of people.

   _____

   _____

   _____

   _____

   _____

4. **Documentation:** Include documentation and examples of team and relationship skills. Ask an advisor, a friend, a supervisor, or an instructor to write a letter of support for you in this area. Keep this letter in your portfolio.

   _____

   _____

   _____

   _____

   _____

13

Develop Positive Habits

LEARNING OUTCOMES

In this chapter, you will learn to

13.1 Use the peak performance success formula

13.2 Describe the top 10 habits of peak performers

13.3 Adapt and change by developing positive habits

13.4 Overcome resistors to making changes

SELF-MANAGEMENT

"It's been a soul-searching journey to get to this point, but I now understand I control my destiny. I make choices every day regarding what new things I will learn, how I will interact with others, and where I will focus my energies. I will be successful because I have the power to become a peak performer in everything I do."

Are you ready for the exciting journey ahead of you? Do you know what your greatest assets are and the areas you want to improve? Only you can determine what kind of person—student, employee, family member, and contributor to society—you will be. You have tremendous power to create your own success. Take a few minutes each morning before you jump out of bed or as you shower to set the tone for the day. Visualize yourself being focused and positive and successfully completing your projects and goals. Imagine yourself overcoming fear and self-defeating habits. See yourself applying all the strategies you've learned and creating positive, long-lasting habits.

JOURNAL ENTRY In **Worksheet 13.1** on page 434, think of a time when you knew what to do but kept repeating negative habits. How would positive visualization have helped you?

T hroughout this text, we have discussed many strategies for doing well in school, your career, and your personal life. You should have a sense of your strengths and areas where you'd like to improve. You have learned how to manage your time, succeed at tests, and develop healthy relationships. Acquiring knowledge and skills is one thing, but actually making these techniques and strategies part of your life is another.

As we've explored, there is no secret to becoming an outstanding athlete or accomplished performer—or to achieving academic excellence. The same principles required to get into Olympic form apply to getting results in school and at work (see **Figure 13.1**). This success formula includes

1. Having a positive attitude that you can succeed (confidence)
2. Setting and focusing on goals (vision)
3. Learning the necessary skills and behaviors (method)
4. Putting all of this into practice—again and again and again (training)

Although steps 1 through 3 are extremely important, practice is what makes the most impact and forms good habits. **Habits** are the behaviors and activities

Figure **13.1**
Peak Performance Success Formula

Success takes time, effort, and determination. *Which components of this formula do you need to focus on to accomplish your desired goals?*

1. Confidence is believing in yourself, knowing your worth, and recognizing you have what it takes to do well. Self-confidence is one of the most important mental qualities you can develop for producing results. When you build on the accomplishments of small victories and successes, you realize that you can achieve almost any goal you set.

2. Vision is mental rehearsal of your victory. You must know clearly what you want to achieve. Be realistic about seeing this vision become a reality. Use encouraging self-talk and imagery. Focus internally, listen to your positive voice, and imagine yourself achieving your goal.

3. Method is the process of achieving your goal and knowing the strategies, techniques, tools, and tactics that produce tangible results. Method involves monitoring your actions and techniques, so that you can modify them to excel consistently.

4. Training is the actual practice and consistent effort required to improve your skills and make them into lasting habits. Training requires the capacity to stay with a vigorous program and hours of rehearsal. You must practice relentlessly even if you often see only small improvements. Practice separates the peak performer from the average person.

you perform unconsciously as a result of frequent repetition. Thoughts wear a path in the neurons of your brain; the more you think certain thoughts and do certain actions, the deeper the path becomes, until those thoughts and behavior are a habit.

Knowing how to develop positive thoughts, attitudes, and behaviors will give you the confidence to take risks, grow, contribute, and overcome setbacks. You have what it takes to keep going, even when you feel frustrated and discouraged. This chapter will show you how to turn strategies from this text into lasting habits.

The 10 Habits of Peak Performers

In Chapter 2, we discussed the importance of emotional maturity for school, job, and life success. You may have a high IQ, talent, skills, and experience but, if you lack emotional maturity and such important qualities as responsibility, effort, commitment, a positive attitude, interpersonal skills, and especially character and integrity, you will have difficulty in all areas of life. However, it is not enough to review essential traits and qualities of emotional maturity. You must commit to making them long-lasting habits. You need to find personal meaning and be willing to learn, observe others, reflect, practice, teach, and model. To create a habit, you must practice and teach deliberately and consistently. Commit yourself to turning the following 10 essential qualities into long-lasting habits (see **Figure 13.2**).

1. **Be honest.** As we have stressed throughout this book, if you lack integrity, all your positive qualities—from skill and experience to intelligence and productivity—are meaningless. Practice the habit of honesty by being truthful, fair, kind, compassionate, and respectful. Doing the right thing is a decision.

2. **Be positive.** Greet each day and every event as opportunities to focus on your strengths and be your own best friend by working for and supporting yourself. Positive thinking is not wishful thinking; it is rational, hopeful thinking. Develop the habit of being positive and optimistic by looking for ways to create a motivated, resourceful state of mind. Look for the best in others and in every situation. Being enthusiastic about routine but necessary tasks at school and work will get you noticed. Throughout this book, you've had an opportunity to practice the ABC Method of Self-Management. You have discovered that your

> **"**If you are going to achieve excellence in big things, you develop the habit in little matters. Excellence is not an exception, it is a prevailing attitude.**"**
>
> COLIN POWELL
> *65th U.S. secretary of state*

THE 10 HABITS OF PEAK PERFORMERS

1. Be honest.
2. Be positive.
3. Be responsible.
4. Be resilient.
5. Be engaged.
6. Be willing to learn.
7. Be supportive.
8. Be a creative problem solver.
9. Be disciplined.
10. Be grateful.

Figure 13.2
The 10 Habits of Peak Performers

Peak performers translate positive qualities into action. *Do you demonstrate these habits consistently?*

thoughts create your feelings, which can affect how you interpret events. Learn to dispel negative thoughts and replace them with realistic, optimistic, and empowering thoughts and behaviors. This habit of optimism will keep you centered, rational, productive, and peaceful, even in the midst of confusion and turmoil.

3. **Be responsible.** You may not always feel like keeping your commitments to yourself or your instructors, friends, co-workers, or supervisors, but meeting obligations is the mark of a mature, responsible person. For example, a major obligation for many students is the timely repayment of student loans. Develop the habit of responsibility by doing what you say you're going to do, showing up, and keeping your agreements.

4. **Be resilient.** Adversity happens to everyone. Even good students sometimes lose papers, forget assignments, miss deadlines, and score low on tests. Don't turn one mistake into a recipe for continued failure. You can't always change circumstances, but you always have a choice about how you rebound and prepare to win next time. The key is to make adversity and setbacks work for you. Take control of how you interpret events, as well as how you react to them. You will learn to reframe your setbacks as stepping-stones to your final goal and energize yourself to take positive action.

5. **Be engaged.** Peak performers do not sit back and wait for life to happen. They are engaged, active, and want to contribute. This means shifting a self-centered "what's in it for me?" attitude to a "how can I be more involved and useful?" attitude. One way to sabotage your classes or career is to expect your instructors or supervisor to make your life interesting. All careers are boring or monotonous at times, and some classes are less than spellbinding. Develop the habit of using your imagination and creativity to make any situation challenging and fun.

6. **Be willing to learn.** Employees can wind up at a dead end if they refuse to learn new skills. Shifts in the economy can result in layoffs for even competent, highly educated, and skilled workers. If you are flexible and willing to learn new skills, you can go to plan B if plan A doesn't work.

7. **Be supportive.** School provides an excellent opportunity to develop empathy and to support, cooperate, and collaborate with people with different backgrounds. Your instructors, advisors, classmates, co-workers, friends, family, and supervisors will go the extra mile to help you if you are respectful, kind, and supportive. Listen to what you say and how you say it. Don't interrupt or criticize—people need to be heard and respected. Use a win/win approach to solve problems. Acknowledge and encourage others' accomplishments and goals.

8. **Be a creative problem solver.** Expand your sense of adventure and originality in problem solving, and learn to think critically and creatively. Challenge your beliefs and try new approaches. Critical thinking also helps you distinguish between an inconvenience and a real problem. Some people spend a great deal of time and energy getting

"We are what we repeatedly do. Excellence, then, is not an act, but a habit."

ARISTOTLE
Greek philosopher

● **Be Willing to Learn**
Many are finding it necessary to further their education after a number of years in the workforce. *What percentage of your fellow students are returning students? What are some of the reasons they are taking classes or pursuing a degree?*

angry at minor annoyances or events they cannot change—such as bad weather, a delayed flight, or a friend who doesn't meet some expectation. A late plane is an inconvenience; a plane crash is a real problem. Critical thinking helps you put events in perspective and "wakes up" your creative mind. Instead of postponing, ignoring, or complaining, you actively engage in exploring solutions.

9. **Be disciplined.** Peak performers do what needs to be done, not simply what they want to do. They keep up on assignments, set goals, and carve out time throughout the day to focus on priorities. Discipline demands mental and physical conditioning, planning, and effort. Using discipline and self-control, you know how to manage your time, stress, money, and emotions, especially anger. As Benjamin Franklin said, "Anger always has its reasons, but seldom good ones." Getting angry rarely solves problems, but it can create big ones. Through discipline and awareness, you can overcome impulsive reactions and learn to use critical thinking before reacting in haste.

10. **Be grateful.** Life often seems like a comparison game, with competition for grades, jobs, relationships, and money. Sometimes you may feel that your life is lacking. Reflect on your blessings and talents, not on how your life compares with others'. Focus on what you have, not on what you don't have. Learn to listen to, appreciate, and renew your body, mind, and spirit. Appreciating your body means taking time to rest, exercise, and eat healthy foods. Appreciating your mind means spending time reading, visualizing, creatively solving problems, writing, and challenging yourself to learn and be open to new ideas. Appreciating your spirit means finding time for quiet reflection and renewal and making an effort to listen, develop patience, and love others. To develop the habit of gratitude, appreciate what you have in life, and approach each day as an opportunity to serve and grow.

Change Your Habits by Changing Your Attitude

How can you keep a positive attitude when you are discouraged and frustrated? What if some days you have one problem after another? What if your study group or work environment is negative? Is it possible to see life differently?

In Chapter 10, we talked about the tendency to see what we already believe. Whereas we see with our eyes, we perceive with our brain. People have mindsets that filter information. Each of us has attitudes or beliefs about people and events, and these attitudes influence what parts of our perception we allow our brain to interpret and what parts we filter out. Our attitudes shape the way we relate to others and to the world and even how we see ourselves. Go back to the illustration on page 318. Some people see a young woman, and some see an old woman. Of course, both are actually there. Which did you see? The point is that most of us do not see the entire meaning in a situation or have difficulty seeing "the big picture."

Most people resist change. Even when you are aware of a bad habit, it can be difficult to change it. However, the ability to adapt to new situations is not only important in school but also crucial in the workplace. Accountemps, a temporary staffing service for accounting professionals, asked 1,400 executives to rank the

> "Notice that the stiffest tree is most easily cracked, while the bamboo or willow survives by bending in the wind."
>
> BRUCE LEE
> *Actor, martial arts expert*

WORDS TO SUCCEED

characteristics essential for an employee to succeed. From the list, "adapts easily to change" and "motivated to learn new skills" ranked #1 and #2.

Strategies for Creating Positive Change

Habits are learned and can be unlearned. Adopting new habits requires a desire to change, consistent effort, time, and commitment. Try the following strategies for eliminating old, ineffective habits and acquiring positive new ones.

1. **Be willing to change.** As with all learning, you must see the value of developing positive habits. It's easy to make excuses for keeping everything the same, but you must be willing to find reasons to change. Identify your goals: "I want to be more optimistic and get along with people." "I am determined to see problems as challenges and find creative alternatives." "I will no longer be a victim. I have control over my thoughts and behavior." Lasting change requires desire, effort, and commitment.

2. **Focus on the positive.** Are you a glass-half-empty or glass-half-full type of person? Practice the ability to see the good qualities in yourself and others and the positive side of situations. Dispute negative thoughts with critical thinking, and use creative problem solving to explore the best alternatives—for example, "I missed my study group meeting. I'll e-mail my test questions to the group, apologize, and offer to do extra summaries for the next meeting. This situation has reminded me how important it is to check my calendar each morning."

3. **Develop specific goals.** Statements such as "I wish I could get better grades" and "I hope I can study more" are too general and only help you continue bad habits. Goals such as "I will study for 40 minutes, two times a day, in my study area" are specific enough to help you measure your achievement.

4. **Change only one habit at a time.** You will become discouraged if you try to change several things about yourself at once. If you have decided to study for 40 minutes, two times a day, in your study area, then do this for a month, then 2 months, then 3, and so on and it will become a habit. After you have made one change, move on to the next. Perhaps you want to exercise more, give better speeches, or get up earlier. When completing **Personal Evaluation Notebook 13.1,** assess your habits, and put a star by the areas you most want to work on.

5. **Start small.** Realize that consistently taking small steps each day will produce major results. Sometimes the smallest changes make the biggest difference. For example, don't put off starting an exercise program because you don't have time for a long workout. Instead, walk to class rather than driving, or take a walk at lunch. Similarly, by being just a little more organized, finding small ways to be kind and supportive, and doing just a little more than what is expected of you are simple steps that can lead to positive change.

6. **Use visualization and affirmations to imagine success.** Imagine yourself progressing through all the steps toward your desired goal. For example, see yourself sitting at your desk in your quiet study area. Affirm, "I am calm and able to concentrate. I enjoy studying and feel good about completing projects." Before you get up in the morning, imagine your day unfolding effortlessly: "I am positive and focused and will accomplish everything on my to-do list."

Personal Evaluation Notebook

Make a Commitment to Learn and Apply Positive Habits

Read the following questions about the habits for success that we have discussed in this text. Answer each question by circling either Yes or No as each statement applies to you. For the statements you circle Yes, answer the follow-up questions to describe how you are making them a habit.

Yes/No   **1.**   Have you created a study area that helps you concentrate? If so, where is it?

Yes/No   **2.**   Do you make learning physical? How?

Yes/No   **3.**   Do you preview each chapter before you read it? What elements do you look at?

Yes/No   **4.**   Do you preview other chapters? If so, how has this helped you understand the material?

Yes/No   **5.**   Do you rewrite your notes before class? How long does this usually take?

Yes/No   **6.**   Do you outline your papers? Which outlining method works best for you?

Yes/No   **7.**   Do you proofread your papers several times? What types of mistakes do you usually catch?

Yes/No   **8.**   Do you rehearse your speeches until you are confident and well prepared? How many times do you usually practice?

Yes/No   **9.**   Do you attend every class? If not, how many classes have you missed in the past 30 days?

Yes/No   **10.**   Do you sit in the front of the class? If not, where do you normally sit?

Yes/No   **11.**   Do you listen attentively and take good notes? Which class is the most challenging to follow?

Yes/No   **12.**   Do you review your notes within 24 hours? Do you usually do it right after class or later in the day?

Yes/No   **13.**   Do you get help early, if necessary? Who has been the most helpful?

Yes/No   **14.**   Do you participate in class and ask questions? Are you usually comfortable or uneasy doing this?

Yes/No   **15.**   Have you developed rapport with each of your instructors? Which instructor(s) do you feel most comfortable asking for additional guidance?

(continued)

Personal Evaluation Notebook

Make a Commitment to Learn and Apply Positive Habits (concluded)

Yes/No   16.   Have you joined a study team? For which classes?

Yes/No   17.   Do you study and review regularly each day? How many minutes do you usually devote to this task?

Yes/No   18.   Do you complete tasks and assignments first and then socialize? Has this ever caused tension with your friends or family?

Yes/No   19.   Do you recite and restate to enhance your memory skills? Do you prefer to do so out loud or on paper?

Yes/No   20.   Do you take advantage of campus and community activities? Which activities do you enjoy the most?

Yes/No   21.   Can you create a motivated, resourceful state of mind? What do you say to yourself or think about to stay motivated?

Yes/No   22.   Do you know how to solve problems creatively? What technique(s) seems to work the best for you?

Yes/No   23.   Do you use critical thinking in making decisions? Up to which level of Bloom's Taxonomy (knowledge, comprehension, application, analysis, synthesis, or evaluation) do you think you've mastered?

Yes/No   24.   Do you exercise daily? Describe your fitness routine.

Yes/No   25.   Do you maintain your ideal weight? What is your ideal weight?

Yes/No   26.   Do you keep your body free of harmful substances and addictions? What substances are readily available to you that you choose to abstain from?

Yes/No   27.   Do you support your body by eating healthy foods? Which healthy foods do you enjoy not simply because they are good for you?

Yes/No   28.   Do you practice techniques for managing your stress? What works for you?

Yes/No   29.   Have you developed an effective budget? When is it hardest to stay within your budget?

Yes/No   30.   Do you take the time for career planning? What are you doing to plan ahead?

If you answered No to many of these questions, don't be alarmed. When old habits are ingrained, it's difficult to change them. Select at least one of the habits you answered No to. Determine what you can do today to turn it into a positive habit.

7. **Observe and model others.** How do successful people think, act, and relate to others? Do students who get good grades have certain habits that contribute to their success? Research indicates that successful students study consistently in a quiet area. They regularly attend classes, are punctual, and sit in or near the front row. Model this behavior until it feels comfortable and natural. Form study groups with good students who are motivated and have effective study habits.

8. **Be aware of your thoughts and behaviors.** For example, you may notice that the schoolwork you complete late at night is not as thorough as the work you complete earlier in the day. Awareness of this pattern may prompt you to change your schedule for schoolwork. You may notice that you feel less stressed in the morning when you take 10 minutes at night to pack your bag, lay out clothes, and check the next day's events.

9. **Reward yourself.** Increase your motivation with specific payoffs for making a positive change. Suppose you want to reward yourself for studying for a certain length of time in your study area or for completing a project. You might decide, "After I outline this chapter, I'll watch television for 20 minutes," or "When I finish reading these two chapters, I'll call a friend and talk for 10 minutes." The reward should always come after achieving the results and be limited in duration.

10. **Be patient and persistent.** Lasting change requires a pattern of consistent behavior. With time and patience, the change will begin to feel comfortable. Don't become discouraged and give up if you haven't seen a complete change in your behavior in a few weeks. Give yourself at least a month. If you fall short one day, get back on track the next. Don't expect to get all *A*'s after a few weeks of studying longer hours. Lasting change requires time.

Overcome Resistance to Change

The following are some obstacles that everyone, even peak performers, may encounter. (See **Figure 13.3** on page 424.) Recognize and confront these resistors to create lasting change:

- **Lack of awareness.** Due to daily pressures, you may not recognize the need to make changes until there is a crisis. This concept is best demonstrated by the boiled-frog syndrome. Neurobiologist Robert Ornstein explained that, if you put a frog in a pot of water and heat the water very slowly, the frog remains in the pot. The frog does not detect the gradual change in temperature until it boils to death. Sometimes you may be so preoccupied by daily pressures that you are unaware of the signals your body is giving you. In a sense, you become desensitized to the "pain." Take time each day to reflect about the state of your mind, body, and spirit, and look for signs of gradual pain, such as a deterioration in grades or morale. Don't wait for a crisis to recognize the need for change.

- **Fear of the unknown.** Change creates uncertainty. Some people even choose the certainty of misery over the uncertainty of pleasure. Fear blocks creativity, causes the imagination to run wild, and makes everyday frustrations look

Take 3 minutes to develop a positive habit:
- What bad habit would you like to change, or what positive habit do you want to adopt?
- What three things do you need to do or change in order to work toward making this a habit?
- Write the new habit and the three things on a sticky note, and put it on your mirror. Realize that making it a habit will take continual practice—and more than just 3 minutes!

What else can you do in 3 minutes?
- Give yourself a mental pep talk by using affirmations and visualization.
- Turn off all unnecessary lights and unused electronics.
- Balance your checkbook.

catastrophic: "I don't like my living situation and it's affecting my grades, but who knows what kind of roommate I would get if I asked for a change." or "I'd like to take a computer class, but I don't know if I could do the work." When you face a new and fearful situation, such as a public speaking class or a new roommate, be positive and optimistic.

- **Familiarity and comfort.** Old habits become comfortable, familiar parts of your life, and giving them up leaves you feeling insecure. For example, you want to get better grades and know you study best in a quiet area. However, you have always read your assignments while watching television. Be open to trying new ideas and methods.

- **Independence.** You may believe that making personal changes means you are giving in to others and losing your independence. Instead, see yourself as part of a team of people working together to achieve a common goal.

- **Security.** You feel secure with your beliefs, and may feel some of the new ideas you are learning may challenge that security. The old saying "knowledge is power" is definitely true and helps you overcome insecurities.

- **Tradition.** There may be expectations for your future based on your experiences at home: "I was always expected to stay home, raise my family, and take a job only to help supplement the family income. My desire for a college education and career of my own contradicts family tradition. My sister says I'm selfish to go back to school at this time in my life." If a change in

Figure 13.3
Courage to Overcome

These peak performers demonstrated discipline, dedication, and a positive attitude to reach their goals despite obstacles. *What stands in your way of realizing your goals? What steps could you take to overcome obstacles?*

Elizabeth Garrett Anderson

Although rejected by medical schools because she was female, she still became the first female member of the British Medical Association.

Abraham Lincoln

Although raised in poverty and teased because of his appearance, he was still elected president of the United States.

Glen Cunningham

Although doctors believed he would never walk again after he was severely burned at age 3, in 1934 he set the world's record for running a mile in just over 4 minutes.

direction benefits you personally (and possibly professionally), then the important people in your life will also benefit and should support your decisions.

- **Embarrassment.** You may fear that a new situation will embarrass you: "Will I feel embarrassed being in classes with younger students? Can I hold up my end of the team projects and class discussions? I haven't had a math course in 20 years, and my study skills are rusty." Remember that learning is all about trial and error.

- **Responsibility.** You may believe the demands on your time are too great to allow for making changes: "I am overwhelmed by the responsibility of working, going to school, and caring for my family. Sometimes it would be easier if someone would just tell me what to do." It's essential to use time-management strategies to ensure you are accomplishing what you need to and identifying areas to change.

- **Environment.** You may believe your physical environment is too constricting: "My place is not supportive for studying. Our home is noisy, and there is no place where I can create a study area. My husband and children say they are proud of me, but they complain about a messy house and resent the time I spend studying." It's important to negotiate when and where you can get your work done, such as at established quiet times or in the library.

- **Cost.** Your personal finances may limit your ability to make changes: "It's too expensive to go to college. Tuition, textbooks, a computer, day care, and supplies all add up. Is it worth it? Maybe I should be saving for my children's education instead." Evaluate all your available resources and make sure you know where your money is going to determine what you can change.

- **Difficulty.** People can and do change. Changing habits is a simple, three-step process:

  1. *Discard what doesn't work.* First, unlearn and discard old ideas, thoughts, and habits in order to learn more positive habits.

  2. *Replace it with what does work.* Replace old habits with new habits.

  3. *Practice! Practice! Practice!* You can learn new habits, but you must consciously apply and practice them. In a sense, you must "freeze" new patterns through consistent repetition.

See **Peak Progress 13.1** on applying the Adult Learning Cycle to developing positive habits.

Contract for Change

Most people talk about changing, wishing they could be more positive or organized, but few put their commitment in writing. Many find it useful to take stock of what

Tracy is the most unmotivated person Cameron knows, yet she's been her best friend since first grade. They've done everything together—soccer, summer jobs, and college roommates. With one more year to go, Cameron is looking forward to applying to law school and is focusing on studying for the LSAT exam, while Tracy is focusing on who won last night's celebrity dancing contest.

- How can Tracy's lack of motivation affect Cameron's success?
- Can Tracy become a motivated person? What can Cameron do or say to help her create and focus on important goals?
- If you were Cameron, would you stay best friends with Tracy?

THINK *FAST*

Copyright © 2012 The McGraw-Hill Companies

Peak Progress

Applying the Adult Learning Cycle to Developing Positive Habits

The Adult Learning Cycle can help you change your behavior and adopt long-lasting positive habits.

1. **RELATE. Why do I want to learn this?** I know that practicing positive habits and creating long-lasting changes will help me succeed in school, work, and life. What are some of my positive habits, and which ones do I need to change or improve? Do I display the 10 habits of a peak performer?

2. **OBSERVE. How does this work?** I can learn a lot about positive habits by watching others and trying new things. I will observe positive, motivated people who know how to manage their lives. What do they do? Are their positive habits obvious? I will also observe people with negative habits to learn from their mistakes.

3. **REFLECT. What does this mean?** I will gather information by going to workshops and taking special classes. I will focus on the 10 habits of a peak performer and create strategies for incorporating them into my routine. I will think about and test new ways of breaking out of old patterns, negative self-talk, and self-defeating behaviors. I will look for connections and associations with time management, stress and health issues, and addictive behaviors.

4. **DO. What can I do with this?** I will focus on and practice one habit for 1 month. I will reward myself when I make progress. I will focus on my successes and find simple, practical applications for using my new skills. Each day, I will take small steps. For example, I will spend more of my social time with my friends who like to hike and do other positive things that I enjoy, instead of hanging out with friends who just like to drink.

5. **TEACH. With whom can I share this?** I will share my progress with family and friends and ask if they have noticed a difference.

Something becomes a habit only when it is repeated, just as the Adult Learning Cycle is more effective the more times you go through it.

common resistors, or barriers, keep them from meeting their goals. Write a contract with yourself for overcoming your barriers. State the payoffs of meeting your goals. Refer back to your mission statement and goals in Chapter 3, using them to help you determine the positive changes you want to make. Use **Personal Evaluation Notebook 13.2** to begin drafting a personal commitment contract to achieve the "habit" of success.

Personal Evaluation Notebook

13.2

Commitment Contract

Complete the following statements in your own words.

1. I most want to change _____

_____

_____

_____

2. My biggest barrier is _____

_____

_____

_____

3. The resources I will use to be successful are _____

_____

_____

_____

4. I will reward myself by _____

_____

_____

_____

5. The consequences for not achieving the results I want will be _____

_____

_____

_____

Date _____

Signature _____

TAKING CHARGE

Summary

In this chapter, I learned to

- **Live the peak performance success formula.** I know that success comes from having confidence, setting and envisioning my goals, learning skills and behaviors, and practicing.

- **Strive to become a peak performer.** Peak performers are successful because they develop and practice good habits. They are honest, responsible, resilient, engaged, willing to learn, supportive, disciplined, and grateful. They have positive attitudes and creatively solve problems.

- **Develop a positive attitude.** I approach tasks with a can-do attitude. Enthusiasm and a positive attitude help me focus on my strengths and create the thoughts and behaviors that produce the results I want.

- **Embrace change and develop positive habits.** I know that adapting to change is important to my success. I will create positive habits by developing specific goals, focusing on one habit at a time, taking small steps each day, and remaining positive and persistent. I know that developing positive habits takes time.

- **Avoid and overcome resistors and fears.** Fear of the unknown, insecurities, embarrassment, and overwhelming responsibilities are just some of the obstacles to my progress if I don't focus on positive outcomes.

- **Make a commitment.** I have made a commitment to turn the strategies I have learned into lasting habits. I have put my commitment in writing by developing a commitment contract.

Performance Strategies

Following are the top 10 tips for developing good habits:

- Commit to changing self-defeating behaviors.
- Set realistic goals and specify behaviors you want to change.
- Assess and monitor your thoughts that create feelings.
- Dispute irrational thoughts and describe events objectively.
- Work on one habit at a time, focusing on success.
- Be resilient and get back on track after setbacks.
- Use affirmations and visualization to stay focused.
- Reward yourself for making improvements.
- Observe your progress and make appropriate changes until you achieve the results you want.
- Surround yourself with support and positive influences.

Tech for Success

Take advantage of the text's Web site at **www.mhhe.com/ferrett8e** for additional study aids, useful forms, and convenient and applicable resources.

- **Inspiration.** In this text, you have read about many peak performers who have overcome major obstacles to get where they are today. Who truly represents a peak performer to you? If the person is even relatively well known chances are you will find his or her story online. Spend at least a few minutes searching and reading about what makes this person stand out. Do you recognize any of the 10 habits?

- **A log of positive habits.** Create a Word or an Excel document. Every time you use 1 of the 10 habits of peak performers, log it in your document. Eventually, this will create an ideal list of personal examples, which you can relay to a future employer. Keep a copy in your Career Development Portfolio.

Study Team Notes

Career*in* focus

Rick Torres
CARPENTER

Related Majors: Mathematics, Bookkeeping,
Computer-Aided Design

Good Habits in the Workplace

Rick Torres is a carpenter who, like one-third of the carpenters in the United States, works as an independent contractor. This means Rick is self-employed and does a variety of carpentry jobs for homeowners, from building decks to completing remodeling jobs.

Rick starts by figuring out how to accomplish each task. Then he gives the customer a written time and cost estimate, purchases materials, completes the work, and hauls away construction debris. He needs basic math skills to provide an accurate estimate and calculate the amount of materials required for the job. Bookkeeping skills also help Rick keep track of his earnings and prepare to pay quarterly taxes. Carpentry work is often strenuous and requires expertise with large tools, such as power saws and sanders; the handling of heavy materials; and prolonged standing, climbing, bending, and kneeling. Rick often works outdoors and enjoys the flexibility and physical activity of his work.

Through the years, Rick has learned that good habits are essential to his future. Rick gains new customers through word of mouth. Customers pass his name on to others because he is reliable and has excellent skills. Rick's business has been successful because he cultivates positive attitudes and is committed to providing quality service. He shows up on time for appointments, is courteous, and follows through with his commitments. Occasionally, Rick works for neighborhood low-income projects. He sometimes hires younger carpenters to work with him and enjoys teaching them old tricks and new methods of construction.

CRITICAL THINKING What might be the result of poor work habits for a carpenter working as an independent contractor?

Peak Performer
PROFILE

Ben Carson, M.D.

Ben Carson's life is a testament to having a positive attitude, motivation, and integrity. Despite major obstacles, he has become a world-renowned neurosurgeon and author who has touched many lives.

Overcoming the disadvantages of growing up in an economically depressed neighborhood in Detroit, Carson has lived by the words "no excuses." As a child, when difficult situations would confront him or his brother, his mother would ask, "Do you have a brain? Then you can think your way out of it." Carson did just that.

During the 1950s, Carson's mother worked multiple domestic jobs to keep the family afloat. Though life at home was challenging, days at school were even more so. Carson recalls, "There was an unspoken decree that the black kids were dumb." His mother knew better. When the two brothers brought home failing grades, she turned off the TV and required the boys to read two books a week and write reports. Eventually, Carson rose to the top of his class and went on to graduate from Yale University and the University of Michigan School of Medicine.

However, one biographer wrote that, during Carson's youth, his temper made him seem "most qualified for putting someone else in the hospital." It was only after a life-threatening confrontation that Carson realized his choices were "jail, reform school—or the grave."

Today Carson is the director of pediatric neurosurgery at Johns Hopkins Medical Institutions. Even working under primitive conditions in South Africa in 1997, Carson succeeded against the odds when he separated 11-month-old conjoined twins who were joined at the head. The man who was tagged "dummy" now saves the lives of children whom others label as hopeless.

PERFORMANCE THINKING Explain how attitude played a part in Ben Carson's success. What are some of the habits he established in his childhood that contributed to his future achievements?

CHECK IT OUT Ben Carson continues his service of helping others through the Carson Scholars Fund (**www.carsonscholars .org**). The foundation's mission is to promote the joy of reading and to recognize and reward students in grades 4–11 who strive for academic excellence and demonstrate a strong commitment to their community. "THINK BIG" is Carson's philosophy, which promotes outstanding academic achievement and dedication to helping others.

Starting Today

At least one strategy I learned in this chapter that I plan to try right away is

_____

_____

_____

What changes must I make in order for this strategy to be most effective?

_____

_____

_____

Review Questions

Based on what you have learned in this chapter, write your answers to the following questions:

1. Name the 10 habits of a peak performer.

_____

_____

2. What are three strategies for creating positive change in your life?

_____

_____

3. Why is adapting to change so critical to job success?

_____

_____

4. Describe one resistor to change you have experienced and how you overcame it.

_____

_____

5. Why is practice important to changing a habit?

_____

_____

To test your understanding of the chapter's concepts, complete the chapter quiz at **www.mhhe.com/ferrett8e.**

Spreading Good Habits

In the Classroom

Craig Bradley is a welding student. He never liked high school, but his mechanical ability helped him get into a trade school. He wants to be successful and knows this is a chance for him to get a good job. Both of Craig's parents worked, so he and his sister had to get themselves off to school and prepare many of their own meals. Money has always been tight, and he hardly ever receives encouragement for positive behavior. He has never learned positive study or work habits.

1. What kind of study plan can you suggest to Craig to build his confidence and help him succeed?

_____

_____

2. What strategies in this chapter can help him develop positive, lasting habits?

_____

_____

In the Workplace

Craig is now working in a large farm equipment manufacturing plant. He has just been promoted to general supervisor in charge of welding and plumbing. He is a valued employee and has worked hard for several years for this promotion. Craig wants to ensure his success in his new job by getting training in motivation, team building, quality customer service, and communication skills.

3. What suggestions do you have for Craig to help him train his staff in good habits?

_____

_____

4. What strategies in this chapter can help him be more successful?

_____

_____

Applying the ABC Method of Self-Management

In the Journal Entry on page 415, you were asked to think of a time when you knew what to do but kept repeating negative habits. How would positive visualization have helped you?

_____

_____

_____

Now apply the ABC Method of Self-Management. How is the outcome different?

A = Actual event:

_____

_____

_____

B = Beliefs:

_____

_____

_____

C = Challenge:

_____

_____

_____

PRACTICE SELF-MANAGEMENT

For more examples of learning how to manage difficult situations, see the "Self-Management Workbook" section of the Online Learning Center Web site at **www.mhhe.com/ferrett8e.**

Developing Positive Habits

On the following lines, list five habits you would like to change into positive behavior. Focus on changing one habit at a time for a successful transition. Then, in the following chart, list the steps you will need to take, the barriers standing in your way, and the methods by which you can overcome these barriers to reach your goal.

POSITIVE HABITS YOU WANT TO DEVELOP

1. _____

2. _____

3. _____

4. _____

5. _____

Steps	Barriers	Methods to Overcome Barriers
1.		
2.		
3.		
4.		
5.		

Overcoming Resistance to Change

Complete the following statements in your own words.

1. I resist _____

2. I resist _____

3. I resist _____

4. I resist _____

5. I resist _____

6. I resist _____

7. I resist _____

8. I resist _____

9. I resist _____

10. I resist _____

For each item you listed, write a strategy for overcoming your resistance to change.

1. _____

2. _____

3. _____

4. _____

5. _____

6. _____

7. _____

8. _____

9. _____

10. _____

Planning Your Career

Developing good planning habits will benefit your career. Use the following form to create a career action plan. Add this page to your Career Development Portfolio.

Career objective:_____

What type of job?_____

When do you plan to apply?_____

Where is this job?_____

- City _____

- State _____

- Company _____

Whom should you contact?_____

How should you contact?_____

- Phone _____

- Letter _____

- E-mail _____

- Walk-in _____

Why do you want this job?_____

Resources available:_____

Skills applicable to this job:_____

Education: _____

- Internship _____

- Courses taken _____

- Grade point average _____

- References _____

14

Explore Majors and Careers

LEARNING OUTCOMES

In this chapter, you will learn to

14.1 Explore majors and careers

14.2 Determine your values, interests, abilities, and skills

14.3 Assemble a Career Development Portfolio

14.4 Prepare for the job-hunting process

14.5 Take charge of your career development

SELF-MANAGEMENT

" *I'm not certain if the major I chose will lead to the job I want. One of my biggest fears is that I'll be stuck in a dead-end job and won't have an interesting career. What if I spent all this time and money and still can't get a good job?* "

Have you ever wondered if you're learning the skills and developing the qualities that will help you get and keep the job you want? Sometimes it's difficult to see the connection between college and the world of work. Have you ever taken a class and wondered how it relates to real life and if it will help you be more successful? How do you integrate all you are learning to make it meaningful and personal? In this chapter, you will learn steps for exploring college majors and careers. You will see that career planning is an exciting, lifelong process. You will also learn how to translate the information, experiences, and skills you are acquiring in school into a useful Career Development Portfolio.

JOURNAL ENTRY In **Worksheet 14.1** on page 474, write down one of the classes you are currently taking, and list at least three skills you will acquire in this class that will benefit you in your career.

Early Roman philosopher Plotinus of Delphi (AD 205–270) recognized three main universal career concerns:

- Who am I?
- What shall I do?
- What shall become of me?

You will be continually challenged to understand who you are and what you want in life. In this rapidly changing world, you may have a chance to do many kinds of work. Studies show that the average working American will have 3 to 5 careers and 10 to 12 jobs during his or her lifetime. Many of the career opportunities that will be available in 10 years don't even exist today. Thus, career planning is more than just picking a profession. It involves learning about yourself and what you want out of life.

In this chapter, we will examine ways to choose a college major and explore careers. The strategies in this chapter, including step-by-step instructions on how to assemble a Career Development Portfolio, will help you create new career opportunities in response to your ever-changing needs, desires, and interests.

Connecting School and Job Success

The path to career success began the day you started classes. As you have read in this text, the same habits, attitudes, and personal qualities required for school success are also required for job success. The same strategies—assessing yourself, knowing your learning style, thinking critically, creatively solving problems, effectively communicating, and establishing healthy relationships—apply to career exploration and planning, no matter what your college major is.

Exploring and Choosing a Major

In our society, people are identified by their profession. For example, adults often ask each other, "What do you do for a living?" In college, the question may be "What is your major?" A college major helps define who you will become professionally. It is a declaration of academic purpose and gives many students structure and goals. It provides entry into an academic department and fellowship with instructors and other students.

Some students know from an early age what their major will be. They may have known for years that they want to be an engineer, a writer, a business owner, a nurse, or a computer programmer. For many students, choosing a college major is daunting. Some students

- Have many interests, so it is difficult to narrow them to one major
- Have not assessed their interests, values, or goals
- Have not explored the wide range of majors at their school

- Have difficulty making decisions
- Fear they will get stuck with a major they won't like
- Fear a major will lead to a career they dislike
- Are influenced by family expectations
- Are unsure of the job market
- Know they like a specific subject area but don't know what they can do with it

If you are unsure of your college major, you're not alone. On some campuses, "undeclared" is the largest major. The average student changes majors three times. Community colleges are experiencing a growth in students who want to change careers or learn new skills. Many students already have a 4-year degree but now want to learn cooking, woodworking, real estate, nursing, firefighting, or fashion design. What you want to do at 18 may be very different from what you want to do at 40, 50, or 60. The strategies for choosing a major are similar to those for choosing a career:

1. **Assess yourself.** Since major and career planning begins with self-assessment, return to Chapter 1 and review the assessment tools. People are happiest when they do work that is consistent with their values, interests, abilities, and skills (which we will discuss further in this chapter). When your job is an extension and expression of who you are, you experience joy and fulfillment.

2. **Meet with a career counselor at your school.** Counselors are trained to offer and interpret self-assessment tools and interest inventories. They can help you clarify values, talents, and skills; offer insight into your interests, personality type, and goals; and help you link majors with careers.

3. **Talk with your support system.** Discuss possible majors with family, friends, instructors, other students, and advisors. People who know you best may shed light on your unique abilities and talents.

4. **Explore through college classes.** Taking general education classes is a great way to experience various disciplines, get to know instructors and students, and still meet college requirements.

5. **Explore through the course catalog.** Review the catalog to find a major you didn't know existed. Pick at least two majors you'd like to research further.

6. **Go to the academic department.** Go to the departments of majors you are interested in, and gather more information, such as the requirements, the job outlook, and possible careers.

7. **Take classes or workshops.** Many schools provide assessments to determine interests, traits, and self-understanding. Sometimes alumni are invited to speak at campus events.

8. **Gain experience.** Get involved through internships, volunteer work, part-time jobs, and service learning activities offering hands-on experience (see **Peak Progress 14.1** on page 442). On- and off-campus jobs help you explore possible major and career interests. Also join clubs, participate in extracurricular activities, seek out leadership opportunities, and travel with educational tours.

9. **Be creative with your major.** Your school may have an interdisciplinary major, a self-designed major, or a broad liberal arts major that allows you to

Peak Progress

Service Learning

As we discussed in Chapter 4, service learning enables you to use what you are learning in the classroom to solve real-life problems. The service reinforces and strengthens the learning, and the learning reinforces and strengthens the service. You learn about democracy and citizenship while becoming an actively contributing citizen and community member.

Many colleges offer courses that provide service learning opportunities. These courses include structured time for you to reflect on your service and learning experiences through a mix of writing, reading, speaking, listening, and creating in groups and individual work. This fosters the development of personal qualities—empathy, personal values, beliefs, awareness, self-esteem, self-confidence, and social responsibility. Credit is awarded for learning, not for a required number of service hours.

Service learning has many benefits:

- It gives you opportunities to use newly acquired skills and knowledge in real-life situations.
- It fills a need for volunteer support in the community and uses that need as a foundation for participants to examine themselves, their society, and their future.
- It tracks progress toward preset learning objectives and goals (as well as the intangible ones).
- The service performed is valuable and significant for the community.
- You feel empowered by contributing to your community.

Service learning experiences can be personally rewarding and enriching, and they are important points in a portfolio or resumé. As employers assess equally qualified job applicants, they look for experiences, skills, or qualities that make one candidate stand out. Service learning opportunities may also allow you to work with administrators and community members you might not have otherwise met, giving you job contacts and mentors who may open doors for you in the future.

Source: Adapted from "What Is Service-Learning?" Corporation for National and Community Service, www.learnandserve.gov; "Four Things Faculty Want to Know About!" Mark Cooper, Florida International University, www.fiu.edu/~time4chg/Library/fourthings.html.

take a wide range of courses in areas that interest you. Many employees are looking for liberal arts graduates who are skilled in writing, critical thinking, reasoning, and creative problem solving and can work well with diverse groups.

10. **Relax and reflect.** Be proactive about exploring various majors, but also listen to your inner wisdom and what makes you happy and fulfilled. In Chapter 2, we reviewed Maslow's hierarchy of needs, which identifies what motivates people and gives their actions meaning. Self-actualization is the process of fulfilling your potential, becoming everything you are capable of, and experiencing satisfaction and joy. Achieving self-actualization requires listening to your inner voice.

Consult with your advisor to determine an optimal time line. If you delay too long, you may discover that some of your courses won't count toward your selected major and other courses still need to be taken. You may also find that your GPA isn't high enough to get into a preferred program and courses you "tried out" but struggled with have pulled down your average.

Finally, remind yourself that getting a college degree in anything will help launch your career. There are no guarantees, but a college degree—plus hard work, additional experience and skills, and positive habits and qualities—go a long way toward creating opportunities.

Values, Interests, Abilities, and Skills

As we discussed in relation to self-assessment, it's important to determine your values, interests, innate abilities, and already acquired skills to help you decide which career direction you want to take and thus which major course of study you should pursue.

VALUES

Values are the worth or importance you attach to various factors in your life. They are formed in early childhood and are influenced by parents, teachers, the environment, and your culture. Your values can reflect your self-esteem, optimism, self-control, and ability to get along with others. You will be much happier if your career reflects your values. Complete **Personal Evaluation Notebook 14.1** on page 444 to determine your personal values and the values important to your career.

INTERESTS

Interests are the activities and subjects that draw you in and cause you to feel comfortable, enthusiastic, or passionate. Psychologist John L. Holland explored interests and their relation to college major and career choice. His theory suggests that career choice often reflects personality type and that most people fit into one of six occupational personality types, which are largely determined by their interests. Revisit Chapter 1 and review your personality assessments. Then read Holland's types and see if you fall into one or two of the categories:

- *Realistic.* Realistic people have athletic or mechanical ability and prefer to work with objects, machines, tools, plants, or animals or to be outdoors. They like to work with their hands. Possible careers include architect, optician, surveyor, laboratory technician, automotive mechanic, mail carrier, engineer, chef, and bus or truck driver.
- *Investigative.* Investigative people like to observe, learn, investigate, analyze, evaluate, or solve problems. They enjoy academic and scientific challenges. Possible careers include computer operator, pilot, mathematics teacher, surgical technician, doctor, economist, and chemist.
- *Artistic.* Artistic people have creative, innovative, or intuitive abilities and like to work in unstructured situations. Many are flamboyant and imaginative. Possible careers include actor, commercial artist, public relations representative, editor, decorator, fashion designer, and photojournalist.
- *Social.* Social people like to work with people—to inform, enlighten, help, train, develop, or cure. They have strong verbal and written skills. Possible careers include social worker, minister, psychologist, parole officer, instructor, school superintendent, rehabilitation therapist, and hair stylist.
- *Enterprising.* Enterprising people enjoy leading—influencing, persuading, performing, or managing to meet organizational goals or achieve economic

> **"** Mostly I just followed my inner feelings and passions . . . and kept going to where it got warmer and warmer, until it finally got hot . . . Everybody has talent. It's just a matter of moving around until you've discovered what it is. **"**
>
> GEORGE LUCAS
> *Director*

WORDS TO SUCCEED

Personal Evaluation Notebook

14.1

Your Values

Your values influence what will satisfy you in a career. By each value, rank them as

1 = Not that important   2 = Somewhat important   3 = Most important

Overall Values	**Rank**
Security	_____
Helping others	_____
Recognition	_____
Collaborating with others	_____
Serving religious or spiritual beliefs	_____
Adventure	_____
Variety	_____
Serving community/national/international concerns	_____
Artistic/creative expression	_____
Personal growth and learning	_____
Focusing on family	_____
Others	_____

Specific Factors You Value in a Career	**Rank**
High salary	_____
Great deal of freedom/autonomy	_____
Flexible working hours	_____
Opportunities for advancement	_____
Good vacation/benefits	_____
Supportive co-workers	_____
Working with others	_____
Working alone	_____
Telecommuting/working at home	_____
Working outdoors	_____
Social environment	_____
Job status	_____
Clean and comfortable working environment	_____
Others	_____

Take note of the factors you rated "3," as these values are most important to you.

gain. Possible careers include small business owner, communications consultant, college department head, stockbroker, sales representative, restaurant manager, and motivational speaker.

- *Conventional.* Conventional people like to work with data, have clerical or numerical abilities, are detail-oriented, and follow directions well. They like working with numbers and facts and enjoy bringing situations to closure. Possible careers include accountant, business teacher, court reporter, credit manager, secretary, military officer, office manager, and title examiner.

ABILITIES

Abilities are the qualities that are an intrinsic part of who you are. They are innate talents or gifts, which can be developed to their maximum potential through study and practice. You may have the ability to understand mathematics, play many musical instruments, resolve conflict, or handle a crisis calmly.

SKILLS

Skills are capabilities you have learned and developed. They often have a more technical connotation than abilities. Some skills are job-specific, such as operating a bulldozer, conducting lab tests, or editing manuscripts. **Transferable skills** are those that can be used in a variety of careers, such as negotiating, analyzing data, preparing presentations, effectively managing people or resources, and using technology.

It's important to identify your skills to see how they can be developed throughout your career. Read the following broad list of skills, and determine the areas in which you excel. What careers using these skills might you like to explore?

People	Data	Mechanical
Instructing	Analyzing	Handling
Supervising	Coordinating	Setting up
Negotiating	Comparing	Driving/operating
Entertaining	Computing	Tending
Persuading	Compiling	Selecting

Exploring Careers

After assessing your personal values and what you are looking for in a career, you can determine what opportunities lie ahead. You may be starting out at the bottom or taking courses to prepare for a promotion or new responsibilities. As mentioned earlier, the strategies for choosing a major also apply to determining a career path. Also investigate these resources:

- *Career center.* Career center personnel can give you information about career trends, opportunities, salaries, and job availability.
- *Library.* Your school or local library has many resources, such as the *Dictionary of Occupational Titles, The Guide for Occupational Exploration,* and the classic *What Color Is Your Parachute?* by Richard Bowles.

- *Professional organizations.* Visit the Web sites of professional organizations in your field of interest and consider joining. Students often can join at a discount. Find out what you would receive with a membership, such as magazines, reports, journals, and access to job listings. At the Web site or in journals, look for individuals who have received promotions or contributed to the field. See if any are local or provide contact information. Most professionals enjoy talking to young people who are entering their field and are happy to offer advice.

- *Your network.* Personal contacts are excellent ways to explore careers and find a job. As we discussed in Chapter 4, networking provides access to people who can serve as mentors and connect you to jobs and opportunities. Create and cultivate personal and professional contacts. Talk with instructors, advisors, counselors, and other students. Collect business cards and e-mail addresses. (See **Worksheets 14.4** and **14.5** on potential questions to ask during informational interviews with professionals and hiring managers.)

- *Government organizations.* Several organizations, such as the U.S. Department of Labor, track job statistics, predict future opportunities, and provide employment guidance, such as SCANS. The *Occupational Outlook Handbook* (go to the Bureau of Labor Statistics Web site at **www.bls.gov/oco**) lists the outlook for hundreds of types of jobs and provides employment guidance, such as job search and application methods, places to learn about job openings, and resumé and job interview tips. See **Peak Progress 14.2** on using the Adult Learning Cycle when exploring majors and careers.

Peak Progress

14.2

Applying the Adult Learning Cycle to Exploring Majors and Careers

1. **RELATE. Why do I want to learn this?** Write down the top three things that are important to you in a career, such as independence, high visibility, flexible hours, ability to work from home, and management opportunities. Compare those wishes with your personality type. Which careers that fit your personality offer these features?

2. **OBSERVE. How does this work?** Explore three potential opportunities for learning more about this career, such as acquaintances in the field, instructors, professional organizations, and introductory courses.

3. **REFLECT. What does this mean?** Based on your research, does this career still appeal to you? What are the drawbacks? Are they significant enough to outweigh the positives? Did any related professions come to light?

4. **DO. What can I do with this?** If the career choice still looks promising, identify three ways you can

gain experience or related skills require for the profession, such as joining a club or securing an internship. Construct a time line for accomplishing those tasks.

5. **TEACH. Whom can I share this with?** Relay your impressions and reservations to your family, your friends, or fellow students who are also career searching. Some will ask you questions that will make you think about where you are in selecting a major and what your next steps should be. You will also enlighten others by sharing the resources you are using.

If you conclude that you are still undecided, explore other career options and retry some or all of the steps. Practice visualization when you need help focusing. Eventually, you will find a career path that suits your personality and interests.

Building a Career Development Portfolio

A Career Development Portfolio is a collection of documents that highlights your strengths, skills, and competencies. It includes grades, summaries of classes, certificates, letters of recommendation, awards, lists of activities, inventories you've taken, and samples of written work. A portfolio can help you connect what you have learned in school to your current or future work, and it organizes documentation that demonstrates you have the necessary education, skills, competencies, and personal qualities to perform a job.

Even if you have little work experience, this documentation can give you an edge when applying for a job. For example, Janet convinced an employer to hire her based on her portfolio: She showed the manager samples of her work and the certificates she had earned. Jake used his portfolio to receive a promotion based on documentation of his skills and experiences.

Your Career Development Portfolio helps you

- Plan and design your educational program and postgraduate learning
- Describe how your experiences have helped you grow professionally
- Document skills and accomplishments in and out of the classroom
- Link what you can do with what an employer is looking for
- Identify areas you want to augment or improve
- Record and organize experiences for your resumé and job interviews
- Express talents creatively and artistically
- Justify college credit for prior learning and military, internship, or life experiences
- Prepare for a job change

When Should You Start Your Portfolio?

You can start your portfolio at any time—the sooner the better. If you completed assessments, journal entries, and worksheets at the end of each chapter in this text, then you've already started your portfolio. Ideally, you will begin your portfolio during your first term or year in school. During each term, make copies of papers or other coursework to add to your portfolio. Make note of courses related to your career interests. If you have a work-study job or an internship related to your career goal, include records of your experiences, any written work, and letters of recommendation in your Career Development Portfolio. By the time you graduate, you will have a tool that is distinctly personal and persuasive.

A sample planning guide appears in **Figure 14.1** on page 448. Students in both 2- and 4-year schools can use this guide. Students in a 2-year school can use freshman and sophomore years for the first year, junior and senior years for the second year. Modify the planning guide to fit your needs.

How to Organize and Assemble Your Portfolio

The steps for organizing and assembling your portfolio will vary, depending on your purpose and your school's guidelines. You may be developing your portfolio as a

Figure 14.1

Career Development Portfolio Planning Guide

This planning guide will help you review your skills and maintain your Career Development Portfolio as you move toward your career goal. This and a modified plan for a 2-year degree can be found at the book's Web site at **www.mhhe.com/ ferrett8e.** *What other strategies can you use to prepare for your career?*

Freshman Year

- Begin your Career Development Portfolio.
- Explore and join clubs, and get involved on campus.
- Assess your interests, skills, values, goals, and personality.
- Go to the career center at your school, and explore majors and careers.
- Set goals for your first year.
- Explore college majors and minors.
- Explore the community.
- Network with professors and students. Get good grades.
- Keep a journal. Label the first section "Self-Assessment." Begin to write your autobiography.
- Label another section "Exploring Careers."

Sophomore Year

- Add to your Career Development Portfolio.
- Start a file about careers and majors.
- Choose a major.
- Review general education requirements.
- Continue to explore resources in the community.
- Build your network.
- Join clubs and take a leadership role.
- Read articles and books about your major area.
- Find a part-time job or volunteer your time.
- Start or update your resumé.
- Explore internships and co-op programs.
- Add a section to your journal called "Job Skills and Qualities."

Junior Year

- Update and expand your Career Development Portfolio.
- Gain more job experience.
- Write and submit a major contract, outline your program, and apply for graduation.
- Join student organizations and professional organizations, and add to your network.
- Develop relationships with faculty, administrators, and other students.
- Identify a mentor or someone you can model to achieve your goals.
- Start to read the journal of your profession.
- Obtain an internship, or gain additional job experience.
- Update your journal with job tips and articles about your field.
- Update your resumé.
- Visit the career center on campus for help with your resumé, internships, and job opportunities.

Senior Year

- Refine your Career Development Portfolio.
- Put your job search into high gear. Go to the career center for advice.
- Read recruitment materials. Schedule interviews with companies.
- Update and polish your resumé and print copies. Write cover letters.
- Actively network! Keep a list of contacts and their telephone numbers.
- Join professional organizations and attend conferences.
- Start sending out resumés and attending job fairs.
- Find a mentor to help you with your job search and career planning.
- Meet with an evaluator or advisor to review graduation requirements.
- Log interviews in your journal or notebook.

general documented system of achievements and professional growth, as a graduation requirement for your major, or for a more specific reason, such as obtaining credit for prior learning experiences.

After you have identified your purpose, determine the best way to show your portfolio to others. This, too, may depend on your school's or profession's expectations. You may be required to develop a digital portfolio rather than a physical one—or both. You need several materials for creating a physical copy of your portfolio:

- Three-ring notebook
- Sheet protectors to hold documents and work samples
- Labels and tabs
- Box to store work samples and information

When developing a physical copy of your portfolio, make sure to print copies on high-quality, durable paper.

Elements of Your Portfolio

As mentioned, if you need to submit your portfolio to your school for review or evaluation, you probably have to follow established guidelines. If not, the following sections describe elements that apply to most portfolios.

TITLE, OR COVER, PAGE

Include a title page with the title of your document, your name, the name of the college, and the date. See **Figure 14.2** for an example. (If you are reproducing your

Sample Title Page	Sample Contents Page	
	CONTENTS	
	Introduction	1
CAREER DEVELOPMENT PORTFOLIO	List of Significant Life Experiences	2
	Analysis of Accomplishments	3
	Inventory of Skills and Competencies	5
	Inventory of Personal Qualities	6
	Documentation	7
	Work Philosophy and Goals	9
	Resumé	11
Kim Anderson	Samples of Work	13
Louis College of Business	Summary of Transcripts	17
September 20, 2011	Credentials, Certificates, Workshops	18
	Bibliography	25
	Appendix	27

Figure 14.2

Career Development Portfolio Elements

The presentation of your Career Development Portfolio reflects your personality and makes a valuable first impression. *What elements could be modified to better reflect your field of study?*

portfolio to submit for evaluation, you can include an additional title page printed on heavy card stock. You can also put your own logo or artwork on the cover to make it unique.)

CONTENTS PAGE

On the contents page, list the sections of the portfolio. You can make a draft when you start your portfolio, but it will be the last item you finish, so that the page numbers and titles are correct. See **Figure 14.2** for an example of a contents page.

INTRODUCTION

In the introduction, discuss the purpose of your portfolio and the goals you are trying to achieve with its development. This is similar to a book's preface, which summarizes the purpose and main features. See **Figure 14.3** for an example of an introduction page.

LIST OF SIGNIFICANT LIFE EXPERIENCES

The next section of your portfolio is a year-by-year account of your significant life experiences (turning points). It is a chronological record, or time line. Resources to consult include family members, friends, photo albums, and journals. Don't be concerned about what you learned, but concentrate on experiences that are important because you

- Found the experience enjoyable (or painful)
- Learned something new about yourself

Figure **14.3**

Sample Introduction Page

The introduction highlights the purpose and goals of the portfolio. *What is the purpose of this sample?*

INTRODUCTION

The Career Development Portfolio I am submitting reflects many hours of introspection and documentation. The purpose of this portfolio is to gain college credit for similar courses I completed at Wake View Community College. I am submitting this portfolio to Dr. Kathryn Keys in the Office of Prior Learning at Louis College of Business.

I recently made a career change and want to enter the marketing field. The reason for the change is personal growth and development. I had an internship in marketing and know I will excel in this area. I plan to complete my degree in business administration at Louis College of Business. Eventually, I want to work my way up to store manager or director of marketing at a large store.

This portfolio contains

- List of significant life experiences
- Analysis of accomplishments
- Inventory of skills and competencies
- Inventory of personal qualities
- Documentation
- Work philosophy and goals
- Resumé
- Samples of work
- Summary of transcripts
- Credentials, certificates, workshops
- Bibliography
- Appendix

- Achieved something you value
- Received recognition
- Expended considerable time, energy, or money

This section can also be written as an autobiography. It can include

- Graduation and formal education
- Jobs/promotions
- Marriage/divorce and other events in your family
- Special projects
- Volunteer work
- Training and workshops
- Self-study or reentry into college
- Extensive travel
- Hobbies and crafts
- Military service

ANALYSIS OF ACCOMPLISHMENTS

Once you have completed your list of significant life experiences, you are ready to identify and describe what you learned and how you learned it. Specifically, what have you learned in terms of knowledge, skills, competencies, and values and how can you demonstrate the learning? When possible, include evidence or a measurement of the learning. Review your list of significant experiences, looking for patterns, themes, or trends. Did these experiences

- Help you make decisions?
- Help you clarify and set goals?
- Help you learn something new?
- Broaden your view of life?
- Accept diversity in people?
- Help you take responsibility?
- Increase your confidence and self-esteem?
- Result in self-understanding?
- Change your attitude? Your values?

INVENTORY OF SKILLS AND COMPETENCIES

Use your completed Career Development Portfolio worksheets, inventories from the career center, and activities in this text to record your skills and competencies. Your college may also provide a list of specific courses, competencies, or categories. You can also use SCANS as a guide. (See **Figure 14.4** on page 452.) Complete **Personal Evaluation Notebook 14.2** to determine your transferable skills.

Also, as you take each college course, determine what skills you are learning in the classroom may translate to job skills. For example, long-term budgeting goals learned in a personal finance course can be helpful in managing project budgets on the job. Keep a list of these courses and skills.

Personal Evaluation Notebook  **14.2**

Transferable Skills

1. What transferable skills do you have?

   _____

   _____

2. What specific content skills do you have that indicate a specialized knowledge or ability, such as plumbing, computer programming, or cooking?

   _____

   _____

3. List your daily activities and determine the skills involved in each. Then consider what you like about the activities, such as the environment, interactions with others, or a certain emotional reaction—for example, "I like bike riding because I am outdoors with friends, and the exercise feels great."

Activity	Skills Involved	Factors
Bike riding	Balance, stamina, discipline	Being outdoors
_____	_____	_____
_____	_____	_____
_____	_____	_____
_____	_____	_____

INVENTORY OF PERSONAL QUALITIES

SCANS lists important personal qualities for success in the workplace: responsibility, a positive attitude, dependability, self-esteem, sociability, integrity, and self-control. Your personal qualities will set you apart from others in the workplace. In

Figure **14.4**
SCANS Skills

Acquiring these skills and competencies will help you succeed throughout your career. *Which of these skills do you need to develop?*

Basic Skills: reading, writing, listening, speaking, and math

Thinking Skills: critical thinking, creative problem solving, knowing how to learn, reasoning, and mental visualization

Personal Qualities: responsibility, positive attitude, dependability, self-esteem, sociability, integrity, and self-management

Interpersonal Skills: teaches others, team member, leadership, works well with diverse groups, and serves clients and customers

Information: acquires, evaluates, organizes, maintains, and uses computers

Systems: understands, monitors, corrects, designs, and improves systems

Resources: allocates time, money, material, people, and space

Technology: selects, applies, maintains, and troubleshoots

Personal Evaluation Notebook

Inventory of Personal Qualities

Indicate how you have learned and demonstrated each of the SCANS qualities. Next indicate how you would demonstrate them to an employer. Add personal qualities you think are important. Use additional pages if needed.

1. Responsibility: _____

_____

_____

2. Positive attitude: _____

_____

_____

3. Dependability: _____

_____

_____

4. Self-esteem: _____

_____

_____

5. Sociability: _____

_____

_____

6. Integrity: _____

_____

_____

7. Self-control: _____

_____

_____

Personal Evaluation Notebook 14.3, use critical thinking to explore ways you've demonstrated your personal qualities.

DOCUMENTATION

For your Career Development Portfolio, document each of the SCANS skills, competencies, and personal qualities. Indicate how and when you learned each. Write the names of people who can vouch that you have these skills, competencies, and personal qualities. Include letters of support and recommendation. These letters can be from your employer, co-workers and community members, and clients or customers expressing their appreciation. Your skills and competencies may have been learned in college, vocational training programs, community service, on-the-job training, or travel.

WORK PHILOSOPHY AND GOALS

Your work philosophy is a statement about how you approach work. It can also include changes you believe are important in your career field. For example, the following statement defines one student's educational goals: "My immediate educational goal is to graduate with a certificate in fashion design. In 5 years, I plan to earn a college degree in business with an emphasis in marketing." The following examples illustrate career goals:

- To hold a leadership role in fashion design
- To upgrade my skills
- To belong to at least one professional organization

Expand on your short-term, medium-range, and long-term goals. Include a mission statement and career objectives. (Recall the discussion of creating a mission statement in Chapter 1. See also **Figure 14.5.**) You may also write your goals according

Figure 14.5
Sample Mission Statement

As discussed in Chapter 1, a mission statement reveals your aspirations, states your philosophy on work and life, and reflects your highest values. *What other types of personal information can your mission statement reveal?*

Name **Anna Marcos**

My mission is to use my talent in fashion design to create beauty and art. I want to influence the future development of fashion. I seek to be a lifelong learner because learning keeps me creative and motivated. In my family, I want to build strong, healthy, and loving relationships. At work, I want to build creative and open teams. In life, I want to be kind, helpful, and supportive. I will live each day with integrity and be an example of outstanding character.

Long-Term Goals
Career goals: I want to own my own fashion design company.
Educational goals: I want to teach and lead workshops.
Family goals: I want to be a supportive parent.
Community goals: I want to belong to different community organizations.
Financial goals: I want to earn enough money to live comfortably and provide my family with the basic needs and more.

Medium-Range Goals
Career goals: I want to be a manager of a fashion company.
Educational goals: I want to earn a college degree in business and marketing.

Short-Term Goals
Career goals: I want to obtain an entry-level job in fashion design.
Educational goals: I want to earn a certificate in fashion design.

to the roles you perform. What do you hope to accomplish in each area of your life? Consider the following questions:

- Do I want to improve my skills?
- Do I want to change careers or jobs?
- Do I want to become more competent in my present job or earn a promotion?
- Do I want to spend more time in one or more areas of my life?
- Do I want to learn a new hobby or explore areas of interest?
- Do I want to become more involved in community service?
- Do I want to improve my personal qualities?
- Do I want to improve my human relations skills?
- Do I want to spend more time with my family?

Return to Chapter 3 and review Personal Evaluation Notebook 3.3: Looking Ahead. Reflect on what you wrote, and update it. How has it changed in just a few weeks? Make it a habit to reflect on what you are learning in class and connect it to work and life. How are these experiences changing the way you see yourself, others, and the world? How are they changing your values, interests, and goals? When you finish college, record these questions in your portfolio and update it often.

RESUMÉ

The purpose of a resumé is to show your strengths, accomplishments, and skills and their connections to an employer's needs. Your resumé is almost always the first contact an employer will have with you, since many companies initially screen potential candidates through online applications. You want it to stand out, highlight your skills and competencies, look professional, and, ideally, fit on one page. Several online services can help you format your resumé, design it to fit the needs of specific professions, link it to hiring companies, and allow you to create your own home page. Also, resumé classes may be offered in the career center. See **Figure 14.6** on page 456 for a sample resumé.

Even if you aren't actively looking for a job right now, it's good practice to have at least a draft resumé in your portfolio to build on. This will make creating a polished version an easier task. Although your resumé's final format and content may depend on the preferences of your prospective employers or career field, you will most likely include the following components:

1. **Personal information.** Include your name, address, phone number, and e-mail address. If you have a temporary or school address, also include a permanent address and phone number. Don't include marital status, height, weight, health, interests, a picture, or hobbies unless they are relevant to the job. Keep your resumé simple.

2. **Job objective.** Include a job objective if you will accept only a specific job. You may be willing to accept various jobs in a company, especially if you're a new graduate with little experience. If you decide not to list a job objective, use your cover letter to relate your resumé to the specific job for which you are applying.

3. **Work experience.** List the title of your last job first, dates worked, and a brief description of your duties. Don't clutter your resumé with needless detail or

Figure 14.6
Sample Resumé

An effective resumé should be clear, concise, and eye-catching to create the best possible first impression. *What is the most important element of your resumé?*

CAITLYN J. JENSEN

1423 10th Street
Arlin, Minnesota 52561
(320) 555-2896
cjjensen@att.net

JOB OBJECTIVE: To obtain an entry-level position as a travel agent

WORK EXPERIENCE
University Travel Agency, Arlin, Minnesota
Tour Guide, August 2009–present
- Arrange tours to historic sites in a four-state area. Responsibilities include contacting rail and bus carriers, arranging for local guides at each site, making hotel and restaurant reservations, and providing historical information about points of interest.

- Develop tours for holidays and special events. Responsibilities include event planning, ticketing, and coordination of travel and event schedules.

- Specialized tour planning resulted in 24 percent increase in tour revenues over the preceding year.

Arlin Area Convention Center
Intern Tourist Coordinator, December 2008–June 2009
- Established initial contact with prospective speakers, coordinated schedules, and finalized all arrangements. Set up database of tours using dBase IV.

- Organized receptions for groups up to 250, including reserving meeting rooms, contacting caterers, finalizing menus, and preparing seating charts.

EDUCATION
Arlin Community College, Arlin, Minnesota
  Associate of Arts in Business, June 2010
  Magna Cum Laude graduate

Cross Pointe Career School, Arlin, Minnesota
  Certificate in Tourism, June 2008

HONORS AND AWARDS
Academic Dean's List
Recipient of Arlin Rotary Scholarship, 2008

CAMPUS AND COMMUNITY ACTIVITIES
Vice President, Tourist Club, 2009–2010
Co-chaired 2009 home-tour fundraising event for Big Sisters

PROFESSIONAL MEMBERSHIP
Arlin Area Convention and Visitors Bureau

REFERENCES
Available upon request.

---

irrelevant jobs. You can elaborate on specific duties in your cover letter and in the interview.

4. **Educational background.** List your highest degree first, school attended, dates, and major field of study. Include educational experience that may be relevant to the job, such as certification, licensing, advanced training, intensive seminars, and summer study programs. Don't list individual classes on your resumé. Your cover letter can mention any classes that relate directly to the job you are applying for.

5. **Awards and honors.** List awards and honors that are related to the job or indicate excellence. In addition, you may want to list other qualifications related to the job, such as fluency in another language.

6. **Campus and community activities.** List activities that show leadership abilities and willingness to contribute.

7. **Professional memberships and activities.** List professional memberships, speeches, or research projects connected with your profession.

8. **References.** Gather three to five references, including employment, academic, and character references. Ask instructors for a general letter before you leave their last class or soon after. Fellow members of professional associations, club advisors, a coach, and students who have worked with you on projects can also provide good character references. See **Figure 14.7** for a sample request for a recommendation. Ask your supervisor for a letter before you leave a job. Be sure to ask your references for permission to use their names and contact information. Don't print your references on the bottom of your resume. It's best to include "References available upon request" and list them on a separate sheet of paper. Provide that list only if asked to do so. You may not want your references to be called until you have an interview. Include letters of recommendation in your Career Development Portfolio. See **Figure 14.8** on page 458 for an example.

May 2, 2011

Professor Eva Atkins
Chair of the Fashion Department
Green Briar Business Institute
100 North Bank Street
Glenwood, New Hampshire 03827

Dear Professor Atkins:

I was a student of yours last term in Fashion Design and earned an A in your class. I am currently assembling my Career Development Portfolio so I can apply for summer positions in the fashion business. Would you please write a letter of recommendation addressing the following skills and competencies?

- My positive attitude and enthusiasm
- My ability to work with diverse people in teams
- My computer and technical skills
- My skills in design and art

I have also included my resumé, which highlights my experience, my GPA, and selected classes. If it is convenient, I would like to stop by your office next week and pick up this letter of recommendation. Your advice and counsel have meant so much to me over the last three years. You have served as an instructor, an advisor, and a mentor. Thank you again for all your help and support. Please call or e-mail me if you have questions.

Sincerely,

Susan Sanchos

Susan Sanchos
242 Cherry Lane
Glenwood, New Hampshire 03827
Home phone: (304) 555-8293
e-mail: susans@edu.glow.com

Figure 14.7
Request for a Letter of Recommendation

Instructors, advisors, coaches, and previous employers are ideal candidates to ask for a letter of recommendation. *Whom might you ask to write a letter of recommendation?*

Take 3 minutes to draft (or update) your resumé:

- What employment experiences and responsibilities should you list?
- List your education history and GPA (if exemplary).
- Which honors and related activities should you include? Every few weeks, return to your resumé and flesh it out further, updating it with new experiences.

What else can you do in 3 minutes?

- Call the career center to find out what resources it offers in your field of study.
- Contact local businesses to see if they offer internship opportunities.
- Make a list of people who could give you a letter of recommendation.

SAMPLES OF WORK

Think of how you can visually demonstrate your expertise in your field. Work samples can include articles, portions of a book, artwork, fashion sketches, drawings, photos of work, poetry, pictures, food demonstrations, brochures, job descriptions, and performance reviews. Include samples of flyers or digital samples of music or media projects on CD or DVD.

SUMMARY OF TRANSCRIPTS

Include a copy of all transcripts of college work.

CREDENTIALS, CERTIFICATES, AND WORKSHOPS

Include a copy of credentials and certificates. List workshops, seminars, training sessions, conferences, continuing education courses, and other examples of lifelong learning.

Figure 14.8
Letter of Recommendation

In your portfolio, include letters of recommendation from a variety of people, highlighting your many strengths and experiences. *How might a letter of recommendation be instrumental in securing a job interview?*

August 12, 2011

Mr. Jason Bently
University Travel Agency
902 Sunnybrae Lane
Pinehill, New Mexico 88503

Dear Mr. Bently:

It is a pleasure to write a letter of support for Ms. Mary Anne Myers. I have worked with Mary Anne for five years at Computer Divisions Corporation. We were part of the same project team for two years and worked well together. For the last year, I have been her supervisor at Computer Divisions. Mary Anne is a team player and works well with a variety of people. She is also well prepared knowledgeable, and hardworking. Recently, a major report was due and Mary Anne worked several weekends and nights to meet the deadline.

Mary Anne has a positive attitude and is willing to tackle any assignment. She is self-motivated and creative. In 2008 she won our Creative Employee Award for her new marketing design. Mary Anne is also an excellent listener. She takes the time to build rapport and listen to customers and, as a result, many repeat customers ask for her by name.

Mary Anne is a lifelong learner. She is attending classes for her college degree in the evenings, and she regularly takes additional training in computers.

I highly recommend Mary Anne Myers. She is an excellent employee. Call or e-mail me if you have questions.

Sincerely,
Joyce Morocco
Joyce Morocco, MBA
Computer Divisions Corporation
388 Maple Street
Midland, New Mexico 85802
Office Phone: (606) 555-3948
e-mail: joycem@CDCorp.com

BIBLIOGRAPHY

Include a bibliography of books you have read that pertain to your major, career goals, or occupation.

APPENDIX

Include internships, leadership experiences in clubs and sports, volunteer work, service to the community, and travel experiences related to your goals. You can also include awards, honors, and certificates of recognition.

PORTFOLIO COVER LETTER

If you are submitting your portfolio for review, include a cover letter that indicates the purpose of the submission (such as to prove previous experiences or college credit), a list of the documents enclosed, a brief review, and a request for a response (such as an interview or acceptance). See **Figure 14.9** for an example of a portfolio cover letter.

Overcome the Barriers to Portfolio Development

The biggest barrier to portfolio development is procrastination. The idea of a portfolio may sound good, but you also think of these excuses:

- It's a lot of work and I don't have the time.
- I wouldn't know where to start.
- I'll do it when I'm ready for a job.
- I don't have enough work samples.

737 Grandview Avenue
Euclid, Ohio 43322

October 2, 2011

Dr. Kathryn Keys
Director of Assessment of Prior Learning
Louis College of Business
333 West Street
Columbus, Ohio 43082

Dear Dr. Keys:

I am submitting my portfolio for credit for prior learning. I am applying for credit for the following courses:

Marketing 201   Retail Marketing
Management 180   Introduction to Management
Business Writing 100   Introduction to Business Writing

I completed my portfolio while taking the course Special Topics 350. My experiences are detailed in the portfolio and I believe they qualify me for six units of college credit. I look forward to meeting you to discuss this further. I will call your office next week to arrange an appointment. If you have questions, please call me at (202) 555-5556.

Sincerely,
Kim Anderson
Kim Anderson

Figure 14.9
Portfolio Cover Letter

Since your portfolio showcases your variety of experiences, your cover letter should pinpoint the reason you are presenting it for review at this time. *What are some possible reasons for submitting your portfolio for review?*

A Career Development Portfolio is an ongoing process. It takes time to develop your work philosophy, goals, documentation of skills and competencies, and work samples. If you are resisting or procrastinating, work with a partner or study group. Together you can organize supplies, brainstorm ideas, review each other's philosophies and goals, and assemble the contents.

Planning the Job Hunt

As discussed earlier in this chapter, many resources are available when you begin your search for a job: the career center and career counselor, instructors, mentors, and alumni. Also, numerous Internet sites match employers with future employees. Most major employers list their job openings on their Web sites. Review job descriptions posted by potential employers to see what types of jobs they often have available and what types of qualifications they are looking for. This can also help you determine if you need to redesign or enhance your portfolio to fulfill certain requirements.

There is no set time to do certain activities. Even so, whether you are a 2-year, 4-year, or transfer student, you will want to put your job search in high gear during your senior or final year.

Submitting a Cover Letter

A cover letter is a written introduction; it should state what job you are applying for and what you can contribute to the company. Try to learn to whom you should address your cover letter. Often, a call to the personnel office will yield the correct name and title. Express enthusiasm, and highlight how your education, skills, and experience relate to the job and will benefit the company.

Submit your cover letter along with your resumé and, if applicable, parts of your portfolio. Follow up with a phone call in a week or two to verify that your resumé was received. Ask if additional information is needed and when a decision will be made.

As you develop your portfolio, include good examples of helpful cover letters. See **Figure 14.10** for a sample cover letter.

Interviewing

The resumé and cover letter open the door, but the job interview is when you can clearly articulate why you are the best person for the job. Many of the tips discussed in this text about verbal and nonverbal communication skills will be extremely important during your job interview. Here are some interview strategies for making full use of these and other skills:

1. **Be punctual.** A good first impression is important and can be lasting. If you arrive late, you have already said a great deal about yourself. Be sure you know the interview's time and location. Allow time for traffic and parking.
2. **Be professional.** Know the interviewer's name and title, including the pronunciation of the interviewer's name. Don't sit down until the interviewer does. Never call anyone by his or her first name unless you are asked to.

July 1, 2011

Dr. Sonia Murphy
North Clinic Health Care
2331 Terrace Street
Chicago, Illinois 69691

Dear Dr. Murphy:

Mr. David Leeland, Director of Internship at Bakers College, gave me a copy of your advertisement for a medical assistant. I am interested in being considered for the position.

Your medical office has an excellent reputation, especially regarding health care for women. I have taken several courses in women's health and volunteer at the hospital in a women's health support group. I believe I can make a significant contribution to your office.

My work experiences and internships have provided valuable hands-on experience. I set up a new computer-designed program for payroll in my internship position. In addition to excellent office skills, I also have clinical experience and people skills. I speak Spanish and have used it often in my volunteer work in hospitals.

I have paid for most of my college education. My grades are excellent, and I have been on the dean's list in my medical and health classes. I have also completed advanced computer and advanced office procedures classes.

I will call you on Tuesday, July 22, to make sure you received this letter and to find out when you might be able to arrange an interview.

Sincerely,

Julia Andrews

Julia Andrews
Green Briar Business Institute
242 Cherry Lane
Chicago, Illinois 69692
Home phone: (304) 555-5593
e-mail: juliaa@edu.BakersC.com

Figure 14.10
Sample Cover Letter

A good cover letter captures the employer's attention (in a positive way) and shows how your qualifications connect to what is being sought for the position. *Whom might you ask to review your cover letter before you send it?*

- **If You Post It, It Will Come . . . Back to Haunt You**
  Sites such as Facebook, MySpace, Twitter, and LinkedIn are often reviewed by companies as they check the background of job candidates. What may seem as a harmless, humorous video on YouTube today may be the reason you are turned down for a job tomorrow. *Have you posted anything online that you would not want a potential employer to see?*

3. **Dress appropriately.** In most situations, you will be safe if you wear clean, pressed, conservative business clothes in a neutral color. Your nails and hair should be clean, trimmed, and neat. Keep makeup light and wear little jewelry. Don't carry a large purse, a backpack, books, a coat, or a hat. Leave extra clothing in an outside office, and simply carry a pen, a pad of paper, and a small folder with extra copies of your resumé and references.

4. **Learn about the company.** The Internet makes researching employers easy, as most companies have a Web site, even if just for informational purposes. Be prepared and show that you know about the company. What product(s) does it make? How is it doing? What is the competition? Refer to the company when you give examples.

5. **Learn about the position.** Before you interview, request a job description from the personnel office. What kind of

● Maintain Eye Contact
Look the hiring manager in the eye, remain calm and confident during your interview, and be prepared to explain how you can contribute to the company. *What typical interview questions should you be prepared to answer?*

employee—and with what skills—is the company looking for? You will likely be asked why you are interested in the job. Be prepared to answer with a reference to the company.

6. **Relate your experience to the job.** Use every question as an opportunity to show how your skills relate to the job. Use examples from school, previous jobs, internships, volunteer work, leadership in clubs, and experiences growing up to indicate that you have the personal qualities, aptitudes, and skills needed at the new job.

7. **Be honest.** Although it is important to be confident and stress your strengths, honesty is equally important. Someone will verify your background, so do not exaggerate your accomplishments, grade point average, or experience.

8. **Focus on how you can benefit the company.** Don't ask about benefits, salary, or vacations until you are offered the job. During a first interview, try to show how you can contribute to the organization. Don't appear too eager to move up through the company or suggest you are more interested in gaining experience than in contributing to the company.

9. **Be poised and relaxed.** Avoid nervous habits, such as tapping your pencil, playing with your hair, or covering your mouth with your hand. Watch language such as *you know, ah,* and *stuff like that.* Don't smoke, chew gum, fidget, or bite your nails.

10. **Maintain comfortable eye contact.** Look people in the eye and speak with confidence. Your eyes reveal much about you; use them to show interest, confidence, poise, and sincerity. Use other nonverbal techniques, such as a firm handshake, to reinforce your confidence.

11. **Practice interviewing.** Consider videotaping a mock interview. Most college campuses have this service available through the career center or media department. Rehearse questions and be prepared to answer directly.

Marketing "Me"

Practice for an interview by completing the following:

- My traits that help me be successful are
- I'm experienced in
- I'm knowledgeable about
- I'm capable of operating the following
- I can contribute to this company because

12. **Anticipate question types.** Expect open-ended questions, such as "What are your strengths?" "What are your weaknesses?" "Tell me about your best work experience," and "What are your career goals?" Decide in advance what information is pertinent and reveals your strengths—for example, "I learned to get along with a diverse group of people when I worked for the park service."

13. **Close the interview on a positive note.** Thank the interviewer for his or her time, shake hands, and say you are looking forward to hearing from him or her.

May 29, 2011

Mr. Henry Sanders
The Mountain View Store
10 Rock Lane
Alpine, Montana 79442

Dear Mr. Sanders:

Thank you for taking the time yesterday to meet with me concerning the position of sales representative. I enjoyed meeting you and your employees, learning more about your growing company, and touring your facilities. I was especially impressed with your new line of outdoor wear. It is easy to see why you lead the industry in sales.

I am even more excited about joining your sales team now that I have visited with you. I have the education, training, enthusiasm, and personal qualities necessary to succeed in business. I am confident I would fit in with your staff and make a real contribution to the sales team.

Thank you again for the interview and an enjoyable morning.

Sincerely,

John A. Bennett

John A. Bennett
124 East Buttermilk Lane
LaCrosse, Wisconsin 54601
Home phone: (608) 555-4958
e-mail: johnb@shast.edu

Figure 14.11

Sample Follow-Up Letter

A follow-up letter is another opportunity to set yourself apart from other job candidates. *What should you include in your follow-up letter?*

14. **Send a thank-you letter.** A follow-up letter (not e-mail) is especially important. Surprisingly, few jobseekers actually send one. A thank-you note shows gratitude, and most employers think a person who appreciates an opportunity will appreciate the job. It reminds the interviewer about you and gives you a chance to reiterate your interest in the position and company and to add anything you forgot to mention previously. Send thank-you notes to every person involved in the interview: the hiring manager, administrative assistant, human resources personnel, and others who were especially helpful. If you are hand writing the letter, use nice stationery or a card and write neatly. If typing the note, include a legible signature at the bottom. Send the thank-you note no later than 1 day after your interview. See **Figure 14.11** for a sample follow-up letter.

15. **Determine what's next.** Although you may be eager for a response, do not bombard the employer with e-mails and phone calls. Ask the human resources manager (or the hiring manager during the interview) how the company notifies candidates about the hiring process. Some organizations send a letter that declines further interest, or others have so many interviews that, unfortunately, they do not call unless you are a selected candidate. The interview process can be lengthy, so it's wise to explore many potential opportunities.

Take Charge of Your Career

If we learned anything from the economic downturn that hit the past decade, it's that few (if any) jobs are guaranteed. At some time in your career, possibly even now, you may find yourself suddenly out of work and needing new skills or

> **"**Don't go around saying the world owes you a living. The world owes you nothing. It was here first.**"**
>
> MARK TWAIN
> *Author*

WORDS TO SUCCEED

experiences to make you an attractive job candidate. Also, when jobs are eliminated, the remaining employees must take on more work, along with responsibility for managing themselves and their work progress. Salary increases and advancement are based on performance and production, rather than seniority.

However, there are steps you can take concerning your education, planning, and assessment and documentation of skills that can keep you marketable and prepare you for whatever career opportunities come your way:

1. **Conduct a personal performance review.** Don't wait for your annual review to assess how you are achieving your goals, whether established by your boss or self-imposed. Map your performance and productivity each month. Continually ask yourself, "How have I added value to the company? What can I do to contribute?"

2. **Keep your portfolio and resumé up to date.** Add examples of successful assignments and team projects that you can use to demonstrate your skills and performance to your current or a potential employer. Every few months, check your resumé and update it with new personal information, education, and responsibilities. You never know when a good opportunity will arise and your resumé needs to be in someone's in-box immediately.

3. **Watch job trends.** Technology has affected and will continue to shape future job opportunities. How will it affect the field you are pursuing? Will you need more training? Is it opening up new kinds of jobs? Watch related fields where growth is predicted. For example, government actions and the focus on clean energy and global environmental issues are expected to fuel the creation of "green" jobs (also known as green-collar jobs) in various industries. According to the Clean Edge research firm, by 2019, the global biofuels market, wind power, and solar energy will have expanded and may hit over $100 billion in revenues in each area. Other trends in employment will result from demographic changes, such as growth in the elderly and very young populations (in 2007, the United States experienced the greatest baby boom to date). Read the business section of the newspaper or the local business journal to see what trends and opportunities your community is experiencing.

4. **Look over the horizon.** As the global economy grows and companies expand overseas, you may find exciting opportunities in other countries. If relocation is an option for you, consider what additional skills would be useful, such as the ability to speak and write in other languages and knowledge of other customs and cultures.

5. **Further your education.** See if your employer offers additional training in job skills or related topics, such as conflict resolution, diversity, team building, communication, or motivation. Does your employer provide tuition reimbursement if you take academic courses online or from a local college?

Must the courses be directly tied to the job or advanced certification? Determine which degrees or certifications would make you a more knowledgeable professional and more valuable to an employer. See if related workshops or seminars are available locally or online.

An employee who learns new skills, cross-trains in various positions, and has excellent human relations skills will be sought after and promoted. Complete **Personal Evaluation Notebook 14.4** on page 466 to assess how your skills have improved during just the past few months.

6. **Keep networking.** Not only does networking help you land your first job, but you'll attain many subsequent jobs based on whom you know. It is rare today for someone to spend 30 years at one company, which was commonplace just a few decades ago. As people change employers, they build substantial contacts at related companies. Your colleague who is leaving today for a higher position at another company may hire you away tomorrow. Show genuine interest in your colleagues and clients, and support their work. Get involved in professional organizations, and join online business sites that link you with other professionals in your field.

7. **Be your own "career coach."** The most important person you report to is the one you see in the mirror. Only you know what type of work keeps you motivated and makes you passionate about contributing day after day. This is *your* career and *your* life—only you can make the best of it by learning to endure the challenging times, overcoming setbacks, gaining valuable knowledge, and being a better person from the experience. What Hsi-Tang Chih Tsang, renowned Zen master, said 1,200 years ago is still true: "Although gold dust is precious, when it gets in your eyes it obstructs your vision." If you focus on your values, positive personal qualities, and mission in life, you will attain whatever you deem precious—and will become a true peak performer.

> **"**It's easy to make a buck. It's a lot tougher to make a difference.**"**
>
> TOM BROKAW
> *Journalist*

Personal Evaluation Notebook

14.4

Assessment Is Lifelong

Read the following skills. Then rate your skill level on a scale of 1 to 5 (1 being poor and 5 being excellent). Refer back to **Personal Evaluation Notebook 1.1** in Chapter 1, and compare it with your answers here. Have you improved your skills and competencies?

	Excellent		Satisfactory		Poor
Skills	5	4	3	2	1
1. Reading			_____		
2. Writing			_____		
3. Speaking			_____		
4. Mathematics			_____		
5. Listening			_____		
6. Critical thinking and reasoning			_____		
7. Decision making			_____		
8. Creative problem solving			_____		
9. Visualization			_____		
10. Knowing how to learn			_____		
11. Personal qualities (honesty, character, responsibility)			_____		
12. Sociability			_____		
13. Self-management and self-control			_____		
14. Self-esteem and confidence			_____		
15. Management of time, money, space, and people			_____		
16. Interpersonal, team, and leadership skills			_____		
17. Working well with cultural diversity			_____		
18. Organization and evaluation of information			_____		
19. Understanding systems			_____		
20. Understanding technology			_____		
21. Commitment and effort			_____		

(continued)

Personal Evaluation Notebook

Assessment Is Lifelong (*concluded*)

Assess your results. What are your strongest skills? What skills need the most improvement?

Do you have a better understanding of how you learned these skills and competencies? Do you know how to document and demonstrate them?

Following are six broad skill areas that can be transferred to many situations or jobs:

- Communication skills
- Human relations skills
- Organization, management, and leadership skills
- Technical and mechanical skills
- Innovation and creativity skills
- Research and planning skills

How would each of these skill areas relate to your major or career choice? What other skill areas might your major or career choice include?

TAKING CHARGE

Summary

In this chapter, I learned to

- **Explore potential majors and career paths.** To determine my major course of study, I consult with available resources, such as a career counselor, family, and friends; explore the college catalog; visit academic departments; and participate in classes, workshops, internships, and service learning opportunities.

- **Assess my values, interests, abilities, and skills.** What I value helps me identify what I will value in a future career. I have certain interests that may lead me in one occupational direction. I have innate abilities that help me succeed in certain areas. I also have acquired transferable skills that apply to many different fields.

- **See the value of Career Development Portfolios.** My portfolio helps me assess, highlight, and demonstrate my strengths, skills, and competencies. Starting my portfolio early helps me get organized and gives me a chance to update, edit, and add to it throughout my college experience and into my career.

- **Organize essential elements.** Assembling my portfolio in a three-ring notebook and box helps me collect and organize work samples, information, lists, examples, transcripts, credentials, certificates, workshop experiences, and documentation of personal qualities.

- **List significant life experiences and accomplishments.** I include such experiences as formal education, special classes and projects, volunteer work and service learning, jobs, travel, hobbies, military service, special recognition, and accomplishments and events that helped me learn new skills or something about myself or others. I list books I have read that pertain to my major or career or that have helped me develop a certain philosophy.

- **Document skills and competencies.** I connect essential skills to school and work, and I look for transferable skills. I document critical thinking, interpersonal, computer, financial, and basic skills related to school and job success. When appropriate, I include samples of my work.

- **Create an effective resumé.** My resumé is an essential document that helps me highlight my education, work experience, awards, professional memberships, and campus and community activities.

- **Write a cover letter, and prepare for an interview.** My cover letter succinctly communicates my interest in and qualifications for a specific job. I prepare for an interview by researching the company and the job requirements and practicing responses to anticipated questions. I am on time for the interview, well groomed, and dressed appropriately. I focus on how I can contribute to the company, using personal examples and positive body language. I end the interview on a positive note, ask about follow up, and thank the hiring manager immediately in a letter.

- **Take charge of my career.** I realize that job opportunities are constantly changing, and I must be proactive by continually assessing my performance and abilities, keeping my portfolio and resumé up to date, and watching job trends for new opportunities and ways to improve my skills. I continue to cultivate personal contacts that benefit me personally and professionally, and I know only I can determine what's important to me in a career and life. I take the time to learn more about career opportunities, and I observe workplace trends, especially needs for additional education and training.

Performance Strategies

Following are the top 10 tips for planning a career:

- Determine what you value in life and a career.
- Know how to connect essential work skills and competencies to school and life and how to transfer skills.
- Assemble your portfolio, and frequently review, assess, and update it.
- Document skills, competencies, and personal qualities in your portfolio.
- Include essential elements in your portfolio, such as a resumé, transcripts, and a list of accomplishments.
- Value, document, and demonstrate service learning and volunteer work on campus and in the community.
- Use your portfolio to reflect on your work philosophy and life mission, as well as to set goals and priorities.
- Prepare for the job-hunting and interview process early.
- Be prepared for changes in job opportunities and expectations.
- Take personal responsibility for directing your career.

Tech for Success

Take advantage of the text's Web site at **www.mhhe.com/ferrett8e** for additional study aids, useful forms, and convenient and applicable resources.

- **Your resumé online.** Most potential employers are willing (and many prefer) to receive your resumé and supporting documents via e-mail or through a Web site, either the company's or an employment service. Programs and services are available to help you develop your portfolio online. Some include virtual space for storing digital files, such as graphic images, video, and PowerPoint presentations. Your school may use its preferred source for developing a portfolio, so consult your advisor as you get started.

- **Job search Web sites.** Job search sites, such as monster.com and hotjobs.com, require you to type your resumé into their format, which then feeds into their search engine. When you start your job hunt, it's worth investigating these and more specialized sites that cater to the field you are pursuing. Also, check out any professional organizations in the field, as they may also provide job listings online.

Study Team Notes

Steven Price
SOCIAL STUDIES TEACHER/LEGISLATOR

Related Majors: Education, Social Studies, Political Science

Career Planning Is Lifelong

Steven Price taught social studies at a high school. With an avid interest in politics, Steven soon developed a strong curriculum for teaching government and current affairs. He was well known in the district for his innovative classes in which students researched and debated local issues and then voted on them.

Throughout the years, Steven remained active in a local political party. Each year, he could be counted on to help hand out flyers and canvass neighborhoods before the September primaries and November elections. One year, a party member suggested that Steven run for state legislator.

Steven took the offer seriously. After 21 years of teaching, he felt ready for a change. He had enjoyed being in the classroom, especially when his students shared his passion for politics. However, he felt that, as a state legislator, he could more directly bring about changes in his community. He took a leave of absence from his teaching job. He filed the appropriate papers and worked hard with a campaign manager to get his name out to the voters in his district. Because Steven had already prepared a Career Development Portfolio over the years, the manager was able to use the collected information to promote Steven.

Using his years of experience teaching government and current affairs, Steven felt rejuvenated and excited as he worked on his political campaign. His lifelong commitment to politics paid off when he won the election! He was glad he had taken the risk. The career change was a positive move for both Steven and his community.

CRITICAL THINKING What might have happened to Steven if he had not taken the risks of moving to a different career?

Peak Performer

PROFILE

Ursula Burns

As you contemplate any future career, it's important to consider what you value, what you enjoy doing, and how those important factors should play a role in your decisions. Ursula Burns, CEO of Xerox and the first African American woman to be named CEO of a Fortune 500 company, exemplifies someone who worked through that process to determine what career area to pursue.

Burns grew up on the Lower East Side of Manhattan in a low-income housing project where crime and poverty were rampant. Burns claims that, when she was a child, her mother's constant hard work and attitude kept her unaware of her family's poverty. Her mother, Olga, ran an at-home day care, took in ironing, and raised three children alone. As Burns says, "She gave us courage. She gave us will and love. I can still hear her telling me that where you are is not who you are."

This advice followed Burns throughout her long career. From a young age, she excelled in mathematics. When it came time for college, she went to the library to research top-paying jobs for people with math or science degrees. Acknowledging her strengths and interests, Burns ultimately decided to pursue a degree in mechanical engineering instead of other degrees her teachers thought she should consider. She attended the Polytechnic Institute of New York and earned her graduate degree from Columbia University.

Burns quickly worked her way up the corporate ladder, beginning as an engineering intern for Xerox in

1980. Her work ethic and straightforward approach to business earned her respect in the company. In 2009, she was named CEO of the $17 billion corporation. Since her appointment, the company's stock price has increased 36 percent, and she was named among *BusinessWeek*'s Top 20 Inspirational Leaders, placing her amid the likes of Bill Gates and former president Bill Clinton. She has also been chosen by President Barack Obama to help direct the national STEM program, which focuses on providing equal science, technology, engineering, and mathematics education to all students. Ultimately, Burns will not only make a tremendous impact on the performance of a multibillion-dollar company but also help shape the nation's curriculum and global leadership position in the fields of science and technology.

PERFORMANCE THINKING Which values and interests are important to you? How are they reflected in the job or career you are studying for? Do your strengths and personal qualities coincide with the skills and abilities needed for success in this career? Are there alternate career areas you should also explore? How does Ursula Burns's mother's advice, "Where you are is not who you are," apply to your life?

CHECK IT OUT Read *BusinessWeek*'s list of qualities possessed by inspirational leaders (**www.businessweek.com/managing/content/dec2009/ca20091217_472500.htm**). Keep track of your score as indicated in the directions. Are you acting as an inspirational leader? In what ways could you become more of a leader in your classes or school organizations? Which traits of the 20 profiled leaders do you most want to develop?

Starting Today

At least one strategy I learned in this chapter that I plan to try right away is

_____

_____

_____

What changes must I make in order for this strategy to be most effective?

_____

_____

_____

Review Questions

Based on what you have learned in this chapter, write your answers to the following questions:

1. Why is it important to determine your values during career planning?

_____

_____

2. Define *transferable skill* and give an example.

_____

_____

3. What is a purpose of a Career Development Portfolio?

_____

_____

4. Name at least four elements that should be included in a portfolio.

_____

_____

5. What information should be included in a resumé?

_____

_____

To test your understanding of the chapter's concepts, complete the chapter quiz at **www.mhhe.com/ferrett8e.**

Exploring Careers

In the Classroom

Maria Lewis likes making presentations, enjoys working with children, and is a crusader for equality and the environment. She also values family, home, and community. Making a lot of money is less important to her than making a difference and enjoying what she does. Now that her children are grown, she wants to complete a college degree. However, she is hesitant because she has been out of school for many years.

1. How would you help Maria with her decision?

_____

_____

2. What careers would you have Maria explore?

_____

_____

In the Workplace

Maria completed a degree in childhood development. She has been a caregiver at a children's day care center for 2 years. She enjoys her job but feels it is time for a change. If she wants to advance in her field, she has to travel and go into management. She wants more time off to spend with her family, write, and become more involved in community action groups. Maria would like to stay in a related field. She likes working with children but also enjoys giving presentations and workshops and writing. She has thought about consulting, writing, or starting her own small business.

3. What strategies in this chapter would help Maria with her career change?

_____

_____

4. What one habit would you recommend to Maria to help her plan her career?

_____

_____

Applying the ABC Method of Self-Management

In the Journal Entry on page 439, you were asked to write down one of the classes you are currently taking and list at least three skills you will acquire in this class that will benefit you in your career:

_____

_____

_____

Now think about a class you are taking that doesn't seem to relate directly to your career plans. Use the ABC Method to analyze what you are learning in that class and how it benefits you, either today or later on.

A = Actual event:

_____

_____

_____

B = Beliefs:

_____

_____

_____

C = Challenge:

_____

_____

_____

Use visualization to help you achieve the results you want. See yourself creating a portfolio that helps you organize the information you're learning and relate it to job success. Think of the confidence you'll have when you've developed a resumé and practiced for job interviews. See yourself focused with a vision and purpose and working in a job you love.

PRACTICE SELF-MANAGEMENT

For more examples of learning how to manage difficult situations, see the "Self-Management Workbook" section of the Online Learning Center Web site at **www.mhhe.com/ferrett8e.**

Checklist for Choosing a Major

Use the Adult Learning Cycle to explore majors and career opportunities.

RELATE

- What are the most important criteria for my future career, such as independence, high visibility, flexible hours, ability to work from home, and management opportunities?
- What is my personality type and/or temperament?
- Do the careers that fit my personality offer these features?
- What skills do I already have that would be useful or necessary?

OBSERVE

- Do I know anyone currently working in this field whom I could interview or talk to?
- Which instructors at my school would be most knowledgeable about the field? Who are the most approachable and available to advise me?
- What are the major professional organizations in this field? Have I explored their Web sites for additional information? Can I join these organizations as a student? Would it be worth the investment?
- Which courses should I be enrolled in now or next semester that will further introduce me to this area?
- I've visited the career center at my school and have talked with my advisor and/or a career counselor about:

REFLECT

- What positives am I hearing?
- What drawbacks am I hearing?
- What education and skills will be necessary for me to pursue this major and career?
- Are there related professions that seem appealing?

DO

- I've constructed a time line for gaining experience in this area that includes tasks such as
  - Securing an internship; to be secured by
  - Joining a student club; to be involved by
  - Participating in related volunteer activities; to be accomplished by
  - Getting a related part-time job; to be hired by
  - Other:

TEACH

- I have relayed my impressions to my family and/or friends. Some of their questions/responses are
- I have talked with fellow students about their major and career search. Some tips I have learned from them are
- The most important resources I have found that I would recommend to others are

As of now, the major/career I would like to continue exploring is

Preparing Your Resumé

To prepare for writing your resumé, start thinking about the information you will include. On the following lines, summarize your skills and qualifications, and match them to the requirements of the job you are seeking. Use proactive words and verbs. Here are some examples:

- *Organized* a group of after-school tutors for math and accounting courses
- *Wrote* and *published* articles for the school newspaper
- *Participated* in a student academic advisory board
- *Developed* a new accounting system
- *Managed* the petty cash accounts for the PTA
- *Created* PowerPoint presentations for a charity benefit

You should not be discouraged if you have only a few action phrases to write at this time. Add to your list as you continue your studies and become an active participant in school activities and with your courses of study.

SKILLS AND QUALIFICATIONS

1. _____

2. _____

3. _____

4. _____

5. _____

6. _____

7. _____

8. _____

9. _____

10. _____

Informational Interview: What's the Job Like?

List the types of jobs you think you would like. Then list people you know in those types of jobs. Ask family, friends, neighbors, or instructors, or contact the alumni office or local Rotary or chamber of commerce to see if they can arrange an interview. The purpose of each interview is to find out about the person's career and what the job is really like. You will also be establishing a contact for the future. Remember to send a thank-you note after each interview.

Following is a list of potential questions to ask.

Person interviewed _____ Date _____

Job title _____ Contact e-mail _____

1. Why did you choose your career? _____
   _____
   _____

2. What do you do on a typical day? _____
   _____
   _____

3. What do you like best about your job? _____
   _____
   _____

4. What do you like least? _____
   _____
   _____

5. What classes, internships, jobs, certifications, or experiences do you wish you had explored when you were in college? _____
   _____
   _____

6. If you had to do it again, would you choose the same job? If not, what would you do differently? _____
   _____
   _____

7. What advice can you give me for planning my career? _____
   _____
   _____

Informational Interview: Who Are You Looking For?

Make a list of the types of jobs you think you would like. Then list local companies that may hire for those kinds of positions. Check out their Web sites to see what types of positions are available and job descriptions, so that you understand their general responsibilities and qualifications. Find out who the hiring managers are (or if they have a human resources department). Contact this person to request an informational interview. Following is a list of potential questions to ask. (Remember to send a thank-you note after each interview.)

Person interviewed _____ Date _____

Job title _____ Contact e-mail _____

1. What specific skills and education do you want in a candidate for this position?

   _____

   _____

2. What two or three traits or qualities are very important in this position?

   _____

   _____

3. What are the difficult aspects of this position?

   _____

   _____

4. Are there areas of professional development in this position?

   _____

   _____

5. What is generally the beginning salary for this position?

   _____

   _____

6. What could I be doing right now that would make me more marketable for your company?

   _____

   _____

Exploring Careers

Go to the library or career center and find careers you've never heard of or are interested in exploring. Do the following exercises. Then add this page to your Career Development Portfolio.

1. Use the Internet to explore at least one career. List the career and skills, education, and abilities needed to be successful.

   _____

   _____

   _____

2. What is the long-term outlook for this career? Is it a growing field? How does technology impact it?

   _____

   _____

   _____

3. List your skills and interests. Then list the careers that match these skills and interests. Create names for careers if they are unusual.

Skills/Interests	Possible Careers
_____	_____
_____	_____
_____	_____

4. Review your list of skills and interests. What stands out? Do you like working with people or accomplishing tasks? Think of as many jobs as you can that relate to your skills and interests. Your skills and interests are valuable clues about your future career.

   _____

   _____

   _____

5. Describe an ideal career that involves the skills you most enjoy using. Include the location of this ideal career and the kinds of co-workers, customers, and employees you would encounter.

   _____

   _____

   _____

Glossary

A

abilities Innate talents or gifts that can be enhanced through study and practice.

academic advisor An educational advisor who assists students in the development of meaningful educational plans compatible with the attainment of their life goals.

acronym A word formed from the first letter of a series of other words.

acrostic A made-up sentence in which the first letter of each word stands for something.

affirmation Positive self-talk or an internal thought that counters self-defeating thought patterns with positive, hopeful, or realistic thoughts.

anorexia nervosa An eating disorder that involves a pathological fear of weight gain leading to faulty eating patterns, malnutrition, and usually excessive weight loss.

assertive communication Expressing oneself in a direct and civil manner.

attentive listening A decision to be fully focused with the intent of understanding the speaker.

B

binge drinking Excessive consumption of alcohol within a short duration of time.

blogging Writing personal reflections and commentary on a Web site, often in a journal format and including hyperlinks to other sources.

body smart People who have physical and kinesthetic intelligence; have the ability to understand and control their bodies; and have tactical sensitivity, like movement, and handle objects skillfully.

bulimia nervosa An eating disorder that involves binge eating and purging through forced vomiting and/or the use of laxatives.

C

character Attributes or features that make up and distinguish an individual and are considered constant and relatively noncontroversial by most people.

cheating Using or providing unauthorized help.

chunking Breaking up long lists of information or numbers to make them easier to remember.

civility Interacting with others with respect, kindness, and good manners.

codependency A psychological condition or a relationship in which a person is controlled or manipulated by another who is affected by an addictive condition.

Common ground

common ground A basis of mutual interest or similarities of core values.

communication Giving and receiving ideas, feelings, and information.

comprehension Understanding main ideas and details.

convergent thinking The ability to look at several unrelated items and bring order to them.

creators People who tend to be innovative, flexible, spontaneous, creative, and idealistic.

critical thinking A logical, rational, systematic thought process that is necessary to understand, analyze, and evaluate information in order to solve a problem or situation.

D

decision making Determining or selecting the best or most effective answer or solution.

decoding The process of breaking words into individual sounds.

deductive reasoning Drawing conclusions based on going from the general to the specific.

depression An emotional state marked especially by sadness, inactivity, difficulty in thinking and concentration, a significant increase or decrease in appetite and time spent sleeping, feelings of dejection and hopelessness, and sometimes suicidal tendencies.

directors People who are dependable, self-directed, conscientious, efficient, decisive, and results-orientated.

discrimination Treating someone differently based on a characteristic.

divergent thinking The ability to break apart an idea into many different ideas.

diversity Differences in gender, race, age, ethnicity, sexual orientation, physical ability, learning styles and learning abilities, social and economic background, and religion.

E

emotional intelligence The ability to understand and manage oneself and relate effectively to others.

empathy Understanding and having compassion for others.

ethics The principles of conduct that govern a group or society.

evaluator A person in an advising center who performs degree checks and reviews transcripts and major contracts.

external locus of control The belief that success or failure is due to outside influences, such as fate, luck, or other people.

extrovert A person who is outgoing, social, optimistic, and often uncomfortable with being alone.

F–I

feeler A person who is sensitive to the concerns and feelings of others, values harmony, and dislikes creating conflict.

formal outline A traditional outline that uses Roman numerals and capital letters to highlight main points.

habits Behaviors performed as a result of frequent repetition.

homophobia An irrational fear of gays and lesbians.

important priorities Essential tasks or activities that support a person's goals and that can be scheduled with some flexibility.

inductive reasoning Generalizing from specific concepts to broad principles.

inference Passing from one statement, judgment, or datum considered as true to another whose truth is based on that of the former.

informal outline A free form of outline that uses dashes and indenting to highlight main points.

integrity Firm adherence to a code of moral values.

interests Activities and subjects that cause you to feel comfortable, excited, enthusiastic, or passionate.

internal locus of control The belief that control over life is due to behavior choices, character, and effort.

Internet A vast network of computers connecting people and resources worldwide.

internship An advanced student or graduate program, usually in a professional field, that provides students with supervised practical experience.

interpreting Developing ideas and summarizing the material.

introvert A person who tends to like time alone, solitude, and reflection and prefers the world of ideas and thoughts.

intuitive People who are more comfortable with theories, abstraction, imagination, and speculation.

J–L

judgers People who prefer orderly, planned, and structured learning and working environments.

Learning and Study Strategies Inventory (LASSI) A self-assessment system that looks at attitude, interest, motivation, self-discipline, willingness to work hard, time management, anxiety, concentration, test strategies, and other study skills to gather information about learning and studying attitudes and practices.

logic smart People who have logical/mathematical intelligence; like numbers, puzzles, and logic; and have the ability to reason, solve problems, create hypotheses, and think in terms of cause and effect.

M

maturity The ability to control impulses, to think beyond the moment, and to consider how words and actions affect others.

memorization The transfer of information from short-term memory into long-term memory.

mentor A role model who takes a special interest in another's goals and personal and professional development.

mind map A visual, holistic form of note taking that starts with the main idea placed in the center of a page and branches out with subtopics through associations and patterns.

mindfulness The state of being totally in the moment and part of the process.

mission statement A written statement focusing on desired values, philosophies, and principles.

mnemonic A memory trick.

motivation An inner drive that moves a person to action.

multitasking Performing many tasks, jobs, or responsibilities simultaneously.

music smart People who have rhythm and melody intelligence; the ability to appreciate, perceive, and produce rhythms.

N

networking Exchanging information or services for the purpose of enriching individuals, groups, or institutions.

nontraditional students Students who do not go directly from high school to college, but return later in life.

note taking A method of creating order and arranging thoughts and materials to help a person retain information.

O

ongoing activities Necessary "maintenance" tasks that should be managed carefully, so that they don't take up too much time.

outdoor smart People who have environmental intelligence and are good at measuring, charting, and observing animals and plants.

P

paraphrase To restate another's ideas in your own words.

peak performer A person who is successful and desires to pursue a lifetime of learning.

people smart People who have interpersonal intelligence; like to talk and work with people, join groups, and solve problems as part of a team; and have the ability to work with and understand people, as well as to perceive and be responsive to the moods, intentions, and desires of other people.

perceiver A person who prefers flexibility and spontaneity and likes to allow life to unfold.

picture smart People who have spatial intelligence; like to draw, sketch, and visualize information; and have the ability to perceive in three-dimensional space and re-create various aspects of the visual world.

plagiarism To steal and pass off the ideas or words of another as one's own.

problem solving Creating or identifying potential answers or solutions to a question or problem.

procrastination Deliberately putting off tasks.

professional advisors Professional and peer staff who answer questions, help students register, and instruct students about deadlines and other important information.

R

racial profiling Using racial or ethnic characteristics to determine whether a person is likely to commit a particular type of crime or illegal act.

rapport The ability to find common ground with another person based on respect, empathy, and trust.

recall The transfer of information from long-term memory into short-term memory.

reflect To think about something in a purposeful way with the intention of creating new meaning.

reframing Choosing to see a situation in a new way.

resilient Able to recover from or adjust easily to misfortune or change.

retention The process of storing information.

S

self smart People who have interpersonal and inner intelligence and the ability to be contemplative, self-disciplined, and introspective.

self-assessment Recognition of the need to learn new tasks and subjects, relate more effectively with others, set goals, manage time and stress, and create a balanced and productive life.

self-esteem How you feel about yourself; sense of self worth.

self-management A thought process that involves techniques you can use to help you manage your thoughts and behaviors, remain focused, overcome obstacles, and succeed.

sensors People who learn best from their senses and feel comfortable with facts and concrete data.

sexism A belief or an attitude that one gender is inferior or less valuable.

sexting Exchanging sexually explicit material, often via cell phone.

skills Capabilities that have been learned and developed.

supporter A person who tends to be cooperative, honest, sensitive, warm, and understanding.

T

thinker A person who likes to analyze problems using facts and rational logic.

traditional student A student 18 to 25 years old, usually going from high school directly to college.

transferable skills Skills that can be used in a variety of careers.

trivial activities Nonessential activities that are completely discretionary and do not directly support a person's goals.

U–W

urgent priorities Tasks or activities that support a person's goals and must be accomplished by a specified date or time to avoid negative consequences.

values Worth or importance you attach to various factors in your life.

visualization The use of imagery to see goals clearly and envision engaging successfully in new, positive behavior.

Web site A collection of mechanisms used to locate, display, and access information available on the Internet.

wellness To live life fully with purpose, meaning, and vitality.

word smart People who have verbal/linguistic intelligence; like to read, talk, and write about information; and have the ability to argue, persuade, entertain, and teach with words.

Additional Credits

Features Guide

Personal Evaluation Notebook
Acronyms and Acrostics, 228
Activities and Clubs, 124
Appreciating Diversity, 400
Assertive Communication Role-Playing, 384
Assessment Is Lifelong, 466
Attentive Listening, 156
Being Observant, 220
Brainstorming Notes, 317
Character and Ethics, 47
Committing to Exercise, 353
Commitment Contract, 427
Conflict Resolution, 389
Controlling Stage Fright and Writer's
    Block, 295
Decision-Making Application, 319
Essay Test Preparation, 257
The Four-Temperament Profile, 20
Getting Proper Rest, 352
Healthy Relationships, 395
How Much Time Do You Spend?, 79
Inductive Versus Deductive Reasoning, 314
Interruptions!, 94
Inventory of Personal Qualities, 453
Keeping Your Life Goals in Balance, 99
Learning Style Inventory, 14
Learning Styles and Memory, 227
Looking Ahead: Your Goals, 80
Make a Commitment to Learn and Apply
    Positive Habits, 421
Memory Assessment, 226
Mind Sets, 318
Money In/Money Out, 132
Multiple Intelligences, 18
Needs, Motivation, and Commitment, 53
Nine-Dot Exercise, 316
Observing Conflict, 388
Patterns in Relationships, 393
Peak Performance Self-Assessment Test, 10
Am I a Positive Person?, 4
Preparing Research Papers, 280
Procrastination, 92
Reviewing Your Health, 350
Self-Talk and Affirmations, 55
Skills and Personal Qualities, 48
Solving Problems and Making Choices, 321
Test Anxiety, 261
Test Taking, 247
That's Not Fair (Use), 288
Think it Through, 309
Time Log, 78
Transferable Skills, 452
Using a Mind Map to Enhance Memory, 223
Using Critical Thinking to Solve
    Problems, 311

Using the SQ3R Reading System, 185
A Walk Down Memory Lane, 229
What Do You Want to Be Called?, 401
Your Daily Energy Levels, 88
Your Values, 444

Peak Progress
The ABC Method of Self-Management, 7
Applying the Adult Learning Cycle to
    Self-Control, 50
Applying the Adult Learning Cycle to
    Becoming a Better Communicator, 498
Applying the Adult Learning Cycle to
    Becoming a Better Reader, 182
Applying the Adult Learning Cycle to
    Becoming an Attentive Listener, 155
Applying the Adult Learning Cycle to
    Creating a Healthier Lifestyle, 357
Applying the Adult Learning Cycle to
    Developing Positive Habits, 426
Applying the Adult Learning Cycle to
    Increasing Your Memory Skills, 219
Applying the Adult Learning Cycle to
    Improving Your Public Speaking, 294
Applying the Adult Learning Cycle to
    Improving your Test-Taking Skills and
    Reducing Test Anxiety, 263
Applying the Adult Learning Cycle to
    Managing Financial Resources, 136
Applying the Adult Learning Cycle to
    Overcoming Math and Science
    Anxiety, 329
Applying the Adult Learning Cycle to
    Taking Control of Your Time and
    Life, 90
Applying the Adult Learning Cycle to
    Exploring Majors and Careers, 446
Asking Questions, 312
Checklist for Incorrect Test Answers, 252
Checklists for Writing Papers and Giving
    Speeches, 289
Creative Ideas Checklist, 324
Differences Between High School and
    College, 57
Digital Reading Material, 191
E-mail Etiquette with Instructors, 386
Eating Disorders, 351
Eating for Health and Energy, 347
Evaluating Online Information, 290
Explore Your Community's Resources, 129
Formal (Traditional) Versus Informal
    (Creative) Outlines, 157
From Knowledge to Evaluation, 308
Getting the Most Out of a Class Lecture, 163
How to Form a Study Group, 119

How to Generate Topic Ideas, 278
How to Say No, 96
Investing Your Time in High-Priority Items:
    The 80/20 Rule, 82
Important Words in Essay Questions, 256
Look It Up! Using the Dictionary, 194
Making Small Talk, 391
Online Learning, 98
Online Writing, 285
Overcoming Writers' Block, 283
Party with a Plan, 358
Preparing for a Performance
    Appraisal, 260
Problem-Solving Checklist, 328
Reading for Different Courses, 187
Reading with Children Around, 200
Remembering Names, 231
Service Learning, 442
Setting Goals, 56
Short-Term and Long-Term Memory, 221
Skills for School and Career, 60
Socially Acceptable Technology, 382
Special Strategies for Math and Science
    Tests, 251
Staying Safe, 124
Stress Leads to Burnout, 354
Taking Note of Special Challenges, 166
Taking Online Exams, 249
Team Players, 402
Thinking about Diversity, 399
To Highlight or Not to Highlight?, 189
Using Technology at School, 125
Using Test Results, 252
Using Your Textbook, 190
What Kind of Student/Worker Are You?, 61
Writing Citations, 286
Writing Do's: The Seven C's of Effective
    Writing, 284

Career in Focus
Setting Business Goals, 34
Positive Attitudes at Work, 66
Focus on Tasks, 102
Benefits of Community Resources, 142
Listening in the Workplace, 170
Keeping Up-to-Date, 204
Integrating Learning Styles, 236
Tests in the Workplace, 266
Communication Skills, 298
Creativity at Work, 332
Preventing Stress and Fatigue at
    Work, 370
Team Building at Work, 406
Good Habits in the Workplace, 430
Career Planning is Lifelong, 470

Peak Performer Profile

Scott Adams, 333
Christiane Amanpour, 67
Mark Herzlich, Jr., 371
Ursula Burns, 471
Ben Carson, M.D., 431
David Diaz, 237
Matthew Friedman and Adam Scott, 143
Malcolm Gladwell, 103
Christy Haubegger, 407
Toni Morrison, 299
Blake Mycoskie, 35
Ellen Ochoa, 267
Anna Sui, 171
Sonia Sotomayor, 205

Case Study

Conquering Fear of Failure, 335
Coping with Anxiety, 266
Developing Attentive Listening Skills, 173
Effective Reading Habits, 207
Exploring Careers, 473
Getting Motivated, 69
Increasing Your Energy Level, 373
Juggling Family and School, 105
Learning Communication Skills, 301
Making a Commitment, 37
Overcoming Memory Loss, 239
Spreading Good Habits, 433
Successful Teamwork, 409
Using Resources, 145

Worksheets

Analyzing Chapters, 213
Apply Bloom's Taxonomy, 337

Applying the ABC Method of Self-Management, 38, 70, 106, 146, 174, 208, 240, 270, 302, 336, 374, 410, 434, 474
Applying the Four-Temperament Profile, 41
Appreciating Diversity, 412
Are You Assertive, Aggressive, or Passive?, 413
Attitudes and Reading, 209
Breaking Barriers to Reading, 215
Checklist for Choosing a Major, 475
Community Resources, 148
Creating a Reading Outline, 212
Creating the Ideal Team, 40
Daily Prioritizer and Planner: Your To-Do List, 111
Developing Positive Habits, 435
Different Types of Reading, 210
Exam Schedule, 271
I Am What I Eat, 377
Informational Interview: What's the Job Like?, 477
Informational Interview: Who Are You Looking For?, 478
Learning Styles and Motivation, 73
Listening Self-Assessment, 175
Map Out Your Goals, 110
Memory, 241
Mental Pictures, 243
Mind Map a Lecture, 176
Mind Map Your Text, 214
Month/Semester Calendar, 113
Monthly Budget, 149
My Time Management Habits, 107
Networking, 147
Overcoming Resistance to Change, 436
Practice Goal Setting, 109

Practice Paraphrasing, 303
Preparing for Critical Thinking, 338
Preparing for Tests and Exams, 272
Preparing Your Resumé, 476
My Learning Style, Personality Types, and Temperament, 39
My Reinforcement Contract, 71
Self-Esteem Inventory, 72
Stress Performance Test, 375
Study Team Relationships, 411
Summarize and Teach, 211
Time Wasters, 108
Use the Cornell System of Note Taking, 177
Weekly Planner, 112
You Can Solve the Problem: Sue's Decision, 339

Career Development Portfolio

Applying Memory Skills, 244
Assessing and Demonstrating Your Critical Thinking Skills, 341
Assessing Your Relationship Skills, 414
Assessing your Skills and Competencies, 274
Assessment of Personal Qualities, 74
Autobiography, 41
Demonstrating Competencies, 216
Demonstrating Your Time-Management Skills, 114
Exploring Careers, 479
Inventory of Interests, 378
Listening and Note Taking in the Workplace, 178
Managing Resources, 150
Planning Your Career, 437
Your Writing and Speaking Skills, 304

Index

Reference books appear in Annotated Instructor's Edition only.

A

ABC Method of Self-Management, 7
Abilities, 445
Academic advisor, 117
Accompanying Web site. *See* Companion
  Web site
Accountant and financial planner, 34
Acquaintance rape, 366
Acronym, 225, 228
Acrostics, 225, 228, 235
Acrostics online, 235
Adams, Scott, 333
Addictions, 357–361
Admissions, records, and
  registration, 120
Adult learning cycle, 27–28
  attentive listener, 155
  communication, 398
  financial resources, 136
  habits, 426
  healthier lifestyle, 357
  lifelong learning, 28–29
  majors and careers, 446
  math and science anxiety, 329
  memory skills, 219
  public speaking, 294
  reading, 182
  self-control, 50
  test taking, 263
  time management, 90
Advising center, 120
Aerobic exercise, 351
Affirmation, 6, 54–55
Aggressive people, 383
AIDS/HIV, 364, 365
Alcohol, 348
Alcohol abuse, 357–358
ALEKS, 331
Alexander, Lloyd, 252
Ali, Muhammad, 315
All-or-nothing thinking, 313
Allen, David, 101
Alumni association, 123
Amanpour, Christiane, 67
Americans with Disabilities Act, 126
Analysis, 308
Analyzer, 21, 24
Anderson, Elizabeth Garrett, 424
Anorexia nervosa, 351
Application, 308
Aristotle, 418
Armstrong, Thomas, 17, 18

Art of Critical Reading, The (Mather/
  McCarthy), 188
Artistic people, 443
Asking questions, 312
Assertiveness, 356, 383, 384
Association, 225
Athletic programs and centers, 123
Attentive listening, 152–156, 381
Attitude, 51–53, 199–200, 398
Auditory learner, 13, 16
Autobiography, 41

B

Bailey, Covert, 346
Balancing family and work, 95–97
Baron, Renee, 26
Behaviors, 398
Belanoff, Patricia, 282
Bell, Eric Temple, 251
Bibliography, 279
Bibliography card, 279
Bill paying online, 141
Binge drinking, 358
Biography. *See* Career in focus; Peak
  performer profile
Birth control, 364–366
Blink (Gladwell), 103
Bloom, Benjamin, 306
Bloom's taxonomy, 306–307, 333
Bodily/kinesthetic intelligence, 17
Body language, 381
Bolles, Nelson, 440
Books, 289
Books online, 141
Brain function, 12
Brainstorming, 278, 315
Brainstorming notes, 317
Break projects into smaller
  tasks, 86, 91
Breathing methods, 355
Briggs, Katherine, 20
Brokaw, Tom, 465
Bubble tests, 250
Buddha, 49
Budget, 130–131, 132, 149
Bulimia nervosa, 351
Burke, Edmund, 188
Burnout, 354
Burns, Ursula, 471
Business professionals, 129
Byrd, Richard E., 139

C

Caffeine, 347, 349
Calendar, 83, 113
Cancer, 345, 346
Capsule biography. *See* Career in focus; Peak
  performer profile
Career center, 122, 445
Career development portfolio, 447–460.
  See also Career development portfolio
  (exercises)
    analysis of accomplishments, 451
    appendix, 459
    bibliography, 459
    contents page, 450
    cover letter, 459
    credentials, certificates, workshops, 458
    documentation, 453–454
    introduction, 450
    inventory of personal qualities, 452–453
    inventory of skills and competencies, 451
    list of significant life experiences, 450–451
    organization/assemblage, 447–449
    planning guide, 448
    reasons for, 447
    resumé, 455–457
    samples of work, 458
    summary of transcripts, 458
    title, or cover, page, 449–450
    when to start, 447
    work philosophy and goals, 454–455
Career development portfolio (exercises)
    assessing your skills and competencies,
      274
    assessment of personal qualities, 74
    autobiography, 41
    career action plan, 437
    careers, 479
    critical thinking skills, 341
    demonstrate competencies, 216
    interests, inventory of, 378
    listening/note taking in workplace, 178
    memory skills, 244
    relationship skills, 414
    resource management, 150
    time management skills, 114
    writing and speaking skills, 304
Career development portfolio elements, 449
Career development portfolio planning
  guide, 448
Career in focus
    accountant and financial planner, 34
    carpenter, 430

firefighter, 370
food scientist, 102
human resources director, 298
information technology specialist, 204
journalist, 236
marine biologist, 406
physical therapist, 266
psychologist, 170
restaurant owner, 332
sales representative, 66
school social worker, 142
social studies teacher/legislator, 470
Careers. *See* Majors and careers
Carpenter, 430
Carson, Ben, 431
Carter, Stephen, L., 45
Case studies
anxiety, 269
attentive listening skills, 173
careers, 473
commitment, 37
communication skills, 301
energy level, 373
fear of failure, 335
habits, 433
juggling family and school, 105
memory loss, 239
motivation, 69
reading habits, 207
resources, using, 145
teamwork, 409
Cell phone, 86
Chamber of Commerce, 129
Change. *See* Habits
Character, 45
Cheating, 45, 260–262
Chin, Beverley, 249
Chlamydia, 365
Chunking, 226
Cigarette smoking, 358–359
Citing sources, 283–285, 286–287
City Web site, 130
Civility, 45
Closed question, 312
Clubs, 119, 124
Codependency, 361
Coffee, 349
College vs. high school, 57
Combination note-taking system, 158–159, 161
Commitment contract, 427
Committed time, 77
Common ground, 380
Communication, 350. *See also* Relationships
Community of Writers, A (Elbow/Belanoff), 282
Community resources, 129–130, 148
Commuter students, 127–128
Compound interest, 135
Comprehension, 308

Compulsive gambling, 360
Conclusion (paper/speeches), 281
Confidence, 50–51, 416
Conflict resolution, 385–388
Constructive criticism, 388–390
Contextual clues, 195
Contraceptives, 364
Contract for change, 425–427
Conventional people, 445
Cornell system of note taking, 155–156, 158
Counseling center, 122
Courage to overcome, 424
Cover letter, 460, 461
Covey, Stephen, 101, 420
Craigslist, 382
Crazy Busy, Overstretched, Overbooked, and About to Snap! (Hallowell), 355
Creative ideas checklist, 324
Creative problem solving, 314–323
Creator, 25
Credit card debt, 131, 136
Credit counseling, 138
Credit report, 135
Crisis center, 130
Critical thinking and problem solving, 5–6, 305–341
creative ideas checklist, 324
creative problem solving, 314–323
critical thinking qualities, 310–312
critical thinking skills, 306–307
errors in judgment, 312–313
math and science applications, 323–329
problem-solving checklist, 328
problem-solving steps, 307–308
strategies, 309–312
Critical thinking qualities, 310–312
Critical thinking skills, 306–307
Criticism, 388–390
Cultural understanding, 397
Cunningham, Glen, 424
Cyberbullying, 382
Cyberstalking, 382

Daily energy levels, 88
Daily prioritizer and planner, 111
Daily to-do list, 83
Dante, 154
Date rape, 366
Day care, 96
Debold, Elizabeth, 153
Debt counseling, 138
Decisions, Decisions: The Art of Effective Decision Making (Welch), 308
Decoding, 199
Deductive reasoning, 311, 314
Deep breathing, 355
Definitions (glossary), 480–482
Depression, 361–362

Dewar, James, 389
Diabetes, 345
Diaz, David, 237
Dictionary, 194
Dietary Guidelines for Americans, 346
Differentiation through Learning Styles and Memory (Sprenger), 224
Digital readers, 191
"Dilbert," 333
Director, 25–26
Disabilities, students with, 126–127
Discipline, 419
Discouraged, 60–62
Discretionary time, 77
Discrimination, 397, 398
Distracted driving, 361
Distraction, 224
Diversity, 396–402
Dropping out, 62
Drucker, Peter, 276
Drug abuse, 359–360
Dryden, John, 425
Dyslexia, 199

E

eBay, 382
e-birthday card, 405
E-mail etiquette, 386
Eating disorders, 351
Eating habits, 377
Ebbinghaus's forgetting curve, 165
Edison, Thomas, 30
Edit, 282–285
Education, 58–59
80/20 rule, 82–83
Einstein, Albert, 314
Einstein's riddle, 314
Elbow, Peter, 282
Electronic journal, 33
Ellerbee, Linda, 399
Ellis, Albert, 8
Embarrassment, 425
Emergency kit, 128
Emerson, Ralph Waldo, 130
Emotional health, 361–363
Emotional intelligence, 44
Emotional Intelligence (Goleman), 44
Emotional maturity, 44
Empathy, 387
Employment interview, 460–463
English speakers of other languages (ESL), 196
Enneagram Made Easy, The (Baron/Wagele), 26
Enterprising people, 443–445
Environmental intelligence, 17
Errors in judgment, 312–313
Essay tests, 254–257
Ethics, 45

Ethics information, 65
Evaluating online information, 290
Evaluation, 308
Evaluator, 120
Exam schedule, 271
Exchange programs, 122–123
Exercises. *See* Career development portfolio
    (exercises); Personal evaluation
    notebook; Worksheets
Expectations, 57
Experiential Learning (Kolb), 27
External locus of control, 47
Extrovert, 19, 21
Eye contact, 291, 390, 462

F

Facebook, 382, 461
Fact-finding question, 312
Failure, 322–323
Fair use, 288
Fear of the unknown, 423
Feedback question, 312
Feeler, 20, 21
Fill-in-the-blank tests, 254
Final draft, 282–283
Financial aid, 131, 133–134
Financial resources, 130–139
Firefighter, 370
Five-part reading system, 181–183, 185–187
Flu (influenza), 345
Follow-up letter, 463
Follow-up question, 312
Food scientist, 102
Forbes, Malcolm, 58
Ford, Henry, 167
Formal outline, 157
Forms, 198–199
Four-temperament profile, 20–26
    analyzer, 21, 24
    creator, 25
    director, 25–26
    personal evaluation notebook, 22–23
    supporter, 24–25
*Frames of Mind: The Theory of Multiple
    Intelligences* (Gardner), 17, 18
France, Anatole, 219
Franklin, Benjamin, 90, 419
Freewriting, 278, 283
Friedman, Matthew, 143

G

Galbraith, John Kenneth, 348
Gambling, 360
Gardner, Howard, 17, 18
Genital herpes, 365
Genital warts, 365
Gide, Andrew, 180

Gladwell, Malcolm, 103
Glossary, 480–482
Goal setting, 56, 109
Goal-setting examples, 65
Goal-setting flowchart, 110
Goals, 80–81
Goldberg, Natalie, 283
Golden rule, 45
Goleman, Daniel, 44
Gonorrhea, 365
Government officials, 129
Government organizations, 446
Grateful, 419
Green jobs, 464

H

Habits, 415–437
    adult learning cycle, 426
    attitude, 419–420
    contract for change, 425–427
    creating positive change, 420–423
    defined, 416–417
    inspiration, 429
    online, 429
    peak performers, of, 417–419
    resistance to change, 423–426, 436
Hallowell, Edward, 355
Halo effect, 313
Haubegger, Christy, 407
Haveson, Randy, 358
Health and wellness, 343–378
    addictions, 357–361
    adult learning cycle, 357
    alcohol abuse, 357–358
    awareness and prevention, 345
    birth control, 364–366
    cigarette smoking, 358–359
    codependency, 361
    connecting mind, body, spirit, 344–345
    depression, 361–362
    drug abuse, 359–360
    eating disorders, 351
    eating habits, 377
    emotional health, 361–363
    illegal drug use, 359
    rape, 366–367
    STIs, 364, 365
    strategies, 346–353
    stress management, 353–356
    stress performance test, 375–376
    suicide, 362–363
Health care, 129
Health center, 122
Healthy foods, 346
Helping organizations, 130
Herpes, 365
Herstein, I. N., 306
Herzlich, Mark, Jr., 371
Hierarchy of needs, 52

High-energy time, 87–88, 93
High school vs. college, 57
Higher education, 58–59
Highlighting, 189
Hippocrates, 19
HIV, 364, 365
H1N1 flu, 345
Holland, John L., 443
Holmes, Oliver Wendall, 328
Holt, John, 306
Holtz, Lou, 7
Homophobia, 397
Houses of worship, 129
How to Ace Any Test (Chin), 249
*How to Get Control of Your Time and Your
    Life* (Lakein), 76
How to Study in College (Pauk), 155
Hsi-Tang Chih Tsang, 465
Human resources director, 298
Humor, 381, 391
Huxley, Aldous, 232

I

"I" statement, 49, 387
Iacocca, Lee, 152
Identity theft, 131, 135
Illegal drug use, 359
Important priorities, 81
Incivility, 45
Inclusion, 401
Incorrect test answers, 252
Inductive reasoning, 311, 314
Influenza, 345
Informal outline, 157
Information technology specialist, 204
Informational interview
    what's the job like, 477
    who are you looking for, 478
Instructors, 118
Instructor's visual presentation, 169
Integrating College Study Skills
    (Sotiriou), 160
Integrity, 45
Integrity and Civility (Carter), 45
Intelligence, 16–18
Interests, 443
Interests, inventory of, 378
Internal locus of control, 47
International and exchange programs,
    122–123
Interpersonal intelligence, 17–18
Interruptions, 93–95
Intrapersonal intelligence, 17
Introduction (paper/speeches), 281
Introvert, 19, 21
Intuitive, 19, 21
Inventory of interests, 378
Investigative people, 443
Irrational thoughts, 293

J

James, William, 27
Job interview, 460–463
Job placement services, 129
Job-related satisfiers, 52
Job search Web sites, 469
Job trends, 464
Jobs. *See* Majors and careers
Johnson, Lady Bird, 290
Jordan, Michael, 62
Journal, 316, 356
Journalist, 236
Judger, 20, 21, 316
Juggling family, school, job, 95–97
Jung, Carl, 5, 19

K

Kaiser, Henry, 451
Kinesthetic learner, 16
King, Martin Luther, Jr., 327
Kitt, Eartha, 447
Knowledge, 308
Kolb, David, 27

L

Lakein, Alan, 76
L'Amour, Louis, 225
Laptop, 164
Last Lecture, The (Pausch), 97
Last-minute study tips, 257–258
Laughter, 356
Learn to Be an Optimist (MacDonald), 344
Learned Optimism (Seligman), 63
Learning a new language, 195–196
Learning center, 121
Learning disability, 127
Learning style
    auditory learner, 13, 16
    instructor's teaching style, and, 29–30
    kinesthetic learner, 16
    personality type, and, 20–26
    time management, and, 89–90
    visual learner, 13
    worksheet, 39
Learning style inventory, 14–15
Lectures, 163
Lee, Bruce, 419
Left-brain dominant, 12
Letter of recommendation, 457, 458
Library, 121–122, 287–289, 445
Life goals, 99
Lincoln, Abraham, 45, 424
LinkedIn, 461
Listening, 152–156, 381
Listening self-assessment, 175
Loans, 133
Local newspapers, etc., 130

Locus of control, 47
Logical/mathematical intelligence, 17
Lombardi, Vince, 258
Loneliness, 362
Long-term memory, 221
Love/belonging needs, 52
Lucas, George, 443
Luft, Lorna, 361

M

Macaulay, Thomas, 46
MacDonald, Lucy, 344
Main body (paper/speeches), 281
Maintenance time, 77
Majors and careers, 439–479
    adult learning cycle, 446
    career development portfolio. *See* Career
        development portfolio
    choosing a major, 440–442
    cover letter, 460, 461
    exploring careers, 445–446
    job interview, 460–463
    skills, 60
    take charge of your career, 463–465
    values, interests, abilities, skills,
        443–445
Malcolm X, 200
Management gurus, 101
Mann, Merlin, 101
Manuals, 197–198
Marijuana, 359
Marine biologist, 406
Maslow, Abraham, 52
Maslow's hierarchy of needs, 52
Mason, Douglas, 218
Matching tests, 254
Math and science anxiety, 327–328, 329
Math and science applications, 323–329
Math and science tests, 251
Mather, Peter, 188
Maturity, 44
MBTI, 20
McCarthy, Rita, 188
Mediterranean diet food pyramid, 347
Memorization, 221
Memory Doctor, The (Mason/Smith), 218
Memory process, 218–221
Memory skills, 217–244
    adult learning cycle, 219
    memory process, 218–221
    memory strategies, 222–231
    mind map, 223
    names, 231
    obstacles, 232
    questions to answer, 232–233
    short-term/long-term memory, 221
    summarize, review, reflect, 231–232
Memory strategies, 222–231
Mental pictures, 243

Mentor, 118
Method, 416
Method-of-place technique, 227
Michener, James, 282
Mind map, 156, 158, 160, 223, 278, 283
Mind set, 318
Mini-vacation, 355
Mission statement, 8–9, 454
Mission statement business cards, 33
Mnemonic devices, 225
*Money Book for the Young, Fabulous &
    Broke, The* (Orman), 135
Money in/money out, 132
Month/semester calendar, 113
Monthly budget, 130–131, 132, 149
Morgenstern, Julie, 83
Morrison, Toni, 299
Motivation, 51–53
Motivation cycle, 54
Motivational strategies, 54–58
Multicultural centers, 122
Multiple-choice tests, 253
Multiple intelligences, 16–18
Multitasking, 30
Musical intelligence, 17
Mycoskie, Blake, 35
Myers, Isabel Briggs, 20
Myers-Briggs Type Indicator (MBTI), 20
MyPyramid, 348
MySpace, 461

N

Nabokov, Vladimir, 276
Native American students, financial
    aid, 134
Negative attitude, 51–52
Negative labeling, 313
Negative thoughts, 354
Networking, 118–120, 147, 385, 446, 465
*New Earth: Awakening to Your Life's Purpose,
    A* (Tolle), 465
New Guide to Rational Living, A (Ellis), 8
New language, 195–196
News online, 203
Nine-dot exercise, 316, 330
9 Steps to Financial Freedom (Orman), 135
New language, 195–196
Nontraditional students, 128
Note cards, 162, 228
Note taking, 154–167
    assess/review your notes, 164–166
    combination system, 158–159, 161
    Cornell system, 155–156, 158
    mind map, 156, 158, 160
    obstacles, 166–167
    shortcuts, 164
    strategies, 159–164, 166–167
    writing process, 278–279
Note-taking shortcuts, 164

O

Obesity, 345
Objective tests, 253–254
Obstacles. *See* Overcoming obstacles
Occupational Outlook Handbook, 446
Ochoa, Ellen, 267
Ongoing activities, 82
Online discussion groups, 65
Online exams, 249
Online information, evaluating, 290
Online learning, 98
Online search, 290–291
Online self-assessments, 33
Online tutors, 265
Online writing, 285
Open-book tests, 254
Open-ended question, 312
Oral presentations. *See* Writing and speeches
Organization, 88–89
Organizing from the Inside Out (Morgenstern), 83
Orientation guide, 126
Orman, Suze, 135
Ornstein, Robert, 423
Outliers (Gladwell), 103
Outline, 157, 188, 279, 280
Over-the-counter medication abuse, 359–360
Overcoming Barricades to Reading (Teele), 189
Overcoming Math Anxiety (Tobias), 259
Overcoming obstacles
    cheating, 260–262
    communication, 392
    discouraged, 60–62
    interruptions, 93–95
    learning style/instructor's teaching style, 29–30
    make it simple, 30–31
    memory, 232
    note taking, 166–167
    positive mind shifts, 62–63
    procrastination, 91–93
    reading difficulties, 199
    test anxiety, 258–260

P

Papers and speeches. *See* Writing and speeches
Paraphrasing, 154
Pareto principle, 82
Party with a Plan, 358
Passive-aggressive people, 383
Passive people, 383
Patience, 423
Pauk, Walter, 155
Pausch, Randy, 97
Payday loans, 137
Peak Performance competency wheel, 9
Peak Performance learning pyramid, 27

Peak Performance self-assessment test, 10–11
Peak Performance success formula, 416
Peak performer, 2–3
Peak Performer Profile
    Adams, Scott, 333
    Amanpour, Christiane, 67
    Burns, Ursula, 471
    Carson, Ben, 431
    Diaz, David, 237
    Friedman, Matthew, 143
    Gladwell, Malcolm, 103
    Haubegger, Christy, 407
    Herzlich, Mark, Jr., 371
    Morrison, Toni, 299
    Mycoskie, Blake, 35
    Ochoa, Ellen, 267
    Scott, Adam, 143
    Sotomayer, Sonia, 205
    Sui, Anna, 171
Peer pressure, 362
Peers, 118
Pell grants, 133
Penn, William, 76
People resources, 117–120
Perceiver, 20, 21, 316
Perceptual distortion, 315
Performance appraisal, 260
Performance strategies
    career planning, 469
    creative thinking and problem solving, 331
    emotional intelligence/personal qualities, 65
    habits, 429
    healthy lifestyle, 369
    lifelong learner, 33
    memory, 235
    note taking, 169
    papers and speeches, 297
    reading, 203
    relationships, 405
    resource maximization, 141
    test taking, 265
    time management, 101
Periodicals, 289
Persistence, 310, 423
Personal digital assistant (PDA), 86
Personal evaluation notebook
    acronyms/acrostics, 228
    activities and clubs, 124
    assertive communication role-playing, 384
    assessment is lifelong, 466–467
    attentive listening, 156
    brainstorming notes, 317
    character and ethics, 47
    commitment contract, 427
    conflict, 388, 389
    critical thinking, 311
    daily energy levels, 88

decision-making application, 319–320
diversity, 400
essay test preparation, 257
four-temperament profile, 22–23
goals, 80–81
habits, 421–422
health and wellness, 350
inductive vs. deductive reasoning, 314
interruptions, 94
learning style inventory, 14–15
learning styles and memory, 227
life goals, 99
memory assessment, 226
mind map, 223
mind set, 318
money in/money out, 132
multiple intelligences, 18
needs, motivation, and commitment, 53
nine-dot exercise, 316
observation, 220
peak performance self-assessment test, 10–11
personal qualities, inventory of, 453
physical exercise, 353
plagiarism vs. fair use, 288
positive person, 4
procrastination, 92
relationships, 393, 395
research papers, 280
rest, 352
self-talk and affirmations, 55
skills and personal qualities, 48
socially acceptable names, 401
solving problems/making choices, 321–322
SQ3R reading system, 185–187
test anxiety, 261–262
test taking, 247
think it through, 309
time, how spent, 79
time log, 78, 79
transferable skills, 452
values, 444
walk down memory lane, 229–230
Personal mission statement, 8–9
Personal motivation, 51–53
Personal performance review, 464
Personal responsibilities, 48
Personal time-out, 101
Personality type, 19–20, 39
Physical activity, 351
Physical exercise, 353
Physical therapist, 266
Physiological needs, 52
Picasso, Pablo, 425
Plagiarism, 45, 283, 288
Planner, 84–85, 112
PLUS loans, 133
Podcasts, 164
Political parties, 129
Portfolio cover letter, 459

Positive attitude, 51, 93, 199–200, 309–310
Positive mind shifts, 62–63
Positive person, 4
Positive self-talk, 390
Positive time, 97
Powell, Colin, 417
PowerPoint presentations, 293
Prejudice, 398
Prescription and over-the-counter
    medication abuse, 359–360
Priorities, 81–82
Problem solving. *See* Critical thinking and
    problem solving
Problem-solving checklist, 328
Problem-solving steps, 307–308
Procrastination, 91–93, 459
Professional organizations, 446
Program resources, 120–123
Project board, 87
Projection, 313
Prompters, 292
Proofreading, 285
Psychological Types (Jung), 19
Psychologist, 170
Public speaking. *See* Writing and speeches
Public speaking strategies, 291–292

Q

Quiet time, 94

R

Racial profiling, 397
Rap, 225
Rape, 366–367
Rapport, 380–382
Readers' Guide to Periodical Literature,
    278, 289
Reading, 179–216
    adult learning cycle, 182
    attitude, 199–200
    different courses, 187
    five-part reading system, 181–183,
        185–187
    forms, 198–199
    importance, 180
    manuals, 197–198
    new language, 195–196
    obstacles, 199–201
    reviewing strategies, 190–193
    sample notes, 192
    speed, 199
    SQ3R reading system, 183–184
    strategies, 184, 188–190
    tasks involved, 180
    technical material, 196–197
    vocabulary building, 193–195
    when children are around, 201
Realistic people, 443

"Really Achieving Your Childhood Dreams"
    (Pausch), 97
Reasoning, 310–312
Recite, 228
Recreation center, 129
Reference materials, 289
Reflection, 6–7
Reframing, 58
Reinforcement contract, 71
Relationships, 379–414
    adult learning cycle, 398
    assertiveness, 383, 384
    communication/rapport, 380–382
    conflict resolution, 385–388
    criticism, 388–390
    diversity, 396–402
    health and wellness, 352
    instructors/advisors, 383–385, 386
    obstacles, 392
    people you live with, 394–396
    romantic, 392–394
    sexual harassment, 402–403
    shyness, 390–392
    small talk, 391
Remembering names, 231
Request for letter of recommendation, 457
Research, 287–291
Research papers, 280. *See also* Writing and
    speeches
Resilience, 60
Resistance to change, 423–425, 436
Resource maximization, 115–150
    additional online/information services,
        123–126
    community resources, 129–130
    commuter students, 127–128
    financial resources, 130–139
    people resources, 117–120
    program resources, 120–123
    returning students, 128–129
    students with disabilities, 126–127
    yourself as resource, 139
Respect, 381
Responsibility, 46–49
Rest, 352
Restaurant owner, 332
Resumé, 455–457, 476
Resumé online, 469
Returning students, 128–129
Review, 285–287
Reviewing strategies, 190–193
Revise, 282
Reward yourself, 58, 93, 423
Rhyme, 225
Rhythms, 225
Right-brain dominant, 12
Rohn, Jim, 83
Romantic relationships, 392–394
Roommate, 394
Roosevelt, Eleanor, 51
Rowan, Carl T., 121

S

Safety, 124
Safety and security needs, 52
Sagan, Carl, 314
Salaries, 59
Sales representative, 66
Sample tests, 248
Sandburg, Carl, 93
Saving money, 135–137
Saying no, 95, 96
SBA, 129–130
SCANS, xx–xxi, 9
SCANS skills, xx–xxi, 452
Scantron tests, 250
Schedule of classes, 126
Scholarships and grants, 133
School. *See* Majors and careers
School catalog, 125
School newspaper, 126
School social worker, 142
Schopenhauer, Arthur, 81
Schweitzer, Albert, 440
Scott, Adam, 143
Secretary's Commission on Achieving
    Necessary Skills (SCANS), xx–xxi, 9
Security/police department, 123
Self-actualization, 52
Self-assessment, 3–5
Self-control, 49–50
Self-esteem, 50
Self-esteem inventory, 72
Self-esteem needs, 52
Self-evaluation. *See* Personal evaluation
    notebook
Self-management, 1, 3–11
Self-talk, 55
Seligman, Martin, 63
Selye, Hans, 353
Semester calendar, 101
Seneca, Lucius Annaeus, 83
Sense of humor, 356
Sensor, 19, 21
Service learning, 123, 442
Setting goals, 56
7 Habits of Highly Effective People, The
    (Covey), 420
*7 Kinds of Smart: Identifying and
    Developing Your Many Intelligences*
    (Armstrong), 17
Sexism, 397
Sexting, 382
Sexual harassment, 402–403
Sexually transmitted infections (STIs), 364,
    365
Short-term memory, 221
Shyness, 390–392
Simplicity, 30–31
Skills, 445
Skills for school and career, 60
SLS, 133

Small Business Administration (SBA), 129–130
Small talk, 391
Smileys, 386, 405
Smith, Spencer, 218
Smoking, 358–359
Snacks, 128
Snap judgment, 313
Social people, 443
Social studies teacher/legislator, 470
Socially acceptable technology, 382
Sotiriou, Peter, 160
Sotomayer, Sonia, 205
Spatial intelligence, 17
Specialized libraries, 122
Specialized reading, 196–199
Speech anxiety, 292–294, 295
Speech evaluation form, 293
Speeches. *See* Writing and speeches
Spell check, 297
Sperry, Roger, 12
Sprenger, Marilee, 224
SQ3R reading system, 183–184, 185–187
Stacking technique, 226–227
Stafford and Perkins loans, 133
Stereotype, 313, 398
STIs, 364, 365
Stored memory, 235
Strategies. *See* Performance strategies
Stress management, 353–356
Stress performance test, 375–376
Stress-reduction techniques, 294
Student activities office, 122–123
Student union, 123
Students with disabilities, 126–127
Study group, 119
Stuwe, T. C., 308
Success, 416
Sui, Anna, 171
Suicide, 362–363
Summarize on your computer, 169
Summarizing out loud, 190
Summary. *See* Performance strategies
Supplemental loans for students (SLS), 133
Support groups, 130
Support system, 63, 355
Supporter, 24–25
Supportive people, 92–93
Sweeping generalization, 313
Swine flu, 345
Synthesis, 308
Syphilis, 365

T

Taking notes. *See* Note taking
Taxonomy of Educational Objectives (Bloom), 306
Team, 402
Technical material, 196–197

Technology, 125
Teele, Sue, 189
Temperament. *See* Four-temperament profile
10,000 hour rule, 103
Terminology (glossary), 480–482
Test anxiety, 258–260, 261–262
Test taking, 245–274
    adult learning cycle, 263
    cheating, 260–262
    essay tests, 254–257
    fill-in-the-blank tests, 254
    incorrect test answers, 252
    last-minute study tips, 257–258
    matching tests, 254
    math and science tests, 251
    multiple-choice tests, 253
    objective tests, 253–254
    online exams, 249
    open-book tests, 254
    questions to answer, 252
    strategies, 246–252
    test anxiety, 258–260, 261–262
    true/false tests, 253
Text Web site. *See* Companion Web site
Textbook accompaniments, 265
Textbooks, 191
Texting: 260, 361
Thackeray, William Makepeace, 281
Thank-you note, 463
Their Own Way: Discovering and Encouraging Your Child's Personal Learning Style (Armstrong), 18
Thesis statement, 278
Thinker, 20, 21
Thoreau, Henry David, 315
Time log, 78, 79
Time management, 75–114
    adult learning cycle, 90
    80/20 rule, 82–83
    interruptions, 93–95
    juggling family, school, job, 95–97
    learning style, 89–90
    priorities, 81–82
    procrastination, 91–93
    strategies, 83–89
    time log, 78, 79
Time wasters, 108
Tipping Point, The (Gladwell), 103
To-do list, 83
Tobias, Sheila, 259
Tolle, Eckhart, 465
TOMS, 35
Topic generation, 278
Tradition, 424
Training, 416
Transferable skills, 452
Trichomoniasis, 365
Trivial activities, 82
True/false tests, 253
Turnitin, 288

Twain, Mark, 463
Twitter, 382, 461
2-1-1, 130

U

Ultimate Fit or Fat, The (Bailey), 346
Unhealthy addictions, 357–361
United Way, 130
Unwarranted assumption, 313
Urgent priorities, 81

V

Values, 443, 444
Verbal/linguistic intelligence, 17
Veterans' programs, 133
Vision, 416
Visual aids, 297
Visual cues, 165
Visual learner, 13
Visualization, 6, 55
Vocabulary building, 193–195
von Oech, Roger, 322

W

Wagele, Elizabeth, 26
Washington, Booker T., 2
Washington, Denzel, 357
Water, 348
Web sites and textbooks, 141
Weekly planner, 112
Welch, David, 308
Whack on the Side of the Head, A (von Oech), 322
What Color is Your Parachute? (Bolles), 440
Wilde, Oscar, 218
Wilson, Earl, 138
Win-win solutions, 49
Winfrey, Oprah, 392
Word parts, 195
Work-study program, 133
Worksheets
    assertive, aggressive, passive?, 413
    attitudes and reading, 209
    Bloom's taxonomy, 337
    community resources, 148
    Cornell system of note taking, 177
    critical thinking, 338
    daily prioritizer and planner, 111
    diversity, 412
    eating habits, 377
    exam schedule, 271
    goal setting, 109
    goal-setting flowchart, 110
    habits, 434–436
    informational interview (what's the job like), 477

informational interview (who are you looking for), 478
learning style, 39
learning styles and motivation, 73
listening self-assessment, 175
majors and careers, 474–478
memory, 240–243
mental pictures, 243
mind map, 176, 214
month/semester calendar, 113
monthly budget, 149
networking, 147
papers and speeches, 302, 303
paraphrasing, 303
personality type, 39
problem solving, 339–340
reading, 209–215
reading online, 212
reinforcement contract, 71
resistance to change, 436
resumé, 476

self-esteem inventory, 72
stress performance test, 375–376
summarize and teach, 211
team, 40
team relationships, 411
temperament, 39
test taking, 270–273
time management habits, 107
time wasters, 108
weekly planner, 112
Wright, Steven, 193
Write it down, 222
Writer's block, 283, 295
Writing and speeches, 275–304
    checklist, 289
    citations, 283–285, 286–287
    evaluating online information, 290
    importance, 276
    online writing, 285
    plagiarism vs. fair use, 288
    PowerPoint presentations, 293

public speaking strategies, 291–292
research, 287–291
seven C's of effective writing, 284
speech anxiety, 292–294, 295
topic generation, 278
writer's block, 283, 295
writing process. *See* Writing process
Writing Down the Bones: Freeing the Writer Within (Goldberg), 283
Writing process
    edit, 282–285
    organize, 279–280
    prepare, 276–279
    review, 285–287
    write, 281
Writing pyramid, 281

Y

"You" statement, 387
YouTube, 461

Your School's Resources

Check your school's Web site, look through the catalog, or go to student services to determine which resources are available, especially those that are of particular interest to you and your needs. In the "Notes" section, include information such as location, office hours, fees, and so on. *These services are for you, so use them!*

Resource	Notes	Contact/phone/e-mail
Activities/Clubs Office		
Adult and Re-entry Center		
Advising Center		
Alumni Office		
Art Gallery/Museum		
Bookstore		
Career Center/Employment Services		
Chaplain/Religious Services		
Child Care Center		
Cinema/Theater		
Computer Lab(s)		
Continuing Education		
Disability Center (learning or physical disabilities)		
Distance Learning		
Financial Aid		
Health Clinic		
Honors Program		
Housing Center		
Information Center		
Intramural Sports		
Language Lab		

(continued)

Resource	Notes	Contact/phone/e-mail
Learning Center		
Library Services		
Lost and Found		
Math Lab		
Multicultural Center		
Off-Campus Housing and Services		
Ombudsman/Conflict Resolution		
Performing Arts Center		
Photography Lab		
Police/Campus Security		
Post Office/Delivery Services		
Printing/Copying Center		
Registration Office		
School Newspaper		
Student Government Office		
Study Abroad/Exchange		
Testing Center		
Tutorial Services		
Volunteer Services		
Wellness and Recreation Center/Gymnasium		
Work-Study Center		
Writing Lab		
Other:		
Other:		
Other:		

7. (a) 9.7, (b) 22.7, (c) 42.5
9. -0.68 V
11. 1×10^{-7}
13. 10
15. (a) H_2 and $AgCl$, (b) 0.2000, (c) 0.32 A

17. (a) 0.175, (b) 0.73, (c) 54
19. (a) 11.5, (b) 10.0, (c) 8.96
21. 0.00050-M
23. 0.00050-M
25. 9.5×10^{-6} cm^2/s

CHAPTER 11   Spectrophotometry

1. (a) 2, 0, (b) infinite
3. (a) 0.0043, (b) 0.124, (c) 0.301, (d) 1.00, (e) 2.00
5. (a) 28, (b) 78, (c) 98
7. (a) 1×10^7, (b) 3×10^{17}
9. 0.060
11. 2.06
13. 4.97

15. (a) -21.7, (b) -4.3, (c) -2.9, (d) -5.4, (e) -100
17. (a) 0.301, (b) 10, 50
19. (a) 0.54 %, (b) 0.14 %
21. 1.8×10^9
23. MX_2
25. 6.63

CHAPTER 13   Solvent Extraction

1. (a) 90.9, (b) 97.2
3. 15.69
5. (a) 6.2×10^{-6}, (b) 3.1×10^{-4}, 6.2×10^{-3}, 6.2×10^{-2}, 0.31, and 0.62
7. 10
9. (b) 4.00, 4.76, 5.00, 5.24, 6.00, 6.50. At pH 4.00, 99 % of M^{2+} is extracted along with 1 % of N^{2+}

11. HA: 9.1, 5.0, 0.91, 0.10, 0.010, 0.0010, 0.00010; HB: 10^3, 10^3, 10^3, 10^3, 990, 909, 500. At pH 9 about 99.9 % of HB is extracted along with only 0.1 % of HA

CHAPTER 16   Analog Electronics

1. (a) 10^{10} electrons; (b) 1.6×10^{-9} coulombs; (c) 16 μA
3. 10 ohms
5. (a) 0.2 mA, (b) 1 kΩ, (c) 3 V, (d) 8 A, (e) 20 MΩ, (f) 1000 V

7. (a) 60 kΩ, (b) 10 kΩ, (c) 10 kΩ, (d) 22.5 kΩ

CHAPTER 17   Digital Electronics and Computers

1. (a) 110000, (b) 11000011, (c) 110, (d) 101
3. 4, 16, 6.3
   5, 32, 3.1
   6, 64, 1.6

7, 128, 0.78
8, 256, 0.39
9, 512, 0.20
10, 1024, 0.10

5. (a)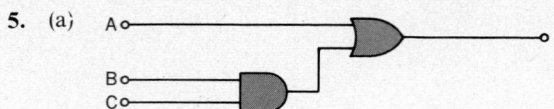

(b)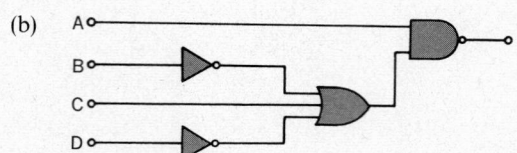

(c)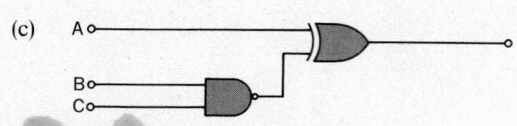

(d)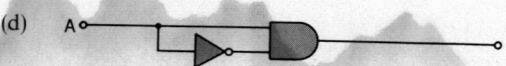

7.

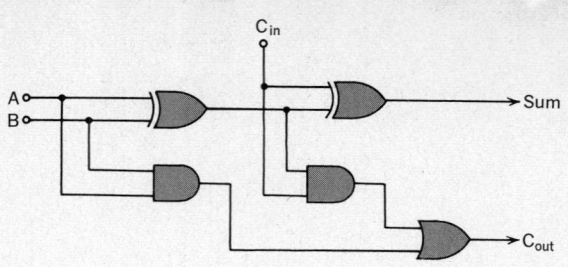

9.

Y	DZM	X
	INA	Y
	JMP	Y
X	—	

Location	Contents
0	030003_8
1	020000_8
2	100000_8
3	—

Index

Absolute method, in polarography, 288
Absolute stability constant, 138
Absorbance, 309
Absorption, self, in fluorescence, 340
Absorption of radiant energy by molecules, 298
Absorption spectra, 328
Absorptivity, 309
Accuracy, 39
Acetate, distribution of species as function of pH, 126
Acid-base:
  calculations, nature of approximations in, 106
  dissociation, 73
  dissociation constants, 80
    (table), 502
  indicators, 88
    (table), 91
  neutralization, 75
  species, distribution of as function of pH, 126
Acids:
  definition, 73
  dissociation of, 73
  dissociation constants of, 80
    (table), 502
  solvent extraction of, 362
Activity, 77
Activity coefficients, 78
  (table), 79
Adder:
  analog, 464
  digital, 486
Addition, binary, 475, 486
Adsorbability of solutes, factors in, 426
Adsorption, 165, 425
  indicators, 165
    (table), 167

Adsorption (*cont.*)
  of ions on precipitates, 187
  isotherm, 425
Aging of precipitates, 192
Amino acids:
  determination of by GLC, 421
  separation of by paper chromatography, 435
Ampere, 26, 444
Amperometric titration, 289
Amplification factor, 459
Amplifiers, operational, 456
  current-to-voltage converter, 460
  differential, 464
  differentiator, 467
  follower-with-gain, 459
  integrator, 466
  inverter, 461
  summing, 464
  voltage follower, 457
Analog-to-digital conversion, 477
Analog information, 472
Analytical chemistry, 1
AND function, 482
Angstrom unit, 297
Anion exchange resins, 428
Anion interferences in flame photometry, 354
Anode, definition, 263
Anodic waves, in polarography, 287
Arithmetic unit, 492
Arsonic acids, 186
Aspirator-burner, 351
Assembly-language programming, 496
Asymmetry potential, of glass electrode, 244
Atomic absorption spectrophotometer (diagram), 356
Atomic weights (table), 510

Atomization, in flame photometry, 351
Automatic titrator, 468
Autoprotolysis constant, 80
Average deviation, 46
Avogadro's number, 6

Balancing equations, 23
Band spectra, 349
Bases:
  definition, 73
  dissociation of, 74
  dissociation constants of, 80
    (table), 502
BASIC, 497
Beer's law, 307
  deviations from, 309
Benzidine, 185
α-Benzoin oxime, 184
Beta-ray ionization detector, 417
Binary addition, 475, 486
Binary-decimal correspondence, 475
Binary digits, 476
Binary number system, 474
Binomial distribution, in Craig extraction, 371
Bit, 476
Bouguer-Beer law, 307
Bouguer's law, 306
Bromide, titration with silver ion, 161
Brønsted acid-base theory, 73
Buffer:
  capacity, 98
  definition, 96
  metal ion, 150
  physiological, 99
  selection of, 98
Buffers for pH standards (table), 250
Burner, for flame photometry, 351

Calomel electrode, 215
Capacitance, 445
Capillary column, 408
Carbonate titrations, 123
Carrier gas in GLC, 406
Cathode:
  definition, 263
  mercury, 268
Cathodic waves, in polarography, 286
Cation enhancement, in flame photometry, 354
Cation exchange resins, 427
Cells (for grouping data), 41
Central processing unit, 492
Central tendency, 45
Chelate compounds, 181
Chelate rings, 133
Chelates:
  separation of metal by GLC, 421
  solvent extraction of metal, 363
Chelometric titrations, 136
Chelons, 136
Chloride:
  titration with mercuric ion, 151
  titration with silver ion, 160
Chopper, beam:
  in atomic absorption spectrophotometer, 357
  in spectrophotometer, 323
Chromate, as indicator in chloride titration with silver
    ion, 162

Chromatography:
  classification, 385
  definition, 385
Chromophore, 305
Closed-loop control, 497
Coefficient of variation, 47
Colloids:
  adsorption on, 187
  coagulation of, 188
  lyophilic, 188
  particle size of, 186
Column, in GLC, 407
Common, 444
Common-ion effect on solubility, 168
Complementary colors, 298
Complexes:
  effect on chelometric titrations, 144
  effect on potentials, 219
  effect on solubility of precipitates, 179
Computation rules, 64
Computers, 489
Concentration overpotential, 266
Concentrations of solutions, 5
Confidence interval of the mean, 49
Confidence limits, 49
Conjugate acid-base pair, 73
Continuous information, 472
Continuous spectra, 348
Control charts, 58
Controlled potential coulometry, 273
Controlled potential electrolysis, 270
Control limits, 59
Conventions for electrochemical cells, 210
Coordination number, 132
Coprecipitation, 193
  minimization of, 195
Core memory, 491
Coulomb, 26, 444
Coulometer, 273
Coulometric titration, 274
Countercurrent extraction, 368
Craig apparatus, 376
Craig extraction, 367
  as model for continuous separation processes, 378
Crystalline precipitates, purity, 193
Cupferron, 184
Curdy precipitates, purity, 194
Current, 433
Current-to-voltage converter, 460
Cyanide, titration with silver, 153

Dark current, in spectrophotometers, 321
DC arc, as emission source, 349
Debye-Hückel limiting law, 171
Debye-Hückel theory, 78
Decimal-binary correspondence, 475
Decomposition potential, 264
Degrees of freedom, 49
Detectors for GLC, 409
  for spectrophotometry, 318
Dextrans, as gel filtration materials, 431
Differential amplifier, 464
Differential detector, 409
Differential spectrophotometry, 321
Differentiator, 467
Diffraction grating, 315
Diffusion coefficients in GLC, 394

Diffusion current, 280, 283
Digital-to-analog conversion, 480
Digital computers, 489
Digital information, 472
Digital logic, 481
Dimethylglyoxime, 184
Diphenylamine, as oxidation-reduction indicator, 231
Diphenylcarbazide, 152
Diphenylcarbazone, 152
Discrete information, 472
Dissociation constants of acids and bases, 80
  (table), 502
Distribution coefficient:
  in GLC, 288
    correlation with vapor pressure of solute, 404
    effect on retention, 403
  in solvent extraction, 361
Distribution ratio:
  in ion exchange, 429
  in solvent extraction, 362
Dithizone, in solvent extraction of metals, 364
Diverse-ion effect on solubility, 170
Doppler broadening, 349
Double monochromator, 317
Drift, 411
Dropping mercury electrode, 278, 281

Eddy diffusion, 394
EDTA, 136
  distribution of species as function of pH, 138
Effective bandwidth (monochromators), 317
Effective solubility product constant, 173
Effective stability constant, 141
EGTA, 147
Electrode(s):
  of the first kind, 240
  of the second kind, 240
  of the third kind, 241
Electrogravimetry, 263
Electrolysis, 26, 262
Electrolytic cell, 263
Electromagnetic spectrum, 296, 298
Electroneutrality condition, 107
Electronic energy, 299
Emission spectroscopy, 348
Equilibrium:
  acid-base, 72
  adsorption, 425
  complex formation, 133
  ion exchange, 428
  oxidation-reduction, 205
  precipitation, 157
  solvent extraction, 360
Equilibrium constant, 76
Equivalence point, 15
Equivalent, 6
Equivalent weight, 7
Eriochrome Black T, 148
Errors, 36
  constant, 37
  determinate, 36
  of the first kind, 56
  indeterminate, 38
  of measurement, 454
  proportional, 37
  of the second kind, 56
  in spectrophotometry, 325

Ethylenediaminetetraacetic acid, 136
Ethyleneglycol-bis-(β-aminoethyl ether)-N,
  N'-tetraacetic acid, 147
Exclusive OR function, 486
Extraction constant of metal chelates, 365

Factor weight solution, 22
Farad, 446
Faraday, 26
Faraday's law, 273
Feasibility of titrations:
  acid-base, 93
  complex formation, 143
  oxidation-reduction, 227
  precipitation, 162
Feedback, 458
  in double-beam spectrophotometer, 324
Ferric ion, as indicator in titration of silver with
  thiocyanate, 163
Ferroin, as oxidation-reduction indicator, 231
Ferrous ion, titration of with ceric ion, 220
Flame ionization detector, 416
Flameless atomic absorption spectrophotometry, 358
Flame photometer (diagram), 352
Flame temperature, in flame photometry, 350
Fluorescein, as adsorption indicator, 166
Fluorescence, 301, 339
Follower, 457
Follower-with-gain, 459
Formality, 9
Formal potential, 218
Formation constant, 133
Formula weight, 9
FORTRAN, 497
Free energy, 77
Frequency, 297
Frequency distributions, 40
Frequency polygon, 42
Freundlich equation, 425
F-test (variance ratio test), 52
Full-adder, 487
F-values (table), 53

Gain, 459
Galvanic cells, 205
Gas-liquid chromatography (GLC):
  apparatus, 386
  applications, 418
  theory, 388
Gates:
  AND, 482
  NAND, 484
  NOR, 484
  NOT, 481
  OR (IOR), 483
  XOR, 486
Gaussian distribution, in solvent extraction, 376
Gaussian distribution curve, 43
Gelatinous precipitates, purity of, 194
Gel filtration, 431
Gel permeation, 431
Gels, 188
Glass electrode, 242
Gradient elution, in liquid chromatography, 434
Gram-atomic weight, 6
Gram-molecular weight, 6
Gravimetric analysis, 15, 19, 167

Gravimetric factor, 19
Ground, 444
    virtual, 461

Half-adder, 486
Half-reaction, 24
Half-wave potential, 284
Hardware, definition of, 496
Height equivalent of a theoretical plate (HETP), 389
Helium, as carrier gas in GLC, 415
Henderson-Hasselbalch equation, 85
Henry's law, 388
Histogram, 42
Hollow-cathode discharge tube, 357
Homologous series, retention volumes of in GLC, 418
Hydrogen discharge tube, as ultraviolet source, 314
Hydrogen electrode, 207
Hydrogen sulfide, in precipitation of metal ions, 175
Hydrolysis, 75, 81
    effect on chelometric titrations, 146
    effect on solubility of precipitates, 177
Hydronium ion, 74
8-Hydroxyquinoline, 182
    in solvent extraction of metals, 363

Ideal chromatography, 393
Ignition of precipitates, 198
Ilkovic equation, 283
Inclusive OR function, 483
Indicator blank, 92
Indicator electrode, 239, 240
Indicators:
    acid-base, 88, 91
    adsorption, 165, 167
    metallochromic, 147
    for precipitation titrations, 162
    redox, 228, 229
Indirect analysis, 21
Inert electrodes, 217
Infinite population, 43
Infrared spectra, 301
Integral detector, 409
Integration, in quantitative GLC, 419
Integrator-amplifier, 466
Interferences, in flame photometry, 354
Internal standard, in flame photometry, 353
Inverter amplifier:
    analog, 461
    digital, 481
Iodide, titration of with silver ion, 161
Ion exchange equilibrium, 428
    resins, 426
Ionic strength, 171
Ion pairs, in solvent extraction, 366
Ion-selective electrodes, 246
IOR function, 483
Isosbestic point (footnote), 310
IUPAC conventions, in electrochemistry, 209

Kirchhoff's laws, 447
    current, 448
    voltage, 449

Levelling effect, 74
Lewis acid-base theory, 132
Liebig titration, 153
Ligand, 132

Limit of detection, in GLC, 412
Linear chromatography, 392
Line spectra, 349
Liquid, stationary, in GLC, 408
Liquid junction potential, 209
Liquid-liquid partition chromatography, 430
Liquid load, effect on retention in GLC, 403
Liquid-membrane electrodes, 247
Logarithms (table), 521
Longitudinal diffusion, 394

Machine-language programming, 493, 496
Macro sample, 4
Magnetic tape, 495
Major constituent, 4
Mass balance equation, 109
Matrix effects, in atomic absorption spectrophotometry, 358
Maxima (polarographic), 284
Maximum suppressors, 284
Mean, 44, 45
Measurement error, 454
Median, 45
Membrane electrodes, 242
Memory, computer, 491
Mercuric ion, titration of chloride with, 151
Mercury, determination of by flameless atomic absorption, 358
Mercury electrode, for metal ions, 241
Metal ion buffers, 150
Metallic electrodes, 240
Metallochromic indicators, 147
Methyl orange, as acid-base indicator, 89
Micron, 297
Micro sample, 4
Migration current, 282
Milliequivalent, 11
Millimole, 11
Minicomputer, 490
Minor constituent, 4
Mixed crystals, 193
Mohr method, 162
Molar absorptivity, 309
Molarity, 9
Mole, 6
Monochromator, 314
Mull, 335
Multicomponent analysis, in spectrophotometry, 331
Multiplication, binary, 475, 489

NAND function, 484
Nanometer, 297
Natural width (spectral lines), 349
Nernst equation, 211
Nernst glower, 314
Neutral salt effect, on solubility, 170
Ninhydrin, 435
Nitrogen, as carrier gas in GLC, 417
Nitrophenol, as acid-base indicator, 88
α-Nitroso-β-naphthol, 184
Noise, 411
Nominal wavelength, 317
Nonaqueous titrations, 101
Nonequilibrium in mass transfer, 395
Nonideal chromatography, 393
NOR function, 484
Normal distribution curve, 43

Normal error curve, 44
Normality, 9
NOT function, 481
Nucleation, 188
Null hypothesis, 52

Occlusion, 193
Off-line computer, 495, 498
Ohm, 446
Ohm's law, 447
On-line computer, 495, 498
Open-tubular column, 408
Operational amplifiers, 456
Optical wedge, 324
OR function:
    Inclusive (IOR), 483
    Exclusive (XOR), 486
Organic precipitants for inorganic ions, 181
    (table), 184
Oxalate, distribution of species as function of pH,
    127
Oxidation number, 23
Oxidation-reduction equilibria, 205
Oxidation-reduction indicators, 228
    (table), 229
Oxine, 182

Paneth-Fajans-Hahn rule, 187
Paper chromatrography, 435
Paper tape, 495
    punch, 495
    reader, 495
Peak-to-peak noise level of detector, 412
Peptization, 188
Percent transmittance, 309
Peripherals, computer, 494
Pesticides, determination of by GLC, 422
pH:
    calculations, 82
    definition, 82
    effect on chelometric titrations, 138
    effect on solubility of precipitates, 172
    measurement with glass electrode, 242
    potentiometric determination of, 249
1, 10-Phenanthroline, as oxidation-reduction indicator,
    231
Phenolphthalein, as acid-base indicator, 89
Phosphate, distribution of species as function of pH,
    129
Phosphorescence, 301, 340
Photometric error, 327
Photometric titration, 335
Photomultiplier tube, 319
Phototube, 319
Pilot-ion method, 288
Poised solution, 226
Polarogram, 280
Polarography, 278
Polyacrylamides, as gel filtration materials, 431
Polyprotic acids, 118
    titration curves, 120
Postprecipitation, 197
Potassium bromide, matrix in infrared
    spectrophotometry, 335
Potential, 444
Potential buffers, 270
Potentiometric titration, 239

Potentiometric titration (*cont.*)
    automatic, 257
    manual, 253
Potentiometry, 239
Potentiostat, 271
Power, radiant, 309
Precipitate electrodes, 249
Precipitates:
    particle size of, 186
    purity of, 192
Precipitation:
    equilibria, 157
    from homogeneous solution, 196
    separations by, 167
    titrations, 159
Precision, 39
Pressure broadening, 349
Primary standard, 16
Prism, 314
Programmed flow in GLC, 404
Programmed temperature in GLC, 406
Programming languages:
    assembly, 496
    BASIC, 497
    FORTRAN, 497
    machine, 493, 496
Propagation of errors, 60
Proton condition, 112
Pseudocountercurrent extraction, 368
Pyrolysis gas chromatography, 421

Q-test, 56
Qualitative analysis, 3
Quantitative analysis, 3
Quenching, self, in fluorescence, 340
Quinaldic acid, 184
8-Quinolinol, 182
Q-values (table), 56

Radiation interferences in flame photometry, 354
Range, 46
Rayleigh diffraction limit, 315
Reference electrode, 215, 239
Register, computer, 492
Rejection of data, 54
Rejection quotient, Q, 56
    (table), 56
Relative average deviation, 47
Replica grating, 316
Residual current, 268, 279, 282
Resistance, 446
    parallel, 452
    series, 450
Resolution (in chromatography), 399
Retention time, 391
Retention volume, 401
    corrected, 402
R_f value, 436
Rotational energy, 299

Salmonella, characterization by pyrolysis gas
    chromatography, 421
Salt bridge, 205
Sampling, 3
Sampling systems in GLC, 406
Scale expansion, 463
    in differential spectrophotometry, 321

Selectivity coefficient, in ion exchange, 429
Semimicro sample, 4
Sensitivity of detector, in GLC, 410
Separation:
    by chromatography, 383, 424
    by electrolysis, 268
    by precipitation, 167
    by solvent extraction, 360
Separation factor (in chromatography), 401
Significance testing, 52
Significant figures, 63
Silver ion, titration of cyanide with, 153
Silver-silver chloride electrode, 215
Single electrode potential, 206
Sodium nitroprusside, 152
Sodium tetraphenylboron, 185
Software, computer, 496
Solid-state electrodes, 249
Solubility, 157
    factors affecting, 167
Solubility product constant, 157
Solvent, effect on solubility, 168
Solvents, for ultraviolet-visible region (table), 334
Sorption, 430
Spectrofluorometer, 341
Spectrophotometer:
    amplifier, 319
    detector, 318
    double-beam, 323
    monochromator, 314
    readout, 320
    sample container, 318
    single-beam, 312
    source, 313
Stability constant, 133
Stability of detector, in GLC, 411
Standard addition, in polarography, 288
Standard deviation, 44, 47
Standardization of solutions, 16
Standard potential, 209
Standard state, 77
Stannous ion, titration of with ceric ion, 224
Stoichiometric point, 15
Stoichiometry, 5
Stray light (monochromators), 316
Student's t, 49
    (table), 50
Subtractor amplifier, 464
Sulfides, separation of metal, 175
Summing amplifier, 464
Summing point, 464
Superficially porous supports, in liquid
        chromatography, 439
Supersaturation, 189
Supporting electrolyte, 282
Supports, in GLC columns, 407
Suspensoids, 188

t (Student's), 49
    (table), 50

Teleprinter, 494
Temperature:
    effect in GLC, 404
    effect on solubility, 168
Tetraphenylarsonium chloride, 185
Theoretical plate, 389
    calculating number of, 390
Thermal conductivities of gases (table), 416
Thermal conductivity detector, 414
Thermistor, 414
Thermobalance, 199
Thermocouple, 319
Thin layer chromatography, 436
Thionalide, 184
Titer, 13
Titration curves:
    acid-base, 83
    amperometric, 290
    complex formation, 143
    oxidation-reduction, 220
    photometric, 336
    potentiometric, 253
    precipitation, 161
Titrator, automatic, 468
Titrimetric analysis, 14, 18
Trace constituent, 4
Transmittance, 309
Triethylenetetramine, 135
Truth table, 481
Tungsten lamp, 313

Ultraviolet spectra, 304

van Deemter equation, 397
Variability, 46
Variance, 47
Variance-ratio test, 52
Velocity of light, 297
Vibrational energy, 299
Virtual ground, 461
Volhard method, 163
Volt, 444
Voltage, 444
Voltage divider, 451
Voltage follower, 457
Voltammetry, 278
von Weimarn ratio, 189

Water hardness titration, 150
Wavelength, 297
Wave number, 297
Weight percent, 5
Wheatstone bridge, 455
    with thermal conductivity detector, 415
Word, computer, 491

XOR function, 486

Zero suppression, 463

3rd
EDITION

QUANTITATIVE ANALYSIS

R. A. Day, Jr.
Emory University

A. L. Underwood
Emory University

Prentice-Hall, Inc., Englewood Cliffs, New Jersey

Library of Congress Cataloging in Publication Data

Day, Reuben Alexander, 1915–
   Quantitative analysis.

   Includes bibliographies.
    1. Chemistry, Analytic—Quantitative.
I. Underwood, Arthur Louis, 1924–   joint author.
II. Title.
QD101.2.D37 1974   545   73-17387
ISBN 0-13-746537-8

PRENTICE-HALL INTERNATIONAL, INC., *London*

PRENTICE-HALL OF AUSTRALIA, PTY. LTD., *Sydney*

PRENTICE-HALL OF CANADA, LTD., *Toronto*

PRENTICE-HALL OF INDIA PRIVATE LIMITED, *New Delhi*

PRENTICE-HALL OF JAPAN, INC., *Tokyo*

Contents

Preface   *ix*

1

Introduction
1

Analytical Chemistry   *1*
Quantitative Analysis   *3*

2

**Review of
Stoichiometry**
5

Concentrations of Solutions   *5*
Titrimetric and Gravimetric Methods   *14*
Illustrative Problems   *16*

3

**Errors and
the Treatment of
Analytical Data**
35

Introduction   *35*
Errors   *36*
Distribution of Random Errors   *39*
Statistical Treatment of Finite Samples   *45*
Control Charts   *58*
Propagation of Errors   *60*
Significant Figures and Computation Rules   *63*

iii

4

Acid-base Equilibria 72

Introduction   *72*
Brønsted Treatment of Acids and Bases   *73*
Dissociation Constants   *76*
Calculations of *p*H Values of Aqueous Solutions   *82*
Acid-Base Titration Curves   *87*
Acid-Base Indicators   *88*
Feasibility of Acid-Base Titrations   *93*
Buffer Solutions   *96*
Physiological Buffers   *99*
Nonaqueous Titrations   *101*
Approximations in Acid-Base Calculations   *106*

5

Acid-base Equilibria in Complex Systems 118

Polyprotic Acids   *118*
Distribution of Acid-Base Species
as a Function of *p*H   *126*

6

Complex Formation Titrations 132

Stability of Complexes   *133*
Chelometric Titrations   *136*
Metal Ion Buffers   *150*
Titrations Involving Unidentate Ligands   *151*

7

Solubility Equilibria 157

The Solubility Product Constant   *157*
Precipitation Titrations   *159*
Indicators for Precipitation Titrations Involving Silver   *162*
Separations by Precipitation   *167*
Factors Affecting Solubility   *167*
Organic Precipitants   *181*
Formation and Properties of Precipitates   *186*
Particle Size   *186*
Purity of Precipitates   *192*
Ignition of Precipitates   *198*

iv

8

Oxidation-Reduction Equilibria 205

Galvanic Cells   *205*
Approximations in Redox Equilibria Calculations   *217*
Titration Curves   *220*
Feasibility of Redox Titrations   *227*
Redox Indicators   *228*
Structural Chemistry of Redox Indicators   *230*

9

Potentiometric Methods of Analysis 239

Indicator Electrodes   *240*
Direct Potentiometry   *249*
Potentiometric Titrations   *253*

10

Other Electrical Methods of Analysis 262

Electrolysis   *262*
Coulometric Analysis   *272*
Polarography   *278*
Amperometric Titrations   *289*

11

Spectrophotometry 296

Introduction   *296*
The Electromagnetic Spectrum   *296*
The Interaction of Radiant Energy with Molecules   *298*
Infrared Spectrophotometry   *301*
Ultraviolet and Visible Spectra   *304*
Quantitative Aspects of Absorption   *305*
Instrumentation for Spectrophotometry   *312*
Errors in Spectrophotometry   *325*
Applications of Spectrophotometry   *328*
Photometric Titrations   *335*
Fluorescence   *339*

12

Flame Emission and Atomic Absorption Spectroscopy 348

Flame Emission Spectroscopy
(Flame Photometry)   *348*
Atomic Absorption Spectroscopy   *355*

13

**Solvent
Extraction
360**

Introduction   *360*
Distribution Law   *360*
Examples of Solvent Extraction Equilibria   *362*
Extraction Systems Involving Ion Pairs and Solvates   *366*
Craig Pseudocountercurrent Extraction   *367*

14

**Gas-liquid
Chromatography
383**

Introduction   *383*
Definition and Classification of Chromatography   *385*
Basic Apparatus for GLC   *386*
Theory of GLC   *388*
Experimental Aspects of GLC   *406*
Applications of GLC   *418*

15

**Liquid
Chromatography
424**

Introduction   *424*
Phase Distribution Processes   *425*
Conventional Liquid Chromatography Techniques   *433*
Modern Liquid Chromatography   *437*

16

**Analog
Electronics
442**

Introduction   *442*
Basic Electronics   *443*
Operational Amplifiers   *456*

17

**Digital
Electronics
and Computers
472**

Introduction   *472*
Digital and Analog Information   *472*
Binary Number System   *474*
Analog-to-Digital and Digital-to-Analog Conversion   *476*
Digital Logic for Control   *481*
Digital Logic for Computation   *486*
Small Computers   *489*

Appendix I   Tables of Equilibrium Constants and Oxidation Potentials   *501*

Appendix II   Table of Atomic Weights   *510*

Appendix III   Table of Formula Weights   *513*

Appendix IV   The Literature of Analytical Chemistry   *515*

Appendix V   Four-Place Table of Logarithms   *521*

Appendix VI   Answers to Odd-Numbered Problems   *524*

Index   *529*

Preface

Analytical chemistry continues to be taught in a variety of ways at different schools. It would be foolish to attempt to write a textbook for all of the undergraduate courses that are offered from the freshman to the senior year. The broad acceptance of our previous edition by teachers at various types of institutions has suggested that the same approach may be useful again, viz., to develop a book for our own students at Emory University while providing flexibility for other course formats.

At Emory, we have three one-quarter undergraduate analytical courses. The first comes in the third quarter of the freshman year, following the usual two-quarter general chemistry sequence; this covers errors and the treatment of data, volumetric and gravimetric analysis, potentiometry, and spectrophotometry.

A second analytical course is offered for students who select chemistry as a college major but who do not expect to become professional chemists. The majority of these are premedical and predental students; some anticipate graduate work in biomedical fields such as physiology, pharmacology, or microbiology. Biology majors may also take this course. Most of these students are juniors who have had a year of organic chemistry; some have had a one-quarter course in physical chemistry designed for the nonprofessional majors. That portion of the book, roughly half, which is not covered in the first course, is completed here. Some schools offer a course similar to ours in the sophomore year, some in the senior year; this is not a matter of great importance. What is important is that this is probably the last exposure to analytical chemistry for most of the students, although some of them will undoubtedly encounter analytical problems in their later careers.

Thus, despite their limited backgrounds, they ought to see something of modern analytical chemistry.

Our third undergraduate analytical course is primarily for professional students, and it is given mainly to seniors who have completed a full year of physical chemistry. A few first-year graduate students also take this course. Our textbook is not written with these students in mind, although many of them find it useful as a starting point for reading more advanced material.

In revising the text we have made the following major changes. The treatment of chromatography has been greatly expanded, with a chapter devoted to gas-liquid chromatography and another to liquid chromatography, including recent advances. A short chapter on flame emission and atomic absorption spectroscopy has been added, as well as a brief treatment of fluorescence. A section on ion-selective electrodes has been included in the chapter on potentiometric methods. We have introduced new chapters on analog and digital electronics and computers. Although these are elementary, the material is more than superficially descriptive and should provide a meaningful introduction to these topics.

To make room for new topics, the treatment of several old ones has been shortened. All of the material on precipitation has been collected in one chapter, with less space devoted to the formation and properties of precipitates. The coverage of electroanalytical chemistry has been limited to a few of the more widely used techniques. All of this material, including redox equilibria, is collected in three consecutive chapters.

As with the previous editions, we have included a large number of problems, some to provide drill and some to challenge the comprehension of the material; a *Teacher's Manual* with worked-out solutions is available. A companion *Laboratory Manual* designed to accompany the text is also available.

We wish to express our appreciation to the many users of the second edition who have made numerous helpful suggestions. We are especially grateful to Professor Stanley Deming, who has prepared the chapters on "Analog Electronics" and "Digital Electronics and Computers."

R. A. Day, Jr.
A. L. Underwood

1 Introduction

ANALYTICAL CHEMISTRY

It used to be possible to subdivide chemistry into several clear and well-defined branches—analytical, inorganic, organic, physical, and biological. Although there was always a certain overlap among these simple categories, it was not difficult to define the branches in terms that were acceptable to most chemists. It was generally fairly clear into which category any particular chemist fitted, and a label such as "organic chemist" usually implied a reasonably clear picture of the sorts of things such a chemist did.

One of the most prominent trends in chemistry over the past ten or twenty years has been a general blurring of the borders of its branches; actually, the boundaries between chemistry itself and other major sciences such as physics and biology are considerably less clear than they used to be. Fields such as chemical physics, biophysical chemistry, physical organic chemistry, geochemistry, and chemical oceanography have achieved recognition in at least a vague way, although precise definitions of these fields are exceedingly difficult to formulate.

During all of this change, chemistry courses in the undergraduate curriculum have largely retained their traditional titles, but they have undergone major changes in content. For example, it is not at all unusual to find such topics as molecular spectroscopy and chemical kinetics in organic chemistry courses. Solution thermodynamics, kinetics of electrode processes, and electronics appear in analytical courses at some schools. In most cases, the college freshman course has undergone drastic change, and interesting changes at the high school level have been initiated.

Analytical chemistry is as old, and as new, as the science of chemistry itself. It may be fairly said that analytical research, as opposed broadly to synthetic, ushered in the change from magic and alchemy to quantitative, scientific chemistry. Analytical work led directly to the revolution that over-threw the phlogiston theory, and rational experiments that would place chemistry on a sound basis of fact and theory became possible with the increasing use of the analytical balance. Careful analyses led to the laws of definite and multiple proportions, and made possible Dalton's great achievement—an atomic hypothesis grounded in fact rather than mystical speculation.

The late nineteenth and early twentieth centuries saw developments in organic and physical chemistry and in physics that were bound to dwarf other fields. During this time many analytical chemists concerned themselves with the chemical composition of various materials which were important in the commerce of a simple industrial society. In many universities, analytical chemistry was taught as a routine, cookbook subject, although a small number of excellent men kept the field alive as a science.

Roughly since World War 2, an increasing sophistication of research in all areas of chemistry, physics, and biology and an explosive technological development have combined to create analytical problems which demand increasingly sophisticated knowledge and instrumentation for their solution. Typical examples of such problems are determining traces of impurities at the part per billion level in ultrapure semiconductor materials, deducing the sequence of some twenty different amino acids in a giant protein molecule, detecting traces of unusual molecules in the polluted atmosphere of a smog-bound city, determining pesticide residues at the part per billion level in food products, and determining the nature and concentration of complex organic molecules in, say, the nucleus of a single cell.

The solutions to a host of problems such as these have been developed by research workers of the most diverse backgrounds. For example, a biochemist received the Nobel Prize for working out the amino acid sequence in the protein insulin, and physicists were actively involved in the first semi-conductor analyses by mass spectrometry. Research workers in many fields are constantly confronted by analytical problems, and in many cases they work out their own solutions. It is interesting to note that in a recent year, nearly 60 % of the papers in the journal *Analytical Chemistry* were authored by people who did not consider themselves to be analytical chemists. The papers originated in a wide variety of laboratories associated with medical schools, hospitals, oceanographic institutes, agricultural experiment stations, physics departments, and many more.

The trends of recent years have drawn analytical chemistry into the forefront of research in many exciting areas, but this very intimacy has blurred the borders of the discipline and made it nearly impossible in many cases to decide what an analytical chemist is. In this connection we may quote from the Fisher Award Address of Prof. David N. Hume:[1]

[1] D. N. Hume, *Anal. Chem.*, **35**, 29A (1963).

One of the most difficult problems facing the analytical chemist today is explaining to others just what analytical chemistry is. Much of the difficulty derives from the changes in the nature of the profession and the fact that a given word may have a whole spectrum of meanings.... The increasing complexity of modern chemistry is to some extent the cause of this confusion, as is the fact that a chemist seldom works in only one branch of the subject, more often combining the techniques and approaches of several.

With this extensive overlap into a variety of fields, what distinguishes the analytical chemist from all others working in these areas? The analytical chemist has, usually, more interest in the methods and techniques in their own right. Physical, organic, and biochemists often need to develop new analytical methods for their own purposes, but their primary interests do not lie in the method itself. To the analytical chemist, developing the methods is the challenging part of the research. Because of his interest in the method per se, the analytical chemist is likely to be skeptical of data presented without a full disclosure of experimental details, and he retains a critical attitude toward results which some workers would like to accept so as to get on with other things. The analytical chemist deals with real, practical systems, and much of his effort is expended in an attempt to apply sound theory to actual chemical situations.

QUANTITATIVE ANALYSIS

We have tried to explain what analytical chemistry is like and what analytical chemists do. With this in mind, what topics are to be considered in an introductory textbook? Obviously the beginning student cannot engage immediately in activities such as determining the sequence of amino acids in a protein. It is reasonable to introduce him first to somewhat traditional topics which are still important, although frequently not of current research interest. The general chemistry course prepares him for these topics in a fairly adequate way, because they are based largely on simple stoichiometry and equilibrium principles. In addition, today's student can expect an earlier introduction to modern topics and a more sophisticated approach to many traditional topics than was common a few years ago. Nevertheless, principles are basically unchanged and as such must be mastered before a full appreciation of current problems can be gained.

Quantitative analysis is concerned with the determination of the quantity of a particular substance present in a sample. Qualitative analysis deals with the identification of substances. Although the beginning student seldom performs a complete quantitative analysis of a sample, it is important that he understand what a complete analysis entails. A chemical analysis actually consists of four steps: (1) sampling, that is, selecting a representative sample of the material to be analyzed; (2) conversion of the desired constituent into a form suitable for measurement; (3) measurement; and (4) calculation and interpretation of the measurements. Often the beginner carries out only steps three and four since these are usually the easiest ones.

The laboratory method employed in the measurement step of an analysis has led to further subdivisions in quantitative analysis: *titrimetric* (*volumetric*), *gravimetric*, and *instrumental*. A *titrimetric* analysis involves the measurement of the volume of a solution of known concentration which is required to react with the substance determined. In a *gravimetric* analysis, the measurement is one of weight; for example, the chloride in a sample may be determined by the precipitation of silver chloride, which is then dried and weighed. The term *instrumental* analysis is used rather loosely, originally referring to the use of some instrument in the measurement step. Actually, instruments may be used in any or all steps of the analysis, and, strictly speaking, burets and analytical balances are instruments. The widespread use of instrumentation in all phases of analysis has all but erased the traditional boundaries around what was known as instrumental analysis.

Another classification of analytical chemistry may be based upon the size of the sample which is available for analysis. The subdivisions are not clearcut, but merge imperceptibly into one another, and are roughly as follows: when a sample weighing more than 0.1 g is available, the analysis is spoken of as *macro*; *semimicro* analyses are performed on samples of perhaps 10 to 100 mg; *micro* analyses deal with samples weighing from 1 to 10 mg; and *ultramicro* analyses involve samples of the order of a microgram (1 μg = 10^{-6} g). A more or less parallel classification considers the relative amount of the *desired constituent* in the sample rather than the size of the sample itself. Constituents are considered *major* if they amount to more than about 1% of the sample, and *minor* from 0.01 to 1%. Finally, a constituent present to the extent of less than about 0.01% is considered a *trace* constituent. Instrumental measurements achieve their greatest significance in analyses for minor and trace constituents. In his early work with gravimetric and volumetric methods, the beginning student will deal mainly with major constituents of macro samples, although extensions of the classical techniques have led to the impossibility of clearly delimiting their usefulness in a brief discussion.

The beginning student should profit from the introductory course in quantitative analysis. In the laboratory, he will become familiar with the tools and instruments of the analytical chemist which will be of service to him in all other areas of chemistry. He will see the point of view of the analyst and will be exposed to the rigors of exacting quantitative work. This will generate, it is hoped, an understanding of the utility and limitations of many of the tools used by all chemists. From his study of theoretical topics, the student should gain an understanding of the principles underlying laboratory procedures and instruments. Since principles are principles, regardless of the course in which they are taught, the material learned here will broaden the student's knowledge of chemistry as a whole. Once the student has learned this introductory material and has increased his background in mathematics, physics, and physical chemistry, he will be able to appreciate more fully the work which analytical chemists are doing today.

2 Review of Stoichiometry

The branch of chemistry which deals with the weight relations between elements and compounds in chemical formulas and equations is called *stoichiometry*. Stoichiometric calculations are described thoroughly in general chemistry courses. Hence we shall review this topic briefly, emphasizing only examples commonly encountered in analytical chemistry.

CONCENTRATIONS OF SOLUTIONS

Since solutions are frequently employed in performing analyses, it is desirable to express concentrations in units that are convenient for calculations. In quantitative analysis, the systems of *molarity* and *normality* are most frequently employed, although the formality system is useful in many instances. The *percent by weight* system is sometimes employed to express approximate concentrations of laboratory reagents.

Weight Percent

This system specifies the number of grams of solute per 100 grams of solution. Mathematically this is expressed as follows:

$$P = \frac{w}{w + w_0} \times 100$$

where P = percent by weight solute, w = number of grams of solute, and w_0 = number of grams of solvent.

5

The following examples illustrate the weight percent system of concentration.

Example 1. 5.0 g of NaOH is dissolved in 45 g of water. (1 g of water is approximately 1 ml.) Calculate the weight percent NaOH in the solution.

$$P = \frac{5.0}{5.0 + 45} \times 100$$

$$P = 10\%$$

Example 2. Concentrated aqueous HCl has a density of 1.19 g/ml and is 37% by weight HCl. How many milliliters of the acid should be taken to obtain 3.65 g of HCl?

$$1.19 \text{ g/ml} \times 0.37 = 0.44 \text{ g of HCl/ml}$$

$$\frac{3.65 \text{ g}}{0.44 \text{ g/ml}} = 8.3 \text{ ml}$$

Moles and Equivalents

Atomic and molecular weights are relative quantities which depend on the arbitrary assignment of a weight to some atom. For many years chemists set the atomic weight of oxygen as it occurs in nature at exactly 16.0000, and the molecular weight of O_2 at 32.0000. Since the gram is the usual unit of mass employed in the laboratory, we say that the gram-atomic weight of oxygen is 16.0000 g. The gram-molecular weight of O_2 is 32.0000 g. Since 1961, the atomic weight scale has been based on the carbon-12 isotope set at exactly 12.0000. On this scale the atomic weight of oxygen is 15.9994, but for our purposes we can round this off to 16.0000.

The gram-atomic weight of any element, such as 22.99 g of sodium, contains 6.023×10^{23} (Avogadro's number) of atoms. The gram-molecular weight of any substance, such as 44 g of CO_2, contains Avogadro's number of molecules. We refer to Avogadro's number of atoms, molecules, or ions as a *mole* of particles. Thus a mole of methyl alcohol, CH_3OH, weighs 32 g and contains 6.023×10^{23} molecules.

Chemical reactions take place between *integral* numbers of atoms, molecules, ions, or moles, but only occasionally does one mole of substance A react with one mole of substance B. In acid-base reactions, one mole of an acid may react with one, two, or three moles of a base. For example, hydrochloric, sulfuric, and phosphoric acids may react with hydroxyl ions as follows:

$$HCl + OH^- \longrightarrow H_2O + Cl^-$$

$$H_2SO_4 + 2 OH^- \longrightarrow 2 H_2O + SO_4^{2-}$$

$$H_3PO_4 + 3 OH^- \longrightarrow 3 H_2O + PO_4^{3-}$$

These equations say that one mole of hydrochloric acid reacts with one mole of OH^- ion, whereas one mole of sulfuric acid reacts with two moles of OH^- ion; and one mole of phosphoric acid reacts with three moles of OH^- ion. The term *equivalent* was introduced many years ago to define the quantity of acid which reacts with a single mole of OH^- ion. One-half mole of sulfuric acid and one-third mole of phosphoric acid react with one mole of OH^- ion and are called equivalents of these acids. For HCl the mole and equivalent are the same. In similar fashion an equivalent of a base is defined as the quantity of base which reacts with one mole of H^+. From these definitions it should be obvious that one equivalent of a base reacts with one equivalent of an acid.

The terms *equivalent* and *equivalent weight* are also used in oxidation-reduction reactions. Consider, for example, the following three reactions:

$$Ag^+ + e \longrightarrow Ag$$

$$Cu^{2+} + 2e \longrightarrow Cu$$

$$Al^{3+} + 3e \longrightarrow Al$$

These equations say that one mole of Ag^+ reacts with one mole of electrons, one mole of Cu^{2+} reacts with two moles of electrons, and one mole of Al^{3+} reacts with three moles of electrons. An equivalent of aluminum is defined as one-third of a mole, and of copper, one-half of a mole. An equivalent and a mole of silver are the same. For substances which furnish electrons, an equivalent is taken as the quantity which furnishes one mole of electrons.

There are two important points which should be noted about the use of the equivalent. First, the equivalent weight of a substance depends upon the chemical reaction which the substance undergoes. Since many compounds can undergo more than a single reaction with other substances, a compound can have more than one equivalent weight. For example, the permanganate ion can undergo the following reactions:

$$MnO_4^- + e \longrightarrow MnO_4^{2-} \tag{1}$$

$$MnO_4^- + 4H^+ + 3e \longrightarrow MnO_2 + 2H_2O \tag{2}$$

$$MnO_4^- + 8H^+ + 4e \longrightarrow Mn^{3+} + 4H_2O \tag{3}$$

$$MnO_4^- + 8H^+ + 5e \longrightarrow Mn^{2+} + 4H_2O \tag{4}$$

The equivalent weight of a permanganate salt, such as $KMnO_4$, is its molecular weight divided by one, three, four, or five, depending upon which of the above reactions occurs.

The reaction of phosphoric acid with a base can be stopped when the following reaction has occurred:

$$H_3PO_4 + OH^- \longrightarrow H_2O + H_2PO_4^-$$

The equivalent weight of the acid is the same as the molecular weight. But the reaction can be carried on further:

$$H_3PO_4 + 2\,OH^- \longrightarrow 2\,H_2O + HPO_4{}^{2-}$$

Here the equivalent weight is one-half the molecular weight. In aqueous solutions it is not feasible to titrate the third hydrogen; if the reaction could be carried out, the equivalent weight of the acid would be one-third of the molecular weight.

The second point is that although the equivalent weight is usually equal to or less than the molecular weight, there are examples in which it is greater than the molecular weight. For example, MnO on ignition in air is converted into Mn_3O_4, which in turn can be determined by reaction with a reducing agent such as sodium oxalate. The equation is:

$$6\,MnO + O_2 \longrightarrow 2\,Mn_3O_4$$

Using the concept of oxidation numbers (page 23), it is seen that manganese changes from $+2$ in MnO to $+2\frac{2}{3}$ in Mn_3O_4. Hence, each manganese atom loses on the average two-thirds of an electron, and the equivalent weight of MnO is $70.93/\frac{2}{3} = 106.4$. Of course, no manganese atom actually loses two-thirds of an electron. Mn_3O_4 may be considered as $MnO_2 \cdot 2\,MnO$; thus one of the three manganese atoms loses two electrons, making an average of two-thirds electron per manganese atom.

In precipitation and complex formation reactions we shall not use the term equivalent. The equivalent weight in such reactions can be defined in more than one way and confusion may result. We shall use only moles in stoichiometric calculations involving such reactions.

The following are some examples illustrating the calculations of equivalent weights.

Example 1. What is the equivalent weight of SO_3 used as an acid in aqueous solution?

SO_3 does not directly furnish hydrogen ions, but it does so indirectly through the reaction with water:

$$SO_3 + H_2O \longrightarrow H_2SO_4 \longrightarrow 2\,H^+ + SO_4{}^{2-}$$

Hence one molecule of SO_3 is responsible for two H^+, and

$$\text{E.W.} = \frac{\text{M.W.}}{2} = \frac{80.07}{2}$$

$$\text{E.W.} = 40.04 \text{ g/eq}$$

Example 2. Calculate the equivalent weight of KHC_2O_4 as an acid and as a reducing agent. As an acid the reaction is

$$HC_2O_4{}^- \longrightarrow H^+ + C_2O_4{}^{2-}$$

As a reducing agent the reaction is

$$C_2O_4^{2-} \longrightarrow 2\,CO_2 + 2e$$

The equivalent weight as an acid is the same as the molecular weight, since one H^+ is furnished per molecule. As a reducing agent the molecule loses two electrons. Hence:

Acid: $\text{E.W.} = \dfrac{\text{M.W.}}{1} = 128.13 \text{ g/eq}$

Reducing agent: $\text{E.W.} = \dfrac{\text{M.W.}}{2} = 64.07 \text{ g/eq}$

Molarity, Normality, and Formality

The concentration systems *molarity*, *normality*, and *formality* are based on the volume of solution and hence are convenient to use in laboratory procedures where the volume of solution is measured. The three systems are defined as follows:

Molarity = number of moles of solute per liter of solution.

Normality = number of equivalents of solute per liter of solution.

Formality = number of formula weights of solute per liter of solution.

The formality system has become more widely used in recent years. It is useful in avoiding confusion over the concentrations of various species in solution when dissociation or complex formation occurs. The formula weight is the summation of the atomic weights of all the atoms in the chemical formula of a substance. The formula of acetic acid is CH_3COOH and the gram-formula weight is 60.05 g. If one-tenth of a gram-formula weight of the acid is dissolved in exactly one liter of solution, the solution is 0.1000 Formal in acetic acid. Because of dissociation, the concentration of acid molecules is about 0.099 Molar, and the concentrations of hydrogen and acetate ions are each about 0.001 Molar. Similarly, a solution which is 0.100-F in $FeCl_3$ may have various molar concentrations of such species as Fe^{3+}, $FeCl^{2+}$, $FeCl_2^+$, etc. In this text we shall use the formality system whenever there is a possibility of confusion over the concentrations of various species in solution. Mathematically, we express molarity and normality as:

$$M = \frac{\text{moles}}{V}$$

$$N = \frac{\text{eq}}{V}$$

where M = molarity, N = normality, and V = volume of solution in liters. Since

$$\text{moles} = \frac{\text{g}}{\text{M.W.}}$$

and

$$eq = \frac{g}{\text{E.W.}}$$

where g = grams of solute, M.W. = molecular weight, and E.W. = equivalent weight, it follows that

$$M = \frac{g}{\text{M.W.} \times V}$$

and

$$N = \frac{g}{\text{E.W.} \times V}$$

These equations may be solved for grams of solute, giving

$$g = M \times V \times \text{M.W.}$$

and

$$g = N \times V \times \text{E.W.}$$

We have seen that the equivalent and molecular weights are usually related by a simple whole number relationship. We can write

$$\text{E.W.} = \frac{\text{M.V.}}{n}$$

where n = number of hydrogen ions furnished or taken up in the case of acids and bases, or the number of electrons gained or lost in the case of redox reagents, etc. Hence, the relation between molarity and normality is

$$N = \frac{n \times g}{\text{M.W.} \times V}$$

or

$$N = n \times M$$

If n is one or greater, as is usually the case, the normality is equal to or greater than the molarity.

In practical quantitative measurements the volumes of solutions are normally of the order of a few thousandths of a liter. The number of equivalents or moles involved is small, frequently of the order of a few thousandths of an equivalent or mole. Hence, it is convenient to adopt a smaller unit, both for the quantity of solute and for the volume of solution. The unit *milliliter*, one thousandth of a liter is a familiar one. Similarly, the terms *milliequivalent* and *millimole* mean simply one-thousandth of an equivalent or of a mole, respectively, that is,

$$1000 \text{ milliequivalents (abbr. meq)} = 1 \text{ equivalent}$$

$$1000 \text{ millimoles (abbr. mmol)} = 1 \text{ mole}$$

Note that normality and molarity can be expressed in either the larger or the smaller units; the numerical value is unchanged. Thus, a solution containing 0.00200 equivalents in 0.00500 liters also contains 2.00 meq in 5.00 ml, and the normality is

$$N = \frac{0.00200 \text{ eq}}{0.00500 \text{ l}} = \frac{2.00 \text{ meq}}{5.00 \text{ ml}} = 0.400$$

It should be noted also that the equivalent weight can be expressed with either the large or the small units. The equivalent weight of NaOH is 40.00 g/eq and 40.00 mg/meq. It should be evident that

$$N = \frac{mg}{E.W. \times ml}$$

Consider the following typical calculations.

Example 1. A sample of pure As_2O_3 weighing 4.0136 g is dissolved in 800.0 ml of solution, producing arsenious acid:

$$As_2O_3 + 3 H_2O \longrightarrow 2 H_3AsO_3$$

Calculate the normality of the solution if the reaction involving arsenic is:

$$H_3AsO_3 + H_2O \longrightarrow H_3AsO_4 + 2 H^+ + 2e$$

Note that each arsenic atom loses two electrons. Since each As_2O_3 contains two arsenic atoms, it is responsible for furnishing four electrons. The equivalent weight of As_2O_3 is one-fourth the molecular weight. Hence,

$$N = \frac{4013.6 \text{ mg}}{197.82/4 \text{ mg/meq} \times 800.0 \text{ ml}}$$

$$N = 0.1014 \text{ meq/ml}$$

Example 2. Calculate the number of grams of Na_2CO_3 in 3.9 l of a 0.170-N solution. The reaction is

$$2 H^+ + CO_3^{2-} \longrightarrow H_2CO_3$$

The equivalent weight of Na_2CO_3 is one-half the molecular weight or $105.99/2 = 53.0$ g/eq. Hence

$$g = 3.9 l \times 0.170 \text{ eq/l} \times 53.0 \text{ g/eq}$$

$$g = 35$$

Example 3. Concentrated hydrochloric acid has a density of 1.19 g/ml and contains 37 % HCl by weight. Calculate the number of milliliters of the concentrated acid required to prepare 2.50 l of a 0.100-M solution. (A 0.100-M solution is also 0.100-N since HCl is a monoprotic acid.)

In 2.50 l of a 0.100-M solution there are

$$2500 \text{ ml} \times 0.100 \text{ mmol/ml} = 250 \text{ mmol}$$

In each ml of concentrated HCl there are

$$\frac{1190 \text{ mg/ml} \times 0.37}{36.5 \text{ mg/mmol}} = 12.1 \text{ mmol/ml}$$

Hence

$$\frac{250 \text{ mmol}}{12.1 \text{ mmol/ml}} = 21 \text{ ml}$$

Example 4. In what volume of solution should 30.00 g of pure NaCl be dissolved to prepare a 0.2000-F solution? Note that NaCl is completely dissociated and the solution is 0.2000-M in each Na^+ and Cl^-.

$$F = \frac{g}{\text{F.W.} \times V}$$

$$V = \frac{g}{\text{F.W.} \times F}$$

$$V = \frac{30.00 \text{ g}}{58.44 \text{ g/F.W.} \times 0.2000 \text{ F.W./l}}$$

$$V = 2.567 \text{ l}$$

Example 5. Concentrations of solutions are often adjusted by dilution. In such cases, there must be the same quantity of solute (mmol or meq) in the final solution as in the original solution. In other words

$$V_2 \times N_2 = V_1 \times N_1$$

where the subscript 1 refers to the original solution, 2 to the final solution. Molarity could be substituted for normality.

500 ml of a 1.250-N solution is diluted to 2500 ml with water. What is the normality of the final solution?

$$2500 \times N_2 = 500 \times 1.250$$

$$N_2 = 0.250 \text{ meq/ml}$$

Example 6. How many grams of solid $Na_2C_2O_4$ should be added to 250 ml of a 0.200-M solution of $KHC_2O_4 \cdot H_2C_2O_4$ in order that the normality of the solution as a reducing agent be four times that as an acid?

The $C_2O_4^{2-}$ ion is oxidized to CO_2, the oxidation number of carbon changing from $+3$ to $+4$. Hence, the equivalent weight of $Na_2C_2O_4$ is one-half the molecular weight.

The equivalent weight of $KHC_2O_4 \cdot H_2C_2O_4$ as an acid is one-third the molecular weight since three hydrogens are furnished by each molecule. As a reducing agent the equivalent weight is one-fourth the molecular weight since two $C_2O_4^{2-}$ ions are furnished, each of which loses two electrons.

Let $w = \text{mg } Na_2C_2O_4$ needed

$$\text{Total meq as reducing agent} = \frac{w}{67.0} + (250 \times 0.200 \times 4)$$

$$\text{Total meq as acid} = 250 \times 0.200 \times 3$$

Therefore (note that the volume cancels),

$$\frac{w}{67.0} + (250 \times 0.200 \times 4) = 4(250 \times 0.200 \times 3)$$

$$\frac{w}{67.0} + 200 = 600$$

$$w = 26,800 \text{ mg} \quad \text{or} \quad 26.8 \text{ g}$$

Titer

Still another method of expressing concentration that is frequently used in analytical chemistry is the *titer*. The units of titer are weight per volume, but the weight is usually that of some reagent with which the solution will react rather than that of the solute itself. For example, if 1.00 ml of a hydrochloric acid solution will exactly neutralize 4.00 mg of sodium hydroxide, the concentration of the acid solution can be expressed as a sodium hydroxide titer of 4.00 mg/ml. Titer (T) can be easily converted to normality, as seen from the following relations:

$$T = \frac{\text{mg}}{\text{ml}}, \qquad N = \frac{\text{mg}}{\text{ml} \times \text{E.W.}}$$

Thus

$$T = N \times \text{E.W.}$$

The equivalent weight employed in the transformation is that of the substance with which the solution reacts, not the solute. In the example above, if the titer of the hydrochloric acid solution is 4.000 mg/ml of sodium hydroxide, the normality is obtained upon dividing by 40.00 mg/meq, the equivalent weight of sodium hydroxide, giving a normality of 0.1000 meq/ml.

Example 1. What is (a) the NH_3 titer of a 0.120-N solution of HCl; (b) the BaO titer of the same solution?

(a)
$$T = 0.120\frac{\text{meq}}{\text{ml}} \times 17.0\frac{\text{mg}}{\text{meq}}(NH_3)$$

$$T = 2.04\frac{\text{mg}}{\text{ml}}(NH_3)$$

(b)
$$T = 0.120 \frac{meq}{ml} \times \frac{153.4}{2} \frac{mg}{meq} (BaO)$$

$$T = 9.2 \frac{mg}{ml} (BaO)$$

This means that 1 ml of the HCl solution will neutralize 2.04 mg of NH_3 or 9.2 mg of BaO.

Example 2. A solution of NaOH has an oxalic acid (M.W. 126.0) titer of 9.45 mg/ml. Calculate the normality of the NaOH solution. (Oxalic acid furnishes two hydrogen ions.)

$$N = \frac{9.45 \text{ mg/ml}}{63.0 \text{ mg/meq}}$$

$$N = 0.150 \text{ meq/ml}$$

TITRIMETRIC AND GRAVIMETRIC METHODS

In quantitative analysis the principal application of stoichiometry is in calculating the percentage purity of a sample. We shall consider here examples from classical titrimetric and gravimetric methods. The following is a brief review of terminology from these areas.

In a *titrimetric* analysis we measure the volume of a solution of known concentration required to react with the desired constituent. The solution of known concentration is called a *standard solution*. The process of determining the volume is known as a *titration*. For many years the term *volumetric* analysis has been used rather than titrimetric. However, from a rigorous standpoint the term *titrimetric* is probably preferable because volume measurements need not be confined to titrations. In certain analyses, for example, one might measure the volume of a gas. The standard solution used in a titration is called the *titrant*.

The chemical reactions which may serve as the basis for titrimetric determinations are conveniently grouped into four types, as follows:

1.   Acid-base, or neutralization

$$H_3O^+ + OH^- \longrightarrow 2 H_2O$$

2.   Oxidation-reduction (redox)

$$Fe^{2+} + Ce^{4+} \longrightarrow Fe^{3+} + Ce^{3+}$$

3. Precipitation

$$Ag^+ + Cl^- \longrightarrow AgCl\downarrow$$

4. Complex formation

$$Ag^+ + 2\,CN^- \longrightarrow Ag(CN)_2^-$$

Of the host of known chemical reactions, relatively few can be used as the basis for titrations. Normally a reaction should satisfy certain requirements before it can be employed. First, it must proceed according to a definite chemical equation, with no side reactions. Second, it should proceed essentially to completion when equivalent amounts of reactants are mixed. If this requirement is met, there will be a large, abrupt change in the concentration of the substance titrated when an equivalent amount of titrant is added. Third, there must be a way of converting this sudden change into a signal which the analyst can detect. For many titrations, chemical substances called *indicators* are available which respond to the appearance of excess titrant by changing color. Fourth, it is desirable that the reaction be rapid, so that the titration can be completed in a few minutes.

In a titration involving, say, the reaction of A with titrant B, the point at which an equivalent amount of B has been added is termed the *equivalence* or *stoichiometric point*. In contrast, the point in the titration where the indicator changes color is termed the *end point*. It is desirable, of course, that the end point be as close as possible to the equivalence point. Choosing indicators to make these two points coincide (or correcting for the difference between the two) is one of the important aspects of volumetric analysis.

If the measurement step in an analysis involves a determination of weight, the analysis is termed *gravimetric*. Classically, precipitation has been the principal method used to separate the desired constituent before the final measurement of weight. A separation of some kind inevitably attends every gravimetric determination, and the following requirements should be met in order that a gravimetric method be successful.

1. The separation process should be sufficiently complete so that the quantity of desired constituent left behind is analytically undetectable (usually 0.1 mg or less in determining a major constituent of a macro sample).

2. The substance weighed should have a definite composition and should be pure, or very nearly so. Otherwise erroneous results may be obtained.

Electrolysis is another important method of separating and determining substances gravimetrically. The technique can also be employed as a "titrimetric" technique. The stoichiometry is discussed in the next section.

ILLUSTRATIVE PROBLEMS

It is important to keep in mind the units of concentration systems we will employ. These are:

Normality: meq/ml or eq/l

Molarity: mmol/ml or moles/l

Titer: mg/ml or g/l

Percent by weight: dimensionless

It should also be recalled that at the equivalence point of a titration the equivalents (or milliequivalents) of, say, substance A equal the equivalents (or milliequivalents) of substance B.

Standardization of Solutions

The process by which the concentration of a solution is accurately ascertained is known as *standardization*. A standard solution can sometimes be prepared by dissolving a known weight of the desired solute in a definite volume of solution. This method is not generally applicable, however, since relatively few chemical reagents can be obtained in sufficiently pure form to meet the analyst's demand for accuracy. Those few substances which *are* adequate in this regard are called *primary standards*. More commonly, a solution is standardized by titrating it against a weighed portion of a primary standard.

Example 1. A sample of pure Na_2CO_3 weighing 0.3542 g is dissolved in water and titrated with a solution of hydrochloric acid. A volume of 30.23 ml is required to reach the methyl orange end point, the reaction being

$$Na_2CO_3 + 2\,HCl \longrightarrow 2\,NaCl + H_2O + CO_2$$

Calculate the normality of the acid.

We know that

$$\text{meq } HCl = \text{meq } Na_2CO_3$$

The equivalent weight of Na_2CO_3 is one-half the molecular weight, or $105.99/2 = 53.00$. Hence

$$V_{HCl} \times N_{HCl} = \frac{\text{mg } Na_2CO_3}{\text{E.W. } Na_2CO_2}$$

$$30.23 \times N_{HCl} = \frac{354.2}{53.0}$$

$$N_{HCl} = 0.2211 \text{ meq/ml}$$

Example 2. A sample of pure sodium oxalate, $Na_2C_2O_4$, weighing 0.2856 g is dissolved in water, sulfuric acid is added, and the solution is titrated at 70°C, requiring 45.12 ml of a $KMnO_4$ solution. The end point is overrun and back-titration is carried out with 1.74 ml of a 0.1032-N solution of oxalic acid. Calculate the normality of the $KMnO_4$ solution.

The reaction, written ionically, is

$$5 C_2O_4{}^{2-} + 2 MnO_4{}^- + 16 H^+ \longrightarrow 2 Mn^{2+} + 10 CO_2 + 8 H_2O$$

We know that

meq permanganate = meq oxalate

or

$$meq\ KMnO_4 = meq\ Na_2C_2O_4 + meq\ H_2C_2O_4$$

$$V_{KMnO_4} \times N_{KMnO_4} = \frac{mg\ Na_2C_2O_4}{E.W.\ Na_2C_2O_4} + V_{H_2C_2O_4} \times N_{H_2C_2O_4}$$

Since the oxalate ion loses two electrons in the above reaction, the equivalent weight of $Na_2C_2O_4$ is one-half its molecular weight, or $134.00/2 = 67.00$. Hence

$$45.12 \times N_{KMnO_4} = \frac{285.6}{67.00} + 1.74 \times 0.1032$$

$$N_{KMnO_4} = 0.0985\ meq/ml$$

Example 3. Suppose in Example 2 the normality of the oxalic acid solution was not known. Instead, the volume ratio of the two solutions was known to be

$$1.000\ ml\ H_2C_2O_4 = 1.048\ ml\ KMnO_4$$

Calculate the normalities of the $KMnO_4$ and $H_2C_2O_4$ solutions.

The volume of oxalic acid can be converted to its equivalent volume of permanganate:

$$1.74 \times 1.048 = 1.82\ ml\ KMnO_4$$

The volume of $KMnO_4$ used by the $Na_2C_2O_4$ is

$$45.12 - 1.82 = 43.30\ ml$$

The normality can then be calculated:

$$43.30 \times N_{KMnO_4} = \frac{285.6}{67.00}$$

$$N_{KMnO_4} = 0.0985\ meq/ml$$

The normality of the $H_2C_2O_4$ is obtained as follows:

$$1.000 \times N_{H_2C_2O_4} = 1.048 \times 0.0985$$

$$N_{H_2C_2O_4} = 0.1032\ meq/ml$$

Titrimetric Analysis of Samples

To analyze a sample of unknown purity, the analyst weighs accurately a portion of the sample, dissolves it appropriately, and titrates it with a standard solution. He then knows that

$$\text{meq titrant} = \text{meq desired constituent}$$

From the normality and volume of titrant, the milliequivalents of the desired constituent are obtained. To express the results as a percentage, the milliequivalents of desired constituent are converted to weight and divided by the weight of the sample:

$$\% = \frac{\text{mg of desired constituent}}{\text{mg of sample}} \times 100$$

or

$$\% = \frac{V(\text{ml}) \times N(\text{meq/ml}) \times \text{E.W.(mg/meq)}}{\text{weight of sample (mg)}} \times 100$$

Note the cancellation of units to give percentage, which is dimensionless.

Example 1. A sample of iron ore weighing 0.6428 g is dissolved in acid. The iron is reduced to the ferrous state and titrated with 36.30 ml of a 0.1052-N solution of an oxidizing agent. (a) Calculate the percentage of iron (Fe) in the sample. (b) Express the percentage as FeO, Fe_2O_3, and Fe_3O_4.

(a) Iron is oxidized from Fe^{2+} to Fe^{3+}, losing one electron. Hence the equivalent weight of iron is 55.847 g/eq or mg/meq.

$$\% \, Fe = \frac{36.30 \text{ ml} \times 0.1052 \text{ meq/ml} \times 55.847 \text{ mg/meq}}{642.8 \text{ mg}} \times 100$$

$$\% \, Fe = 33.18$$

(b) To express the percentages in terms of an oxide, the equivalent weight of the oxide is substituted for that of iron in the expression above. Since each iron atom loses one electron, the equivalent weights of the oxides are:

$$FeO: \quad \frac{71.85}{1} = 71.85$$

$$Fe_2O_3: \quad \frac{159.69}{2} = 79.85$$

$$Fe_3O_4: \quad \frac{231.54}{3} = 77.18$$

18

Alternatively, the percentage of FeO can be calculated from the percentage of Fe:

$$\% \, FeO = \% \, Fe \times \frac{E.W. \, FeO}{E.W. \, Fe}$$

The student should confirm that $\%FeO = 42.69$, $\%Fe_2O_3 = 47.44$, and $\%Fe_3O_4 = 45.85$.

Example 2. It is found that 23.76 ml of 0.0491-M $AgNO_3$ is required to titrate a sample of impure KCN weighing 0.3642 g. The reaction is

$$Ag^+ + 2 \, CN^- \longrightarrow Ag(CN)_2{}^-$$

Calculate the percentage of KCN in the sample.
    At the equivalence point

$$mmol \, KCN = 2 \times mmol \, Ag^+$$

$$mmol \, KCN = 2 \times 23.76 \, ml \times 0.0491 \, mmol/ml$$

$$mmol \, KCN = 2.333$$

$$\% \, KCN = \frac{2.333 \, mmol \times 65.12 \, mg/mmol}{364.2 \, mg} \times 100$$

$$\% \, KCN = 41.7$$

Gravimetric Analysis of Samples

In the usual gravimetric analysis a precipitate is weighed, and from this value the weight of the desired constituent is computed. The term *gravimetric factor* is frequently employed, this factor being the number of grams of the desired constituent in 1 g (or the equivalent of 1 g) of the substance weighed. Multiplication of the weight of the precipitate by the gravimetric factor gives the number of grams of the desired constituent in the sample. Division by the weight of the sample and multiplication by 100 gives the percentage of the desired constituent:

$$\frac{Weight \, of \, precipitate \times gravimetric \, factor}{Weight \, of \, sample} \times 100 = \%$$

The following examples illustrate the calculation of gravimetric factors and the calculation of the percentage purity of a sample.

Example 1. Calculate the following gravimetric factors: (a) Cl in AgCl, (b) FeO in Fe_2O_3, (c) $KHC_2O_4 \cdot H_2C_2O_4$, from CaO.

(a) One mole of AgCl, 143.32 g, contains one mole of Cl atoms, 35.453 g. Hence one gram of AgCl contains

$$\frac{35.453}{143.323} = 0.24736 \text{ g Cl}$$

Letting the chemical symbols represent the atomic or molecular weights, this gravimetric factor is usually written

$$\frac{Cl}{AgCl}$$

(b) One mole of Fe_2O_3, 159.691 g, is equivalent to two moles of FeO. By this we mean that two moles of FeO are required to make one mole of Fe_2O_3. Hence the gravimetric factor is:

$$\frac{2 \text{ FeO}}{Fe_2O_3} = \frac{2(71.846)}{159.691} = 0.89981$$

Two points should be noted in setting up a gravimetric factor. First, the molecular weight of the desired constituent is in the numerator; that of the substance weighed is in the denominator. Second, the number of molecules or atoms appearing in the numerator and denominator must be chemically equivalent.

(c) The salt potassium tetraoxalate, $KHC_2O_4 \cdot H_2C_2O_4$, can be determined by precipitating the oxalate as calcium oxalate and then igniting the latter compound to calcium oxide. The abbreviated reactions are:

$$KHC_2O_4 \cdot H_2C_2O_4 + 2 \text{ Ca}^{2+} \longrightarrow 2 \text{ CaC}_2O_4 \longrightarrow 2 \text{ CaO}$$

Hence, two molecules of CaO are produced from one molecule of the tetraoxalate, and the factor needed to calculate the weight of tetraoxalate from the weight of calcium oxide is:

$$\frac{KHC_2O_4 \cdot H_2C_2O_4}{2 \text{ CaO}} = \frac{218.17}{2(56.08)} = 1.9452$$

Example 2. A 0.5483 g sample of iron ore is dissolved in acid, all the iron oxidized to Fe^{3+}, and then excess ammonia is added to precipitate $Fe(OH)_3$. The precipitate is filtered, washed, and ignited to Fe_2O_3. The latter compound weighs 0.2456 g. Calculate (a) the percentage of Fe in the ore and (b) the percentage expressed as Fe_3O_4.

(a) The gravimetric factor for Fe in Fe_2O_3 is

$$\frac{2 \text{ Fe}}{Fe_2O_3} = \frac{2 \times 55.847}{159.69} = 0.6994$$

Hence

$$\% \text{ Fe} = \frac{0.2456 \times 0.6994}{0.5483} \times 100$$

$$\% \text{ Fe} = 31.33$$

(b) The gravimetric factor for converting Fe_2O_3 to Fe_3O_4 is

$$\frac{2\ Fe_3O_4}{3\ Fe_2O_3} = \frac{2 \times 231.54}{3 \times 159.69} = 0.9666$$

Hence

$$\% \ Fe_3O_4 = \frac{0.2456 \times 0.9666}{0.5483} \times 100$$

$$\% \ Fe_3O_4 = 43.30$$

Example 3. *Indirect Analysis.* Two components in a mixture can be determined from two sets of independent analytical data. Two equations containing the two unknowns are set up and the equations solved simultaneously. The following is an illustration.

A 0.7500-g sample containing both NaCl and NaBr is titrated with 0.1043-M $AgNO_3$, using 42.23 ml. A second sample of the same weight is treated with excess silver nitrate, and the mixture of AgCl and AgBr is filtered, dried, and found to weigh 0.8042 g. Calculate the percentages of NaCl and of NaBr in the sample.

Let x = mmol of NaCl and y = mmol of NaBr. Then:

$$x + y = \text{total mmol} = 42.23 \text{ ml} \times 0.1043 \text{ mmol/ml}$$

$$x + y = 4.405$$

Also x = mmol AgCl and y = mmol AgBr produced. Hence

$$AgCl\ x + AgBr\ y = 804.2$$

$$143.32\ x + 187.78\ y = 804.2$$

Solving gives

$$x = 0.517 \text{ and } y = 3.888$$

Then

$$\% \ NaCl = \frac{0.517 \text{ mmol} \times 58.443 \text{ mg/mmol}}{750.0 \text{ mg}} \times 100 = 4.03$$

$$\% \ NaBr = \frac{3.888 \text{ mmol} \times 102.90 \text{ mg/mmol}}{750.0 \text{ mg}} \times 100 = 53.34$$

It should be noted that in solving this expression for y, it is necessary to divide by the difference in molecular weights of AgCl and AgBr. The closer these two weights are to each other, the greater effect an error in the experimental data (say in the weight of the combined precipitates) will have on the value of y and correspondingly of x. In other words, the reliability of the procedure is greatly reduced if the two molecular weights are very close to the same value.

When a sample is a mixture of *only two* substances, such as NaCl and NaBr, only one measurement need be made in order to calculate the percentage of each constituent. In effect, the second equation is provided by the fact that the sum of the percentages of the two compounds must total 100.

Factor Weight Solutions

It is possible to adjust the normality of a standard solution and the weight of sample taken for analysis so that the number of milliliters used in a titration equals the percentage of the desired constituent (or a factor thereof). This is of particular advantage in laboratories where many determinations of the same constituent are made. The following are examples of the calculations.

Example 1. What weight of sample should be taken for analysis so that the volume of 0.1074-N NaOH used for titration equals the percentage of potassium acid phthalate in the sample. The latter compound has the formula

and is abbreviated KHP. The molecular and equivalent weights are the same, 204.22.

$$\% \text{ KHP} = \frac{\text{ml NaOH} \times 0.1074 \text{ meq/ml} \times 204.22 \text{ mg/meq}}{\text{mg sample}} \times 100$$

Since $\%$ KHP = ml NaOH, these two terms cancel and

$$\text{mg sample} = 0.1074 \times 204.22 \times 100$$

$$\text{mg sample} = 2193$$

$$\text{g sample} = 2.193$$

Example 2. Samples containing arsenic weighing 0.8000 g are titrated with a standard iodine solution. What should be the normality of the iodine in order that each ml of titrant represents one-half percent As_2O_3 in the sample.

Arsenic is oxidized from the $+3$ to the $+5$ oxidation state, losing two electrons. Hence the equivalent weight of As_2O_3 is $197.84/4 = 49.46$ mg/meq.

$$\% \text{ As}_2\text{O}_3 = \frac{\text{ml I}_2 \times \text{N}_{\text{I}_2} \times 49.46}{800} \times 100$$

$$0.500 = \frac{1.00 \times \text{N}_{\text{I}_2} \times 49.46}{800} \times 100$$

$$\text{N}_{\text{I}_2} = 0.0809 \text{ meq/ml}$$

Balancing Oxidation-Reduction Equations

We shall describe briefly the oxidation number and the half-reaction methods for balancing redox equations. Both methods are presented in most general chemistry texts today.

Oxidation Number Method

In this method oxidation numbers are assigned to atoms in the reactants and products, and any changes in these numbers are attributed to a loss or gain of electrons. The number of electrons gained by the oxidizing agent is made equal to the number lost by the reducing agent by selecting appropriate coefficients for these two reactants.

Although the assignment of oxidation numbers can be made on an arbitrary basis, it is convenient to select the numbers as follows:

1. In ionic compounds the oxidation number is taken to be the same as the number of electrons gained or lost by the elements in forming the ion. For example, in sodium chloride, Na^+Cl^-, the oxidation number (also called oxidation state) of sodium is $+1$, that of chlorine -1. In zinc oxide, ZnO, zinc is taken as $+2$, oxygen as -2.

2. In covalent compounds of known structure, where electrons are shared by two atoms, the electrons are counted as belonging to the more electronegative of the two atoms. In HCl, for example, chlorine is assigned a number of -1, hydrogen a number of $+1$. In a covalent bond between like atoms, such as Cl_2, one electron is assigned to each atom, making the oxidation number of each Cl atom zero. The oxidation number of any elemental substance, such as Na, H_2, O_3, P_4, etc., is zero.

In assigning oxidation numbers in compounds containing hydrogen, it is customary to start with hydrogen as $+1$. The only exception occurs in ionic hydrides, such as Na^+H^-, where it is taken as -1. Oxygen is next assigned a value of -2 except in peroxides, such as H_2O_2, where the value must be -1 if hydrogen is $+1$.

It should be noted that the algebraic sum of oxidation numbers in a neutral molecule is zero. Similarly, in a complex ion the sum of the oxidation numbers of the atoms must equal the charge of the ion. For example, in the ion HPO_4^{2-}, the oxidation numbers are $H = +1$, $0 = -2$, and $P = +5$, giving the sum $+1 + 5 + 4(-2) = -2$.

The following examples illustrate the use of the oxidation number method to balance equations. Since the reactions occur in aqueous solution, we may need to add H^+, OH^-, or H_2O to balance oxygen and hydrogen atoms.

Example 1. Potassium permanganate, $KMnO_4$, oxidizes oxalic acid, $H_2C_2O_4$, in acid solution to form manganous ion, Mn^{2+}, and carbon dioxide, CO_2:

$$MnO_4^- + H_2C_2O_4 \longrightarrow Mn^{2+} + CO_2$$

Balance the equation adding H^+ and H_2O as needed.

Note that the oxidation number of manganese changes from $+7$ in MnO_4^- to $+2$ in Mn^{2+}. Hence each MnO_4^- ion gains five electrons. The oxidation number of carbon changes from $+3$ in $H_2C_2O_4$ to $+4$ in CO_2, a loss of one electron per carbon atom. Since each $H_2C_2O_4$ molecule contains two carbon atoms, the molecule loses two electrons. We can equate the electrons gained and lost by taking 2 MnO_4^- ions for each 5 $H_2C_2O_4$ molecules. Hence we write:

$$2\,MnO_4^- + 5\,H_2C_2O_4 \longrightarrow 2\,Mn^{2+} + 10\,CO_2 \qquad (1)$$

Next we balance the ionic charge by placing H^+ ions where needed. We need six plus charges on the left to make the charge $+4$ on each side of the arrow. The process is completed by adding eight molecules of water to the right side to balance the oxygen and hydrogen atoms.

$$2\,MnO_4^- + 5\,H_2C_2O_4 + 6\,H^+ \longrightarrow 2\,Mn^{2+} + 10\,CO_2 + 8\,H_2O \qquad (2)$$

Example 2. Chromate ion, CrO_4^{2-}, oxidizes sulfite ion, SO_3^{2-}, to sulfate, SO_4^{2-}, and is reduced to chromite, CrO_2^-, in basic solution:

$$CrO_4^{2-} + SO_3^{2-} \longrightarrow CrO_2^- + SO_4^{2-}$$

Balance the equation adding water and OH^- as needed.

Note that the oxidation number of chromium changes from $+6$ to $+3$, a gain of three electrons. Sulfur changes from $+4$ to $+6$, a loss of two electrons. Hence we write:

$$2\,CrO_4^{2-} + 3\,SO_3^{2-} \longrightarrow 2\,CrO_2^- + 3\,SO_4^{2-}$$

Next balance the ionic charge by placing two hydroxyl ions on the right side of the equation. The addition of one molecule of water to the left completes the balancing.

$$2\,CrO_4^{2-} + 3\,SO_3^{2-} + H_2O \longrightarrow 2\,CrO_2^- + 3\,SO_4^{2-} + 2\,OH^-$$

Half-Reaction Method

A redox equation can be balanced by writing separate reactions for the oxidizing and reducing agents. These "half-reactions" are balanced by adding electrons where needed. The numbers of electrons gained and lost in the two reactions are made the same, and the two equations are added to give the desired result.

Example 1. Balance the following equation for the reaction which occurs in aqueous acid.

$$MnO_4^- + C_2O_4^{2-} \longrightarrow Mn^{2+} + CO_2$$

Add H_2O and H^+ where needed.

First treat the oxidizing agent:

$$MnO_4^- \longrightarrow Mn^{2+}$$

Add water to the right to balance the oxygen:

$$MnO_4^- \longrightarrow Mn^{2+} + 4\,H_2O$$

Add H^+ to the left to balance hydrogen:

$$MnO_4^- + 8\,H^+ \longrightarrow Mn^{2+} + 4\,H_2O$$

The charge is balanced by placing five electrons on the left:

$$MnO_4^- + 8\,H^+ + 5e \longrightarrow Mn^{2+} + 4\,H_2O \qquad (1)$$

Second, treat the reducing agent:

$$C_2O_4^{2-} \longrightarrow 2\,CO_2$$

This is balanced except for the charge. Add two electrons to the right:

$$C_2O_4^{2-} \longrightarrow 2\,CO_2 + 2e \qquad (2)$$

Multiply Eq. (1) by 2 and Eq. (2) by 5, and add to give the final balanced equation:

$$2\,MnO_4^- + 5\,C_2O_4^{2-} + 16\,H^+ \longrightarrow 2\,Mn^{2+} + 10\,CO_2 + 8\,H_2O$$

Example 2. Balance the following reaction in basic solution:

$$Cr(OH)_3 + IO_3^- \longrightarrow I^- + CrO_4^{2-}$$

First treat the reducing agent:

$$Cr(OH)_3 \longrightarrow CrO_4^{2-}$$

Add H_2O to the left and H^+ to the right:

$$Cr(OH)_3 + H_2O \longrightarrow CrO_4^{2-} + 5\,H^+$$

Since we wish the equation to show OH^- ions rather than H^+ ions, we can add $5\,OH^-$ to both sides. This yields:

$$Cr(OH)_3 + H_2O + 5\,OH^- \longrightarrow CrO_4^{2-} + 5\,H_2O$$

or

$$Cr(OH)_3 + 5\,OH^- \longrightarrow CrO_4^{2-} + 4\,H_2O$$

Now balance the charge by adding three electrons to the right:

$$Cr(OH)_3 + 5\,OH^- \longrightarrow CrO_4{}^{2-} + 4\,H_2O + 3e \tag{1}$$

Next treat the oxidizing agent similarly, giving:

$$IO_3{}^- + 6\,H^+ \longrightarrow I^- + 3\,H_2O$$

$$IO_3{}^- + 6\,H_2O \longrightarrow I^- + 3\,H_2O + 6\,OH^-$$

$$IO_3{}^- + 3\,H_2O + 6e \longrightarrow I^- + 6\,OH^- \tag{2}$$

Multiply Eq. (1) by 2 and add it to Eq. (2), giving:

$$2\,Cr(OH)_3 + IO_3{}^- + 4\,OH^- \longrightarrow 2\,CrO_4{}^{2-} + I^- + 5\,H_2O$$

Electrolysis

As previously mentioned, a substance may be determined by using the technique of electrolysis; the procedure can be either gravimetric or titrimetric. The classical gravimetric determination of copper consists of depositing the metal on a previously weighed cathode. The increase in weight of the cathode gives the quantity of copper in the sample. In the titrimetric technique, called *coulometry*, the amount of a substance in solution is determined by measuring the quantity of electricity required to react with it completely. The quantity of electricity which brings about one equivalent of chemical change at an electrode is called a *faraday*. One equivalent of chemical change corresponds to the loss or gain of one mole of electrons. Hence, in electrical units, the faraday is equal to 96,500 coulombs of charge:

$$6.023 \times 10^{23} \text{ electrons/faraday} \times 1.60 \times 10^{-19} \text{ coulombs/electron}$$

$$= 96,500 \text{ coulombs/faraday}$$

It should also be recalled that the unit of current, the ampere, is defined as one coulomb per second. By measuring the current and time required for a reaction to go to completion, the chemist can calculate the number of coulombs and hence the number of equivalents of the desired substance in solution.

The following examples illustrate the calculations involved in analytical procedures.

Example 1. A 1.200-g sample containing lead was dissolved, and the lead oxidized electrolytically, and deposited on the anode as PbO_2. The reaction is

$$Pb^{2+} + 2\,H_2O \longrightarrow PbO_2 + 4\,H^+ + 2e$$

A constant current of 0.500 ampere was employed and the lead dioxide weighed

0.2309 g. (a) Calculate the percentage of Pb in the sample. (b) How many minutes are required for the electrolysis?

(a) The percentage lead is given by

$$\frac{0.2309 \times Pb/PbO_2}{1.200} \times 100 = 16.67\%$$

(b) Since two electrons are required to produce one PbO_2, the equivalent weight of PbO_2 is one-half the molecular weight. Hence

$$\text{meq } PbO_2 = \frac{230.9 \text{ mg}}{239.2/2 \text{ mg/meq}} = 1.931$$

Since 1 eq = 96,500 coul, 1 meq = 96.5 coul. And

$$96.5 \text{ coul/meq} \times 1.931 \text{ meq} = 186.3 \text{ coul required}$$

Hence

$$\frac{186.3 \text{ coul}}{0.500 \text{ coul/s}} = 372.6 \text{ sec or } 6.21 \text{ min}$$

Example 2. A sample of copper ore weighing 2.132 g is dissolved in acid and the copper electrolyzed:

$$Cu^{2+} + 2e \longrightarrow Cu$$

If 8.04 minutes are required for the electrolysis using a constant current of 2.00 amperes, calculate the percentage of copper in the ore.

The meq of copper is given by

$$\frac{8.04 \text{ min} \times 60 \text{ sec/min} \times 2.00 \text{ coul/sec}}{96.5 \text{ coul/meq}} = 10.0$$

Since 1 mmol Cu = 2 meq, the sample must contain 5.00 mmol Cu. Hence the percentage is

$$\% \text{ Cu} = \frac{5.00 \text{ mmol} \times 63.54 \text{ mg/mmol}}{2132 \text{ mg}} \times 100$$

$$\% \text{ Cu} = 14.9$$

REFERENCES

M. J. SIENKO, *Stoichiometry and Structure*, W. A. Benjamin, Inc., New York, 1964.

C. PIERCE and R. N. SMITH, *General Chemistry Workbook*, 4th ed., W. H. Freeman and Co., San Francisco, 1971.

C. B. KREMER and J. S. ARENTS, *Theory and Problems of Modern General Chemistry*, Thomas Y. Crowell Co., New York, 1965.

A. J. FRANK, *Quantitative Concepts in General Chemistry*, Charles E. Merrill Publishing Co., Columbus, Ohio, 1971.

1. Explain the advantages of molar and equivalent methods of expressing concentration over physical methods, such as weight percent.

2. What is the advantage of the formality system of concentration?

3. What are the equivalent weights of the following anhydrides? Write the reactions of the anhydrides with water. P_2O_5, N_2O_3, BaO, Cl_2O, Cl_2O_7, and Na_2O.

4. Explain the effect that the following errors would have on the standardization of a sodium hydroxide solution with pure potassium acid phthalate (KHP). Would the error cause the normality to be high or low, or would it have no effect?
    (a) The buret containing NaOH is read too quickly, not allowing time for drainage.
    (b) The initial reading of the NaOH buret is recorded as 1.90 when it is actually 2.10.
    (c) The weight of KHP is recorded as 0.6234 g when it is actually 0.6324 g.
    (d) The sample is dissolved in 100 ml of water although the directions called for only 50 ml.

5. Repeat Question 4 for the analysis of an impure sample of KHP by titration with standard base. Explain the effects of the errors on the percentage of KHP in the sample.

6. Balance the following half reactions in aqueous acid:
    (a) $MnO_4^- \longrightarrow Mn^{3+}$
    (b) $Cr_2O_7^{2-} \longrightarrow Cr^{3+}$
    (c) $H_3AsO_3 \longrightarrow H_3AsO_4$
    (d) $PH_3 \longrightarrow HPO_3^{2-}$
    (e) $S_2O_3^{2-} \longrightarrow SO_4^{2-}$

7. Balance the following half reactions in aqueous base:
    (a) $MnO_4^- \longrightarrow MnO_2$
    (b) $O_2 \longrightarrow OH^-$
    (c) $Cu_2O \longrightarrow Cu(OH)_2$
    (d) $CrO_4^{2-} \longrightarrow Cr(OH)_3$
    (e) $Sn^{2+} \longrightarrow SnO_3^{2-}$

8. Balance the following equations, adding H_2O and H^+ where needed. Where basic medium is indicated, show OH^- ions rather than H^+ ions. Use either the oxidation number or half reaction method, as you prefer.
    (a) $H_2O_2 + MnO_4^- \longrightarrow Mn^{2+} + O_2$
    (b) $SO_3^{2-} + Br_2 \longrightarrow SO_4^{2-} + Br^-$
    (c) $I_2 \longrightarrow IO_3^- + I^-$ (basic)
    (d) $Mn^{2+} + BiO_3^- \longrightarrow MnO_4^- + Bi^{3+}$
    (e) $HO_2^- + CrO_2^- \longrightarrow CrO_4^{2-}$ (basic)
    (f) $Al + NO_3^- \longrightarrow AlO_2^- + NH_3$ (basic)
    (g) $MnO_4^- + VO^{2+} \longrightarrow VO_3^- + Mn^{2+}$
    (h) $C_7H_8O + Cr_2O_7^{2-} \longrightarrow C_7H_8O_2 + Cr^{3+}$
    (i) $SbH_3 + Cl_2O \longrightarrow H_4Sb_2O_7 + Cl^-$
    (j) $FeS + NO_3^- \longrightarrow Fe^{3+} + NO + S$
    (k) $MnO_4^- + CN^- \longrightarrow MnO_2 + CNO^-$ (basic)
    (l) $UO_5^{2-} \longrightarrow UO_2^{2+} + O_2$
    (m) $Zn + NO_3^- \longrightarrow Zn^{2+} + NH_4^+$
    (n) $Fe + ClO_4^- \longrightarrow Fe^{3+} + Cl_2$
    (o) $Pt + NO_3^- + Cl^- \longrightarrow PtCl_6^{2-} + NO_2$
    (p) $VO_2^+ + V^{2+} \longrightarrow VO^{2+}$
    (q) $S_2O_3^{2-} + I_2 \longrightarrow S_4O_6^{2-} + I^-$

(r) $I^- + Cr_2O_7^{2-} \longrightarrow I_2 + Cr^{3+}$

(s) $Cl^- + MnO_4^- \longrightarrow Cl_2 + Mn^{2+}$

(t) $MnO_4^- + Mn^{2+} \longrightarrow MnO_2$ (basic)

PROBLEMS   (*Note:* For redox agents the oxidized and reduced forms are given at the end of the problem. For example, $MnO_4^- - Mn^{2+}$ means that permanganate was reduced to manganous ion in the reaction about which the calculation is to be made.)

1. *Molarity and normality.* (a) Calculate the molarity of each of the following solutions:
   (1) 6.00 g of NaOH in 0.200 l of solution.
   (2) 0.315 g of $H_2C_2O_4 \cdot 2H_2O$ in 50.0 ml of solution.
   (3) 21.03 g of CaO in 2.00 l of solution.
   (4) 49.0 mg of H_2SO_4 in 10.0 ml of solution.
   (5) 34.06 g of NH_3 in 5.00 l of solution.
   (b) Calculate the normality of each of the above solutions, assuming: $H_2C_2O_4 \cdot 2H_2O = 2 H^+$; $CaO = 2 H^+$; $H_2SO_4 = 2 H^+$; $NH_3 = 1 H^+$; $NaOH = 1 H^+$.

2. *Molarity and normality.* (a) Calculate the molarity of each of the following solutions:
   (1) 3.95 g $KMnO_4$ in 3.00 l solution.
   (2) 14.71 g $K_2Cr_2O_7$ in 200.0 ml solution.
   (3) 2.171 g I_2 in 750.0 ml solution.
   (4) 623.2 mg $Na_2S_2O_3 \cdot 5H_2O$ in 30.00 ml solution.
   (b) Calculate the normality of each of the above solutions if the reactants and products are as follows:

   $MnO_4^- - Mn^{2+}$; $Cr_2O_7^{2-} - Cr^{3+}$; $S_2O_3^{2-} - S_4O_6^{2-}$; $I_2 - I^-$

3. *Formality and molarity.* (a) Calculate the formalities of the following solutions:
   (1) 7.40 g $NaNO_3$ in 1.20 l solution.
   (2) 23.2 g $CaCl_2$ in 2.04 l solution.
   (3) 36.6 mg K_2SO_4 in 2.50 ml solution.
   (b) Assuming that the salts in part (a) are completely dissociated in aqueous solution, calculate the molarities of each of the ionic species.

4. *Titer.* Express the titer of the following solutions in mg/ml. (a) 0.150-*N* HCl in terms of CaO, $Ca(OH)_2$, Na_2O, and NaOH. (b) 0.240-*N* NaOH in terms of HCl, $HClO_4$, H_2SO_4, and acetic acid, $HC_2H_3O_2$. (c) 0.0200-*M* $KMnO_4$ in terms of FeO, Fe_2O_3, and As_2O_3. Reactions: $MnO_4^- - Mn^{2+}$; $Fe^{2+} - Fe^{3+}$; $AsO_3^{3-} - AsO_4^{3-}$. (d) 0.120-*M* $Na_2C_2O_4$ in terms of $KMnO_4$ and $K_2Cr_2O_7$. Reactions: $MnO_4^- - Mn^{2+}$; $Cr_2O_7^{2-} - Cr^{3+}$; $C_2O_4^{2-} - CO_2$.

5. *Density and molarity.* Calculate the molarity of the following solutions: (a) HCl, density 1.057 g/ml, 12.0% HCl by weight; (b) NH_4OH, density 0.954 g/ml, 11.6% NH_3 by weight; (c) $HClO_4$, density 1.242 g/ml, 34.0% $HClO_4$ by weight; (d) H_2SO_4, density 1.30 g/ml, 32.6% SO_3 by weight.

6. *Dilution of solutions.* (a) 150.0 ml of a 0.1200-*M* solution is diluted to 200.0 ml. What is the molarity of the final solution? (b) What volume of water would be added to 500 ml of a 0.200-*M* solution to make the molarity 0.125? Assume volumes are additive. (c) What volume of 0.5000-*M* solution of NaOH should be added to

100 ml of a 0.0800-M NaOH solution to make the resulting solution 0.200-M? Assume the volumes are additive. (d) 40.0 ml of 0.150-M HCl is mixed with 60.0 ml of 0.200-M NaOH. Is the resulting solution acidic, basic, or neutral? Calculate the molarity of the reactant which is in excess.

7. *Molarity.* It is found that 16.00 ml of a solution containing Ni^{2+} is required to react with 0.5210 g of pure KCN according to the equation

$$Ni^{2+} + 4\,CN^- \longrightarrow Ni(CN)_4{}^{2-}$$

Calculate the molarity of the nickel solution.

8. *Molarity.* Calculate the molarity of ethyl alcohol in a liquor which is labeled "80 Proof." The term *proof* is defined as twice the percentage by volume of pure ethyl alcohol at 60°F. (80 proof means 40% by volume alcohol.) The densities at 60°F are: alcohol 0.80 g/ml; water 1.00 g/ml.

9. *Parts per million.* Phosphate concentration in water is usually expressed as parts per million PO_4 by weight (ppm PO_4). Thus a solution containing one milligram of $PO_4{}^{3-}$ in one liter (one kilogram) of aqueous solution has a concentration of 1 ppm PO_4. What is the molarity of a 1.9 ppm PO_4 solution?

10. *Standardization.* From the following data calculate the normalities of the acid and base solutions: weight of potassium acid phthalate (KHP), 100% pure, = 0.8234 g; volume of base used = 41.34 ml; volume of acid used in back-titration = 0.72 ml; 1.000 ml acid = 0.976 ml base.

11. *Standardization.* A sample of pure iron wire weighing 0.2602 g is dissolved in hydrochloric acid. The iron is reduced to Fe^{2+} and titrated with 43.26 ml of potassium dichromate in acid solution. Calculate the normality of the dichromate solution. Reactions: $Fe^{2+} - Fe^{3+}$; $Cr_2O_7{}^{2-} - Cr^{3+}$.

12. *Chemical equivalents.* Complete the following blanks so that the quantities of the two substances are chemically equivalent. (a) 98.92 mg As_2O_3 = _____ ml of 0.2000-N I_2; (b) 654 mg $KHC_2O_4 \cdot H_2C_2O_4$ = _____ ml of 0.150-N $KMnO_4$; (c) 50.0 ml of 0.0250-M $K_2Cr_2O_7$ = _____ mg Fe_2O_3; (d) 40.0 ml of 0.200-M $C_2O_4{}^{2-}$ = _____ ml of 0.200-M $MnO_4{}^-$ Reactions: $AsO_3{}^{3-} - AsO_4{}^{3-}$; $I_2 - I^-$; $C_2O_4{}^{2-} - CO_2$; $Cr_2O_7{}^{2-} - Cr^{3+}$; $MnO_4{}^- - Mn^{2+}$; $Fe^{2+} - Fe^{3+}$.

13. *Sample size.* A student wishes to weigh out a sufficiently large sample so that he will use about 30 ml of a 0.10-N reagent for titration. How many grams should he take if the sample is (a) pure KHP, (b) 35% KHP, (c) 40% Na_2CO_3; (d) 25% $Na_2C_2O_4$? Reactions: $CO_3{}^{2-} - H_2CO_3$; $C_2O_4{}^{2-} - CO_2$.

14. *Titrant concentration.* If a 1.0-N base solution is employed as a titrant, what size sample containing about 30% KHP should be taken so that the volume of titrant used will be about 40 ml? (b) Repeat the calculation for 0.010-N base. (c) Suggest why titrants are usually about 0.1 to 0.2-N.

15. *Titrimetric analysis.* A 2.045-g sample of an impure acid required 38.34 ml of 0.0984-N base for titration. Calculate the percentage purity as (a) KHP, (b) $H_2C_2O_4$, (c) $H_2C_2O_4 \cdot 2H_2O$. Oxalic acid, $H_2C_2O_4$, furnishes 2 H^+.

16. *Titrimetric analysis.* A 20.00 ml sample of vinegar having a density of 1.055 g/ml requires 40.34 ml of 0.3024-N base for titration. Calculate the percentage of acetic acid ($HC_2H_3O_2$) in the sample.

17. *Titrimetric analysis.* A 1.600-g sample of an acid having an equivalent weight of 80.0 is titrated with standard base. It is found that the percentage purity is exactly 50.0 times the normality of the base. What volume of base was used in the titration?

18. *Titrimetric analysis.* An ore contains 25.0% Fe_2O_3 and 12.0% Fe_3O_4. What volume of 0.120-N oxidizing agent is required to titrate a 0.600-g sample of the ore? Reaction: $Fe^{2+} - Fe^{3+}$.

19. *Titrimetric analysis.* An ore can be analyzed for MnO_2 by adding excess pure sodium oxalate, $Na_2C_2O_4$, in acid medium. The following reaction occurs:

$$MnO_2 + C_2O_4^{2-} + 4 H^+ \longrightarrow Mn^{2+} + 2 CO_2 + 2 H_2O$$

The excess oxalate is titrated with standard $KMnO_4$, the oxalate being oxidized to CO_2 and the permanganate reduced to Mn^{2+}. Given the following data: weight sample = 1.000 g; weight $Na_2C_2O_4$ = 0.4020 g; volume of 0.1000-N $KMnO_4$ = 20.00 ml. Calculate the percentage of MnO_2 in the sample.

20. *Percentage purity.* Repeat the calculation in Problem 19, but report the percentage as (a) oxygen; (b) manganese.

21. *Titrimetric analysis.* The silver in a 1.000-g sample is determined by first precipitating the silver as Ag_2CrO_4. The precipitate is dissolved in acid, excess KI added, and the chromate oxidizes iodide to iodine. The I_2 requires 30.00 ml of 0.0950-M $Na_2S_2O_3$ for titration. Calculate the percentage of silver in the sample. Reactions: $CrO_4^{2-} - Cr^{3+}$; $I^- - I_2$; $Na_2S_2O_3 - Na_2S_4O_6$.

22. *Sulfur in steel.* The sulfur in a steel sample is determined by oxidation to SO_3 and absorption of the SO_3 in standard base. The SO_3 from a 0.800-g sample of steel is absorbed in 50.00 ml of 0.0500-N NaOH, and the excess base requires 26.34 ml of 0.0600-N acid for titration. Calculate the percentage of sulfur in the steel.

23. *Percentage purity.* A student found that a sample contained 10.0% S. He was told to report his result as SO_3 rather than S. By what factor should he multiply the percentage S to obtain percentage SO_3?

24. *Kjeldahl analysis.* In a Kjeldahl analysis for nitrogen, the element is converted into NH_3 which is then distilled into a measured volume of standard acid. Excess acid is titrated with standard base. The ammonia from a 1.325-g sample of fertilizer is distilled into 50.00 ml of 0.2030-N H_2SO_4, and 25.32 ml of 0.1980-N NaOH is required for back-titration. Calculate the percentage of nitrogen (N) in the sample.

25. *Calcium in blood.* Calcium can be determined in blood by precipitating CaC_2O_4, dissolving the precipitate in sulfuric acid, and titrating the oxalate with $KMnO_4$. The reactions are: $C_2O_4^{2-} - CO_2$; $MnO_4^- - Mn^{2+}$. 10.0 ml of blood from a patient is diluted to 50.0 ml in a volumetric flask. A 20.0 ml sample from the flask is treated with oxalate to precipitate CaC_2O_4. The precipitate is redissolved and titrated with 1.25 ml of 0.00400-N $KMnO_4$. Calculate the concentration of calcium ions in the blood. Express this as milligrams of Ca^{2+} per 10.0 ml of blood.

26. *Titrimetric analysis.* A sample of impure KI weighing 0.6125 g is dissolved in water, the solution acidified, and 20.00 ml of 0.0500-M KIO_3 (an excess) added. The following reaction occurs (unbalanced):

$$IO_3^- + I^- + H^+ \longrightarrow I_2 + H_2O$$

The iodine is boiled off, the solution cooled, and an excess of pure KI is added to react with the unused KIO_3. The iodine produced is titrated with 25.34 ml of 0.1023-N thiosulfate. The following reaction occurs (unbalanced):

$$I_2 + S_2O_3^{2-} \longrightarrow I^- + S_4O_6^{2-}$$

Balance the equations and calculate the percentage of KI in the sample.

27. *Titration.* In Problem 26 how many milliliters of the same thiosulfate solution would have been required to titrate the iodine which was boiled off?

28. *Titration.* A 0.2608-g sample consists of only $Na_2C_2O_4$ and KHC_2O_4. It requires 50.00 ml of 0.0800-N $KMnO_4$ for titration in acid solution. In an acid-base titration a 0.2608-g sample of the same material requires how many milliliters of a 0.1600-N solution of NaOH? Reactions: $C_2O_4^{2-} - CO_2$; $MnO_4^- - Mn^{2+}$; $HC_2O_4^- - CO_2$.

29. *Factor weight solution.* What should be the normality of a solution of an oxidizing agent so that the volume (ml) of titrant divided by 2 gives the percentage Fe_2O_3 in a 0.5000-g sample of the ore? Reaction: $Fe^{2+} - Fe^{3+}$.

30. *Factor weight solution.* What weight of sample should be taken for analysis so that the volume (ml) of 0.1500-N HCl titrant multiplied by 2 equals the percentage NaOH in the sample?

31. *Stoichiometry.* The hydrogen sulfide in a gas sample is absorbed in water and titrated with 30.00 ml of 0.1000-N I_2 solution. What volume did the H_2S occupy as a gas at STP? Reactions: $H_2S - S$; $I_2 - I^-$.

32. *Titration.* What volume of 0.150-N $KMnO_4$ is required to react with 5.00 ml of H_2O_2 that has a density of 1.01 g/ml and contains 3.00% by weight H_2O_2? Reactions: $MnO_4^- - Mn^{2+}$; $H_2O_2 - O_2$.

33. *Gas volume.* If the reaction in Problem 32 is carried out and the oxygen collected, what volume does it occupy at standard temperature and pressure?

34. *Stoichiometry.* What should be the normality of the permanganate in Problem 32 if the volume of oxygen collected (STP) is exactly twice the volume of permanganate used in the titration?

35. *Stoichiometry.* A 0.500-g sample containing MnO_2 is treated with concentrated HCl producing Cl_2. The chlorine is passed into a solution of KI, and 30.34 ml of 0.0988-N $Na_2S_2O_3$ are required to titrate the liberated iodine. Calculate (a) the percentage of MnO_2 in the sample and (b) the volume occupied by the Cl_2 at STP. Reactions: $MnO_2 - Mn^{2+}$; $Cl^- - Cl_2$; $I^- - I_2$; $Na_2S_2O_3 - Na_2S_4O_6$.

36. *Gravimetric analysis.* A 0.6834-g sample containing chloride is dissolved and the chloride precipitated as AgCl. The precipitate is washed, dried, and found to weigh 0.4281 g. Calculate the percentage chloride in the sample.

37. *Gravimetric analysis.* The lead in a 0.5250-g sample of an ore is precipitated as $PbSO_4$. The dried precipitate weighs 0.4264 g. Calculate (a) the percentage of lead (Pb) in the ore and (b) the percentage expressed as Pb_3O_4.

38. *Gravimetric analysis.* The phosphorus in a sample of phosphate rock weighing 0.5428 g is precipitated as $MgNH_4PO_4 \cdot 6H_2O$ and ignited to $Mg_2P_2O_7$. If the ignited precipitate weighs 0.2234 g, calculate (a) the percentage of P_2O_5 in the rock and (b) the weight of the precipitate of $MgNH_4PO_4 \cdot 6H_2O$.

39. *Gravimetric analysis.* Iron is determined in a sample by precipitating $Fe(OH)_3$ and igniting the precipitate to Fe_2O_3. What weight of sample should be taken for analysis so that each milligram of Fe_2O_3 represents 0.100% Fe in the sample?

40. *Atomic weight.* A pure sample of sodium chloride weighing 0.65310 g is dissolved in water and the chloride precipitated as AgCl. If the AgCl precipitate weighs 1.6029 g, calculate the atomic weight of sodium. Assume the atomic weights of chlorine and silver are 35.453 and 107.87, respectively.

41. *Stoichiometry.* A mixture which contains only Fe_2O_3 and Al_2O_3 weighs 0.6200 g. It is treated with H_2, reducing the Fe_2O_3 to Fe. The Al_2O_3 is not changed. The mixture now weighs 0.5321 g. Calculate the percentage of Al in the sample.

42. *Stoichiometry.* A sample containing only $CaCO_3$ and $BaCO_3$ is ignited to CaO and MgO. The mixture of oxides weighs exactly 50.0% as much as the original sample. Calculate the percentages of $CaCO_3$ and $MgCO_3$ in the sample.

43. *Stoichiometry.* A 0.3531-g sample containing only $CaCO_3$ and $MgCO_3$ produced 89.6 ml of CO_2 at STP when treated with HCl. Assuming that all the carbonates reacted completely, how many grams of $CaCO_3$ did the original sample contain?

44. *Stoichiometry.* A certain material contains 20.0% KCl. How many grams of pure NaCl should be added to 1.40 g of this material so that the resulting mixture will contain 15.0% chloride (Cl)?

45. *Gravimetric analysis.* The sodium and potassium in a sample weighing 0.9134 g are converted into NaCl and KCl. The mixture of chlorides weighs 0.5924 g. The chlorides are then treated with sulfuric acid, converting them to Na_2SO_4 and K_2SO_4. The mixture of sulfates weighs 0.7024 g. Calculate the percentages of Na_2O and K_2O in the sample.

46. *Indirect analysis.* A 0.6000-g sample that contains both NaCl and NaBr gives a precipitate of AgCl and AgBr that weighs 0.4482 g. Another 0.6000-g sample is titrated, requiring 26.48 ml of 0.1084-M $AgNO_3$ for complete reaction. Calculate the percentages of NaCl and NaBr in the sample.

47. *Stoichiometry.* A mixture containing only AgCl and AgBr weighs 0.4834 g. It is treated with Cl_2, converting the AgBr to AgCl. The total weight of AgCl is 0.3826 g. Calculate the weight of AgBr in the original sample.

48. *Coulometric analysis.* A 1.00-g sample of an alloy containing copper is dissolved and the copper deposited by electrolysis. It requires 10.0 minutes using a constant current of 4.00 amperes to complete the electrolysis. Calculate the percentage of copper in the sample.

49. *Electrolysis.* Calculate the time in minutes required to deposit the following by electrolysis (100% current efficiency): (a) zinc from 100 ml of a 0.200-M solution of Zn^{2+}, 0.500-ampere current; (b) aluminum from 60 ml of a 0.15-M solution of Al^{3+}, current of 2.0 amperes; (c) lead from 200 ml of a 0.100-M solution of Pb^{2+}, current of 0.600 ampere, lead deposited on anode as PbO_2.

50. *Electrolysis.* Calculate the number of electrons and the time (minutes) required (a) to liberate 336 ml of H_2 (STP), current of 2.00 amperes; (b) to liberate 14.0 liters of O_2 (STP), current of 8.0 amperes; (c) to liberate 1.00 ml of Cl_2 (STP) from a Cl^- solution, current of 0.250 amperes.

51. *Electrolysis.* A solution of copper sulfate is electrolyzed, depositing copper on the cathode and liberating oxygen at the anode. The acid produced during the electrolysis requires 30 ml of 0.15-N NaOH for neutralization. Calculate (a) the weight in grams of copper deposited on the cathode and (b) the average current used if 10 minutes are required for the electrolysis.

3 Errors and the Treatment of Analytical Data

INTRODUCTION

In an experimental science such as chemistry, much effort is expended in gathering data, and as chemistry has developed into a modern science, most of the data have become quantitative, i.e., they derive from measurements. When any scientific measurement is performed, it is necessary to consider the fact that an error has been made, and it is important to develop the ability to evaluate data, learning to draw justified conclusions while rejecting interpretations that are unwarranted because of limitations in the measurements. Although analytical chemists in particular like to emphasize the techniques by which data may be evaluated, it is clear that any chemist may enhance his competence by learning methods which are more reliable than intuition alone in assessing the significance of experimental results. The methods which are most suitable for the treatment of analytical data are powerful, general tools which may be used in many other scientific situations.

Most of the techniques which we shall consider are based upon statistical concepts. There is increasing awareness that statistical methods are efficient in planning experiments that will yield the most information from the fewest measurements and in "boiling down" data so that their significance is concisely presented. Statistics, on the other hand, should not be expected to lessen the necessity of obtaining good measurements, and statistical methods are most powerful when applied to good data.

Statistics and the theory of probability represent an important branch of mathematics which possesses a logical and rigorous structure. Although chemists may profit from study in this field, it is impossible in this textbook to examine the foundations of probability theory and to derive their consequences. We must here accept the conclusions of the mathematicians largely on faith, and then attempt to see how they may be useful to chemists. We may hope to learn how our intuitive judgments of data may be validated by quantitative expressions of their probable reliability, and even what the term "reliability" means in connection with measurements of quantities that are actually unknown. We shall see how sets of data may be compared to learn whether they are *really* different or whether an apparent difference could be attributable not to an assignable cause, but to chance alone. A convenient technique will be described for "keeping track" of repetitive measurements so that correctives can be applied if they begin to wander beyond acceptable deviations. We shall see how errors are propagated through a series of experimental steps and calculations. The student should emerge from this study with a heightened skepticism of data which is moderated by an increased confidence in his ability to draw justified conclusions.

ERRORS

The term *error* as used here refers to the numerical difference between a measured value and the true value. The *true value* of any quantity is really a philosophical abstraction, something that man is not destined to know, although scientists generally feel that there is such a thing and believe that they may approach it more and more closely as their measurements become increasingly refined. In analytical chemistry, it is customary to act as though the true value of a quantity were known when it is believed that the uncertainty in the value is less than the uncertainty in something else with which it is being compared. For example, the percentage composition of a standard sample certified by the National Bureau of Standards may be treated as correct in evaluating a new analytical method; differences between the standard values and the results obtained by the new method are then treated as errors in the latter. Values which we are willing to treat as *true* are generally arrived at by a variety of methods whose limitations and pitfalls are sufficiently different that agreement among them cannot reasonably be ascribed to coincidence. Even so, it is well to remain skeptical about standard, accepted, or certified values, because they stem from experimental measurements performed by human, albeit expert, hands.

Determinate Errors

Errors which can, at least in principle, be ascribed to definite causes are termed *determinate* or *systematic* errors. A given determinate error is generally unidirectional with respect to the true value, in contrast to indeterminate errors, discussed below, which lead to both high and low results with equal probability. Determinate errors are often reproducible, and in many cases they can be predicted by a person who thoroughly understands all the aspects of the measurement. Examples of sources of determinate errors are: a corroded weight, a poorly calibrated buret, an impurity in a reagent, an appreciable solubility of a precipitate, a side reaction in a titration, and heating a sample at too high a temperature.

Determinate errors have been classified as *methodic*, *operative*, and *instrumental* in accordance with their origin in (a) the method of analysis as it reflects the properties of the chemical systems involved, (b) ineptitude of the experimenter, and (c) failure of measuring devices to perform in accordance with required standards.[1] Frequently the source of an error may lie in more than one of these categories. For example, some error may always be expected in weighing a hygroscopic substance, but it may be increased if the analyst has poor balance technique; the environment outside the system may influence the error, as, for example, in the effect of humidity upon the error in weighing a hygroscopic substance.

Constant Errors

Sometimes the magnitude of a determinate error is nearly constant in a series of analyses, regardless of the size of the sample. This may be the case, for example, with an indicator blank that is not corrected for in a series of titrations. Some writers have used the term *additive* for this type of error. The significance of a constant error generally decreases as the size of the sample increases, since usually we are not so interested in the absolute value of an error as in its value relative to the magnitude of the measured quantity. For example, a constant end point error of 0.1 ml in a series of titrations represents a relative error of 10% for a sample requiring 1 ml of titrant, but only 0.2% if 50 ml of titrant is used.

Proportional Errors

The absolute value of this type of error varies with sample size in such a way that the relative error remains constant. A substance that interferes in an analytical method may lead to such an error if present in the sample. For example, in the iodometric determination of an oxidant like chlorate, another oxidizing agent such as iodate or bromate would cause high results if its presence were unsuspected and not corrected for. Taking a larger sample would increase the absolute error, but the relative error would remain constant provided the sample were homogeneous. Errors may be encountered which vary with the size of the sample but not in a strictly linear fashion. Many writers use the term "proportional" for these also, although of course it is not strictly correct for such cases.

Data obtained a number of years ago by Benedetti-Pichler[2] are often quoted to illustrate the interplay of constant and proportional errors and to

---

[1] E. B. Sandell, "Errors in Chemical Analysis," Chapter 2 in I. M. Kolthoff and P. J. Elving, eds., *Treatise on Analytical Chemistry*, Part I, Vol. 1, Interscience Publishers, Inc., New York, 1959.

[2] A. A. Benedetti-Pichler, *Ind. Eng. Chem., Anal. Ed.*, **8**, 373 (1936).

suggest how they may be distinguished. The ideas apply as well to modern measurements of a much more sophisticated type. The data are given in Table 3.1. Samples of potassium alum were dissolved and acidified with

TABLE 3.1   DETERMINATION OF ALUMINUM (as Al_2O_3) IN POTASSIUM ALUM†

$KAl(SO_4)_2$ $\cdot$ 12 H_2O taken, g	Al_2O_3 taken, g	Al_2O_3 found using stock NH_3, g	Differ- ence, g	Al_2O_3 found using distilled NH_3, g	Differ- ence, g
1.0000	0.1077	0.1288	0.0211	0.1087	0.0010
2.0000	0.2154	0.2384	0.0230	0.2178	0.0024
3.0000	0.3231	0.3489	0.0258	0.3258	0.0027
4.0000	0.4308	0.4588	0.0280	0.4352	0.0044

† See reference 2.

proper amounts of hydrochloric acid so that the quantity of ammonia required to precipitate hydrous aluminum oxide was nearly constant. In one set of experiments, ammonia from a stock bottle was used; in the other set, freshly distilled ammonia. In the former case, it is seen that the errors were nearly constant. This was attributed to the fact that coprecipitation of silicic acid, originating from the attack of the old ammonia solution on the glass bottle, was constant because the same volume of ammonia solution was used in each case. In the latter experiments, silicic acid was absent, and the errors, now much smaller, were much more nearly proportional to sample size. These errors were attributed to the presence of water in the ignited precipitate, the quantity of water retained depending upon the quantity of alumina and hence upon sample size. In evaluating a new analytical method, information about the type of errors present and sometimes clues pointing toward their minimization may be obtained simply by varying the size of the sample.

Indeterminate Errors

If a measurement is sufficiently coarse, repetition will yield exactly the same result each time. For example, in weighing a 50-g object to the nearest gram with a good balance, only by extreme negligence could a person obtain different values or a group of people fail to agree. The only reasonable errors in such a measurement would be determinate ones, such as a seriously defective weight. On the other hand, any measurement can be refined to the point where it is mere coincidence if replicates agree to the last recorded digit. Sooner or later, the point is approached where unpredictable and imperceptible factors introduce what appear to be random fluctuations in the measured quantity. In some cases, it may be possible to specify definite variables that are beyond control near the performance limit of an instrument: noise and drift in an electronic circuit, vibrations in a building caused by passing traffic, temperature variations, and the like. Often the inability of the eye to detect slight changes in a readout device may be invoked as a source of error. To be sure, variations which a slipshod person considers random may appear obvious and controllable to a careful onlooker, but nevertheless the point must be reached where anyone, however meticulous, will encounter random errors which he cannot further reduce. These errors are classified as *indeterminate*.

It is tempting at first glance to retreat from indeterminate errors simply by performing coarser measurements. After backing off to the point where scatter in the data ceases to exist, an observer will obtain exactly the same result each time, and superficially this seems as good as recording an additional digit which varies from one time to the next. But this withdrawal from the challenge to push measurements as far as possible is unacceptable to most scientists. More cogent, however, is the fact that the average of a number of fine observations with random scatter is more precise than coarser data which agree perfectly. Data that exhibit random scatter may be subjected to an analysis that does attach significance to the last recorded digit, as we shall see below.

Accuracy and Precision

The terms *accuracy* and *precision*, often used synonymously in ordinary discourse, should be carefully distinguished in connection with scientific data. An accurate result is one that agrees closely with the true value of a measured quantity. The comparison is usually made on the basis of an inverse measure of the accuracy, viz., the error (the smaller the error, the greater the accuracy). The error is most frequently expressed relative to the size of the measured quantity, for example, in percent or in parts per thousand. In view of the nebulous nature of true values, it is clear that accuracy cannot often be ascertained. Precision, on the other hand, refers to the agreement among a group of experimental results, and implies nothing about their relation to the true value. Precise values may well be inaccurate, since an error causing deviation from the true value may affect all of the measurements equally and hence not impair their precision. A determinate error which leads to inaccuracy may or may not affect precision, depending upon how nearly constant it remains throughout a series of measurements.

DISTRIBUTION OF RANDOM ERRORS

After the search for determinate errors has been carried as far as possible and all precautions taken and corrections applied, the remaining fluctuations in the data are found to be random in nature. Results that scatter in a random fashion are best treated by the powerful techniques of statistics. It will now be our goal to show how these techniques are applied and what information they furnish beyond what may be seen by simply inspecting the data.

Frequency Distributions

Table 3.2 contains some actual data obtained by a person who prepared sixty replicate colored solutions and measured their absorbance values with

TABLE 3.2   INDIVIDUAL VALUES, UNORGANIZED

1	0.458	21	0.462	41	0.450
2	0.450	22	0.450	42	0.455
3	0.465	23	0.454	43	0.456
4	0.452	24	0.446	44	0.456
5	0.452	25	0.464	45	0.459
6	0.447	26	0.461	46	0.454
7	0.459	27	0.463	47	0.455
8	0.451	28	0.457	48	0.458
9	0.446	29	0.460	49	0.457
10	0.467	30	0.451	50	0.456
11	0.452	31	0.456	51	0.455
12	0.463	32	0.455	52	0.460
13	0.456	33	0.451	53	0.456
14	0.456	34	0.462	54	0.463
15	0.449	35	0.451	55	0.457
16	0.454	36	0.469	56	0.456
17	0.456	37	0.458	57	0.457
18	0.441	38	0.458	58	0.453
19	0.457	39	0.456	59	0.455
20	0.459	40	0.454	60	0.453

a spectrophotometer. (Absorbance is discussed in a later chapter, but the nature of the measured quantity need not concern us here.) The data in Table 3.2 have not been treated in any way, but are simply listed in the order in which they were obtained. We are here concerned, not with any "correct" result, but only with the relationships of the measured values among themselves. It is apparent that the values in Table 3.2 must be treated in some manner before they can be discussed intelligently. A reader with an exceptionally quick eye may notice that the lowest value is 0.441 and the highest 0.469, and perhaps it is apparent that many values are between 0.45 and 0.46, but on the whole the table is relatively uninstructive. Let us now enumerate some steps that will enable us to interpret the data more fully.

First, we arrange the results in order from lowest to highest. This has been done in Table 3.3. This simple operation discloses information not so readily apparent in the raw data, namely the maximum and minimum values, and, by simple counting, the middle or median value. This is still an inadequate

TABLE 3.3 INDIVIDUAL VALUES ARRANGED IN ORDER

1	0.441	21	0.454	41	0.457
2	0.446	22	0.455	42	0.458
3	0.446	23	0.455	43	0.458
4	0.447	24	0.455	44	0.458
5	0.449	25	0.455	45	0.458
6	0.450	26	0.455	46	0.459
7	0.450	27	0.456	47	0.459
8	0.450	28	0.456	48	0.459
9	0.451	29	0.456	49	0.460
10	0.451	30	0.456	50	0.460
11	0.451	31	0.456	51	0.461
12	0.451	32	0.456	52	0.462
13	0.452	33	0.456	53	0.462
14	0.452	34	0.456	54	0.463
15	0.452	35	0.456	55	0.463
16	0.453	36	0.456	56	0.463
17	0.453	37	0.457	57	0.464
18	0.454	38	0.457	58	0.465
19	0.454	39	0.457	59	0.467
20	0.454	40	0.457	60	0.469

presentation of the data, however; the mind does not grasp the meaning of sixty numbers on a piece of paper, regardless of how they are arranged. We need more compactness in order to make practical use of the data.

The second step involves condensing the data by grouping them into cells. We divide the range from the lowest to the highest value into a convenient number of intervals or *cells* and then count the number of values falling within each cell. Strictly, this process involves some loss of information, but this is more than compensated by the increased efficiency with which the significance of the condensed data may be perceived. In order to proceed, we must first decide upon the number of cells to be used and choose their boundaries. Usually the range is divided into equal intervals, and sometimes confusion is avoided by choosing cell boundaries halfway between possible observed values. In the present case, the absorbance was recorded to three decimal places, and we choose cell boundaries such as 0.4605 so that none of the values coincides with a boundary. Judgment is required in selecting the number of cells: 13 to 20 are sometimes recommended, but 10 or even fewer may be preferable if the number of values to be grouped is small, say, less than 250. A fairly satisfactory grouping of our data into eight cells is shown in Table 3.4.

A glance at Table 3.4 shows that information buried in Tables 3.2 and 3.3 is now obvious. Thus, although the values range from 0.441 to 0.469, we see immediately that very few results are below 0.448 or above 0.464.

Next, we may devise a pictorial representation of the frequency distribution. This step is actually unnecessary, and it is rarely performed except for teaching purposes or for popular presentation of what might otherwise

TABLE 3.4 GROUPING OF INDIVIDUAL VALUES INTO CELLS

Cell midpoint	Cell boundaries	Number of values
	0.4405	
0.4425		1
	0.4445	
0.4465		3
	0.4485	
0.4505		11
	0.4525	
0.4545		21
	0.4565	
0.4585		14
	0.4605	
0.4625		7
	0.4645	
0.4665		2
	0.4685	
0.4705		1
	0.4725	

be "dry" data to laymen. Two types of graphs are shown in Fig. 3.1: The *histogram* consists of contiguous columns of heights proportional to the frequencies, erected upon the full widths of the cells; the *frequency polygon* is constructed by plotting frequencies at cell midpoints and connecting the points with straight lines.

FIGURE 3.1   Histogram and frequency polygon for absorbance measurements of 60 replicate solutions.

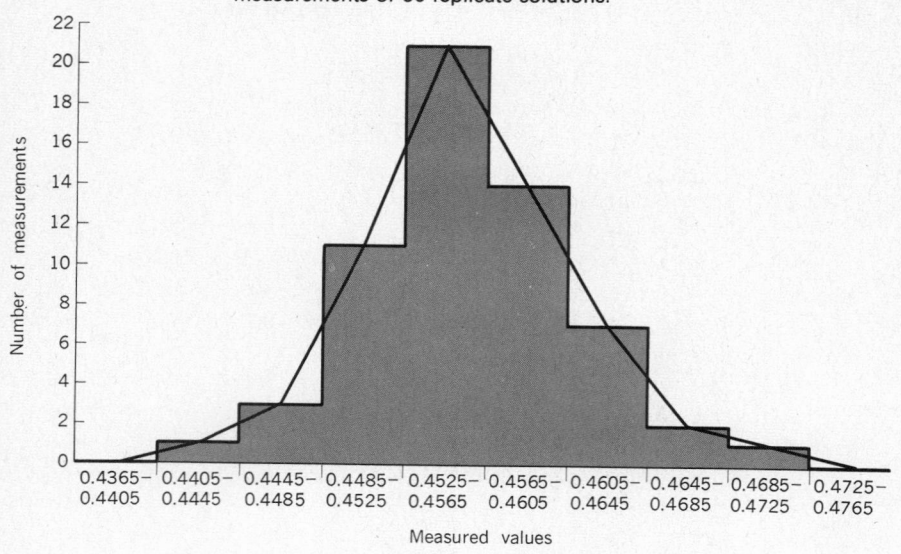

42

The Normal Error Curve

The limiting case approached by the frequency polygon as more and more replicate measurements are performed is the *normal* or *Gaussian* distribution curve, shown in Fig. 3.2. This curve is the locus of a mathematical function which is well-known, and it is more easily handled than the less ideal and more irregular curves that are often obtained with a smaller number of observations. Data are often treated as though they were normally distributed in order to simplify their analysis, and we may look upon the normal error curve as a model which is approximated more or less closely by real data. It is supposed that there exists a "universe" of data made up of an infinite number of individual measurements, and it is actually this "infinite population" to which the normal error function pertains. A finite number of replicate measurements is considered by statisticians to be a sample drawn in a random fashion from a hypothetical infinite population; thus the sample is at least hopefully a representative one, and fluctuations in its individual values may be considered to be normally distributed, so that the terminology and techniques associated with the normal error function may be employed in their analysis.

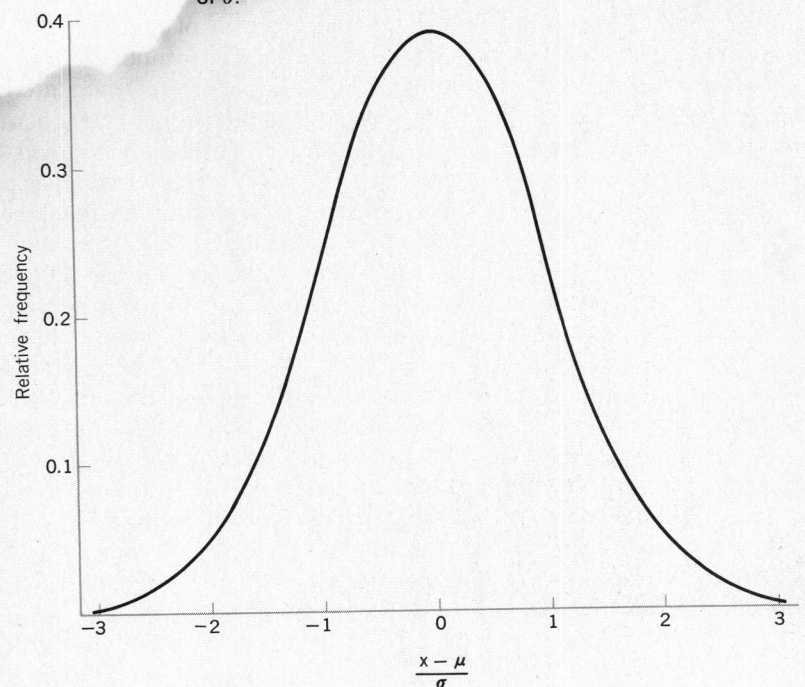

FIGURE 3.2 Normal distribution curve; relative frequencies of deviations from the mean for a normally-distributed infinite population; deviations $(x - \mu)$ are in units of σ.

The equation of the normal error curve may be written for our purposes as follows:

$$y = \frac{1}{\sigma\sqrt{2\pi}} e^{-(x-\mu)^2/2\sigma^2}$$

Here y represents the relative frequency with which random sampling of the infinite population will bring to hand a particular value x. The quantities μ and σ, called the population parameters, specify the distribution. μ is the *mean* of the infinite population, and since we are not here concerned with determinate errors, we may consider that μ gives the correct magnitude of the measured quantity. It is clearly impractical to determine μ by actually averaging an infinite number of measured values, but we shall see below that a statement can be made from a finite series of measurements regarding the probability that μ lies within a certain interval. To the extent of our confidence in having eliminated determinate errors, such a statement approaches an assessment of the true value of the measured quantity. σ, which is called the *standard deviation*, is the distance from the mean to either of the two inflection points of the distribution curve, and may be thought of as a measure of the spread or scatter of the values making up the population; σ thus relates to precision. π has its usual significance and e is the base of the natural logarithm system. The term $(x - \mu)$ represents simply the extent to which an individual value x deviates from the mean.

The distribution function may be normalized by setting the area under the curve equal to unity, representing a total probability of one for the whole population. Since the curve approaches the abscissa asymptotically on either side of the mean, there is a small but finite probability of encountering enormous deviations from the mean. A person who happened to encounter one of these in performing a series of laboratory observations would be unfortunate indeed; some of us who have faith in never obtaining such a "wild" result in our own work are inclined to the view that the normal distribution as a model for real data breaks down, and that only the central region of the distribution curve is pertinent when applied to scientific measurements by competent workers. The area under the curve between any two values of $(x - \mu)$ gives the fraction of the total population having magnitudes between these two values. It may be shown that about two-thirds (actually 68.26%) of all the values in an infinite population fall within the limits $\mu \pm \sigma$, while $\mu \pm 2\sigma$ includes about 95% and $\mu \pm 3\sigma$ practically all (99.74%) of the values. Happily, then, small errors are more probable than large ones. Since the normal curve is symmetrical, high and low results are equally probable once determinate errors have been dismissed.

When a worker goes into the laboratory and measures something, we suppose that his result is one of an infinite population of such values that he might obtain in an eternity of such activity; then the chances are roughly 2 to 1 that his measured values will be no further than σ from the mean of the infinite population, and about 20 to 1 that his result will lie in the range

$\mu \pm 2\sigma$. In practice, of course, we can never find σ for an infinite population, but the standard deviation of a finite number of observations may be taken as an estimate of σ. Thus we may predict something about the likelihood of occurrence of an error of a certain magnitude in the work of a particular individual once he has performed enough measurements to permit estimation of the characteristics of his particular infinite population.

STATISTICAL TREATMENT OF FINITE SAMPLES

Although there is no doubt as to its mathematical meaning, the normal distribution of an infinite population is a fiction so far as real laboratory work is concerned. We must now turn our attention to techniques for handling scientific data as we obtain them in practice.

Measures of Central Tendency and Variability

The *central tendency* of a group of results is simply that value about which the individual results tend to "cluster." For an infinite population, it is μ, the mean of such a sample. The *mean* of a finite number of measurements, $x_1, x_2, x_3, \ldots, x_n$, is often designated $\bar{x}$ to distinguish it from μ. Of course $\bar{x}$ approaches μ as a limit when n, the number of measured values, approaches infinity. Calculation of the mean involves simply averaging the individual results:

$$\bar{x} = \frac{x_1 + x_2 + x_3 + \cdots + x_n}{n} = \frac{\sum_{i=1}^{i=n} x_i}{n}$$

The mean is generally the most useful measure of central tendency. It may be shown that the mean of n results is $\sqrt{n}$ times as reliable as any one of the individual results. Thus there is a diminishing return from accumulating more and more replicate measurements: The mean of four results is twice as reliable as one result in measuring central tendency; the mean of nine results is three times as reliable; the mean of twenty-five results, five times as reliable, etc. Thus, generally speaking, it is inefficient for a careful worker who gets good precision to repeat a measurement more than a few times. Of course the need for increased reliability, and the price to be paid for it, must be decided on the basis of the importance of the results and the use to which they are to be put.

The *median* of an odd number of results is simply the middle value when the results are listed in order; for an even number of results, the median is the average of the two middle ones. In a truly symmetrical distribution, the mean and the median are identical. Generally speaking, the median is a less efficient measure of central tendency than is the mean, but in certain instances it may be useful, particularly in dealing with very small samples.

Since two parameters, μ and σ, are required to specify a frequency distribution, it is clear that two populations may have the same central tendency

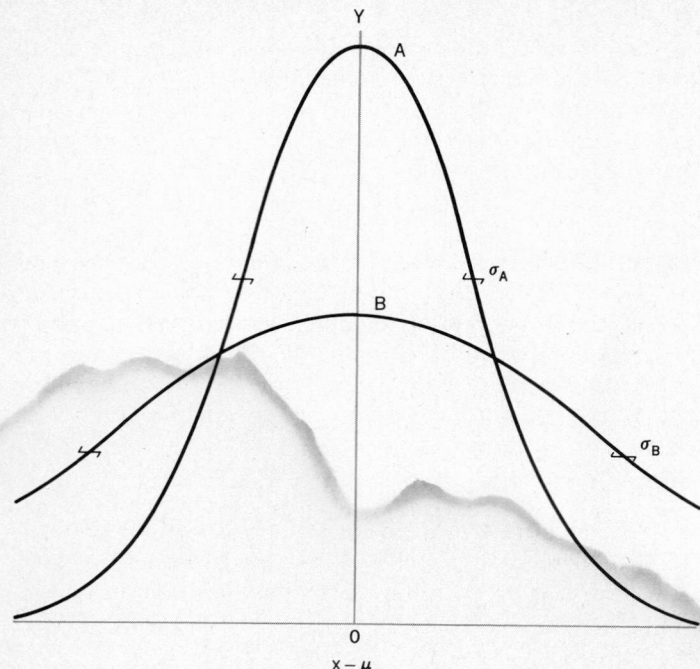

FIGURE 3.3 Two populations with the same central tendency μ, but different variability.

but differ in "spread" or *variability* (or, as some say, *dispersion*), as suggested in Fig. 3.3. For a finite number of values, the simplest measure of variability is the *range*, which is the difference between the largest and smallest values. Like the median, the range is sometimes useful in small sample statistics, but generally speaking it is an inefficient measure of variability. Note, for example, that one "wild" result exerts its full impact upon the range, whereas its effect is diluted by all of the other results in the better measures of variability noted below.

The *average deviation* from the mean is often given in scientific papers as a measure of variability, although strictly it is not very significant from a statistical point of view, particularly for a small number of observations. For a large group of data which are normally distributed, the average deviation approaches 0.8σ. To calculate the average or mean deviation, one simply finds the differences between individual results and the mean, regardless of sign, adds these individual deviations up, and divides by the number of results:

$$\text{Average deviation} = \bar{d} = \frac{\sum\limits_{i=1}^{i=n} |x_i - \bar{x}|}{n}$$

Often the average deviation is expressed relative to the magnitude of the measured quantity, for example as a percentage:

$$\text{Relative average deviation } (\%) = \frac{\bar{d}}{\bar{x}} \times 100 = \frac{\sum\limits_{i=1}^{i=n} |x_i - \bar{x}|/n}{\bar{x}} \times 100$$

Because analytical results are often expressed as percentages (e.g., percent iron in an iron ore sample), it may be confusing to report relative deviations on a percentage basis, and it is preferable to use parts per thousand instead of percent (parts per hundred):

$$\text{Relative average deviation (ppt)} = \frac{\sum\limits_{i=1}^{i=n} |x_i - \bar{x}|/n}{\bar{x}} \times 1000$$

The *standard deviation* is much more meaningful statistically than is the average deviation. The symbol s is used for the standard deviation of a finite number of values; σ is reserved for the population parameter. The standard deviation, which may be thought of as a root mean square deviation of values from their average, is calculated using the formula:

$$s = \sqrt{\frac{\sum\limits_{i=1}^{i=n} |x_i - \bar{x}|^2}{n - 1}}$$

If n is large (say 50 or more), then, of course, it is immaterial whether the term in the denominator is $n - 1$ (which is strictly correct) or n. When the standard deviation is expressed as a percentage of the mean, it is called the *coefficient of variation*, v:

$$v = \frac{s}{\bar{x}} \times 100$$

The *variance*, which is s^2, is fundamentally more important in statistics than is s itself, but the latter is much more commonly used in treating chemical data.

For the data in Tables 3.2, 3.3, and 3.4 the following measures of central tendency and variability were calculated:

Mean: $\bar{x} = 0.456$

Median: $M = 0.456$

Range: $R = 0.028$

Average deviation: $\bar{d} = 0.0038$

Relative average deviation: $\dfrac{\bar{d}}{\bar{x}} \times 1000 = 8.3$ ppt

Standard deviation: $s = 0.0052$

Coefficient of variation: $v = \dfrac{s}{\bar{x}} \times 100 = 1.1\%$

The following example illustrates the calculation of the above terms in the case of a determination of the normality of a solution.

Example. The normality of a solution is determined by four separate titrations, the results being 0.2041, 0.2049, 0.2039, and 0.2043. Calculate the mean, median, range, average deviation, relative average deviation, standard deviation and the coefficient of variation.

Mean: $\bar{x} = \dfrac{0.2041 + 0.2049 + 0.2039 + 0.2043}{4}$

$\bar{x} = 0.2043$

Median: $M = \dfrac{0.2041 + 0.2043}{2}$

$M = 0.2042$

Range: $R = 0.2049 - 0.2039$

$R = 0.0010$

Average deviation: $\bar{d} = \dfrac{(0.0002) + (0.0006) + (0.0004) + (0.0000)}{4}$

$\bar{d} = 0.0003$

Relative average deviation: $\dfrac{\bar{d}}{\bar{x}} \times 1000 = \dfrac{0.0003}{0.2043} \times 1000$

$= 1.5$ ppt

Standard deviation: $s = \sqrt{\dfrac{(0.0002)^2 + (0.0006)^2 + (0.0004)^2 + (0.0000)^2}{4 - 1}}$

$s = 0.0004$

Coefficient of variation: $v = \dfrac{0.0004}{0.2043} \times 100$

$v = 0.2\%$

Student's *t*

We have seen that, given μ and σ for the normal distribution of an infinite population, a precise statement can be made regarding the odds of drawing from the population an observation lying outside certain limits. But in practical work, we deal with finite numbers of observations, and we know not μ and σ, but rather $\bar{x}$ and s, which are only estimates of μ and σ. Since these estimates are subject to uncertainty, what we really have is a sort of blurred distribution curve on which to base any predictions we wish to make. This naturally widens the limits corresponding to any given odds that an individual observation will fall outside such limits. An English chemist, W. S. Gosset, writing under the pen name of Student, studied the problem of making predictions based upon a finite sample drawn from an unknown population and published a solution in 1908.[3] The theory of Student's work is beyond the scope of this book, but we may accept it as soundly based and see how it may be used in chemistry. The quantity t (often called Student's t) is defined by the expression

$$\pm t = (\bar{x} - \mu)\frac{\sqrt{n}}{s}$$

Tables of t values relating to various odds or probability levels and for varying degrees of freedom may be found in statistical compilations; a portion of such a table is reproduced here in Table 3.5. *Degrees of freedom* in the present connection are one less than n, the number of observations.[4] The t values are calculated to take into account the fact that $\bar{x}$ will not in general be the same as μ and to compensate the uncertainty in using s as an estimate of σ. Values of t such as those in Table 3.5 are used in several statistical methods, some of which are outlined below.

Confidence Interval of the Mean

By rearranging the equation above which defines t, we obtain the so-called confidence interval of the mean, or confidence limits:

$$\mu = \bar{x} \pm \frac{ts}{\sqrt{n}}$$

We might use this to estimate the probability that the population mean, μ, lies within a certain region centered at $\bar{x}$, the experimental mean of our

---

[3] *Biometrika*, **6**, 1 (1908).

[4] Degrees of freedom may be defined as the number of individual observations that could be allowed to vary under the condition that $\bar{x}$ and s, once determined, be held constant. For example, once the mean is obtained and we decide to keep it constant, all but one observation can be varied; the last one is fixed by $\bar{x}$ and all of the other x_i values, and the degrees of freedom then equal $n - 1$. In general, if s is calculated from the same number of observations as were used to calculate $\bar{x}$ (which would normally be the case in treating analytical data), then the degrees of freedom equal $n - 1$.

TABLE 3.5 SOME VALUES OF STUDENT'S t

No. of observations, n	No. of degrees of freedom, $n-1$	50%	90%	Probability levels 95%	99%
2	1	1.000	6.314	12.706	127.32
3	2	0.816	2.920	4.303	9.925
4	3	0.765	2.353	3.182	5.841
5	4	0.741	2.132	2.776	4.604
6	5	0.727	2.015	2.571	4.032
7	6	0.718	1.943	2.447	3.707
8	7	0.711	1.895	2.365	3.500
9	8	0.706	1.860	2.306	3.355
10	9	0.703	1.833	2.262	3.250
11	10	0.700	1.812	2.228	3.169
21	20	0.687	1.725	2.086	2.845
∞	∞	0.674	1.645	1.960	2.576

measurements. It is more usual in treating analytical data, however, to adopt an acceptable probability and then find the limits on either side of $\bar{x}$ to which we must go in order to be assured that we have embraced μ. It may be seen in Table 3.5 that t values increase as n, the number of observations, decreases. This is reasonable, since the smaller n becomes, the less information is available for estimating the population parameters. Increases in t exactly compensate for the lessening information.

The following example illustrates the use of Table 3.5.

Example. A chemist determined the percentage iron in an ore, obtaining the following results: $\bar{x} = 15.30$, $s = 0.10$, $n = 4$.

(a) Calculate the 90% confidence interval of the mean.
From Table 3.5, $t = 2.353$ for $n = 4$. Hence:

$$\mu = 15.30 \pm \frac{2.353 \times 0.10}{\sqrt{4}}$$

$$\mu = 15.30 \pm 0.12$$

(b) Calculate the 99% confidence interval of the mean.
From Table 3.5, $t = 5.841$ for $n = 4$. Hence:

$$\mu = 15.30 \pm \frac{5.841 \times 0.10}{\sqrt{4}}$$

$$\mu = 15.30 \pm 0.29$$

The meaning of confidence intervals is sometimes confused by the beginning student. The correct interpretation, using part (a) of the example above, is as follows: Suppose the chemist repeats the analysis ten times, each time performing four determinations and calculating an interval as illustrated above. He would obtain ten intervals, such as 15.30 ± 0.12, 15.28 ± 0.14, 15.33 ± 0.11, etc. He could expect nine of these ten intervals to embrace the population mean, μ. It is a common misconception that 90% of the experimental means would lie within the interval 15.30 ± 0.12. Predicting the interval within which future $\bar{x}$ values will lie is a different statistical problem which can be treated only with another sort of limits which are much wider than the confidence limits discussed here.

In some cases where analyses have been repeated extensively, a chemist may have a reliable estimate of the population standard deviation, σ. In this case there is no uncertainty in the value of σ, and the confidence interval is given by

$$\mu = \bar{x} \pm \frac{Z\sigma}{\sqrt{n}}$$

where Z is simply the value of t at $n = \infty$ (Table 3.5). Note that in the example above the confidence interval for part (a) would be given by

$$15.30 \pm \frac{1.645 \times 0.10}{\sqrt{4}} = 15.30 \pm 0.08$$

The interval is narrower since the uncertainty in σ has been removed.

It is possible to calculate a confidence interval from the range, R, of a series of measurements, using the relationship

$$\mu = \bar{x} \pm c_n R$$

Values of c_n for various numbers of observations and probability levels have been tabulated; some of these are given in Table 3.6. The values of c_n are based upon estimates of s obtained from the range. It should be emphasized that, while it is easy to calculate a confidence interval from the range, an

TABLE 3.6   SOME VALUES OF c_n FOR CALCULATING CONFIDENCE INTERVALS FROM THE RANGE

Number of observations	Probability levels 95%	99%
2	6.353	31.828
3	1.304	3.008
4	0.717	1.316
5	0.507	0.843
6	0.399	0.628

occasional large error will have an undue impact upon the result. The range is normally used in this way only when dealing with a very small number of observations, say, ten or less.

Testing for Significance

Suppose that a sample is analyzed by two different methods, each repeated several times, and that the mean values obtained are different. Statistics, of course, cannot say which value is "right," but there is a prior question in any case, namely, is the difference between the two values significant? It is possible simply by the influence of random fluctuations to get two different values using two methods; but it is likewise possible that one (or even both) of the methods is subject to a determinate error. There is a test, using Student's t, that will tell (with a given probability) whether it is worthwhile to seek an assignable cause for the difference between the two means. It is clear that the greater the scatter in the two sets of data, the less likely it is that differences between the two means are real.

The statistical approach to this problem is to set up the so-called *null hypothesis*. This hypothesis states, in the present example, that the two means are identical. The t-test gives a *yes* or *no* answer to the correctness of the null hypothesis with a certain confidence such as 95 or 99 %. The procedure is as follows: Suppose a sample has been analyzed by two different methods, yielding means $\bar{x}_1$ and $\bar{x}_2$ and standard deviations s_1 and s_2; n_1 and n_2 are the number of individual results obtained by the two methods. The first step is to calculate a t value using the formula

$$t = \frac{|\bar{x}_1 - \bar{x}_2|}{s} \sqrt{\frac{n_1 n_2}{n_1 + n_2}}$$

(This procedure presupposes that s_1 and s_2 are the same; there is a test for this, noted below.) Second, enter a t table such as Table 3.5 at a degree of freedom given by $(n_1 + n_2 - 2)$ and at the desired probability level. If the value in the table is greater than the t calculated from the data, the null hypothesis is substantiated; i.e., $\bar{x}_1$ and $\bar{x}_2$ are the same with a certain probability. If the t value in the table is less than the calculated t, then by this test the null hypothesis is incorrect and it might be profitable to look for a reason to explain the difference between $\bar{x}_1$ and $\bar{x}_2$.

If s_1 and s_2 are really different, a much more complicated procedure, which is not discussed here, must be used. Usually in analytical work involving methods that would by ordinary common sense be considered comparable, s_1 and s_2 are about the same. A test is available for deciding whether a difference between s_1 and s_2 is significant: This is the *variance-ratio* or *F-test*. The procedure is simple: Find the ratio $F = s_1^2/s_2^2$, placing the larger s value in the numerator so that $F > 1$; then go to a table of F values. If the F value in the table is less than the calculated F value, then the two standard deviations are significantly different, otherwise they are not. Some sample F values are given in Table 3.7 for a probability level of 95%. The F-test may be used to determine the validity of the simple t-test described here, but it may also be of interest in its own right to determine whether two analytical procedures yield significantly different precision.

TABLE 3.7 F VALUES AT THE 95% PROBABILITY LEVEL

$n-1$ for smaller s^2			$n-1$ for larger s^2			
	3	4	5	6	10	20
3	9.28	9.12	9.01	8.94	8.79	8.66
4	6.59	6.39	6.26	6.16	5.96	5.80
5	5.41	5.19	5.05	4.95	4.74	4.56
6	4.76	4.53	4.39	4.28	4.06	3.87
10	3.71	3.48	3.33	3.22	2.98	2.77
20	3.10	2.87	2.71	2.60	2.35	2.12

Sometimes it may be of interest to compare two results, one of which is considered a priori to be highly reliable. An example of this might be a comparison of the mean $\bar{x}$ of several analyses of an NBS sample with the value certified by the National Bureau of Standards. The goal would be not to pass judgment upon the Bureau, but to decide whether the method employed gave results that agreed with the Bureau's. In this case, the Bureau's value is taken as μ in the equation defining Student's t, and a t value is calculated using $\bar{x}$, n, and s for the analytical results at hand. If the calculated t value is greater than that in the t table for $n-1$ degrees of freedom and the desired probability, then the analytical method in question gave a mean value significantly different from the NBS value; otherwise, differences in the two values would be attributable to chance alone.

The following examples illustrate the foregoing points.

Example 1. A sample of soda ash (Na_2CO_3) is analyzed by two different methods giving the following results for the percentage of Na_2CO_3:

Method 1	Method 2
$\bar{x}_1 = 42.34$	$\bar{x}_2 = 42.44$
$s_1 = 0.10$	$s_2 = 0.12$
$n_1 = 5$	$n_2 = 4$

(a) Are s_1 and s_2 significantly different? Apply the variance-ratio, or F test:

$$F = \frac{s_2^2}{s_1^2} = 1.44$$

Consult Table 3.7 under column $n-1 = 3$ (since $s_2 > s_1$) and row $n-1 = 4$, finding $F = 6.59$. Since $6.59 > 1.44$, the standard deviations are not significantly different.

(b) Are the two means significantly different? Calculate a t value (either s_1 or s_2 may be used):

$$t = \frac{|42.34 - 42.44|}{0.10} \sqrt{\frac{5 \times 4}{5 + 4}}$$

$$t = 1.491$$

Consult Table 3.5 at degrees of freedom $n_1 + n_2 - 2 = 7$, finding t for the 95% probability level $= 2.365$. Since $1.149 < 2.365$, the null hypothesis is correct and the difference is not significant.

Example 2. A chemist analyzes a sample of iron ore furnished by the Bureau of Standards and obtains the following results: $\bar{x} = 10.52$, $s = 0.05$, $n = 10$. The Bureau's value for this sample is 10.60% Fe. Are the results significantly different?

Calculate t from the equation

$$\mu = \bar{x} \pm \frac{ts}{\sqrt{n}}$$

$$10.60 = 10.52 \pm \frac{t \times 0.05}{\sqrt{10}}$$

$$t = 5.06$$

In Table 3.5, at degrees of freedom $= 9$ and 95% probability level $t = 2.262$. Since $5.06 > 2.262$ the results are significantly different from the Bureau's value.

Criteria for Rejection of an Observation

Sometimes a person performing measurements is faced with one result in a set of replicates which seems to be out of line with the others, and he then must decide whether to exclude this result from further consideration. This problem is encountered in beginning analytical chemistry courses, later in physical chemistry laboratory work, and even in advanced research, although hopefully with lessening frequency as the student progresses. It is a generally accepted rule in scientific work that a measurement is to be automatically rejected when it is known that an error was made; this is a determinate situation with which we are not concerned here. It should be noted that it is incorrect (but all too human) to reject results which were subject to known errors only when they appear to be discordant. The only way to avoid an unconscious introduction of bias into the measurements is to reject every result where an error was known to be made, regardless of its agreement with the others. The problem to which we address ourselves here is a different one: How do we decide whether to throw out a result which appears discordant when there is no known reason to suspect it?

If the number of replicate values is large, the question of rejecting one value is not an important one; first, a single value will have only a small effect upon the mean, and second, statistical considerations give a clear answer regarding the probability that the suspected result is a member of the same population as the others. On the other hand, a real dilemma arises when the number of replicates is small: The divergent result exerts a significant effect upon the mean while at the same time there are insufficient data to permit a real statistical analysis of the status of the suspected result.

The many different recommendations that have been promulgated by various writers attest to the conclusion that the question of rejecting or retaining one divergent value from a small sample really cannot satisfactorily be answered. Some of the more widely recommended criteria for rejection are considered below, and the student is referred to the excellent discussion by Blaedel, et al.,[5] and interesting briefer commentaries by Laitinen[6] and Wilson.[7]

In the first place, it is necessary to decide how large the difference between the suspected result and the other data must be before the result is to be discarded. If the minimum difference is made too small, valid data may be rejected too frequently; this is said to be an "error of the first kind." On the other hand, setting the minimum difference too high leads to "errors of the second kind," viz., too frequent retention of highly erroneous values. The various recommendations for criteria of rejection steer one course or another between the Scylla and Charybdis of these two types of errors, some closer to one and some closer to the other.

The *2.5 d rule* is applied as follows:

1. Compute the mean and the average deviation of the "good" results.

2. Find the deviation of the suspected result from the mean of the "good" ones.

3. If the deviation of the suspected result from the mean of the "good" ones is at least 2.5 times the average deviation of the "good" results, then reject the suspected result. Otherwise retain it.

Strictly, the limit for rejection is too low with the 2.5 d rule: Valid data are rejected too often (errors of the first kind). The degree of confidence often quoted for the rule is based upon large sample statistics extended to small samples without proper compensation.

The *4 d rule* is used in the same manner as the 2.5 d rule above. This rule likewise leads to errors of the first kind, although obviously not so frequently. There is no statistical justification for using either the 2.5 d or the 4 d rule,

[5] W. J. Blaedel, V. W. Meloche, and J. A. Ramsey, *J. Chem. Ed.*, **28**, 643 (1951).

[6] H. A. Laitinen, *Chemical Analysis*, McGraw-Hill Book Company, New York, 1960, p. 574.

[7] E. B. Wilson, Jr., *An Introduction to Scientific Research*, McGraw-Hill Book Company, New York, 1952, p. 256.

although both are widely recommended. It should be noted that these rules are meant to apply to the rejection of only one result from a group of four to eight, not to one out of three, two out of five, etc.

The *Q-test*, described by Dean and Dixon,[8] is statistically correct, and it is very easy to apply. When the Q-test calls for rejection, confidence is high (90%) that the suspected result was indeed subject to some special error. Using the Q-test for rejection, errors of the first kind are highly unlikely. However, when applied to small sets of data (say, three to five results), the Q-test allows rejection only of results that deviate widely, and hence leads frequently to errors of the second kind (retention of erroneous results). Thus, the Q-test provides excellent justification for the rejection of grossly erroneous values, but it does not eliminate the dilemma with suspicious but less deviant values. The reason for this, of course, is that with small samples only crude guesses of the real population distribution are possible, and thus sound statistics lends assurance only to the rejection of widely divergent results.

The Q-test is applied as follows:

1. Calculate the range of the results.

2. Find the difference between the suspected result and its nearest neighbor.

3. Divide the difference obtained in step 2 by the range from step 1 to obtain the rejection quotient, Q.

4. Consult a table of Q values. If the computed value of Q is greater than the value in the table, the result can be discarded with 90% confidence that it was indeed subject to some factor which did not operate on the other results.

Some Q values are given in Table 3.8.

TABLE 3.8 VALUES OF REJECTION
QUOTIENT, Q

Number of observations	$Q_{0.90}$
3	0.90
4	0.76
5	0.64
6	0.56
7	0.51
8	0.47
9	0.44
10	0.41

[8] R. B. Dean and W. J. Dixon, *Anal. Chem.*, **23**, 636 (1951).

The following example illustrates the application of the above tests.

Example. Four results obtained for the normality of a solution are 0.1014, 0.1012, 0.1019, and 0.1016. Apply the above tests to see if the 0.1019 result can be discarded.

(a) Compute the mean and average deviation of the three "good" results:

Results	Deviations (ppt)
0.1014	0.0
0.1012	2.0
0.1016	2.0
Average: 0.1014	Average: 1.3

(b) Compute the deviation of the suspected result from the mean of the three "good" results:

$$0.1019 - 0.1014 = 0.0005 \text{ or } 5.0 \text{ ppt}$$

Using the 2.5 d rule,

$$2.5 \times 1.3 = 3.3 < 5.0 \text{ (discard)}$$

Using the 4.0 d rule,

$$4.0 \times 1.3 = 5.2 > 5.0 \text{ (do not discard)}$$

Using the Q-test,

$$Q = \frac{0.1019 - 0.1016}{0.1019 - 0.1012}$$

$$Q = \frac{0.0003}{0.0007}$$

$$Q = 0.43$$

Since $Q < 0.76$ (Table 3.8), do not discard.

As noted above, the Q-test affirms the rejection of a value at a confidence level of 90%. Willingness to reject a result with less confidence would make possible a Q-test which allowed retention of fewer deviant values (errors of the second kind). While this appears superficially attractive, there are valid reasons for conservatism in rejecting measurements. Actually, low confidence levels (say 50%) are scarcely meaningful when only a small number of observations is involved. Further, although to many students in introductory courses laboratory measurements are only exercises, it must be remembered that the collection of data is a scientific enterprise with a purpose, and the matter must be discussed as though it were important. The worker who has carefully conceived his measurement and executed it painstakingly, and who has reason to hope that the outcome will be significant, will not quickly throw his work away. He will be more likely to repeat the measurement until the dilemma of the discordant result has evaporated through the operation of two factors: Dilution of any one result by all of the others will lessen its significance, and, as the number of observations increases, statistical evaluation of the suspected result will become more meaningful.

A sort of compromise between outright rejection and the retention of a suspected value is sometimes recommended, viz., reporting the median of all the results rather than a mean either with or without the deviant value. The median is influenced by the *existence* of one discordant result, but it is not affected by the *extent* to which the result differs from the others. For a sample containing three to five values, Blaedel et al. recommend testing the suspected value with the *Q*-test and rejecting it if the test allows this; if not, the median is reported rather than the mean. Some writers, e.g., Wilson, recommend that the highest and lowest values both be rejected and the mean of the others reported: "The best procedure to use depends on what is known about the frequency of occurrence of wild values, on the cost of additional observations, and on the penalties for the various types of error. In the absence of special arguments, the use of the interior average ... would appear to be good practice."[9] It may be noted that this interior average and the median are necessarily identical in the special case where there are just three results.

CONTROL CHARTS

The control chart method was originally developed as a system for keeping track of quality during large-scale manufacturing operations. Often a production run is too large to permit individual inspection of each item (say, razor blades or ball bearings), and in some cases the quality test is destructive (as in measuring the stress required to break an object) and hence cannot be applied to each specimen produced by a company. In such cases, some sort of spot-checking of a few of the samples coming off the production line is necessary, and judgment is required to decide whether the manufacturing process is under control or whether a costly shutdown is justified in order to seek the cause of a deviation from the specifications in the tested results. The control chart method has also proved useful in keeping track of the performance of analytical methods in busy laboratories where the same types of samples are repeatedly analyzed day after day over long periods of time. The method tends to distinguish with a high degree of efficiency definite trends or periodically recurring anomalies from random fluctuations. The control chart method can be discussed only briefly here; the interested

---

[9] E. B. Wilson, Jr., *loc. cit.*, p. 257.

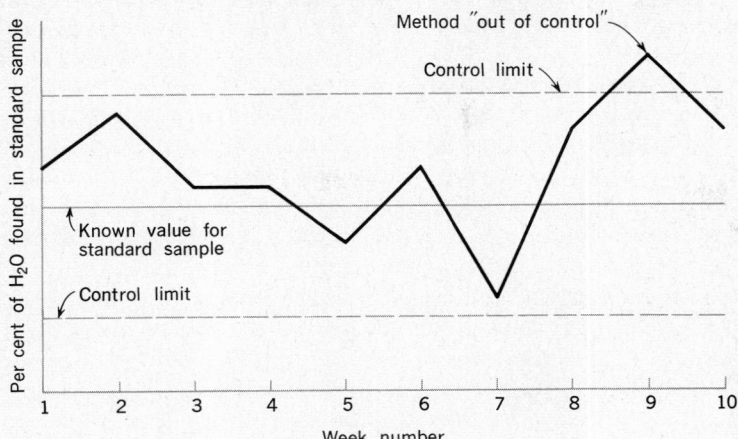

FIGURE 3.4   Control chart.

reader is referred to books on the subject[10,11] and several briefer discussions.[12-15]

Let us suppose that a company manufactures some chemical material, and that as part of the quality control program, the analytical laboratory performs each day a certain analysis on samples bled from the plant output, perhaps for percent water in the product. Let us further suppose that the laboratory checks its water determination each day by running a standard sample of known water content through the analytical procedure. We are interested here in how the control chart for the laboratory analysis is set up and used. The plant could also use a control chart method, based upon the laboratory reports, for monitoring the quality of the product, but here we are concerned with the laboratory's checking its own analytical method.

The control chart for the analysis is set up as follows (see Fig. 3.4). The percent water in the standard sample is indicated on the chart by a horizontal line. The standard sample is analyzed every day, and the average of five weekly results is plotted, week after week, on the chart. Also placed on the chart are the *control limits*. Analytical results falling outside these limits are considered to result from the operation of some definite factor which is worth investigating and correcting. When results fall within the limits, the method is "under control," and fluctuations are only random and indeterminate. (The analogous conclusion with a production control chart is that,

[10] E. L. Grant, *Statistical Quality Control*, 2nd ed., McGraw-Hill Book Company, New York, 1952.
[11] W. A. Shewhart, *Economic Control of Quality of Manufactured Product*, D. Van Nostrand Co., New York, 1931.
[12] H. A. Laitinen, *loc. cit.*, p. 560.
[13] E. B. Wilson, Jr., *loc. cit.*, p. 263.
[14] G. Wernimont, *Ind. Eng. Chem.*, *Anal. Ed.*, **18**, 587 (1946).
[15] J. A. Mitchell, *Ibid.*, **19**, 961 (1947).

when samples test outside the control limits, there is justification for shutting down the process and looking for the trouble.) Clearly, the control limits must be set in an arbitrary manner; one must decide how large must be the probability of an assignable cause for a deviant result before he is willing to say that something is wrong with the analysis. It seems usual in practice to set the control limits at the expected value $\pm 3s$; there is no fundamental aspect of probability theory demanding this, but apparently experience has shown that these are sound limits economically as a basis for action. Sometimes two sets of control limits are placed on the chart, "inner limits" at about $\pm 2s$ to warn of possible trouble, and "outer limits" of $\pm 3s$ demanding a corrective. (Actually, the chances are 1 in 20 that an observation subject only to random scatter will lie outside limits of $\pm 1.96\sigma$; 99.7 % of a group of results should fall within the $\pm 3\sigma$ limits unless a definite cause is operating on the analysis.) If the analysis is one that has been performed many times, the laboratory may have a value for s which is a good estimate of σ. Otherwise, the control limits can be established temporarily on the basis of an s value obtained from a few results, and then adjusted later as more data become available. Parallel control charts for ranges, standard deviations, etc., may be employed to help the laboratory personnel keep track of the precision of an analytical method.

PROPAGATION OF ERRORS

Usually the numerical result of a measurement is not of interest in its own right, but rather is used, sometimes in conjunction with several other measurements, to calculate the quantity which is actually desired. Attention is naturally focused upon the precision and accuracy of the final, computed quantity, but it is instructive to see how errors in the individual measurements are propagated into this result. A rigorous treatment of this problem requires more space than is available and mathematics beyond that presupposed for this book. An interesting elementary approach has been given by Waser,[16] and the interested student may find the elements of a more sophisticated treatment discussed briefly by Wilson[17] and by Shoemaker and Garland.[18] A discussion with particular emphasis on analytical chemistry has been given by Benedetti-Pichler.[19]

Determinate Errors

Consider a computed result, R, based upon the measured quantities A, B, and C. Let α, β, and γ represent the absolute determinate errors in A, B,

[16] J. Waser, *Quantitative Chemistry*, rev. ed., W. A. Benjamin, Inc., New York, 1964, p. 371.

[17] E. B. Wilson, Jr., *loc. cit.*, p. 272.

[18] D. P. Shoemaker and C. W. Garland, *Experiments in Physical Chemistry*, McGraw-Hill Book Company, New York, 1962, p. 30.

[19] A. A. Benedetti-Pichler, *Ind. Eng. Chem., Anal. Ed.*, **8**, 373 (1936).

and C, respectively, and let ρ represent the maximum resulting error in R. To see how the errors are transmitted through addition and subtraction, suppose that $R = A + B - C$. Changing each quantity by the amount of its error, we may write

$$R + \rho = (A + \alpha) + (B + \beta) - (C - \gamma)$$

or

$$R + \rho = (A + B - C) + (\alpha + \beta + \gamma)$$

Subtracting $R = A + B - C$ gives

$$\rho = \alpha + \beta + \gamma$$

Now suppose, on the other hand, that multiplication and division are involved, i.e., let $R = AB/C$. Again insert the appropriate errors:

$$R + \rho = \frac{(A + \alpha)(B + \beta)}{C - \gamma} = \frac{AB + \alpha B + \beta A + \alpha \beta}{C - \gamma}$$

Let us neglect $\alpha\beta$, since it may be supposed that the errors are very small compared with the measured values. Then subtracting $R = AB/C$ gives

$$\rho = \frac{AB + \alpha B + \beta A}{C - \gamma} - \frac{AB}{C}$$

Placing the right-hand terms over a common denominator gives

$$\rho = \frac{\alpha BC + \beta AC + \gamma AB}{C(C - \gamma)}$$

It is now convenient to consider the relative error, ρ/R, by dividing by $R = AB/C$, which leads, after appropriate cancellation, to

$$\frac{\rho}{R} = \frac{\alpha BC + \beta AC + \gamma AB}{AB(C - \gamma)}$$

Since γ is very small compared with C, this reduces to:

$$\frac{\rho}{R} = \frac{\alpha}{A} + \frac{\beta}{B} + \frac{\gamma}{C}$$

Thus it is found that determinate errors are propagated as follows:

1. Where addition or subtraction is involved, the *absolute* determinate errors are transmitted directly into the result.

2. Where multiplication or division is involved, the *relative* determinate errors are transmitted directly into the result.

Indeterminate Errors

In the case of determinate errors, it was reasonable to assume, at least for the purpose of illustration, that each measurement of some quantity A was attended by a definite error α; we were able to work with the errors of individual measurements. Indeterminate errors, on the other hand, are manifested by scatter in the data when a measurement is performed more than once. In considering the propagation of indeterminate errors, then, we must inquire how scatter in measurements of quantities A, B, C, etc., is translated into random variation in the final result R.

Suppose again that $R = A + B - C$ on the one hand, and that $R = AB/C$ on the other. The result of statistical theory is:

1. In addition or subtraction, the variances (squares of the standard deviations) of the measured values are additive in determining the variance of the result, i.e., for $R = A + B - C$, $s_R^2 = s_A^2 + s_B^2 + s_C^2$.

2. With multiplication or division, the squares of the relative standard deviations are transmitted, i.e., for $R = AB/C$,

$$\left(\frac{s_R}{R}\right)^2 = \left(\frac{s_A}{A}\right)^2 + \left(\frac{s_B}{B}\right)^2 + \left(\frac{s_C}{C}\right)^2$$

Consideration of error propagation leads to a conclusion of prime importance. This conclusion, although intuitively obvious to experienced workers, should be pointed out for beginners: Thought should be given to the attainable precisions and accuracies of the various measurements in a multistep operation. Once the weakest link in the operation is found, then the care taken in the other steps should be adjusted so that the result will not be impaired while at the same time valuable labor and time will not be uselessly expended.

For example, suppose that an error of ten parts per thousand is expected in a certain analysis for the percentage of some constituent in a sample because of the known limitations of a certain instrument. Then for this analysis, it would be a waste of time to weigh out a starting sample of 10 g to the nearest 0.0001 g, even though the balance might be capable of this. A weighing to the nearest 0.1 g would represent ten parts per thousand and would then be adequate, although admittedly a cautious person might well prefer to weigh to the nearest 0.01 g just to be on the safe side. In this example, it is supposed that multiplication and division are involved in calculating the result; e.g., a formula of this sort might be used:

$$\% \text{ of constituent} = \frac{\text{Instrument reading} \times \text{some factor}}{\text{Weight of sample}}$$

Where addition or subtraction is used, the *absolute* rather than the relative errors must be considered. For example, suppose that a 50-g vessel is weighed; then a sample of 0.1 g is added to it, and the weighing is repeated. If the weight of the sample is desired to a part in a thousand, then weighing to the nearest 0.0001 g is required, even though this represents precision of 1 part in 500,000 so far as the weight of the container is concerned.

SIGNIFICANT FIGURES AND COMPUTATION RULES

Significant Figures

When a computation is made from experimental data, the error or uncertainty in the final result can be calculated by the procedures just described. A widely used procedure for making a crude estimate of this uncertainty involves the use of *significant figures*. The principal advantage of this procedure is that it is less laborious than the calculations of actual uncertainties, particularly those based on indeterminate errors. The principal disadvantage is that only a rough estimate of uncertainty is obtained. In most situations encountered in analyses, an estimate is all that is needed, and hence significant figures are widely used.

Most scientists define significant figures as follows: All digits that are certain plus one which contains some uncertainty are said to be significant figures.[20] For example, in weighing an object on an analytical balance, the figures 10.746 can be recorded with certainty. The fourth decimal is estimated by reading a pointer scale or a vernier, and the final weight recorded as 10.7463. The last digit is uncertain, probably to ± 1 in a single reading, or ± 2 if a difference of two readings is involved. The six digits in this weight are all significant figures.

It is important to use only significant figures in expressing analytical data. The use of too many or too few figures may mislead another person with respect to the precision of the experimental data. If a volume is recorded as 1.234 ml, for example, it would be understood that the graduations on the buret were in 0.01-ml intervals and that the third decimal was estimated by reading between the graduations. The same volume read on an ordinary 50-ml buret could be estimated only to the second decimal, since the graduations are in 0.1-ml intervals. Hence the reading should have no more than three figures, say, 1.23 ml.

The digit zero may or may not be a significant figure, depending upon its function in the number. In a buret reading of, say, 10.06 ml, both zeros are measured and are therefore significant figures; the number contains four significant figures. Suppose the foregoing volume is expressed in liters,

---

[20] Note that in terms of this definition it is improper to say, as do many authors, that "one should use the appropriate number of significant figures." Rather, one should say that only significant figures should be recorded. One can record too many digits, but not too many significant figures.

that is, 0.01006 l. We do not increase the number of significant figures by changing the unit of volume. The function of the initial zero is to locate the decimal point; hence, initial zeros are not significant. Usually a zero is also placed before the decimal, as 0.01006, and this also is not significant. Terminal zeros are significant. For example, a weight of 10.2050 g has six significant figures. When it is necessary to use terminal zeros merely to locate the decimal properly, powers of ten may be used to avoid confusion with regard to the number of significant figures. For example, a weight of 24.0 mg expressed as micrograms should not be written as 24,000. The last two zeros are not significant, and this is indicated by writing the numbers as 24.0×10^3 or 2.40×10^4.

Computation Rules

As previously mentioned, the analytical chemist uses his experimental data to compute a final result. We would like to examine now the rules which are suggested to insure that the final result contains only the number of digits justified by the uncertainties in the data.

In considering the propagation of uncertainties in a series of calculations, the chemist treats them as though they were determinate errors. The reason for this deserves some detailed comment. In practice a chemist does not always push his measurements to the point where indeterminate errors are seen because, in many real analyses, the precision of the final result is determined largely by factors such as sample inhomogeneity and losses or contamination. If experience has shown that such errors amount to several parts per thousand, there is no point in weighing a sample to better than a part per thousand or so. In such a case it may often turn out that the last digit in the sample weight will not show random scatter at all, but rather will assume one of only two or three possible values. For example, in weighing a sample to the nearest 0.1 mg, the operator will ordinarily make no effort to estimate vernier readings to any better than 0.05 mg, regardless of the capability of his particular balance. Thus, in rounding these to the nearest 0.1 mg, he would expect to be in error no more than 0.1 mg unless some special accident occurred. If he records a weight of, let us say, 0.1036 g, the operator is reasonably certain that the correct value to four decimal places is 0.1035, 0.1036, or 0.1037. These, of course, are not randomly distributed numbers. Rather, the maximum error, once decided upon, is treated as a determinate error with respect to its propagation through a series of computations. In treating this propagation, it is usual not to count upon even partial cancellation of the errors in the various measured quantities, but rather to predict the errors in the result on the most pessimistic grounds. Actually, of course, the final computed results will tend to show random scatter because of the unpredictable cancellation of errors in the various measurements and the operation of unknown factors. Thus, we find in practice that the errors in individual measurements are treated as though they were determinate, while at the same time the final results are subjected to a statistical analysis of random errors.

Addition and Subtraction

The rule suggested here is to keep only as many decimal places as occur in that one of the numbers which has the fewest decimals. Consider the following example.

Example. Add properly the following numbers: 50.1 ± 0.1, 1.36 ± 0.02, and 0.5182 ± 0.0001.

Treating the uncertainties as determinate, the maximum uncertainty in the final result is:

$$\rho = 0.1 + 0.02 + 0.0001 \cong 0.1$$

Hence only one decimal place is justified in the final result. Following the rule suggested, we obtain:[21]

50.1	50.1
1.36	1.4
0.5182	0.5
	Sum = 52.0

There are three significant figures in the answer, with an uncertainty of at least ± 1 in the last digit. This is a good approximation of the result obtained by actual propagation of the uncertainties.

Multiplication and Division

The rule suggested here is to retain in each term and the final result a number of digits which will indicate a relative uncertainty no greater than that of the term with the greatest relative uncertainty. This rule is derived from the fact that relative determinate errors are transmitted directly into the result in the operations of multiplication and division. Consider the following examples.

Example 1. Calculate the following, giving the maximum uncertainty in the final result:

$$\frac{(10.00 \pm 0.02) \times (5.000 \pm 0.001)}{2.50 \pm 0.01}$$

The relative uncertainties are:

10.00	2.0 ppt
5.000	0.2 ppt
2.50	4.0 ppt
	Sum = 6.2 ppt

---

[21] In rounding off numbers, drop the last digit if it is less than 5: 4.33 becomes 4.3. If the last digit is greater than 5, increase the preceding digit by one: 4.36 becomes 4.4. If the digit to be dropped is 5, round the preceding digit to the nearest even number: 4.35 becomes 4.4; 4.65 becomes 4.6. This procedure avoids a tendency to round in one direction only.

Hence the uncertainty in the final result is 6.2 ppt. The final result, 20.0000 . . . , should be properly rounded off to express this relative uncertainty. If two zeros are retained, 20.00, an uncertainty of at least ± 0.01 is implied. The relative uncertainty is 0.5 ppt, less than we actually have. If the number is written 20.0, an uncertainty of at least ± 0.1 is indicated. This is a relative uncertainty of 5.0 ppt, close to our value of 6.2. If the number is written 20, the uncertainty is ± 1 with a relative value of 50 ppt, obviously too high. Hence the rule says to retain one zero, 20.0, this giving an uncertainty closest to that portion of the data which has the greatest relative uncertainty.

The approximate nature of significant figures can be seen from the above example. In rounding off numbers in this fashion, one obtains only an estimate of the uncertainty in the final result. An extreme case is that in which all the uncertainties are of equal magnitude. For example, suppose the above calculation had been

$$\frac{(10.00 \pm 0.04) \times (5.00 \pm 0.02)}{2.50 \pm 0.01}$$

All three relative uncertainties are 4.0 ppt, making a total of 12 ppt in the final result. Expressing the number as 20.0, as our rule would suggest, means that the uncertainty in the last digit is as large as ± 2.

The following example involves a calculation of percentage purity from typical titrimetric data. It illustrates the fact that the chemist knows some of the uncertainties from his experience with the measurements which were made.

Example 2. The percentage chromium is calculated from a titration as follows:

$$\% \, Cr = \frac{40.64 \text{ ml} \times 0.1027 \text{ mmol/ml} \times (51.996 \text{ mg/mmol}/3)}{346.4 \text{ mg}} \times 100$$

$$\% \, Cr = 20.883096 \ldots$$

How should the final $\% \, Cr$ be expressed?

The chemist would estimate the uncertainties as follows:

$$40.64 \pm 0.04 \text{ ml} \quad \text{or} \quad 1 \text{ ppt}$$

$$0.1027 \pm 0.0001 \quad \text{or} \quad 1 \text{ ppt}$$

$$51.996 \pm 0.001 \quad \text{or} \quad 0.02 \text{ ppt}$$

$$346.4 \pm 0.2 \quad \text{or} \quad 0.6 \text{ ppt}$$

He would round off his answer as 20.88 since this implies a relative uncertainty reasonably close to 1 ppt. A more exact analysis shows that the sum of the uncertainties is actually 3 ppt, indicating that the actual uncertainty in the final digit of our result is about ± 6.

The student may have noted that the number of significant figures in the final result of multiplication and division is normally the same as that portion of the data which contains the least number of significant figures. Sometimes such a rule is cited for this operation. The ultimate criterion in rounding off an answer in multiplication and division, however, is the relative uncertainty, not the number of significant figures in the data. For example, the results 9.99% and 10.01% each imply a relative uncertainty of about 1 ppt, but the first result contains three significant figures; the second contains four.

REFERENCES

C. A. BENNETT and N. S. FRANKLIN, *Statistical Analysis in Chemistry and the Chemical Industry*, John Wiley & Sons, Inc., New York, 1954.

E. B. WILSON, Jr., *An Introduction to Scientific Research*, McGraw-Hill Book Company, New York, 1952.

R. LANGLEY, *Practical Statistics*, Dover Publications, Inc., New York, 1970.

H. D. YOUNG, *Statistical Treatment of Experimental Data*, McGraw-Hill Book Company, New York, 1962.

H. C. BATSON, *An Introduction to Statistics in the Medical Sciences*, Burgess Publishing Co., Minneapolis, 1956.

W. J. DIXON and F. J. MASSEY, Jr., *Introduction to Statistical Analysis*, 2nd ed., McGraw-Hill Book Company, New York, 1957.

QUESTIONS

1. Student A reported three values for the normality of a solution as 0.12, 0.12, and 0.12, with a precision of 0.0 ppt. Student B reported 0.1243, 0.1237, and 0.1240 with a precision of 5.0 ppt. Comment on the merit of the two reports.

2. Explain whether the following errors are determinate or indeterminate and whether they affect the accuracy or the precision of the measurement. If the error is determinate, tell whether it is methodic, operative, or instrumental, and how it could be eliminated.
   (a) The analytical weights are corroded.
   (b) The analyst unknowingly spatters some solution from his flask during a titration.
   (c) A sample picks up moisture during a weighing.
   (d) A reagent is used which contains some of the substance being determined.
   (e) The buret is misread once.
   (f) A student uses the wrong equivalent weight in his calculations.

3. Explain clearly the meaning of the following terms: mean, median, standard deviation, range, central tendency, average deviation, variability, variance, coefficient of variation, relative average deviation, degrees of freedom, null hypothesis, and Student's t.

4. Two students determined the volume ratio of an acid and base solution. Student *A* reported his precision as 0.0 ppt, and Student *B* obtained 1.0 ppt. How should their work be compared? What can be said about the accuracy of each student's results?

5. Explain clearly the meaning of a confidence interval of 95 %.

6. Explain clearly how to test two sets of results to determine if they differ significantly.

7. Why can no definite answer be given regarding the rejection of a discordant result? Why aren't confidence levels of 50 % used in applying the *Q*-test?

8. Explain how errors are propagated in the operations of addition-subtraction and of multiplication-division. What is the difference in the cases of determinate and indeterminate errors?

9. Show that the conclusions regarding propagation of errors are consistent with the rules for rounding off numbers so that only significant figures are recorded.

10. Criticize this statement from a text: "Remind the student if he gives too many significant figures, he is making an erroneous scientific statement."

11. Explain briefly the nature of the statistical problem involved in deciding whether to retain or reject a suspicious value in a small series of replicate measurements. What may be wrong with using the so-called 2.5 *d* rule in this connection? With the *Q*-test?

12. Explain what are meant by *additive* and *proportional* determinate errors. Suppose a certified sample whose "true" composition is known is used to check out a new analytical method. How could you tell whether an observed determinate error is proportional or additive?

13. You are in charge of the clinical laboratory in a large hospital. Explain briefly how you would set up a control chart for blood calcium analyses so you could tell at a glance how well your technicians were doing on this determination.

PROBLEMS

(Unless otherwise indicated, it is to be understood that any weight or volume involves the difference of two readings.)

1. *Precision.* Refer to the Table of Atomic Weights. Assume that the uncertainty in the last digit of each value is ± 1. (a) The weight of which element is known with the greatest precision? the least precision? (b) Express these precisions in parts per thousand.

2. *Mean, median, etc.* Analysts *A* and *B* reported the following percentages of iron in the same sample: *A*: 20.48, 20.55, 20.58, 20.60, 20.53, and 20.50; *B*: 20.44, 20.64, 20.56, 20.70, 20.38, and 20.52. For each set of results, calculate the mean, median, range, average deviation, relative average deviation (ppt), standard deviation, and coefficient of variation. Also calculate the 99 % confidence intervals, first from the standard deviations, and second from the ranges. What can you say about the work of the two analysts?

3. *Accuracy of analysis.* The Bureau of Standards' value for the percentage of iron in the sample in Problem 2 is 20.45 %. Calculate the absolute and relative errors of analysts *A* and *B*.

4. *Testing for significance.* Two sets of results for the percentage of manganese in an ore are obtained using two methods of analysis.

Method 1	Method 2
$\bar{x} = 10.56$	$\bar{x} = 10.64$
$s_1 = 0.10$	$s_2 = 0.12$
$n_1 = 11$	$n_2 = 11$

(a) Are the standard deviations significantly different? (b) Are the two means significantly different?

5. *Testing for significance.* Repeat Problem 4 for the case where the mean for method 2 is 10.70 rather than 10.64.

6. *Testing for significance.* Repeat Problem 4 for $s_1 = 0.05$ and $s_2 = 0.06$.

7. *Testing for significance.* Repeat Problem 4 for $n_1 = 5$ and $n_2 = 6$.

8. *Rejection of a result.* A student obtained the following results for the normality of a solution: 0.1031, 0.1033, 0.1032, and 0.1040. (a) Can the last result be rejected according to the Q-test? (b) What value should be used for the normality? (c) Calculate the 99% confidence interval of the mean.

9. *Rejection of a result.* A student obtained the following results for the percentage chloride in a sample: 30.44, 30.52, 30.60, and 30.12. (a) Can the last result be rejected according to the Q-test? (b) What value should be used for the percentage chloride in the sample? (c) Calculate the 95% confidence interval of the mean.

10. *Rejection of a result.* A student obtained the following three results for the normality of a solution: 0.1043, 0.1041, and 0.1045. What is (a) the highest and (b) the lowest value a fourth result could be without being discarded by the Q-test?

11. *Rejection of a result.* A student obtained the following values for the normality of a solution: 0.1141, 0.1140, 0.1148, and 0.1142. Can the third result be discarded by the Q-test? A fifth result was run and a value of 0.1141 was obtained. Can the third result now be discarded? Explain.

12. *Testing for significance.* An analyst develops a new method for chloride. He analyzes a sample from the Bureau of Standards and obtains the following data: mean of four results = 16.72%; standard deviation = 0.08. The Bureau's value is 16.62%. Are the results significantly different at the 95% level?

13. *F-test.* Two students are given the same sample to analyze. Student A makes seven determinations and obtains a standard deviation of 0.08. Student B makes six determinations with a standard deviation of 0.05. Does the difference in standard deviations imply a significant difference in the techniques of the two students?

14. *Errors.* A student obtained the following results for the percentage chloride in a sample:

g sample	% chloride
0.5372	21.64
0.5168	21.62
0.6425	21.66
0.4235	21.58

The correct percentage is 21.42. What can you say about the existence of a determinate error in the student's method of analysis?

15. *Confidence interval of the mean.* It is known from past experience that the standard deviation for a method used to determine manganese in an ore is 0.12. A sample is analyzed by this method, giving a result of 9.56% manganese. Calculate the confidence interval of the mean if the analysis is based on (a) a single determination, (b) four determinations, and (c) nine determinations.

16. *Precision.* (a) The uncertainty in each reading on an analytical balance is ± 0.1 mg. How large a sample should be taken for analysis so that the uncertainty in the sample weight is no more than 1 ppt? (b) The uncertainty in each reading of a buret is ± 0.02 ml. How large a volume should be used in a titration so that the uncertainty in the volume is no more than 1 ppt?

17. *Precision.* Repeat Problem 16 for the following conditions: (a) A microbalance is used; the uncertainty in each reading being ± 0.001 mg. (b) A microburet is used; the uncertainty in each reading being ± 0.002 ml.

18. *Precision.* An analyst wishes to weigh a sample of 20 mg to within 1 ppt. What is the maximum uncertainty in each balance reading that can be tolerated?

19. *Precision.* The readings on a rough balance can be made to within ± 1 g. How large a sample should be taken for analysis to insure an uncertainty of no more than 1%?

20. *Relative error.* Answer the following: (a) An error of 0.4% is how many parts per 1000? (b) An error of 0.5% is how many parts per 500? (c) An error of 0.2% is how many parts per 2000?

21. *Relative error.* Assuming an uncertainty of ± 1 in the last digit, how should the number 50 be expressed to indicate an uncertainty no more than (a) 1%, (b) 0.2%, (c) 0.1%, and (d) 5%?

22. *Relative error.* The error in an analysis is known to be at least 1%. A 0.4-g sample is to be analyzed. What is the maximum uncertainty that can be allowed in the sample weight so that the relative error is no more than 1%?

23. *Significant figures.* How many significant figures does each of the following numbers contain? (a) 0.003080; (b) 6.023×10^{23}; (c) 96,500; (d) 4.80×10^{-10}; (e) 999; (f) 1000.

24. *Precision.* If the uncertainty in the last digit of each number in Problem 23 is ± 1, what is the relative uncertainty in each number in ppt?

25. *Parts per million.* If a drinking water contains 1.5 parts per million of NaF, how many liters of water can be fluoridated with 1 lb of NaF?

26. *Propagation of errors.* Calculate the following properly, giving the maximum uncertainties:

(a) $(10.54 \pm 0.04) + (18.26 \pm 0.02) - (8.35 \pm 0.03)$

(b) $\dfrac{(10.12 \pm 0.02) \times (5.06 \pm 0.02)}{2.50 \pm 0.01}$

27. *Significant figures.* Express the results of the following calculations using only significant figures:

(a) $\dfrac{2.52 \times 4.10 \times 15.04}{6.15 \times 10^4}$
(b) $\dfrac{3.10 \times 21.14 \times 5.10}{0.001120}$

(c) $\dfrac{51.0 \times 4.03 \times 10^{-4}}{2.512 \times 0.002034}$
(d) $\dfrac{0.0324 \times 8.1 \times 2.12 \times 10^2}{0.00615}$

(e) $213.64 + 4.4 + 0.3244$

28. *Sample size.* A sample contains about 10% of the ion B^{2-}. B^{2-} is determined by precipitating the compound A_2B. A has an atomic weight about twice that of B. If the uncertainty in determining the weight of the precipitate is not to exceed 1 ppt on a balance sensitive to 0.1 mg, what size sample should be taken for analysis?

29. *Significant figures.* How should the percentage of (a) Cl in AgCl and (b) Fe in Fe_2O_3 be properly expressed, assuming that the uncertainties in the atomic weights of the elements are ± 1 in the last decimal?

30. *Errors.* A student analyzed a sample of soda ash weighing 0.4240 g which contained 50.00% Na_2CO_3. He used 40.10 ml of 0.1000-N acid for titration. (The equivalent weight of Na_2CO_3 is 53.00.) Calculate (a) the absolute error, (b) the relative error in ppt.

31. *Errors.* A student analyzed a sample for chloride by precipitating and weighing AgCl. A 1.000-g sample gave him 0.8000 g of AgCl. (a) Calculate the percentage of chloride in the sample. (b) If the student by mistake used the atomic weight of Cl as 35.345 instead of the correct value of 35.453, what was his relative error in ppt?

4 Acid-Base Equilibria

INTRODUCTION

Acid-base equilibrium is an extremely important topic throughout chemistry and in other fields, like agriculture, biology, and medicine, which utilize chemistry. Titrations involving acids and bases are widely employed in the analytical control of many products of commerce, and the ionization of acids and bases exerts an important influence upon metabolic processes in the living cell. Acid-base equilibrium, as it is taught in analytical chemistry courses, offers the inexperienced student opportunity to broaden his understanding of chemical equilibrium and to gain the confidence to apply this understanding to a wide variety of problems.

In the evaluation of a reaction which is to serve as the basis for a titration, one of the most important aspects is the extent to which the reaction proceeds toward completion near the equivalence point. Stoichiometric calculations, which have been considered previously, do not take into account the position of equilibrium toward which a chemical reaction tends. In stoichiometry, one calculates maximal yields of products (or consumption of reactants) with the implicit assumption that the reaction proceeds to completion, whereas in actuality the realization of completeness may require that one of the reactants be present in large excess or that a reaction product be removed from the mixture. Titrimetry by its very nature generally precludes forcing a reaction to completion by a large excess of reactant, and we shall see that the feasibility of a titration depends, at least in part, upon the position of equilibrium established when equivalent quantities of reactants have been mixed. Although our main goal in this chapter will be the understanding of acid-base titrations, other important aspects of acid-base chemistry will be discussed at appropriate points.

BRØNSTED TREATMENT OF ACIDS AND BASES

Although substances with acidic and basic properties had been known for hundreds of years, the quantitative treatment of acid-base equilibria became possible after 1887, when Arrhenius presented his theory of electrolytic dissociation. In water solution, according to Arrhenius, acids dissociate into hydrogen ions and anions, and bases dissociate into hydroxyl ions and cations:

$$\text{Acid}: HX \rightleftharpoons H^+ + X^-$$

$$\text{Base}: BOH \rightleftharpoons OH^- + B^+$$

By applying to these dissociations the principles of chemical equilibrium which had been well systematized before the turn of the century, the behavior of acids and bases in aqueous solution could be quantitatively described, at least approximately. The Debye-Hückel theory (1923) permitted a refined treatment that was even better.

In 1923, Brønsted presented a new view of acid-base behavior which retained the soundness of the Arrhenius equilibrium treatment but which was conceptually broader and facilitated the correlation of a much larger body of information.[1] In Brønsted terms, an acid is any substance that can give up a proton, and a base is a substance that can accept a proton. The hydroxyl ion, to be sure, is such a proton acceptor and hence a Brønsted base, but it is not unique; it is one of many species that can exhibit basic behavior. When an acid yields a proton, the deficient species must have some proton affinity, and hence it is a base. Thus in the Brønsted treatment we encounter "conjugate" acid-base pairs:

$$\underset{\text{acid}}{HB} \rightleftharpoons H^+ + \underset{\text{base}}{B}$$

The acid HB may be electrically neutral, anionic, or cationic (e.g., HCl, HSO_4^-, NH_4^+), and thus we have not specified the charges on either HB or B.

As the elemental unit of positive charge, the proton possesses a charge density which makes its independent existence in a solution extremely unlikely. Thus, in order to transform HB into B, a proton acceptor (i.e., another base) must be present. Often, as in the dissociation of acetic acid in water, this base may be the solvent itself:

$$HOAc \rightleftharpoons H^+ + OAc^-$$
$$H_2O + H^+ \rightleftharpoons H_3O^+$$
$$\overline{\underset{\text{acid}_1}{HOAc} + \underset{\text{base}_2}{H_2O} \rightleftharpoons \underset{\text{acid}_2}{H_3O^+} + \underset{\text{base}_1}{OAc^-}}$$

[1] The same ideas were proposed independently by Lowry in 1924; some writers speak of the Brønsted-Lowry theory.

The interaction of the two conjugate acid-base pairs (designated by subscripts 1 and 2) leads to an equilibrium in which some of the acetic acid molecules have transferred their protons to water. The protonated water molecule or hydrated proton, H_3O^+, may be called a "hydronium ion," but it is usually designated simply "hydrogen ion" and often written "H^+."[2]

Water is not the only solvent to which acids can transfer their protons, and we may write a general ionization equation, where S is any solvent capable of accepting a proton:

$$HB + S \rightleftharpoons HS^+ + B$$

The species HS^+ is the solvated proton (H_3O^+ in water solution, H_2OAc^+ in glacial acetic acid, $H_3SO_4^+$ in sulfuric acid, $C_2H_5OH_2^+$ in ethanol, etc.). One of the important contributions of Brønsted theory is its emphasis on the role of the solvent in the ionization of acids and bases. We may suppose that an acid has a certain intrinsic "acidity" if we wish, but the Brønsted treatment makes clear that the extent to which such an acid is ionized in solution depends importantly upon the basicity of the solvent. Thus perchloric acid, $HClO_4$, is a strong acid, completely ionized, in water solution, but it is only slightly ionized in nonaqueous sulfuric acid.

If HB is inherently a stronger acid than HS^+, it will transfer its proton to the solvent; in other words, the position of the equilibrium in the reaction $HB + S \rightleftharpoons HS^+ + B$ will lie toward the right. If HB is very much stronger than HS^+, the equilibrium will lie far to the right, and HB will be essentially 100% dissociated. A series of different acids, all of which are very much stronger than the solvated proton, will dissociate completely; such solutions will be brought to a level of acidity governed by the acid strength of HS^+. This is known as the *leveling effect*. Thus, in aqueous solution the acids perchloric, nitric, and hydrochloric are equally strong, whereas in the less basic solvent, glacial acetic acid, the three acids are not leveled, and perchloric is stronger than the other two.

In Brønsted terms, the dissociation of bases is treated in a similar fashion except that here the process is promoted by the *acidity* of the solvent. Again, the general case may be formulated as the interaction of two conjugate pairs:

$$SH \rightleftharpoons S^- + H^+$$
$$B + H^+ \rightleftharpoons BH^+$$
$$\overline{B + SH \rightleftharpoons BH^+ + S^-}$$
$$\text{base}_1 \quad \text{acid}_2 \quad \text{acid}_1 \quad \text{base}_2$$

An example is $NH_3 + H_2O \rightleftharpoons NH_4^+ + OH^-$. As with acids, bases may be of any charge type (neutral, cationic, or anionic). The charges have been

---

[2] The proton in aqueous solution may actually be more heavily hydrated than H_3O^+. For example, a species $H_9O_4^+$ ($H_3O^+ \cdot 3\ H_2O$ or $H^+ \cdot 4\ H_2O$) has been postulated on the basis of the infrared spectra of strong acid solutions, studies of the extraction of strong acids from water into certain organic solvents, and other experimental evidence. For an interesting review, see H. L. Clever, *J. Chem. Educ.*, **40**, 637 (1963).

placed in the above equations simply to show that the base and its conjugate acid differ by one. If the solvent is sufficiently acidic, we may again encounter a leveling effect in which a series of bases are brought to a level of basicity in solution determined by the species S^-. In water, for example, so-called basic anhydrides like CaO yield OH^- by a process which may be written:

$$O^{2-} + H_2O \rightleftharpoons 2\,OH^-$$

In anhydrous sulfuric acid sulfates are analogous to the basic anhydrides in the aqueous system:

$$SO_4{}^{2-} + H_2SO_4 \rightleftharpoons 2\,HSO_4{}^-$$

Neutralization reactions involving strong acids and bases in the various solvents become, in Brønsted terms, simply reactions between the cation and the anion of the solvent because of the leveling effect. Water, for example, dissociates as follows:

$$2\,H_2O \rightleftharpoons H_3O^+ + OH^-$$

One of the two water molecules in the equation acts as an acid, the other as a base, which is to say that water is *amphoteric*. Neutralization of strong acids and bases is simply the reverse of this self-dissociation or autoprotolysis reaction:

$$H_3O^+ + OH^- \rightleftharpoons 2\,H_2O$$

Likewise, in liquid ammonia solution, strong acids and bases are leveled to $NH_4{}^+$ and $NH_2{}^-$, respectively, and neutralization may be written

$$NH_4{}^+ + NH_2{}^- \rightleftharpoons 2\,NH_3$$

In sulfuric acid as a solvent, the reaction becomes

$$H_3SO_4{}^+ + HSO_4{}^- \rightleftharpoons 2\,H_2SO_4$$

The Brønsted treatment offers the conceptual advantage of unifying a number of acid-base processes which, in other terms, may appear different. Hydrolysis, for example, need no longer be distinguished as a special process. The hydrolysis of a salt, like sodium acetate, is simply the dissociation reaction of the acetate ion as a base:

$$OAc^- + H_2O \rightleftharpoons HOAc + OH^-$$

It may be seen that it will be a property of a conjugate acid-base pair that a strong acid has a weak conjugate base and vice versa. Thus chloride ion, the conjugate base of the strong acid hydrochloric, is too weak a base to abstract protons from water, and hydrolysis of the chloride ion is negligible.

Using this introduction as a basis, we shall refer repeatedly to the Brønsted ideas throughout this chapter.

DISSOCIATION CONSTANTS

Chemical Equilibrium

When reactive chemical substances are mixed together, the products of the reaction are formed at a rate which decreases with time until finally it becomes equal to the rate at which the products react to form the starting substances. Consider a reaction:

$$A + B \rightleftharpoons C + D$$

When A and B are mixed, they react to form C and D. The rate of this reaction progressively decreases, while the rate at which C and D react to form A and B increases, until, when the two rates become equal, there is no further net change in the quantities of A, B, C, and D in the system. It is then said that the system is in a state of equilibrium. The rate at which equilibrium is attained is of the order of a microsecond for the dissociation that occurs when acetic acid is mixed with water. On the other hand, a mixture of hydrogen and oxygen, standing at room temperature, would change little in thousands of years unless the reaction were catalyzed, even though at equilibrium H_2O is greatly favored over H_2 and O_2. If a reaction is to be useful as part of an analytical method, obviously its rate must be reasonably fast under the conditions employed. This is often the case with the relatively simple reactions involving ions in solution, although not necessarily so. The best proof that a system is in equilibrium is a demonstration that a mixture of the same composition is obtainable by mixing reactants A and B as by mixing products C and D.

The Equilibrium Constant

The law of chemical equilibrium states that the activities of reactants and products for the general reaction

$$a\,A + b\,B \rightleftharpoons c\,C + d\,D$$

will attain values at equilibrium such that the quotient given below will be a constant at a given temperature:

$$\frac{a_C^c \times a_D^d}{a_A^a \times a_B^b} = K_{eq}$$

The constant, K_{eq}, is called the equilibrium constant. We may accept the equilibrium law as an experimental fact at this time, although it is derivable from thermodynamic principles which the student encounters in physical chemistry courses. The terms a_C^c, a_D^d, etc., represent the activities of the species C, D, etc., raised to the powers indicated by the coefficients in the balanced chemical equation.

Activity

The concept of activity may be explained to the student in a rigorous fashion only after he has encountered partial molal free energy or chemical potential in thermodynamics. However, he is probably acquainted with the concept of free energy, the measure of the driving force of a chemical reaction and the maximum work that can be obtained at constant temperature and pressure. This change in free energy for the transfer of one mole of a given substance from a state of activity a_1 to activity a_2 is given by:

$$\Delta G = 2.3RT \log \frac{a_2}{a_1}$$

In the case of solutions, the volumes must be so large that the transfer does not change the concentrations.

It is evident that the change in free energy is determined by the *ratio* of the two activities. Hence, to define an individual activity it is customary to adopt an *arbitrary* reference or *standard state* and to assign to it an activity of unity at any given temperature and pressure. The customary choices are as follows:

1. For a perfect gas the standard state is one atmosphere, and the activity is then the same as the pressure of the gas. For a real gas the standard state is that in which the so-called fugacity is unity.[3] Since at low pressures the real gas approaches ideal behavior, making fugacity and pressure approximately equal, we will take the pressure of a gas as its activity. Thus,

$$\frac{a}{P} = 1 \quad \text{when} \quad P \longrightarrow 0$$

2. The activity of a pure liquid or solid (in its most stable crystalline state) acting as a solvent for other substances is unity. That is, the standard state is a mole fraction of unity, where X is the mole fraction of the solvent.

$$\frac{a}{X} = 1 \quad \text{when} \quad X \longrightarrow 1$$

If the activity of the liquid or solid is changed by dissolving in it a solute,

---

[3] The fugacity is the same as the vapor pressure when the vapor is a perfect gas, and it may be regarded as an "ideal" or "corrected" vapor pressure.

the activity of the solvent is still given by the mole fraction. In most examples that we shall encounter, it will still be acceptable to take a value of unity as the activity of the solvent. For example, a liter of a 0.1-M aqueous solution of a solute contains 0.1 mole of that solute and about 55.3 moles of water. The mole fraction of water is thus about $55.3/55.4 \cong 1$. The possible effect of the solute upon the activity of water will be ignored in our calculations.

3. The activity of a solute is the same as its molality in very dilute solution, where ideal behavior may be assumed. That is,

$$\frac{a}{m} = 1 \quad \text{when} \quad m \longrightarrow 0$$

where m is the molality.[4] Here, as for a real gas, the standard state is a hypothetical one in which the solute is at 1 molal concentration (1 atmosphere pressure), but the environment about the solute would be the same as that of an ideal solution. In dilute solutions the behavior of the solute does approach ideal, and we use molality for activity for such solutions.

Activity Coefficient

In solutions where the activity of a solute is expressed as concentration, deviations from ideal solution behavior are generally expressed in terms of the *activity coefficient*, γ, defined as

$$a = \gamma m$$

The more nearly ideal a solute behaves, the closer to unity is γ, and hence the closer activity is to concentration. According to our chosen standard state, as $m \to 0$, $\gamma \to 1$ and $a \to m$. For solutions of electrolytes the activity coefficient is a measure of the deviation from ideality because of ion-ion interactions. Such interactions are general, not just between the specific ions undergoing chemical reaction. For instance, the activities of ions such as Ag^+ and Cl^- in the formation of a precipitate of AgCl are lowered by the addition of a nonreacting electrolyte such as potassium nitrate. Debye and Hückel interpreted this diminished activity in terms of electrostatic interactions of the ions: Clustering of NO_3^- about the Ag^+ and of K^+ around the Cl^- tends to shield the Ag^+ and Cl^- from each other and thus hampers the effectiveness of these ions in forming AgCl.

Either the activity or the activity coefficient could be made dimensionless, but generally it is the activity coefficient which is so treated. Since our limiting definition is $a/m = 1$, it seems logical to make the units of activity the same as those of molality, thereby making the activity coefficient dimensionless.

---

[4] This is also defined in terms of mole fraction, i.e., $a/X = 1$ when $X \to 0$, where X is the mole fraction solute. Since in very dilute solution molality becomes proportional to mole fraction, either definition can be used.

It should also be noted that in analytical chemistry most concentrations are expressed in the molarity system rather than molality. Since these two systems are very nearly the same in dilute aqueous solution, we shall use molarity in place of molality.

Equations arising from the theoretical treatment of Debye and Hückel permit the calculation of activity coefficients in solutions which are not too concentrated, and various physicochemical techniques may be employed to measure them. Some values of activity coefficients of typical electrolytes are given in Table 4.1 to give the student an idea of the magnitude of the error

TABLE 4.1 MEAN MOLAL ACTIVITY COEFFICIENTS OF ELECTROLYTES AT 25°C

Molality	0.001	0.005	0.01	0.05	0.1	0.5
HCl	0.97	0.93	0.90	0.83	0.80	0.76
HCl (0.01 M) in NaCl)	—	—	0.87	0.82	0.78	0.76
HNO$_3$	0.97	0.93	0.90	0.82	0.79	0.72
H$_2$SO$_4$	0.83	0.64	0.54	0.34	0.27	0.15
KOH	—	0.93	0.90	0.81	0.76	0.67
NaCl	0.97	0.93	0.90	0.82	0.78	0.68
CaCl$_2$	0.89	0.79	0.73	0.57	0.52	0.52
K$_2$SO$_4$	—	0.78	0.71	0.53	0.44	0.26
CuSO$_4$	0.74	0.53	0.41	0.21	0.16	0.07

involved in using molar concentration in place of activity. It may be seen in the table that the activity of an electrolyte such as HCl depends not only on the concentration of this solute itself but also upon the presence of other ions such as those of NaCl. It may also be noted that activity coefficients are lowered when the electrical charges of the ions are increased; compare, for example, the values for comparable concentrations of NaCl and CuSO$_4$.

In general, the presence of ions will have a lesser effect upon the activity of a neutral molecule than upon that of another electrolyte. However, ions do influence molecules to some degree by interacting with existing dipoles or even inducing them.

Throughout this text we shall use molar concentrations as though they were activities in most of the calculations we make. It is rare that activity coefficients are known in the complex, concentrated solutions encountered in analytical chemistry. Furthermore, many of the answers we seek regarding, for example, the feasibility of a titration, can be obtained by approximate calculations. We shall make a practice, however, of reminding the student that activities should be used in equilibrium calculations, and we shall point out instances where activity effects may appreciably affect the answer we are seeking.

Dissociation Constants of Acids and Bases

Autoprotolysis Constant of Water

Equilibrium constants for dissociation reactions like those discussed earlier are often given distinctive names. The equilibrium constant for the self-dissociation of a solvent is often called the *autoprotolysis constant*. In the case of water, this constant is designated K_w.

$$2\,H_2O \rightleftharpoons H_3O^+ + OH^-$$

$$K_w = [H_3O^+][OH^-]$$

We have simply written the equilibrium constant for the dissociation reaction, using molar concentrations for the activities of H_3O^+ and OH^- and unity for the activity of water, H_2O. K_w is sometimes called the *ion product* or the *ion product constant* of water. At room temperature (25°C), the value of K_w is 1.01×10^{-14}. In pure water, $[H_3O^+] = [OH^-] = 1.0 \times 10^{-7}$-$M$. In acidic solutions, $[H_3O^+] > 1.0 \times 10^{-7}$ and, correspondingly, $[OH^-] < 1.0 \times 10^{-7}$. In basic solution, the situation is reversed, and $[OH^-] > [H_3O^+]$.

Dissociation Constants of Acids and Bases

With strong acids that are essentially completely dissociated, such as HCl, the concentration of undissociated molecules, [HCl], is negligible, and $[H_3O^+]$ is readily calculated from the quantity of HCl introduced into the solution. On the other hand, with weak acids, which are only partially dissociated, we must work with appropriate equilibrium constants in order to calculate $[H_3O^+]$.

For the dissociation of a weak acid HB, we may write:

$$HB + H_2O \rightleftharpoons H_3O^+ + B$$

where HB and B are a conjugate acid-base pair with their charges unspecified for generality. Then, again using molar concentrations to approximate activities and taking $a_{H_2O} = 1$, we obtain for the equilibrium expression:

$$K_a = \frac{[H_3O^+][B]}{[HB]}$$

K_a is called the *dissociation constant* (or sometimes the *acidity constant*) of the acid HB.

Similarly, for the dissociation of a weak base B,

$$B + H_2O \rightleftharpoons HB + OH^-$$

we may obtain a dissociation constant K_b,

$$K_b = \frac{[HB][OH^-]}{[B]}$$

There is a simple relation between K_a and K_b for a conjugate pair. From the autoprotolysis constant of water, we obtain by rearrangement

$$[OH^-] = \frac{K_w}{[H_3O^+]}$$

Substitution of this for $[OH^-]$ in the above K_b expression yields

$$K_b = \frac{[HB]K_w}{[B][H_3O^+]}$$

But note that $[HB]/[B][H_3O^+] = 1/K_a$, where K_a is the dissociation constant of the conjugate acid of the base in question. Thus, in general for an acid-base pair,

$$K_b = \frac{K_w}{K_a}$$

or

$$K_a \times K_b = K_w$$

Hence it is really unnecessary to tabulate dissociation constants for both acids and bases; one can always be obtained from the other. For convenience, however, both K_a and K_b values are given in Table I, Appendix I, with conjugate acid-base pairs shown side by side.

Hydrolysis reactions of salts of weak acids or bases, which are treated as a distinct topic in many books, are viewed in Brønsted terms as ordinary dissociation reactions, and there is no need to designate a special "hydrolysis constant." Thus the equilibrium constant for the hydrolysis of, say, sodium acetate,

$$OAc^- + H_2O \rightleftharpoons HOAc + OH^-$$

which some writers designate K_h, is found in Table I, Appendix I, simply as K_b for acetate ion, the conjugate base of acetic acid. Similarly, the hydrolysis of ammonium chloride,

$$NH_4^+ + H_2O \rightleftharpoons H_3O^+ + NH_3$$

is viewed as the dissociation of the acid NH_4^+, and the equilibrium constant is K_a for this species, the conjugate acid of the base ammonia. In the hydrolysis of sodium acetate and of ammonium chloride, Na^+ and Cl^- ions, respectively, do not participate in any acid-base equilibrium; hence, they are not included in the equation above for the hydrolysis reactions.

CALCULATIONS OF pH VALUES OF AQUEOUS SOLUTIONS

pH and Other p-Functions

The concentrations of H_3O^+ and OH^- ions as encountered in typical analytical situations such as titrations vary over many orders of magnitude. Thus, in 0.1-M HCl, the concentration of H_3O^+ is 10^{-1}-M (0.1-M), and the hydroxyl concentration is 10^{-13}-M (0.0000000000001-M). In 0.1-M NaOH solution, $[H_3O^+] = 10^{-13}$-M. Cumbersome decimals of this sort are avoided, and numbers are obtained which are much more manageable graphically, by defining a logarithmic function of the hydrogen ion concentration. In order to obtain in usual aqueous solutions numbers on a positive scale, the function pH is defined as a negative logarithm:

$$pH = -\log [H_3O^+] = \log \frac{1}{[H_3O^+]}$$

Thus a hydrogen ion concentration of 1.0×10^{-1}-M corresponds to a pH value of 1.00, and a hydrogen ion concentration of 1.0×10^{-13} becomes pH = 13.00. Such numbers, ranging from, say, 0 or 1 up to perhaps 13 or 14 are conveniently plotted on titration curves as seen later in this chapter. In a later chapter, it is seen that the electromotive force developed by certain galvanic cells is more directly related to the logarithmic function than to the hydrogen ion concentration itself.

The student should note that the digit before the decimal point in a pH value is not really a significant figure in the usual sense, but is merely obtained from the position of the decimal point in the original hydrogen ion concentration. For example, a hydrogen ion concentration expressed as 1.00×10^{-5}-M implies a precision of measurement of 1 part in 100; the 10^{-5} term merely fixes the decimal point, and in the corresponding pH value of 5.00..., the digit is related only to the position of the decimal point in the original number. The student may, as an exercise, show the manner in which an error in y is transformed into an error in x, given a function like $x = 10^y$ ($y = \log x$). For our purposes, pH values will ordinarily be given to two decimal places.

It is often convenient to define other p-functions analogous to pH, for example, $pOH = -\log [OH^-]$, $pK_a = -\log K_a$, or $pAg = -\log [Ag^+]$. Note that since $[H_3O^+][OH^-] = K_w = 1.0 \times 10^{-14}$, then $pH + pOH = pK_w = 14$.

Strong-Acid, Strong-Base Titration

Let us now consider the calculations involved in obtaining the pH of a solution of a strong acid titrated with a strong base. We are interested in whether such a reaction goes to completion as it must to fulfill one of the requirements for volumetric analysis (page 15). It is convenient and instructive to construct a *titration curve*, a plot of pH against the milliliters of titrant. We shall do this in the next section (page 87) after completing the calculations.

Strong acids and strong bases are completely ionized in water solutions. Hence the hydrogen or hydroxyl ion concentration can be calculated directly from the stoichiometric concentration of acid or base that has been added. At the equivalence point the pH is determined by the extent to which water dissociates, that is, the pH is 7.00 at 25°C. All calculations made in this section are approximate. See page 106 for a complete treatment of the nature of these approximations. Consider the following calculation:

Example. 50.0 ml of 0.100-M HCl is titrated with 0.100-M NaOH. Calculate the pH at the start of the titration and after the addition of 10.0, 50.0, and 60.0 ml of titrant.

(a) *Initial pH.* HCl is a strong acid and is completely dissociated. Hence

$$[H_3O^+] = 0.100$$

$$pH = 1.00$$

(b) *pH after the addition of 10.00 ml of base.* The reaction which occurs during the titration is

$$H_3O^+ + OH^- \rightleftharpoons 2\,H_2O$$

The equilibrium constant, which we shall designate K_t, is $1/K_w$ or 1.0×10^{14}. This is a very large constant, meaning that the reaction goes well to completion. We start with $50.0 \text{ ml} \times 0.100 \text{ mmol/ml} = 5.00 \text{ mmol}$ of H_3O^+ and add $10.0 \text{ ml} \times 0.100 \text{ mmol/ml} = 1.00 \text{ mmol OH}^-$. Assuming that the reaction goes to completion, we have $5.00 - 1.00 = 4.00$ mmol excess H_3O^+ in 60.0 ml of solution. Hence

$$[H_3O^+] = \frac{4.00 \text{ mmol}}{60.0 \text{ ml}} = 6.67 \times 10^{-2} \text{ mmol/ml}$$

$$pH = 2 - \log 6.67 = 1.18$$

The pH values for other volumes of titrant can be calculated in a similar fashion.

(c) *pH at the equivalence point.* The equivalence point is reached when 50.0 ml of NaOH has been added. Because the salt formed in the reaction (NaCl) is neither acidic nor basic in water solution (not hydrolyzed), the solution is neutral: $[H_3O^+] = [OH^-] = 1.0 \times 10^{-7}$. Hence the pH is 7.00, as in pure water.

(d) *pH after addition of 60.0 ml of base*. At this point $60.0 \text{ ml} \times 0.100 \text{ mmol/ml}$ $= 6.00$ mmol of OH^- has been added. We have $6.00 - 5.00 = 1.00$ mmol excess OH^- in 110 ml of solution. Hence

$$[OH^-] = \frac{1.00 \text{ mmol}}{110 \text{ ml}} = 9.1 \times 10^{-3} \text{ mmol/ml}$$

$$pOH = 3 - \log 9.1 = 2.04$$

$$pH = 14.00 - 2.04 = 11.96$$

Weak-Acid, Strong-Base Titration

Let us now consider the titration of a weak acid with a strong base. The calculations will also apply to the titration of a weak base with a strong acid. Again we shall make approximations. See page 108 for a complete treatment of the nature of these approximations.

Example. 50.0 ml of a 0.100-*M* solution of a weak acid, HB, $K_a = 1.0 \times 10^{-5}$, is titrated with 0.100-*M* NaOH. Calculate the *pH* at the start of the titration and after the addition of 10.0, 50.0, and 60.0 ml of titrant.

The following equilibria are involved in this example:

1.   Dissociation of the weak acid:

$$HB + H_2O \rightleftharpoons H_3O^+ + B^- \qquad K_a = 1.0 \times 10^{-5}$$

2.   Dissociation of the weak base:

$$B^- + H_2O \rightleftharpoons HB + OH^- \qquad K_b = 1.0 \times 10^{-9}$$

3.   Dissociation of water:

$$2 H_2O \rightleftharpoons H_3O^+ + OH^- \qquad K_w = 1.0 \times 10^{-14}$$

4.   In addition, the reaction during titration is simply the reverse of reaction (2):

$$HB + OH^- \rightleftharpoons B^- + H_2O \qquad K_t = 1.0 \times 10^9$$

In any solution all of the above equilibria are established simultaneously. The constants are interrelated, as we might expect: $K_a \times K_b = K_w$ and $K_t = 1/K_b$. We can make our calculations using any one of the above equilibria. We shall choose the one which is most convenient for our purposes.

(a) *Initial pH*. Since HB is weakly dissociated and produces one B^- and one H_3O^+ upon dissociation, we assume that

$$[H_3O^+] = [B^-]$$

and

$$[HB] = 0.100 - [H_3O^+] \cong 0.100$$

It is simplest to use the expression for K_a:

$$\frac{[H_3O^+][B^-]}{[HB]} = 1.0 \times 10^{-5}$$

$$\frac{[H_3O^+]^2}{0.10} = 1.0 \times 10^{-5}$$

$$[H_3O^+] = 1.0 \times 10^{-3}$$

$$pH = 3.00 - \log 1.0 = 3.00$$

(b) *pH after addition of 10.0 ml of base.* We assume that the titration reaction [(4) above] goes well to completion since $K_t = 1.0 \times 10^9$. We start with $50.0 \times 0.100 = 5.00$ mmol HB and add $10.0 \times 0.100 = 1.00$ mmol OH$^-$. Upon reaction we have 4.00 mmol HB in excess and have produced 1.00 mmol of B$^-$. Hence

$$[HB] = \frac{4.00}{60.00} - [H_3O^+] \cong \frac{4.00}{60.0}$$

$$[B^-] = \frac{1.00}{60.0} + [H_3O^+] \cong \frac{1.00}{60.0}$$

These terms may be substituted in the expression for either K_a or K_b. Since we are looking for the hydrogen ion concentration, it is simplest to use K_a:

$$\frac{[H_3O^+](1.00/60.0)}{(4.00/60.0)} = 1.0 \times 10^{-5}$$

Note that the volume of the solution cancels. Hence

$$[H_3O^+] = 4.0 \times 10^{-5}$$

$$pH = 5 - \log 4.0 = 4.40$$

The above calculation is sometimes set up in a manner that seems different at first glance but which really amounts to the same thing. Rearrange the K_a expression so that it is explicit in $[H_3O^+]$, take logarithms of both sides of the equation, and multiply by -1:

$$\frac{[H_3O^+][B^-]}{HB} = K_a$$

$$[H_3O^+] = K_a \times \frac{[HB]}{[B^-]}$$

$$-\log[H_3O^+] = -\log K_a - \log\frac{[HB]}{[B^-]}$$

$$pH = pK_a - \log\frac{[HB]}{[B^-]}$$

This equation explicitly shows that the pH is a function of pK_a and the ratio of acid concentration to that of the salt, or conjugate base. Since HB and B^- are present in the same volume of solution, the volume cancels and the ratio of mmols is the same as the ratio of molar concentrations. This logarithmic form of the ionization expression frequently appears in biochemistry and physiology textbooks under the designation *Henderson-Hasselbalch equation*. For a weak base B and its conjugate acid HB^+, the corresponding expression is

$$pOH = pK_b - \log\frac{[B]}{[BH^+]}$$

(c) *pH at the equivalence point.* 50.0 ml of NaOH has been added and 5.00 mmol of B^- has been formed, i.e., $[B^-] = 0.050\text{-}M$. The concentrations of HB, H_3O^+ and OH^- are not known, but we know that $[HB] \cong [OH^-]$ since equivalent amounts of acid and base have been added. It is most convenient to use the expression for K_b, solve for the pOH, and then calculate the pH.

$$\frac{[HB][OH^-]}{[B^-]} = K_b = 1.0 \times 10^{-9}$$

$$\frac{[OH^-]^2}{0.050} = 1.0 \times 10^{-9}$$

$$[OH^-]^2 = 5.0 \times 10^{-11}$$

$$2\,pOH = 11 - \log 5 = 10.30$$

$$pOH = 5.15$$

$$pH = 8.85$$

(d) *pH after the addition of 60.0 ml of base.* This is 10.0 ml, or 1.00 mmol, past the equivalence point. The pH is calculated from the excess strong base, that is

$$[OH^-] \cong \frac{1.00\text{ mmol}}{110\text{ ml}} = 9.1 \times 10^{-3}$$

$$pOH = 2.04$$

$$pH = 11.96$$

The OH^- ion produced by B^- in the reaction

$$B^- + H_2O \rightleftharpoons HB + OH^-$$

is negligible since the reaction is suppressed by the excess strong base.

As previously mentioned it is convenient and instructive to construct titration curves in considering the equilibrium aspects of acid-base reactions. The pH values calculated in the previous section, plus a number of additional ones, are shown in Table 4.2 and are plotted against the milliliters of NaOH in

TABLE 4.2 TITRATION OF A STRONG ACID AND A WEAK ACID WITH NaOH (50.0 ml of 0.100-M acid titrated with 0.100-M NaOH)

ml NaOH	Volume of solution	pH, HCl	pH, HB‡
0.00	50.0	1.00	3.00
10.00	60.0	1.18	4.40
20.00	70.0	1.37	4.82
25.00	75.0	1.48	5.00
30.00	80.0	1.60	5.18
40.00	90.0	1.95	5.60
49.00	99.0	3.00	6.69
49.90	99.9	4.00	7.70
†49.95	99.95	4.30	8.00
50.00	100.0	7.00	8.85
†50.05	100.05	9.70	9.70
50.10	100.10	10.00	10.00
51.00	101.0	11.00	11.00
60.00	110.0	11.96	11.96
70.00	120.0	12.23	12.23

† Assuming twenty drops per milliliter, these values are one drop before and one drop after the equivalence point.
‡ $K_a = 1.0 \times 10^{-5}$.

Fig. 4.1. The most striking features of these graphs are the very gradual changes in pH both before and after the equivalence point and the large "break" near the equivalence point for the addition of only a few drops of titrant. It will be noted that the magnitude of the change in pH at the equivalence point is less for a weak acid than for a strong acid. Titration curves for several weak acids are also shown in Fig. 4.1, where it can be seen that the weaker the acid, the smaller is the change in pH at the equivalence point. This is brought about by the fact that the neutralization reaction is not as complete at the equivalence point for a weak acid as it is for a stronger acid. In other words, the equilibrium constant, K_t for the reaction

$$HB + OH^- \rightleftharpoons B^- + H_2O$$

is smaller the weaker the acid HB. We shall see that the magnitude of this break relates to the sharpness of an indicator color change and hence to the precision with which the titration end point can be determined.

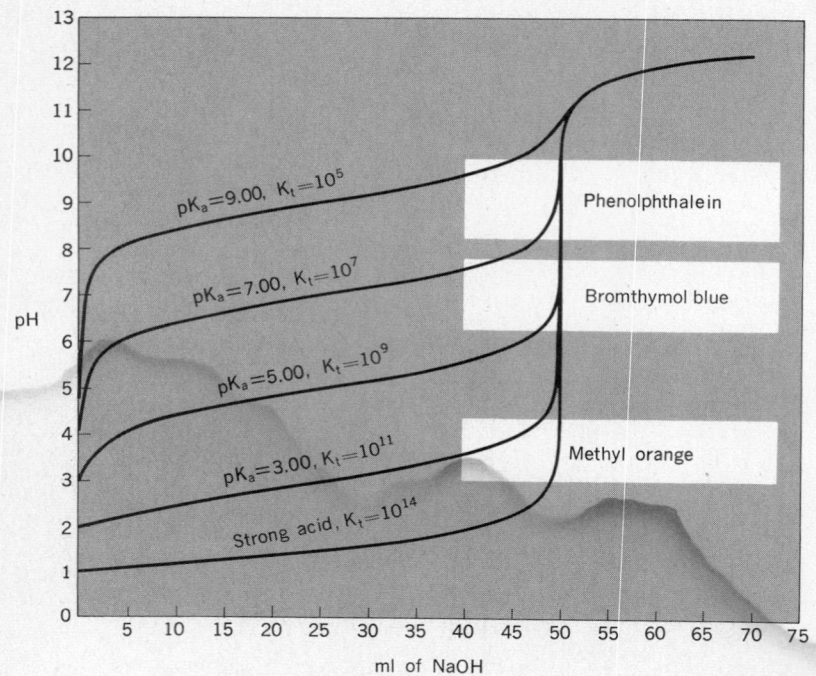

FIGURE 4.1 Typical acid-base titration curves: 50.00 ml of 0.1000-M monoprotic acid titrated with 0.100-M NaOH; pK_a values of the acids are shown on the curves.

ACID-BASE INDICATORS

The analyst takes advantage of the large change in pH that occurs in titrations in order to determine when the equivalence point is reached. There are many weak organic acids and bases in which the undissociated and ionic forms show different colors. Such molecules may be used to determine when sufficient titrant has been added and are termed *visual indicators*. A simple example is *para*-nitrophenol, which is a weak acid, dissociating as follows:

The undissociated form is colorless, but the anion, which has a system of

88

alternating single and double bonds (a conjugated system), is yellow. Molecules or ions having such conjugated systems absorb light of longer wavelengths than comparable molecules in which no conjugated system exists. The light absorbed is often in the visible portion of the spectrum, and hence the molecule or ion is colored (see Chapter 11).

The well-known indicator phenolphthalein (below) is a diprotic acid and is colorless. It dissociates first to a colorless form and then, on losing the

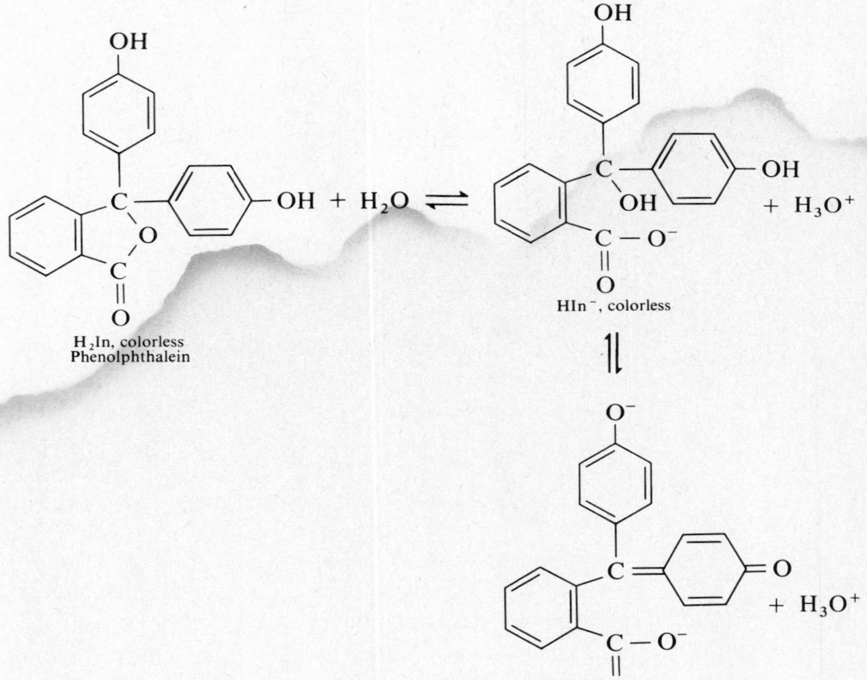

H$_2$In, colorless
Phenolphthalein

HIn$^-$, colorless

In^{2-}, red

second hydrogen, to an ion with a conjugated system; a red color results. Methyl orange, another widely used indicator, is a base and is yellow in the molecular form. Addition of a hydrogen ion gives a cation which is pink in color.

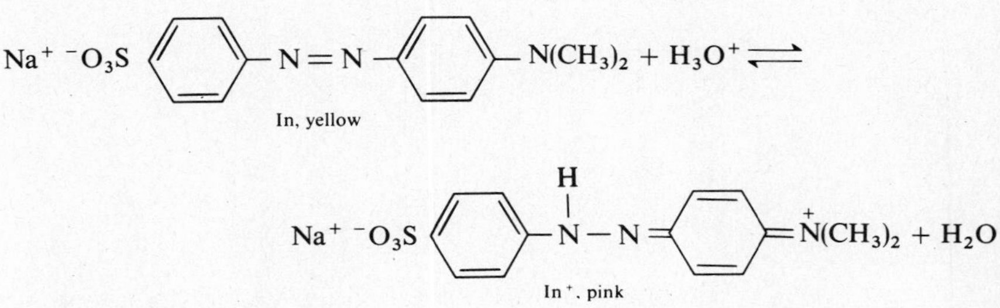

In, yellow

In$^+$, pink

For simplicity, let us designate an acid indicator as HIn, a basic indicator as InOH. The ionization expressions are

$$HIn + H_2O \rightleftharpoons H_3O^+ + In^-$$

$$InOH \rightleftharpoons In^+ + OH^-$$

The dissociation constant of the acid is

$$K_a = \frac{[H_3O^+][In^-]}{[HIn]}$$

In the logarithmic form, this becomes

$$pH = pK_a - \log\frac{[HIn]}{[In^-]}$$

Let us for illustration assume that the molecule HIn is red in color and the ion In⁻ is yellow. Both forms are present, of course, in a solution of the indicator, their relative concentrations depending upon the pH. The color that the human eye detects depends upon the relative amounts of the two forms. Obviously, in solutions of low pH, the acid HIn predominates and we would expect to see only a red color. In solutions of high pH, In⁻ should predominate and the color should be yellow. At intermediate pH values, where the two forms are in about equal concentrations, the color might be orange.

Suppose that the pK_a of HIn is 5.00 and that a few drops of HIn are added to a solution of a strong acid which is being titrated with a strong base. The quantity of HIn added is so small that the amount of titrant used by HIn can be considered negligible. Now let us follow the ratio of the two colored forms as the pH changes during the titration. This is shown in Table 4.3. Let

TABLE 4.3 RATIO OF COLORED FORMS OF INDICATOR AT VARIOUS pH VALUES

pH solution	Ratio: [HIn]/[In⁻]	Color
1	10,000:1	Red
2	1000:1	Red
3	100:1	Red
4	10:1	Red ⎫
5	1:1	Orange ⎬ Range
6	1:10	Yellow ⎭
7	1:100	Yellow
8	1:1000	Yellow

us also assume that the solution appears red to the eye when the ratio of $[HIn]/[In^-]$ is as large as $10:1$, and yellow when this ratio is $1:10$ or less. In such a case, the minimum change in pH, designated ΔpH, required to cause a color change from red to yellow is two units:

$$
\begin{aligned}
\text{Red:} \quad & pH_r = pK_a - \log 10/1 = 5 - 1 \\
\text{Yellow:} \quad & pH_y = pK_a - \log 1/10 = 5 + 1 \\
\hline
& \Delta pH = pH_r - pH_y = (5 - 1) - (5 + 1) = -2
\end{aligned}
$$

This minimum change in pH required for a color change is referred to as the "indicator range." In our example, the range is 4 to 6. At intermediate pH values, the color shown by the indicator is not red or yellow but some shade of orange. At pH 5, the pK_a of HIn, the two colored forms are in equal concentrations, that is, HIn is half-neutralized. Frequently one hears terminology such as "An indicator which changed color at pH 5 was employed." This means that the pK_a of the indicator is 5, and the range is approximately from pH 4 to 6.

TABLE 4.4   SOME ACID-BASE INDICATORS

Indicator	Color change with increasing pH	pH range
Picric acid	Colorless to yellow	0.1–0.8
Thymol blue	Red to yellow	1.2–2.8
2,6-Dinitrophenol	Colorless to yellow	2.0–4.0
Methyl yellow	Red to yellow	2.9–4.0
Bromphenol blue	Yellow to blue	3.0–4.6
Methyl orange	Red to yellow	3.1–4.4
Bromcresol green	Yellow to blue	3.8–5.4
Methyl red	Red to yellow	4.2–6.2
Litmus	Red to blue	4.5–8.3
Methyl purple	Purple to green	4.8–5.4
Para-nitrophenol	Colorless to yellow	5.0–7.0
Bromcresol purple	Yellow to purple	5.2–6.8
Bromthymol blue	Yellow to blue	6.0–7.6
Neutral red	Red to yellow	6.8–8.0
Phenol red	Yellow to red	6.8–8.4
para-α-Naphtholphthalein	Yellow to blue	7.0–9.0
Phenolphthalein	Colorless to red	8.0–9.6
Thymolphthalein	Colorless to blue	9.3–10.6
Alizarin yellow R	Yellow to violet	10.1–12.0
1,3,5-Trinitrobenzene	Colorless to orange	12.0–14.0

Table 4.4 lists some acid-base indicators together with their approximate ranges. Note that the ranges are roughly one to two pH units, in general agreement with the assumption we made above. Actually the range may not be symmetrical about the pK of the indicator, since a higher ratio may

be required for the observer to see one form than is required to see the other. It should also be noted that various indicators change color at widely different pH values. It is necessary for the analyst to select the proper indicator for his titration.

Selection of Proper Indicator

In Fig. 4.1 the shaded areas are the indicator ranges of methyl orange (3.1 to 4.4) and phenolphthalein (8.0 to 9.6). It is apparent that as a strong acid is titrated, the large break in the curve at the equivalence point is sufficient to span the ranges of both these indicators. Hence either indicator would change color within one or two drops of the equivalence point, as would any other indicator changing color between pH 4 to 10.

In the titration of weaker acids, the choice of indicators is much more limited. For an acid of pK_a 5, approximately that of acetic acid, the pH is higher than 7 at the equivalence point and the change in pH is relatively small. Phenolphthalein changes color at approximately the equivalence point and is a suitable indicator.

In the case of a very weak acid, for example, $pK_a = 9$, no large change in pH occurs in the vicinity of the equivalence point. Hence a large volume of base would be required to change the color of an indicator, and the equivalence point could not be detected with the usually desired precision.

As a general rule, then, one should select an indicator which changes color at approximately the pH at the equivalence point of the titration. For weak acids, the pH at the equivalence point is above 7 and phenolphthalein is the usual choice. For weak bases, where the pH is below 7, methyl red (4.2 to 6.2) or methyl orange is widely used. For strong acids and strong bases, methyl red, bromthymol blue, and phenolphthalein are suitable.

Indicator Errors

There are at least two sources of errors in the determination of the end point of a titration using visual indicators. One occurs when the indicator employed does not change color at the proper pH. This is a determinate error and can be corrected by the determination of an *indicator blank*. The latter is simply the volume of acid or base required to change the pH from that at the equivalence point to the pH at which the indicator changes color. The indicator blank is usually determined experimentally.

A second error occurs in the case of very weak acids (or bases) where the slope of the titration curve is not great and hence the color change at the end point is not sharp. Even if the proper indicator is employed, an indeterminate error occurs and is reflected in a lack of precision in deciding exactly when the color change occurs. The use of a nonaqueous solvent (page 101) may improve the sharpness of the end point in such cases.

In order to sharpen the color change shown by some indicators, mixtures of two indicators, or of an indicator and an indifferent dye, are sometimes used. The familiar "modified methyl orange" for carbonate titrations is a mixture of methyl orange and the dye xylene cyanole FF. The dye absorbs some of the wavelengths of light that are transmitted by both colored forms, thus cutting down on the overlapping of the two colors. At an intermediate pH, the methyl orange assumes a color which is almost complementary to that of xylene cyanole FF, and the solution thus appears gray. This color change is more easily detected than the gradual change of methyl orange from yellow to red through a number of shades of orange. Many mixtures of two indicators have been recommended for improved color changes.

FEASIBILITY OF ACID-BASE TITRATIONS

We have previously mentioned that for a chemical reaction to be suitable for use in a titration, the reaction must be complete at the equivalence point. The degree of completeness of the reaction determines the size and sharpness of the vertical portion of the titration curve. The larger the equilibrium constant, the more complete the reaction, the larger the break in the titration curve, and the easier it is to locate the equivalence point with good precision. The completeness of the reaction is related to the practical feasibility of the titration. Theoretically, it may be possible to locate the equivalence point of a reaction which does not go well to completion, but practically, this may be a difficult problem.

The equilibrium constant for the titration of a strong acid with a strong base is quite large:

$$H_3O^+ + OH^- \rightleftharpoons 2\,H_2O \qquad K_t = \frac{1}{K_w} = 1 \times 10^{14}$$

We have noted the large ΔpH which occurs at the equivalence point, 5.20 units for $\Delta V = 0.10$ ml, and have pointed out that because of this large break several indicators could be used to determine the equivalence volume with a precision of a few parts per thousand. Hence we say that the titration is *feasible*.

How large must the equilibrium constant be for a titration to be feasible? It is difficult to give an unequivocal answer to this question. The concentrations of the substance titrated and the titrant influence the magnitude of ΔpH, and under certain circumstances an analyst might be satisfied with less precision than we specified above. However, if we are given a specific set of conditions to be met, we can make a rather simple calculation to determine the magnitude of K_t. It is generally desired that essentially all of the substance titrated be converted into product at or near the equivalence point. It is also desirable that the pH change by one or two units for the addition of a few drops of titrant at the equivalence point if a visual indicator is to be employed. The following example illustrates a calculation of K_a for a weak acid and K_t for the titration for a specific statement as to feasibility requirements.

Example. 50 ml of 0.10-M HA is titrated with 0.10-M strong base. (a) Calculate the minimum value of K_t so that, when 49.95 ml of titrant has been added, essentially all of HA has reacted and the pH changes by 2.00 units on the addition of two more drops (0.10 ml) of titrant. (b) Repeat the calculation for $\Delta pH = 1.00$ unit.

(a) the pH 0.05 ml beyond the equivalence point can be calculated as follows:

$$[OH^-] = \frac{0.05 \times 0.10}{100.05} = 5 \times 10^{-5} - M$$

$$pOH = 4.30$$

$$pH = 9.70$$

If ΔpH is to be 2.00 units, the pH 0.05 ml before the equivalence point should be 7.70. At this point, if the reaction is complete, we have only 1 ppt of HA unreacted. Hence

$$pH = pK_a - \log \frac{[HA]}{[A^-]}$$

$$7.70 = pK_a - \log \frac{1}{1000}$$

$$pK_a = 4.70$$

$$K_a = 2 \times 10^{-5}$$

$$K_t = \frac{K_a}{K_w} = \frac{2 \times 10^{-5}}{1 \times 10^{-14}} = 2 \times 10^9$$

(b) If $\Delta pH = 1.00$, then

$$8.70 = pK_a - \log \frac{1}{1000}$$

$$pK_a = 5.70$$

$$K_a = 2 \times 10^{-6}$$

$$K_t = 2 \times 10^8$$

Effect of Concentration

The magnitude of ΔpH at the equivalence point also depends upon the concentrations of the substance titrated and the titrant. The effect of concentration upon the change in pH for the strong-acid, strong-base titration is shown in Fig. 4.2. The ΔpH decreases as the concentration of substance titrated and titrant decrease.

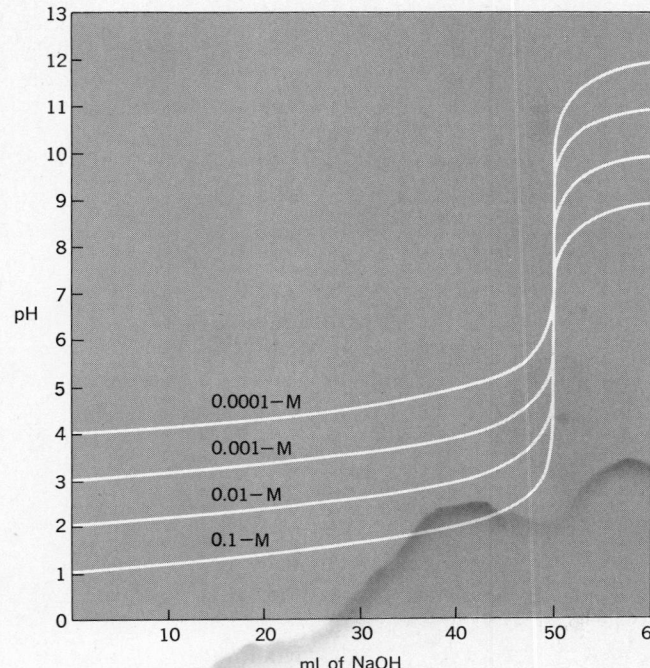

pH

ml of NaOH

FIGURE 4.2 Effect of concentration on titration curves of strong acids with strong bases. 50 ml acid titrated with base of same molarity.

For weak acids the effect of concentration as well as the magnitude of K_a on ΔpH is shown in Table 4.5. The following conclusions can be drawn:

1. The smaller the value of K_a, the higher the pH at the equivalence point and the smaller ΔpH.

TABLE 4.5 ΔpH FOR TITRATION OF WEAK ACID, HA, WITH 0.1-M STRONG BASE

K_a of Ha	mmol HA titrated	Initial volume, ml	pH, 0.05 ml before eq. pt.	pH at eq. pt.	pH, 0.05 ml after eq. pt.	ΔpH for 0.10 ml
	2.5	75	7.70	8.70	9.70	2.00
	2.5	50	7.70	8.76	9.82	2.12
1×10^{-5}	2.5	25	7.70	8.85	10.00	2.30
	5.0	75	8.00	8.80	9.60	1.60
	5.0	50	8.00	8.85	9.70	1.70
	5.0	25	8.00	8.91	9.82	1.82
5×10^{-6}	2.5	75	8.00	8.85	9.70	1.70
1×10^{-6}	2.5	75	8.70	9.20	9.70	1.00
5×10^{-7}	2.5	75	9.00	9.35	9.70	0.70
†1×10^{-7}	2.5	75	9.70	9.70	9.70	0.00

† Usual approximate calculations.

95

2.   (a) Increasing the amount of HA titrated in the same initial volume decreases ΔpH. However, this increases the volume of titrant required, rendering a given error in determining the end point a smaller relative error. (b) If the same amount of HA is titrated but the initial volume is decreased, ΔpH is increased. This is caused primarily by the fact that excess titrant is in a smaller volume. (See below.)

3.   Increasing the concentration of titrant increases ΔpH. This decreases the volume of titrant required, thus making a given error a larger relative error.

For the titration of a given amount of a certain weak acid, the procedure recommended to increase ΔpH is as described above in 2(b). Starting with a smaller volume, that is, an increased concentration of HA, will sharpen the break at the equivalence point while using the same volume of titrant.

As a general rule it can be said that a precision of a few parts per thousand can be obtained in the titration of a 0.03-M solution of a weak acid or base of dissociation constant as low as 1×10^{-6}, using 0.1-M titrant. This corresponds to a value of K_t of 1×10^8. Still weaker acids or bases may be titrated with sacrifice of precision in determining the end point.

A salt of a weak acid, that is, a Brønsted base, can be titrated feasibly with a strong acid if the acid itself is too weak for feasible titration. For example, an acid HA, with $K_a = 1 \times 10^{-9}$, is too weak for feasible titration. The dissociation constant of the conjugate base A^- is 1×10^{-5}, since (page 81)

$$K_a \times K_b = 1 \times 10^{-14}$$

Hence, A^- can be titrated feasibly with a strong acid. Similar conclusions can be drawn for the titration of salts of weak bases.

BUFFER SOLUTIONS

A solution which resists large changes in pH when an acid or base is added or when the solution is diluted is called a *buffer solution*. A solution containing a conjugate acid-base pair is an example of a buffer. The acid reacts with any hydroxyl ions added to the solution, and the conjugate base combines with hydrogen ions. Consider, for example, a solution of acetic acid and sodium acetate. Hydrogen and hydroxyl ions are removed by the reactions:

$$HOAc + OH^- \rightleftharpoons OAc^- + H_2O$$

$$OAc^- + H_3O^+ \rightleftharpoons HOAc + H_2O$$

The pH is dependent upon the logarithm of the ratio of acid to salt (base),

$$pH = pK_a - \log \frac{[HOAc]}{[OAc^-]}$$

and it is necessary to change this ratio by a factor of 10 to change the pH by one unit. The flat portion of the titration curve (Fig. 4.1) for weak acids results from the buffering action just described. It should also be noted in the above equation for pH that dilution should have no effect on pH, at least theoretically, since the volume terms cancel out.

The effectiveness of a buffer solution in resisting change in pH per unit of strong acid or base added is greatest when the ratio of buffer acid to salt is unity. In the titration of a weak acid this point of maximum effectiveness is reached when the acid is half-neutralized, or the $pH = pK_a$. This can be seen from the following calculation:

Example. Calculate the slope of the titration curve of the weak acid, HA, titrated with OH^-, and find its minimum value. Let a = original mmol of HA and b = mmol of OH^- added. Then

$$[HA] = \frac{(a-b)}{v}$$

$$[A^-] = \frac{b}{v}$$

where v is the volume of solution.

$$pH = pK_a - \log\frac{a-b}{b} = pK_a - \log(a-b) + \log b$$

Differentiating, the slope is

$$\frac{dpH}{db} = \frac{0.43}{a-b} + \frac{0.43}{b} = \frac{0.43a}{b(a-b)}$$

To find the minimum value of the slope, differentiate the above expression and equate to zero,

$$\frac{d^2pH}{db^2} = -\frac{0.43a(a-2b)}{b^2(a-b)^2} = 0$$

$$b = \frac{a}{2}$$

That is, $[HA] = [A^-]$, and at this point $pH = pK_a$.

It may be instructive to examine Table 4.6 which shows the change in pH produced during the titration of two different amounts of acetic acid at intervals of 1 mmol of added base. It is apparent that at the start of the titration the solution is not well buffered, and the pH rises rapidly as base is added. This explains the initial rapid rise in the titration curves of weak acids shown in Fig. 4.1. The rate of rise in pH decreases, passes through a minimum at $pH = pK_a$, and then slowly increases again. At the equivalence point, a large change occurs since the acid is exhausted and the solution is no longer buffered.

TABLE 4.6   CHANGE IN pH DURING TITRATION OF ACETIC ACID

mmol OH$^-$ added to 10 mmol HOAc	pH†	ΔpH	mmol OH$^-$ added to 20 mmol HOAc	pH†	ΔpH
0	2.87	—	0	2.72	—
1	3.79	0.92	1	3.46	0.74
2	4.14	0.35	2	3.79	0.33
3	4.37	0.23	3	3.99	0.20
4	4.56	0.19	9	4.65	—
5	4.74	0.18	10	4.74	0.09
6	4.92	0.18	11	4.83	0.09
7	5.11	0.19	12	4.92	0.09
8	5.34	0.23	18	5.69	—
9	5.69	0.35	19	6.02	0.33
10	8.87	3.18	20	9.02	3.00

† Calculated for 100 ml volume, assuming no change in volume as base added.

Concentrated solutions of strong acids and bases resist large changes in pH, and the titration curves are flat over a wide range of pH (Fig. 4.1). However, such solutions are sometimes not regarded as buffers in the strictest sense, since the pH is markedly changed by dilution.

The capacity of a buffer is a measure of its effectiveness in resisting changes in pH upon the addition of acid or base. The greater the concentrations of the acid and conjugate base, the greater is the capacity of the buffer. This is evident from Table 4.6 in that twice as much base is required to increase the pH of the more concentrated solution from 3.79 to 4.74 than is needed for the more dilute solution. Buffer capacity can be defined more quantitatively as the number of moles of strong base required to change the pH of one liter of solution by one pH unit. The term "range" of a buffer is ill-defined, but it is evident from Table 4.6 that little buffering action is obtained if the acid-salt ratio is greater than 9 to 1 or less than 1 to 9.

In preparing a buffer of a desired pH, the analyst should select an acid-salt (or base-salt) system in which the pK_a of the acid is as close as possible to the desired pH. By this selection, the ratio of acid to salt is near unity, and maximal effectiveness against increase or decrease in pH is obtained. The actual concentrations of acid and salt employed depend upon the desired resistance to change in pH. These points are illustrated in the following example.

Example.   (a) It is desired to prepare 100 ml of a buffer of pH 5.00. Acetic, benzoic, and formic acids and their salts are available for use. Which acid should be used for maximum effectiveness against increase or decrease in pH? What acid-salt ratio should be used?

The pK_a values of these acids are: acetic, 4.74; benzoic, 4.18; and formic, 3.68. The pK_a of acetic is closest to the desired pH, and this acid and its salt should be used.

Then

$$pH = pK_a - \log \frac{[HOAc]}{[OAc^-]}$$

$$5.00 = 4.74 - \log \frac{[HOAc]}{[OAc^-]}$$

Taking antilogs $[HOAc]/[OAc^-] = 1/1.8$, or the salt-to-acid ratio should be 1.8 to 1. This is the molar ratio, not the ratio of grams.

(b) If it is desired that the change in pH of the buffer be no more than 0.10 unit for the addition of 1 mmol of either acid or base, what minimum concentrations of the acid and salt should be used?

Since there is less acid present than salt, a greater change in pH will result if base is added. Hence if we calculate on the basis that base is added, the condition will be more than satisfied for the addition of acid. Thus if

$$x = \text{mmol acid originally present}$$

$$1.8x = \text{mmol salt originally present}$$

If 1 mmol OH^- is added, then

$$x - 1 = \text{mmol acid remaining}$$

$$1.8x + 1 = \text{mmol salt}$$

Then

$$5.10 = 4.74 - \log \frac{x-1}{1.8x+1}$$

Solving gives $x = 6.6$ mmol, and $1.8x = 11.9$ mmol. The molar concentrations are then, $[HOAc] = 0.066$ mmol/ml, and $[OAc^-] = 0.119$ mmol/ml.

PHYSIOLOGICAL BUFFERS

It is of interest to point out that the principles of acid-base chemistry discussed in this chapter are of direct significance in such fields as biochemistry and physiology. The great physiologist Claude Bernard was the first to emphasize that the fluids of the body provide an "internal environment" in which the body cells live and perform their many functions protected from the inconstancy of the external environment. Living tissues are extremely sensitive to changes in the composition of the fluids that bathe them, and the regulatory mechanisms within the body which maintain the constancy of the internal environment comprise one of the most important phases in the study of the biological sciences.

A very important aspect of this regulation is the maintenance of a nearly constant pH in the blood and other fluids of the body. Substances that are acidic or alkaline in character are ingested in the diet and are formed continually by metabolic reactions, but the pH of the blood normally remains constant within about 0.1 pH unit (7.35 to 7.45).

The two principal routes for the elimination of acids from the body are the lungs and kidneys. It is estimated that in one day the normal human adult eliminates the equivalent of about 30 liters of 1-M acid by way of the lungs, and about 100 ml of 1-M acid through the kidneys.[5] To handle such large amounts of acid, the normal adult has enough buffers in his approximately 5 liters of blood to absorb about 150 ml of 1-M acid. The proton acceptors found in tissues, such as the muscles, can handle about five times as much acid as the blood buffers.

The principal buffers in the blood are proteins, bicarbonate, phosphates, hemoglobin (HHb), and oxyhemoglobin (HHbO$_2$). Carbon dioxide is formed metabolically in the tissues and is carried away by the blood primarily as bicarbonate ion. A typical reaction is

$$H_2O + CO_2(aq) + Hb^-(aq) \rightleftharpoons HHb(aq) + HCO_3^-$$

$$\underset{\text{base}}{} \qquad \underset{\text{acid}}{} \qquad \underset{\longrightarrow \text{ to lungs}}{}$$

Note that H_2CO_3 is a stronger acid ($pK_{a_1} = 6.1$ under conditions in the blood) than is hemoglobin ($pK_a = 7.93$); hence the above reaction tends to go to the right. In the blood, at pH 7.4, the ratio of bicarbonate to free CO_2 can be calculated from the equation

$$7.4 = 6.1 - \log \frac{[CO_2]}{[HCO_3^-]}$$

The ratio $[HCO_3^-]/[CO_2]$ is about 20 to 1, showing that the predominant form in the blood is bicarbonate ion.

In the lungs carbon dioxide is released by the reaction

$$HCO_3^-(aq) + HHbO_2(aq) \rightleftharpoons HbO_2^-(aq) + H_2O + CO_2(g)$$

$$\underset{\longrightarrow \text{ to tissues}}{} \qquad \qquad \underset{\longrightarrow \text{exhaled}}{}$$

When blood is oxygenated in the lungs, hemoglobin is converted into oxyhemoglobin. Since oxyhemoglobin is a stronger acid ($pK_a = 6.68$) than hemoglobin, this facilitates the conversion of HCO_3^- to CO_2 by the above reaction.

The phosphate buffer system is found mostly in the red cells. Its reaction is

$$H_2PO_4^- + H_2O \rightleftharpoons HPO_4^{2-} + H_3O^+$$

The pK_a of $H_2PO_4^-$ is about 7.2; hence, this system exhibits its maximal effectiveness very close to physiological pH.

---

[5] W. R. Frisell, *Acid-Base Chemistry in Medicine*, The Macmillan Co., New York, 1968.

Disturbances in the pH of the blood are seen clinically in certain diseases. For example, untreated diabetes sometimes give rise to an acidosis which may be fatal. Kidney failure, or chronic nephritis, leads to retention of $H_2PO_4^-$ and an increase in the amount of carbon dioxide in the blood:

$$H_2PO_4^- + HCO_3^- \rightleftharpoons HPO_4^{2-} + H_2O + CO_2$$

NONAQUEOUS TITRATIONS

Consider an acid, HB, which we wish to titrate with base, say NaOH. We have discussed the feasibility of this titration in terms of the "strength" of HB, using its dissociation constant, K_a, as a measure. But, as pointed out earlier, in terms of the Brønsted theory, K_a is really a measure of the tendency of HB to transfer a proton to the solvent, water:

$$HB + H_2O \rightleftharpoons H_3O^+ + B$$

That is, K_a is not a measure of an "intrinsic" acid strength of HB, because the basicity of water is also involved in this reaction. The same acid might dissociate to a much greater degree in a more basic solvent, say an organic amine:

$$HB + RNH_2 \rightleftharpoons RNH_3^+ + B$$

That is, there will be a greater concentration of solvated protons in the latter solvent. Thus it might appear that if HB were too weak an acid to be titrated feasibly in aqueous solution, we could enhance its "acidity" and hence its "titratibility" by choosing a solvent more basic than water.

Actually, in a practical sense, this is often the case, but the above discussion is misleading as it stands. In fact, dissociation is not at all necessary for successful acid-base titrations. Excellent titrations have been performed in nonpolar solvents like benzene or chloroform which do not promote dissociation to any appreciable extent. Indeed, it is *not* the greater basicity of the organic amine that makes it a better solvent than water for the titration of the very weak acid, HB. It is a better solvent for this titration because it is a *weaker acid* than water. In the aqueous system the titration reaction is

$$HB + OH^- \rightleftharpoons H_2O + B^- \qquad K_t = \frac{K_a}{K_w} \qquad (1)$$

Water is a product of the titration reaction, and furthermore it is present in large excess. Thus, to the extent that water is acidic, it competes against the acid we wish to titrate and prevents the titration reaction from going to completion unless HB is itself sufficiently strong. This can be seen from the constant K_t; the constant is larger the larger K_a and the smaller the autoprotolysis constant of the solvent. In general terms, we wish the following reaction to go to completion:

$$HB + S^- \rightleftharpoons HS + B^- \qquad K_t = \frac{K_a}{K_{auto}} \qquad (2)$$

Here HS is the solvent, S^- the conjugate base, and K_{auto} the autoprotolysis constant of the solvent. If HS is a weaker acid than water, K_t for reaction (2) will be larger than K_t for reaction (1). It often happens that the solvent is also more basic than water, but it is not correct to fixate upon this latter aspect.

In any case, we find that many titrations of weak acids and bases which are not feasible in water solution can be performed in other solvents. A variety of solvents have now been studied, and various methods of end-point detection are available. Much of the work is empirical because we do not have acidity scales in all of these solvents as we have for water. But even on this basis, the field of nonaqueous titrations has become important in analytical chemistry.

Solvent Systems

Several classifications of solvents have been proposed. Laitinen[6] considers four types. *Amphiprotic* solvents possess both acidic and basic properties as does water. They undergo autoprotolysis, and, as we noted above, the degree to which the titration reaction goes to completion is a function of this reaction. Some, such as methanol and ethanol, have acid-base properties comparable to water and, along with water, are called *neutral* solvents. Others, called *acid* solvents, such as acetic acid, formic acid, and sulfuric acid, are much stronger acids and weaker bases than water. *Basic* solvents such as liquid ammonia and ethylenediamine have greater basicity and weaker acidity than water.

Aprotic, or inert, solvents are neither appreciably acidic nor basic and hence show little or no tendency to undergo autoprotolysis reactions. Examples are benzene, carbon tetrachloride, and chloroform.

Another group of solvents, called basic solvents, have a strong affinity for protons but are not appreciably acidic. Examples are ether, pyridine, and various ketones. Pyridine, for example, can accept a proton from an acid such as water:

On the other hand, pyridine has no tendency to furnish a proton. Consequently, no autoprotolysis reaction can be written.

[6] H. A. Laitinen, *Chemical Analysis*, McGraw-Hill Book Company, New York, 1960, p. 60.

A fourth class of solvents would be those with acidic but no basic properties. No examples of such solvents are known.

Differentiating Ability of a Solvent

We have previously pointed out that water levels the mineral acids perchloric, hydrochloric, and nitric (page 74). That is, in aqueous solution these acids appear equally strong. However, in an acidic solvent such as acetic acid, the greater strength of perchloric acid over, say, hydrochloric, allows it to be titrated in a separate step from the latter acid. Of the two equilibria,

$$HClO_4 + HOAc \rightleftharpoons H_2OAc^+ + ClO_4^- \tag{1}$$

$$HCl + HOAc \rightleftharpoons H_2OAc^+ + Cl^- \tag{2}$$

the first goes much farther to the right than the second. Hence, in a titration of a mixture of the two acids in acetic acid solvent, two breaks in the titration curve are found, and the acids are said to be *differentiated*.

There are two properties of the solvent which determine its leveling or differentiating ability. One is the intrinsic acid-base character of the solvent, and the second is the autoprotolysis constant. For example, water is sufficiently strong a base to level HCl and $HClO_4$, but not HCl and HOAc. The latter two acids are differentiated in aqueous solution. Acetic acid is a weaker base than water and differentiates $HClO_4$ and HCl. Ammonia, however, is a stronger base than water and levels not only HCl and $HClO_4$ but also HCl and HOAc. An inert solvent, having no appreciable acidic or basic properties, exerts no leveling effect and hence is very suitable for differentiating mixtures of compounds of varying acidity.

We have previously pointed out that the neutralization of a strong acid with a strong base in aqueous solution is simply the reverse of the auto-protolysis reaction of the solvent:

$$H_3O^+ + OH^- \rightleftharpoons 2 H_2O$$

The K_t for this reaction is $1/K_w = 1 \times 10^{14}$. The magnitude of this constant determines the size of the break at the equivalence point or the useful range over which breaks in titration curves can be detected. For the titration of 0.1-N reagents, the steep break is about 6 pH units, from pH 4 to 10. Below pH 4 and above pH 10 water levels acids and bases which are dissolved in it. These two pH extremes correspond to concentrations of H_3O^+ and OH^- of 10^{-4}-M each.

Consider ethanol, C_2H_5OH ($pK_{auto} = 19.5$) as a solvent. The autoprotolysis constant is 3×10^{-20} and hence K_t for the reaction of strong acid with strong base,

$$C_2H_5OH_2^+ + OC_2H_5^- \rightleftharpoons 2 C_2H_5OH$$

is $1/K_{auto}$ or 3×10^{19}. Reasoning as in the case of water above, the large break in the titration curve would occur between the limits of 10^{-4}-M strong acid and strong base. That is, the useful pH range in ethanol is roughly $19.5 - 2 \times 4 = 11.5$ units, almost twice the useful range of water. In general, we can conclude that the useful pH range for a solvent in differentiating acids and bases is greater the smaller the autoprotolysis constant.

Dielectric Constant

Another property of a solvent which is of importance in nonaqueous titrations is the dielectric constant. In amphiprotic solvents the dissociation of a weak acid into separate ions is thought to occur as follows:

$$HB + HS \underset{}{\overset{1}{\rightleftarrows}} \underset{\text{ion pair}}{\{H_2S^+B^-\}} \underset{}{\overset{2}{\rightleftarrows}} \underset{\text{separate ions}}{H_2S^+ + B^-}$$

The first step is called ionization, and the product is called an *ion-pair*. In the second step, complete separation of the ion occurs. Solvents with high dielectric constants encourage complete dissociation into ions by lessening the energy required for the process. In solvents of low dielectric constant, considerable ion-pairing occurs.

The acidity of an ion such as NH_4^+ is not greatly affected by the dielectric constant of the solvent since no ion-pair production occurs:

$$NH_4^+ + H_2O \rightleftarrows \{NH_3H_3O^+\} \rightleftarrows NH_3 + H_3O^+$$

On the other hand, the autoprotolysis constant of the solvent is increased, the larger the dielectric constant:

$$HS + HS \rightleftarrows \{H_2S^+S^-\} \rightleftarrows H_2S^+ + S^-$$

since charge separation does occur.

Generally, a high dielectric constant is desirable for amphiprotic solvents. A factor of prime importance is solubility; a high dielectric constant generally favors the solubility of polar reagents and samples. Water is a unique solvent in having a very high dielectric constant and a relatively small autoprotolysis constant.

Completeness of the Titration Reaction

In general we represent the titration of a weak acid, HX, with the solvent anion (base), S^-, as follows:

$$HX + S^- \rightleftarrows HS + X^-$$

In solvents of low dielectric constant where ion-pair formation may occur, we can represent the reaction as

$$H^+X^- + M^+S^- \rightleftarrows HS + M^+X^-$$

From Le Chatelier's principle we can conclude that the reaction goes further to completion the more highly dissociated the ion pairs H^+X^- and M^+S^- and the more highly associated the ion pairs of the salt M^+X^-. In addition, the lower the autoprotolysis constant of the solvent, the larger K_t for the titration reaction. Concentration factors (page 94) also are to be considered in nonaqueous systems.

Titrants

Perchloric acid is by far the most widely used acid for the titration of weak bases, because it is a very strong acid which is readily available. It is normally obtained commercially as 72% $HClO_4$ by weight, the remainder being water; this is an azeotrope of $HClO_4$ and H_2O, and it represents approximately the composition $HClO_4 \cdot H_2O$, which some writers formulate as hydronium perchlorate $H_3O^+ ClO_4^-$. Weak bases are titrated most often in glacial acetic acid solution. In such cases, the titrant is perchloric acid, say 0.1-M, in the same solvent. Because the presence of water may be deleterious (see above), the desired quantity of 72% $HClO_4$ is mixed with acetic acid, and then acetic anhydride is added in approximately the correct amount to react with the water estimated to be present. The product of this reaction is, of course, acetic acid.

A somewhat larger variety of strong bases are used, including alkali hydroxides, tetraalkylammonium hydroxides, and sodium or potassium methoxide or ethoxide. Common solvents for these bases are lower alcohols and mixtures of benzene with methanol or ethanol.

Normally the effect of temperature upon measured titrant volumes can be ignored with aqueous solutions under ordinary room temperature variations. Organic solvents such as acetic acid, benzene, or methanol, on the other hand, have fairly large coefficients of thermal expansion, and the volume changes may not be negligible if the titrant is at a different temperature from that at which it was standardized. Correction for the effect of a temperature change upon the volume of titrant may be made by means of an equation of the type

$$V_t = V_0(1 + \alpha t + \beta t^2 + \gamma t^3)$$

where V_0 is the volume at 0°C and V_t the volume at t°C. Values of α, β, and γ for various liquids may be found in handbooks. Practically, β and γ are usually small enough so that βt^2 and γt^3 may be ignored. Suppose the titrant were at 30°C when an unknown was titrated, whereas it had been standardized at 25°C. Neglecting the higher-order terms in the above equation and eliminating V_0 between the two temperatures involved gives

$$V_{25} = V_{30} \times \frac{1 + 25\alpha}{1 + 30\alpha}$$

Using a handbook value for α, the volume of titrant that would have been consumed had the titration been performed at 25°C can be readily calculated. For a mixed solvent such as benzene-methanol, a value for α may be used, weighted according to the volume fractions or the mole fractions of the two solvents in the mixture (if the mixture is nonideal, an exact, theoretically valid value of α cannot be calculated from the information that is normally available, but an adequate value can be obtained with weighted means).

End-Point Detection

A number of visual indicators are available, generally under trivial names such as cresol red, methyl red, azo violet, and crystal violet. The rationale of indicator selection is not on a good theoretical base, and the choice is often best made on the basis of experience, trial-and-error, or reference to analogous cases which may be found in the literature.

Potentiometric end-point methods (Chapter 9) are frequently employed, although, in general, electrode behavior in nonaqueous solvents is not well understood. Again, the safest approach is to see what other workers have used in similar situations. Other instrumental end points such as conductometric and photometric (Chapter 11) have been used successfully.

Applications

The number of compounds which have been titrated in nonaqueous media is much too large for listing here. Very weak acids, such as phenols, have been titrated in ethylenediamine. Carboxylic acids are sufficiently strong so that only moderately basic solvents such as methanol or ethanol can be employed. Nonaqueous titrations have become important in the pharmaceutical industry. For example, most of the well-known sulfa drug group can be determined by titration as acids (the acidity is conferred by the sulfonamide group, $-SO_2-NH-$) with alkali methoxide in benzene-methanol or dimethylformamide solution.

Weak bases, such as amines, amino acids, and anions of weak acids, have been titrated in glacial acetic acid solution using perchloric acid. Alkaloids have very weak basic properties and can be titrated in acidic or inert solvents.

The solvent methyl isobutyl ketone, a basic but not acidic solvent, has been used for the titration of a wide range of acids and bases. It has been used to differentiate a five-component acid mixture: perchloric, hydrochloric, salicylic, acetic, and phenol. This mixture ranges from the strongest mineral acid, perchloric, to phenol, a very weak acid. The titrant for acids is a solution of tetrabutylammonium hydroxide in isopropanol; for the titration of bases, perchloric acid dissolved in dioxane is usually employed.

APPROXIMATIONS IN ACID-BASE CALCULATIONS

In our calculations of the pH of aqueous solutions of acids and bases we made frequent assumptions and approximations to simplify the problem at hand.

Most of these assumptions are valid and the approximate answers we obtained are accurate enough for our purposes in determining the feasibility of titrations. Nevertheless, it is worthwhile to examine more critically the shortcuts we have taken. A much better understanding of all aspects of acid-base equilibria should be gained by such a study.

The general approach normally used is to find a set of equations sufficient in principle to permit the calculation of the concentration of each chemical species in a solution. This means we need as many equations as unknowns. But when we obtain in a particular case more equations than can be solved simultaneously with convenience, we shall invoke our chemical knowledge to simplify the mathematical problem. Frequently, for example, we shall be able to drop certain terms because, as chemists, we know that they are negligible. Once we have obtained approximate answers, we can substitute them in our original equations and see the actual magnitude of the error introduced by the approximations.

We shall consider the same types of solutions we encountered in the titrations of strong and weak acids.

Solutions of Strong Acids or Bases

Consider the following example:

Example. Calculate the concentrations of all species in a 0.10-M solution of HCl. This strong acid is completely ionized, i.e., $[HCl] = 0$. There are three species which will be present in the solution: H_3O^+, OH^-, and Cl^-. Thus we need three equations in order to determine the concentrations of these ions. We always have available the autoprotolysis constant of water,

$$[H_3O^+][OH^-] = K_w \tag{1}$$

Secondly, it is always required that there be an equal number of positive and negative charges in any solution (beakers of aqueous solutions might jump across the room if this were not the case), so we may write the *electroneutrality condition*:

$$[H_3O^+] = [OH^-] + [Cl^-] \tag{2}$$

Since HCl is completely ionized, our third equation (which we may call a *mass balance* on chloride) is simply

$$[Cl^-] = 0.10 \tag{3}$$

Substituting (3) into (2), we obtain

$$[H_3O^+] = [OH^-] + 0.10$$

But we recognize that water is a very weak acid compared with HCl (also, of course, a very weak base, if you wish), and thus $[OH^-]$ is very small, smaller, indeed, than the 10^{-7}-M found in pure water, because the ionization of water is repressed by the

H_3O^+ from the strong acid HCl. Thus we neglect $[OH^-]$ as compared with $[Cl^-]$ $= 0.10\text{-}M$ and obtain

$$[H_3O^+] = [OH^-] + 0.10 \cong 0.10$$

From Eq. (1) it is now readily obtained that

$$[OH^-] = \frac{K_w}{[H_3O^+]} = \frac{1.0 \times 10^{-14}}{1.0 \times 10^{-1}} = 1.0 \times 10^{-13}$$

Thus the pH of the solution is 1.00 and its pOH is 13.00.

The approximation made above, that $[H_3O^+] = [Cl^-]$, is obviously all right in reasonably concentrated HCl solutions. Consider, however, a $10^{-10}\text{-}M$ solution of HCl. This same approximation would lead to $[H_3O^+] = [Cl^-] = 10^{-10}\text{-}M$. That is, we would have added HCl (albeit a tiny amount) to neutral water of pH 7 and made it alkaline (pH 10)! A correct solution in this situation would be developed as follows

$$[H_3O^+] = [OH^-] + [Cl^-]$$

Since from Eq. (1), $[OH^-] = K_w/[H_3O^+]$,

$$[H_3O^+] = \frac{K_w}{[H_3O^+]} + [Cl^-]$$

Substituting 1.0×10^{-14} for K_w and 10^{-10} for $[Cl^-]$, we could solve the equation for $[H_3O^+]$. This is a quadratic equation, which we obviously would avoid except in situations where $[OH^-]$ and $[Cl^-]$ were of comparable magnitude and neither could be neglected. This would clearly be the case if the HCl concentration were not far from $10^{-7}\text{-}M$. Roughly, if it is greater than $10^{-6}\text{-}M$, the quadratic need not be solved; if it is less than $10^{-8}\text{-}M$, the pH can safely be based upon the ionization of water alone, and it will be very close to 7.0.

With solutions of strong bases such as NaOH or KOH, the pH is calculated in essentially the same manner. Here we directly obtain $[OH^-]$ rather than $[H_3O^+]$, but one is readily converted to the other via K_w.

Weak Acids or Bases

Consider the following example:

Example. Calculate the concentrations of all species in a 0.10-M solution of the weakly ionized acetic acid. The species in the solution are: H_3O^+, OH^-, HOAc, and OAc^-. With four unknown concentrations, the problem requires four equations. Three are already familiar: The autoprotolysis constant of water, the electroneutrality condition, and the ionization constant of the weak acid.

$$[H_3O^+][OH^-] = K_w \tag{1}$$

$$[H_3O^+] = [OH^-] + [OAc^-] \tag{2}$$

$$\frac{[H_3O^+][OAc^-]}{[HOAc]} = K_a \tag{3}$$

The fourth equation is obtained by writing what is termed a *mass balance* on acetate: that is, all of the acetic acid introduced into the solutions ends up as HOAc and OAc$^-$:

$$[HOAc] + [OAc^-] = 0.10 \tag{4}$$

In seeking a simple solution for these equations, we may first, recognizing that acetic acid, although weak, is appreciably acidic, decide to neglect [OH$^-$] as compared with [OAc$^-$]. Thus Eq. (2) becomes

$$[H_3O^+] = [OH^-] + [OAc^-] \cong [OAc^-]$$

Also, since acetic acid is weak, [OAc$^-$] is small compared with [HOAc]. Thus Eq. (4) becomes

$$[HOAc] + [OAc^-] \cong [HOAc] = 0.10$$

Substitution of the modified (2) and (4) into (3) gives

$$\frac{[H_3O^+]^2}{0.10} = K_a = 1.8 \times 10^{-5}$$

Whence

$$[H_3O^+]^2 = 1.8 \times 10^{-6}$$

$$[H_3O^+] = 1.34 \times 10^{-3}\text{-}M$$

We may then obtain from (1),

$$[OH^-] = 7.5 \times 10^{-12}\text{-}M$$

and from (2),

$$[OAc^-] = 1.34 \times 10^{-3}\text{-}M$$

Now we may check the assumptions of neglecting [OH$^-$] in Eq. (2) and [OAc$^-$] in Eq. (4). Equation (2) becomes

$$[H_3O^+] = [OH^-] + [OAc^-]$$

$$1.34 \times 10^{-3} \cong 7.5 \times 10^{-12} + 1.34 \times 10^{-3}$$

This is obviously a good approximation. Equation (4) becomes

$$[HOAc] + [OAc^-] = 0.10$$

$$0.10 + 0.00134 \cong 0.10$$

The relative error incurred here (which is so small that we cannot calculate it without disregarding significant figures) is

$$\frac{0.00134}{0.10} \times 100 = 1.3\%$$

Weak Acid Plus Salt

Let us next consider the situation in which a strong base is added to a weak acid solution in less than equivalent amount. This is illustrated by the following example:

Example. 50 ml of 0.20-M NaOH is added to 50 ml of 0.40-M HOAc. Calculate the concentrations of all the species in the solution. In the presence of the excess acetic acid, we may assume that the neutralization reaction goes practically to completion, so that we end up with $50 \times 0.20 = 10$ mmol of NaOAc and $(50 \times 0.40) - (50 \times 0.20) = 10$ mmol of HOAc in a final volume of 100 ml. The solution contains the five species: H_3O^+, OH^-, HOAc, OAc^-, and Na^+. The required five equations are:

$$\frac{[H_3O^+][OAc^-]}{[HOAc]} = K_a \tag{1}$$

$$[H_3O^+][OH^-] = K_w \tag{2}$$

$$[Na^+] + [H_3O^+] = [OAc^-] + [OH^-] \tag{3}$$

$$[HOAc] + [OAc^-] = \frac{50 \times 0.40}{100} = 0.20 \tag{4}$$

$$[Na^+] = \frac{50 \times 0.20}{100} = 0.10 \tag{5}$$

The following approximations are appropriate. In the charge balance Eq. (3), since the solution is acidic we may consider that $[OH^-]$ is negligible. Thus $[Na^+] + [H_3O^+] = [OAc^-]$. Substituting $[Na^+] = 0.10$ into this, we obtain $0.10 + [H_3O^+] = [OAc^-]$. But HOAc is a weak acid, and we may assume that $[H_3O^+]$ is small as compared with 0.10. Thus $[OAc^-] \cong 0.10$. Now substitute this into the acetate mass balance (4), to obtain $[HOAc] + 0.10 = 0.20$ and $[HOAc] = 0.10$. Substitution into (1) yields

$$\frac{[H_3O^+] \times 0.10}{0.10} = K_a = 1.8 \times 10^{-5}$$

$$[H_3O^+] = 1.8 \times 10^{-5}\text{-}M$$

Also,

$$[OH^-] = 5.5 \times 10^{-10}$$

The assumptions may be checked. Equation (3) gives

$$0.10 + 1.8 \times 10^{-5} \cong 0.10 + 5.5 \times 10^{-10}$$

The left-hand term differs from the right by only 0.0185 %. Equation (4) gives simply $0.10 + 0.10 = 0.20$.

Salt of a Weak Acid

Finally, let us consider the case of a salt of a weak acid (it could just as well be the salt of a weak base), such as sodium acetate. This situation results at the equivalence point of a titration or from dissolving the salt in water.

Example. Calculate the concentrations of all species in a 0.10-M solution of sodium acetate, NaOAc.

As pointed out earlier, the acetate ion is the base, but Na^+ cannot be ignored because it will appear in the charge balance (electroneutrality condition). Thus there are five species to be considered: H_3O^+, OH^-, HOAc, OAc^-, and Na^+. The five equations are the K_a expression for acetic acid, the ion product expression for water, the charge balance, a mass balance on acetate, and a mass balance on sodium:[7]

$$\frac{[H_3O^+][OAc^-]}{[HOAc]} = K_a \tag{1}$$

$$[H_3O^+][OH^-] = K_w \tag{2}$$

$$[Na^+] + [H_3O^+] = [OH^-] + [OAc^-] \tag{3}$$

$$[HOAc] + [OAc^-] = 0.10 \tag{4}$$

$$[Na^+] = 0.10 \tag{5}$$

Because OAc^- is a weak base, $[OH^-]$ will be small, and since this is a basic solution, $[H_3O^+]$ will likewise be small. Thus Eq. (3) simplifies to $[Na^+] = [OAc^-]$. In Eq. (4) we assume, again because OAc^- is a weak base, that [HOAc] is small, and we obtain $[OAc^-] = 0.10$. We wish now to go to Eq. (1) and solve for $[H_3O^+]$, but notice that we do not have as yet a number to substitute into (1) for [HOAc]. Generally, this situation arises when the charge balance equation includes ions present in major concentration (compare with the charge balance equation of the previous problem). The term we wish is low and is negligible compared with the large concentration of

---

[7] One of our equations could be the K_b expression for acetate ion, but we could not elect to use for three of our equations this K_b and both the K_a of acetic acid and K_w. The equations must be independent, and it is recalled that $K_a \times K_b = K_w$. Thus only two of these three expressions can be used.

salt ions. However, a useful expression can be obtained as follows: Add Eqs. (3) and (4),

$$[Na^+] + [H_3O^+] + [HOAc] = [OH^-] + 0.10$$

Since $[Na^+] = 0.10$, this becomes

$$[H_3O^+] + [HOAc] = [OH^-] \qquad (6)$$

Some writers refer to this equation as the *proton condition*. It may also be arrived at by considering the major species H_2O and OAc^- and noting that other species with excess protons (H_3O^+ and HOAc) must have formed at the expense of the proton deficient species, OH^-. Now, since the solution is basic and $[H_3O^+]$ is small, we may write:

$$[HOAc] = [OH^-]$$

Substitution into Eq. (1) then yields

$$\frac{[H_3O^+] \times 0.10}{[OH^-]} = K_a$$

But

$$[OH^-] = \frac{K_w}{[H_3O^+]}$$

Thus

$$\frac{[H_3O^+]^2 \times 0.10}{K_w} = K_a$$

$$[H_3O^+]^2 = \frac{K_w \times K_a}{0.10} = \frac{1.0 \times 10^{-14} \times 1.8 \times 10^{-5}}{1.0 \times 10^{-1}}$$

$$= 1.8 \times 10^{-18}$$

$$[H_3O^+] = 1.34 \times 10^{-9}\text{-}M$$

Also, $[OH^-] = 7.5 \times 10^{-6}\text{-}M$. To check our approximations, Eq. (6) becomes

$$1.34 \times 10^{-9} + 7.5 \times 10^{-6} = 7.5013 \times 10^{-6}$$

Thus, neglecting 1.34×10^{-9} as compared with 7.5×10^{-6} introduced an error of only about 0.017%.

H. A. LAITINEN, *Chemical Analysis*, McGraw-Hill Book Company, New York, 1960.

L. G. SILLEN, "Graphic Presentation of Equilibrium Data," I. M. KOLTHOFF, "Concepts of Acids and Bases," S. BRUCKENSTEIN and I. M. KOLTHOFF, "Acid-base Strength and Protolysis Curves in Water," and I. M. KOLTHOFF and S. BRUCKENSTEIN, "Acid-base Equilibria in Nonaqueous Solutions," Chapters 8, 11, 12, and 13. Part 1, Vol. 1, of *Treatise on Analytical Chemistry*, I. M. Kolthoff and P. J. Elving, eds., Interscience Publishers, Inc., New York, 1959.

J. N. BUTLER, *Ionic Equilibrium, A Mathematical Approach*, Addison-Wesley Publishing Co., Inc., Reading, Mass., 1964.

WALTER HUBER, *Titrations in Nonaqueous Solvents*, Academic Press, New York, 1967.

QUESTIONS

1. Sketch a graph of hydrogen ion concentration (ordinate) vs volume of alkali (abscissa) for the neutralization of 50 ml of 0.10-M HCl with 0.10-M NaOH. How would the graph look if solid NaOH were used and the volume remained constant? Does the ordinate ever reach zero?

2. Plot the function $y = \log x$. Comment on any relation of the shape of this plot to the shape of a titration curve. Calculate the pH after the addition of 0.00, 0.01, 0.10, 1.00, and 10.0 ml of 0.10-M NaOH to 100 ml of water, and plot the graph. Does this look like part of a titration curve?

3. Plot the pH vs the logarithm of the ratio of the concentrations of acetic acid to acetate ion during the neutralization of 10 mmol of acetic acid with NaOH. What is the significance of the pH value when the logarithm of the ratio is zero?

4. Derive the error in y resulting from an error in x, where the function is $x = 10^y$ or $y = \log x$.

5. If one calculates the pH of a 10^{-6}-M solution of a weak acid, $K_a = 1 \times 10^{-10}$, with the usual approximations, the result is a pH of 8. What is the fallacy in this calculation? What is the correct pH?

6. A student once asked if pH could be defined as the logarithm of the volume of solution required to furnish one mole of hydrogen ion. Is this correct? Explain.

7. What is the significance of a negative pH or pOH? of a pH or pOH greater than 14?

8. The ion product constant of water, K_w, is about 10^{-12} at 100°C. What is the pH of pure water at 100°C?

9. If the change in pH per change in volume of titrant is plotted against the volume of titrant (strong acid vs strong base), what is the shape of the curve? Check your conclusion with Fig. 9.3(b).

10. A student standardized a solution of sodium hydroxide against a standard solution of hydrochloric acid using methyl orange as the indicator (no indicator blank). He then titrated a potassium acid phthalate unknown with the base using phenolphthalein indicator. Were his results high, low, or correct? Explain.

11. Plot log C (ordinate, from -9 vertically to zero) vs pH (0 to 12) for a 0.01-M solution of HOAc in water, letting C be the following: [HOAc], [OAc$^-$], [H$^+$], and [OH$^-$]. Comment on the utility of such a plot.

12. Given the following acids, bases, and indicators. Answer the questions below.

Acid	pK_a	Base	pK_b	Indicator
HA	strong	MOH	strong	I (acid) pK_a = 5
HB	4.85	NOH	8.70	II (base) pK_b = 5
HC	9.30	ROH	3.80	III (acid) pK_a = 9
HD	8.70	VOH	3.70	

(a) Which titrations are feasible (0.10-M solutions)? (1) HB with NaOH; (2) HC with NaOH; (3) NOH with HCl; (4) VOH with HCl; (5) D$^-$ with HCl; (6) B$^-$ with HCl; (7) N$^+$ with NaOH; (8) R$^+$ with NaOH.

(b) For those titrations in part (a) which are feasible choose the proper indicator (or indicators).

(c) Which salt solution has a pH of 7? (1) NaA; (2) NaC; (3) MCl; (4) VCl.

(d) Which is the strongest acid, HB, HC, or HD?

(e) Which is the weakest conjugate acid, N$^+$, R$^+$, or V$^+$?

PROBLEMS

1. pH. Convert the following values of hydrogen ion concentrations to pH: (a) 0.0050; (b) 0.10; (c) 1.0; (d) 10; (e) 4.0×10^{-8}; (f) 8.0×10^{-14}.

2. pOH. Convert the following values of hydroxide ion concentration to pH: (a) 2.0×10^{-4}; (b) 1.0; (c) 10; (d) 0.40; (e) 4.0×10^{-15}; (f) 5.0×10^{-10}.

3. *Hydrogen ion concentration.* Convert the following to hydrogen ion concentration: (a) $pH = -0.70$; (b) $pH = +0.70$; (c) $pH = 4.74$; (d) $pH = 10.30$; (e) $pOH = -0.30$; (f) $pOH = 14.40$; (g) $pOH = 8.26$; (h) $pOH = 1.70$.

4. pH *calculations.* Calculate the pH of the following solutions: (a) 20 g of NaOH in 200 ml of solution; (b) 0.0365 g of HCl in 2.00 l of solution; (c) 600 mg of HOAc in 50.0 ml of solution; (d) 1.7 g of NH$_3$ in 0.20 l of solution; (e) 100 ml of solution containing 10.0 mmol of HOAc and 10.0 mmol of NaOAc; (f) 100 ml of solution containing 10.0 mg of HOAc and 10.0 mg of NaOAc; (g) 82 mg of NaOAc in 10.0 ml of solution; (h) 0.0535 g of NH$_4$Cl in 10.0 ml of solution; (i) 10^{-10} moles of HCl in 1 liter of solution; (j) 12 g of NaHSO$_4$ in 1 liter of solution.

5. *Mixtures of solutions.* Calculate the pH of the following solutions. Assume the volumes are additive. (a) 60 ml of 0.10-M formic acid + 40 ml of 0.15-M NaOH; (b) 80 ml of 0.080-M NH$_3$ + 20 ml of 0.16-M HCl; (c) 50 ml of 0.10-M HCl × 50 ml of 0.08-M NaOH; (d) 40 ml of 0.15-M HCl + 60 ml of 0.10-M NaOH; (e) 50 ml of 0.10-M HOAc + 50 ml of 0.12-M NaOH; (f) 50 ml of HCl, $pH = 2.00$, + 50 ml of pure water; (g) 50 ml of NaOH, $pOH = 2.00$, + 50 ml of NaOH, $pOH = 4.00$; (h) 50 ml of HCl, $pH = 2.00$, + 50 ml of NaOH, $pH = 8.00$; (i) 50 ml of 0.10-M NaCN + 50 ml of 0.10-M HCl; (j) 60 ml of 0.10-M NH$_4$Cl + 40 ml of 0.05-M NaOH.

6. *Degree of dissociation.* A weak acid, HX, is 2.0% dissociated in 0.10-M solution. (a) Calculate the dissociation constant of the acid. (b) Calculate the percentage dissociation in a 0.05-M solution. (c) At what concentration is the acid 1.0% dissociated?

7. *Dissociation constant.* A weak base, BOH, has a molecular weight of 125 g/mole. A solution prepared by dissolving 0.500 g of BOH in 50.0 ml of solution has a pH of 11.30. Calculate the dissociation constant of BOH.

8. *Dissociation constant.* The pH of a 0.10-M solution of the salt NaY (salt of the weak acid HY) is 8.30. Calculate the dissociation constant of HY.

9. *Strong and weak acids.* A chemist wishes to prepare 500 ml of a solution of pH 2.30 by dissolving an acid in water. Calculate the number of grams required if the acid is (a) HCl; (b) formic acid; (c) benzoic acid.

10. *Strong acid.* Calculate the volume of 0.10-M HCl required to change the pH of 100 ml of water from 7.00 to 4.00.

11. *Mixtures of solutions.* Calculate the pH of solutions resulting from mixing equal volumes of the following solutions of strong electrolytes: (a) pH 1.00 + pH 2.00; (b) pH 1.00 + pH 3.00; (c) pH 1.00 + pH 5.00; (d) pH 1.00 + pH 13.00; (e) pH 1.00 + pH 14.00; (f) pH 5.00 + 9.00.

12. *Approximations.* Calculate the concentrations of the various species in the following solutions, writing all exact equations and making the appropriate assumptions: (a) 0.02-M HOAc + an equal volume of 0.05-M NaOAc; (b) 0.02-M NaCN; (c) 0.02-M HCl + an equal volume of 0.02-M NaF.

13. *Mixtures of solutions.* An analyst wishes to prepare 100 ml of a solution of pH 12.60 from solutions of HCl, pH = 0.70, and NaOH, pH = 13.60. How many milliliters of each solution should be mixed to give the desired solution. Assume the volumes are additive.

14. *Hydrolysis.* Calculate the percentage hydrolysis of the following in 0.10-M solutions: (a) F^-; (b) CO_3^{2-} (to HCO_3^-); (c) S^{2-} (to HS^-); (d) NH_4^+.

15. *Hydrolysis.* The pH of a solution of NH_4Cl is 5.28. Calculate the concentration of NH_4^+ in the solution.

16. *Derivations.* Derive the following expressions for calculating the pH of a solution at the specified conditions: (a) Equivalence point in the titration of a weak acid HA with NaOH:

$$pH = \tfrac{1}{2}pK_w + \tfrac{1}{2}pK_a + \tfrac{1}{2}\log[A^-]$$

(b) Equivalence point in the titration of a weak base BOH with HCl:

$$pH = \tfrac{1}{2}pK_w - \tfrac{1}{2}pK_b - \tfrac{1}{2}\log[B^+]$$

(c) Solution of a weak acid HA:

$$pH = \tfrac{1}{2}pK_a - \tfrac{1}{2}\log[HA]$$

17. *Approximations.* Calculate the pH of the following solutions in two ways: (1) Use the approximation as done on page 85, where $[OAc^-]$ was neglected; (2) do not neglect $[OAc^-]$ and solve the complete quadratic. Note the differences in the answers by the two procedures. (a) 0.10-M dichloroacetic acid; (b) 0.10-M sodium bisulfate; (c) 0.10-M chloroacetic acid; (d) 0.10-M formic acid; (e) 0.10-M acetic acid.

18. *Approximations.* On page 107 the hydroxide ion concentration was neglected in calculating the *p*H of 0.10-*M* HCl. Calculate the error in making this same approximation for the following HCl solutions: (a) 1.0×10^{-6}-*M*; (b) 5.0×10^{-7}-*M*; (c) 2.0×10^{-7}-*M*; (d) 1.0×10^{-7}-*M*.

19. *Weak acid + salt.* How many grams of sodium formate, $NaHCO_2$, should be added to 500 ml of a 0.050-*M* solution of formic acid to make the *p*H = 4.00?

20. *Weak base + salt.* A solution contains 5.4 g of NH_4Cl in 125 ml of solution. How many grams of NH_3 should be added to the solution to make the *p*H = 9.56?

21. *Fraction neutralized.* A solution of formic acid is titrated with NaOH. Calculate the *p*H when the following percentages of the acid have been neutralized: (a) 25%; (b) 33%; (c) 50%; (d) 75%; (e) 99%; (f) 99.9%; (g) 99.99%.

22. *Fraction neutralized.* A solution of ammonia is titrated with HCl. Calculate the percentage of base neutralized at the following *p*H values: (a) 9.86; (b) 9.56; (c) 9.26; (d) 8.96; (e) 6.26.

23. *Common ion effect.* 50.00 ml of 0.10-*M* HOAc is titrated with 0.10-*M* NaOH. Calculate the hydroxide ion concentration produced by the reaction

$$OAC^- + H_2O \longrightarrow HOAc + OH^-$$

after the addition of (a) 49.90, (b) 50.00, (c) 50.10, and (d) 51.00 ml of NaOH.

24. *Titration.* A student is to titrate a sample containing the weak acid HA, $pK_a = 5.00$. By mistake he stops the titration at *p*H 7.00. If his sample contains 30.0% HA, what percentage will he find?

25. *Titration.* A 0.50-g sample containing 20% HOAc is titrated with 0.100-*M* NaOH. The volume of solution at the equivalence point is 100 ml. The titration is stopped at a *p*H 0.50 units higher than the *p*H at the equivalence point. How much excess base is added?

26. *Titration curve.* 40.00 ml of 0.0900-*M* HCl is diluted to 100 ml and titrated with 0.1000-*M* NaOH. Calculate the *p*H after the addition of the following volumes of titrant: (a) 0.00; (b) 10.00; (c) 18.00; (d) 30.00; (e) 35.95; (f) 36.00; (g) 36.05; (h) 40.00 ml.

27. *Titration curve.* Repeat Problem 26 for the titration of 40.00 ml of 0.0900-*M* NH_3 with 0.1000-*M* HCl.

28. *Titration.* 3.0 mmol of Na_2CO_3 are dissolved in 90 ml of water and titrated with 0.10-*M* HCl. The reaction is

$$CO_3{}^{2-} + 2\,H^+ \longrightarrow H_2CO_3$$

Calculate the *p*H (a) at the equivalence point, and (b) two drops (0.10 ml) beyond the equivalence point. (c) Choose a suitable indicator. (d) Would you expect the end point to be very sharp?

29. *Feasibility of titration.* 30 ml of 0.10-*M* NaOAc is diluted to 70 ml and titrated with 0.10-*M* HCl. Calculate the *p*H at the equivalence point and two drops (0.10 ml) beyond. Is the titration feasible?

30. *Indicator.* The pH range of an indicator HIn is 1.60 units. The ratio of $[HIn]/[In^-]$ required so that only the acid color is seen is the same as the ratio of $[In^-]/[HIn]$ required to see only the basic color. What percentage of the indicator must be in the HIn form for the eye to detect only the acid color?

31. *Titration.* A 0.900-g sample containing a weak acid HX (M.W. = 75.00) is dissolved in 60.00 ml of solution and titrated with 0.1000-M NaOH. When half of the acid is neutralized, the pH is 5.00; at the equivalence point the pH is 8.85. Calculate the percentage of HX in the sample.

32. *Buffer solution.* A buffer solution is prepared by dissolving 6.0 g of acetic acid and 16.4 g of sodium acetate in 1.0 liter of solution. (a) Calculate the pH of the buffer. (c) Calculate the pH of the solution which results when the following are added to separate 100 ml portions of the buffer: (1) 5.0 mmol of HCl; (2) 5.0 mmol of NaOH; (3) 400 mg of NaOH; (4) 730 mg of HCl; (5) 480 mg of NaOH.

33. *Buffer solution.* It is desired to prepare a buffer of pH 5.00. Three weak acids and their salts are available: A, $K_a = 2 \times 10^{-5}$; B, $K_a = 5 \times 10^{-5}$; C, $K_a = 5 \times 10^{-6}$. Calculate the ratio of acid to salt required for each acid to prepare such a buffer.

34. *Buffer solutions.* The three buffers of pH 5.00 (Problem 33) are prepared with the component in larger concentration being 0.20-M in each solution. Calculate the changes in pH which result when 5.00 mmol of (a) hydroxide ion and (b) hydrogen ion are added to 200 ml of each buffer.

35. *Buffer solution.* A buffer solution is prepared from an acid, HA, $K_a = 5 \times 10^{-5}$, and its salt. The concentration of HA in the buffer is 0.25-M. To 100 ml of the buffer is added 5.0 mmol of NaOH, and the pH of the resulting solution is 5.60. What was the pH of the original buffer?

36. *Buffer solution.* It is desired to prepare 200 ml of a buffer solution of pH 9.49 using NH_3 and NH_4Cl such that the change in pH will not be greater than 0.12 pH units for the addition of 1.0 mmol of either H^+ or OH^-. What weight of NH_4Cl and what volume of 1.0-M NH_3 should be used to prepare the buffer?

37. *Ion trapping.* A model used to explain the absorption of a drug, such as aspirin (a weak acid), is as follows:

Membrane

Blood plasma		Stomach
$pH = 7.4$		$pH = 1.0$

$H^+ + Asp^- \rightleftharpoons HAsp \rightleftharpoons HAsp \rightleftharpoons H^+ + Asp^-$

It is assumed that ions such as H^+ and Asp^- do not penetrate the membrane, but that the undissociated form, HAsp, equilibrates freely across the membrane. At equilibrium the concentration of HAsp is the same on both sides of the membrane, but there is more *total drug* on the side where the degree of dissociation is greater. This mechanism is known as *ion trapping*.

Aspirin is a weak acid with a pK_a of 3.5. Calculate the ratio of total drug, $[HAsp] + [Asp^-]$, in the blood plasma to total drug in the stomach, assuming the above model is correct.

5

Acid-Base Equilibria in Complex Systems

In the previous chapter we confined our attention to acids and bases which furnish or react with a single hydrogen ion. An acid which furnishes only one proton is called a *monoprotic* acid. Carbonic acid, H_2CO_3, is a *diprotic* acid, H_3PO_4 is triprotic, etc.; in general, acids which furnish two or more protons are called *polyprotic*. Phosphoric acid, H_3PO_4, is one of the most important polyprotic acids, since phosphates are involved in buffers in the body fluids of living systems.

As might be expected, the equilibrium calculations involving polyprotic acids are more complex than those of monoprotic acids. Reasonable assumptions can be made, however, which enable the chemist to make good approximations of the pH values of solutions of such acids and their salts. The purpose of this chapter is to examine a few of the more important calculations which involve equilibria of polyprotic acids and their salts.

POLYPROTIC ACIDS

A solution of the diprotic acid H_2B contains two acids, H_2B and HB^-, dissociating as follows:

$$H_2B + H_2O \rightleftharpoons H_3O^+ + HB^- \qquad K_{a_1} = \frac{[H_3O^+][HB^-]}{[H_2B]}$$

$$HB^- + H_2O \rightleftharpoons H_3O^+ + B^{2-} \qquad K_{a_2} = \frac{[H_3O^+][B^{2-}]}{[HB^-]}$$

With a triprotic acid (e.g., phosphoric, H_3PO_4), there are three stages of dissociation; occasionally, even a tetraprotic acid is encountered, the best-known example being the chelon ethylenediaminetetraacetic acid (EDTA) which is discussed in detail in Chapter 6. A complete treatment of all of the equilibria involved in solutions of polyprotic acids and their several salts is complicated and beyond the scope of this text. However, for many purposes, fairly valid approximations may be made which greatly simplify the treatment.

Usually the successive K_a values for a polyprotic acid differ by several orders of magnitude, as may be seen in Table I, Appendix I. As a result, the pH of a solution of an acid H_2B can usually be calculated accurately enough by considering only K_{a_1} and ignoring the further stages of dissociation. The problem thus reduces to one that we have already considered. Similarly, the K_b values of the conjugate bases usually differ sufficiently to permit a fairly good calculation of the pH of a B^{2-} solution on the basis of K_{b_1} alone. (Recalling the relationship for a conjugate pair, $K_a \times K_b = K_w$, the student should note that K_{b_1} for the species B^{2-} is K_w/K_{a_2} and that K_{b_2} is K_w/K_{a_1}, where K_{a_1} and K_{a_2} are the successive constants for the acid H_2B.) The student may acquire a better "feeling" for this matter after reading the next section of this chapter on distribution of species as a function of pH.

Let us next consider the pH of a solution in which the intermediate species HB^- predominates. This might have been obtained simply by dissolving the salt $NaHB$ in water, or by mixing equimolar quantities of H_2B and $NaOH$. Suppose we calculate the pH of a 0.10-M solution of $NaHB$ for the case where K_{a_1} and K_{a_2} are 1.0×10^{-3} and 1.0×10^{-7}, respectively. There are three equilibria that may be considered, the dissociations of the two acids H_2B and HB^- as written above, and the dissociation of water. The equilibrium expressions for these processes may be combined in various ways, but it is most convenient to focus attention upon the fate of the principal species HB^-. This ion can react in three ways, all of which are of course acid-base reactions in the Brønsted sense.

Disproportionation:

$$HB^- + HB^- \rightleftharpoons H_2B + B^{2-} \qquad K = \frac{K_{a_2}}{K_{a_1}} = 1.0 \times 10^{-4}$$

Dissociation as a base:

$$HB^- + H_2O \rightleftharpoons H_2B + OH^- \qquad K_{b_2} = \frac{K_w}{K_{a_1}} = 1.0 \times 10^{-11}$$

Dissociation as an acid:

$$HB^- + H_2O \rightleftharpoons H_3O^+ + B^{2-} \qquad K_{a_2} = 1.0 \times 10^{-7}$$

From the magnitudes of the constants of the three reactions, it is evident that the first reaction (disproportionation) proceeds farthest to the right. This suggests that we might neglect the amounts of H_2B and B^{2-} formed by the second and third reactions as compared with the quantities formed by the first one. Thus, at least approximately, we may write[1]

$$[H_2B] \cong [B^{2-}]$$

Note that the product of the two dissociation constants contains these two terms:

$$K_{a_1} \times K_{a_2} = \frac{[H_3O^+]^2[B^{2-}]}{[H_2B]}$$

Thus

$$[H_3O^+]^2 = K_{a_1} \times K_{a_2}$$

$$[H_3O^+] = \sqrt{K_{a_1} \times K_{a_2}}$$

or

$$pH = \tfrac{1}{2}(pK_{a_1} + pK_{a_2})$$

In our example, this gives a pH value of 5.00 for the solution of NaHB.

Titration Curves of Polyprotic Acids

As previously mentioned, the pH of a solution of an acid, H_2B, can be calculated accurately enough by considering only K_{a_1}, provided K_{a_1} is several orders of magnitude larger than K_{a_2}. Let us calculate the titration curve of an acid for which this is true. Then we shall consider an example where the two constants are closer in value.

> **Example.** 50.0 ml of 0.100-M H_2B is titrated with 0.100-M NaOH. The ionization constants are: $K_{a_1} = 1 \times 10^{-3}$, $K_{a_2} = 1 \times 10^{-7}$. Calculate the pH at various stages of the titration, using the usual approximation methods, and plot the titration curve.

---

[1] The magnitude of the error involved in this approximation can be obtained readily as follows. Write the charge balance and the mass balance for the species obtainable from H_2B. Adding the two equations will give

$$[H_2B] + [H_3O^+] = [B^{2-}] + [OH^-] \tag{a}$$

Since the solution is acidic, $[H_3O^+] > [OH^-]$, and we may assume that

$$[H_2B] + [H_3O^+] = [B^{2-}] \tag{b}$$

Noting that $[HB^-]$ is about 0.10-M and substituting this into the expression for K_{a_1}, we get

$$[H_3O^+] = 0.01\,[H_2B] \tag{c}$$

Substitution of (c) into (b) gives

$$1.01\,[H_2B] = [B^{2-}]$$

Hence, in our particular problem, the error in this approximation is 1%.

(a) *Initial p*H. Consider only the first step in dissociation:

$$H_2B + H_2O \rightleftharpoons H_3O^+ + HB^-$$

$$\frac{[H_3O^+]^2}{0.10} = 1 \times 10^{-3}$$

$$[H_3O^+] = 1 \times 10^{-2}$$

and

$$pH = 2.00$$

(b) *p*H *after addition of 10.0 ml of base.*

$$mmol\ H_2B = 50.0 \times 0.100 - 10.0 \times 0.100 = 4.00$$

$$mmol\ HB^-\ formed = 10.0 \times 0.100 = 1.00$$

$$pH = pK_{a_1} - \log \frac{[H_2B]}{[HB^-]}$$

$$pH = 3.00 - \log \frac{4.00}{1.00}$$

$$pH = 2.40$$

The *p*H at other points up to the first equivalence point is calculated in the same manner.

(c) *p*H *at first equivalence point.* 50.0 ml of base has been added and the species HB^- is the predominant one. The *p*H is readily approximated (see page 120) by the expression

$$pH = \tfrac{1}{2}(pK_{a_1} + pK_{a_2})$$

Hence

$$pH = \tfrac{1}{2}(3.00 + 7.00)$$

$$pH = 5.00$$

(d) *p*H *during titration of* HB^- : *60.0 ml of base added.* The second acid, HB^-, is now being neutralized,

$$HB^- + OH^- \rightleftharpoons H_2O + B^{2-}$$

and the *p*H is calculated from the dissociation constant for HB^-,

$$HB^- + H_2O \rightleftharpoons H_3O^+ + B^{2-} \qquad K_{a_2} = 1 \times 10^{-7}$$

$$pH = pK_{a_2} - \log \frac{[HB^-]}{[B^{2-}]}$$

Here

$$\text{mmol } HB^- = 50.0 \times 0.100 - 10 \times 0.100 = 4.00$$

$$\text{mmol } B^{2-} = 10.0 \times 0.100 = 1.00$$

$$pH = 7.00 - \log \frac{4.00}{1.00}$$

$$pH = 6.40$$

The pH at other points up to the second equivalence point is calculated in the same manner.

(e) pH *at second equivalence point.* 100 ml of base has been added. The pH can be approximated by considering the first step in the hydrolysis of B^{2-},

$$B^{2-} + H_2O \rightleftharpoons HB^- + OH^-$$

$$[B^{2-}] = \frac{50.0 \times 0.100}{150} = 0.0333\text{-}M$$

$$\frac{[HB^-][OH^-]}{[B^{2-}]} = \frac{K_w}{K_{a_2}}$$

Since

$$[HB^-] \cong [OH^-]$$

$$\frac{[OH^-]^2}{0.0333} = \frac{1 \times 10^{-14}}{1 \times 10^{-7}}$$

$$[OH^-] = 5.8 \times 10^{-5}$$

$$pOH = 4.24$$

$$pH = 9.76$$

Values beyond the second equivalence point are calculated from the amount of excess base.

The titration curve is shown in Fig. 5.1, curve A, where two distinct breaks are evident. In the same figure (curve B) is shown the curve for a diprotic acid in which the ratio of K_{a_1} to K_{a_2} is 10^2. In this case only a slight tendency toward a break at the first equivalence point can be seen. In curve C for H_2SO_4, where both the H_2SO_4 and HSO_4^- dissociate extensively ($K_{a_2} = 0.012$), the shape is essentially the same as that for a monoprotic strong acid.

In general, one can conclude that the successive constants of a polyprotic acid must differ by a factor of about 10^4, or the pK_a values must differ by 4,

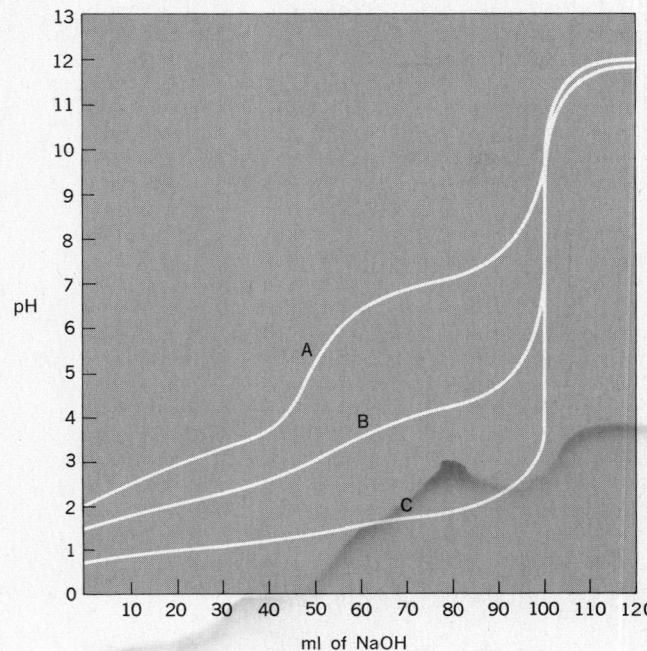

FIGURE 5.1   Titration curves for diprotic acids. A, $K_{a_1}/K_{a_2} = 10^4$; B, $K_{a_1}/K_{a_2} = 10^2$; C, H_2SO_4, K_{a_1} large, $K_{a_2} = 0.012$.

in order for a reasonably good break to occur between the two stages of the titration. Maleic and phosphoric acids have pK_a values differing by 4.3 and 5.1 units, respectively, and hence give two breaks. In the case of sulfurous acid, the two pK_a values differ by 3.4 units, and the break is not extremely sharp. Phosphoric acid has pK_a values of 2.12, 7.12, and 12.32. The break at the first equivalence point, about pH 4.62, is a good one and can be detected with an indicator such as methyl red. At the second equivalence point, about pH 9.72, the break is good but not as sharp as the first since the acid $H_2PO_4^-$ is somewhat weak. Phenolphthalein can be used to detect this equivalence point. The third acid, HPO_4^{2-}, is too weak for feasible titration (page 93). The value of K_t for the reaction

$$HPO_4^{2-} + OH \rightleftharpoons PO_4^{3-} + H_2O$$

is only $4.8 \times 10^{-13}/1.0 \times 10^{-14} = 4.8 \times 10^1$.

Titration of Carbonates

The first pK_a of carbonic acid is 6.34 and the second 10.36, making the difference 4.02 units. We might expect a fair break between the two curves in this case, but K_{a_1} is so small that the break at the first equivalence point is poor. Usually the carbonate ion is titrated as a base with a strong acid titrant, in which case two fair breaks are obtained, as shown in Fig. 5.2,

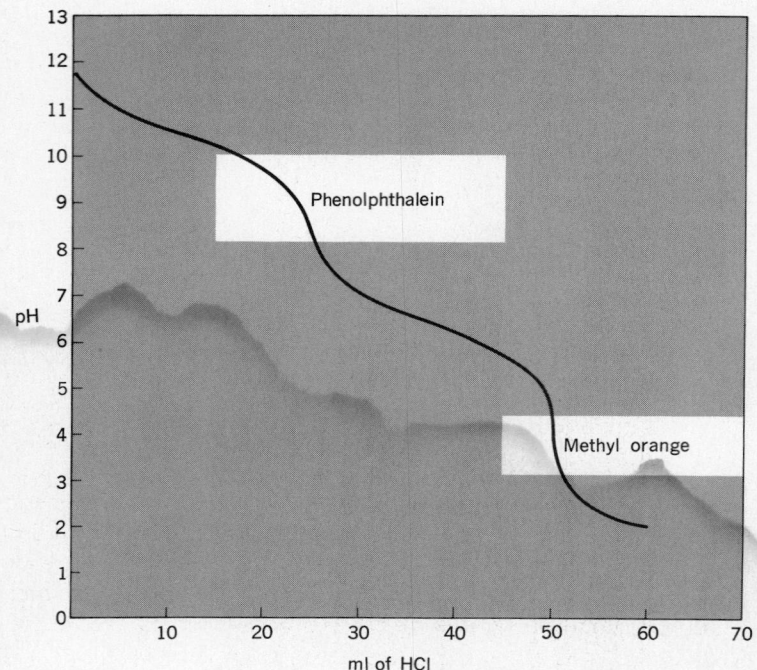

FIGURE 5.2   Titration   curve   of Na_2CO_3;
2.5 mmol Na_2CO_3 titrated with 0.10-M HCl.

corresponding to the reactions

$$CO_3^{2-} + H_3O^+ \rightleftharpoons HCO_3^- + H_2O$$

$$HCO_3^- + H_3O^+ \rightleftharpoons H_2CO_3 + H_2O$$

Phenolphthalein is a suitable indicator for the first end point and methyl orange for the second. Usually samples containing only sodium carbonate (soda ash) are neutralized to the methyl orange end point, and excess acid is added. Carbon dioxide is then removed by boiling, and the excess acid is titrated with standard base. The end point is not sharp unless carbon dioxide is removed.

Mixtures of carbonate and bicarbonate, or of carbonate and hydroxide, can be titrated with acid to the two end points mentioned above. From the volumes used to each end point it is possible to identify the components of such mixtures and to determine fairly accurately the amount of each constituent. In Table 5.1 are listed the relations between the volumes of acid used to the two end points for single components and mixtures. Here v_1 is the volume of acid used from the start of the titration to the phenolphthalein

TABLE 5.1 VOLUME RELATIONS IN CARBONATE TITRATIONS

Substance	Relation for qualitative identification	Millimoles of substance present	
NaOH	$v_2 = 0$		$M \times v_1$
Na_2CO_3	$v_1 = v_2$		$M \times v_1$
$NaHCO_3$	$v_1 = 0$		$M \times v_2$
$NaOH + Na_2CO_3$	$v_1 > v_2$	NaOH:	$M(v_1 - v_2)$
		Na_2CO_3:	$M \times v_2$
$NaHCO_3 + Na_2CO_3$	$v_1 < v_2$	$NaHCO_3$:	$M(v_2 - v_1)$
		Na_2CO_3:	$M \times v_1$

end point, and v_2 is the volume from the phenolphthalein to methyl orange end point, corrected for indicator blank. The molarity of the acid is designated by M. The student should be able to verify these relationships, recalling that sodium hydroxide is completely neutralized at either the phenolphthalein or methyl orange end points. The mixture of sodium hydroxide and sodium bicarbonate is not considered since in solution these two compounds react to form either a mixture of carbonate and hydroxide, bicarbonate and carbonate, or carbonate alone, depending upon the relative amounts of the two compounds in the sample.

The following example illustrates the use of the two indicator method for analyzing a mixture of the above bases.

Example. A 0.6234-g sample that might contain NaOH, Na_2CO_3, $NaHCO_3$, or a mixture of $NaOH + Na_2CO_3$ or $Na_2CO_3 + NaHCO_3$ is titrated with 0.1062-M HCl by the two-indicator method. It is found that 40.38 ml of the acid are required to reach the phenolphthalein end point. Methyl orange is then added to the solution and the titration continued using an additional 12.83 ml of the acid. (a) Identify the base or mixture of bases in the sample. (b) Calculate the percentage of each in the sample.

(a) Since 40.38 ml > 12.83 ml, the sample must contain NaOH and Na_2CO_3.

(b) The volume of titrant used by Na_2CO_3 in the second step is 12.83 ml. An equal volume must have been used in the first step. Hence the volume used by the NaOH is $40.38 - 12.83 = 27.55$ ml.

Then

$$\% \, Na_2CO_3 = \frac{12.83 \times 0.1062 \times 106.0}{623.4} \times 100 = 23.17$$

and

$$\% \, NaOH = \frac{27.55 \times 0.1062 \times 40.00}{623.4} \times 100 = 18.77$$

DISTRIBUTION OF ACID-BASE SPECIES
AS A FUNCTION OF pH

It is convenient for various purposes to be able to see at a glance the status of dissociation of common acid-base species as a function of pH. Graphs which show this enable us to determine which of several possible species predominate at a given pH, and they aid in selecting the regions of buffer effectiveness for mixtures of acids or bases and their salts. For example, the pH of blood plasma is held at about 7; it might be of interest to know whether plasma phosphate exists as H_3PO_4, $H_2PO_4^-$, HPO_4^{2-}, PO_4^{3-}, or as some mixture of these species at physiological pH. The type of graph we discuss below can provide answers to such questions almost instantly. This is illustrated in the following example:.

Example 1. In a solution of acetic acid, calculate the fraction present as HOAc molecules and as OAc^- ions at various pH values. Draw an appropriate graph.

Let c_a represent the *total* concentration of all species arising from acetic acid, ionized or not (this is sometimes called the *analytical concentration*, and it is simply a mass balance as used above):

$$c_a = [HOAc] + [OAc^-]$$

From the dissociation constant expression for HOAc, we obtain

$$[OAc^-] = \frac{[HOAc]K_a}{[H_3O^+]}$$

Substitution into the expression for c_a gives

$$c_a = [HOAc] + \frac{[HOAc]K_a}{[H_3O^+]}$$

$$c_a = [HOAc]\left\{1 + \frac{K_a}{[H_3O^+]}\right\}$$

$$\frac{[HOAc]}{c_a} = \frac{1}{1 + (K_a/[H_3O^+])} = \frac{[H_3O^+]}{[H_3O^+] + K_a}$$

$[HOAc]/c_a$ is the fraction of total acetate present in the undissociated form. By a similar approach, it may be shown that the fraction of the acetic acid in the dissociated form is given by

$$\frac{[OAc^-]}{c_a} = \frac{K_a}{[H_3O^+] + K_a}$$

Graphs of these fractions vs pH are shown in Fig. 5.3. Notice that at a pH roughly two units below pK_a, practically all of the acetate (about 99 %) is in the undissociated form, HOAc, and that the acid is almost completely dissociated at a pH of $(pK_a + 2)$. At the intersection of the two curves, $[OAc^-]/c_a = [HOAc]/c_a = 0.5$ and $pH = pK_a$ or $[H_3O^+] = K_a$.

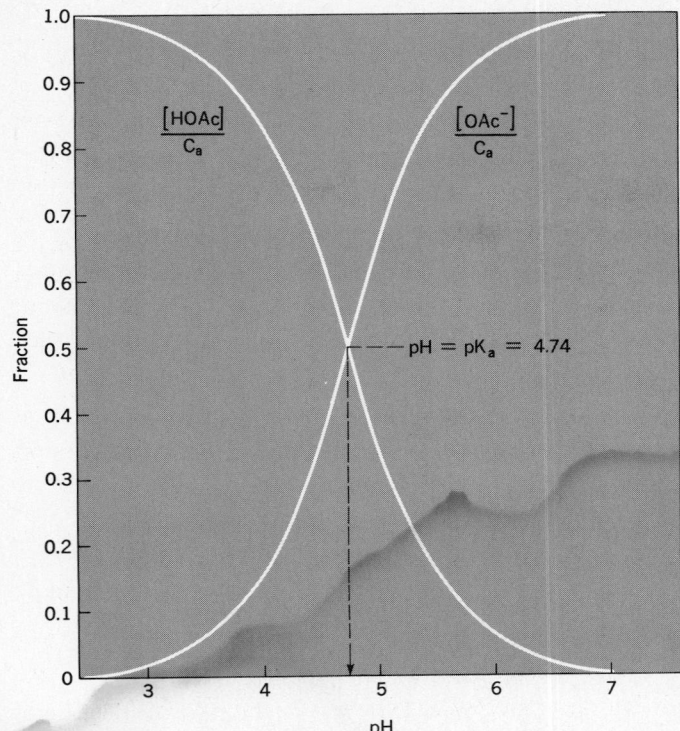

FIGURE 5.3 Distribution of acetate species as a function of pH.

Example 2. In a solution of the dibasic acid, oxalic, (H_2Ox), calculate the fractions present as H_2Ox molecules and as HOx^- and Ox^- ions as a function of pH. Draw appropriate graph.

Here the analytical concentration is given by

$$c_a = [H_2Ox] + [HOx^-] + [Ox^{2-}]$$

We also have the two dissociation expressions:

$$K_{a_1} = \frac{[H_3O^+][HOx^-]}{[H_2Ox]}$$

$$K_{a_2} = \frac{[H_3O^+][Ox^{2-}]}{[HOx^-]}$$

Rearrangement of the two K_a expressions gives

$$[HOx^-] = \frac{[H_2Ox]K_{a_1}}{[H_3O^+]}$$

$$[Ox^{2-}] = \frac{[HOx^-]K_{a_2}}{[H_3O^+]} = \frac{[H_2Ox]K_{a_1}K_{a_2}}{[H_3O^+]^2}$$

127

Substitution into the expression for the analytical concentration yields

$$c_a = [H_2Ox] + \frac{[H_2Ox]K_{a_1}}{[H_3O^+]} + \frac{[H_2Ox]K_{a_1}K_{a_2}}{[H_3O^+]^2}$$

Whence

$$c_a = [H_2Ox]\left\{1 + \frac{K_{a_1}}{[H_3O^+]} + \frac{K_{a_1}K_{a_2}}{[H_3O^+]^2}\right\}$$

$$\frac{[H_2Ox]}{c_a} = \frac{1}{1 + \dfrac{K_{a_1}}{[H_3O^+]} + \dfrac{K_{a_1}K_{a_2}}{[H_3O^+]^2}}$$

$$\frac{[H_2Ox]}{c_a} = \frac{[H_3O^+]^2}{[H_3O^+]^2 + [H_3O^+]K_{a_1} + K_{a_1}K_{a_2}}$$

With no more difficulty, the expressions for the fractions present as HOx^- and Ox^{2-} can be derived.

$$\frac{[HOx^-]}{c_a} = \frac{[H_3O^+]K_{a_1}}{[H_3O^+]^2 + [H_3O^+]K_{a_1} + K_{a_1}K_{a_2}}$$

$$\frac{[Ox^{2-}]}{c_a} = \frac{K_{a_1}K_{a_2}}{[H_3O^+]^2 + [H_3O^+]K_{a_1} + K_{a_1}K_{a_2}}$$

Fractions of total oxalate present as H_2Ox, HOx^-, and Ox^{2-} are shown as functions of pH in Fig. 5.4.

FIGURE 5.4 Distribution of oxalate species as a function of pH.

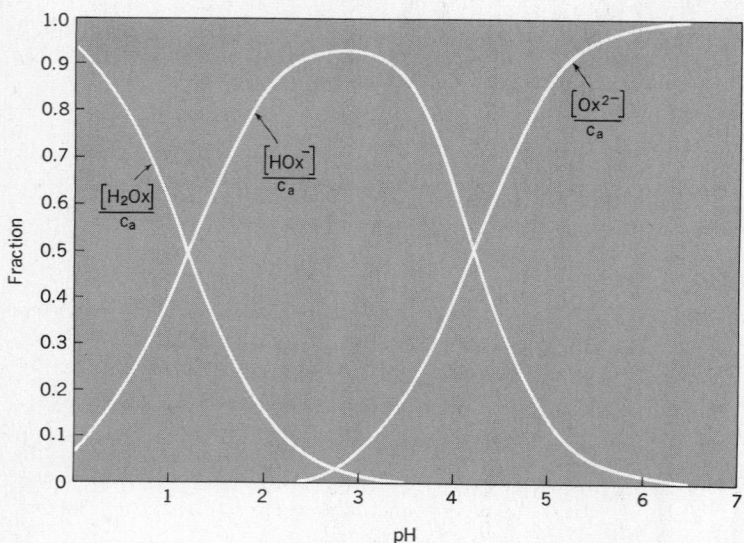

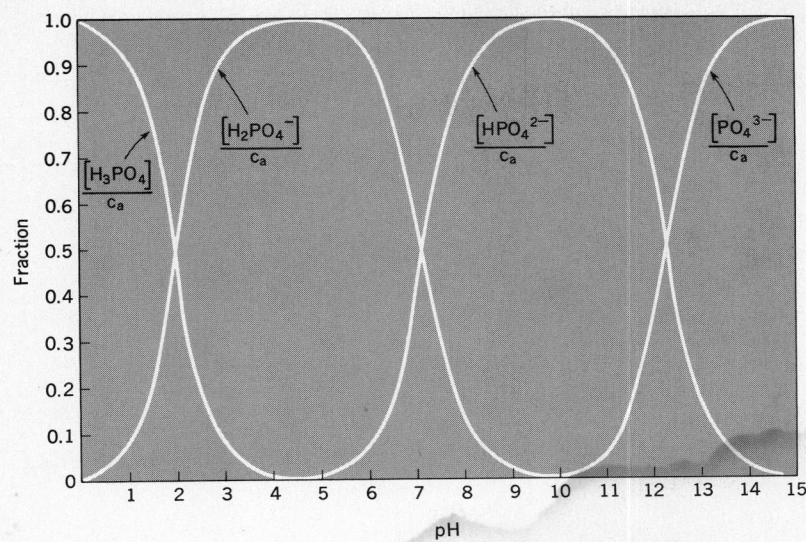

FIGURE 5.5 Distribution of phosphate species as a function of pH.

Derivation of similar equations for tri- or even tetraprotic acids, H_3B or H_4B, is more tedious but no more difficult than the above. Figure 5.5 shows the distribution of phosphoric acid species as a function of pH. It may be seen that below pH 5 or so, the only species present in significant concentration are H_3PO_4 and its first dissociation product, $H_2PO_4^-$. Thus the pH of an H_3PO_4 solution can be safely calculated on the basis of the first dissociation constant, as though the acid were monoprotic. As a matter of fact, at no pH are more than two species present in appreciable amount. In the case of oxalic acid, the two pK_a values are closer than are any pair of H_3PO_4 values; however, only in the pH range 2.5 to 3.0 are all three species discernible in Fig. 5.4 and even here one of the three is predominant.

REFERENCES

H. A. LAITINEN, *Chemical Analysis*, McGraw-Hill Book Company, New York, 1960.

J. N. BUTLER, *Ionic Equilibrium, A Mathematical Approach*, Addison-Wesley Publishing Co., Inc., Reading, Mass., 1964.

T. R. BLACKBURN, *Equilibrium, A Chemistry of Solutions*, Holt, Rinehart, and Winston, Inc., New York, 1969.

QUESTIONS   1. Plot curves such as shown in Fig. 5.4 for the following acids: (a) carbonic; (b) phthalic; (c) citric. Point out the best buffering range for each acid and the principal components of the solution in these pH ranges.

129

2. Write all equations needed to calculate the concentrations of all the species in a 0.10-M solution of NaH_2PO_4. Write the proton condition expression.

3. Given that the three pK_a values of H_3PO_4 are 2.12, 7.21, and 12.32, at which of the following pH's will the concentration of the HPO_4^{2-} species be greatest? (a) 12.32; (b) 15; (c) 7.21; (d) 10; (e) 4.0. Explain.

4. A solution of H_3PO_4 is titrated with NaOH. At the first equivalence point which of the following approximations is most valid? (a) $[H_2PO_4^-] \cong [H_3PO_4]$; (b) $[H_2PO_4^-] \cong [HPO_4^{2-}]$; (c) $[H_3PO_4] \cong [HPO_4^{2-}]$; (d) $[H_2PO_4^-] \cong [PO_4^{3-}]$. Justify your answer.

5. To 100 ml of a 0.10-M solution of H_3PO_4 is added 100 ml of 0.15-M NaOH. In the resulting solution which of the following approximations is most valid? (a) $[H_2PO_4^-] \cong [HPO_4^{2-}]$; (b) $[H_2PO_4^-] \cong [H_3PO_4]$; (c) $[H_3PO_4] \cong [HPO_4^{2-}]$; (d) $[H_2PO_4^-] \cong [PO_4^{3-}]$.

6. If v_1 and v_2 are the volumes of acid used in the titration of carbonate mixtures as indicated in Fig. 5.2, answer the following:
   (a) In a certain titration it is found that $2v_1 = v_2$. What can you conclude about the composition of the sample?
   (b) If the sample contains an equal number of moles of NaOH and Na_2CO_3, what is the relation between v_1 and v_2?
   (c) If the sample contains twice as many moles of Na_2CO_3 as $NaHCO_3$, what is the relation between v_1 and v_2?
   (d) If the sample contains 3 millimoles of NaOH and 4 millimoles of $NaHCO_3$, what is the relation between v_1 and v_2?

PROBLEMS

1. *Mixtures of solutions.* Calculate the pH of the following solutions. Assume the volumes are additive. (a) 50 ml of 0.12-M H_3PO_4 + 60 ml of 0.20-M NaOH; (b) 50 ml of 0.10-M Na_3PO_4 + 50 ml of 0.20-M HCl; (c) 3.00 mmol of Na_2CO_3 + 40 ml H_2O + 60 ml of 0.10-M HCl; (d) 40 ml of 0.020-M H_2CO_3 + 20 ml of 0.080-M NaOH; (e) 50 ml of 0.10-M Na_3PO_4 + 50 ml of 0.30-M HCl; (f) 40 ml of 0.10-M NaH_2PO_4 + 50 ml of 0.080-M NaOH.

2. *Titration curve.* 50.00 ml of 0.100-M H_3PO_4 is titrated with 0.100-M NaOH. (a) Calculate the pH after the addition of the following volumes of titrant: (a) 0.00; (b) 10.00; (c) 25.00; (d) 50.00; (e) 65.00; (f) 75.00; (g) 100.00; (h) 110.00 ml. Plot the titration curve. (b) Select suitable indicators for stopping the titration at the first and second equivalence points.

3. *Derivation.* Derive the following expression for the pH at the first equivalence point in the titration of a mixture of two weak acids: HA, the stronger, K_{a_1}, concentration C_1; HB, the weaker, K_{a_2}, concentration C_2:

$$pH = \tfrac{1}{2}(pK_{a_1} + pK_{a_2}) - \tfrac{1}{2}\log\frac{C_2}{C_1}$$

4. *Phosphate solutions.* It is known that the total concentration of all phosphate species in solutions A and B is 0.10-M each. The pH values of the two solutions are: $A = 7.21$ and $B = 6.91$. Calculate (a) the concentration of HPO_4^{2-} ions in solution A and (b) the concentration of HPO_4^{2-} ions in solution B. (c) 17 millimoles of NaOH are added to 1 liter of solution B. Calculate the pH of the resulting

solution. (d) 17 millimoles of HCl are added to another liter of solution B. Calculate the pH of the resulting solution.

5. *Carbonate mixtures.* A sample that may be Na_2CO_3, NaOH, $NaHCO_3$, or mixtures thereof uses 40 ml of 0.10-M HCl for titration to the phenolphthalein end point. (a) If the sample contains an equal number of millimoles of Na_2CO_3 and NaOH, how many milliliters will be required to go from the phenolphthalein to the methyl orange end point? (b) If the sample contains an equal number of moles of Na_2CO_3 and $NaHCO_3$, how many milliliters will be required to go from the phenolphthalein to the methyl orange end point?

6. *Carbonate mixtures.* A sample that may be a sodium carbonate-bicarbonate or sodium carbonate-sodium hydroxide mixture is titrated using the two-indicator method. A 1.000-g sample required 32.24 ml of 0.2000-M HCl to reach the phenolphthalein end point and an additional 12.84 ml to reach the methyl orange end point. Identify the mixture and calculate the percentage of each component.

7. *Carbonate mixtures.* A 1.000-g sample of a carbonate mixture required 16.58 ml of 0.1500-M HCl to reach the phenolphthalein end point and an additional 33.16 ml to reach the methyl orange end point. Identify the mixture and calculate the percentage of each component.

8. *Carbonate mixtures.* A sample of pure $NaHCO_3$ weighing 0.840 g is dissolved in water, and 0.240 g of pure NaOH is added to the solution. The solution is then diluted to 200 ml in a volumetric flask. A 50-ml aliquot is titrated with 0.1000-M HCl using phenolphthalein indicator. How many milliliters are required? What volume will be required if methyl orange is used as the indicator?

9. *Carbonate mixtures.* A 1.000-g sample consisting of $NaHCO_3$, Na_2CO_3, and impurities is analyzed as follows: It is first titrated to the phenolphthalein end point, 20.00 ml of 0.1000-M HCl being required. To this solution is added a 50.00 ml portion of 0.1000-M NaOH. Then Ba^{2+} ions are added to precipitate $BaCO_3$. The precipitate is separated by filtration and the filtrate titrated with 0.1000-M HCl using phenolphthalein indicator. 15.00 ml of acid is required. Calculate the percentages of Na_2CO_3 and $NaHCO_3$ in the sample.

10. *Carbonate mixtures.* Carbonate mixtures are sometimes analyzed by titrating two samples of the same size, one using phenolphthalein, the second using methyl orange as the indicator. If V_p is the volume of acid used with phenolphthalein and V_m that with methyl orange, answer the following: (a) What is the relation between V_p and V_m if the mixture contains an equal number of moles of NaOH and Na_2CO_3? (b) What is the relation between V_p and V_m if the mixture contains twice as many moles of $NaHCO_3$ as Na_2CO_3?

11. *Carbonate mixtures.* A sample consists of only NaOH and Na_2CO_3. A portion weighing 0.3720 g requires 40.00 ml of 0.1500-M HCl for titration to the phenolphthalein end point. What additional volume will be required to reach the methyl orange end point?

12. *Carbonate mixtures.* A 0.4640-g sample consisting of only $NaHCO_3$ and Na_2CO_3 is dissolved in 50.0 ml of solution and titrated with standard HCl, using methyl orange indicator. The normality of the solution is found to be 0.140-N. What normality will be found if phenolphthalein is used as the indicator?

6 Complex Formation Titrations

One of the types of chemical reactions which may serve as the basis of a titrimetric determination is that which involves the formation of a complex. An example is the reaction of silver ion with cyanide ion to form the very stable $Ag(CN)_2{}^-$ complex:

$$Ag^+ + 2 CN^- \rightleftharpoons Ag(CN)_2{}^-$$

The complexes we wish to consider in this chapter are formed by the reaction of a metal ion, a cation, with an anion or neutral molecule. The metal ion in the complex is called the *central atom*, and the group attached to the central atom is called a *ligand*. The number of bonds formed by the central metal atom is called the *coordination number* of the metal. In the complex above, silver is the central metal atom with a coordination number of two, and cyanide is the ligand.

The reaction by which a complex is formed can be regarded as a Lewis acid-base reaction with the ligand acting as the base, donating a pair of electrons to the cation, which is the acid. The bond formed between the central metal atom and the ligand is often covalent, but in some cases the interaction may be one of coulombic attraction. Some complexes undergo substitution reactions very rapidly and the complex is said to be *labile*. An example is

$$\underset{\text{light blue}}{Cu(H_2O)_4{}^{2+}} + 4 NH_3 \rightleftharpoons \underset{\text{dark blue}}{Cu(NH_3)_4{}^{2+}} + 4 H_2O$$

The reaction goes readily to the right by the addition of ammonia to the

132

aquo-complex; addition of a strong acid which neutralizes the ammonia shifts the equilibrium rapidly back to the aquo-complex. Some complexes undergo substitution reactions only very slowly and are said to be *nonlabile* or *inert*. Almost all complexes formed by cobalt and chromium in the $+3$ oxidation state are inert, whereas most of the other complexes of the first series of transition metals are labile.

Molecules or ions which act as ligands generally contain an electronegative atom, such as nitrogen, oxygen, or one of the halogens. Ligands which have only one unshared pair of electrons, for example $:NH_3$, are said to be *unidentate*. Ligands which have two groups capable of forming two bonds with the central atom are said to be *bidentate*. An example is ethylene diamine, $NH_2CH_2CH_2NH_2$, where both nitrogen atoms have unshared electron pairs. Cupric ion forms a complex with two molecules of ethylene diamine as follows:

$$Cu^{2+} + 2\,NH_2CH_2CH_2NH_2 \rightleftharpoons \left[\begin{array}{c} CH_2 \diagup {}^{NH_2} \diagdown \quad \diagup {}^{NH_2} \diagdown CH_2 \\ \quad\quad Cu \\ CH_2 \diagdown {}_{NH_2} \diagup \quad \diagdown {}_{NH_2} \diagup CH_2 \end{array} \right]^{2+}$$

Heterocyclic rings formed by the interaction of a metal ion with two or more functional groups in the same ligand are called *chelate rings*; the organic molecule is a *chelating* agent, and the complexes are called *chelates* or *chelate* compounds.

STABILITY OF COMPLEXES

Let us write in a general manner the formation of a water soluble metal complex as

$$M + L \rightleftharpoons ML$$

where M is the central metal cation, L the ligand, and ML the complex. The stability of the complex is measured by the equilibrium constant of the above reaction:

$$K_s = \frac{[ML]}{[M][L]}$$

where K_s is the *stability* or *formation* constant of the complex. Sometimes the reaction is written as the dissociation of the complex

$$ML \rightleftharpoons M + L$$

and the equilibrium constant is called the *instability* or *dissociation* constant. The stability and instability constants are obviously reciprocals of one another. We shall use only stability constants in our discussion in this chapter.

For a feasible titration of a metal with a ligand the complex formed should be stable, that is, the value of K_s should be large. Note that the titration reaction is simply the reaction forming the complex; hence, the equilibrium constant we have called K_t (page 83) is here the same as K_s. Also the form of the constant is the same as that for the titration of a weak acid, such as acetic, with a strong base:

$$HOAc + OH^- \rightleftharpoons OAc^- + H_2O \qquad K_t = \frac{[OAc^-]}{[HOAc][OH^-]}$$

$$M + L \rightleftharpoons ML \qquad K_t = K_s = \frac{[ML]}{[M][L]}$$

We have seen (page 96) that an acid-base reaction with a K_t of about 10^8 is sufficiently complete at the equivalence point for a feasible titration. We can conclude that a reaction yielding a complex of the form ML with a stability constant of at least 10^8 should also give a feasible titration.

Stepwise Formation Constants

The reaction of cations with ligands such as ammonia usually proceeds stepwise. For example, the formation of the complex ion $Cu(NH_3)_4^{2+}$ proceeds in four steps:

$$Cu^{2+} + NH_3 \rightleftharpoons Cu(NH_3)^{2+} \qquad K_1 = 1.3 \times 10^4 \tag{1}$$

$$Cu(NH_3)^{2+} + NH_3 \rightleftharpoons Cu(NH_3)_2^{2+} \qquad K_2 = 3.2 \times 10^3 \tag{2}$$

$$Cu(NH_3)_2^{2+} + NH_3 \rightleftharpoons Cu(NH_3)_3^{2+} \qquad K_3 = 8.0 \times 10^2 \tag{3}$$

$$Cu(NH_3)_3^{2+} + NH_3 \rightleftharpoons Cu(NH_3)_4^{2+} \qquad K_4 = 1.3 \times 10^2 \tag{4}$$

Considering the overall reaction

$$Cu^{2+} + 4NH_3 \rightleftharpoons Cu(NH_3)_4^{2+}$$

$$K = \frac{[Cu(NH_3)_4^{2+}]}{[Cu^{2+}][NH_3]^4} = K_1 K_2 K_3 K_4 = 4.3 \times 10^{12}$$

the equilibrium constant seems large enough to provide a feasible titration. The titration of a strong acid with ammonia, $H_3O^+ + NH_3 \rightleftharpoons NH_4^+ + H_2O$, where the K_t is 1.8×10^9, is feasible. However, as shown in Fig. 6.1, the titration of strong acid with ammonia yields a good break around the equivalence point, whereas the titration of Cu^{2+} with ammonia does not.

It may be seen in Fig. 6.1 that the break in the copper titration would be better if the pCu ($pCu = -\log[Cu^{2+}]$) remained lower in the early stages of the titration, as does the pH in the H_3O^+ titration. For example, 75% of the way to the equivalence point, if the ratio of $[Cu^{2+}]$ to $[Cu(NH_3)_4^{2+}]$ were

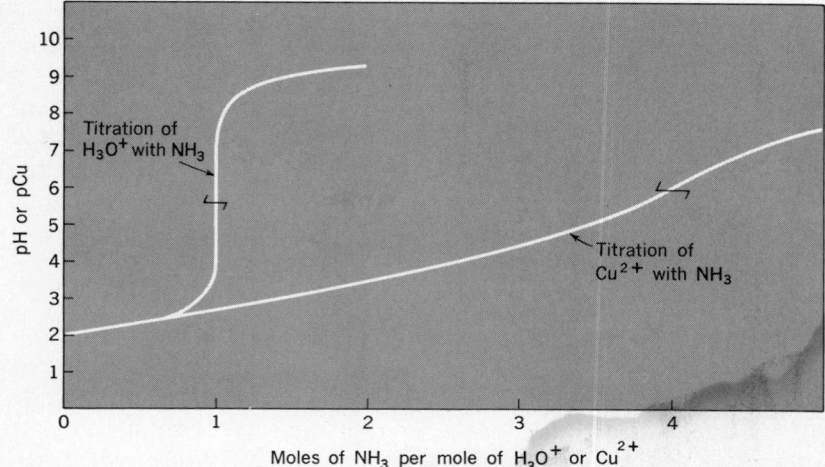

FIGURE 6.1 Titration of strong acid and of cupric ion with ammonia calculated for 10^{-2}-M H_3O^+ and Cu^{2+}, assuming no volume change.

close to 1:3, the pCu would be about 2.6, whereas in fact it is about 4.5 at this point. The reason that the pCu is too high lies in the fact that all of the added ammonia has not been used to form the complex $Cu(NH_3)_4^{2+}$. Rather, lower complex species such as $Cu(NH_3)^{2+}$ have formed, lowering the free $[Cu^{2+}]$ below a desirable value for a feasible titration. Such behavior is predictable from the formation constants of the individual steps given above. It is seen, for example, that there is less tendency for $Cu(NH_3)^{2+}$ to add a second ammonia than for free Cu^{2+} to bind the first one. It is sometimes said in a frivolous vein, that the titration would be feasible if one could titrate with little sacks, each containing four ammonia molecules; a cupric ion would then take four ammonia molecules or none, and the difficulty arising from the lower complexes would be averted.

The chemical equivalent of these little sacks can indeed be obtained. Consider, for example, the compound triethylenetetramine, a quadridentate ligand, often abbreviated "trien." Here, four nitrogen atoms are linked by ethylene bridges in a single molecule which can satisfy copper's normal coordination number of four in one step:

$$\begin{bmatrix} & CH_2CH_2 & \\ H_2N & & NH-CH_2 \\ & Cu & \\ H_2N & & NH-CH_2 \\ & CH_2CH_2 & \end{bmatrix}^{2+}$$

It may be supposed that the formation of the first nitrogen-copper bond brings the other nitrogens of the trien molecule into such proximity that the formation of additional bonds involving these nitrogens is much more probable than the formation of bonds between the copper and other trien molecules. Similarly, it is unlikely that one trien molecule will coordinate with more than one copper. Thus, under ordinary conditions, the stoichiometry of complex formation in this system is $1 \, Cu^{2+} : 1$ trien. The resulting five-membered rings shown in the structural formula are relatively free of strain. The complex is very stable, as shown by its formation constant:

$$Cu^{2+} + trien \rightleftharpoons Cu(trien)^{2+} \qquad K = \frac{[Cu(trien)^{2+}]}{[Cu^{2+}][trien]} = 2.5 \times 10^{20}$$

Thus trien is a good titrant for copper: The ligand and the complex ion are both soluble in water, only a $1:1$ complex is formed, the equilibrium constant for the titration reaction is large, and the reaction proceeds rapidly.

Only a few metal ions such as copper, cobalt, nickel, zinc, cadmium, and mercuric form stable complexes with nitrogen ligands such as ammonia and trien. Certain other metal ions, e.g., aluminum, lead, and bismuth, are better complexed with ligands containing oxygen atoms as electron donors. Certain chelating agents which contain both oxygen and nitrogen are particularly effective in forming stable complexes with a wide variety of metals. Of these, the best known is ethylenediaminetetraacetic acid, sometimes designated (ethylenedinitrilo)-tetraacetic acid, and often abbreviated EDTA:

$$
\begin{array}{ccc}
HOOCCH_2 & & CH_2COOH \\
& \diagdown\,NCH_2CH_2N\,\diagup & \\
HOOCCH_2 & & CH_2COOH
\end{array}
$$

The term *chelon* (pronounced "key-loan") has been proposed as a generic name for the entire class of reagents including polyamines such as trien, polyaminocarboxylic acids such as EDTA, and related compounds that form stable, water-soluble, $1:1$ complexes with metal ions and which hence may be employed as titrants for metals. The complexes, a special class of chelate compounds, are called *metal chelonates*, and the titrations are termed *chelometric titrations*. Chelons have practically revolutionized the analytical chemistry of many of the metallic elements, and they are of great importance in many fields.

CHELOMETRIC TITRATIONS

The suitability of chelons such as EDTA as titrants for metal ions has been mentioned above. We wish here to examine some of the equilibria involved in these titrations, consider end-point techniques, and show some representative applications. Our discussion will be limited largely to EDTA.

EDTA is potentially a sexidentate ligand which may coordinate with a metal ion through its two nitrogens and four carboxyl groups. It is known from infrared spectra and other measurements that this is the case, for example, with the cobaltous ion, which forms an octahedral EDTA complex whose structure is somewhat as shown below:

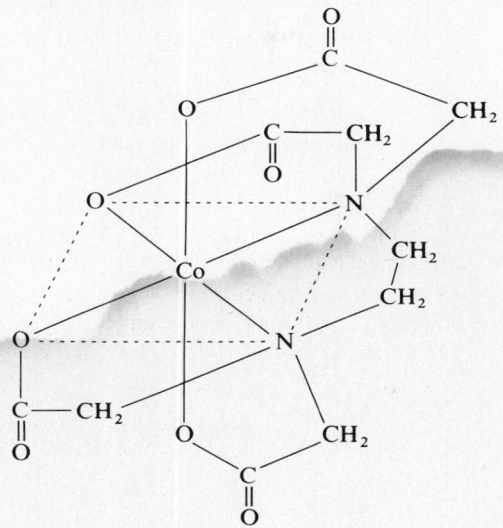

In other cases, EDTA may behave as a quinquedentate or quadridentate ligand having one or two of its carboxyl groups free of strong interaction with the metal.

For convenience, the free acid form of EDTA is often abbreviated H_4Y. The above cobalt complex is then written CoY^{2-}, and other complexes become CuY^{2-}, FeY^-, CaY^{2-}, etc. In solutions which are fairly acidic, partial protonation of EDTA without complete rupture of the metal complex may occur, leading to species such as $CuHY^-$; but under the usual conditions all four hydrogens are lost when the ligand is coordinated with a metal ion. At very high pH values, hydroxyl ion may penetrate the coordination sphere of the metal and complexes such as $Cu(OH)Y^{3-}$ may exist.

Equilibria Involved in EDTA Titrations

We may consider a metal ion such as Cu^{2+}, which is seeking electrons in its reactions, to be analogous to an acid like H_3O^+, and the EDTA anion Y^{4-}, which is an electron donor, to be a base. Then the reaction $Cu^{2+} + Y^{4-} \rightleftharpoons CuY^{2-}$ is analogous to an ordinary neutralization reaction, and it should be a simple matter to calculate pCu values under various conditions, calculate titration curves, discuss feasibility, etc. As a matter of fact, however, the situation is more complicated than this because of the intrusion of other equilibria into the titration situation. We shall discuss some of these in the sections below.

The Absolute Stability or Formation Constant

It is customary to tabulate for various metal ions and various chelons such as EDTA, values of the equilibrium constants for reactions formulated as follows:

$$M^{n+} + Y^{4-} \rightleftharpoons MY^{-(4-n)} \qquad K_{abs} = \frac{[MY^{-(4-n)}]}{[M^{n+}][Y^{4-}]}$$

K_{abs} is called the *absolute stability constant* or the *absolute formation constant*. Values of some of these constants may be found in Table 3, Appendix I.

The pH Effect

The four dissociation constants of the acid H_4Y are as follows:

$$H_4Y + H_2O \rightleftharpoons H_3O^+ + H_3Y^- \qquad K_{a_1} = 1.02 \times 10^{-2}$$

$$H_3Y^- + H_2O \rightleftharpoons H_3O^+ + H_2Y^{2-} \qquad K_{a_2} = 2.14 \times 10^{-3}$$

$$H_2Y^{2-} + H_2O \rightleftharpoons H_3O^+ + HY^{3-} \qquad K_{a_3} = 6.92 \times 10^{-7}$$

$$HY^{3-} + H_2O \rightleftharpoons H_3O^+ + Y^{4-} \qquad K_{a_4} = 5.50 \times 10^{-11}$$

The distributions of the five EDTA species as functions of pH are shown in Fig. 6.2. It may be seen that only at pH values greater than about 12 does

FIGURE 6.2   Distribution of EDTA species as a function of pH.

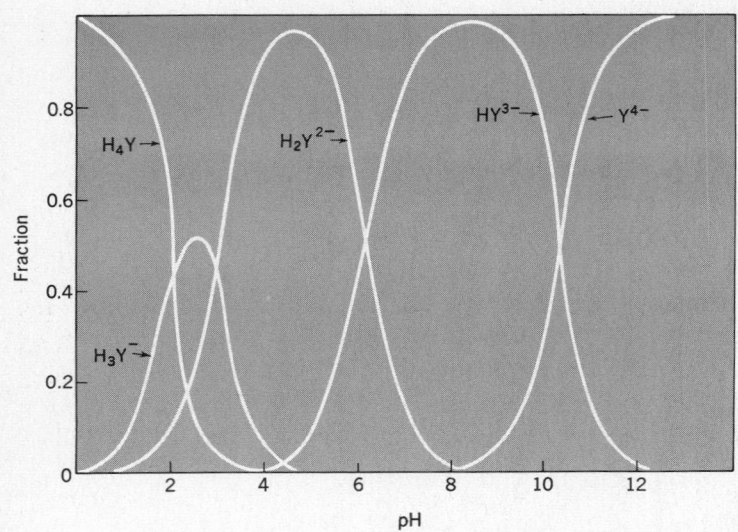

most of the EDTA exist as the tetra-anion Y^{4-}. At lower pH values, the protonated species HY^{3-}, etc., predominate. We may consider that H_3O^+, then, competes with a metal ion for EDTA, and it is clear that the real tendency to form the metal chelonate at any particular pH value is not discernible directly from K_{abs}. For example, at pH 4 the predominant EDTA species is H_2Y^{2-}, and the reaction with a metal such as copper may be written

$$Cu^{2+} + H_2Y^{2-} \rightleftharpoons CuY^{2-} + 2H^+$$

Obviously as the pH goes down, the equilibrium is shifted away from the formation of the chelonate CuY^{2-}, and we may expect that there will be a pH value below which the titration of copper with EDTA will not be feasible. We wish to be able to estimate what this value is. Clearly a calculation will involve K_{abs} and the appropriate K_a values of EDTA. Actually, as shown below, it is possible to estimate very easily the minimal pH for a feasible metal ion titration from the K_{abs} value and a simple graph.

The expression for the fraction of EDTA in the Y^{4-} form can be obtained in the same manner as was done for oxalic acid (page 127). The total concentration of all species, i.e., the analytical concentration c_a, is given by

$$c_a = [Y^{4-}] + [HY^{3-}] + [H_2Y^{2-}] + [H_3Y^-] + [H_4Y]$$

Substituting for the concentrations of the various species in terms of the dissociation constants and solving for the fraction in the Y^{4-} form gives:

$$\frac{[Y^{4-}]}{c_a} = \frac{K_{a_1}K_{a_2}K_{a_3}K_{a_4}}{[H_3O^+]^4 + [H_3O^+]^3 K_{a_1} + [H_3O^+]^2 K_{a_1}K_{a_2} + [H_3O^+]K_{a_1}K_{a_2}K_{a_3} + K_{a_1}K_{a_2}K_{a_3}K_{a_4}}$$

Giving the fraction of EDTA in the Y^{4-} form the symbol α_4, we may write

$$\frac{[Y^{4-}]}{c_a} = \alpha_4$$

or

$$[Y^{4-}] = \alpha_4 c_a$$

The value of α_4 may obviously be calculated at any desired pH for any chelon whose dissociation constants are known. Shortcuts may be taken in the calculation; for example, it is obvious that at very high pH values, the term containing $[H_3O^+]^4$ will be negligible. In any case, the work has already been done, and graphs or tables showing α values as functions of pH for a number of chelons may be found in the literature.[1] Because the values

[1] For example, see C. N. Reilley, R. W. Schmid, and F. S. Sadek, *J. Chem. Educ.*, **36**, 555 (1959).

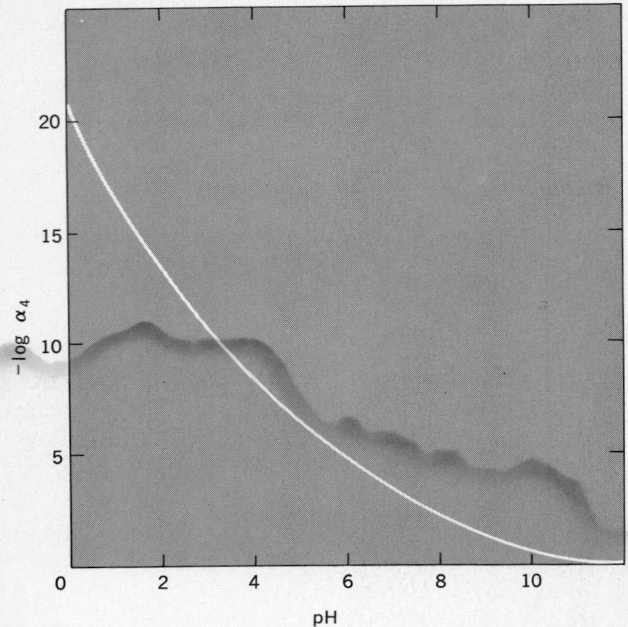

FIGURE 6.3 Variation of $-\log \alpha_4$ with pH for EDTA.

extend over a wide range of magnitudes, $-\log \alpha_4$ is usually plotted vs pH. Such a graph for EDTA is shown in Fig. 6.3. Some values are also given in Table 6.1.

Substitution of $\alpha_4 c_a$ in the absolute stability constant expression given above yields

$$K_{\text{abs}} = \frac{[\text{MY}^{-(4-n)}]}{[\text{M}^{n+}]\alpha_4 c_a}$$

VALUES OF α_4 FOR EDTA

pH	α_4	$-\log \alpha_4$
2.0	3.7×10^{-14}	13.44
2.5	1.4×10^{-12}	11.86
3.0	2.5×10^{-11}	10.60
4.0	3.3×10^{-9}	8.48
5.0	3.5×10^{-7}	6.45
6.0	2.2×10^{-5}	4.66
7.0	4.8×10^{-4}	3.33
8.0	5.1×10^{-3}	2.29
9.0	5.1×10^{-2}	1.29
10.0	0.35	0.46
11.0	0.85	0.07
12.0	0.98	0.00

or

$$K_{abs}\alpha_4 = \frac{[MY^{-(4-n)}]}{[M^{n+}]c_a} = K_{eff}$$

K_{eff} is called the *effective* or *conditional stability constant*. Unlike K_{abs}, K_{eff} varies with pH because of the pH dependence of α_4. In certain regards K_{eff} is more immediately useful than K_{abs}, because it shows the actual tendency to form the metal chelonate at the pH value in question. Although K_{eff} values are not customarily tabulated, it is apparent that they may be estimated readily from values of K_{abs}, which are found in tables of constants, and α_4 values obtained from tables such as Table 6.1.

It may be noted that, as the pH goes down, α_4 becomes smaller, and hence K_{eff} becomes smaller. Remember that α_4 is the fraction of EDTA in the Y^{4-} form. Thus, at pH values above 12 or so, where EDTA is essentially completely dissociated, α_4 approaches unity ($-\log \alpha_4$ approaches zero), and K_{eff} approaches K_{abs}.

Normally the solutions of metal ions to be titrated with EDTA are buffered so that the pH will remain constant despite the release of H_3O^+ as the complexes are formed. Thus there is usually a definite basis for estimating K_{eff}, and with this value at hand, it is easy to calculate the titration curve, from which a judgment of feasibility may be made just as with acid-base titrations. The pH is often adjusted to as low a value as consistent with feasibility in order to gain selectivity in the titrations. At very low pH values, only metal ions which form very stable EDTA complexes are titrated. Furthermore, the hydrolysis of many metal ions leads to undesirable effects, sometimes even precipitation, if the pH is too high (see below).

Example 1. 50.0 ml of a solution which is 0.0100-M in Ca^{2+} and buffered at pH 10.0 is titrated with a 0.0100-M EDTA solution. Calculate values of pCa at various stages of the titration and plot the titration curve.

K_{abs} for CaY^{2-} is 5.0×10^{10}. Referring to Table 6.1 α_4 at pH 10.0 is 0.35. Hence K_{eff} is $5.0 \times 10^{10} \times 0.35 = 1.8 \times 10^{10}$.

(a) *Start of titration.*

$$[Ca^{2+}] = 0.0100\text{-}M$$

$$pCa = -\log[Ca^{2+}] = 2.00$$

(b) *After addition of 10.0 ml of titrant.* There is a considerable excess of Ca^{2+} at this point, and with a K_t value of the order of 10^{10}, we may assume that the reaction goes to completion. Thus,

$$[Ca^{2+}] = \frac{(0.50 - 0.10)\text{ mmols}}{60.0\text{ ml}} = 0.0067\text{-}M$$

$$pCa = 2.17$$

Similar calculations can be made at various intervals before the equivalence point. In the vicinity of the equivalence point, more accurate calculations can be made by not assuming complete reaction, i.e., by taking into account calcium ions produced by dissociation of CaY^{2-}, and solving the usual quadratic equation. The data in Table 6.2 were calculated by the approximate method.

(c) *Equivalence point.*

$$[Ca^{2+}] = c_a$$

$$[CaY^{2-}] = \frac{0.500 \text{ mmol}}{100 \text{ ml}} = 5.0 \times 10^{-3}\text{-}M$$

$$K_{eff} = \frac{5.0 \times 10^{-3}}{[Ca^{2+}]^2} = 1.8 \times 10^{10}$$

$$[Ca^{2+}] = 5.2 \times 10^{-7}$$

$$pCa = 6.28$$

(d) *After addition of 60.0 ml titrant.* Excess EDTA = 0.100 mmol

$$c_a = \frac{0.100 \text{ mmol}}{110 \text{ ml}} = 9.1 \times 10^{-4}\text{-}M$$

$$[CaY^{2-}] = \frac{0.500 \text{ mmol}}{110 \text{ ml}} = 4.55 \times 10^{-3}\text{-}M$$

$$\frac{4.55 \times 10^{-3}}{[Ca^{2+}]9.1 \times 10^{-4}} = 1.8 \times 10^{10}$$

$$[Ca^{2+}] = 2.8 \times 10^{-10}$$

$$pCa = 9.55$$

TABLE 6.2 TITRATION OF 50.0 ml OF 0.0100-M Ca^{2+} WITH 0.0100-M EDTA

ml EDTA	$[Ca^{2+}]$	pCa	% Ca^{2+} reacted
0.00	0.0100	2.00	0.0
10.0	0.0067	2.17	20.0
20.0	0.0043	2.37	40.0
30.0	0.0025	2.60	60.0
40.0	0.0011	2.96	80.0
49.0	1.0×10^{-4}	4.00	98.0
49.9	1.0×10^{-5}	5.00	99.8
50.0	5.2×10^{-7}	6.28	100.0
50.1	2.8×10^{-8}	7.55	100.0
60.0	2.8×10^{-10}	9.55	100.0

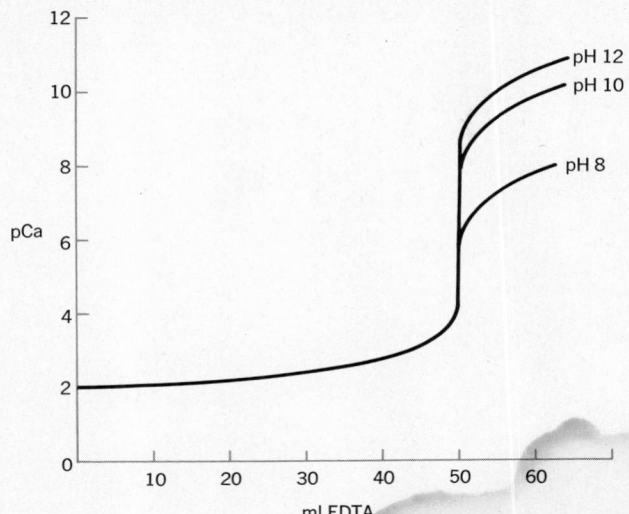

FIGURE 6.4 Titration curves: 50 ml 0.0100-M Ca^{2+} titrated with 0.0100-M EDTA at pH 8, 10, and 12.

The data for this titration are given in Table 6.2, and the titration curve is plotted in Fig. 6.4. The titration curve is of familiar shape, with a sharp break in the value of pCa at the equivalence point. Also shown in the figure are curves for the titration done in solutions of pH 8 and pH 12. In these solutions the values of K_{eff} (same as K_t for the titration) are 2.6×10^8 and 4.9×10^{10}, respectively. Note that the curves are the same up to the equivalence point. The larger break is obtained at high pH since K_{eff} is larger in solutions of low hydrogen ion concentration. At low pH K_{eff} becomes so small that the titration is not feasible.

The magnitude of K_{eff} or K_t required for a feasible titration can be calculated as was done for an acid-base titration (page 94). The following example is an illustration.

Example 2. 50 ml of 0.010-M M^{2+} is titrated with 0.010-M EDTA. Calculate the value of K_{eff} so that when 49.95 ml of titrant has been added, essentially all of M^{2+} has reacted, and the pM changes by 2.00 units on the addition of two more drops (0.10 ml) of titrant.

One drop before the equivalence point 0.4995 mmol of EDTA has been added. We started with $50 \times 0.010 = 0.50$ mmol of M^{2+}. There must remain 0.00050 mmol. Hence

$$[M^{2+}] = \frac{0.00050 \text{ mmol}}{99.95 \text{ ml}} = 5 \times 10^{-6}\text{-}M$$

$$pM = 5.30$$

If $\Delta pM = 2.00$ units, then $pM = 7.30$ and $[M^{2+}] = 5 \times 10^{-8}\text{-}M$ when 50.05 ml of titrant is added. At this point

$$c_a = \frac{0.05 \times 0.010}{100.05} \cong 5 \times 10^{-6}$$

$$[MY^{2-}] \cong \frac{0.5}{100} \cong 5 \times 10^{-3}$$

Hence

$$K_{eff} = \frac{5 \times 10^{-3}}{(5 \times 10^{-8})(5 \times 10^{-6})}$$

$$K_{eff} = K_t = 2 \times 10^{10}$$

The student should confirm that, for $\Delta pM = 1.00$, K_{eff} should be 2×10^9.

The Complex Effect

Substances other than the chelon titrant which may be present in the metal ion solution may form complexes with the metal and thus compete against the desired titration reaction. Actually, such complexing is sometimes used deliberately to overcome interferences, in which case the effect of the complexer is called *masking*. For example, nickel forms a very stable complex ion with cyanide, $Ni(CN)_4^{2-}$, whereas lead does not. Thus, in the presence of cyanide, lead can be titrated with EDTA without interference from nickel, despite the fact that the stability constants for NiY^{2-} and PbY^{2-} are nearly the same (log K_{abs} values are 18.6 and 18.3, respectively).

With certain metal ions that hydrolyze readily, it may be necessary to add complexing ligands in order to prevent precipitation of the metal hydroxide. As mentioned above, the solutions are frequently buffered, and buffer anions or neutral molecules such as acetate or ammonia may form complex ions with the metal. Just as the interaction of hydrogen ions with Y^{4-} lowers K_{eff}, so it is lowered by ligands which complex the metal ion. If the stability constants for all the complexes are known, then the effect of the complexers upon the EDTA titration reaction can be calculated. For example, Zn^{2+} forms four complexes with ammonia:

$$Zn^{2+} + NH_3 \rightleftharpoons Zn(NH_3)^{2+} \qquad K_1 = 190$$

$$Zn(NH_3)^{2+} + NH_3 \rightleftharpoons Zn(NH_3)_2^{2+} \qquad K_2 = 210$$

$$Zn(NH_3)_2^{2+} + NH_3 \rightleftharpoons Zn(NH_3)_3^{2+} \qquad K_3 = 250$$

$$Zn(NH_3)_3^{2+} + NH_3 \rightleftharpoons Zn(NH_3)_4^{2+} \qquad K_4 = 110$$

If we designate the total or analytical concentration of all species containing zinc as c_{Zn}, then

$$c_{Zn} = [Zn^{2+}] + [Zn(NH_3)^{2+}] + [Zn(NH_3)_2^{2+}] + [Zn(NH_3)_3^{2+}] + [Zn(NH_3)_4^{2+}]$$

$$c_{Zn} = [Zn^{2+}]\{1 + K_1[NH_3] + K_1K_2[NH_3]^2 + K_1K_2K_3[NH_3]^3$$

$$+ K_1K_2K_3K_4[NH_3]^4\}$$

Let us designate the fraction of zinc in the uncomplexed form as β_4:

$$\frac{[Zn^{2+}]}{c_{Zn}} = \beta_4$$

or

$$[Zn^{2+}] = \beta_4 c_{Zn}$$

The term β_4 is simply the reciprocal of the terms in the bracket of the equation for the total concentration of all species containing zinc. It can be evaluated from the various equilibrium constants and the concentration of NH_3.

For the reaction of Zn^{2+} with EDTA in the presence of ammonia,

$$Zn^{2+} + Y^{4-} \rightleftharpoons ZnY^{2-}$$

$$K_{abs} = \frac{[ZnY^{2-}]}{[Zn^{2+}][Y^{4-}]} = \frac{[ZnY^{2-}]}{\beta_4 c_{Zn} \alpha_4 c_a}$$

$$K_{abs}\alpha_4\beta_4 = K_{eff} = \frac{[ZnY^{2-}]}{c_{Zn}c_a}$$

The following is an example illustrating the calculation of K_{eff} in a solution which contains ammonia.

Example. Given the four constants, K_1, K_2, K_3, and K_4, for the reaction of Zn^{2+} with NH_3 (above) and that K_{abs} for the reaction of Zn^{2+} with EDTA is 1.8×10^{16}. Calculate the value of K_{eff} for the reaction of Zn^{2+} with EDTA in a buffer of pH 9.0. Assume that the concentration of free NH_3 in the buffer is 0.10-M.

The value of β_4 is given by

$$\beta_4 = \frac{1}{1 + 190 \times 0.10 + 190 \times 210 \times (0.10)^2 + 190 \times 210 \atop \times 250 \times (0.10)^3 + 190 \times 210 \times 250 \times 110 \times (0.10)^4}$$

$$\beta_4 = 8.3 \times 10^{-6}$$

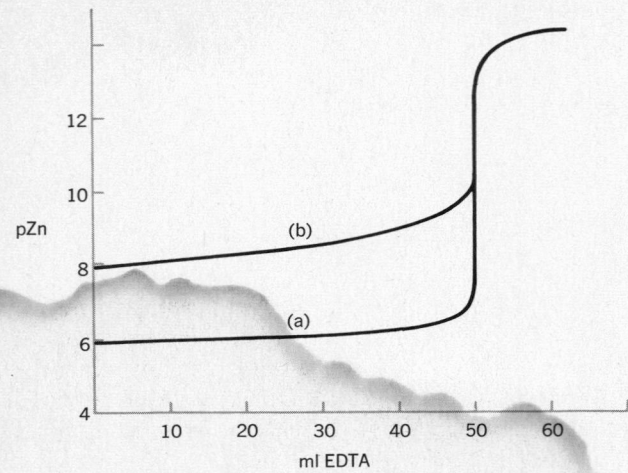

FIGURE 6.5 Titration of 0.0010-M Zn^{2+} with 0.0010-M EDTA at pH 9; (a) 0.010-M in NH_3, (b) 0.10-M in NH_3.

At pH 9.0, α_4 is 5.1×10^{-2}. Hence

$$K_{\text{eff}} = K_{\text{abs}} \times \alpha_4 \times \beta_4$$

$$K_{\text{eff}} = 1.8 \times 10^{16} \times 0.051 \times 8.3 \times 10^{-6}$$

$$K_{\text{eff}} = 7.6 \times 10^9$$

The effect of the concentration of ammonia on the titration curve of Zn^{2+} with EDTA at pH 9.0 is shown in Fig. 6.5. It can be seen that the break at the equivalence point is smaller the higher the concentration of ammonia. It may be noted that the addition of too much buffer is a common error in EDTA titrations, the resulting complexing action often worsening the end point unnecessarily.

Hydrolysis Effect

Hydrolysis of metal ions may compete with the chelometric titration process. Raising the pH makes this effect worse by shifting toward the right equilibria of the type

$$M^{2+} + H_2O \rightleftharpoons M(OH)^+ + H^+$$

Extensive hydrolysis may lead to the precipitation of hydroxides which react only slowly with EDTA even when equilibrium considerations favor the formation of the metal chelonate. Frequently, the appropriate hydrolysis constants for metal ions are not at hand, and hence these effects often cannot be calculated accurately. But of course there is much empirical information which serves experienced persons in deciding how high the pH may be for

EDTA titrations of various metal ions. Solubility product constants may sometimes be used to predict where precipitation may occur, although often these constants are quite inaccurate in the case of metal hydroxides.

Sometimes precipitation is actually utilized as a sort of masking in order to circumvent a particular interference. For example, at pH 10, both calcium and magnesium are titrated together with EDTA, only the sum of the two being obtainable. But, if strong base is added to raise the pH above 12 or so, $Mg(OH)_2$ precipitates and calcium alone can be titrated.

Chelons Other Than EDTA

Many other chelons have been synthesized. A few of these offer advantages over EDTA in particular situations, although none is so frequently used. The all-nitrogen chelons such as triethylenetetramine, mentioned in the introduction of this chapter, are more selective than EDTA. For example, copper can be titrated with trien in the presence of nickel, zinc, and cadmium, whereas with EDTA these metals interfere.

Ethylene glycol-bis-(β-aminoethyl ether)-N,N'-tetraacetic acid (EGTA) (below) forms a much more stable chelonate with calcium than with magnesium (log K_{abs} = 11.0 vs 5.4), whereas with EDTA, as noted above, the stabilities are much more nearly the same (log K_{abs} = 10.7 vs 8.7). Thus

$$HOOCCH_2\diagdown \atop HOOCCH_2\diagup NCH_2CH_2-O-CH_2CH_2-O-CH_2CH_2N{\diagup CH_2COOH \atop \diagdown CH_2COOH}$$

Ethylene glycol-bis-(β-aminoethyl ether)-N,N'-tetraacetic acid (EGTA)

calcium can be titrated selectively with EGTA in the presence of magnesium, whereas only the sum of the two can be obtained with EDTA unless the magnesium is precipitated as noted before.

Indicators for Chelometric Titrations

When EDTA was first introduced as a titrant, there was a dearth of good visual indicators, and various instrumental end-point techniques were frequently employed. The latter are still valuable in certain situations, but a wide variety of good visual indicators is now available, and usually the visual titrations are the more convenient. We have seen above, using calcium as an example, that there is a large and abrupt break in pM in the vicinity of the equivalence point in a feasible chelometric titration. We wish to convert this into a color change just as acid-base indicators respond to pH changes by changing color. A variety of chemical substances, often called *metallochromic indicators*, are now available for this purpose. Whereas all pH indicators need respond only to hydrogen ion, for chelometric titrations we need a series of substances responsive to pMg, pCa, pCu, etc., although often one indicator may be useful with more than one metal ion.

Basically, the metallochromic indicators are colored organic compounds which themselves form chelates with metal ions. The chelate must have a different color from the free indicator, of course, and if large indicator blanks are to be avoided and sharp end points obtained, the indicator must release the metal ion to the EDTA titrant at a pM value very close to that of the equivalence point. This may be considered as analogous to the action of an indicator acid in releasing hydrogen ion to hydroxide ion in the titration of an acid. A complete treatment of the equilibria involved is somewhat more complicated than the analogous discussion of acid-base indicators, however, because of the circumstance that the common metallochromic indicators also have acid-base properties and respond as pH indicators as well as indicators for pM. Thus, in order to specify the color that a metallochromic indicator will assume in a certain solution, we generally must know both the pH value and the pM value for the particular metal ion which is present. A thorough discussion of the equilibria involved in the action of metallochromic indicators has been given by Reilley and Schmid.[2] We shall present here a somewhat simplified discussion of one indicator, Eriochrome Black T, and then simply note some of the others which are available.

The structure of Eriochrome Black T is shown below:

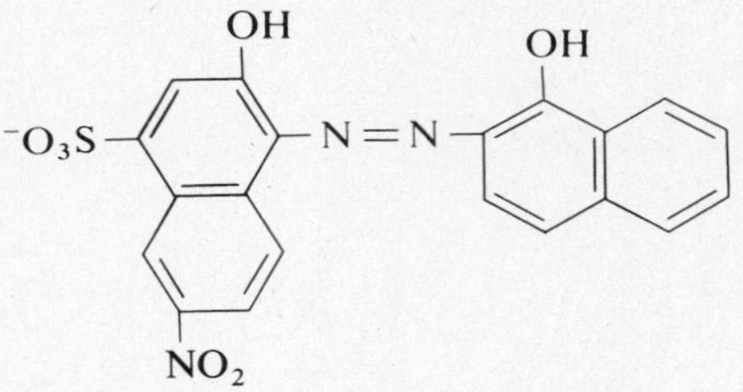

Metal chelates are formed with this molecule by loss of hydrogen ions from the phenolic —OH groups and the formation of bonds between the metal ions and the oxygen atoms as well as the azo group. The molecule is usually represented in abbreviated form as a tribasic acid, H_3In. The sulfonic acid group is shown in the figure above as ionized; this is a strong acid group which is dissociated in aqueous solution regardless of pH, and thus the structure shown is that of the ion H_2In^-. This form of the indicator is red. The pK_a value for the dissociation of H_2In^- to form HIn^{2-} is 6.3. The latter species is blue. The pK_a value for the ionization of HIn^{2-} to form In^{3-} is 11.6; the latter ion is a yellowish-orange color. The indicator forms stable 1:1 complexes, which are wine-red in color, with a number of cations, such as Mg^{2+}, Ca^{2+}, Zn^{2+}, and Ni^{2+}. Many EDTA titrations are performed in buffers of pH 8 to 10, the range in which the predominant form of Eriochrome Black T is the blue HIn^{2-} form.

[2] C. N. Reilley and R. W. Schmid, *Anal. Chem.*, **31**, 887 (1959).

The reaction which results in the color change can be written

$$MIn^- + HY^{3-} \rightleftharpoons MY^{2-} + HIn^{2-}$$

red blue

In order for the color change to occur at the proper value of pM, the stability of the MIn^- complex must be less than that of MY^{2-} so that the metal releases the indicator when only a slight excess of EDTA is added.

Eriochrome Black T is a suitable indicator for the titration of Zn^{2+} with EDTA in ammonia buffers of pH 9. The equilibrium constant for the reaction

$$Zn^{2+} + HIn^{2-} \rightleftharpoons ZnIn^- + H^+$$

is about 22. That is,

$$\frac{[ZnIn^-][H^+]}{[Zn^{2+}][HIn^{2-}]} = 22$$

or

$$[Zn^{2+}] = \frac{[ZnIn^-][H^+]}{22[HIn^{2-}]}$$

At the end point of the titration, the ratio of $[ZnIn^-]$ to $[HIn^{2-}]$ is about 1 to 10. Hence the zinc ion concentration at pH 9 is

$$[Zn^{2+}] = \frac{1 \times 10^{-9}}{22 \times 10}$$

$$[Zn^{2+}] = 5 \times 10^{-12}$$

$$pZn = 11.3$$

Note in Fig. 6.5 that this value of pZn occurs on the steep portion of the titration curve. Hence the color change occurs very close to the equivalence point of the titration.

The complex formed between calcium ion and Eriochrome Black T is not extremely stable, and the color change occurs prematurely in the titration of Ca^{2+} with EDTA. A number of other indicators are known which can be used for various cations. These are discussed in the article of Reilley and Schmid to which we previously referred.

Applications of Chelometric Titrations

There is much detailed information about chelometric titrations that cannot be given in a chapter of this length but which should be looked into before undertaking a particular application. For example, certain indicators may be "blocked" by traces of heavy metals too small to interfere otherwise. Some metal ion-EDTA reactions as well as metal-indicator reactions are slow at room temperature. There is a wealth of information about masking interference for particular sorts of samples. The choice of indicator may not be obvious. Some indicator-metal complexes are quite insoluble. At least, however, a person who has studied this chapter should be able to read the available literature.

The EDTA titration has virtually replaced the former tedious gravimetric analyses for many metals in a variety of samples. One of the most important applications in terms of the number of analyses performed is the EDTA water hardness titration, which has replaced the crude titration of hardness with soap. The total hardness, roughly calcium plus magnesium for most waters, is determined by a single titration with EDTA using Eriochrome Black T or Calmagite, usually at pH 10 in an ammonia buffer. The EDTA is generally standardized against calcium carbonate as a primary standard.

Potentiometric EDTA titrations with a mercury indicator electrode are explained in Chapter 9, and photometric titrations of metal ions with EDTA are discussed briefly in Chapter 11.

METAL ION BUFFERS

We saw in Chapter 4 that certain systems containing Brønsted conjugate acid-base pairs resisted pH changes upon the addition of strong acids or bases. Such systems are said to be buffered. An analogous buffering action with respect to changes in pM is established in solutions containing a metal complex and excess complexing agent.

Consider the equilibrium involving a metal ion M, a ligand L, and a complex ML, where the charges are omitted for convenience:

$$M + L \rightleftharpoons ML$$

$$K_{eff} = \frac{[ML]}{[M][L]}$$

Solving for [M] and then taking logs, we obtain

$$[M] = \frac{1}{K_{eff}} \times \frac{[ML]}{[L]}$$

$$\log [M] = \log \frac{1}{K_{eff}} + \log \frac{[ML]}{[L]}$$

$$pM = \log K_{eff} - \log \frac{[ML]}{[L]}$$

Compare this with the Henderson-Hasselbalch equation (Chapter 4, page 85).

It is seen that the pM of such a solution is fixed by the value of K_{eff} and the molar ratio of metal complex to free ligand. Introduction of additional metal ion to the solution will lead to formation of more ML; in other words, the solution resists the lowering of pM that would otherwise occur if L were absent. Similarly, removal of metal ion will be resisted by the dissociation of ML, and metal ion can be drained by some other reaction without a large rise in pM so long as the capacity of ML to furnish metal ion is not exhausted.

Metal ion buffers have found application in biology and biochemistry in studies of enzyme systems whose catalytic activity exhibits a metal ion dependence. Just as pK_a must be considered in the analogous case of pH buffers, a metal ion buffer will be most efficient if log K_{eff} is nearly the same as the desired pM value.

TITRATIONS INVOLVING UNIDENTATE LIGANDS

Because of the stepwise formation of successive complexes as noted above, unidentate ligands are only rarely suitable for the titration of metal ions. However, there are a few examples of important titrations based upon such ligands, and we shall consider briefly the two best-known cases.

Titration of Chloride with Mercuric Ion

The mercuric ion-chloride system is unusual in that the last two of the successive complexes in the formation of $HgCl_4^{2-}$ are of much lesser stability than the first two, as shown by the successive formation constants given below:[3]

$$Hg^{2+} + Cl^- \rightleftharpoons HgCl^+ \qquad K_1 = \frac{[HgCl^+]}{[Hg^{2+}][Cl^-]} = 10^{6.74}$$

$$HgCl^+ + Cl^- \rightleftharpoons HgCl_2 \qquad K_2 = \frac{[HgCl_2]}{[HgCl^+][Cl^-]} = 10^{6.48}$$

$$HgCl_2 + Cl^- \rightleftharpoons HgCl_3^- \qquad K_3 = \frac{[HgCl_3^-]}{[HgCl_2][Cl^-]} = 10^{0.85}$$

$$HgCl_3^- + Cl^- \rightleftharpoons HgCl_4^{2-} \qquad K_4 = \frac{[HgCl_4^{2-}]}{[HgCl_3^-][Cl^-]} = 10^{1.0}$$

Thus in the titration of a chloride solution with an ionized mercuric salt such as mercuric nitrate or perchlorate, there is a sudden drop in pHg (pHg = $-$log $[Hg^{2+}]$) when the formation of $HgCl_2$ is essentially complete.

[3] A. Johnson, I. Quarfort, and L. G. Sillen, *Acta Chem. Scand.*, **1**, 461, 473 (1947).

One of the common indicators for this titration is sodium nitroprusside, $Na_2Fe(CN)_5NO$. This compound forms a white precipitate of mercuric nitroprusside, and the end point is taken as the appearance of a white turbidity in the formerly homogeneous solution. The pHg at the equivalence point of the titration is not so low as might otherwise be expected because of the consumption of mercuric ion in the following reaction:

$$Hg^{2+} + HgCl_2 \rightleftharpoons 2\,HgCl^+ \qquad K = \frac{K_1}{K_2} \cong 1.8$$

Actually, the mercuric nitroprusside precipitate is first seen somewhat after the equivalence point, and a correction must be applied in order to obtain the best results. The correction is not really the same as an indicator blank run with distilled water, because the above reaction does not then take place appreciably. The correction depends upon the final concentration of mercuric chloride, and hence varies with the quantity of sample and the final volume. The acidity of the solution also affects the correction, and there is further variation which depends upon the rate at which the titration is performed and the manner in which the individual analyst views the turbid solution. Typical correction values are given by Kolthoff and Stenger;[4] for example, where the final solution is 100 ml of 0.025-M $HgCl_2$, the correction is roughly 0.2 ml. An advantage of this particular method lies in the fact that the titration may be performed in solutions which are quite acidic, and it works well even in fairly dilute solution, for example, at levels of chloride (e.g., 10 mg per liter) which frequently occur in natural waters.

Certain organic compounds which form colored complexes with mercuric ion have also been employed as indicators for the mercurimetric titration of chloride. The best known are diphenylcarbazide (colorless) and diphenylcarbazone (orange), which form intense violet mercuric complexes. With these indicators, it has been found important to control the pH of the solution being titrated. According to Roberts,[5] diphenylcarbazide performs best at pH 1.5 to 2.0, while Clark[6] found that diphenylcarbazone is best employed at pH 3.2 to 3.3.

It should be pointed out that bromide, thiocyanate, and cyanide may be determined by mercurimetric titration, although there is no advantage over the usual titrations of these ions with silver nitrate. Nitroprusside cannot be used as the indicator in the thiocyanate titration because the appearance of the mercuric nitroprusside precipitate is obscured by the slightly soluble mercuric thiocyanate. In this case, the usual indicator is ferric ion, which acts by the formation of red complexes with thiocyanate such as $FeSCN^{2+}$.

[4] I. M. Kolthoff and V. A. Stenger, *Volumetric Analysis*, 2nd ed., Vol. II, Interscience Publishers, Inc., New York, 1947, p. 332.

[5] I. Roberts, *Ind. Eng. Chem., Anal. Ed.*, **8**, 365 (1936).

[6] F. E. Clark, *Anal. Chem.*, **22**, 553 (1950).

The titration of iodide with mercury is largely unsatisfactory. The complex HgI_4^{2-} forms during the titration; later, a red precipitate of HgI_2 appears through the reaction

$$Hg^{2+} + HgI_4^{2-} \rightleftharpoons 2\,HgI_2$$

The appearance of this precipitate has been used as an end point, but actually it occurs much too early.

Titration of Cyanide with Silver Ion

Another titration of some practical importance involving a unidentate ligand and a metal ion is the so-called Liebig titration of cyanide with silver nitrate. The basis of the method is the formation of the very stable complex ion, $Ag(CN)_2^-$:

$$2\,CN^- + Ag^+ \rightleftharpoons Ag(CN)_2^-$$

The equilibrium constant for this reaction as written is about 10^{21}, and this is the only silver-cyanide complex of appreciable stability. Originally, the end point was based upon the appearance of turbidity due to the precipitation of silver cyanide, which may be written as

$$Ag^+ + Ag(CN)_2^- \rightleftharpoons 2\,AgCN$$

or

$$Ag^+ + Ag(CN)_2^- \rightleftharpoons Ag[Ag(CN)_2]$$

This precipitation occurs after $[CN^-]$ has dropped to a low value, although a calculation based upon the appropriate equilibria shows that it actually comes a little too early, corresponding to an end-point error of the order of 0.2 parts per thousand. This error is small enough to be accepted, but there is an additional problem: Silver cyanide precipitated locally is slow to redissolve as the solution is stirred, and it is time consuming to perform the titration carefully. Also, there is some difficulty in seeing the silver cyanide precipitate.

In the Deniges modification of Liebig's method, iodide ion is added as the indicator. Precipitated silver iodide is bulky and easy to see, and it is less soluble than silver cyanide and hence precipitates in place of the latter at the end point. This end point occurs, however, too early in the titration. For this reason, ammonia is added which, by forming the soluble species $Ag(NH_3)_2^+$, retards the precipitation of silver iodide until a more propitious time; ammonia does not prevent the formation of the much more stable $Ag(CN)_2^-$, and hence does not interfere with the titration reaction.

G. SCHWARZENBACH and H. FLASCHKA, *Complexometric Titrations*, Trans. by H. M. N. H. Irving, Methuen and Co., Ltd., London, 1969.

A. RINGBOM, *Complexation in Analytical Chemistry*, Interscience Publishers, New York, 1963.

H. A. LAITINEN, *Chemical Analysis*, McGraw-Hill Book Company, New York, 1960.

H. F. WALTON, *Principles and Methods of Chemical Analysis*, 2nd ed., Prentice-Hall, Inc., Englewood Cliffs, N.J., 1964.

J. N. BUTLER, *Ionic Equilibrium, A Mathematical Approach*, Addison-Wesley Publishing Co., Inc., Reading, Mass., 1964.

QUESTIONS

1. Explain the meaning of the following terms: (a) complex, (b) chelon, (c) quadridentate ligand, (d) chelating agent, (e) labile complex, (f) masking, (g) trien, and (h) metallochromic indicator.

2. Why is the titration of Cu^{2+} with NH_3 not feasible? Why is the titration of I^- with Hg^{2+} not satisfactory?

3. Explain why the concept of an effective stability constant is useful in chelometric titrations.

4. Why is the pH of the solution an important factor in the selection of an indicator for a chelometric titration?

5. Why cannot sodium nitroprusside be used as the indicator for the titration of SCN^- with Hg^{2+}?

6. What effect does the concentration of the substance titrated have on a titration curve such as that shown in Fig. 6.4? What is the effect of the titrant concentration?

7. Given the acid H_3X, dissociation constants K_{a_1}, K_{a_2}, and K_{a_3}. Write the expression for α_3.

8. Given: $M + Y \rightleftharpoons MY$; K_{abs} is the stability constant. Show that the following relation holds:

$$pM + pY - pMY = pK_{abs}$$

PROBLEMS

1. *Standardization.* A sample of pure $CaCO_3$ weighing 0.4206 g is dissolved in hydrochloric acid and the solution diluted to 500.0 ml in a volumetric flask. A 50.0 ml aliquot requires 38.84 ml of an EDTA solution for titration. Calculate the formality of the EDTA solution and the number of grams of $Na_2H_2Y \cdot 2H_2O$ (M.W. = 372.2) required to prepare one liter of the solution.

2. *Titrimetric analysis.* A 100-ml sample of water is titrated with 12.24 ml of the EDTA solution in Problem 1. Calculate the degree of hardness of the water in parts per million of $CaCO_3$. Recall that 1 ppm is 1 mg/liter.

3. *Liebig method.* A 0.6250-g sample containing NaCN is dissolved in water and then concentrated ammonia and some KI solution are added. The solution required

24.32 ml of 0.1033-M $AgNO_3$ for titration. Calculate the percentage of NaCN in the sample.

4. *Liebig method.* A sample weighing 0.4340 g and containing only NaCN and KCN required 38.42 ml of 0.1022-M $AgNO_3$ for titration. Calculate the percentage of KCN in the sample.

5. *Titer.* The $MgCO_3$ titer of an EDTA solution is 1.240 mg/ml. Calculate (a) the formality of the EDTA and (b) the $CaCO_3$ titer of the EDTA.

6. *Value of α.* Verify the values of α_4 for EDTA given in Table 6.1 at pH 2, 6, and 10.

7. *Values of pM.* Calculate the following: (a) pMg of a 0.02-F solution of $Mg(NO_3)_2$ solution; (b) pCu of a 0.005-F $CuCl_2$ solution; (c) pCa of a 1.0-F $CaCl_2$ solution; (d) pZn of a 0.00025-F $ZnSO_4$ solution, (e) pNa of a 0.001-F Na_2SO_4 solution.

8. *Titration.* Calculate the value of pM at the equivalence point for the titration of 1.00 mmol of each of the following metals with EDTA at pH 5.0. The final volume in each case is 100 ml. (a) Ni^{2+}; (b) Mn^{2+}; (c) Sr^{2+}.

9. *Calculation of K_{eff}.* (a) Calculate the value of β_4 for the reaction of Cu^{2+} with ammonia in a solution in which the concentration of free NH_3 is 0.10-M. (b) Calculate the value of K_{eff} for the reaction of copper with EDTA in a buffer of pH 9.0 where the concentration of free NH_3 is 0.10-M.

10. *Titration curve.* 50.00 ml of a solution which is 0.0100-F in a metal ion, M^{2+}, and buffered at pH 10.0 is titrated with 0.0100-F EDTA. The value of K_{abs} for MY^{2-} is 2.0×10^{12}. Calculate the values of pM when the following volumes of titrant are added: (a) 0.00, (b) 25.0, (c) 49.9, (d) 50.0, (e) 50.1, and (f) 55.0 ml.

11. *Titration curve.* Repeat Problem 10 at pH 8 and 12. Comment on the sharpness of the end point to be expected at the different pH values.

12. *Feasibility of titration.* (a) 50.0 ml of a 0.010-F solution of a cation N^{2+} is titrated with 0.010-F EDTA. Calculate the value of K_{eff} for the formation of NY^{2-} so that when 49.95 ml of titrant is added essentially all of N^{2+} is reacted and that pN changes by 1.00 unit on the addition of 0.10 ml of additional titrant. (b) Repeat the calculation for 0.10-F solutions.

13. *Metal ion buffer.* A metal ion buffer is prepared which contains 3.00 mmol of ZnY^{2-} and 6.00 mmol of Y^{4-} per 100 ml of solution. The pH is 8.00. Calculate (a) the pM of the buffer and (b) the pM of the solution after 2.00 mmol of Zn^{2+} is added to 100 ml of the buffer.

14. *Titrations.* Given the following data:

Complex	Metal log K_{abs}	pH	Chelon, L $-\log \alpha$
ML	18.00	3.00	20.00
NL	13.30	5.00	10.00
QL	9.70	7.00	5.00
RL	7.00	9.00	2.00
SL	3.00	10.00	1.00

(a) Calculate the value of K_{eff} for QL at pH 9.00. (b) 2.0 mmol of metal N is titrated with chelon L at pH 9.00. Calculate the value of pN at the equivalence point where the volume is 100 ml. (c) 50 ml of 0.20-F solution of M is titrated with 0.10-F L at pH 7.00. Calculate the value of pM after the addition of 50 ml of L. (d) Metal M is titrated with chelon L in a solution buffered at pH 5.00 with an acetic acid-acetate buffer. If $\log K_{eff}$ is 5.00, what is the value of $-\log \beta$?

7

Solubility Equilibria

Precipitation reactions have been widely used in classical analytical chemistry both for titrations and for separating a sample into its component parts. Newer techniques have supplanted many of the older methods, but precipitation is still an important technique in many analytical procedures. In this chapter we shall first discuss precipitation titrations and then the use of precipitation as a separation technique. Included in the latter discussion will be the factors which influence the size and purity of particles of a precipitate.

THE SOLUBILITY PRODUCT CONSTANT

The equilibrium constant expressing the solubility of a precipitate in water is the familiar *solubility product constant*. For a precipitate of silver chloride, the equilibrium constant of the reaction

$$AgCl(s) \rightleftharpoons Ag^+(aq) + Cl^-(aq)$$

is

$$K = \frac{a_{Ag^+} a_{Cl^-}}{a_{AgCl}}$$

The activity of solid AgCl is constant and by convention we take it to be unity (page 77). The solid is only slightly soluble; hence the concentrations of Ag^+ and Cl^- ions are small and, unless large concentrations of other ions are present, activities can be approximated by molarities, giving

$$K_{sp} = [Ag^+][Cl^-]$$

The constant K_{sp} is called the solubility product constant.

The proper equilibrium expressions for a few other salts are given below:

Salt	K_{sp}
$BaSO_4$	$[Ba^{2+}][SO_4{}^{2-}]$
Ag_2CrO_4	$[Ag^+]^2[CrO_4{}^{2-}]$
CaF_2	$[Ca^{2+}][F^-]^2$
$Al(OH)_3$	$[Al^{3+}][OH^-]^3$

A general expression for the salt A_xB_y ionizing as follows:

$$A_xB_y = xA^{y+} + yB^{x-}$$

is

$$K_{sp} = [A^{y+}]^x[B^{x-}]^y$$

Calculation of K_{sp} from Solubility

The numerical value of a solubility product constant can be readily calculated from the solubility of the compound. The calculation can be reversed, of course, and the solubility calculated from the K_{sp}. If the ions of the precipitate undergo reactions such as hydrolysis or complex formation, the calculations are more complicated. Such cases will be considered in a later section. Typical computations are illustrated in the following examples:

Example 1. The solubility of barium sulfate (M.W. = 233) at 25°C is 0.00023 g per 100 ml of solution. Calculate the value of K_{sp}.

The solubility is 0.23 mg/100 ml or 0.0023 mg/ml. The molarity is

$$\frac{0.0023 \text{ mg/ml}}{233 \text{ mg/mmol}} = 1.0 \times 10^{-5} \text{ mmol/ml}$$

Since each mmol of $BaSO_4$ yields 1 mmol of Ba^{2+} and 1 mmol of $SO_4{}^{2-}$,

$$[Ba^{2+}] = [SO_4{}^{2-}] = 1.0 \times 10^{-5}$$

$$K_{sp} = [Ba^{2+}][SO_4{}^{2-}] = [1.0 \times 10^{-5}]^2 = 1.0 \times 10^{-10}$$

Example 2. The solubility of silver chromate (M.W. = 332) is 0.0279 g per 1 at 25°. Calculate K_{sp}, neglecting hydrolysis of the chromate ion.

The molarity of Ag_2CrO_4 is

$$\frac{0.0279 \text{ g/l}}{332 \text{ g/mol}} = 8.4 \times 10^{-5} \text{ mol/l}$$

Since each Ag_2CrO_4 yields two Ag^+ ions and one $CrO_4{}^{2-}$ ion,

$$[Ag^+] = 2 \times 8.4 \times 10^{-5} = 1.7 \times 10^{-4}$$

$$[CrO_4{}^{2-}] = 8.4 \times 10^{-5}$$

Therefore

$$K_{sp} = [Ag^+]^2[CrO_4{}^{2-}] = [1.7 \times 10^{-4}]^2[8.4 \times 10^{-5}]$$

$$K_{sp} = 2.4 \times 10^{-12}$$

It should be noted that one can judge on inspection the relative molar solubilities of two compounds from their solubility product constants only if they are the same type of compounds, that is, both the type AB or AB_2, etc. The solubility product constants of both AgCl and $BaSO_4$ are about 1×10^{-10}, and hence both are soluble to the extent of 1×10^{-5} mole per l. However, a compound of the type AB_2 with the same molar solubility would have a small solubility product constant, 4×10^{-15}.

PRECIPITATION TITRATIONS

Titrations involving precipitation reactions are not nearly so numerous in volumetric analysis as those involving redox or acid-base reactions. In fact, in a beginning course examples of such titrations are usually limited to those involving precipitation of silver ion with anions such as the halogens and thiocyanate. One of the reasons for the limited use of such reactions is the lack of suitable indicators. In some cases, particularly in the titration of dilute solutions, the rate of reaction is too slow for convenience of titration. As the equivalence point is approached and the titrant is added slowly, a high degree of supersaturation does not exist and the precipitation may be very slow. Another difficulty is that the composition of the precipitate is frequently not known because of coprecipitation effects. Although the latter can be minimized or partially corrected for by processes such as aging the precipitate, this is not possible in a direct titration involving the formation of a precipitate.

We shall limit our discussion here to precipitation titrations involving silver salts with particular emphasis on the indicators which have been successfully employed in such titrations.

Titration Curves

Titration curves for precipitation reactions can be constructed and are entirely analogous to those for acid-base and complex titrations. The following example illustrates the calculations involved, using the titration of chloride ion with silver ion.

Example. 50.0 ml of 0.100-M NaCl solution are titrated with 0.100-M AgNO$_3$. Calculate the chloride ion concentration at intervals during the titration and plot pCl vs ml of AgNO$_3$. pCl $= -\log[\text{Cl}^-]$, and K_{sp} of AgCl $= 1 \times 10^{-10}$.

(a) *Start of titration.* Since

$$[\text{Cl}^-] = 0.100 \text{ mmol/ml}$$

$$p\text{Cl} = 1.00$$

(b) *After addition of 10.0 ml AgNO$_3$.* Since the reaction goes well to completion,

$$[\text{Cl}^-] = \frac{[(50.0 \times 0.100) - (10.0 \times 0.100)] \text{ mmol}}{(50.0 + 10.0) \text{ ml}}$$

$$[\text{Cl}^-] = 0.067 \text{ mmol/ml}$$

$$p\text{Cl} = 1.17$$

(c) *After addition of 49.9 ml AgNO$_3$.*

$$[\text{Cl}^-] = \frac{[(50.0 \times 0.100) - (49.9 \times 0.100)] \text{ mmol}}{(50.0 + 49.9) \text{ ml}}$$

$$[\text{Cl}^-] = 1.00 \times 10^{-4} \text{ mmol/ml}$$

$$p\text{Cl} = 4.00$$

In these calculations we have disregarded the contribution of chloride ions to the solution by the solubility of the precipitate. This approximation is valid except within one or two drops of the equivalence point.

(d) *Equivalence point.* This point is reached when 50.0 ml of AgNO$_3$ have been added. There is neither excess chloride nor silver ion, and the concentration of each is given by the square root of K_{sp}.

$$[\text{Ag}^+] = [\text{Cl}^-]$$

$$[\text{Cl}^-]^2 = 1.0 \times 10^{-10}$$

$$[\text{Cl}^-] = 1.0 \times 10^{-5}$$

$$p\text{Cl} = 5.00$$

(e) *After addition of 60.0 ml of AgNO$_3$.* The concentration of excess silver ion is

$$[\text{Ag}^+] = \frac{[(60.0 \times 0.100) - (50.0 \times 0.100)] \text{ mmol}}{(50.0 + 60.0) \text{ ml}}$$

$$[\text{Ag}^+] = 9.1 \times 10^{-3}$$

$$p\text{Ag} = 2.04$$

Since

$$pCl + pAg = 10.00$$

$$pCl = 7.96$$

The data for this titration are given in Table 7.1 and the titration curve is plotted in Fig. 7.1. The curves for the titration of iodide and of bromide ions with silver are also plotted in this figure. The break in the curve at the equivalence point is greatest for the titration of iodide, since silver iodide is the least soluble of the three salts. Note that the value of K_t for the titration reaction

$$Ag^+ + X^- \rightleftharpoons AgX(s)$$

TABLE 7.1   TITRATION OF 50 ml OF 0.10-M NaCl WITH 0.10-M AgNO$_3$

ml AgNO$_3$	[Cl$^-$]	%Cl$^-$ pptd.	pCl
0.0	0.10	0.0	1.00
10.0	0.067	20.0	1.17
20.0	0.043	40.0	1.37
30.0	0.025	60.0	1.60
40.0	0.011	80.0	1.96
49.0	0.0010	98.0	3.00
49.9	1.0×10^{-4}	99.8	4.00
50.0	1.0×10^{-5}	100	5.00
50.1	1.0×10^{-6}	100	6.00
51.0	1.0×10^{-7}	100	7.00
60.0	1.1×10^{-8}	100	7.96

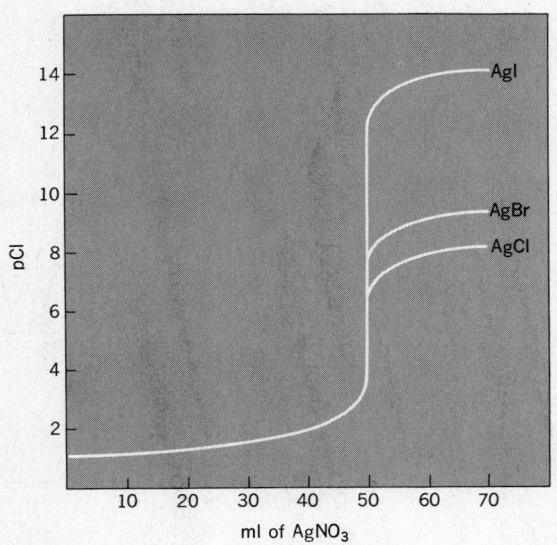

FIGURE 7.1   Titration curves of NaCl, NaBr, and NaI. 50 ml of 0.1-M salt titrated with 0.1-M AgNO$_3$.

is the reciprocal of K_{sp}. For the three salts shown in Fig. 7.1 the values of K_t are: AgCl, 1×10^{10}; AgBr, 2×10^{12}; AgI, 1×10^{16}.

The magnitude of K_t required for a feasible precipitation titration can be calculated as was done previously for acid-base (page 93) and complex titrations (page 143). The following example illustrates this.

Example. 50 ml of 0.10-M NaX is titrated with 50 ml of 0.10-M AgNO$_3$. Calculate the value of K_t and that of K_{sp} for AgX so that when 49.95 ml of titrant has been added essentially all of X$^-$ has reacted, and the pX changes by 2.00 units on the addition of two more drops (0.10 ml) of titrant. NaX is a completely dissociated salt, and the titration reaction is

$$Ag^+ + X^- \rightleftharpoons AgX(s) \qquad K_t = 1/K_{sp}$$

One drop before the equivalence point, 4.995 mmol of Ag$^+$ has been added. We started with $50 \times 0.10 = 5.0$ mmol of X$^-$. Hence 0.0050 mmol remains and

$$[X^-] = \frac{0.0050 \text{ mmol}}{99.95 \text{ ml}} \cong 5 \times 10^{-5}\text{-}M$$

$$pX = 4.30$$

If $\Delta pX = 2.00$, then $pX = 6.30$ and $[X^-] = 5 \times 10^{-7}\text{-}M$ when the volume of titrant is 50.05 ml. Since

$$[Ag^+] = \frac{0.05 \times 0.10}{100.05} \cong 5 \times 10^{-5}$$

$$K_t = \frac{1}{(5 \times 10^{-5})(5 \times 10^{-7})}$$

$$K_t = 4 \times 10^{10} \quad \text{and} \quad K_{sp} = 2.5 \times 10^{-11}$$

The student should confirm that for $\Delta pX = 1.00$, K_t should be 4×10^9.

INDICATORS FOR PRECIPITATION TITRATIONS INVOLVING SILVER

Formation of a Colored Precipitate:
The Mohr Method

Just as an acid-base system can be used as an indicator for an acid-base titration, the formation of another precipitate can be used to indicate the completion of a precipitation titration. The best-known example of such a case is the so-called *Mohr* titration of chloride with silver ion, in which chromate ion is used as the indicator. The first permanent appearance of the reddish silver chromate precipitate is taken as the end point of the titration.

It is necessary, of course, that the precipitation of the indicator occur at or near the equivalence point of the titration. Silver chromate is more soluble (about 8.4×10^{-5} moles/liter) than silver chloride (about 1×10^{-5} mole/liter). If silver ions are added to a solution containing a large concentration of chloride ions and a small concentration of chromate ions, silver chloride will first precipitate; silver chromate will not form until the silver ion concentration increases to a large enough value to exceed the K_{sp} of silver chromate. One can readily calculate the concentration of chromate that will lead to precipitation of silver chromate at the equivalence point where $p\text{Ag} = p\text{Cl} = 5.00$. Since the K_{sp} of Ag_2CrO_4 is 2×10^{-12}, and $[Ag^+] = 1 \times 10^{-5}$ at the equivalence point, then

$$[Ag^+]^2[CrO_4{}^{2-}] = 2 \times 10^{-12}$$

$$[CrO_4{}^{2-}] = \frac{2 \times 10^{-12}}{(1 \times 10^{-5})^2} = 0.02\text{-}M$$

Such a high concentration cannot be used in practice, however, since the yellow color of chromate ion makes it difficult to observe the formation of the colored precipitate. Normally a concentration of 0.005 to 0.01-M chromate is employed. The error caused by using such a concentration is quite small. It can be corrected by running an indicator blank or by standardizing the silver nitrate against a pure chloride salt under conditions identical to those used in the analysis.

The Mohr titration is limited to solutions with pH values from about 6 to 10. In more alkaline solutions silver oxide precipitates. In acid solutions the chromate concentration is greatly decreased, since $HCrO_4{}^-$ is only slightly ionized. Furthermore, hydrogen chromate is in equilibrium with dichromate:

$$2\,H^+ + 2\,CrO_4{}^{2-} \rightleftharpoons 2\,HCrO_4{}^- \rightleftharpoons Cr_2O_7{}^{2-} + H_2O$$

A decrease in chromate ion concentration makes it necessary to add a large excess of silver ions to bring about precipitation of silver chromate, and thus leads to large errors. Dichromates are, in general, fairly soluble.

The Mohr method can also be applied to the titration of bromide ion with silver, and also cyanide ion in slightly alkaline solutions. Adsorption effects (page 193) make the titration of iodide and thiocyanate ions not feasible. Silver cannot be titrated directly with chloride, using chromate indicator. The silver chromate precipitate, present initially, redissolves only slowly near the equivalence point. However, one can add excess standard chloride solution, and then back-titrate, using the chromate indicator.

Formation of a Colored Complex:
The Volhard Method

The Volhard method is based on the precipitation of silver thiocyanate in nitric acid solution, with ferric ion employed to detect excess thiocyanate ion:

$$Ag^+ + SCN^- \rightleftharpoons AgSCN$$

$$Fe^{3+} + SCN^- \rightleftharpoons FeSCN^{2+} \text{ (red)}$$

The method can be used for the direct titration of silver with standard thiocyanate solution, or for the indirect titration of chloride ion. In the latter case, an excess of standard silver nitrate is added, and the excess is titrated with standard thiocyanate. Other anions, such as bromide and iodide, can be determined by the same procedure. Anions of weak acids, such as oxalate, carbonate, and arsenate, the silver salts of which are soluble in acid, can be determined by precipitation at higher pH and filtration of silver salt. The precipitate is then dissolved in nitric acid and the silver titrated directly with thiocyanate.

The Volhard method is widely used for silver and chloride because of the fact that the titration can be done in acid solution. In fact, it is desirable to employ an acid medium to prevent hydrolysis of the ferric ion indicator. Other common methods for silver and chloride require a nearly neutral solution for successful titration. Many cations precipitate under such conditions, and hence interfere in these methods. Mercury is the only common cation that interferes with the Volhard method. In fact, mercury can be determined by titration with thiocyanate, since mercuric thiocyanate is a very slightly dissociated compound. High concentrations of colored cations, such as cobaltous, nickelous, and cupric, cause difficulty in observation of the end point. Nitrous acid interferes in the titration, since it reacts with thiocyanate to produce a transitory red color.

In the direct titration of silver with thiocyanate there are two sources of error, both of which are minor. In the first place, the silver thiocyanate precipitate adsorbs silver ions on its surface (page 193), thereby causing the end point to occur prematurely. This difficulty can be largely overcome by vigorous stirring of the mixture near the end point. Secondly, the color change which marks the end point occurs at a concentration of thiocyanate slightly in excess of the concentration of the equivalence point. The magnitude of this error is of the order of a few hundredths of a percent.

In the indirect method a more serious error is encountered if the silver salt of the anion being determined is more soluble than silver thiocyanate. Silver chloride, for example, is more soluble than silver thiocyanate, and the chloride tends to redissolve according to the reaction

$$AgCl + SCN^- \rightleftharpoons AgSCN + Cl^-$$

The equilibrium constant of this reaction is given by the ratio of the solubility product constant of silver chloride to that of silver thiocyanate. Since the former constant is larger than the latter, the foregoing reaction has a strong tendency to proceed from left to right. Thus thiocyanate can be consumed not only by excess silver ions, but also by the silver chloride precipitate itself. If this occurs, low results will be obtained in the chloride analysis. This reaction can be prevented, however, by filtering off the silver chloride or adding nitrobenzene before titration with thiocyanate.[1] The nitrobenzene apparently forms an oily coating on the silver chloride surface, preventing the reaction with thiocyanate. Another method of decreasing this error is to use a sufficiently high concentration of ferric ion (about 0.2-M) so that the end point color is reached at a lower concentration of thiocyanate.[2] A smaller amount of silver chloride is then redissolved and there is still a sufficiently high concentration of the red $FeSCN^{2+}$ complex to be visible. Swift et al.[2] found that the end-point error was reduced to 0.1 % by this procedure.

In the determination of bromide and iodide by the indirect Volhard method, the reaction with thiocyanate does not cause any trouble, because silver bromide has about the same solubility as silver thiocyanate and silver iodide is considerably less soluble.

Adsorption Indicators

When a colored organic compound is adsorbed on the surface of a precipitate, modification of the organic structure may occur, and the color may be greatly changed and may become more intense. This phenomenon can be used to detect the end point of precipitation titrations of silver salts. The organic compounds thus employed are referred to as "adsorption indicators."

The mechanism by which such indicators work is different from any we have discussed so far. Fajans,[3] who discovered the fact that fluorescein and some substituted fluoresceins could serve as indicators for silver titrations, explained the process as follows. When silver nitrate is added to a solution of sodium chloride, the finely divided particles of silver chloride tend to hold to their surface (adsorb) some of the excess chloride ions in the solution. These chloride ions are said to form the primarily adsorbed layer and thus cause the colloidal particles of silver chloride to be negatively charged. These negative particles then tend to attract positive ions from the solution to form a more loosely held secondary adsorption layer:

$$(AgCl) \cdot Cl^- \quad \vdots \quad M^+$$

Primary   Secondary   Excess chloride
layer   layer

If one continues to add silver nitrate until silver ions are in excess, these ions will displace chloride ions in the primary layer.[4] The particles then

[1] J. R. Caldwell and H. V. Moyer, *Ind. Eng. Chem.*, *Anal. Ed.*, **7**, 38 (1935).

[2] E. H. Swift, G. M. Arcand, R. Lutwack, and D. J. Meier, *Anal. Chem.*, **22**, 306 (1950).

[3] K. Fajans and O. Hassel, *Z. Elektrochem.*, **29**, 495 (1923); see also I. M. Kolthoff, *Chem. Rev.*, **16**, 87 (1935), and K. Fajans, Chapter 7 of *Newer Methods of Volumetric Analysis*, W. Bottger, ed., D. Van Nostrand and Co., New York, 1938.

[4] A precipitate tends to adsorb most readily those ions that form an insoluble compound with one of the ions in the lattice. Thus silver or chloride ions will be more readily adsorbed by a silver chloride precipitate than will, say, sodium or nitrate ions.

become positively charged, and anions in the solution are attracted to form the secondary layer:

$$(AgCl) \cdot Ag^+ \; \vdots \quad X^-$$

| Primary layer | | Secondary layer | Excess silver |

Fluorescein is a weak organic acid, which we may represent as HFl. When fluorescein is added to the titration flask, the anion, Fl^-, is not adsorbed by colloidal silver chloride as long as chloride ions are in excess. However, when silver ions are in excess the Fl^- ions can be attracted to the surface of the positively charged particles, as

$$(AgCl) \cdot Ag^+ \vdots Fl^-$$

The resulting aggregate is pink, and the color is sufficiently intense to serve as a visual indicator.

A number of factors must be considered in choosing a proper adsorption indicator for a precipitation titration. These are summarized below.

1. Since the surface of the precipitate is the "active agent" in the operation of the indicator, the precipitate should not be allowed to coagulate into large particles and settle to the bottom of the titration flask. Coagulation of a silver chloride precipitate will occur at the equivalence point, where neither chloride nor silver ions are in excess, unless a substance such as dextrin is present. Dextrin acts as a "protective colloid," keeping the precipitate highly dispersed. In the presence of dextrin the color change is reversible, and if the end point is overrun, one can back-titrate with a standard chloride solution.

2. The degree to which different indicator ions are adsorbed varies considerably, and an indicator must be chosen that is not too strongly or too weakly adsorbed. Ideally, adsorption should start just before the equivalence point is reached and increase rapidly at the equivalence point. Some indicators are so strongly adsorbed that they will actually displace the primarily adsorbed ion well before the equivalence point is reached. Eosin, for example, cannot be used for titration of chloride with silver because of this effect. On the other hand, eosin can be used for the titration of iodide or bromide with silver, since these two anions are so strongly adsorbed that eosin does not displace them. If the indicator is too weakly adsorbed, the end point will occur, of course, after the equivalence point is passed.

3. Adsorption indicators are weak acids or bases, and thus the pH of the titration medium is of importance. The dissociation constant of fluorescein, for example, is about 10^{-7}. In solutions more acidic than $pH\,7$, the concentration of the Fl^- anion is so small that no color change is observed. Fluorescein can be used only in the pH range of about 7 to 10. On the other hand, derivatives of fluorescein that are stronger acids can be used in solutions of lower pH. For example, dichlorofluorescein has dissociation constant of about 10^{-4} and can be used in the pH range 4 to 10. The anion of dichloro-fluorescein also is more strongly adsorbed than the anion of fluorescein. Eosin (tetrabromofluorescein) is a still stronger acid and can be used in bromide or iodide titrations even at a pH of 2.

4. It is preferable that the indicator ion be of opposite charge to the ion added as the titrant. Adsorption of the indicator will then not occur until excess titrant is present. For the titration of silver with chloride, methyl violet, the chloride salt of an organic base, can be employed. The cation is not adsorbed until excess chloride ions are present and the colloid is nega-tively charged. It is possible to use dichlorofluorescein in this case, but the indicator should not be added until just before the equivalence point.

A list of some adsorption indicators is given in Table 7.2.

TABLE 7.2 SOME ADSORPTION INDICATORS

Indicator	Ion titrated	Titrant	Conditions
Dichlorofluorescein	Cl^-	Ag^+	pH 4
Fluorescein	Cl^-	Ag^+	pH 7–8
Eosin	Br^-, I^-, SCN^-	Ag^+	pH 2
Thorin	SO_4^{2-}	Ba^{2+}	pH 1.5–3.5
Bromcresol green	SCN^-	Ag^+	pH 4–5
Methyl violet	Ag^+	Cl^-	Acid solution
Rhodamine 6 G	Ag^+	Br^-	Sharp in presence of HNO_3 up to 0.3-M
Orthochrome T	Pb^{2+}	CrO_4^{2-}	Neutral 0.02-M solution
Bromphenol blue	Hg_2^{2+}	Cl^-	0.1-M solution

SEPARATIONS BY PRECIPITATION

Precipitation is a very valuable method for separating a sample into its component parts, and until recent years it was the analyst's most widely used separation technique. The process involved is one in which the substance being separated is used to construct a new phase—the solid precipitate. The discussion of this section will be devoted to a consideration of the equilibrium between the solid and its saturated solution. We shall consider the factors which affect solubility and hence the completeness of the separation that can be effected.

FACTORS AFFECTING SOLUBILITY

The important factors that affect the solubility of crystalline solids are temperature, nature of the solvent, and the presence of other ions in the solution. In the latter category are included ions that may be common or not common to ions in the solid, and ions that form slightly ionized molecules or complex ions with ions of the solid.

Temperature

Most of the inorganic salts in which we are interested increase in solubility as the temperature is increased. It is usually advantageous to carry out the operations of precipitation, filtration, and washing with hot solutions. Particles of large size may result, filtration is faster, and impurities are dissolved more readily. Therefore directions frequently call for employing hot solutions in those cases where the solubility of the precipitate is still negligible at the higher temperature. However, in the case of a fairly soluble compound, such as magnesium ammonium phosphate, the solution must be cooled in ice water before filtration. Quite an appreciable amount of this compound would be lost if the solution were filtered while hot.

The student may recall that lead chloride is separated from silver and mercurous chlorides in the qualitative analysis scheme by treatment with hot water. The lead salt dissolves at elevated temperature leaving the other two salts in the precipitate.

Solvent

Most inorganic salts are more soluble in water than in organic solvents. Water has a large dipole moment and is attracted to both cations and anions to form hydrated ions. We have already noted, for example, that the hydrogen ion in water is completely hydrated, forming the H_3O^+ ion. All ions are undoubtedly hydrated to some extent in water solutions, and the energy released by interaction of the ions and the solvent helps overcome the attractive forces tending to hold the ions in the solid lattice. The ions in a crystal do not have so large an attraction for organic solvents, and hence the solubilities are usually smaller than in water. The analyst can frequently utilize the decreased solubility in organic solvents to separate two substances which are quite soluble in water. For example, a dried mixture of calcium and strontium nitrates can be separated by treatment with a mixture of alcohol and ether. Calcium nitrate dissolves, leaving strontium nitrate. Potassium can be separated from sodium by precipitating K_2PtCl_6 from an alcohol-water mixed solvent.

Common-Ion Effect

A precipitate is generally more soluble in pure water than in a solution which contains one of the ions of the precipitate. In a solution of silver chloride, for example, the product of the concentrations of silver and chloride ions cannot exceed the value of the solubility product constant, 1×10^{-10}. In pure water, each ion has a concentration of 1×10^{-5}-M, but if sufficient silver nitrate is added to make the silver ion concentration 1×10^{-4}-M, the chloride ion concentration must decrease to a value of 1×10^{-6}-M. The reaction

$$Ag^+ + Cl^- \rightleftharpoons AgCl\downarrow$$

is forced to the right by excess silver ion, resulting in the precipitation of additional salt, and decreasing the quantity of chloride remaining in the solution.

The importance of the common-ion effect in bringing about complete precipitation in quantitative analyses is readily apparent. In carrying out precipitations, the analyst always adds some excess of the precipitating agent to insure complete precipitation. In washing a precipitate where solubility losses may be appreciable, a common ion may be used in the wash liquid to diminish solubility. The ion should be that of the precipitating agent, of course, not the ion sought. Likewise, the salt used in the wash water should be such that any excess is removed by volatilization when the precipitate is finally heated to constant weight.

In the presence of a large excess of common ion, the solubility of a precipitate may be considerably greater than the value predicted by the solubility product constant. This effect will be discussed later. In general, directions call for adding about 10 % excess precipitating agent.

The effect of a common ion on the solubility of a precipitate is illustrated in the following calculations.

Example. Calculate the molar solubility of CaF_2 in (a) water, (b) 0.010-M $CaCl_2$, (c) 0.010-M NaF solution, given the K_{sp} as 4×10^{-11} and neglecting hydrolysis of the fluoride ion.

(a) The equilibrium is

$$CaF_2(s) \rightleftharpoons Ca^{2+} + 2\,F^-$$

Let s = molar solubility of CaF_2. The mass balances are

$$[Ca^{2+}] = s$$

$$[F^-] = 2s$$

Since

$$[Ca^{2+}][F^-]^2 = K_{sp}$$

$$(s)(2s)^2 = 4 \times 10^{-11}$$

and

$$s = 2.1 \times 10^{-4}\,\text{mol/l}$$

(b) In 0.010-M $CaCl_2$ the mass balances are

$$[Ca^{2+}] = 0.010 + s$$

$$[F^-] = 2s$$

Hence,

$$(0.01 + s)(2s)^2 = 4 \times 10^{-11}$$

Since $s \ll 0.01$, this becomes

$$4s^2 = 4 \times 10^{-9}$$

$$s = 3.2 \times 10^{-5} \, \text{mol/l}$$

(c) The mass balances are

$$[Ca^{2+}] = s$$

$$[F^-] = 0.01 + 2s$$

Hence,

$$(s)(0.01 + 2s)^2 = 4 \times 10^{-11}$$

Since $2s \ll 0.01$, this becomes

$$s = 4 \times 10^{-7} \, \text{mol/l}$$

Note the extensive reduction in solubility brought about by the common ion. It should also be noted that excess F^- has a greater effect than excess Ca^{2+}.

Diverse-Ion Effect

It has been found that many precipitates show an increased solubility when salts that contain no ions in common with the precipitate are present in the solution. The effect is referred to by various names, such as *diverse-ion*, *neutral salt*, or *activity* effect. The data in Table 7.3 illustrate the magnitude of this increased solubility for silver chloride and barium sulfate in potassium nitrate solutions. It is seen that in 0.010-M KNO_3 the solubility of AgCl is increased from the value in water by about 12 %, and that of $BaSO_4$ by about 70 %.

It was pointed out earlier (page 79) that we were justified in substituting molarity for activity only in very dilute solutions, where activity coefficients are approximately unity. In more concentrated solutions of electrolytes, activity coefficients decrease rapidly because of greater attraction between oppositely charged ions. The effectiveness of the ions in maintaining equilibrium conditions is thus decreased and additional precipitate must dissolve

TABLE 7.3 SOLUBILITY OF AgCl AND BaSO₄ IN KNO₃ SOLUTIONS†

Molarity KNO₃	Molarity AgCl × 10⁵	Molarity BaSO₄ × 10⁵
0.000	1.00	1.00
0.001	1.04	1.21
0.005	1.08	1.48
0.010	1.12	1.70

† From data of S. Popoff and E. W. Neuman, *J. Phys. Chem.*, **34**, 1853 (1930); and E. W. Neuman, *J. Am. Chem. Soc.*, **55**, 879 (1933). The K_{sp} of each salt was taken as 1×10^{-10}.

to restore this activity. The solubility product expression for AgCl is

$$a_{Ag^+} \times a_{Cl^-} = K_{sp}^\circ$$

where K_{sp}° is the equilibrium constant in terms of activities. In terms of concentrations this becomes

$$\gamma_{Ag^+}[Ag^+] \times \gamma_{Cl^-}[Cl^-] = K_{sp}^\circ$$

or

$$[Ag^+][Cl^-] = \frac{K_{sp}^\circ}{\gamma_{Ag^+}\gamma_{Cl^-}} = K_{sp}$$

It is apparent that the smaller the activity coefficients of the two ions, the larger is the product of the molar concentrations of the ions (K_{sp}). This increase in solubility is greater for BaSO₄ than for AgCl, since activity coefficients of bivalent ions decrease more rapidly than those of univalent ions, as the electrolyte concentration is increased. In very dilute solutions the activity coefficients approach unity, and K_{sp} is approximately the same as K_{sp}°.

The following example illustrates a calculation that the chemist can make in estimating activity effects on solubilities.

Example. Calculate the K_{sp} of BaSO₄ in 0.010-M KNO₃ solution and compare with the experimental value from Table 7.3. Use the Debye-Hückel limiting law to estimate activity coefficients.[5]

The Debye-Hückel expression for the activity coefficient of an ion in water at 25°C is

$$-\log \gamma_i = 0.5Z_i^2\sqrt{\mu}$$

where μ, the ionic strength, is given by

$$\mu = \tfrac{1}{2}\sum C_i Z_i^2$$

[5] P. Debye and E. Hückel, *Physik. Z.*, **24**, 185 (1923).

Z_i is the charge on the ion and C_i is the concentration. The ionic strength in this case can be calculated on the basis of the KNO_3 alone, since the concentrations of Ba^{2+} and SO_4^{2-} are so small. Hence

$$\mu = \tfrac{1}{2}[0.01(1)^2 + 0.01(-1)^2] = 0.01$$

The K_{sp} expression above in logarithmic form is

$$\log K_{sp} = \log K_{sp}^\circ - \log \gamma_{Ba^{2+}} - \log \gamma_{SO_4^{2-}}$$

or

$$\log K_{sp} = \log K_{sp}^\circ + 0.5(2)^2\sqrt{0.01} + 0.5(-2)^2\sqrt{0.01}$$

$$\log K_{sp} = -10.0 + 4\sqrt{0.01} = -10.0 + 0.4 = -9.6$$

and

$$K_{sp} = 2.5 \times 10^{-10}$$

From Table 7.3, $K_{sp} = 2.9 \times 10^{-10}$.

The diverse-ion effect does not cause serious problems for the analyst since conditions are normally chosen so as to make the loss from solubility negligibly small. It is rarely necessary to make a precipitation from a salt solution of very high concentration, and in such a case an estimate of the increased solubility can be made as illustrated above. Errors from other sources are normally more important.

Effect of pH

The solubility of the salt of a weak acid depends upon the pH of the solution. Some of the more important examples of such salts in analytical chemistry are oxalates, sulfides, hydroxides, carbonates, and phosphates. Hydrogen ion combines with the anion of the salt to form the weak acid, thereby enhancing the solubility of the salt. We shall limit our discussion in this section to solutions which are fairly acidic, so that the hydrogen ion concentration is not changed appreciably as the salt dissolved.

Let us consider first the simplest case, that of a salt MA of the weak acid HA. The equilibria to be considered are

$$MA(s) \rightleftharpoons M^+ + A^-$$

$$HA + H_2O \rightleftharpoons H_3O^+ + A^-$$

As we did previously (page 126), let us designate c_a as the total (analytical) concentration of all species related to the acid HA.

$$c_a = [A^-] + [HA]$$

$$c_a = [A^-]\left\{\frac{[H_3O^+] + K_a}{K_a}\right\}$$

The fraction in the A^- form is

$$\frac{[A^-]}{c_a} = \frac{K_a}{[H_3O^+] + K_a} = \alpha_1$$

Hence

$$[A^-] = \alpha_1 c_a$$

The latter expression can be substituted in the K_{sp} giving

$$K_{sp} = [M^+][A^-] = [M^+]\alpha_1 c_a$$

or

$$\frac{K_{sp}}{\alpha_1} = K_{\text{eff}} = [M^+]c_a$$

We have designated K_{eff} as the effective solubility product constant, in agreement with the terminology used on page 141 for the effective stability constant of complexes. The value of K_{eff} varies with pH because of the pH-dependence of α_1.

The student should be able to show that, for a salt MA_2, the relation is

$$K_{\text{eff}} = \frac{K_{sp}}{\alpha_1^2} = [M^{2+}]c_a^2$$

and that for a diprotic acid, H_2A, the concentration of A^{2-} is given by $\alpha_2 c_a$, where

$$\alpha_2 = \frac{K_{a_1}K_{a_2}}{[H_3O^+]^2 + [H_3O^+]K_{a_1} + K_{a_1}K_{a_2}}$$

$$K_{\text{eff}} = \frac{K_{sp}}{\alpha_2} = [M^{2+}]c_a$$

The following examples illustrate some calculations based on the relations just described.

Example 1. Calculate the molar solubility of CaF_2 in an HCl solution, $pH = 3.00$, given that K_{sp} of $CaF_2 = 4 \times 10^{-11}$, and K_a of HF $= 6 \times 10^{-4}$.

First evaluate α_1:

$$\alpha_1 = \frac{6 \times 10^{-4}}{6 \times 10^{-4} + 1 \times 10^{-3}} = 0.38$$

$$\alpha_1^2 = 0.14$$

Hence

$$K_{eff} = \frac{4 \times 10^{-11}}{0.14} = 2.9 \times 10^{-10}$$

Let s = molar solubility of CaF_2. The mass balances are

$$[Ca^{2+}] = s$$

$$c_F = [HF] + [F^-] = 2s$$

and

$$(s)(2s)^2 = 2.9 \times 10^{-10}$$

$$s = 4.2 \times 10^{-4} \text{ mol/l}$$

Example 2. Calculate the solubility of CaC_2O_4 in an HCl solution of pH 3.00, given $K_{sp} = 2 \times 10^{-9}$, $K_{a_1} = 6.5 \times 10^{-2}$, $K_{a_2} = 6.1 \times 10^{-5}$.

$$\alpha_2 = \frac{6.5 \times 10^{-2} \times 6.1 \times 10^{-5}}{6.5 \times 10^{-2} \times 6.1 \times 10^{-5} + 6.5 \times 10^{-2} \times 10^{-3} + (10^{-3})^2}$$

$$\alpha_2 = 0.057$$

Hence,

$$K_{eff} = \frac{2 \times 10^{-9}}{0.057} = 3.5 \times 10^{-8}$$

The mass balances are

$$[Ca^{2+}] = s$$

$$c_{Ox} = s$$

Then

$$s^2 = 3.5 \times 10^{-8}$$

$$s = 1.9 \times 10^{-4} \text{ mol/l}$$

The separation of metal sulfides, based upon the control of pH, has been used for many years in the qualitative analysis scheme. The metals which form the less soluble sulfides (Group II) are precipitated by H_2S in about 0.10-M HCl. Then the pH is raised to precipitate the metals of Group III. Hydrogen sulfide is a diprotic acid, and the expression for α_2 (above) is applicable. However, since the two acid constants are so small ($K_{a_1} = 1 \times 10^{-7}$, $K_{a_2} = 1 \times 10^{-15}$), the two terms in the denominator containing the acid constants are negligible compared to the square of the hydrogen ion concentration. The expression becomes (approximately)

$$\alpha_2 \cong \frac{K_{a_1}K_{a_2}}{[H_3O^+]^2}$$

Also in strongly acidic solution, the analytical concentration of hydrogen sulfide is approximately

$$c_S = [H_2S] + [HS^-] + [S^{2-}] \cong [H_2S]$$

Hence the sulfide ion concentration, $\alpha_2 c_S$, becomes

$$[S^{2-}] = \frac{[H_2S]K_{a_1}K_{a_2}}{[H_3O^+]^2}$$

Since a saturated solution of H_2S is about 0.10-M, this gives

$$[S^{2-}] = \frac{1 \times 10^{-23}}{[H_3O^+]^2}$$

This is the usual expression employed to show how the sulfide ion concentration can be varied by changing the hydrogen ion concentration. The following example illustrates the separation of two metals by employing this principle.

Example 3. 100 ml of a solution that is 0.10-M in both Cu^{2+} and Mn^{2+} and 0.20-M in H_3O^+ is saturated with H_2S.

(a) Show which metal sulfide precipitates. K_{sp} of CuS is 4×10^{-38}, of MnS 1×10^{-16}.

The sulfide concentration is given by

$$[S^{2-}] = \frac{1 \times 10^{-23}}{(0.20)^2} = 2.5 \times 10^{-22}$$

The K_{sp} of CuS is greatly exceeded but that of MnS is not:

$$(0.10)(2.5 \times 10^{-22}) = 2.5 \times 10^{-23} \gg 4 \times 10^{-38}$$

$$= 2.5 \times 10^{-23} \ll 1 \times 10^{-16}$$

Hence CuS precipitates, but MnS does not.

(b) What must be the hydrogen ion concentration for MnS to start to precipitate? The sulfide ion concentration needed in order for $[Mn^{2+}][S^{2-}]$ to equal the K_{sp} of MnS is

$$(0.10)[S^{2-}] = 1 \times 10^{-16}$$

$$[S^{2-}] = 1 \times 10^{-15}$$

Hence,

$$1 \times 10^{-15} = \frac{1 \times 10^{-23}}{[H_3O^+]^2}$$

$$[H_3O^+] = 1 \times 10^{-4}\text{-}M$$

The following example illustrates the separation of two metal hydroxides by control of pH.

Example 4. Calculate the pH at which the following hydroxides begin to precipitate if the solution is 0.1-M in each cation: $Fe(OH)_3$, $K_{sp} = 1 \times 10^{-36}$; and $Mg(OH)_2$, $K_{sp} = 1 \times 10^{-11}$.

Ferric hydroxide:

$$[Fe^{3+}][OH^-]^3 = 1 \times 10^{-36}$$

$$(0.1)[OH^-]^3 = 1 \times 10^{-36}$$

$$[OH^-]^3 = 1 \times 10^{-35}$$

$$3pOH = 35$$

$$pOH = 11.7$$

$$pH = 2.3$$

Magnesium hydroxide:

$$[Mg^{2+}][OH^-]^2 = 1 \times 10^{-11}$$

$$(0.1)[OH^-]^2 = 1 \times 10^{-11}$$

$$[OH^-]^2 = 1 \times 10^{-10}$$

$$2pOH = 10.0$$

$$pOH = 5.0$$

$$pH = 9.0$$

Thus, if an acidic solution containing these two ions is slowly neutralized with base, ferric hydroxide will precipitate first. This precipitate can be separated by filtration before the pH is sufficiently high to precipitate magnesium hydroxide. In actual practice, however, the ferric hydroxide precipitate is likely to be contaminated by magnesium hydroxide. This arises from the fact that in the region where the two solutions mix, the solubility product constant of magnesium hydroxide may be temporarily exceeded. The magnesium hydroxide may not redissolve as the solution is stirred, and the separation is then not a clean one. Usually a buffer solution of intermediate pH is employed to diminish the local increase in hydroxyl ion concentration. Better still, the pH can be gradually increased by the hydrolysis of a substance such as urea. (See discussion of precipitation from homogeneous solution, page 196.)

Effect of Hydrolysis

In the previous section we limited our discussion to solutions of fairly high acidity, such that the anion of the weak acid did not change the pH appreciably. Let us now consider the case in which the salt of a weak acid is dissolved, not in strong acid, but in water. The problem is more complex than the previous one since the change in hydrogen ion concentration may be of considerable magnitude.

For simplification let us consider that whatever the amount of salt MA which dissolves, the anion is completely hydrolyzed:

$$A^- + H_2O \rightleftharpoons HA + OH^-$$

This is a good approximation if HA is very weak and if MA is not very soluble, i.e., if both K_a and K_{sp} are small. It should be noted that the lower the concentration of A^-, the more complete the hydrolysis reaction.

Let us further consider two extremes, depending upon the magnitude of the K_{sp}:

1. The solubility is so low that the pH of water is not changed appreciably by the hydrolysis.

2. The solubility is sufficiently large so that hydroxyl ion contribution of water can be neglected.

These cases are illustrated in the following example.

Example. Calculate the molar solubilities in water of (a) CuS, $K_{sp} = 4 \times 10^{-38}$, and (b) MnS, $K_{sp} = 1 \times 10^{-16}$. Consider the hydrolysis reaction

$$S^{2-} + H_2O \rightleftharpoons HS^- + OH^-$$

(a) Since the solubility of CuS is so low, we shall neglect the OH^- produced by hydrolysis, taking $[OH^-] = 1 \times 10^{-7}$. Hence

$$\alpha_2 = \frac{1 \times 10^{-22}}{(1 \times 10^{-7})^2 + (1 \times 10^{-7})(1 \times 10^{-7}) + 1 \times 10^{-22}}$$

$$\alpha_2 = 5 \times 10^{-9}$$

$$K_{eff} = \frac{4 \times 10^{-38}}{5 \times 10^{-9}} = 8 \times 10^{-30}$$

Letting s = solubility, the mass balances are

$$[Cu^{2+}] = s$$

$$c_S = s$$

Hence,

$$s^2 = 8 \times 10^{-30}$$

$$s = 3 \times 10^{-15}$$

(b) Since the hydrolysis is complete, we can write the reaction as

$$MnS(s) + H_2O \rightleftharpoons Mn^{2+} + HS^- + OH^-$$

the equilibrium constant for which is given by

$$K = \frac{K_{sp}K_w}{K_{a_2}} = \frac{1 \times 10^{-16} \times 1 \times 10^{-14}}{1 \times 10^{-15}}$$

$$K = 1 \times 10^{-15}$$

Letting s = solubility, then

$$[Mn^{2+}] = s$$

$$[HS^-] = s$$

$$[OH^-] = s$$

Hence,

$$s^3 = 1 \times 10^{-15}$$

$$s = 1 \times 10^{-5}$$

The cation of a salt can undergo hydrolysis just as can the anion, and this will also increase the solubility. Typical hydrolytic reactions of ferric ion are

$$Fe^{3+} + HOH \rightleftharpoons FeOH^{2+} + H^+$$

$$FeOH^{2+} + HOH \rightleftharpoons Fe(OH)_2^+ + H^+$$

Many metals have been found to form ionic species containing more than one metal atom, as, for example

$$2\,Fe^{3+} + 2\,H_2O \rightleftharpoons Fe_2(OH)_2^{4+} + 2\,H^+$$

In the case of aluminum, species such as $Al_6(OH)_{15}^{3+}$ have been postulated to explain certain experimental data.

Because of the complexity of these processes, we shall not consider the topic further here.

Effect of Complexes

The solubility of a slightly soluble salt is also dependent upon the concentration of substances which form complexes with the cation of the salt. The effect of hydrolysis, mentioned above, is an example in which the complexing agent is hydroxyl ion. The complexing agents normally considered under a heading such as this are neutral molecules and anions, both foreign and common to the precipitate.

One of the best-known examples in analytical chemistry is the effect of ammonia on the solubility of the silver halides, especially silver chloride. Silver chloride can be dissolved in ammonia, and this fact is utilized in separating silver from mercury in the first group of the traditional qualitative analysis scheme. Silver ion forms two complexes with ammonia,

$$Ag^+ + NH_3 \rightleftharpoons Ag(NH_3)^+ \qquad K_1 = 2.3 \times 10^3$$

$$Ag(NH_3)^+ + NH_3 \rightleftharpoons Ag(NH_3)_2^+ \qquad K_2 = 6.0 \times 10^3$$

Designating β_2 as the fraction of silver in the uncomplexed form as we did for zinc (page 145):

$$\beta_2 = \frac{1}{1 + K_1[NH_3] + K_1 K_2[NH_3]^2} = \frac{[Ag^+]}{c_{Ag}}$$

where c_{Ag} is the analytical concentration of silver. Since

$$K_{sp} = [Ag^+][Cl^-]$$

$$K_{sp} = \beta_2 c_{Ag}[Cl^-]$$

or

$$\frac{K_{sp}}{\beta_2} = K_{eff} = c_{Ag}[Cl^-]$$

The following example illustrates a calculation of the effect of complexes on the solubility of AgCl.

Example. Calculate the molar solubility of AgCl in 0.010-M NH_3. (This is the final concentration of free NH_3 molecules in the solution.) Given K_{sp} of AgCl $= 1.0 \times 10^{-10}$ and stability constants: $K_1 = 2.3 \times 10^3$, $K_2 = 6.0 \times 10^3$.
Evaluating β_2:

$$\beta_2 = \frac{1}{1 + 2.3 \times 10^3(10^{-2}) + 1.4 \times 10^7(10^{-2})^2}$$

$$\beta_2 = 7.1 \times 10^{-4}$$

$$K_{eff} = \frac{1.0 \times 10^{-10}}{7.1 \times 10^{-4}} = 1.4 \times 10^{-7}$$

Letting $s =$ molar solubility

$$s = c_{Ag} = [Cl^-]$$

Hence

$$s^2 = 1.4 \times 10^{-7}$$

$$s = 3.7 \times 10^{-4} \text{ mol/l}$$

Many precipitates form soluble complexes with the ion of the precipitating agent itself. In such a case, the solubility first decreases because of the common-ion effect, passes through a minimum, and then increases as complex formation becomes appreciable. Silver chloride forms complexes with both silver and chloride ions, such as

$$AgCl + Cl^- \rightleftharpoons AgCl_2^-$$

$$AgCl_2^- + Cl^- \rightleftharpoons AgCl_3^{2-}$$

and

$$AgCl + Ag^+ \rightleftharpoons Ag_2Cl^+$$

In addition, there is a certain amount of undissociated AgCl molecules in solution. Figure 7.2 shows the solubility of AgCl in NaCl and $AgNO_3$ solutions. It is interesting to note that AgCl is actually more soluble in

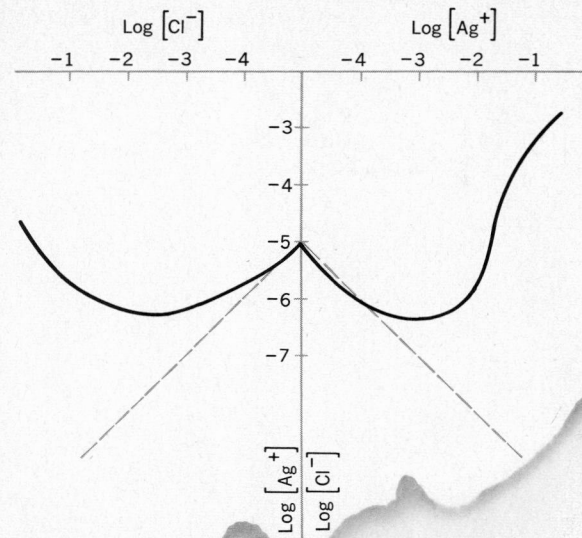

Log [Cl⁻]

Log [Ag⁺]

FIGURE 7.2 Solubility of AgCl in solutions of NaCl and AgNO₃. (From H. F. Walton, *Principles and Methods of Chemical Analysis*, 2nd ed., Prentice-Hall, Inc., Englewood Cliffs, N.J. Used by permission of the author and publisher.)

$0.1\text{-}M$ $AgNO_3$ and in $1\text{-}M$ NaCl than it is in water. It is because of such effects that only a reasonable excess (usually about 10%) of precipitating agent is used in quantitative precipitations.

ORGANIC PRECIPITANTS

Many inorganic ions can be precipitated with certain organic reagents called "organic precipitants." A number of these reagents are useful not only for separations by precipitation, but also by solvent extraction. This topic will be discussed in some detail in Chapter 13.

Most of the organic precipitants, about which our discussion will be centered, combine with cations to form *chelate* rings. We discussed such compounds in Chapter 6, where the emphasis was on reagents which form stable 1:1 complex ions which remain in solution and which could be employed as titrants for metals. Here, we shall be concerned with neutral metal chelate compounds. There are a few examples of organic precipitants which form saltlike precipitates with metal ions and we shall consider them briefly also.

Reagents Forming Chelate Compounds

Generally speaking, most of the better-known organic precipitants which form chelate compounds with cations contain both an acidic and a basic (electron-donating) functional group. The metal, interacting with both of these groups, becomes itself one member of a heterocyclic ring. From the strain theory of organic chemistry it is expected that rings of this type would be mainly five- and six-membered. Hence, the acidic and basic functional groups in the organic molecule must be situated in position with respect to each other which permit the closure of such rings.

8-Hydroxyquinoline (often called 8-quinolinol, or "oxine") forms insoluble compounds with a number of metal ions, aluminum for one. The formation of this compound may be formulated as follows:

Aluminum replaces the acidic hydrogen of the hydroxyl group. At the same time, the previously unshared pair of electrons on the nitrogen is donated to the aluminum, thereby forming a five-membered ring.

A neutral chelate compound of the type described is essentially organic in nature. The metal ion becomes simply one of the members of an organic ring structure, and its usual properties and reactions are no longer readily demonstrable. With the reservation in mind that exceptions can be found, we may state generally that such chelate compounds are insoluble in water but soluble in less polar solvents such as chloroform or carbon tetrachloride. We shall see in Chapter 13 that this differential solubility may be utilized in effecting separations by extraction processes, and in Chapter 11 we shall mention briefly the use of chelates in colorimetric analysis. At this point, we wish to consider only the precipitation of metal ions by these organic reagents.

Let us consider first the advantages offered by organic precipitants.

1. Many of the chelate compounds are very insoluble in water, as noted above, so that metal ions may be quantitatively precipitated.

2. The organic precipitant often has a large molecular weight. Thus a small amount of metal may yield a large weight of precipitate.

3. Some of the organic reagents are fairly selective, yielding precipitates with only a limited number of cations. Certain people once thought that we should ultimately have available an absolutely specific reagent for each cation. Although there is little optimism in this regard today, modern research has demonstrated that a sound knowledge of the chemistry of ions in solution makes such specificity seem less necessary. By controlling such factors as pH and the concentration of masking reagents, the selectivity of an organic reagent can often be greatly enhanced.

4. The precipitates obtained with organic reagents are often coarse and bulky, and hence easily handled.

5. In some cases a metal can be precipitated with an organic reagent, the precipitate collected and dissolved, and the organic molecule titrated, furnishing an indirect volumetric method for the metal.

8-Hydroxyquinoline can be quantitatively brominated with a bromate-bromide mixture. Methods of this type are available for only a few organic precipitants because of the difficulty in finding organic oxidations which satisfy the general requirements for titrations. Since most organic precipitants are weak acids and bases (too weak to be titrated in water), it is sometimes possible to titrate the organic molecule in nonaqueous media.[6]

We must also consider certain disadvantages in the use of organic precipitants.

1. The low solubility of the metal chelate compounds was listed as an advantage. However, the very limited aqueous solubility of most organic reagents themselves is often troublesome. It is generally necessary to add at least a slight excess of the precipitant, and thus the danger of contaminating the precipitate with excess reagent is often a real one. Occasionally, but not always, the excess reagent can be washed out of the precipitate with a solvent such as hot water or alcohol.

2. Many of the organic precipitates do not have good weighing forms, largely because of uncertainty in the drying process. Some of the most attractive of the organic precipitants can be used only for separations, not for determinations, because of this difficulty in drying to a product of definite composition. Some of the metal chelates tend to volatilize at the temperatures required to remove water. In other cases, decomposition of the organic molecule sets in before drying to constant weight has been assured.

3. A minor disadvantage is the fact that the precipitates are not easily wet by water, and hence tend to float on the surface of the solution and to creep up the sides of glass vessels. This trouble can be alleviated by addition of a small amount of wetting agent to the solution before filtration.

A list of a few of the more widely used organic precipitants is given in Table 7.4.

Reagents Forming Saltlike Precipitates

Some organic precipitants form salts rather than chelate complexes with inorganic ions. Oxalic acid is well known in analytical processes for its use in the precipitation of calcium; calcium oxalate is a typical insoluble salt.

[6] C. H. Hill, Han Tai, A. L. Underwood, and R. A. Day, Jr., *Anal. Chem.*, **28**, 1688 (1956).

TABLE 7.4 SOME COMMON ORGANIC PRECIPITANTS

Compound	Chelate with metal of valence n	Comments
$CH_3-C=N-OH$ $CH_3-C=N-OH$ Dimethyl glyoxime		Principally used for determination of nickel.
8-Hydroxyquinoline		Precipitates many elements but can be used for group separations by controlling pH
α-Nitroso-β-naphthol		Principally used for precipitation of cobalt in presence of large amounts of nickel.
Cupferron		Mainly used for separations, such as iron and titanium from aluminum.
α-Benzoin oxime		Good reagent for copper. Also precipitates bismuth and zinc.
Thionalide		Used for precipitation and determination of elements of H_2S group.
Quinaldic acid		Used for determination of cadmium, copper and zinc.

There are a number of such organic compounds which form precipitates with both cations and anions, and we shall describe here a few of the ones most widely used in quantitative analysis.

Sodium Tetraphenyl Boron

This compound has the formula

$$Na^+B(C_6H_5)_4{}^-$$

and has found widest use in precipitating potassium ion. If the precipitation is carried out in a cold solution of about 0.1-M HCl, only $NH_4{}^+$, Hg^{2+}, Rb^+, and Cs^+ interfere. At pH 6.5 in the presence of EDTA, the mercuric ion does not interfere. The precipitate can be dried and weighed, or dissolved in acetone and titrated with perchloric acid.

Benzidine

This compound is used primarily for the precipitation of sulfate ion. Its reaction with sulfuric acid is shown below:

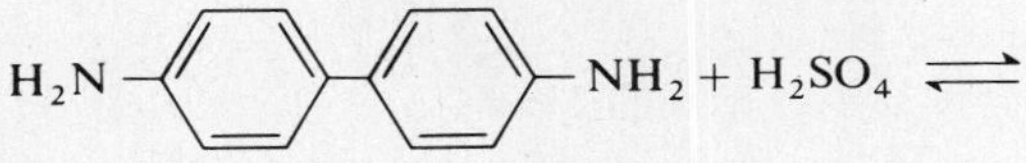

Benzidine

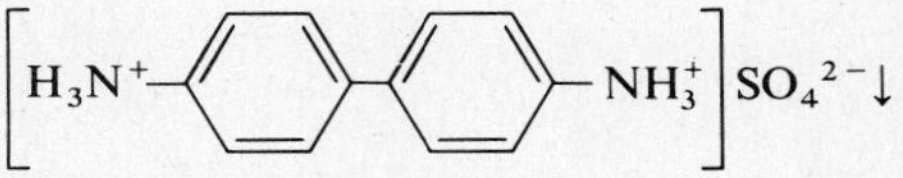

Benzidine sulfate

The precipitate may be weighed as such or suspended in water and titrated with standard base using phenolphthalein indicator. It is the benzidinium ion, an acid, which reacts with base.

Tetraphenylarsonium Chloride

This compound is used to precipitate a number of metals from sodium chloride solutions as the tetraphenylarsonium salt of the complex ion. An example is

$$(C_6H_5)_4As^+Cl^- + TlCl_4{}^- \rightleftharpoons (C_6H_5)_4AsTlCl_4\downarrow + Cl^-$$

Tetraphenylarsonium
chloride

This precipitate with thallium can be weighed as such. Other metals which form precipitates include tin, gold, zinc, platinum, mercury, and cadmium.

Arsonic Acids

Arsonic acids have the structure

$$R-As{\displaystyle{\nearrow \text{OH} \atop \searrow \text{OH}}}=O$$

where R is an organic group, especially phenyl, p-hydroxyphenyl, and n-propyl. These acids precipitate quadrivalent metal ions such as tin, thorium, and zirconium from acid media. The precipitates contain two moles of the acid per mole of quadrivalent cation, and these are generally ignited to the oxides before weighing.

FORMATION AND PROPERTIES OF PRECIPITATES

In our discussion of precipitation thus far we have considered only the equilibrium which exists between an ionic solid and a solution of the ions. We wish now to consider the rate at which solid particles are built from ions into particles sufficiently large to separate from the solution as a precipitate. This study will give us an insight into the factors which influence the nature and size of the solid particles, as well as the purity of the precipitate. We shall learn how the analyst can exercise some control over the size and purity of precipitates. The substance finally weighed in a gravimetric analysis must be pure, or nearly so, for the analysis to be valid. Hence this aspect of precipitation is of great importance in analytical chemistry.

PARTICLE SIZE[7]

Let us consider the process of precipitation of a salt AB, starting with the ions A^+ and B^- in aqueous solution. The ions are of the order of a few Angstrom units (10^{-8} cm) in diameter. When the solubility product is surpassed, A^+ and B^- ions begin clinging together, forming a crystal lattice and growing sufficiently large to be pulled to the bottom of the container by the force of gravity. As a general rule, it is said that a particle (spherical) must have a diameter greater than roughly 10^{-4} cm before it will settle from solution as a precipitate. During the growth process the particle passes through the colloidal range. Particles with diameters of about $10^{-4} - 10^{-7}$ cm are said to be *colloids*. We can represent the precipitation process as

$$\begin{array}{ccccc} \text{Ions in solution} & \rightarrow & \text{colloidal particles} & \rightarrow & \text{precipitate} \\ (10^{-8}\,\text{cm}) & & (10^{-7} - 10^{-4}\,\text{cm}) & & (>10^{-4}\,\text{cm}) \end{array}$$

[7] An excellent summary of this topic at a more advanced level is given by H. A. Laitinen, *Chemical Analysis*, McGraw-Hill Book Company, 1960, p. 117.

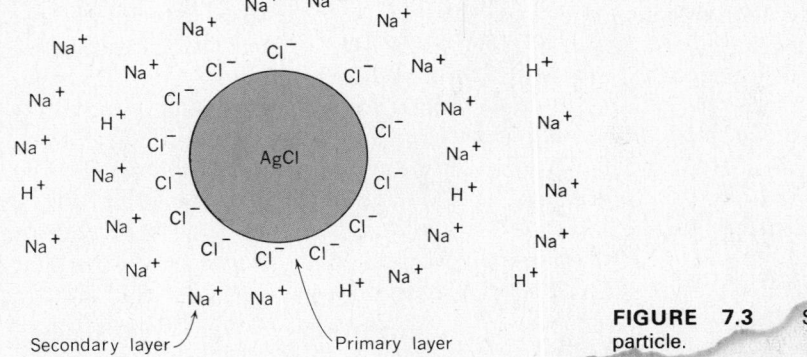

FIGURE 7.3 Schematic picture of colloidal particle.

There are two important properties of colloids which are of importance in the precipitation process.

1. Very small particles may be more soluble than large particles.
2. Colloidal particles are electrically charged.

A small particle has a large surface-to-mass ratio. Ions on the surface tend to *adsorb* other ions from the solution, causing the particles to acquire an electrical charge. For example, suppose a drop of silver nitrate is added to a sodium chloride solution and the solubility product constant of AgCl is surpassed. When the first particles grow to colloidal size, there are a large number of Ag^+ and Cl^- ions on the surfaces. In the solution are Na^+, Cl^-, and NO_3^- ions. The surface Ag^+ ions attract Cl^- and NO_3^- ions from the solution, and the surface Cl^- ions attract Na^+ ions. As a general rule (Paneth-Fajans-Hahn), the ion in the solution which is more strongly adsorbed is the one in common to the lattice, in this case the chloride ion.[8] Thus the surface of the particle acquires a layer of chloride ions, and the particles becomes negatively charged. The process is represented schematically in Fig. 7.3. The chloride ions are said to form the *primary layer*; they in turn attract sodium ions, forming a secondary layer. The secondary layer is held more loosely than is the primary layer.

Since colloidal particles all carry the same charge (negative in this case), they repel one another and resist combining to form larger particles that will settle from the solution. The particles can be made to *coagulate* (or *flocculate*), that is, to cohere and form larger clumps of material that will settle from the solution, by removal of the charge contributed by the primary layer. In the example of silver chloride, which was cited above, coagulation can be achieved by further addition of silver nitrate until equivalent amounts of silver and chloride ions are present. Since silver ions are more strongly

---

[8] If no common ion is present, this rule says that the ion in solution that forms the least soluble compound with one of the lattice ions is the most strongly adsorbed.

attracted to the primary layer of chloride ions than are sodium ions, they replace sodium ions in the secondary layer and then "neutralize" the negative charge contributed by the primary layer. Stripped of their charge, the particles immediately cohere and form clumps of material which are sufficiently large to settle from the solution. Some colloids when coagulated, carry down large quantities of water, giving a jelly-like precipitate. Such materials are termed *gels* or *hydrogels* if water is the solvent. The solid material is also referred to as an *emulsoid*, or said to be *lyophilic*, meaning that it has a strong affinity for the solvent. (If water is the solvent, the term *hydrophilic* is used.) Ferric and aluminum hydroxides and silicic acid are familiar examples of emulsoids. A colloid that has only a small affinity for water is called a *suspensoid*, or said to be *lyophobic*, and when coagulation takes place very little solvent is retained. Silver chloride is this type of material, and the small amount of water that is retained upon coagulation of silver chloride is easily removed by drying above 100°C. The water retained by an emulsoid, such as ferric hydroxide, is much more strongly held, and high temperatures are required for complete dehydration.

Coagulation of colloidal dispersions can be brought about by ions other than those of the precipitate itself. When coagulation of a colloid occurs, the coagulating ions may be dragged down with the precipitate. If these ions are dissolved when a precipitate is washed, the solid particles will go back into a colloidal dispersion and pass through the filter. Such a process of dispersing an insoluble material into a liquid as a colloid is termed *peptization* and must be avoided in quantitative procedures. When peptization may occur, an electrolyte is dissolved in the wash water to replace the ions which are washed away. Dilute nitric acid is added for this reason to the water used to wash a silver chloride precipitate. When the precipitate is dried, any nitric acid retained by the silver chloride is volatilized and does not interfere in the analysis.

The Precipitation Process

When the solubility product constant of a compound is exceeded and precipitation begins, a number of small particles, called nuclei, are formed. Subsequent precipitation can take place on these initially formed particles, with the particles growing in size until large enough to settle from the solution. The particle size distribution of the precipitate is determined by the relative rates of the two processes, the formation of nuclei, called *nucleation*, and the growth of nuclei. It is apparent that, if the rate of nucleation is small compared to the rate of growth of nuclei, fewer particles are finally produced, and these particles are of relatively large particle size. Such a material is more easily filterable and frequently purer than is the case with small particles. Hence the analyst tries to adjust conditions during precipitation so that the rate of nucleation is relatively small in order that the particle size will be large.

According to Ostwald,[9] the relationship between solubility and temperature of a solid dissolved in a liquid can be expressed as in Fig. 7.4. The normal

---

[9] W. Ostwald, *Z. physik. Chem.*, Leipzig, **22**, 289 (1897).

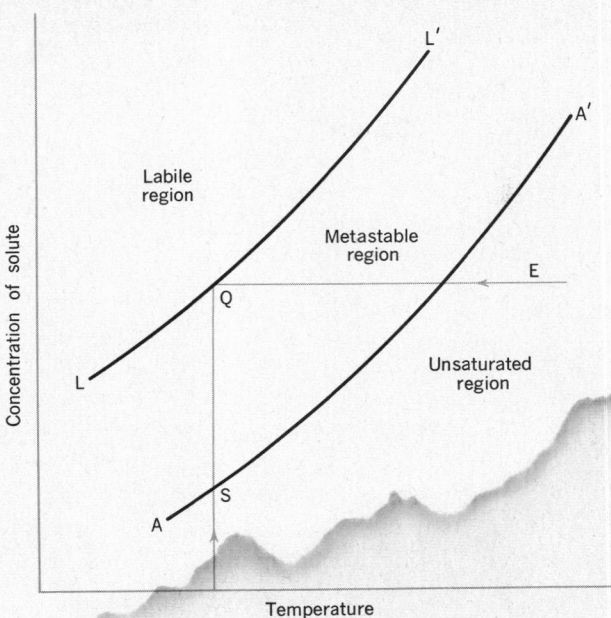

FIGURE 7.4 Solubility curves.

solubility curve is represented by curve AA'. The region between AA' and LL' is a *metastable* one; a solution having conditions of temperature and concentration represented by this region is *supersaturated*. The system is not at equilibrium, and precipitation will occur if a crystal of the solid is added to the solution (seeding). The concentration of solute will decrease to the equilibrium value given by the curve AA'. Ostwald proposed that beyond a certain degree of supersaturation, the solution becomes *labile*, that is, subject to spontaneous formation of nuclei and subsequent precipitation without the necessity of seeding. This limit is represented by the curve LL'.

At a certain temperature, say T_1, precipitation can be described as follows: As the concentration of solute increases, say by mixing two reagents, the solution becomes saturated at point S on curve AA'. If supersaturation occurs, the concentration continues to rise into the metastable region between S and Q. When the concentration reaches Q, nucleation begins spontaneously and precipitation begins. Note that the same point could be reached by lowering the temperature along the line EQ. The degree of supersaturation at point Q is given by $Q - S$; the relative supersaturation is given by the ratio $(Q - S)/S$.

Von Weimarn Ratio

Von Weimarn[10] studied thoroughly the relationship between the size of particles of a precipitate and the rate of precipitation. He proposed that the

---

[10] P. P. von Weimarn, *Chem. Rev.*, **2**, 217 (1926).

initial rate of precipitation is proportional to the relative supersaturation

$$\text{Initial rate of precipitation} = K\frac{Q-S}{S}$$

where Q is the total concentration of substance momentarily produced in solution by mixing the reactants, S is the solubility of the macro crystals, and K is a constant. The term $Q-S$ represents the degree of supersaturation at the moment precipitation begins, and the larger this term, the more rapid is the initial growth of particles, that is, the greater is the number of nuclei formed. The term S in the denominator represents the force resisting precipitation, or causing the precipitate to redissolve. The greater the value of S, the smaller will be the ratio, and the smaller will be the number of nuclei formed. Since the analyst is interested in obtaining large particles, he should try to adjust conditions to make the ratio $(Q-S)/S$ as small as possible.

Actually, the von Weimarn expression is only approximate, but it serves as an excellent guide to the selection of conditions of precipitation. Before discussing these conditions, let us examine the expression more closely. We have already seen that the solubility S may depend upon the size of the particles, and although we have indicated above that the solubility of macro crystals should be employed in the ratio, actually one should consider S as the solubility of the nuclei that are first formed as precipitation begins. In most cases such data are unavailable, but in the case of barium sulfate it has been found that particles as small as 0.04 μ or less are about one thousand times as soluble as large particles.[11] It has also been found that hard substances, of high surface tension, show a greater increase in solubility when the particles are of micro size than do soft substances, of low surface tension. While no data are available for silver chloride, this substance does form soft crystals, and it can be assumed that its solubility is fairly independent of particle size. With these facts in mind, let us consider the precipitation of barium sulfate and of silver chloride. The solubility product constants of the two salts are about the same, yet silver chloride precipitates as a coagulated colloid and barium sulfate as a crystalline substance.

Example. Calculate the value of $(Q-S)/S$ for $BaSO_4$ and for $AgCl$ under the following conditions:

(a) 100 ml of 0.1-M Na_2SO_4 with 0.05 ml of 0.1-M $BaCl_2$ added.

(b) 100 ml of 0.1-M NaCl solution with 0.05 ml of 0.1-M $AgNO_3$ added (K_{sp} of each salt is 1×10^{-10}).

The momentary concentration of each salt is

$$Q = \frac{0.05 \text{ ml} \times 0.1 \text{ mmol/ml}}{100 \text{ ml}} = 5 \times 10^{-5} \text{ mmol/ml}$$

Since $[SO_4{}^{2-}] = 0.1$, $[Ba^{2+}] = S = 1 \times 10^{-9}$ (S is the same for AgCl).

[11] M. L. Dundon and E. Mack, *J. Am. Chem. Soc.*, **45**, 2479 (1923); M. L. Dundon, *J. Am. Chem. Soc.*, **45**, 2658 (1923).

Thus for AgCl, where S of micro particles is about the same as that for macro particles,

$$\frac{Q - S}{S} = \frac{5 \times 10^{-5} - 1 \times 10^{-9}}{1 \times 10^{-9}} = 50,000$$

However, for $BaSO_4$, S is about 1000 times 1×10^{-9}, or 1×10^{-6}. Thus

$$\frac{Q - S}{S} = \frac{5 \times 10^{-5} - 1 \times 10^{-6}}{1 \times 10^{-6}} = 49$$

Thus under the same conditions of precipitation, many more nuclei of silver chloride are formed than of barium sulfate. The silver chloride particles are extremely small, become electrically charged, and remain in the form of a colloidal dispersion. The barium sulfate particles are fewer in number and of much larger size. Further precipitation results in a continued growth of these few particles until a well-formed crystalline solid separates from the solution.

Hydroxides of metals such as aluminum and iron are very insoluble and separate from solution as gelatinous precipitates. A calculation of $(Q - S)/S$ for ferric hydroxide (K_{sp} of 1×10^{-36}), under the same conditions as in the last example, gives a value of about 1×10^7. In other words, an extremely large number of nuclei are formed, with a subsequent aggregation of these tiny particles (carrying a large amount of water) into a gelatinous precipitate.

The three compounds discussed above, barium sulfate, silver chloride, and ferric hydroxide, are typical examples of the three types of precipitates encountered in gravimetric analysis: crystalline, curdy, and gelatinous. All three compounds are crystalline internally, that is, there is a regular arrangement of the ions inside the solid particles, as shown by X-ray examination.[12] However, only barium sulfate appears crystalline to an observer, since the particles are large and have well-defined crystal faces. Silver chloride and ferric hydroxide appear to be amorphous because they are made up of a large number of tiny crystals, clumped together in a curd or gel, with no apparent crystal faces.

We can now summarize the conditions of precipitation which the analyst can employ to obtain particles as large as possible. It is necessary to decrease the value of $(Q - S)/S$, and this can be done by decreasing Q or increasing S. While it is possible to decrease Q sufficiently to bring about a large decrease in the ratio (using extremely dilute solutions as with barium sulfate above), an unduly long time may be required for precipitation. In practice, one routinely brings about a moderate decrease in Q by using reasonably dilute solutions and adding the precipitating agent slowly. It is frequently possible to increase the value of S markedly and thus effect a large decrease in the ratio. This can be done by taking advantage of the factors that may

---

[12] A gel such as ferric hydroxide may be amorphous when first precipitated, but gradually becomes crystalline upon standing.

increase solubility: temperature, pH, or the use of complexing agents. Precipitations are quite commonly carried out at elevated temperatures for this reason. Salts of weak acids, such as calcium oxalate and zinc sulfide, are better precipitated in weakly acidic, rather than in alkaline, solution.[13] Barium sulfate is better precipitated in 0.01 to 0.05-M hydrochloric acid solution since the solubility is increased by formation of the bisulfate ion. A compound such as ferric hydroxide is so insoluble that even in acidic solution the value of $(Q - S)/S$ is still so large that a gelatinous precipitate results. However, a dense precipitate of iron as the basic formate can be obtained by homogeneous precipitation (page 196).

In addition to controlling the conditions during the actual precipitation process, the analyst has one other recourse after the precipitate is formed. This is to *digest*, or *age*, the precipitate, that is, to allow the precipitate to stand in contact with the mother liquor, frequently at elevated temperature, for some time before filtration. The small particles of a crystalline substance, such as barium sulfate, being more soluble than the larger ones, dissolve more readily making the solution supersaturated with respect to the larger particles. In order to establish equilibrium with respect to the larger particles, additional material must leave the solution and enter the solid phase. The ions now deposit on the larger particles, causing these particles to grow even larger. Thus, the larger particles grow at the expense of the smaller ones. This process, sometimes called "Ostwald ripening," is useful for increasing the particle size of crystalline precipitates, but not for curdy or gelatinous precipitates. The latter are either so insoluble, or the small particles do not differ sufficiently in solubility from the larger ones, that no appreciable growth in size occurs. Even with crystalline precipitates it is necessary to employ conditions which increase solubility if a beneficial effect is to be attained in a reasonable time. This is the reason for the frequent use of elevated temperatures during digestion.

Thus to obtain a precipitate of large particle size, precipitation is carried out by slow mixing of dilute solutions under conditions of increased solubility of the precipitate. Crystalline precipitates are normally digested at elevated temperature before filtration to further increase particle size.

PURITY OF PRECIPITATES

One of the most difficult problems that faces the analyst in employing precipitation as a means of separation and gravimetric determination is obtaining the precipitate in a high degree of purity. We wish to look now at the ways in which a precipitate can become contaminated, and to see what conditions the analyst can employ to minimize contamination during the precipitation

---

[13] The solubility should not be increased to such an extent that precipitation is incomplete, of course. Frequently, precipitation is started under conditions of increased solubility. After most of the precipitate is formed, the solubility is lowered to insure complete precipitation.

process. We shall also examine methods that can be employed to increase the purity of the precipitate after precipitation has been carried out.

Coprecipitation

The process by which a normally soluble substance is carried down during the precipitation of the desired precipitate is called *coprecipitation*. For example, when sulfuric acid is added to a solution of barium chloride containing a small amount of nitrate ions, the precipitate of barium sulfate is found to contain barium nitrate. It is said that the nitrate is coprecipitated with the sulfate.

Coprecipitation may occur by the formation of *mixed crystals* or by the adsorption of ions during the precipitation process. In the former case, which occurs only infrequently, the impurity actually enters the crystal lattice of the precipitate. In the latter case, adsorbed ions are dragged down with the precipitate during the process of coagulation. A better discussion of coprecipitation which results from adsorption can be given in terms of the three types of precipitates previously described: crystalline, curdy, and gelatinous.

Crystalline Precipitates

A crystalline precipitate, such as barium sulfate, sometimes adsorbs impurities when the particles are small. As the particles grow in size, the impurity may become enclosed in the crystal. This type of contamination is called *occlusion* to distinguish it from the case where the solid does not grow around the impurity. Occluded impurities cannot be removed by washing the precipitate.

There are several things that the analyst can do to minimize coprecipitation with crystalline precipitates. If he is aware of the presence of an ion that readily coprecipitates, he can decrease (but not completely eliminate) the amount of coprecipitation by the method of addition of the two reagents. If it is known that either the sample or the precipitant contains a contaminating ion, the solution containing this ion can be added to the other solution. In this way the concentration of the contaminant is kept at a minimum during the early stages of precipitation.

After a crystalline precipitate is formed, the analyst can still increase the purity. If the substance can be readily redissolved (as salts of weak acids in stronger acids), it can be filtered, redissolved, and reprecipitated. The contaminating ion will be present in a lower concentration during the second precipitation, and consequently a smaller amount will be coprecipitated.

A substance such as barium sulfate is not readily redissolved, but its purity can be improved by the process of aging or digestion. We have already seen that during aging the particle size is increased. At the same time impurities held by these small particles are redissolved and are not readsorbed appreciably by the larger particles. Also during aging the lattice becomes more compact, probably by ions dissolving at the corners and edges and redepositing in an orderly fashion. During this perfection process, occluded impurities may be expelled, and since the number of surface ions has decreased, very little impurity is readsorbed.

Curdy Precipitates

Impurities are adsorbed by the primary particles of a substance such as silver chloride in the same manner as by particles of barium sulfate. However, silver chloride particles do not grow beyond colloidal dimensions, and they finally precipitate as a coagulated colloid. The resulting curd is still made up of fine particles that have not grown together to form an extensive lattice structure. Thus curdy precipitates do not enclose, or occlude, foreign ions as do crystalline precipitates. The impurities on the surfaces of the tiny particles can normally be washed off, since the particles are not firmly bound to one another, and the wash liquid can penetrate to all parts of the curd. As previously mentioned, peptization of the particles must be avoided, and hence the wash liquid must contain a volatile electrolyte.

Digestion of a curdy precipitate is not normally employed for purification because there are no occluded impurities. However, a silver chloride precipitate is usually heated and allowed to stand for one or two hours in contact with the mother liquor containing nitric acid in order to promote coagulation of the colloidal particles. The primary particles do not grow larger during digestion, although it is thought that in some cases colloids form loose agglomerates by sharing the "jackets" of water by which they are surrounded.

Gelatinous Precipitates

We have seen in our previous discussion that the primary particles of a gelatinous precipitate are much larger in number and of much smaller dimensions than those of crystalline or curdy precipitates. The surface area exposed to the solution by such a precipitate is extremely large. A large quantity of water is adsorbed, of course, rendering the precipitate gelatinous, and also the adsorption of foreign ions can be quite extensive. Since the flocculated primary particles do not readily grow into larger crystals, the impurities are not occluded, as with barium sulfate, but are held by adsorption on the surface of the tiny particles.

The electric charge of the primary particles of substances such as ferric and aluminum hydroxides is primarily a function of the pH of the solution, since hydrogen and hydroxyl ions are readily adsorbed by such precipitates. Ferric hydroxide is positively charged at pH values less than about 8.5 and negatively charged at higher pH values. Thus anions tend to be coprecipitated by secondary adsorption at low pH, cations at high pH. This point is important in processes involving the separation of iron from other cations by precipitation of the hydrous oxide. In analyses of minerals such as limestone, where calcium and magnesium are present, iron is precipitated at as low a pH as possible to avoid coprecipitation of these cations.

Washing and reprecipitation can be employed to increase the purity of a gelatinous precipitate once it has been formed. Digestion is not beneficial, since the precipitate is so slightly soluble that the particles have little tendency to grow in size. Washing is normally employed, and, as with curdy precipitates, a volatile electrolyte must be present to avoid peptization. Reprecipitation is employed with a precipitate such as ferric hydroxide. The hydroxide is filtered, washed, and then redissolved in dilute hydrochloric acid. The concentration of impurities is lower in the new solution, and when the precipitate is reformed by raising the pH, a smaller degree of contamination results. The dissolving and reprecipitation, with intervening filtration, can be repeated several times, but usually one reprecipitation insures a sufficiently pure precipitate. This procedure, as previously mentioned, can also be employed for purification of crystalline precipitates that can be readily dissolved in acids. Calcium oxalate and magnesium ammonium phosphate are usually treated in this manner in the limestone analysis.

Summary

We can now summarize the procedures that can be employed to minimize coprecipitation.

1. *Method of addition of the two reagents.* This can be used to control the concentration of impurity and the electric charge carried by the primary particles of precipitate. In the case of hydrous oxides the charge can be controlled by using the proper pH.

2. *Washing.* With curdy and gelatinous precipitates one must have an electrolyte in the wash solution to avoid peptization.

3. *Digestion.* This is of considerable benefit to crystalline precipitates, of some benefit to curdy precipitates, but not used for gelatinous precipitates.

4. *Reprecipitation.* This is used where the precipitate is readily redissolved, primarily for hydrous oxides and crystalline salts of weak acids.

5. *Separation.* The impurity may be separated or its chemical nature changed by some reaction before the precipitate is formed.

6. *Use of conditions that lead to large particle size* (page 191). This point needs further clarification. It would be expected that conditions which lead to large particles would result in a purer precipitate since the surface area of the particles is then relatively small. This is found to be true if the precipitation is sufficiently slow (next section), but it is not true under the usual conditions of precipitation. We have seen how crystalline precipitates, formed under conditions leading to large particles, can occlude impurities during their growth. Such impurities are not readily removed by washing, but digestion is beneficial. Therefore it is sometimes recommended that a crystalline substance be precipitated from reasonably concentrated solutions at room temperature, the solution then diluted and the precipitate digested under conditions of increased solubility. An electrolyte may be added and

the digestion performed at elevated temperature for this purpose. The precipitate is then first formed in a finely divided state, with impurities held on the surfaces of the small particles, not occluded. Upon digestion, Ostwald ripening occurs, leading finally to both large and pure particles. Kolthoff and Sandell[14] obtained large particles of calcium oxalate in this manner in the presence of iodate ions. Less iodate was coprecipitated using this procedure than when the compound was precipitated under conditions of increased solubility and then digested.

Precipitation from Homogeneous Solution

When a precipitant is added to a solution, even when the solution is dilute and well stirred, there will always be some local regions of high concentration. However, by using a procedure in which the precipitant is produced as the result of the reaction *taking place in the solution*, such local effects can be avoided. This technique is usually called *precipitation from homogeneous solution*, and it can lead to both large and pure particles of a precipitate. The best-known example of this method is the use of the hydrolysis of urea to increase the pH and precipitate hydrous oxides, or salts of weak acids. Urea hydrolyzes according to the equation

$$CO(NH_2)_2 + H_2O \longrightarrow CO_2 + 2\,NH_3$$

The hydrolysis is slow at room temperature but is fairly rapid at 100°. Thus the pH can be well controlled in effecting separation by controlling the temperature and duration of heating. Also, the carbon dioxide liberated as bubbles prevents "bumping." Precipitation is usually complete in one to two hours. During this slow growth the particles have time to attain a large size without imperfections occurring in the lattice structure, and therefore the amount of occluded impurity is minimized.

The precipitation of a number of compounds used for gravimetric analysis has been carried out by this technique. Willard and Chan[15] recommend the precipitation of calcium oxalate by neutralizing an acid solution of calcium, containing excess oxalate, by hydrolysis of urea. The precipitate is not contaminated by magnesium or phosphate after only one precipitation. Barium sulfate can be precipitated in this manner by hydrolyzing dimethyl sulfate[16] or sulfamic acid to generate sulfate ions. The data in Table 7.5 show that much less calcium is coprecipitated with barium sulfate when the latter is precipitated homogeneously. Other ions that have been generated homogeneously include: chloride, from chlorohydrin; phosphate, from ethyl phosphate; and oxalate, from ethyl oxalate.

[14] I. M. Kolthoff and E. B. Sandell, *J. Phys. Chem.*, **37**, 443, 459 (1933).

[15] H. H. Willard and F. L. Chan, See *Elementary Quantitative Analysis*, by H. H. Willard and N. F. Furman, D. Van Nostrand Co., New York, 1940, p. 344.

[16] P. J. Elving and R. E. Van Atta, *Anal. Chem.*, **22**, 1375 (1950).

TABLE 7.5   COPRECIPITATION OF CALCIUM WITH BARIUM SULFATE†

Precipitant	Ca added, mg	Ca in precipitate, mg
Dilute H_2SO_4	5.4	3.4
Sulfamic acid	100	0.4
Ethyl sulfate	100	0.6

† Reprinted by permission from H. F. Walton, *Principles and Methods of Chemical Analysis*, Prentice-Hall, Inc., Englewood Cliffs, N.J., 2nd ed., 1964.

Hydrous oxides are gelatinous whether formed under ordinary analytical conditions or homogeneously. However Willard and his co-workers[17] have obtained dense precipitates of iron and aluminum by precipitation with urea in the presence of certain anions. The succinate ion is best for aluminum, and formate is best for iron. The precipitates are of indefinite composition but contain basic salts of aluminum and succinate or of iron and formate. Coprecipitation of foreign ions is less than when the hydrous oxides are precipitated by addition of ammonia. The aluminum precipitate has been found to lose water more readily than the hydrous oxide.[18] Normally, a temperature of about 1100° is required for ignition of hydrous alumina, but the precipitate obtained using urea-succinate reaches constant weight at about 650°.

Postprecipitation

The process by which an impurity is deposited *after* the precipitation of the desired substance is termed *postprecipitation*. This process differs from coprecipitation principally in the fact that the amount of contamination increases, the longer the desired precipitate is left in contact with the mother liquor. When there is a possibility that postprecipitation may occur, directions call for filtration to be made shortly after the desired precipitate is formed.

Postprecipitation occurs when the solution is supersaturated with a foreign substance that precipitates very slowly. For example, zinc sulfide does not readily precipitate from solutions containing zinc ion, hydrogen ion (0.1 to 0.2-M), and saturated with hydrogen sulfide. However, if mercuric sulfide is precipitated under the same conditions in the presence of zinc, over 90 % of the zinc comes down as the sulfide within twenty minutes. Apparently zinc sulfide forms very stable supersaturated solutions. When mercuric sulfide is present, sulfide ions are strongly adsorbed at the interface of the solid and solution. The solubility product constant of zinc sulfide is exceeded to an even greater extent at the interface than in the bulk of the solution, and the rate of precipitation is increased.

Magnesium oxalate forms stable, supersaturated solutions, and unless precautions are taken, postprecipitates on calcium oxalate when calcium

[17] H. H. Willard, *Anal. Chem.*, **22**, 1372 (1950).
[18] T. Dupuis and C. Duval, *Anal. Chem. Acta*, **3**, 191 (1949).

and magnesium are separated by precipitation of the latter compound. Post-precipitation can be avoided by using as high acidity as possible and filtering off the calcium precipitate within one or two hours after precipitation.

IGNITION OF PRECIPITATES

In any gravimetric procedure involving precipitation, one must finally convert the separated substance into a form suitable for weighing. It is necessary that the substance weighed be pure, stable, and of definite composition for the results of the analysis to be accurate. Even if coprecipitation has been minimized, there still remains the problem of complete removal of water and of any electrolytes added to the wash water. Some precipitates are weighed in the same chemical form as that in which they precipitate. Others undergo chemical changes during ignition, and these reactions must go to completion for correct results. The procedure used in this final step depends both upon the chemical properties of the precipitate and upon the tenacity with which water is held by the solid.

Some precipitates can be dried sufficiently for analytical determination without resort to high temperature. For example, magnesium ammonium phosphate hexahydrate, $MgNH_4PO_4 \cdot 6 H_2O$, is sometimes dried by washing with a mixture of alcohol and ether and drawing air over the precipitate for a few minutes.[19] Generally, however, such a procedure is used only when considerable difficulty is encountered upon ignition of the precipitate. It is not usually recommended because of the danger of incomplete removal of water by washing. Water that merely *adheres* to the precipitate is removed, but water that is adsorbed or occluded (or water of hydration) is not removed by washing.

Some precipitates lose water readily in an oven at temperatures of 100° to 130°. Silver chloride does not adsorb water strongly and is normally dried in this manner for ordinary analytical work. In the determination of atomic weights, however, it has been found necessary to fuse silver chloride to remove the last traces of water.

Ignition at high temperature is required for complete removal of water that is occluded or very strongly adsorbed, and for complete conversion of some precipitates to the desired compound. Water can become enclosed within a particle during crystal growth and is then expelled only at high temperatures, probably by the crystal's bursting from the steam pressure generated. Gelatinous precipitates, such as the hydrous oxides, adsorb water quite strongly and must be heated to very high temperatures to remove water completely. Hydrous silica and alumina are well-known examples of precipitates that require very high ignition temperatures. The ignition of calcium

---

[19] H. A. Fales, *Inorganic Quantitative Analysis*, Century Co., New York, 1925, p. 22; J. P. Mehlig, *J. Chem. Ed.*, **12**, 288 (1935).

oxalate to calcium oxide involves an example of a chemical change that requires a high temperature for complete reaction. At about 880° the dissociation pressure of calcium carbonate reaches one atmosphere, but the rate of decomposition is rather slow at this temperature. Therefore, it is usually recommended that temperatures in the range of 1100° be employed.

Errors other than incomplete removal of water or volatile electrolytes can occur during ignition. One of the most serious is reduction of the precipitate by carbon when filter paper is employed. Substances that are very easily reduced, such as silver chloride, are never filtered on paper; filtering crucibles are always employed. Students frequently encounter trouble with precipitates of barium sulfate and ferric oxide. Unless the paper is burned off with a plentiful supply of air, these precipitates will be reduced. Magnesium ammonium phosphate is also easily reduced when ignited to the pyrophosphate. This substance is frequently collected on a porcelain filter crucible to avoid using filter paper.

Precipitates can be over-ignited, leading to decomposition and to substances of indefinite composition. Errors can also result from an ignited precipitate's reabsorbing water or carbon dioxide upon cooling. Crucibles should be properly covered and kept in a desiccator while cooling.

The Thermobalance

Until recent years very few careful studies had been made of the ignition temperatures required for different precipitates. In 1944 Chevenard[20] designed a balance, called a *thermobalance*, which allows a sample to be weighed while it is actually in a furnace. The balance is sensitive to 0.2 mg, and the temperature of the furnace can be measured to within about 1° between room temperature and 1100°. Duval[21] has used this balance to study the ignition of a large number of precipitates of analytical interest. The data are recorded in the form of a graph of weight of the precipitate against temperature. Such a graph is called a pyrolysis curve. It is evident that one should ignite a sample in a temperature range where the curve is flat, that is, where the weight is constant over a wide temperature range. The pyrolysis curves for a few substances are shown in Fig. 7.5. The curves for calcium and magnesium oxalates are particularly interesting. The monohydrate $CaC_2O_4 \cdot H_2O$ is stable at 100° and then loses water up to about 226°. Up to 398° the form CaC_2O_4 is stable, and then the oxalate loses carbon monoxide abruptly to form $CaCO_3$. The carbonate is stable in the range of about 420° to 600°, and then the dissociation to calcium oxide commences. The weight finally becomes constant at about 850°. Magnesium oxalate differs in its behavior in that it loses carbon monoxide and dioxide simultaneously, forming magnesium oxide directly with no intermediate carbonate.

[20] P. Chevenard, X. Wache, and R. de la Tullaye, *Bull. Soc. chim.* (5), **11**, 41 (1944).

[21] C. Duval, *Inorganic Thermogravimetric Analysis*, 2nd ed., Elsevier Publishing Co., New York, 1963.

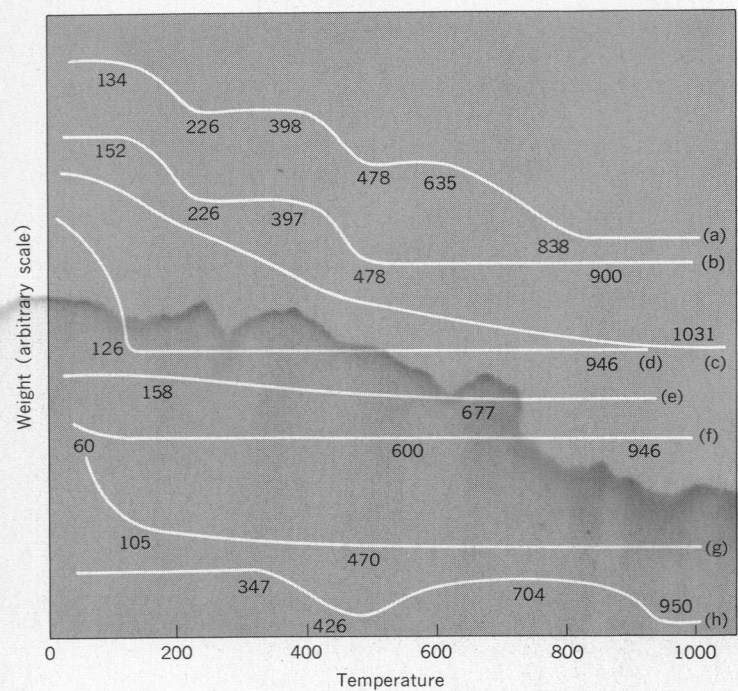

FIGURE 7.5 Pyrolysis curves: (a) CaC_2O_4, (b) MgC_2O_4, (c) Al_2O_3, precipitated by aqueous NH_3, (d) Al_2O_3, precipitated by urea, (e) $BaSO_4$, (f) AgCl, (g) Fe_2O_3, (h) CuSCN. (Taken by permission from C. Duval, *Inorganic Thermogravimetric Analysis*, 2nd ed., Elsevier Publishing Co., New York, 1963.)

REFERENCES

H. A. LAITINEN, *Chemical Analysis*, McGraw-Hill Book Company, New York, 1960.

D. L. LEUSSING, "Solubility," and J. F. COETZEE, "Equilibria in Precipitation Reactions and Precipitation Lines," Chapters 17 and 19, Part 1, Vol. 1, of *Treatise on Analytical Chemistry*, I. M. Kolthoff, P. J. Elving, and E. B. Sandell, eds., Interscience Publishers, Inc., New York, 1959.

M. L. SALUTSKY, "Precipitates: Their Formation, Properties, and Purity," Chapter 18, Part 1, Vol. 1, of *Treatise on Analytical Chemistry* (see preceding reference).

L. GORDON, M. L. SALUTSKY and H. H. WILLARD, *Precipitation from Homogeneous Solution*, John Wiley & Sons, Inc., New York, 1959.

H. F. WALTON, *Principles and Methods of Chemical Analysis*, 2nd ed., Prentice-Hall, Inc., Englewood Cliffs, N.J., 1964.

QUESTIONS   **1.**   What effect do the concentrations of the reacting ions have upon the titration curve of the precipitation reaction such as Cl^- with Ag^+? Show this by roughly sketching curves for 0.1-, 0.01-, and 0.001-M solutions, the titrant being the same concentration.

2. Why is the chance of error in the Volhard determination of chloride much greater than in the determination of bromide or iodide?

3. Explain clearly the mechanism by which adsorption indicators work. What is the function of dextrin? Why must the pH of the solution be controlled?

4. Explain how the following errors would affect the indicated determination, that is, will the error make the result high, low, or have no effect? (a) Chloride (Mohr), solution at pH of 2; (b) chloride (Volhard), failure to add nitrobenzene; (c) chloride (Fajans), eosin used as the indicator; (d) bromide (Mohr), $AgNO_3$ standardized against NaCl, no indicator blank.

5. Point out the various factors that affect the solubility of inorganic crystals and explain how each factor operates.

6. Explain why the following statements are true:
   (a) Silver chloride is more soluble in 1-M potassium nitrate than in water.
   (b) Silver chloride is more soluble in 1-M hydrochloric acid than in water.
   (c) Silver chloride is more soluble in 1-M ammonia than in water.
   (d) Silver chloride is less soluble in 0.001-M hydrochloric acid than in water.
   (e) Ferrous hydroxide is less soluble in 0.1-M ammonia than in water.
   (f) Zinc hydroxide is more soluble in 0.1-M ammonia than in water.
   (g) Calcium fluoride is more soluble at pH 3 than at pH 4.
   (h) Silver chromate is less soluble in 0.001-M silver nitrate than in 0.001-M potassium chromate.

7. Compare metal chelate precipitates and strictly inorganic precipitates with regard to their properties. What are some of the advantages and disadvantages of these organic precipitants?

8. Make plots of pAg vs pCl and of pAg vs $pCrO_4$ for the precipitation of AgCl and Ag_2CrO_4. Note the difference in the two plots.

9. Suggest experimental methods by which you could determine whether a substance is temporarily suspended, a colloid, or in true solution.

10. Explain why small particles of some substances are more soluble than large particles. How does the analyst make use of this property to improve analytical methods?

11. Explain the following:
    (a) Barium sulfate is washed with water, whereas the wash water for silver chloride contains a little nitric acid.
    (b) Barium sulfate is digested following precipitation, but this procedure is not used for silver chloride or ferric hydroxide.

12. A precipitate of ferric hydroxide is contaminated with magnesium hydroxide. What is the best way to get rid of the impurity?

13. The sulfate ion in a solution is to be precipitated by the addition of lead. The sulfate solution also contains small amounts of nitrate, chloride, and perchlorate ions. Which of these ions is most likely to be coprecipitated? Explain. How could you minimize coprecipitation?

14. The oxalate ion in a solution which contains a small amount of sulfate is to be precipitated as calcium oxalate. What conditions of precipitation would you use to minimize coprecipitation?

15. What conditions should be used to precipitate a sulfide, such as ZnS, in order to obtain as large particles as possible?

16. When is postprecipitation likely to occur? Will zinc sulfide be more likely to postprecipitate on mercuric sulfide or on barium sulfate? Explain.

17. Point out possible errors in the final step of igniting and weighing a precipitate.

PROBLEMS

1. *Solubility product constant.* Calculate the solubility product constants from the given solubilities: (a) AgI, 0.00235 mg/l; (b) $Mg(OH)_2$, 0.000793 g/100 ml; (c) $Ag_2C_2O_4$, 3.28 mg/100 ml.

2. *Solubility.* From the solubility product constants listed in the appendix, calculate the following solubilities in water, neglecting such effects as hydrolysis: (a) $PbSO_4$ in mg/ml; (b) CaF_2 in g/100 ml; (c) $Cu(IO_3)_2$ in mg/100 ml.

3. *Solubility.* Calculate the molar solubilities of the following, neglecting such effects as hydrolysis: (a) $BaSO_4$ in 0.01-F K_2SO_4; (b) MgF_2 in 0.20-F NaF; (c) $Ag_2C_2O_4$ in 0.001-F $AgNO_3$.

4. *Effect of pH.* Calculate the molar solubilities of the following: (a) $Mg(OH)_2$ at pH 12.30; (b) CdS at pH 1.70, solution saturated with H_2S; (c) ZnS at pH 0.60, solution saturated with H_2S.

5. *Effect of pH.* Calculate the molar solubilities of the following: (a) CaF_2 in HCl, pH = 1.70; (b) CaC_2O_4 in HCl, pH = 2.30; (c) MgF_2 in HCl, pH = 3.00.

6. *Effect of complexes.* Calculate the solubilities in g/100 ml of the following: (a) AgCl in 1.0-M NH_3; (b) AgBr in 4.0-M NH_3; (c) AgI in 15-M NH_3.

7. *Calculation of pX.* Calculate the following: (a) pCl of 0.02-F NaCl; (b) pBr of 0.05-F $CaBr_2$; (c) pI of 0.001-F MgI_2; (d) pCl of 0.01-F $CrCl_3$.

8. *Mixtures.* Calculate the values of pCl and pAg of the solutions made by mixing (a) 75 ml of 0.10-F NaCl + 25 ml of 0.12-F $AgNO_3$; (b) 40 ml of 0.10-F NaCl + 60 ml of 0.15-F $AgNO_3$; (c) 40 ml of 0.15-F NaCl + 60 ml of 0.10-F $AgNO_3$.

9. *Mixtures.* Repeat Problem 8 substituting (a) NaBr for NaCl and calculating pBr and pAg; (b) NaI for NaCl and calculating pI and pAg.

10. *Mixtures.* (a) Calculate the value of pCl of a solution made by mixing 50 ml of HCl, pCl = 2.00, with 50 ml of HCl, pCl = 4.00. (b) Calculate the value of pAg in a solution made by mixing equal volumes of a solution of $AgNO_3$, pAg = 1.70, and of NaCl, pCl = 2.00.

11. *Titration.* A 50-ml aliquot of 0.10-F NaBr is titrated with 0.10-F $AgNO_3$. Calculate the value of pBr at 49.9 and 50.1 ml of titrant. Repeat the calculation for the titration of NaI. Compare the changes in pBr and pI with that of pCl (Table 7.1), and interpret the differences in terms of the equilibrium constants for the titration reactions.

12. *Approximations.* A 50-ml sample of a 0.10-F solution of the salt NaX is titrated with 0.10-F $AgNO_3$ forming the precipitate AgX. Calculate the value of pX after the addition of 49.9 ml of titrant two ways: first neglecting the solubility of AgX, and second, not neglecting the solubility. Use the following values for the K_{sp} of AgX: (a) 1×10^{-6}; (b) 1×10^{-8}; (c) 1×10^{-10}.

13. *Solubility.* 50 ml of 0.060-F K_2CrO_4 is mixed with 50 ml of 0.080-F $AgNO_3$. Calculate the following: (a) the solubility of Ag_2CrO_4 in the solution in moles per liter; (b) the concentrations of the following ions: Ag^+, CrO_4^{2-}, K^+, and NO_3^-.

14. *Equivalence point.* (a) Calculate the value of pAg and $pCrO_4$ at the equivalence point in the titration of Ag^+ with CrO_4^{2-}. (b) Show that the following relations are true at the equivalence point of this titration: $3\,pAg = pK_{sp} - \log 2$ and $2\,pCrO_4 = pK_{sp} + \log 2$.

15. *Equilibrium constants.* Calculate the equilibrium constants for the following reactions:

$$AgSCN(s) + Cl^-(aq) \rightleftharpoons AgCl(s) + SCN^-(aq)$$

$$AgSCN(s) + Br^-(aq) \rightleftharpoons AgBr(s) + SCN^-(aq)$$

Why does this reaction cause trouble in the indirect Volhard method for chloride but not for bromide?

16. *Error in the Mohr method.* 5.00 mmol of NaCl are dissolved in 50.0 ml of a solution that is 0.0100-F in K_2CrO_4. This solution is titrated with 0.100-F $AgNO_3$ to the formation of a precipitate of Ag_2CrO_4. Calculate (a) the value of pCl at which the precipitation of Ag_2CrO_4 begins; (b) the error in the titrations. (c) Repeat (a) and (b) except that the initial chromate ion concentration is 0.0001-F.

17. *Fraction precipitated.* Urea is added to 100 ml of a 0.10-F solution of $MgCl_2$, and the pH is gradually raised by boiling the solution. Calculate the pH values when 50, 90, 99.9, and 99.99 % of the magnesium is precipitated. Assume the temperature is 25°C.

18. *Sulfide precipitation.* (a) Calculate the pH required just to prevent the precipitation of CdS from a solution which is 0.050-M in Cd^{2+} and is saturated with H_2S. (b) What should the pH be if it is desired to lower the concentration of Cd^{2+} to 10^{-6}-M by precipitating CdS?

19. *Solubility.* To 60 ml of 0.10-F NaCl is added 40 ml of 0.16-F $AgNO_3$. (a) Calculate the number of milligrams of Cl^- not precipitated. (b) The precipitate is washed with 75 ml of water at room temperature. Assuming solubility equilibrium is reached, how many milligrams of AgCl dissolve in the wash water?

20. *Separations.* It is desired to separate two metals M^{2+} and N^+ by precipitation of their sulfides from a solution which is 0.10-M in H^+ and saturated with H_2S. What is the minimum ratio of the K_{sp} of MS to that of N_2S in order that the concentration of N^+ be reduced to 10^{-6}-M without precipitating M^{2+} from a 0.10-M solution?

21. *Hydrolysis.* Calculate the molar solubilities in water of the following, taking into account hydrolysis of the anion: (a) calcium carbonate; (b) barium chromate; (c) silver chromate; (d) zinc sulfide; (e) silver sulfide.

22. *Buffer solution.* Magnesium hydroxide is precipitated from an NH_3-NH_4Cl buffer. What must be the concentration of NH_3 to precipitate all but 0.1 mg of magnesium from 100 ml of a solution which is 0.02-M in NH_4Cl?

23. *Buffer solution.* 50 ml of 0.01-M RCl_2 is mixed with 50 ml of an NH_3-NH_4Cl buffer, precipitating the hydroxide $R(OH)_2$. The buffer is 0.10-M in NH_3 before the mixing. If it is found that a minimum of 1.00 g of NH_4Cl must be dissolved in the buffer before mixing just to prevent precipitation, what is the K_{sp} of $R(OH)_2$?

24. *Complexes.* If exactly 1.00 liter of 3.0-M NH_3 (final concentration) is required to dissolve 4.00 mmol of the silver salt AgX, what is the K_{sp} of the salt?

25. *Complexes.* One mmol of AgCl is dissolved in 500 ml of ammonia, the final concentration of NH_3 being 0.50-M. Calculate the concentration of uncomplexed Ag^+ ions in the solution.

26. *Sulfide precipitation.* 100 ml of a solution that is 0.10-M in Cu^{2+} and 0.10-M in H^+ is saturated with H_2S. Calculate the milligrams of copper left in the solution, taking into account the fact that the precipitation of CuS produces hydrogen ions.

27. *Precipitation.* A solution which is 0.05-M in Sr^{2+} and 0.10-M in Ca^{2+} is treated with solid Na_2CO_3, first precipitating $SrCO_3$. What percentage of the Sr^{2+} is precipitated when $CaCO_3$ begins to precipitate?

28. *Complexes.* The successive stepwise formation constants for $Cd(NH_3)_4^{2+}$ are as follows: $k_1 = 550$, $k_2 = 162$, $k_3 = 23.5$, and $k_4 = 13.5$. Calculate the molar solubility of CdS in a 0.10-M solution of ammonia, calculating first α_2 for the anion, β_4 for the cation, and then the solubility.

29. *Solubility.* (a) Show that the molar solubility of the salt MX, where

$$MX \rightleftharpoons M^{2+} + X^{2-}$$

is given by

$$s = \sqrt{\frac{K_{sp} \times K_{a_1} \times K_{a_2} + K_{sp} \times K_{a_1}[H^+] + K_{sp}[H^+]^2}{K_{a_1} \times K_{a_2}}}$$

Here K_{a_1} and K_{a_2} are the two dissociation constants of the acid H_2X. (b) Some texts give the following expression for the solubility of a metal sulfate, MSO_4, in acid media:

$$s = \sqrt{\frac{K_{sp} \times K_{a_2} + K_{sp}[H^+]}{K_{a_2}}}$$

How do you rationalize this expression with that in part (a)?

30. *Solubility.* (a) Calculate the molar solubility of $BaSO_4$ in 0.10-M HCl using the expression in Problem 29(b) above. (b) Repeat part (a) using the expression in Problem 29(a) above. Take K_{a_1} for H_2SO_4 to be 10. (c) Repeat part (b) taking K_{a_1} for H_2SO_4 to be 100.

8 Oxidation-Reduction Equilibria

Chemical reactions which involve oxidation-reduction are more widely used in titrimetric analyses than acid-base, complex formation, or precipitation reactions. In this chapter we wish to discuss the equilibrium aspects of such reactions. We shall discuss how equilibrium constants are obtained, titration curves calculated, indicators selected, and how the feasibility of a titration is determined.

GALVANIC CELLS

The equilibrium constant of an oxidation-reduction (redox) reaction can be evaluated from the potential of an appropriate galvanic cell. An example of a galvanic cell is shown in Fig. 8.1. The cell consists of two single *electrodes* (half-cells), one a strip of zinc dipping into a 1-M solution of a zinc salt, the other a strip of copper dipping into a 1-M solution of a copper salt. Wires from the metal strips lead to an ammeter (or voltmeter). The circuit is completed by connecting the two solutions with a so-called "salt bridge." This may be an inverted U-tube containing a solution of a salt, such as potassium chloride, with an agar plug at each end.

Each of the two metals has an inherent tendency to lose electrons. We can represent this by the half-reactions

$$\underset{\text{reductant}}{\text{Zn}} \rightleftharpoons \underset{\text{oxidant}}{\text{Zn}^{2+}} + 2e$$

$$\underset{\text{reductant}}{\text{Cu}} \rightleftharpoons \underset{\text{oxidant}}{\text{Cu}^{2+}} + 2e$$

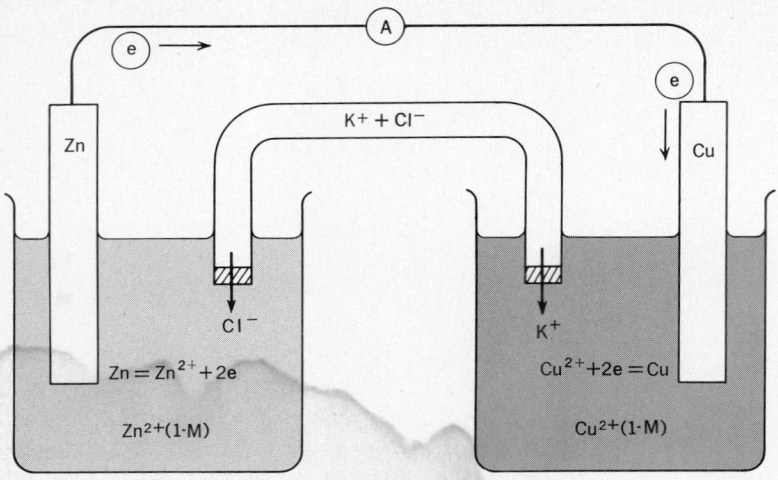

FIGURE 8.1 A galvanic cell.

The metal atoms, for example zinc, tend to leave the strip and enter the solution as ions. In the process the zinc is *oxidized* since it *loses* electrons; electrons are left on the surface of the metal strip. Zinc ions tend to leave the solution and deposit as atoms on the strip, *gaining* electrons and undergoing *reduction*. We say that zinc atoms act as the *reductant*, or reducing agent, and zinc ions act as the *oxidant*, or oxidizing agent. The $Zn-Zn^{2+}$ system is called a "redox couple," and a redox reaction involves the exchange of electrons between two redox couples. An electrostatic force, or difference in potential, is set up at each electrode, at the interface of the solid and liquid phases. This potential, called a "single electrode potential," is a measure of the tendency of the redox couple to lose or gain electrons.

If the cell pictured in Fig. 8.1 is short-circuited by means of an external wire connecting the two electrodes, electrons will flow spontaneously through the wire from zinc to copper. Zinc is oxidized at one electrode and copper is reduced at the other. The two solutions must remain electrically neutral, and here the salt bridge comes into play, completing the electrical circuit inside the cell. Chloride ions, Cl^-, diffuse into the right-hand solution, and K^+ into the left. A current flows through the whole system, carried by electrons in the metallic conductors and ionic migration through the solutions. If the process is allowed to continue, the current will gradually diminish as Zn^{2+} builds up in the zinc electrode and Cu^{2+} is depleted in the other solution, until finally the system will come to equilibrium, both half-cells at the same potential, the current down to zero. The cell reaction is

$$Zn + Cu^{2+} \longrightarrow Zn^{2+} + Cu$$

From the direction of electron flow we note that the $Zn-Zn^{2+}$ redox couple has a greater tendency to lose electrons than does the $Cu-Cu^{2+}$ couple.

206

Instead of "shorting" the cell into a heavy wire (in which case all of the energy is dissipated as heat), we can use the energy to light a flashlight bulb, run a small motor, or to do other useful things. And of course electrochemical cells or "batteries" are employed for many practical purposes outside the laboratory. These cells are called *galvanic* (as opposed to *electrolytic* cells, which we shall consider in a later chapter). A galvanic cell is one in which some of the energy released spontaneously in a chemical reaction is converted into electrical energy and thereby made available for performing work.

At present we are not interested in the action of a galvanic cell in furnishing electrical energy. Rather, we are interested in the magnitude of the potential difference between the two electrodes, because from this value we can obtain the equilibrium constant of the cell reaction. If, in the outer circuit of our cell, the ammeter is replaced by a potentiometer, the potential, or voltage, of the cell can be measured. When a potentiometer is used, an opposing voltage is applied to that of the cell, and the potential just required to prevent the cell reaction from occurring is measured. For analytical purposes, measurements must be made in this manner to minimize the current flow through the cell which will change the concentrations of ions in solution.

The Hydrogen Electrode:
Standard Potentials

If we measure the potential of the cell in Fig. 8.1, we find that the value is 1.10 V (volts). We can also determine experimentally that the zinc electrode is negative with respect to copper, meaning that electrons will flow from zinc to copper if we short-circuit the cell as discussed above.

The quantity we have measured is the *difference* in potential between the zinc and copper redox systems. We do not know the absolute value of either single electrode potential; in order to measure the tendency of one redox couple to lose or gain electrons, we must introduce another couple for the purpose of comparison. Since definite potential values are convenient to use, the chemist arbitrarily assigns a value to a certain single electrode. All other single electrodes are then referred to this standard by measuring the emf of galvanic cells in which one electrode is the standard and the other the electrode in question.

The redox couple selected as the reference is $H_2 - H^+$:

$$2\,H^+ + 2e \rightleftharpoons H_2$$

This couple is assigned a potential of exactly zero volts at all temperatures when the pressure of hydrogen gas is one atmosphere and the hydrogen-ion activity is unity. Physically, the electrode is somewhat as suggested schematically in Fig. 8.2. A platinum surface, rough so as to have a large area, provides an electrical connection to the external circuit and serves as a catalyst for the combination of H atoms formed in the electron transfer step.

If we set up a cell in which one electrode is $Zn - Zn^{2+}$ (1-M) and the other is the standard hydrogen electrode, we find that the potential at 25°C is

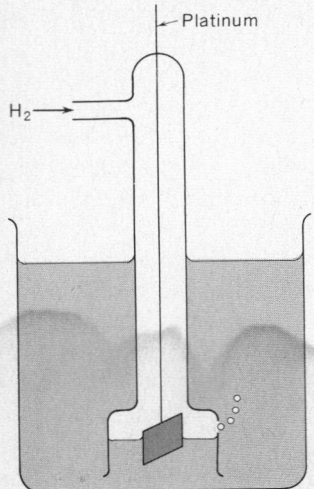

- Platinum

$H_2 \rightarrow$

FIGURE 8.2 Hydrogen electrode.

0.76 V. We also can determine that the polarity of the zinc electrode is negative, hydrogen positive. If we set up another cell consisting of the $Cu-Cu^{2+}$ (1-M) electrode and the standard hydrogen, we find that the potential is 0.34 V, with copper positive and hydrogen negative. We say that the standard potential of the $Zn-Zn^{2+}$ couple is 0.76 V and that of the $Cu-Cu^{2+}$ couple is 0.34 V referred to the hydrogen electrode. By international agreement the electrode reactions are written as reduction (left to right):

$$Zn^{2+} + 2e \rightleftharpoons Zn \qquad E^\circ = -0.76 \text{ V}$$

$$2\,H^+ + 2e \rightleftharpoons H_2 \qquad E^\circ = 0.00 \text{ V}$$

$$Cu^{2+} + 2e \rightleftharpoons Cu \qquad E^\circ = +0.34 \text{ V}$$

The voltages are given positive or negative signs in accordance with experimentally determined polarities with respect to hydrogen. Zinc is more negative than hydrogen; this means that the reaction

$$Zn + 2\,H^+ \longrightarrow Zn^{2+} + H_2$$

will occur spontaneously rightward if both H^+ and Zn^{2+} are at unit activity; zinc loses electrons to hydrogen in this reaction. On the other hand, hydrogen is more negative than copper, the reaction

$$H_2 + Cu^{2+} \longrightarrow 2\,H^+ + Cu$$

occurring spontaneously rightward if both ions are at unit activity and the pressure of H_2 is one atmosphere.

208

Note that we used the term *standard* potential and the symbol $E°$ to represent it. By a standard potential is meant the potential of a single electrode in which each reactant is at unit activity. Recall that a substance having an activity of unity is said to be in its "standard state." On page 77 we listed the conventions which are used to define the standard states of pure and impure liquids and solids, gases, and soluble electrolytes.

A list of standard potentials is given in Table 4 of Appendix I. All reactions in this table are written as reduction in accordance with the recommendations of the International Union of Pure and Applied Chemistry. The signs are also in accordance with the recommendations of this body. We shall follow this manner of writing half-reactions throughout the text. However, the student may encounter other texts which write reactions as

$$Zn \rightleftharpoons Zn^{2+} + 2e$$

saying that the "oxidation" potential is $+0.76$ V. There is nothing wrong in this procedure, but care should be taken to be sure that the sign is changed.

Representation of Galvanic Cells

Instead of drawing pictures such as Fig. 8.1, we normally use a schematic representation of cells. We depict the cell of Fig. 8.1 as follows:

$$Zn|Zn^{2+}(1-M)| \quad |Cu^{2+}(1-M)|Cu$$
$$E_1 \qquad E_{j_1} \; E_{j_2} \qquad E_r$$

A vertical line (sometimes a "slant" when made with a typewriter) indicates a phase boundary across which we suppose that a potential exists. The emf of this cell is the algebraic sum of four potential differences, one across each metal-solution interface and one at each end of the salt bridge. That is,

$$E_{cell} = E_1 + E_{j_i} + E_{j_2} + E_r$$

The two potentials at the metal-solution interfaces are single electrode potentials, as discussed above. The potentials at the interfaces of the solutions and the salt bridge are called *liquid junction potentials*, abbreviated E_j.

Liquid Junction Potentials

Suppose we could prepare a quiet interface between pure water and a solution of hydrochloric acid, perhaps by very gently sliding out an ultrathin partition separating the two liquids. Immediately, hydrogen and chloride ions would move from the HCl solution into the water, and if we waited long enough, a uniform HCl concentration would prevail throughout. Stirring, of course, would speed the mixing, but we are not going to do that. Now, although both cations and anions migrate across the boundary, a potential will develop at the interface because hydrogen ions move much more rapidly

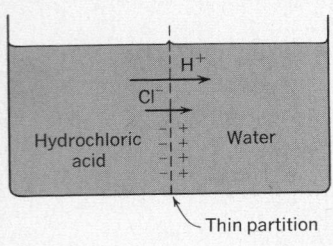

Thin partition **FIGURE 8.3** Development of a liquid junction potential.

than do chloride ions. Thus there is a slight tendency for a charge separation, as depicted in Fig. 8.3, with the water side of the interface positive and an excess of negative charge on the HCl side. This potential, once established, will itself act upon the migrating ions, decelerating the faster ones and speeding up the slower ones. Thus we may visualize a "steady-state" situation, at least for a certain length of time, involving a constant charge separation.

A liquid junction potential may be expected to develop at any interface between two ionic solutions of different compositions as a result of the tendencies of different ions to diffuse at different rates across the boundary. It is possible to calculate the liquid junction potential for a simple case, but in complex electrolyte mixtures the value is generally unknown. Junction potentials may vary over a considerable range and can be quite appreciable in some cases, but typically they are of the order of a few millivolts (thousandths of a volt). The junction potential is minimized by using a salt bridge in which the electrolyte is quite concentrated and the cation and the anion have comparable mobilities. Potassium and chloride ions represent such a case, and salt bridges of saturated aqueous potassium chloride are widely used.

It is necessary to prevent the KCl solution from running out of the salt bridge, and for this purpose the ends are plugged with a porous material that soaks up solution and permits migration of ions but acts as a barrier to the heavy flow of a liquid stream. Small wads of cotton were used at one time; currently, thin disks of porous glass or small plugs of agar gel are often employed.

In our emf calculations, we shall neglect liquid junction potentials. This is done primarily because we usually do not know what they are, but in fact the errors we incur in this manner are negligible for most purposes.

Conventions

To represent the reaction which occurs in a galvanic cell if the cell is allowed to discharge spontaneously, proceed as follows:

1. Write the half-reaction for the right-hand electrode, with electrons on the left. For the cell in Fig. 8.1 this is

$$Cu^{2+} + 2e \rightleftharpoons Cu \qquad E_r^\circ = +0.34 \text{ V}$$

Also record the standard potential.

2. Write the half-reaction and standard potential for the left-hand electrode in the same manner:

$$Zn^{2+} + 2e \rightleftharpoons Zn \qquad E_1^\circ = -0.76 \text{ V}$$

3. If necessary, multiply one or both of the equations by proper integers so that the number of electrons is the same in both equations. Since $n = 2$ for both the copper and the zinc couples, this is unnecessary in the present example. Do not multiply the potentials; these are experimental values which do not depend upon how the equations are written.

4. Subtract the left-hand half-reaction from the right-hand half-reaction, and also subtract the potentials:

$$Cu^{2+} + 2e \rightleftharpoons Cu \qquad\qquad E_r^\circ = +0.34 \text{ V}$$

$$Zn^{2+} + 2e \rightleftharpoons Zn \qquad\qquad E_1^\circ = -0.76 \text{ V}$$

$$Cu^{2+} + Zn \rightleftharpoons Cu + Zn^{2+} \qquad E_{cell}^\circ = +1.10 \text{ V}$$

5. The sign of the emf, E_{cell}°, gives the polarity of the right-hand electrode. In the present example, the copper electrode is positive, the zinc electrode negative.

6. The sign of the E_{cell}° indicates the direction of spontaneous reaction. If the sign is positive, the reaction goes from left to right as written. In the cell of Fig. 8.1, cupric ion is reduced to copper metal and zinc metal is oxidized to zinc ion when the cell discharges. A negative sign indicates, of course, that the reaction proceeds from right to left.

Students sometimes ask what would happen if they had written the cell in the reverse manner, that is, with zinc as the right-hand electrode and copper the left. If the procedure just outlined is followed, the cell potential will be -1.10 V, but the cell reaction will be reversed. Hence, the conclusions regarding the direction of spontaneous reaction and polarity of the electrodes are the same as before. It is true that, for a cell such as ours, the direction of spontaneous reaction would be obvious ahead of time to most chemists. In cases where this is so, many people would probably formulate the cell in such a way that E_{cell}° came out positive. The rationale for this is that we read English from left to right, and it is convenient if the direction of spontaneous change comes out the same way we read. But there is no reason to endorse this; indeed, when we consider the effect of concentrations upon the cell emf values, we shall see that the sign of E_{cell}° may not be obvious ahead of time.

The Nernst Equation

The potential of a galvanic cell depends upon the activities of the various species which undergo reaction in the cell. The equation which expresses this relationship is called the Nernst equation, after the physical chemist, Nernst, who in 1889 first used the equation to express the relation between the potential of a metal-metal ion electrode and the concentration of the ion in solution.

In a chemical reaction such as

$$aA + bB \rightleftharpoons cC + dD$$

the change in free energy is given by the equation

$$\Delta G = \Delta G° + 2.3RT \log \frac{a_C^c \times a_D^d}{a_A^a \times a_B^b}$$

where $\Delta G°$ is the free energy change when all the reactants and products are in their standard states (unit activity). R is the gas constant, 8.314 joules/degree-mole, and T is the absolute temperature.

The free energy change, or work done, by driving Avogadro's number of electrons through a voltage E is $(Ne)E$, where N is Avogadro's number and e is the charge on the electron. The product Ne is 96,500 coulombs, called one faraday, or F. Hence,

$$\Delta G = -nFE$$

where n is the number of moles of electrons involved in the reaction. If all reactants and products are in their standard states, this becomes

$$\Delta G° = -nFE°$$

Hence

$$-nFE = -nFE° + 2.3RT \log \frac{[C]^c[D]^d}{[A]^a[B]^b}$$

where concentrations are substituted for activities. This can be written as

$$E = E° - \frac{2.3RT}{nF} \log \frac{[C]^c[D]^d}{[A]^a[B]^b}$$

At 298°K the equation becomes

$$E = E° - \frac{0.059}{n} \log \frac{[C]^c[D]^d}{[A]^a[B]^b}$$

This is the form in which we commonly use the Nernst equation. Note that at equilibrium, $E = 0$, $\Delta G = 0$, and the logarithmic term is the equilibrium constant. Hence,

$$\Delta G° = -2.3RT \log K$$

or

$$E^\circ = \frac{0.059}{n} \log K$$

If we know the standard potentials of two redox couples, we can calculate the equilibrium constant for the reaction between the couples using the above equation. We can then judge whether the reaction goes sufficiently to completion to be useful in a titrimetric procedure. Before considering titrations, we will illustrate the application of the Nernst equation, as well as other points covered thus far.

Example 1. A cell is set up as follows:

$$Fe|Fe^{2+}(a = 0.1)||Cd^{2+}(a = 0.001)|Cd$$

(a) Write the cell reaction. (b) Calculate the voltage of the cell, the polarity of the electrodes, and the direction of spontaneous reaction. (c) Calculate the equilibrium constant of the cell reaction.

(a) The electrode reactions and standard potentials are

$$
\begin{aligned}
Cd^{2+} + 2e &\rightleftharpoons Cd & E_r^\circ &= -0.40 \text{ V} \\
Fe^{2+} + 2e &\rightleftharpoons Fe & E_1^\circ &= -0.44 \text{ V} \\
\hline
\text{Subtracting, } Fe + Cd^{2+} &\rightleftharpoons Fe^{2+} + Cd & E_{cell}^\circ &= +0.04 \text{ V}
\end{aligned}
$$

(b) The cell potential can be calculated from the single electrode potentials:

$$E_r = -0.40 - \frac{0.059}{2} \log \frac{1}{0.001} = -0.49 \text{ V}$$

$$E_1 = -0.44 - \frac{0.059}{2} \log \frac{1}{0.1} = -0.47 \text{ V}$$

Thus

$$E_r - E_1 = -0.02 \text{ V}$$

Alternatively, the cell potential can be evaluated from the expression

$$E_{cell} = E_{cell}^\circ - \frac{0.059}{2} \log \frac{a_{Fe^{2+}}}{a_{Cd^{2+}}}$$

$$E_{cell} = +0.04 - \frac{0.059}{2} \log \frac{0.1}{0.001}$$

$$E_{cell} = +0.04 - 0.06 = -0.02 \text{ V}$$

Therefore the cell reaction, as written above, tends to occur spontaneously from right to left at the given activities. The cadmium electrode is negative, the iron positive.

Note that if both ions are at unit activity, $E°_{cell} = +0.04$ V, and the direction is from left to right. The polarities of the electrodes are reversed also.

(c) The equilibrium constant is given by

$$E°_{cell} = \frac{0.059}{n} \log K$$

$$+0.04 = \frac{0.059}{2} \log K$$

$$\log K = 1.36$$

$$K = 23$$

As a further illustration, consider the following example.

Example 2. Calculate the potential of the following cell, giving the polarities of the electrodes and the direction of spontaneous reaction. Calculate the equilibrium constant of the cell reaction.

$$Pt, H_2(0.9 \text{ atm})|H^+(0.1\text{-}M|\,|KCl(0.1\text{-}M), AgCl|Ag$$

The electrode reactions are

$$
\begin{array}{ll}
2\,AgCl + 2e \rightleftharpoons 2\,Ag + 2\,Cl^- & E°_r = 0.22 \text{ V} \\
2\,H^+ + 2e \rightleftharpoons H_2 & E°_l = 0.00 \text{ V} \\
\hline
2\,AgCl + H_2 \rightleftharpoons 2\,H^+ + 2\,Ag + 2\,Cl^- & E°_{cell} = +0.22 \text{ V}
\end{array}
$$

$$E_{cell} = +0.22 - \frac{0.059}{2} \log \frac{(a_{H^+})^2(a_{Ag})^2(a_{Cl^-})^2}{(a_{AgCl})^2(a_{H_2})}$$

In accordance with our conventions regarding activities:

$a_{AgCl} = 1$, since AgCl is a pure solid.
$a_{H_2} = 0.9$, since this is the partial pressure of the gas in atmospheres.
$a_{H^+} = 0.1$, since this is a soluble electrolyte.
$a_{Ag} = 1$, since silver is a pure solid.
$a_{Cl^-} = 0.1$, since this is a soluble electrolyte.

Substituting these values and solving gives

$$E_{cell} = +0.34 \text{ V}$$

Hence the silver-silver chloride electrode is positive and the reaction is spontaneous left to right.

The equilibrium constant is given by

$$0.22 = \frac{0.059}{2} \log K$$

$$\log K = 7.46$$

$$K = 2.9 \times 10^7$$

Laboratory Reference Electrodes

The hydrogen electrode is inconvenient for routine, practical measurements in the laboratory. It requires a tank of compressed gas which is heavy and awkward, explosive mixtures of hydrogen and air may be formed, and the catalytic platinum surface is easily poisoned, i.e., contaminated with adsorbed substances that inhibit catalytic activity. Thus, in the laboratory, more convenient reference electrodes are commonly employed for measuring the potentials of other half-cells. The potentials of these reference electrodes have themselves been measured against the standard hydrogen electrode. Regardless of what reference electrode is actually employed, it is customary to report any potential as though it had been measured against the standard hydrogen electrode. The commonest reference electrodes are the calomel and the silver-silver chloride electrodes.

One form of the calomel electrode is shown schematically in Fig. 8.4. The half-reaction may be written:

$$Hg_2Cl_2 + 2e \rightleftharpoons 2\,Hg + 2\,Cl^-$$

The basic redox couple, $Hg_2^{2+} + 2e \rightleftharpoons 2\,Hg$, establishes a potential which depends upon the activity of mercurous ions, but since mercurous chloride is a slightly soluble electrolyte, the mercurous activity depends upon the concentration of chloride ions. Most commonly the solution is saturated with potassium chloride; in this case, the single electrode potential of the calomel electrode (called an S.C.E. for saturated calomel electrode) is $+0.2458$ V at $25°C$ as determined against a standard hydrogen electrode. If the potassium chloride is 1-M, the potential is $+0.2847$ V; this is sometimes called a standard or normal calomel electrode.

The silver-silver chloride electrode is analagous to the calomel in that the basic redox couple, $Ag^+ + e \rightleftharpoons Ag$, establishes a potential determined by the chloride ion activity via the slightly soluble salt AgCl. Physically, the

FIGURE 8.4   Calomel electrode.

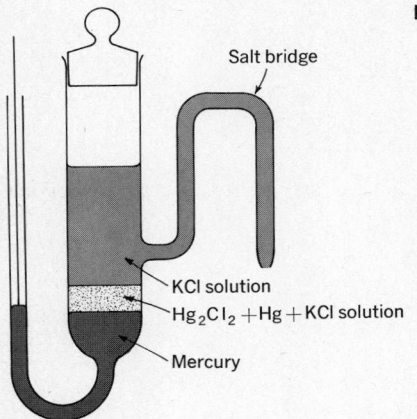

Salt bridge

KCl solution

$Hg_2Cl_2 + Hg + KCl$ solution

Mercury

electrode is usually a spiral of silver wire coated with an adherent layer of AgCl obtained by anodizing the metal in a chloride solution. The coated wire dips into a potassium chloride solution. The overall half-reaction may be written

$$AgCl + e \rightleftharpoons Ag + Cl^-$$

For chloride ion at unit activity, the standard single electrode potential is +0.2221 V at 25°C.

The following example illustrates the use of a reference electrode.

Example. (a) The potential of a cell made up of an electrode of unknown potential and a standard calomel electrode is 1.04 V, with the calomel electrode positive. Calculate the potential of the unknown electrode referred to the hydrogen electrode.

If we consider our cell as having the unknown electrode on the left, calomel on the right, we must give a positive sign to the potential. That is,

$$E_{cell} = E_r - E_1$$

$$+1.04 = +0.28 - E_1$$

$$E_1 = -0.76 \text{ V}$$

(b) In a second measurement with another unknown electrode, the potential of the cell is found to be 0.06 V, with the calomel negative. Calculate the potential of the unknown electrode referred to hydrogen.

In this case, if the calomel is the right-hand electrode as before, the potential of the cell must be written −0.06 V. Hence

$$-0.06 = 0.28 - E_1$$

$$E_1 = +0.34 \text{ V}$$

The relation between these potentials is shown schematically in Fig. 8.5.

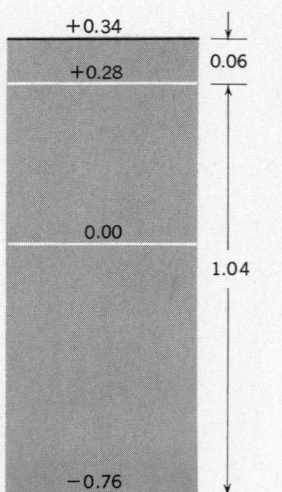

FIGURE 8.5   Potential relations.

Inert Electrodes

So far most of our examples of redox systems have consisted of metals in equilibrium with their ions. There are many important examples of redox systems involving only different oxidation states of ions in solution. A familiar example is the ferric-ferrous system,

$$Fe^{3+} + e \rightleftharpoons Fe^{2+}$$

A solution of ferric and ferrous ions is a possible source of electrons, but some metal must be inserted into the solution to act as a conductor. A metal such as platinum is normally used because it is not easily attacked by most solutions. The platinum is said to be an *inert* electrode, since it does not enter into the reaction.

A cell made up of the ferric-ferrous and ceric-cerous systems is written as

$$Pt \mid Fe^{3+}(x\text{-}M) + Fe^{2+}(y\text{-}M) \parallel Ce^{4+}(a\text{-}M) + Ce^{3+}(b\text{-}M) \mid Pt$$

The student should confirm that the standard potential of this cell as written is $+0.84$ V, and that ceric ion oxidizes ferrous ion spontaneously if the concentration of each reactant is $1\text{-}M$.

APPROXIMATIONS IN REDOX EQUILIBRIA CALCULATIONS

We have seen that the equilibrium constant of a redox reaction can be calculated from standard electrode potentials. From the equilibrium constant we can calculate the degree of completion of a redox reaction at the equivalence point, and thereby decide on the feasibility of the titration. We shall now consider this application of potential data to redox titrations, calculating the potential at different stages during the titration. It will be convenient to construct a titration curve as we did for acid-base titrations. Here we shall plot potential vs milliliters of titrant.

Before considering the details of such calculations, it is important that we examine some of the limitations of the use of potential data in this regard. We have previously mentioned that it was necessary for us to make approximations for the activities of chemical species in redox titrations.

Complex Redox Reactions

The mechanism of many redox reactions is complex, and we do not know the exact nature of the reaction determining the potential at an electrode surface. For example, the reaction for the reduction of dichromate ion to chromic ion is

$$Cr_2O_7{}^{2-} + 14\,H^+ + 6e \rightleftharpoons 2\,Cr^{3+} + 7\,H_2O$$

The standard potential, $+1.33$ V, is obtained indirectly, not from galvanic cell measurements. The reaction above simply represents the correct stoichiometry. It is thought that the reaction proceeds in steps through an unstable intermediate which is then converted into the products. The Nernst expression

$$E = 1.33 - \frac{0.059}{6} \log \frac{[Cr^{3+}]^2}{[Cr_2O_7^{2-}][H^+]^{14}}$$

is not followed. Actually, the potential is practically independent of the concentration of chromic ions.

The same behavior is found with other complex redox systems, the permanganate-manganous system being one important example. With reactions which involve a large number of hydrogen ions, it is normally found that the potential is strongly dependent upon the hydrogen ion concentration, although the dependence cannot be predicted from the coefficients in the balanced equations. Hence, calculations of the potentials of such systems on the basis of these equations give incorrect results. In many cases, however, the error is small, and conclusions regarding the feasibility of a titration may not be invalidated.

Formal Potentials

We have pointed out earlier that it is customary to substitute concentration (molarity) for activity of a soluble electrolyte, and that this assumption can lead to considerable error, particularly in solutions which contain high concentrations of highly charged ions. For example, we express the potential of the ceric-cerous redox couple using the Nernst equation as

$$E = E° - 0.059 \log \frac{[Ce^{3+}]}{[Ce^{4+}]}$$

It would appear from the equation that the potential is independent of the nature and concentration of other electrolytes in the solution. Actually, the value found for $E°$ varies from $+1.23$ V in 1-M HCl to $+1.70$ V in 1-M HClO$_4$, and it varies with the concentration of a given acid. A similar effect is found with many other systems. The potential of the ferric-ferrous systems is $+0.700$ V in 1-M HCl and $+0.732$ V in 1-M HClO$_4$.

There are two reasons for this behavior. First, the activity coefficients of the simple (uncomplexed) ions vary with the electrolyte concentration of the solution. Properly, one should write

$$E = E° - 0.059 \log \frac{a_{Ce^{3+}}}{a_{Ce^{4+}}} = E° - 0.059 \log \frac{\gamma_{Ce^{3+}}[Ce^{3+}]}{\gamma_{Ce^{4+}}[Ce^{4+}]}$$

or

$$E = E° - 0.059 \log \frac{\gamma_{Ce^{3+}}}{\gamma_{Ce^{4+}}} - 0.059 \log \frac{[Ce^{3+}]}{[Ce^{4+}]}$$

and

$$E = E_f^\circ - 0.059 \log \frac{[Ce^{3+}]}{[Ce^{4+}]}$$

Here E_f° is the value of E at unit concentrations of the uncomplexed ions and is called the *formal potential* of the redox couple (see below). The formal potential varies with the ionic strength of the solution since the latter affects the activity coefficients. It also includes any liquid junction potential between the two half-cells.

Second, the occurrence of reactions such as complex formation and hydrolysis will affect the concentrations of the ions and thereby change the potential. Ceric and cerous ions undoubtedly form complexes with anions, as

$$Ce^{4+} + X^- \rightleftharpoons CeX^{3+}$$

$$Ce^{3+} + X^- \rightleftharpoons CeX^{2+}$$

where X^- represents an anion. The extent of this complexing is normally not the same, that is, the formation constant of the ceric and cerous complexes are not equal. Hence, a solution prepared by dissolving an equal number of moles of a ceric salt and a cerous salt in hydrochloric acid does not have equal concentrations of simple ceric and cerous ions. The concentrations of the simple ions are also different from those obtained by dissolving the salts in sulfuric acid or nitric acid.

Another example of the effect of the medium upon a potential is the ferrocyanide-ferricyanide couple:

$$Fe(CN)_6{}^{3-} + e \rightleftharpoons Fe(CN)_6{}^{4-} \qquad E^\circ = +0.356 \text{ V}$$

The potential of a system containing equal formal concentrations of the two ions varies with the concentration of HCl as follows: 1.0-M, $+0.71$ V; 0.1-M, $+0.56$ V; 0.01-M, $+0.48$ V. Both of these anions associate with hydrogen ions to form acids, but the hydroferrocyanic acids are weaker than the hydroferricyanic acids. Hence, as the hydrogen ion concentration is increased, the above equilibrium is shifted to the right and the potential increases.

It is obvious that even if a true standard potential is known, it is erroneous to use this value for a solution containing a high concentration of electrolytes. Hence many chemists prefer to use values called "formal potentials" rather than standard potentials. Swift[1] defines a formal potential as that potential shown by a redox couple in which the concentration of each reactant is one formal and the concentrations of any other constituents of the solution are specified. For example, the values quoted above for the ceric-cerous and

[1] E. H. Swift, *Introductory Quantitative Analysis*, Prentice-Hall, Inc., Englewood Cliffs, N.J., 1950, p. 109.

ferrocyanide-ferricyanide couples are all formal potentials. Such potentials are subject, of course, to direct experimental measurement; hence they are normally of more practical value to the analytical chemist than are standard potentials. Titrations are frequently carried out in the presence of high electrolyte concentrations, and calculations based on formal potentials give in such cases much better agreement with experiment than those based on standard potentials.

It is often difficult to measure a standard potential, and many so-called "standard potentials" found in the literature are actually formal potentials. Table 5, Appendix I, in reality contains both types, but our calculations based upon these values will normally be sufficiently accurate for our purposes. In our examples, no false conclusions regarding feasibility of titrations will be drawn. We shall call attention to any case in which it is important to consider formal potentials. A short list of formal potentials is given in Table 5, Appendix I.

TITRATION CURVES

Titration of Ferrous with Ceric Ion

Let us now consider the following example:

Example. Five millimoles of a ferrous salt are dissolved in 100 ml of sulfuric acid solution and titrated with 0.10-F ceric sulfate. Calculate the potential of an inert electrode in the solution at various intervals in the titration and plot a titration curve. Use 0.68 V as the formal potential of the Fe^{2+}–Fe^{3+} system in sulfuric acid and 1.44 V for the Ce^{3+}–Ce^{4+} system.

(a) *Start of titration.* The potential is determined by the ferrous-ferric ion ratio, that is,

$$E = 0.68 - 0.059 \log \frac{[Fe^{2+}]}{[Fe^{3+}]}$$

However, we do not know the ferric ion concentration, this being dependent upon how the ferrous salt was prepared, how much has been oxidized by air, etc. Let us assume that no more than 0.1 % of the iron remains in the ferric state, that is, the ferrous to ferric ion ratio is 1000 to 1. For such a condition the potential can be calculated:

$$E = 0.68 - 0.059 \log 1000$$

$$E = 0.50 \text{ V}$$

(If the ferric ion concentration were actually zero, what would be the value of the potential?)

(b) *10-ml ceric solution added.* We now have mixed our two redox systems and allowed them to react and reach equilibrium,

$$Fe^{2+} + Ce^{4+} \rightleftharpoons Fe^{3+} + Ce^{3+}$$

We can calculate the potential from the expression for either redox system, that is,

$$E = 0.68 - 0.059 \log \frac{[\mathrm{Fe}^{2+}]}{[\mathrm{Fe}^{3+}]}$$

$$E = 1.44 - 0.059 \log \frac{[\mathrm{Ce}^{3+}]}{[\mathrm{Ce}^{4+}]}$$

The system is at equilibrium, that is, each redox couple has the same potential.[2] It is simpler at this stage of the titration to use the expression for the ferric-ferrous system since we can estimate the concentrations of these two ions more readily than that of the ceric ion as seen below:

$$[\mathrm{Fe}^{2+}] = \left\{ \frac{4}{110} + x \right\} \mathrm{mmol/ml}$$

$$[\mathrm{Fe}^{3+}] = \left\{ \frac{1}{110} - x \right\} \mathrm{mmol/ml}$$

$$[\mathrm{Ce}^{3+}] = \left\{ \frac{1}{110} - x \right\} \mathrm{mmol/ml}$$

$$[\mathrm{Ce}^{4+}] = x \,\mathrm{mmol/ml}$$

The value of x can be calculated, of course, from the equilibrium constant of the reaction. Assuming that the reaction goes well to completion, x is small and may be disregarded in estimating the ferric and ferrous ion concentrations. Hence

$$E = 0.68 - 0.059 \log \frac{4/110}{1/110}$$

or

$$E = 0.64 \,\mathrm{V}$$

(Note that the volume term cancels, that is, the potential is independent of volume.)

Values of the potential of all other points before the equivalence point are calculated in the same manner. In Table 8.1 is a list of such values, and these are plotted in Fig. 8.6. Note that the potential rises slowly in the earlier stages of the titration and begins to increase more rapidly as the equivalence point is approached.

---

[2] Some students ask why this is so. They have become accustomed to calculating the potential of a galvanic cell and think that the potentials of the two half-cells are different. They usually are, but at equilibrium the galvanic cell potential is zero, meaning that the two single electrodes have the same potential, here designated by E. In the titration we are placing the two reagents in the same container and allowing them to come to equilibrium. The solution has only one potential and it can be calculated from either redox system. This is the potential you would observe if you made your titration solution one half of the galvanic cell, and the other electrode was the standard hydrogen electrode.

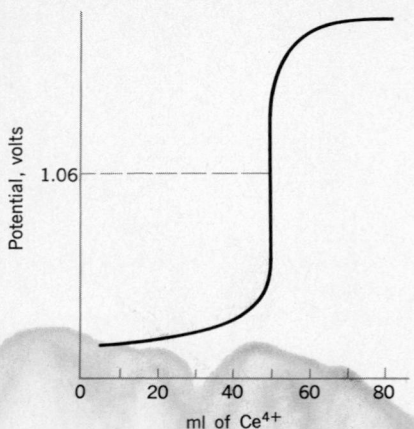

Potential, volts

1.06

0   20   40   60   80

ml of Ce⁴⁺

FIGURE 8.6   Titration of ferrous with ceric ion.

TABLE 8.1   REDOX POTENTIAL DURING TITRATION OF 5 mmol OF Fe^{2+} WITH 0.1-M Ce^{4+}

ml Ce^{4+}	mmol Fe^{2+} unoxidized	% Fe^{2+} oxidized	E, volts
0.00	5.00	0	—
10.00	4.00	20	+0.64
20.00	3.00	40	0.67
30.00	2.00	60	0.69
40.00	1.00	80	0.72
45.00	0.50	90	0.74
49.50	0.05	99	0.80
49.95	0.005	99.9	0.86
50.00	—	100	1.06
	mmol excess Ce^{4+}		
50.05	0.005		+1.26
50.50	0.05		1.32
51.00	0.10		1.34
55.00	0.50		1.38
60.00	1.00		1.40

(c) *Equivalence point.* This point is reached when 50 ml of ceric solution are added. The concentrations of the reactants and products are then

$$[Fe^{2+}] = [Ce^{4+}] = x$$

$$[Fe^{3+}] = [Ce^{3+}] = \frac{5}{150} - x$$

If either of the following expressions is employed, it is necessary to evaluate x, using the equilibrium constant in order to calculate the potential:

$$E = 0.68 - 0.059 \log \frac{[Fe^{2+}]}{[Fe^{3+}]}$$

$$E = 1.44 - 0.059 \log \frac{[Ce^{3+}]}{[Ce^{4+}]}$$

Notice, however, that if the two equations are added, giving

$$2E = 2.12 - 0.059 \log \frac{[Fe^{2+}][Ce^{3+}]}{[Fe^{3+}][Ce^{4+}]}$$

the logarithmic term is zero, since at the equivalence point

$$[Fe^{2+}] = [Ce^{4+}] \quad \text{and} \quad [Fe^{3+}] = [Ce^{3+}]$$

Hence

$$2E = 2.12 \quad \text{or} \quad E = 1.06 \text{ V}$$

For any reaction in which the number of electrons lost by the reductant is the same as the number gained by the oxidant, the potential at the equivalence point is simply the arithmetic mean of the two standard potentials:

$$E_{\text{eq pt}} = \frac{E_1^\circ + E_2^\circ}{2}$$

(d) *60-ml ceric solution added.* After the addition of 60 ml of titrant, the concentrations are

$$[Fe^{2+}] = x$$

$$[Fe^{3+}] = \left\{ \frac{5}{160} - x \right\} \text{mmol/ml}$$

$$[Ce^{3+}] = \left\{ \frac{5}{160} - x \right\} \text{mmol/ml}$$

$$[Ce^{4+}] = \left\{ \frac{1}{160} + x \right\} \text{mmol/ml}$$

It is now the ferrous ion concentration that must be evaluated from the equilibrium constant. Hence, it is more convenient to employ the expression for the ceric-cerous system:

$$E = 1.44 - 0.059 \log \frac{[Ce^{3+}]}{[Ce^{4+}]}$$

Noting that x is small, we write

$$E = 1.44 - 0.059 \log \frac{5/160}{1/160} = 1.40 \text{ V}$$

Other values beyond the equivalence point are calculated in the same manner. The curve is plotted in Fig. 8.6, where its similarity to a strong-base titration curve may be seen. A large change in potential occurs in the vicinity of the equivalence point of the titration. The data are given in Table 8.1.

Titration of Stannous with Ceric Ion

Let us consider now an example where the reductant loses two electrons while the oxidant gains one.

Example. Calculate the potential at the equivalence point in the titration of stannous ion with ceric ion:

$$Sn^{2+} + 2\,Ce^{4+} \rightleftharpoons Sn^{4+} + 2\,Ce^{3+}$$

The potential is given by either of the following expressions:

$$E = 0.15 - \frac{0.059}{2} \log \frac{[Sn^{2+}]}{[Sn^{4+}]}$$

or

$$E = 1.44 - 0.059 \log \frac{[Ce^{3+}]}{[Ce^{4+}]}$$

Multiplying the first equation by 2 and adding it to the second gives

$$3E = 1.74 - 0.059 \log \frac{[Sn^{2+}][Ce^{3+}]}{[Sn^{4+}][Ce^{4+}]}$$

The logarithmic term is zero since at the equivalence point[3]

$$[Ce^{4+}] = 2[Sn^{2+}] \quad \text{and} \quad [Ce^{3+}] = 2[Sn^{4+}]$$

Hence

$$E = \frac{1.74}{3} = 0.58 \text{ V}$$

For the case in which one redox system gains or loses one electron and the other

---

[3] Remember that the concentrations are molarities. Obviously, the number of equivalents of ceric ion is the same as that of stannous ion. But there are twice as many moles of ceric as of stannous ion.

loses or gains two, the potential of the equivalence point is

$$E = \frac{E_1^\circ + 2E_2^\circ}{3}$$

where E_1° is the standard potential of the first system and E_2° that of the second. It should be noted that the titration curve is not symmetrical about the equivalence point in this case as it is in the titration of ferrous with ceric ion. This is always true when the two redox systems exchange a different number of electrons per molecule.

A completely general expression for the potential at the equivalence point can be derived in the same manner that we have employed here (see Problem 6).

Titration of Other Redox Couples

Figure 8.7 shows the variation of potential with fraction of reagent in the oxidized form for several redox couples. The curves for couples with oxidation potentials greater than 1 V have been plotted on a scale to the right of those couples with potentials less than 1 V. This is done to emphasize the fact that a single titration curve is a combination of two of the branches plotted here.

In comparing Fig. 8.7 with the titration curves for acid-base reactions, one should keep in mind the fact that the acid-base properties of our solvent, water, are quite different from the redox properties. Protons are rapidly transferred to H_2O to form H_3O^+, and just as easily they passed along to some other base to regenerate water. Likewise, removal of a proton to form OH^- does not alter water irreversibly. But the addition of electrons to water is a different matter:

$$2\,H_2O + 2e \longrightarrow 2\,OH^- + H_2$$

Hydrogen, not very soluble in water, tends to escape from the solution as a gas. Moreover, even if it remained and tried to reduce something else, many of its reactions are slow under ordinary conditions. The same sort of considerations arise when water is oxidized to O_2.

Thus we do not ordinarily encounter a leveling effect in redox titrations. Reducing agents stronger than H_2 would be leveled to the power of that reagent; similarly, stronger oxidants than O_2 would be consumed in aqueous solution. But, because H_2 and O_2 are not suitable titrants in aqueous redox systems, we generally avoid reagents that oxidize or reduce water, at least those which do so at an appreciable rate. Thus, in common redox titrations, each reagent exerts its own characteristic reactivity, with no mediation by the solvent.

Several points about Fig. 8.7 should be noted.

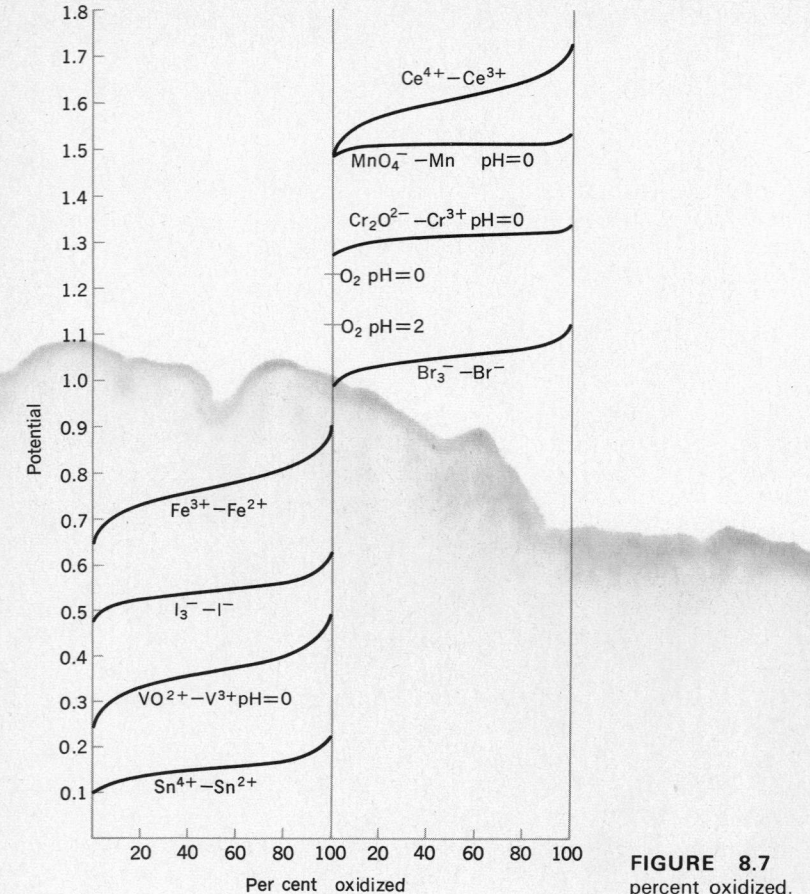

FIGURE 8.7 Variation of potential with percent oxidized.

1. The change in potential at the equivalence point in the titration of, say, ferrous ion depends upon the oxidant used. The oxidants are not leveled by water as pointed out before.

2. The shape of a curve depends upon the value of n, the number of electrons gained or lost by the oxidant or reductant. Note that the ferrous-ferric curve ($n = 1$) is steeper than the stannic-stannous curve ($n = 2$). Also note the flatness of the permanganate and dichromate curves, where n is 5 and 6, respectively. The shape of a titration curve will obviously be determined by that of the two halves which make up the curve.

3. The curves are asymptotic to the vertical axis at zero and 100 % oxidation. The curves are flattest near the midpoints (50 % oxidation), which corresponds to the standard potential for a couple such as Fe^{3+}-Fe^{2+}. The stabilization of the potential in this region is analogous

to buffering action of an acid-base pair about the pH region which corresponds to the pK_a. A redox couple is said to be *poised* in this region where the potential is stabilized.

4. In Fig. 8.7 the potential of the reaction

$$O_2 + 4H^+ + 4e \rightleftharpoons 2H_2O$$

is indicated at pH 0 and 2. Redox couples with standard potentials more positive than these values should not be stable in water at pH 0 and 2. Solutions of these couples are usually stable, however, since the reactions with water to liberate oxygen are generally slow.

FEASIBILITY OF REDOX TITRATIONS

The magnitude of the equilibrium constant required for a feasible redox titration can be calculated as was done previously for acid-base (page 94), complex (page 143), and precipitation titrations (page 162). The following example illustrates this.

Example. For the redox reaction

$$Ox_1 + Red_2 \rightleftharpoons Red_1 + Ox_2$$

where

$$Ox_1 + e \rightleftharpoons Red_1 \qquad E_1^\circ$$

$$Ox_2 + e \rightleftharpoons Red_2 \qquad E_2^\circ$$

(a) Calculate the value of the equilibrium constant for the following conditions: 50 ml of 0.10-M Red_2 is titrated with 0.10-M Ox_1. When 49.95 ml of titrant is added, essentially all of Red_2 has reacted. On the addition of two more drops (0.10 ml) of titrant, the value of $pRed_2$ changes by 2.00 units.

(b) What is the difference in standard potentials of the two redox couples for this value of K_t?

(a) We start with $50 \times 0.10 = 5.0$ mmol of Red_2, and at 49.95 ml of titrant 0.0050 mmol remains unreacted. Hence

$$[Red_2] = \frac{0.0050 \text{ mmol}}{99.95 \text{ ml}} \cong 5 \times 10^{-5}\text{-}M$$

$$pRed_2 = 4.30$$

For a change of 2.00 units, $pRed_2 = 6.30$ and $[Red_2] = 5 \times 10^{-7}$-$M$ when the volume of titrant is 50.05 ml. The other concentrations are:

$$[Ox_1] = \frac{0.05 \times 0.10}{100.05} \cong 5 \times 10^{-5}$$

$$[Red_1] = [Ox_2] \cong \frac{5 \text{ mmol}}{100.05 \text{ ml}} \cong 5 \times 10^{-2}\text{-}M$$

Hence

$$K_t = \frac{(5 \times 10^{-2})(5 \times 10^{-2})}{(5 \times 10^{-5})(5 \times 10^{-7})}$$

$$K_t = 1 \times 10^8$$

(b) Since

$$E_1^\circ - E_2^\circ = \frac{0.059}{1} \log K$$

$$E_1^\circ - E_2^\circ = 0.059 \log 1 \times 10^8$$

$$E_1^\circ - E_2^\circ = 0.47 \text{ V}$$

Note that in this example the number of electrons, n, is 1 for both redox couples. See problems 15 and 16 for calculations involving other values of n.

REDOX INDICATORS

There are several types of indicators which may be used in redox titrations:

1.   A colored substance may act as its own indicator. For example, potassium permanganate solutions are so deeply colored that a slight excess of this reagent in a titration can be easily detected.

2.   A *specific* indicator is a substance which reacts in a specific manner with one of the reagents in a titration to produce a color. Examples are starch, which forms a deep-blue color with iodine, and thiocyanate ion, which forms a red color with ferric ion.

3.   External, or *spot test*, indicators were once employed when no internal indicator was available. The ferricyanide ion was used to detect ferrous ion by formation of ferrous ferricyanide (Turnbull's blue) on a spot plate outside the titration vessel.

4.   The redox potential can be followed during a titration and the equivalence point detected from the large break in the titration curve. Such a procedure is called potentiometric titration (see Chapter 9), and the titration curve may be plotted manually, or automatically recorded.

5.   Finally, an indicator which itself undergoes oxidation-reduction may be employed. We shall refer to such a substance as a true redox indicator, and it is with such a reagent that the rest of our discussion is concerned.

For simplicity, let us designate the redox couple as follows:

$$\underset{\text{Color A}}{\text{In}^+} + e \rightleftarrows \underset{\text{Color B}}{\text{In}}$$

where one electron is gained by the oxidant and no hydrogen ions are involved in the reaction. Let us also say that the colors of the oxidized and reduced forms are different, as indicated above. The equation for the potential of this system is

$$E = E_i^\circ - 0.059 \log \frac{[\text{In}]}{[\text{In}^+]}$$

where E_i° is the standard potential of the indicator couple.

Let us now assume that, if the ratio $[\text{In}]/[\text{In}^+]$ is 10 to 1 or greater, only color B can be seen by the eye. (See page 90 for similar treatment of acid-base indicators.) Also, if the ratio is 1 to 10 or smaller, only color A is observed. That is,

$$\text{Color B}: E = E_i^\circ - 0.059 \log 10/1 = E_i^\circ - 0.059$$
$$\text{Color A}: E = E_i^\circ - 0.059 \log 1/10 = E_i^\circ + 0.059$$

Subtracting,
$$\Delta E = \pm 2 \times 0.059 = \pm 0.12 \text{ V}$$

Thus a change in potential of about 0.12 V is required to bring about a change in color of the indicator, if our assumptions are reasonable.

Table 8.2 lists some true redox indicators with the colors observed and the "transition" potentials of the redox couple. The latter are the formal potentials of the systems in the media indicated and are usually of more practical value than the standard potentials. In many cases the oxidized and reduced forms of the indicator are weak acids or bases and their concentrations depend on the pH of the solution. In this case the equation given above is not strictly correct and the formal potentials, often called transition potentials in the case of indicators, are more properly employed.

TABLE 8.2   TRANSITION POTENTIALS OF SOME REDOX INDICATORS

Indicator	Color of reductant	Color of oxidant	Transition potential, volts	Conditions
Phenosafranine	Colorless	Red	+0.28	1-M acid
Indigo tetrasulfonate	Colorless	Blue	0.36	1-M acid
Methylene blue	Colorless	Blue	0.53	1-M acid
Diphenylamine	Colorless	Violet	0.76	1-M H$_2$SO$_4$
Diphenylbenzidine	Colorless	Violet	0.76	1-M H$_2$SO$_4$
Diphenylaminesulfonic acid	Colorless	Red-violet	0.85	Dilute acid
5,6-Dimethylferroin			0.97	1-M H$_2$SO$_4$
Erioglaucin A	Yellow-green	Bluish-red	0.98	0.5-M H$_2$SO$_4$
5-Methylferroin			1.02	1-M H$_2$SO$_4$
Ferroin	Red	Faint blue	1.11	1-M H$_2$SO$_4$
Niroferroin	Red	Faint blue	1.25	1-M H$_2$SO$_4$

Selection of Indicator

Obviously an indicator should change color at or near the equivalence potential. If the titration is feasible, there will be a large change in potential at the equivalence point, and this should be sufficient to bring about the change in color of the indicator. The following example illustrates more precisely the procedure that may be followed to select the proper indicator.

Example. (a) In the titration of ferrous iron with ceric sulfate in 1-M sulfuric acid, what indicator should be used? We have calculated the potential at the equivalence point to be 1.06 V (page 223). Referring to Table 8.2, it is seen that ferroin, with a transition potential of 1.11 V, is a suitable indicator. The standard potential of ferroin is 1.06 V, but the color change occurs at 1.11 V since it is necessary to have more of the indicator in the oxidized form (light blue) than the reduced form (dark red).

(b) Ferrous iron is titrated with an oxidizing agent in a sulfuric-phosphoric acid medium. What should be the transition potential of an indicator which changes color when all but 0.1 % of ferrous ion is oxidized to ferric?

The formal potential of the ferric-ferrous couple in 1-F H_2SO_4 and 0.5-F in H_3PO_4 is 0.61 V. Hence

$$E = 0.61 - 0.059 \log \frac{[Fe^{2+}]}{[Fe^{3+}]}$$

$$E = 0.61 - 0.059 \log \frac{1}{1000}$$

$$E = 0.61 + 0.18 = 0.79 \text{ V}$$

The indicator diphenylaminesulfonic acid is frequently used when iron is titrated with potassium dichromate in sulfuric-phosphoric acid media. Note (Table 8.2) that its transition potential is 0.85 V, and hence it changes color when even less than 0.1 % of Fe^{2+} remains unoxidized.

STRUCTURAL CHEMISTRY OF REDOX INDICATORS

The redox indicators to which we have referred in this chapter are organic molecules that undergo structural changes upon being oxidized or reduced. There are fewer such indicators than there are acid-base indicators, and their chemistry has not been as widely studied. Nevertheless, the structural changes which account for the different colors are known for a number of substances. We shall consider only two examples here, sodium diphenylaminesulfonate and ferrous orthophenanthroline (ferroin).

Diphenylamine was one of the first redox indicators to be widely used in volumetric analysis. Since this compound is difficultly soluble in water, and since tungstate ion and mercuric chloride interfere with its action, the barium or sodium salt of diphenylaminesulfonic acid is more commonly used. The reduced form of this indicator is colorless, the oxidized form a deep violet. The mechanism of the color change has been shown to be as follows, using diphenylamine as the example:[4]

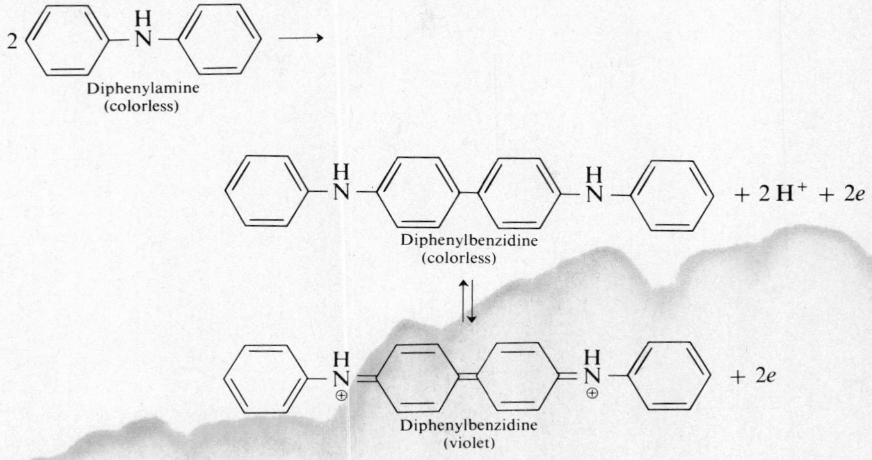

Diphenylamine
(colorless)

Diphenylbenzidine
(colorless)

$+ 2H^+ + 2e$

Diphenylbenzidine
(violet)

$+ 2e$

The presence of a long conjugated system, such as that in the diphenyl-benzidine ion, leads to absorption of light in the visible region, and hence the ion is colored.

The indicator ferroin is the ferrous complex of the organic compound 1,10-phenanthroline,

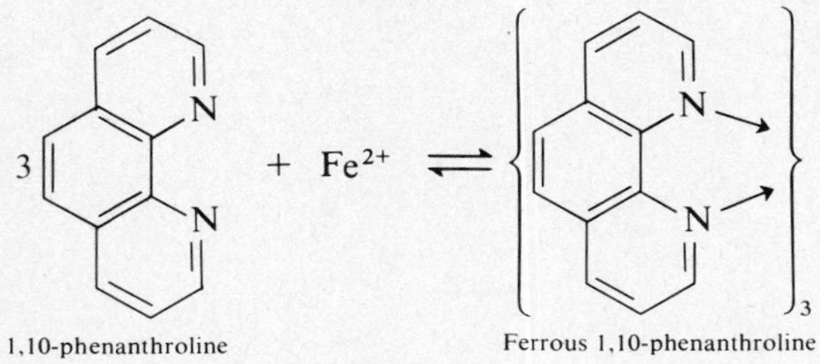

3 1,10-phenanthroline $\quad + Fe^{2+} \rightleftharpoons$ Ferrous 1,10-phenanthroline

Each of two nitrogen atoms in 1,10-phenanthroline has an unshared pair of electrons that can be shared with the ferrous ion. Three such molecules of the organic compound attach themselves to the metallic ion to form a blood-red complex ion. The ferrous ion can be oxidized to ferric, and the latter ion also forms a complex with three molecules of 1,10-phenanthroline. The color of the ferric complex is light blue, and hence a sharp color change occurs when ferrous is oxidized to ferric in the presence of 1,10-phenanthroline:

$$Ph_3Fe^{3+} + e \rightleftharpoons Ph_3Fe^{2+} \qquad E° = 1.06 \text{ V}$$

light blue $\qquad$ dark red

[4] I. M. Kolthoff and L. A. Sarver, *J. Am. Chem. Soc.*, **52**, 4179 (1930).

The indicator is prepared by mixing equivalent quantities of ferrous sulfate and 1,10-phenanthroline. The complex salt is called *ferroin*; the complex salt of ferric ions is called *ferriin*. As previously mentioned, the color change occurs at about 1.11 V, since the color of ferroin is so much more intense than that of ferriin.

Substituted 1,10-phenanthrolines also form complexes with ferrous and ferric ions and act as redox indicators. The redox potentials are different from that of the ferroin-ferriin system. A few examples are included in Table 8.2, where a partial list of redox indicators is given.

REFERENCES

J. J. LINGANE, *Electroanalytical Chemistry*, 2nd ed., Interscience Publishers, Inc., New York, 1958.

H. A. LAITINEN, *Chemical Analysis*, McGraw-Hill Book Company, New York, 1960.

H. F. WALTON, *Principles and Methods of Chemical Analysis*, Prentice-Hall, Inc., Englewood Cliffs, N.J., 1964.

R. G. BATES, "Electrode Potentials," and F. R. DUKE, "Oxidation-Reduction Equilibria and Titration Curves," Chapters 9 and 16, Part 1, Vol. 1, of *Treatise on Analytical Chemistry*, I. M. Kolthoff, P. J. Elving, and E. B. Sandell, eds., Interscience Publishers, Inc., New York, 1959.

QUESTIONS

1. Consult the table of redox potentials in the appendix. Which is the strongest oxidant in the table? the weakest? Which is the strongest reductant? the weakest?

2. List the following in order of decreasing strength as reductants (all unit activity): Pb, Au, Cl^-, Fe^{2+}, Cu^+, Ag, Fe, and Ca.

3. Repeat Question 2 for the following oxidants: Ba^{2+}, Fe^{2+}, Au^+, Zn^{2+}, Ce^{4+}, Fe^{3+}, Pb^{2+}, and O_2.

4. Which is the better oxidant (unit activity), I_2 or H_3AsO_4? Explain how the titration of H_3AsO_3 with I_2 is carried out feasibly.

5. Explain why the leveling effect is not observed with redox reagents as with acids and bases.

6. The standard potential of the ferrous-ferric couple is $+0.77$ V, whereas that of the ferroin-ferriin couple is $+1.06$ V. Which complex is the more stable (has the larger stability constant), ferroin or ferriin? Explain.

7. Suppose we chose to write redox reactions as

$$Zn \rightleftharpoons Zn^{2+} + 2e$$

with $E° = +0.76$ V. If we followed the same conventions for obtaining the cell reaction (as on page 210), what changes in the conclusions drawn from the sign of $E°$ are necessary?

8. If the saturated calomel electrode were adopted as the primary reference electrode and assigned a value of zero volts, what would be the potentials of the following couples?

$$2\,H^+ + 2e \rightleftharpoons H_2$$

$$K^+ + e \rightleftharpoons K$$

$$MnO_4^- + 8\,H^+ + 5e \rightleftharpoons Mn^{2+} + 4\,H_2O$$

9. Draw a graph plotting the potential on the vertical axis and pH on the horizontal axis for the following redox couples:

$$2\,H^+ + 2e \rightleftharpoons H_2$$

$$O_2 + 4\,H^+ + 4e \rightleftharpoons 2\,H_2O$$

$$MnO_4^- + 8\,H^+ + 5e \rightleftharpoons Mn^{2+} + 4\,H_2O \text{ (up to } pH\text{ 6)}$$

$$MnO_4^- + 4\,H^+ + 3e \rightleftharpoons MnO_2 + 2\,H_2O \text{ (above } pH\text{ 8)}$$

$$Ce^{4+} + e \rightleftharpoons Ce^{3+}$$

$$Sn^{2+} + 2e \rightleftharpoons Sn \text{ (up to } pH\text{ 4)}$$

10. Which of the ions in the previous question should not be stable in water solutions? How does pH affect the stabilities? Why are such solutions apparently stable in spite of these data?

11. The following relationship is given in some texts:

$$\log K = 16.9nE°$$

Show that this is the same relationship we derived in this chapter.

PROBLEMS   For simplicity in arithmetical calculations, round off 0.059 to 0.06 in all problems. (The answers given in the book have been obtained using 0.06.)

1. *Cell potentials.* Calculate the potentials of the following cells. Write the cell reaction, and determine the polarities of the electrodes.

   (a) $Fe|Fe^{2+}(1\text{-}M)\,||Cd^{2+}(0.001\text{-}M)|Cd$

   (b) $Fe|Fe^{2+}(0.002\text{-}M)|\,|Cd^{2+}(0.2\text{-}M)|Cd$

   (c) $Zn|Zn^{2+}(0.2\text{-}M|\,|Cr^{3+}(10^{-4}\text{-}M)|Cr$

   (d) $Zn|Zn^{2+}(0.001\text{-}M)|\,|Cr^{3+}(0.1\text{-}M)|Cr$

(e) $$Ag|AgCl, HCl(0.01\text{-}M)|H_2(1\text{-atm}), Pt$$

(f) $$Pt|Fe^{2+}(0.1\text{-}M) + Fe^{3+}(10^{-5}\text{-}M)| \; |Cr^{3+}(10^{-5}\text{-}M) + Cr_2O_7^{2-}(0.1\text{-}M) \\ + H^+(1\text{-}M)|, Pt$$

(g) $$Ag|AgCl, HCl(1.0\text{-}M)| \; |KCl(0.1\text{-}M), Hg_2Cl_2|Hg$$

(h) $$Pt, H_2(0.64 \text{ atm})|HCl(0.01\text{-}M)|Cl_2(1\text{-atm}), Pt$$

2. *Hydrogen electrode.* Derive an equation relating the potential of the hydrogen electrode to the *pH* of the solution. Consider the hydrogen gas pressure as 1 atm. What is the potential at *pH* 7? in a 0.01-*M* solution of NaOH?

3. *Equilibrium constant.* Calculate the equilibrium constant for the reduction of ferric ion by stannous to form ferrous and stannic ions. What is the concentration of ferric ion in a solution containing stannous, stannic, and ferrous ions each at a concentration of 0.2-*M*?

4. *Cell potential.* A platinum electrode is placed in the solution of the previous problem. This is made one electrode of a cell, the other half being a standard hydrogen electrode. What is the voltage of the cell? Calculate this from both redox couples, showing that both have the same potential.

5. *Single electrode potential.* Suppose one could lower the ferric ion concentration in a solution to only one ion per liter of solution. (a) If the ferrous ion concentration is 0.5-*M*, what is the potential of the ferric-ferrous redox couple? (b) How low would the ferric ion concentration need to be in order for the potential of the couple to be -2.00 V, the ferrous ion concentration being 0.1-*M*?

6. *Equivalence point.* Show that the potential at the equivalence point in the titration of Red_1 with Ox_2 is

$$E = \frac{aE_1^\circ + bE_2^\circ}{a + b}$$

where

$$Ox_1 + ae \rightleftharpoons Red_1 \quad E_1^\circ$$

and

$$Ox_2 + be \rightleftharpoons Red_2 \quad E_2^\circ$$

7. *Equivalence point.* Show that the potential at the equivalence point in the titration of ferrous ion with permanganate is

$$E = \frac{E_1^\circ + 5E_2^\circ}{6} - 0.08 \, pH$$

where E_1° is the standard potential of the ferric-ferrous couple and E_2° is that of the permanganate-manganous couple.

8. *Mixtures of solutions.* In the following examples the solutions are mixed and the reaction reaches equilibrium. A platinum electrode is inserted in the solution

making a half-cell. This half-cell is connected to a standard hydrogen electrode and the potential measured. In each case calculate the potential. (a) 50 ml of 0.10-M Fe^{3+} + 50 ml of 0.10-M Sn^{2+}. (b) 50 ml of 0.20-M Fe^{3+} + 50 ml of 0.08-M Sn^{2+}. (c) 40 ml of 0.06-M Fe^{2+} + 16 ml of 0.05-M B^{4+} where B^{4+} + $3e \rightleftharpoons B^+$, $E° = +1.30$ V. (d) 50 ml of 0.12-M Fe^{2+} + 50 ml of 0.10-M $Cr_2O_7^{2-}$, $[H^+] = 1.00$-M. (e) 40 ml of 0.25-M Sn^{2+} + 10 ml of 0.10-M MnO_4^-, $[H^+] = 1.0$-M.

9. *Reference electrode.* The potential of a cell made up of an electrode of unknown potential and a standard calomel is 0.90 V. The calomel electrode is positive. Calculate the potential of the unknown electrode referred to hydrogen.

10. *pH-Cell potential.* Given the cell

$$Pt, H_2(1 \text{ atm})|H^+(x - M)| \, |KCl(1\text{-}M), Hg_2Cl_2|Hg$$

(a) Derive an equation relating the potential of this cell to the pH of the solution in the left-hand electrode. (b) 50 ml of 0.10-M acetic acid is placed in the left-hand electrode. What is the potential of the cell? (c) 50 ml of 0.10-M NaOH is added to the acetic acid in part (b). After equilibrium is reached, what is the potential of the cell?

11. *Dissociation constant.* The following cell has a potential of 0.82 V; the calomel electrode is positive.

$$Pt, H_2(1 \text{ atm})|NaX(0.10\text{-}M)| \, |KCl(1\text{-}M), Hg_2Cl_2|Hg$$

NaX is the salt of the weak acid HX. Its presence determines the hydrogen ion concentration in the hydrogen electrode. Calculate the dissociation constant of HX.

12. *Buffer solution.* The same cell as in Problem 11 is set up, except that the solution in the hydrogen electrode is 0.10-M in HX and 0.050-M in NaX. Calculate the potential of the cell.

13. *Weak base.* Calculate the potential of the following cell:

$$Pt, H_2(1 \text{ atm})|BOH(0.10\text{-}M)| \, |KCl(sat), Hg_2Cl_2|Hg$$

BOH is a weak base, $K_b = 5 \times 10^{-4}$.

14. *Concentration cell.* Calculate the potential of the following cell:

$$Pt, H_2(1 \text{ atm})|H^+(0.10\text{-}M)| \, |H^+(0.0010\text{-}M)|H_2(1 \text{ atm}), Pt$$

15. *Feasibility of titration.* For the redox titration

$$A^{2+} + 2 M^{3+} \rightleftharpoons A^{4+} + 2 M^{2+}$$

(a) Calculate the value of the equilibrium constant for the following conditions: 50 ml of 0.10-M A^{2+} is titrated with 0.20-M M^{3+}. When 49.95 ml of titrant is added essentially all of A^{2+} has reacted. On addition of two more drops (0.10 ml) of titrant, the value of pA changes by 2.00 units. (b) What is the difference in standard potentials of the two redox couples for this value of K_t?

16. *Feasibility of titration.* Repeat Problem 15 for the titration

$$A^{2+} + N^{4+} \rightleftharpoons A^{4+} + N^{2+}$$

Use 0.10-M A^{2+} and 0.10-M N^{4+}.

17. *Feasibility of titration.* (a) Calculate the equilibrium constant for the titration

$$Fe^{2+} + B^{3+} \rightleftharpoons Fe^{3+} + B^{2+}$$

where the standard potential of the B^{3+}–B^{2+} system is +1.07 V. Do you expect the titration to be feasible? (b) Calculate the number of milligrams of Fe^{2+} which remain unoxidized when 5.0 mmol of Fe^{2+} are titrated with 0.10-M B^{3+}, one drop (0.05 ml) in excess. The final volume is 100 ml.

18. *Indicator.* The indicator ferroin shows a color change at +1.11 V. The standard potential is +1.06 V. Calculate the percentage of the indicator in the oxidized form at the potential of the color change. A one-electron change is involved.

19. *Stability constant.* A solution is prepared by mixing 30 ml of 0.10-M Hg^{2+} with 70 ml of 0.10-F EDTA. The pH of the solution is 4.00. Into the solution are inserted a mercury and a standard calomel electrode giving the cell:

$$Hg|Hg^{2+} + EDTA| \,|KCl(1\text{-}M), Hg_2Cl_2|Hg$$

The potential of the cell is 0.17 V and the calomel electrode is negative. Calculate the value of K_{abs} for the reaction

$$Hg^{2+} + Y^{4-} \rightleftharpoons HgY^{2-}$$

20. *Titration.* 8.00 mmol of Fe^{2+} are dissolved in 100 ml of solution and titrated with 0.10-M B^{4+}, where B^{4+} + 2$e \rightleftharpoons$ B^{2+}, $E° = +1.28$ V. Calculate the potential of the solution referred to hydrogen (a) after the addition of 10.0 ml of titrant, (b) at the equivalence point, and (c) after the addition of 60.0 ml of titrant. (d) Calculate the ratio of ferric to ferrous ions at the equivalence point. (e) What percent of the ferrous ion remains unoxidized at the equivalence point?

21. *Titration.* 3.00 mmol of Fe^{2+} are titrated with 0.025-M Cr$_2$O$_7^{2-}$, the final volume being 100 ml and the hydrogen ion concentration 1-M. Calculate the number of milligrams of Fe^{2+} remaining when 0.10 ml of titrant is in excess.

22. *Direction of reaction.* Given the following redox couples and standard potentials:

$$A^{4+} + e \rightleftharpoons A^{3+} \qquad E° = 1.10 \text{ V}$$

$$B^{4+} + 2e \rightleftharpoons B^{2+} \qquad E° = 1.04 \text{ V}$$

(a) Calculate the equilibrium constant for the reaction

$$2\,A^{4+} + B^{2+} \rightleftharpoons 2\,A^{3+} + B^{4+}$$

(b) What is the direction of spontaneous reaction when each reactant and product is at unit activity? What is the value of $\Delta G°$? (c) What is the direction of spontaneous reaction and value of ΔG at the following activities: $A^{3+} = 0.10$, $B^{4+} = 0.10$, $A^{4+} = 0.001$, and $B^{2+} = 0.01$? (d) Repeat (c) for the following activities: $A^{3+} = 0.10$, $B^{4+} = 0.001$, $A^{4+} = 0.001$, and $B^{2+} = 0.10$.

23. *Equilibrium constant.* (a) Refer to the table of standard potentials and calculate the equilibrium constant for the reaction:

$$H_2(g) + \tfrac{1}{2} O_2(g) \rightleftharpoons H_2O(l)$$

(b) Calculate the value of $\Delta G°$ at 25°C. (c) How do you account for the fact that H_2 and O_2 can be mixed at 25°C and no reaction is noticeable?

24. *Equilibrium constant.* An excess of pure copper turnings is added to a 0.16-M solution of Ag^+. Calculate the final concentration of Ag^+ after equilibrium is reached. Assume the equilibrium concentration of Cu^{2+} is 0.08-M. Explain.

25. *Equilibrium constant.* Suppose a strip of pure copper is placed in 100 ml of 1-M HCl which contains no cupric ions. Assume the following reaction reaches equilibrium

$$Cu + 2 H^+ \rightleftharpoons Cu^{2+} + H_2(g)$$

Calculate (a) the number of copper atoms which dissolve and (b) the milliliters (STP) of H_2 gas produced.

26. *Direction of reaction.* Suppose a strip of copper is placed in 100 ml of an HCl solution which is 0.1-M in cupric ions. Assume the pressure of H_2 gas is 1 atm. What will the hydrogen ion concentration need to be for the reaction in Problem 25 to proceed spontaneously to the right. Is such a concentration possible?

27. *Solubility product constant.* Calculate the K_{sp} of AgCl using only data found in the table of standard potentials.

28. *Solubility product constant.* Excess hydrochloric acid is added to a silver nitrate solution, the final chloride ion concentration being 0.010-M. The silver ion concentration in the solution is determined by inserting a silver electrode and measuring the potential of this electrode against a standard calomel electrode. The potential of the cell is found to be 0.050 V, with the silver electrode positive. Calculate the K_{sp} of AgCl.

29. *Standard potential from K_{sp}.* Given that the K_{sp} of CuBr is 6×10^{-9}, calculate the standard potential of the redox couple

$$Cu^{2+} + Br^- + e \rightleftharpoons CuBr(s)$$

30. *Disproportionation.* (a) From the table of standard potentials, determine whether the following disproportionation occurs spontaneously or not when all reactants are at unit activity:

$$3 Br_2(aq) + 3 H_2O \rightleftharpoons BrO_3^- + 5 Br^- + 6 H^+$$

(b) Calculate the equilibrium constant of the reaction.

31. *Disproportionation.* In basic solution the reaction in Problem 30 is

$$3\,Br_2(aq) + 6\,OH^- \rightleftharpoons BrO_3^- + 5\,Br^- + 3\,H_2O$$

(a) Calculate the equilibrium constant for this reaction. (b) Calculate the *p*H at which the reaction is spontaneous. The activities of Br_2, BrO_3^-, and Br^- are each unity.

32. *Disproportionation.* (a) Refer to the table of standard potentials and calculate whether or not cuprous ion disproportionates (unit activities):

$$2\,Cu^+ \rightleftharpoons Cu^{2+} + Cu$$

(b) Calculate the equilibrium constant for this reaction. (c) How large a concentration of Cu^+ ions can exist in equilibrium with Cu^{2+} ions at 1-*M* concentration?

33. *Complex formation.* (a) Calculate the potential of the following cell:

$$Ag|Ag^+(0.010\text{-}M)|\,|H^+(1.0\text{-}M)|H_2(1\text{ atm}), Pt$$

(b) Ammonia is added to the left-hand electrode until the final concentration of uncomplexed NH_3 is 1.0-*M*. Calculate the potential of the cell.

9 Potentiometric Methods of Analysis

Since the potential of a galvanic cell depends upon the activities of ionic species in the cell solution, the measurements of cell potentials are of considerable importance in analytical chemistry. In many cases a cell can be devised so that its potential depends upon the concentration of a single ionic species in the solution. One of the electrodes of the cell must be such that its potential depends upon the concentration of the ion being determined; it is called an *indicator electrode*. The other electrode is a reference, such as calomel, whose potential is known and remains constant during the measurement.

There are two methods used in making experimental measurements. First, a single measurement of the potential of the cell is made; this is sufficient to determine the concentration of the ion of interest. Second, the ion may be titrated and the potential measured as a function of the volume of titrant. The first method is called *direct potentiometry* and has been used principally in the measurement of pH of aqueous solutions. Today it is also widely applied to the determination of other ions through the use of *ion-selective electrodes*. The second method, called *potentiometric titration*, employs the measurement of potential to detect the equivalence point of a titration. It can be applied to all types of reactions we have found suitable for titrimetric analyses.

Direct potentiometric measurements are very useful for determining the activity of a species in an equilibrium mixture, since the equilibrium is not disturbed by the measurement. For example, the pH of a 0.10-F solution of acetic acid might be measured and the hydrogen ion concentration found to be 0.0013-M. On the other hand, if the solution is titrated, we will find that the concentration is 0.10-M. The titration yields stoichiometric information on

239

the number of available protons, whereas the direct measurement gives the equilibrium concentration of protons in the solution.

Direct potentiometric measurements must be very precise to give the degree of accuracy usually demanded by the analyst. The method is rapid and is readily adapted to automatic continuous-flow analyses used in many industrial plants.

In this chapter we shall first discuss the types of indicator electrodes which are available for various ions. The measurement of pH by direct potentiometry will be examined in some detail. Then we shall discuss the application of potentiometric methods to the four types of reactions used in titrimetric analyses.

INDICATOR ELECTRODES

Metallic Electrodes

Some metals, such as silver, mercury, copper, and lead, can act as indicator electrodes when they are in contact with a solution of their ions. For example, the potential developed at a piece of silver wire dipping in a solution of silver nitrate varies with the activity of silver ion in accordance with the prediction of the Nernst equation. Apparently reversible electron transfer takes place between the metal surface and the ions in solution:

$$Ag^+ + e \rightleftharpoons Ag \qquad E° = +0.80 \text{ V}$$

and the potential is given by the equation

$$E = 0.80 - 0.059 \log \frac{1}{a_{Ag^+}}$$

Electrodes of this type, in which the ion exchanges electrons directly with the metal, are called "electrodes of the first kind."

A number of metals, such as nickel, cobalt, chromium, and tungsten, do not give reproducible potentials when used as electrodes. Such metals are harder and more brittle than those which do behave satisfactorily. It is thought that crystal deformations and oxide coatings may account for this behavior.

The silver-silver chloride electrode, discussed previously as a reference electrode (page 215), is an example of an "electrode of the second kind." The potential is a function of the activity of chloride ions in the solution. The equilibrium can be written

$$AgCl(s) + e \rightleftharpoons Ag + Cl^- \qquad E° = +0.22 \text{ V}$$

and the potential is given by

$$E = 0.22 - 0.059 \log \frac{1}{a_{Cl^-}}$$

In an electrode of the second kind, the ions in solution, Cl^- in this case, do not exchange electrons directly with the metal electrode. Rather, they regulate the concentration of silver ions which exchange electrons with the metal surface.

A widely used "electrode of the third kind" is the mercury-EDTA electrode. It was observed by Reilley and Schmid[1] that the potential of a mercury electrode responds reversibly to other metal ions in solution in the presence of the mercury-EDTA complex. We can represent the electrode system as follows (using M^{2+} as the metal of interest):

$$Hg|M^{2+} + MY^{2-} + HgY^{2-} + Hg^{2+}$$

A small amount of HgY^{2-} is added to the solution. Some of it dissociates to give Hg^{2+} ions, but since the complex is so stable, most of the mercury remains in the form of HgY^{2-}. The metal to be determined must form a weaker EDTA complex than does mercury. Hence, M^{2+} will not remove an appreciable amount of Y^{4-} from Hg^{2+}. Letting K_{HgY} and K_{MY} represent the stability constants of the two complexes, we can derive a relation between the potential and the concentration of M^{2+} as follows. First mercuric ions exchange electrons with the metal:

$$Hg^{2+} + 2e \rightleftharpoons Hg \qquad E^\circ = +0.85 \text{ V}$$

$$E = 0.85 - \frac{0.059}{2} \log \frac{1}{[Hg^{2+}]}$$

If we substitute for $[Hg^{2+}]$ from the expression for K_{HgY} and for $[Y^{4-}]$ using the expression for K_{MY}, we obtain the equation

$$E = 0.85 - 0.03 \log \frac{K_{HgY}[MY^{2-}]}{K_{MY}[HgY^{2-}][M^{2+}]}$$

Let us assume we are titrating M^{2+} with Y^{4-}. Near the equivalence point the term $[MY^{2-}]$ becomes essentially constant. The terms K_{HgY} and K_{MY} are constants, and the concentration of the mercury complex, $[HgY^{2-}]$, is constant throughout the titration since the complex is so stable. Hence, the equation above becomes

$$E = K - 0.03 \log \frac{1}{[M^{2+}]}$$

or

$$E = K - 0.03 \, p\text{M}$$

The term K is a composite of all the constant terms.

[1] C. N. Reilley and R. W. Schmid, *Anal. Chem.*, **30**, 947 (1958); R. W. Schmid and C. N. Reilley, *J. Am. Chem. Soc.*, **78**, 5513 (1956).

The mercury electrode has proved applicable to the potentiometric determination of about thirty metal ions, either by direct or back-titration procedures. Potentials are established rather rapidly with the electrode since all the species except mercury itself are in solution.

An inert metal, such as platinum or gold, serves well as the indicator electrode for redox couples such as $Fe^{3+} + e \rightleftharpoons Fe^{2+}$ (page 217). The function of the metal is simply to transfer electrons; it does not itself enter into the redox reaction. The potential developed is a function of the ratio of the concentrations of the oxidized and reduced forms of the redox couple.

Care must be taken in the use of platinum in the presence of strong oxidizing agents, especially in solutions that contain a high concentration of chloride ions. Platinum is more readily oxidized in the presence of chloride ions because of the formation of the stable $PtCl_4^{2-}$ complex. There is also danger in using platinum in the presence of very strong reducing agents such as chromous ion. The latter ion can reduce hydrogen ion in acid solution, and the reaction, which is normally slow, is catalyzed by platinum.

Membrane Electrodes

Membrane electrodes differ in principle from the metal electrodes we have just discussed. No electrons are given up by, or to, the membrane. Rather, a membrane allows certain kinds of ions to penetrate it, but excludes others. The glass electrode, used for determining pH, is the most widely known example of a membrane electrode. It was observed many years ago that a potential is developed at a thin glass membrane which separates two solutions of different hydrogen ion concentration. Furthermore, with certain types of glass, the potential developed is dependent on the difference in concentrations of hydrogen ions on either side of the membrane and is not affected, at least appreciably, by the presence of other ions in the solutions. The glass electrode has been widely studied, and the results have led to the development of glasses which respond selectively to ions other than hydrogen. In addition, other types of membranes have been proposed and are now commercially available for the analytical determination of a number of ions.

We shall consider the glass electrode in some detail since it has been so thoroughly studied. Then we shall look briefly at liquid membrane and solid-state electrodes.

The Glass Electrode for the Measurement of pH

The usual commercial glass electrode consists of a thin glass bulb containing an internal reference electrode, usually silver-silver chloride. The activity of hydrogen ion inside the bulb is kept constant. The bulb is immersed in a solution whose pH is to be determined and the electrode is connected to a reference, such as calomel, via a salt bridge. A schematic diagram of the electrode is shown in Fig. 9.1, where a setup for potentiometric titrations is given. A small hole in the bottom of the calomel electrode acts as the salt bridge by allowing KCl to flow through.

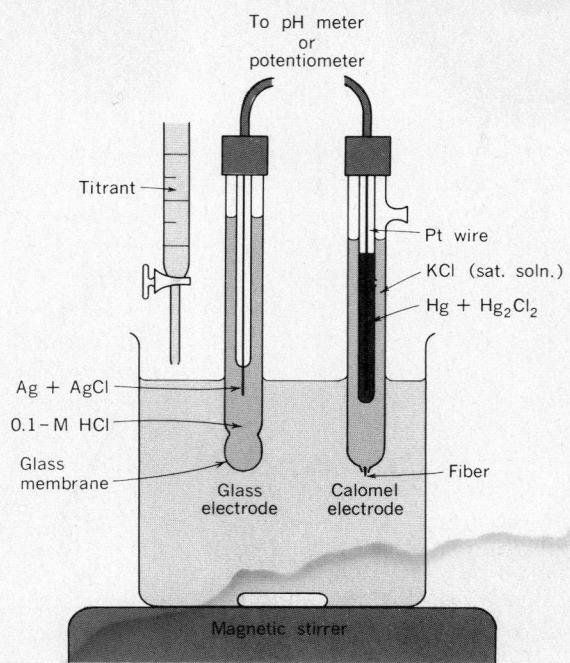

Titrant

To pH meter
or
potentiometer

Pt wire

KCl (sat. soln.)

Hg + Hg$_2$Cl$_2$

Ag + AgCl

0.1 - M HCl

Glass
membrane

Glass
electrode

Calomel
electrode

Fiber

Magnetic stirrer

FIGURE 9.1 Apparatus for potentiometric titration.

The cell can be represented as follows:

$$Ag|AgCl, HCl\,(0.1\text{-}M)|Glass|H^+(x-M)||KCl\,(sat.), Hg_2Cl_2|Hg$$

$\underbrace{\qquad\qquad}_{\text{Glass electrode}}$ $\underbrace{\qquad}_{\substack{\text{Test}\\\text{solution}}}$ $\underbrace{\qquad\qquad}_{\substack{\text{Calomel}\\\text{electrode}}}$

Note that we have simply placed a reference electrode in each of the two solutions separated by the glass membrane. Since the potentials of the two reference electrodes remain constant, any change in the potential of the cell must come from the potential developed across the glass membrane. It is found experimentally that the potential of this cell follows the relation

$$E = k + 0.0591\,pH$$

at 25°C and over a pH range of 0 to 10–12, depending upon the composition of the glass and of the test solution.

Compared with other indicator electrodes for hydrogen ions, the glass electrode has several advantages. First, no foreign substance need be added to the solution whose pH is being measured. Second, substances that are easily oxidized or reduced can be present in the solution being measured without interfering. Such substances might react with hydrogen, for example, in the hydrogen electrode. Third, the electrode can be made quite small, so that very small volumes of solutions can be measured. Fourth, there is no catalytic surface susceptible to poisoning as in the hydrogen electrode. Finally, sparingly buffered solutions can be measured accurately, and the electrode is well suited for continuous measurements.

The glass membrane is somewhat fragile, but this is not a serious disadvantage. One effect that can lead to a serious error, however, is the diffusion of ions other than hydrogen through the membrane in solution of high pH. In a strongly basic solution, where the concentration of hydrogen ions is very low, the diffusion of other cations, such as sodium, becomes appreciable. If the membrane is made of soda-lime glass, this effect is sufficient to invalidate completely measurements in solutions of pH greater than about 10.0. It is possible to correct a pH reading for this effect. Manufacturers of glass electrodes furnish a chart of "sodium ion corrections" for use in solutions of pH greater than 10. In recent years other types of glass have been developed that do not show an appreciable error in solutions up to a pH of about 12.5.[2] These glasses contain a high percentage of lithium oxide in place of sodium oxide and are often referred to as "lithium glasses."

An error also occurs with the glass electrode in very acidic solutions ($pH < 0$). This is thought to be caused by a change in activity of water in the glass membrane brought about by the transfer of H_3O^+ ions through the membrane.

The high resistance of the glass membrane makes it necessary to employ a "pH meter" in order to measure the potential. Many commercial models of pH meters are on the market today. These meters are used principally in connection with a glass electrode, but they can be used, of course, with other electrodes. Such meters have a scale that reads directly in pH units. This scale is first calibrated by immersing the electrodes in a buffer solution of known pH and adjusting the scale to read this value. The same scale can be used for direct reading in millivolt units.

Two different glass electrodes are not likely to give exactly the same potential reading when immersed in the same solution. In fact a small potential may be developed at a glass membrane even if the same solution is on both sides of the membrane. It is thought that this effect results from "strains" in the glass, and it is often referred to as an "asymmetry potential." Because of this effect, it is necessary to calibrate the scale using a buffer, as described above, and it is necessary to repeat this calibration if one glass electrode is replaced by another.

Theory of the Glass-Membrane Potential

A number of proposals have been made to explain the mechanism by which the glass electrode functions. Considerable information has been gained from the efforts mentioned above to reduce the "sodium-ion error" by changing the composition of the glass.

[2] G. A. Perley, *Anal. Chem.*, **21**, 391, 394, 559 (1949).

Glass consists of a negatively charged silicate network containing small cations, principally sodium ions. Other cations, such as hydrogen, can enter the glass by displacing sodium ions, but negative ions are repelled by the negatively charged silicate network. Not all glass membranes give the response to pH mentioned before; quartz and pyrex glass are practically insensitive to changes in pH. The glass commonly used for many years in commercial glass electrodes is "Corning 015," which has the approximate composition (mole percent) Na_2O, 22, CaO, 6, and SiO_2, 72. The electrical resistance of this glass is relatively low and the glass is sensitive only to hydrogen ions up to a pH of about 10. The lithium glasses mentioned above were developed in an attempt to minimize the alkaline error.

It is known that a glass membrane must be soaked in water before it becomes operative. The outer surface of the glass becomes hydrated when the glass is soaked; the inner surface is already hydrated. It is thought that the glass membrane has the following general structure:

E_i	E_d	E_d	E_e
Internal solution $a_{H^+} = a_1$	Inner hydrated gel $\leftarrow 10^{-4}$ mm$\rightarrow$	Dry glass layer $\leftarrow 0.1$ mm$\rightarrow$	Outer hydrated gel $\leftarrow 10^{-4}$ mm$\rightarrow$	External solution $a_{H^+} = a_2$

Surface occupied by H^+ — Surface occupied by H^+

There is a center layer of dry glass sandwiched between two layers of silicic acid gel. These gels are formed by water molecules penetrating into the surface of the silicate lattice. In the process the following reaction occurs:

$$H^+(aq) + Na^+Gl^-(s) \rightleftharpoons Na^+(aq) + H^+Gl^-(s)$$

This is the type of reaction which occurs with cation exchange resins (page 426); the protons are free to move and exchange with other ions, but the silicate lattice is fixed.

At the inner and outer surfaces of the glass membrane, *boundary* potentials E_i and E_e are developed. The explanation for the potential is similar to that of a liquid junction potential (page 209). At the interface between the gel and solution hydrogen ions tend to migrate in the direction of lesser hydrogen-ion activity. The external and internal potentials are given by the expressions:

$$E_e = k_1 + 0.059 \log \frac{(a_2)_1}{(a_2)_s}$$

$$E_i = k_2 + 0.059 \log \frac{(a_1)_1}{(a_1)_s}$$

where $(a_2)_1$ and $(a_1)_1$ are the hydrogen ion activities in the two solutions on either side of the membrane; $(a_2)_s$ and $(a_1)_s$ are the corresponding activities in the gels.

If the two gel surfaces have the same number of sites from which protons can leave, then $k_1 = k_2$ and $(a_1)_s = (a_2)_s$. Hence, the total boundary potential, E_b, is given by

$$E_b = E_e - E_i = 0.059 \log \frac{(a_2)_1}{(a_1)_1}$$

In the glass electrode $(a_1)_1$ is constant. Hence,

$$E_b = k + 0.059 \log (a_2)_1$$

This is the same equation found experimentally for the glass electrode (above).

Potential differences are also developed at the boundaries between the dry glass layer and the inner and outer gel layers. These potentials are developed by the tendencies of sodium and hydrogen ions to migrate in the direction of lesser activity. Sodium ions are unhydrated and loosely bound in the dry glass layer; they can move from the silicate framework toward the gel layers. At the same time, hydrogen ions tend to move toward the dry glass layer, and since hydrogen and sodium ions have different mobilities, a potential difference is developed. It is thought that these *diffusion* potentials, designated E_d in the diagram above, are equal and opposite in sign; hence they cancel. The potential across the glass membrane is therefore dependent only on the difference in hydrogen ion activities in the inner and outer solutions,

$$E = k + 0.059 \log a_2$$

Ion-Selective Glass Electrodes

In recent years glass membranes have been developed which are selective for a given cation, just as the conventional glass electrode is selective for hydrogen ions. For example, glass electrodes are now available commercially for sodium, potassium, lithium, and silver ions. These electrodes are not *specific* for a given ion, but rather they possess a certain *selectivity* for a given ion and for that reason are called *ion-selective* electrodes.

We have already mentioned how the composition of the glass reduced the sodium-ion error of the ordinary glass electrode at high pH. Eisenman and his collaborators[3] studied the influence of alkali metal ions and hydrogen ions on the glass membrane potential as a function of the composition of the glass. They found, for example, that a glass composed of 28% Na_2O, 5% Al_2O_3, and 68% SiO_2 shows a selective response to potassium ions down to an activity of 10^{-4}. A glass with a composition of 15% Li_2O, 25% Al_2O_3, and 60% SiO_2 can be used to determine lithium in the presence of both sodium and potassium ions.

Eisenman related the glass-electrode response to the ion-exchange

[3] See G. Eisenman, *Advances in Analytical Chemistry and Instrumentation*, Vol. 4, John Wiley & Sons, New York, 1965, p. 213, for a summary of this work.

properties of the glass surface. For example, suppose the following exchange reaction occurs at a glass surface:

$$H^+Gl^-(s) + Na^+(aq) \rightleftharpoons Na^+Gl^-(s) + H^+(aq)$$

The boundary potential depends upon the activities of both sodium and hydrogen ions. In addition, sodium ions are able to penetrate the gel and influence the diffusion potential. The diffusion potentials do not cancel as in the case we discussed earlier. Instead, the total potential is given by the expression

$$E = k + 0.059 \log \left\{ \underbrace{(a_{H^+})_{aq}}_{\text{Term } A} + \underbrace{K_{ex}\left(\frac{U_{Na}}{U_H}\right)(a_{Na^+})_{aq}}_{\text{Term } B} \right\}$$

where U_{Na} and U_H are measures of the mobility of sodium and hydrogen ions in the gel, and K_{ex} is the equilibrium constant of the ion-exchange reaction above.

Note that if term B in the equation above is small (K_{ex} small), the potential is dependent mainly on the hydrogen-ion activity. This is the case for the ordinary pH-sensitive glass electrode. On the other hand, if the term B is large (K_{ex} large) and term A is small, the potential is largely a function of the sodium ion activity. It can be seen that the selectivity of the glass electrode is related to the cation exchange selectivity of the glass surface.

Commercial ion-selective electrodes are very similar in construction to the glass electrode. The internal reference electrode is usually silver-silver chloride and the filling solution is the chloride salt of the cation to which the electrode is most responsive. It should be remembered that all these electrodes are responsive to some degree to hydrogen ions and must be used at sufficiently high pH that the term A in the above equation is quite low.

Liquid-Membrane Electrodes

These electrodes employ as the membrane a water-immiscible liquid which will selectively bond the ion being determined. An example is the calcium-ion electrode which uses a cation exchanger that contains a phosphoric acid group. The exchanger has a greater tendency to bond calcium than most other cations. A schematic representation and a drawing of the commercial electrode are shown in Fig. 9.2. The liquid exchanger is held between two porous glass or plastic membranes. It separates the test solution from the internal solution; the latter contains a fixed concentration of calcium chloride and a silver-silver chloride electrode.

At each interface the following reaction occurs:

$$Ca^{2+}(aq) + Ex^{2-} \rightleftharpoons CaEx$$

The potentials developed at the two interfaces are given by

$$E_e = k_1 + \frac{0.059}{2} \log \frac{(a_1)_{aq}}{(a_1)_{Ex}}$$

$$E_i = k_2 + \frac{0.059}{2} \log \frac{(a_2)_{aq}}{(a_2)_{Ex}}$$

where $(a_1)_{aq}$ and $(a_2)_{aq}$ are the activities of calcium ion in the aqueous solutions and $(a_1)_{Ex}$ and $(a_2)_{Ex}$ are the activities in the exchanger phase. Normally the latter activities are equal. Hence the total potential is given by

$$E = E_e - E_i = k + \frac{0.059}{2} \log \frac{(a_1)_{aq}}{(a_2)_{aq}}$$

Since $(a_2)_{aq}$ is fixed, this becomes

$$E = k + \frac{0.059}{2} \log (a_1)_{aq}$$

The calcium electrode is about 3000 times more selective for calcium than for sodium or potassium. Its selectivity ratio for calcium over magnesium is about 200, and for calcium over strontium about 70. It is independent of pH in the range 5.5 to 11, and it can be used to determine calcium ion concentrations as low as 10^{-5}-M.

Several other ion-selective membrane electrodes are available, including anion-exchange membranes for anions such as nitrate, chloride, and perchlorate. An electrode which responds to several divalent cations is used to measure water hardness.

FIGURE 9.2 Liquid membrane electrode. (a) Schematic. (b) Commercial electrode. (Courtesy of Orion Research Inc., Cambridge, Mass.)

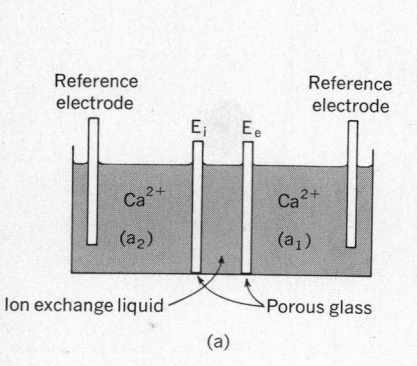

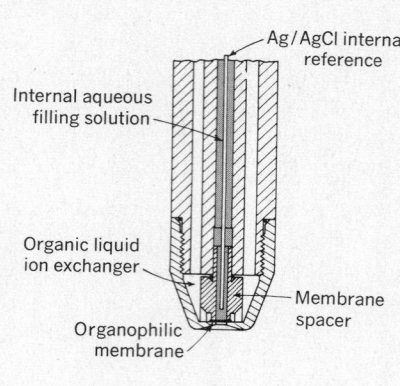

Solid-State and Precipitate Electrodes

Solid materials which are selective to anions, just as glass is selective to cations, have been used successfully as membrane electrodes in recent years. A *solid-state* electrode has a membrane in the form of a single crystal or a pellet of the compound which contains the anion to be determined. A *precipitate* electrode is prepared by suspending a finely divided insoluble salt in an inert semiflexible matrix from which a membrane can be fabricated.

The most successful solid-state electrode is that used to determine fluoride ion. A single crystal of lanthanum fluoride acts as the membrane. The crystal is doped with a rare earth element, europium (II), to increase its electrical conductivity. The electrode responds to fluoride ion down to concentrations of about 10^{-5}-M. It is a thousand times more selective for fluoride than the other common anions. Hydroxide ion does interfere and the electrode is limited in use over the pH range of about 0–8.5. Other successful solid-state electrodes are available for chloride, bromide, iodide, sulfide, cyanide, and thiocyanate ions. In these electrodes the membrane is a cast pellet of an insoluble salt of the anion, such as silver chloride for chloride ions.

A precipitate electrode which is selective for iodide can be prepared by polymerizing silicone rubber in the presence of an equal weight of finely divided silver iodide. After the mixture has solidified, it is sealed in the bottom of a glass tube. Inside the tube is placed a silver-silver iodide electrode dipping in a solution of potassium iodide. Barium sulfate suspended in paraffin is used in a similar manner to prepare an electrode sensitive to sulfate ions.

DIRECT POTENTIOMETRY

Potentiometric Determination of pH

As previously mentioned, one of the principal applications of direct potentiometry is the determination of the pH of aqueous solutions. We wish now to examine briefly the meaning of the term pH as it is measured experimentally by direct potentiometry. A complete discussion of this topic has been given by Bates.[4]

The term pH was defined by Sorensen in 1909 as the negative logarithm of the hydrogen ion *concentration*. It was later realized that the emf of galvanic cells used to measure pH was dependent upon the *activity* of hydrogen ions rather than the *concentration*. Hence the definition of pH was taken to be

$$pH = -\log a_{H^+}$$

This definition is satisfactory from a theoretical standpoint, but the quantity cannot be measured experimentally. There is no way to measure unambiguously the activity of a single ion species. (In thermodynamic terms it is

---

[4] R. G. Bates, *Determination of pH: Theory and Practice*, John Wiley & Sons, New York, 1964.

said that pH is proportional to the work required to transfer hydrogen ions reversibly from the solution examined to one in which the activity of hydrogen ions is unity. No experiment can be performed in which hydrogen ions are transferred without at the same time transferring negative ions.)

The quantity measured potentiometrically is actually neither concentration nor activity of hydrogen ion. It is therefore preferable to define pH in terms of the emf of the cell employed for the measurement. For example, suppose that such a cell consisted of a suitable reference electrode connected by a salt bridge to the solution being treated, in which a hydrogen electrode was immersed:

$$\text{Reference} \, \| \text{H}^+(x\text{-}M) | \text{H}_2, \text{Pt}$$

The equation relating the potential of this cell to pH is

$$E = E_{ref} + 0.059 pH$$

Strictly speaking, this equation should also contain a term E_j, the liquid junction potential, which may be small with an appropriate salt bridge, but not zero. Hence the equation should read

$$E = E_{ref} + 0.059 pH + E_j$$

where E_{ref} is the potential of the reference electrode. Calling $E_{ref} + E_j$ a constant, k, this becomes

$$E = k + 0.059 pH$$

or

$$pH = \frac{E - k}{0.059}$$

The above equation contains two unknowns, pH and k; hence it cannot be used to evaluate both quantities. It is necessary to assign arbitrarily a pH value to some standard buffer in order to fix a practical scale of pH.

The Bureau of Standards determines the pH of certain buffers by careful measurements of selected cells, using reasonable assumptions regarding activity coefficients.[5] Table 9.1 contains a few examples of the buffers recommended by the Bureau. It would be possible, of course, to define a pH scale, according to the equation

$$E = k + 0.059 pH$$

using a single buffer. However, the term k is not strictly constant over a wide

[5] R. G. Bates, *op. cit.*; an excellent summary is given by H. F. Walton, *Principles and Methods of Chemical Analysis*, 2nd ed., Prentice-Hall, Inc., Englewood Cliffs, N.J., 1964, pp. 246–248.

TABLE 9.1 pH VALUES OF NBS STANDARD BUFFERS*

Composition	25°C	pH 30°C	40°C
$KH_3(C_2O_4)_2 \cdot 2H_2O(0.05\text{-}M)$†	1.68	1.69	1.70
KHC_4O_6(sat. at 25°C)	3.56	3.55	3.54
$KHC_8H_4O_4(0.05\text{-}M)$	4.01	4.01	4.03
$KH_2PO_4(0.025\text{-}M) + Na_2HPO_4(0.025\text{-}M)$	6.86	6.85	6.84
$Na_2B_4O_7 \cdot 10H_2O(0.001\text{-}M)$	9.18	9.14	9.07
$Ca(OH)_2$ (sat. at 25°C)†	12.45	12.30	11.99

* R. G. Bates in *Treatise on Analytical Chemistry*, Part I, Vol. I, I. M. Kolthoff and P. J. Elving, eds., The Interscience Encyclopedia, Inc., New York, 1959, p. 375.
† Secondary standards; the other four are primary standards.

pH range largely because of changes in E_j with changes in composition of the solution. It is therefore recommended that a pH standard be chosen which is close to that of the unknown. Even better, two standards, one on either side of the unknown, are recommended.

It is possible to arrange experimental conditions so that the term k is constant to about ± 1 mV over the pH range 2 to 10. This leads to an uncertainty in the value of pH of about ± 0.01 to 0.02 units. Hence it is not possible to obtain significant pH numbers to any greater precision than this by potentiometric measurement.

Most pH measurements made by analytical chemists and biochemists employ a glass electrode connected to a calomel reference electrode by a potassium chloride salt bridge. Assuming that one of the Bureau of Standards buffers is used to standardize the pH meter, just what does the measured, or practical, pH number mean? This question is thoroughly discussed in an article by Feldman.[6] The pH measured will not be exactly equal to $-\log a_{H^+}$, but under ordinary conditions it will be nearly so. By "ordinary conditions" we mean:

1. The ionic strength of the test solution is less than about 3.

2. No unusual ions of exceptional mobility are present in the solution, e.g., very large organic ions, highly hydrated lithium ion, etc.

3. The pH range is about 2 to 10.

4. There are no charged suspensions, such as clays, soils, or ion-exchange resins in the test solution. The meaning of pH measurements near cell surfaces in biological systems may be questionable. Measurements of pH on protein solutions apparently give reasonable results.

Care must be taken in calculating hydrogen-ion concentration from a

[6] I. Feldman, *Anal. Chem.*, **28**, 1859 (1956).

practical pH measurement. In order to make such a calculation it is necessary to know something about the activity coefficient of hydrogen ion:

$$p\text{H} \cong -\log a_{\text{H}^+} = -\log [\text{H}^+]\gamma_{\text{H}^+}$$

If the value of γ_{H^+} is taken as unity, very large errors may result, depending upon the ionic strength of the solution as well as other factors. It is estimated that, at an ionic strength of 0.16, the value of interest in biological chemistry, the magnitude of the error in determining the concentration of hydrogen ion is about 25 % if it is assumed that $[\text{H}^+] = a_{\text{H}^+}$.

Determination of Concentrations of Other Ions

The potential of any indicator electrode is apparently dependent on the activity rather than the concentration of the ion to which it is sensitive. If the concentration of an ion is to be determined by direct potentiometry, the total ionic strength of the sample and standard solutions must be similar. For example, suppose calcium ion is being determined with a calcium ion-selective electrode. The potential is given by

$$E = k + \frac{0.059}{2} \log a_{\text{Ca}^{2+}}$$

$$E = k + \frac{0.059}{2} \log \gamma_{\text{Ca}^{2+}}[\text{Ca}^{2+}]$$

$$E = k + \frac{0.059}{2} \log \gamma_{\text{Ca}^{2+}} + \frac{0.059}{2} \log [\text{Ca}^{2+}]$$

If the ionic strength is held constant, the activity coefficient, $\gamma_{\text{Ca}^{2+}}$, remains constant for all concentrations of calcium ion. The second term on the right side of the equation is constant and can be combined with k, giving

$$E = k' + \frac{0.059}{2} \log [\text{Ca}^{2+}]$$

In practice it is customary to prepare a calibration curve of potential versus the logarithm of the concentration of the ion being determined, with the ionic strength held constant. A salt to which the electrode is not sensitive is added to both the standards and the test solution. The plot is linear if the ionic strength is constant; otherwise it is nonlinear. The potential of the unknown solution, at the same ionic strength as the standards, is measured and the concentration determined from the calibration curve. In the determination of unbounded calcium in serum, the standards and unknowns are diluted with 0.15-M NaCl. The measurement gives only the unbound calcium, not that which is complexed.

POTENTIOMETRIC TITRATIONS

In a potentiometric titration, the end point is detected by determining the volume at which a relatively large change in potential occurs as the titrant is added. Figure 9.1 shows a schematic experimental setup for such a titration, using a glass electrode as an example of an indicator electrode. The method can be employed for all the reactions used for titrimetric purposes: acid-base, redox, precipitation, and complex formation. The proper indicator electrode is selected; a reference electrode, such as calomel, completes the cell. The titration may be performed manually, or the procedure may be automated. We shall consider the various techniques under three headings, recognizing that all variants cannot be discussed in a book of this sort: manual potentiometric titrations, automatic recording of the titration curve, and automatic titrant shut-off at the end point.

In manual titrations the potential is measured after the addition of each successive increment of titrant, and the resulting readings are plotted on graph paper versus the volume of titrant to give a titration curve such as shown in Fig. 9.3(a). In many cases, a simple potentiometer could be used. However, if the glass electrode is involved, as in most acid-base titrations, a measuring device with a high input impedance is required because of the high resistance of the glass; typically, a commercial pH meter is employed. Because these pH meters have become so common, they are widely utilized for all sorts of titrations, even where their use is not obligatory.

Once the titration curve is at hand, a subjective element enters the procedure. The analyst must determine where the curve is steepest, normally by some sort of inspection. He may draw a vertical line through the steep portion of the curve and find the intersection of this line with the volume axis. There must be some uncertainty in this procedure, and this will, of course, be reflected in the ultimate volume reading. For a reaction which goes well to completion, the titration curve is so steep near the equivalence point that the uncertainty is small; for a reaction with a small equilibrium constant, the precision with which an end point may be reproduced becomes poorer.

Figure 9.3(b) shows a plot of the slope of a titration curve, that is, the change in potential with change in volume ($\Delta E/\Delta V$) against volume of titrant. The resulting curve rises to a maximum at the equivalence point. The volume at the equivalence point is determined by dropping a vertical line from the peak to the volume axis. There is some uncertainty, of course, in locating exactly the peak in the curve. The more complete the reaction, the sharper the peak, and hence the more accurate the location of the equivalence point.

Figure 9.3(c) shows a plot of the change in the slope of a titration curve ($\Delta^2 E/\Delta V^2$) against the volume of titrant. At the point where the slope $\Delta E/\Delta V$ is a maximum, the derivative of the slope is zero. The end point is located by drawing a vertical line from the point at which $\Delta^2 E/\Delta V^2$ is zero to the volume axis. The portion of the curve joining the maximum and minimum values of $\Delta^2 E/\Delta V^2$ is steeper the more complete the titration reaction.

The curves shown in Figs. 9.3(a), (b), and (c) are for "symmetrical" reactions, that is, reactions in which 1 mole of titrant reacts with 1 mole of the substance titrated. Examples of acid-base, redox, and precipitation reactions that are symmetrical are

$$H_3O^+ + OH^- \longrightarrow 2H_2O$$

$$Ag^+ + Cl^- \longrightarrow AgCl\downarrow$$

$$Fe^{2+} + Ce^{4+} \longrightarrow Fe^{3+} + Ce^{3+}$$

For such reactions the midpoint of the steep portion of the curve in Fig. 9.3(a) corresponds to the equivalence point (see page 223). Likewise, the peak in the curve of Fig. 9.3(b) as well as the zero value of the second derivative in Fig. 9.3(c) occur exactly at the equivalence point.

For nonsymmetrical reactions such as

$$2\,Ag^+ + CrO_4^{2-} \longrightarrow Ag_2CrO_4\downarrow$$

and

$$Sn^{2+} + 2\,Ce^{++} \longrightarrow Sn^{4+} + 2\,Ce^{3+}$$

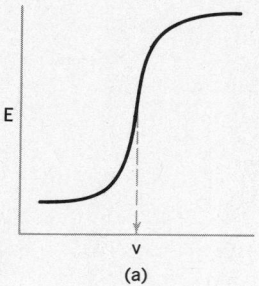

(a)

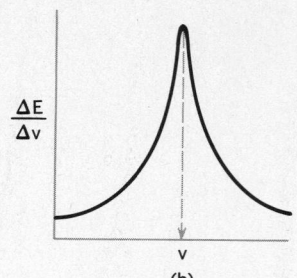

(b)

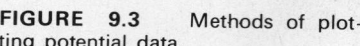

FIGURE 9.3 Methods of plotting potential data.

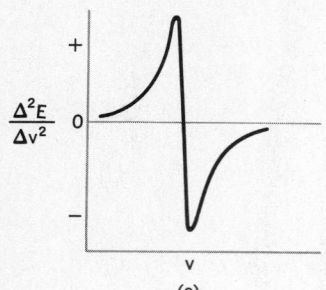

(c)

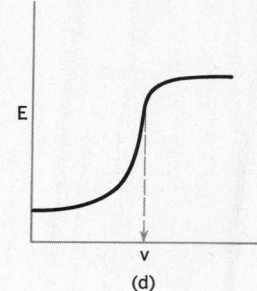

(d)

TABLE 9.2 POTENTIAL READINGS NEAR THE EQUIVALENCE POINT

ml titrant	E(mV)	$\Delta E/\Delta V$/0.1 ml	$\Delta^2 E/\Delta V^2$
24.70	210		
		12	
24.80	222		+6
		18	
24.90	240		+102
		120	
25.00	360		+120
		240	
25.10	600		−224
		16	
25.20	616		−7
		9	
25.30	625		

the equivalence point does not occur at the midpoint of the curve of Fig. 9.3(d). The potential at the equivalence point in the titration of stannous (E_1°) with ceric ion (E_2°) is $(2E_1^\circ + E_2^\circ)/3$ (see page 224). Similarly, the maximal value of $\Delta E/\Delta V$ for a nonsymmetrical reaction does not coincide exactly with the equivalence point. Nevertheless, the maximum is usually taken as the end point of a titration. The error made by this procedure is quite small.

It is possible to locate the end point by a simple systematic method based upon the actual data without resorting to a graph. Only potential readings near the equivalence point need be recorded. Some definite increment of volume, say 0.10 ml, is selected and a number of readings is taken, 0.10 ml apart, on either side of the equivalence point. An example is given in Table 9.2, where the values of the first and second derivatives are included. It can be seen from the second derivative values that the slope changes sign, and hence goes through the value zero, between 25.00 and 25.10 ml of titrant. The volume at which the value of zero is reached is closer to 25.00 than to 25.10, since the reading of $+120$ is closer to zero than is -224. Since 0.10 ml caused a total change in the second derivative of $344[+120 - (-224)]$, the fraction $(120/344) \times 0.10$ ml is the approximate number of milliliters in excess of 25.00 necessary to bring the second derivative to the value zero. Hence the calculated volume at the equivalence point is

$$V = 25.00 + 0.10\left(\frac{120}{120 + 224}\right) = 25.035 \text{ ml}$$

By a very simple experimental modification, values of $\Delta E/\Delta V$, the change in potential with change in volume of titrant, may be obtained directly. These values can be plotted as shown in Fig. 9.3(b), or the volume corresponding to the maximal value of $\Delta E/\Delta V$ may be obtained from inspection of the data.

No reference electrode is required for this method. Two indicator electrodes are employed, but one is kept separated from the main body of solution

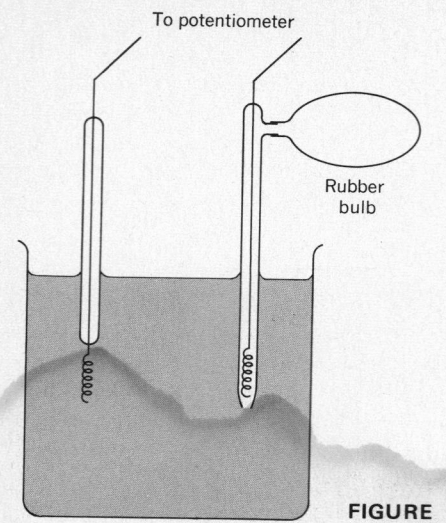

To potentiometer

Rubber
bulb

FIGURE 9.4   Apparatus for differential titration.

until a potential reading has been taken. A simple device that can be used for performing such a titration is shown in Fig. 9.4. One electrode is in the body of the solution, the other inside a small glass tube that dips into the same solution. When the solutions inside and outside of the tube are uniform in composition, there is no difference in potential between the electrodes. When titrant is added to the main body of the solution, however, a difference in potential develops, since the solution inside the tube no longer has the same composition as that outside. The potential difference is noted, and then the solution is expelled from the tube by squeezing the rubber bulb so that the composition becomes uniform again. The potential difference falls to zero as bulk solution is sucked into the tube. The volume of solution in the tube must, of course, be kept small compared to the total volume of solution titrated. The method is rapid and the results can be accurate.

Automatic Recording of Titration Curves

Recording potentiometers have become commonplace in chemistry laboratories. With typical "recorders," as they are called, voltages from many different origins can be plotted with pen and ink as a function of time. The voltage developed across a resistor in a circuit of inherently very high resistance, as encountered in glass-electrode setups, cannot be fed directly to a recorder for reasons that are beyond the scope of this book. Suffice it here to say that it is necessary to "match" the input impedance of the recorder with the impedance of the voltage source. The circuitry of most modern pH meters does this. Thus the student who is not interested in instrumentation per se can simply note that with relatively inexpensive commercially available "black boxes," one may take the potential between the electrodes during a potentiometric titration and feed this to a recorder. Since the recorder plots voltage versus time, it is obvious that a potentiometric titration curve can be recorded provided the titrant is added at a constant rate. Thus, to record automatically a potentiometric titration curve, it is clear that one requires an electrode setup, as in manual titrations, plus an impedance matching device, a recorder, and a constant-flow buret. Commercial pH meters serve for the impedance matching and many are fitted with terminals for wires connecting with the recorder. Constant-flow burets usually rely, not upon gravity feed as with ordinary burets, but upon the action of a motor-driven plunger in a syringe type of assembly. Such devices are available commercially. Rapid stirring, usually accomplished with a magnetic stirrer, is important in order to maintain a uniform concentration in the solution during the titration.

After the titration curve has been recorded, the analyst faces the same problem of selecting the end point as with graphs plotted manually. On the other hand, while the titration is in progress, he is free to perform other tasks, perhaps preparing the next sample for titration, and thus time may be saved. The continuous nature of the recording insures that features of the curve will be seen which might be missed in a manual titration unless points were taken at very close intervals. A real disadvantage of recording, at least with the typical titrant flow rates, lies in the fact that the titration reaction must be rapid. In a manual titration, if the reaction is slow, the operator can wait for a steady reading before adding the next increment of titrant, and although it may try his patience, the titration will work. With automatic recording, the potentials may never reach equilibrium values at any stage of the titration, the recorded curve may be distorted, and a large potential break may appear before the equivalence point is actually reached.

Automatic Titrant Shut-Off

Finally, potentiometric titrations can be completely automated so that the buret is mechanically shut off at the end point. In some cases the buret is a conventional one and the meniscus is read in the usual manner. The drive mechanism of a syringe buret can be fitted with a revolution counter that provides direct digital readout.

One type of automatic titrator titrates the sample to a pre-set potential. The difference between the indicator and reference electrodes at the equivalence point is determined ahead of time, and the instrument is then set to shut off the buret at this potential. Even with good stirring, mixing is not instantaneous, and it is necessary to provide for restarting the titrant flow if the buret shuts off too soon due to a high local concentration of titrant around the indicator electrode. End point "anticipation" is provided for by positioning the delivery tip of the buret very close to the indicator electrode.[7] Then the solution adjacent to the electrode is at a more advanced stage of titration than is the bulk of the solution. Thus the electrode reaches the equivalence potential somewhat early, and the delivery of titrant is stopped

[7] J. J. Lingane, *Electroanalytical Chemistry*, 2nd ed., Interscience Publishers, Inc., New York, 1958, p. 159.

too soon. However, as the solution becomes uniform in concentration through further stirring, the potential drops back, and the buret is turned on again. This process is repeated until the entire solution reaches the equivalence potential. A human operator does the same sort of thing in a visual titration when he adds titrant rapidly in the early stages and then dropwise as fleeting color changes are seen near the equivalence point.

Another type of automatic titrator, developed by Malmstadt and Fett,[8] is based upon electronic differentiation. It is possible, by using a resistance-capacitance network with the right time constant, to construct an electronic circuit which produces a voltage that is proportional to the derivative (with respect to time) of a voltage which is fed into it. By combining two such circuits and including appropriate amplification, Malmstadt was able to trigger a relay system that shut off a buret when the second derivative of the voltage input from the electrodes changed sign. (Electronically, the second derivative is more suitable than the first derivative for actuating such a relay.) At constant titrant flow, differentiation with respect to time is equivalent to differentiation with respect to volume of titrant. Actually the commercial instrument based upon Malmstadt's ideas (E. H. Sargent Co.) employs an ordinary gravity-feed buret, but near the equivalence point (the only region of interest, really) the hydrostatic head is constant enough.

For a person with an occasional titration to perform, automatic titrators have little to offer. On the other hand, a laboratory with hundreds of samples to titrate each week, a repetitive and boring task, may find them nearly indispensable. The titrator cannot do anything that people cannot do, but it is cheaper than people and it does not complain about its work provided it is properly serviced.

REFERENCES

J. J. LINGANE, *Electroanalytical Chemistry*, 2nd ed., Interscience Publishers, Inc., New York, 1958.

R. G. BATES, "Concept and Determination of *p*H," Chapter 10, Part 1, Vol. 1, of *Treatise on Analytical Chemistry*, I. M. Kolthoff, P. J. Elving, and E. B. Sandell, eds., Interscience Publishers, Inc., New York, 1959.

G. EISENMAN, ed., *Glass Electrodes for Hydrogen and Other Cations*, Marcel Dekker, New York, 1967.

R. G. BATES, "Electrometric Methods of *p*H Determination," Vol. 3-A of *Standard Methods of Chemical Analysis*, F. J. Welcher, ed., D. Van Nostrand, Inc., New York, 1966.

G. A. RECHNITZ, "New Directions for Ion Selective Electrodes," *Anal. Chem.*, 41, 109A (1969).

QUESTIONS

1. Explain how the glass electrode functions as an indicator electrode for hydrogen ions.

2. What two assumptions are involved in the establishment of the conventional scale of *p*H? What is the uncertainty with which one can measure *p*H numbers?

[8] H. V. Malmstadt and E. R. Fett, *Anal. Chem.*, **26**, 1348 (1954); **27**, 1757 (1955); **29**, 1901 (1957).

3. Describe the various types of membrane electrodes. Explain what is meant by an "ion-selective" electrode.

4. Give examples of electrodes of the first, second, and third kinds.

5. Explain how the molarity of an ion such as Na^+ is determined experimentally with an ion-selective electrode. Why is the ionic strength of the solution important?

6. Explain how the mercury electrode serves as an indicator electrode for various metal ions.

7. What are the advantages of potentiometric titration over direct potentiometry?

8. Will the pH reading of a soda-lime glass electrode be too high or too low in 0.1-M NaOH? Explain.

PROBLEMS   (In problems using the Nernst equation, 0.059 can be rounded off to 0.06.)

1. *Potentiometric titration.* A 30.0-ml aliquot of 0.100-M HCl is diluted to 100 ml and titrated with 0.100-M NaOH. (a) Calculate the pH of the solution after the addition of the following volumes of titrant: 0.00, 10.0, 15.0, 29.0, 29.9, 30.0, 30.1, 31.0, and 40.0. (b) Calculate the potential readings one would obtain in a potentiometric titration using a cell which consists of a hydrogen-saturated calomel electrode pair. Plot the curve: potential vs ml of titrant.

2. *Potentiometric titration.* Repeat Problem 1 substituting acetic acid for hydrochloric.

3. *First and second derivatives.* From the data of Problems 1 and 2 plot $\Delta E/\Delta V$ and $\Delta^2 E/\Delta V^2$ vs volume of titrant.

4. *Potentiometric titration.* 2.00 mmol of Sn^{2+} are dissolved in 60 ml of solution and titrated with 0.10-M Ce^{4+} using a platinum-saturated calomel electrode pair. Calculate the potential after the addition of the following volumes of titrant: 0.00, 10.0, 20.0, 39.9, 40.0, 40.1, and 50.0. Plot the titration curve.

5. *Equivalence point.* Given the following potential readings near the equivalence point of a titration:

Volume titrant, ml	Potential, mV
31.10	270
31.20	280
31.30	300
31.40	520
31.50	540
31.60	550

Calculate the volume at the equivalence point.

6. *Membrane electrode.* A liquid-membrane electrode is used to determine the concentration of calcium ion in a solution. The potential reading obtained with this electrode and a reference dipping into a solution which is 0.010-M in Ca^{2+} is 0.250 V. In the same cell a solution of unknown concentration gives a reading of

0.271 V. The ionic strengths of the two solutions are the same. Calculate the concentration of calcium ion in the unknown.

7. *Measurement of* pH. Derive an equation relating the potential of the following cell to pH:

$$Ag|AgCl, HCl(0.010\text{-}M)| |H^+(x - M)|H_2(1 \text{ atm}), Pt$$

8. *Measurement of* pH. Show that the potential of the following cell

$$M|M^{2+}| |KCl(1\text{-}M), Hg_2Cl_2|Hg$$

is related to the pH of the solution in the left-hand electrode according to the equation

$$E = k + 0.06pH$$

where k is a constant. Assume that M^{2+} forms a slightly soluble hydroxide, $M(OH)_2$, and that the concentration of M^{2+} depends on the hydroxide-ion concentration as expressed by the solubility product constant.

9. *Complex formation.* A sample of 4.0 mmol of M^{2+} is titrated with X^- according to the reaction

$$M^{2+} + X^- \rightleftharpoons MX^+$$

The potential of the cell

$$Hg|Hg_2Cl_2, KCl(1\text{-}M)| |M^{2+}|M$$

is 0.00 V at the equivalence point. Given that for $M^{2+} + 2e \rightleftharpoons M$, $E° = +0.48$ V, calculate the equilibrium constant for the formation of the MX^+ complex. The volume at the equivalence point is 100 ml.

10. *Potential-*pH. How many grams of HCl should be dissolved in 1 liter of solution so that the potential reading obtained with a standard calomel-hydrogen electrode pair is 0.40 V? The calomel electrode is positive.

11. *Potential-*pH. A standard calomel-hydrogen electrode pair is inserted in a solution of HCl and a potential of 0.322 V was measured. When these electrodes were inserted in a solution of NaOH, the reading was 1.096 V. The hydrogen electrode is negative. How many milliliters of each solution should be mixed in order to prepare 100 ml of a solution that would give a reading of 1.036 V with the same electrodes?

12. *Buffer solution.* What should be the ratio of acetic acid to sodium acetate in a buffer so that the potential reading obtained in the cell of Problem 7 is 0.64 V. The hydrogen electrode is negative.

13. *Nernst equation.* A platinum and standard calomel electrode pair is placed in a solution which contains stannic and stannous ions. The potential reading is 0.07 V, with the calomel electrode positive. Calculate the ratio of stannic to stannous ions in the solution.

14. *Titrimetric analysis.* A 2.00-g sample of an acid HA, M.W. of 120, is dissolved in 50.0 ml of water and titrated with 0.200-M NaOH using a standard calomel-hydrogen electrode pair. The potential reading is 0.58 V when half of the acid is neutralized and 0.82 V at the equivalence point. The hydrogen electrode is negative. Calculate the percentage of HA in the sample.

15. *Redox titration.* A 50.0-ml aliquot of 0.100-M Fe^{2+} is titrated potentiometrically with 0.100-M Ce^{4+}, using a standard calomel-platinum electrode pair. When the potential reading is 0.55 V, how many milliliters of the ceric solution have been added? The polarity of the platinum electrode is positive.

16. *Quinhydrone electrode.* The so-called "quinhydrone electrode" is an indicator electrode for hydrogen ions. A platinum electrode is inserted in the test solution which is saturated with quinhydrone, a 1:1 compound of quinone and hydroquinone. The redox couple is

$$+ 2\,H^+ + 2e \rightleftharpoons \qquad E° = 0.70\text{ V}$$

Derive an equation relating the *pH* of a solution to the potential of the following cell:

$$\text{Pt,}\,|H^+(x\text{-}M) + H_2Q + Q|\,|KCl(1\text{-}M), Hg_2Cl_2|Hg$$

H_2Q stands for hydroquinone and Q for quinone. You can assume that the dissociation of quinhydrone produces an equal number of moles of quinone and hydroquinone.

17. *Quinhydrone electrode.* Answer the following questions about the quinhydrone electrode described in Problem 16. (a) What is the polarity of the calomel electrode at *pH* 4? (b) At *pH* 9? (c) At what *pH* is the potential of the cell zero? (d) At high *pH* some H_2Q is neutralized and the ratio of H_2Q to Q is no longer unity. Suppose the electrode is used to measure the *pH* of a solution which actually has a *pH* of 12.00. Will the *pH* value obtained with the electrode be above 12, below 12, or exactly 12?

18. *Mercury electrode.* Calculate the potential of the mercury indicator electrode at the equivalence point for the titration of 5.0 mmol of Ni^{2+} with EDTA at *pH* 5.00. Assume that the volume at the equivalence point is 100 ml and the concentration of HgY^{2-} is 0.010-M.

19. *Precipitation titration.* A 50-ml portion of 0.10-M $AgNO_3$ is titrated with 0.10-M NaCl using a silver indicator electrode. (a) Calculate the potential of the indicator electrode after the addition of 49.9, 50.0, and 50.1 ml of titrant. (b) Repeat (a) substituting NaBr for NaCl. (c) Repeat (a) substituting NaI for NaCl. Note the dependence of the potential change on the solubility of the silver halide.

20. *Precipitation titration.* Consider the possibility of titrating a mixture of chloride, bromide, and iodide, each 0.10-M, with silver nitrate. Calculate the percentage of iodide unprecipitated when AgBr begins to precipitate, and the percentage of bromide unprecipitated when AgCl begins to precipitate. Sketch roughly a titration curve of potential, or *p*Ag, vs milliliters of titrant.

10

Other Electrical Methods of Analysis

The field of electrochemistry is a vast one, with a wide variety of techniques and applications employing complicated and sophisticated instrumentation. Some of the techniques have analytical applications, while others are of interest primarily in providing fundamental information on the nature of electrode processes. A detailed study of the entire field is obviously beyond the scope of an introductory text. Excellent treatments can be found in the book of Delahay[1] and in the chapters by Reilley and by Reilley and Murray[2] in a treatise.

The subject of potentiometry discussed in Chapter 9 is an example of an electrical method of analysis. In this chapter we shall discuss the topics of electrolysis, polarography, and amperometric titrations. These are the more classical techniques which are still widely applicable to analytical problems.

ELECTROLYSIS

Introduction

We saw in Chapter 8 that a galvanic cell can act as a source of electrical energy. If the electrodes are short-circuited, the cell reaction occurs

---

[1] P. Delahay, *New Instrumental Methods in Electrochemistry*, Interscience Publishers, New York–London, 1954.

[2] I. M. Kolthoff and P. J. Elving, eds., *Treatise on Analytical Chemistry*, Part I, Vol. 4, Interscience Publishers, Inc., New York, 1963, Chapters 42 and 43.

spontaneously. For example, in the cell below

$$\overset{\ominus}{Cu}|Cu^{2+}(1-M)||Ag^{+}(1-M)|\overset{\oplus}{Ag}$$

the electrode and cell reactions are

$$
\begin{array}{ll}
2\,Ag^{+} + 2e \rightleftharpoons 2\,Ag & E^{\circ} = +0.80\ V \\
Cu^{2+} + 2e \rightleftharpoons Cu & E^{\circ} = +0.34\ V \\
\hline
2\,Ag^{+} + Cu \rightleftharpoons 2\,Ag + Cu^{2+} & E^{\circ}_{cell} = +0.46\ V
\end{array}
$$

In the spontaneous reaction copper displaces silver, forming cupric ions and metallic silver. However, if a battery with a voltage greater than 0.46 V is connected to the cell, with its negative pole connected to the copper and the positive to silver, the foregoing reaction will take place from right to left. That is, copper will deposit at the left-hand electrode, and silver will dissolve at the right-hand electrode. The electrode reactions are being forced to take place in the opposite direction to that indicated in the galvanic formulation above, and the cell is electrolytic. An ordinary storage battery, used to start an automobile, acts as a galvanic cell. A discharged battery that is being re-charged by application of a higher voltage acts as an electrolytic cell. Note that copper is the negative electrode and silver the positive electrode regard-less of the direction of electron flow. However, in the galvanic cell, copper is the anode because it is oxidized, and silver is the cathode because it is reduced. In the electrolytic cell, copper is the cathode and silver the anode. The term *electrolysis* embraces all the phenomena occurring at the electrodes of an electrolytic cell as the reactions take place.

Electrolysis is used in analytical chemistry to separate substances from one another. Some substances may be deposited during electrolysis, whereas others are not. The electric current may be regarded as the precipitating agent, and the procedure is called *electrogravimetry*. Another application of electrolysis is called *coulometric* analysis. The quantity of electricity required to oxidize or reduce a substance is measured, and the method may be re-garded as a titrimetric method in which electrons act as the titrant.

Electrogravimetry

The apparatus normally used to deposit a substance from solution is shown schematically in Fig. 10.1. Two platinum electrodes are inserted in the solution, here a solution of copper sulfate, and an external voltage is applied. Once electrolysis is started, copper is deposited on the cathode and oxygen is liberated at the anode.[3] The products of electrolysis form a galvanic cell whose potential opposes the applied voltage. This potential is called the

---

[3] The initial products at the electrodes can be predicted from redox potentials. The substance most readily reduced (most positive potential) will react at the cathode; the one most readily oxi-dized (most negative potential) will react at the anode.

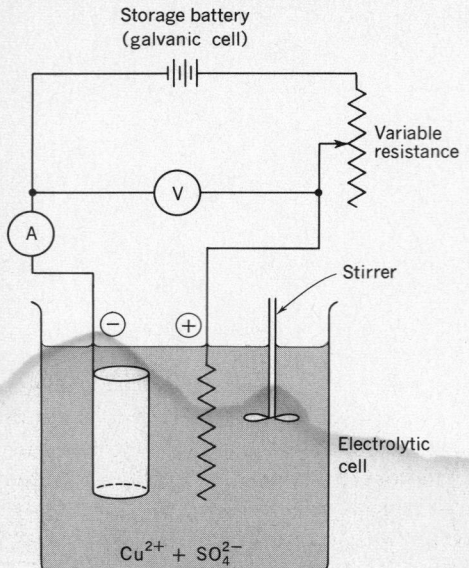

Storage battery
(galvanic cell)

Variable
resistance

V

A

Stirrer

Electrolytic
cell

$Cu^{2+} + SO_4^{2-}$

FIGURE 10.1 Apparatus for electrolysis.

equilibrium decomposition voltage of the cell, or sometimes the "back emf." The decomposition potential for equilibrium conditions is readily calculated by the methods of Chapter 8. Consider the following example.

Example. Calculate the equilibrium decomposition voltage of a 0.1-*M* solution of copper sulfate; two platinum electrodes are employed and the solution is 1-*M* in hydrogen ion.

The products of electrolysis are copper at the cathode and oxygen at the anode. The products form a galvanic cell, which we represent as

$$Cu|Cu^{2+}(0.1\text{-}M) + H^+(1\text{-}M) + H_2O|O_2, Pt$$

The electrode reactions are

$$2\,H^+ + \tfrac{1}{2}O_2 + 2e \rightleftharpoons H_2O \qquad E_a^\circ = +1.23$$
$$\underline{Cu^{2+} + 2e \rightleftharpoons Cu \qquad\qquad\quad E_c^\circ = +0.34}$$
$$Cu + 2\,H^+ + \tfrac{1}{2}O_2 \rightleftharpoons Cu^{2+} + H_2O \qquad E_a^\circ - E_c^\circ = 0.89$$

Here we have designated by E_a° and E_c° the standard potentials of the reactions that take place at the anode and cathode. Let us call the equilibrium decomposition potential E_d. Then

$$E_d = 0.89 - \frac{0.059}{2} \log \frac{a_{Cu^{2+}}}{a_{O_2}^{1/2} \times a_{H^+}^2}$$

According to our usual assumptions,[4]

$$a_{Cu^{2+}} = 0.1$$

$$a_{H^+} = 1$$

$$a_{O_2} = p_{O_2} = 1$$

Therefore

$$E_d = 0.89 - \frac{0.059}{2} \log 0.1 = 0.92 \text{ V}$$

The decomposition voltage changes during the electrolysis, of course, since concentration changes occur. The voltage can be calculated by the last equation under any given conditions. It should be apparent that as the concentration of copper decreases, the concentration of hydrogen ion increases, and the decomposition voltage increases. That is, a higher voltage is required to force the reactions to occur as the amount of copper in the solution decreases.

In addition to the equilibrium decomposition voltage, sufficient voltage must be applied in order to overcome the resistance of the cell, that is, to force the ions to migrate to the electrodes. This voltage is given by Ohm's law. If the resistance of the cell is 2 ohms, for example, and it is desired to pass a current of $\frac{1}{2}$ A, the additional voltage requirement is

$$E = I \times R$$

$$E = 0.5 \times 2 = 1.0 \text{ V}$$

It is apparent that if a larger current is desired, a larger voltage must be applied.

If the voltage initially applied to the cell is merely the equilibrium value, no net current flows, of course, and the concentration of cupric ions remains 0.1-M. In order for a finite current to flow, the voltage must be greater than the equilibrium, or *reversible*, value and the difference, $E - E_d = \eta$, is commonly called the *overvoltage* or *activation overpotential*.[5] This overpotential is caused by some slow kinetic process in the electrode reactions. An electrode is said to be *polarized*, implying a deviation of the potential of the electrode from its reversible value.

---

[4] Oxygen is liberated on the platinum below the surface of the solution. Hence its pressure must be atmospheric, plus a slight hydrostatic pressure, in order for bubbles to be liberated.

[5] H. A. Laitinen, *Chemical Analysis*, McGraw-Hill Book Company, New York, 1960, uses the term *voltage* to refer to a cell, and *potential* to refer to a single electrode. We shall use the terms *overvoltage* and *overpotential* in this same context.

As current flows, the concentration of cupric ions in the portion of solution in contact with the electrode becomes less than the value we used above, 0.1-M. This decrease in concentration at the electrode-solution interface occurs even though the solution is stirred vigorously. It is practically impossible to replenish the volume element adjacent to the electrode rapidly enough to keep the concentration uniform throughout the solution. The ions in the immediate vicinity of the electrode are, of course, the ones in equilibrium with the electrode. The concentration of these ions at the surface rather than the concentration in the bulk of the solution should be used in calculating the equilibrium decomposition potential. Since the former concentration is lower than the latter, the actual value of E_d is greater than that which we calculated above. This additional potential is often referred to as "concentration polarization," although this is really a misnomer since the electrode is presumably acting reversibly with respect to the activity of cupric ions at the surface. Many chemists refer to this term today as "concentration overpotential."

The magnitude of the concentration overpotential is normally small in solutions that are well stirred and under conditions such that the applied voltage is not far above the equilibrium decomposition voltage. The activation overpotential can be quite large, especially in cases where a gas is liberated at an electrode. Hydrogen and oxygen are the two gases normally encountered in electrolysis with water solutions. It is thought that several steps are involved in the liberation of these gases, one of which is slow and requires an additional potential to force it to occur at a reasonable rate. The magnitude of activation overpotential depends upon the nature of the electrode material, the physical state of the electrode surface, the temperature, and the current density (amperes per square centimeter of surface). Increasing the temperature decreases the overpotential, whereas increasing the current density increases overpotential.

The actual voltage required for electrolysis can be considered as the sum of three terms: (1) the reversible or equilibrium decomposition voltage, (2) the activation and concentration overpotentials, and (3) the IR drop through the solution. If we let ω_c and ω_a represent the overpotential terms at the cathode and anode, respectively, then the voltage required for electrolysis, E_{app}, is given by

$$E_{app} = (E_a - E_c) + (\omega_c + \omega_a) + IR$$

Current-Voltage Curves

It is instructive to consider the relationship between the voltage applied to an electrolytic cell and the current that flows through the cell. Let us consider two cases: one in which the electrodes are in equilibrium with ions in solution; one in which the electrodes are inert at the start of the electrolysis. As an example of the first type we may take the cell described on page 263:

$$Cu|Cu^{2+}(1\text{-}M)||Ag^+(1\text{-}M)|Ag$$

If the cell acts as a galvanic cell, the reaction

$$2\,Ag^+ + Cu \rightleftharpoons Cu^{2+} + 2\,Ag$$

tends to occur from left to right. The potential is 0.46 V. Now suppose that a variable external voltage is applied to this cell, with the applied voltage opposing that of the silver-copper cell. If the applied voltage is less than 0.46 V, the cell reaction occurs from left to right according to the equation above. The cell still acts as a galvanic cell. At applied voltages greater than 0.46 V, however, the cell is electrolytic, the reaction above being forced to take place from right to left. Thus copper is plated out at the cathode, and silver dissolves at the anode. At an applied voltage of exactly 0.46 V, no current flows through the cell; this point corresponds to the usual measurement of the cell voltage using a potentiometer. This relation is plotted in Fig. 10.2. Below the voltage of 0.46 V, the current is given a negative sign, and above 0.46 V, it is given a positive sign. The decomposition voltage has a discrete value in this case, 0.46 V. Above this voltage the cell reaction, that is, the reverse of the spontaneous reaction, starts to take place.

As an example of the second type of cell, let us take the cell on page 264, that is, a solution of copper sulfate with two platinum electrodes. The cell is

$$Cu|Cu^{2+}(0.1\text{-}M) + H^+(1\text{-}M) + H_2O|O_2, Pt$$

For the purpose of the present discussion we may disregard the effects of concentration and activation overpotentials, and focus our attention on the equilibrium decomposition potential. We calculated on page 265 that the equilibrium decomposition voltage of this cell is 0.92 V. If we now apply a

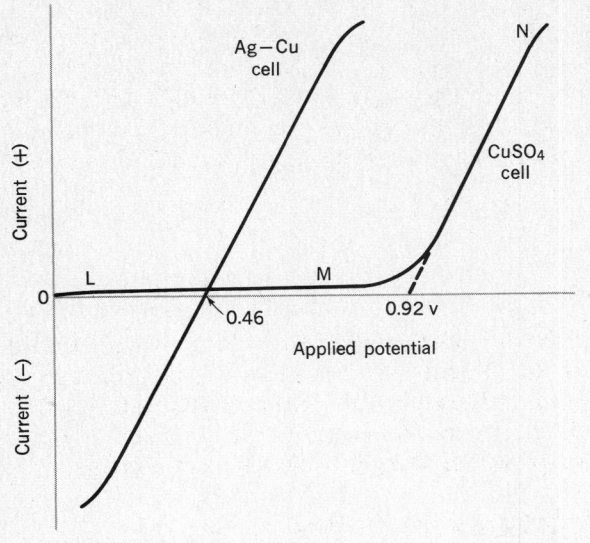

FIGURE 10.2 Current-voltage curves (schematic).

voltage smaller than 0.92 V, the cell cannot operate as a galvanic cell since there are as yet no products of electrolysis. Hence we expect the current to be zero. Actually, a small "residual current" flows, as shown in Fig. 10.2. This current gradually increases along LM as the value of 0.92 V is approached. The curve is rounded near the point M, and then the current increases rapidly along MN.[6] The current I is given by Ohm's law, $I = E/R$, where R is the cell resistance in ohms, and E is the "effective" voltage. The effective voltage is that voltage above the decomposition voltage. The decomposition voltage is taken as the point of intersection of the extrapolated portion of MN with the voltage axis. Note that there is no discrete voltage at which the cell reaction begins, as there was in the case of the silver-copper cell above. A slight reaction is apparently occurring at all voltages along the line LM. This behavior is characteristic of cells in which one or more of the electrodes is not in equilibrium with the solution as the voltage is first applied.

The residual current is sometimes attributed to the electrolysis of trace impurities in the solution. With a dropping mercury electrode (page 278) the residual current is due chiefly to the charging of the mercury-solution interface; the mercury surface increases continuously as the drop grows, and the process is somewhat like charging a condenser of continuously increasing area. With solid electrodes of constant area, it is thought that the first small amounts of metal deposited are not sufficient to cover the electrode surface completely. In the example above, the activity of the copper metal is variable until the voltage nears the equilibrium decomposition value. Here sufficient copper is deposited to cover completely the electrode surface, the electrode becoming a copper electrode and the activity of copper becoming constant (unity). Extensive studies have been made on the deposition of metals from extremely dilute solutions, and evidence has been found to support this explanation.[7] However, a completely satisfactory theoretical treatment of the process has not been made.[8]

Separations by Electrolysis

Separations from Hydrogen

Many metals that are less readily reduced than hydrogen ion can be deposited from aqueous solutions by increasing the pH, using an electrode which has a high hydrogen activation overpotential, or using a mercury cathode. The first two factors make the reduction of hydrogen ion more difficult (E more negative), and the third makes the reduction of the metal ion easier (E more positive). The mercury cathode is particularly advantageous

---

[6] Actually there is some nonlinearity in the rising portion of the curve, since the oxygen overpotential is a function of current density.

[7] L. B. Rogers, et al., *J. Electrochem. Soc.*, **98**, 447, 452, 457 (1951); *Trans. Electrochem. Soc.*, **95**, 25, 33, 129 (1949).

[8] See *Treatise on Analytical Chemistry*, Part I, Vol. 4, I. M. Kolthoff and P. J. Elving, eds., Interscience Publishers, Inc., New York, 1963, pp. 2441–2443.

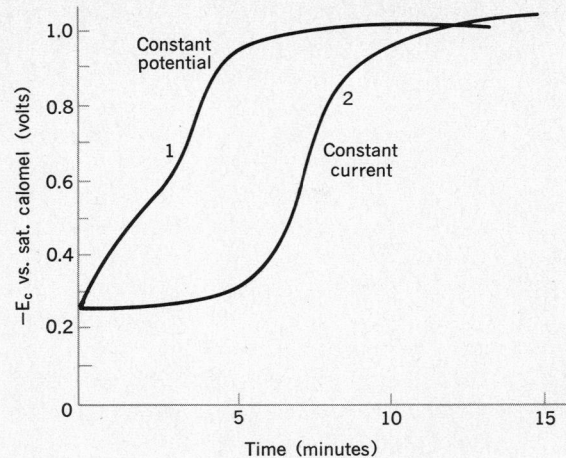

FIGURE 10.3 Change of cathode potential during electrolysis. (After J. J. Lingane, *Electroanalytical Chemistry*, 2nd ed., Interscience Publishers, Inc., New York, 1958.)

for the deposition of active metals from acid solutions, both because of amalgamation and because of the high activation overpotential of hydrogen on mercury. Approximately one-third of the elements are deposited, either completely or partially, in the mercury cathode.[9]

Separation of Metals by Electrolysis

The separation of two metals from one another by depositing one electrolytically while leaving the other in solution is sometimes a difficult problem. The difficulty arises in the fact that as one substance is deposited, the cathode potential becomes more negative and may reach a sufficiently negative value to deposit the second substance. The separation of two metals, one of which has a greater and the other a smaller affinity for electrons than hydrogen ion, is experimentally simple. The separation of copper and nickel is a familiar example of this. In acid solution, copper is deposited while nickel remains in solution. The cathode potential becomes more negative as the copper concentration decreases (Fig. 10.3), and finally hydrogen is evolved at the cathode. Since the hydrogen ion concentration is quite large and since hydrogen ion is formed at the anode, the potential does not become appreciably more negative. The electrolysis is stopped, and the cathode is weighed to determine the amount of copper. The solution containing nickel is then neutralized with ammonia and the electrolysis continued. The *p*H is now sufficiently high that nickel is reduced more readily than hydrogen ion. In this manner the two metals are separated and also determined by electrolysis.

In order to separate two metals, both of which have greater (or smaller) electron affinities than hydrogen ion, it is necessary to control the cathode potential to prevent this electrode from becoming sufficiently negative to

---

[9] J. A. Maxwell and R. P. Graham, *Chem. Rev.*, **46**, 471 (1950).

reduce the second metal before the deposition of the first is complete. The apparatus shown in Fig. 10.1 cannot be used. A more elaborate apparatus, described in the next section, is necessary to maintain a good control over the cathode potential.

The action of the hydrogen ion-hydrogen redox system in preventing the cathode potential from becoming very negative is often referred to as "potential buffering." Other redox systems act in the same way and have been employed as "potential buffers." For example, the ferric-ferrous system,

$$Fe^{3+} + e \rightleftharpoons Fe^{2+}$$

limits the cathode potential to a value no more negative than $+0.77$ V if the concentrations of the two ions are equal. If no substance is present that is more readily oxidized than ferrous ion, the latter is oxidized at the anode, and since ferric ion is reduced at the cathode, a fairly constant ratio of the two ions is maintained.

Controlled Potential Electrolysis

In carrying out an electrolysis using the apparatus shown in Fig. 10.1 there are two techniques that are commonly used. In the *constant potential* method the applied voltage is set at the desired value and left there during the electrolysis. The current is allowed to decrease during the run. In the *constant current* method the applied voltage is increased during the electrolysis in order to maintain the current at the selected value. With both of these techniques the cathode potential rapidly becomes more negative and a second metal may be deposited also. This is shown in Fig. 10.3 where a plot is given of the cathode potential against time during an electrolysis of copper from a tartrate solution.[10] Curve 1 was obtained when the applied voltage was held constant at 2.00 V. Curve 2 was obtained when the current was held constant at 1.00 A. In both cases the cathode potential becomes more negative by about 0.75 V in a short interval of time. The negative drift of the cathode potential is stopped at about -1.00 V by evolution of hydrogen.

It is evident from these examples that the cathode potential must be prevented from becoming so negative if the desired separation is to be achieved. It is necessary to measure the cathode potential with reference to an external electrode throughout the electrolysis. Then the applied voltage can be decreased as the electrolysis proceeds, thereby "controlling" the cathode and preventing its becoming any more negative than is necessary to deposit the desired metal. The apparatus shown in Fig. 10.4 can be used for this purpose. The electrolysis circuit is the same as that in Fig. 10.1, but a reference electrode (in this case a saturated calomel) is inserted in the solution and the difference in potential between the reference and cathode is measured with a potentiometer. The tip of the salt bridge from the calomel

---

[10] J. J. Lingane, *Electroanalytical Chemistry*, Interscience Publishers, Inc., New York, 2nd ed., 1958, p. 217.

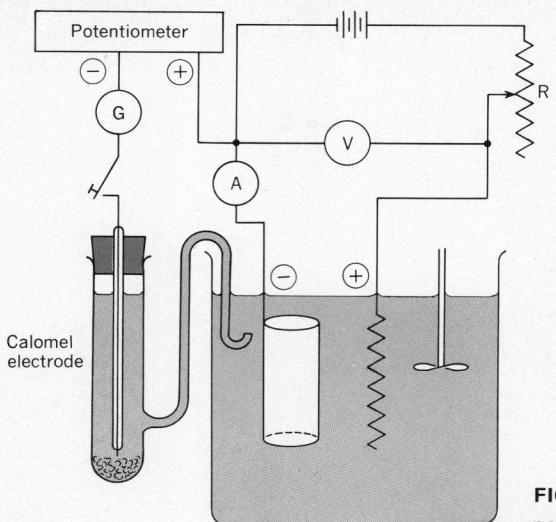

FIGURE 10.4 Apparatus for measuring cathode potential.

electrode is placed very close to the cathode and on the side away from the anode. In this manner the calomel-cathode voltage is affected least by the flow of current between the cathode and anode (IR drop).

In using this apparatus, one first selects a "limiting" value of the cathode potential, this value being sufficiently negative to deposit quantitatively one metal without depositing any of the second. The difference between this value and that of the reference electrode is then calculated and this voltage is set on the potentiometer. Then whenever the cathode is at the desired potential the galvanometer does not deflect when the key is tapped. If the cathode is more positive or negative than the desired value, the galvanometer shows a deflection, and the applied voltage can be adjusted accordingly. At the start of the electrolysis the applied voltage is adjusted by the rheostat R to give the desired current. The potential of the cathode is much more positive than the limiting value at this time, but it becomes more negative rapidly, as was shown in the example in Fig. 10.3. As the limiting potential is approached, careful control is required to prevent the cathode from becoming too negative. This requires the constant attention of the operator if the control is manual. The key is tapped and R is adjusted to make the galvanometer deflection zero. A few moments later the key is tapped again and the applied voltage is again decreased to keep the deflection zero.

Electronic instruments, called *potentiostats*, are available which automatically adjust the applied voltage, and the constant attention of the operator is not necessary.[11] Figure 10.5 shows the change of the total applied voltage during the electrolysis of copper from a tartrate solution (see reference 10 and Fig. 10.3). A potentiostat was used and the cathode potential was limited to

[11] *Ibid.*, p. 308.

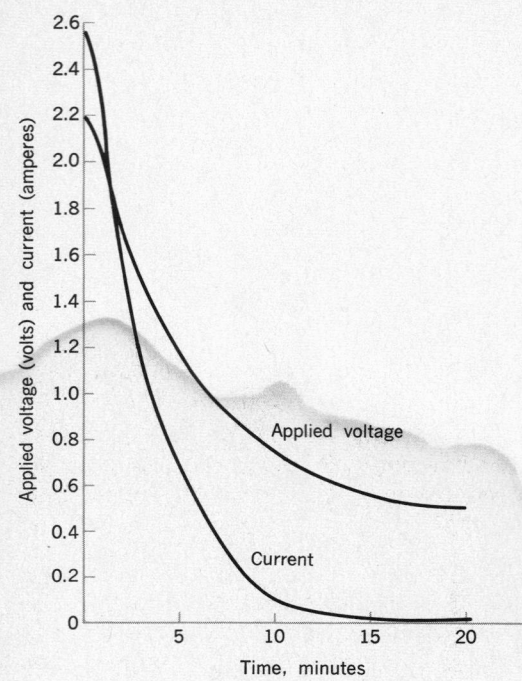

FIGURE 10.5 Change in applied voltage and current during controlled potential electrolysis of copper from a tartrate solution. (After J. J. Lingane, *Electroanalytical Chemistry*, 2nd ed., Interscience Publishers, Inc., New York, 1958.)

-0.36 V versus a saturated calomel electrode. The potentiostat continuously decreased the applied voltage from 2.2 V to 0.48 V. The current decreased continuously from an initial value of 2.6 A to 0.03 A after 17 minutes, and finally to less than 0.01 A after 30 minutes.[12] Under appropriate conditions, the current-time curve obeys the relation[13]

$$i_t = i_0 10^{-kt}$$

where i_0 is the initial current, i_t is the current at time t, and k is a constant. On the other hand, the current may remain nearly constant in the early stages of the electrolysis if the cathode potential is only slightly more negative than the equilibrium value. However, if the potential is more negative by at least 0.10 V than the equilibrium value, then the above equation is generally followed from the start of the electrolysis.

COULOMETRIC ANALYSIS

As previously mentioned, the quantity of a substance in solution may sometimes be determined by measuring the number of coulombs required

[12] *Ibid.*, p. 223.
[13] *Ibid.*, p. 224.

to react with it completely. According to Faraday's second law, one equivalent of any substance requires 96,500 coulombs of electricity for complete reaction. By measuring the number of coulombs required for reaction, the analyst can calculate the number of equivalents of the substance undergoing the reaction. A fundamental requirement for accurate results is a current efficiency of 100 %, that is, only a single reaction must occur, with no "side reactions." Two experimental approaches are commonly used in coulometric analysis: The potential of the working electrode is controlled, or a constant current is employed. Further discussion is based on these two approaches.

Controlled Potential Coulometry

The technique of controlled potential electrolysis has been previously described. As applied here to a cathodic process, a potentiostat is set to give the desired limiting potential, thereby allowing only the desired reaction to take place. The electrolysis is then run until the current falls to zero. No indicator is necessary, the electrolysis ceasing when the current reaches zero.

Coulometers

A number of types of coulometers have been employed in controlled potential coulometry. The silver coulometer is one of the oldest. Silver is deposited on a platinum electrode from a silver nitrate solution and the electrode is then weighed. The oxidation of iodide ion to iodine electrolytically is also a classical example. In this case the iodine is determined by titration. Such methods are usually slow and inconvenient for routine analytical work.

The hydrogen-oxygen coulometer has been widely used because of its simplicity and the fact that it is direct reading. The current is passed through a sodium sulfate solution and the evolved hydrogen and oxygen are collected in a single bulb. The volume is read directly on a buret and the coulombs calculated. The device designed by Lingane[14] can be adapted for measurements from a large number down to about 10 coulombs with an accuracy of ±0.1 %.

A number of mechanical and electronic devices which perform the function of integrating the current-time curve have been developed and are described in some detail by Lingane.[15] A very convenient integrator has been described by Wise[16] and by Bard and Solon.[17] This instrument integrates the current-time function by feeding the IR drop across a standard resistor into a voltage-to-frequency converter whose pulsed output is counted electronically by a scaling circuit with digital readout. The device is capable of a high degree of accuracy and can be used over a wide range of coulomb values.

[14] *Ibid.*, p. 453.

[15] *Ibid.*, pp. 340–350. Also see Laitinen, *Chem. Anal.*, pp. 2500–2503.

[16] E. N. Wise, *Anal. Chem.*, **34**, 1181 (1962).

[17] A. J. Bard and E. Solon, *Anal. Chem.*, **34**, 1181 (1962).

Applications

Controlled potential coulometry has been shown by research workers to be applicable to the determination of a wide variety of substances. However, the technique has not been widely applied to practical analyses. The principal reason for this is the availability of techniques such as polarography and voltammetry which can usually be used for the same determination. The latter techniques are generally faster and require simpler apparatus.

Constant-Current Coulometry— Coulometric Titrations

In contrast to controlled potential coulometry, coulometric titrations have been widely applied to practical analyses. The technique employs constant current rather than controlled potential. The number of coulombs used in the reaction is calculated from the value of the current and the time required for complete reaction. Some type of indicator is required to tell when the reaction is complete. The substance determined can react directly at the electrode, or with a reagent which is generated at an electrode.

Direct Process

In a *direct* or *primary* process, the substance being determined reacts directly at the cathode or anode of the electrolytic cell. Only a relatively few substances have been determined by a primary coulometric titration. The reason is evident from our previous discussion of the constant current technique. If the unknown substance reacts directly at one of the electrodes, the potential of that electrode changes fairly quickly as the reaction proceeds, and it very soon reaches a value where a second reaction begins. The current efficiency is no longer 100 % and the analysis is invalidated.

Indirect Process

In an *indirect*, or *secondary*, method the substance to be determined reacts with a reagent which is generated by the electrolytic cell. This is a much more practical technique because it is relatively easy to obtain 100 % current efficiency. This method is used in practically all coulometric titrations.

The potential of the working electrode is kept fairly constant by maintaining a high concentration of the substance which is undergoing the electrode reaction to generate the titrant. For example, in the coulometric titration of ferrous ion, electrolytically generated ceric ion can be used.[18] Cerous ion, from which ceric ion is generated by anodic oxidation, is present in large concentration, and hence the anode potential is kept from becoming sufficiently positive for oxygen to be evolved. At the start of the electrolysis, ferrous ion is directly oxidized at the anode; then the potential becomes more positive, reaching a value sufficiently positive to oxidize cerous to ceric ion.

[18] N. H. Furman, W. D. Cooke, and C. N. Reilley, *Anal. Chem.*, **23**, 945 (1951).

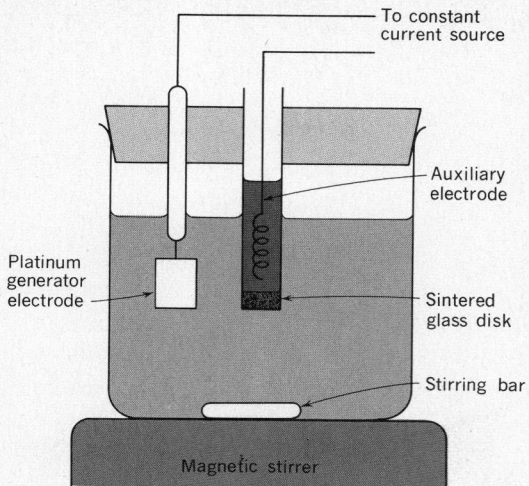

To constant
current source

Auxiliary
electrode

Platinum
generator
electrode

Sintered
glass disk

Stirring bar

Magnetic stirrer

FIGURE 10.6   Cell for coulometric titration.

The ceric ion in turn oxidizes any remaining ferrous ion in the body of the solution. The quantity of electricity used is the same, of course, as if the ferrous ion alone were directly oxidized at the anode. If the direct oxidation of ferrous ion were attempted, however, oxygen would be liberated before the oxidation of ferrous ion were complete, and the analysis would not be valid.

Experimental Techniques

(a) *Detection of the end point.* Since a coulometric titration is no different in principle from any ordinary titration, the same methods for detecting the end point can be employed. Methods which have been used include: visual, potentiometric, amperometric, conductometric, and photometric techniques. We shall not discuss these techniques further except to point out that, when the end-point method employs electrodes, there are then two pairs of electrodes in the solution. The electrolysis circuit itself contains a *generator* (working) and an *auxiliary* electrode; if the potentiometric technique is used, the other two are the indicator and reference electrodes.

(b) *Cells.* A typical cell[19] in which the generator electrode is a solid metal, such as platinum, is shown in Fig. 10.6. The platinum generator electrode is placed directly in the test solution, but the auxiliary electrode is in a separate tube, the bottom of which is a sintered glass disk. This isolation of the auxiliary electrode prevents products formed here from interfering with the analysis.

(c) *Constant-current sources.* A constant-current source is often referred to as a *galvanostat.* One of the simplest types is a high-voltage battery connected to the electrolysis cell through a large series resistance. More convenient and precise are automatically regulated constant-current supplies. Many of these

[19] J. J. Lingane and A. M. Hartley, *Anal. Chim. Acta*, **11**, 475 (1954).

have been described in the literature and several are available commercially.[20] These are generally electromechanical or electronic regulators. They are capable of maintaining constant currents of 1 to 100 mA or more with a precision of ± 0.01 to $\pm 0.1\%$. Several of these are described in detail by Lingane.[21]

(d) *Measurement of time.* It is necessary to measure the time required for a coulometric titration to within $\pm 0.1\%$. The timer should be turned off and on by the same switch that is used to close the electrolysis circuit. If several off-on cycles are employed in detecting the end point, the error in the time measurement accumulates and can become large. Ordinary stop-clocks are generally not satisfactory because there is a lag in the starting and stopping of the motor. Clocks with solenoid-operated brakes are precise to ± 0.01 seconds per operation, but are somewhat higher priced than ordinary laboratory timers.

The accuracy of a timer also depends upon the variation in the frequency of the line voltage. Generally such variations lead to errors of less than 0.2% but the error can be appreciable.[22]

(e) *External generation of titrant.* Occasionally difficulties are encountered in coulometric titrations because of undesired electrode reactions with certain substances in the test solution. For example, the titration of acids with electrolytically generated base involves the formation of hydroxyl ion at the cathode by the reaction

$$2\,H_2O + 2e \rightleftharpoons H_2 + 2\,OH^-$$

This cannot be carried out in the presence of substances which reduce more readily at the cathode than hydrogen ion. However, the titrant can be generated outside the titration vessel and allowed to flow into the vessel where it reacts with the substance being determined. A simplified version of the apparatus suggested by DeFord, Johns, and Pitts[23] is shown in Fig. 10.7. This illustrates the generation of hydroxide ion at the cathode of the generator cell by electrolysis of a solution such as sodium sulfate. Many other titrants have been previously generated in a similar fashion.

Applications

As previously mentioned, coulometric titrations have found widespread applications to practical analytical problems. A large number of titrants have been generated[24] for the purpose of carrying out acid-base, redox, pre-

[20] Laitinen, *Chem. Anal.*, p. 2497.

[21] Lingane, *Elec. Chem.*, pp. 499–511.

[22] *Ibid.*, p. 511.

[23] D. D. DeFord, J. N. Pitts, and C. J. Johns, *Anal. Chem.*, **23**, 938, 941 (1951); see also N. Bett, W. Cook, and G. Morris, *Analyst*, **79**, 607 (1954).

[24] See *Treatise on Analytical Chemistry*, Kolthoff and Elving, eds., p. 2516 for an extensive table; and Lingane, *Elec. Chem.*, pp. 536–616 for a detailed discussion of various applications.

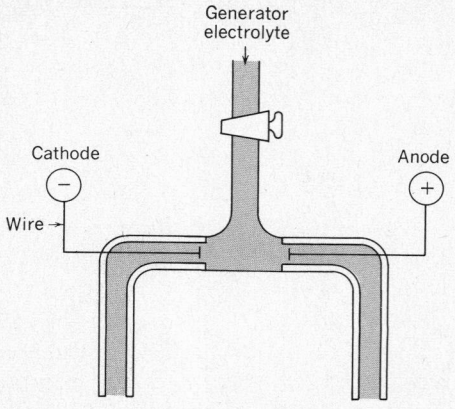

Cathode

Anode

Wire →

$2H_2O + 2e \rightarrow H_2 + 2OH^-$ $H_2O \rightarrow \frac{1}{2}O_2 + 2H^+ + 2e$ **FIGURE 10.7**   Cell for external generation of titrant.

cipitation, and complex formation reactions. In principle, any titration that can be carried out by classical volumetric techniques can also be done coulometrically provided the titrant can be generated with 100% current efficiency. Some common reagents such as permanganate and thiosulfate cannot be generated electrolytically, but other reagents, such as bromine, silver(II), and copper(I), which are unstable and difficult to employ as standard solutions can be generated and employed as needed by the coulometric technique.

Coulometric titrations are comparable in precision and accuracy to classical volumetric titrations and are more easily automated. With simple instrumentation, the precision in measuring the number of coulombs is of the order of $\pm 0.1\%$ and this can be improved considerably if more sophisticated apparatus is employed. Sample sizes from 100 mg down to a few hundredths of a microgram in volumes of 10 to 50 ml have been employed. Excellent results have even been reported with solution volumes as small as 10 μl.[25]

The reason that the method can be employed for such small samples can be seen as follows:

$$96{,}500 \text{ coulombs} = 1 \text{ equivalent}$$

$$1 \text{ coulomb} = 0.00001036 \text{ equivalent or } 10.36 \text{ microequivalents}$$

Since a quantity of electricity as small as 0.1 coulomb can be determined with a precision of about 1 ppt, 1.036 microequivalents can be determined with equal precision. For a substance of equivalent weight 100, this means a precision of about 0.1 μg.

[25] R. Schreiber and W. D. Cooke, *Anal. Chem.*, **27**, 1475 (1955).

POLAROGRAPHY

When an electrolysis is carried out using a microelectrode and a current-voltage curve is recorded, the process is called *polarography* (or *voltammetry*), and the current-voltage curve is called a *polarogram*. A limiting (diffusion) current is obtained which is proportional to the concentration of the electroactive species in the bulk of the solution. Analytical applications are widespread, and the technique is considered to be of major importance in quantitative analysis. The originator of the technique, Jaroslav Heyrovsky, received the Nobel Prize for this work.

Potential Requirements

A typical experimental set-up for determining a polarogram is shown in Fig. 10.8. The cathode is a dropping mercury electrode, a narrow glass capillary from which very small drops of mercury grow and fall. This is a *micro*electrode, in contrast to the anode, which is a calomel electrode of normal, or *macro*, size. The test solution contains a cadmium salt at low concentration (0.001-M) and potassium chloride at a concentration of 0.1-M.

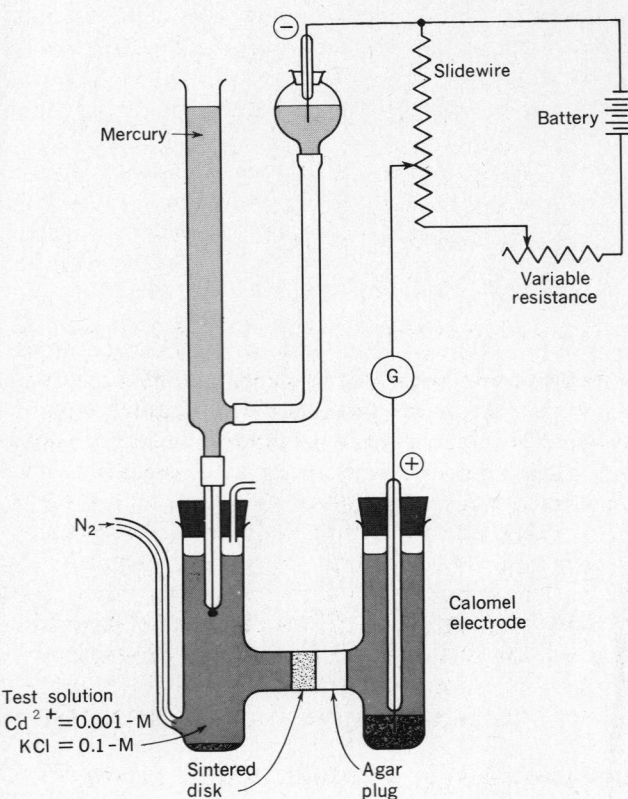

FIGURE 10.8 Apparatus for polarography using H-cell with dropping mercury electrode.

Mercury

Slidewire

Battery

Variable resistance

G

N$_2$

Calomel electrode

Test solution
Cd^{2+} = 0.001 - M
KCl = 0.1 - M

Sintered disk

Agar plug

The solution is not stirred. The voltage applied to the cell is varied by use of a calibrated slide wire, and the current is read on a galvanometer. These conditions should be contrasted with those used in ordinary electrogravimetric methods discussed on page 263.

We have seen that the voltage applied to an electrolytic cell is given by

$$E_{app} = (E_a - E_c) + (\omega_a + \omega_c) + IR$$

Let us consider the magnitude of these terms when the voltage applied is sufficiently large to cause cadmium to be reduced at the cathode. Because the cathode is very small, the current is correspondingly small, normally only a few microamperes. Thus, unless the cell resistance is very large, the IR term is negligible. For example, if the value of I is·5 μA and R is as large as 100 ohms, the IR term is only 0.5 mV.

As cadmium is reduced at the cathode, mercury reacts with chloride ions at the anode to produce mercurous chloride. The reaction, written with electrons on the left, is

$$Hg_2Cl_2 + 2e \rightleftharpoons 2 Hg + 2 Cl^- \qquad E_a = +0.25 \text{ V (sat.)}$$

Since such a small current flows, the concentration of chloride ions is not changed appreciably, and hence the term E_a remains constant. The overpotential term at the anode, ω_a, is negligibly small since the current is small and the electrode is large. Hence the total anode potential, $E_a + \omega_a$, is constant at $+0.25$ V.

It is apparent that any change in the applied voltage must be reflected in a corresponding change in the total cathode potential, $E_c - \omega_c$. In our present example,

$$E_{app} = 0.25 - (E_c - \omega_c) + 0$$

if the applied voltage is increased by, say, 0.20 V, the term $E_c - \omega_c$ becomes 0.20 V more negative. In other words the applied voltage is a direct measure of the cathode potential. In polarography, voltages are commonly referred to the saturated calomel electrode rather than to the hydrogen electrode. Thus an applied voltage of 1.00 V usually means that the cathode is -1.00 V with respect to the saturated calomel electrode.

The Polarogram

The current-voltage curve, or polarogram, for the electrolysis being considered is shown in Fig. 10.9. Along LM a small residual current flows. Near M the decomposition voltage of the cell is reached and the current increases rapidly with further increase in voltage. The cell reaction that is occurring is

$$Cd^{2+} + 2 Hg + 2 Cl^- \rightleftharpoons Cd + Hg_2Cl_2$$

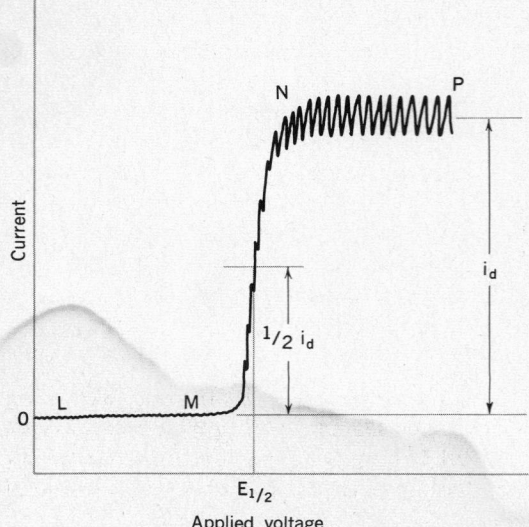

FIGURE 10.9   Typical polarogram.

The cadmium is dissolved in the mercury as an amalgam. Along the portion of the curve MN the concentration of cadmium ions at the electrode interface drops to a smaller value than the concentration in the body of the solution, since the solution is not stirred. This difference in concentration (concentration gradient) causes cadmium ions to move toward the cathode by the process of diffusion. The rate of diffusion is proportional to the concentration gradient,

$$\text{Rate of diffusion} \propto [Cd^{2+}]_{bulk} - [Cd^{2+}]_{interface}$$

As point N is approached, the concentration of cadmium ions at the interface falls to a very low value, and between N and P the concentration is so small it can be considered negligible. Hence, the rate of diffusion becomes constant and is given by

$$\text{Rate of diffusion} = k_1[Cd^{2+}]_{bulk}$$

where k_1 is the proportionality constant. Since the current is proportional to the rate of diffusion,

$$i_d = k[Cd^{2+}]$$

where i_d is the so-called *diffusion current* and $[Cd^{2+}]$ represents the concentration in the body of the solution. The current, i_d, is sometimes referred to as a diffusion-controlled limiting current. The current oscillates from practically zero to a maximum value as the mercury drop grows and falls

280

(Fig. 10.9). The average current is readily determined by damping the galvanometer.

Along the diffusion current plateau (NP) the microelectrode is said to be polarized because its potential can be changed by a relatively large amount without appreciably changing the current. The electrode reaction is still reversible; the effect is one of concentration overpotential. (If the electrode reaction is irreversible, the effect is one of activation overpotential.)

Since the concentration of cadmium ions can be determined from the value of the diffusion current, the method is of obvious interest to analytical chemists. Much of our later discussion will be devoted to the techniques used to convert current measurements into concentration.

The Dropping-Mercury Electrode

As previously mentioned, the microelectrode used in polarography is the dropping-mercury electrode (abbreviated DME). Mercury is forced through a very fine capillary from which small drops grow and fall at regular intervals of about 3 to 5 seconds. The drop time can be adjusted by varying the height of the mercury reservoir (Fig. 10.8).

There are several advantages that the DME possesses over a solid microelectrode, such as platinum. In the first place, the surface exposed to the solution is reproducible, smooth, and continually renewed. This makes it possible to obtain highly reproducible current-voltage curves, independent of the previous use of the electrode. Second, the DME furnishes ideal conditions for obtaining a completely diffusion-controlled limiting current. The diffusion layer remains quite thin because of the periodic dropping of the mercury which stirs the solution sufficiently to destroy the concentration gradient. The current does tend to decrease with time, of course, as the concentration of the electroactive species decreases at the mercury-solution interface. This is more than compensated, however, by the increase in surface area and the movement of the surface toward the bulk of the solution as the drop grows. The current falls when the drop falls, and hence an oscillation is observed. This oscillation is so uniform, however, that the average current can be observed as readily as a steady current. The average current assumes a steady, reproducible value very quickly as the applied voltage is changed. With solid electrodes the current does not become steady until sufficient time has elapsed to establish a steady state of diffusion and convection.

The third advantage of the DME results from the high overpotential of hydrogen on mercury and the fact that many metals form amalgams with mercury, thereby decreasing the tendency of the metal to redissolve. Hence, it is possible to reduce from aqueous solutions many metals which are more active than hydrogen. For example, polarograms have been obtained even for the alkali metals. Mercury is not equally useful as an anode material, since it is rather readily oxidized. An unlimited current increase, caused by the anodic dissolution of mercury, occurs about $+0.4$ V vs SCE. A platinum anode can be used up to the potential at which water is oxidized (about $+1.4$ V vs SCE).

The Residual Current

As shown in Fig. 10.9, a small residual current flows along LM as the applied voltage is increased. This current may be regarded as the sum of two components: (1) a faradaic current resulting from the electrolysis of trace impurities in a solution and (2) a "charging" or "capacity" current resulting from the charging of the mercury drop and the electrical double layer around its surface. The faradaic current can be minimized by purification of the reagents employed in the test solution. The charging current cannot be eliminated. It can be either positive or negative, depending upon the potential at the mercury surface. At potentials more positive than about -0.5 V, the mercury surface is positively charged with respect to the solution. As the area of the drop grows, electrons flow from the mercury reservoir toward the calomel electrode. This is conventionally called a negative, or anodic, current since electrons are flowing in the same direction as if an oxidation were occurring at the mercury drop. At potentials more negative than -0.5 V, the surface is negatively charged and the growth of a drop leads to a flow of electrons into the mercury from the calomel electrode. This is called a positive, or cathodic, current. At approximately -0.5 V (the exact value depends upon the nature and concentration of ions in the solution), the mercury surface is uncharged and this point is called the *electrocapillary zero* of mercury.

The Migration Current

It has been pointed out previously that there are three methods for accomplishing mass transport: migration, diffusion, and convection. In polarography, conditions are adjusted so that the limiting current is controlled principally by diffusion. Convection is minimized by not stirring the solution, and the migration current is minimized by the addition of a *supporting electrolyte*, the potassium chloride in Fig. 10.8. The migration current results from the attraction of positive ions by the cathode and negative ions by the anode. All ions in the solution contribute to the migration current, the fraction of current carried depending upon the concentration and mobility of the particular ion. In the absence of KCl, cadmium ions reach the electrode by migration and diffusion and the limiting current is about twice as large as the diffusion current alone. Addition of KCl lowers the limiting current, which becomes constant when the concentration of this electrolyte is about 50 times that of the cadmium. Potassium ions are attracted to the cathode but do not contribute to the current because they are not reduced at the potential required to reduce cadmium ions. The latter ions contribute negligibly to the conduction through the solution and hence reach the cathode by the force of diffusion alone.

The supporting electrolyte also serves to lower the resistance of the cell, thereby decreasing the IR drop to a very low value. As a general rule, polarographic conditions call for the supporting electrolyte to be 50 to 100 times the concentration of the reducible ion.

The Diffusion Current

In spite of the complex geometry of the DME, theoretical treatment of the diffusion current has been very successful. Ilkovic, in 1934, derived the following equation for the average diffusion current at a DME:

$$i_d = 607 n D^{1/2} C m^{2/3} t^{1/6}$$

The term i_d is the average diffusion current in microamperes, n is the number of faradays per mole of reactant, D is the diffusion coefficient (cm^2/s), C is the concentration (millimolar), m is the mass of mercury flowing per second (mg/s), and t is the drop time (s). The constant 607 is a combination of natural constants including the faraday; the value is slightly temperature-dependent and the figure given here is for 25°C. The principal importance of the Ilkovic equation is that it shows in a quantitative manner the influence of many factors on the diffusion current.

It is convenient to divide the factors in the Ilkovic equation into two parts:

(1) $nCD^{1/2}$, which is determined by the properties of the solution
(2) $m^{2/3}t^{1/6}$, which is dependent upon the characteristics of the capillary

The first part contains the concentration of the electroactive species. We have previously mentioned that the diffusion current is proportional to concentration, and this is the factor of primary interest to the analytical chemist. The term n, of course, is a property of the solute, the number of faradays per mole of reactant. The diffusion coefficient D is also a property of the solute in a given solvent. For simple ions this factor is related to the equivalent conductance and charge of the ion as well as to the temperature. The diffusion current increases with increase in temperature, this being about 2 % per degree for the DME. Hence, to insure an error no greater than $\pm 1\%$ in the diffusion current, the temperature should be controlled to within ± 0.5°C.

The second part, $m^{2/3}t^{1/6}$, can be evaluated by measuring the mass of mercury flowing through the capillary per second and the drop time in the diffusion current region. Currents obtained with different capillaries can be compared when this factor is known. The proportionality between the diffusion current and $m^{2/3}t^{1/6}$ does not hold at very short drop times. It is usually recommended that this time be adjusted to three to five seconds per drop. The surface tension of mercury and hence the drop time varies with the potential of the microelectrode. For practical purposes the drop time can be considered approximately constant from 0 to about -1.0 V. At more negative potentials this term decreases much more rapidly and this must be taken into account in calculating diffusion currents. All other factors being constant, the diffusion current is found to depend upon the effective pressure on the dropping mercury. The current should be proportional to the square root of the height of the mercury column if the process is diffusion controlled.

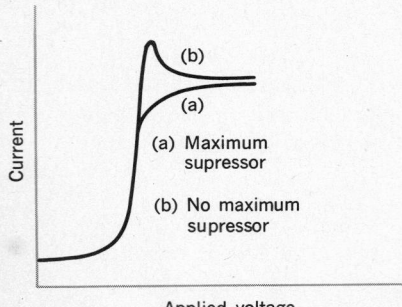

Current

(b)

(a)

(a) Maximum
   supressor

(b) No maximum
   supressor

Applied voltage   **FIGURE   10.10**   Maximum on polarographic wave.

Maxima

The current-voltage curves obtained with a dropping-mercury electrode frequently have maxima, such as the one shown in Fig. 10.10. The shapes of maxima vary from sharp peaks to rounded humps. Both the height and shape depend upon the concentration of the reducible substance, the concentration and charge of the supporting electrolyte, and the drop time of the capillary. Maxima are not observed with a stationary platinum electrode if one waits for the current to become steady.

For a maximum to occur it is evident that the concentration of the reducible substance at the electrode interface must be increased by some process other than diffusion. There is some reason to believe that this added factor is an absorption on the growing drop. At any rate, maxima must be eliminated to insure that the current is dependent strictly upon diffusion and is proportional to the concentration of the electroactive substance. Maxima can normally be eliminated by surface-active agents such as gelatin or the ions of certain dyes. Gelatin, at a concentration of 0.002 to 0.01 %, Triton X-100, a commercial surface-active agent, and methyl red are particularly useful as maxima suppressors.

The Half-Wave Potential

The potential at which the current in a polarographic cell is one-half the diffusion current (that is, where $i = \frac{1}{2}i_d$) is called *the half-wave potential* and is given the symbol $E_{1/2}$ (see Fig. 10.9). In other words, at the half-wave potential, one-half of the ions that reach the cathode during a given time are reduced. The half-wave potential is approximately the same as the standard potential of the redox couple.

The equation of the polarographic wave is

$$E = E_{1/2} - \frac{0.059}{n} \log \frac{i}{i_d - i}$$

where i is the current at any point on the curve and i_d is the diffusion current. A plot of E vs $\log i/(i_d - i)$ gives a straight line with a slope of $-0.059/n$ if the reaction proceeds reversibly (see Fig. 10.11). The value of n, the number

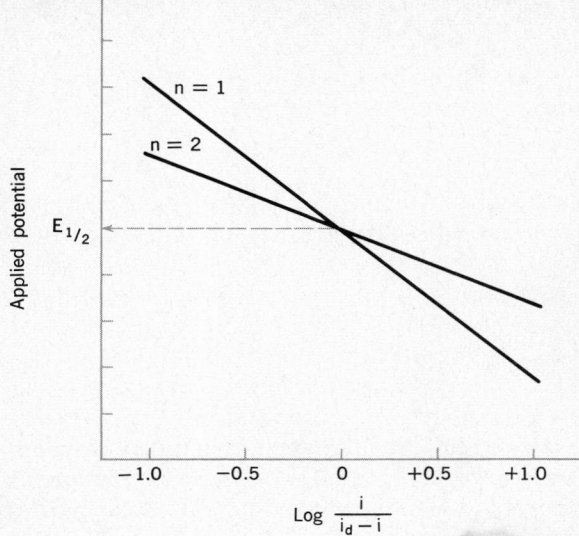

FIGURE 10.11 Plot of $\log i/(i_d - i)$ vs E_{app} for polarographic wave.

of electrons gained by the reductant, can be determined from the slope. If the value of n thus determined corresponds to the theoretical value and if the plot is a straight line, the reaction is regarded as proceeding reversibly. Practically, any reaction proceeding at a finite rate is, of course, irreversible in the strict sense. If the activation overpotential is very small, however, the above equation may be obeyed to within a small experimental error, and this is taken to be "reversible" behavior.

The half-wave potential can be determined from a plot such as that in Fig. 10.11. This is the potential at which the term $\log i/(i_d - i)$ is equal to zero, that is, the current is one-half the diffusion current. The half-wave potential, like the standard potential, is characteristic of the particular redox system. It is independent of the concentration of the electroactive species in the solution, and thus it can be used for qualitative identification of an unknown substance. This is seldom used as a method of identification, however, unless the number of possible substances is quite limited. There are many substances that have almost the same values of half-wave potentials, and they could not be distinguished from one another by such a measurement.

Applications

There are many substances that can be reduced or oxidized to yield well-defined polarographic waves. The concentrations of such substances in solution can be determined by the polarographic technique. We shall briefly summarize here the types of substances which give polarographic waves, as well as the types of waves formed, following the classification of Kolthoff and Laitinen.[26]

[26] I. M. Kolthoff and H. A. Laitinen, *pH and Electro Titrations*, John Wiley & Sons, Inc., New York, 1941, p. 148.

Cathodic Waves

Many inorganic cations, anions, and neutral molecules, as well as a large number of organic molecules, undergo reduction at a dropping-mercury electrode and yield *cathodic* waves.

1. Inorganic cations. A cation such as copper, which is more easily reduced than hydrogen ion, readily yields a cathodic wave in water solution. Cations which are less readily reduced than hydrogen may also yield waves even at low *p*H values, since the activation overpotential of hydrogen on mercury is large and since the activity of the metal is reduced through amalgamation. Polarographic waves of very active metals, such as the alkali and alkaline earth metals, can be obtained under certain conditions. Very negative potentials are required, and hence the hydrogen-ion concentration must be low and the cation of the supporting electrolyte must not be reduced more readily than the cation whose polarogram is desired. Salts of a tetraalkylammonium hydroxide, such as tetramethylammonium bromide, are used as supporting electrolytes since they are not decomposed until about -2.6 V vs SCE. The half-wave potential of sodium ion in 50% ethanol with 0.1-M tetraethylammonium hydroxide as the supporting electrolyte is -2.07 V.

2. Inorganic anions. Since diffusion is the process by which an ion reaches the microelectrode, the ion does not have to be of opposite charge to the electrode. Hence, anions may be reduced at the cathode and cations may be oxidized at the anode. The most important inorganic anions which give cathodic waves are the anions which contain oxygen, such as iodate, bromate, nitrate, tellurite, selenite, and permanganate. Hydrogen ions are involved in the reduction process, and hence the half-wave potentials are strongly dependent upon *p*H. In well-buffered solutions the waves are reproducible and the diffusion current is proportional to the concentration of the reducible anion.

3. Neutral molecules. Oxygen, sulfur dioxide, nitric oxide, cyanogen, carbon disulfide, and hydrogen peroxide are examples of uncharged inorganic substances which are reduced at the DME. The reduction of oxygen occurs at potentials more negative than about -0.2 V vs SCE, and the resulting waves may interfere with those of other substances. For this reason, dissolved oxygen is normally removed from a test solution by deaerating the solution with an inert gas such as nitrogen. The reduction of oxygen yields two waves of about equal height, corresponding to the following two reactions:

$$O_2 + 2\,H_2O + 2e \longrightarrow H_2O_2 + 2\,OH^-$$

$$H_2O_2 + 2e \longrightarrow 2\,OH^-$$

The polarographic method is an important one for the determination of oxygen.

Numerous organic molecules give cathodic waves, and the field of organic polarography is a large one. Organic groups which are reducible at the

DME include the carbonyl (aldehydes, ketones, and quinones), nitro, nitroso, diazo, amine oxide, epoxide, peroxide, carbon-halogen, and carbon-carbon double bond in conjugated systems. The reductions are generally irreversible, but the current is usually proportional to concentration, enabling the analyst to use the method for quantitative determinations.

Anodic Waves

Some inorganic and organic substances may be directly oxidized at the DME to produce anodic waves. A few examples are ferrous and ferrocyanide ions, hydroquinone, mercaptans, and enediols. A second type of anodic wave is observed with substances which form either an insoluble salt or a stable complex with mercurous or mercuric ions. Mercury is oxidized according to the reaction (right to left)

$$Hg_2^{2+} + 2e \rightleftharpoons 2\,Hg \qquad E° = +0.80 \text{ V}$$

when the dropping-mercury anode becomes about 0.45 V more positive than the SCE. If an anion which forms an insoluble salt or a stable complex with mercurous ion is in the solution, the foregoing oxidation is facilitated, that is, a less positive potential is required to dissolve the mercury. Chloride ion, for example, forms insoluble mercurous chloride at the anode according to the reaction

$$Hg_2Cl_2 + 2e \rightleftharpoons 2\,Hg + 2\,Cl^- \qquad E° = +0.28 \text{ V}$$

and the potential required for oxidation is considerably less positive than it is in the absence of chloride ions. As mercurous ions are produced at the anode, mercurous chloride precipitates, thereby lowering the chloride concentration at the electrode interface. Chloride ions then diffuse to the electrode, and the current is dependent upon the concentration of chloride ions in the body of the solution. A linear relationship is found between the diffusion current and the concentration of chloride ions. Other halide ions, sulfate, thiosulfate, cyanide, and thiocyanate are a few examples of anions which can be determined by the use of such anodic waves.

Polarographic Techniques

The polarographic method is commonly employed to determine concentrations in the range of 10^{-4}- to 10^{-2}-M. Under favorable conditions, concentrations as low as 10^{-6}-M can be detected. Errors of about $\pm 2\%$ are to be expected, although these may be reduced by a factor of ten in special circumstances. Since the concentration is proportional to the diffusion current, the main problem in polarographic analysis is to measure this current accurately.

Correction must be made, of course, for the residual current. This can be measured separately on a solution which contains the supporting electrolyte alone, and subtracted from the average current which is measured on the diffusion current plateau at the same voltage. When a recording polarograph is used, the portion of the residual current curve (*LM* in Fig. 10.9) is extrapolated, and a line parallel to it is drawn through the value of the limiting current (*NP* in Fig. 10.9). This procedure is simpler than the first one, but is less exact, particularly when the plateau of the wave is not closely parallel to the residual current.

There are a number of procedures which can be used to obtain concentration values from diffusion currents.[27] In the *absolute method* the concentration is calculated from the diffusion current using the Ilkovic equation. The diffusion current constant, *I*, defined as

$$I = 607nD^{1/2} = \frac{i_d}{Cm^{2/3}t^{1/6}}$$

can be evaluated by measuring the diffusion current at a known concentration and by determining *m* and *t* for the capillary used. Once *I* is evaluated and $m^{2/3}t^{1/6}$ is known, the analyst needs to run only one polarogram to determine the concentration of a solution.

There are several *comparative* methods which have been widely used. A calibration curve can be prepared by measuring the diffusion currents of a series of standard solutions. The current is plotted against concentration to give a straight line. The diffusion current of the unknown is measured and the concentration read from the graph. The *pilot-ion* method compares the diffusion current produced by the substance of interest with the current produced in the same solution by a second substance, called the *pilot ion*. The unknown and pilot ions must have sufficiently different half-wave potentials so that two well-defined waves are obtained in a solution containing both ions.

In the *method of standard addition* a known quantity of the substance being determined is added to a definite volume of the solution of unknown concentration. The calculation is illustrated in the example below.

Example. A lead solution of unknown concentration is found to give a diffusion current of 4.00 μA. To 10.0 ml of the unknown are added 10.0 ml of a standard solution of lead, the concentration being 0.0020-*M*. The diffusion current of the new solution is found to be 6.00 μA. Calculate the concentration of the unknown.

Since the current is directly proportional to concentration, we can write, letting c = molarity of the unknown,

(a) $4.00 = kc$

(b) $6.00 = k\dfrac{10.0 \times c + 10.0 \times 0.0020}{20}$

Solving for c gives

$$c = 0.0010\text{-}M$$

[27] See J. K. Taylor, *Ind. Eng. Chem., Anal. Ed.*, **19**, 368 (1947) for a detailed evaluation of various methods.

The method of standard addition is independent of the characteristics of the capillary and hence is useful where different capillaries must be employed. The method gives good results and is particularly advantageous for occasional determinations where time does not allow the preparation and examination of many standard solutions.

AMPEROMETRIC TITRATIONS

Since the diffusion current is proportional to the concentration of the electroactive species, the polarographic technique can be used to follow a titration involving this substance. The applied voltage is set on the diffusion plateau where the current is proportional to concentration. One or both electrodes may be polarized.

In the technique where one electrode is polarized, the diffusion current, corrected for dilution, is plotted against the volume of titrant. The type of titration curve obtained depends upon whether the substance titrated or titrant, or both, give diffusion currents at the applied voltage. For the reaction

$$A + B \rightleftharpoons AB$$

where A is the substance titrated and B the titrant, the curve shown in Fig. 10.12(b) is obtained for the titration carried out at E_1 [Fig. 10.12(a)]. At this potential only A is reducible. Since the concentration of A drops as the titrant is added, the diffusion current decreases up to the equivalence point and then levels off. If the titration is carried out at E_2 [Fig. 10.12(a)], the titration curve shown in Fig. 10.12(c) is obtained. At this potential both A and B are reducible; hence, beyond the equivalence point, the current increases as excess B is reduced.

There is a second technique in which both electrodes are polarizable. Two identical electrodes are employed and a small constant voltage is impressed across the pair. There are numerous examples of such titrations, and various shapes of titration curves can be obtained.[28]

The amperometric technique has been particularly useful for determining the end points of titrations involving precipitation and complex formation reactions. In many cases, suitable indicators are lacking and the amperometric method can be employed if either reactant gives a diffusion current. Substances which cannot be titrated potentiometrically may yield well-defined diffusion currents and hence be suitable for amperometric titration. The two-electrode technique has been employed with a number of redox systems and a very important use is the titration of water with the Karl Fischer reagent.[29]

As in ordinary polarography, the substance titrated is usually in the

[28] See pages 280–295 of footnote 10.

[29] Many practical examples of amperometry are given in a chapter by J. Jordan and J. H. Clausen in *Handbook of Analytical Chemistry*, L. Meites, ed., McGraw-Hill Book Company, New York, 1963, pp. 5–155.

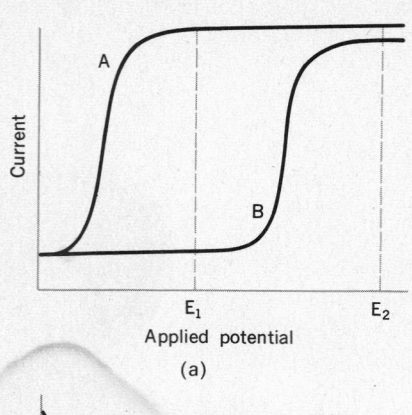

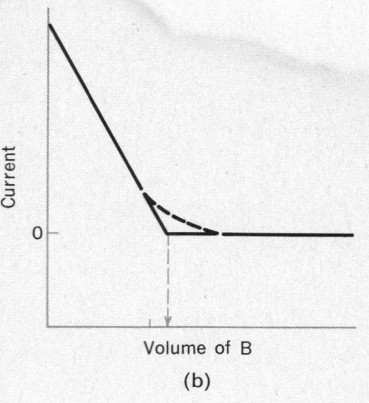

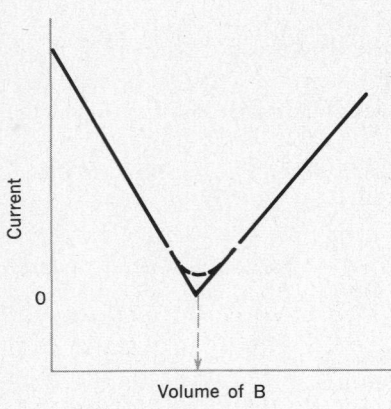

FIGURE 10.12 (a) Polarograms of substance titrated and of titrant. (b) Amperometric titration of A with B at E_1. (c) Amperometric titration of A with B at E_2.

concentration range of 0.10- to 0.0001-M. The diffusion current should be corrected for the effect of dilution by multiplying the current reading by the factor $(v_1 + v_2)/v_1$, where v_1 is the original volume of the solution titrated

290

and v_2 is the volume of titrant added. This correction can be minimized by making the titrant concentration at least ten times that of the substance titrated. A microburet is employed to keep the error small in determining the volume of titrant. The overall error in amperometric techniques is often as small as 0.1 %, and it is generally smaller than that which can be obtained with polarographic techniques. For best results, the indicator current is plotted and the end point determined by linear extrapolation.

As compared with potentiometric, amperometric titrations share with photometric (Chapter 11, page 335) the advantage that the measured quantity is directly proportional to concentration; hence the end point may be found by a linear extrapolation from points far from the equivalence point, where the reaction goes essentially to completion.

REFERENCES

C. N. REILLEY, "Fundamentals of Electrode Processes," and C. N. REILLEY and R. W. MURRAY, "Introduction to Electrochemical Techniques," Chapters 42 and 43, Part 1, Vol. IV, of *Treatise on Analytical Chemistry*, I. M. Kolthoff, P. J. Elving, and E. B. Sandell, eds., Interscience Publishers, Inc., New York, 1963.

I. M. KOLTHOFF and J. J. LINGANE, *Polarography*, Vols. I and II, Interscience Publishers, Inc., New York, 1952.

A. J. BARD, ed., *Electroanalytical Chemistry*, Vols. I–V, Marcel Dekker, Inc., New York, 1967.

L. MEITES, *Polarographic Techniques*, 2nd ed., Interscience Publishers, New York, 1965.

J. O'M. BOCKRIS and A. K. N. REDDY, *Modern Electrochemistry*, Vols. I and II, Macdonald, London, 1970.

QUESTIONS

1. Predict the first products of electrolysis in the following cells. Each electrolyte is 0.1-M and the solution is 0.1-M in H^+.

Cathode	Electrolyte	Anode
Pt	KCl	Pt
Pt	NaI	Cu
Cu	$CuSO_4$	Cu
Pt	$FeCl_3$	Hg
Pt	$H_2C_2O_4$	Pt

2. Is the flow of current through a cell the result or cause of the electrode reactions? Criticize the statement: "The current was increased until the electrode reactions began."

3. In the lead storage battery one electrode is made of lead, the other of lead dioxide, and the electrolyte is sulfuric acid. Write the reactions which occur at each electrode when the battery acts as a galvanic cell. Which electrode is negative?

4. Distinguish between activation and concentration overpotential. Under what conditions are these terms negligible? What is meant by a *polarized* electrode?

5. Explain how some metals which are more active than hydrogen can be deposited by electrolysis from acidic solutions.

6. Constant potential electrolysis can be used to separate copper and nickel in an acidic solution of the two metals, but it cannot be used to separate silver and copper. Explain the difference.

7. Compare the problem of separating two metals (more active than hydrogen) by electrolysis with that of separating two metals which form insoluble hydroxides by fractional precipitation.

8. Explain why an indirect coulometric titration is more practical than a direct one.

9. Suppose some H_2O_2 is formed at the anode of a hydrogen-oxygen coulometer and then is reduced at the cathode. Does the coulometer give high, low, or correct results? Explain.

10. Point out the differences between the experimental conditions used in ordinary electrogravimetry and in polarography.

11. Explain why the total cathode potential $(E_c - \omega_c)$ is the only term affected by a change in the applied voltage under polarographic conditions.

12. Explain what is meant by a "completely polarized" electrode. Can the reaction at such an electrode be reversible?

13. What are the advantages of the DME over a solid microelectrode? Compare the usefulness of the DME as a cathode and as an anode.

14. Explain what is meant by the terms (a) charging current and (b) migration current.

15. Consider the amperometric titration of A with B where

$$A + B \rightleftharpoons AB$$

Sketch the titration curve at a potential where (a) B gives a diffusion current, A does not; and (b) A gives an anodic, and B a cathodic diffusion current.

16. Suppose the reaction of A with B to form AB is essentially complete before the reaction of C with B to form CB begins. A solution containing both A and C is titrated with B. Simply sketch the shapes of the amperometric titration curves (one electrode polarizable) at a potential where (a) A and B give diffusion currents, C does not; (b) C gives a diffusion current, A and B do not; and (c) B and C give diffusion currents, A does not.

PROBLEMS

(0.059 may be rounded off to 0.06 for convenience.)

1. *Decomposition voltage.* Calculate the equilibrium decomposition voltages of the following electrolytes, all with platinum electrodes: (a) 1.0-*F* H_2SO_4, (b) 0.10-*F* H_2SO_4, and (c) 0.010-*F* H_2SO_4.

2. *Decomposition voltage.* Calculate the equilibrium decomposition voltages of the following cells:

(a) $\overset{\ominus}{Pt}|Cu^{2+}(0.1\text{-}M) + H^+(0.01\text{-}M) + H_2O|\overset{\oplus}{Pt}$

(b) $\overset{\ominus}{Pt}|Na^+(0.1\text{-}M) + H^+(0.02\text{-}M) + Cl^-(0.01\text{-}M), AgCl|\overset{\oplus}{Ag}$

(c) $\overset{\ominus}{Pt}|Ag^+(0.1\text{-}M) + H^+(0.01\text{-}M)|\overset{\oplus}{Ag}$

(d) $\overset{\ominus}{Pt}|Ag^+(0.2\text{-}M) + H^+(0.2\text{-}M)|\overset{\oplus}{Pt}$

3. *Decomposition voltage.* What is the value of the equilibrium decomposition voltage of the cell in 2(d) after the electrolysis has proceeded until the concentration of Ag^+ has been reduced to 0.00010-M? Note the increase in H^+ concentration.

4. *Applied voltage.* What voltage must be applied to a pair of smooth platinum electrodes immersed in a 0.010-M solution of Ag^+ in order for the initial current to be 0.50 A? The H^+ concentration is 1-M, the cell resistance 0.40 ohm, and the overpotential terms at the cathode and anode are 0.10 V and 0.85 V, respectively.

5. *Electrolysis.* A solution which is 0.20-M in Cu^{2+} and 0.10-M in H^+ is electrolyzed between platinum electrodes. (a) Assuming that the overpotential term for hydrogen is negligible, what is the concentration of cupric ions when hydrogen begins to be liberated at the cathode? (b) Repeat (a) but assume that the overpotential term for hydrogen is 0.50 V.

6. *Overpotential-pH.* A solution which is 0.10-M in Zn^{2+} has a pH of 1.00. It is electrolyzed using platinum electrodes. (a) Assuming the overpotential term for H_2 is zero, what is the first product at the cathode? (b) If the overpotential term for H_2 is 0.85 V, what is the concentration of Zn^{2+} when H_2 begins to be liberated? (c) Repeat (b) except that the solution has a pH of 4.00 instead of 1.00.

7. *Effect of pH.* (a) Theoretically, what must be the pH of a solution so that the concentration of cadmium can be reduced by electrolysis to 10^{-6}-M before evolution of hydrogen? Assume the overpotential for hydrogen is zero. (b) Repeat (a) for manganese. (c) Repeat (a) for magnesium.

8. *Effect of overpotential.* Repeat Problem 7 except that the overpotential for hydrogen is 0.40 V.

9. *Overpotential.* Calculate the overpotential term for hydrogen to allow the concentration of Zn^{2+} to be reduced to 10^{-6}-M by electrolysis before evolution of H_2 from a solution of pH 4.30.

10. *Mercury cathode.* Calculate the pH of a solution so that the concentration of Mn^{2+} can be reduced to 10^{-6}-M by electrolysis before evolution of H_2 for the following conditions: (a) no overpotential; (b) 1.0-V overpotential; (c) mercury cathode, 1.0-V overpotential, activity of manganese in the amalgam = 10^{-6}-M.

11. *Cathode potential.* If a cathode having a potential of +0.52 V is actually in equilibrium with a 0.10-M solution of Cu^{2+}, what is the activity of metallic copper on the surface of the electrode?

12. *Controlled potential electrolysis.* In a controlled potential electrolysis of a silver solution, the cathode potential reaches a value of +0.10 V when the silver-ion concentration in the body of the solution is 10^{-3}-M. (a) What is the overpotential term at the cathode? (b) What is the concentration of silver ions actually in equilibrium with the electrode surface?

13. *Potential buffer.* What should be the ratio of the concentrations of ferric to ferrous ions in a potential buffer in order to limit the cathode potential to +0.83 V?

14. *Internal electrolysis.* An electrolysis carried out by short-circuiting a galvanic cell is called an *internal electrolysis.* Suppose it is desired to separate copper from

nickel in a solution which is 0.10-M in each Cu^{2+} and Ni^{2+}. The following cell can be used:

$$Cu|Cu^{2+}(0.10\text{-}M) + Ni^{2+}(0.10\text{-}M)\|Pb^{2+}(0.10\text{-}M|Pb$$

The cell is short-circuited and allowed to run down. (a) Calculate the potential of the cathode at the end of the electrolysis. (b) What should the cathode potential be in order to deposit nickel? (c) What is the final concentration of Cu^{2+}?

15. *Coulometric titration.* The concentration of a hydrochloric acid solution is determined by coulometric titration using a platinum cathode and a silver anode. (a) What are the products at the two electrodes? (b) If 10.00 ml of acid is electrolyzed and a weight of 0.2158 g of silver is deposited in a silver coulometer, what is the molarity of the acid? (c) If the titration is done at constant current, what must the current be in order for the reaction to be complete in ten minutes?

16. *Coulometer.* Calculate the volume of hydrogen plus oxygen (STP) that should be produced per coulomb in a hydrogen-oxygen coulometer. What volume would this be if the gas is saturated with water vapor at 25°C and the pressure is 740 mm of mercury?

17. *Microelectrolysis.* Suppose a cadmium solution is electrolyzed in the cell shown in Fig. 10.8 for 5.00 minutes, the diffusion current being 1.00 μA. Calculate (a) the number of micrograms of cadmium deposited at the cathode and (b) the number of micrograms of mercurous chloride formed at the anode. (c) Calculate the time in hours that would be required to reduce the concentration of cadmium in 10 ml of solution from 0.0010-M to 0.0009-M by electrolysis at a current of 1.0 μA.

18. *Half-wave potential.* A metal ion is reduced polarographically, the diffusion current being 10 μA. The following currents were obtained at the indicated potentials (all negative): 0.444 V, 1.0 μA; 0.465 V, 2.0 μA; 0.489 V, 4.0 μA; 0.511 V, 6.0 μA; 0.535 V, 8.0 μA; 0.556 V, 9.0 μA. Calculate (a) the half-wave potential and (b) the value of n.

19. *Diffusion current.* The diffusion current constant of zinc in 0.10-M KCl is 3.42. What diffusion current in microamperes is obtained with a 0.00200-M solution of Zn^{2+} using a capillary with a drop time of (a) 3.00 sec. (b) 4.00 sec. and (c) 5.00 sec? Assume for each drop time that one drop of mercury weighs 5.00 mg.

20. *Pilot-ion method.* The ratio of diffusion current constants of cadmium to lead is 0.924. A polarogram is run on a solution of unknown lead concentration, the cadmium ion concentration being 0.0014-M. The diffusion currents are: lead 4.40 μA, cadmium 6.20 μA. Calculate the concentration of lead in the unknown.

21. *Method of Standard Addition.* A lead solution of unknown concentration gives a diffusion current of 6.00 μA. To 5.0 ml of this solution are added 10 ml of a 0.0020-M solution of Pb^{2+}, and the polarogram is run again giving a diffusion current of 18 μA. Calculate the concentration of the unknown lead solution.

22. *Diffusion current.* A 0.0014-M solution of Pb^{2+} gives a diffusion current of 4.2 μA. What should be the concentration of another lead solution so that when equal volumes of the two are mixed the diffusion current will be 12 μA?

23. *Method of Standard Addition.* The following is a modification of the Method of Standard Addition. A 5.00-ml portion of a lead solution of unknown concentration

is diluted to 25.0 ml and a polarogram run, the diffusion current being 0.40 μA. Another 5.00-ml portion of the same lead solution is mixed with 10.0 ml of a 0.00100-M solution of lead, the mixture diluted to 25.0 ml, the polarogram run, and the wave height is 2.00 μA. Calculate the concentration of the unknown solution.

24. *Polarographic analysis.* A sample containing 10.0 % $CdCl_2$ is to be dissolved and the solution diluted to 100 ml in a volumetric flask. A polarogram is to be recorded using 10.0 ml of the solution. What is the largest sample that can be taken so that the diffusion current does not exceed 20 μA? The diffusion-current constant of cadmium is 3.50, and the value of $m^{2/3}t^{1/6}$ for the capillary is 1.20.

25. *Diffusion coefficient.* A certain metal undergoes reduction by taking up two electrons. The average diffusion current of a 0.00200-M solution of the metal is 12.0 μA and the value of $m^{2/3}t^{1/6}$ for the capillary is 1.60. Calculate the diffusion coefficient of the metal.

11 Spectrophotometry

INTRODUCTION

Chemists have long used color as an aid in the identification of chemical substances. Spectrophotometry may be thought of as an extension of visual inspection in which a more detailed study of the absorption of radiant energy by chemical species permits greater precision in their characterization and quantitative measurement. Replacing the human eye with other detectors of radiation permits the study of absorption outside the visible region of the spectrum, and frequently spectrophotometric experiments can be performed automatically. In current usage, the term spectrophotometry suggests the measurement of the extent to which radiant energy is absorbed by a chemical system as a function of the wavelength of the radiation, as well as isolated absorption measurements at a given wavelength. In order to understand spectrophotometry, we need to review the terminology employed in characterizing radiant energy, consider in an elementary fashion the interaction of radiation with chemical species, and see in a general way what the instruments do. The student should understand that this chapter is only an introduction to the broad subject of spectrophotometry, and that it is possible to go much more deeply into nearly every topic that is mentioned here.

THE ELECTROMAGNETIC SPECTRUM

Various experiments in the physics laboratory are best interpreted in terms of the idea that light is propagated in the form of transverse waves. By

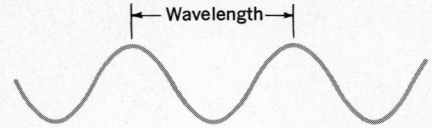

Wavelength

FIGURE   11.1   Transverse wave.

appropriate measurements, these waves may be characterized with regard to wavelength, velocity, and the other terms which may be used to describe any wave motion. In Fig. 11.1, it is indicated that the *wavelength* refers to the distance between two adjacent crests (or troughs) of the wave. The reciprocal of the wavelength, which is the number of waves in a unit length, is referred to as the *wave number*. The wave front is moving with a certain *velocity*. The number of complete cycles or waves passing a fixed point in a unit time is termed the *frequency*. The relationship of these properties is as follows, using the symbols λ for wavelength, $\bar{v}$ for wave number, v for frequency, and c for the velocity of light:

$$\frac{1}{\lambda} = \bar{v} = \frac{v}{c}$$

The velocity of light is about 3×10^{10} cm/s. Various units are employed for wavelength, depending upon the region of the spectrum: For ultraviolet and visible radiation, the angstrom unit and the nanometer are widely used, while the micron is the common unit for the infrared region. A micron, μ, is defined as 10^{-6} m (meters), and a nanometer,[1] nm, is 10^{-9} m, or 10^{-7} cm. One angstrom unit, Å, is 10^{-10} m or 10^{-8} cm. Thus there are ten angstrom units in one nanometer. Wave number is often used by chemists as a frequency unit because it has convenient numerical values ($\bar{v}$ and v are related by a constant factor, c, the velocity of light); the common unit of wave number is the reciprocal centimeter, cm^{-1}.

Luminous bodies such as the sun or an electric bulb emit a broad spectrum comprising many wavelengths. Those wavelengths associated with *visible light* are capable of affecting the retina of the human eye and hence give rise to the subjective impressions of vision. But much of the radiation emitted by hot bodies lies outside the region where the eye is sensitive, and we speak of the *ultraviolet* and *infrared* regions of the spectrum which lie on either side of the visible. The entire electromagnetic spectrum is classified approximately as shown in Fig. 11.2.

Within the visible region of the spectrum, persons with normal color vision are able to correlate the wavelength of light striking the eye with the subjective sensation of color, and color is indeed sometimes used for convenience in designating certain portions of the spectrum, as shown in the rough classification in Table 11.1.

[1] The term *millimicron*, mμ, is synonymous with nanometer and is still widely used by chemists.

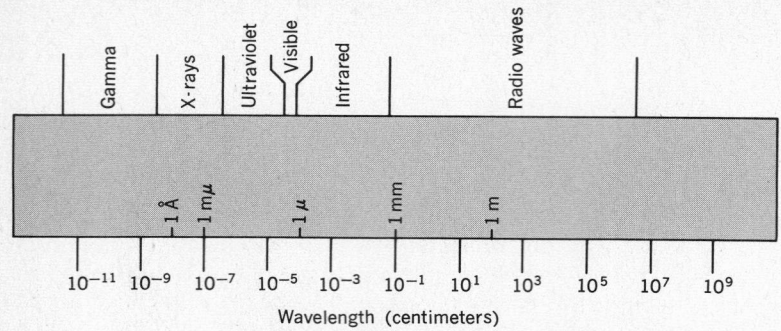

FIGURE 11.2 Approximate classification of electromagnetic spectrum.

TABLE 11.1 VISIBLE SPECTRUM AND COMPLEMENTARY COLORS

Wavelength, nm	Color	Complementary color
400–435	Violet	Yellow-green
435–480	Blue	Yellow
480–490	Green-blue	Orange
490–500	Blue-green	Red
500–560	Green	Purple
560–580	Yellow-green	Violet
580–595	Yellow	Blue
595–610	Orange	Green-blue
610–750	Red	Blue-green

We "see" objects by means of either transmitted or reflected light. When "white light," containing a whole spectrum of wavelengths, passes through a medium such as a colored glass or a chemical solution which is transparent to certain wavelengths but absorbs others, the medium appears colored to the observer. Since only the transmitted waves reach the eye, their wavelengths dictate the color of the medium. This color is said to be *complementary* to the color that would be perceived if the absorbed light could be inspected, because the transmitted and absorbed light together make up the original white light. Similarly, opaque colored objects absorb some wavelengths and reflect others when illuminated with white light.

THE INTERACTION OF RADIANT ENERGY WITH MOLECULES

The wave theory of light explains many optical phenomena such as reflection, refraction, and diffraction, but there are other experimental results, such as the photoelectric effect, that are best interpreted in terms of the idea that a beam of light is a stream of particulate energy packets called photons. Each of these particles possesses a characteristic energy which is related to the frequency of the light by the equation

$$E = h\nu$$

where h is Planck's constant. Light of a certain frequency (or wavelength) is associated with photons, each of which possesses a definite quantity of energy. As explained below, it is the quantity of energy possessed by a photon which determines whether a certain molecular species will absorb or transmit light of the corresponding wavelength.

In addition to the ordinary energy of translational motion, which is not of concern here, a molecule possesses internal energy which may be subdivided into three classes. First, the molecule may be rotating about various axes, and possess a certain quantity of *rotational energy*. Second, atoms or groups of atoms within the molecule may be vibrating, that is, moving periodically with respect to each other about their equilibrium positions, conferring *vibrational energy* upon the molecule. Finally, a molecule possesses *electronic energy*, by which we mean the potential energy associated with the distribution of negative electric charges (electrons) about the positively charged nuclei of the atoms.

$$E_{int} = E_{elec} + E_{vib} + E_{rot}$$

One of the basic ideas of quantum theory is that a molecule may not possess any arbitrary quantity of internal energy, but rather, it can exist only in certain "permitted" energy states. If a molecule is to absorb energy and be raised to a higher energy level, it must absorb a quantity appropriate for the transition. It cannot absorb an arbitrary quantity of energy determined by the experimenter and linger in an energy state intermediate between its permitted levels. This quantization of molecular energy, coupled with the concept that photons possess definite quantities of energy, sets the stage for selectivity in the absorption of radiant energy by molecules. When molecules are irradiated with many wavelengths, they will abstract from the incident beam those wavelengths corresponding to photons of energy appropriate for permitted molecular energy transitions, and other wavelengths will simply be transmitted.

The rotational energy levels of a molecule are quite closely spaced, as indicated schematically in Fig. 11.3. Thus pure rotational transitions require relatively little energy and are induced by radiation of very low frequency (long wavelength). It is in the far infrared and "microwave" regions of the spectrum (wavelengths of perhaps 100 μ to 10 cm) that absorption of radiation is correlated with changes in rotational energy alone. Studies of absorption in this region have contributed fundamental information regarding molecular structure but have found relatively little application in analytical chemistry.[2]

[2] J. H. Goldstein, "Microwave Spectrophotometry," Chapter 62, Part I, Vol. 5, of *Treatise on Analytical Chemistry*, I. M. Kolthoff and P. J. Elving, eds., Interscience Publishers, Inc., New York, 1964.

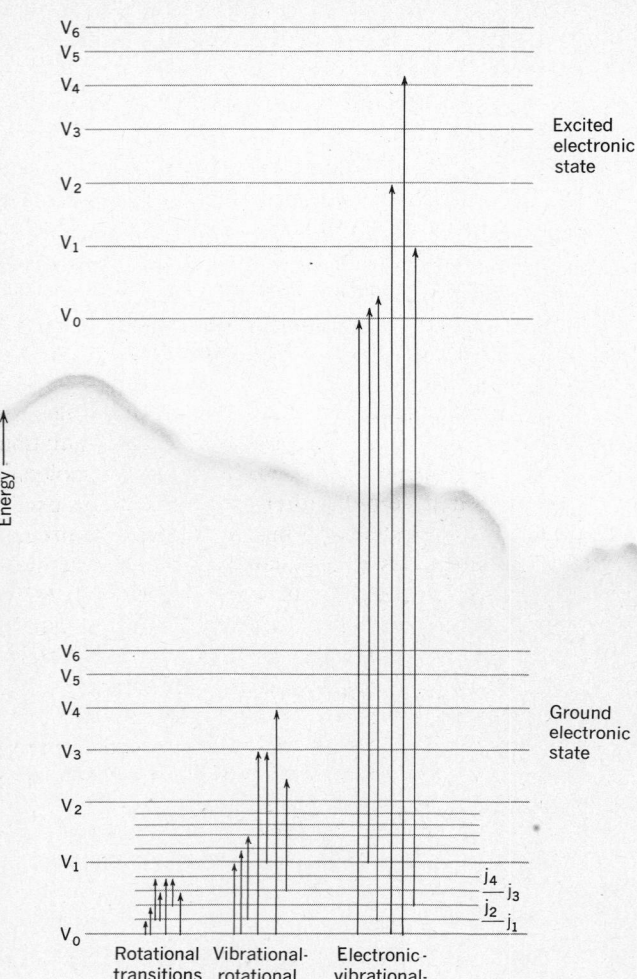

Energy →

V_6
V_5
V_4
V_3 — Excited electronic state
V_2
V_1
V_0

V_6
V_5
V_4 — Ground electronic state
V_3
V_2
V_1
j_4
j_3
j_2
j_1
V_0

Rotational transitions Vibrational-rotational transitions Electronic-vibrational-rotational transitions

FIGURE 11.3 Schematic energy level diagram. Two electronic levels are shown: V_0, V_1, etc. are vibrational levels, and a few rotational levels represented by j values are shown.

Vibrational energy levels are farther apart (Fig. 11.3), and more energetic photons are required if absorption is to increase the vibrational energy of a molecule. Absorption due to vibrational transitions is seen in the infrared region of the spectrum, roughly from 2 to 100μ. Pure vibrational changes are not observed, however, because rotational transitions are superimposed upon them. Thus a typical vibrational absorption spectrum is composed of complex bands rather than single lines. In practice, an infrared absorption spectrum consists, not of discrete lines as might be supposed from Fig. 11.3, but rather of a broad envelope extending over a wavelength span, because of distortion of molecular energy levels by neighboring molecules and because of the inability of the instrument to resolve closely spaced lines.

300

Absorption of visible light and ultraviolet radiation increases the electronic energy of a molecule. That is, the energy contributed by the photons enables electrons to overcome some of the restraint of the nuclei and move out to new orbitals of higher energy. Vibrational and rotational effects are super-imposed upon the electronic change, but the region where the absorption is found is determined by the electronic energy levels of the molecule. The vibrational and rotational changes introduce "fine structure" into the spectrum, so that the absorption involves a band of wavelengths rather than a single line. The individual lines making up the band are usually not resolved under experimental conditions, and the observed visible or ultraviolet absorption spectrum generally consists of peaks exhibiting a smooth curvature.

Once the absorption has been recorded, the fate of the excited molecules is usually not of interest in ordinary spectrophotometry for analytical purposes, but we may briefly note, for the curious student, that the molecule tends not to remain in the excited state but rather to get rid of the excess energy. Commonly, the energy is degraded into heat by a stepwise process involving collisions with other molecules. (This heat is not noticeable in an ordinary spectrophotometric experiment.) Sometimes the energy is re-emitted as radiation, usually of longer wavelength than was originally absorbed; this phenomenon is known as *fluorescence* (if there is a detectable time delay in reemission, the term *phosphorescence* is used). Fluorescence can lead to errors in absorption measurements if the reemitted radiation reaches the detector of the instrument. Finally, in some cases the absorbed energy may cause the molecule to dissociate into free radicals or ions, which may then proceed through a complicated series of reactions.

INFRARED SPECTROPHOTOMETRY

Infrared spectrophotometry is very important in modern chemistry, especially in the area of organic chemistry. It has become a routine tool for identifying compounds and detecting functional groups, and for quantitative analysis of complex mixtures. Commercial instruments which record infrared spectra became available after World War II, and since then great progress has been made in the design of instruments for routine use.

The utility of infrared spectrophotometry originates in the fact that the energy absorbed in the infrared region depends upon such factors as the masses of atoms and the strengths of the bonds which hold them together. A diatomic molecule such as HCl has only one mode of vibration, the stretching and shortening of the H—Cl bond. The resistance to stretching and hence the frequency of radiation required to excite the vibration is characteristic of the particular arrangement of atoms in the molecule. Most groups, such as C—H, O—H, C=O, etc., have associated with them certain bands in the infrared which vary only slightly from molecule to molecule. Such bands are called *group frequencies*, a representative list of which is shown in Table 11.2.

TABLE 11.2 INFRARED GROUP FREQUENCIES

Group		Frequency, cm⁻¹	Wavelength, μ
OH	Alcohol	3580–3650	2.74–2.79
	H-bonded	3210–3550	2.82–3.12
	Acid	2500–2700	3.70–4.00
NH	Amine	3300–3700	2.70–3.03
CH	Alkane	2850–2960	3.37–3.50
	Alkene	3010–3095	3.23–3.32
	Alkyne	3300	3.03
	Aromatic	∼3030	∼3.30
C≡C	Alkyne	2140–2260	4.42–4.76
C=C	Alkene	1620–1680	5.95–6.16
	Aromatic	∼1600	∼6.25
C=O	Aldehyde	1720–1740	5.75–5.81
	Ketone	1675–1725	5.79–5.97
	Acid	1700–1725	5.79–5.87
	Ester	1720–1750	5.71–5.86
C≡N	Nitrile	2000–2300	4.35–5.00
NO₂	Nitro	1500–1650	6.06–6.67

The infrared spectrum in Fig. 11.4 shows some of the group frequencies in ethanol.

In addition to the motion involved in stretching a bond, molecules have other modes of vibration. For example, a linear triatomic molecule such as CO_2 has four normal modes of vibration, shown in Fig. 11.5. The stretching mode can be symmetric or asymmetric, and in addition, two bending modes are possible. Although there are four modes of vibration, only two absorption peaks are found in the infrared. One occurs at 2330 cm⁻¹ for the asymmetric

FIGURE 11.4 Infrared spectrum of ethanol.

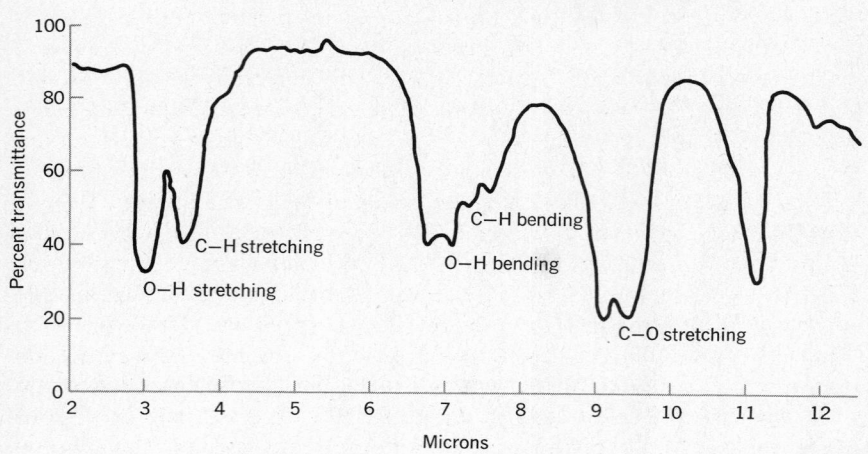

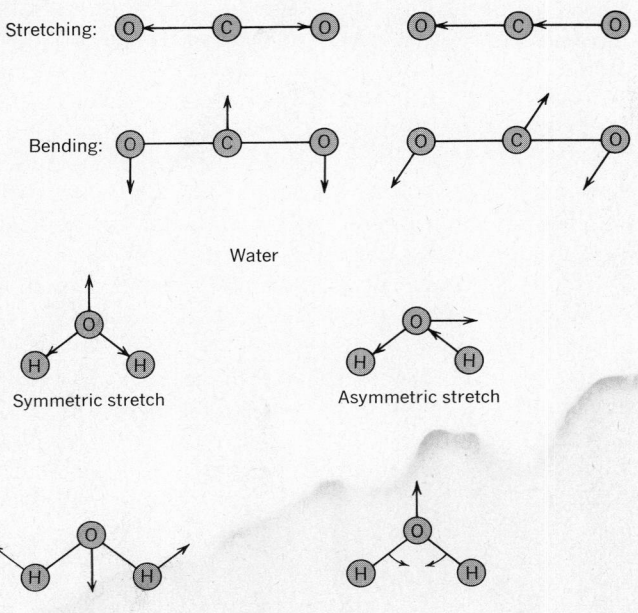

CARBON DIOXIDE

Stretching:

Bending:

Water

Symmetric stretch　　　　　Asymmetric stretch

Scissoring

FIGURE　11.5　　Vibrational modes in CO_2 and H_2O.

stretch, and one at 667 cm⁻¹ for the bending mode. The symmetric stretch does not change the dipole moment of the molecule and is said to be infrared inactive. The two bending modes are identical in energy and produce only one peak.

Water is a nonlinear molecule with three vibrational modes shown in Fig. 11.5. The symmetric stretch gives a peak at 3650 cm⁻¹, the asymmetric stretch at 3760 cm⁻¹, and the bending mode at 1595 cm⁻¹.

Infrared spectra of most organic compounds are so complex that a complete assignment of all absorption bands to particular vibrational modes is seldom made. The complexity arises from the multitude of vibrations that can occur in molecules which contain many atoms and several types of bonds, as well as by interactions among vibrational modes of adjacent bonded atoms. The complexity of a spectrum is actually an advantage in qualitative identifications and in establishing the structure of a compound. For example, in the so-called "fingerprint" region of the spectrum (1500–700 cm⁻¹; 6.7–14μ), the absorption pattern is frequently complex because of the interaction of vibrations of various single bonds. Small differences in structure may result in significant changes in the spectra observed, and absorption in this region is probably unique for every molecular species. The region is extremely useful for the purposes of identifying a molecule.

As previously mentioned, absorption spectra in the ultraviolet and visible regions generally consist of one or a few broad absorption bands, as shown in Fig. 11.6. All molecules can absorb radiation in the UV-visible region because they contain electrons, both shared and unshared, which can be excited to higher energy levels. The wavelengths at which absorption occurs depends upon how firmly the electrons are bound in the molecule. The electrons in a single covalent bond are tightly bound, and radiation of high energy, or short wavelength, is required for their excitation. For example, alkanes, which contain only C—H and C—C single bonds, show no absorption above 160 nm. Methane shows a peak at 122 nm (Table 11.3) which is designated a σ-σ* transition. This means that an electron in a sigma-bonding orbital is excited to a sigma antibonding orbital.

If a molecule contains an atom such as chlorine which has unshared electron pairs, a nonbonding electron can be excited to a higher energy level. Since nonbonding electrons are not as tightly bound as are sigma-bonding electrons, the absorption takes place at longer wavelengths. Note that such a transition occurs in CH_3Cl at 173 nm (Table 11.3), and that the transitions in CH_3Br and CH_3I occur at even longer wavelengths. This is because the electrons are held less tightly by bromine and iodine. The transition described here is designated n-σ* to indicate that a nonbonding electron is raised to a σ-antibonding orbital.

Electrons in double or triple bonds are rather easily excited to higher pi-orbitals. A transition is designated pi-pi* when a pi-electron is raised from a pi-bonding orbital to a pi-antibonding orbital. The absorption of energy in such a transition is usually stronger than σ-σ* transitions. In conjugated molecules, i.e., those containing a series of alternating double bonds, the absorption is shifted to longer wavelengths, as can be seen in Table 11.3. Such molecules are described by writing resonance structures, saying that the electron is more "delocalized" than if it were confined to one bond between two atoms. The shift to longer wavelengths reflects the fact that the electron in a conjugated system is less tightly bound than one in a nonconjugated system.

It has been found that pi-pi* transitions in molecules which contain unsaturated groups are very similar irrespective of the atoms which make

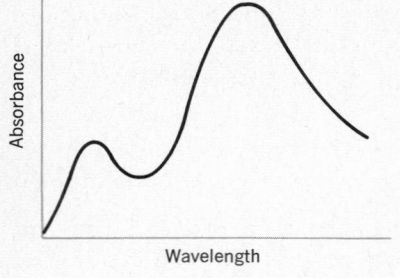

FIGURE 11.6 Visible or ultraviolet absorption spectrum.

TABLE 11.3 SOME ELECTRONIC TRANSITIONS IN ORGANIC MOLECULES

Compound	Wavelength, nm
Single bonds:	
CH_4	122
$CH_3—CH_3$	135
CH_3Cl	173
CH_3Br	204
CH_3I	258
CH_3OH	184
CH_3OCH_3	184
Double bonds:	
$CH_2=CH_2$	162
$—(CH=CH)_2—$	217
$—(CH=CH)_3—$	258
$—(CH=CH)_4—$	300
$—(CH=CH)_5—$	330
$(CH_3)_2C=O$	190, 280
$CH_3CH=CH—CHO$	217
$CH_2=CH—CH=CH—CHO$	263
Triple bonds:	
$HC≡CH$	178
$HC≡N$	175

up the double bonds. Note (Table 12.3) that the absorptions in acetylene, $H—C≡C—H$, and hydrogen cyanide, $H—C≡N$, occur at about the same wavelengths. The same is true for the two conjugated systems $—C=C—C=C—$ and $—C=C—C=O$, both giving peaks around 217 nm. Many years ago the association betweeen unsaturation and the absorption of light was recognized by organic chemists, and the term *chromophore* was introduced to describe the role of such groups as $C=C$, $C=O$, and $N=N$ in shifting the absorption of light toward the visible region.

Most applications of ultraviolet and visible spectrophotometry to organic compounds are based on n-pi* or pi-pi* transitions and hence require the presence of chromophoric groups in the molecule. These transitions occur in the region of the spectrum (about 200 nm to 700 nm) which is convenient to use experimentally. Commercial UV-visible spectrophotometers usually operate from about 220 to 1000 nm. The qualitative identification of organic compounds in this region is much more limited than in the infrared. This is because the absorption bands are broad and lacking in detail. However, certain functional groups, such as carbonyl, nitro, and conjugated systems, do show characteristic peaks, and useful information can often be obtained concerning the presence or absence of such groups in the molecule.

QUANTITATIVE ASPECTS OF ABSORPTION

Absorption spectra can be obtained using samples in various forms, e.g., gases, thin films of liquids, solutions in various solvents, and even solids.

Most analytical work involves solutions, and we wish here to develop a quantitative description of the relationship between the concentration of a solution and its ability to absorb radiation. At the same time, we must realize that the extent to which absorption occurs will depend also upon the distance traversed by the radiation through the solution. As we have seen, absorption also depends upon the wavelength of the radiation and the nature of the molecular species in solution, but for the time being we may suppose that we can control these.

Bouguer's (Lambert's) Law

The relationship between the absorption of radiation and the length of the path through the absorbing medium was first formulated by Bouguer (1729), although it is sometimes attributed to Lambert (1768). Let us subdivide a homogeneous absorbing medium such as a chemical solution into imaginary layers, each of the same thickness. If a beam of monochromatic radiation (i.e., radiation of a single wavelength) is directed through the medium, it is found that each layer absorbs an equal fraction of the radiation, or each layer diminishes the radiant power of the beam by an equal fraction. Suppose, for example, that the first layer absorbed half of the radiation incident upon it. Then the second layer would absorb half of the radiation incident upon *it*, and the radiant power emerging from this second layer would be one-fourth that of the original power; from the third layer, one-eighth, etc.

Bouguer's finding may be formulated mathematically as follows, where P_0 is the incident radiant power and P is the power emergent from a layer of medium b units thick:

$$-\frac{dP}{db} = k_1 P$$

The minus sign indicates that the power decreases with absorption. For the student who is unfamiliar with calculus, we may express this equation verbally as: The decrease in radiant power per unit thickness of absorbing medium is proportional to the radiant power. For the student who has studied calculus, let us rearrange the above equation to

$$-\frac{dP}{P} = k_1 \, db$$

and integrate between limits P_0 and P and 0 and b:

$$-\int_{P_0}^{P} \frac{dP}{P} = k_1 \int_0^b db$$

$$-(\ln P - \ln P_0) = k_1 b$$

$$\ln P_0 - \ln P = k_1 b$$

$$\ln \frac{P_0}{P} = k_1 b$$

Usually the equation is written with base-10 logarithms, which simply changes the constant:

$$\log \frac{P_0}{P} = k_2 b$$

A verbal statement of this equation might be: The power of the transmitted radiation decreases in an exponential fashion as the thickness of the absorbing medium increases arithmetically. Some writers consider this integration step to be a "derivation" of Bouguer's law, but actually the two formulations are equivalent representations of what we are here taking as an experimental finding.

Bouguer's law appears to describe correctly, without exception, the absorption of monochromatic radiation by various thicknesses of a homogeneous medium. The student can convince himself that the law applies strictly only with monochromatic radiation by considering an extreme case. Pass two wavelengths through a medium, one of which is absorbed appreciably and the other not at all. According to Bouguer's law, if we allow the thickness of the medium to increase indefinitely, then the transmitted radiant power should approach zero. But it cannot fall to zero if an appreciable fraction is not absorbed at all.

It may be noted that Bouguer's law takes the same form as other familiar functions such as the rate expression for first-order kinetics or radioactive decay, and the compound interest law.

Beer's Law

The relationship between the concentration of an absorbing species and the extent of absorption was formulated by Beer in 1859. Beer's law is analogous to Bouguer's law in describing an exponential decrease in transmitted radiant power with an arithmetic increase in concentration. Thus,

$$-\frac{dP}{dc} = k_3 P$$

which upon integration and conversion to ordinary logarithms becomes

$$\log \frac{P_0}{P} = k_4 c$$

Beer's law is strictly applicable only for monochromatic radiation and where the nature of the absorbing species is fixed over the concentration range in question. We shall comment further on this point in connection with so-called "deviations" from Beer's law.

Combined Bouguer-Beer Law

Bouguer's and Beer's laws are readily combined into a convenient expression. We note that, in studying the effect of changing concentration upon absorption, the path length through the solution would be held constant but the measured results would depend upon the magnitude of the constant value. In other words, in Beer's law as written above, $k_4 = f(b)$. Similarly, in Bouguer's law, $k_2 = f(c)$. Substitution of these fundamental relationships into Bouguer's and Beer's laws gives

$$\log\frac{P_0}{P} = f(c)b \quad \text{and} \quad \log\frac{P_0}{P} = f(b)c$$
(Bouguer)   (Beer)

The two laws must apply simultaneously at any point, so that

$$f(c)b = f(b)c$$

or, separating the variables,

$$\frac{f(c)}{c} = \frac{f(b)}{b}$$

Now, the only condition under which two functions of independent variables can be equal is that they both equal a constant:

$$\frac{f(c)}{c} = \frac{f(b)}{b} = K$$

or

$$f(c) = Kc \quad \text{and} \quad f(b) = Kb$$

Substitution into either the Bouguer or the Beer expression yields the same result:

$$\log\frac{P_0}{P} = f(c)b = Kbc$$

$$\log\frac{P_0}{P} = f(b)c = Kbc$$

Nomenclature and Units

Unfortunately, the development of the nomenclature regarding the Bouguer-Beer law has not been systematic, and a confusing array of terms appears in the literature. In analytical chemistry, the tendency in the United States has been to adopt recommendations of a Joint Committee on Nomenclature in Applied Spectroscopy, established by the Society for Applied Spectroscopy and the American Society for Testing Materials (ASTM).[3]

[3] For the report of this committee, see H. K. Hughes et al., *Anal. Chem.*, **24**, 1349 (1952).

The symbols P_0 and P as used here are recommended for the incident and transmitted radiant powers, respectively.[4] The term $\log(P_0/P)$ is called the *absorbance* and given the symbol A. Other terms which have been used synonymously with absorbance and which the student may encounter in the literature are *extinction*, *optical density*, and *absorbancy*.

The symbol b is accepted for the length of the path through the absorbing medium; it is ordinarily expressed in centimeters. Other writers have used the letter l for the same quantity, and, more rarely, the letters d or t.

Two different units for c, the concentration of absorbing solute, are often used, grams per liter and moles per liter. It is apparent that the value of the constant (designated K above) in the Bouguer-Beer law will depend upon which concentration system is used. When c is in grams per liter, the constant is called the *absorptivity*, symbol a. When c is in moles per liter, the constant is the *molar absorptivity*, symbol ε. Thus, in the recommended system, the Bouguer-Beer law may take two forms:

$$A = abc_{g/1} \quad \text{or} \quad A = \varepsilon bc_{\text{moles}/1}$$

It is apparent that $\varepsilon = a \times$ M.W., where M.W. refers to the molecular weight of the absorbing substance in the solution. Other designations for a are *specific extinction*, *extinction coefficient*, *Bunsen coefficient*, and *specific absorption*. Similarly, some writers call ε the *molar extinction coefficient*, *molecular extinction*, and various other names.

The *transmittance*, $T = P/P_0$, is simply the fraction of the incident power which is transmitted by a sample. The *percent transmittance*, $\%T = P/P_0 \times 100$, is also encountered. If $A = \log(P_0/P)$ and $T = P/P_0$, then $A = \log(1/T)$. Since, from Beer's law, absorbance is directly proportional to concentration, it is clear that transmittance is not; $\log T$ must be plotted vs c to obtain a linear graph. Figure 11.7 shows the situation. Analytical chemists prefer absorbance plots, but the student should be familiar with transmittance because it is encountered frequently. The detectors of most instruments generate a signal which is linear in transmittance, because they respond linearly to radiant power. Thus, if an instrument is to be read in absorbance units, there must be a logarithmic scale on the readout device or the signal must be altered logarithmically by an electronic circuit or in some mechanical fashion.

Deviations from the Bouguer-Beer Law

According to the Bouguer-Beer law (or, as many writers say, simply Beer's law), a plot of absorbance vs molar concentration will be a straight line of slope εb. Frequently, however, measurements on real chemical

---

[4] Many writers use I_0 and I for these terms, standing for *intensity* of the beam, but in ordinary spectrophotometers the quantity actually measured is the rate at which radiant energy is absorbed at the detector; this is best called "radiant power." Such units as watts or ergs per second might be employed, but in spectrophotometry we deal with a ratio (P/P_0) or the logarithm of a ratio ($\log P_0/P$), and the units cancel.

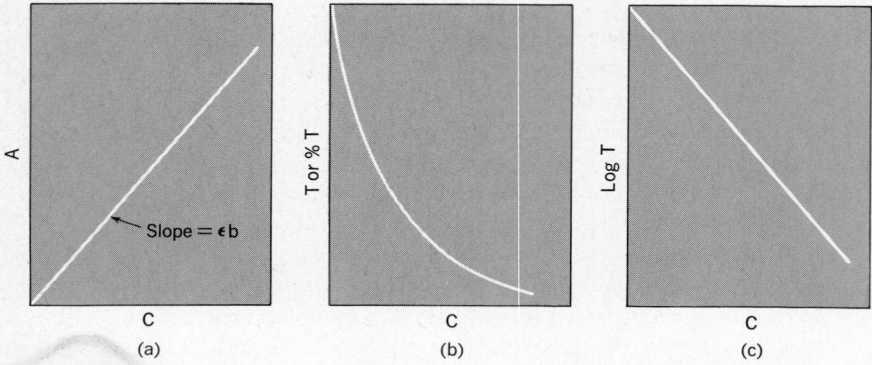

FIGURE 11.7 Appearance of Beer's law plots.

systems yield Beer's law plots which are not linear over the entire concentration range of interest. Such curvature suggests that ε is not a constant, independent of concentration, for such systems, but closer consideration leads to a somewhat more sophisticated view. The value of ε is expected to depend upon the nature of the absorbing species in solution and upon the wavelength of the radiation. Most deviations from Beer's law encountered in analytical practice are attributable to failure or inability to control these two aspects, and hence may be called apparent deviations because they reflect experimental difficulties more than any inadequacy of Beer's law itself.[5]

Consider, for example, absorbance measurements on a series of solutions of a weak acid, HB. The degree of dissociation of HB (fraction ionized) varies with the quantity of HB introduced into each solution if the final volumes are the same. Under this circumstance, it is possible to encounter either positive or negative Beer's law deviations, depending upon the ε-values of the two species, HB and B^-, at the wavelength employed. Since the fraction of the material present as B^- decreases with increasing analytical concentration of HB, a negative deviation from Beer's law will be seen if $\varepsilon_{B^-} > \varepsilon_{HB}$. On the other hand, if $\varepsilon_{HB} > \varepsilon_{B^-}$, a positive deviation will result. The system should follow Beer's law at a wavelength[6] where $\varepsilon_{HB} = \varepsilon_{B^-}$.

[5] There is another class of deviations which may be considered *real* rather than apparent, but they are not likely to be encountered in analytical chemistry. For example, it is shown in the theory of optics that ε for a substance in solution will change with changes in the refractive index of the solution. Since changes in refractive index attend concentration changes, Beer's law should not hold, even ideally. However, this effect is very small and is generally well within the experimental errors of spectrophotometry. Another real deviation from Beer's law sometimes occurs when relatively strong radiation passes through a medium containing only a few absorbing molecules. Under these conditions, all of the molecules may be elevated to higher energy states by only a fraction of the available photons, and hence there will be no opportunity for further absorption regardless of how many more photons may be available. This situation, known as *saturation*, is ordinarily not encountered in analytical practice.

[6] A wavelength where two or more species in equilibrium with one another have the same ε-value is called an *isosbestic point*.

310

These deviations from Beer's law may be circumvented, not only by performing measurements at the isosbestic wavelength (which lowers the sensitivity because ε-values generally are not maximal here), but by adjusting all of the solutions to a very low pH by addition of strong acid so as to repress the ionization of HB, or by addition of sufficient strong alkali to transform all of the material into B^-.

Many examples of this sort of Beer's law deviation are known. The general viewpoint here is that there is nothing wrong with Beer's law, that ε-values for individual species are constant over a wide concentration range, and that the deviations are predictable from a knowledge of the equilibria in which these species participate. Equilibria involving ions are often sensitive to added electrolytes, and failure to control the ionic strength may create problems in spectrophotometry. Temperature and various other factors may further complicate the situation.

Even with systems that are "well-behaved" chemically, deviations from Beer's law may occur because of characteristics of the instruments used in measuring absorbance values. In days past, such deviations sometimes resulted from fatigue effects in detectors, nonlinearity in amplifiers and readout devices, and instability in the sources of radiant energy. These problems have largely been solved in modern spectrophotometric instruments.

We pointed out earlier that the Bouguer-Beer law demands monochromatic radiation. Because ε values depend upon wavelength, measured absorbance values reflect the wavelength distribution in the radiation, which, in a practical spectrophotometer, is never strictly monochromatic. Think again of an absorbing solution as a series of imaginary layers of equal thickness. Now if heterochromatic radiation passes through the first layer, the more strongly absorbed wavelengths are abstracted from the beam to a greater extent than the others. Thus the radiation impinging upon the second layer will be richer in the less strongly absorbed wavelengths, and the second layer will not absorb the same fraction of the radiation incident upon it as did the first layer. Since the Bouguer-Beer law states that each layer will absorb an equal fraction, deviation from the law will clearly result.[7]

Although it must be pointed out that instrumental characteristics can lead to deviations from the Bouguer-Beer law, it is a practical fact that the better modern spectrophotometers are capable of performing well in this regard. This is not the case with the colorimeters or filter photometers which employ broad band-pass filters to isolate the desired radiation and which are still widely used in clinical and control laboratories. Further, good spectrophotometers can be operated in such a way as to lose some of their fine characteristics. Thus the student should file away in the back of his mind the warning to check before assuming the Bouguer-Beer law to hold for a particular chemical system with a particular instrument.

[7] A mathematical analysis of this type of deviation may be found in L. Meites and H. C. Thomas, *Advanced Analytical Chemistry*, McGraw-Hill Book Company, New York, 1958, p. 255.

INSTRUMENTATION FOR SPECTROPHOTOMETRY

A spectrophotometer is an instrument for measuring the transmittance or absorbance of a sample as a function of wavelength; measurements on a series of samples at a single wavelength may also be performed. Such instruments may be classified as manual or recording, or as single or double beam. In practice, single-beam instruments are usually operated manually and double-beam instruments generally feature automatic recording of absorption spectra, but it is possible to record a spectrum with a single-beam instrument. An alternative classification is based upon the spectral region, and we speak of infrared or ultraviolet spectrophotometers, etc. A complete understanding of spectrophotometers requires a detailed knowledge of optics and electronics which is far beyond the scope of this book. It is possible, though, for the student at this stage to understand what the instruments do. By combining this general, fundamental understanding with detailed instructions furnished in the form of "manuals" by the manufacturers, the chemist can obtain good data with modern spectrophotometers. Manually operated, single-beam spectrophotometers will be discussed first, because this provides the background for appreciating the capabilities of the more complex instruments.

Single-Beam Spectrophotometers

The essential components of a spectrophotometer, which are shown schematically in Fig. 11.8, are the following:

1. A continuous source of radiant energy covering the region of the spectrum in which the instrument is designed to operate.

2. A monochromator, which is a device for isolating a narrow band of wavelengths from the broad spectrum emitted by the source (of course, strict monochromaticity is not attained).

3. A container for the sample.

4. A detector, which is a *transducer* that converts radiant energy into an electrical signal.

5. An amplifier and associated circuitry which renders the electrical signal appropriate for readout.

6. A readout system on which is displayed the magnitude of the electrical signal.

Both single- and double-beam spectrophotometers, and instruments which operate in various regions of the spectrum, all have these essential components, although the details are quite different in the several cases. In accord with the goal set forth above, we shall discuss these components briefly.

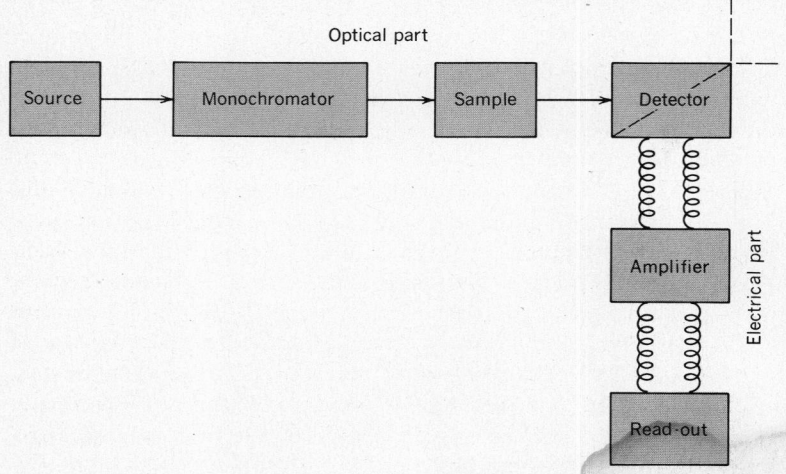

FIGURE 11.8 Block diagram showing components of a single-beam spectrophotometer. Arrows represent radiant energy, coiled lines electrical connections. The optical part and the electrical part of the instrument meet at the detector, a transducer which converts radiant energy into electrical energy.

Source

The usual source of radiant energy for the visible region of the spectrum as well as the near infrared and near ultraviolet is an incandescent lamp with a tungsten filament. Under ordinary operating conditions, the output of this tungsten lamp is adequate from about 325 or 350 nm to about 3μ. The energy emitted by the heated filament varies greatly with wavelength, as shown in Fig. 11.9. The energy distribution is a function of the temperature of the filament, which depends in turn upon the voltage supplied to the lamp; an increase in operating temperature increases the total energy output and

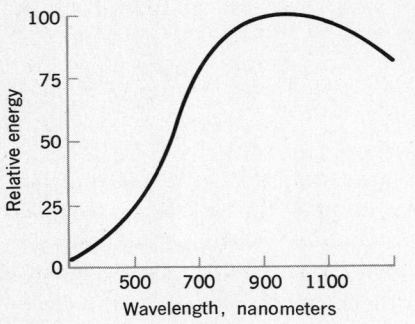

FIGURE 11.9 Relative output of a typical tungsten lamp as a function of wavelength.

313

shifts the peak of Fig. 11.9 to shorter wavelength. Thus the voltage to the lamp should be a stable one; a 6-V storage battery with a well-maintained charge is sometimes employed, whereas a regulated power supply is incorporated into some instruments. The heat from a tungsten lamp may be troublesome in an instrument; often the lamp housing is water-jacketed to prevent warming of the sample or of other instrument components.

Below about 325 to 350 nm, the output of a tungsten lamp is inadequate for spectrophotometers, and a different source must be used. Most common is a hydrogen (or deuterium) discharge tube, which is used from about 185 to 375 or 400 nm. When a discharge between two electrodes excites emission by a sample of a gas such as hydrogen, a discontinuous line spectrum characteristic of the gas is obtained provided the pressure is relatively low. As the hydrogen pressure is increased, the lines broaden and eventually overlap, until at relatively high pressures, a continuous spectrum is emitted. The pressure required in a hydrogen discharge tube is lower than that with certain other gases; also the tube runs cooler. Such tubes are conveniently small—about the size of common radio tubes. The envelope is usually glass, but a quartz window is provided to pass the ultraviolet radiation. A high-voltage power supply is required for gaseous discharge tubes. In a number of spectrophotometers, provision is made for interchanging tungsten and hydrogen discharge sources in order to cover the visible and ultraviolet regions through which the instruments operate.

The source for infrared spectrophotometers, which commonly operate from about 2 to 15μ, is usually the Nernst glower. This is a small rod of ceramic appearance fabricated from a special mixture of metal oxides, with platinum leads sealed into the ends. The rod is nonconducting at room temperature, but it is brought into a conducting state when heated, after which a flow of current maintains a glow which is rich in infrared radiation.

Monochromator

This is an optical device for isolating from a continuous source a beam of radiation of high spectral purity of any desired wavelength. The essential components of a monochromator are a slit system and a dispersive element. Radiation from the source is focused upon the entrance slit, then collimated by a lens or mirror so that a parallel beam falls upon the dispersing element, which is either a prism or a diffraction grating. By mechanically turning the prism or grating, various portions of the spectrum produced by the dispersive element are focused on the exit slit, whence, by a further optical path, they encounter the sample.

The student may recall from elementary physics the action of a prism in dispersing white light into a spectrum. When a beam of light passes through the interface between two different media, such as air and glass, bending takes place which is called *refraction*. The extent of the bending depends upon the index of refraction of the glass. This index of refraction varies with the wavelength of the light; the blues are bent more than the reds, as shown in

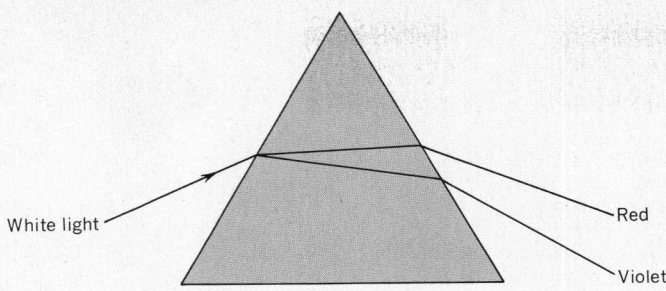

White light

Red

Violet

FIGURE 11.10 Dispersion of white light by a prism.

Fig. 11.10. As a result of the variation of refractive index with wavelength, the prism is able to disperse or spread out a beam of white light into a spectrum, in which the various colors making up the white light may be recognized separately. Infrared and ultraviolet radiation are dispersed in the same manner, but here the words *light* and *color* are not used and the prism material is not glass. The material of choice represents a compromise between dispersive power and transparency in the desired wavelength region, along with several other factors. Spectrophotometers covering mainly the visible region of the spectrum have glass prisms, whereas quartz is the prism material for instruments covering the ultraviolet and near infrared as well as the visible; infrared spectrophotometers commonly have prisms of rock salt.

The spectral purity of the emergent radiation from the monochromator depends upon the dispersive power of the prism and the width of the exit slit. At first thought, one might suppose that monochromaticity could be approached as closely as desired by merely decreasing the slit width sufficiently, but this is not the case. Eventually the slit becomes so narrow that diffractive effects at its edges only create a loss of radiant power with no increase in spectral purity (this is the so-called "Rayleigh diffraction limit"); actually, before this limit is approached in a typical spectrophotometer, the narrowed slit is passing insufficient energy to activate the detector.

With prism monochromators, a given slit width does not yield the same degree of monochromaticity throughout the spectrum. The wavelength dependence of the dispersion of a prism is such that the wavelengths in the spectrum are not spread out uniformly. The dispersion is greater for the shorter wavelengths, and hence wider slits may here achieve the same degree of spectral purity as would narrower slits at longer wavelengths.

Figure 11.11 is a schematic diagram of the optical system of a particular single-beam spectrophotometer with a quartz prism. The back of the prism is coated with a reflective metallized surface so that the radiation actually passes twice through the dispersive element. This not only enhances the dispersion but also is of great geometric convenience.

A diffraction grating (reflection) is made by ruling on a polished metal surface, such as aluminum, a large number of parallel lines. For the infrared region there are about 1500–2500 lines per inch; for the ultraviolet and

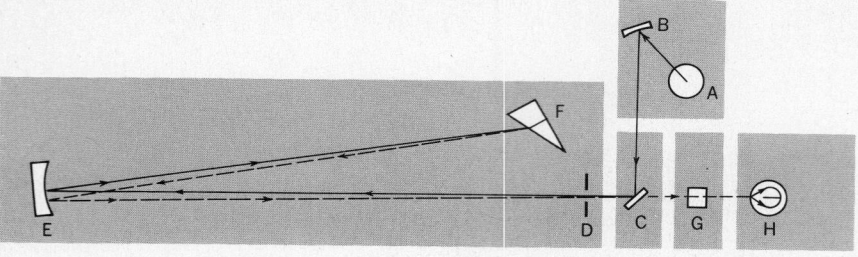

FIGURE 11.11 Schematic diagram of optical system of Beckman model DU spectrophotometer. *A*, light source; *B*, *C*, mirrors; *D*, slit; *E*, collimating mirror; *F*, quartz prism with reflecting back surface; *G*, cell; *H*, phototube. (Courtesy of Beckman Instruments, Inc.)

visible regions, about 15,000–30,000 lines per inch. When light is reflected from this surface, that which strikes the rulings is dissipated by scattering; the unruled portions reflect regularly, acting as individual light sources. Overlapping of the waves from these sources establishes an interference pattern which results in the dispersion of the reflected light into its component wavelengths. The student is referred to elementary physics texts for a full explanation of this phenomenon.

The machines for ruling the lines on a grating must be constructed to very close tolerances, and original gratings are expensive. Much cheaper, and much more widely used, are *replica gratings*, large numbers of which can be prepared from a single master grating. The original is coated with a plastic material, which, after hardening, is stripped off to yield a replica. The plastic is made reflective by evaporating a film of metal, generally aluminum, onto the ruled face; the grating is mounted in the monochromator in such a way that rotation allows various portions of the spectrum to illuminate the exit slit.

Gratings differ from prisms in rendering a uniform dispersion throughout the entire spectrum; in other words, a single slit width yields the same degree of monochromaticity of the emergent radiation throughout the spectrum. Figure 11.12 shows the optical path through a widely used grating instrument.

As mentioned earlier, the radiation emergent from a monochromator is not monochromatic, although it is much more nearly so than is the original source. The wavelength distribution is somewhat as shown in Fig. 11.13. The terminology employed in describing the width of the band shown in the figure is not entirely standard, and advertisements for instruments often quote figures for "band width" without specifying what is meant. A particular terminology which is widely understood is shown in the figure.

A problem in monochromators is so-called "stray light," by which is meant radiation of unspecified wavelengths which is reflected about inside the monochromator and which may find its way to the exit slit. In good instruments, this is minimized by using dull black surfaces and by inserting

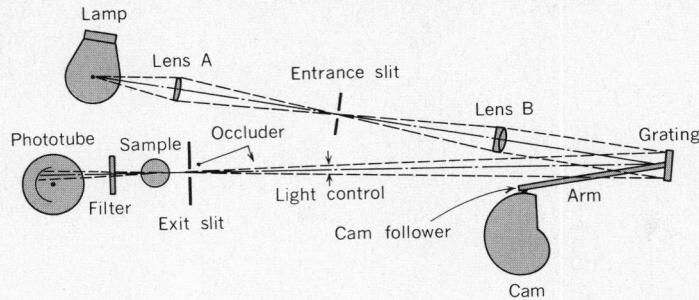

FIGURE 11.12 Schematic diagram of optical system of Spectronic 20. (Courtesy of Bausch and Lomb, Inc.)

baffles in appropriate positions. It is cut to an extremely low level in the finer instruments which employ double monochromators, generally combining both prism and grating. With ordinary instruments, spurious absorbance readings due to stray light may be obtained in spectral regions where very little energy of the desired wavelengths is available.

Until quite recently, instruments without true monochromators were widely used for absorbance measurements, mainly in the visible region, in laboratories where a low initial investment, simplicity, and speed were more important than the quality of the results. These instruments, designated

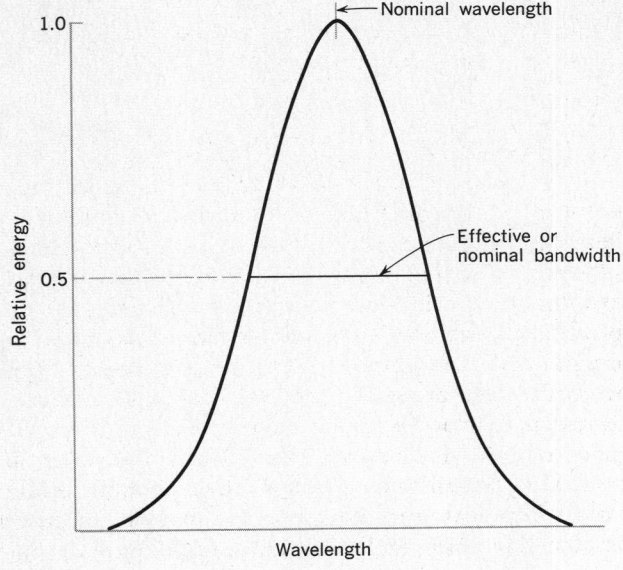

FIGURE 11.13 Wavelength distribution of the energy emergent from a monochromator.

filter photometers, utilized colored glass filters to isolate fairly broad wave-length bands from the source. They served admirably for many routine analyses, but they are rapidly being displaced by inexpensive grating spectrophotometers.

Sample Container

Most spectrophotometry involves solutions, and thus most sample containers are cells for placing liquids in the beam of the spectrophotometer. The cell must transmit radiant energy in the spectral region of interest; thus glass cells serve in the visible region, quartz or special high-silica glasses in the ultraviolet, and rock salt in the infrared. It must be remembered that the cell, which in a sense is merely a container for the sample, is actually more than this; when in position, it becomes part of the optical path through the spectrophotometer, and its optical properties are important. In less expensive instruments, cylindrical test tubes are sometimes used as sample containers. It is important that such tubes be positioned reproducibly by marking one side of the tube and facing the mark in the same direction whenever it is placed in the instrument. The better cells have flat optical surfaces. The cells must be filled so that the light beam goes through the solution, with the meniscus entirely above the beam. Cells are generally held in position by kinematic design of the holder or by spring clips which ensure reproducible positioning in the cell compartment of the instrument.

Typical visible and ultraviolet cells have path lengths of 1 cm, but a wide variety is available, ranging from very short paths, fractions of a millimeter, up to 10 cm or even more. Special microcells may be obtained, by means of which minute volumes of solution yield an ordinary path length, and adjustable cells of variable path length are also available, particularly for infrared work. The variety of infrared cells currently on the market is beyond the scope of this discussion. Problems in the infrared are different from those in the ultraviolet and visible regions. Because solvents which are infrared-transparent are not available, the tendency is to run concentrated solutions at short path lengths (0.1 mm or even less) to minimize absorption by the solvent, and the cells are thus quite different from those employed at shorter wavelengths.

Detector

In a detector for a spectrophotometer, we desire high sensitivity in the spectral region of interest, linear response to radiant power, a fast response time, amenability to amplification, and high stability or low "noise" level, although in practice it is necessary to compromise among these factors. Higher sensitivity, for example, can be bought only at the expense of increased noise. The types of detection that have been most widely used are based upon photochemical change (mainly photographic), the photoelectric effect, and thermal effects. Photography is no longer used in ordinary spectrophoto-metry; generally speaking, photoelectric detectors are employed in the visible and ultraviolet regions and detectors based upon thermal effects are used in the infrared.

The commonest photoelectric detector is the *phototube*. This is an evacuated envelope, with a transparent window, containing a pair of electrodes across which a potential is maintained. The surface of the negative electrode is photosensitive, i.e., electrons are ejected from this surface when it is irradiated with photons of sufficient energy. The electrons are accelerated across the potential difference to the positive electrode, and a current flows in the circuit. Whether or not electrons are emitted depends upon the nature of the cathode surface and the frequency of the radiation; the number of electrons emitted per unit time, and hence the current, depends upon the radiant power. A variety of phototubes are available which differ in the material of the cathode surface (also in the transparent window) and hence in their response to radiation of various frequencies. A number of spectrophotometers provide for interchanging detectors so as to maintain a good response over a broad wavelength range.

Photomultiplier tubes are more sensitive than ordinary phototubes because of high amplification accomplished with the tube itself. Such a tube has a series of electrodes, each at a progressively more positive potential than the cathode. The geometry of the tube is such that the primary photoelectrons are focused into a beam and accelerated to an electrode which is, say, 50 to 90 V more positive than the cathode. The bombardment of this electrode (or dynode, as it is called) releases many more secondary electrons which are accelerated to a third, more positive, electrode, etc., for perhaps ten stages. A regulated high-voltage power supply, furnishing about 500 to 900 V, is required to operate the tube; a number of batteries in series can also be used. The output of the photomultiplier may be still further amplified with an external electronic amplifier. The enhanced sensitivity of this detector permits narrower slit widths in the monochromator and hence better resolution of spectral fine structure.

The common infrared detector is the thermocouple. The student may recall the thermoelectric effect: If two dissimilar metals are joined at two points, a potential is developed if the two junctions are at different temperatures. Heating of one of the junctions by the infrared radiation is thus the basis of detection. This junction is specially designed to have a low heat capacity so that it will be warmed appreciably by radiant energy of the power encountered in the instrument.

Amplification and Readout

It is beyond the scope of this text to discuss the detailed electronics of amplification and readout as they are accomplished in various spectrophotometers. To give an idea of what may be involved, we may briefly consider one possibility. Let us place a large load resistor in series with a phototube, as shown schematically in Fig. 11.14. Suppose the radiant power supplied to the cathode is such that a current of one microampere (10^{-6} A)

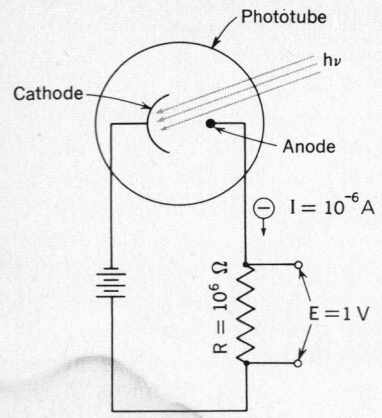

Phototube

Cathode

hν

Anode

$I = 10^{-6}$ A

$R = 10^6$ Ω

$E = 1$ V

FIGURE 11.14 Simple phototube circuit (see text).

flows in the circuit. If the resistor has a value of one megohm (10^6 ohms) as shown in the figure, then according to Ohm's law the voltage across the resistor, $E = IR$, is $10^{-6} \times 10^6 = 1$ V. Although 1 V is a fair voltage, it cannot be measured by connecting an ordinary voltmeter across the resistor. As soon as such a connection is made, the meter becomes part of the circuit, establishing a parallel shunt around the resistor. Since the resistance of a typical voltmeter is very low as compared with 10^6 ohms, most of the current bypasses the large resistance and flows through the meter, and the voltage across the resistor, although measured correctly as it is, is no longer 1 V, but perhaps only a few millivolts.

The problem may be handled by applying the voltage across the load resistor to the control grid of a vacuum tube. The grid circuit of such a tube draws very little current, and thus the voltage holds up as it should. Small changes in grid potential are translated by the vacuum tube into large changes in plate current. The amplified output may be taken to a meter for direct reading, or it may be "bucked out" by another voltage under the control of the operator, with the meter used as a null device. The amplified signal may also be fed to a recording potentiometer.

Operation of a Single-Beam Spectrophotometer

We shall first describe the usual mode of operation of a typical manually operated, single-beam spectrophotometer, and then examine briefly some possible variations on the common procedure.

Ordinary Operation

Typically, there is an opaque shutter, controlled by the operator, which may be placed in front of the phototube so that the tube is in darkness. With this shutter in position, a small current ("dark current") flows in the phototube circuit due to thermal emission of electrons by the cathode or perhaps a

320

small leakage in the tube. By means of a knob on the instrument, the operator cancels out the dark current and sets the scale on the instrument to read infinite absorbance (zero transmittance). Next, with the wavelength set at the desired value and a cell containing a reference solution in the beam (the reference may be the pure solvent, a "blank" from an analytical procedure, etc.), the shutter is removed to expose the detector. Now, by adjusting the radiant power to the detector by means of the monochromator slit control, and/or by changing electronically the gain of the amplifier, the instrument scale is set to read zero absorbance (100% transmittance). With a scale thus established, the sample solution is placed in the beam and its absorbance or transmittance is read off. (The scale is generally linear in transmittance, but most instruments have an absorbance scale alongside the transmittance scale and either one can be read.)

The scale, set up as described above, must be reestablished whenever the wavelength is changed, in order to compensate for the variation of source output with wavelength and the wavelength-dependence of the detector response, as well as any absorption by the reference solution or the cell. It is good practice to check the dark current and reference solution settings frequently because of possible drift in the circuit and in the output of the source. Usually two cells are used, one for the reference solution and one for the samples to be measured; it is obvious that these cells should be matched with regard to path length and optical qualities.

Differential Measurements

Ordinarily the reference solution in spectrophotometry is the pure solvent or a "blank" solution of some kind which contains little or none of the substance being determined. Using this reference and the dark current adjustment, a scale is set up as described above and shown in the upper part of Fig. 11.15. Also shown along the scale are the absorbance and transmittance values of two solutions, one an unknown which is to be measured and the other a standard solution containing a known quantity of the substance being determined.

FIGURE 11.15   Scale expansion in differential spectro-photometer.

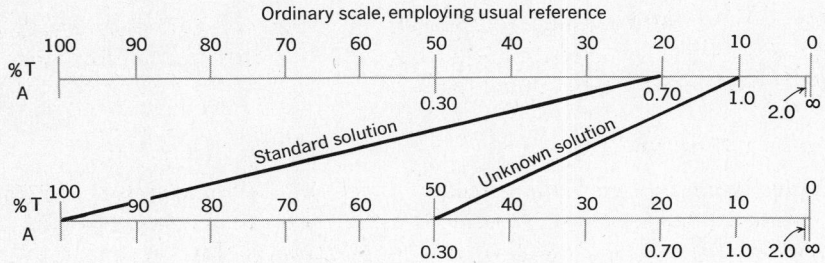

Ordinary scale, employing usual reference

Expanded scale, employing reference which reads 0.70 A on ordinary scale

Now we must recognize that the instrument does not know anything about the sort of solution that is in the beam. All it is capable of is to produce a reading of zero absorbance (100 % T) when a certain radiant power falls upon the detector and the amplification of the electronic circuit is appropriate. Thus the instrument can be set to read zero absorbance with a strongly absorbing solution, instead of the usual reference in the beam, by opening the slits of the monochromator and/or increasing the gain of the amplifier. Suppose, then, that we place the standard solution shown in Fig. 11.15 in the beam and set the absorbance reading at zero. As we have attempted to show in the figure by the lower scale and the lines tying it to the upper scale, we have now accomplished essentially a scale expansion. What was only a small portion of the upper scale becomes a much larger portion of the lower scale. Note that the difference in absorbances of the two solutions is 0.30 units in each case, but 0.30 units is a much larger portion of the lower scale than the upper. Hence we may expect that a constant instrumental error will result in a smaller relative concentration error. Actually, in some cases the error can be reduced to as little as a part per thousand, and the spectrophotometric measurement (normally not this good; see below) can compete with ordinary titrimetric and gravimetric techniques, which are usually considered more precise. Several applications of differential spectrophotometry have been given by Bastian,[8] and a detailed mathematical analysis of the technique and its errors has been developed by Hiskey.[9]

To see more clearly how the error is reduced in differential spectrophotometry, let us consider an example. Suppose we wish to determine copper by measuring the absorbance of blue cupric solutions. Let us simply assume, to establish a specific basis for our discussion, that a solution with a copper concentration of 2 mg per ml (solution A) can be measured against a pure water reference with an error of 1 %. Now consider the error if a solution containing 20 mg of copper per ml (solution B) were measured, using as a reference, not water, but another cupric solution containing 18 mg of copper per ml (solution C). The concentration difference between B and C is the same as the difference between solution A and water. Thus, if Beer's law is obeyed, the foregoing two measurements will give rise to the same absorbance value and the same error. In other words, supposing solution B were our unknown solution, we could determine how much it differed from solution C with a 1 % error. But we know *accurately* the concentration of solution C, because it is a carefully prepared reference solution (by *accurately*, we mean that no spectrophotometric error is involved). Thus, so far as errors in spectrophotometry are concerned, the concentration of solution B can be determined with an error of only 0.1 %. (In measuring solution A versus water, the error is $0.02/2 \times 100 = 1$ %; if B is measured against C, the error is still $0.02/2 \times 100 = 1$ %, but the error in the absolute concentration of B is only $0.02/20 \times 100 = 0.1$ %.)

[8] R. Bastian et al., *Anal. Chem.*, **21**, 972 (1949); **22**, 160 (1950); **23**, 580 (1951).
[9] C. F. Hiskey et al., *Anal. Chem.*, **21**, 1440 (1949); **22**, 1464 (1950); **23**, 506 (1951); **23**, 1196 (1951); **24**, 342 (1952).

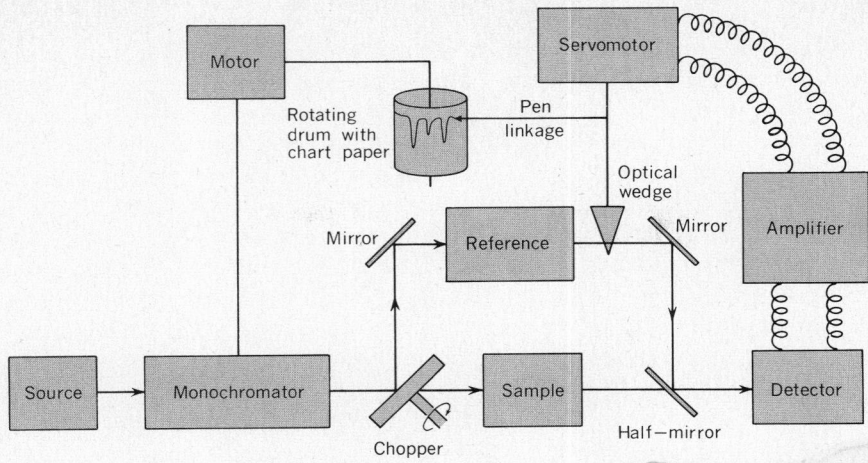

FIGURE 11.16 Schematic diagram of a possible double-beam optical null recording spectrophotometer.

The differential approach not only leads to lower errors, as explained above, but also permits the extension of spectrophotometry to the analysis of solutions which would be too highly absorbing for ordinary measurements.

It is possible to achieve even greater precision by setting both ends of the scale with standard solutions in the beam. In other words, the $100\% \, T$ is set as described above using a standard solution more dilute than the unknown, but the $0\% \, T$ is set, not with a shutter in the beam, but with a more concentrated standard solution. Reilley and Crawford, whose definitive paper[10] should be consulted for further details, refer to this as the "method of ultimate precision."

Double-Beam Spectrophotometers

Recording spectrophotometers which automatically plot the absorbance of a sample as a function of wavelength are almost always double-beam instruments. It is far beyond the scope of this text to present a full discussion of these marvelous devices which have practically revolutionized the taking of absorption spectra for modern chemists, but it is obligatory at least to give an idea of what they do. The student should realize that, easy as they may be to operate, these instruments are extremely complicated. We shall discuss here one type of instrument, the optical null type, and that only briefly and in very general and schematic terms. Reference should be made to Fig. 11.16 throughout this discussion. The figure is not intended to represent any particular real instrument, but it is presented only to give the student an idea of the sort of thing that the instrument makers have been able to do for chemists.

[10] C. N. Reilley and C. M. Crawford, *Anal. Chem.*, **27**, 716 (1955).

Radiation from the source passes through a monochromator as in a single-beam instrument and encounters a chopper. The chopper, driven by a synchronous motor (not shown in the figure), is a rotating mirror of such shape and such placement that it permits the beam to pass straight through during half of its period of rotation. During the other half the beam encounters a reflective surface that turns it through a right angle, directing it upward in the figure. The direction may be changed again by other stationary mirrors as desired. Thus we now have two beams, from the same source, which are not steady but pulsate at a frequency determined by the chopper. One beam is passing while the other is blocked, and they alternate perhaps many times a second. One beam next passes through the sample while the other encounters a reference solution. The beams are then recombined so that they both fall upon a single detector.

Now as the chopper rotates, the detector "sees" first one beam, then the other. Suppose the monochromator is set at a wavelength where the sample does not absorb. Then the sample beam and the reference beam are of equal power, and the detector sees the same thing, regardless of the position of the chopper. A steady, constant power impinges upon the detector, and the electrical output of the detector circuit is a voltage which does not vary with time, in other words, a dc voltage. Now the signal from the detector is fed to an amplifier, and the important characteristic of this amplifier is that it is an ac amplifier which is tuned to the frequency of the chopper. The dc voltage from the detector is not amplified, and the output of the amplifier is inadequate to do anything in the instrument.

Let us now change the wavelength so that the sample absorbs. Now the radiant power in the reference beam is greater than in the sample beam, and the detector, looking first at one and then the other, generates an electrical signal which reflects this pulsation in radiant power. This signal is an ac voltage, a square wave, actually, superimposed upon the dc signal mentioned above. The amplifier amplifies this ac voltage, which is then fed to a motor (a so-called "servo").

The motor drives an "optical wedge" or "variable-density wedge" into the reference beam. This wedge is a special device which blocks part of the beam and diminishes the radiant power in a smoothly progressive fashion as it moves. Now, when the wedge has moved so as to attenuate the reference beam to the same extent as the sample absorption has attenuated the sample beam, then once again the detector sees the same thing regardless of where the chopper is in its rotational period. Thus the electrical signal is again dc, the amplifier output falls off, and the motor stops. This is an example of "feedback"; the imbalance which set the servomotor in motion has "committed suicide." The position of the optical wedge at this point is reflected mechanically by the position of a pen which moves up and down on a piece of chart paper.

If we drive the monochromator with a motor which also moves the chart paper at right angles to the pen motion, we are then able to obtain a plot of wavelength vs optical wedge position which becomes wavelength vs transmittance or absorbance if the wedge is shaped properly and the chart paper is appropriately calibrated.

Real instruments are more complicated than we have suggested above and in the figure. For example, there may be a slit servomotor controlling the radiant power from the monochromator, and we have not indicated how an imbalance signal tells the motor which way to move the wedge. While some instruments operate on an optical null principle as discussed here, there are others which employ an electrical null that is quite different.

These instruments are extremely complicated, but they have been engineered so well that anyone can operate them by merely inserting samples and pushing buttons. Obtaining the top performance of which the instrument is capable, however, requires more knowledge than this. Most chemists must strike a compromise between the extremes of total ignorance and devoting a lifetime to the study of instrumentation. Unfortunately, the compromise in many cases falls so far toward the side of ignorance that data are obtained which are no better than a less expensive instrument could have furnished, and the instrument may even be needlessly damaged.

ERRORS IN SPECTROPHOTOMETRY

Errors in spectrophotometric measurements may arise from a host of causes, some of which have been anticipated in the discussion of instrumentation above. Many can be countered by care and common sense. Sample cells should be clean. Certain substances, e.g., proteins, sometimes adsorb very strongly on the cell and are washed out only with difficulty. Fingerprints may absorb ultraviolet radiation. The positioning of the cells in the beam must be reproducible. Gas bubbles must not be present in the optical path. The wavelength calibration of the instrument should be checked occasionally, and drift or instability in the circuit must be corrected. It must not be assumed that Beer's law holds for an untested chemical system. Sample instability may lead to errors if the measurements are not carefully timed.

The concentration of the absorbing species is of great importance in determining the error after all other controllable errors have been minimized. It is intuitively reasonable that the solution being measured should not absorb practically all of the radiation nor should it absorb hardly any. We might expect, then, that the error in a spectrophotometric determination of concentration would be minimal at some intermediate absorbance value away from the extreme ends of the scale. An expression can be derived from Beer's law which shows where this minimum error occurs.

Recall that

$$A = \log \frac{P_0}{P} = \frac{1}{2.3} \ln \frac{P_0}{P} = \varepsilon bc$$

Let the relative error in concentration be $dc/c = dA/A$. We want to obtain an expression for dc/c and then inquire where this expression has a minimum.

Differentiating Beer's law, $A = (1/2.3) \ln (P_0/P)$, we obtain

$$dA = \frac{1}{2.3} d \ln \frac{P_0}{P} = \frac{(-P_0/P^2)\, dP}{2.3(P_0/P)}$$

Dividing numerator and denominator by P_0/P yields

$$dA = -\frac{(1/P)\, dP}{2.3} = -\frac{dP}{2.3P}$$

Dividing both sides by A,

$$\frac{dA}{A} = -\frac{dP}{2.3PA}$$

From Beer's law, $P = P_0 \times 10^{-A}$; substitution into the above equation gives

$$\frac{dA}{A} = -\frac{dP}{2.3AP_0 \times 10^{-A}} = \frac{dc}{c}$$

It is convenient to normalize the equation by setting $P_0 = 1$, corresponding to the customary actual operation of setting the instrument to $100\% \ T$ or zero absorbance with a reference solution in the beam. This gives

$$\frac{dc}{c} = -\frac{dP}{2.3A \times 10^{-A}}$$

Now the minimum in dc/c occurs when the term, $A \times 10^{-A}$, is at a maximum. To find this maximum, we differentiate and set the derivative equal to zero:

$$\frac{d(A \times 10^{-A})}{dA} = 10^{-A} - 2.3A \times 10^{-A} = 0$$

or

$$10^{-A}(1 - 2.3A) = 0$$

If 10^{-A} is zero, A is infinite, and the error is infinite. Setting the other term equal to zero,

$$1 - 2.3A = 0$$

$$2.3A = 1$$

$$A = \frac{1}{2.3} = 0.43$$

An absorbance value of 0.43 corresponds to 36.8% transmittance. (The student who is familiar with calculus may notice that the absorbance of 0.43 could, so far as we have actually shown above, represent either a maximum or a minimum error. Such a student will know that the first derivative may be tested for this; it turns out that we are dealing with a minimum error.)

The term dP in the equations above, following the usual practice in calculus, may be taken as an approximation of ΔP, the error in P. This is often called the *photometric error*, and for our purposes simply represents the uncertainty in reading the instrument scale. This uncertainty is considered constant in the present discussion, and it is probably roughly so with many actual instruments. To find the relative error in concentration as a function of the photometric error at the optimal concentration, substitute 0.43 for A in the above equation for dc/c:

$$\frac{dc}{c} = -\frac{dP}{2.3 \times 0.43 \times 10^{-0.43}} = -2.72\,dP$$

Thus, if a 1% error were made in reading the instrument, the relative error in c would be 2.72% at best; with absorbance values above and below 0.43, it would be even larger. Photometric errors may range from 0.1% to several percent, depending upon the instrument employed.

The relative error in concentration resulting from a 1% photometric error is plotted against percent transmittance in Fig. 11.17. The curve approaches infinity at both 0 and 100% T, passes through a minimum at 36.8% T, but is actually not very far from minimal over a fair range, say 10 to 80% T (absorbance values of about 0.1 to 1.0).

The student who has difficulty in visualizing why there should be a minimum in the error curve, or in following the calculus treatment above, could think of the situation this way: Refer to Fig. 11.7(b). A given error in measuring %T gives a small error, Δc, in concentration at very low concentrations, because the %T vs c curve is very steep. But, where c is very low, a

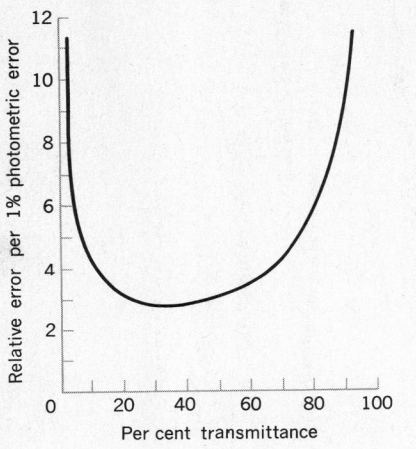

FIGURE 11.17 Error curve.

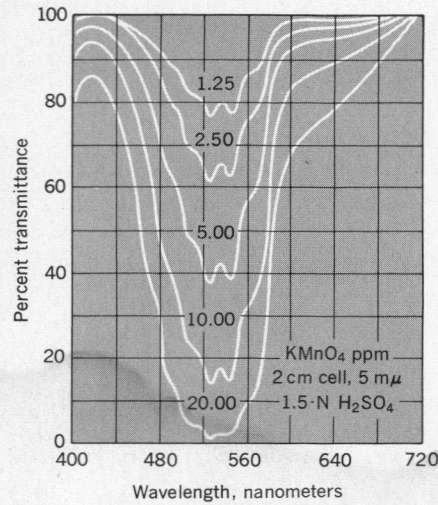

FIGURE 11.18 Transmittance-wavelength curves for solutions of potassium permanganate. (M. G. Mellon, ed., *Analytical Absorption Spectroscopy*, John Wiley & Sons, Inc., New York, 1950. Used by permission of the author and publisher.)

small error in c becomes a large relative error, $\Delta c/c$. At high concentrations, the same error in $\%T$ represents a much larger absolute error in c, because the $\%T$ vs c curve is much flatter. Somewhere in between, there will be a point where these two effects meet to give a minimal relative error, $\Delta c/c$. This happens to fall at $36.8\% T$.

In the error treatment above, it was supposed that the error in measuring transmittance was constant, independent of the value of the transmittance; the error was considered to arise entirely from uncertainty in reading the instrument scale. In some of the best modern instruments, on the other hand, the limiting factor in the accuracy lies elsewhere, usually in the "noise" level of the detector circuit. In such cases, dP is not constant, and a different error function is obtained which is minimal, not at $36.8\% T$ but at a lower T value. Actually, with a complex instrument it may be difficult to decide which of several factors limits the accuracy. Thus the way in which dP varies with P may not be clear, and it may not be legitimate to calculate a $\%T$ value corresponding to minimal error.[11] With one of the well-known, high-quality, modern instruments, the Cary Model 14 recording spectrophotometer, the minimal error is said to occur at about $10\% T (A = 1)$.[12]

APPLICATIONS OF SPECTROPHOTOMETRY

Plotting Spectrophotometric Data

Absorption spectra are most frequently plotted as $\%T$ vs wavelength (λ), A or ε vs λ, and $\log A$ or $\log \varepsilon$ vs λ. Comparison of these plots may be

[11] R. P. Bauman, *Absorption Spectroscopy*, John Wiley & Sons, Inc., New York, 1962, p. 376.

[12] *Instructions for Cary Recording Spectrophotometer Model 14*, Applied Physics Corporation, Monrovia, Calif., p. 5.

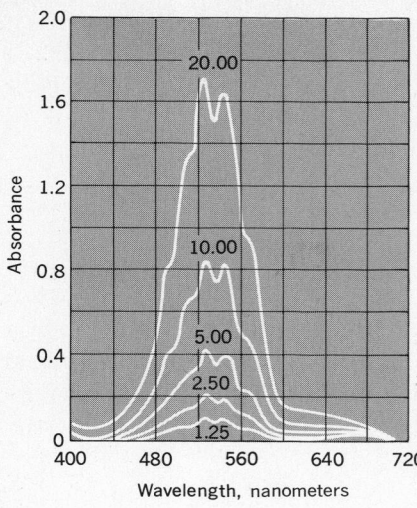

FIGURE 11.19 Absorbance-wavelength curves for solutions of potassium permanganate. (M. G. Mellon, ed., *Analytical Absorption Spectroscopy*, John Wiley & Sons, Inc., New York, 1950. Used by permission of the author and publisher.)

made clear by reference to Figs. 11.18, 11.19, and 11.20. Analytical chemists generally prefer absorbance to $\%T$ for the ordinate. Note that a minimum in $\%T$ corresponds to a maximum in A. The two curves are not mirror images, however, because A and $\%T$ are related logarithmically $[A = \log(1/T)]$. Sometimes ε-values are calculated from absorption data and plotted against λ.

It may be seen from Fig. 11.19 that the shape of the absorption spectrum depends upon the concentration of the solution if the ordinate is linear in absorbance. That is, the curves in Fig. 11.19 are not superimposable by simple vertical displacement. This is clear from Beer's law, $A = \varepsilon bc$, which shows that changing the concentration changes the absorbance at each

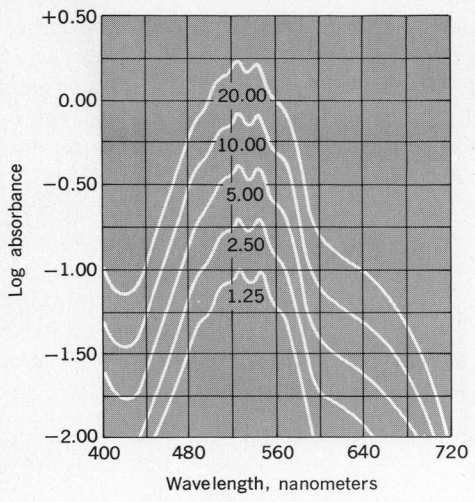

FIGURE 11.20 Log absorbance-wavelength curves for solutions of potassium permanganate. (M. G. Mellon, ed., *Analytical Absorption Spectroscopy*, John Wiley & Sons, Inc., New York, 1950. Used by permission of the author and publisher.)

wavelength by a constant *multiple*. On the other hand, as seen in Fig. 11.20, the shape of the curve is independent of concentration if the ordinate is log A. That this should be the case is seen by taking logarithms of both sides of the Beer's law equation:

$$\log A = \log(\varepsilon bc) = \log \varepsilon + \log b + \log c$$

Now the concentration term is *added* rather than multiplied, and hence increasing the concentration adds a constant increment to log A at each wavelength across the spectrum. The curve for the higher concentration is thus displaced upward, but could be superimposed upon the lower one by a simple vertical movement. The same ε vs λ plot should be obtained regardless of concentration provided the system follows Beer's law at all wavelengths. It is common practice, particularly among organic chemists, to plot log ε vs λ.

Identification of Chemical Substances

The student is familiar with simple color tests which are used for indentification purposes. The purple color of permanganate solutions, the blue of copper, the yellow of chromate, and many others might be mentioned. The absorption spectrum of a compound, determined with a spectrophotometer, may be considered as a more elegant, objective, and reliable indication of identity. The spectrum is another physical constant, so to speak, which along with melting point, refractive index, and other properties, may be used for characterization. Like the others, absorption spectra are not infallible proof of identity, but simply represent another tool available for intelligent application.

It must be remembered that an absorption spectrum depends upon not only the chemical nature of the compound in question but also other factors. Changing the solvent often results in shifts in absorption bands. The shape of a band and particularly the appearance of "fine structure" may well depend upon instrument characteristics such as the resolution of the monochromator, the amplifier gain, and the rate of scan as it relates to inertia in the recorder. Treating a recording spectrophotometer as a "black box" can lead to peculiar absorption spectra.

Spectra of many thousands of compounds and materials have been recorded, and locating the proper ones for comparison in connection with a particular problem may be extremely difficult. Several catalogues and compilations are available.[13] Increasingly, large laboratories are employing machine data-handling techniques to store and retrieve spectra as well as other important information.

[13] For example, H. M. Hershenson, *Ultraviolet and Visible Absorption Spectra: Indexes for 1930–1954 and 1955–1959*, Academic Press, New York, 1956 and 1961; R. A. Friedel and M. Orchin, *Ultraviolet Spectra of Aromatic Compounds*, John Wiley & Sons, Inc., New York, 1951.

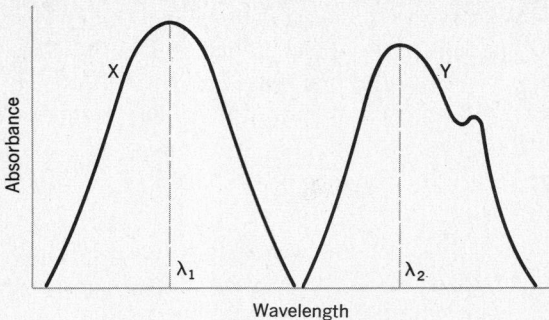

FIGURE 11.21 Spectra of *X* and *Y*, no overlapping.

Multicomponent Analysis

A spectrophotometer cannot *analyze* a sample. It becomes a useful tool only after the sample has been treated in such a way that the measurement is interpretable in unambiguous terms. In many cases, however, it is not necessary that each individual component of a complex sample be isolated from all others. In spectrophotometry, for example, it is sometimes possible to measure more than one constituent in a single solution. Let us suppose a solution to contain two absorbing constituents, X and Y. The complexity of the situation depends upon the absorption spectra of X and Y.

Case 1

The spectra do not overlap, or at least it is possible to find a wavelength where X absorbs and Y does not and a similar wavelength for measuring Y. Figure 11.21 shows such a situation. The constituents X and Y are simply measured at the wavelengths λ_1 and λ_2, respectively.

Case 2

One-way overlap of the spectra: As shown in Fig. 11.22, X does not interfere with the measurement of Y at λ_2, but Y does absorb appreciably along with X at λ_1. The approach to this problem is simple in principle. The concentration of Y is determined directly from the absorbance of the solution

FIGURE 11.22 One-way overlap of spectra.

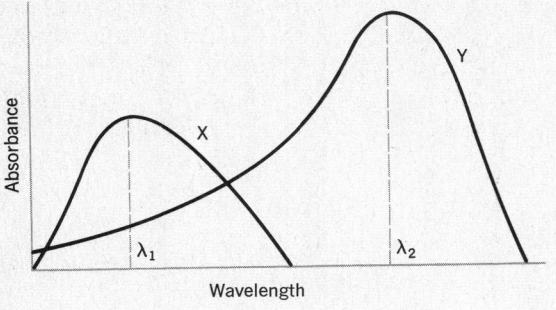

331

at λ_2. Then the absorbance contributed at λ_1 by this concentration of Y is calculated from the previously known molar absorptivity of Y at λ_1. This contribution is subtracted from the measured absorbance of the solution at λ_1, yielding the absorbance due to X, whose concentration is then calculated in the usual manner.

Case 3

Two-way overlap of the spectra: When no wavelength can be found where either X or Y absorbs exclusively, as suggested in Fig. 11.23, it is necessary to solve two simultaneous equations in two unknowns. Let

$$A_1 = \text{measured absorbance at } \lambda_1$$

$$A_2 = \text{measured absorbance at } \lambda_2$$

$$\varepsilon_{X_1} = \text{molar absorptivity of X at } \lambda_1$$

$$\varepsilon_{X_2} = \text{molar absorptivity of X at } \lambda_2$$

$$\varepsilon_{Y_1} = \text{molar absorptivity of Y at } \lambda_1$$

$$\varepsilon_{Y_2} = \text{molar absorptivity of Y at } \lambda_2$$

$$C_X = \text{molar concentration of X}$$

$$C_Y = \text{molar concentration of Y}$$

$$b = \text{path length}$$

Since the total absorbance is the sum of the contributions of the individual absorbing constituents of the solution:

$$A_1 = \varepsilon_{X_1}bC_X + \varepsilon_{Y_1}bC_Y$$

$$A_2 = \varepsilon_{X_2}bC_X + \varepsilon_{Y_2}bC_Y$$

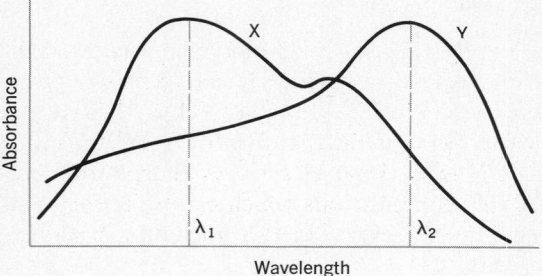

FIGURE 11.23 Two-way overlap of spectra.

C_X and C_Y are the only unknowns in these equations and hence their values can be readily determined. The ε-values must be known, of course, from measurements on pure solutions of X and Y at the two wavelengths.

Equations can be set up in principle for any number of components provided absorbance values are measured at as many wavelengths. However, the importance of small errors in measurement is magnified as the number of components increases, and in practice this approach is generally limited to two- or possibly three-component systems. An exception to this is possible if a computer is available. Then, particularly if the spectrum is recorded, it becomes not too difficult to "over-determine" the system (i.e., take absorbance values at many more wavelengths than there are components) and by a rapid series of successive approximations obtain reliable values for a large number of components.

Preparation of Samples
for Spectrophotometric Analysis

So far we have said little about chemistry in this chapter. But seldom will the analyst receive a sample which is ready to be measured without some sort of pretreatment. Often separations of interfering substances are necessary; some of the available techniques are considered in later chapters.

Many organic compounds absorb in the ultraviolet region of the spectrum, and pretreatment then involves only separation of interferences. Some elements in the periodic table absorb strongly in the visible or ultraviolet, at least in certain oxidation states, and the preliminary steps may involve redox reactions as well as separations. Manganese, for example, is often determined spectrophotometrically after oxidation to Mn(VII) by means of persulfate or periodate:

$$2\,Mn^{2+} + 5\,S_2O_8{}^{2-} + 8\,H_2O \longrightarrow 2\,MnO_4{}^- + 10\,SO_4{}^{2-} + 16\,H^+$$

The purple $MnO_4{}^-$ solution is measured at about 525 nm. Chromium is determined similarly after oxidation to Cr(VI).

Development of absorption by means of inorganic reagents is occasionally possible. For example, iron may be determined by means of the red color obtained by treating ferric solutions with thiocyanate:

$$Fe^{3+} + SCN^- \longrightarrow (FeSCN)^{2+}$$

The system is complicated by the tendency to form higher complexes such as $[Fe(SCN)_2]^+$. Other examples of colored complexes formed with inorganic reagents are the blue tetraammine copper complex, $[Cu(NH_3)_4]^{2+}$, and the several complex heteropoly acids such as phosphomolybdic, $H_3P(Mo_3O_{10})_4$ $\cdot 29\,H_2O$, which are used to determine elements such as phosphorus and silicon. Iodide ion forms yellowish complex ions which exhibit absorption maxima in the ultraviolet region with several metals, including bismuth, antimony, and palladium (e.g., $PdI_4{}^{2-}$).

The colored complexes formed by metal ions with organic reagents offer the most impressive variety of spectrophotometric methods, and they are especially useful in the field of trace analysis. Most of these complexes are of the chelate type which were discussed more fully elsewhere (pages 133 and 181). We mention here only a few points of special interest regarding their adaptation to spectrophotometric analysis.

In some regards, the low aqueous solubility of many of the metal chelate compounds is disadvantageous, but on the other hand, extraction of metals into nonaqueous solvents by means of chelating agents may lead to very powerful analytical methods. In favorable cases, it may be possible to concentrate the metal, separate it from interferences, and develop the absorbing system in a single step. For example, the chelates of 8-hydroxyquinoline (oxine, page 182) with such metals as aluminum, ferric iron, cadmium, gallium, lead, and copper are soluble in chloroform, and extractions with this solvent generally precede the spectrophotometric determination. By controlling the pH of the aqueous phase and by adding complexing agents which mask certain metal ions, the extraction can be made quite selective. Reasonable absorbance values are generally obtained with chloroform solutions whose metal concentrations are of the order of a few micrograms per milliliter.[14]

The solvent used in spectrophotometric procedures poses a problem in some regions of the spectrum. The solvent must not only dissolve the sample but also must not absorb appreciably in the region in which the determination is made. Water is an excellent solvent in that it is transparent throughout the visible region and down to a wavelength of about 200 nm in the ultraviolet. However, since water is a poor solvent for many organic compounds, organic solvents are commonly employed for these substances. The transparency cutoff points in the ultraviolet region of a number of solvents are listed in Table 11.4. Aliphatic hydrocarbons, methanol, ethanol, and diethyl ether are transparent to ultraviolet radiation and are frequently employed as solvents for organic compounds.

TABLE 11.4   SOLVENTS FOR ULTRAVIOLET AND VISIBLE REGIONS

Solvent	Approximate transparency minimum, nm	Solvent	Approximate transparency minimum, nm
Water	190	Chloroform	250
Methanol	210	Carbon tetrachloride	265
Cyclohexane	210	Benzene	280
Hexane	210	Toluene	285
Diethyl ether	220	Pyridine	305
p-Dioxane	220	Acetone	330
Ethanol	220	Carbon disulfide	380

[14] See E. B. Sandell, *Colorimetric Determination of Traces of Metals*, 3rd ed., Interscience Publishers, Inc., New York, 1959, for spectrophotometric methods for most inorganic ions.

There is no single solvent which is transparent throughout the infrared region. Carbon tetrachloride is useful up to 7.6μ, and carbon disulfide up to 15μ. Not all substances are soluble in these solvents, however, and other liquids with more restricted ranges must be used. Water exhibits strong absorption in the infrared and must be avoided. Rock-salt cells are frequently employed in the infrared region, and water tends to dissolve the salt.

Because of the problems encountered in working with solutions in the infrared, various other techniques have been employed. Liquids can be measured directly, using a very thin film placed between rock-salt plates. Another technique employs a liquid *mull*, made by dispersing the sample in a viscous hydrocarbon, such as the mineral oil Nujol. Still another employs solid potassium bromide which is highly transparent to infrared radiation. The finely ground sample is mixed homogeneously with potassium bromide and pressed into a small pellet. The pellet can be placed directly in the beam of a spectrophotometer and absorption measurements made.

PHOTOMETRIC TITRATIONS

Various properties of a solution may be measured in order to assess the progress of a titration toward the equivalence point. We have seen, for example, in Chapter 9 that the potential of an indicator electrode may be used for this purpose, and we have described another end-point technique, amperometric, in Chapter 10. The absorbance of a solution may likewise be measured during the course of a titration; we have available, then, still another end-point technique which may be useful in certain circumstances. Our discussion of photometric titrations will be brief; a more complete treatment may be found in two reviews which also provide a guide to the recent literature.[15,16]

As a matter of fact, visual titrations are really photometric in nature. "The color change reflects a change in the absorption of light by the solution, accompanying changes in the concentrations of absorptive species. In a visual titration, one actually employs all of the features of an automatic photometric titrator: Light passes through the solution to the eye, which is a photosensitive transducer responding with a signal to the brain. The brain is analogous to the circuitry of an instrument which amplifies the signal and otherwise renders it appropriate for transmission to an electromechanical shutoff system; traversing a motor neuron, the signal triggers a muscular response that closes the buret to terminate the titration. In visual titrations, the most complicated and expensive instruments of all—people—act as automatic photometric titrators."[16]

Photometric titrations often possess advantages of sensitivity of end-point

[15] J. B. Headridge, *Photometric Titrations*, Pergamon Press, New York, 1961.

[16] A. L. Underwood, "Photometric Titrations," a chapter in *Advances in Analytical Chemistry and Instrumentation*, Vol. 3, C. N. Reilley, ed., Interscience Publishers, Inc., New York, 1964, p. 31.

detection and circumvention of interferences over visual titrations. Further, they are not restricted to the wavelength region where the human eye responds, and they are fairly easily automated. In comparison with potentiometric titrations, the photometric approach is often advantageous for borderline cases of titrations which are approaching nonfeasibility. While the potential of an indicator electrode responds to the logarithm of a concentration (or a concentration ratio), the absorbance of a solution is directly proportional to concentration. If the equilibrium constant of a titration reaction is undesirably small, concentrations will not change as rapidly as one would like in the vicinity of the equivalence point, and the potential, because of the logarithmic compression, will change even less rapidly. The absorbance, on the other hand, will change just as rapidly as the concentration. This is not a unique advantage of photometric titrations, of course. The same consideration applies to amperometric and other end points which are obtained by linear extrapolation.

Just as with amperometric titrations (Chapter 10, page 289), it is necessary to correct measured absorbance values for dilution if the volume of titrant is appreciable compared with the initial volume of the solution.

Titrations without Indicators

Sometimes a substance directly involved in the titration reaction absorbs appreciably at an accessible wavelength, and the titration can be followed spectrophotometrically without adding an indicator. The shapes of the

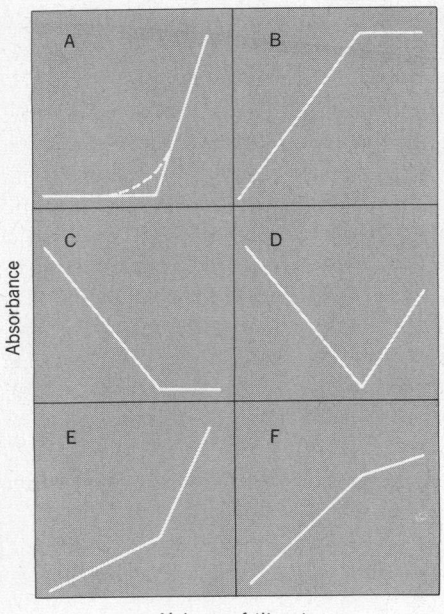

FIGURE 11.24 Typical photometric titration curves: (A) $\varepsilon_t > \varepsilon_s = \varepsilon_p$ (usually $\varepsilon_s = \varepsilon_p = 0$); ($B$) $\varepsilon_p > \varepsilon_s$, $\varepsilon_t = 0$; (C) $\varepsilon_s > \varepsilon_p$; $\varepsilon_t = 0$; (D) $\varepsilon_s > \varepsilon_p$, $\varepsilon_t > 0$; (E) $\varepsilon_p > \varepsilon_s$; $\varepsilon_t > \varepsilon_p$; ($F$) $\varepsilon_p > \varepsilon_s$, $\varepsilon_t < \varepsilon_p$. ε_s, ε_p, and ε_t are the molar absorptivities of the substance titrated, reaction product, and titrant, respectively.

titration curve are predictable from the ε-values of the chemical species concerned. Some typical photometric titration curves of this type are shown in Fig. 11.24. If the titration reaction is appreciably incomplete in the vicinity of the equivalence point, the curve will become rounded, as shown by the dotted portion of curve *A* in Fig. 11.24. The end point is then located by the intersection of extrapolated straight lines drawn through points taken sufficiently before and after the rounded portion. Titration curves of this sort are easily calculated: One simply computes the concentrations of absorbing species at any point using the equilibrium constant of the reaction; then the contribution of each species to the absorbance of the solution is calculated from Beer's law, using known ε-values and path length.

Titrations with Indicators and the Titration of Mixtures

In cases where none of the species involved in the titration reaction absorbs sufficiently, an indicator may be added to the solution. Figure 11.25 shows an example of an indicator titration, a chelometric titration of cupric ion with EDTA using the metallochromic indicator pyrocatechol violet. In this titration, a wavelength was selected where the free indicator absorbs more strongly than the copper-indicator complex. We see in the figure, first the reaction of free cupric ion with EDTA, which does not affect the absorbance of the solution at this wavelength. Then, as the end point is approached, copper is pulled away from the indicator by the titrant, and the absorbance rises as free indicator accumulates, until finally all of the copper has been titrated and the absorbance becomes constant again.

Figure 11.26 shows a photometric titration of a mixture of bismuth and copper with EDTA. At the wavelength selected, the cupric-EDTA chelate absorbs strongly, while the other species (Bi^{3+}, bismuth-EDTA chelate, and EDTA) have ε-values of zero. The bismuth chelate is much more stable than the cupric one. Thus, as EDTA is added to the Bi^{3+}-Cu^{2+} mixture, the bismuth chelate is formed first. When $[Bi^{3+}]$ has been reduced to a very low value, the cupric-EDTA chelate begins to form, and, because this is the strongly absorbing species, the absorbance begins to rise. After the copper end point, the curve levels off as excess, nonabsorbing EDTA is added.

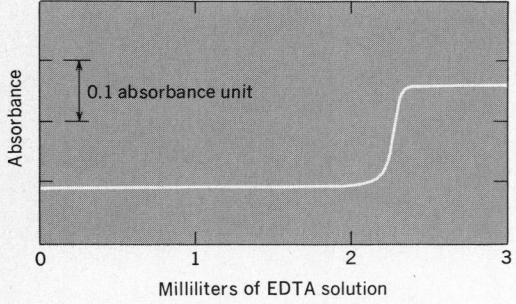

FIGURE 11.25 Titration of copper with EDTA, using pyrocatechol violet indicator: 14.01 mg of copper in 150 ml titrated with 10^{-1}-*M* EDTA at 440 nm (Data of T. M. Robertson.)

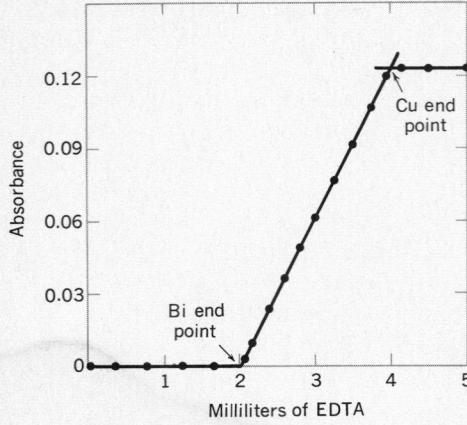

FIGURE 11.26 Titration of bismuth-copper mixture with EDTA; 41.8 mg of bismuth and 13.1 mg of copper in 100 ml (each 2×10^{-3}-M) buffered at pH 2, titrated at 745 nm with 10^{-1}-M EDTA.

Instrumentation

The simplest approach to a photometric titration is to titrate in a flask or beaker on the laboratory bench, taking samples out of the titration vessel for absorbance measurements as the titration proceeds. Of course the samples must be returned each time, and this technique is inconvenient for more than an occasional single titration. On the other hand, any good spectrophotometer can be used without modification, and it is more obvious to a beginner exactly what is going on than might be the case if more elaborate instrumentation were employed.

Sometimes it is possible to fit a spectrophotometer with a modified cell compartment so that a titration vessel such as a beaker can be positioned in the light beam. It is convenient to stir by means of a magnetic stirrer underneath the compartment. The buret tip is introduced into the solution through a hole in the cover of the cell compartment; care must be taken that this arrangement be light-tight.

With a recording spectrophotometer, it is possible to record absorbance vs time at a constant wavelength. If titrant is introduced into a titration vessel in the sample beam at a constant flow rate, if adequate stirring is provided, and also if the titration reaction is rapid, then the plot of absorbance vs time readily becomes a photometric titration curve. With relatively simple on-the-spot modification, the output signal of a manual spectrophotometer can be recorded; thus an expensive double beam recording instrument is not really required for this application.

Finally, photometric titrators which terminate titrant flow at the end point are on the market. The operator merely sets up and starts the titration, and then later reads a buret. We described briefly in Chapter 9 an automatic potentiometric titrator based upon double electronic differentiation of the voltage from a pair of electrodes. Now the first derivatives of photometric titration curves like those in Fig. 11.24 exhibit the sigmoid shape associated

338

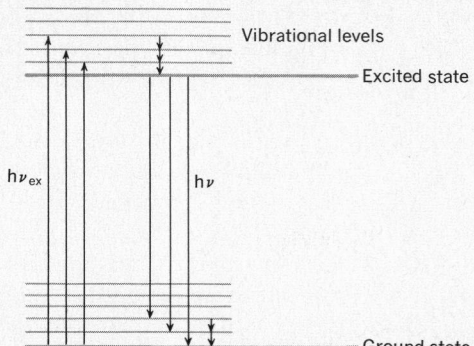

Vibrational levels

Excited state

$h\nu_{ex}$ $h\nu$

Ground state   **FIGURE 11.27**   Energy diagram for fluorescence.

with a typical potentiometric titration. By differentiating electronically a signal arising from a photodetector and then feeding this into the circuit of the existing potentiometric titrator, an instrument was devised for automatic photometric titration. Of course it was necessary to add to the potentiometric titrator not only an additional differentiating circuit but also optical components, source, photodetector, etc.[17]

FLUORESCENCE

As mentioned early in this chapter (page 301), once absorption of radiation has occurred, the energy may be reemitted as radiation usually of longer wavelength than was originally absorbed. This phenomenon, known as *fluorescence*, can be used for the analysis of many inorganic and organic species. It offers advantages in its high sensitivity and specificity, and it has found many applications in the field of biochemistry.

Principles

The absorption process which leads to fluorescence usually involves a pi-pi* transition (page 304) in a complex organic molecule. The process is represented schematically in Fig. 11.27. The molecule absorbs radiation, labeled $h\nu_{ex}$, raising the electron from the ground state to an excited state. In this higher-energy level, the molecule can be in one of several vibrational states. The molecule loses vibrational energy through collisions with solvent molecules, falling to the lowest vibrational level in the excited state. In this lowest level the probability of return to the ground state by emission of a photon is greatest. Fluorescence always involves a transition from the lowest vibrational level of the excited state; the electron can return to any of several vibrational levels of the ground state. In the ground state, the

[17] H. V. Malmstadt and C. B. Roberts, *Anal. Chem.*, **28**, 1408 (1956).

molecule loses energy and returns to the lowest vibrational level by collisions with solvent molecules. Both the absorption and emission of radiation occurs over a band of wavelengths, just as in ultraviolet and visible spectrophotometry.

Generally, the exciting radiation is in the ultraviolet region; the emitted radiation is usually in the visible region, although it may be in the ultraviolet region. The lifetime in the excited state is about 10^{-8} s and emission of fluorescent radiation occurs with practically no time delay. The ground and excited states are "singlets," meaning that the electron pair in the molecular orbital have paired spins. In certain cases the electron in the excited state can cross over to a "triplet" state (electron spins not paired) before the transition back to the ground state occurs. In this case the transition is much less probable than before, and the lifetime of the excited triplet state may be of the order of 10^{-4} to several seconds. Emission of radiation may persist for some time after the exciting radiation is discontinued, and the phenomenon is then called *phosphorescence.*

The molecular structure of a compound strongly influences its fluorescent behavior. Aromatic and heterocyclic compounds, particularly those which contain electron-donating groups, such as —OH and —NH$_2$, tend to fluoresce strongly. Other groups, such as —Br, —I, —NO$_2$, and —COOH, tend to inhibit fluorescence. It is thought that heavy atoms such as bromine and iodine cause a greater chance of a singlet excited state changing over to a triplet, thus decreasing the probability of fluorescence occurring.

If the concentration of the fluorescent compound is small, the power (intensity), F, of the fluorescent light is directly proportional to concentration, c,

$$F = kc$$

A plot of the fluorescent power vs concentration gives a straight line if the concentration is sufficiently low that the absorbance ($A = abc$) is less than about 0.01–0.05. The linear relationship usually holds for concentrations up to a few parts per million, depending upon the emitting species. At higher concentrations the fluorescent power lies below an extrapolation of the straight-line plot. One reason for this behavior is that at high concentrations the distribution of exciting radiation is not uniform. The first layers of solution may absorb a much larger fraction of the radiation than layers at greater depth in the solution. In dilute solutions, where, for example, at least ninety percent of the radiation is transmitted, the distribution of the absorbed light is much more uniform.

Two other factors contribute to the negative deviation from the linear plot. One is called *self-quenching*; at high concentrations the excited molecules may lose energy by collisions among themselves, rather than by fluorescence. The other is *self-absorption*; if the fluorescent radiation is absorbed by a molecule in its ground state, the intensity of the fluorescent light is decreased as it passes through the solution.

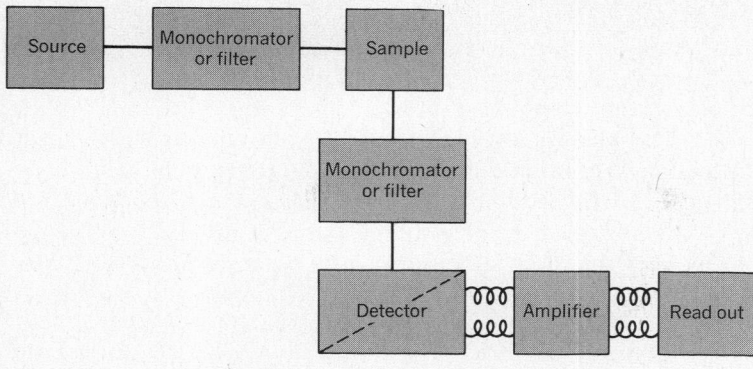

FIGURE 11.28 Block diagram showing components of a fluorometer or spectrofluorometer.

Measurement of Fluorescence

A number of instruments have been described for measuring fluorescence. All of these operate on the same principle; they differ in types of components, degree of sophistication, and performance characteristics. The basic design is shown in Fig. 11.28. The source is usually a mercury vapor lamp or a xenon arc lamp. The mercury vapor lamp produces an intense line spectrum. Since most fluorescent molecules absorb a variety of wavelengths of ultraviolet light, a line source is generally suitable. The xenon arc lamp produces a continuous spectrum over the range of about 250–600 nm, with the peak intensity at about 470 nm.

The ultraviolet light from the source passes through a filter or monochromator to allow selection of the wavelength for excitation. Instruments called *fluorometers* employ filters at this point as well as in the fluorescent beam. *Spectrofluorometers* employ a monochromator, usually a grating, to select the desired wavelength.

The exciting radiation then enters the sample solution which is held in a glass or quartz cell. Fluorescent radiation is emitted in all directions and must be separated from the incident radiation for measurement. This is done most conveniently by measuring the fluorescence at right angles to the incident beam. A spectrofluorometer contains a second monochromator which permits the selection of the wavelength of maximum emission.

The fluorescent radiation next reaches a detector. Since the fluorescent signal is of low intensity, it must be amplified. Usually a photomultiplier tube (page 319) is used, and its output is further amplified with an external electronic amplifier. Finally, some readout device (page 320) is employed.

Applications

Fluorescent procedures have been used successfully for the determination of both organic and inorganic substances and have proved especially useful for biological systems. The fluorometric method is inherently more sensitive than methods based on the absorption of radiation. The reason for this is the fact that the power of the fluorescent light, F, can be measured independently of the power of the incident radiation, P_o. The sensitivity of a fluorescent measurement can be increased by increasing P_o, or by amplifying the signal produced by the fluorescent radiation. In spectrophotometry the absorbance is dependent on the ratio of P_o and P. Increasing P_o increases P proportionately and does not affect the absorbance. Amplification of the detector signal also affects P_o and P and does not affect the absorbance. Determinations at the part per billion level are fairly common with fluorescent methods.

Inorganic substances can be measured by converting them to species which are fluorescent. For example, the chelating agent, 8-hydroxyquinoline (page 182), forms fluorescent compounds with metals such as beryllium, aluminum, and zinc and has been used in their determinations. Inorganic anions have been determined by their "quenching" effect, that is, their ability to decrease fluorescence. Iodide ion is an effective quencher, apparently competing with the fluorescent material for the excitation energy.

There are many applications of fluorometric methods to organic compounds, including such substances as enzymes, vitamins, and steroids. A summary of over one hundred different substances has been given by Weissler and White.[18]

A number of factors other than concentration may affect the intensity of fluorescent light. Among these are pH, temperature, and the concentration of foreign ions. Calibration curves are normally prepared using the same conditions which are employed in the determination of an unknown sample.

REFERENCES

R. P. BAUMAN, *Absorption Spectroscopy*, John Wiley & Sons, Inc., New York, 1962.

J. R. DYER, *Applications of Absorption Spectroscopy of Organic Compounds*, Prentice-Hall, Inc., Englewood Cliffs, New Jersey, 1965.

C. E. WHITE and R. J. ARGAUER, *Fluorescence Analysis: A Practical Approach*, Marcel Dekker, Inc., New York, 1970.

S. UDENFRIEND, *Fluorescence Assay in Biology and Medicine*, Vol. 2, Academic Press, Inc., New York, 1962.

"Ultraviolet Spectra," Vols. 1–62, "Infrared Prism Spectra," Vols. 1–36, and "Standard Infrared Grating Spectra," Vols. 1–16, *The Sadtler Standard Spectra*, Sadtler Research Laboratories, Philadelphia.

U. V. Atlas of Organic Compounds, Vols. 1–4, Plenum Press, New York.

[18] A. Weissler and C. E. White in *Handbook of Analytical Chemistry*, L. Meites, ed., McGraw-Hill Book Company, New York, 1963.

1. Explain how a molecule absorbs radiant energy. Compare the absorption of light in the far infrared and microwave region with that in the ultraviolet portion of the spectrum. Explain how fluorescence occurs.

2. Explain the following terms: wavelength, wave number, frequency, micron, nanometer, Angstrom unit, complementary color, fine structure, chromophore.

3. Define the following: absorbance, absorptivity, transmittance, molar extinction coefficient, optical density, specific extinction, isosbestic point.

4. Why are most applications of UV and visible spectrophotometry based on n-pi* or pi-pi* transitions?

5. Distinguish between real and apparent deviations from Beer's law. Under what circumstances does one get positive deviations from Beer's law in the case of a weak acid?

6. What are the essential components of a spectrophotometer? Describe the function of each.

7. Describe the sources of radiation used for the ultraviolet, visible, and infrared regions of the spectrum.

8. Describe the two types of monochromators used in spectrophotometers, giving the advantages and disadvantages of each.

9. Describe how phototubes, photomultiplier tubes, and thermocouples serve as detectors of radiation.

10. Explain how a differential measurement reduces the error in spectrophotometry.

11. Describe the operation of a double-beam, optical-null spectrophotometer.

12. What is the advantage of plotting the logarithm of the absorbance rather than the absorbance against wavelength?

13. In a so-called Ringbom plot, the percent absorptance $(100 - \%T)$ is plotted against the log (base 10) of the concentration. Sketch such a curve for a colored compound.

14. Show that the following relation holds for a Ringbom plot (Question 13):

$$\frac{dc/c}{dP} = \frac{230}{\text{slope}} = \frac{\% \text{ relative error}}{1\% \text{ photometric error}}$$

where the slope is that of the Ringbom curve.

15. A worker reported that a substance could be determined spectrophotometrically in the range of 0 to 15 ppm with an accuracy of ± 0.08 ppm. Criticize this statement.

16. A plot of absorbance vs concentration at constant b gives a straight line if Beer's law is obeyed. What property of the line is represented by the absorptivity? Why are photometric measurements of concentration usually carried out at the maximum value of the absorptivity?

17. Describe the effect of stray light on a photometric titration curve. How would the error compare at high and low absorbances?

18. What are the advantages of the fluorescent method for analytical processes?

19. Why does a plot of fluorescent power vs concentration vary from linearity at high concentrations of solute?

1. *Absorbance.* The scale on a spectrophotometer extends from 1 to 100% transmittance. (a) What are the values of the absorbances at these two extremes? (b) If the percent transmittance is actually zero, what is the value of the absorbance?

2. *Absorbance.* If the absorbance were defined in terms of natural rather than common logarithms, what would be the values of the absorbance in part (a) of the previous problem? What would be the absorbance of a solution which has a transmittance of 36.8%?

3. *Absorbance.* Convert the following values of percent transmittance to absorbance: (a) 99, (b) 75, (c) 50, (d) 10, and (e) 1.0.

4. *Transmittance.* Convert the following values of absorbance to percent transmittance: (a) 0.01, (b) 0.10, (c) 0.30, (d) 0.70, (e) 1.00, (f) 1.50, and (g) 2.00.

5. *Transmittance.* The percent transmittance of a solution in a 2.0-cm cell is 60. Calculate the percent transmittance of this solution in cells of the following lengths: (a) 5.0, (b) 1.0, and (c) 0.10 cm.

6. *Absorptivity.* The absorbance of a solution containing 5.0×10^{-3} g/l of a solute in a 1.00-cm cell is 1.00. Calculate (a) the absorptivity and (b) the molar absorptivity if the molecular weight of the solute is 125 g/mol.

7. *Wavelength-frequency.* (a) If the wavelength of certain radiation is 1.0 nm, calculate the frequency in wave numbers (cm^{-1}). (b) Calculate the frequency in hertz (cycles per second) of radiation which has a wavelength of 10 angstrom units.

8. *Molar absorptivity.* A solution contains 3.0 mg of iron per liter. The iron is converted into a complex with 1,10-phenanthroline and the absorbance of the solution in a 2.0-cm cell is 1.20. The molecular weight of the complex is 596. Calculate (a) the absorptivity and (b) the molar absorptivity of the ferrous complex.

9. *Dilution.* A compound of molecular weight 125 has a molar absorptivity of 2.5 $\times 10^5$. How many grams of this compound should be dissolved in exactly one liter of solution so that after a 200-fold dilution the resulting solution will give an absorbance reading of 0.60 in a 1.0-cm cell?

10. *Molecular weight.* A sample of an amine of unknown molecular weight is converted into the amine picrate (a 1:1 addition compound) by treatment with picric acid (M.W. = 229). Most amine picrates have about the same molar absorptivities, $\log \varepsilon = 4.13$ at 380 nm in 96% ethanol. A solution of the amine picrate was prepared by dissolving 0.0300 g of the material in exactly one liter of 95% ethanol. The absorbance of the solution in a 1.00-cm cell at 380 nm is 0.800. Estimate the molecular weight of the unknown amine.

11. *Analysis.* A 1.00-g sample of steel is dissolved in nitric acid and the manganese oxidized to permanganate with potassium periodate. The solution is made up to 250 ml in a volumetric flask and found to have an absorbance which is 1.50 times as great as that of a 0.00100-M solution of $KMnO_4$. Calculate the percentage of manganese in the steel.

12. *Analysis.* A 0.500-g sample of steel is dissolved in acid, and the manganese oxidized to permanganate. The solution is made up to 100 ml in a volumetric flask and the absorbance at 520 nm in a 2.0-cm cell is 0.62. The molar absorptivity of permanganate at 520 nm is 2235. Calculate the percentage of manganese in the steel.

13. *Blood volume.* The blood volume of a man can be measured by injecting a known amount of a harmless dye into a vein and determining the concentration of the dye after it has been well mixed by circulation. The blood volume is obtained by dividing the plasma volume by the fractional volume of plasma in the blood.

In a certain determination, 1.00 ml of Evans blue is injected into a 75-kg man. Ten minutes later a blood sample is withdrawn from the man. The blood is centrifuged to separate the plasma from the cells, and it is found that the plasma makes up 53% of the blood volume. The absorbance of the plasma in a 1.00-cm cell, using a blank as a reference, is 0.380.

Another 1.00-ml sample of the same Evans blue solution is diluted to exactly one liter in a volumetric flask. Then 10.0 ml of this solution is further diluted to 50.0 ml in a volumetric flask. The absorbance of the fully diluted solution is 0.200, against the same reference as above. Calculate the man's blood volume in liters.

14. *Photometric error.* If the error in determining concentration is to be 0.50% in a solution which gives an absorbance reading of 0.60, what must the photometric error be?

15. *Relative error.* Calculate the error in determining concentration per 1% photometric error for the following values of percent transmittance: (a) 1.0, (b) 10, (c) 50, (d) 80, and (e) 99.

16. *Relative error.* The molar absorptivity of the compound A (M.W. = 125) at 480 nm is 2500. What weight of sample containing about 1.5% of A should be taken for analysis so that maximum accuracy may be obtained in the photometric determination of A? The solution is finally diluted to 100 ml and the cell used is 1.00 cm in length.

17. *Differential measurement.* In a conventional spectrophotometric measurement a standard solution which is 0.0010-M in compound X gives an absorbance reading of 0.699. An unknown solution of X reads A = 1.000. If the standard solution is used as the reference with A = 0.000, answer the following: (a) What is the absorbance of the unknown? (b) What are the differences in $\%T$ of the two solutions in the two methods of measurement?

18. *Differential measurement.* Solution A, concentration c, gives an absorbance reading against a blank of 0.30. (a) Calculate the absorbance readings of solutions B, C, and D of concentrations $2c$, $3c$, and $4c$, respectively. (b) Calculate the percentage transmittances of the four solutions and the differences between A and B, B and C, and C and D. (c) If A is used as the reference and is set to give an absorbance of 0.000, repeat the calculations of parts (a) and (b).

19. *Differential measurement.* A solution of concentration c has an absorbance of 0.4343 when the reference is the pure solvent. (a) What is the relative error in c if the photometric error is 0.20%? (b) If a solution whose concentration is $3c$ is used as the reference and one of $4c$ is measured, what is the relative error in the latter concentration, the photometric error being the same as in (a)?

20. *Multicomponent analysis.* The absorption spectra of two colored substances A and B are determined and the following data obtained in a 1.00-cm cell:

Solution	Concentration	A at 450 nm	B at 700 nm
A alone	5.0×10^{-4}-M	0.800	0.100
B alone	2.0×10^{-4}-M	0.100	0.600
A + B	Unknown	0.600	1.000

Calculate the concentrations of A and B in the unknown solution.

21. *Stability of a complex.* When a large excess of the ion X^- is added to a solution of the metal M^{2+} the complex MX_3^- is formed. The concentrations of other complex species can be considered negligible. The MX_3^- complex absorbs strongly at 350 nm, where other species absorb negligibly. A solution which is 5.0×10^{-4}-F in M^{2+} is made 0.20-F in X^-, and the absorbance at 350 nm is found to be 0.80 in a 1.00-cm cell. Another 5.0×10^{-4}-F solution of M^{2+} is made 0.0025-F in X^- and the absorbance at 350 nm found to be 0.64 in the same cell. Assuming that all of the M^{2+} is converted into the complex in the first solution but not in the second, calculate the stability constant of MX_3^-.

22. *Method of continuous variations.* The formula of a complex formed by a reaction such as $M + nX \rightleftharpoons MX_n$ can be determined by the method of continuous variations. The absorbances of a series of solutions of varying composition are measured at the wavelength at which the complex shows its maximum absorptivity. The number of moles of M and X is kept constant, while the mole fractions of the reactants are varied.

The following data were obtained for the reaction of M and X. Solution A is 0.0100-F in M; solution B is 0.0100-F in X. The absorbances can be assumed to be a measure of the concentration of MX_n.

Solution	ml A	ml B	Absorbance
1	10.00	0.00	0.000
2	9.00	1.00	0.133
3	7.00	3.00	0.400
4	5.00	5.00	0.667
5	3.00	7.00	0.932
6	2.00	8.00	0.800
7	1.00	9.00	0.400
8	0.00	10.00	0.00

Plot the absorbance against mole fraction X, and calculate the formula of the complex from the mole fraction at which the maximum absorbance is obtained.

23. *Mole-ratio method.* The formula of the complex MX_n can also be determined by the mole-ratio method. Solutions are prepared in which the concentration of M is held constant and that of X is varied. The absorbance of MX_n is measured.

The following data were obtained by mixing solution A, 0.0100-F in M, solution B, 0.0100-F in X, and solution C, 0.100-F in $HClO_4$.

ml A	ml B	ml C	Absorbance
4.00	0.00	16.00	0.000
4.00	1.00	15.00	0.125
4.00	3.00	13.00	0.375
4.00	4.00	12.00	0.500
4.00	5.00	11.00	0.625
4.00	6.00	10.00	0.750
4.00	10.00	6.00	1.000
4.00	12.00	4.00	1.000

Plot the absorbances against the ratio of moles of X to moles of M. Calculate the formula of the complex from the mole ratio at which the absorbance reaches a maximum and levels off.

24. *Photometric titration.* Lead forms a chelate PbY^{2-} with EDTA, the log of whose stability constant is 18.3. This chelate has an absorption maximum at 240 nm, with a molar absorptivity of 6500. Suppose 100 ml of a 5.0×10^{-5}-F solution of a lead salt is titrated with a 1.0×10^{-3}-F EDTA solution. The lead solution is buffered at pH 3.00. The length of the path through the titration cell is 3.0 cm. Calculate the absorbance of the solution at the following volumes of titrant, correcting for dilution: (a) 1.00, (b) 2.00, (c) 4.00, (d) 5.00, (e) 6.00, and (f) 8.00 ml. Plot the titration curve.

25. *pK of an indicator.* Exactly 1.00 mmol portions of an indicator, a weak acid, HIn, and its salt NaIn are dissolved in 1.00-l volumes of various buffer solutions. The absorbances of the resulting solutions are measured at 650 nm in a 1.00-cm cell and found to be:

pH	Absorbance
12.00	0.840
11.00	0.840
10.00	0.840
7.00	0.588
2.00	0.000
1.00	0.000

Calculate the molar absorptivities of HIn and In^- at 650 nm and calculate the pK_a of the indicator.

26. *pK of an indicator.* A solution of a weak acid indicator HA is prepared by dissolving 3.0 mmol of the acid in 10.0 l of solution. The following values of the absorbances were measured in a 1.00-cm cell in various buffers.

pH	Absorbance
1.00	0.150
2.00	0.150
4.70	0.500
11.00	1.200
12.00	1.200

Assuming that at low pH the principal species in the solution is HA and at high pH the principal species is A^-, calculate the pK_a of the indicator.

12

Flame Emission and Atomic Absorption Spectroscopy

Flame emission spectroscopy (or flame photometry, as it is often called) involves the measurement of radiant energy emitted by an excited atom population. In atomic absorption spectroscopy, the absorption of radiant energy by atoms in the ground state is measured. The two methods are often discussed together for convenience, despite their fundamental difference, because the flame is common to both: whether emission or absorption is to be measured, the required atom population is usually obtained from the sample by means of the flame.

FLAME EMISSION SPECTROSCOPY (FLAME PHOTOMETRY)

Emission Spectroscopy

Flame photometry is a branch of emission spectroscopy, a major field which represents, in a sense, the other side of the coin from spectrophotometry or absorption spectroscopy. In absorption studies, at least for analytical purposes, the fate of the excited species is not of interest (unless it involves a process that interferes with the absorption measurement, as fluorescence might). In emission spectroscopy, the sample is excited by various means, and the emission of radiation by excited species as they revert to lower energy states is measured.

Types of Emission Spectra

There are three major types of spectra emitted by excited substances. Incandescent solids emit *continuous spectra* which are characterized by the absence of discrete lines. That is to say, a graph showing emitted energy as a function of frequency or wavelength does not exhibit sharp peaks. An example is the radiation from the hot tungsten filament in a light bulb, as shown in Fig. 11.9; the spectral distribution of the energy approximates that of a black-body radiator.

Excited molecules in the gas phase emit *band spectra*. When a molecule in an excited electronic state of energy, E_2, undergoes a transition to a state of lower energy, E_1, a photon of energy $h\nu$ is emitted, where

$$h\nu = E_2 - E_1$$

But within each electronic state, the molecule may exist in a number of vibrational-rotational substates of slightly different energies. Hence the radiation from a large assembly of excited molecules comprises a number of frequencies which are grouped into bands. Each band corresponds to a transition from one excited electronic state to another electronic state of lower energy. The slightly different frequencies within each band result from the multiplicity of vibrational and rotational states within each electronic energy level. We saw a similar situation with regard to absorption in Chapter 11. The individual frequencies which make up a band may not be resolved by the particular instrument employed to examine the spectrum, in which case only an envelope over the individual lines is actually recorded.

Excited atoms or monatomic ions in the gaseous state emit *line spectra*. Vibrational and rotational "fine structure" is absent from the spectra of monatomic species, and the emission spectrum is a series of individual frequencies or lines corresponding to transitions between various electronic energy levels.

A spectral line is not a line in the mathematical sense of having no width. There is a *natural width*, of the order of 10^{-4}Å, which results from the probability distribution associated with each electronic energy level of an atom. Observed lines, in both emission and absorption, are considerably wider than this as a result of additional factors. *Doppler broadening*, of the order of 10^{-2}Å at typical flame temperatures, reflects the different velocity components of the atoms along the line of observation; the Doppler effect is discussed in elementary physics textbooks. *Pressure broadening*, which in flames is typically of the same order of magnitude as Doppler broadening, results from perturbations of the energy levels of an absorbing or emitting atom by neighboring atoms or molecules. Lines observed in flame work are generally between 10^{-2} and 10^{-1}Å in width. Measuring an actual line profile requires spectroscopic apparatus of higher resolving power than would be used for analytical work.

Methods of Excitation

In this chapter, we are concerned with excitation in a flame, but it may be mentioned that other methods are used as well. The dc arc, for example, is very common in emission spectroscopy. An electrical arc is struck between two electrodes, using a voltage of perhaps 200 to 300 V. The electrodes are often graphite rods, to one of which the sample is applied in some manner. For instance, a depression may be machined into one end of a rod to hold a drop of sample solution. The rod is dried in an oven or under an infrared lamp. When an arc is formed between this rod and a second electrode, sufficient energy is provided to volatilize the sample residue, dissociate it into atoms, and excite these atoms, at least for many of the elements. Examination of the radiant energy emitted from the arc will disclose that it comprises discrete frequencies (or wavelengths) that serve to identify components of the sample. Under very carefully standardized conditions, quantitative analysis may be possible by measuring the radiant power at appropriate wavelengths, but there are many problems in quantitative emission spectroscopy with arc sources. Although very high temperatures are attained in the arc (say, 4000 to 8000°), all of the sample components may not be volatilized uniformly, and the time dependence of the emission spectrum may be tricky. Further, an arc tends to wander about as it plays upon an electrode surface, and much flickering is observed as well. Ac arcs, operated at 1000 V or more, are somewhat steadier than dc arcs. High-voltage sparks are also used to excite spectra in some cases.

Flame Sources

Of the common sources used in emission spectroscopy, the flame is the least energetic and excites the fewest elements—about fifty of the metallic ones. But where it is applicable, the flame has notable advantages over arc or spark excitation. A well-regulated flame is a much more stable source than an arc or spark. Further, the emission spectrum of an element in a flame is relatively simple. Only a few of the lines that are seen in an arc spectrum are found in flame emission. This places a much lighter burden upon the resolving power of the monochromator with regard to interferences, that is, it is easier to find an emission line for a particular element which does not have lines of other elements as near neighbors.

Temperature

The temperature of the flame is obviously one of the most important variables in flame photometry. This is determined by the nature of the fuel and its rate of supply, the supply of air or oxygen, and the design of the burner. Some of the less expensive instruments employ a Meker burner in which ordinary city gas burns in air. Temperatures are not much over 1500° in the hottest portion of the flame, and relatively few elements such as the alkali metals are excited. Hydrogen-oxygen flames are widely employed in better instruments; temperatures well over 2000° are attainable, providing sufficient energy for most purposes, and the flame itself produces very little background radiation to interfere with the observation of desired spectral lines.

Sample Introduction

Several arrangements are possible for introducing the sample solution into the flame. Instruments that employ a Meker burner generally have a separate atomization chamber in which the sample solution, introduced through a funnel, is broken up into fine droplets by the action of a blast of air. The geometry of the chamber is such that large drops are removed by the walls or by special baffles. The fine mist is swept by the air stream into the base of the burner where it mixes with the burner gases and is carried into the flame. This type of atomizer is uneconomical with regard to sample consumption, which may be as high as 20 or 30 ml per min; much of the sample never reaches the flame.

The other common arrangement, which is better for many purposes, employs an integral aspirator-burner with which the sample solution is sprayed directly into the flame. Such a burner is depicted schematically in Fig. 12.1.

The flow of oxygen through the constricted tip of the inner annulus draws sample solution from a small beaker up through the capillary. At the tip of the capillary, the column of liquid encounters strong shear forces which disperse it into droplets that are carried directly into the flame by the rushing gases. The fuel, most commonly hydrogen, is supplied through an outer annulus. Sample consumption is comparatively low, perhaps 0.5 to 2 ml per min. Over a period of time, there may be a tendency for an encrustation of solid salts to form near the capillary tip. This of course may affect the rate of sample feed through the capillary. This rate is also sensitive to variations in the viscosity of the sample solutions. Thus, for the most accurate work, it may be helpful to force the solution through the capillary at a constant flow rate. This is easily accomplished using a motor-driven hypodermic syringe connected to the bottom of the capillary with a section of plastic tubing.

FIGURE   12.1   Schematic diagram of an integral aspirator-burner.

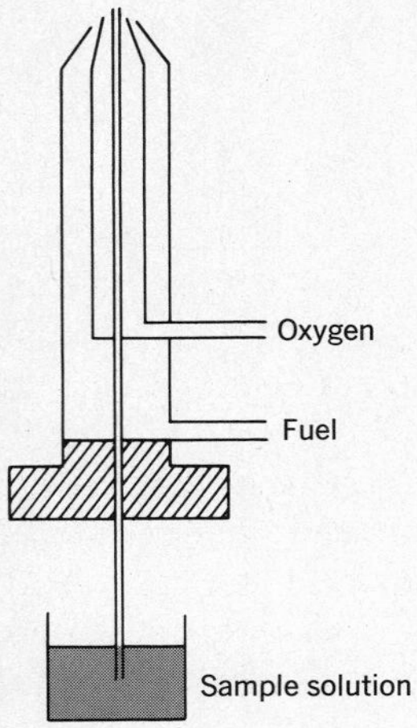

Instrumentation

Figure 12.2 shows in block form the components of a basic, research-level flame photometer. Commercial instruments over a wide price range represent compromises with regard to one or another of the components in order to provide adequate capability under marketable conditions for applications of varying difficulty and sophistication. For example, in determining sodium using a low-temperature flame, only a few lines of the alkali and alkaline earth metals appear in the emission spectrum. Thus an inexpensive filter of colored glass could serve to transmit the desired sodium frequency to the detector while blocking the radiation emitted by, say, potassium or calcium, and an expensive monochromator would not be needed.

The scanning monochromator and recorder are convenient for evaluating baseline effects arising from the flame background emission and for examining lines from several elements. But a less expensive arrangement is possible in which a monochromator is manually set for a certain wavelength. A background reading is obtained by introducing distilled water or some sort of analytical "blank" into the flame, and then the sample is measured at the same wavelength. A simple electrical meter would then be used in place of the recorder.

If sensitivity is not a problem, the photomultiplier tube may be replaced by an ordinary phototube. This simplifies the circuitry because a high-voltage power supply is no longer required to operate the detector. Flow meters for the fuel and oxygen are not essential if the pressures are well regulated, the aspirator is clean, and standards are run frequently along with the unknown samples.

FIGURE   12.2   Block diagram of a flame photometer.

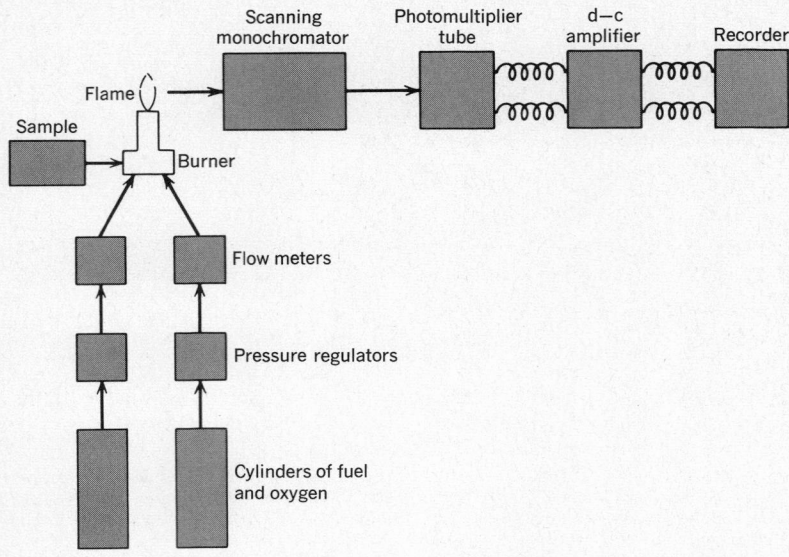

Some instruments provide for a direct comparison of the radiant power emitted by two elements in the sample, thereby permitting the use of an *internal standard* to minimize the effects of variation in sample feed and fluctuations in the flame. For example, suppose sodium analyses were being performed. A constant quantity of a lithium salt might be added to all of the standard and unknown sodium solutions. The choice of lithium would be based upon its similarity to sodium in its response to excitational variations and the unlikelihood of its occurrence in the particular set of unknowns at hand. The radiation emitted in one direction from the flame passes to a filter that transmits only the yellow sodium line to a detector. Radiation emitted in another direction goes to a filter that transmits only the lithium line, and thence to a second detector. A measuring circuit compares the two detector signals. The calibration curve for such a case would be a graph with the ratios of sodium-to-lithium emissions plotted against the sodium concentrations of the standard solutions.

Problems

The sequence of events required to produce an emission spectrum in the flame is almost forbidding enough to suggest that quantitative flame photometry should not work. Droplets of sample solution must evaporate; the resulting tiny solid particles must dissociate into atoms; the atoms must be excited. All of these processes occur within a distance of a few cm as the sample droplets are being carried upward at a high velocity by the flame gases. Actually, it is more critical than this, because the optical system does not examine the whole flame but sees only the radiation from a region lying a certain distance above the burner tip. With the proper illumination, one may see unevaporated sample droplets issuing in profusion from the top of the flame. The flame gases are diluted by inrushing air as a result of the low pressure created by high velocity. There is at no point a stable, equilibrium atom population of the sort that might be obtained by holding the sample in a furnace for a sufficient time.[1] Thus the observed emission intensity depends upon a series of kinetic effects—rate of evaporation, rate of dissociation, etc.

It turns out, however, that flame photometry does work provided conditions are very carefully controlled. Under the best circumstances, deviations of the order of perhaps 2% may be seen in replicate analyses. But there are many traps for the unwary, and errors of 50 or 100% are probably far more common than many people realize.

Interferences

We shall list briefly some of the commonest problems in quantitative flame photometry.

[1] The furnace as a stable source for emission spectroscopy has in fact been considered by various people; technical problems—materials of construction, techniques for sample introduction, contamination from one sample to another—remain to be overcome. Certain makeshift approaches such as heating the sample electrically on a graphite rod are being used to some extent.

1. Radiation from other elements. Perhaps no two spectral lines have exactly the same wavelength, but some are very close together. Whether emission by one metal will interfere in determining another will depend upon how close the lines are and the quality of the monochromator. With a good instrument, it is usually possible to measure an element without interference of this type, but with inexpensive filter instruments this is often not the case. Band spectra emitted by excited molecules formed in the combustion process may also represent a problem in some cases.

2. Cation enhancement. In high-temperature flames, some of the metal atoms may ionize, e.g.,

$$Na \rightleftharpoons Na^+ + e$$

The ion has an emission spectrum of its own, with different frequencies from those of the atomic spectrum. Thus ionization decreases the radiant power of atomic emission. Sometimes a second metal, say potassium in this example, represses by its own ionization the ionization of the first (sodium). It is as though the partial pressure of free electrons had been increased in the above equilibrium. The sodium atom emission is thereby enhanced. Sodium analyses on unknown samples containing varying quantities of potassium are thus subject to errors. One solution to this problem would be addition of a large quantity of a potassium salt to all of the solutions—unknowns and standards—so as to swamp out variations from one sample to another.

3. Anion interference. Many examples of this are known. For instance, phosphate and sulfate ions lower the emission of calcium well below the level found for, say, calcium chloride solutions. Little is known of the detailed mechanism; presumably the solid residue resulting from solvent evaporation is less readily dissociated into atoms than is calcium chloride. Again, the swamping technique is often useful. For example, addition of 0.1-M EDTA to the solutions overcomes the effects of at least 0.01-M phosphate and sulfate on the emission from 6×10^{-4}-M calcium.[2] Addition of a large excess of phosphate or sulfate would also overcome the effects of variations in these ions from sample to sample, but in this case EDTA is more satisfactory. For some reason which is not known, EDTA not only counters the effect of the other anions, but also enhances calcium emission, leading to improved sensitivity.[2]

Because our goal in this chapter is to provide a brief introduction to flame photometry without unduly lengthening the book, there are many aspects which are not considered here. Anyone undertaking a flame photometric analysis should do a great deal of reading and exercise the utmost attention to detail in preparing standard and unknown solutions in the laboratory. Matrix effects are very important, that is to say, the overall composition of a solution may have a large effect upon the emission intensity of a particular element.

[2] A. C. West and W. D. Cooke, *Anal. Chem.*, **32**, 1471 (1960).

Applications

The important applications of flame photometry involve analyses that are difficult or impossible to perform in any other way, at least where speed is much more important than accuracy. For many years the main forte of flame photometry was analysis for alkali metals, mainly sodium and potassium, and to a lesser extent, the alkaline earths, primarily calcium. Analyses for these ions became important in connection with electrolyte balance studies in physiology and in clinical chemistry laboratories. The alkali metals form few compounds containing chromophores to provide a basis for ultraviolet or visible spectrophotometry, they are not electroactive at reasonable potentials for electroanalytical techniques such as polarography, and they form few insoluble compounds. Thus flame photometry has been exceedingly useful in studies involving these elements. It is too early to state whether it will be supplanted in the future by other methods such as potentiometry with ion-selective electrodes, but at least for some time to come, flame photometry will probably continue to be important in biomedical research, agronomy, water analysis, nutrition studies, and other areas where alkali metals must be determined.

It would be incorrect to leave the student with the impression that flame photometry has been applied only to the alkali metals. Many other examples may be found in the literature involving perhaps fifty of the metallic elements. Lead in gasoline samples can be determined by spraying the gasoline directly into the flame. In many cases, metals have been extracted as chelates into organic solvents which are then subjected to flame photometry. Matrix effects are limited by the extraction process, and thus interferences are often minimal with this technique. Sensitivity is often greater with organic solvents than with water. The enhancement of metal emission probably results largely from a smaller droplet size and more rapid evaporation of the solvent, with a small contribution from the slightly higher flame temperature.

ATOMIC ABSORPTION SPECTROSCOPY

In a typical flame, most of the atoms by far are in the ground electronic state rather than in an excited state. For example, with regard to the transition that leads to the yellow sodium line at 589 nm, the ratio of excited atoms to ground state atoms at 2700° is about 6×10^{-4}. Further, the number of excited atoms varies exponentially with temperature, whereas, with so few atoms excited, the ground state population is practically constant over a reasonable temperature range. (Note that this argument neglects the effect of temperature on evaporation and dissociation.) In 1955, Walsh pointed out these facts and suggested that improved analytical methods might be possible based upon absorption of radiation by ground state atoms in the flame.[3] This

[3] A. Walsh, *Spectrochim. Acta*, 7, 108 (1955).

technique was developed rapidly during the 1960s. Unhappily, some of the early workers as well as the instrument manufacturers propounded overly optimistic views concerning interferences in atomic absorption. While it is true that the flame is no longer an excitation source, one may still expect kinetic effects related to evaporation and dissociation in the formation of the ground state atom population. Nevertheless, experience has proved that atomic absorption is a very useful technique for determining small quantities of a number of metals.

Instrumentation

Figure 12.3 shows in schematic form the basic components of an atomic absorption spectrophotometer. It might be supposed that a continuous source such as those discussed in Chapter 11 could be used, but in practice this is not done. Absorption lines due to atomic species are much narrower than the bands encountered in ordinary spectrophotometry. If the band of radiation provided by a monochromator is much wider than the absorption line, then much of the radiation has no chance of being absorbed, and sensitivity will suffer. If the band pass of the monochromator is diminished enough to yield reasonable absorbance values, then an extremely intense continuous source is required in order to furnish enough energy in the very narrow wavelength region passed by the monochromator to operate the detector system. Thus the common source in atomic absorption is the one originally suggested by Walsh,[3] viz., the hollow-cathode discharge tube. This tube contains an anode and a hollow, cylindrical cathode in an inert gas atmosphere (often argon) at low pressure. The tube is operated with a power supply that furnishes several hundred volts. Atoms of the gas are ionized in the electrical discharge, and collisions of the energetic ions with the cathode surface dislodge atoms of the metal which are excited. This results in the emission of a line spectrum of the metal which appears as a glow within the hollow cathode space.

A suitable line in the emission spectrum of the source is selected for the analysis. This line, a so-called resonance line, represents a transition from an excited atomic state to the ground state, and it thus represents the correct

FIGURE 12.3 Components of an atomic absorption spectro-photometer.

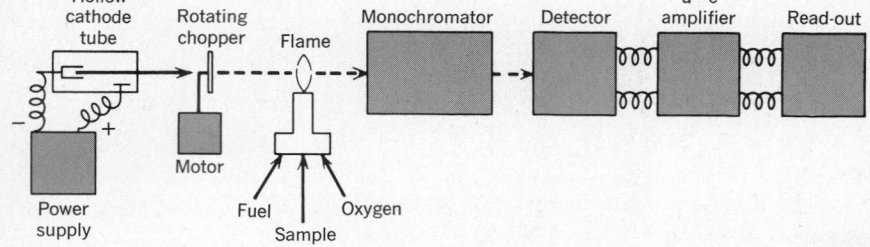

frequency for absorption by ground state atoms in the flame. Hollow-cathode emission lines are very sharp—narrower in general than absorption lines in the flame—and are thus well suited to atomic absorption work. The only requirement of the monochromator is that other lines in the spectrum of the source, arising from the metal cathode and the inert gas, not be transmitted to the detector. This permits the use of a fairly inexpensive monochromator. Perhaps the major disadvantage of the hollow-cathode source is that a different tube is required for each metal determined.[4] Demountable tubes can be constructed in which various metal cathodes can be interchanged, but the nuisance of pumping out the air each time the tube is opened has precluded their extensive use. After evacuation, bleeding-in the inert gas to the correct pressure is an additional problem. Thus sealed tubes, a different one for each metal, are commonly used. Some commercial instruments provide for a rapid and convenient switch from one tube to another.

The flame in atomic absorption is itself an emitting source just as it is in flame photometry, and the detector responds to radiation from the flame as well as from the hollow-cathode source. Yet, if uncorrected, this would obviously interfere with absorption measurements: if radiation emitted from the flame and unabsorbed radiation from the hollow-cathode source were not distinguished, then absorbance values would be too low and would be subject to the annoying fluctuations of flame emission. This problem is eliminated by the combination of the beam chopper with the tuned amplifier shown in Fig. 12.3. Only an ac electrical signal whose frequency is the same as that of the pulsating beam created by the chopper is amplified; unamplified signals are below the sensitivity of the readout device and go unnoticed. If emission from the flame were steady, it would give rise to only a dc signal at the detector, and even if not, it is improbable that more than a tiny component would have the correct frequency to be amplified.

Most atomic absorption spectrophotometers are single-beam instruments. Double-beam design compensates for source and detector fluctuations but not for the major source of noise and instability, the flame itself. Single-beam operation is the same as described in Chapter 11: P_o is determined with distilled water or an analytical blank sprayed into the flame, and then P is measured with the sample. The Bouguer–Beer law applies as in any spectrophotometry. Special burners which provide a long path length through the flame have been devised to improve the sensitivity via Bouguer's law. Radiation may be passed several times through the flame by means of a mirror arrangement, or a fishtail burner shape may provide a long path.

Applications

Atomic absorption has gained very rapid acceptance and is now a very widely used analytical tool. There are several advantages as compared with flame emission:

---

[4] This is not strictly correct; in some cases, the cathode can be fabricated from an alloy so that emission lines of several metals may be obtained from a single tube.

1. Because absorption depends upon the ground state population, the sensitivity may be higher, especially for elements that are difficult to excite (zinc, for example, may be determined down to 0.5 ppm, while the lower limit in emission is perhaps 500 ppm or so).

2. Ground state population is much less sensitive to flame temperature than excited population.

3. Interference from spectral lines of other elements and flame background emission is minimized by the beam-chopping technique.

But it should be remembered that the same sequence of events as in flame emission—atomization, evaporation, and dissociation—occurs in atomic absorption, and many interferences operate at these steps, particularly dissociation. The gross composition of the sample may have a great effect upon the ground state population of a particular trace metal in the flame. Proper attention to such matrix effects in preparing standard solutions as well as unknown samples is very important.

Atomic absorption spectrophotometry is too widely used to permit a survey of applications in this chapter. Procedures may be found in the literature for determining forty or more metals in a wide variety of samples that are important in industry, agriculture, medicine, oceanography, and many other fields. Basic studies, for example, on the distribution of lead in the environment, involving plants, soils, animal tissues, and urine samples, depend very heavily upon atomic absorption. Mercury, which represents an unusual example, is discussed more fully later.

Applications of atomic absorption may also be found in which the primary goal is not an immediate analysis but rather a better understanding of flame processes. For example, Cook et al. measured ground state atom populations by atomic absorption at various heights above the burner tip. These data, along with temperature and emission measurements, provided a clear explanation for many reported discrepancies involving enhancement and suppression effects in flame photometry.[5]

Flameless Atomic Absorption

The determination of mercury at low concentrations represents an important exception to the use of the flame to obtain an atom population for atomic absorption. Mercury ions in solution are easily reduced to metallic mercury, and the element is sufficiently volatile to yield an atomic vapor without recourse to high temperature. The solution containing mercury salts is treated with a reducing agent such as stannous chloride, and the finely divided metallic mercury is volatilized by bubbling air through the solution. The vapor is swept by the air stream into an absorption cell with quartz windows where the attenuation of a mercury line (253.7 nm) is measured.

---

[5] J. H. Gibson, W. Grossman, and W. D. Cooke, *Anal. Chem.*, **35**, 266 (1963).

The source is an ordinary mercury vapor lamp. As the air bubbling is continued, the absorbance rises to a maximum value and then diminishes. It is convenient to record absorbance as a function of time so that the maximum is easily found. Although there is no obvious theoretical reason to expect it, the maximal absorbance is proportional to the mercury concentration of the original solution. The method is effective well into the nanogram level.

REFERENCES

J. A. DEAN, *Flame Photometry*, McGraw-Hill Book Company, New York, 1960.

I. M. KOLTHOFF and P. J. ELVING, eds., *Treatise on Analytical Chemistry*, Part 1, Vol. 6, Chapter 65, Interscience Publishers Division of John Wiley & Sons, New York, 1965.

J. A. DEAN and T. C. RAINS, eds., *Flame Emission and Atomic Absorption Spectrometry*, Vols. 1–3, Marcel Dekker, Inc., New York, 1969.

R. HERRMANN and C. Th. J. ALKEMADE, *Chemical Analysis by Flame Photometry*, 2nd ed., trans. by P. T. Gilbert, Interscience Publishers, New York, 1963.

W. T. ELWELL and J. A. F. GIDLEY, *Atomic Absorption Spectrophotometry*, Pergamon Press, New York, 1966.

J. RAMIREZ-MUNOZ, *Atomic Absorption Spectroscopy*, Elsevier Publishing Co., New York, 1968.

J. W. ROBINSON, *Atomic Absorption Spectroscopy*, Marcel Dekker, Inc., New York, 1966.

13 Solvent Extraction

INTRODUCTION

The partition of solutes between two immiscible liquids offers many attractive possibilities for analytical separations. Even where the primary goal is not analytical but rather preparative, solvent extraction may be an important step in the sequence that leads to a pure product in the organic, inorganic, or biochemical laboratory. Although complicated apparatus is sometimes employed, frequently only a separatory funnel is required. Often a solvent extraction separation can be accomplished in a few minutes. The technique is applicable over a wide concentration range, and has been used extensively for the isolation of extremely minute quantities of carrier-free isotopes obtained by nuclear transmutation as well as industrial materials produced by the ton. Solvent extraction separations are usually "clean" in the sense that there is no analog of coprecipitation with such systems. Aside from its intrinsic interest, there is an important reason for discussing solvent extraction in this text: We shall use a particular approach to solvent extraction, the Craig pseudocountercurrent technique, as a model to aid our understanding of chromatographic processes in Chapter 14.

DISTRIBUTION LAW

When a solute distributes itself between two immiscible liquids, there is a definite relationship between the solute concentrations in the two phases at equilibrium. Nernst gave the first clear statement of the distribution law when he pointed out in 1891 that a solute will distribute itself between two immiscible liquids in such a way that the ratio of concentrations at equilibrium is constant at a particular temperature:

$$\frac{[A]_1}{[A]_2} = \text{constant}$$

$[A]_1$ represents the concentration of a solute A in the liquid phase 1.

Although this relationship holds fairly well in certain cases, in reality it is inexact. Strictly, in thermodynamic terms, it is the activity ratio rather than the concentration ratio that should be constant. The activity of a chemical species in one phase maintains a constant ratio to the activity of the same species in the other liquid phase:

$$\frac{a_{A_1}}{a_{A_2}} = K_{D_A}$$

Here a_{A_1} represents the activity of solute A in phase 1. The true constant K_{D_A} is called the *distribution coefficient* of species A.

Sometimes it is necessary or desirable to take into account the chemical complications in extraction equilibria. For example, consider the distribution of benzoic acid between the two liquid phases benzene and water. In the aqueous phase, benzoic acid is partly ionized,

$$HBz + H_2O \rightleftharpoons H_3O^+ + Bz^-$$

In the benzene phase, benzoic acid is partially dimerized by hydrogen bonding in the carboxyl groups,

$$2\,HBz \rightleftharpoons (HBz)_2$$

Each particular species, HBz, Bz^-, $(HBz)_2$, will have its own particular K_D value. The system water, benzene, and benzoic acid may then be described by three distribution coefficients:

$$K_{D_{HBz}} = \frac{a_{HBz_{org}}}{a_{HBz_{aq}}}$$

$$K_{D_{Bz^-}} = \frac{a_{Bz^-_{org}}}{a_{Bz^-_{aq}}}$$

$$K_{D(HBz)_2} = \frac{a_{(HBz)_2\,org}}{a_{(HBz)_2\,aq}}$$

Now it happens that the benzoate ion in fact remains almost totally in the aqueous phase, and the benzoic acid dimer exists only in the organic phase. Further, in a practical experiment, the chemist will usually want to know where the "benzoic acid" *is*, not whether part of it is ionized or dimerized. Also, he will be more interested in how much is there than in its thermodynamic activity. He would be better served, then, by an expression combining the concentrations of all the species in the two phases:

$$D = \frac{\text{total benzoic in organic phase}}{\text{total benzoic in aqueous phase}}$$

$$= \frac{[HBz]_{org} + 2[(HBz)_2]_{org}}{[HBz]_{aq} + [Bz^-]_{aq}}$$

The ratio D is called the *distribution ratio*.

It is clear that D will not remain constant over a range of experimental conditions. For example, raising the pH of the aqueous phase will lower D by converting benzoic acid into benzoate ion, which does not extract into benzene. The addition of any electrolyte may affect D by changing activity coefficients. However, the distribution ratio is useful when its value is known for a particular set of conditions.

EXAMPLES OF SOLVENT EXTRACTION EQUILIBRIA

In this section we shall consider examples illustrating the manner in which equilibrium expressions may be manipulated to obtain equations which show the factors upon which D values depend.

Partition of a Weak Acid

Consider a weak acid, HB. Assume for simplicity that the acid is monomeric in both solvent phases, and that the anion of the acid does not penetrate the organic phase. The pertinent equilibrium expressions then are:

$$D = \frac{[HB]_{org}}{[HB]_{aq} + [B^-]_{aq}} \tag{1}$$

$$K_{D_{HB}} = \frac{[HB]_{org}}{[HB]_{aq}} \tag{2}$$

$$K_a = \frac{[H_3O^+]_{aq}[B^-]_{aq}}{[HB]_{aq}} \tag{3}$$

Rearranging (3) gives

$$[B^-]_{aq} = K_a\frac{[HB]_{aq}}{[H_3O^+]_{aq}}$$

and substitution into (1) yields

$$D = \frac{[\mathrm{HB}]_{\mathrm{org}}}{[\mathrm{HB}]_{\mathrm{aq}} + (K_a[\mathrm{HB}]_{\mathrm{aq}}/[\mathrm{H_3O^+}]_{\mathrm{aq}})}$$

or

$$D = \frac{[\mathrm{HB}]_{\mathrm{org}}}{[\mathrm{HB}]_{\mathrm{aq}}\{1 + (K_a/[\mathrm{H_3O^+}]_{\mathrm{aq}})\}}$$

Referring to (2), we see that

$$D = \frac{K_{D_{\mathrm{HB}}}}{1 + (K_a/[\mathrm{H_3O^+}]_{\mathrm{aq}})}$$

Thus we have derived an expression showing explicitly the dependence of the distribution ratio upon the distribution coefficient of the weak acid, its ionization constant, and the pH of the aqueous phase. It might well be that we could capitalize upon inherent differences in the values of the appropriate constants to effect the separation of a mixture of acids by regulating the pH of the aqueous phase.

Extraction of a Metal as a Chelate Compound

Many important separations of metal ions have been developed around the formation of chelate compounds with a variety of organic reagents. As an example, consider the reagent 8-quinolinol (8-hydroxyquinoline), often referred to by the trivial name "oxine,"

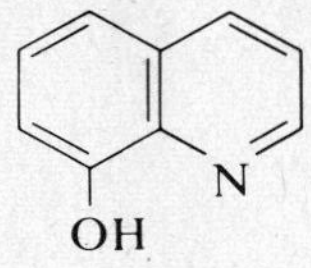

This reagent forms neutral, water-insoluble, chloroform- or carbon tetrachloride-soluble molecules with metal ions; the cupric oxinate chelate may be depicted as follows:

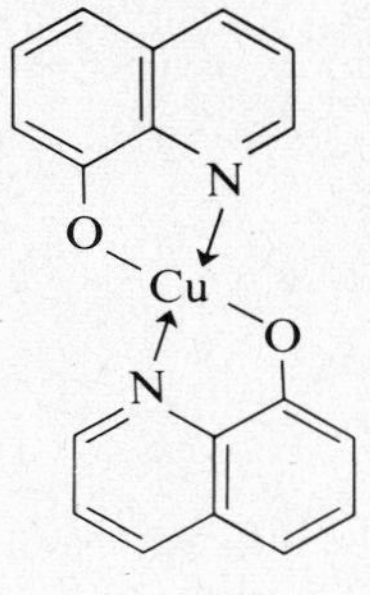

If we abbreviate oxine as HOx, we may write the chelation reaction as

$$Cu^{2+} + 2\,HOx \rightleftharpoons Cu(Ox)_2 + 2\,H^+$$

Another very important chelating agent for the solvent extraction of metal ions is diephenylthiocarbazone or "dithizone,"

$$\begin{array}{c}
C_6H_5 \\
| \\
NH-NH \\
S=C \\
\diagdown \\
N=N \\
| \\
C_6H_5
\end{array}$$

The chelation reaction may be written as

$$M^{n+} + n\,HDz \rightleftharpoons M(Dz)_n + n\,H^+$$

Consider the extraction of an aqueous solution of the metal ion M^{n+} with an organic solvent containing a chelating agent HX. A distribution ratio may be written for the metal:

$$D = \frac{C_{M_{org}}}{C_{M_{aq}}}$$

where C_M is the total metal concentration regardless of what form it is in. Let us assume for simplicity (but not a bad assumption in many actual cases) that the only metal in the organic phase is present as the chelate, MX_n, i.e., $C_{M_{org}} = [MX_n]_{org}$. Also, let us ignore possible lower complexes such as MX or MX_{n-1} which may exist in the aqueous phase. (A large excess of HX would perhaps insure the validity of this assumption.) Thus

$$C_{M_{aq}} = [M^{n+}]_{aq} + [MX_n]_{aq}$$

If the partition of the chelate greatly favors the organic phase, which is frequently the case, we may neglect $[MX_n]_{aq}$ as compared with $[M^{n+}]_{aq}$, and thus we may write

$$D = \frac{[MX_n]_{org}}{[M^{n+}]_{aq}}$$

Rearranging the distribution coefficient expression for the chelate gives

$$[MX_n]_{org} = K_{D_{MXn}}[MX_n]_{aq}$$

and substitution into the expression for D yields

$$D = \frac{K_{D_{MXn}}[MX_n]_{aq}}{[M^{n+}]_{aq}} = \frac{K_{D_{MXn}}}{[M^{n+}]_{aq}/[MX_n]_{aq}}$$

Next, consider the formation constant of the chelate in the aqueous phase:

$$M^{n+} + n\,X^- \rightleftharpoons MX_n$$

$$K_f = \frac{[MX_n]_{aq}}{[M^{n+}]_{aq}[X^-]^n_{aq}} \quad \text{or} \quad [M^{n+}]_{aq} = \frac{[MX_n]_{aq}}{K_f[X^-]^n_{aq}}$$

and the acid dissociation of the chelating agent:

$$HX + H_2O \rightleftharpoons H_3O^+ + X^-$$

$$K_a = \frac{[H_3O^+]_{aq}[X^-]_{aq}}{[HX]_{aq}} \quad \text{or} \quad [X^-]_{aq} = \frac{K_a[HX]_{aq}}{[H_3O^+]_{aq}}$$

Thus,

$$[M^{n+}]_{aq} = \frac{[MX_n]_{aq}[H_3O^+]^n_{aq}}{K_f K_a^n [HX]^n_{aq}}$$

and

$$\frac{[M^{n+}]_{aq}}{[MX_n]_{aq}} = \frac{[H_3O^+]^n_{aq}}{K_f K_a^n [HX]^n_{aq}}$$

Returning to the expression for D, we obtain

$$D = \frac{K_{D_{MX_n}} K_f K_a^n [HX]^n_{aq}}{[H_3O^+]^n_{aq}}$$

Next consider the distribution coefficient for the chelating agent:

$$K_{D_{HX}} = \frac{[HX]_{org}}{[HX]_{aq}} \quad \text{or} \quad [HX]_{aq} = \frac{[HX]_{org}}{K_{D_{HX}}}$$

Then

$$D = \frac{K_{D_{MX_n}} K_f K_a^n [HX]^n_{org}}{K_{D_{HX}}^n [H_3O^+]^n_{aq}}$$

This equation gives the distribution ratio for the metal in terms of (a) constants $K_{D_{MX_n}}$, $K_{D_{HX}}$, K_f, and K_a which are properties of the particular compounds involved in the selected system, and (b) variables $[H_3O^+]_{aq}$ and $[HX]_{org}$ which are subject to experimental manipulation for a particular system. Let us lump together the constants into an *extraction constant*, K_{ex}:

$$\frac{K_{D_{MX_n}} K_f K_a^n}{K_{D_{HX}}^n} = K_{ex}$$

Then

$$D = \frac{K_{ex}[HX]_{org}^n}{[H_3O^+]_{aq}^n}$$

Taking logarithms,

$$\log D = \log K_{ex} + n \log [HX]_{org} - n \log [H_3O^+]_{aq}$$

or

$$\log D = \log K_{ex} + n \log [HX]_{org} + n\, pH$$

Thus a plot of $\log D$ vs pH should be a straight line with a slope of n and an intercept on the $\log D$ axis of $\log K_{ex} + n \log [HX]_{org}$. The higher the charge on the metal ion, the steeper the slope of the line. Varying the concentration of the chelating agent shifts the curves along the pH axis.

Note that no term involving metal concentration appears in the final equation. One of the attractive aspects of solvent extraction (unlike, say, precipitation) is the fact that it works all the way from tracer levels up to macro quantities.

Of course, the constants K_f and $K_{D_{MX_n}}$ vary from one metal ion to another. This is the basis for separation by extraction of aqueous solutions with organic solvents containing chelating agents.

EXTRACTION SYSTEMS INVOLVING ION PAIRS AND SOLVATES

Generally, simple metal salts tend to be more soluble in a highly polar solvent like water than in organic solvents of much lower dielectric constant. Many ions are solvated by water, and the energy of solvation contributes to the disruption of the crystal lattice of the solid salt. Furthermore, less work is required to separate ions of opposite charge in a high-dielectric solvent. Usually, then, the formation of an uncharged species is necessary if an ion is to be extracted from water into an organic solvent. We have seen an example of this in the extraction of metals converted into neutral chelates of 8-quinolinol. The metal ion is bound in the chelate by definite chemical bonds, often largely covalent in character.

Sometimes, on the other hand, an uncharged species extractable into an organic solvent is obtained through the association of ions of opposite charge. In point of fact, it must be admitted that it is difficult to draw a line between an ion pair and a neutral molecule. Probably if the components stay together in water, it will be called a molecule; if the components are separated in water sufficiently that an entity cannot be detected, this entity will be called an ion pair if it does show up in a nonpolar solvent.

A common example of an extraction system involving ion-pair formation in the organic phase is found in the use of tetraphenylarsonium chloride to extract permanganate, perrhenate, and pertechnetate from water into chloroform. The species which passes into the organic phase is an ion pair, $[(C_6H_5)_4As^+, ReO_4^-]$. Similarly, the extraction of uranyl ion, UO_2^{2+}, from aqueous nitrate solutions into solvents such as ether (an important process in uranium chemistry) involves an association of the type $[UO_2^{2+}, 2\,NO_3^-]$. It is believed that the uranyl ion is solvated by ether as well as by water, a fact which doubtless facilitates penetration of the organic phase by an ion pair which then takes on more of the character of the solvent.

It has been known for many years that ferric iron can be extracted into ether from strong hydrochloric acid solution. This process is useful for the separation of bulk quantities of iron prior to the determination of other elements in ferrous alloys. Despite extensive study, the system water-ether-HCl-Fe^{3+} is still not completely understood. There is evidence that the extractable species is an ion pair of the type $[H_3O^+, Fe(H_2O)_2Cl_4^-]$; other equilibria may intrude, such as solvation of both proton and ferric ion by ether:

$$H_3O^+ + C_4H_{10}O \rightleftharpoons C_4H_{10}OH^+ + H_2O$$

$$Fe(H_2O)_2Cl_4^- + 2\,C_4H_{10}O \rightleftharpoons Fe(C_4H_{10}O)_2Cl_4^- + 2\,H_2O$$

Thus under certain conditions the species in the ether phase may be $[C_4H_{10}OH^+, Fe(C_4H_{10}O)_2Cl_4^-]$. The system is undoubtedly complicated, and mixtures of various solvated ion pairs probably participate under the usual conditions of the extraction.

CRAIG PSEUDOCOUNTERCURRENT EXTRACTION

In an ideal separation by solvent extraction, all of the desired substance would end up in one solvent and all the interfering substances in the other. Such all-or-none transfer from one solvent to another is rare, and we are much more likely to encounter mixtures of substances that differ only somewhat in their tendencies to pass from one solvent into another. Thus one transfer does not lead to a clean separation. In such cases, we must consider how best to combine a number of successive partial separations until we eventually achieve the desired degree of purity.

In considering how two phases may be brought together repetitively, four levels of complexity may be distinguished.[1] First would be the simple, one-shot contact as mentioned above. Second, one phase could be brought repeatedly into contact with fresh portions of a second phase. This would be applicable where one substance remained quantitatively in one phase, while another substance was distributed between the two phases. An example might be repeated extraction of an aqueous solution with successive portions

[1] H. A. Laitinen, *Chemical Analysis*, McGraw-Hill Book Company, New York, 1960, p. 472.

of an organic solvent. The Soxhlet extractor would fall in this category, as would the technique of reprecipitation in gravimetric analysis.

Third, one phase may move while in contact with a second phase which remains stationary. The moving phase may move continuously, as in the various chromatographic techniques, or in a series of equilibrium steps, as in the Craig apparatus described below. Some techniques of this type have been designated "countercurrent," but this is not really the case, since only one phase moves. The term "pseudocountercurrent" is sometimes applied to such processes.

Fourth, we list true countercurrent methods, in which both phases move, continually in contact with each other, in opposite directions. Fractional distillation is an example of a true countercurrent process: Refluxing liquid runs continuously down the distilling column in contact with rising vapors. Countercurrent processes are extensively employed by chemical engineers in large-scale plant operations. Because of experimental difficulties as well as problems in the theoretical treatment, however, they are not nearly so common in the research laboratory as techniques in the third category.

In the brief treatment of this chapter, we shall be restricted to a thorough discussion of only the Craig pseudocountercurrent extraction process. As previously mentioned, this technique will be used as a model to aid our understanding of chromatographic processes in Chapter 14.

Basic Idea of the Craig Experiment

Consider an aqueous solution containing 1000 mg of some solute in a separatory funnel. Let it be a simple solute whose partition is uncomplicated by ionization, dimerization, etc. Add to the funnel an equal (for convenience) volume of an immiscible organic solvent. Also, for simplicity, suppose that the distribution coefficient of the solute is unity. Now, after equilibration, there will be 500 mg of the solute in the aqueous phase and 500 mg in the organic phase.

Next, take a second funnel and transfer the lighter liquid (say the organic phase) from the first funnel into it. Then add fresh aqueous solvent to this organic phase in the second funnel and add fresh organic phase to the first funnel. Now shake both funnels until equilibration is achieved. There will then be 250 mg of the solute in each layer in each funnel.

As the student probably suspects by now, we next secure a third funnel, and transfer the organic solution from the second funnel into the third and also introduce a fresh portion of the aqueous solvent. We replace the organic layer in the second funnel using the organic phase from the first one, and we add fresh organic phase to the latter. Then all three funnels are shaken to secure equilibrium.

After two or three transfers, it becomes easier to keep track of what is going on by introducing a simple schematic representation. Portions of aqueous and organic solvent are represented by boxes, and where an aqueous box adjoins an organic box we have equilibration of the phases. Within this box, we give the weight of solute present in that phase. Thus the first step is depicted as follows:

funnel 0

fresh org	fresh org	fresh org		
		1000 mg	fresh aq	fresh aq

The two phases in funnel 0 then equilibrate:

funnel 0

fresh org	fresh org	org 500 mg		
		aq 500 mg	fresh aq	fresh aq

In the second step noted above, we have performed one transfer ($n = 1$), and the resulting situation may be represented by:

funnel 0 funnel 1

fresh org	fresh org	500 mg		
	500 mg	fresh aq	fresh aq	fresh aq

Equilibration then takes place, giving:

funnel 0   funnel 1

fresh org	org 250 mg	org 250 mg		
	aq 250 mg	aq 250 mg	fresh aq	fresh aq

In effect, we are pushing the top row of boxes toward the right with each transfer.

For the third step, where n, the number of transfers, is 2, the resulting situation is

funnel 0 funnel 1 funnel 2

fresh org	fresh org	250 mg	250 mg		
	250 mg	250 mg	fresh aq	fresh aq	fresh aq

After equilibration the distribution is as follows:

funnel 0   funnel 1   funnel 2

...	fresh org	org 125 mg	org 250 mg	org 125 mg			...
...		aq 125 mg	aq 250 mg	aq 125 mg	fresh aq	fresh aq	...

Note that the number of funnels is one more than the number of transfers, and hence the first funnel is labeled number 0. Let us write diagrams for two more steps, after equilibration takes place: fourth step, $n = 3$

funnel 0   funnel 1   funnel 2   funnel 3

fresh org	org 62.5 mg	org 187.5 mg	org 187.5 mg	org 62.5 mg	
	aq 62.5 mg	aq 187.5 mg	aq 187.5 mg	aq 62.5 mg	fresh aq

fifth step, $n = 4$

	0	1	2	3	4	
	31.25	125	187.5	125	31.25	
	31.25	125	187.5	125	31.25	

Perhaps we have carried this far enough to see what is happening: As the number of transfers is increased, the solute spreads out through more and more funnels, but it is "bunching up" toward the center (because $K_D = 1$) and the fraction of the solute in the extreme funnels is decreasing.

It may also be surmised that for a different solute with a distribution coefficient, not 1, but favoring the aqueous phase, the peak concentration would not appear in the middle funnel but rather toward the left in our diagram. Likewise, a solute relatively more soluble in the organic layer would peak toward the right of the center.

Binomial Distribution in the Craig Extraction

Let us now formulate a more general mathematical treatment of the Craig countercurrent distribution. Actually, the mathematics is not difficult. In the first step of the treatment above, we distributed the solute between the two phases according to the distribution coefficient:

$$K_D = \frac{[\text{solute}]_{\text{org}}}{[\text{solute}]_{\text{aq}}}$$

If we started with weight W of solute, and weight w went over into the organic layer, then

$$K_D = \frac{w/V_{\text{org}}}{(W - w)/V_{\text{aq}}}$$

where V is the volume of the phase. To simplify, let the volumes be the same, so that

$$K_D = \frac{w}{W - w}$$

Rearranging and solving for W,

$$K_D W - K_D w = w$$

$$K_D W = K_D w + w$$

$$W = \frac{w + K_D w}{K_D} = \frac{w(1 + K_D)}{K_D}$$

Now the fraction of the solute in the organic phase, f_{org}, is given by

$$f_{\text{org}} = \frac{w}{W} = \frac{w}{w(1 + K_D)/K_D} = \frac{K_D}{1 + K_D}$$

Similarly, f_{aq} is

$$f_{\text{aq}} = \frac{W - w}{W} = \frac{\{w(1 + K_D)/K_D\} - w}{w(1 + K_D)/K_D} = 1 - \left\{ \frac{w K_D}{w(1 + K_D)} \right\} = \frac{1}{1 + K_D}$$

In the apparatus that Craig developed, and in the formulations encountered in the literature, the lighter phase (here, organic) is transferred from vessel 0 to vessel number 1. Fresh organic phase is then introduced into 0, and fresh aqueous phase into 1. After equilibration of the two vessels,

$$f_{\text{orgo}} = \left(\frac{1}{1 + K_D}\right)\left(\frac{K_D}{1 + K_D}\right)$$

(The fraction $1/1 + K_D$ was present in the aqueous layer in the vessel after the first equilibration, as shown above, and the fraction $K_D/1 + K_D$ passed over into the fresh organic solvent upon equilibration. Thus the product of the two fractions gives the fraction of the original W now present in the organic layer of vessel 0.) Likewise,

$$f_{\text{aqo}} = \left(\frac{1}{1 + K_D}\right)\left(\frac{1}{1 + K_D}\right)$$

(At the beginning of this step, the fraction $1/1 + K_D$ was present in the aqueous layer, as shown above, and the fraction $1/1 + K_D$ *of that* is what remains after equilibration with fresh organic phase.) Also,

$$f_{\text{org}_1} = \left(\frac{K_D}{1 + K_D}\right)\left(\frac{K_D}{1 + K_D}\right)$$

and

$$f_{\text{aq}_1} = \left(\frac{K_D}{1 + K_D}\right)\left(\frac{1}{1 + K_D}\right)$$

We have gone through these steps to make certain that the student understands what is happening. Actually, it is easier finally to consider the total solute in each vessel instead of focusing upon the two phases separately, although we may add what is in the two phases to get the total. Let us work this out for vessels 0, 1, and 2 where $n = 2$, including for practice all stages up to $n = 2$.

$n = 0$

$$f_0 = \left(\frac{K_D}{1 + K_D}\right) + \left(\frac{1}{1 + K_D}\right) = \frac{1 + K_D}{1 + K_D} = 1$$

$$\underset{\substack{\text{Organic} \\ \text{phase}}}{} \underset{\substack{\text{Aqueous} \\ \text{phase}}}{}$$

Since, where $n = 0$, all of the solute is in this vessel, the fraction contributed by the organic phase and the fraction in the aqueous phase must add up to 1.

$n = 1$

$$f_0 = \left(\frac{1}{1 + K_D}\right)\left(\frac{K_D}{1 + K_D}\right) + \left(\frac{1}{1 + K_D}\right)\left(\frac{1}{1 + K_D}\right) = \frac{1}{1 + K_D}$$

$$f_1 = \left(\frac{K_D}{1 + K_D}\right)\left(\frac{K_D}{1 + K_D}\right) + \left(\frac{K_D}{1 + K_D}\right)\left(\frac{1}{1 + K_D}\right) = \frac{K_D}{1 + K_D}$$

Here, $f_0 + f_1 = 1$, and we may confirm our result:

$$\frac{1}{1 + K_D} + \frac{K_D}{1 + K_D} = \frac{1 + K_D}{1 + K_D} = 1$$

$n = 2$

$$f_0 = \left(\frac{1}{1 + K_D}\right)\left(\frac{1}{1 + K_D}\right) = \left(\frac{1}{1 + K_D}\right)^2$$

$$f_1 = \left(\frac{1}{1 + K_D}\right)\left(\frac{K_D}{1 + K_D}\right) + \left(\frac{K_D}{1 + K_D}\right)\left(\frac{1}{1 + K_D}\right) = 2\left(\frac{1}{1 + K_D}\right)\left(\frac{K_D}{1 + K_D}\right)$$

$$f_2 = \left(\frac{K_D}{1 + K_D}\right)\left(\frac{K_D}{1 + K_D}\right) = \left(\frac{K_D}{1 + K_D}\right)^2$$

Now, examine the above fractions:

$$f_0 = \left(\frac{1}{1 + K_D}\right)^2$$

$$f_1 = 2\left(\frac{1}{1 + K_D}\right)\left(\frac{K_D}{1 + K_D}\right)$$

$$f_2 = \left(\frac{K_D}{1 + K_D}\right)^2$$

The alert student will note that these three terms are the terms in the expansion of the binomial

$$\left(\frac{1}{1 + K_D} + \frac{K_D}{1 + K_D}\right)^2$$

In general, for any number of transfers, n, it may be shown that the fractions of the total solute to be found in the various vessels $0, 1, 2, \ldots, n$ are given by the terms in the expression of the binomial

$$\left(\frac{1}{1 + K_D} + \frac{K_D}{1 + K_D}\right)^n$$

In working with the formulas above, we assumed equal volumes of the two phases. In general, where the volumes are not necessarily equal (but the same in all vessels), it may be shown that the fractions of solute in the various vessels are given by the terms in the expansion of the binomial

$$\left(\frac{1}{1 + E} + \frac{E}{1 + E}\right)^n$$

where

$$E = K_D \times \frac{V_{\text{upper}}}{V_{\text{lower}}}$$

and V_{upper} and V_{lower} are the volumes of upper and lower phases, respectively.

If n is not small, expansion of the binomial becomes tedious. Fortunately, mathematical tables are available where it is worked out. Any single term in the binomial expansion can be obtained directly, using the formula

$$f_{n,r} = \left(\frac{n!}{r!(n-r)!} \right) \left(\frac{1}{1+K_D} \right)^n K_D^r$$

where $f_{n,r}$ is the fraction of solute in the rth tube after n transfers. Some writers use the form

$$f_{n,r} = \frac{n! K_D^r}{r!(n-r)!(1+K_D)^n}$$

FIGURE 13.1 Theoretical distributions for solute with distribution coefficient $K_D = 1$ after various numbers of transfers (n) in a Craig experiment.

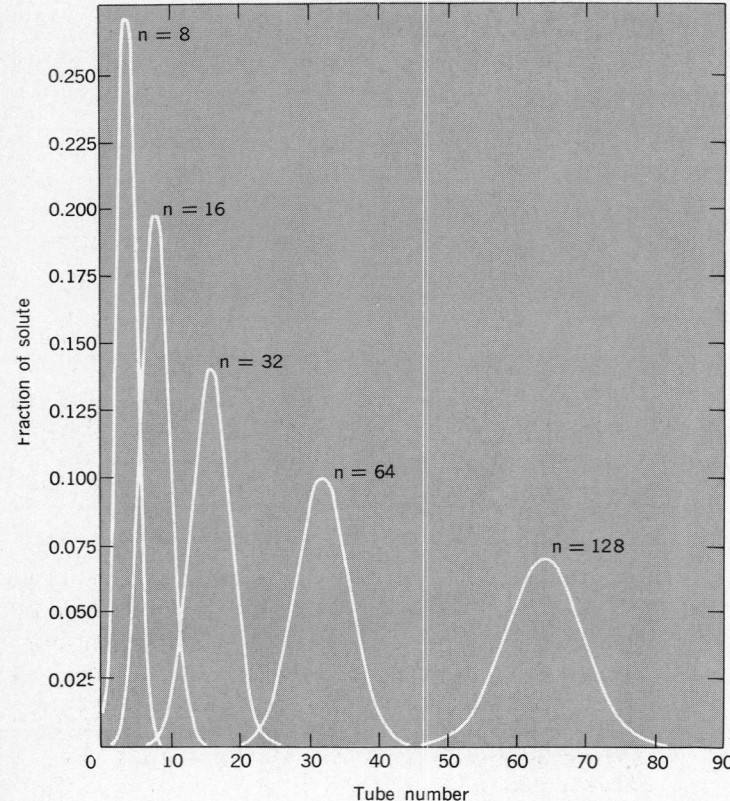

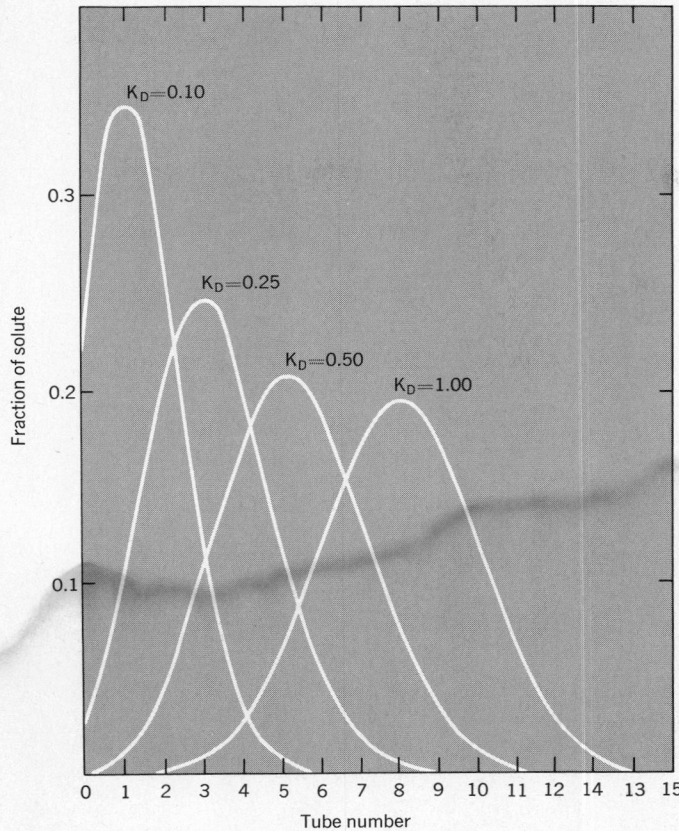

FIGURE 13.2 Theoretical distributions for various values of the distribution coefficient, K_D, in a 16-transfer Craig experiment.

During a series of successive transfers, a solute moves through the vessels of a Craig apparatus as a sort of wave of diminishing amplitude. The solute spreads through more and more vessels as n increases, but at the same time the fraction of the vessels which contain the solute decreases. Figure 13.1 shows theoretical distributions of solute for various numbers of transfers, n, for the case where $K_D = 1$ and $V_{org} = V_{aq}$.

For a given number of transfers, substances with different distribution coefficients are distributed differently. Figure 13.2 shows theoretical distributions after sixteen transfers for various values of the distribution coefficient. We see in the figure that solutes with different K_D values are beginning to separate after the particular number of transfers indicated, but that separation is not complete in any case. This means that for these solutes more stages would be required in order to obtain pure components in quantitative yield.

It may be seen from the mathematical treatment given above why it is said that a Craig distribution is a *binomial* one. (Other types commonly encountered are *Gaussian*, as we saw in Chapter 3 for the distribution of random errors, and Poisson distributions.) However, as the number of transfers increases, the binomial distribution approximates more and more closely the Gaussian. (Poisson distributions also tend to Gaussian as n increases.) When n becomes large, say 50, although there is no definite demarcation, a Gaussian treatment is sufficiently accurate for describing a Craig distribution, and it is more convenient than the more cumbersome binomial theorem for such cases. The approximate equations then are:

$$r_{max} = \frac{nK_D}{K_D + 1}$$

$$f_{max} = \frac{1}{\sqrt{2\pi n K_D/(1 + K_D)^2}}$$

$$f_x = f_{max} \times e^{-[x^2/[2nK_D/(1 + K_D)^2]]}$$

where r_{max} is the number of the tube containing the maximal quantity of the solute, f_{max} is the fraction of solute in this tube, f_x is the fraction of solute in a tube x tubes distant from r_{max}, and e is the base of natural logarithms. To use these equations for the case of unequal volumes of the two phases, simply replace K_D by E as defined earlier in the chapter.

Apparatus for Craig Extraction

For a large number of transfers, say 100 or 1000, manual operation with separatory funnels would be impossible in a practical sense. Craig, who expounded both the theory and practice of this type of extraction process, developed apparatus to take much of the labor out of the procedure. The typical Craig apparatus is based upon glass units shaped as shown in Fig. 13.3. Although most people think in terms of vigorous shaking to equilibrate two liquid phases, Craig showed that a gentle sloshing of one liquid over another was actually more effective; further, troublesome emulsions were often avoided by the less vigorous technique. Thus it was unnecessary to adhere to the usual separatory funnel shape when designing a more auto-mated apparatus. In the unit shown in Fig. 13.3, the two liquids are equilibrated by gently rocking the apparatus about twenty times, and the phases are allowed to separate. The apparatus is then rotated as indicated in the figure so that the cell is in a vertical position, whereupon the upper phase runs out of the equilibrium tube and into a temporary holding tube. Obviously the volume of the lower phase must be such that the solvent interface occurs at the level of the run-off side arm. When the cell is returned to a horizontal position, the lighter phase runs out of the holding tube and into the

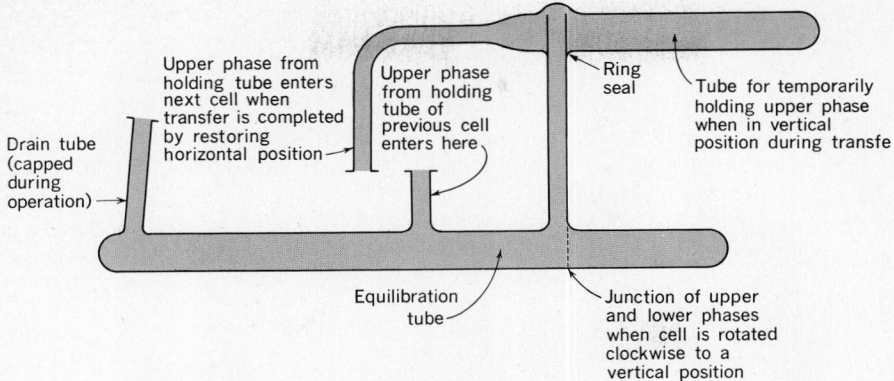

Upper phase from
holding tube enters
next cell when
transfer is completed
by restoring
horizontal position

Upper phase
from holding
tube of
previous cell
enters here

Ring
seal

Tube for temporarily
holding upper phase
when in vertical
position during transfe

Drain tube
(capped
during
operation)

Equilibration
tube

Junction of upper
and lower phases
when cell is rotated
clockwise to a
vertical position

FIGURE   13.3   Typical glass cell for Craig apparatus.

equilibration tube of the next cell in line. (The liquid is prevented from returning to the equilibration tube whence it came by the design of the cell in the
area labeled "ring seal" in the figure.)

A battery of cells is clamped firmly to a metal frame so that all may be
rocked and tilted together. The liquid-tight joints between adjacent cells are
held together by spring clamps. In practice, the lower phase is introduced
into all of the cells at the beginning of the experiment. The solute mixture
to be separated is placed in the first cell (number 0) in either phase. A solvent
reservoir and metering device introduces the appropriate volume of the
lighter phase into the first cell after each transfer. In the simpler instruments,
the rocking and tilting are done manually by the operator. Larger outfits
with as many as 1000 cells are operated by a motorized robot so that the
entire distribution experiment requires no attention once it is set in motion.
Two commercial Craig machines are shown in Figs. 13.4 and 13.5.

After the distribution has been completed, the bank of cells is tilted so
that the liquids in the cells may be collected from the drain tubes shown in
Fig. 13.3. If the experiment is a preparative one, the pooled solvents from
tubes containing the desired solute may be evaporated to obtain the desired
material. In an analytical run, the solutions from the individual cells may
be analyzed by appropriate means, for example, by spectrophotometry,
titrimetry, or measurement of refractive index.

Applications of Craig Extraction

Many of the applications of the Craig extraction process are found in the
biochemical area. It has proved particularly useful for separating peptides
in the molecular weight range of about 500 to 5000. Some antibiotics and
certain hormones are polypeptides, and several examples of successful
purification by the Craig method may be found. Crude tyrocidin from a
bacterial source was separated after 673 transfers into three major components (A, B, and C) and several minor ones; 1600 transfers on component A

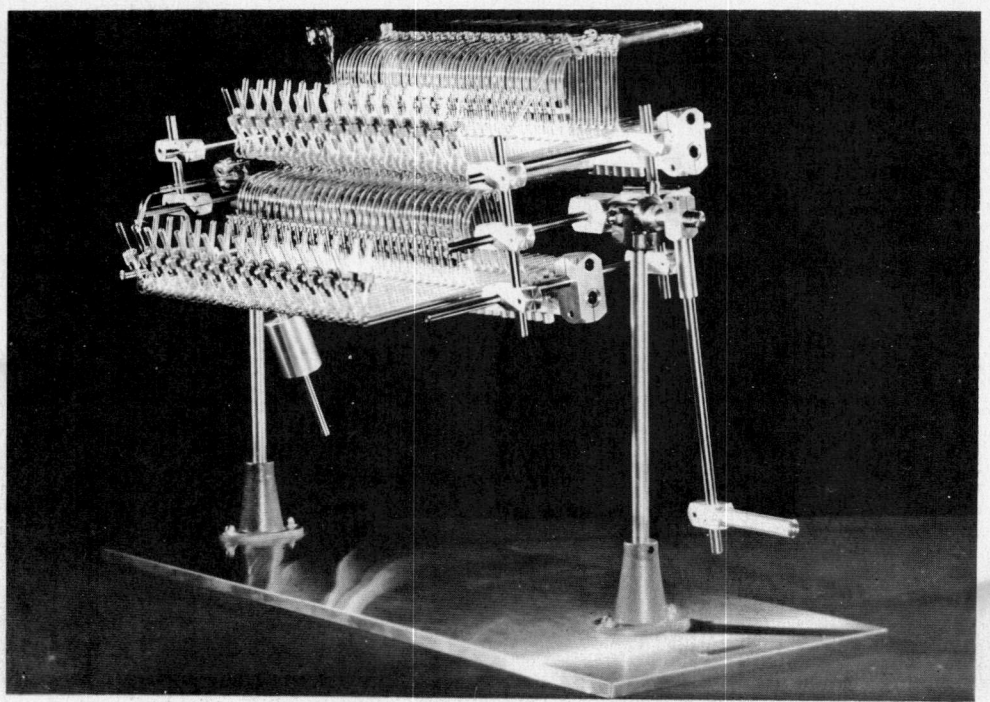

FIGURE 13.4 Manually operated 60-cell Craig Countercurrent Distribution Apparatus. The cells are arranged in two banks of thirty each. (Courtesy of H. O. Post Scientific Instrument Co., Inc.)

led to a crystallizable material, and 2140 more transfers eliminated the last trace of a particularly troublesome impurity. Peptide hormones from the posterior lobe of the pituitary gland have been fractionated by Craig extraction; distribution between 2-butanol and $0.1\text{-}M$ aqueous acetic acid was employed in the final purification of synthetic oxytocin and in comparing this product with the naturally occurring hormone, and similar work was done on vasopressin. Craig distribution has been employed for isolating and characterizing ACTH (adrenocorticotrophic hormone) from the anterior pituitary. Although proteins present many difficulties, some have been successfully handled by the Craig technique, notably insulin, ribonuclease, lysozyme, and the serum albumins. The technique is used for purification of many pharmaceutical preparations. Chemists other than biochemists have been slow to adopt the technique. Only a few inorganic applications appear in the literature.

Craig Extraction as a Model
for Continuous Separation Processes

In the Craig extraction experiment, the heavier liquid phase remains stationary, while the lighter phase is transported down the series of cells,

FIGURE 13.5   1000-Cell Craig Countercurrent Distribution Instrument for automatic operation. The instrument can also be operated as two 500-cell units running concurrently. Driving mechanism is on the right-hand side under the table, with a driving shaft extending through the table top to the instrument. The unit is enclosed in a fume hood with glass doors and removable sides and top to afford access. (Courtesy of H. O. Post Scientific Instrument Co., Inc.)

carrying solutes with it to various extents in accord with their partition properties. In chromatography, which we shall consider in Chapter 14, there is likewise a stationary and a moving phase (not necessarily both liquid). But here the moving phase flows continuously, and equilibrium is not actually attained at any time during the experiment. This leads to great difficulty in formulating the separation process mathematically, and the difficulty appears in the form of complicated equations with many correction factors and adjustable parameters. It is easy for the student to lose sight of what is going on in such processes. In the Craig experiment, on the other hand, the intermittent flow of the moving phase permits equilibration in each step of the overall process, and as we have seen above, the theoretical treatment is not unusually difficult. The Craig extraction process then, while it is by no means real chromatography, is useful as a teaching tool in explaining chromatography to beginners. We shall try to show the similarities and differences in more detail in the next chapter.

H. IRVING and R. J. P. WILLIAMS, "Liquid-Liquid Extraction," Chapter 31, Part 1, Vol. 3, p. 1309, of *Treatise on Analytical Chemistry*, I. M. Kolthoff and P. J. Elving, eds., Interscience Publishers, Inc., New York, 1961.

D. DYRSSEN, J. O. LILJENZIN, and J. RYDBERG, eds., *Solvent Extraction Chemistry*, Interscience Publishers Division of John Wiley & Sons, Inc., New York, 1967.

G. H. MORRISON and H. FREISER, *Solvent Extraction in Analytical Chemistry*, John Wiley & Sons, Inc., New York, 1957.

J. STARY, *The Solvent Extraction of Metal Chelates*, The Macmillan Co., New York, 1964.

C. J. O. R. MORRIS and P. MORRIS, *Separation Methods in Biochemistry*, Interscience Publishers, Inc., New York, 1963.

QUESTIONS

1. Distinguish between the distribution coefficient and distribution ratio.

2. Consider a substance which does not behave in a simple fashion, but rather participates in equilibria such as dissociation or dimerization, so that its distribution between two liquid phases is not adequately described by a K_D value. We might then employ a distribution ratio, D, in describing its behavior in a Craig experiment. If D were not independent of the analytical concentration of the substance (Why might it not be?), what would be the effect upon the shape of the Craig distribution curve?

3. Suppose you wish to extract an organic compound from water using 100 ml of ether. You are told to perform the extraction in one of the following ways: (a) Do a single extraction using the 100-ml portion of ether, or (b) Divide the ether into two 50-ml portions and perform two successive extractions. Which method should you use to obtain the larger amount of the desired compound? Explain

4. Expansion of the binomial $(x + y)^4$ gives

$$x^4 + 4x^3y + 6x^2y^2 + 4xy^3 + y^4$$

Assume that these terms represent the fractions of solute in tubes 0, 1, 2, 3, and 4 of a Craig extraction experiment where $x = y = \frac{1}{2}$. Show that this expression gives the same fraction of solute in tube $2(6x^2y^2)$ as the expression on page 374 for $n = 4$ and $r = 2$. Recall that $K_D = 1$.

5. The stability constants of complex ions can be determined by a solvent extraction method. A chelating agent is employed and the distribution ratio D is determined as a function of the concentration of the complexing agent in the aqueous phase. Consider a metal ion, M^{2+}, which forms a chelate MT_2 with HT, and a complex ion MX^+ with X^-. Derive an expression relating the distribution ratio to the concentration of X^-, involving the stability constant K_s, for the reaction

$$M^{2+} + X^- \rightleftharpoons MX^+$$

You can assume that MT_2 is the only metal-containing species in the organic phase and that it exists predominantly in that phase. Also assume that no appreciable complexing occurs between M^{2+} and HT in the aqueous phase.

6. Repeat Question 5, except that the complexing agent is HX, rather than X^-. That is, the constant desired is for the reaction

$$M^{2+} + HX \rightleftharpoons MX^+ + H^+$$

1. *Solvent extraction.* The distribution ratio (organic/aqueous) for the extraction of solute A from water into ether is 10.0. (a) If 100 ml of water containing 1.00 g of A is shaken with 100 ml of ether, what percentage of A is extracted into ether? (b) If the aqueous phase is extracted twice with 50-ml portions of ether, what percentage of A is extracted?

2. *Distribution ratio.* 100 ml of a solution which is 0.100-F in the weak acid HA is extracted with 25.0 ml of ether. After the extraction a 25.0-ml aliquot of the aqueous phase required 20.0 ml of 0.0500-M NaOH for titration. Calculate the distribution ratio of HA, organic to aqueous.

3. *Solvent extraction.* The distribution ratio of iodine between an organic solvent and water is 8.00. If 50.0 ml of 0.100-M aqueous iodine is shaken with 100 ml of this organic solvent until equilibrium is reached, how many milliliters of 0.0600-M $Na_2S_2O_3$ are required to titrate a 10.0-ml aliquot of the organic phase?

4. *Distribution ratio.* When an aqueous solution of ferric chloride in HCl is shaken with twice its volume of ether containing HCl, 99 % of the iron is extracted. Calculate the distribution ratio (organic to aqueous) of the compound.

5. *Craig extraction.* The distribution coefficient for the extraction of solute A from water into an organic solvent is 10 (organic/aqueous). 1.00 g of A is dissolved in water and placed in tube 0 of a Craig extraction apparatus and extracted with the organic solvent. The organic phase is transferred from tube 0 to tube 1, and so on. (a) Calculate the fraction of A remaining in tube 0 after five transfers. (b) Calculate the fraction of A in tubes 1, 2, 3, 4, and 5.

6. *Craig extraction.* Repeat Problem 5 except that the value of K_D is 100.

7. *Distribution ratio.* Two extractions with 20-ml portions of an organic solvent removed 89 % of a solute from 100 ml of an aqueous solution. Calculate the distribution ratio (organic/aqueous) of the solute.

8. *Extraction of a metal chelate.* A chelating agent, HT, dissolved in an organic solvent extracts a metal, M^{2+}, from an aqueous solution according to the reaction

$$M^{2+}(aq) + 2\,HT(org) \rightleftharpoons MT_2(org) + 2\,H^+(aq)$$

The equilibrium constant for this reaction is 0.010. (a) Identify this equilibrium constant in terms of other constants (page 365). (b) Calculate the pH values at which 1, 25, 50, 75, and 99.9 % of the metal is extracted into the organic phase. 10 ml of the aqueous solution is shaken with 10 ml of a 0.010-M solution of HT. Assume that the concentration of the metal is so small that the concentration of HT in the aqueous phase is negligible. (c) Plot the results, percent extracted vs pH.

9. *Extraction of a metal chelate.* Repeat Problem 8 for a metal, N^{2+}, where the K of the extraction reaction is 1.0×10^{-6}. Suggest a pH at which metals M^{2+} and N^{2+} could be separated quantitatively by solvent extraction.

10. *Extraction of a metal chelate.* A certain metal ion is extracted by a chelating agent as in Problems 8 and 9. The concentration of the chelating agent in the organic phase is 0.010-M. The following data are obtained:

pH	1	2	3	4	5
D	10^{-8}	10^{-4}	1	10^4	10^8

Make a plot of log D vs pH (page 366) and evaluate n and K.

11. *Separation of acids.* Given two acids, HA and HB, with the following distribution coefficients and dissociation constants:

	K_D	K_a
HA	10	1×10^{-5}
HB	1000	1×10^{-10}

Calculate the distribution ratios of the two acids at pH values 4, 5, 6, 7, 8, 9, and 10. Assuming that the ratio of the two D's needs to be 10^6 to 1 for a quantitative extraction of HB without extracting HA appreciably, what is the lowest pH (roughly) at which such a separation can be accomplished?

12. *Acid dissociation constant.* An acid, HX, has a distribution ratio of 10 between an organic solvent and water. At pH 5.0, half of the acid is extracted into the organic solvent. Calculate the dissociation constant of HX.

14

Gas-Liquid Chromatography

INTRODUCTION

The resolution of mixtures into their components is important in all of the branches of chemistry and no less so in the many other fields where chemical techniques are employed in solving a wide variety of problems. Thus the impact of a powerful and versatile separation technique will be felt throughout much of modern science. In this connection, the significance of chromatography can scarcely be overstated. Utilizing chromatographic methods, separations in many cases are accomplished much more rapidly and effectively than before, and many separations are routinely successful which would never have been attempted by other techniques. Unparalleled breakthroughs in biochemistry—for example, in our understanding of the structure and function of enzymes and other proteins—have stemmed directly from the application of chromatography to biological research. Evaluating air and water pollution, determining pesticide residues on fruits and vegetables, identifying and classifying bacteria, monitoring respiratory gases during anesthesia, searching for organic compounds and living organisms on other planets, determining metabolic pathways and mechanisms of action of drugs —a list of all such studies based upon chromatography would be a lengthy one indeed.

Although forerunners can be found in the nineteenth century, it is generally considered that a paper published in 1906 by Michael Tswett, a lecturer in botany at the University of Warsaw, provided the first description in nearly modern terms of a chromatographic separation.[1] Tswett described the

[1] M. Tswett, *Ber. Deut. Botan. Ges.*, **24**, 235 (1906).

383

resolution of the chlorophylls and other pigments in a plant extract as follows:

> If a petroleum ether solution of [crude] chlorophyll is filtered through a column of adsorbent (I use mainly calcium carbonate which is packed firmly into a narrow glass tube), then the pigments are resolved from top to bottom into various colored zones according to an adsorption sequence, where the more strongly adsorbed pigments displace the more weakly adsorbed ones and force them further downward. This separation becomes practically complete if, following the pigment solution, a stream of pure solvent is passed through the column. Like a spectrum of light rays, the different components of the pigment mixture are systematically resolved on the calcium carbonate column and can be identified and also determined quantitatively. Such a preparation I term a chromatogram, and the corresponding method the chromatographic method.

Although the term chromatography is derived from Greek words meaning "color" and "write," the color of the compounds is obviously incidental to the separation process; Tswett himself anticipated applications to a wide variety of chemical systems. Had his work been immediately seized upon and extended, several sciences might have progressed more rapidly. As it was, chromatography remained dormant until about 1931, when separations of plant carotene pigments were reported by the prominent organic chemist Kuhn. This research attracted more attention, and adsorption chromatography became widely used in the field of natural product chemistry.

More recently, there have been four major developments: ion-exchange chromatography in the late 1930s, partition chromatography in 1941, gas chromatography in 1952, and gel-filtration chromatography in 1959. In addition to these major advances, which provided additional mechanisms to adsorption for distributing solutes between stationary and mobile phases, there have also appeared modifications in the geometry of the chromatographic system, as in paper and thin-layer chromatography.

Theoretical developments which permit a thorough understanding of the chromatographic process and hence clarify the factors which determine column performance appeared first in connection with gas chromatography. But certain of these insights have proved, with suitable adjustments, to be equally helpful in understanding chromatography where the moving phase is a liquid. Thus there began about 1968 a revolution in liquid chromatography which promises new speed and efficiency in the separation of nonvolatile compounds which do not lend themselves to the gas chromatographic approach.

Because of its great practical importance in many research areas, chromatography is a fast-moving field. Efforts continue along many lines, of which we may mention a few: better detectors, new column-packing materials, improved interfacing with other instruments (such as the mass spectrometer) which serves to identify the separated components, new data processing techniques based upon computers, and new mathematical models which provide additional insight into the nature of the process. Our goal in this book is to present a basic introduction which will acquaint the student with the nature of the chromatographic process, explain in simple terms what the instruments fundamentally do, and show some of the applications which have made chromatography indispensible in so many fields.

DEFINITION AND CLASSIFICATION OF CHROMATOGRAPHY

Although the meaning of the term is largely understood by chemists, a good definition of chromatography is difficult to formulate. It is a collective term applied to methods which appear diverse in some regards but share certain common features. A definition should emphasize that components of the sample are distributed between two phases, but this alone is inadequate because we do not wish the term to embrace all separation processes. Keulemans' definition serves as well as any:

> Chromatography is a physical method of separation, in which the components to be separated are distributed between two phases, one of these phases constituting a stationary bed of large surface area, the other being a fluid that percolates through or along the stationary bed.[2]

The stationary phase may be either a solid or a liquid, and the moving phase may be either a liquid or a gas. Thus all of the known types of chromatography fall into the four categories that are shown in Table 14.1, viz., liquid-solid, gas-solid, liquid-liquid, and gas-liquid.

TABLE 14.1   SUMMARY OF TYPES OF CHROMATOGRAPHY

Stationary Phase	Solid		Liquid	
Moving Phase	Liquid	Gas	Liquid	Gas
Examples	Tswett's original chromatography with petroleum ether solutions and $CaCO_3$ columns. Ion-exchange chromatography.	Gas-solid chromatography or GSC.	Partition chromatography on silica gel columns. Paper chromatography.	Gas-liquid chromatography or GLC.

In all of the chromatographic techniques, the solutes to be separated migrate along a column (or, as in paper or thin-layer chromatography, the

[2] A. I. M. Keulemans, *Gas Chromatography*, 2nd ed., Reinhold Publishing Corp., New York, 1959, p. 2.

physical equivalent of a column), and of course the basis of the separation lies in different rates of migration for the different solutes. We may think of the rate of migration of a solute as the result of two factors, one tending to move the solute and the other to retard it. In Tswett's original process, the tendency of solutes to adsorb on the solid phase retarded their movement, while their solubility in the moving liquid phase tended to move them along. A slight difference between two solutes in the firmness of their adsorption and in their interaction with the moving solvent becomes the basis of a separation when the solute molecules repeatedly distribute between the two phases over and over again throughout the length of the column.

In this chapter we consider gas-liquid chromatography or GLC, by far the more important form of gas chromatography. In the next chapter, we shall describe chromatographic techniques where the moving phase is a liquid.

BASIC APPARATUS FOR GLC

To orient readers who are totally unfamiliar with gas chromatography, we shall first describe the apparatus and technique of GLC briefly and in general terms. Then we shall consider the theory, next indicate more fully the functions of the components of the apparatus, and finally give some illustrative applications which show the power and versatility of the method.

Figure 14.1 is a schematic diagram of a common type of basic GLC instrument. Although gas chromatographs can become very complicated if additional features are included, the basic instrument is a fairly simple one. The moving phase in GLC is a gas, most commonly helium, hydrogen, or nitrogen. The choice of carrier gas depends primarily upon the characteristics of the detector, as we shall see later. The user buys a cylinder of the compressed gas and attaches his own reducing value to it. Commercial gas chromatographs usually provide an additional regulating valve for good control of the pressure at the inlet of the column. With instruments of the type shown, employing the thermal conductivity detector, the carrier gas passes through one side of the detector and then enters the column. Near the column inlet is a device whereby samples may be introduced into the carrier gas stream. The samples may be gases or volatile liquids. The injection port is heated so that liquid samples are quickly vaporized. Samples of a few microliters of liquid or a few milliliters of gas are commonly introduced through a rubber septum by means of a hypodermic syringe.

The gas stream next encounters the column, which is mounted in a constant-temperature oven. This is the heart of the instrument, the place where the basic chromatographic process takes place. Columns vary widely in size and packing material. A common size is 6 feet long and $\frac{1}{4}$ inch internal diameter, made of copper or stainless steel tubing; to save space, it may be U-shaped or coiled into a spiral. The tubing is packed with a relatively inert, pulverized solid material of large surface area, frequently diatomaceous

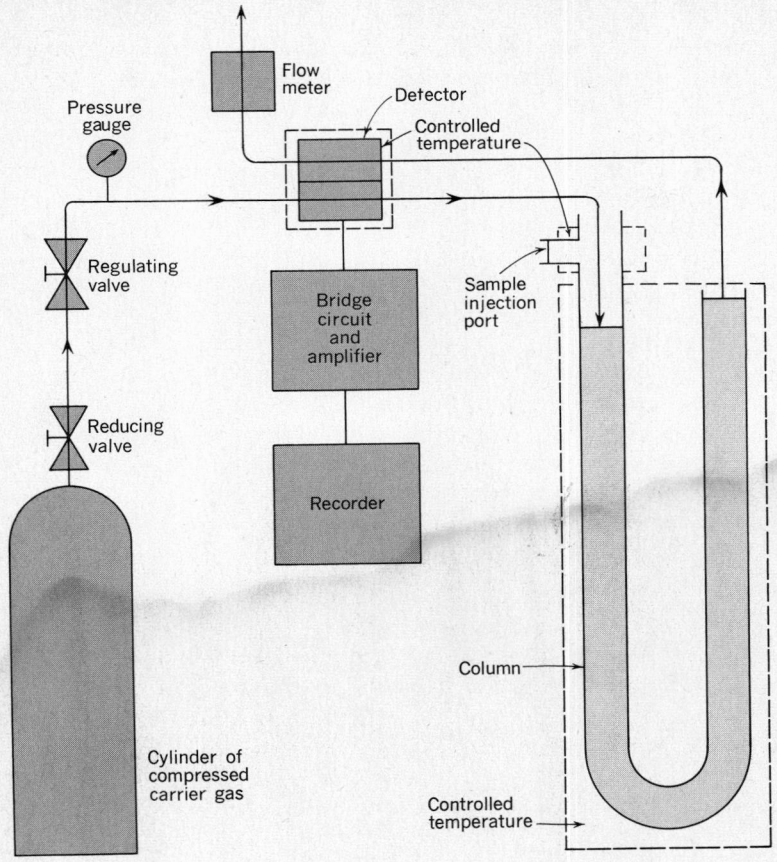

FIGURE 14.1 Schematic diagram of a gas chromatograph with thermal conductivity detector. Large arrows indicate direction of gas flow.

earth or firebrick. The solid, however, is actually only a mechanical support for a liquid; before it is packed into the column, it is impregnated with the desired liquid which serves as the real stationary phase. This liquid must be stable and nonvolatile at the temperature of the column, and it must be appropriate for the particular separation.

After emerging from the column, the gas stream passes through the other side of the detector. Elution of a solute from the column thus sets up an imbalance between the two sides of the detector which is recorded electrically. The carrier gas flow rate is important, and usually a flow meter of some sort is provided. There may be another regulating valve at the outlet end of the system, although normally the emerging gases are vented at atmospheric pressure. Because continual exposure of laboratory workers to the vapors of chromatographed compounds may be unwise even though the samples are usually small, attention should be paid to ventilation at the outlet of the instrument. Provision can be made to trap separated solutes as they emerge from the column if this is required for further investigation.

THEORY OF GLC

The Theoretical Plate Concept

It is suggested that the reader review the Craig countercurrent solvent extraction distribution in Chapter 13; we shall approach GLC in essentially the same manner. Suppose we have a series of small chambers as shown in Fig. 14.2, each containing a portion of a nonvolatile liquid which serves as the stationary phase. Let us introduce into the first chamber a sample of the mobile phase, a gas such as nitrogen, containing vapor of an organic compound, say benzene. If the liquid is a suitable one for our purpose, some of the benzene will dissolve in it, and some will remain in the space above it. Now Henry's law, in its usual form, states that the partial pressure exerted by a solute in dilute solution is proportional to its mole fraction. Thus, for the equilibrium distribution of benzene between liquid and vapor phases in our chamber, we may write:

$$p_{\text{benzene}} = kX_{\text{benzene}}$$

where p_{benzene} is the partial pressure of benzene in the vapor phase, X_{benzene} is the mole fraction of benzene in the liquid, and k is a constant. In gas chromatography, partial pressure and mole fraction are often replaced by concentration terms which yield a dimensionless *distribution coefficient, K*:

$$K = \frac{\text{Concentration of benzene in liquid phase, wt/ml}}{\text{Concentration of benzene in gas phase, wt/ml}} = \frac{C_L}{C_G}$$

It is customary for the liquid term to be the numerator. K is also called a *partition coefficient* by many writers.

FIGURE 14.2   Imaginary chambers for a Craig model of a GLC experiment.

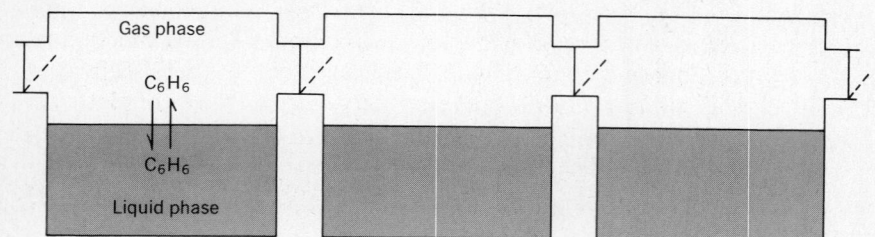

Now let us perform the same sort of operation that we employed in the Craig extraction. Transfer the gas (nitrogen plus benzene vapor) from the first chamber into the second one, where it encounters fresh liquid that contains no benzene. Introduce fresh nitrogen containing no benzene into the first chamber. Wait until equilibrium has been established in both chambers. Then transfer the gas from the second chamber into the third and from the first into the second, and introduce fresh nitrogen into the first. As the transfers proceed, the benzene will become distributed through the chambers in the same manner as a solute in the Craig solvent extraction system, illustrated in Fig. 13.1. The position of the benzene band on the horizontal axis will depend upon the number of transfers, the value of K, and the relative volumes of vapor and liquid in the individual chambers (cf. discussion accompanying Fig. 13.1). Just as we saw in the Craig experiment, a second compound, say toluene, could be separated from benzene in this gas-liquid system if the K values for the two compounds were different, provided sufficient stages were employed (cf. Fig. 13.2). After a large number of transfers, the binomial distribution will become virtually the symmetrical Gaussian one.

There is a major difference in practice between Craig solvent extraction and chromatography which should be pointed out, although it is not important with regard to the principle involved. With the Craig apparatus, it is customary to stop when the desired separation has been achieved and drain the solutions from the tubes containing the solutes. In modern chromatography, on the other hand, the flow of the mobile phase is continued until the solutes have migrated the entire length of the column whence they emerge, one after the other, to enter the detector. The practice of terminating the Craig process as soon as possible simply reflects the more cumbersome nature of the apparatus and the time-consuming character of the process.

The equilibrium chambers in the apparatus described above are called *theoretical plates*, a term which originated in distillation theory and was later carried over into chromatography. Each cell in the Craig apparatus is a plate in this sense. Now a chromatographic column operates under conditions of continuous flow of the moving phase, and equilibrium is not attained at any point in the column. However, after traversing a certain length of column, a mixture will have been subjected to the same degree of fractionation as would have been achieved in one equilibrium step. That length of column which accomplishes this is called the *height equivalent of a theoretical plate* or HETP. The total length of a column divided by HETP is the number, n, of theoretical plates in the column,[3] and it is customary to rate column performance in terms of number of plates. A good column will have more plates than a poor column of the same length. The great efficiency of GLC for performing difficult separations lies in the fact that large numbers of plates are

[3] The reader should note that n in this chapter is the number of *plates*, while in Chapter 13, n was the number of *transfers* in the Craig solvent extraction experiment. Sometimes our goal of avoiding confusion in the use of symbols conflicts with our desire to conform to the commonest usage as found elsewhere in the literature.

fairly easily obtained with columns of reasonable length; columns with a couple of thousand plates may be only five or six feet long. (To give an idea of the power of the chromatographic technique, it may be noted that columns for fractional distillation are likewise rated in terms of theoretical plates; a fairly good 6-ft conventional distilling column may have something of the order of twenty or thirty plates.[4])

In gas chromatography, samples are injected as rapidly as possible, so that a substance is placed on the column as a narrow "plug." However, just as in the Craig extraction technique, when the substance moves along it spreads out through more and more plates but occupies a progressively smaller fraction of the total number of plates which it has encountered. In other words, as we increase the number of plates, the absolute width of the elution band increases, but there is a decrease in width relative to the total base of the operation. In this perspective, elution bands look narrow as they emerge from a good column, broad from a poor column.

Calculation of the Number of Theoretical Plates

It is often desirable to evaluate a chromatographic column by measuring n, the number of theoretical plates. With a Craig apparatus, the plates may simply be counted. But this cannot be done with a column, because the plates are now imaginary; a theoretical plate is a mental concept, part of a model developed to explain the chromatographic process in familiar terms. We can determine the apparent number of plates, however, because the model implies a relationship between the characteristics of a chromatographic elution band and the number of plates in the column. The mathematical derivation of an equation for calculating n from a chromatogram is beyond the scope of this book,[5] but the general idea is intuitively reasonable, and the result is a very simple formula. In the Craig extraction scheme, we were able to calculate how a solute distributed itself through a known number of tubes. We may readily imagine that, if we had known instead the characteristics of the distribution, we might have turned our thinking around and calculated the number of tubes. Similarly, as implied in the preceding paragraph, the time required to elute a solute from a column and the width of the elution band should enable us to calculate n.

Figure 14.3 shows a Gaussian elution band and the parameters which are used to calculate n. The time from injection of the sample to the appearance of

---

[4] The direct comparison of numbers of plates in distillation and chromatography is not quite fair unless it is qualified as follows. In a fractional distillation, all of the plates in the column are utilized throughout the experiment. In chromatography, on the other hand, after the sample components have migrated along the column, that portion of the column already traversed might just as well not be there any longer. Thus chromatography basically requires more plates than distillation. But these plates are so readily obtained that, even taking this factor into account, chromatographic columns are ordinarily far more efficient than distilling columns.

[5] The interested reader may find a derivation in O. E. Schupp, III, *Gas Chromatography*, Vol. 13 of E. S. Perry and A. Weissberger, eds., *Technique of Organic Chemistry*, Interscience Publishers Division of John Wiley & Sons, Inc., New York, 1968, pp. 39–46.

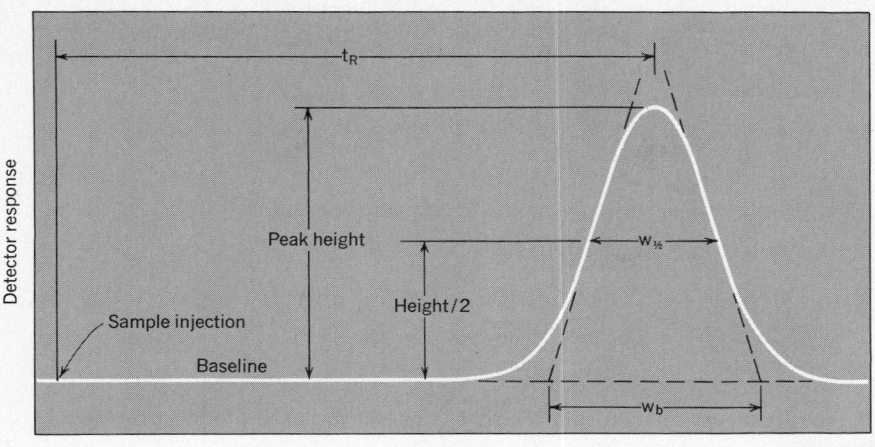

FIGURE 14.3 Chromatographic elution band showing measurement of t_R and w for estimating n, the number of theoretical plates.

the peak of the elution band at the detector is called the *retention time*, t_R. The formula for calculating n from t_R and the bandwidth depends upon where the width is measured. The two commonest ways are given here. If the width is measured halfway between the baseline and the top of the band, we may designate it as $w_{1/2}$. Then the formula for obtaining n is:

$$n = 5.54\left(\frac{t_R}{w_{1/2}}\right)^2$$

If the width is measured at the baseline using the construction shown in the figure, we designate it w_b; the formula then becomes:

$$n = 16\left(\frac{t_R}{w_b}\right)^2$$

In the latter case, tangents to the band are drawn at the two inflection points; the width, w_b, is the distance between the intersections of these tangents with the baseline. The two formulas give comparable results, and the choice is a matter of personal preference. Although there may be some difficulty in locating accurately the inflection points of an elution band, the slopes of the tangents are not highly sensitive to this error.

If a mixture of several compounds with different K values is injected into the chromatograph, then of course several elution bands will be recorded. These will show different retention times, but the bandwidths will also be different; thus comparable (although probably not identical) n values will be calculated from the several bands. A component with a larger K value will spend more time in the liquid phase and hence take longer to be eluted. Referring to a Craig type of model with discrete plates, we should say that more transfers would be required to elute such a compound. But the band is also broadened thereby, so that theoretically the n value should be the same as that obtained for an earlier band.

For the purpose of determining n, the units for the abscissa in Fig. 14.3 make no difference. Thus, although t_R is defined as a time, we may actually measure distances on the recorder chart paper in centimeters or millimeters; of course, t_R and w must be measured in the same units.

The number of plates in a given column is found to vary with sample size in a fairly regular way. Overloading of any column leads to a deterioration of performance and poor separations. To obtain a value for n, sometimes extrapolation to zero sample size is performed on a graph of measured n-values vs sample size.

Nonideal Behavior:
The van Deemter Equation

GLC as Linear Nonideal Chromatography

The plate model based upon a Craig type of solute distribution between gas and liquid phases, with equilibrium attained prior to each transfer from one plate to the next, represents what is sometimes called *linear ideal chromatography*. Linear in this connection means that the distribution coefficient, K, is independent of solute concentration; thus a graph of concentration in the liquid phase vs concentration in the gas phase is a straight line (Fig. 14.4, curve 1a). Such a graph is often called an *isotherm*. In general, a linear isotherm leads to a symmetrical elution band as shown by curve 1b in Fig. 14.4. A departure from Henry's law behavior, shown by a nonlinear isotherm

FIGURE 14.4 Linear and nonlinear isotherms (a) and the shapes of the corresponding elution bands (b).

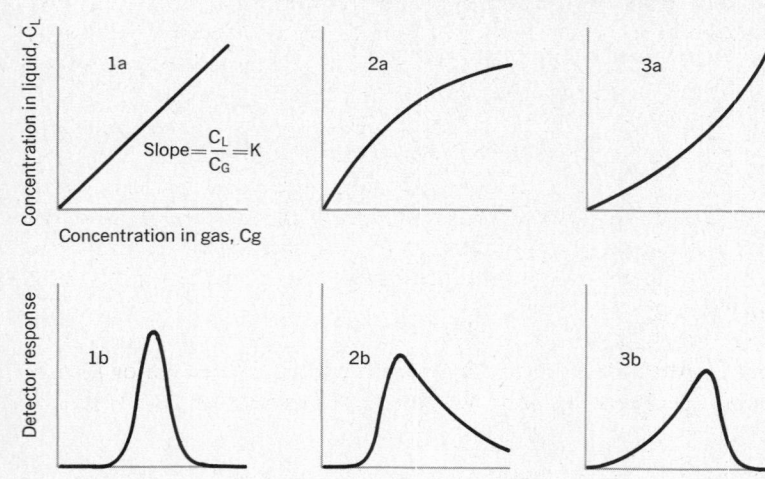

(Fig. 14.4, curves 2a and 3a), leads to a skewed elution band (Fig. 14.4, curves 2b and 3b). Referring to curves 2a and 2b, we may interpret the asymmetric elution band as follows: Where the solute concentration is high, a greater fraction of solute remains in the gas phase than is the case at lower concentrations. As a result, solute at the peak will move faster through the column, and hence the peak will tend to catch up to the leading edge of the elution band and leave a long tail at the trailing edge.

Nonlinear isotherms of the type shown in Fig. 14.4, curve 2a, are common in adsorption equilibria, and thus skewed elution bands with tailing as shown in curve 2b are often encountered in gas-solid chromatography and in liquid adsorption chromatography. At the low concentrations normally employed in GLC, deviations from Henry's law do not generally occur, and thus GLC commonly provides an example of linear chromatography.

Ideal behavior, on the other hand, is not attainable in any actual chromatographic process. First, ideality would require that the sample be placed initially in only the first plate. This can be done in the Craig apparatus, but in a column, where HETP may be only a fraction of a millimeter, it is impossible with a finite sample. Second, ideal chromatography would require a column whose packing was perfectly uniform in regard to particle size and shape, liquid loading, and geometric array; further, the velocity of the moving phase would have to be the same everywhere in the column. Third, in ideal chromatography, equilibrium would always exist at all points in the column between the stationary and moving phases with regard to the solute distribution; because the flow of the moving phase is continuous, this means that equilibration would have to be instantaneous. Finally, ideal chromatography would require that the solute move along the column as a result only of the motion of the moving phase; that is to say, the solute could not spread out in the column by its own tendency to diffuse.

Thus, under the usual conditions, GLC provides an example of *linear nonideal chromatography*. Departures from the requirements for the ideal process as listed in the paragraph above result in elution bands which are broader than the hypothetical bands for an ideal case. A detailed theoretical consideration of the kinetic factors which lead to this band broadening has given considerable insight into the nature of the chromatographic process in real columns. Not only has this been intellectually satisfying; practical improvements have resulted in terms of better separations in less time, and these have spilled over from GLC to revitalize liquid chromatography as well. A mathematical analysis of chromatographic theory is far beyond the scope of this text, but the principal factors are understandable in qualitative terms. We may summarize these for what insights they provide and leave the details to the experts.

The pioneering treatment of nonideal behavior in GLC was presented in 1956 by van Deemter et al.[6] These workers considered three major factors that caused band broadening when a solute, initially a narrow plug, migrated

[6] J. J. van Deemter, E. J. Zuiderwig, and A. Klinkenberg, *Chem. Eng. Sci.*, **5**, 271 (1956).

along a column. An equation was derived containing three terms which represented the contributions of these three factors to HETP.

Eddy Diffusion

The first factor, which is usually called eddy diffusion, arises from the multiplicity of pathways for a gas flowing through a column which is packed with particles of various sizes and shapes arranged in an irregular manner. As it flows through the channels among the packing particles, the carrier gas divides into many streams which may merge and again split in a complex manner as the gas follows a myriad of routes through the column. Likewise, solute molecules, as they move along with the flowing carrier gas, will follow many paths, some shorter and some longer than the average distance. This means that the original solute plug will spread out, some molecules reaching the detector sooner, some later, with many at an average time. The magnitude of the contribution of eddy diffusion to band broadening ought to depend upon the size of the packing particles, their shape, and the uniformity of their distribution in the column.

There has been some dispute about the importance of eddy diffusion which appears now to be settled. Perhaps this factor was more severe with the column packing materials and techniques of the earlier years of GLC. Measurements with very carefully packed columns have suggested that it is less important than early workers supposed. Apparently, in a good column most of the pathways actually followed by the gas are about the same length. Also, it has been proposed that lateral diffusion of solute from one portion of the gas stream to an adjacent one might counter the effect of eddy diffusion upon the solute profile. Furthermore, it appears that some of the band broadening formerly attributed to eddy diffusion actually occurred outside the column, for example in the glass wool that was sometimes used to plug the end of the column, in the tubing that led from the column to the detector, and in the detector itself. It now seems clear that eddy diffusion may be only a very small factor in a well-designed gas chromatograph with a good column, and indeed it may be practically negligible as compared with other band broadening factors. Nevertheless, eddy diffusion is worth noting because it is negligible only if rendered so by proper attention to details in the design and fabrication of the chromatograph and the column.

Longitudinal Diffusion

The second factor contributing to band broadening is longitudinal diffusion of the solute in the gas phase. Solute molecules tend to diffuse along concentration gradients, and thus a solute band moving along a column will broaden as molecules spread into the regions of lower concentration ahead of the band and behind it. Solute molecules spend part of their time in the gas phase and part in the liquid phase, but diffusion is much faster in gases than in liquids (diffusion coefficients in the gas phase are typically of the order of 10^5 times as great as in liquids). Thus diffusion in the liquid phase is generally considered negligible in GLC. Diffusion takes time, and thus the contribution of diffusion to band broadening will increase with the length of time required to elute the band from the column. Hence the diffusion term in the van Deemter equation involves the velocity of the carrier gas, becoming smaller as the velocity increases.

Nonequilibrium in Mass Transfer

The last factor in nonideality arises from the fact that equilibrium cannot be attained for the distribution of the solute between stationary and mobile phases in the face of continuous flow of the carrier gas. Using C_L and C_G for solute concentrations in the liquid and gas phases, respectively, we may write Henry's law as:

$$C_L = KC_G$$

But Henry's law describes an equilibrium situation, and for cases where there is insufficient time for equilibration, we must write:

$$C_L = KC_G \times f(t)$$

where $f(t)$ is some function of time which reflects the kinetics of the mass transfer process between the two phases. When t is large, i.e., when equilibrium is approached, then of course $f(t)$ must approach unity so as to yield Henry's law.

The band broadening that arises from the fact that equilibration is not instantaneous is depicted in Fig. 14.5, where both ideal and nonideal solute distributions are shown. The ideal case (upper portion of Fig. 14.5) is simply a Craig distribution, where equilibrium is attained in all of the plates before transfers are made. The lower part of Fig. 14.5 illustrates the case where the gas phase is moving continuously, equilibrium is never attained at any point, and hence in general $C_L \neq KC_G$. Where the front of the solute zone in the gas phase encounters fresh liquid, some of the solute dissolves in the liquid but, because we do not wait for equilibrium, $C_L < KC_G$. The result is that some of the solute which would have been retarded by the liquid phase if equilibrium had been attained actually continues to migrate along the column with the carrier gas. At the other extreme, the rear of the gas-phase solute zone, solute cannot leave the liquid rapidly enough to equilibrate with the fresh carrier gas, and $C_L > KC_G$. In other words, part of the solute is retarded to a greater degree by the stationary liquid than would have been the case if equilibration had been instantaneous. This nonideal behavior continues as the solute traverses the entire length of the column, with the obvious result that the elution band is broader than it would otherwise have been.

The extent of band broadening arising from the slow mass transfer kinetics depends upon the time available for the process to move toward equilibrium. Thus the nonequilibrium term in the van Deemter equation ought to involve the carrier gas velocity and, in contrast with the longitudinal

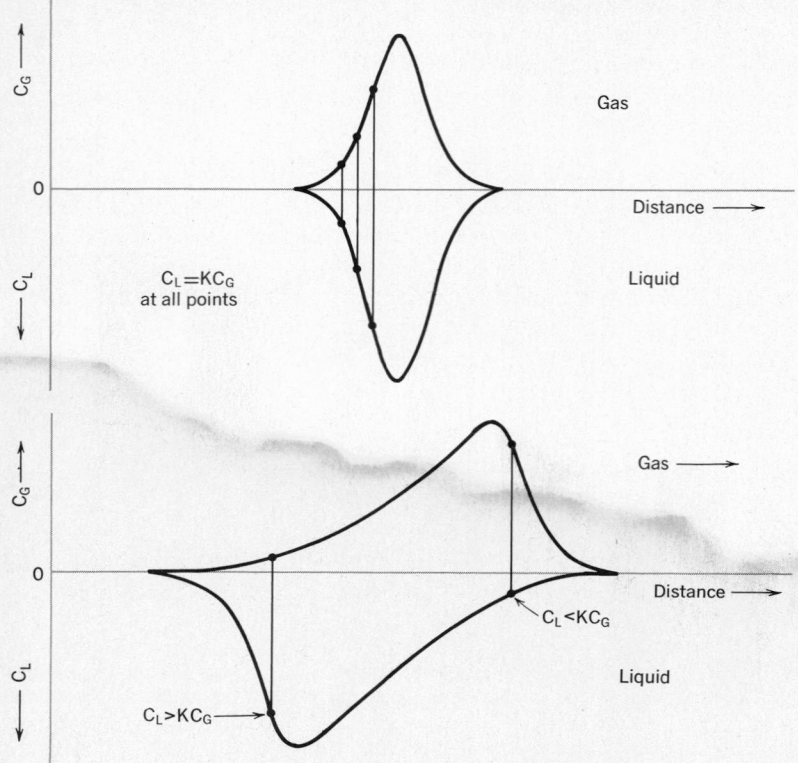

$C_L = KC_G$
at all points

Gas

Distance

Liquid

Gas

Distance

$C_L < KC_G$

Liquid

$C_L > KC_G$

FIGURE 14.5 Band broadening caused by non-equilibrium in mass transfers: Concentration profiles in gas and liquid phases for a solute zone within a column. Upper: ideal distribution assuming instantaneous equilibration. Lower: actual distribution resulting from finite rate of mass transfer.

diffusion term considered above, it should become larger as the velocity increases. Furthermore, we might expect that solute in a thin film of liquid would be closer to equilibrium with the moving gas stream than would be the case for solute which had penetrated deep pools of liquid. Thus the magnitude of the nonequilibrium term should depend upon the quantity of liquid with which the solid support is impregnated and the manner of its distribution within the nonuniform pores of the solid. In addition, the nonequilibrium term contains the diffusion coefficient of the solute in the liquid phase. The faster the solute molecules can move along concentration gradients in the liquid to and from the interface with the gas, the closer will be the approach to equilibrium in the mass transfer process, and the less the band spreading attributable to this factor.

The van Deemter Equation

Consideration of the three factors discussed above led to the following equation:

$$HETP = 2\lambda d_p + \frac{2\gamma D_G}{u} + \frac{8kd_f^2}{\pi^2(1 + k)^2 D_L}u$$

where:

λ is a dimensionless parameter measuring the irregularity of the column packing;

d_p is the diameter of the packing particles;

γ is a correction factor accounting for the irregularity of diffusion pathways through the packing material;

D_G is the diffusion coefficient of the solute in the gas phase;

u is the linear velocity of the carrier gas;

k is a constant for a particular solute and a particular column;

d_f is the "effective film thickness," a measure of the liquid loading of the packing material; and

D_L is the diffusion coefficient of the solute in the liquid phase.

Theoretically minded people have scrutinized the three terms in the van Deemter equation very carefully and have proposed extensions of these as well as additional factors in order to gain a better understanding of the chromatographic process. Such work, which involves sophisticated mathematics, is far beyond the scope of an introductory textbook. The van Deemter equation as given here focuses attention upon the major factors which cause band broadening and serves quite well, for the interested reader, as a takeoff point for understanding the further refinements that have followed.

The van Deemter equation is often seen in the abbreviated form:

$$HETP = A + \frac{B}{u} + Cu$$

where:

A represents the eddy diffusion term;

B/u represents the longitudinal diffusion term; and

Cu represents the nonequilibrium in mass transfer term.

A graph of HETP vs u is a branch of a hyperbola, as shown in Fig. 14.6. The dashed construction on the graph depicts the contributions of the A, B/u,

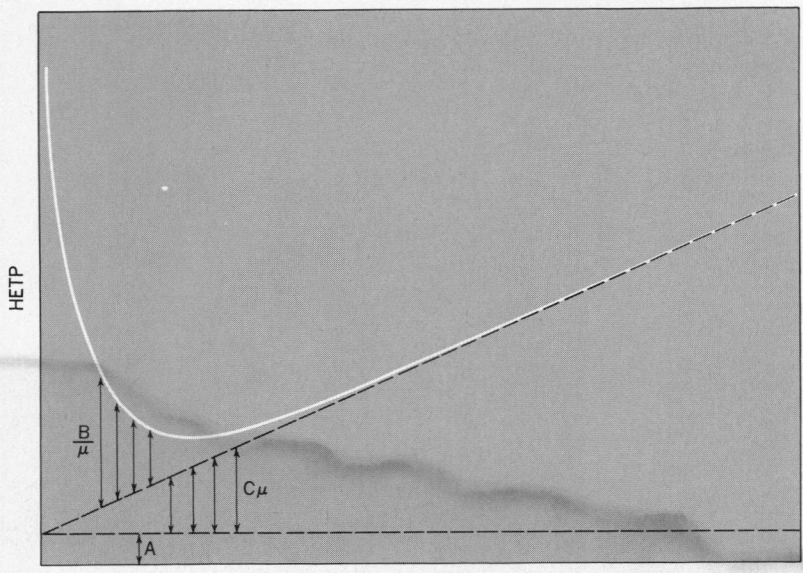

HETP

$\frac{B}{\mu}$

$C\mu$

A

Carrier gas velocity, u

FIGURE 14.6 Schematic depiction of the van Deemter equation, HETP = $A + B/u + Cu$. Note that the contribution of the A term to HETP is independent of velocity, that B/u increases as velocity decreases, and that Cu predominates at high velocities.

and Cu terms to HETP at various carrier gas velocities. The A term remains constant, independent of velocity. At very low velocities, most of the band broadening is due to longitudinal diffusion, while at high velocities, the increasing departure from equilibrium in the mass transfer process becomes dominant. There is an optimal velocity where the best balance of these factors is obtained, i.e., where HETP is a minimum or the number of plates in the column is a maximum. The minimum in the graph is a rather shallow one, and in practice it is not necessary to locate it exactly; it is obviously advantageous, however, to be in the right neighborhood.

Although more recent work has led to a more sophisticated understanding of the processes that occur in the column, the van Deemter equation as presented here is fairly good, at least with regard to predicting the shape of a graph of HETP vs u. Curves very similar to the one shown in Fig. 14.6 are in fact obtained in the laboratory. Such curves are not calculated because values are generally not at hand for the parameters such as λ and γ in the van Deemter equation. A, B, and C are easily obtained from experimental data by measuring HETP at three carrier gas velocities and setting up three equations in three unknowns. The values will vary greatly from one sort of column to another; the following have been presented as typical for packed columns of the sort commonly used in analysis:[7]

$$A \cong 0 - 1 \text{ mm}$$

$$B \cong 10 \text{ mm}^2/\text{s}$$

$$C \cong 0.001 - 0.01 \text{ s}$$

$$\text{HETP}_{\min} \cong 0.5 - 2 \text{ mm}$$

$$u_{\text{opt}} \cong 1 - 10 \text{ cm/s}$$

In summary, the plate theory of chromatography enables us to calculate a very useful measure of column performance, viz., the number of theoretical plates or, if we wish, HETP. This is very simply done using one of the formulas on page 391. But the plate theory in itself does not suggest how the performance of a column may be improved. The so-called rate theory, as exemplified by the van Deemter equation, on the other hand, gives definite factors such as particle size, liquid loading, and carrier gas velocity over which we have some control by which improved performance may be obtained.

Resolution

In general, the positions of elution bands on the horizontal axis of the chromatogram and their widths will determine how complete a separation of the starting mixture has been accomplished. Although samples may have many components, we suppose that one pair of these will be the most difficult to separate and confine our discussion of resolving mixtures to two-component systems.

The *resolution*, R, of two components is often defined as follows, using the terms shown in Fig. 14.7:

$$R = \frac{2(t_{R_2} - t_{R_1})}{w_{b_1} + w_{b_2}}$$

Alternatively, if the widths are measured halfway between the baseline and the tops of the bands, the equation becomes:

$$R = \frac{2(t_{R_2} - t_{R_1})}{1.699(w_{1/2_1} + w_{1/2_2})}$$

Often, for two bands which are close together, the widths are about the same; in that case, the 2 can be removed from the numerator and one of the w terms dropped from the denominator.

[7] A. B. Littlewood, *Gas Chromatography: Principles, Techniques, and Applications*, 2nd ed., Academic Press, New York, 1970, p. 202.

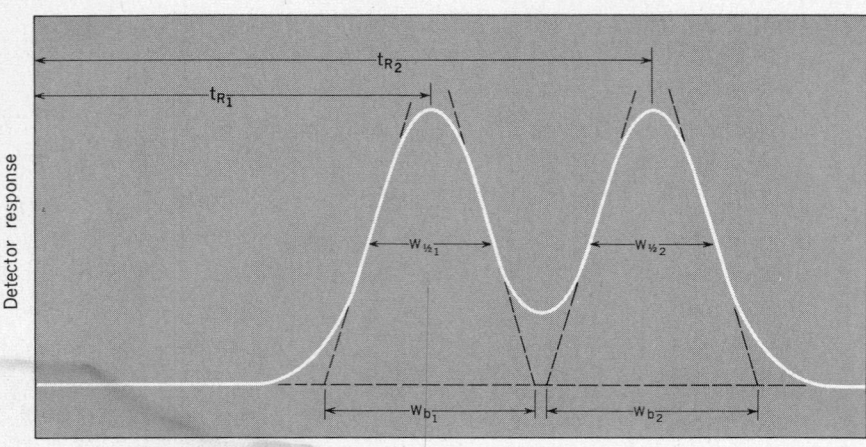

FIGURE 14.7 Measurements used to calculate the resolution, R, of two peaks.

If $R = 1.5$, the two solutes are virtually completely separated; there will be only 0.3% overlap of the two elution bands. If $R = 1$, the separation is adequate for most analyses; the overlap is about 2%. As R decreases below 1, the overlap becomes progressively more severe until, at about $R = 0.75$ (50% overlap), the separation becomes unsatisfactory for most purposes. For quantitative analysis by GLC, the area under a solute peak is the best measure of the quantity of that solute in the sample. Complete resolution of a mixture is not required for this. If overlap is not too great and if the peaks are symmetrical, fairly good estimates of the areas can be made. This can be extended by computer methods for analyzing a complex shape into a family of discrete peaks. Of course, whatever technique is used, some point will be reached beyond which good results cannot be obtained. It then becomes necessary to consider the factors that determine resolution in order to improve the situation.

Length of Column

The number of theoretical plates in a column, everything else being the same, is proportional to its length, and hence one of the obvious ways to improve resolution is to employ a longer column. The separation of two peaks, $t_{R_2} - t_{R_1}$, is directly proportional to the distance that the two solutes migrate, whereas the width of an elution band increases directly with the square root of the distance. Thus, as we lengthen a column, two bands will separate faster than they broaden, so to speak, and resolution will improve. There are limitations, however, on column length, of which we may mention two. If a column is too long, the pressure required to give a reasonable carrier gas flow rate is excessive. Second, the longer the column, the longer will be the

400

time required for elution. The efficiency of a busy laboratory handling many samples might be better served by improving the resolution in some manner that did not lead to great increases in t_R values. Nevertheless, if preliminary experiments with an ordinary column, perhaps 4 to 6 feet long, showed a fair separation with a particular sort of sample, then it might be sensible to employ a somewhat longer column, say 8 or 10 feet, in order to achieve a really good separation.

Separation Factor

If a satisfactory separation is not obtained with a good column of reasonable length after careful attention to operating parameters such as temperature (see below) and carrier gas flow rate, then the best approach is usually to try a different stationary liquid phase. In other words, if logical attempts to achieve resolution by narrowing the solute bands fail, then we must move the peaks farther apart by changing the K values for the solutes.

The ratio of retention times, t_{R_2}/t_{R_1}, is called the *separation factor*, S (some writers use S.F. and some α for this ratio). Usually the ratio of retention times is about the same as the ratio of the K values for the two solutes. Thus:

$$S = \frac{t_{R_2}}{t_{R_1}} \cong \frac{K_2}{K_1}$$

Note that S is not the same thing as the resolution, R. The ratio of retention times, measured at the peaks of the elution bands, does not in itself describe the effectiveness of the separation, because it tells nothing about the widths of the bands. However, it may be shown, as we might expect intuitively, that there is a relation between R and S if the number of theoretical plates in the column is taken into account:

$$R = \frac{n^{1/2}(S-1)/S}{4}$$

Taking $R = 1$, which as noted earlier represents a fairly good separation of two solutes, we may plot the number of plates required vs the separation factor, S, which yields the curve shown in Fig. 14.8. The curve approaches the ordinate axis asymptotically, reflecting the fact that, if $S = 1$, no separation is possible however long the column. As S increases above 1, the number of plates required decreases rapidly. In other words, if we can promote a rather small increase in S by changing the liquid phase, it may be far more effective in improving the resolution than even a large increase in the length of the column.

Factors in Retention

For many purposes, the *retention volume* of a solute, V_R, is more convenient than the retention time. The retention volume is the product of the retention

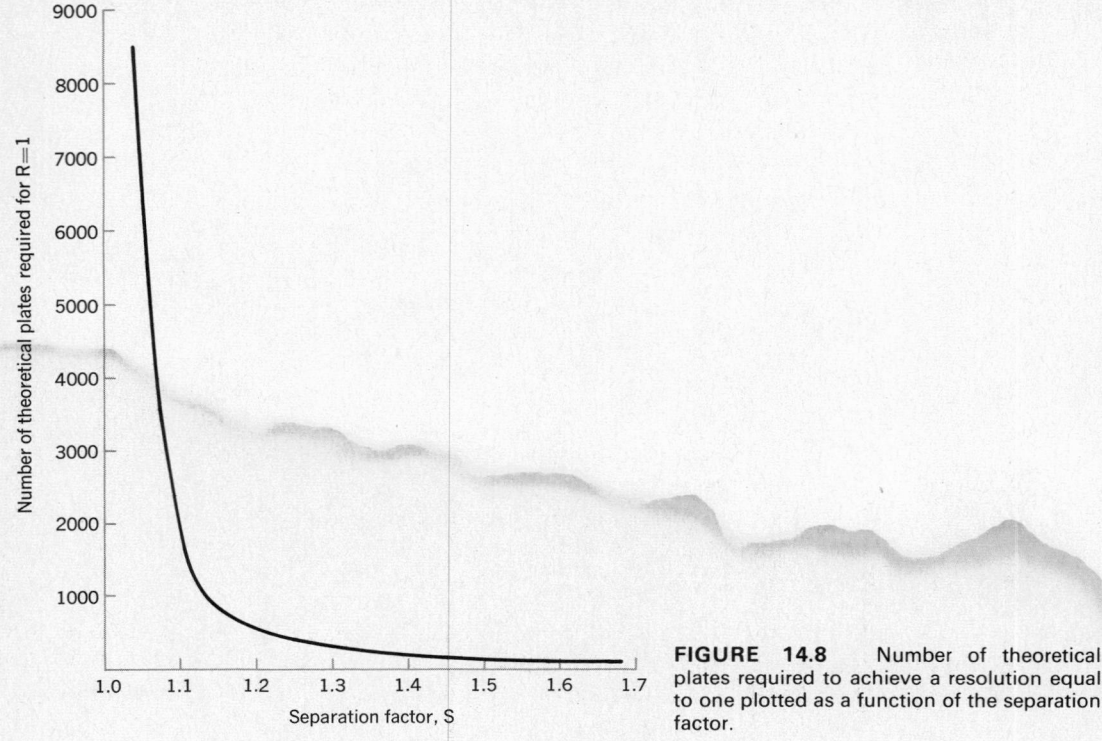

FIGURE 14.8 Number of theoretical plates required to achieve a resolution equal to one plotted as a function of the separation factor.

time and the carrier gas flow rate; since there is an inverse relation between flow rate and retention time, V_R is independent of flow rate. The flow rate is ordinarily measured at a point beyond the column, as shown in Fig. 14.1. This measured value, F, should be corrected to account for the fact that the column is at a different temperature than the flow meter; a further correction is required if the flow meter introduces moisture into the gas or creates an appreciable pressure drop of its own. If F_c is the corrected flow rate, then:

$$V_R = t_R \times F_c$$

Because the gas is compressible, its velocity is not uniform throughout the column—the gas moves faster near the outlet end—and V_R should be corrected to an average column pressure to yield the *corrected retention volume*, V_R°. The corrections are not discussed in detail in this text, but they may be found in the books on gas chromatography listed in the bibliography.

Consider a compound which does not interact with the stationary phase, i.e., $K = 0$. This compound is not retarded by the liquid in the column, but its retention time is not zero; some time, which we may call t_G, will be required simply to wash the compound through the column. Using the same corrections as above, we may calculate a corrected retention volume, V_G°, for such a compound. This volume should amount to the same thing as the space within the column which is available to the gas, i.e., the portion of the column which is not occupied by the packing material and its liquid load. Other terms such as "interstitial volume" and "void volume" have been used for the analogous space in other forms of chromatography such as ion exchange.

The fixed gases of the air are not appreciably soluble in most organic liquids that are used as stationary phases. Thus it is easy to obtain t_G by injecting a little air along with the sample. The thermal conductivity detector responds to air, and a small blip called the "air peak" appears on the recorder chart, from which V_G° can be calculated. (The other common detector, the flame ionization detector, does not respond to the gases of the air; another approach is then required.)

Distribution Coefficient and Liquid Load

Let V_L be the volume of the liquid phase in the column, and recall the distribution coefficient:

$$K = \frac{C_L, \text{wt/ml}}{C_G, \text{wt/ml}}$$

Now when the peak of an elution band for some solute appears at the detector, we suppose that half of that solute is still in the column and half has been eluted in a volume of $V_R^\circ - V_G^\circ$. Then we may cancel the weight terms in the above equation and write:

$$K = \frac{1/V_L}{1/(V_R^\circ - V_G^\circ)} = \frac{V_R^\circ - V_G^\circ}{V_L}$$

whence:

$$KV_L = V_R^\circ - V_G^\circ$$

and

$$V_R^\circ = V_G^\circ + KV_L$$

More rigorous derivations of this equation and a discussion of the assumptions involved may be found in monographs on gas chromatography.

V_G° is often quite small compared with V_R°. Thus it is frequently the case that the retention volume for a solute is almost directly proportional to the quantity of liquid phase in the column. Similarly, with a given liquid loading, the retention volume will vary directly with K. In other words, the experimenter has considerable control over retention in his choice of the liquid phase and the quantity used in preparing the column.

It may be noted that the time corresponding to a given retention volume is also under the control of the operator via the flow rate, but, as we have seen, the analysis time cannot be shortened at will in this manner without the penalty of poorer resolution. With certain types of mixtures, it may be advantageous to vary the flow rate during the chromatographic run, starting with a low value for optimal resolution of solutes whose K values are small and close together, and continuously increasing the flow rate to accelerate the elution of laggard solutes which are easily resolved but are spending more time than necessary in the column. This technique is known as "programmed flow gas chromatography."

Temperature

Virtually every aspect of GLC is sensitive to temperature to some extent. The volume of the liquid phase and hence also the gas space in the column, the viscosity of the carrier gas and therefore the inlet pressure required for a given flow rate, diffusion coefficients of solutes—these are a few examples of factors which may be affected to some degree by the column temperature. But we are particularly interested here in the often very pronounced direct effect of temperature upon solute retention. The usual effect of a temperature increase is to lower the value of the distribution coefficient K; in other words, at the higher temperature, a solute is driven out of the liquid phase in accord with the general rule that an increase in temperature lowers the solubility of a gas in a liquid. Decreasing K in turn decreases the retention time and the retention volume. The magnitude of the effect depends upon the nature of the solute and of the liquid phase and the temperature region investigated, but roughly the change in retention volume is of the order of a few percent, say 3 to 12%, per degree. An analysis, then, is completed most rapidly at the highest column temperature compatible with the desired separation and sample stability.

On the other hand, the separation factor for a pair of solutes is generally larger the lower the temperature. As a crude rule of thumb, the higher the temperature the more similar the behavior of two compounds in a GLC column. Thus the column temperature selected for an analysis ought to be low enough to achieve the necessary separation, but no lower than this so as not to waste time.

For a series of solutes which interact in the same manner with the liquid phase, for instance an homologous series, the distribution coefficients generally bear an inverse relation to the vapor pressures; the larger the vapor pressure, the smaller is K. In general, the lower the boiling point of a solute, the greater will be its vapor pressure at a given temperature. Thus the components of a mixture of such solutes will emerge from a column in order of increasing boiling points. (If some of the solutes interact in specific ways with the stationary liquid, e.g., by hydrogen bonding, then this simple rule may not hold.)

Figure 14.9(a) shows a chromatogram of a hydrocarbon mixture obtained in the ordinary manner with the column held at a certain temperature. The temperature selected was a compromise: it was too high to yield an optimal separation of the lower compounds in the hydrocarbon series and too low

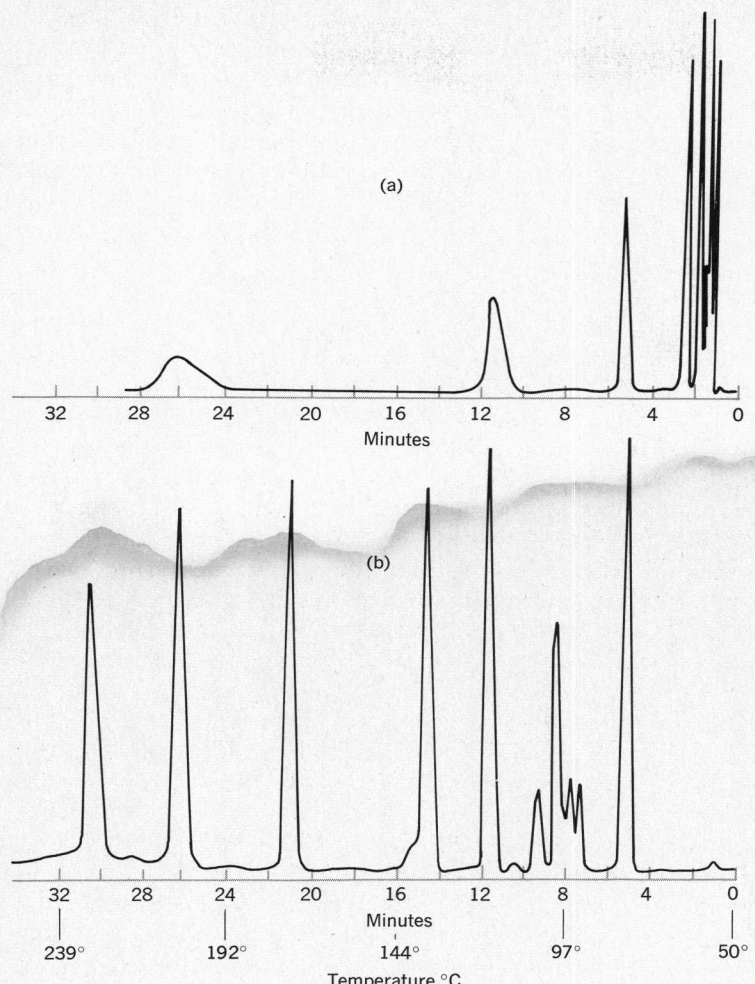

(a)

32 28 24 20 16 12 8 4 0
Minutes

(b)

32 28 24 20 16 12 8 4 0
Minutes

239°   192°   144°   97°   50°

Temperature °C.

FIGURE 14.9   Gas chromatograms of a mixture
of normal hydrocarbons. (a) Isothermal chromatogram
of the following mixture at 168°C: (1) pentane, (2)
hexane, (3) heptane, (4) 1-octene, (5) decane, (6)
1-dodecene, (7) 1-tetradecene. (b) Programmed
temperature chromatogram of the same mixture.
(Reprinted from *Anal. Chem.*, **30**, 1157 (1956);
copyright by the American Chemical Society. Reprinted by permission of the copyright owner.)

for the higher molecular weight compounds. A much nicer chromatogram
of the same mixture is seen in Fig. 14.9(b): resolution is better, and in fact a
number of impurities in the hydrocarbons that were mixed to prepare the
sample may be seen which do not show up in curve (a). All of the bands have
about the same shape, which facilitates quantitative measurements; peak

405

number 7 which was very low in curve (a) is now higher above the baseline, representing a better signal-to-noise ratio for improved quantitative accuracy. Curve (b) was obtained by the technique of *programmed temperature GLC*. Here the temperature of the column was raised during the chromatographic run, starting at a temperature that was suitable for the lower members of the series, and finishing at a higher temperature where the elution of the higher boiling components was more satisfactory. The effect is rather similar to that of programming the flow rate as mentioned in the section above. Various temperature-time functions have been studied, but the commonest by far for ordinary work is a linear program: the temperature increases linearly with time at so many degrees per minute. Modern chromatographs often provide for this capability, and the operator can select on the panel an initial temperature, a rate of increase, and a final temperature.

EXPERIMENTAL ASPECTS OF GLC

Having seen what gas-liquid chromatography is, and after considering the theory, we may now discuss briefly some of the more practical aspects which will make the gas chromatograph less of a mysterious "black box."

Carrier Gas

Various gases have been used in GLC, for example, hydrogen, helium, nitrogen, argon, carbon dioxide, and even water vapor. The lighter gases, hydrogen and helium, permit more longitudinal diffusion of solutes, which tends to lower column efficiency, particularly at lower flow rates. Thus nitrogen might be a better choice of carrier gas in order to accomplish a really difficult separation. In addition, it is cheaper than helium and safer in the laboratory than hydrogen. However, there is another consideration, viz., the characteristics of the detector. It is obviously desirable that the response of the detector to the components of the sample differ greatly from its response to the ever-present carrier gas. In the case of the thermal conductivity cell, which is one of the most widely used detectors, this requirement is much better met by the lighter gases, hydrogen and helium, as we shall see below. Thus, with instruments employing this detector, helium is by far the commonest carrier gas in the United States, while in Europe, where helium is very expensive, hydrogen is more widely used. With the flame ionization detector, which has become a rather common one in recent years, nitrogen is probably the most widely used carrier gas.

Sampling System

Liquid samples, typically ranging from a small fraction of a μl to perhaps 25 μl or more, are usually injected through a rubber septum by means of a hypodermic syringe. Special syringes delivering various volumes in the microliter range are on the market, sometimes equipped with mechanical devices that aid in reproducing sample size. Gaseous samples may also be injected, or they may be introduced by means of various gas-sampling devices designed for commercial chromatographs. The injection technique is important : the sample should be introduced as a sharp "plug" rather than being slowly bled into the carrier gas stream. Slow injection leads to much more band spreading than is necessary; actually HETP calculated from the elution peak as described above is a function of the injection rate. Good injection technique requires practice.

It is important that the size of the sample not be too large for the apparatus. Overloading has an extremely deleterious effect upon column efficiency. The lower limit of sample size is determined by the detector : so far as the column is concerned, the smaller the sample the better. The sensitivity of the detector determines how small a sample can be handled.

The temperature at the injection port is very important. If a liquid sample evaporates slowly, the result is similar to that caused by injecting too slowly. The injection port is usually heated independently of the heating unit surrounding the column, and generally it should be held at a temperature above the boiling points of the sample components. On the other hand, the temperature should be below a level where the compounds would decompose.

Column

The stationary phase in GLC is a liquid, but it cannot be allowed simply to slosh around inside a tube. The liquid must be immobilized, preferably in the form of a thin layer of large surface area. This is most commonly accomplished by impregnating a ground-up solid material with the liquid phase before the column is packed. The solid should be chemically inert toward the substances which will be chromatographed, stable at the operating temperature, and of large surface area per unit weight. The pressure drop required for desirable gas flow rates should not be excessive. Mechanical strength is desirable so that the particles will not break and alter the particle size distribution with handling. Most of the solids employed as supports in GLC are highly porous, but the characteristics of the pores are very important. For example, the pores in silica gel tend to be narrow ; they fill up with the liquid and provide insufficient area of gas-liquid interface. The active adsorbents such as activated charcoal and silica gel are poor solid supports. Even when coated with the liquid film, these solids adsorb sample components, causing "tailing" of the elution bands as shown in curve 2b of Fig. 14.4. The commonest solid support materials are diatomaceous earth (a deposit formed on ocean bottoms from the siliceous shells of a certain type of algae) and firebrick. The materials are ground and carefully graded with respect to particle size and often subjected to various chemical pretreatments to improve their surface qualities. The preparation of the solid, its impregnation with the liquid phase, and the final packing into copper, stainless steel, or glass columns used to be an art that was cultivated by chromatographers. Today, it is much more common to buy ready-made columns from the manufacturers who have made available a wide variety of very good columns.

There is another type of column for GLC called the open-tubular or capillary column. This is a long, thin tube of glass or other material such as stainless steel, perhaps 0.1 to 1 mm in diameter, sometimes several hundred feet long, coiled up to save space. The inner surface is coated with a very thin layer of the stationary liquid phase, just that quantity which will adhere as a film on the glass or metal; there is no column packing in the usual sense. The pathways through the column are practically the same length for all molecules of the sample, and hence eddy diffusion is virtually zero in open-tubular columns. The very thin liquid film, containing no deep, stagnant pools, promotes a rapid approach to equilibrium in the partition process. The columns are very long, and it has been argued that they are not much more efficient than packed columns of comparable length would be. On the other hand, packed columns of that length would require relatively enormous pressure drops to attain reasonable flow rates. Because of the very light liquid loading, open-tubular columns can handle only very small samples, and their widespread use awaited the development of very sensitive detectors. Very impressive separations are often obtained with these columns. Open-tubular is perhaps preferable to capillary in designating such columns; the tubing is not fine enough to be considered a capillary in the original sense of hair-like.

The stationary liquid phase must be selected with the particular separation problem in mind. The liquid should have a very low vapor pressure at the column temperature; a common rule of thumb suggests a boiling point at least 200° above the temperature to which the liquid will be subjected. The two important reasons for desiring low volatility are, first, loss of liquid will eventually destroy the column, and second, the detector will respond to the vapor of the stationary phase with resulting drift of the recorder baseline and lowered sensitivity toward the components of the analytical sample. Some commercial gas chromatographs have dual columns to compensate for the effect of liquid bleed on the detector, but even here, excessive volatility is undesirable.

Obviously the liquid phase should be thermally stable at the column temperature, and, except in special cases, it should not react chemically with the sample components. The liquid must have an appreciable solvent power for the sample. Recalling the old rule that "like dissolves like," it may be stated rather crudely that generally there should be some chemical resemblance between the liquid substrate and the solutes to be separated. Thus the saturated hydrocarbon squalane ($C_{30}H_{62}$, mol. wt. 423, boiling pt. about 350°) is a good liquid phase for the separation of low molecular weight alkanes on a column that will not be heated above about 150°. For the separation of aromatic hydrocarbons, the aromatic liquid benzyldiphenyl, useful up to about 120°, is sometimes recommended. A polyglycol column might be used to separate a mixture of alcohols. Of course it is not required that the stationary liquid match the solutes functional group for functional group, and sometimes one liquid phase will serve for the separation of a variety of mixtures. This has led to the designation "general purpose" for some columns, although this is misleading in that no liquid phase provides completely general effectiveness for separating all classes of solutes. Examples of general purpose liquids are silicone oils and greases, useful for a wide variety of nonpolar solutes, and polyethyleneglycols (Carbowaxes), widely used for mixtures of polar solutes. Lists of liquid phases, recommended temperature limits, and the types of compounds for whose separation they are useful may be found in monographs on GLC.

The quantity of liquid substrate applied to the solid support is important. If too much liquid is present, solutes spend too much time diffusing through the liquid phase, and the separation efficiency is lowered. Too little liquid allows solutes to interact with the solid itself, in which case adsorption may cause "tailing" and consequent overlapping of elution bands.

Detector

The separation process occurs in the column, and hence this component must be considered the heart of the instrument. On the other hand, the separation would be of little value without some way to detect and measure the separated solutes as they emerge from the column.

Two types of detectors are commonly distinguished, integral and differential. An integral detector provides at any instant a measure of the total quantity of eluted material which has passed through it up to that time. The first paper on GLC[8] described an example of an integral detector. A mixture of fatty acids was chromatographed, and the effluent gas from the column was bubbled through an aqueous solution containing a pH indicator. When an acid emerged from the column, the pH of the solution dropped, the indicator changed color, and a light beam of appropriate wavelength passing through the solution was attenuated by absorption. The resulting change in the electrical signal from a photodetector activated a relay which turned on a buret containing sodium hydroxide. The addition of the base restored the pH of the solution to its original value, and hence the indicator to its original color, whereupon the buret was automatically shut off. The volume of titrant was recorded as a function of time, and the resulting chromatogram, of the type shown in Fig. 14.10(a), consisted of a series of steps, each representing the titration of one of the acids in the original mixture. The quantity of each acid was easily found by measuring the height of the corresponding step. This detector, which seems crude and clumsy by hindsight, was useful at the time because it was easily assembled from available components, and it served its purpose very nicely at the birth of GLC. But integral detectors have been largely supplanted by differential detectors; the latter are found on the overwhelming majority of modern gas chromatographs, and it is these that we wish to emphasize in this chapter.

Differential detectors yield the familiar chromatograms consisting of peaks rather than steps, as shown in Fig. 14.10(b). Two major classes may be distinguished: first, those which measure the *concentration* of a solute by

[8] A. T. James and A. J. P. Martin, *Biochem. J.*, **50**, 679 (1952).

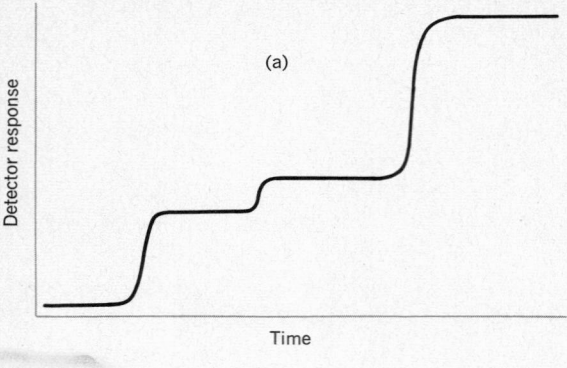

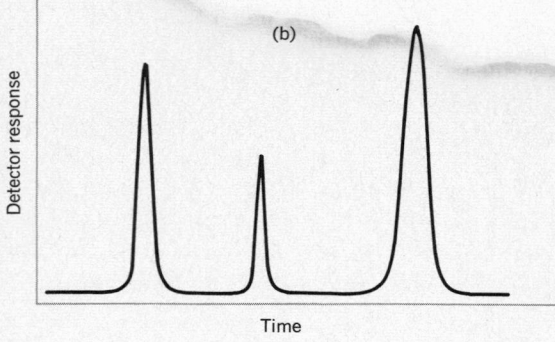

FIGURE 14.10 Comparison of chromatograms obtained with (a) integral and (b) differential detectors.

means of some physical property of the effluent gas stream, and second, those which respond to the solute directly and hence measure its *mass flow rate*. This distinction will be clarified as we examine one example of each type of differential detector. First, though, we list some general detector characteristics which are useful in evaluating any detector.

1. Sensitivity. As explained below, the sensitivity of the detector represents an important limitation upon the smallest quantity of a solute that can be determined by GLC, and the increased demand for trace analyses in many different fields has stimulated the development of more sensitive detectors. For example, our growing awareness of the impact of trace contaminants upon biological ecosystems has provided a market for very sensitive detectors in studies of water pollution and pesticide residues in food products. It is possible for detector sensitivity to have a direct economic, political, or legal implication. For example, certain Federal agencies are empowered to establish permissible levels of various poisons in foods. However, an important exception was legislated: the so-called Delaney clause requires a level of zero for any compound which is known to be carcinogenic in man or experimental animals. Now zero means zero to a politician, but to an analytical chemist it means a quantity smaller than he can detect with available methodology. It is perhaps not coincidental that the growing agitation by spokesmen for the food industry to repeal the Delaney clause has paralleled the increasing sensitivity of GLC and other analytical techniques. It may be argued that a level of zero means nothing outside the context of a particular analytical method employing a specified instrument.

Various measures of detector sensitivity are found in the literature, but basically, for our purpose, we may consider the sensitivity as the slope of a curve showing detector response as a function of the quantity measured, as shown in Fig. 14.11. A general expression for the sensitivity, then, is

$$S = \frac{\Delta R}{\Delta Q}$$

as shown in the figure below.

2. *Stability.* The baseline of a chromatogram is subject to short-term fluctuations of a largely random nature which are called "noise." A longer range upward or downward trend in the baseline is called "drift." Noise and drift, illustrated in Fig. 14.12, may originate in various instrument components such as amplifiers or recorders and in fluctuations of the carrier gas flow rate. Drift is seen in programmed temperature operation if the column reaches a temperature where the stationary liquid volatilizes. Much of the problem is eliminated by good circuit design, high-quality components, and

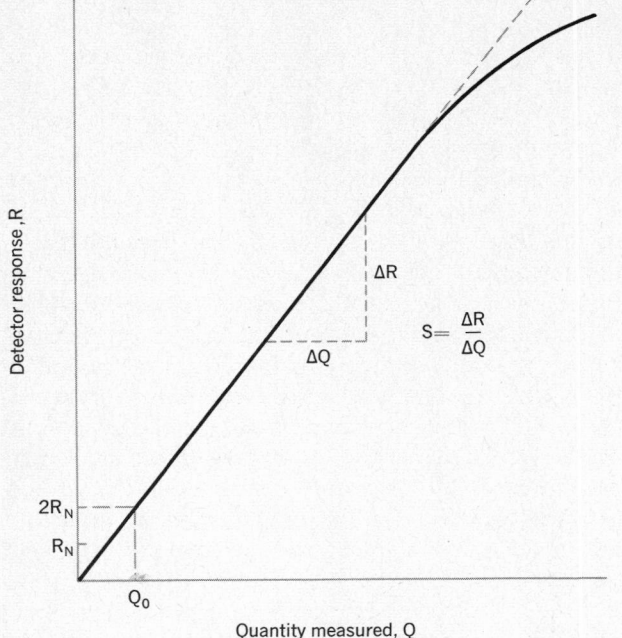

FIGURE 14.11 Detector response curve showing the definition of the sensitivity, S, and the relationship of peak-to-peak noise level, R_N, to limit of detection, Q_o.

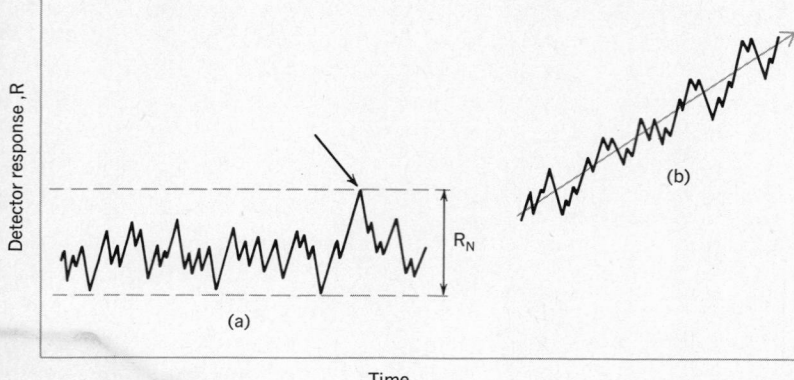

FIGURE 14.12 Expanded baselines. Left-hand portion illustrates noise and shows the measurement of the peak-to-peak noise level, R_N; the peak marked by the arrow might be ignored in estimating R_N (see text). Right-hand portion illustrates short-term noise superimposed upon upward drift.

proper operation of the chromatograph. There will always be, however, an inherent detector noise level which, along with the sensitivity, sets the lower limit for the quantity of a solute that can be detected.

The basic problem can be easily understood in qualitative terms. Suppose a solute elution band is too small to be measured accurately. Perhaps the first thing to come to mind is this: why not increase the amplification in order to enlarge the elution band on the recorder chart? The answer is, this can be done but there is a limitation upon the benefit to be derived from it because the noise is amplified too. The smallest elution band that can be distinguished from noise peaks corresponds to the limit of detection for a solute. This becomes essentially a statistical problem: how much larger than the random baseline fluctuations must an elution band be in order to yield acceptable odds that we shall identify it correctly as an elution band and not confuse it with noise. This is a problem not unlike some of those encountered in Chapter 3; we need to estimate the level beyond which a recorder deflection is probably not noise but rather is due to a definite cause, viz., the sample. Various analyses of this problem have been presented in the literature, and various recommendations may be found. Perhaps the commonest advice is to take, as the limit of detection, that quantity of a solute which gives an elution band whose height is twice the peak-to-peak noise level. The peak-to-peak noise level, R_N, is explained in Fig. 14.12.

The relationship among sensitivity, noise level, and limit of detection may be formulated as follows. Recalling the definition of sensitivity,

$$S = \frac{\Delta R}{\Delta Q}$$

if we associate the limit of detection, Q_o, with twice the peak-to-peak noise level, $2 \times R_N$, then we may write

$$S = \frac{2R_N}{Q_o}$$

or

$$Q_o = \frac{2R_N}{S}$$

In other words, low noise level and high sensitivity are favorable detector attributes with regard to the limit of detection.

Unusually large noise peaks such as the peak marked by the arrow in Fig. 14.12 occur infrequently. If such peaks are excluded in estimating R_N, then the limit of detection will appear to be better. Along with this goes, of course, an increased risk of reporting an analytical result for a solute when, in fact, a noise peak was measured.

3. Linearity. The ideal detector response would be linear with respect to the quantity measured, Q. This is the case with commonly used detectors within certain concentration limits, but eventually, as shown in Fig. 14.11, the response generally falls off.

4. Versatility. It is obviously advantageous that a detector respond to a wide variety of chemical compounds. None of the components of a sample would then be overlooked, nor would it be necessary to change detectors in order to handle various types of samples.

5. Response time. The detector should respond rapidly to the presence of the solute, or, as it is sometimes said, there should be a small "time constant." The total response time for a chromatograph is a function not only of the detector itself, but also of inertia in other components, for example, the recorder.

6. Chemical activity. In many cases, this is not an important factor, but sometimes solutes which have been separated by GLC are subjected to further study. For example, a mass spectrum or an infrared spectrum may be desired in order to identify the solute with certainty. In that event, it is obviously important that the solute not be decomposed in the detection process.

There are additional desiderata which may be classed as nonfunctional but which may be important in certain circumstances, such as low cost, simplicity, safety, and ability to withstand abuse.

The geometry of the detector and the pathway to it is very important. Solutes which have been separated in the column must not remix in the tubing leading to the detector nor inside the detector itself. A small volume within the detector is also conducive to a fast response. Stagnant pockets of gas must be avoided, and the dead volume between the column and the detector should be as small as possible.

Thermal Conductivity Detector

One of the most widely used detectors for general purpose GLC is the thermal conductivity cell. This device contains either a heated metal filament (generally platinum, a platinum-rhodium alloy, or tungsten) or a thermistor. Thermistors are small beads prepared by fusing a mixture of metal oxides, generally of manganese, cobalt, nickel, and traces of other metals. There is usually a thin protective layer of glass on the surface, and fine platinum alloy wires provide electrical connections. The important property of thermistors in the present context is an unusually large temperature coefficient of electrical resistance.

The heated detector element, filament or thermistor, under steady-state conditions, adopts a certain temperature determined by the heat supplied to it and the rate at which it loses heat to the walls of the chamber which surrounds it. Although a small amount of heat is lost through radiation and by conduction through the metal electrical leads, the temperature of the element is determined primarily by the thermal conductivity of the gas in the space between the element and the walls. Detection is based upon the fact that different gases have different thermal conductivities. When the composition of the gas changes, the temperature of the element changes, and this is reflected by a change in the electrical resistance of the element.

As shown schematically in Fig. 14.1, the detector generally has two sides, each with its own element. The pure carrier gas traverses one side of the detector, which is ahead of the sample injection port, while the column effluent flows through the other side. This is seen in more detail in Fig. 14.13, where one type of detector employing thermistors is illustrated schematically.

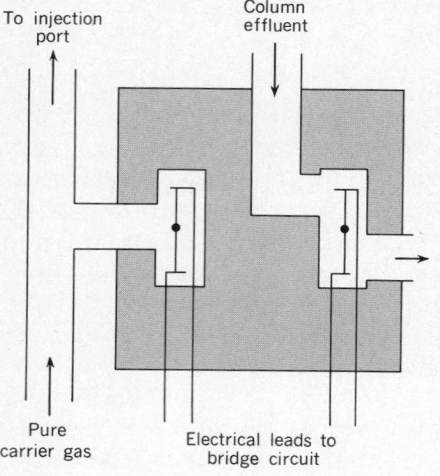

To injection port

Column effluent

Pure carrier gas

Electrical leads to bridge circuit

FIGURE 14.13 Schematic diagram of a thermal conductivity cell. The black dots are thermistor beads.

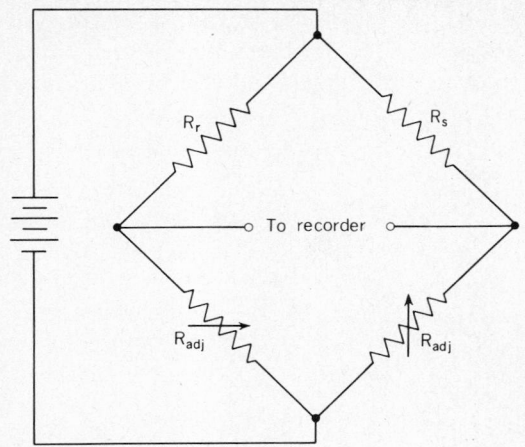

FIGURE 14.14 Wheatstone bridge circuit for thermal conductivity detector. R_r and R_s are the resistive elements in the reference and sample sides of the detector. R_{adj} is adjustable by the operator in order to balance the bridge.

As we said, the detector elements are simply electrical resistances selected for their unusually large temperature coefficients of resistance. Thus the circuitry associated with the thermal conductivity detector is exactly what one would expect from elementary physics regarding resistance measurements. The two resistances in the two sides of the detector are two arms of a Wheatstone bridge circuit, as shown in Fig. 14.14. Before the injection of the sample into the chromatograph, pure carrier gas is flowing through both sides of the detector; the adjustable resistors are set so that the bridge is balanced, which establishes the baseline on the recorder chart. Now, after injection, when a solute emerges from the column, the value of R_s in Fig. 14.14 changes, while the other resistances remain the same. The bridge goes out of balance, and a voltage appears across the leads labelled "to recorder" in the figure. After the solute has passed through the detector, the bridge returns to its original balance. Thus a record of the voltage across the bridge vs time will exhibit a peak as shown in Fig. 14.3 for the elution of each separated component of the sample. Basically, the thermal conductivity detector responds to changes in the concentration of a solute in the carrier gas stream, reflecting the way in which the thermal conductivity of the gas mixture depends upon the concentration.

Helium is an attractive carrier gas in conjunction with the thermal conductivity cell because its thermal conductivity, like that of hydrogen, is much greater than that of most organic compounds, while it does not represent an explosion hazard. Thus the appearance of an eluted solute at the detector causes a much greater change in the temperature of the resistive element than would be the case, say, with nitrogen as the carrier gas. This implies, of course, a greater sensitivity in detection, or a lower limit of detection. A few thermal conductivity values are given in Table 14.2.

The thermal conductivity detector is relatively simple and inexpensive, rugged, and reliable. Its sensitivity is adequate for many purposes. The sensitivity may be increased by operating the elements at a higher temperature by furnishing a larger bridge current, but this involves a tradeoff with regard to the life expectancy of the elements. This detector, in general, is non-destructive; i.e., solutes may be recovered unchanged and subjected to further investigation. As may be inferred from Table 14.2, the response is not the same for all compounds, and accurate quantitative work requires calibration with known quantities of the various solutes.

TABLE 14.2   THERMAL CONDUCTIVITIES OF SOME GASES AND ORGANIC VAPORS†

Hydrogen	5.34
Helium	4.16
Methane	1.09
Nitrogen	0.75
Ethane	0.73
n-Butane	0.56
Ethanol	0.53
Benzene	0.44
Acetone	0.42
Ethyl acetate	0.41
Chloroform	0.25
Carbon tetrachloride	0.22

† Values are calories per second conducted through a 1-cm layer of gas 1 m² in area at 100°C, with a temperature gradient of 1°C per cm.

Flame Ionization Detector

This detector was developed in response to the need, in certain applications, for higher sensitivity and faster response time than are provided by the thermal conductivity cell. The sensitivity of a detector depends upon not only its type but also upon the specific design and the manner in which it is operated. Thus a definite numerical comparison is difficult, but very roughly we may state that the flame ionization detector is several hundred to a thousand times as sensitive as the thermal conductivity detector. This detector is in very wide use, although perhaps it still runs second to thermal conductivity in actual numbers. The circuitry associated with the flame ionization detector is more complicated than the simple bridge circuit just discussed and gas chromatographs equipped with this detector are more expensive. Not only is the detector fast and sensitive, it is fairly stable, linear over a wide solute range, and responsive to almost all organic compounds. It is unresponsive to many inorganic compounds, including water.

The general principle of the flame ionization detector is as follows. The thermal energy in a hydrogen flame is sufficient to cause many molecules to ionize. The effluent gas from the column is mixed with hydrogen and burned at the tip of a metal jet in an excess of air. A potential is applied between the jet itself and a second electrode located above or around the flame. Ordinarily the jet is the positive electrode. When ions are formed in the flame, the gas

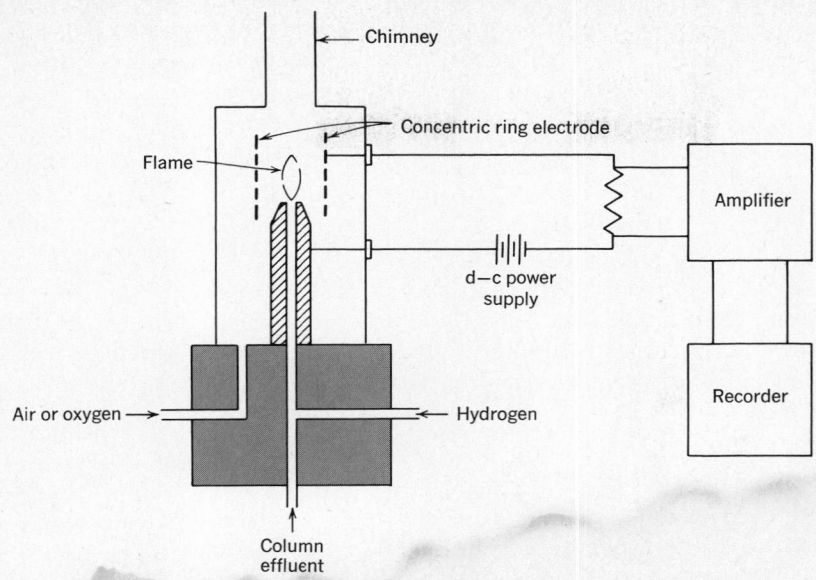

Chimney

Concentric ring electrode

Flame

Amplifier

d—c power
supply

Recorder

Air or oxygen →

← Hydrogen

Column
effluent

FIGURE   14.15   Schematic diagram of a flame ionization detector and the associated circuitry.

space between the two electrodes becomes more conducting, and an increased current flows in the circuit. This current passes through a resistor, the voltage across which is amplified to yield a signal which is fed to a recorder. Hydrogen may serve as the carrier gas, although it is more common to use nitrogen, in which case hydrogen is fed into the gas stream just ahead of the burner. Major aspects of the setup are shown in schematic form in Fig. 14.15.

With the flame ionization detector, the concentration of ions in the space between the electrodes and hence the magnitude of the current depends upon the rate at which solute molecules are delivered to the flame. A given weight of solute reaching the flame in unit time will yield the same detector response regardless of the degree of dilution by the carrier gas. This is the basis for the statement that this detector responds, not to solute concentration, but rather to the mass flow rate of solute. It should also be noted that the flame ionization detector is destructive of the sample components, in contrast with detectors such as the thermal conductivity cell which respond to some physical property of the gas related to solute concentration.

Although flame ionization is the most common, it may be mentioned that detectors are available in which solute molecules are ionized by radioactive sources. In one of these, the β-ray ionization detector, the source is a β-emitter such as tritium (^3H) or ^{99}Sr. The kinetic energy of the β-particle is much greater than that required to ionize a solute molecule; thus a series of ions is produced by one collision after another as each β-particle travels through the gas flowing through the detector. Isotopes which emit α-particles have also been employed as ionization sources. Attention must be given to

417

safety with these detectors: along with the dangerous voltages associated with ionization detectors, the radioactive source represents a potential health hazard in the event of leakage or inadequate shielding.

Still other types of detectors may be found in monographs on GLC and in the current research literature.

APPLICATIONS OF GLC

In discussing the theory of GLC, we emphasized that the column was a separation tool, but the gas chromatograph as a whole, because of the detection and recording of elution bands, is an analytical instrument which provides both qualitative and quantitative information about the components of a sample.

Identification of Compounds

With a particular column, and with all of the variables such as temperature and flow rate carefully controlled, the retention time or retention volume of a solute is a property of that solute, just as its boiling point or refractive index is a property. This implies that retention behavior could be used to identify a compound. It must be stated, however, that this is not the forte of the gas chromatograph. Instruments such as the mass spectrometer, the infrared spectrophotometer, and the n.m.r. spectrometer provide far more information about the nature of an unknown compound. In fact, for an analyst starting from scratch, with no information about the sample or whence it came, it would be virtually impossible to identify the components by their retention times alone. The thousands of known compounds simply provide too many possibilities from which to choose. In such a case, the best approach utilizes the capabilities of two instruments. For example, the chromatograph is used to separate the components of the sample mixture, and these are then introduced consecutively into the mass spectrometer. Various interfacing devices for accomplishing this automatically have been described. Frequently the mass spectral data are handled by a computer which prints out possible identities of the compounds.

On the other hand, the analyst is not always faced with a totally unknown sample. The source of the sample and its history may permit reasonable guesses regarding some of the components. In such a case, a comparison of retention times with those of known compounds may confirm the identities of some of the components. Such an identification is quite likely to be correct if spiking the sample with a known compound does not lead to an additional elution band with several different columns at several temperatures.

Within an homologous series, say a series of normal alkanes, the logarithm of the retention volume is a linear function of the number of carbon atoms if the experiment is very carefully performed. Such a plot is shown in Fig. 14.16(a). Graphs of the sort shown in Fig. 14.16(b) may be useful in establishing the series in which an unknown compound belongs.

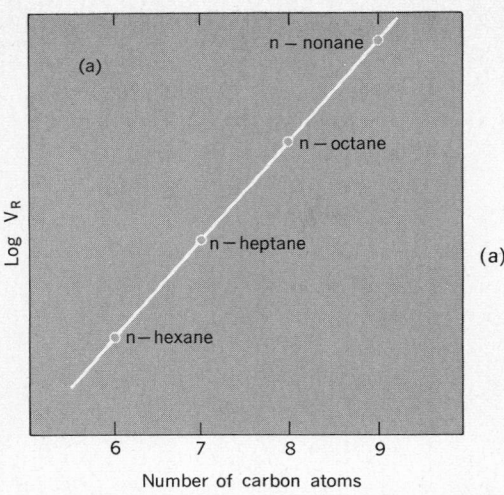

(a)

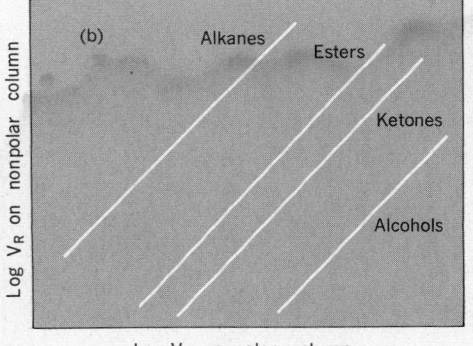

(b)

FIGURE 14.16 Identification of organic compounds by retention volume measurements.

Quantitative Analysis

Quantitative analysis by GLC depends upon the relationship between the quantity of a solute and the size of the resulting elution band. In general, with differential detectors (which are almost always employed), the best measure of the quantity of a solute is the area under the elution band. Solutes with very low retention times yield sharp, narrow bands, in which case the height of the band may be an adequate measurement. Otherwise, some sort of integration is required to obtain the area. The detector sensitivity is different for various compounds; this may be inferred from Table 14.2 for the thermal conductivity cell, and the same is true for other types of detectors. Thus there is no way to relate the area of an elution band to quantity of solute other than by calibration with known samples. Once this is done, we may write

$$
\begin{array}{ccc}
\text{Quantity of} & = & \text{Calibration} \\
\text{a solute} & & \text{factor}
\end{array}
\times
\begin{array}{c}
\text{Area under} \\
\text{elution band}
\end{array}
$$

The units in which the area is measured make no difference provided the calibration factor is appropriate.

Various integrative methods may be applied to the measurement of the area under an elution band, of which we may mention a few examples. A planimeter may be employed. The baseline is extrapolated under the peak, and a stylus on a movable arm is traced around the enclosed area; a dial with a vernier device yields a number that is proportional to the area. The elution band may be cut out of the chart paper with scissors and weighed on an analytical balance. The weight will be proportional to the area provided the paper is uniform. Still another method involves construction of a triangle by extending the baseline and drawing tangents through the inflection points as shown in Fig. 14.3. The area of the triangle is found by measuring its base and its height and applying the usual formula, area = base × height/2. It is assumed that the area of the triangle is the same as the area under the elution band.

Various devices which provide an integral readout may be obtained as accessories to laboratory recorders, in some cases from the recorder manufacturers. The ball-and-disc integrator is an example of these.

Although in many cases the analyst may wish to examine a recorded chromatogram, it is unnecessary to have such a record so far as integration per se is concerned. Thus electronic devices have been developed which accept the detector signal directly and provide an integrated output. By an analog-to-digital conversion, this output may be transformed into a suitable input for a digital computer. The computer may then print out a complete record of the analysis including retention times, areas under elution bands, percentages of the components in the sample, and other information of interest.

Applicability of GLC

There are far too many applications of GLC to permit, in the available space, anything more thorough than listing a few examples. Each year thousands of papers are published in which GLC is at least mentioned, and the technique has spread outside of chemistry into many other fields.

The major limitation is volatility. The sample must have an appreciable vapor pressure at the temperature of the column, and this immediately eliminates many kinds of samples. An actual count is impossible, but it has been estimated that perhaps 20 % of the known chemical compounds can be handled directly in a gas chromatograph. Biologists use GLC extensively, but unfortunately many of the most important biological compounds are insufficiently volatile, including amino acids, peptides, proteins, vitamins, coenzymes, carbohydrates, and nucleic acids. Sometimes, however, it is possible to convert nonvolatile sample components into volatile derivatives which can then be chromatographed. Obviously a difficult or time-consuming preliminary chemical step would nullify the speed and simplicity of the chromatographic analysis; hence there is a continuous search for reagents and reaction conditions which will derivatize all of the components of the sample quickly, cleanly, and quantitatively. For example, many studies have been directed toward the preparation of volatile amino acid derivatives. These involve both reactions of the carboxyl group, such as the formation of methyl or other alkyl esters, and reactions of the amino group, such as the formation of the trifluoroacetyl derivative. In recent years, volatile trimethylsilyl derivatives of acids, alcohols, amines, monosaccharides, and many other compounds have been studied extensively.

The technique called "pyrolysis gas chromatography" has become quite common in studies of nonvolatile polymeric materials such as tars, paints, rubber, synthetic films and fibers, and various sorts of plastics. The sample is heated very rapidly to a high temperature in a nonoxidizing atmosphere, and the gaseous products of the thermal decomposition are swept into the chromatographic column. In some cases the products are known compounds, but frequently the chromatogram is complex with many bands which are not identified. Despite the difficulty of a complete chemical interpretation, such a chromatogram may be reproducible and highly characteristic of the starting material, and it may be used in a manner somewhat analogous to the use of fingerprints. An interesting application of this technique is the identification of bacteria. In one example, the characterization of Salmonella organisms was described.[9] The cultured cells were harvested, washed free of culture medium, and centrifuged. The wet, packed cells were freeze-dried, and a sample of about 80 μg of the dried bacteria was subjected to pyrolysis GLC. Forty-seven species of Salmonella were correctly classified by examination of the chromatograms. Correlations were observed between GLC bands and groupings based upon traditional serological and biochemical classification tests. It is thought that some of the characteristic GLC band patterns arise from species differences in the hexose sugars of the bacterial cell wall.

Most inorganic samples are not sufficiently volatile to permit the direct application of GLC, although some work has been done at very high temperatures using molten salts or eutectic mixtures as the stationary liquid phase. Halides of some elements such as tin, titanium, arsenic, and antimony are fairly volatile and have been separated by GLC. A number of metals such as beryllium, aluminum, copper, iron, chromium, and cobalt have been subjected to GLC in the form of fairly volatile chelate compounds with acetylacetone and its fluorinated derivatives.[10] For example, aluminum, iron, and copper have been determined in alloys by dissolution of the sample followed by extraction of the metals into a chloroform solution of trifluoroacetylacetone which is then chromatographed.[11] Relative errors of the order of 0.2 to 3% were reported.

GLC figures prominently in efforts to monitor and control the distribution of pollutants in the environment. For example, the U.S. Environmental

[9] E. Reiner, et al., *Anal. Chem.*, **44**, 1058 (1972).

[10] R. W. Moshier and R. E. Sievers, *Gas Chromatography of Metal Chelates*, Pergamon Press, Oxford, 1965.

[11] R. W. Moshier and J. E. Schwarberg, *Talanta*, **13**, 445 (1966).

Protection Agency operates an extensive program for monitoring pesticide levels in soils throughout the country; the goal is to establish a baseline showing exactly where we are at the present time so that trends in the future can be interpreted meaningfully. Details vary, but the general approach involves extracting the soil sample with an organic solvent and chromatographing the extract in an instrument with a very sensitive detector. Similar programs are underway for crops, water, fish, and wildlife, and GLC is important in all of these.

Although it is perhaps more fun to discuss unusual applications and those which relate to popularly relevant subjects, the chemistry student should also keep in mind that thousands of chromatograms are recorded every day in laboratories where GLC is a routine analytical tool.

REFERENCES

C. E. BENNETT, S. DAL NOGARE, and L. W. SAFRANSKI, "Chromatography: Gas," Chapter 37, Part 1, Volume 3 of *Treatise on Analytical Chemistry*, I. M. Kolthoff and P. J. Elving, eds., Interscience Publishers, Inc., New York, 1961.

A. B. LITTLEWOOD, *Gas Chromatography: Principles, Techniques, and Applications*, 2nd ed., Academic Press, New York, 1970.

R. A. JONES, *An Introduction to Gas-Liquid Chromatography*, Academic Press, New York, 1970.

O. E. SCHUPP, 3, *Gas Chromatography*, Volume 13 of *Technique of Organic Chemistry*, E. S. Perry and A. Weissberger, eds., Interscience Publishers Division of John Wiley & Sons, Inc., New York, 1968.

S. DAL NOGARE and R. S. JUVET, JR., *Gas-Liquid Chromatography*, Interscience Publishers, Inc., New York, 1962.

H. P. BURCHFIELD and E. E. STORRS, *Biochemical Applications of Gas Chromatography*, Academic Press, New York, 1962.

J. H. PURNELL, *Gas Chromatography*, John Wiley & Sons, Inc., New York, 1962.

A. I. M. KEULEMANS, *Gas Chromatography*, 2nd ed., Reinhold Publishing Corp., New York, 1959.

QUESTIONS

1. Explain clearly what is meant by "height equivalent of a theoretical plate" in connection with a continuous-flow separation process such as gas-liquid chromatography.

2. By discussing the factors that contribute to band spreading in a GLC column, show that it is reasonable to expect that there will be an optimal carrier gas velocity.

3. Glass microbeads which are virtually perfect spheres perhaps 50 or 100 micrometers in diameter can be obtained. The beads have a very small surface area as compared with porous materials of the same particle size. A very thin coating of liquid will adhere to the surface of the glass. Several people have experimented with columns packed with these beads for GLC. The spherical particles pack into columns in a more uniform manner than do the irregularly shaped particles of typical porous packing materials. Knowing what you do about GLC, and considering the statements above regarding glass microbeads, what would you predict about the

advantages and disadvantages of glass microbead columns for GLC, as compared with columns where the support for the liquid phase is a porous solid of the usual type?

4. Using the peaks numbered 5, 6, and 7 in the chromatogram shown in Fig. 14.9(a), obtain three estimates of the number of theoretical plates in the column. The column was four feet long. Obtain estimates of HETP, in millimeters, for this column under the operating conditions that were used. (1 in = 2.54 cm.)

5. Show by a simple sketch what the baseline would look like in a programmed temperature GLC experiment where the initial temperature is very low and the final temperature is high enough to volatilize the stationary liquid appreciably. The instrument is a single-column chromatograph with no provision for baseline compensation.

6. Silver nitrate, $AgNO_3$, is soluble in certain organic liquids. Consider a column where the stationary phase is a certain liquid, say benzyl cyanide. What effect might the addition of silver nitrate to the liquid phase have upon the retention times of low molecular weight olefins?

7. Suppose a manufacturer redesigned his thermal conductivity detector, taking advantage of the latest improvements in materials and fabrication methods. In the new detector, the peak-to-peak noise level was found to be half of what it was in the old one, and the sensitivity had been doubled. What was the effect of these improvements upon the limit of detection for a certain organic compound?

8. Let us say that you are a skilled chromatographer and you have just hired an inexperienced person to work in your laboratory. The newcomer runs a chromatogram on a sample that you yourself have run many times. What in the appearance of the chromatograms might suggest to you that he had injected the sample too slowly?

15 Liquid Chromatography

INTRODUCTION

In this chapter, we shall consider several forms of chromatography where the moving phase is a liquid. Perhaps 80% of all chemical compounds are better handled in solution than in the gas phase, largely because of volatility limitations. Thus liquid chromatography is potentially more important than gas chromatography, although the latter will retain its dominant position where volatile compounds are involved. Historically, liquid chromatography was invented first, but the theoretical ideas and the modern instrumentation that led to highly efficient performance were developed first in GLC. In 1968 or so, an effort began to upgrade liquid chromatography utilizing concepts, particularly the kinetic approach, which had been successful in GLC. This process continues, and its rapid pace makes liquid chromatography today one of the most exciting aspects of analytical chemistry.

We shall first examine the phase distribution processes that are involved in the common forms of liquid chromatography. Next, to provide perspective in which to view recent developments, we shall briefly consider the conventional mode of operation. Finally, we shall describe modern practice as it has evolved so far. Concepts presented in the last chapter will be useful in this one, and we shall refer to these rather than presenting a self-contained theoretical treatment here.

Adsorption

Imagine a solid material with a clean, dry surface. Now if this surface is exposed to a fluid—gas, pure liquid, or solution—there is generally a tendency for molecules of gas, solvent, or solute to interact with the surface. If the solid material is very finely divided or is highly porous, in other words, if there is a large surface area, then the extent of adsorption may be appreciable. For example, if a good adsorbent is introduced into a vessel containing a gas, the decrease in pressure as the surface attracts gas molecules is easily measurable. An atom, ion, or molecule in the surface layer of a solid, unlike its counterparts in the interior, does not have neighboring particles on all sides. Thus residual attractive forces are exerted upon components of the fluid which bathes the surface, and the free energy of the system may be minimized if such components concentrate at the interface. In certain systems under certain conditions, the adsorbed layer may be only one molecule thick; frequently, however, the adsorbed molecules can in turn hold others so that a multimolecular layer is built up. In the case of the adsorption of ions on the surfaces of ionic solids, the force involved is an obvious electrostatic one. In other cases, van der Waals forces (dipole-dipole, dipole-induced dipole, and London forces) are responsible for adsorption.

If a solution containing a solute is placed in contact with a solid adsorbent, that solute will distribute itself between the two phases, with the position of equilibrium determined by the affinity of the surface for the solute, the affinity of the surface for the solvent (i.e., the solvent competes with the solute for available surface sites), and the affinity of the solvent for the solute.

Adsorption Equilibrium

The isotherm which describes an adsorption equilibrium is usually non-linear. Many systems follow the Freundlich equation, at least if the concentration is not too high; this may be given in the form

$$C_S = K C_L^{1/n}$$

where C_S is the concentration of an adsorbed solute on a solid phase in equilibrium with a solution of solute concentration C_L. Typical units for C_S are mmol of solute per g of adsorbent, and for C_L, molarity. K and n are constants. If n were equal to 1, the Freundlich equation would resemble other equilibrium expressions such as Henry's law or the equation for the distribution coefficient in solvent extraction. But in general $n > 1$, and hence a graph of C_S vs C_L, which is called an adsorption isotherm, resembles curve 2a in Fig. 14.4. Taking logarithms of both sides of the Freundlich equation yields

$$\log C_S = \log K + \frac{1}{n} \log C_L$$

which suggest that a graph of $\log C_S$ vs $\log C_L$ is a straight line of slope $1/n$ and an intercept of $\log K$ on the $\log C_S$ axis.

K and n are constants only for a given system and, of course, only for a stated temperature. They vary with the nature of the adsorbent and its surface character and with the solvent and the solute. K is more sensitive than is n to changes in the nature of the solute, and separations based upon adsorption depend largely upon differences in the K values for various solutes. As we saw in the last chapter, nonlinear isotherms are associated with skewed chromatographic elution bands; frequently the bands obtained with adsorption columns resemble curve 2b in Fig. 14.4, although at very low concentrations, where the isotherm may approximate linearity, fairly symmetrical bands are sometimes seen.

Variability in the surface properties of commercial adsorbents has been a problem for chromatographers. In some cases, simply washing an adsorbent such as alumina with acid or alkali considerably modifies its behavior, and the temperature at which it is dried may also be very important. Different batches of adsorbents, even those from the same producer, may exhibit troublesome variability. In recent years, the marketing of specially prepared adsorbents which are tested and labelled "for chromatography" has been helpful.

A few general rules regarding the adsorbability of a solute may be stated. Everything else the same, the more polar a compound, the more strongly will it be adsorbed from solution. Other factors equal, high molecular weight favors adsorption. The nature of the solvent from which adsorption occurs is very important: the more polar the solvent, the stronger is its tendency to occupy surface sites in competition with the solute, and hence the less the adsorption of the solute.

A wide variety of adsorbents have been employed in various applications. Among the more common ones are sucrose, starch, cellulose, calcium carbonate, magnesium carbonate, silica gel, alumina, and charcoal.

Ion Exchange

Ion Exchange Resins

A wide variety of materials, both natural and synthetic, organic and inorganic, exhibit ion exchange behavior, but in the research laboratory, where uniformity from one batch to another is important, the preferred ion exchangers are usually synthetic materials known as ion exchange resins. The resins are prepared by introducing ionizable groups into an organic polymer matrix. The commonest matrix is a copolymer of styrene and divinylbenzene.

The polymerization of styrene yields a linear polymer:

$CH = CH_2$ $\cdots\cdots -CH-CH_2-CH-CH_2-CH-CH_2-CH- \cdots\cdots$

Styrene   Polystyrene

The addition of the bifunctional monomer divinylbenzene to the polymerization mix, on the other hand, links together the polystyrene chains and yields a material with a three-dimensional network structure:

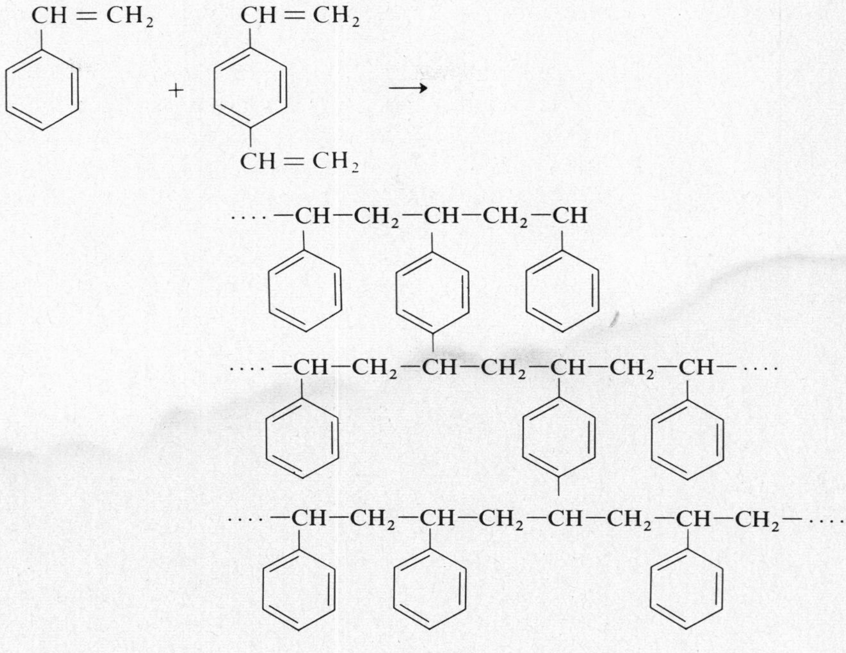

By varying the divinylbenzene content, the degree of cross-linking can be controlled quite reproducibly. General purpose resins usually contain 8 to 12% divinylbenzene; a resin with, say, 8% divinylbenzene is said to be "8% cross-linked." The resins are made in the form of spherical beads by the process of emulsion polymerization. The bead diameter is controlled; this is usually in the range of 0.1 to 0.5 mm, although other sizes can be made for special purposes.

To prepare a typical cation exchange resin, the polymer is sulfonated to introduce $-SO_3H$ groups into the aromatic rings. Because these sulfonic acid groups are highly polar, the polymer thus acquires a high affinity for water. When the resin particles are suspended in water, they increase in size because of the water uptake. This swelling is limited, of course, by the cross-linking; a linear (noncross-linked) polymer would swell indefinitely until it finally yielded a molecular dispersion in solution.

The arylsulfonic acids are strong acids. Thus these groups are ionized when water penetrates the resin beads:

$$R-SO_3H + H_2O \rightleftharpoons R-SO_3^- + H_3O^+$$

But, unlike ordinary electrolytes, here the anion is permanently attached to the immovable polymer matrix, and it cannot migrate through the aqueous phase within the pores of the resin. This fixation of the anion in turn restricts the mobility of the cation, H_3O^+. Electrical neutrality is maintained within the resin, and H_3O^+ will not leave the resin particle unless it is replaced by some other cation. The exchange is stoichiometric; i.e., one H_3O^+ is replaced by one Na^+, two H_3O^+ by one Ca^{2+}, etc. As we discuss below, ion exchange is an equilibrium process, and seldom does it go to completion; but regardless of the extent to which it proceeds, the stoichiometry is exact in that one positive charge leaves the resin for each one which enters.

The introduction of basic groups into the polymer yields anion exchange materials. One of the common strong base anion exchangers may be represented as

$$R \underset{}{\overset{}{\bigcirc}} CH_2 - \overset{\overset{\displaystyle CH_3}{|}}{\underset{\underset{\displaystyle CH_3}{|}}{N^+}} - CH_3 \qquad X^-$$

where X^- is an anion such as OH^-, Cl^-, or NO_3^-. The exchangeable ion, i.e., the ion which is not fixed to the polymer matrix, is called the "counter ion."

Ion-Exchange Equilibrium

Suppose a resin containing the exchangeable counter ion B is placed in a solution containing ion A of the same charge. The exchange reaction takes place,

$$\underset{\text{Solution}}{A} + \underset{\substack{\text{Resin} \\ \text{phase}}}{RB} \rightleftarrows \underset{\substack{\text{Resin} \\ \text{phase}}}{RA} + \underset{\text{Solution}}{B}$$

and equilibrium will be attained with some of each ion in the resin phase and some in solution, for which we may write an equilibrium constant,

$$K = \frac{a_{A_r} \times a_{B_s}}{a_{B_r} \times a_{A_s}}$$

where a_{A_r} represents the activity of ion A in the resin phase and a_{A_s} its activity in the solution outside the resin pores. This expression can be written

$$K = \frac{X_{A_r} \times (B)_s}{X_{B_r} \times (A)_s} \times \frac{\gamma_{A_r} \times \gamma_{B_s}}{\gamma_{B_r} \times \gamma_{A_s}}$$

or

$$K = Q \times \frac{\gamma_{A_r} \gamma_{B_s}}{\gamma_{B_r} \gamma_{A_s}}$$

where X_{A_r} and X_{B_r} are the concentrations in mole fraction in the resin phase, parentheses mean molal concentrations in the external solution, and γ is the activity coefficient. The term Q is called the concentration quotient, or "practical selectivity coefficient." Some workers use the term "selectivity coefficient" to refer to the product of Q and the activity coefficient ratio of the ions in solution:

$$Q_\gamma = Q\frac{\gamma_{B_s}}{\gamma_{A_s}} = K\frac{\gamma_{B_r}}{\gamma_{A_r}}$$

At low concentrations of the ions in solution, $Q_\gamma \cong Q$ since the activity coefficients approach unity.

It is clear why Q_γ values are called selectivity coefficients: If Q_γ is large, the resin is showing a preference for ion A; if Q_γ is small, the selectivity of the resin favors ion B. We may never speak of the tendency of a resin to pick up a certain ion without noting that there is already another ion in the resin, that is, we should consider, not the tendency for the resin to pick up ion A in an absolute sense, but rather the tendency to pick up A at the expense of ion B. The tendency to pick up ion A will be different if the resin phase contains some other ion C instead of B as the counter ion.

However, we can put a certain ion on a resin and then compare a series of other ions using this as a reference. For the ions in this series we may simply write distribution ratios:

$$D = \frac{\text{Concentration of an ion in the resin}}{\text{Concentration of the same ion in solution}}$$

The conventional units of D are

$$\frac{\text{Amount/kg of dry resin}}{\text{Amount/l of solution}}$$

The "amount" term may be in mg, mols, or whatever, since its units cancel in the D ratio.

A distribution ratio with different units is sometimes used, with the symbol D_V.

$$D_V = \frac{\text{Amount/l of resin bed}}{\text{Amount/l of solution}}$$

The conversion factor for D to D_V is the so-called bed density, ρ,

$$D_V = D \times \rho$$

where ρ is in kg of dry resin per liter of resin bed.

The significant aspect of ion exchangers is, of course, their selectivity, i.e., D values are different for various ions, and hence separations may be accomplished by ion exchange.

Neutral molecules can find their way into the pores of an ion exchange resin, but they are not subject to forces so strong as those acting on ions, and in general they can be washed out by water or some other solvent. Solutes in the resin which are not so strongly held as ions are said to be "sorbed"; the pick-up of such solutes by the resin is called "sorption." Sorption can sometimes be used to effect separations, but in this discussion we are concerned only with legitimate ion exchange. Of course the sign of the charge on an ion is important in selectivity, but this is so obvious as to be trivial. A cation cannot participate in exchange on an anion exchange resin; it might find its way into the resin pores by some sort of general electrolyte sorption, but it would not be strongly held and could be washed out with water.

In a series of ions which have the proper sign to act as true counter ions, the magnitude of the charge is important. Normally, the resin prefers the ion of higher charge. Thus the extent of exchange with, say, H_3O^+, would decrease in the order

$$Th^{4+} > Al^{3+} > Ca^{2+} > Na^+$$

provided proper allowance was made for other factors such as concentration. There are exceptions to this, but it is a good rule of thumb under ordinary conditions.

With a series of ions of the same charge, the resin still shows selectivity. For example, with the alkali metals, the following order is generally found with cation exchange resins:

$$Cs^+ > Rb^+ > K^+ > Na^+ > Li^+$$

The important factor here is probably the radius of the ion; the smaller an ion of given charge, the more strongly it will be held by the resin. At first glance, the above order may not appear consistent with this statement, which would imply that Cs^+ is a smaller ion than Li^+. The usual values of ionic radii, however, are obtained by X-ray diffraction studies of solid crystals, and these "crystallographic" or "naked" radii are not the right ones to use here. The ions in solution are hydrated, and it is the radius of the hydrated ion that determines the ion exchange behavior. Such hydrated radii are much more difficult to measure, but estimates are available. While the naked radius of Li^+ is 0.68 A, the hydrated radius is about 10 A; the naked and hydrated radii for Cs^+ are 1.65 A and 5.05 A, respectively.

Liquid-Liquid Partition

If a solution of sodium silicate is acidified under the proper conditions, the precipitated silicic acid takes the form of a gel, a hydrophilic network structure which contains a large quantity of water. If this water is then driven out by heating the gel to an appropriate temperature, the silica which remains is a hard solid with a highly porous structure of very large surface area which is known as silica gel. Silica gel has a high affinity for water and is widely used as a desiccant. In 1941, Martin and Synge employed silica gel as a solid support to immobilize water as the stationary phase in a chromatographic column.[1] With a mixture of n-butanol and chloroform as the moving phase, acetylated amino acids were separated on this column. The basis for the separation was considered to be partition of the solutes between the stationary water phase and the mobile organic phase, the same process utilized in Craig's countercurrent solvent extraction technique adapted to the chromatographic mode. This particular form of chromatography was not widely adopted because shortly after it was proposed, a variant known as paper chromatography appeared which was more convenient in view of the technological limitations upon chromatography in the 1940s. Liquid-liquid partition chromatography in columns is returning, however, in a newer form which will be mentioned later.

Gel Filtration

The process of gel filtration is also known as gel permeation and molecular exclusion. Chromatography based upon this process is widely used in biochemistry to separate proteins and other macromolecules, and in industrial laboratories to characterize synthetic polymers. The most important column-packing materials are cross-linked dextrans and polyacrylamides, sold under the trade names Sephadexes and Bio-Gels, respectively.

When certain bacteria grow on substrates containing sucrose, they synthesize polysaccharides called dextrans. Dextrans are linear polymers of D-glucose with a small amount of cross-linking between adjacent chains; a typical molecular weight is of the order of 75,000. Additional cross-links can be introduced artificially by means of various chemical reagents to yield a network structure in which the pore size is controlled. The commercial materials are offered in the form of small beads of stated diameters with designations that reflect the pore sizes.

The glucose residues in the cross-linked dextrans are hydrophilic, and when the beads are placed in an aqueous solution, there is an appreciable uptake of water which is called the "water regain." This is accompanied by the swelling of the particles to form the Sephadex gel. The process with which we are now concerned is the distribution of solutes between an aqueous phase within the gel particles and an external aqueous phase. At first glance, transferring a solute from water into water is no process at all. But selectivity with regard to different solutes is achieved on the basis of the pore size. A small molecule may freely enter the gel phase, in other words, the water within the particles is available. In a column operation, this will have a retarding effect because molecules which are able to penetrate the gel will spend part of their time sheltered from the moving phase. On the other hand, the internal water phase will not be available for a large molecule that cannot

[1] A. J. P. Martin and R. L. M. Synge, *Biochem. J.*, **35**, 91 (1941).

penetrate the pores, and such a molecule will not experience retardation by the stationary phase. In between, there will be molecules of intermediate size which can penetrate some of the larger pores and will then be retarded in some degree.

Let V_R be the retention volume for a solute in a chromatographic experiment with a Sephadex column. Let V_o be the interstitial volume or void volume, i.e., the volume within the column which is available for the moving phase (this is analogous to V_G in the last chapter), and let V_L be the volume of the water within the gel particles which is available for accepting solutes. Then we can write an equation of the same sort that we had in GLC:

$$V_R = V_o + KV_L$$

where K has the form of a distribution coefficient. If a solute is completely excluded from the interior of the gel particle, then $K = 0$ and $V_R = V_o$; colored marker substances which approximate this behavior are available from the Sephadex supplier. For a solute which can freely enter the gel particle, there should be no preference for water inside or outside the gel, and hence $K = 1$ and $V_R = V_o + V_L$. For molecules of intermediate size which can penetrate the gel to some extent but not freely, K values should fall between 0 and 1. If sieving based upon molecular size were the only phenomenon occurring, then K values greater than 1 would never be encountered. In fact, however, such values are sometimes obtained, suggesting that solutes may interact with the dextran matrix itself; effects such as adsorption, hydrogen bonding, and ion exchange would explain such behavior. Figure 15.1 shows the manner in which solute elution volume typically varies with molecular weight.

The polyacrylamide gels are prepared by copolymerizing acrylamide, $H_2N-CO-CH=CH_2$, with methylenebisacrylamide,

$$H_2N-CO-CH=CH-CH_2-CH=CH-CO-NH_2,$$

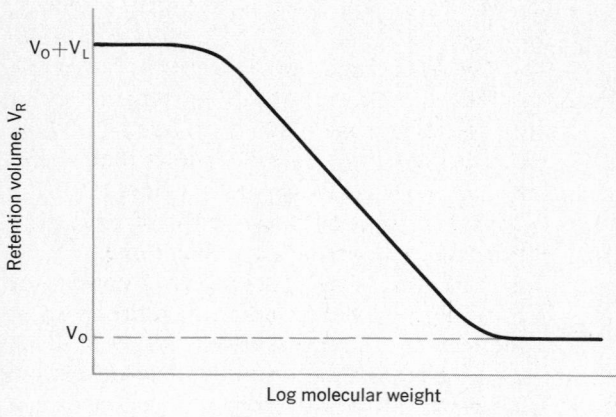

Retention volume, V_R

V_o+V_L

V_o

Log molecular weight

FIGURE 15.1 Relation between retention volume and molecular weight for solutes on a gel filtration column.

the latter providing cross-linking. The polymer, which is produced in the form of spherical beads, hydrates readily when soaked in water because of the polar amide groups. Bio-Gel columns are similar to Sephadex with regard to their general applicability.

Recently, gel filtration materials into which ionizable groups have been deliberately introduced have appeared on the market. Presumably the ion exchange aspect offers additional selectivity over that provided by molecular exclusion alone for the separation of solutes which are ionic. Materials are also now available which are suitable for use with certain organic solvents rather than water, extending gel filtration further into organic chemistry.

CONVENTIONAL LIQUID CHROMATOGRAPHY TECHNIQUES

We saw in the last chapter that the gas chromatograph is a complete analytical instrument in the sense that components of the sample are not only separated but are measured as well. Liquid chromatography developed earlier, in a period when speed and automation were not major concerns in the laboratory and before the "systems" approach had been applied to analytical instrumentation. The great power of liquid chromatography as a separation tool was recognized forty years ago, but the idea of building an efficient analytical instrument around it goes back only four or five years. These recent developments will be better appreciated if we examine briefly the conventional approach, which, as a matter of fact, is still widely used.

Various sizes of columns may be employed, the major consideration being adequate capacity to accept the sample without overloading the stationary phase. It is a common rule of thumb that the length of the column should be at least ten times its diameter. For a typical case, let us say that we have a column 20 cm long and 1 or 2 cm in diameter, something like the one shown in Fig. 15.2. The packing material, an adsorbent like alumina or perhaps an ion exchange resin, had probably been added in the form of a suspension in a portion of the moving phase and allowed to settle into a wet bed with a little liquid remaining above the surface. Now by opening the stopcock, the liquid level is allowed to fall just to the top of the bed, and then a small portion of sample solution (a few tenths of a milliliter up to perhaps a couple of milliliters) is carefully pipetted onto the top of the bed. The liquid reservoir is positioned, and the flow of the mobile phase is started. The desired flow rate is obtained by gravity alone, by inserting the outlet end of the column into an evacuated vessel as shown in the figure, or by pumping liquid in at the top of the column. A typical flow rate might be a few tenths of a milliliter per minute, possibly faster if the separation were not a difficult one.

The effluent solution is collected in a series of fractions of convenient volume. The solution may drip into a graduated cylinder which the operator dumps into a beaker or test tube each time a certain volume, say 5 or 10 ml, has accumulated. It is not uncommon for the chromatographic elution process to require several hours, even all day or overnight. In such a case, a

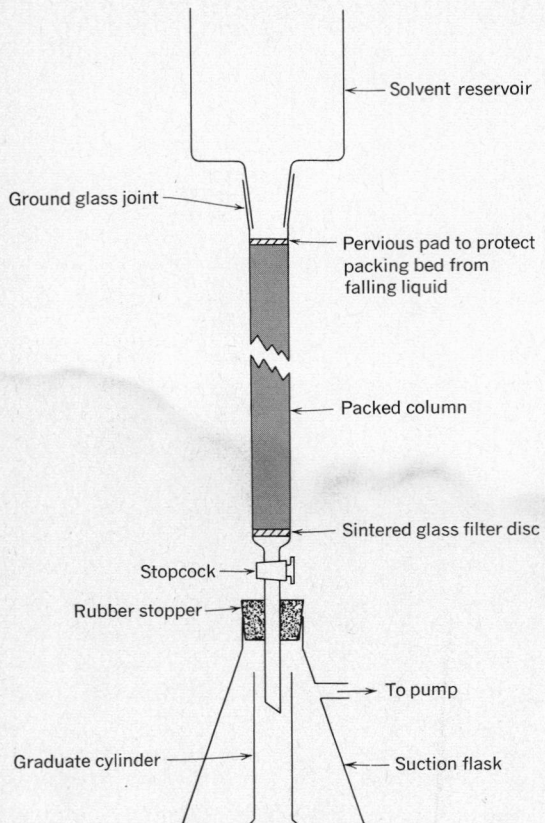

Solvent reservoir

Ground glass joint

Pervious pad to protect
packing bed from
falling liquid

Packed column

Sintered glass filter disc

Stopcock

Rubber stopper

To pump

Graduate cylinder

Suction flask

FIGURE 15.2 Possible setup for conventional liquid chromatography.

mechanical device called a fraction collector is convenient. The operator sets up a series of tubes on a turntable which positions a new tube under the column when the desired volume has been collected in the previous one; activation can be based upon time, drop counting, or the deflection of a light beam by the rising meniscus in the tube.

It sometimes happens that no single moving phase is well suited for the elution of all of the components of a sample. In adsorption, for example, a fairly nonpolar solvent may be ideal for eluting some of the less polar solutes, whereas the more polar solutes may then show an inordinately long retention. In such a case, the technique of gradient elution may be useful. The composition of the mobile phase is changed continuously by allowing a more polar solvent to flow into the reservoir containing the less polar one, whence the mixture flows to the column. The reservoir is stirred. Figure 15.3 shows such an arrangement schematically. Now the laggard solutes will move along faster as the eluting power of the solvent mixture increases. Bands with serious "tailing" may be sharpened, since the tail sees a stronger solvent than the front of the band. The result of gradient elution is rather similar to that of

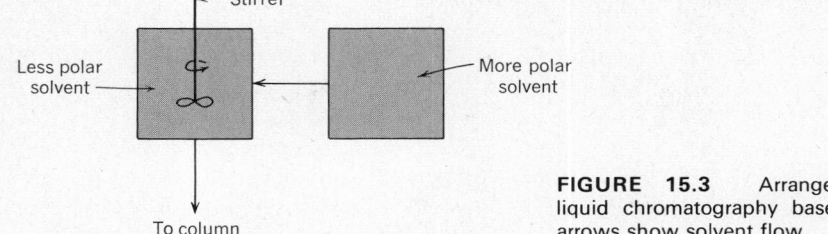

FIGURE 15.3 Arrangement for gradient elution in liquid chromatography based upon adsorption. Large arrows show solvent flow.

temperature programming in GLC, which was mentioned in the last chapter.

The individual fractions of the effluent solution are examined by whatever means is appropriate—spectrophotometry, polarography, radioactive assay, titrimetry, etc.—to locate the desired components of the sample and to determine their quantities.

As seen above, the conventional column operation is slow and tedious, and it is poorly suited to automation and modern methods of data processing. It is not totally without merit, however; for example, fairly large columns can be used which have sufficient capacity for preparative-scale work. But for handling large numbers of analytical samples, recent developments enable us to do better. Before describing these developments, we shall complete our discussion of conventional liquid chromatography by considering briefly two widely used forms which do not employ a column in the usual sense.

Paper Chromatography

In 1944, again from Martin's laboratory, the separation of a mixture of amino acids was reported using paper chromatography.[2] In this technique, a small volume of sample solution is applied near one end of a strip of filter paper and the spot is allowed to dry (blowing on it with a hair dryer is convenient). The end of the strip is then placed in a trough containing a suitable solvent within a closed chamber. In ascending paper chromatography, the paper is suspended from the top of the chamber so that it dips into the solvent at the bottom, and the solvent creeps up the paper by capillarity. In the descending form, the paper is anchored in a solvent trough at the top of the chamber, and the solvent migrates downward by capillarity assisted by gravity. After the solvent front has moved almost the length of the paper, the strip is removed, dried, and examined. In a successful case, solutes from the original mixture will have migrated along the paper at different rates, forming a series of separated spots. If the compounds are colored, of course the spots can be seen. If not, they must be found in some other way. Some compounds fluoresce, in which case glowing spots may be seen when the paper is held under an ultraviolet lamp. For amino acids, the paper is usually sprayed with a solution of ninhydrin, a reagent which reacts with the amino group

[2] R. Consden, A. H. Gordon, and A. J. P. Martin, *Biochem. J.*, **38**, 224 (1944).

to yield a purple compound. For quantitative analysis, the spots may be cut out with scissors, the solutes leached from the paper by appropriate solvents, and the solutions examined by a suitable technique, often spectrophotometry.

For identification purposes, spots are often characterized by their R_f values. An R_f value is the ratio of the distance moved by a solute to the distance that the solvent front moved during the same time. Identical R_f values for a known and an unknown compound using several different solvent systems provides good evidence that the two are identical, especially if they are run side by side along the same strip of paper.

It sometimes happens that all of the components of a sample cannot be separated using any one solvent system; some components separate better in one system, some in another. Two-dimensional paper chromatography may then be employed. The sample is spotted near one corner of a square filter paper sheet. After migration of the solutes parallel to one edge of the paper using one solvent system, the paper is turned 90°, and a second solvent system carries the solutes into the unused portion of the paper. The pattern of ninhydrin-stained spots that results from applying this technique to the amino acids in a protein hydrolyzate is often called a "fingerprint" of the protein.

It was considered at first that paper chromatography was simply a form of liquid-liquid partition. The hydrophilic cellulose fibers of the paper can bind water; after exposure to a humid atmosphere, filter paper that appears dry may actually contain a large percentage of water, say 20 % or more by weight. Thus the paper was considered to be the analog of a column containing a stationary aqueous phase. Solutes then were partitioned between this water and the moving immiscible organic solvent. It was soon realized, however, that this model was too simple. Separations were obtained where the moving phase was miscible with water or in some cases was itself an aqueous solution. Thus, although liquid-liquid partition may indeed play a role in some cases, the mechanism of paper chromatography is often more complicated than that. Interactions between solutes and the cellulose support are probably involved, for example, adsorption and hydrogen bonding. Carboxyl and other ionizable groups are introduced into cellulose during the pulping and bleaching operations of paper manufacture, and hence the paper may also act as an ion exchanger.

Thin-Layer Chromatography

Thin-layer chromatography or TLC, like paper chromatography, is inexpensive and simple to perform. It has an advantage of speed over paper chromatography: the process may require only a half hour or so, whereas a typical separation on paper requires several hours. TLC is very popular and is used routinely in many laboratories.

The separation medium is a layer perhaps 0.1 to 0.3 mm thick of an adsorbent solid on a glass, plastic, or aluminum plate. A typical plate is 8 × 2 in. Typical solids are alumina, silica gel, and cellulose. Workers used to prepare their own plates by coating the glass with an aqueous suspension of the solid, which usually contained a binder such as plaster of paris, and then drying the plates in the oven. Precoated glass plates and sheets of plastic and aluminum foil which can be cut to size with scissors are commercially available, and probably the majority of workers use these today.

The sample, generally a mixture of organic compounds, is applied near one end of the plate as a small volume of solution, usually a few microliters containing microgram quantities of the compounds. A hypodermic syringe or a small glass pipet may be used. The sample spot is dried, and then the end of the plate is dipped into a suitable moving phase. The solvent moves up the thin layer of solid on the plate, and as it moves, sample solutes are carried along at rates which depend upon their solubilities in the moving phase and their interactions with the solid. After the solvent front has migrated perhaps 10 cm, the plate is dried and examined for solute spots as in paper chromatography. A two-dimensional run using two different moving phases is often performed; here a square plate is used rather than a narrow one. The separation may be followed by a quantitative determination; where a spot is located, the adsorbent can be scraped from the plate with a spatula, the solute eluted from the solid material with a suitable solvent, and the concentration of the solution determined by a technique such as spectrophotometry.

MODERN LIQUID CHROMATOGRAPHY

Although a theoretical consideration of liquid chromatography can become very complicated, our purpose here requires a brief and qualitative treatment. Fortunately, it is possible to understand recent developments in these terms. Let us look at the situation in the following manner. We have been "spoiled" by GLC. We have become accustomed to chromatography where excellent separations required only a few minutes; perhaps integrations were performed electronically and a computer printed out complete analyses. After this experience, we are no longer content with the conventional technique when we encounter nonvolatile samples which require liquid moving phases. Several hours to elute a sample, assaying eluate fractions one at a time, one or two samples a day—out of the question! Yet we need the power of chromatography for increasingly difficult separations. So we must speed it up and at least partly automate it. How shall we do this?

The first thing that comes to mind is to increase the flow rate; solutes will elute faster. Gravity will no longer suffice, and we shall need a pump, along with plumbing connections that do not leak under high pressure. But there is more to consider than this. It has been well known for years that high flow rates in liquid chromatography are incompatible with good separations. Recalling the last chapter, we suspect that kinetic factors are responsible for this. So we need more than a pump: we must consider how to overcome the increasing departure from equilibrium that accompanies the increased flow rate, and this leads into the area of column technology.

In comparing liquid chromatography with GLC, it is instructive to consider the three terms in the van Deemter equation:

$$\text{HETP} = A + \frac{B}{u} + Cu$$

A, the eddy diffusion term, is probably small, and we shall not expect to benefit greatly by improvements here. Smaller diameter of the column packing particles tends to lessen A, but smaller particles are more difficult to pack uniformly, a factor which operates in the opposite direction. In seeking a big improvement in column efficiency, we must turn to factors other than eddy diffusion. (But this is not the whole story on particle size, because the size may also affect the nonequilibrium term in the van Deemter equation, as we shall note below.)

In GLC, the B/u term was very important at low carrier gas flow rates. This is not the case in liquid chromatography because of the fact that diffusion coefficients of solutes in the liquid phase are very much smaller than in gases. Thus low flow rates in liquid chromatography are not deleterious so far as the separation itself is concerned, although we take no comfort in this. We are interested in faster flow rates, not slower ones, in our quest for high performance which includes speed as well as good separations. For all practical purposes, we may neglect the effect of longitudinal diffusion in liquid chromatography.

There is only one factor left: If we want high-speed liquid chromatography that is also highly efficient with regard to the resolution of solutes, it becomes crucial to obtain faster mass transfer of solutes between stationary and moving phases. One possibility is to raise the temperature. If the sample is stable at, say 80°, we may operate the column at this temperature and get somewhat faster mass transfer kinetics than at room temperature. The higher temperature also lowers the viscosity of the liquid, with the result that the desired flow rate may be obtained with a smaller pressure drop. But only small gains are made in this way. The major breakthrough to date has been the development of new column packing materials.

The old packing materials are porous solids—silica gel, diatomaceous earth, ion-exchange resin beads, etc.—which have deep pores that fill with stagnant portions of mobile phase. Diffusion of solutes through such pores is slow and represents the major obstacle to high-speed operation. Grinding the solid to a smaller particle size would counter this problem, but a dramatic improvement would require a very small size. With such packing, it would be difficult to obtain the desired flow rate with inlet pressures provided by present pumps; moreover, it would be very difficult to pack the columns uniformly. Nevertheless, experts in liquid chromatography do anticipate developments along this line:

> ... future developments of column packings will involve the use of very small porous particles (2–5 μ). The next big development in column technology will be in overcoming experimental difficulties in packing homogeneous columns of these very small

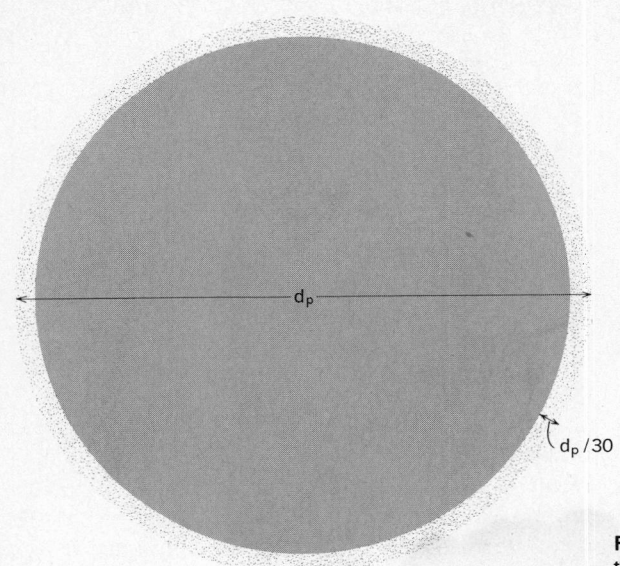

FIGURE 15.4 Schematic section through the center of a porous layer bead.

particles. Column pressures needed to operate columns of these small particles probably will not need to exceed 10,000 psi.[3]

At the present time, the best performance available is provided by new packing materials known as "superficially porous supports" or "porous layer beads." These are commercially available under tradenames such as Zipax (E. I. du Pont de Nemours and Co., Inc.) and Corasil (Waters Associates). The porous layer beads represent an ingenious combination of large overall particle size for easy column packing and low pressure drop with very small pore depth for rapid equilibration. Each bead is an impervious sphere of glass or siliceous material of some sort, 30 to 50 μ in diameter, with a thin surface coating of porous material, as shown schematically in Fig. 15.4. With Zipax, the surface layer is made up of bonded spherical microbeads, each about 200 nm in diameter. The interstices in this partly fused bead structure are large enough to permit solute molecules free access to a very thin film of stationary liquid. The Zipax surface is a very weak adsorbent; this material is intended primarily as a support for a stationary liquid phase. Corasil I has a very thin layer of silica gel bonded to the surface of a glass bead. It has been used as a support for a liquid phase as well as an adsorbent for liquid-solid chromatography. Corasil II has a thicker silica gel layer and was developed primarily as an adsorbent. Materials are also available for ion-exchange chromatography; these comprise a thin, porous outer shell of an

[3] J. J. Kirkland, *Anal. Chem.*, **43**, 36A (1971).

ion exchange medium over a solid, nonporous core. Interesting packing materials have been developed where molecules which play somewhat the role of a stationary liquid are chemically bonded to a silica matrix; the purpose is to eliminate deterioration of liquid loaded columns resulting from solubility of the stationary phase in the mobile liquid and from stripping due to shear forces at high carrier velocities.

Figure 15.5 shows how HETP varies with mobile phase velocity, with the typical behavior in GLC also shown for contrast. The point noted earlier, viz., longitudinal diffusion is not a problem at low velocities in the liquid case, may be seen in the figure. It may also be seen that the price for a fast flow rate, in terms of increased HETP, is not so bad as might have been expected; the curve almost levels off at very fast velocities. Possibly this relates to the occurrence of turbulent flow at high carrier velocities.

The new packing materials have led to the development of liquid chromatographs which are operated in much the same manner as gas chromatographs. Small samples are injected, picked up by the flowing liquid carrier stream, and carried to columns which are typically 50 to 100 cm long and 2 or 3 mm in internal diameter. Typical flow rates are 1 or 2 ml per min, requiring pressures of 500 to several thousand psi, depending upon the column. The column effluent passes through a detector, the output of which is recorded as in GLC. With superficially porous supports, sample capacities are small, and very sensitive detectors are required. Two types are in common use, one based upon the absorption of ultraviolet radiation by sample components, the other upon measurement of refractive index. The former is generally the more sensitive but not universally applicable, while the latter is less sensitive but responds to a larger number of compounds. Figure 15.6 shows a chromatogram obtained with such an instrument.

Modern liquid chromatography is in its infancy, but because it promises so much, it is an active field and rapid advances may be expected. Particu-

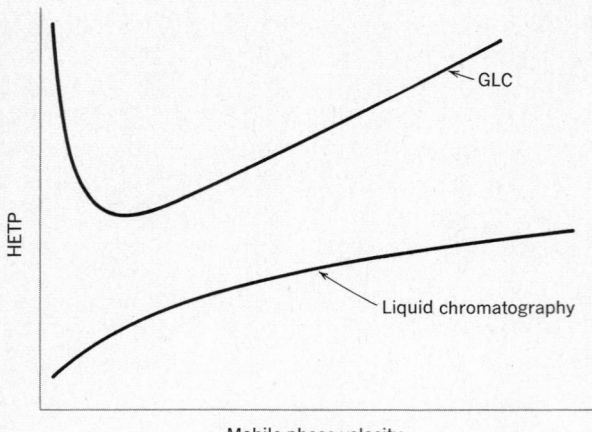

FIGURE 15.5 Typical graphs of HETP vs mobile phase velocity for gas and liquid chromatography.

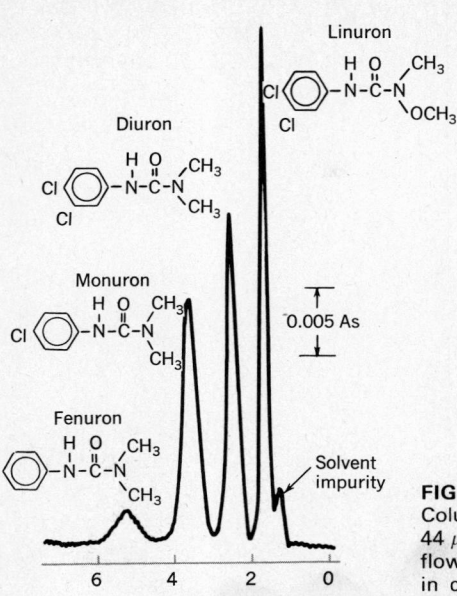

FIGURE 15.6 Separation of substituted urea herbicides. Column = 50 cm, 2.1 mm i.d., 1.0% β,β'-oxydipropionitrile on 37–44 μ controlled surface porosity support; carrier = di-n-butyl ether; flow rate = 1.14 cc/min; sample 1 μl of a solution of 67 μg/ml each in carrier. (Courtesy of the publisher of the *Journal of Chromatographic Science*.)

larly important would be detectors of high sensitivity and broader applicability than the present ultraviolet detector. Many chemists would like to see high-efficiency operation on a preparative scale, but basically there is a conflict between capacity for large samples and optimization for high-speed separations, and there may be disappointments. However, some degree of scale-up is certainly possible.

REFERENCES

J. J. KIRKLAND, ed., *Modern Practice of Liquid Chromatography*, Wiley-Interscience Division of John Wiley & Sons, Inc., New York, 1971.

F. HELFFERICH, *Ion Exchange*, McGraw-Hill Book Company, New York, 1962.

E. W. BERG, *Physical and Chemical Methods of Separation*, McGraw-Hill Book Company, New York, 1963, Chaps. 4, 6, 10, 11.

H. A. LAITINEN, *Chemical Analysis*, McGraw-Hill Book Company, New York, 1960, Chap. 25.

I. M. KOLTHOFF and P. J. ELVING, eds., *Treatise on Analytical Chemistry*, Part 1, Vol. 3, Interscience Publishers, New York, 1961, Chaps. 33, 34, 35, 36.

J. G. KIRCHNER, *Thin-Layer Chromatography*, Vol. XII of E. S. Perry and A. Weissberger, eds., *Technique of Organic Chemistry*, Interscience Publishers Division of John Wiley & Sons, New York, 1967.

L. FISCHER, *An Introduction to Gel Chromatography*, Part II of T. S. Work and E. Work, eds., *Laboratory Techniques in Biochemistry and Molecular Biology*, Vol. I, North-Holland Publishing Co., Amsterdam, 1970.

16 Analog Electronics

INTRODUCTION[1]

As a student taking a course in analytical chemistry, you are probably wondering why you should be introduced to electronics. Your main objective is, after all, the study of analytical chemistry. To help answer this question, let us look once again at the final two basic steps in an analysis, *measurement* and *calculation*.

Fundamental to all types of analytical measurements upon chemical systems is the transformation of chemical information (such as *p*H, transmittance, etc.) into some other information medium (such as voltage, numbers, etc.) as suggested[2] in Fig. 16.1. The subsequent operations that are carried out on this transformed information belong to the calculational step of an analysis. Consider, for example, the measurement of hydrogen ion activity. Ordinarily, the experimenter calibrates his *p*H meter with one or two standard buffer solutions, places the electrodes in the solution to be "measured," and reads the value of *p*H from the meter. The "calculation" involved, though trivial, consists of taking the antilog of the negative of the indicated *p*H to arrive at a value of the hydrogen ion activity.

A few minutes' reflection will suggest that the calculational part of the

[1] This chapter contributed by Stanley N. Deming, Assistant Professor of Chemistry, Emory University.

[2] For a discussion of measurement transducers and the transformation of information, see C. G. Enke, "Data Domains—An Analysis of Digital and Analog Instrumentation Systems and Components," *Anal. Chem.*, **43**(1), 69A (1971).

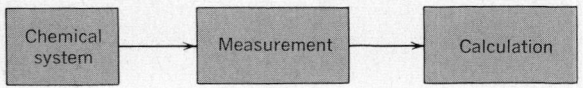

FIGURE 16.1 Final sequence of events in a quantitative analysis.

analysis is done not just by the experimenter but also by the *p*H meter, and it is really not all that trivial. The operations involved in the calibration step set certain "electronic constants" that the *p*H meter multiplies by and adds to the electrical signal coming from the glass electrode. The *p*H meter is, in fact, performing a rather sophisticated calculation on the signal before it reaches the meter.

The calculation step of a quantitative analysis begins just after the signal has been transformed from the chemical domain and extends until the question of "how much?" has been answered. The entire history of chemical instrumentation, especially the last decade, has seen the entry point for human interaction progress away from the measurement step more and more toward the final stages of calculation.

Thus, the answer to the question raised at the beginning of this chapter is that the use of electronics in analytical chemistry has significantly reduced the amount of work a chemist must do in the measurement and calculation steps of an analysis. The subject of this chapter and the next is the exploration of various of the electronic methods used to simplify the experimenter's duties.

BASIC ELECTRONICS

Current

The conduction of electricity from one point to another is accomplished most frequently by the movement of negatively charged electrons. For this reason, chemists quite naturally imagine a "flow of negative charge" when they think of electrical *current*. Physicists and electrical engineers, however, prefer to think of the more abstract "flow of positive charge." Because much of the electrical and electronic literature is phrased in terms of the flow of positive charge (positive current), it is well to understand why this concept is used and how it is related to negative current.

In the early days of electrical research, two types of electricity were recognized. Quite arbitrarily, one type of electricity was called *positive*, the other type *negative*. Physicists and electrical engineers chose to develop the explanations and theories of electricity and electronics with the arbitrary convention that positive electricity be used as the reference. Thus, current was described as a flow of positive charge.

Electricity of one type repels other electricity of the same type but attracts electricity of the opposite type. When electrons were discovered, they were found to be attracted by positive electricity; electrons, therefore, must have a negative charge.

It is perhaps unfortunate for chemists that the types of electricity were not oppositely named or that negative electricity was not used as the reference.

The concept of negative current has a physical meaning in most circuits: for example, the conduction of electricity by photoelectrons across a phototube. The cases in which positive current has a physical meaning are less common. However, either concept can be used to describe the flow of electricity. No difficulty arises if it is realized that positive current flowing in one direction is electrically equivalent to negative current flowing in the opposite direction.

Current is measured in *amperes* (A) which have units of coulombs sec^{-1} and express the rate of flow of electricity. A *coulomb* is 1/96,500 mole of charge. Currents found in most chemical instrumentation are usually less than an ampere, commonly on the order of milliamperes (mA) and not infrequently microamperes (μA). The symbol for current is I or i.

Example 1. A microammeter indicates a current flow of 16 μA in a circuit. How many electrons per second is this?

$$16 \, \mu A = 1.6 \times 10^{-5} \frac{\text{coulombs}}{\text{sec}} \times \frac{1 \text{ mole } e}{9.65 \times 10^4 \text{ coulombs}}$$

$$\times \frac{6.02 \times 10^{23} e}{\text{mole } e} = 1.0 \times 10^{14} \, e/\text{sec}$$

Example 2. How long will it take to deposit one mole of silver on an electrode assuming a constant current of 1 ampere?

$$1 \text{ mole Ag} = \frac{1 \text{ mole Ag}}{9.65 \times 10^4 \text{ coulombs}} \times \frac{1 \text{ coulomb}}{\text{sec}} \times T \text{ sec}$$

$$T = 9.65 \times 10^4 \text{ sec or almost 27 hours}$$

Voltage

Voltage, often referred to as *potential*, is defined as a difference in electrical potential energy between two points. This difference in potential is expressed in joules coulomb^{-1} and a special unit, the *volt* (V), is used to represent it. If it requires 67 joules of energy to move one coulomb of positive charge from point 1 to point 2, the voltage at the second point is 67 V greater than it is at the first point.

Voltage measurements are relative and depend upon what point is chosen as the reference. To avoid confusion, voltage measurements are usually specified with reference to the potential of the earth (*earth* or *ground*, represented as ⏚), an instrument's chassis (*chassis ground*, ⌐⊤⊤⌐), or some common point in the circuit (*common ground*, represented as ▽).

Voltages found in most chemical instrumentation range from kilovolts (for powering photomultiplier tubes) to millivolts (from electrodes) and less. The symbol for electrical potential is E. A source of voltage is represented as ——⊣|⊦|⊦——⁺—— . The plus and minus signs are often omitted. Voltage sources are usually assumed to have the capability of delivering current.

Example. Two batteries each have potential differences of 1.5 V between their positive and negative terminals.

(a) If the positive terminal of one battery is connected to the negative terminal of the other battery, what is the potential difference between the unconnected terminals?

1.5 V — Point 1 — Point 2 — 1.5 V — Point 3

Point 3 is 1.5 V more positive than point 2, which is 1.5 V more positive than point 1. Therefore, the potential difference between the unconnected terminals must be 3.0 V.

(b) If the positive terminal of one battery is connected to the positive terminal of the other battery, what is the potential difference between the unconnected terminals?

1.5 V — Point 1 — Point 2 — 1.5 V — Point 3

Point 3 is 1.5 V more *negative* than point 2, which is 1.5 V more positive than point 1. Therefore, the potential differences between the unconnected terminals must be 0.0 V.

Capacitance

Figure 16.2 shows two flat metal plates separated some distance from each other and connected through wires and a switch to a battery, a source of voltage and current. Assume that initially there is no potential difference between the two plates. When the switch is closed, positive current will flow through the battery and out onto the upper plate giving it a more positive charge. Positive current will also flow in the lower part of the circuit but from the lower plate into the battery. The current will diminish as the charge on the plates builds up and becomes repulsive to the addition of more like charge. If the switch remains closed until equilibrium is established (i.e., until there is no longer any net flow of current in the circuit), upon opening the switch it will be found that the voltage difference between the two metal plates is the same as the voltage of the battery.

FIGURE   16.2   Capacitor connected to a battery.

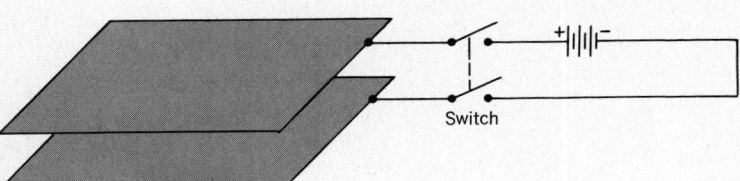

Switch

Metal plates

For a given voltage, the amount of charge that is stored depends upon the exact geometry of the plates—in particular, their surface area and distance of separation. It has been found experimentally that the amount of charge stored on a given capacitor is proportional to the voltage applied to it:

$$q = CE$$

where q is the charge in coulombs and C is a proportionality constant called *capacitance* with units of coulombs volt^{-1}. In honor of Michael Faraday, this set of units is called the *farad*. Capacitances found in chemical instrumentation range from millifarads (mF) in power supplies to picofarads (pF)[3] in very high frequency circuits. Capacitance is represented as ——⊣⊢—— .

Example. How long must a 1 μA current flow to charge a 1 μF capacitor to 20 volts?

$$1 \times 10^{-6}\,\text{F} = \frac{1 \times 10^{-6}\,\text{coulomb sec}^{-1} \times T\,\text{sec}}{20\,\text{V}}$$

$$T = 20\,\text{sec}$$

Resistance

Resistance (R) is well named: it is simply a resistance to the flow of electric current. It is expressed in units of *ohms* (Ω) and is defined by a relationship between current and voltage. If a potential E across a portion of a circuit causes a current i to flow through it, then the resistance of that portion of the circuit is given by

$$R\,(\text{ohms}) = \frac{E\,(\text{joules coulomb}^{-1})}{i\,(\text{coulombs sec}^{-1})}$$

Resistance values in chemical instrumentation range from essentially zero to many millions of ohms and more. If no current flows between two points that have different potentials, the resistance between the two points is infinite. The symbol for resistance or *resistors* (devices that have a resistance) is ——WWWW—— . Kilohms (kΩ) is often used as an abbreviation for 1×10^3 ohms. Megohms (MΩ) indicates 1×10^6 ohms.

Example. A 12-volt battery is connected to a light bulb that is to be used as a light source in a spectrophotometer. The current flowing through the circuit is found to be 0.5 amperes. What is the resistance of the light bulb?

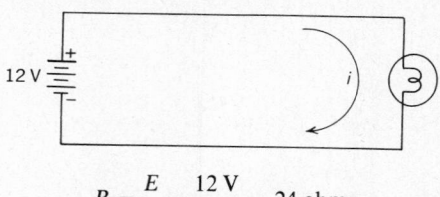

$$R = \frac{E}{i} = \frac{12\,\text{V}}{0.5\,\text{A}} = 24\,\text{ohms}$$

[3] Pico $= 10^{-12}$.

Ohm's Law

The equation that defines resistance is known as *Ohm's law*. It is usually stated in a form that emphasizes current rather than resistance:

$$i \text{ (amperes)} = \frac{E \text{ (volts)}}{R \text{ (ohms)}}$$

Still another form emphasizes voltage: it states that the voltage drop across a resistance is equal to the product of that resistance and the current flowing through it.

$$E = iR$$

Example 1. A constant-current source for use in coulometry is to be constructed from a 12-V battery, a resistor and an electrolytic cell. If a 1.20-kΩ resistor is used, what will be the resulting current? (Assume the resistance of the electrolytic cell is negligible.)

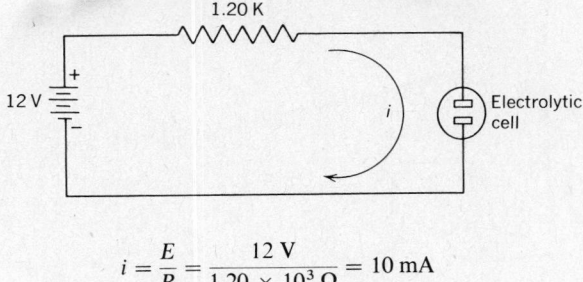

$$i = \frac{E}{R} = \frac{12 \text{ V}}{1.20 \times 10^3 \, \Omega} = 10 \text{ mA}$$

Example 2. A current of 1 μA is generated by light striking a phototube. If this current is made to flow through a 1 MΩ resistor, what is the voltage across the resistor?

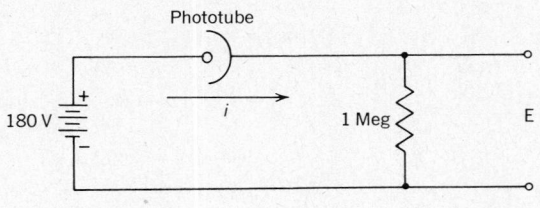

$$E = iR = 1 \times 10^{-6} \text{ A} \times 1 \times 10^6 \text{ ohms} = 1 \text{ V}$$

Kirchhoff's Laws

Kirchhoff's laws are useful in the analysis of more complicated circuits. The laws are really just common sense combined with restatements of the conservation of energy.

447

Kirchhoff's Current Law

The algebraic summation of currents entering a junction equals zero.

The mathematical statement of Kirchhoff's current law requires that signs be given to the currents involved. Some confusion might result unless it is realized that all currents refer to the flow of positive charge. The sign simply indicates whether the current is flowing into or out of a junction. Positive current flowing *into* a junction is algebraically *positive*, whereas positive current flowing *out of* a junction is algebraically *negative*.

For the junction,

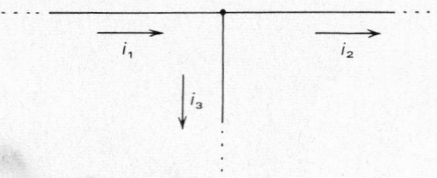

Kirchhoff's current law states that

$$+i_1 - i_2 - i_3 = 0$$

where the i's refer to the magnitudes of the positive currents and the signs preceding them indicate the direction of current flow with respect to the junction. Rearranging the above equation to make all signs positive puts all of the currents entering the junction on one side of the equation and all of the currents leaving on the other side:

$$i_1 = i_2 + i_3$$

That is, the amount of current entering a junction exactly equals the amount of current leaving that junction.

Example. What are the values of i_1, i_2, i_3, and i_4 in the circuit

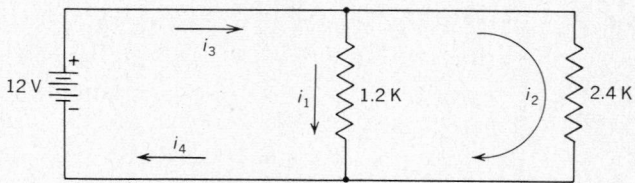

Kirchhoff's current law applied to the two junctions gives:

$$+i_3 - i_1 - i_2 = 0$$

$$+i_1 + i_2 - i_4 = 0$$

or

$$i_3 = i_1 + i_2$$

$$i_4 = i_1 + i_2$$

The currents i_3 and i_4 can be calculated if i_1 and i_2 are determined.

The voltage difference between the junctions is 12 V. Thus, the voltage across each resistor must be the same. Using Ohm's law gives

$$i_2 = \frac{12 \text{ V}}{2.4 \times 10^3 \text{ ohms}} = 5 \text{ mA}$$

$$i_1 = \frac{12 \text{ V}}{1.2 \times 10^3 \text{ ohms}} = 10 \text{ mA}$$

$$i_3 = i_4 = 15 \text{ mA}$$

Kirchhoff's Voltage Law

The algebraic summation of voltage drops around a closed loop equals zero.

Again, a sign convention is involved. No matter which direction, clockwise or counterclockwise, we choose to go around the loop to calculate the summation, if the potential *increases* as we go past a device, the change is assigned a positive voltage; if the potential *decreases* as we go across a device, the change is assigned a negative voltage. For the circuit

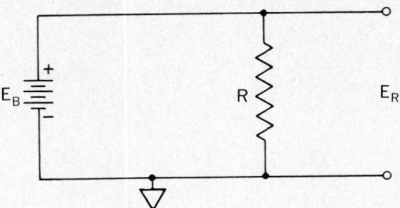

if we go clockwise around the circuit starting at the point tied to common, Kirchhoff's voltage law states that

$$+E_B - E_R = 0$$

or $E_B = E_R$. If Kirchhoff's voltage law did not hold, a point in the loop could have two different potentials, clearly impossible.

Example. What is the value of R in the following circuit if a current of 15 mA flows through it?

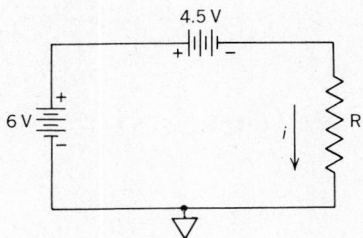

Kirchhoff's and Ohm's laws give

$$+6\,\text{V} - 4.5\,\text{V} - iR = 0$$

$$iR = 1.5\,\text{V}$$

$$R = \frac{1.5\,\text{V}}{1.5 \times 10^{-2}\,\text{A}} = 100\,\text{ohms}$$

Series Resistance

Kirchhoff's laws are useful for analyzing resistances connected in series such as the circuit shown in Fig. 16.3. If the current law is applied to points X, Y, and Z in the circuit, it is found that the current flowing through R_1 must be equal to the current flowing through R_2. Kirchhoff's voltage law indicates that the sum of the voltages across the two resistors must be equal to the voltage of the battery.

$$E_B - iR_1 - iR_2 = 0$$

$$E_B = iR_1 + iR_2$$

Two important conclusions can be drawn from this circuit. Ohm's law states that $E = iR$, where R is the resistance through which a current i is flowing to produce a voltage E. The voltage across the *two* resistors in Fig. 16.3 must equal iR, where R is the value of resistance associated with the two resistors in series.

$$E_B = iR_1 + iR_2 = i(R_1 + R_2) = iR$$

Therefore,

$$R = R_1 + R_2$$

The effective resistance of resistors connected in series is the sum of the individual resistances.

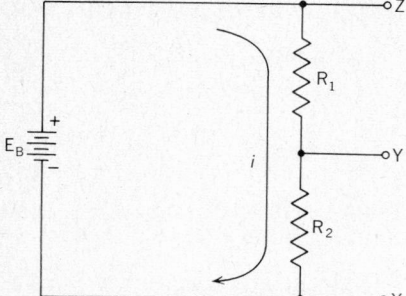

FIGURE 16.3   Series resistances in a circuit.

The second important point concerns the voltage at point Y. Point Y is iR_2 volts more positive than point X. Point Z is $iR_1 + iR_2$ volts more positive than point X.

$$E_Y = iR_2$$

$$E_Z = iR_1 + iR_2 = i(R_1 + R_2)$$

Dividing one into the other gives

$$\frac{E_Y}{E_Z} = \frac{iR_2}{i(R_1 + R_2)} = \frac{R_2}{R_1 + R_2}$$

$$E_Y = E_Z\left(\frac{R_2}{R_1 + R_2}\right)$$

Resistance in series act as a *voltage divider*: the total voltage across the two resistors is divided between them, a portion of it appearing across one resistor, the remainder appearing across the other.

Example. The following circuit is often used to supply voltages to the different stages of a photomultiplier tube; $R_1 = R_2 = \cdots = R_{10} = 100 \text{ k}\Omega$.

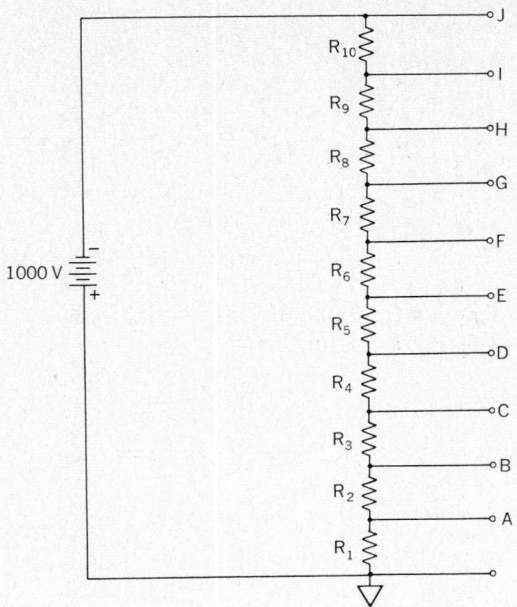

(a) What is the total resistance of the circuit?

$$R = R_1 + R_2 + \cdots + R_9 + R_{10} = 10 \times 100 \text{ k}\Omega = 1 \text{ M}\Omega$$

(b) What is the voltage at point *F* (with reference to common)?
The circuit can be simplified for this computation by combining all resistances below point *F* and all resistances above point *F*. The equivalent circuit is then

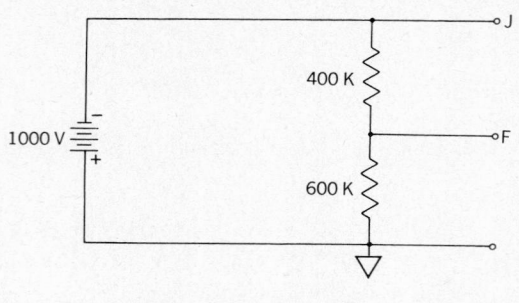

$$E_F = E_J\left(\frac{600\ \text{k}\Omega}{400\ \text{k}\Omega + 600\ \text{k}\Omega}\right) = -1000\ \text{V} \times 0.6 = -600\ \text{V}$$

Parallel Resistance

Kirchhoff's laws are also useful for analyzing resistances connected in parallel such as the circuit shown in Fig. 16.4. Comparison of this figure with Fig. 16.3 indicates that, whereas resistors in series act as a voltage divider, resistors in parallel act as a current divider. In series circuits, the current flowing through each element is the same; in parallel circuits, the voltage across each element is the same.

A relationship for the effective resistance of resistors in parallel can be obtained. Ohm's law gives

$$E_B = i_1 R_1$$

$$E_B = i_2 R_2$$

$$E_B = i_3 R$$

where *R* equals the effective parallel resistance of R_1 and R_2. Rearrangement gives

$$i_1 = \frac{E_B}{R_1}; \qquad i_2 = \frac{E_B}{R_2}; \qquad i_3 = \frac{E_B}{R}$$

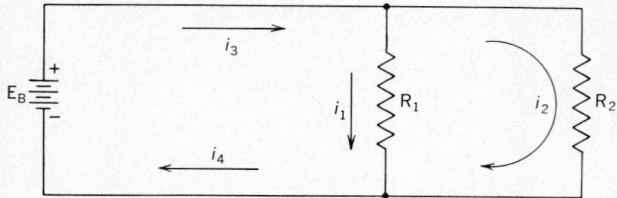

FIGURE 16.4 Parallel resistances in a circuit.

From Kirchhoff's current law,

$$i_3 = i_1 + i_2$$

$$\frac{E_B}{R} = \frac{E_B}{R_1} + \frac{E_B}{R_2}$$

$$\frac{1}{R} = \frac{1}{R_1} + \frac{1}{R_2}$$

The reciprocal of the effective resistance of resistors connected in parallel is the sum of the reciprocals of the individual resistances.

For the special case of just two resistors connected in parallel,

$$R = \frac{R_1 R_2}{R_1 + R_2}$$

Example 1. What currents will flow in the following circuit?

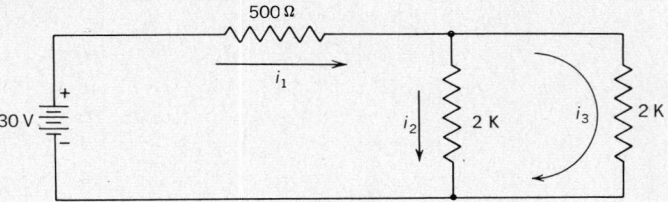

The circuit is most easily treated if the parallel resistors are first combined into an effective resistance.

$$\frac{1}{R} = \frac{1}{2000} + \frac{1}{2000} = \frac{2}{2000}$$

$$R = 1 \text{ k}\Omega$$

This resistance in series with the already present 500 Ω gives a total of 1500 Ω. The current i_1 is then

$$i_1 = \frac{E}{R} = \frac{30 \text{ V}}{1500 \,\Omega} = 20 \text{ mA}$$

The voltage across each of the parallel resistors is

$$E = 30 \text{ V} \left(\frac{1000}{1000 + 500} \right) = 20 \text{ V}$$

$$i_2 = i_3 = \frac{20 \text{ V}}{2000 \,\Omega} = 10 \text{ mA}$$

Kirchhoff's law allows us to check the above calculations.

$$20\,\text{mA} = i_3 = i_1 + i_2 = 10\,\text{mA} + 10\,\text{mA} = 20\,\text{mA}$$

Voltage measurement on a circuit has the effect of adding a parallel resistance to the circuit. Electromechanical meters are really current-measuring devices; an electrical current flowing through the coils of a meter produces a magnetic field that deflects the pointer in proportion to the amount of current. When meters are used for making voltage measurements, a resistor is usually placed in series with the meter to produce a current from the voltage. For purposes of discussion, we will represent the voltmeter as a resistance device.

Suppose a voltmeter is attached to points X and Y in Fig. 16.3. The measurement circuit is shown in Fig. 16.5 in which R_M represents the resistance of the meter. Consider the effect of including R_M in the circuit. If the meter is not present, the voltage at point $Y\,(E_Y)$ is

$$E_Y = iR_2 \quad \text{where} \quad i = \frac{E_B}{R_1 + R_2}$$

With the meter included in the circuit, the voltage at point $Y\,(E'_Y)$ is

$$E'_Y = i\left(\frac{R_2 R_M}{R_2 + R_M}\right) \quad \text{where} \quad i = \frac{E_B}{\left(R_1 + \dfrac{R_2 R_M}{R_2 + R_M}\right)}$$

The error in volts introduced by adding the parallel resistance of the meter can be shown to be directly proportional to a term of the form

$$R_2 - \left(\frac{R_2 R_M}{R_2 + R_M}\right)$$

FIGURE 16.5   Voltmeter connected to a circuit.

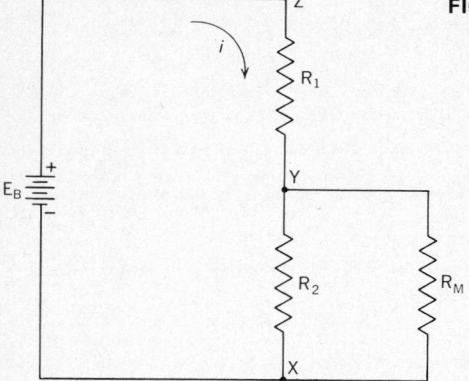

If R_M is very, very large compared to R_2, then $R_M + R_2 \cong R_M$ and the term in parentheses is about equal to R_2. The error $E_Y - E'_Y$ is then very small. If, however, R_M is not large with respect to R_2, the term in parentheses will be less than R_2, and an error results.

When making measurements on a circuit, the measuring device should have as little effect on the circuit as possible. In the case of voltage measurements, the measuring device should have a very high resistance compared to the resistance of the circuit being measured.

Example 2. What is the error of measurement if a 10-kΩ resistance voltmeter is used to measure the voltage between points X and Y in the following circuit?

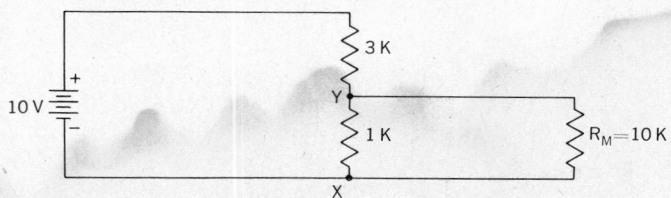

Without the meter,

$$E_Y = 10 \text{ V} \left(\frac{1 \text{ k}\Omega}{1 \text{ k}\Omega + 3 \text{ k}\Omega} \right) = 2.50 \text{ V}$$

With the meter, the parallel resistance reduces to

$$R = \frac{1 \text{ k}\Omega \times 10 \text{ k}\Omega}{1 \text{ k}\Omega + 10 \text{ k}\Omega} = \frac{10 \text{ k}\Omega}{11}$$

$$E'_Y = 10 \text{ V} \left(\frac{10/11}{10/11 + 3} \right) = 10 \text{ V} \left(\frac{10}{43} \right) = 2.33 \text{ V}$$

$$E_Y - E'_Y = 2.50 - 2.33 = 0.17 \text{ V}$$

Wheatstone Bridge

The familiar *Wheatstone bridge* is a circuit that makes use of series and parallel resistances. The bridge circuit is drawn in Fig. 16.6 to emphasize the series and parallel aspects of the circuit (see Fig. 14.14 for a more common representation). Bridge circuits are frequently used to produce voltages from a sensor that changes resistance as a function of the phenomenon to which it responds. The voltage is generated as a difference between points X and Y in Fig. 16.6.

Because R_1 and R_3 as well as R_2 and R_s act as series resistance voltage dividers, if

$$\frac{R_3}{R_1 + R_3} = \frac{R_s}{R_2 + R_s}$$

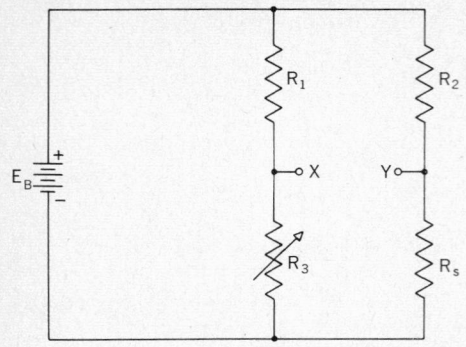

FIGURE 16.6 Wheatstone bridge circuit.

then

$$E_X = E_Y = E_B\left(\frac{R_3}{R_1 + R_3}\right) = E_B\left(\frac{R_s}{R_2 + R_s}\right)$$

and $E_Y - E_X = 0$. R_3 is usually adjustable to allow this condition to be achieved for various initial values of R_s. Once R_3 has been set, if the value of R_s increases, E_Y will increase and $E_Y - E_X$ will become more positive. If R_s decreases, $E_Y - E_X$ will become more negative. The relationship is not strictly linear but is quite good for small changes in R_s. The voltage across X and Y is thus a measure of the resistance of R_s which in turn is related to the phenomenon being studied.[4] The voltage can be measured with a high-resistance voltmeter or it can be fed to other electronic circuitry for further processing.

> **Example.** A thermistor decreases its resistance approximately 100 ohms/C° near 25°C, the temperature at which its resistance is 10 kΩ. If $R_1 = R_2 = R_3 = 10$ kΩ and $E_B = 10$ V in Fig. 16.6, what is the voltage change per C° between points X and Y?

$$E_X = 10 \text{ V} \left(\frac{10 \text{ k}\Omega}{10 \text{ k}\Omega + 10 \text{ k}\Omega}\right) = 5.000 \text{ V}$$

$$E_Y = 10 \text{ V} \left(\frac{9.9 \text{ k}\Omega}{10.0 \text{ k}\Omega + 9.9 \text{ k}\Omega}\right) = 4.975 \text{ V}$$

$$E_Y - E_X = 4.975 \text{ V} - 5.000 \text{ V} = -25 \text{ mV/C}°$$

OPERATIONAL AMPLIFIERS

Operational amplifiers are sophisticated electronic devices that have found wide use in instrumentation systems. They are called "operational amplifiers" because, first, they are amplifiers, and second, they can be used to

---

[4] For an excellent discussion of the transformation of information from one data domain to another, see C. G. Enke, *Anal. Chem.*, **43**(1), 69A (1971).

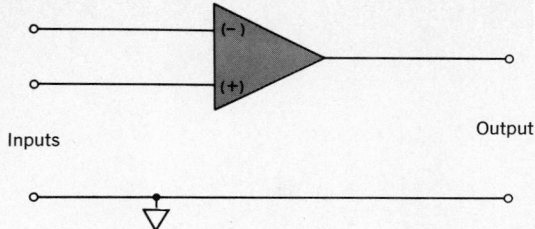

FIGURE 16.7 Symbolic representation of an operational amplifier.

perform mathematical operations on a signal by the addition of simple circuit components to their inputs and outputs. A description of the internal circuitry of operational amplifiers is beyond the scope of this chapter. However, an understanding of basic electronics, a knowledge of operational amplifier characteristics, and common sense are sufficient to study operational amplifiers and their use in chemical instrumentation. The operational amplifier configurations presented in this chapter are by no means comprehensive but are illustrative of their wide applicability.

Operational amplifiers, or "op amps" as they are often called, can be thought of as electronic modules with the following characteristics:

1. Two inputs, designated *inverting* (−) and *noninverting* (+), with a very high internal resistance between them.

2. One output capable of producing voltages from about −10 V to +10 V and delivering currents of up to a few milliamperes.

3. A desire to have no current flowing into its inputs.[5]

4. The capability of *decreasing* its output voltage if positive current enters the *inverting* input (hence, the name "inverting input").

5. The capability of *increasing* its output voltage if positive current enters the *noninverting* input (hence, the name "noninverting input").

Figure 16.7 shows an operational amplifier as it is normally represented. The inputs are usually designated as (−) and (+), but if the designations are not present, the upper input (or the single input if only one is shown) is taken to be the inverting input. Figure 16.7 also includes the portion of the circuit that is common to both the inputs and the output.

Voltage Follower

Two characteristics of the operational amplifier, its desire to have essentially no current flow into its inputs and its capability of providing several milliamperes output current, immediately suggest one use. As seen in a previous section, voltmeters should have a very high input resistance so they

---

[5] In practice, a small but finite amount of current must flow. This is of the order of a microampere or less, and it can often be ignored.

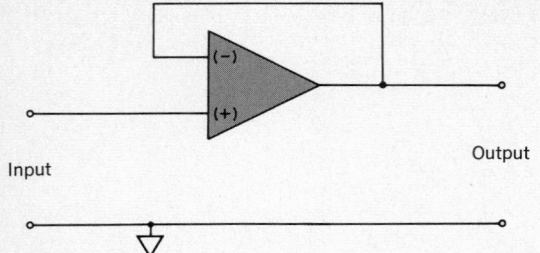

Input

Output

FIGURE 16.8 Voltage follower configuration.

draw negligible current from the circuit being measured and thus do not appreciably alter the true voltage. Most meters, however, require several milliamperes of current to achieve full-scale deflection and are not suitable for the direct measurement of voltage. The operational amplifier has the potential of being an almost ideal interface between the circuit being measured and the meter that is to indicate the voltage.

Consider the operational amplifier configuration in Fig. 16.8 in which the output has been connected directly to the inverting input. The output voltage if *fed back* to the inverting input. If the output and the noninverting input are initially at the same potential, a stable condition exists. No current will flow internally between the inputs because they are at the same voltage.

If the voltage at the noninverting input is increased, a positive current will begin to flow from the noninverting input to the inverting input which is still at the previous potential. The operational amplifier reacts by increasing its output voltage (recall characteristic 5 above) until the output voltage becomes the same as the voltage at the noninverting input. A stable condition is again established in which there is no voltage difference and hence no current flow between the inverting and noninverting inputs. A stable condition also results for decreases in voltage at the noninverting input.

This configuration is called a *voltage follower* because the output voltage is the same as (or follows) the input voltage. The input current is very, very small, but the output current can be several milliamperes. A high-resistance voltmeter capable of measuring voltages from 0 to about $+10$ V is shown in Fig. 16.9.

FIGURE 16.9 High-resistance voltmeter using a voltage follower. Input range = 0 to $+10$ V.

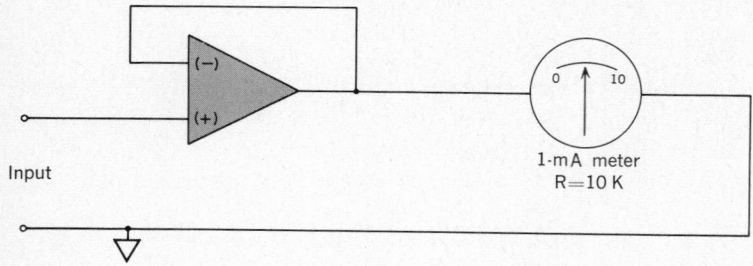

Input

1-mA meter
R=10 K

Amplification factor or *gain,* A is a measure of an amplifier's ability to increase the magnitude of a signal. For voltage amplification, it is defined as the ratio of output voltage to input voltage.

$$A = \frac{E_{out}}{E_{in}}$$

$$E_{out} = A \times E_{in}$$

Amplification is the electrical analog of the mathematical operation of multiplying a variable (E_{in}) by a constant (A).

The voltage gain of the voltage follower is clearly unity. However, it can be made to have a gain greater than unity if a voltage divider is used in the *feedback network.* Figure 16.10 shows a *follower-with-gain.* The voltage at the inverting input is determined by the output voltage and the voltage divider formed by R_1 and R_2.

$$E_{(-)} = E_{out}\left(\frac{R_1}{R_1 + R_2}\right)$$

When the amplifier is "in equilibrium,"

$$E_{(-)} = E_{in}$$

Thus,

$$E_{out} = \left(\frac{R_1 + R_2}{R_1}\right)E_{in}$$

The gain of the circuit is

$$A = \frac{E_{out}}{E_{in}} = \left(\frac{R_1 + R_2}{R_1}\right)$$

FIGURE 16.10   Follower-with-gain.

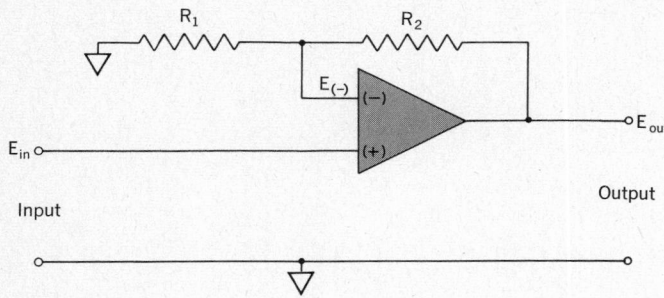

Example. Using the operational amplifier and meter in Fig. 16.9 and any other necessary simple components, design a voltmeter with two full-scale ranges, 0-10 V and 0-1 V.

Two resistors and a switch can be added to an amplifier to give

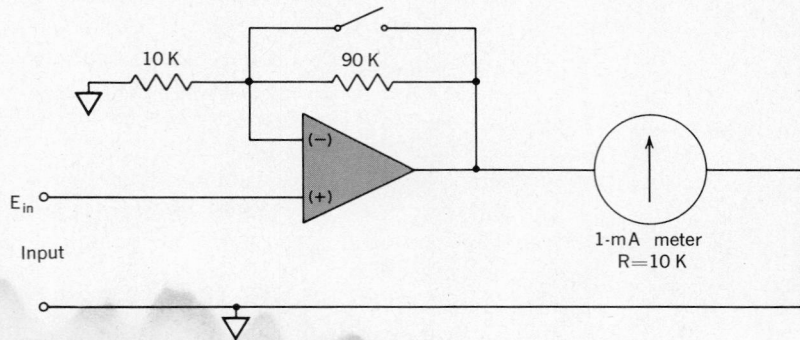

When the switch is closed, $E_{out} = E_{in}$. If E_{in} is 10 V, $E_{out} = 10$ V and $i_M = 1$ mA. When the switch is open,

$$E_{out} = E_{in}\left(\frac{10\text{ k}\Omega + 90\text{ k}\Omega}{10\text{ k}\Omega}\right) = 10\,E_{in}$$

If $E_{in} = 1$ V, $E_{out} = 10$ V and i_M again equals 1 mA.

Current-to-Voltage Converter

Figure 16.11 shows an operational amplifier configuration that is useful for converting signals from the current domain to the voltage domain. The noninverting input is grounded, and a resistor is placed in the *feedback loop* between the output and the inverting input. The resulting configuration is called a *current-to-voltage converter*.

The inverting input is connected to a source of current (i_{in}) that can divide and flow into the amplifier (i_a) and into the feedback loop (i_f). The junction near the inverting input is often called the *summing point* for these currents.

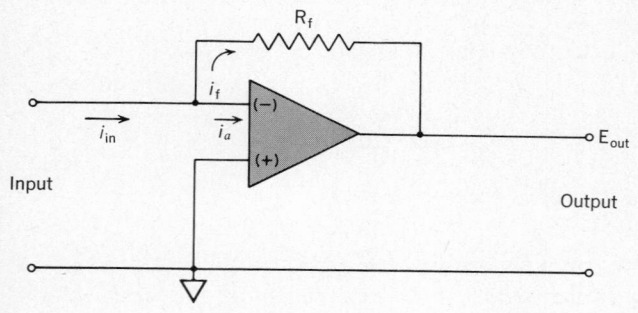

FIGURE 16.11   Current-to-voltage converter.

The amplifier would rather have all of the current flow into the feedback loop than have any of it flow into the inverting input. If positive current flows into the amplifier, the amplifier will react by making its output voltage more negative.

Common sense is useful at this point. The requirements for the amplifier to be stable are that $i_{in} = i_f$, $i_a = 0$. If $i_a = 0$, then no current flows between the inverting and the noninverting inputs, and the voltage difference between them must be zero. Because the noninverting input is connected to common ground, the voltage at the inverting input must be 0 V with respect to common. This is called a *virtual ground* because, although the point is not connected directly to ground, it is at ground potential.

The requirement that $i_f = i_{in}$ implies that the voltage across the feedback resistor must be

$$E_f = i_f R_f = i_{in} R_f$$

with the summing point side of the resistor more positive than the output side. Because the summing point is at virtual ground, the output side of the resistor must be $-E_f$ with respect to common. Thus,

$$E_{out} = E_f = -i_{in} R_f$$

The input resistance of the current-to-voltage converter is very low.

Example. A common use of the current-to-voltage converter is in spectrophotometry, where phototube currents on the order of microamperes must be converted to the level of volts. Design a circuit to convert phototube currents to voltages with a gain of -1 V per μA.

In the following circuit,

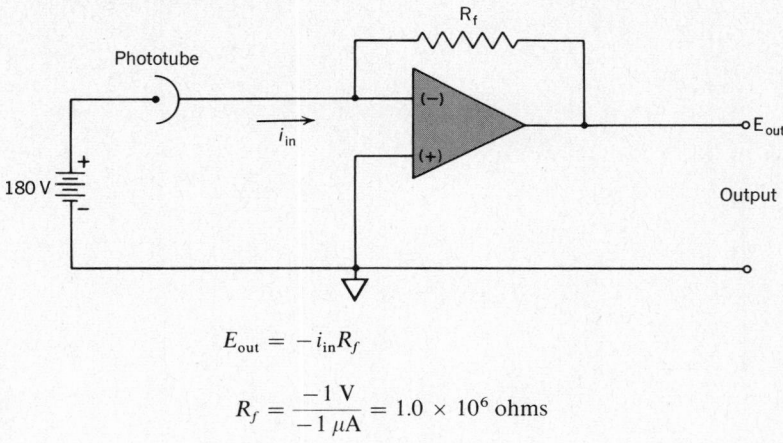

$$E_{out} = -i_{in} R_f$$

$$R_f = \frac{-1 \text{ V}}{-1 \, \mu\text{A}} = 1.0 \times 10^6 \text{ ohms}$$

Inverter Amplifier

Probably the most common operational amplifier configuration is the *inverter amplifier*, so named because it inverts the sign of the input voltage

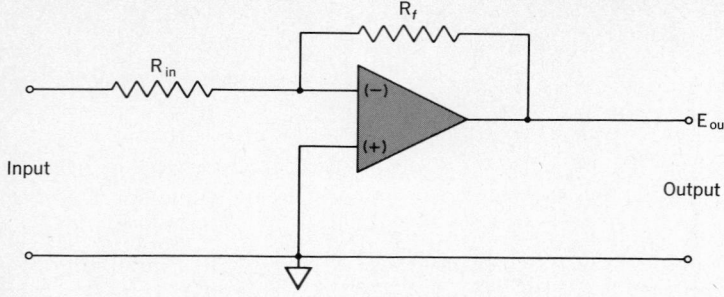

FIGURE 16.12 Inverter amplifier.

while at the same time amplifying that voltage. The inverter is nothing more than a current-to-voltage converter in which the input current has been generated by an input voltage across the input resistor according to Ohm's law. The configuration, illustrated in Fig. 16.12, can be viewed as a voltage-to-voltage converter.

The summing point of this amplifier is at virtual ground, which makes the voltage difference between E_{in} and the summing point the same as the difference between E_{in} and common. The input current is

$$i_{in} = \frac{E_{in}}{R_{in}}$$

The current-to-voltage converter gave us the equation

$$E_{out} = -i_{in} R_f$$

from which the equation for the output voltage of the inverter amplifier can be derived:

$$E_{out} = -\frac{E_{in}}{R_{in}} \times R_F = -E_{in}\left(\frac{R_F}{R_{in}}\right)$$

The voltage amplification factor is

$$A = \frac{E_{out}}{E_{in}} = -\frac{R_F}{R_{in}}$$

and the input resistance is simply R_{in}.

Unlike the follower-with-gain, the inverter can have a gain of less than unity. Another difference, of course, is that it does not retain the sign of the input voltage but instead inverts it. If a sign change is undesirable, the output can be fed to another inverter with a gain of unity.

462

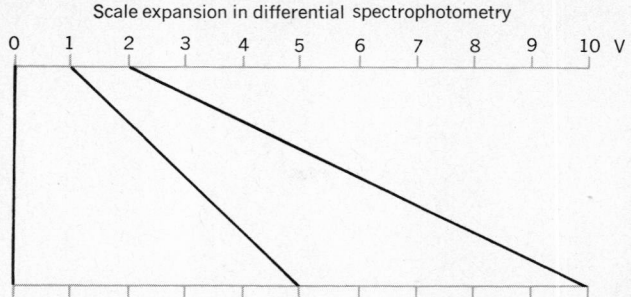

Scale expansion in differential spectrophotometry

FIGURE 16.13 Scale expansion in differential spectrophotometry.

Inverters are often used to accomplish *scale expansion* of signals. Differential measurement in spectrophotometry is an example that has been treated in Chapter 11. The example is reproduced here as Fig. 16.13 using voltages that correspond to the different levels of transmittance. On the upper scale, 0 V corresponds to 0 % T and 10 V corresponds to 100 % T. If the signal of interest lies between 10 and 20 % T, amplification of the original voltage by -5 (inverter amplifier) gives a scale on which 0 % T still corresponds to 0 V, but 20 % T now corresponds to -10 V. The 2-V portion of the scale has been expanded to cover a 10-V range, allowing the signal of interest to be determined with greater accuracy and precision.

The alert student will perceive that scale expansion is most effective when the signal of interest lies at the low end of the scale. Expansion by -5 of a 2-V interval between 7 and 9 V on the original scale would result in a 10-V interval as before, but the interval would be between -35 and -45 V, values that are beyond the capability of most operational amplifiers. To remain within the allowed upper limit of 10 V, the amplification factor that should be used with the 7- to 9-V range is only -1.11. The solution to this apparent dilemma is to *suppress* the unwanted portion of the signal as suggested in Fig. 16.14, that is, make the lower limit of the range of interest correspond to 0 and then amplify. Fortunately, the inverter amplifier is capable of this suppression, as shown in the next section.

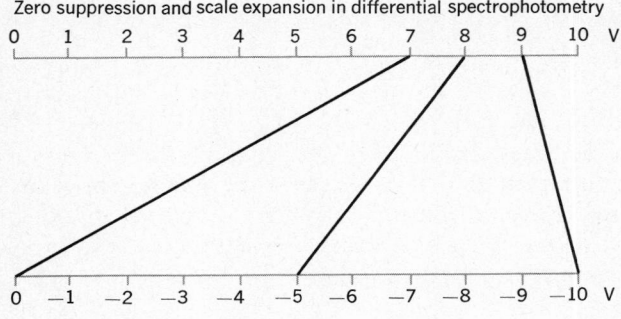

Zero suppression and scale expansion in differential spectrophotometry

FIGURE 16.14 Zero suppression and scale expansion in differential spectrophotometry.

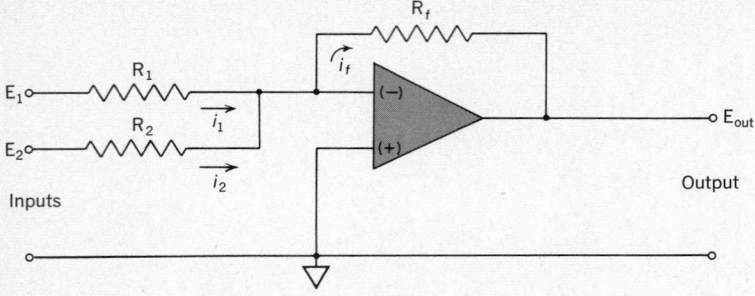

FIGURE   16.15   Summing amplifier.

Summing Amplifier

The inverter is sometimes called a *summing amplifier* or *adder* because of its ability to accept more than one input current at its summing point. Application of Kirchhoff's current law to the circuit in Fig. 16.15 shows that if i_a is to be zero, then

$$i_f = i_1 + i_2$$

$$E_{out} = -i_f R_f = -(i_1 + i_2)R_f = -\left(\frac{E_1}{R_1} + \frac{E_2}{R_2}\right)R_f$$

If the resistances are not equal, the result is a weighted sum

$$E_{out} = -\left(\frac{R_f}{R_1}E_1 + \frac{R_f}{R_2}E_2\right)$$

If the resistors are equal,

$$E_{out} = -(E_1 + E_2)$$

Any number of voltages (currents) can be added using the summing amplifier. The reader should verify that the zero suppression and scale expansion indicated in Fig. 16.14 can be accomplished if E_1 is the signal input, $E_2 = -7$ V, $R_1 = R_2 = 10$ kΩ, and $R_f = 50$ kΩ in Fig. 16.15.

Differential Amplifier

A configuration that may be used to amplify the *difference* between two voltages that have the same sign, the *differential amplifier* or *subtractor*, is diagrammed in Fig. 16.16. Resistors R_2 and R_3 act as a voltage divider for the signal E_2, giving the noninverting input a voltage of

$$E_{(+)} = E_2\left(\frac{R_3}{R_2 + R_3}\right)$$

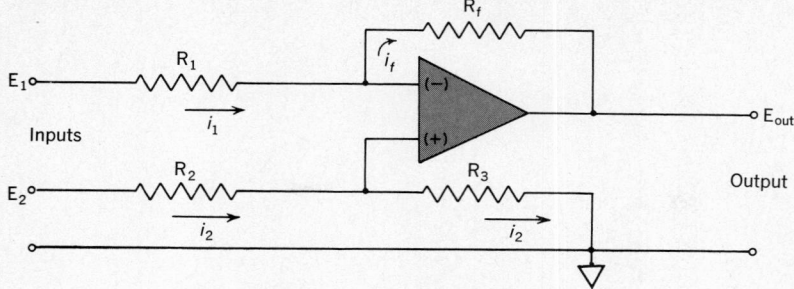

FIGURE 16.16 Differential amplifier.

The inverting input can no longer be considered a virtual ground because, for a stable condition to exist, the inverting input must be at

$$E_2\left(\frac{R_3}{R_2 + R_3}\right)$$

with respect to common.

Again, common sense is useful for the analysis of the circuit. The input current from E_1, i_1, will *not* equal E_1/R_1 because the summing point is not at virtual ground. Instead,

$$i_1 = \frac{E_1 - E_2\left(\dfrac{R_3}{R_2 + R_3}\right)}{R_1}$$

The current flowing through the feedback loop, i_f, must be equal to i_1; therefore E_{out} must be

$$E_{out} = -i_f R_f = -i_1 R_f = -R_f\left[\frac{E_1 - E_2\left(\dfrac{R_3}{R_2 + R_3}\right)}{R_1}\right]$$

with respect to the summing point. When compared to circuit common as the reference,

$$E_{out} = -\frac{R_f}{R_1}\left[E_1 - E_2\left(\frac{R_3}{R_2 + R_3}\right)\right] + E_2\left(\frac{R_3}{R_2 + R_3}\right)$$

$$= -\frac{R_f}{R_1}\left[E_1 - E_2\left(\frac{R_3}{R_2 + R_3}\right)\left(1 + \frac{R_1}{R_f}\right)\right]$$

$$= -\frac{R_f}{R_1}\left[E_1 - E_2\left(\frac{R_3}{R_2 + R_3}\right)\left(\frac{R_f + R_1}{R_f}\right)\right]$$

465

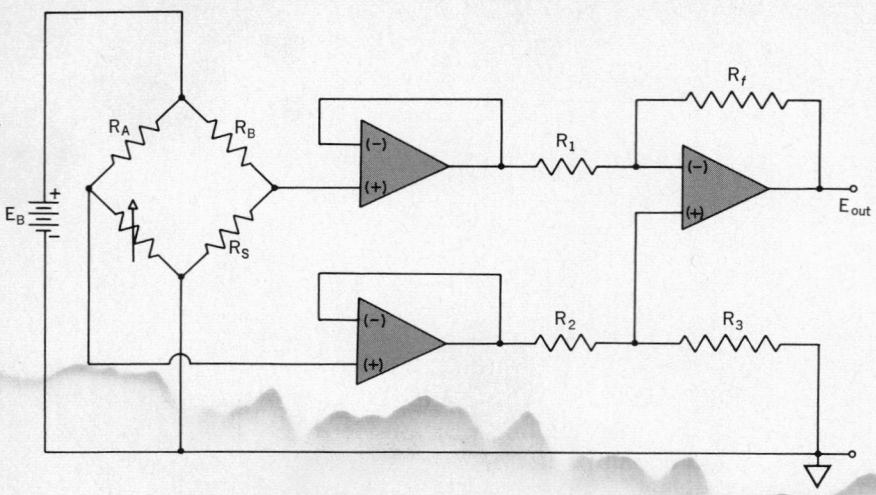

FIGURE 16.17 Differential amplifier used to measure bridge voltage.

This is simplified considerably if $R_1 = R_2$ and $R_3 = R_f$, in which case

$$E_{out} = \frac{-R_f}{R_1}(E_1 - E_2)$$

Finally, if $R_1 = R_f$ and $R_2 = R_3$, then

$$E_{out} = -(E_1 - E_2)$$

One application of the differential amplifier is its use in conjunction with two voltage followers to monitor bridge circuits as indicated in Fig. 16.17.

Integrator

Integration is a mathematical operation that is often used in chemistry. The silver coulometer is a device that integrates current as a function of time. The area under a chromatographic peak is the integral of detector response as a function of time. Operational amplifiers can be used to compute such integrals using the configuration indicated in Fig. 16.18. The output voltage is given by

$$E_{out} = -\frac{1}{C_f} \int_0^t i_1 \, dt = \frac{-1}{R_1 C_f} \int_0^t E_1 \, dt$$

and is most easily understood if it is realized that

$$\int_0^t i_1 \, dt$$

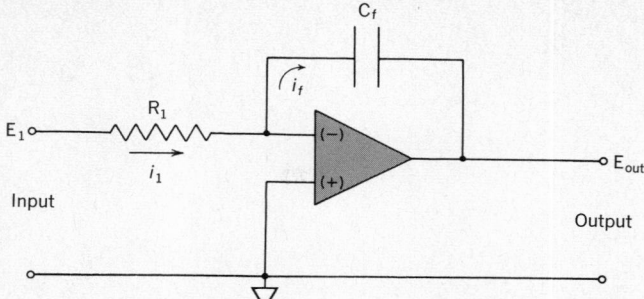

FIGURE 16.18. Integrator.

is the total amount of charge (q) that flows toward the input (and into the feedback loop where it collects on the capacitor) over the time interval of interest. The equation for the integrator is simply a restatement of the fundamental equation for capacitance:

$$E_{out} = \frac{-1}{C_f} \int_0^t i_1 \, dt = \frac{-q}{C_f}$$

The output voltage is inverted to keep the summing point at virtual ground.

Figure 16.19 illustrates the use of an integrator to calculate the area under chromatographic peaks. The peak area is proportional to the distance between the plateaus of the integrated signal on either side of the peak of interest.

Differentiator

Changing the positions of the resistor and capacitor on the integrator in Fig. 16.18 gives the configuration shown in Fig. 16.20, a *differentiator*. The

FIGURE 16.19 Integration of chromatographic peaks using an operational amplifier integrator.

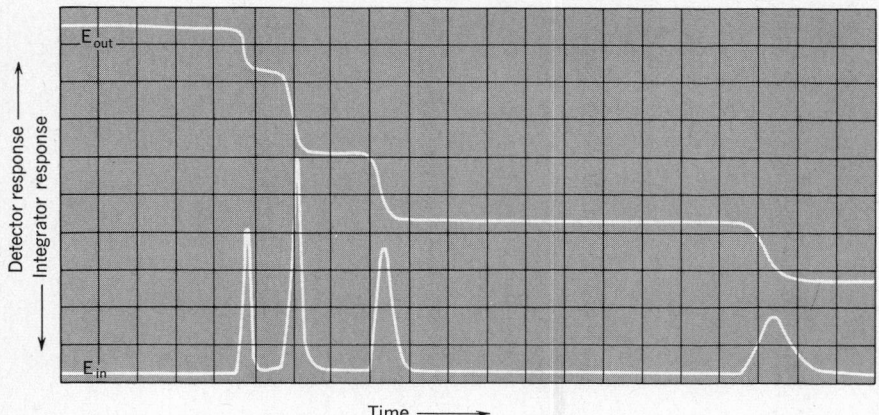

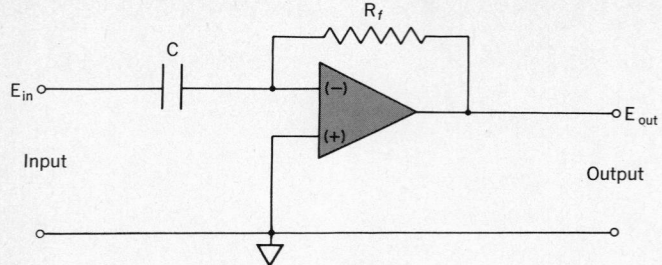

FIGURE 16.20.   Differentiator.

output voltage is proportional to the *rate of change with time* of the input voltage.

$$E_{out} = -R_f C \frac{dE_{in}}{dt}$$

One use of the differentiator has already been described at the end of Chapter 9 where automatic titrations were discussed. The student who has found the equivalence point volume by manual calculation of the second derivative of the titration curve will appreciate the circuit shown in Fig. 16.21.

FIGURE 16.21   Circuit for computing the first and second derivatives of a signal.

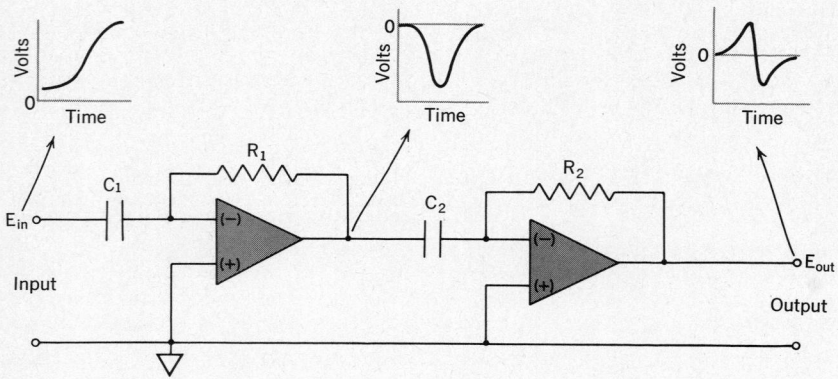

REFERENCES

R. E. LUEG and E. A. REINHARD, *Basic Electronics for Engineers and Scientists*, Intext, Scranton, Pa., 1972.

H. V. MALMSTADT, C. G. ENKE, and E. C. TOREN, JR., *Electronics for Scientists*, Benjamin, New York, 1962.

L. F. PHILLIPS, *Electronics for Experimenters*, John Wiley & Sons, Inc., New York, 1966.

Philbrick Researches, Inc., *Applications Manual for Computing Amplifiers for Modelling, Measuring, Manipulating, and Much Else*, Philbrick, Boston, 1966.

R. G. McKEE, "A Modular Approach to Chemical Instrumentation," *Anal. Chem.*, 42 (11), 91A (1970).

J. S. SPRINGER, "Using Integrated Circuits in Chemical Instrumentation," *Anal. Chem.*, 42 (8), 22A (1970).

H. A. STROBEL, *Chemical Instrumentation: A Systematic Approach*, 2nd ed., Addison-Wesley, Menlo Park, California, 1973.

QUESTIONS

1. A frequent simplifying assumption in electrochemistry is that liquid junction potentials are equal and will cancel each other. Why do they not add together?

2. Assume that the resistance between your hand and a damp metal water pipe is about $1.0\,k\Omega$, the internal resistance of your body is on the order of a few ohms, and the resistance between your other hand and an electrical contact 120 V greater than the water pipe is $1.0\,M\Omega$. If a current as small as $10\,\mu A$ can cause bodily harm, would you voluntarily complete the circuit?

3. Would an inverter amplifier be stable if the inputs were reversed, that is, if the inverting input were grounded and the noninverting input used as the summing point?

4. Give a suitable operational amplifier circuit for converting microampere polarographic currents to voltage.

5. A diode is an electrical device that allows positive current to flow in one direction only.

$$E_1 \longrightarrow\!\!\mid\!\longrightarrow E_2$$
Diode

If and only if E_1 is more positive than E_2, positive current will flow from E_1 to E_2. The following circuit can be used to remember the height of the largest peak in a chromatogram. Why is a voltage follower used?

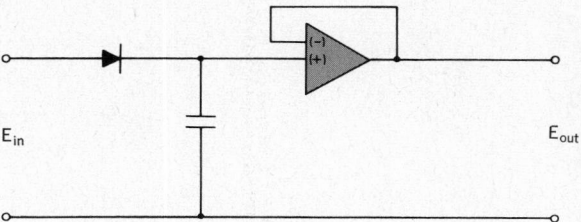

6. The amount of current flowing through a circuit is to be measured by opening the circuit at the point of interest and connecting a meter to the two exposed wires, i.e., the meter is connected in series with the other components. Should the resistance of the meter be high or low to have a minimum effect on the measurement?

PROBLEMS

1. *Current.* Photomultiplier tubes are used to transform photons into electrical currents. Assuming that every photon striking a photomultiplier's photocathodic surface ejects one electron and that each dynode has a gain of 10 (i.e., each electron

that strikes a dynode causes a total of ten electrons to be given off): (a) How many electrons per original photon are ejected from the tenth dynode of a photomultiplier tube? (b) How many coulombs is this? (c) If this charge flows for 10^{-4} seconds, what is the current in amperes?

2. *Capacitance.* One possible circuit containing a source of voltage, a switch, a resistor, and a capacitor is:

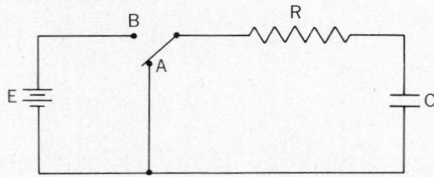

If the switch is moved from *A* to *B*, what will be the voltage across the capacitor *C* as a function of time? What will be the voltage across the resistor as a function of time? (Qualitative answers only.)

3. *Resistance.* What is the resistance of a wire that shows a potential difference of 10 V between its ends when a current of 1 A flows through it?

4. *Ohm's Law.* A phototube can be considered a variable resistor. What is the effective resistance of the phototube in the following circuit if at a given light intensity the voltage across the fixed resistor is 1.0 V?

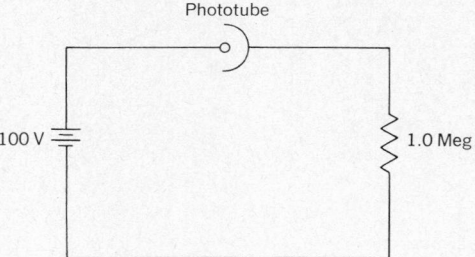

5. *Ohm's Law.* Calculate the value of *X* in each of the following: (a) $R = 10 \text{ k}\Omega$, $E = 2 \text{ V}, i = X$; (b) $E = 3 \text{ V}, i = 3 \text{ mA}, R = X$; (c) $i = 3 \text{ A}, R = 1 \text{ ohm}, E = X$; (d) $E = 12 \text{ V}, R = 1.5 \text{ ohm}, i = X$; (e) $i = 1.5 \text{ } \mu\text{A}, E = 30 \text{ V}, R = X$; (f) $R = 1 \text{ M}\Omega$, $i = 1 \text{ mA}, E = X$.

6. *Kirchhoff's Laws.* What are the values of i_1, i_2, i_3, and i_4 in the following circuit?

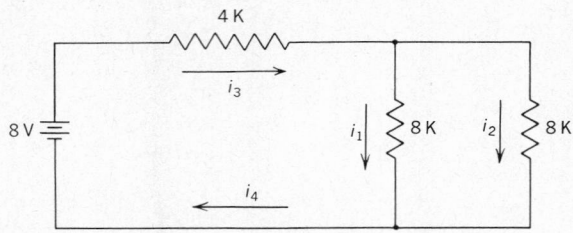

7. *Series and Parallel Resistance.* What is the effective resistance of each of the following circuits?

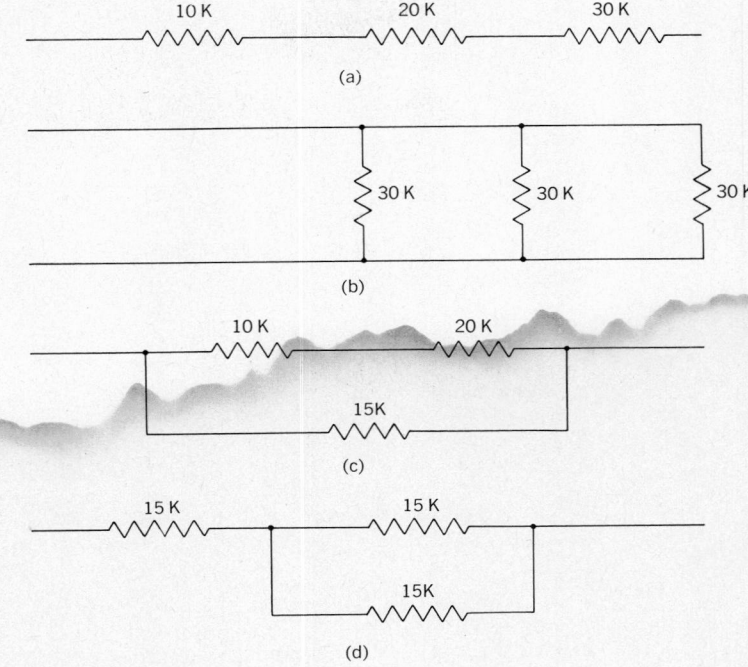

(a)

(b)

(c)

(d)

8. *Zero-Suppression and Scale Expansion.* The output of a spectrophotometer is 0 V at 0% T and -1.0 V at 100% T and is connected through one of two 10-kΩ input resistors to the summing point of an operational amplifier. If 50% T corresponds to 0 V at the amplifier output and 60% T corresponds to $+10$ V: (a) What voltage is connected to the other input resistor? (b) What is the value of the feedback resistor?

9. *Summing Amplifier.* Suppose you have access to a set of balance weights that are kept in a rather unique case—each weight rests on a corresponding switch that closes when the weight is removed from the case. Devise an operational amplifier circuit that could be used with this case to produce a voltage that is proportional to the mass of the object being weighed.

10. *Integrator.* Develop a circuit for use in polarography that will produce an output voltage that varies linearly from 0 V to -3 V in three minutes. (*Hint:* A switch in the feedback loop would be useful for initializing the output to 0 V.)

17

Digital Electronics and Computers

INTRODUCTION[1]

The introduction of operational amplifiers into analytical chemistry in the mid-1950s made a tremendous impact on chemical instrumentation. As op amps became more reliable and less expensive, their use appeared more and more frequently in the chemical literature. The analytical chemist was suddenly able to become his own instrument designer, tailoring his circuitry to meet his needs, and then constructing the instruments from readily available modular components.

The impact of digital circuits began to be felt by analytical chemistry in the mid-1960s. Here was a means of controlling instrumentation and, if computers were involved, of acquiring and processing large amounts of information. It would be difficult to overstate the revolutionary impact computers have had on chemical instrumentation and automation. This chapter presents an introduction to digital computers, their capabilities, their uses in analytical chemistry, and the fundamental concepts behind their operation.

DIGITAL AND ANALOG INFORMATION

In the world around us, there are two different types of information: *continuous* and *discrete*. Analytical chemists are probably most familiar with

---

[1] This chapter contributed by Stanley N. Deming, Assistant Professor of Chemistry, Emory University.

continuous information. Time is an example—it flows smoothly from one instant to the next with no jumps or discontinuities. Pressure, volume, temperature, and voltage are continuous parameters. The strip-chart recorder is an instrument giving an output that is continuous in both voltage and time.

Continuous information is often referred to as *analog* information. The voltage from a glass electrode is *analogous* to the continuously variable hydrogen-ion activity to which the electrode is responding. Phototube current is analogous to the continuously variable intensity of radiation striking its photocathodic surface. The use of the term "analog" to mean "continuous" is somewhat unfortunate because it ignores the existence of electrical signals that are analogous to discrete events—for example, photomultiplier current pulses are analogous to the individual photons causing them. Nonetheless, the term "analog" is commonly used as a synonym for continuous.

Examples of discrete information are readily available in chemistry. Electronic charge is a fundamentally discrete parameter. Oxidation state is (usually) an integral number. Scintillation counters are used in radiochemistry to detect and count the rays emitted from radioactive samples. Discrete information can be expressed by an integer number or count and is, for that reason, often referred to as *digital* information. As an example, low levels of light intensity can be expressed as the number of photons reaching the detector per one-second interval. It is important to realize that "digital" simply refers to something that can be counted—it does not mean that the value must necessarily be expressed in decimal (i.e., base ten) notation.

Although many parameters are continuous, we tend to round off their true values and speak of them as though they were discrete. Thus, we say it is 10:17 p.m. when it might be any time between exactly 10:16:30 and 10:17:30. The pen trace of a strip-chart recorder is seldom read to more than three significant figures, implying a resolution or "discreteness" of about one part in 1000. Rounding off to a discrete value is usually justified either because of experimental uncertainty or because it is cumbersome to manipulate numbers with more significant digits than will eventually be required in the answer.

Perhaps the greatest advantage digital information has over analog information concerns immunity to noise. Our environment is constantly filled with a variety of electromagnetic radiation, the most common of which comes from our power distribution system and has a frequency of 60 hertz. Wires act as antennas and convert some of the electromagnetic radiation into electrical currents which appear as noise in electronic instruments. Depending upon the degree of interference, an analog voltage that should really be 1.000 V may have noise superimposed on it so that it ranges from 1.010 V to 0.990 V. The value observed will depend upon when in the noise cycle the voltage is sampled. Designers of sensitive analog electronic equipment take strong precautions to shield their instruments from this unwanted electromagnetic interference.

Digital information, on the other hand, is commonly stored in switches and is therefore much less susceptible to noise. If the switches are electronic ones, the amount of noise necessary to cause interference is usually greater than 1 V, a degree of noise intensity not usually found in most electronic circuits. The accurate transmission of information over long distances is accomplished more easily for digital data than it is for analog data, again primarily because of noise immunity. An obvious and highly significant advantage of digital information is its complete compatibility with modern digital computers.

BINARY NUMBER SYSTEM

The number system used for most scientific work is the *decimal* system based upon *ten* distinct digits (0, 1, 2, 3, 4, 5, 6, 7, 8, and 9). Each position of the number signifies a different power of the *base*,[2] in this case ten. The position immediately to the left of the decimal point[3] signifies the quantity 10^0 or "ones." The second position to the left of the decimal point indicates 10^1 or "tens," the third position 10^2 or "hundreds," and so on. The digit occupying a particular position signifies how many of these powers of ten are contained in the number. Thus, the decimal number 763 means

$$
\begin{array}{rl}
7 \times 10^2 = & 700 \\
+6 \times 10^1 = & 60 \\
+3 \times 10^0 = & \underline{3} \\
& 763
\end{array}
$$

It has been suggested that the decimal number system is natural for humans in view of the fact that we have ten fingers. By a similar line of reasoning, it can be argued that electronic circuits can work most naturally with the *binary* number system. The binary system is based upon only *two* distinct digits (0 and 1) which can be used to correspond to the *off* and *on* states of electronic switching circuits.

The significance of position and digit is the same in the binary number system as it is in the decimal system, but the base is different. In the binary system, the position immediately to the left of the radix point signifies the quantity 2^0 or "ones." The second position to the left of the radix point indicates 2^1 or "twos," the third position 2^2 or "fours," and so on. Thus, the binary number 110 means

$$
\begin{array}{rl}
1 \times 2^2 = & 4 \\
+1 \times 2^1 = & 2 \\
+0 \times 2^0 = & \underline{0} \\
& 6
\end{array}
$$

---

[2] Also called *radix*.

[3] The general term is *radix point*.

TABLE 17.1 CORRESPONDENCE BETWEEN BINARY AND DECIMAL NUMBER SYSTEMS

Decimal representation	Binary representation
0	0
1	1
2	10
3	11
4	100
5	101
6	110
7	111
8	1000
9	1001
10	1010
11	1011
15	1111
16	10000
32	100000
64	1000000

Table 17.1 gives the equivalence between the binary and decimal number systems for selected values.

Addition in the binary system is similar to that in the decimal system, but simpler because there are only four fundamental possibilities:

$$
\begin{array}{cccc}
0 & 0 & 1 & 1 \\
+0 & +1 & +0 & +1 \\
\hline
0 & 1 & 1 & 10
\end{array}
$$

Addition of two numbers gives the same result whether performed in decimal or binary arithmetic as the following examples show.

$$
\begin{array}{cc}
12 & 1100 \\
+10 & +1010 \\
\hline
22 & 10110
\end{array}
$$

$$
\begin{array}{cc}
39 & 100111 \\
+9 & +1001 \\
\hline
48 & 110000
\end{array}
$$

Multiplication of two numbers gives the same result whether performed in tion table for the binary system:

$$
\begin{array}{cccc}
0 & 0 & 1 & 1 \\
\times 0 & \times 1 & \times 0 & \times 1 \\
\hline
0 & 0 & 0 & 1
\end{array}
$$

Multiplication of two numbers gives the same result whether performed in decimal or binary arithmetic as shown in the following examples.

475

$$
\begin{array}{r}
2 \\
\times 2 \\
\hline
4
\end{array}
$$

$$
\begin{array}{r}
10 \\
\times 10 \\
\hline
00 \\
10 \\
\hline
100
\end{array}
$$

$$
\begin{array}{r}
39 \\
\times 9 \\
\hline
351
\end{array}
$$

$$
\begin{array}{r}
100111 \\
\times 1001 \\
\hline
100111 \\
000000 \\
000000 \\
100111 \\
\hline
101011111
\end{array}
$$

Subtraction and division of binary numbers are analogous to the corresponding operations in the decimal number system.

The *binary digits* 0 and 1 are frequently referred to as *bits*, a contraction that is used for simplicity and for avoiding confusion with decimal digits. Just as the number of decimal digits in a value is a rough measure of its size, so too is the number of binary digits in a value. Thus, 69 is a two-digit number and its binary equivalent, 1000101, is a seven-bit number.

Large binary numbers are difficult to remember: the decimal representation "six-nine" is much easier to keep in mind than its binary equivalent, "one-zero-zero-zero-one-zero-one." However, if the bits in a binary number are grouped in threes starting from the least significant integral position, the decimal equivalent of each group of three bits (see Table 17.1) can be used as a shorthand representation of the binary number. This results in the same representation of the number as in the base eight number system and is often referred to as octal notation.[4]

$$\text{decimal} = 69$$

$$\text{binary} = 1\ 000\ 101$$

$$\text{octal} = 105$$

In most cases, the appropriate numerical base can be inferred from the context in which a value is used. When ambiguity is possible, the appropriate base is usually written as a subscript to the representation. (For example, $69_{10} = 1000101_2 = 105_8$.)

ANALOG-TO-DIGITAL AND DIGITAL-TO-ANALOG CONVERSION

Because of the previously mentioned advantages of handling data in a discrete representation rather than in a continuously variable form, it is often

---

[4] In the example given, it can be verified that $69 = 1 \times 8^2 + 0 \times 8^1 + 5 \times 8^0$.

desirable to transform information from the analog domain to the digital domain. The general technique is called *analog-to-digital* conversion, and devices that perform the conversion are analog-to-digital converters, abbreviated ADCs.

Perhaps the oldest of all analog-to-digital converters is the double-pan balance and its associated weights which together comprise a mass-to-number converter. As we normally perceive it, weight is a continuous quantity. Yet when we speak about weight, we do so in discrete terms. A person is said to weigh 158 pounds, not 157.69328 ... pounds. Laboratory notebooks usually contain records of weights rounded off to the nearest tenth of a milligram. The way we arrive at a particular value for an object's weight is similar in many aspects to the manner in which certain electronic ADCs operate. An understanding of the details of weighing is useful for an understanding of the operation of many other analog-to-digital converters.

Weighing is essentially a series of comparisons: Is the mass of the object being weighed greater than or less than the combined masses of the weights that have been added so far to the other pan of the balance? The results of the comparison are indicated by the pointer of the balance. If the object is heavier, weight is added. If the object is lighter, weight is removed. The process is begun by comparing the object with the heaviest weight of the set and is repeated with consecutively smaller weights until the difference in masses is within the desired resolution.

Imagine that a 733-mg object is to be weighed to the nearest milligram. Instead of using the usual set of weights (1, 2, 2, 5, 10, 20, 20, 50, 100, 200, 200, and 500 milligrams), a more efficient set with values of 1, 2, 4, 8, 16, 32, 64, 128, 256, and 512 milligrams will be used. The weighing sequence is given in Table 17.2. The column at the right indicates which weights were retained and which weights were removed after the comparisons. The total weight of the object may be obtained as follows:

$$
\begin{array}{rcl}
1 \times 512 &=& 512 \text{ mg} \\
+0 \times 256 &=& 0 \\
+1 \times 128 &=& 128 \\
+1 \times 64 &=& 64 \\
+0 \times 32 &=& 0 \\
+1 \times 16 &=& 16 \\
+1 \times 8 &=& 8 \\
+1 \times 4 &=& 4 \\
+0 \times 2 &=& 0 \\
+1 \times 1 &=& \underline{1} \\
& & 733 \text{ mg}
\end{array}
$$

Notice that in this summation each weight's multiplier is derived from Table 17.2 in which a "no" answer corresponds to a 0 and a "yes" answer corresponds to a 1. The binary representation of the weight is 1 011 011 101 or 1335 in octal notation.

Step	New weight added, mg	Total mass of weights, mg	Retain new weight?
1	512	512	yes
2	256	768	no
3	128	640	yes
4	64	704	yes
5	32	736	no
6	16	720	yes
7	8	728	yes
8	4	732	yes
9	2	734	no
10	1	733	yes

Figure 17.1 shows another type of analog-to-digital converter, a voltage-to-number converter. The operational amplifier in Fig. 17.1 is in the summing configuration (see Chapter 16). E_{in} is the voltage that is to be converted and must be between 0 V and about 1000 mV for an accurate conversion. For this example, we will assume that E_{in} is $+733$ mV. The input voltage is transduced into a current, i_{in}, by the 1-kΩ input resistor.

FIGURE 17.1   Voltage-to-number converter.

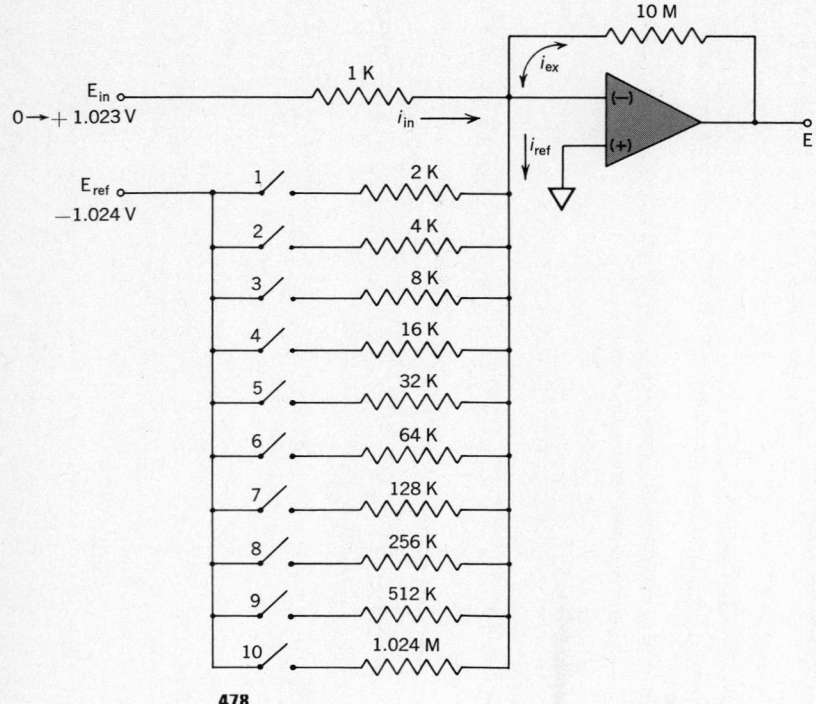

Also connected to the summing point are ten reference resistors with values from $2\,k\Omega$ to $1.024\,M\Omega$. Each of these resistors can be connected through a switch to a $-1.024\,V$ reference voltage. Each resistor that is connected draws a specified amount of positive current away from the summing point. The total of these currents is referred to in Fig. 17.1 as i_{ref}; its value depends upon which switches are closed. If switch 3 is closed, for example, then

$$i_{\text{ref}} = \frac{-1.024\,V}{8\,k} = -0.128\,mA$$

If both switches 3 and 4 are closed,

$$i_{\text{ref}} = \frac{-1.024\,V}{8\,k} + \frac{-1.024\,V}{16\,k}$$

$$= -0.192\,mA$$

Excess positive current, i_{ex}, will flow *into* the summing point if $|i_{\text{in}}| < |i_{\text{ref}}|$ or *out of* the summing point if $|i_{\text{in}}| > |i_{\text{ref}}|$. Therefore, if the output voltage of the operational amplifier is negative, it means i_{ref} should be increased to make it more equal to i_{in}. If the op amp's output is positive, then i_{ref} is too large and should be decreased. The operational amplifier is used as a current comparator in this particular application and is entirely analogous to the pointer on a double-pan balance.

The operation of this device as an analog-to-digital converter is similar to the procedure used to weigh an object. The switch producing the largest reference current is closed first, and the output of the operational amplifier is examined. If the output is negative, insufficient current is being removed from the summing point: That switch is left closed and the switch that produces the next-largest current is tested for its effect. If, on the other hand, the op amp's output is positive, too much current is being removed and the switch that is being tested must be opened before moving on to the next one. Table

TABLE 17.3   CONVERSION SEQUENCE FOR OBTAINING THE VALUE OF A $+733$-mA SIGNAL

Step	Reference current increment, mA	Total reference current, mA	Keep switch closed?
1	0.512	0.512	yes
2	0.256	0.768	no
3	0.128	0.640	yes
4	0.064	0.704	yes
5	0.032	0.736	no
6	0.016	0.720	yes
7	0.008	0.728	yes
8	0.004	0.732	yes
9	0.002	0.734	no
10	0.001	0.733	yes

17.3 shows the switches that remain closed after converting an input voltage of $+733$ mV. Notice that

$$i_{in} = \frac{0.733 \text{ V}}{1 \text{ k}} = 0.733 \text{ mA}$$

$$
\begin{array}{rcl}
1 \times 0.512 &=& 0.512 \text{ mA} \\
+0 \times 0.256 &=& 0.000 \\
+1 \times 0.128 &=& 0.128 \\
+1 \times 0.064 &=& 0.064 \\
+0 \times 0.032 &=& 0.000 \\
+1 \times 0.016 &=& 0.016 \\
+1 \times 0.008 &=& 0.008 \\
+1 \times 0.004 &=& 0.004 \\
+0 \times 0.002 &=& 0.000 \\
+1 \times 0.001 &=& \underline{0.001} \\
& & 0.733 \text{ mA}
\end{array}
$$

The binary representation of the voltage is 1 011 011 101 (1335 octal).

An interesting feature of the analog-to-digital converter shown in Fig. 17.1 is that it contains a *digital-to-analog converter* (abbreviated DAC). Each comparison of the input current with a trial binary number requires that the binary number be converted to an analog current (digital-to-analog conversion), an operation that is carried out by the reference voltage, the reference resistors, and the associated switches.

FIGURE 17.2 Number-to-voltage converter.

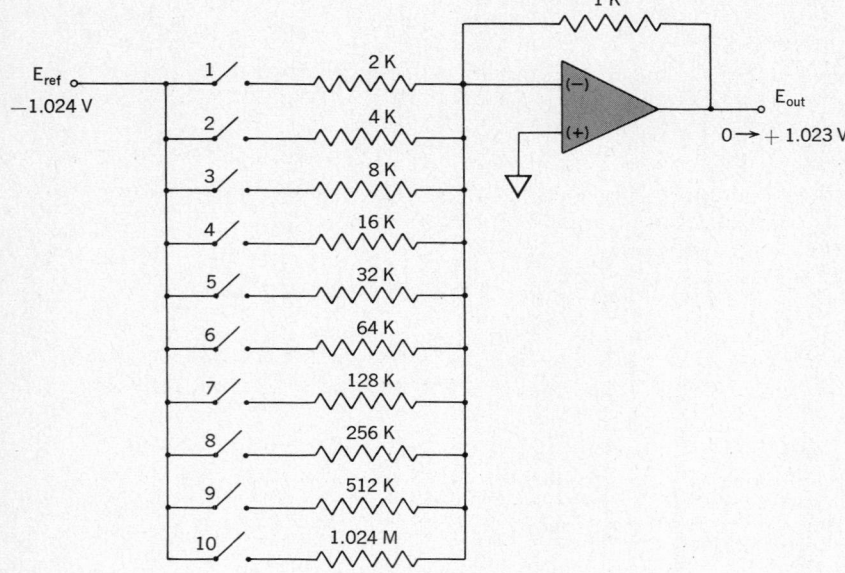

Figure 17.2 is a diagram of a separate digital-to-analog converter that will output a voltage equal in millivolts to the value of a ten-bit binary number set in its switches. Switch 1 corresponds to the most-significant bit (MSB) and switch 10 corresponds to the least-significant bit (LSB). Digital-to-analog converters are used whenever it is necessary to transform information from the digital domain to the analog domain. As an example, many modern electrochemical instruments make use of mathematically generated numerical waveforms which can be converted into voltages or currents by digital-to-analog converters and applied to electrodes.[5]

DIGITAL LOGIC FOR CONTROL

In Chapter 16 it was seen that operational amplifiers are the heart of modern chemical instrumentation involving analog signals. The fundamental building blocks of digital instrumentation are logic gates, devices capable of giving binary 1 or 0 outputs for certain combinations of binary values applied to their inputs. Because the detailed electronic theory necessary to explain the operation of modern logic components is beyond the scope of this chapter, logic gates will be described simply in terms of what they do, not how they do it.

The values 1 and 0 appear frequently in descriptions of digital logic gates. The meaning of these symbols is usually as follows: if something is true, positive, yes, on, good, up, light, etc., it is designated as 1; if something is false, negative, no, off, bad, down, dark, etc., it is assigned the value 0. It should be kept in mind that in practice these logical 1's and 0's are implemented by electrical signals; for example, $+3$ V might correspond to logical 1, and 0 V to logical 0.

The simplest logic gate is the inverter. Its function is to give an output that is the opposite of its single input. If the input is 0, the output will be 1; if the input is 1, the output will be 0. Because there are only two possible binary values, a different but equivalent way of saying this is that the value of the output is *not* the value of the input. For this reason, the inverter is said to perform the logical NOT function. The symbol for the NOT gate is a triangle with a small circle following it[6] as shown below:

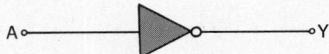

The various combinations of inputs and outputs can be expressed concisely in a "truth table" as shown in Table 17.4 in which column A represents

[5] See, for example, J. B. Flato, *Anal. Chem.*, **44**(11), 75A (1972).

[6] Strictly speaking, the triangle indicates amplification. The circle is used to express an "active low" condition and leads to the concept of "negative logic," a concept that is useful in more sophisticated treatments of logic circuits but confusing to the beginner. Thus, although the circle does not strictly mean inversion, we will nonetheless use it in that sense for this brief introduction to digital logic.

the possible input values and column Y gives the corresponding outputs. When a signal has been inverted, it is often represented as the original symbol followed by a prime. Thus, $Y = A'$ for an inverter.

TABLE 17.4   TRUTH TABLE FOR
                 "NOT" FUNCTION

A	Y
0	1
1	0

Example 1.   A switch is to be used to indicate to a digital logic circuit that the technician is ready to begin a procedure. Use a NOT gate in a circuit that will give a logical 1 output when and only when the switch is closed.

Assume that the voltage levels associated with the 0 and 1 logic levels are 0 V and $+3$ V, respectively. The following circuit will give the desired output.

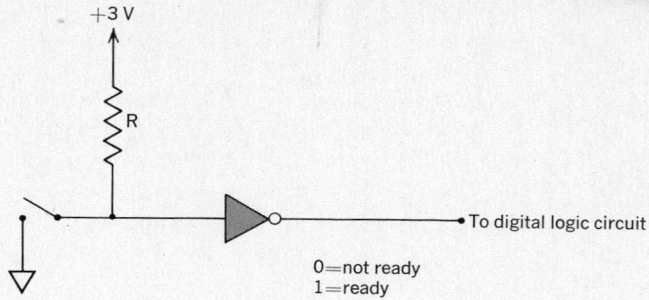

When the switch is open, the input of the inverter is tied to $+3$ V through the resistor R. The input to the gate will be about $+3$ V, which corresponds to a logical 1; the output will be a logical 0. When the switch is closed, the input of the inverter is connected to 0 V, which corresponds to a logical 0; the output will then be a logical 1.

A slightly more complicated logic gate performs the AND function. This gate must have at least two inputs but can have more. The symbol for a two-input AND gate is:

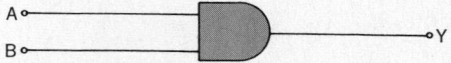

The truth table associated with the AND function is given in Table 17.5. The AND gate produces a 1 output if and only if *both* inputs *A and B* have values of 1. The logical symbol for the AND function is the dot; $Y = A \cdot B$ for a two-input AND gate.

TABLE 17.5 TRUTH TABLE FOR
                "AND" FUNCTION

A	B	Y
0	0	0
0	1	0
1	0	0
1	1	1

Example 2. A computer is connected to an experiment and will begin acquiring data through an analog-to-digital converter when it receives a signal that changes from logical 0 to logical 1. The signal is to be a 1 if and only if the technician is ready *and* the computer is not busy doing something else. Devise a circuit that will output the necessary information to the computer.

Assume that the computer will provide us with a signal that is a logical 0 if it is busy with some other task, or a logical 1 if the computer is available for this task. The circuit shown below will give the required output.

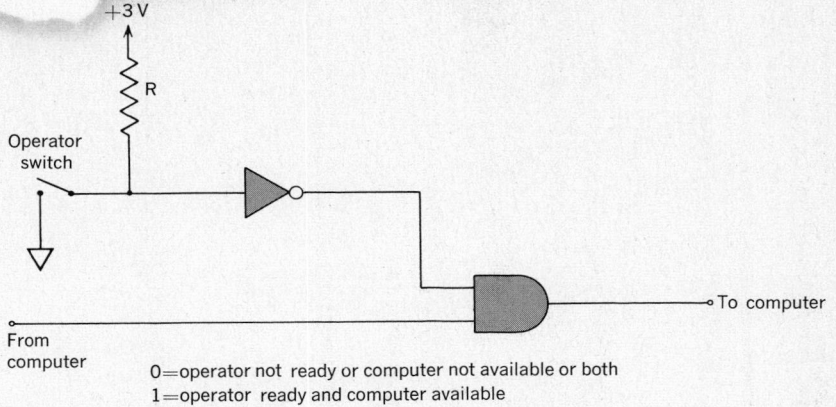

0=operator not ready or computer not available or both
1=operator ready and computer available

Another useful function is implemented by the OR gate. Its operation is such that it will produce a 1 output if at least one of its inputs has a value of 1. The symbol for a two-input OR gate is

Its truth table is shown in Table 17.6. If *either A or B* is a 1, the output will be a 1. This is often referred to as the IOR (INCLUSIVE OR) function because it

TABLE 17.6 TRUTH TABLE FOR
                "INCLUSIVE OR" FUNCTION

A	B	Y
0	0	0
0	1	1
1	0	1
1	1	1

also gives a binary 1 output when A and B are both 1. The logical symbol for the OR function is the cross:[7] $Y = A + B$ for a two-input OR gate.

Example 3. A polarography experiment requires that a "halt" signal be given to a computer if the applied voltage is more negative than -3 V *or* if the current exceeds 1 milliampere. Analog electronic circuits are provided that will close a switch if the applied voltage is more negative than -3 V and provide a signal that is a logical 1 $(+3$ V$)$ if the current is less than 1 milliampere or logical 0 (0 V) if the current exceeds 1 milliampere. Construct a digital logic circuit that will give a logical 1 halt signal at its output.

The OR gate in the following circuit will provide the proper halt signal. Note that an inverter is required to change the sense of the output from the current detector.

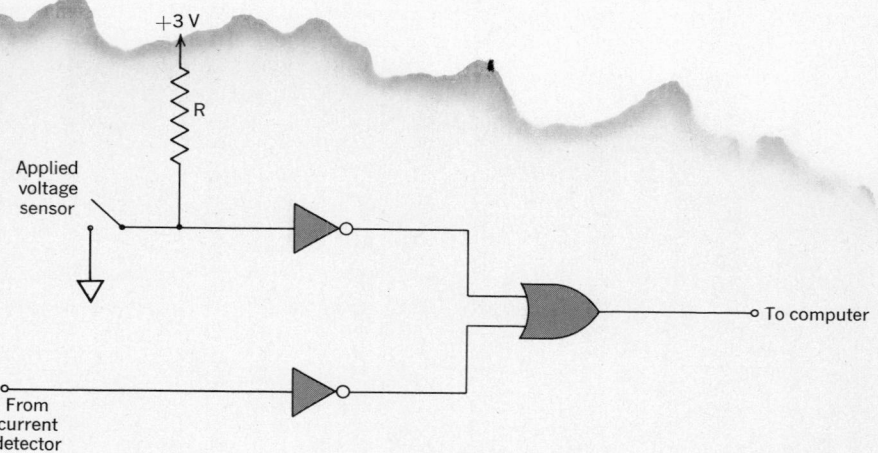

Often the AND and OR functions are combined with the NOT function to give NAND (NOT AND) gates

and NOR (NOT OR) gates

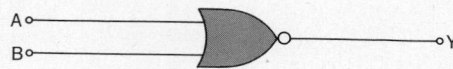

Here the inverter symbol is simply combined with the AND or OR gate by incorporating the circle and omitting the triangle. The NAND and NOR

---

[7] Care should be taken to avoid confusing the arithmetic meaning of the symbols "+" and "·" with their meaning in digital logic. For this discussion, "+" means OR (not "plus" or "and"), "·" means AND (not "times").

operations are written as $Y = (A \cdot B)'$ and $Y = (A + B)'$ respectively. Their truth tables are shown in Tables 17.7 and 17.8.

TABLE 17.7 TRUTH TABLE FOR "NAND" FUNCTION

A	B	Y
0	0	1
0	1	1
1	0	1
1	1	0

TABLE 17.8 TRUTH TABLE FOR "NOR" FUNCTION

A	B	Y
0	0	1
0	1	0
1	0	0
1	1	0

Example 4. A NAND gate can be used to implement the circuit of the previous example as shown below:

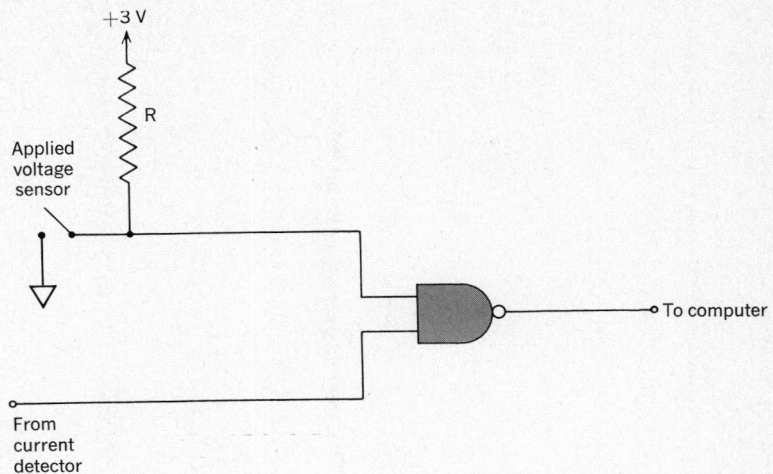

The output of the NAND gate will be 0 when and only when its inputs are both 1 (see Table 17.7). Otherwise, the output will be a 1. This circuit is simpler than the one in the previous example: only one gate is needed here, compared to three gates in the other circuit.

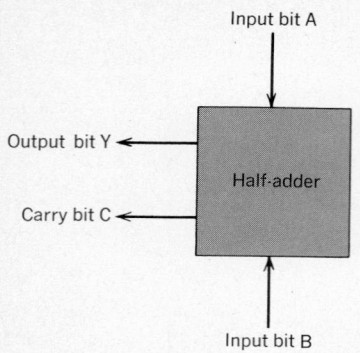

Input bit A

Output bit Y

Half-adder

Carry bit C

Input bit B

FIGURE 17.3 Necessary characteristics of a half-adder.

DIGITAL LOGIC FOR COMPUTATION

Logic gates can also be used to perform mathematical operations on digital information. The *half-adder*, a circuit that will add together two one-bit binary numbers, is one of the fundamental building blocks of digital computation. A review of binary addition suggests that the half-adder should possess the characteristics shown in Fig. 17.3. The device must have two inputs, one input for each of the two bits that are to be added. It must have one output to represent the sum of the addition, and another output to indicate whether or not a carry occurred. A truth table for the half-adder is shown in Table 17.9.

TABLE 17.9 TRUTH TABLE FOR HALF-ADDER

A	B	C	Y
0	0	0	0
0	1	0	1
1	0	0	1
1	1	1	0

Inspection of this truth table shows that the carry output, C, is the same as the logical AND of inputs A and B. Output Y is the result of a function not yet encountered, the XOR (EXCLUSIVE OR) function which produces a binary 1 output if and only if *either* A or B is a binary 1 (but not if A and B are both binary 1). The XOR operation is expressed as $Y = A \oplus B$ and is often represented:

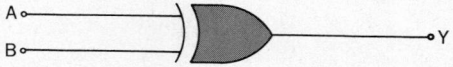

A

B

Y

Its truth table is shown in Table 17.10.

TABLE 17.10 TRUTH TABLE FOR
"EXCLUSIVE OR" FUNCTION

A	B	Y
0	0	0
0	1	1
1	0	1
1	1	0

The XOR function can also be stated, "if A AND the *inverse* of B are both binary 1 OR if B AND the *inverse* of A are both binary 1, then output Y will be a binary 1." Thus, the XOR function can be generated by an appropriate combination of inverters, AND, and OR gates. To obtain "A AND the inverse of B," the following circuit can be used:

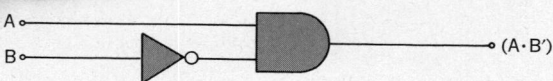

To obtain "B AND the inverse of A,"

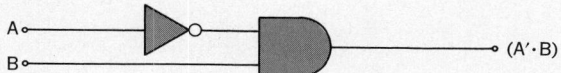

The complete XOR function is obtained by forming the logical OR of the previous two circuits and is shown in Fig. 17.4.

The circuit for the complete half-adder is shown in Fig. 17.5.

The half-adder does not provide for a possible carry input from the addition of the next-less-significant bits of the numbers being added—therefore, it can only be used to add the least-significant bit of each of two numbers. A somewhat more complicated circuit that does take into account a previous carry is the *full-adder* for which the truth table is given in Table 17.11. By

FIGURE 17.4 Implementation of XOR function.

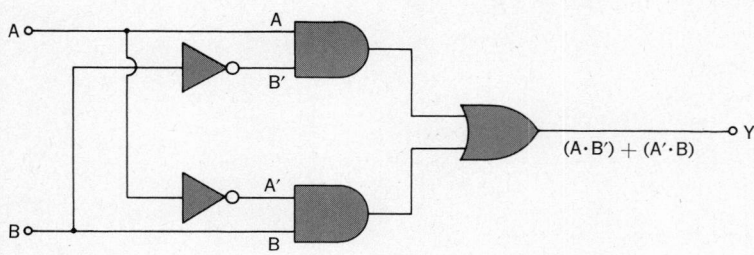

487

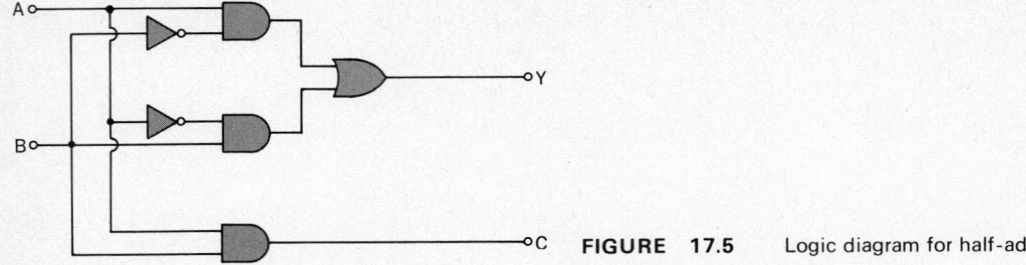

FIGURE 17.5   Logic diagram for half-adder.

TABLE 17.11   TRUTH TABLE FOR FULL-ADDER

Previous carry	A	B	C	Y
0	0	0	0	0
0	0	1	0	1
0	1	0	0	1
0	1	1	1	0
1	0	0	0	1
1	0	1	1	0
1	1	0	1	0
1	1	1	1	1

connecting one half-adder and $n - 1$ full-adders in a sequence, two n-bit numbers can be added as suggested in Fig. 17.6. The following addition could be performed by the circuit shown in Fig. 17.6.

$$
\begin{array}{rr}
C_n\ C_{n-1}\ \cdots\ C_1\ C_0 & \\
A_n\ \ \cdots\ A_2\ A_1\ A_0 & 10010111 \\
B_n\ \ \cdots\ B_2\ B_1\ B_0 & 11011001 \\
\hline
C_n\ Y_n\ \ \cdots\ Y_2\ Y_1\ Y_0 & 101110000
\end{array}
$$

Multiplication can also be carried out with an adder if extra circuits are provided. A review of binary multiplication suggests that it can be accomplished by a series of shifts and additions. One of two n-bit binary numbers

FIGURE 17.6   Block diagram of n-bit adder.

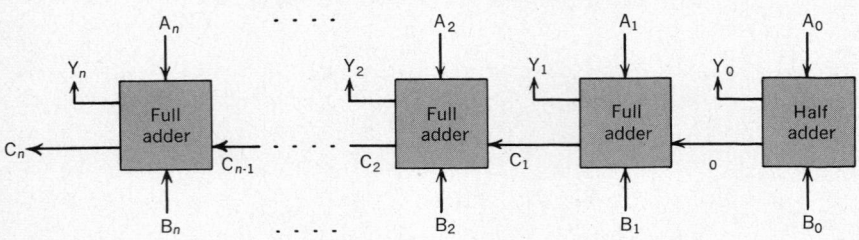

(A) is used to decide when additions are to occur. The other number (B) is applied to the upper side of a $2n$-bit adder. The lower side of the adder is initially equal to 0. The following sequence is repeated n times: (a) if the nth bit to the left of the radix point of number A is equal to a 1, perform an addition (if the bit is 0, no addition takes place); (b) apply the results of the addition to the lower side of the adder; (c) shift the number B one place to the left along the upper side of the adder.

Example. Multiply 101_2 and 011_2 using the above algorithm.[8]

Let 101_2 be the number applied to the adder. Table 17.12 shows the results of the steps in the multiplication. As a check, $101_2 \times 011_2 = 1111_2$ is the same as $5 \times 3 = 15$.

TABLE 17.12   MULTIPLICATION OF 101_2 BY 011_2 BY MEANS OF SHIFTS AND ADDITIONS

	$2n$-bit adder	Decision bit of A	Add?
INITIALLY:			
B (original position)	000101	011	yes
Previous sum	000000	↑	
New sum	000101		
AFTER FIRST ADDITION:			
B (shifted left)	001010	011	yes
Previous sum	000101	↑	
New sum	001111		
AFTER SECOND ADDITION:			
B (shifted left again)	010100	011	no
Previous sum	001111	↑	
New sum	001111		

Result = 001111_2

All other mathematical operations can be accomplished by suitable algorithms that are based ultimately on AND, OR, and NOT functions.

SMALL COMPUTERS

It is possible to design logic circuits that will perform almost any specific task capable of being carried out in the digital realm. We have seen, for example, how it is possible to construct a digital logic device that will add

[8] An *algorithm* is a prescribed set of well-defined rules or procedures for the solution of a problem.

together two binary numbers. With a few modifications, the circuit can be used for multiplication. Other changes could be implemented that would result in subtracters, dividers, magnitude comparators, etc. As the desired task becomes more complex, however, the required circuitry also becomes more complicated. There is a point at which it becomes desirable to use a more versatile instrument, the digital computer. It consists of a modest amount of circuitry yet can be programmed to carry out very complicated tasks. Because it is programmable, the same instrument can be used to perform a variety of tasks (though not necessarily all at the same time), thus obviating the need for several expensive special purpose circuits.

Computers vary in their complexity, from hand-held calculators to the gigantic "number crushers" used for involved calculations. This section deals with one particular class of computers, the so-called "laboratory mini computers." As their name implies, they are not large, but the impact they have made on analytical chemical instrumentation and automation has been tremendous. Because of continual advances in electronic technology, the exact details of various minicomputer operations are rapidly changing. The principles behind the operations, however, have remained (and probably will remain) more or less constant. What follows is a brief introduction to the principles, operation, capabilities, and uses of computers in analytical chemistry.

Figure 17.7 shows a diagrammatic representation of a small computer system. The computer itself is enclosed within dotted lines. The various components of the system are discussed individually.

FIGURE   17.7   Small computer system.

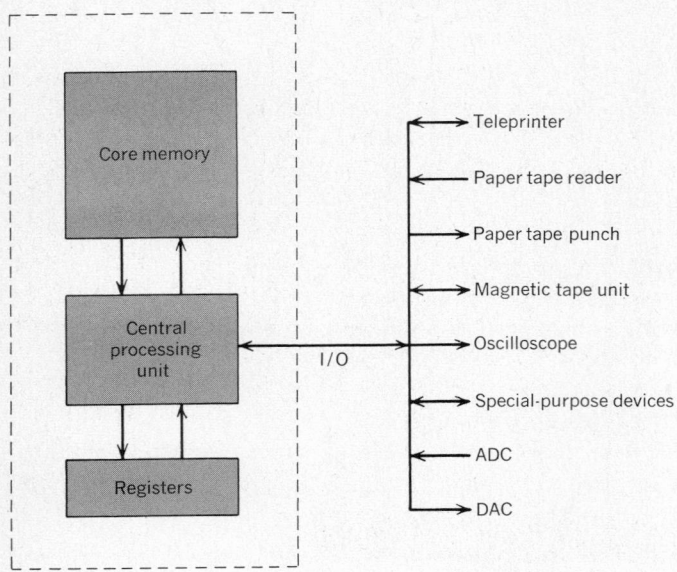

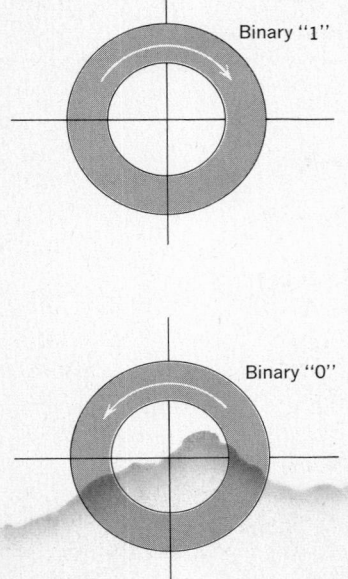

Binary "1"

Binary "0"

FIGURE 17.8 Magnetic cores.

Core Memory

To be effective, computers must be able to remember two kinds of information: *instructions* that tell the computer what to do, and *data* that the computer manipulates. Both kinds of information are stored in *core memory*. Core memory consists of arrays of tiny donuts (or cores) of ferromagnetic material that can be magnetized in either of two directions. Electrical currents applied to wires threaded through the centers of these cores can be used to sense the direction of magnetization (called "reading" information from core memory) or, if the current is large enough, to force the magnetization into one state or the other ("writing" information into core memory). Figure 17.8 shows two cores, one storing a binary 1, the other a 0. The arrows indicate the direction of magnetization.

Core memory is organized into *words* as shown in Fig. 17.9. Just as a word in a language is a group of letters that are treated as a single unit, a "computer word" is a group of bits treated as a unit. Typical word lengths of small computers are 12, 16, and 18 bits. Each bit of the computer word corresponds to an individual magnetic core.

FIGURE 17.9 A 16-bit computer word.

Bit number

15	14	13	12	11	10	9	8	7	6	5	4	3	2	1	0
0	1	0	0	1	1	1	0	1	0	0	1	1	0	1	1

Address	Binary contents
7777	1 101 111 001 110 011
7776	0 000 000 101 111 101
7775	1 111 111 111 010 111
7774	1 010 101 010 101 010
•	•
•	•
•	•
11	1 111 111 111 111 111
10	0 000 000 000 000 000
7	1 101 110 010 110 011
6	0 001 010 011 100 101
5	0 110 111 110 101 100
4	0 011 010 001 000 111
3	1 111 000 111 000 101
2	1 000 111 000 111 010
1	1 010 101 110 011 101
0	0 011 101 111 110 010

FIGURE 17.10 Addresses assigned to 4096-word core memory, each word sixteen bits long.

Each word in core memory is assigned a unique address, numbered from zero upward, usually in octal notation. Figure 17.10 illustrates the structure of core memory for a computer with 4096 16-bit words of core memory.[9]

Registers

As the computer operates, it must keep track of certain separate pieces of information such as the instruction it is executing, the location in memory from which it is to obtain its next instruction, the value of a number that is to be added to another number, etc. This information is stored in devices called *registers* which can be thought of as extra words of memory that are more easily and rapidly accessed than words of core memory. Registers are often connected to circuits such as adders so that computations and logical operations can be performed directly on information contained in them.

Central Processing Unit

The *central processing unit* (CPU), sometimes referred to as the *arithmetic unit* (AU), is the brain center of the computer. It interprets instructions, directs information to and from core memory, carries out arithmetic operations,

[9] An abbreviation often encountered in reference to core memory is the term "K" which stands for 1024. An 8-K core memory contains 8192 words.

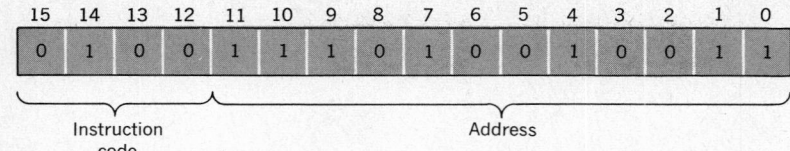

15	14	13	12	11	10	9	8	7	6	5	4	3	2	1	0
0	1	0	0	1	1	1	0	1	0	0	1	0	0	1	1

Instruction code   Address

FIGURE 17.11   Instruction word format.

synchronizes events, loads registers with data, communicates with other devices connected to the computer, etc.

As an illustration of how the central processing unit interacts with core memory and the working registers, let us look at how a 16-bit word-length computer adds two numbers together and saves the result. Memory reference instruction words are usually interpreted in two parts, instruction code and address, as shown in Fig. 17.11. The four bits numbered 15–12 might be used as an instruction code. Bits 11–0 are the address upon which the instruction is to operate. We will consider three possible instruction codes:

1. $0001_2 = 01_8$: load the binary value of the word found at the indicated address into a working register associated with an adder, register X.

2. $0101_2 = 05_8$: add the binary value of the word found at the indicated address to the value contained in register X and place the sum in register X.

3. $0100_2 = 04_8$: store the binary value found in register X at the core memory location indicated by the address part of the instruction.

Assume that the numbers we want to add together, say 625_8 and 13524_8, are stored in memory locations 162_8 and 163_8, and that the sum of these two values is to be placed in memory location 164_8. The following instructions are placed somewhere else in core, say in locations 7324_8, 7325_8, and 7326_8:

Address	Contents
7324_8	010162_8
7325_8	050163_8
7326_8	040164_8

The binary and octal representations of core memory are now as shown in Fig. 17.12. At this point, the contents of location 164_8 are not important. If we cause the computer to begin fetching its instructions from location 7324_8, the following actions will take place.

The instruction word at location 7324_8 is placed in the computer's instruction register. The computer is directed by the instruction to load (code 01_8) the value at location 162_8 into register X. After executing this instruction (a typical execution time is about two microseconds), register X

493

Address	Binary contents	Octal contents
•	•	•
•	•	•
•	•	•
7326	0 1 0 0 000 001 110 100	040164
7325	0 101 000 001 110 011	050163
7324	0 001 000 001 110 010	010162
•	•	•
•	•	•
•	•	•
164	x xxx xxx xxx xxx xxx	xxxxxx
163	0 001 011 101 010 100	013524
162	0 000 000 110 010 101	000625
•	•	•
•	•	•
•	•	•

FIGURE   17.12   Contents of core memory.

contains 000625_8. The central processing unit fetches the next instruction (at location 7325_8) and then adds (code 05_8) the contents of location 163_8 (contents $= 13524_8$) to register X and places the result (14351_8) in register X. The next instruction directs the computer to store (code 04_8) the value contained in the X register at core memory location 164_8. The binary value in location 164_8 will now be 0 001 100 011 101 001, and the task is complete.

We have considered only three of many possible instruction codes that are necessary for a versatile computer. Other codes perform shift operations, testing, logical operations, input-output operations, skips, halts, etc. With proper programming (i.e., the proper sequence of instruction words) the digital computer can be made to perform a wide variety of tasks.

Peripheral Equipment

Digital computers usually consist of a central processing unit, 4 or 8K of core memory, and several registers. Also included are lights and switches that allow information in memory to be manually examined and changed. To be more effective in their communication with the outside world, computers are usually provided with other equipment that simplifies the transfer of information into and out of the computer. These ancillary pieces of equipment are called "input-output" (I/O) devices or "peripherals."

The most common I/O device associated with computer systems is the *teleprinter*. It is basically a typewriter that has the capability of sending and

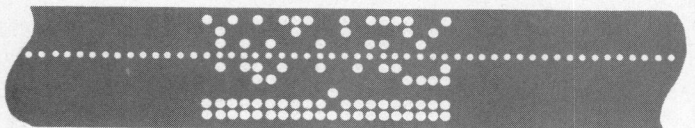

FIGURE 17.13 Punched paper tape.

receiving digital information. When a key is struck, the associated character is converted to a digital code and sent from the teleprinter to the computer. For example, the letter "A" is usually transmitted as 11000001_2. When the teleprinter receives a digital code from the computer, it will print the appropriate character. If the code were 11000010, a "B" would be printed. In this way, information can be rapidly and concisely communicated between the user and the computer.

Another means of communicating information to the computer is with punched paper tape such as that shown in Fig. 17.13. A *paper tape reader* converts the pattern of holes (binary 1) and no-holes (binary 0) into digital information that can be placed in one of the computer's registers and then stored in memory. The complementary device, a *paper tape punch*, accepts digital information and punches it into blank tape.

Paper tape is often used as an intermediate storage medium for digital information. As an example, a gas chromatograph could be connected to an analog-to-digital converter which might convert detector response to a number once every tenth of a second. The ADC could then transfer its digital output to a paper tape punch which would record the detector response on paper tape. Later, the paper tape could be placed in a reader and the information transferred to core memory for processing by a computer. The relationship between the computer and the chromatographic experiment in this example is said to be "off-line," meaning that there is no direct line of communication between them. (Paper tape is used as an intermediate storage medium.) If the ADC were connected directly to the computer, the relationship would then be "on-line," indicating a direct line of communication between the experiment and the computer.

Another storage medium commonly used with small computers is magnetic tape. It is similar in concept to punched paper tape, but rather than retaining data as a pattern of holes and no-holes, magnetic tape records information as tiny spots of magnetized metal oxide. A binary zero is stored as a spot magnetized in one direction; a binary 1 is magnetized in the other direction. Information on magnetic tapes can be "erased," and new information can be written on the tapes. This is not the case with punched paper tape. The density of information (usually expressed in "bits per inch") is greater on magnetic tape than it is on paper tape.

Analog-to-digital and digital-to-analog converters have been discussed previously. Whereas teleprinters, paper tape readers and punches, and magnetic tape units all communicate discrete information, ADCs and DACs are the computer's means of communicating with the analog world. ADCs are used extensively in *data acquisition* applications in which continuous parameters must be input to the computer. DACs are used most commonly in *control* situations in which the computer must specify a value of some parameter in the analog domain.

Other peripheral devices that are found in small computer systems include card readers, line printers, storage oscilloscopes, incremental plotters, magnetic disc storage, and telephone communications equipment. Many of these are usually found only on the bigger systems. Other, less common peripherals are often encountered in systems with special requirements.

Software

All of the physical equipment that make up a computer system is called *hardware. Software* is the programming that directs the operation of the hardware.[10] We have already dealt with the most fundamental level of software, *machine-language programming*, in which instructions are written as groups of 1's and 0's. Programming in machine language is extremely tedious and time consuming but often necessary for some applications.

A higher level of software, *assembly-language programming*, uses mnemonics to express machine language codes. The computer can be programmed[11] to read a series of statements written in assembly language (called a source program) and translate them into their machine-language equivalent (called an object program) which can then be read into the computer and executed. As an example, LDX might be a mnemonic that means "load register X" and correspond to an instruction code of 0001_2. Similarly, ADX might mean "add to register X" (0101_2) and STX could stand for "store register X" (0100_2). The assembly language program

$$LDX \qquad 162$$

$$ADX \qquad 163$$

$$STX \qquad 164$$

would generate the machine code

$$0\ 001\ 000\ 001\ 110\ 010$$

$$0\ 101\ 000\ 001\ 110\ 011$$

$$0\ 100\ 000\ 001\ 110\ 100$$

which could be used to add two numbers together and save the result as discussed earlier in this chapter.

---

[10] One distinction between hardware and software is, "If you can walk up to and kick it, it is hardware; if you cannot, it is software." Another: "If you want to kick it, it is software; if it is all right, it is hardware." (*Research/Development*, November, 1971, p. 14.)

[11] The program is called an *assembler*.

Higher-level languages are usually used for most programming. The most common high-level languages that are used with small computers are FORTRAN and BASIC (or BASIC-like languages). FORTRAN is an abbreviation of FORmula TRANslation and is a very powerful language for mathematical computation. A statement that will add two numbers together might look like

$$A = B + C$$

Assembly-language programs can be linked to FORTRAN programs to provide the higher-level language with the capability of executing special purpose operations (such as controlling ADCs and displaying points on an oscilloscope). As normally implemented on small computer systems, FORTRAN must be translated by a program called a *compiler* first into assembly language and then into machine language. Program changes, even very minor ones, usually require that the whole program be recompiled.

BASIC differs from FORTRAN in that it is an interpretive language. Rather than translate the program into machine language and then run it, BASIC uses its own machine language subprograms to execute the program statements. Program changes are made easily and quickly because there is no need to recompile. A typical BASIC statement might be

$$1 \quad \text{LET } A = B + C$$

Assembly-language programs can also be linked to BASIC.

Applications of Small Computers in Analytical Chemistry

Implicit in all of the preceding discussions has been the assumption that the computer is used in conjunction with some analytical chemical instrument. The off-line and on-line interactions of a computer with a gas chromatograph were discussed previously and are shown diagrammatically in Fig. 17.14(a) and 17.14(b). On-line data acquisition and subsequent processing is a very common use of small computers in analytical laboratories.

The most powerful interaction between computer and experiment is suggested in Fig. 17.14(c). Here the computer not only acquires information from the instrument, but also exerts control over the instrument. The closed-loop control allows the computer to observe information coming from the instrument, make split-second decisions about how best to operate the instrument, and immediately implement this control.

As an example of closed-loop control, a gas chromatograph might have its detector output amplified by an operational amplifier whose gain can be controlled in steps (say 1, 10, 100, etc.) by a computer. The output of this amplifier would be digitized by an ADC and then input to the computer. If the computer senses that a strong chromatographic peak is about to cause the ADC to go off scale, it can decrease the gain of the operational amplifier

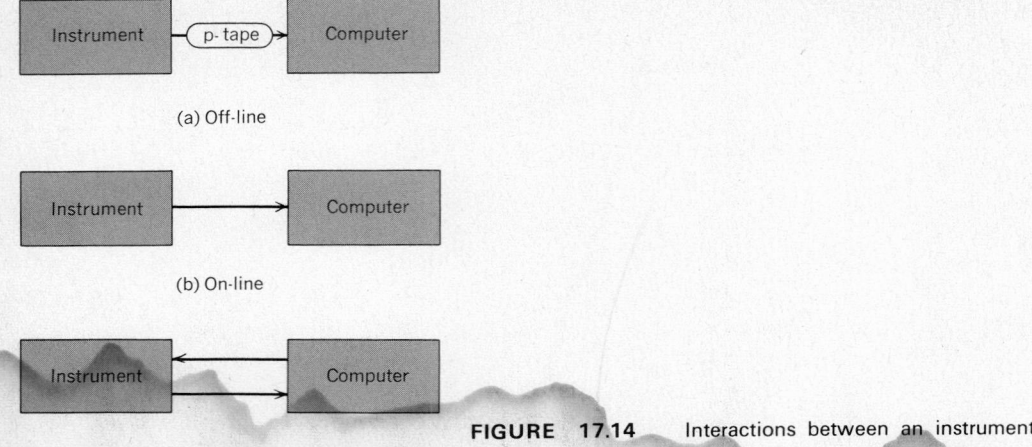

(a) Off-line

(b) On-line

(c) Closed-loop

FIGURE 17.14 Interactions between an instrument and a computer.

and allow valid readings to be obtained. Similarly, if the detector response is near baseline, the gain of the amplifier can be increased to better observe very weak chromatographic peaks. The computer can keep track of what gain is being used at a particular time during data acquisition and multiply or divide the input from the ADC by an appropriate factor to give the actual detector response.

REFERENCES

H. V. MALMSTADT and C. G. ENKE, *Digital Electronics for Scientists*, W. A. Benjamin, Inc., New York, 1969.

R. L. MORRIS and J. R. MILLER, eds., *Designing with TTL Integrated Circuits*, McGraw-Hill Book Company, New York, 1971.

J. S. SPRINGER, "Using Integrated Circuits in Chemical Instrumentation," *Anal. Chem.*, 42(8), 22A (1970).

C. G. ENKE, "Data Domains—An Analysis of Digital and Analog Instrumentation Systems and Components," *Anal. Chem.*, 43(1), 69A (1971).

C. P. SPECTOR, "Analytical Lab Computers," *Industrial Research*, Nov. 1971, p. 40.

R. E. DESSY and D. G. LARSEN, "Minicomputers: Focus on Lab Revolution," *Chem. Eng. News*, Dec. 20, 1971, p. 42.

M. ELECCION, "A/D and D/A Converters," *IEEE Spectrum*, July, 1972, p. 63.

E. ZIEGLER, D. HONNEBERG, and G. SCHOMBURG, "Mulheim Computer System for Analytical Instrumentation," *Anal. Chem.*, 42(9), 51A (1970).

S. P. PERONE, "Computer Applications in the Chemistry Laboratory—A Survey," *Anal. Chem.*, 43, 1288 (1971).

PROBLEMS **1.** *Binary number system.* Perform the following operations in binary arithmetic: (a) $10111 + 11001$; (b) 1101×1111; (c) $100000 - 11010$; (d) $1001011 \div 1111$.

2. *Binary number system.* A tutor offers you a package deal of fifteen one-hour sessions. Payment is to be made as follows: one cent for the first session, two cents for the second session, \$0.04 for the third, \$0.08 for the fourth, and so on. If you had accepted his offer, how much would you have had to pay him?

3. *Digital-to-analog converters.* The resolution of a DAC is a function of the number of bits it will convert. Complete the following table.

No. of bits	Resolution (1 part in)	Resolution (%)
1	$2^1 =$ 2	50
2	$2^2 =$ 4	25
3	$2^3 =$ 8	12.5
4		
5		
6		
7		
8		
9		
10		

4. *Truth tables.* Use truth tables to show the following equivalences: (a) $A \cdot 1 = A$; (b) $A + 1 = 1$; (c) $A \cdot A' = 0$; (d) $A + A' = 1$; (e) $A + B = (A' \cdot B')'$; (f) $A \cdot B = (A' + B')'$.

5. *Logic gates.* Given the signals A, B, C, and D, implement the following circuits with logic gates: (a) $Y = A + (B \cdot C)$; (b) $Y = (A \cdot (B' + C + D'))'$; (c) $Y = A \oplus (B \cdot C)'$; (d) $Y = A \cdot A'$.

6. *Control.* Design a circuit to give a logical 1 output if a chemist is ready, a buret is full, a stopcock is open, and it is between the hours of 8:00 a.m. and 5:00 p.m.

7. *Digital circuits.* Design a circuit for use as a full-adder. (See Table 17.11.)

8. *Computer words.* The designers of a sixteen-bit computer chose five bits for the instruction code of an instruction word and eleven bits for the address. (a) What is the maximum number of different instruction codes the computer could have? (b) How many locations could be directly addressed?

9. *Computer programming.* Assume that DZM (code 0011_2) is a mnemonic that means "deposit zero in the specified address." INA (0010_2) means "increment the contents of the specified address by 1." JMP (1000_2) means "go to the specified address and execute instructions starting there." Write a program, first in assembly language and then in machine language, to deposit zeros in all (or most) of a 16-bit computer's 4-K core memory.

Appendix I

Tables of Equilibrium Constants and Oxidation Potentials

TABLE 1 DISSOCIATION CONSTANTS OF WEAK ACIDS AND BASES (25°C)

Acid	Formula	K_a	pK_a	Conjugate base	K_b	pK_b
Acetic	CH_3COOH	1.8×10^{-5}	4.74	Acetate ion	5.6×10^{-10}	9.26
Ammonium ion	NH_4^+	5.6×10^{-10}	9.26	Ammonia	1.8×10^{-5}	4.74
Anilinium ion	$C_6H_5NH_3^+$	2.2×10^{-5}	4.66	Aniline	4.6×10^{-10}	9.34
Arsenic	H_3AsO_4	5.6×10^{-3}	2.26	Dihydrogen arsenate ion	1.8×10^{-12}	11.74
Dihydrogen arsenate ion	$H_2AsO_4^-$	1.7×10^{-7}	6.77	Monohydrogen arsenate ion	5.9×10^{-8}	7.23
Monohydrogen arsenate ion	$HAsO_4^{2-}$	3×10^{-12}	11.5	Arsenate ion	3×10^{-3}	2.5
Arsenious	H_3AsO_3	6×10^{-10}	9.2	Dihydrogen arsenite ion	1.7×10^{-5}	4.8
Dihydrogen arsenite ion	$H_2AsO_3^-$	3×10^{-14}	13.5	Monohydrogen arsenite ion	3×10^{-1}	0.5
Benzoic	$HC_7H_5O_2$	6.6×10^{-5}	4.18	Benzoate ion	1.5×10^{-10}	9.82
Boric	H_3BO_3	5.8×10^{-10}	9.24	Dihydrogen borate ion	1.7×10^{-5}	4.76
Carbonic	H_2CO_3	4.6×10^{-7}	6.34	Bicarbonate ion	2.2×10^{-8}	7.66
Bicarbonate ion	HCO_3^-	4.4×10^{-11}	10.36	Carbonate ion	2.3×10^{-4}	3.64
Chloroacetic, mono	$CH_2ClCOOH$	1.5×10^{-3}	2.82	Monochloroacetate ion	7×10^{-12}	11.18
Chloroacetic, di	$CHCl_2COOH$	5×10^{-2}	1.3	Dichloroacetate ion	2×10^{-13}	12.7
Chloroacetic, tri	CCl_3COOH	2×10^{-1}	0.7	Trichloroacetate ion	5×10^{-14}	13.3
Chromic	H_2CrO_4	1.8×10^{-1}	0.74	Bichromate ion	5.6×10^{-14}	13.26
Bichromate ion	$HCrO_4^-$	3.2×10^{-7}	6.49	Chromate ion	3.1×10^{-8}	7.51
Citric	$H_3C_6H_5O_7$	8.4×10^{-4}	3.08	Dihydrogen citrate ion	1.2×10^{-11}	10.92
Dihydrogen citrate ion	$H_2C_6H_5O_7^-$	1.8×10^{-5}	4.74	Monohydrogen citrate ion	5.6×10^{-10}	9.26
Monohydrogen citrate ion	$HC_6H_5O_7^{2-}$	4.0×10^{-6}	5.40	Citrate ion	2.5×10^{-9}	8.60
Cyanic	$HOCN$	2×10^{-4}	3.7	Cyanate ion	5×10^{-11}	10.3
Diethylammonium ion	$C_4H_{10}NH_2^+$	7.7×10^{-12}	11.11	Diethylamine	1.3×10^{-3}	2.89
Dimethylammonium ion	$C_2H_6NH_2^+$	1.9×10^{-11}	10.72	Dimethylamine	5.2×10^{-4}	3.28
Ethylammonium ion	$C_2H_5NH_3^+$	1.8×10^{-11}	10.75	Ethylamine	5.6×10^{-4}	3.25

Acid	Formula	K_a	pK_a	Conjugate base	K_b	pK_b
Formic	$HCOOH$	1.8×10^{-4}	3.74	Formate ion	5.6×10^{-11}	10.26
Hydrazinium ion	$N_2H_5^+$	3.3×10^{-9}	8.48	Hydrazine	3.0×10^{-6}	5.52
Hydrocyanic	HCN	7.2×10^{-10}	9.14	Cyanide ion	1.4×10^{-5}	4.86
Hydrofluoric	HF	6×10^{-4}	3.22	Fluoride ion	1.7×10^{-11}	10.78
Hydrogen sulfide	H_2S	1×10^{-7}	7.0	Bisulfide ion	1.1×10^{-7}	7.0
Bisulfide ion	HS^-	1×10^{-15}	15.0	Sulfide ion	10	-1.0
Hypochlorous	$HOCl$	3×10^{-8}	7.5	Hypochlorite ion	3×10^{-7}	6.5
Methylammonium ion	$CH_3NH_3^+$	2×10^{-11}	10.7	Methylamine	5×10^{-4}	3.3
Nitrous	HNO_2	4.5×10^{-4}	3.35	Nitrite ion	2.2×10^{-11}	10.65
Oxalic	$H_2C_2O_4$	6.5×10^{-2}	1.19	Bioxalate ion	1.5×10^{-13}	12.81
Bioxalate ion	$HC_2O_4^-$	6.1×10^{-5}	4.21	Oxalate ion	1.6×10^{-10}	9.79
Phenol	C_6H_5OH	1.3×10^{-10}	9.89	Phenolate ion	7.7×10^{-5}	4.11
Phosphoric	H_3PO_4	7.5×10^{-3}	2.12	Dihydrogen phosphate ion	1.3×10^{-12}	11.88
Dihydrogen phosphate ion	$H_2PO_4^-$	6.2×10^{-8}	7.21	Monohydrogen phosphate ion	1.6×10^{-7}	6.79
Monohydrogen phosphate ion	HPO_4^{2-}	4.8×10^{-13}	12.32	Phosphate ion	2.1×10^{-2}	1.68
Phthalic	$C_6H_4(COOH)_2$	1.3×10^{-3}	2.89	Biphthalate ion	7.7×10^{-12}	11.11
Biphthalate ion	$C_6H_4C_2O_2H^-$	3.9×10^{-6}	5.41	Phthalate ion	2.6×10^{-9}	8.59
Pyridinium ion	$C_5H_5NH^+$	7.1×10^{-6}	5.15	Pyridine	1.4×10^{-9}	8.85
Sulfuric	H_2SO_4	Strong	—	Bisulfate ion	Weak	—
Bisulfate ion	HSO_4^-	1.2×10^{-2}	1.92	Sulfate ion	8.3×10^{-13}	12.08
Sulfurous	H_2SO_3	1.7×10^{-2}	1.77	Bisulfite ion	5.9×10^{-13}	12.23
Bisulfite ion	HSO_3^-	6.2×10^{-8}	7.21	Sulfite ion	1.6×10^{-7}	6.79
Tartaric	$H_2C_4H_4O_6$	9.4×10^{-4}	3.03	Bitartrate ion	1.1×10^{-11}	10.97
Bitartrate ion	$HC_4H_4O_6^-$	2.9×10^{-5}	4.54	Tartrate ion	3.4×10^{-10}	9.46

TABLE 2 STEPWISE FORMATION CONSTANTS OF COMPLEX IONS†

Ligand	Cation	Ionic strength	Temp. °C	K_1	K_2	K_3	K_4
Ammonia	Ag^+	1.0	25	3.37	3.78		
	Cd^{2+}	2.1	25	2.74	2.21	1.37	1.13
	Cu^{2+}	1.0	25	4.27	3.55	2.90	2.18
	Ni^{2+}	1.0	25	2.36	1.90	1.55	1.23
	Zn^{2+}	2.0	30	2.37	2.44	2.50	2.15
Chloride	Ag^+	0.2	25	2.85	1.87	0.32	0.86
	Fe^{3+}	1.0	25	0.62	0.11	-1.40	-1.92
	Hg^{2+}	0.5	25	6.74	6.48	0.85	1.00
	Pb^{2+}	1.0	25	0.88	0.61	-0.40	-0.15
Cyanide	Cd^{2+}	3.0	25	5.48	5.14	4.56	3.58
	Hg^{2+}	0.1	20	18.00	16.70	3.83	2.98
EDTA	Ag^+	0.1	20	7.32			
	Al^{3+}	0.1	20	16.13			
	Ba^{2+}	0.1	20	7.76			
	Ca^{2+}	0.1	20	10.70			
	Cd^{2+}	0.1	20	16.59			
	Co^{2+}	0.1	20	16.21			
	Cu^{2+}	0.1	20	18.79			
	Fe^{2+}	0.1	20	14.33			
	Fe^{3+}	0.1	20	25.1			
	Hg^{2+}	0.1	20	21.80			
	Mg^{2+}	0.1	20	8.69			
	Mn^{2+}	0.1	20	13.58			
	Ni^{2+}	0.1	20	18.56			
	Pb^{2+}	0.1	20	18.3			
	Sr^{2+}	0.1	20	8.63			
	Th^{4+}	0.1	20	23.2			
	TiO^{2+}	0.1	—	17.3			
	VO^{2+}	0.1	20	18.77			
	Zn^{2+}	0.1	20	16.26			
Thiocyanate	Ag^+	4.0	25	4.59	3.70	1.77	1.20
	Fe^{3+}	1.8	18	1.96	2.02	< -0.41	> -0.14
	Ni^{2+}	1.0	20	1.18	0.46	0.17	
Thiosulfate	Ag^+	0.2	20	10.00	3.36		

† Stepwise constants are defined as follows:

$$M^{4+} + X^- \rightleftharpoons MX^{3+} \qquad K_1 = \frac{[MX^{3+}]}{[M^{4+}][X^-]}$$

$$MX^{3+} + X^- \rightleftharpoons MX_2^{2+} \qquad K_2 = \frac{[MX_2^{2+}]}{[MX^{3+}][X^-]} \qquad \text{etc.}$$

TABLE 3   SOLUBILITY PRODUCT CONSTANTS

Compound	Formula	Solubility product constant, K_{sp}
Aluminum hydroxide	$Al(OH)_3$	5×10^{-33}
Barium carbonate	$BaCO_3$	7×10^{-9}
Barium chromate	$BaCrO_4$	2×10^{-10}
Barium fluoride	BaF_2	3×10^{-6}
Barium iodate	$Ba(IO_3)_2$	6×10^{-10}
Barium oxalate	BaC_2O_4	2×10^{-7}
Barium sulfate	$BaSO_4$	1×10^{-10}
Cadmium carbonate	$CdCO_3$	3×10^{-14}
Cadmium oxalate	CdC_2O_4	1×10^{-8}
Cadmium sulfide	CdS	5×10^{-27}
Calcium carbonate	$CaCO_3$	5×10^{-9}
Calcium fluoride	CaF_2	4×10^{-11}
Calcium oxalate	CaC_2O_4	2×10^{-9}
Calcium sulfate	$CaSO_4$	6×10^{-5}
Cupric hydroxide	$Cu(OH)_2$	2×10^{-19}
Cupric iodate	$Cu(IO_3)_2$	1×10^{-7}
Cupric oxalate	CuC_2O_4	3×10^{-8}
Cupric sulfide	CuS	4×10^{-38}
Cuprous bromide	$CuBr$	6×10^{-9}
Cuprous chloride	$CuCl$	3×10^{-7}
Cuprous iodide	CuI	1×10^{-12}
Cuprous thiocyanate	$CuSCN$	4×10^{-14}
Ferric hydroxide	$Fe(OH)_3$	1×10^{-36}
Ferrous hydroxide	$Fe(OH)_2$	2×10^{-14}
Ferrous oxalate	FeC_2O_4	2×10^{-7}
Ferrous sulfide	FeS	4×10^{-19}
Lead carbonate	$PbCO_3$	2×10^{-13}
Lead chloride	$PbCl_2$	1×10^{-4}
Lead chromate	$PbCrO_4$	2×10^{-14}
Lead fluoride	PbF_2	5×10^{-8}
Lead hydroxide	$Pb(OH)_2$	3×10^{-16}
Lead iodate	$Pb(IO_3)_2$	3×10^{-13}
Lead sulfate	$PbSO_4$	2×10^{-8}
Lead sulfide	PbS	3×10^{-28}

TABLE 3 SOLUBILITY PRODUCT CONSTANTS (continued)

Compound	Formula	Solubility product constant, K_{sp}
Magnesium ammonium phosphate	$MgNH_4PO_4$	3×10^{-13}
Magnesium carbonate	$MgCO_3$	3×10^{-5}
Magnesium fluoride	MgF_2	7×10^{-9}
Magnesium hydroxide	$Mg(OH)_2$	1×10^{-11}
Magnesium oxalate	$Mg(C_2O_4)_2$	9×10^{-5}
Manganous hydroxide	$Mn(OH)_2$	4×10^{-14}
Manganous sulfide	MnS	1×10^{-16}
Mercuric sulfide	HgS	3×10^{-52}
Mercurous bromide	Hg_2Br_2	3×10^{-23}
Mercurous chloride	Hg_2Cl_2	6×10^{-19}
Mercurous iodide	Hg_2I_2	7×10^{-29}
Nickel sulfide	NiS	1×10^{-25}
Silver arsenate	Ag_3AsO_4	1×10^{-22}
Silver bromate	$AgBrO_3$	6×10^{-5}
Silver bromide	$AgBr$	4×10^{-13}
Silver carbonate	Ag_2CO_3	8×10^{-12}
Silver chloride	$AgCl$	1×10^{-10}
Silver chromate	Ag_2CrO_4	2×10^{-12}
Silver cyanide	$Ag[Ag(CN)_2]$	2×10^{-12}
Silver hydroxide	$AgOH$	2×10^{-8}
Silver iodate	$AgIO_3$	3×10^{-8}
Silver iodide	AgI	1×10^{-16}
Silver oxalate	$Ag_2C_2O_4$	5×10^{-12}
Silver sulfide	Ag_2S	1×10^{-48}
Silver thiocyanate	$AgSCN$	1×10^{-12}
Strontium carbonate	$SrCO_3$	2×10^{-9}
Strontium fluoride	SrF_2	3×10^{-9}
Strontium oxalate	SrC_2O_4	6×10^{-8}
Strontium sulfate	$SrSO_4$	3×10^{-7}
Thallous chloride	$TlCl$	2×10^{-4}
Thallous sulfide	Tl_2S	1×10^{-22}
Zinc carbonate	$ZnCO_3$	3×10^{-8}
Zinc hydroxide	$Zn(OH)_2$	2×10^{-14}
Zinc oxalate	ZnC_2O_4	3×10^{-9}
Zinc sulfide	ZnS	1×10^{-24}

TABLE 4   STANDARD POTENTIALS†

Redox couple	E^0
$F_2 + 2H^+ + 2e \rightleftharpoons 2HF(aq)$	3.06
$F_2 + 2e \rightleftharpoons 2F^-$	2.87
$O_3 + 2H^+ + 2e \rightleftharpoons O_2 + H_2O$	2.07
$S_2O_8^{2-} + 2e \rightleftharpoons 2SO_4^{2-}$	2.01
$Co^{3+} + e \rightleftharpoons Co^{2+}$	1.82
$H_2O_2 + 2H^+ + 2e \rightleftharpoons 2H_2O$	1.77
$MnO_4^- + 4H^+ + 3e \rightleftharpoons MnO_2 + 2H_2O$	1.70
$PbO_2 + SO_4^{2-} + 4H^+ + 2e \rightleftharpoons PbSO_4 + 2H_2O$	1.69
$Au^+ + e \rightleftharpoons Au$	1.68
$HClO_2 + 2H^+ + 2e \rightleftharpoons HClO + H_2O$	1.64
$HClO + H^+ + e \rightleftharpoons \frac{1}{2}Cl_2 + H_2O$	1.63
$Ce^{4+} + e \rightleftharpoons Ce^{3+}$	1.61
$Bi_2O_4 + 4H^+ + 2e \rightleftharpoons 2BiO^+ + 2H_2O$	1.59
$BrO_3^- + 6H^+ + 5e \rightleftharpoons \frac{1}{2}Br_2 + 3H_2O$	1.52
$MnO_4^- + 8H^+ + 5e \rightleftharpoons Mn^{2+} + 4H_2O$	1.51
$PbO_2 + 4H^+ + 2e \rightleftharpoons Pb^{2+} + 2H_2O$	1.46
$Cl_2 + 2e \rightleftharpoons 2Cl^-$	1.36
$Cr_2O_7^{2-} + 14H^+ + 6e \rightleftharpoons 2Cr^{3+} + 7H_2O$	1.33
$MnO_2 + 4H^+ + 2e \rightleftharpoons Mn^{2+} + 2H_2O$	1.23
$O_2 + 4H^+ + 4e \rightleftharpoons 2H_2O$	1.23
$IO_3^- + 6H^+ + 5e \rightleftharpoons \frac{1}{2}I_2 + 3H_2O$	1.20
$ClO_4^- + 2H^+ + 2e \rightleftharpoons ClO_3^- + H_2O$	1.19
$Br_2(aq) + 2e \rightleftharpoons 2Br^-$	1.09
$Br_2(liq) + 2e \rightleftharpoons 2Br^-$	1.07
$Br_3^- + 2e \rightleftharpoons 3Br^-$	1.05
$VO_2^+ + 2H^+ + e \rightleftharpoons VO^{2+} + H_2O$	1.00
$AuCl_4^- + 3e \rightleftharpoons Au + 4Cl^-$	1.00
$NO_3^- + 4H^+ + 3e \rightleftharpoons NO + 2H_2O$	0.96
$NO_3^- + 3H^+ + 2e \rightleftharpoons HNO_2 + H_2O$	0.94
$2Hg^{2+} + 2e \rightleftharpoons Hg_2^{2+}$	0.92
$AuBr_4^- + 3e \rightleftharpoons Au + 4Br^-$	0.87
$Cu^{2+} + I^- + e \rightleftharpoons CuI$	0.86
$NO_3^- + 2H^+ + e \rightleftharpoons NO_2 + H_2O$	0.80
$Ag^+ + e \rightleftharpoons Ag$	0.80
$Hg_2^{2+} + 2e \rightleftharpoons 2Hg$	0.79
$Fe^{3+} + e \rightleftharpoons Fe^{2+}$	0.77
$PtCl_4^{2-} + 2e \rightleftharpoons Pt + 4Cl^-$	0.73
$Q + 2H^+ + 2e \rightleftharpoons H_2Q$	0.70
$PtBr_4^{2-} + 2e \rightleftharpoons Pt + 4Br^-$	0.58
$MnO_4^- + e \rightleftharpoons MnO_4^{2-}$	0.56
$I_3^- + 2e \rightleftharpoons 3I^-$	0.54
$I_2(s) + 2e \rightleftharpoons 2I^-$	0.54
$Cu^+ + e \rightleftharpoons Cu$	0.52
$4H_2SO_3 + 4H^+ + 6e \rightleftharpoons S_4O_6^{2-} + 6H_2O$	0.51

TABLE 4 STANDARD POTENTIALS (continued)

Redox couple	E^0
$2\,H_2SO_3 + 2\,H^+ + 4e \rightleftharpoons S_2O_3^{2-} + 3\,H_2O$	0.40
$Fe(CN)_6^{3-} + e \rightleftharpoons Fe(CN)_6^{4-}$	0.36
$VO^{2+} + 2\,H^+ + e \rightleftharpoons V^{3+} + H_2O$	0.36
$Cu^{2+} + 2e \rightleftharpoons Cu$	0.34
$Hg_2Cl_2 + 2e \rightleftharpoons 2\,Hg + 2\,Cl^-$	0.28
$IO_3^- + 3\,H_2O + 6e \rightleftharpoons I^- + 6\,OH^-$	0.26
$AgCl + e \rightleftharpoons Ag + Cl^-$	0.22
$HgBr_4^{2-} + 2e \rightleftharpoons Hg + 4\,Br^-$	0.21
$Cu^{2+} + e \rightleftharpoons Cu^+$	0.15
$Sn^{4+} + 2e \rightleftharpoons Sn^{2+}$	0.15
$S + 2\,H^+ + 2e \rightleftharpoons H_2S$	0.14
$CuCl + e \rightleftharpoons Cu + Cl^-$	0.14
$AgBr + e \rightleftharpoons Ag + Br^-$	0.10
$S_4O_6^{2-} + 2e \rightleftharpoons 2\,S_2O_3^-$	0.08
$CuBr + e \rightleftharpoons Cu + Br^-$	0.03
$2\,H^+ + 2e \rightleftharpoons H_2$	0.00
$HgI_4^{2-} + 2e \rightleftharpoons Hg + 4\,I^-$	-0.04
$Pb^{2+} + 2e \rightleftharpoons Pb$	-0.13
$CrO_4^{2-} + 4\,H_2O + 3e \rightleftharpoons Cr(OH)_3 + 5\,OH^-$	-0.13
$Sn^{2+} + 2e \rightleftharpoons Sn$	-0.14
$AgI + e \rightleftharpoons Ag + I^-$	-0.15
$CuI + e \rightleftharpoons Cu + I^-$	-0.19
$Ni^{2+} + 2e \rightleftharpoons Ni$	-0.25
$V^{3+} + e \rightleftharpoons V^{2+}$	-0.26
$PbCl_2 + 2e \rightleftharpoons Pb + 2\,Cl^-$	-0.27
$Co^{2+} + 2e \rightleftharpoons Co$	-0.28
$PbBr_2 + 2e \rightleftharpoons Pb + 2\,Br^-$	-0.28
$PbSO_4 + 2e \rightleftharpoons Pb + SO_4^{2-}$	-0.36
$PbI_2 + 2e \rightleftharpoons Pb + 2\,I^-$	-0.37
$Cd^{2+} + 2e \rightleftharpoons Cd$	-0.40
$Cr^{3+} + e \rightleftharpoons Cr^{2+}$	-0.41
$Fe^{2+} + 2e \rightleftharpoons Fe$	-0.44
$2\,CO_2(gas) + 2\,H^+ + 2e \rightleftharpoons H_2C_2O_4(aq)$	-0.49
$Cr^{3+} + 3e \rightleftharpoons Cr$	-0.74
$Zn^{2+} + 2e \rightleftharpoons Zn$	-0.76
$Mn^{2+} + 2e \rightleftharpoons Mn$	-1.18
$Al^{3+} + 3e \rightleftharpoons Al$	-1.66
$Mg^{2+} + 2e \rightleftharpoons Mg$	-2.37
$Na^+ + e \rightleftharpoons Na$	-2.71
$Ca^{2+} + 2e \rightleftharpoons Ca$	-2.87
$Sr^{2+} + 2e \rightleftharpoons Sr$	-2.89
$Ba^{2+} + 2e \rightleftharpoons Ba$	-2.90
$K^+ + e \rightleftharpoons K$	-2.93
$Li^+ + e \rightleftharpoons Li$	-3.05

† From W. M. Latimer's *Oxidation Potentials*, 2nd ed., Prentice-Hall, Inc., Englewood Cliffs, N.J., 1952.

TABLE 5 SOME FORMAL POTENTIALS

Redox systems	Standard potential	Formal potential	Solution
$Ce^{4+} + e \rightleftharpoons Ce^{3+}$	—	1.23	1-M HCl
		1.44	1-M H_2SO_4
		1.61	1-M HNO_3
		1.7	1-M $HClO_4$
$Fe^{3+} + e \rightleftharpoons Fe^{2+}$	+0.771	0.68	1-M H_2SO_4
		0.700	1-M HCl
		0.732	1-M $HClO_4$
$Cr_2O_7^{2-} + 14\,H^+ + 6e \rightleftharpoons 2\,Cr^{3+} + 7\,H_2O$	+1.33	1.00	1-M HCl
		1.05	2-M HCl
		1.08	3-M HCl
		1.08	0.5-M H_2SO_4
		1.15	4-M H_2SO_4
		1.03	1-M $HClO_4$
$Fe(CN)_6^{3-} + e \rightleftharpoons Fe(CN)_6^{4-}$	+0.356	0.48	0.01-M HCl
		0.56	0.1-M HCl
		0.71	1-M HCl
		0.72	1-M H_2SO_4
		0.72	1-M $HClO_4$
$H_3AsO_4 + 2\,H^+ + 2e \rightleftharpoons H_3AsO_3 + H_2O$	+0.559	0.557	1-M HCl
		0.557	1-M $HClO_4$
$TiO^{2+} + 2\,H^+ + e \rightleftharpoons Ti^{3+} + H_2O$	+0.1	0.04	1-M H_2SO_4
$Pb^{2+} + 2e \rightleftharpoons Pb$	−0.126	−0.14	1-M $HClO_4$
$Sn^{2+} + 2e \rightleftharpoons Sn$	−0.136	−0.16	1-M $HClO_4$
$V^{3+} + e \rightleftharpoons V^{2+}$	−0.255	−0.21	1-M $HClO_4$

Appendix II

Table of Atomic Weights

TABLE OF ATOMIC WEIGHTS (based on the assigned relative atomic mass of $^{12}C = 12$)†

(The following values apply to elements as they exist in materials of terrestrial origin and to certain artificial elements. When used with the footnotes, they are reliable to ±1 in the last digit, or ±3 if that digit is in small type.)

	Symbol	Atomic number	Atomic weight
Actinium	Ac	89	
Aluminum	Al	13	26.9815[a]
Americium	Am	95	
Antimony	Sb	51	121.75
Argon	Ar	18	39.943[b,c,d,g]
Arsenic	As	33	74.9216[a]
Astatine	At	85	
Barium	Ba	56	137.34
Berkelium	Bk	97	
Beryllium	Be	4	9.01213[a]
Bismuth	Bi	83	208.9806[a]
Boron	B	5	10.81[c,d,e]
Bromine	Br	35	79.904[e]
Cadmium	Cd	48	112.40
Calcium	Ca	20	40.08
Californium	Cf	98	
Carbon	C	6	12.011[b,d]
Cerium	Ce	58	140.12
Cesium	Cs	55	132.9055[a]
Chlorine	Cl	17	35.453[c]
Chromium	Cr	24	51.996[c]
Cobalt	Co	27	53.9332[a]
Copper	Cu	29	63.546[c,d]
Curium	Cm	96	

	Symbol	Atomic number	Atomic weight
Dysprosium	Dy	66	162.50
Einsteinium	Es	99	
Erbium	Er	68	167.26
Europium	Eu	63	151.96
Fermium	Fm	100	
Fluorine	F	9	18.9984[a]
Francium	Fr	87	
Gadolinium	Gd	64	157.25
Gallium	Ga	31	69.72
Germanium	Ge	32	72.59
Gold	Au	79	196.9665[a]
Hafnium	Hf	72	173.49
Helium	He	2	4.00260[b,c]
Holmium	Ho	67	164.9303[a]
Hydrogen	H	1	1.0080[b,d]
Indium	In	49	114.82
Iodine	I	53	126.9045[a]
Iridium	Ir	77	192.22
Iron	Fe	26	55.847
Krypton	Kr	36	83.80
Lanthanum	La	57	138.9055[b]
Lawrencium	Lr	103	
Lead	Pb	82	207.2[d,g]
Lithium	Li	3	6.941[c,d,e]
Lutetium	Lu	71	174.97
Magnesium	Mg	12	24.305[c]
Manganese	Mn	25	54.9380[a]
Mendelevium	Md	101	
Mercury	Hg	80	200.59
Molybdenum	Mo	42	95.94
Neodymium	Nd	60	144.24
Neon	Ne	10	20.179[c]
Neptunium	Np	93	237.0482[b]
Nickel	Ni	28	58.71
Niobium	Nb	41	92.9064[a]
Nitrogen	N	7	14.0067[b,c]
Nobelium	No	102	
Osmium	Os	76	190.2
Oxygen	O	8	15.9994[b,c,d]
Palladium	Pd	46	106.4
Phosphorus	P	15	30.9738[a]
Platinum	Pt	78	195.09
Plutonium	Pu	94	
Polonium	Po	84	
Potassium	K	19	39.102
Praseodymium	Pr	59	140.0977[a]
Promethium	Pm	61	
Protactinium	Pa	91	231.0359[a]
Radium	Ra	88	226.0254[a,f,g]
Radon	Rn	86	
Rhenium	Re	75	186.2
Rhodium	Rh	45	102.9055[a]
Rubidium	Rb	37	85.4678[e]
Ruthenium	Ru	44	101.07

	Symbol	Atomic number	Atomic weight
Samarium	Sm	62	150.4
Scandium	Sc	21	44.9559[a]
Selenium	Se	34	78.96
Silicon	Si	14	28.086[d]
Silver	Ag	47	107.868[c]
Sodium	Na	11	22.9898[a]
Strontium	Sr	38	87.62[g]
Sulfur	S	16	32.06[d]
Tantalum	Ta	73	180.9479[b]
Technetium	Tc	43	98.9062[f]
Tellurium	Te	52	127.60
Terbium	Tb	65	158.9254[a]
Thallium	Tl	81	204.37
Thorium	Th	90	232.0381[a]
Thulium	Tm	69	168.9342[a]
Tin	Sn	50	118.69
Titanium	Ti	22	47.90
Tungsten	W	74	183.85
Uranium	U	92	238.029[b,c,e]
Vanadium	V	23	50.9414[b,c]
Wolfram	W	74	183.85
Xenon	Xe	54	131.30
Ytterbium	Yb	70	173.04
Yttrium	Y	39	88.9059[a]
Zinc	Zn	30	65.37
Zirconium	Zr	40	91.22

† *Chemical & Engineering News*, Jan. 26, 1970, p. 39.

[a] Mononuclidic element.

[b] Element with one predominant isotope (about 99 to 100% abundance).

[c] Element for which the atomic weight is based on calibrated measurements.

[d] Element for which variation in isotopic abundance in terrestrial samples limits the precision of the atomic weight given.

[e] Element for which users are cautioned against the possibility of large variations in atomic weight due to inadvertent or undisclosed artificial isotopic separation in commercially available materials.

[f] Most commonly available long-lived isotope; see "Table of Selected Radioactive Isotopes."

[g] In some geological specimens this element has a highly anomalous isotopic composition, corresponding to an atomic weight significantly different from that given.

Appendix III

Table
of Formula Weights

TABLE OF FORMULA WEIGHTS†

$AgBr$	187.779	KCN	65.120
$AgCl$	143.323	K_2CrO_4	194.196
$AgCN$	133.888	$K_2Cr_2O_7$	294.189
Ag_2CrO_4	331.732	$KHC_8H_4O_4(KHP)$	204.229
AgI	234.774	$KHC_2O_4 \cdot H_2C_2O_4$	218.166
$AgNO_3$	169.874	KI	166.006
$AgSCN$	165.952	KIO_3	214.003
Al_2O_3	101.961	$KIO_3 \cdot HIO_3$	390.003
As_2O_3	197.841	$KMnO_4$	158.036
$BaCl_2$	208.24	K_2O	94.203
$BaCO_3$	197.35	KOH	56.109
BaO	153.34	K_2PtCl_6	485.99
$Ba(OH)_2$	171.36	$KSCN$	97.184
$BaSO_4$	233.40	K_2SO_4	174.264
$CaCO_3$	100.09	$MgCl_2$	95.218
CaC_2O_4	128.10	$MgCO_3$	84.320
$CaCl_2$	110.98	MgO	40.310
CaF_2	78.08	$Mg_2P_2O_7$	222.465
CaO	56.08	MnO_2	86.937
$Ca(OH)_2$	74.10	MoO_3	143.94
$CaSO_4$	136.14	$NaBr$	102.899
$Ce(SO_4)_2$	332.24	$NaC_2H_3O_2$	82.035
CO_2	44.010	Na_2CO_3	105.989
Cr_2O_3	151.991	$Na_2C_2O_4$	134.000
$Cu(IO_3)_2$	413.35	$NaCl$	58.443
CuO	79.54	$NaCN$	49.008
$CuSCN$	121.62	$NaHCO_3$	84.007
$FeCO_3$	115.855	NaI	149.894
FeO	71.846	Na_2O	61.979
Fe_2O_3	159.691	$NaOH$	39.997
Fe_3O_4	231.537	Na_2SO_4	142.040
$FeSO_4$	151.907	$Na_2S_2O_3 \cdot 5 H_2O$	248.180
$FeSO_4(NH_4)_2SO_4 \cdot 6 H_2O$	392.135	NH_3	17.031
$FeSO_4C_2H_4(NH_3)_2SO_4 \cdot 4 H_2O$	382.153	NH_4Cl	53.492
$HCOOH$	46.026	$(NH_4)_2C_2O_4$	124.096
$HC_2H_3O_2$	60.053	$(NH_4)_2Ce(NO_3)_6$	548.28
$H_2C_2O_4$	90.036	$(NH_4)_2HPO_4$	132.057
HCl	36.461	$(NH_4)_2SO_4$	132.138
$HClO_4$	100.457	$Ni(C_4H_7O_2N_2)_2$	288.97
HNO_2	47.014	P_2O_5	141.945
HNO_3	63.013	PbO	223.19
H_2O	18.015	PbO_2	239.19
H_3PO_4	97.995	Pb_3O_4	685.57
H_2S	34.080	$PbSO_4$	303.28
H_2SO_3	82.077	SO_2	64.062
H_2SO_4	98.076	SO_3	80.061
$HgCl_2$	271.50	SiO_2	60.084
Hg_2Cl_2	472.09	SnO_2	150.69
KBr	119.011	V_2O_5	181.879
$KBrO_3$	167.008	WO_3	231.85
KCl	74.555	ZnO	81.37
$KClO_3$	122.552	$Zn_2P_2O_7$	304.68
$KClO_4$	138.551		

† No more than three decimals are carried, although in some instances four could be retained according to rules of significant figures.

Appendix IV

The Literature of Analytical Chemistry

People have referred to an "information explosion" which threatens to inundate the scientists in a sea of paper. The volume of published research in chemistry is possibly more than doubling every ten years, and wags are saying that it is easier to repeat work in the laboratory than to find it in the literature. Experts are considering various automated schemes for retrieving information, but it is impossible now to predict what library services may ultimately become available. Meanwhile, the chemist has to get along somehow, and there are ways of finding information in the literature that are more efficient than others. The student should certainly become familiar with the library during his undergraduate years.

The *primary* literature sources are published research papers in a host of journals, American and foreign. Some of these journals of a more general nature publish papers of broad interest, while others attract primarily a narrower readership, say, organic, physical, or analytical chemists. *Secondary* sources include brief abstracts of published papers, articles which review the literature in restricted areas, monographs in which experts describe at length the status of certain fields, treatises and other reference works, and textbooks. The beginning student will normally use mainly secondary sources, but as he pushes closer to the present boundary of knowledge, he should increasingly consult original research papers.

We can present here only a bare introduction to the literature of analytical chemistry. Further, it must be remembered that the research analytical chemist often confronts problems which have never been investigated before;

it would be impossible to define ahead of time the fields in which he might read in order to find approaches to such problems, but it is not unusual to find organic reaction mechanisms, spectroscopy, electronics, and other such "nonanalytical" information brought to bear in analytical problems.

ANALYTICAL JOURNALS

Analyst, dating from 1877, is a publication of the Society for Analytical Chemistry in Great Britain.

Analytical Biochemistry, is a journal which presents applications of analytical chemistry to biochemistry.

Analytical Chemistry, published monthly by the American Chemical Society. Prior to 1947, this was called the Analytical Edition of *Industrial and Engineering Chemistry*, but the yearly volumes are numbered consecutively, without break, dating from 1929.

Analytica Chimica Acta, published by Elsevier Publishing Co. in The Netherlands since 1947. Papers are written in English, French, or German; each has a summary in all three languages.

Analytical Letters, is an international journal for rapid communication, published by Marcel Dekker since 1968.

Chemical Instrumentation is a journal of experimental techniques in chemistry and biochemistry, published by Marcel Dekker, Inc. since 1969.

Chimie Analytique (now called *Analusis*) is the major French journal in the field.

CRC Critical Reviews in Analytical Chemistry presents informed, thorough, up-to-date and critical reviews of important topics in analytical chemistry. It has been published since 1971 by The Chemical Rubber Company.

Journal of Chromatographic Science, published since 1963 by Preston Technical Abstracts Co., Evanston, Ill.

Journal of Chromatography, published since 1958 by Elsevier Publishing Co. in The Netherlands.

Journal of Electroanalytical Chemistry, since 1962, an Elsevier publication dealing with all aspects of theory and practice of electrical methods of analysis.

Separation Science, published since 1966, is an interdisciplinary journal of methods and processes of separation; a Marcel Dekker, Inc. publication.

Talanta, published since 1958 by the Pergamon Press, contains research papers in English, French, and German, with summaries in all three languages.

Zeitschrift für analytische Chemie, dating from 1862, is the principal German analytical journal.

Zhurnal Analitischeskoi Khimii (Journal of Analytical Chemistry of the USSR) is the Russian analytical journal. It is available in English translation from Consultants Bureau, New York.

ABSTRACTS

Chemical Abstracts (Chem. Abstr. or C.A.), published since 1907 by the American Chemical Society, is the outstanding source of information for all fields of chemistry and certain related areas as well. Chemical Abstracts publishes brief abstracts of papers from nearly 10,000 periodicals, and it covers the patent literature as well. It appears biweekly. The abstracts are grouped into 74 sections, such as section 2, analytical chemistry, section 3, general physical chemistry, section 4, surface chemistry and colloids, and section 60, biochemical methods. Annual indexes provide access by subject, authors' names, and chemical formula. Decennial indexes covering 10-year periods, e.g., 1907–16, 1917–26, appeared through 1956; the last collective index covered a five-year period, 1967–71. The nomenclature and list of abbreviations used by C.A. are practically official for writers of American books and journal articles. A thorough search through C.A. is a tedious job, and workers frequently employ shortcuts based upon their experience or upon information obtained from other sources such as reference books, review articles, and monographs. But C.A. is the ultimate source, and information which cannot be found there can probably be best obtained by original work in the laboratory.

Chemisches Zentralblatt, the German abstract journal, dates back to 1830 and hence covers literature published before C.A. began. It is particularly valuable for this period, but has no advantage over C.A. for more recent information.

Analytical Abstracts, published by the Society for Analytical Chemistry, was formerly a section of the now-discontinued *British Abstracts*, appearing now in its own right. This is a short periodical, and a routine scan each month doesn't take much time.

Chemical Titles, published by the American Chemical Society, lists the titles of most papers in the world's chemical literature very promptly. Indexes are prepared on the basis of key words in the titles.

In addition to these more or less general abstract journals, abstracts sometimes appear catering to a particular special field. An example of these is *Gas Chromatography Abstracts* published by the Institute of Petroleum in London. It appears annually, with subject and author indexes.

REVIEWS

Each April, *Analytical Chemistry* publishes along with its regular issue a separate Annual Review issue. In even years, e.g., 1964, 1966, fundamental topics are reviewed, while applied topics are covered in the alternate years. Typical fundamental reviews are gas chromatography, nucleonics, polarographic theory, emission spectrometry, nuclear magnetic resonance, and X-ray diffraction, while titles of applied reviews include clinical analysis,

517

ferrous alloys, and paints and finishes. Each review will normally give hundreds of journal references, organized in some convenient fashion. These are the most comprehensive reviews of the analytical literature, but others are also published; for example, the *Annual Reports* on the progress of chemistry to the Chemical Society of London has an analytical section.

REFERENCE BOOKS AND ADVANCED TEXTS

Probably, at least for a few years, the best single reference work will be *Treatise on Analytical Chemistry*, edited by I. M. Kolthoff, P. J. Elving, and E. B. Sandell and published by Interscience Publishers, a Division of John Wiley & Sons, Inc., New York. Publication began in 1959, and volumes are still appearing. The goal is "to present a concise, critical, comprehensive, and systematic, but not exhaustive, treatment of all aspects of classical and modern analytical chemistry." Publication is in three parts: Part I, Theory and Practice; Part II, Analytical Chemistry of the Elements; Part III, Analysis of Industrial Products.

A second general reference work with a similar goal, *Comprehensive Analytical Chemistry*, edited by C. L. Wilson and D. W. Wilson and published by Elsevier Publishing Co., Amsterdam, began to appear in 1959. Chapters written by experts are well referenced with regard to the original literature.

There is much information of analytical interest in the multivolume series *Technique of Organic Chemistry*, edited by A. Weissberger (John Wiley & Sons, Inc., New York). Volumes have been appearing since 1959.

The following are textbooks of a more or less general nature which are more advanced than the present one.

H. A. LAITINEN, *Chemical Analysis*, McGraw-Hill Book Company, New York, 1960.

L. MEITES and H. C. THOMAS, *Advanced Analytical Chemistry*, McGraw-Hill Book Company, New York, 1958.

S. SIGGIA, *Survey of Analytical Chemistry*, McGraw-Hill Book Company, New York, 1968.

T. B. SMITH, *Analytical Processes: A Physico-Chemical Interpretation*, 2nd ed., Arnold, Ltd., London, 1952.

C. R. N. STROUTS, J. H. GILFILLAN, and H. N. WILSON, *Analytical Chemistry*, Oxford University Press, Inc., New York, 1955.

H. F. WALTON, *Principles and Methods of Chemical Analysis*, 2nd ed., Prentice-Hall, Inc., Englewood Cliffs, N.J., 1964.

In addition, the elementary text *Quantitative Chemical Analysis*, 4th ed., by I. M. KOLTHOFF, E. B. SANDELL, E. J. MEEHAN, and S. BRUCKENSTEIN (The Macmillan Co., New York, 1969) contains an unusual wealth of information for an elementary book.

SOME REPRESENTATIVE BOOKS ON SPECIAL TOPICS

R. N. ADAMS, *Electrochemistry at Solid Electrodes*, Marcel Dekker, Inc., New York, 1969.

M. R. F. ASHWORTH, *Titrimetric Organic Analysis*, Interscience-Wiley, New York, 1964–65.

A. J. BARD, ed., *Electroanalytical Chemistry*, Marcel Dekker, Inc., New York, 1966– (a continuing series).

R. G. BATES, *Determination of pH: Theory and Practice*, John Wiley & Sons, Inc., New York, 1964.

R. P. BAUMAN, *Absorption Spectroscopy*, John Wiley & Sons, Inc., New York, 1962.

E. W. BERG, *Physical and Chemical Methods of Separation*, McGraw-Hill Book Company, New York, 1963.

R. J. BLOCK and G. ZWEIG, *A Practical Manual of Paper Chromatography and Electrophoresis*, Academic Press, New York, 1962.

D. F. BOLTZ, ed., *Colorimetric Determination of Nonmetals*, John Wiley & Sons, Inc., New York, 1958.

S. J. CLARK, *Quantitative Methods of Organic Microanalysis*, Butterworth & Co., Ltd., London, 1956.

W. M. CLARK, *Oxidation-Reduction Potentials of Organic Systems*, The Williams and Wilkins Co., Baltimore, 1960.

F. E. CRITCHFIELD, *Organic Functional Group Analysis*, Pergamon Press, New York, 1962.

R. A. DURST, ed., *Ion-Selective Electrodes, National Bureau of Standards Special Publication 314*, U.S. Government Printing Office, Washington, D.C., 1969.

C. DUVAL, *Inorganic Thermogravimetric Analysis*, 2nd ed., Elsevier Publishing Co., Inc., Amsterdam, 1963.

H. FLASCHKA, *EDTA Titrations*, Pergamon Press, New York, 1959.

J. S. FRITZ and G. S. HAMMOND, *Quantitative Organic Analysis*, John Wiley & Sons, Inc., New York, 1957.

D. GLICK, ed., *Methods of Biochemical Analysis*, John Wiley & Sons, Inc., New York, 1954– (a continuing series).

E. HEFTMANN, *Chromatography*, Reinhold Publishing Corp., New York, 1961.

F. HELFFERICH, *Ion Exchange*, McGraw-Hill Book Company, New York, 1962.

W. F. HILLEBRAND, G. E. F. LUNDELL, H. A. BRIGHT, and J. I. HOFFMANN, *Applied Inorganic Analysis*, 2nd ed., John Wiley & Sons, Inc., New York, 1953.

W. HUBER, *Titrations in Nonaqueous Solvents*, Academic Press, Inc., New York, 1967.

J. J. KIRKLAND, ed., *Modern Practice of Liquid Chromatography*, Wiley-Interscience, New York, 1971.

I. M. KOLTHOFF and J. J. LINGANE, *Polarography*, 2nd ed., Interscience Publishers, Inc., New York, 1952.

I. M. KOLTHOFF and V. A. STENGER, *Volumetric Analysis*, 2nd ed., John Wiley & Sons, Inc., New York, 1942–57.

W. M. LATIMER, *The Oxidation States of the Elements and Their Potentials in Aqueous Solutions*, 2nd ed., Prentice-Hall, Inc., Englewood Cliffs, N.J., 1952.

J. J. LINGANE, *Electroanalytical Chemistry*, 2nd ed., Interscience-Wiley, New York, 1958.

A. B. LITTLEWOOD, *Gas Chromatography: Principles, Techniques, and Applications*, 2nd ed., Academic Press, Inc., New York, 1970.

L. MEITES, *Polarographic Techniques*, 2nd ed., Interscience-Wiley, New York, 1965.

M. G. MELLON, ed., *Analytical Absorption Spectroscopy*, John Wiley & Sons, Inc., New York, 1950.

J. MITCHELL, Jr., I. M. KOLTHOFF, E. S. PROSKAUER, and A. WEISSBERGER, eds., *Organic Analysis*, John Wiley & Sons, Inc., New York, 1953– (a continuing series).

G. H. MORRISON and H. FREISER, *Solvent Extraction in Analytical Chemistry*, John Wiley & Sons, Inc., New York, 1957.

J. P. PHILLIPS, *Automatic Titrators*, Academic Press, New York, 1959.

C. N. REILLEY, ed., *Advances in Analytical Chemistry and Instrumentation*, Interscience-Wiley, New York, 1960– (a continuing series).

O. SAMUELSON, *Ion Exchangers in Analytical Chemistry*, 2nd ed., John Wiley & Sons, Inc., New York, 1962.

E. B. SANDELL, *Colorimetric Determination of Traces of Metals*, 3rd ed., Interscience-Wiley, New York, 1959.

G. SCHWARZENBACH and H. FLASCHKA, *Complexometric Titrations*, trans. by H. M. N. H. IRVING, Methuen & Co., Ltd., London, 1969.

S. SIGGIA and H. J. STOLTEN, *An Introduction to Modern Organic Analysis*, John Wiley & Sons, Inc., New York, 1956.

F. D. SNELL and F. M. BIFFEN, *Commercial Methods of Analysis*, Chemical Publishing Co., Inc., New York, 1964.

H. A. STROBEL, *Chemical Instrumentation: A Systematic Approach to Instrumental Analysis*, 2nd ed., Addison-Wesley, Reading, Mass., 1973.

Appendix V

Four-Place Table
of Logarithms

FOUR-PLACE TABLE OF LOGARITHMS

No.	0	1	2	3	4	5	6	7	8	9
10	0000	0043	0086	0128	0170	0212	0253	0294	0334	0374
11	0414	0453	0492	0531	0569	0607	0645	0682	0719	0755
12	0792	0828	0864	0899	0934	0969	1004	1038	1072	1106
13	1139	1173	1206	1239	1271	1303	1335	1367	1399	1430
14	1461	1492	1523	1553	1584	1614	1644	1673	1703	1732
15	1761	1790	1818	1847	1875	1903	1931	1959	1987	2014
16	2041	2068	2095	2122	2148	2175	2201	2227	2253	2279
17	2304	2330	2355	2380	2405	2430	2455	2480	2504	2529
18	2553	2577	2601	2625	2648	2672	2695	2718	2742	2765
19	2788	2810	2833	2856	2878	2900	2923	2945	2967	2989
20	3010	3032	3054	3075	3096	3118	3139	3160	3181	3201
21	3222	3243	3263	3284	3304	3324	3345	3365	3385	3404
22	3424	3444	3464	3483	3502	3522	3541	3560	3579	3598
23	3617	3636	3655	3674	3692	3711	3729	3747	3766	3784
24	3802	3820	3838	3856	3874	3892	3909	3927	3945	3962
25	3979	3997	4014	4031	4048	4065	4082	4099	4116	4133
26	4150	4166	4183	4200	4216	4232	4249	4265	4281	4298
27	4314	4330	4346	4362	4378	4393	4409	4425	4440	4456
28	4472	4487	4502	4518	4533	4548	4564	4579	4594	4609
29	4624	4639	4654	4669	4683	4698	4713	4728	4742	4757
30	4771	4786	4800	4814	4829	4843	4857	4871	4886	4900
31	4914	4928	4942	4955	4969	4983	4997	5011	5024	5038
32	5051	5065	5079	5092	5105	5119	5132	5145	5159	5172
33	5185	5198	5211	5224	5237	5250	5263	5276	5289	5302
34	5315	5328	5340	5353	5366	5378	5391	5403	5416	5428
35	5441	5453	5465	5478	5490	5502	5514	5527	5539	5551
36	5563	5575	5587	5599	5611	5623	5635	5647	5658	5670
37	5682	5694	5705	5717	5729	5740	5752	5763	5775	5786
38	5798	5809	5821	5832	5843	5855	5866	5877	5888	5899
39	5911	5922	5933	5944	5955	5966	5977	5988	5999	6010
40	6021	6031	6042	6053	6064	6075	6085	6096	6107	6117
41	6128	6138	6149	6160	6170	6180	6191	6201	6212	6222
42	6232	6243	6253	6263	6274	6284	6294	6304	6314	6325
43	6335	6345	6355	6365	6375	6386	6395	6405	6415	6425
44	6435	6444	6454	6464	6474	6484	6493	6503	6513	6522
45	6532	6542	6551	6561	6571	6580	6590	6599	6609	6618
46	6628	6637	6646	6656	6665	6675	6684	6693	6702	6712
47	6721	6730	6739	6749	6758	6767	6776	6785	6794	6803
48	6812	6821	6830	6839	6848	6857	6866	6875	6884	6893
49	6902	6911	6920	6928	6937	6946	6955	6964	6972	6981
50	6990	6998	7007	7016	7024	7033	7042	7050	7059	7067
51	7076	7084	7093	7101	7110	7118	7126	7135	7143	7152
52	7160	7168	7177	7185	7193	7202	7210	7218	7226	7235
53	7243	7251	7259	7267	7275	7284	7292	7300	7308	7316
54	7324	7332	7340	7348	7356	7364	7372	7380	7388	7396
	0	1	2	3	4	5	6	7	8	9

No.	0	1	2	3	4	5	6	7	8	9
55	7404	7412	7419	7427	7435	7443	7451	7459	7466	7474
56	7482	7490	7497	7505	7513	7520	7528	7536	7543	7551
57	7559	7566	7574	7582	7589	7597	7604	7612	7619	7627
58	7634	7642	7649	7657	7664	7672	7679	7686	7694	7701
59	7709	7716	7723	7731	7738	7745	7752	7760	7767	7774
60	7782	7789	7796	7803	7810	7818	7825	7832	7839	7846
61	7853	7860	7868	7875	7882	7889	7896	7903	7910	7917
62	7924	7931	7938	7945	7952	7959	7966	7973	7980	7987
63	7992	8000	8007	8014	8021	8028	8035	8041	8048	8055
64	8062	8069	8075	8082	8089	8096	8102	8109	8116	8122
65	8129	8136	8142	8149	8156	8162	8169	8176	8182	8189
66	8195	8202	8209	8215	8222	8228	8235	8241	8248	8254
67	8261	8267	8274	8280	8287	8293	8299	8306	8312	8319
68	8325	8331	8338	8344	8351	8357	8363	8370	8376	8382
69	8388	8395	8401	8407	8414	8420	8426	8432	8439	8445
70	8451	8457	8463	8470	8476	8482	8488	8494	8500	8506
71	8513	8519	8525	8531	8537	8543	8549	8555	8561	8567
72	8573	8579	8585	8591	8597	8603	8609	8615	8621	8627
73	8633	8639	8645	8651	8657	8663	8669	8675	8681	8686
74	8692	8698	8704	8710	8716	8722	8727	8733	8739	8745
75	8751	8756	8762	8768	8774	8779	8785	8791	8797	8802
76	8808	8814	8820	8825	8831	8837	8842	8848	8854	8859
77	8865	8871	8876	8882	8887	8893	8899	8904	8910	8915
78	8921	8927	8932	8938	8943	8949	8954	8960	8965	8971
79	8976	8982	8987	8993	8998	9004	9009	9015	9020	9025
80	9031	9036	9042	9047	9053	9058	9063	9069	9074	9079
81	9085	9090	9096	9101	9106	9112	9117	9122	9128	9133
82	9138	9143	9149	9154	9159	9165	9170	9175	9180	9186
83	9191	9196	9201	9206	9212	9217	9222	9227	9232	9238
84	9243	9248	9253	9258	9263	9269	9274	9279	9284	9289
85	9294	9299	9304	9309	9315	9320	9325	9330	9335	9340
86	9345	9350	9355	9360	9365	9370	9375	9380	9385	9390
87	9395	9400	9405	9410	9415	9420	9425	9430	9435	9440
88	9445	9450	9455	9460	9465	9469	9474	9479	9484	9489
89	9494	9499	9504	9509	9513	9518	9523	9528	9533	9538
90	9542	9547	9552	9557	9562	9566	9571	9576	9581	9586
91	9590	9595	9600	9605	9609	9614	9619	9624	9628	9633
92	9638	9643	9647	9652	9657	9661	9666	9671	9675	9680
93	9685	9689	9694	9699	9703	9708	9713	9717	9722	9727
94	9731	9736	9741	9745	9750	9754	9759	9763	9768	9773
95	9777	9782	9786	9791	9795	9800	9805	9809	9814	9818
96	9823	9827	9832	9836	9841	9845	9850	9854	9859	9863
97	9868	9872	9877	9881	9886	9890	9894	9899	9903	9908
98	9912	9917	9921	9926	9930	9934	9939	9943	9948	9952
99	9956	9961	9965	9969	9974	9978	9983	9987	9991	9996
	0	1	2	3	4	5	6	7	8	9

Appendix VI

Answers to Odd-Numbered Problems

CHAPTER 2 **Review of Stoichiometry**

1. (a) (1) 0.750, (2) 0.0500, (3) 0.188, (4) 0.0500, (5) 0.400
   (b) (1) 0.750, (2) 0.100, (3) 0.376, (4) 0.100, (5) 0.400
3. (a) (1) 0.0725, (2) 0.102, (3) 0.0840
   (b) (1) both 0.0725, (2) 0.102, 0.204, (3) 0.1680, 0.0840
5. (a) 3.48, (b) 6.50, (c) 4.20, (d) 5.29
7. 0.1250
9. 2.0×10^{-5}
11. 0.1077
13. (a) 0.61, (b) 1.8, (c) 0.40, (d) 0.80
15. (a) 37.67, (b) 8.31, (c) 11.63
17. 10.00 ml
19. 17.39

21. 20.50
23. 2.497
25. 0.251
27. 33.31
29. 0.03131
31. 33.6 ml
33. 99.8 ml
35. (a) 26.1, (b) 33.6 ml
37. (a) 55.48, (b) 61.20
39. 0.699
41. 27.96
43. 0.100 g
45. 12.55 % Na_2O ; 26.02 % K_2O
47. 0.4259 g
49. (a) 129, (b) 22, (c) 107
51. 0.72

CHAPTER 3 **Errors and the Treatment of Analytical Data**

1. (a) Neptunium; palladium
   (b) 0.00042; 0.94
3. (a) Absolute: 0.09 %; relative: 4.4 ppt
5. Means are significantly different (99 %)

7. Means are not significantly different (95 %)
9. (a) No, (b) 30.42, (c) 30.09–30.75
11. No; yes
13. No
15. (a) ±0.24, (b) ±0.12, (c) ±0.078

17. (a) 2.0 mg, (b) 4.0 ml
19. 200 g
21. (a) 50.0, (b) 50.0, (c) 50.00, (d) 50
23. (a) 4, (b) 4, (c) 5, (d) 3, (e) 3, (f) 4
25. 3.0×10^5

27. (a) 2.53×10^{-3}, (b) 2.98×10^5, (c) 4.02, (d) 9.0×10^3, (e) 218.3
29. (a) 24.737, (b) 69.943
31. (a) 19.79, (b) 3.0

CHAPTER 4   Acid-Base Equilibria

1. (a) 2.30, (b) 1.00, (c) 0.00, (d) -1.00, (e) 7.40, (f) 13.10
3. (a) 5.0, (b) 0.20, (c) 1.8×10^{-5}, (d) 5.0×10^{-11}, (e) 5.0×10^{-15}, (f) 2.5, (g) 1.8×10^{-6}, (h) 5.0×10^{-13} (e) 12.00, (f) 2.30, (g) 11.70, (h) 2.30, (i) 5.22, (j) 8.78
5. (a) 8.26, (b) 9.26, (c) 2.00, (d) 7.00 (e) 12.00, (f) 2.30, (g) 11.70, (h) 2.30, (i) 5.22, (j) 8.78
7. 5.0×10^{-5}
9. (a) 0.091, (b) 0.32, (c) 23
11. (a) 1.26, (b) 1.30, (c) 1.30, (d) 7.00, (e) 13.65, (f) 7.00
13. 60 ml HCl; 40 ml NaOH
15. 0.050

17. (a) 1.15, 1.30; (b) 1.46, 1.54; (c) 1.91, 1.94; (d) 2.37, 2.38; (e) 2.87, 2.87
19. 3.1 g
21. (a) 3.26, (b) 3.44, (c) 3.74, (d) 4.22, (e) 5.74, (f) 6.74, (g) 7.74
23. (a) 2.8×10^{-7}, (b) 5.3×10^{-6}, (c) 2.8×10^{-7}, (d) 2.8×10^{-8}
25. 0.01 ml
27. (a) 10.90, (b) 9.68, (c) 9.26, (d) 8.56, (e) 6.41, (f) 5.42, (g) 4.43, (h) 2.54
29. (a) 3.14, (b) 3.10. Not feasible
31. 50.0
33. A : 0.50: B : 0.20: C : 2.0
35. 5.30
37. 7.9×10^3

CHAPTER 5   Acid-Base Equilibria in Complex Systems

1. (a) 9.77, (b) 4.67, (c) 3.93, (d) 11.24, (e) 1.72, (f) 9.77
5. (a) 20 ml, (b) 80 ml
7. $\% \text{Na}_2\text{CO}_3 = 26.36$; $\% \text{NaHCO}_3 = 20.89$

9. $\% \text{Na}_2\text{CO}_3 = 21.20$; $\% \text{NaHCO}_3 = 12.60$
11. 13.33 ml

CHAPTER 6   Complex Formation Titrations

1. 0.01082; 4.027
3. 39.40
5. (a) 0.01471, (b) 1.472 mg/ml
7. (a) 1.70, (b) 2.30, (c) 0.00, (d) 3.60, (e) 2.70
9. (a) 1×10^{-9}, (b) 3.2×10^8

11. pH 8 : 2.00; 2.48; 5.00; 6.15; 7.30; 9.00
pH 12 : 2.00; 2.48; 5.00; 7.30; 9.60; 11.30
13. (a) 14.27, (b) 13.87

CHAPTER 7   Solubility Equilibria

1. (a) 1×10^{-16}, (b) 1×10^{-11}, (c) 5×10^{-12}

3. (a) 1×10^{-8}, (b) 2×10^{-7}, (c) 5×10^{-6}

5. (a) 2.3×10^{-3}, (b) 4.2×10^{-4},
   (c) 2.3×10^{-3}
7. (a) 1.70, (b) 1.00, (c) 2.70, (d) 1.52
9. (a) 1.35, 11.05; 1.30, 11.10;
       6.20, 6.20
   (b) 1.35, 14.65; 1.30, 14.70;
       8.00, 8.00
11. For AgBr: 4.00, 8.40; for AgI:
    4.00, 12.00
13. (a) 7×10^{-6},
    (b) $[Ag^+] = 1.4 \times 10^{-5}$;
    $[NO_3^-] = 0.040$;
    $[CrO_4^{2-}] = 0.010$;
    $[K^+] = 0.060$

15. (a) 1×10^{-2}, (b) 2.5
17. (a) 9.15, (b) 9.50, (c) 10.50,
    (d) 11.00
19. (a) 8.9×10^{-5}, (b) 0.11
21. (a) 1×10^{-4}, (b) 1.8×10^{-6},
    (c) 1.1×10^{-5}, (d) 1.4×10^{-8},
    (e) 3.7×10^{-14}
23. 1.2×10^{-13}
25. 5.7×10^{-10}
27. 20

CHAPTER 8   Oxidation-Reduction Equilibria

1. (a) -0.05 V, left, Cd negative
   (b) $+0.10$ V, right, Cd positive
   (c) -0.04 V, left, Cr negative
   (d) $+0.09$ V, right, Cr positive
   (e) -0.46 V, left, $Pt(H_2)$
        negative
   (f) $+0.89$ V, right, Pt(Cr)
        positive
   (g) $+0.12$ V, right, Hg positive
   (h) $+1.58$ V, right, $Pt(Cl_2)$
        positive
3. 4.7×10^{20}; 9.2×10^{-12}
5. (a) -0.64 V, (b) 6.8×10^{-48}
9. -0.62 V

11. 1×10^{-5}
13. $+0.96$ V
15. (a) 1×10^{11}, (b) $+0.33$ V
17. (a) 1×10^5, No, (b) 0.8
19. 4.8×10^{21}
21. 1.0×10^{-7}
23. (a) 1×10^{41}, (b) -56.5 kcal,
    (c) rate slow
25. (a) 2.8×10^{11}, (b) 1.1×10^{-8}
27. 2.1×10^{-10}
29. $+0.64$ V
31. (a) 1.5×10^{48}, (b) 5.97
33. -0.68 V, (b) -0.25 V

CHAPTER 9   Potentiometric Methods of Analysis

1.

Volume	pH	E, V
0.00	1.52	0.34
10.00	1.74	0.35
15.00	1.89	0.36
29.0	3.11	0.44
29.9	4.11	0.50
30.0	7.00	0.67
30.1	9.89	0.84
31.0	10.88	0.90
40.0	11.85	0.96

5. 31.350
7. $E = -0.34 - 0.06\, pH$
9. 9.1×10^{11}
11. 60 ml HCl; 40 ml NaOH
13. 100
15. 45.5
17. (a) Negative, (b) positive, (c) 7,
    (d) below 12
19. (a) 0.56, 0.50, 0.44; (b) 0.56, 0.43,
    0.30; (c) 0.56, 0.32, 0.08

CHAPTER 10   Other Electrical Methods of Analysis

1. (a) 1.23 V, (b) 1.23 V, (c) 1.23 V
3. 0.65 V

5. (a) 1×10^{-12}-M,
   (b) 2.1×10^{-28}-M